Fodor's

CALIFORNIA

Welcome to California

California's endless wonders, from Yosemite National Park to Disneyland, are both natural and man-made. With the iconic Big Sur coast, dramatic Mojave Desert, and majestic Sierra Nevada mountains, sunny California indulges those in search of great surfing, hiking, and golfing. Other pleasures await, too: superb food in San Francisco, studio tours in Los Angeles, winery visits and spas in Napa and Sonoma. This book was produced in the middle of the COVID-19 pandemic. As you plan your upcoming travels, please confirm that places are still open and let us know when we need to make updates by writing to us: editors@fodors.com.

TOP REASONS TO GO

★ **Stunning Scenery:** Picture-perfect backdrops from the Golden Gate Bridge to redwoods.

★ **Beaches:** For surfing, swimming, or sunbathing, the state's beaches can't be beat.

★ **Cool Cities:** San Francisco, Los Angeles, San Diego, Palm Springs, and more.

★ **Feasts:** Cutting-edge restaurants, food trucks, fusion flavors, farmers' markets.

★ **Wine Country:** Top-notch whites and reds in Napa, Sonoma, and beyond.

★ **Road Trips:** The Pacific Coast Highway offers spectacular views and thrills aplenty.

Contents

Fodor's Features

MAPS

Chapter 1

EXPERIENCE CALIFORNIA

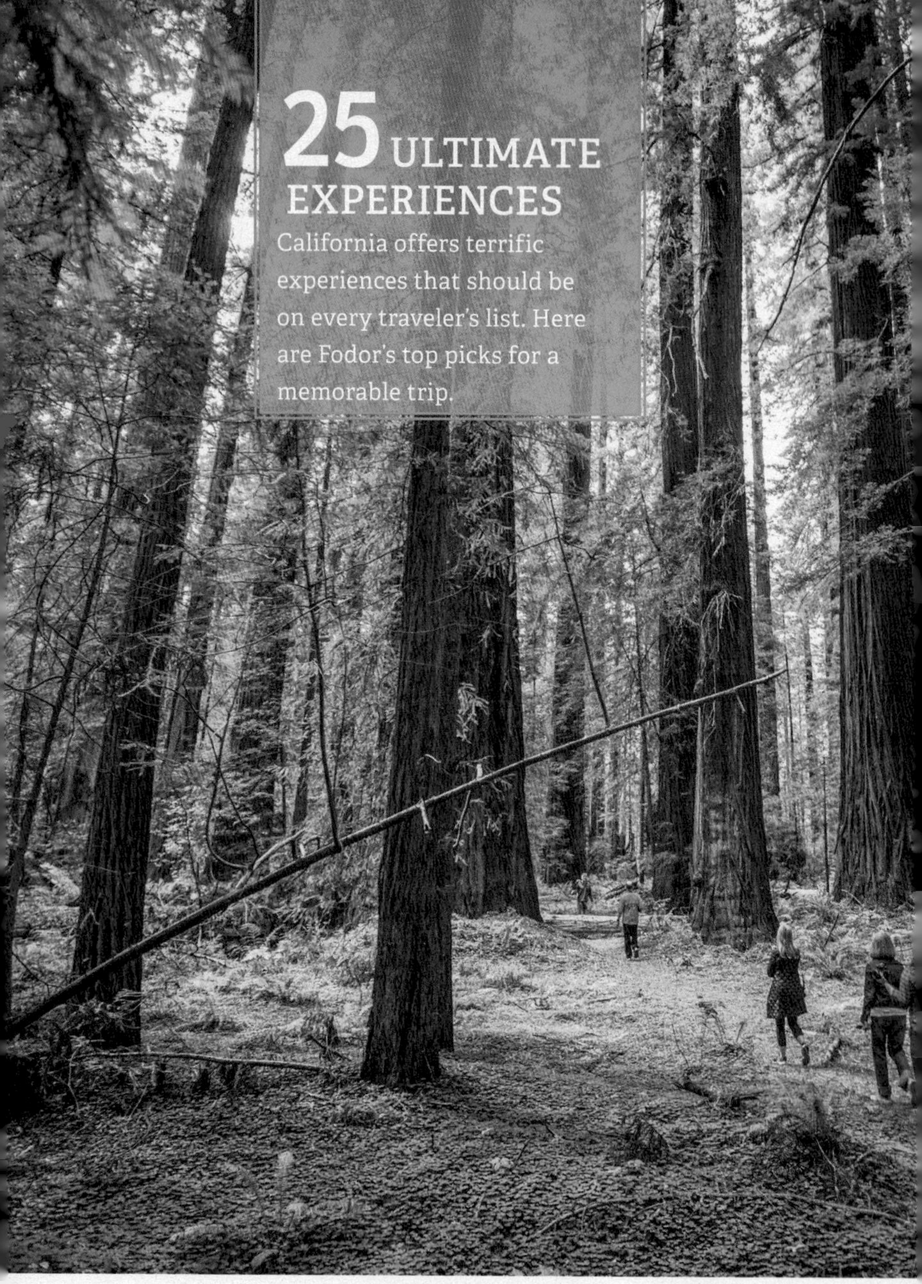

25 ULTIMATE EXPERIENCES
California offers terrific experiences that should be on every traveler's list. Here are Fodor's top picks for a memorable trip.

1 Crane Your Neck at Redwood National and State Parks

Redwood National and State Parks have the tallest trees on Earth (300–400 feet), and hug 40 miles of California coastline. There are countless things to see and do including camping, hiking, fishing, and kayaking. *(Ch. 22)*

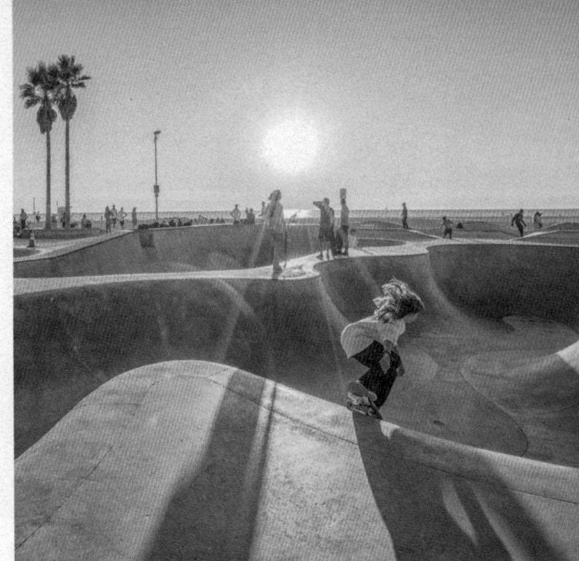

2 Find the Weird at Venice Beach

California's counterculture—bodybuilders at Muscle Beach, head shops on the boardwalk—contrasts with multimillion-dollar homes along the Venice Canals. *(Ch. 6)*

3 Catch Waves in Malibu

Surfrider Beach, a stretch of Malibu that includes the Malibu Pier, is popular with surfers and beach bums. On Zuma Beach, surfers share the water with sea lions. *(Ch. 6)*

4 Suspend Disbelief at Universal Studios

Tour sets like *Jaws* and *Back to the Future*, or visit The Wizarding World of Harry Potter and Jurassic World. *(Ch. 6)*

5 Dive Into History in Chinatown

In San Francisco's Chinatown, the oldest in the United States and the largest outside of Asia, see Chinatown Dragon Gate and Golden Gate Fortune Cookie Factory. *(Ch. 18)*

6 Spot Whales in Monterey

Depending on the season, you can charter boats to witness gray, humpback, and blue whales spyhopping, breaching, and spouting water. *(Ch. 12)*

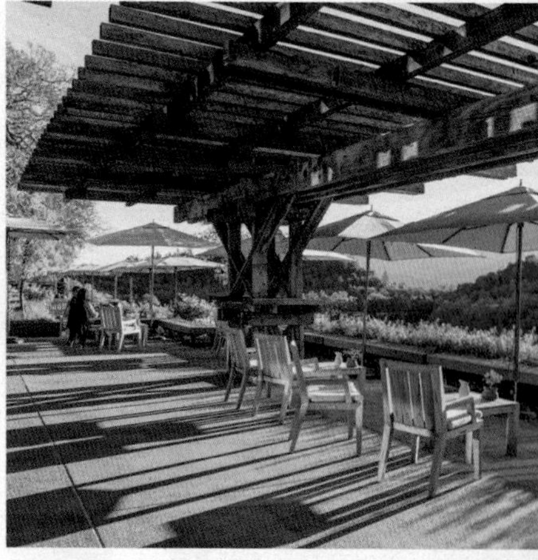

7 Drink All the Wine at a Wine Tasting

Up and down the coast are some of the best winemakers on the planet, and the crown jewels reside in Napa and Sonoma counties. *(Ch. 20)*

8 Hike the Hollywood Sign

The iconic Hollywood sign was originally erected in 1923 and read "Hollywoodland." The easiest path starts from the Griffith Park Observatory. *(Ch. 6)*

9 Cross the Golden Gate Bridge

Opened in 1937, this mile-long suspension bridge connects San Francisco to Marin County and is a stunning display of engineering. *(Ch. 18)*

10 Get a Bird's-Eye View of Palm Springs

Ride the Palm Springs Aerial Tramway—the world's largest rotating tramway. At the top (8,516 feet) are restaurants and hiking trails. *(Ch. 7)*

11 Relive Youth at Disneyland

This truly is the happiest place on Earth. *(Ch. 5)*

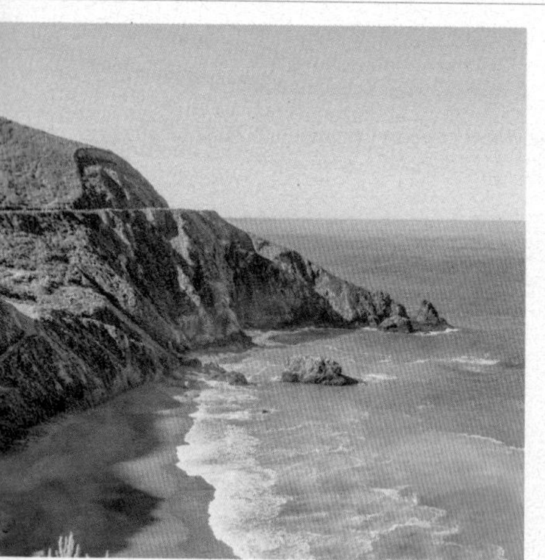

12 Find Jaw-Dropping Vistas at Big Sur

Spectacular Highway 1 winds around the Pacific Ocean amid jagged mountains and redwood trees. *(Ch. 11)*

13 See Wildlife in San Diego

The San Diego Zoo and the San Diego Safari Park showcase wildlife without the claustrophobic animal cages. *(Ch. 4)*

14 Commune with Nature at Yosemite National Park

Yosemite is known for its giant sequoia trees, epic waterfalls, and abundance of wildlife. *(Ch. 14)*

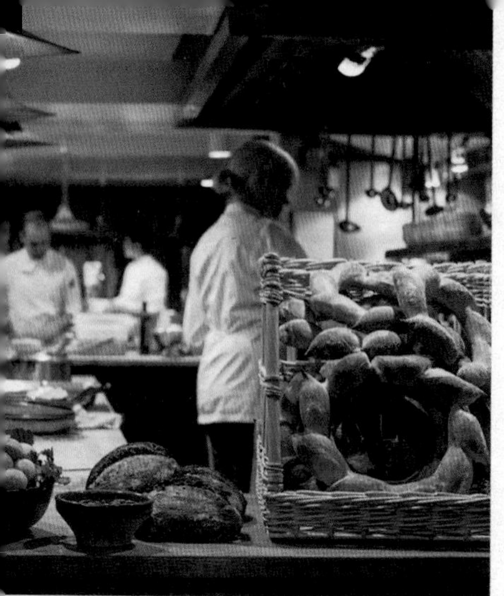

15 Eat Your Way Through Berkeley

Explore Berkeley's campus, and then dine in the nearby Gourmet Ghetto (Shattuck Avenue), where chef Alice Waters got her start. *(Ch. 19)*

16 Camp in Joshua Tree

Just east of Palm Springs is this national park, named for the yucca trees that Mormons named after the biblical Joshua, who raised his hands into the sky. *(Ch. 8)*

17 Traverse Death Valley

One of the hottest places on Earth, Death Valley sits on the eastern edge of California along the border with Nevada. *(Ch. 10)*

18 Old Mission Santa Barbara

The "Queen of Missions"—one of the Central Coast's most photographed structures—also contains superb colonial Spanish/Mexican art. *(Ch. 11)*

19 Ski at Mammoth

Near Yosemite National Park and built on a volcano, California's largest ski resort (roughly 3,500 skiable acres) draws millions of skiers and snowboarders each year. *(Ch. 15)*

20 Witness Greatness in Sport

Check out the San Diego Padres; Los Angeles Lakers or Dodgers; Sacramento Kings; and, in San Francisco, the Giants, '49ers, and Golden State Warriors. *(Ch. 4, 6, 16, 18)*

21 Go to a Show Taping in L.A.

Dozens of sitcoms, talk shows, and game shows film every day in Los Angeles, and you can get tickets to be an audience member. *(Ch. 6)*

22 See a Concert at the Hollywood Bowl

A live music amphitheater built into the side of the Hollywood Hills, the venue is known for its incredible acoustics. *(Ch. 6)*

23 See Stars on the Hollywood Walk of Fame

The first stars were revealed in the early 1960s; today, more than 2,600 dot the pavement. *(Ch. 6)*

24 Experience Opulence at Hearst Castle

Once a celebrity hot spot hosting roaring '20s parties, you can tour the palace's zoo, gold-leaf Roman pool, and priceless art collection. *(Ch. 11)*

25 Get an Adrenaline Rush at Lake Tahoe

Straddling California and Nevada, Lake Tahoe is a summer and winter wonderland for adventure enthusiasts. *(Ch. 17)*

California Today

"Has the Golden State Lost Its Luster?" "Is the California Dream Dead?" So read the rueful headlines upon the early-2021 announcement of California's first-ever population decline (in 2020) and, based on recent census data, the loss of a congressional seat. These articles and similar pieces detailed the supposedly insurmountable obstacles—most notably the high cost of living (especially housing), but also wildfires, drought, crime, traffic congestion, homelessness, COVID-19, and high taxes—fueling out-of-state migration.

So dire were some of the assessments that one might have assumed there was no reason to stay (or come for a visit). This was despite the fact that everything that has lured settlers and tourists from the get-go—among them breathtaking scenery, abundant natural resources, agricultural bounty, and a hospitable climate—remains well in evidence.

Although California, like the rest of the nation and world, faces daunting challenges, the same gloomy predictions (often bearing precisely the same "lost its luster" and "dream dead" headlines) have appeared before: in the middle of the Great Recession (2009), after the first dot-com implosion (2000), all the way back to the gold and silver busts of the 19th century. And guess what? In every instance, the state bounced back, sometimes brilliantly.

Each allegedly ruinous calamity required reinvention, and each time residents rose to the occasion. Based on the past, there's no reason to think that the Golden State won't regain its luster—if it's even been lost.

POPULATION, POTENTIAL

California's birth rate and the pace of migration may have slowed, but they're hardly stagnant. For perspective, consider that the current population of just under 40 million (an eighth of the U.S. total) represents a 2.2 million increase between 2010 and 2020, the third-highest after Texas and Florida. While many residents departing California cite the high cost of living, recent transplants tend to perceive the same potential in the state as previous settlers.

HISTORICAL CONTEXT

By most accounts, the ancestors of California's indigenous peoples migrated from Asia, traversing a land bridge across the Bering Strait that formerly joined what's now Russia and Alaska. Some of these trailblazers continued south to California, flourishing for centuries off the fertile land. Many famous place names—Malibu, Napa, Ojai, Shasta, and Sonoma among them—reflect this heritage.

Millennia later, Spanish explorers ventured north from Mexico searching for gold, with converts to Christianity the quest of 18th-century missionaries. Nineteenth-century miners rushed here from the world over also seeking gold—the state achieved statehood two years after the precious metal's 1848 discovery.

During the 20th century, successive, sometimes overlapping, waves of newcomers followed in their footsteps: real-estate speculators, would-be motion-picture actors and producers, Dust Bowl farmers and migrant workers, Asians fleeing poverty or chasing opportunity, sexual and gender pioneers, artists, dot-commers, and venture capitalists.

POLITICS

The result is a population that leans toward idealism (some say utopianism)—without necessarily being as liberal as voter-registration statistics might lead one to think. (Democrats hold a 2–1 registration advantage over Republicans, the latter essentially tied with "no party preference.") This is Ronald Reagan's old stomping ground after all, and Herbert Hoover's, and Richard Nixon was born here. If you wander into some inland counties, you may see signs proposing a breakaway, more conservative 51st State of Jefferson. Many residents in these areas supported 2021 efforts to recall Governor Gavin Newsom, a liberal Democrat. (Early summer polls indicated the special-election race might be tight, but the governor prevailed by a substantial margin.)

DEMOGRAPHICS

As with politics, despite the stereotype of the blue-eyed, blond surfer, California's population isn't homogeneous either. Latino residents outnumber Whites 39%–36%, with Asians (15%) and African Americans (6%) the next-largest groups. Residents here speak more than 220 languages, making California by far the nation's most linguistically diverse state.

ECONOMICS

Back to California's supposedly desperate situation: keep in mind that, in 2021, the Golden State reported a $75 billion budget *surplus,* hardly numbers to prompt despair and proving the Great Recession doomsayers predicting economic catastrophe way off the mark. California, responsible for 14% of gross domestic product, leads all other states in terms of the income generated by agriculture, tourism, entertainment, and industrial activity. With a gross state product of approximately $3 trillion (median household income about $75,000), by many estimates, California would have the world's fifth-largest economy were it an independent nation.

STILL DREAMIN'

In mid-2021, dueling state-of-the-state analyses appeared within days of each other. A historian's *New York Times* opinion piece described the 2020 census numbers and the loss of the seat in Congress as among recent negative "firsts" for California that had "sapped the collective sense of zealous optimism." The historian also predicted "decades of pain" if politicians don't quickly produce solutions to California's pressing problems.

Two days before the *Times* piece ran, the University of California published a study suggesting pretty much the opposite: that the rate of residents moving out of state is not unusual and isn't something to fret over; that residents, by a 2–1 majority, still believe in the California Dream; and that the state attracts more than half the nation's venture-capital investments, a sign that favorable economic conditions persist.

The naysayers may well be right about California's demise, but if history is any indication, the populace will likely shift gears as necessary. And again the next time it's required.

WHAT'S WHERE

1 San Diego. San Diego's Gaslamp Quarter and early California–theme Old Town have a human scale—but big-ticket animal attractions like the San Diego Zoo pull in visitors.

2 Disneyland and Orange County. A diverse destination with premium resorts and restaurants, strollable waterfront communities, and kid-friendly attractions.

3 Los Angeles. Go for the glitz of the entertainment industry, but stay for the rich arts offerings and cultural communities.

4 Palm Springs and the Desert Resorts. Golf on some of the West's most challenging courses, lounge at fabulous resorts, check out mid-century-modern architectural gems, and trek through primitive desert parks.

5 Joshua Tree National Park. Proximity to major urban areas—as well as world-class rock climbing and nighttime celestial displays—help make this one of the most visited national parks.

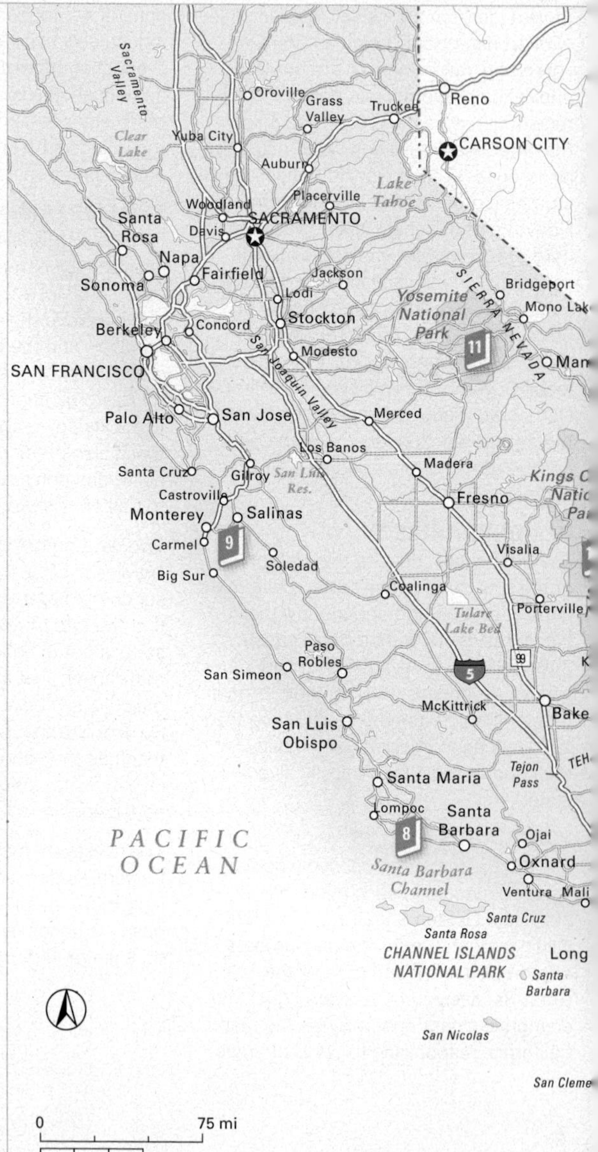

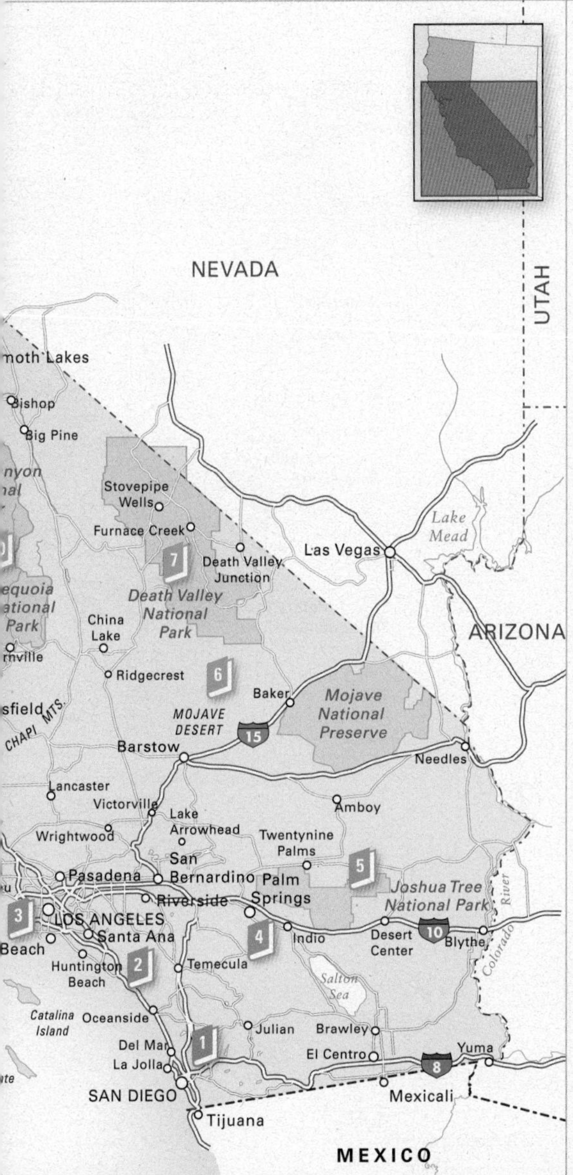

6 Mojave Desert. Material pleasures are in short supply here, but Mother Nature's stark beauty more than compensates.

7 Death Valley National Park. This vast, beautiful national park is often the hottest place in the country.

8 The Central Coast. Three of the state's top stops—swanky Santa Barbara, Hearst Castle, and Big Sur—sit along a scenic 200-mile route. A quick boat trip away lies Channel Islands National Park.

9 Monterey Bay Area. Postcard-perfect Monterey, Victorian-flavored Pacific Grove, and exclusive Carmel all share this stretch of California coast. To the north, Santa Cruz boasts a boardwalk, a UC campus, ethnic clothing shops, and plenty of surfers.

10 Sequoia and Kings Canyon National Parks. The sight of ancient redwoods towering above jagged mountains is breathtaking.

11 Yosemite National Park. The views immortalized by photographer Ansel Adams—towering granite monoliths, verdant glacial valleys, and lofty waterfalls—are still camera-ready.

WHAT'S WHERE

12 Eastern Sierra. In the Mammoth Lakes region, sawtooth mountains and deep powdery snowdrifts create the state's premier conditions for skiing and snowboarding.

13 Sacramento and the Gold Country. The 1849 gold rush that built San Francisco and Sacramento began here, and the former mining camps strung along 185 miles of Highway 49 replay their past to the hilt.

14 Lake Tahoe. With miles of crystalline water reflecting High Sierra peaks, Lake Tahoe is the perfect setting for activities like hiking and golfing in summer and skiing and snowmobiling in winter.

15 San Francisco. To see why many have left their hearts here, you need only explore iconic neighborhoods such as posh Pacific Heights, the Hispanic Mission, and gay-friendly Castro.

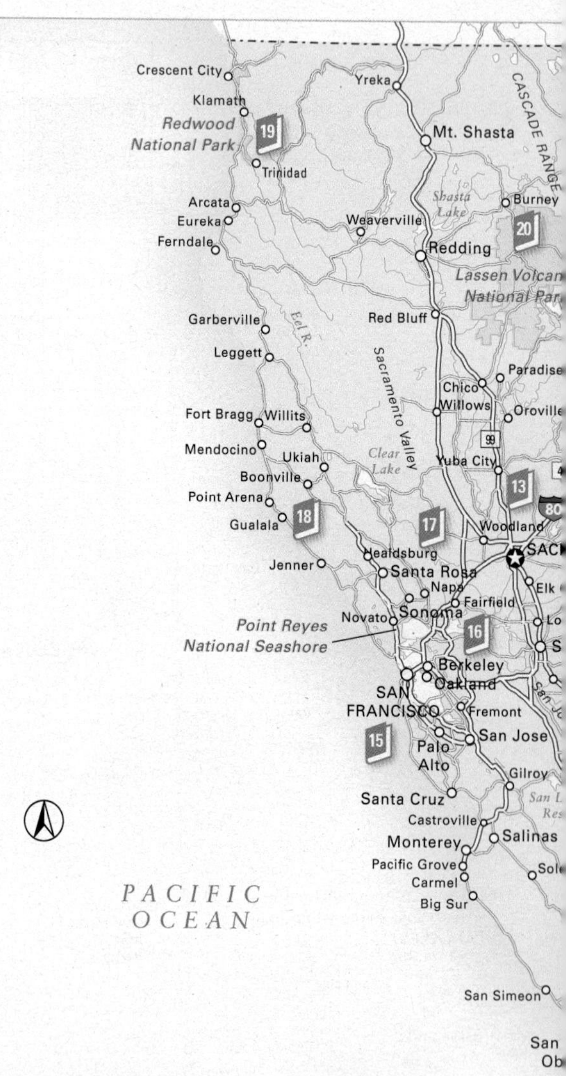

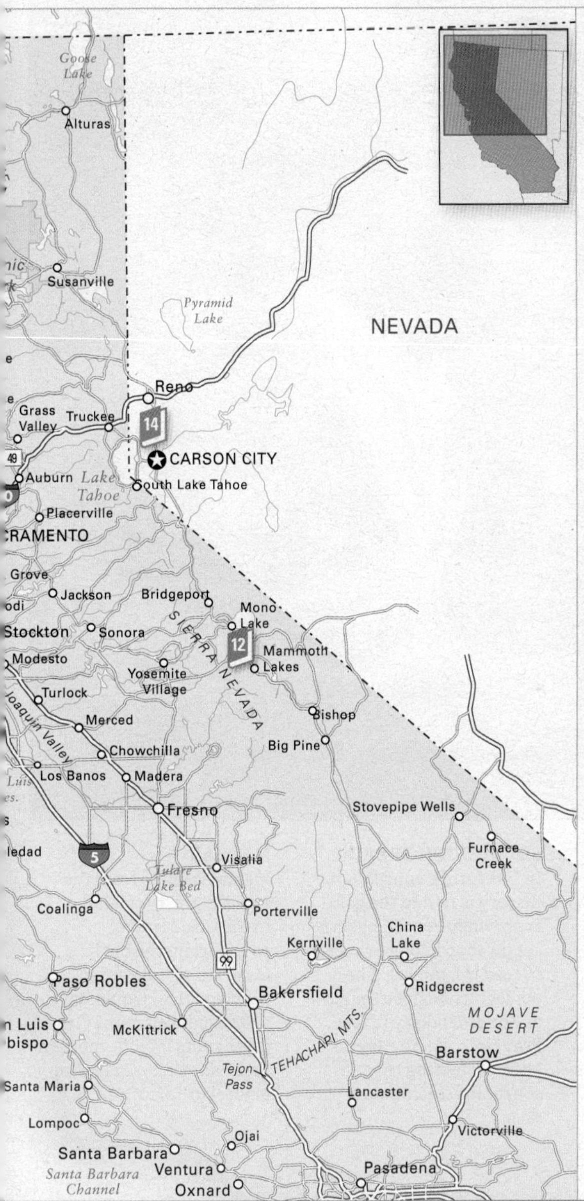

16 The Bay Area. The area that rings San Francisco is nothing like the city—but it is home to some of the nation's great universities, fabulous water views, Silicon Valley, and Alice Waters's Chez Panisse.

17 Napa and Sonoma. By virtue of award-winning vintages, luxe lodgings, and epicurean eats, Napa and Sonoma counties retain their title as *the* California Wine Country.

18 The North Coast. The star attractions here are natural ones, from the secluded beaches and wave-battered bluffs of Point Reyes National Seashore to the towering redwood forests.

19 Redwood National and State Parks. More than 200 miles of trails, ranging from easy to strenuous, allow visitors to spectacular redwood trees in their primitive environments.

20 The Far North. California's far northeast corner is home to snowcapped Mount Shasta, the pristine Trinity Wilderness, and abundant backwoods character.

What to Eat and Drink in California

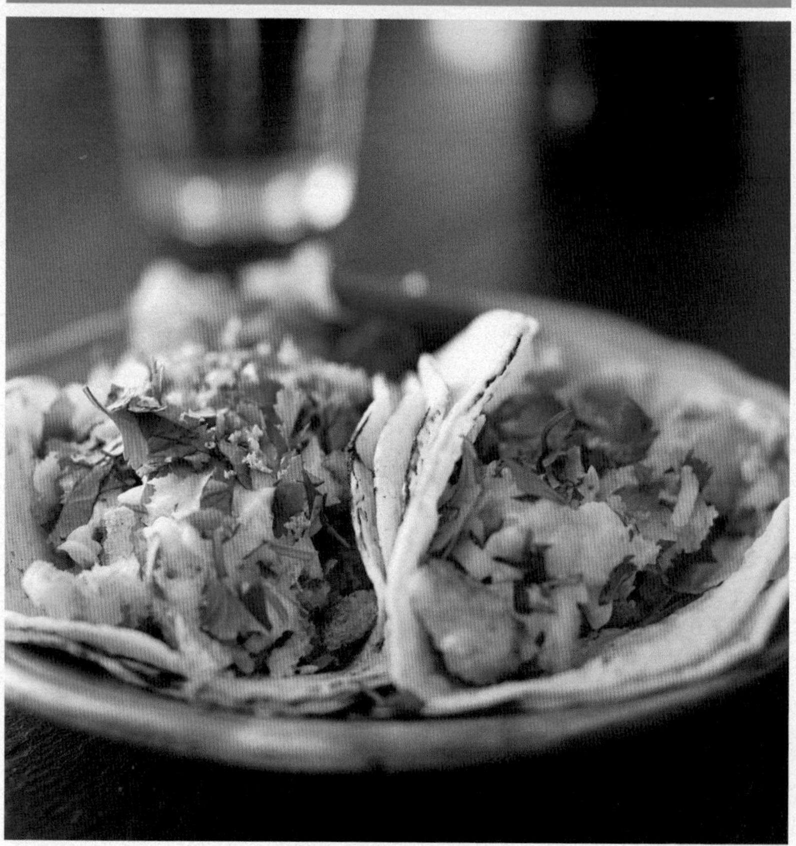

Tacos

TACOS

The Mexican influence on California has taken the taco to all-new heights. For modern/gourmet fare: Guerrilla Tacos in Los Angeles; for fish tacos: Best Fish Taco in Ensenada; for the "Best Taco in California": Nuestro Mexico in Bakersfield; and for simple and classic: La Taqueria in San Francisco.

SOURDOUGH BREAD

In California, sourdough history is tied to the gold rush, when French bakers set up shop in San Francisco to feed the miners. The perfect loaf can be found at Boudin Bakery in San Francisco where they've been perfecting the sourdough recipe since 1849.

MEZCAL

Mezcal is made from the agave plant, typically in Oaxaca, Mexico, so naturally the best Oaxacan restaurant in L.A. (Guelaguetza) would have a top-shelf selection. Other great spots include modern taco joint Petty Cash, and Madre! in Torrance.

Dim sum

WINE AND BEER
California produces world-class wines, but it is also a hotbed of beer making. Check out Stone Brewing in San Diego, Eagle Rock Brewery in L.A., 21st Amendment in San Francisco, or the ultimate classic Sierra Nevada Brewing in Chico.

FRENCH DIP
Not only was the French Dip invented in Los Angeles, two different restaurants claim its origin. Philippe the Original in Downtown opened in 1908 and is a counter-style diner; Cole's also opened in 1908, is (slightly) more upscale, and features a hidden speakeasy in the back of the restaurant.

MAI TAIS
White rum, dark rum, Curaçao liqueur, orgeat syrup, and lime juice. The drink was invented (allegedly) by Victor Bergeron of Trader Vic's in Oakland, California, though Donn Beach (of Don the Beachcomber fame) claims he invented it in the 1930s in Hollywood.

DOUGHNUTS
Doughnuts in Los Angeles have taken on a life of their own with some of the most inventive and creative sweets around. There's the iconic Randy's Donuts; California Donuts covered with Lucky Charms; Blinkie's Donut Emporium filled with Bavarian cream; or Colorado Donuts where doughnut design is Instagram-worthy.

DIM SUM
There are more Asian Americans in the San Gabriel Valley than almost any other locale in the United States, and the food culture here rivals the best restaurants in Asia. The most delicious dim sum (dumplings typically eaten at breakfast) can be had at Din Tai Fung.

KOREAN BBQ
Los Angeles has the largest Korean population outside of Korea, and that fact is very much reflected in the food. For traditional Korean BBQ feasts, check out Park's BBQ, Kobawoo House, or Soot Bull Jeep.

10 Best Wineries in Napa and Sonoma

JOSEPH PHELPS VINEYARDS
In good weather, there are few more glorious tasting spots in the Napa Valley than the terrace at this St. Helena winery. Phelps is known for its Cabernet Sauvignons and Insignia, a Bordeaux blend. The wine-related seminars here are smart and entertaining.

JORDAN VINEYARD AND WINERY
A winery with a knack for discerning hospitality, Jordan produces a single Russian River Valley Chardonnay and an Alexander Valley Cabernet Sauvignon that perennially rank high on lists of best restaurant wines nationwide.

RIDGE VINEYARDS
Oenophiles will be familiar with Ridge, which produces some of California's best Cabernet Sauvignon, Chardonnay, and Zinfandel. You can taste wines made from grapes grown here at Ridge's Healdsburg vineyards, and some from its neighbors, along with wines made at its older Santa Cruz Mountains winery.

ASHES AND DIAMONDS
Record producer Kashy Khaledi opened this winery whose splashy glass-and-metal tasting space evokes classic mid-century modern California architecture. In their restrained elegance, the all- Bordeaux wines by two much-heralded pros hark back to 1960s Napa, too.

THE DONUM ESTATE
Single-vineyard Pinot Noirs exhibiting "power yet elegance" made the reputation of this Carneros District winery also known for smooth, balanced Chardonnays. The three dozen–plus large-scale, museum-quality outdoor sculptures by the likes of Anselm Kiefer add a touch of high culture to a visit.

DOMAINE CARNEROS
The main building was modeled after an 18th-century French château owned by the Champagne-making Taittinger family, one of whose members selected the site of this Napa winery. The experience of sipping sparkling wine on the terrace feels noble indeed.

SILVER OAK
"Only one wine can be your best," was cofounder Justin Meyer's rationale for Silver Oak's decision to focus solely on Cabernet. The winery pours its two yearly offerings (one from Napa, the other from Sonoma) in a glass-walled eco-friendly tasting room in the Alexander Valley.

Inglenook

INGLENOOK
History buffs won't want to miss Inglenook, which was founded in the 19th century by a Finnish sea captain and rejuvenated over the past several decades by filmmaker Francis Ford Coppola. You can learn all about this fabled property on a tour or while tasting in an opulent salon—or just sip peacefully at a wine bar with a picturesque courtyard.

SCHRAMSBERG
The 19th-century cellars at sparkling wine producer Schramsberg hold millions of bottles. On the fascinating tour you'll learn how the bubblies at this Calistoga mainstay are made using the *méthode traditionelle,* and how the bottles are "riddled" (turned every few days) by hand.

IRON HORSE VINEYARDS
Proof that tasting sparkling wine doesn't have to be stuffy, this winery on the outskirts of Sebastopol pours its selections outdoors, with tremendous views of vine-covered hills that make the top-notch bubblies (and a few still wines) taste even better.

10 Best Beaches in San Diego

CORONADO

Often praised for its sparkling sand, the island is home to Hotel del Coronado, a 130-year-old luxury hotel perfect for postbeach snacks; Del Beach, which is open to the public; and Dog Beach where pooches can run free sans leash.

MISSION BEACH

Located near SeaWorld San Diego, Mission Beach is home to a bustling boardwalk that's frequented by walkers, cyclists, and people-watchers. The bay is popular for water sports such as stand-up paddleboarding and Jet Skiing, but the beach is best known for Belmont Park, its oceanfront amusement park.

WINDANSEA BEACH

Seasoned surfers should head to La Jolla's Windansea Beach for powerful waves. Tucked away in a residential area, Windansea's entrance is marked by large rocks that make for a great place to watch or dry out, but recreational swimming is not advised here due to the strong surf.

TORREY PINES STATE BEACH

Situated at the base of a 1,500-acre natural reserve, La Jolla's Torrey Pines State Beach offers a long, narrow stretch of pristine beach framed by picturesque sea cliffs. Beachgoers can add a hike to their itinerary that starts or finishes on the sand, with plenty of lookout areas for great photo ops. Beyond the bluffs, a salt marsh provides seclusion from businesses and their associated street noise.

LA JOLLA SHORES

Pack up the whole family for a beach day in La Jolla Shores, which is known for its calm waves, two parks, and playground. Sea caves and underwater canyons that are part of La Jolla Underwater Park and Ecological Reserve—a marine protected area—attract kayakers and scuba divers.

DEL MAR CITY BEACH

In the upscale coastal neighborhood of Del Mar lie two beach parks that are popular for special events because of their stunning views of the Pacific. Seagrove Park is perched on the hill at the end of 15th Street, with benches for ocean gazing and winding paths along the bluffs. Farther north across the railroad tracks, Powerhouse Park offers easy beach access, a playground area, and a volleyball court.

La Jolla Shores is the best beach in San Diego for water sports.

SWAMI'S STATE BEACH
West of the magnificent Self-Realization Fellowship Temple and Meditation Gardens in Encinitas, this beach draws surfers and yogis in with its Zen vibes, while others treat the steep staircase leading down to the beach as a workout, with a rewarding view of sea cliffs waiting at the bottom. At low tide, shells and other sea creatures are left behind for beachcombers to easily discover.

FLETCHER COVE BEACH PARK
Nestled in the heart of Solana Beach, Fletcher Cove Beach Park doubles as a recreational park and beach access area. Here you'll find a basketball court, playground, lawn area, and picnic tables. A paved ramp leads down to the crescent-shape beach that's flanked by cliffs on both sides. For sweeping views of the ocean, position yourself at one of the lookouts outfitted with seating and/or binoculars—yup, binoculars are waiting for you.

MOONLIGHT STATE BEACH
Fans of active beach days should head to this Encinitas beach. Volleyball courts, picnic tables, and playgrounds line the beach, with a concession stand, equipment rentals, and free Sunday concerts in high season.

BEACON'S BEACH
Follow the windy dirt path laden with switchbacks down to find Beacon's Beach in Encinitas, a well-known beach spot and favorite locals' hangout; on maps it may be labeled Leucadia State Beach. Since its entrance is hidden below sea cliffs on a one-way residential street, Beacon's Beach has an air of exclusivity. With plenty of space to spread out here, you won't have to infringe on sun-worshipping neighbors.

10 Best Photo Ops in San Francisco

THE PAINTED LADIES

Familiar to fans of the 1990s' TV show *Full House*, the so-called Painted Ladies or Seven Sisters are a row of seven colorful and beautifully maintained Queen Anne–style houses just off Alamo Square Park. Take photos at midday for clear city views.

TWIN PEAKS

These two adjacent peaks near Noe Valley are at the near geographic center of San Francisco, with an elevation of 925 feet. Especially pretty (and popular, but chilly) at sunrise and sunset, the peaks provide sweeping 180-degree views of the Bay Area, with a great perspective on downtown San Francisco, the Bay Bridge, and the tips of the Golden Gate Bridge.

THE PALACE OF FINE ARTS

This stirringly lovely terra-cotta–color domed structure on a lagoon near the Marina's yacht harbor has an otherworldly quality about it. Built in 1915 for an exposition, the palace is a San Francisco architect's version of a Roman ruin, and it's been eliciting gasps ever since. It's a popular wedding spot, which is good if you like happy couples in your photos.

LANDS END COASTAL TRAIL

This 4-mile trail winds and twists along the rugged cliffs of San Francisco Bay, offering stunning views of the Golden Gate Bridge and surprisingly woodsy forest. At the 1.3-mile mark, turn left at the wooden staircase to explore Mile Rock Beach and the Lands End Labyrinth. On a clear day, you can see the Golden Gate Bridge in the distance.

THE PRESIDIO
As the gateway to the Golden Gate Bridge, San Francisco's 1,500-acre Presidio is part of the National Park System and offers incredible views of the bridge and the sprawling landscape that surrounds it. The Presidio also abuts Baker Beach, a stretch of sand with an alternative perspective.

MUIR WOODS NATIONAL MONUMENT
Naturalist John Muir wrote, "Most people are on the world, not in it—have no conscious sympathy or relationship to anything about them ..." It's hard not to feel connected as you walk the shaded paths of Muir Woods amid the towering majesty of the redwood groves.

UNION SQUARE
This lively and central location is a great spot to capture cable cars as they rumble by. Also, the towering Dewey Monument pillar, topped triumphantly by Nike, the Greek goddess of victory, is a legitimately beautiful sculpture. Relax on the steps and soak in or photograph the city.

Treasure Island

TREASURE ISLAND
Tiny, man-made Treasure Island is generally off the tourist track, so your photos won't be crowded with selfie-takers. Sitting right in the middle of San Francisco Bay, it offers gorgeous views of the San Francisco skyline, especially at night when everything is lit up.

HAWK HILL
At a high point on the south-facing Marin Headlands, Hawk Hill lies opposite the city with vistas of the Pacific and of the Golden Gate Bridge as it enters San Francisco. True to its name, it's also a great spot for nature watching. Hawk Hill is the site of the autumnal raptor migration and also serves as a habitat for the Mission Blue Butterfly.

BERNAL HEIGHTS
This somewhat stumpy-looking mound rises unenthusiastically above the houses of the surrounding neighborhood. But, pictures taken *from* Bernal Heights Hill offer 360-degree panoramic views. Take a sunset stroll here for stunning San Fran shots.

10 Best Celebrity Hangouts in Los Angeles

THE HOLLYWOOD ROOSEVELT

The Hollywood Roosevelt is one of L.A.'s oldest hotels, and has hosted numerous celebrities and dignitaries in its Spanish Colonial Revival rooms. Set in the heart of Hollywood, it offers a convenient location as well as a number of watering holes, including Tropicana Pool & Café.

THE GROVE

L.A. may be strewn with outdoor malls, but it's The Grove that gets the highest billing, not just for its collection of mid- to high-end shops and restaurants, but also for its next-door neighbor, the Farmers Market. It's also one of the best places to see stars like Lena Headey, Zendaya, and Mario Lopez.

CAFÉ GRATITUDE LARCHMONT

Round out your L.A. vacation with a plant-based meal at local chain Café Gratitude. For a celeb sighting, head to their Larchmont Boulevard location where Jake Gyllenhaal and Beyoncé obligingly declare what they're grateful for before digging in.

PINZ BOWLING CENTER

For a bit of family-friendly fun, head to Pinz in Studio City, where bowling is more than just a game, it's also a neon- and black-light party. Celebrities often pop in here for bowling night, from A-listers like Vin Diesel and Jessica Alba to performers like Bruno Mars and Missy Elliott.

NOBU MALIBU

Nobu is a known A-list hot spot that's hosted everyone from Keanu Reeves to Kendall Jenner. Even if you don't spot a star, it's still worth the trip for its impeccable sushi and sashimi. Be warned, though: mingling with A-listers doesn't come cheap.

TOSCANA

Upscale Brentwood is home to many celebrities, and rustic trattoria Toscana is one of their neighborhood haunts. It may not be L.A.'s best Italian restaurant—for that, check out Osteria Mozza—but for star sightings, it's your best bet.

CHATEAU MARMONT

The Chateau Marmont is possibly L.A.'s best-known celebrity haunt. Come for brunch in the garden terrace or drop in at night for the Hollywood-inspired cocktails. Photos are not allowed.

Catch

CRAIG'S

A West Hollywood dining staple, Craig's plain facade provides a safe haven for the movie industry's most important names and well-known faces like John Legend and Chrissy Teigen. Just keep in mind this joint is always busy, so you might not even get a table. It's a good thing the food is worth the effort.

CATCH

Secure a table at the flora-cluttered Catch in West Hollywood and rub elbows with the likes of David Beckham and the Jenner-Kardashian clan. This eatery is as L.A. as you can get, with its alfresco setting, vegan and gluten-free offerings, and locally and sustainably grown ingredients.

RUNYON CANYON

Out of L.A.'s numerous beautiful hiking spots, Runyon Canyon gets the biggest share of celebrity regulars, probably because it's strategically tucked between the Hollywood Hills, where many stars live, and the Sunset Strip. It's also a great venue for getting some fresh air, not to mention an ideal spot to take panoramic sunset photos.

What to Watch and Read Before Your Trip

MULHOLLAND DRIVE

Surreal, psychotic, and artsy, David Lynch's film paints L.A. as a city of scary fun house turns that blur the lines between reality and cuts from a movie. Such dichotomies exist as well in the two main characters: Betty (Naomi Watts), the blond Midwesterner fresh to L.A., and Rita (Laura Elena Harring), an amnesiac shrouded in darkness and mystery.

TANGERINE

Shot completely with an iPhone camera, this indie film explores the streets of Hollywood with a close lens on a few very moving, human characters. Recently out of prison, a transgender prostitute tries to track down her pimp and his new girlfriend with the help of a friend. It's hard to explain just how much light, humor, and beauty fills this film—you just have to see it for yourself.

THE REVOLT OF THE COCKROACH PEOPLE BY OSCAR ZETA ACOSTA

Based on real events, this story outlines many aspects of east Los Angeles's Chicano movement through protests, marches, and court cases. The main protagonist is based on the fascinating author himself, an activist, lawyer/politician, and key player in the movement.

THE BIRDS

Alfred Hitchcock's 1963 *The Birds* centers around a small Northern Californian town under attack by swarming, possessed birds. Although, you'll never again look at a crow in quite the same way after watching this graphic thriller, it also showcases the beauty of Sonoma County's coast and the charm of Bodega Bay, the town where most of the movie was filmed.

THE GIRLS BY EMMA CLINE

In this nuanced story about coming-of-age in the Sonoma County town of Petaluma, a 14-year-old narrator yearns for excitement, attention and beauty—and falls into the violent, psychological mind-trip of a Charles Manson–like cult. Beautiful and gripping, Cline's novel shares a gritty, late 1960s Sonoma County—one that couldn't be further from the world of Cabernets and Pinots and is instead full of long hair, VW buses, angst, and seduction.

THE GANGSTER WE ARE ALL LOOKING FOR BY LE THI DIEM THUY

The characters of Thuy's novel, based on the author's own childhood, are Vietnamese refugees in the late '70s, adjusting to life in crowded bungalows and apartments of Normal Heights, Linda Vista, and east San Diego.

GUN, WITH OCCASIONAL MUSIC BY JONATHAN LETHEM

Lethem started his career with a captivating but decidedly weird novel set in San Francisco and Oakland. In this sci-fi noir detective story, people rub elbows with talking, man-sized, genetically engineered animals, and everyone lives under a monetized "karma" system like that used in modern-day China to track and influence its citizens.

BURMA SUPERSTAR BY DESMOND TAN AND KATE LEAHY

Burmese food is increasingly popular in San Francisco, where the Burma Superstar restaurant is a hit. This cookbook offers a look into the flavor-packed southeast Asian cuisine.

Chapter 2

TRAVEL SMART

Updated by
Daniel Mangin

★ CAPITAL:
Sacramento

POPULATION:
39.5 million

LANGUAGE:
English

$ CURRENCY:
U.S. dollar

COUNTRY CODE:
1

EMERGENCIES:
911

DRIVING:
On the right

ELECTRICITY:
120–240 v/60 cycles; plugs have two or three rectangular prongs

TIME:
Three hours behind New York

WEB RESOURCES:
www.visitcalifornia.com, www.parks.ca.gov, dot.ca.gov/travel, travel.state.gov

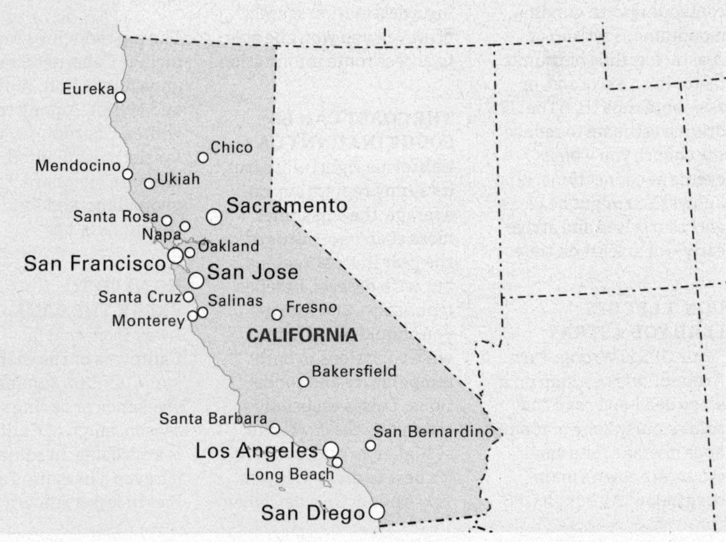

Know Before You Go

To help you prepare for a visit to the vast, diverse, unique state of California, below are tips about driving, destinations, the weather, saving money at restaurants and hotels, wildlife, cannabis tourism, and things to see and do that may save you time or money or increase peace of mind.

ROAD TRIPS TAKE TIME

California has some of the most scenic drives in the world. It's also the third-largest state behind Alaska and Texas and, in square miles, is similar in size to Sweden, Japan, or Paraguay. So, if you want to see all its beaches, deserts, mountains, and forests, you'll need a car—and, perhaps, a bit of patience.

A road trip through even half of the state takes several hours in the best of traffic (frequently not the case), and this doesn't count contending with winding, mountainous terrain or coastal fog. Rule of thumb: factor in an extra 20% or 25% more time than the GPS driving estimate to reduce the chance you'll miss events or connections. Who knows? You might be pleasantly surprised and arrive early—or at least on time.

DON'T LET GPS LEAD YOU ASTRAY

"Your GPS is Wrong: Turn Around," warns a sign on a steep dead-end road that some smartphone mapping apps mistake for a small mountain town's main drag below. Although GPS is generally reliable in cities and suburbs, it's less so in coastal, mountain, and desert areas, including some national and state parks. In addition to referencing the maps in this book, back yourself up with old-school atlases or fold-out paper maps.

If you plot out a trip and begin navigation while your smartphone reception is good, you should still receive turning directions even if you move out of cell range. If you're already out of range when initiating a destination search, however, you won't be able to access route information.

THE COAST CAN BE FOGGY IN SUNNY CA

California rightfully earns its sunny reputation: on average, the sun shines more than two-thirds of the year in most regions, but with deserts, beaches, mountains, and forests, you should prepare for wide variations in both temperature and conditions. This is especially true along the coast and at higher altitudes, where it's best to dress in layers year-round. On a day when it's 85 or 95 degrees inland, the temperature along the coast can be 55 and windy.

In July and August, hot inland temperatures often cause cooler Pacific Ocean air—in the form of fog—to blanket areas nearest the shore. As a rule along the coast: the farther south you go, the drier and hotter the weather tends to be. The farther north, the cooler and wetter you're likely to find it.

"WINE COUNTRY" IS MORE THAN NAPA AND SONOMA

Modern California winemaking got its start in Sonoma County, and Napa Valley wines raised the state's profile worldwide, but with about 4,000 wineries from the Oregon border to San Diego County producing nearly ¾ billion gallons—80-plus percent of the U.S. total—the whole state's pretty much "Wine Country." Tasting rooms abound, even in unlikely places.

The top red-wine grapes include Cabernet Sauvignon, Pinot Noir, Zinfandel, and Merlot. Among the whites, Chardonnay is by far the most planted, with French Colombard, Sauvignon Blanc, and Pinot Gris the runners-up.

NO NEED TO BREAK THE BANK

Away from coastal California or the eastern mountains on summer weekends or during ski season, much of California is affordable. In some cases, it's even a bargain. Tasting fees in lesser-known wine regions, for example, are at least half the price of those in high-profile ones, and some wineries even provide sips for free. In many inland areas, except for the fanciest bed-and-breakfasts, room rates trend way lower than by the shore.

AVOIDING STICKER SHOCK AT RESTAURANTS

Even if you're not dining at temples of haute cuisine, eating out in California can induce sticker shock. There are several ways to avoid this. Have the day's fancy meal at brunch or lunch, when prices tend to be lower. Happy hour, when a restaurant might serve a signature appetizer or smaller version of a famous plate at a lower price, is another option. Even small towns in the interior are likely to have a purveyor or two of gourmet food to go, making picnicking in a park or eating back at your lodging a viable strategy.

AVOIDING STICKER SHOCK AT HOTELS

California's hotels, inns, and resorts are the most expensive from late spring to early fall. The easiest way to avoid sticker shock is to come during winter when, except at ski resorts and a few desert hot spots, prices are the least expensive. Year-round you can save money by traveling midweek, when rates tend to drop. Visiting during the shoulder seasons of mid-to-late spring and mid-to-late fall, when the weather can be nice and the crowds less formidable, can also save you money. Many travelers cut costs by booking a big-city business hotel on the weekend, when rates trend lower (with Sunday often the cheapest night of the week at such places). Conversely, weekend prices at beach or countryside resorts are generally high but sometimes drop midweek.

MAKERS AND MUSEUMS

The state's early-21st-century DIY types birthed what's come to be known as the maker movement, and throughout California you'll see evidence of this artisanal activity. Blue jeans, lasers, Apple computers, sourdough bread, Popsicles, McDonald's, Barbie Dolls, Hollywood movie glamour, and television all emerged from California. Nearly 3,000 museums (more than any other state) honor such accomplishments and more—if you can think of it, there's probably a museum here that celebrates it.

PLAY BALL

Because the weather is basically great year-round, there's a dynamic sports culture in the Golden State. Spectacular (and often free) recreation areas and parks offer opportunities for surfing, skiing, hiking, and biking, among other activities.

If you're more into spectating, California supports more professional sports teams than any other state, including five MLB, four NBA (plus one WNBA), three NFL and NHL franchises, and several (men's and women's) soccer squads. Any day of the week, you can witness athletic greatness at the highest levels.

CALL OF THE WILDLIFE

Off the coast, creatures from gray and humpback whales to blue whales and orcas might come into view, along with sea lions, elephant seals, dolphins, and the occasional shark. Inland forests contain black bears, mountain lions, bobcats, beavers, and foxes. The desert supplies no end of reptiles, and the entire state is a birder's paradise.

Wild animals generally avoid interacting with humans, but contact is not unheard of. Most state and national parks post advice about steering clear of potentially dangerous encounters and what to do if you find yourself in one.

POT IS LEGAL, BUT...

Marijuana is legal in California for medical and recreational purposes. If you're 21 (or 18 with a doctor's order) and have proof of age or medical status, you can acquire and use marijuana, albeit not always in public. The California Cannabis Portal website maintains a searchable database (🌐 *search.cannabis.ca.gov/retailers*) of licensed dispensaries, where cannabis might come as flowers, edibles, and concentrates, among other things. The Cannabis Travel Association (🌐 *www.cannabistravelassociation.org*) promotes "safe and responsible cannabis tourism," and provides general information.

Getting Here and Around

From Los Angeles To:	By Air	By Car
San Diego	55 mins	2 hrs
Death Valley	No flights	5 hrs
San Francisco	1 hr 30 mins	6 hrs
Monterey	1 hr 10 mins	5 hrs
Santa Barbara	50 mins	1 hr 40 mins
Big Sur	No flights	5 hrs 40 mins
Sacramento	1 hr 30 mins	6 hrs

From San Francisco To:	By Air	By Car
San Jose	No flights	1 hr
Monterey	N/A (no nonstops)	2 hrs
Los Angeles	1 hr 30 mins	5 hrs 40 mins
Portland, OR	1 hr 50 mins	10 hrs
Mendocino	No flights	3 hrs
Yosemite NP/ Fresno	1 hr	3 hrs
Lake Tahoe/ Reno	1 hr	3 hrs 30 mins

 Air

Most national and many international airlines fly to California. Flying time to the state is about 6½ hours from New York and 4¾ hours from Chicago. Travel from London to either Los Angeles or San Francisco is 11½ hours and from Sydney approximately 14 hours. Flying between San Francisco and Los Angeles takes about 90 minutes.

From Los Angeles To:	Route	Distance
San Diego	I–5 or I–405	127 miles
Las Vegas	I–10 to I–15	270 miles
Death Valley	I–10 to I–15 to Hwy. 127 to Hwy. 190	260 miles
San Francisco	I–5 to I–580 to I–80	382 miles
Monterey	U.S. 101 to Salinas, Hwy. 68 to Hwy. 1	320 miles
Santa Barbara	U.S. 101	95 miles
Big Sur	U.S. 101 to Hwy. 1	349 miles
Sacramento	I–5	391 miles

 Bus

Greyhound is the primary bus carrier in California. Regional bus service is available in metropolitan areas.

 Car

A car is essential in most of California, the exceptions being parts of its largest cities, where it can be more convenient to use public transportation, taxis, or ride-sharing services. Two main north–south routes run through California: I–5 through the middle of the state, and U.S. 101, a parallel route closer to the coast. Slower but more scenic is Highway 1, which winds along much of the coast.

From north to south, the state's main east–west routes are I–80, I–15, I–10, and I–8. Much of California is mountainous, and you may encounter winding roads and steep mountain grades.

From San Francisco to:	Route	Distance
San Jose	U.S. 101	50 miles
Monterey	U.S. 101 to Hwy. 156 to Hwy. 1	120 miles
Los Angeles	I–80 to I–580 to I–5	382 miles
Portland, OR	I–80 to I–505 to I–5	635 miles
Mendocino	U.S. 101 to Hwy. 128 to Hwy. 1	174 miles
Yosemite NP	I–80 to I–580 to I–205 to Hwy. 120 east	184 miles
Lake Tahoe/ Reno	I–80	220 miles

ROAD CONDITIONS

View current road conditions online or download the easier-to-use Caltrans QuickMap smartphone app. Rainy weather can make driving along the coast or in the mountains treacherous. Some smaller routes over mountain ranges and in the deserts are prone to flash flooding. Many smaller roads over the Sierra Nevada are closed in winter, and if it's snowing, tire chains may be required on routes that are open. Note, though, that most rental-car companies prohibit chain installation on their vehicles. If you disregard this rule, your insurance likely won't cover chains-related damage.

Chains or cables generally cost $30–$75. ■ **TIP→ It's less expensive to purchase chains before you get to the mountains.** On some highways and freeways, uniformed chain installers will apply chains for a fee (around $30), though these installers are not allowed to sell or rent chains. On lesser roads, you're on your own.

RULES OF THE ROAD

All passengers must wear a seat belt at all times. A child must be secured in a federally approved child passenger restraint system and ride in the back seat until at least eight years of age or until the child is at least 4 feet 9 inches tall. Unless indicated, right turns are allowed at red lights after you've come to a full stop. Drivers with a blood-alcohol level higher than 0.08 are subject to arrest.

You must turn on your headlights whenever weather conditions require the use of windshield wipers. Texting on a wireless device is illegal. If using a mobile phone while driving, it must be hands-free and mounted (i.e., it's not legal having it loose on the seat or your lap). For more driving rules, refer to the Department of Motor Vehicles driver's handbook at 🌐 *www.dmv.ca.gov*.

CAR RENTAL

When you reserve a car, ask about cancellation penalties, taxes, drop-off charges (to drop off in another city), and surcharges (for age, additional drivers, or driving across state or country borders).

Train

Amtrak provides rail service within California. On some trips, passengers board motor coaches part of the way.

Essentials

Activities

Athletic Californians often boast that it's possible to surf in the morning and ski in the afternoon (or vice versa) in the Golden State. With thousands of hiking, biking, and horse-riding trails and hundreds of lakes, rivers, and streams for fishing, swimming, and boating—not to mention sandy coastal strands for sunning and surfing and other beaches with dunes or rocks to explore—there's no shortage of outdoor fun to be had. One challenge on many a hiker's bucket list is the Pacific Crest Trail, which travels the length of the state. The National Park Service operates numerous parks and sites in California, and the state park system is robust.

Dining

California has led the pack in bringing natural and organic foods to the forefront of American dining. Though rooted in European cuisine, California cooking sometimes has strong Asian and Latin influences. Wherever you go, you're likely to find that dishes are made with fresh produce and other local ingredients.

The restaurants we list are the cream of the crop in each price category. *Restaurant reviews have been shortened. For full information, visit Fodors.com. For price information, see the Planning sections in each chapter.*

DISCOUNTS AND DEALS

The better grocery and specialty-food stores have grab-and-go sections, with prepared foods on a par with restaurant cooking, perfect for picnicking.

MEALS AND MEALTIMES

Lunch is typically served from 11 or 11:30 to 2:30 or 3, with dinner service starting at 5 or 5:30 and lasting until 9 or later. Restaurants that serve breakfast usually open by 7, sometimes earlier, with some serving breakfast through the lunch hour. Most weekend brunches start at 10 or 11 and go at least until 2.

PAYING

In 2020, most restaurants began taking only credit cards and not cash, though some still don't accept one or the other. In most establishments tipping is the norm, but some include the service in the menu price or add it to the bill. *For guidelines on tipping see Tipping, below.*

RESERVATIONS AND DRESS

It's a good idea to make a reservation when possible. Where reservations are indicated as essential, book a week or more ahead in summer and early fall. Large parties should always call ahead to check the reservations policy. Except as noted in individual listings, dress is informal.

Health/Safety

If you have a medical condition that may require emergency treatment, be aware that many rural and mountain communities have only daytime clinics, not hospitals with 24-hour emergency rooms. Take the usual precautions to protect your person and belongings. In large cities, ask at your lodging about areas to avoid, and lock valuables in a hotel safe when not using them. Car break-ins are common in some larger cities, but it's always a good idea to remove valuables from your car or at least keep them out of sight.

COVID-19

Although COVID-19 brought travel to a virtual standstill for most of 2020 and into 2021, vaccinations have made travel possible and safe again. Remaining requirements and restrictions—including those for non-vaccinated travelers—can, however, vary from one place (or even business) to the next. Check out the websites of the CDC and the U.S. Department of State, both of which have destination-specific, COVID-19 guidance. Also, in case travel is curtailed abruptly again, consider buying trip insurance. Just be sure to read the fine print: not all travel-insurance policies cover pandemic-related cancellations.

THE OUTDOORS

At beaches, heed warnings about high surf and deadly rogue waves, and don't fly within 24 hours of scuba diving. When hiking, stay on trails, and heed all warning signs about loose cliffs, predatory animals, and poison ivy or oak.

Before heading out into remote areas, let someone know your trip route, destination, and estimated time and date of return. Make sure your vehicle is in good condition and equipped with a first-aid kit, snacks, extra water, jack, spare tire, tools, and a towrope or chain. Mind your gas gauge, keeping the needle at above half if possible and stopping to top off the tank whenever you can.

In arid regions, stay on main roads, and watch out for wildlife, horses, and cattle. Don't enter mine tunnels or shafts. Not only can such structures be unstable, but they might also have hidden dangers such as pockets of bad air. Be mindful of sudden rainstorms, when floodwaters can cover or wash away roads and quickly fill up dry riverbeds and canyons. Never place your hands or feet where you can't see them: rattlesnakes, scorpions, and black widow spiders may be hiding there.

Sunscreen and hats are musts, and layered clothing is best as desert temperatures can fluctuate greatly between dawn and dusk. Drink at least a gallon of water a day (three gallons if you're hiking or otherwise exerting yourself). If you have a headache or feel dizzy or nauseous, you could be suffering from dehydration. Get out of the sun immediately, dampen your clothing to lower your body temperature, and drink plenty of water.

Although you might not feel thirsty in cooler, mountain climes, it's important to stay hydrated (drinking at least a quart of water during activities) at high altitudes, where the air is thinner, causing you to breathe more heavily. Always bring a fold-up rain poncho to keep you dry and prevent hypothermia. Wear long pants, a hat, and sturdy, closed-toe hiking boots with soles that grip rock. If you're going into the backcountry, bring a signaling device (such as a mirror), emergency whistle, compass, map, energy bars, and water purifier.

Lodging

With just under 5,600 lodgings, California has inns, motels, hotels, and specialty accommodations to suit every traveler's fancy and finances. Retro motels recalling 1950s roadside culture but with 21st-century amenities are a recent popular trend, but you'll also see traditional motels and hotels, along with luxury resorts and boutique properties. Reservations are a good idea throughout the year but especially so in the summer. On weekends at smaller lodgings, minimum-stay requirements of two or three nights are common, though some places are flexible about this in winter. Some accommodations aren't suitable for children, so ask before you book.

The lodgings we review are the top choices in each price category. *Hotels reviews have been shortened. For full information, visit Fodors.com.* We don't specify whether the facilities cost extra; when pricing accommodations, ask what's included and what costs extra.

Essentials

For price information, see the Planning sections in each chapter.

APARTMENT AND HOUSE RENTALS

You'll find listings for Airbnb and similar rentals throughout California.

BED-AND-BREAKFASTS

California has more than 1,000 bed-and-breakfasts. You'll find everything from simple homestays to lavish luxury lodgings, many in historic hotels and homes. The California Association of Boutique and Breakfast Inns represents 200 member properties you can locate and book through its website.

HOTELS

Some properties allow you to cancel without a penalty—even if you prepaid to secure a discounted rate—if you cancel at least 24 hours in advance. Others require you to cancel a week in advance or penalize you the cost of one night. Small inns and B&Bs are most likely to require you to cancel far in advance. Most hotels allow children under a certain age to stay in their parents' room at no extra charge, but others charge for them as additional adults; find out the cutoff age for discounts.

Money

On the coast, you'll pay top dollar for everything from gas and food to lodging and attractions. Aside from desert and ski resorts, inland prices tend to be lower.

TAXES

The base state sales tax is 7.25%, but local taxes can add as much as 3.25%. Exceptions include grocery-store food items and some takeout. Hotel taxes vary from about 8% to 15%.

Tipping Guidelines for California

Bartender	$1–$3 per drink, or 15%–20% per round
Bellhop	$2–$5 per bag, depending on the level of the hotel
Hotel Concierge	$5–$10 for advice and reservations, more for difficult tasks
Hotel Doorman	$3–$5 for hailing a cab
Valet Parking Attendant	$3–$5 when you get your car
Hotel Maid	$4–$6 per day (either daily or at the end of your stay, in cash)
Waiter	18%–22% (20%–25% is standard in upscale restaurants); nothing additional if a service charge is added to the bill
Skycap at Airport	$2 per bag
Hotel Room-Service Waiter	15%–20% per delivery, even if a service charge was added since that fee goes to the hotel, not the waiter
Tasting-room server	$5–$10 per couple basic tasting, $5–$10 per person hosted seated tasting
Taxi Driver	15%–20%, but round up the fare to the next dollar amount
Tour Guide	15% of the cost of the tour, more depending on quality

Nightlife

The good life in California extends to the evening with skilled mixologists serving up farm-to-bar cocktails in big-city night spots, some of them modeled on speakeasies of yore. Regular ole bartenders provide an additional layer of atmosphere to dives in towns large and small.

Packing

The California lifestyle emphasizes casual wear, and with the generally mild climate you needn't worry about packing cold-weather clothing unless you're going into mountainous areas. Jeans, walking shorts, and T-shirts are acceptable in most situations. Few restaurants require men to wear a jacket or tie, though a collared shirt is the norm at upscale establishments.

Summer evenings can be cool, especially near the coast, where fog often rolls in. Always pack a sweater or light jacket. If you're headed to state or national parks, packing binoculars, clothes that layer, long pants and long-sleeve shirts, sunglasses, and a wide-brimmed hat is wise. Pick up insect repellant, sunscreen, and a first-aid kit once in-state.

Performing Arts

With about 40 million residents, California supplies a built-in audience for touring and homegrown companies from the worlds of dance, opera, theater, comedy, and music of all types. A-list performers appear at venues large and intimate, and numerous cultural festivals fill the calendar. In all the major cities and some smaller ones you'll find a former movie palace or two (or more) converted into a performance venue. Look also for events sponsored by top-tier museums. Wineries throughout the state host concerts during the summer.

Shopping

California is home to world-class shopping in its big cities, where you'll find major designer labels and fine-jewelry establishments represented. The state was the birthplace of the maker movement, and artisans throughout California craft beautiful soaps, clothing from organic cotton, fashion jewelry from recycled products, and other handmade items.

When to Go

Expect high summer heat in the desert areas and low winter temperatures in the Sierra Nevada and other inland mountain ranges.

HIGH SEASON $$$–$$$$

High season lasts from late May through early September (a little later in wine regions and well into winter in desert resorts and ski areas). Expect higher hotel occupancy rates and prices.

LOW SEASON $$

From December to March, tourist activity slows. Except in the mountainous areas, which may see snowfall and an influx of skiers, winters here are mild and hotels are cheaper.

VALUE SEASON $$–$$$

From April to late May and from late September to mid-November the weather is pleasant and hotel prices are reasonable.

Contacts

Air

AIRLINE SECURITY ISSUES

CONTACTS Transportation Security Administration. (*TSA*). *866/289–9673* *www.tsa.gov.*

AIRLINES

CONTACTS Air Canada. *888/247–2262* *www.aircanada.com.* **Alaska Airlines/Horizon Air.** *800/252–7522* *www.alaskaair.com.* **American Airlines.** *800/433–7300* *www.aa.com.* **Delta Airlines.** *800/221–1212 for U.S. reservations, 800/241–4141 for international reservations* *www.delta.com.* **Frontier Airlines.** *801/401–9000* *www.flyfrontier.com.* **JetBlue.** *800/538–2583* *www.jetblue.com.* **Southwest Airlines.** *800/435–9792* *www.southwest.com.* **United Airlines.** *800/864–8331* *www.united.com.*

AIRPORTS

SOUTHERN CALIFORNIA Hollywood Burbank Airport. *818/840–8840* *www.hollywoodburbankairport.com.* **John Wayne Airport.** *949/252–5200* *www.ocair.com.* **Long Beach Airport.** *562/570–2600* *www.lgb.org.* **Los Angeles International Airport.** *855/463–5252* *www.flylax.com.* **Ontario International Airport.** *909/544–5300* *www.flyontario.com.* **San Diego International Airport.** *619/400–2400* *www.san.org.*

NORTHERN CALIFORNIA Oakland International Airport. *510/563–3300* *www.oaklandairport.com.* **Sacramento International Airport.** *916/929–5411* *www.sacramento.aero/smf.* **San Francisco International Airport.** *650/821–8211, 800/435–9736* *www.flysfo.com.* **San Jose International Airport.** *408/392–3600* *www.flysanjose.com.*

Bus

CONTACTS Greyhound. *800/231–2222* *www.greyhound.com.*

Car

INFORMATION Caltrans Current Highway Conditions. *800/427–7623* *quickmap.dot.ca.gov.* **511 Traffic/Transit Alerts.** *511.*

MAJOR RENTAL AGENCIES Alamo. *800/462–5266* *www.alamo.com.* **Avis.** *800/633–3469* *www.avis.com.* **Budget.** *800/218–7992* *www.budget.com.* **Hertz.** *800/654–3131* *www.hertz.com.* **National Car Rental.** *844/382–6875* *www.nationalcar.com.*

ROADSIDE ASSISTANCE American Automobile Association. (*AAA*). *800/222–4357* *www.aaa.com.*

SPECIALTY CAR AGENCIES Enterprise Exotic Car Rentals. *866/458–9227* *exoticcars.enterprise.com.*

Health/Safety

EMERGENCIES Ambulance, fire, police. *911 emergency.*

Reservation Service

CONTACTS California Association of Boutique and Breakfast Inns. (*CABBI*). *800/373–9251* *www.cabbi.com.*

Train

CONTACTS Amtrak. *800/872–7245* *www.amtrak.com.*

Chapter 3

CALIFORNIA'S BEST ROAD TRIPS

Updated by
Daniel Mangin

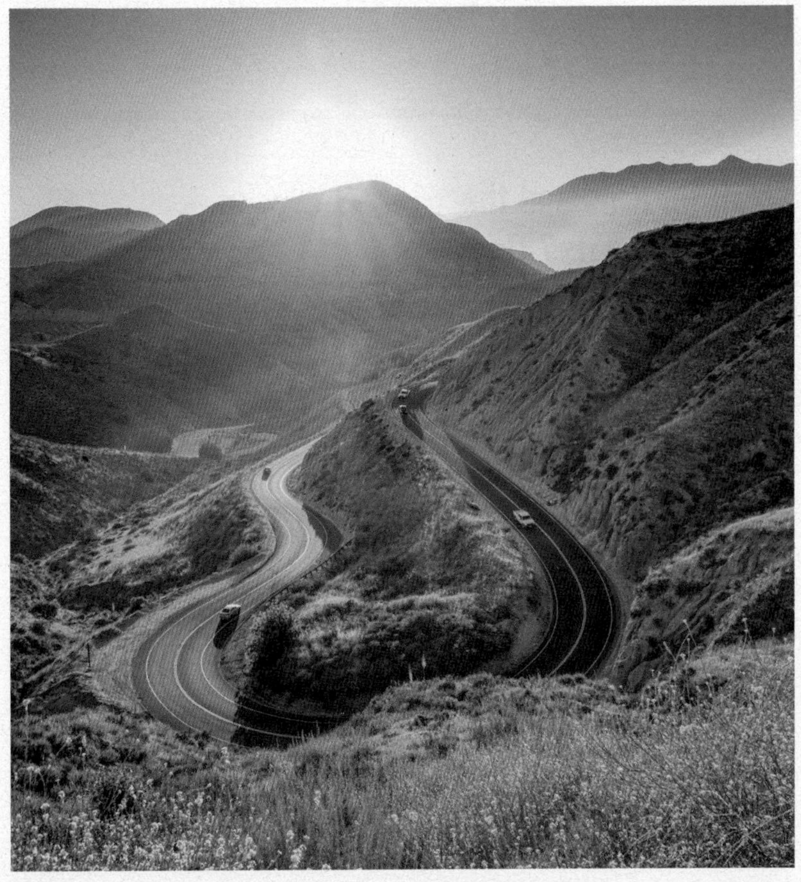

A California visit wouldn't be complete without taking a spin through the state's spectacular scenery. However, adding a road trip to your itinerary is not just a romantic idea: it's often a practical one, too—perhaps linking one urban area with another, say, or sampling some of this massive state's remote areas. Whether you have just a few days or longer to spare, these itineraries will help you hit the road.

SoCal for Kids and the Young at Heart, 7 Days

SoCal offers many opportunities to entertain the kids and the young at heart beyond the Magic Kingdom, this trip's last stop. San Diego's LEGOLAND is a blast for kids 12 and under, and the city's diverse attractions include a water park, the zoo, and several historic districts. Oh yes, and well-groomed La Jolla and other beach towns, too. If you can, fly into San Diego and out of Los Angeles to save time (and maybe money).

Traffic Tip

No matter how carefully you plan, you will inevitably encounter heavy traffic in L.A., Orange County, and San Diego. Follow traffic reports, and load an app that provides real-time traffic advice onto your smartphone Also, allow yourself twice as much time as you think you'll need to negotiate Los Angeles International Airport (LAX).

DAYS 1–2: LEGOLAND

LEGOLAND's hotels are a 35-min drive from the airport.

Arrive at **San Diego** International Airport, pick up your rental car, and settle in at the **LEGOLAND Hotel** or the **Sheraton Carlsbad Resort & Spa**, perhaps taking a dip in the pool. In the late afternoon, drive south along the Pacific Coast Highway (PCH) past popular San Diego County surfing beaches. Stop in Solana Beach or Del Mar for a sunset cocktail, perhaps staying for dinner.

Getting an early start for an action-packed day at **LEGOLAND** is a breeze because both hotels offer direct access to the park. LEGOLAND has a water park and aquarium in addition to LEGO-based rides, shows, and roller coasters. Little ones can live out their fairy-tale fantasies, and bigger ones can spend all day on waterslides, shooting water pistols, driving boats, or water fighting with pirates.

DAY 3: DOWNTOWN SAN DIEGO

Downtown is 35 mins from Carlsbad.

Check out of your LEGOLAND hotel in the late morning, taking the freeway south 35 minutes to **Downtown San Diego.** It'll probably be too early to check in (do it when convenient later in the afternoon), but park your car at your hotel and drop off your bags. Then proceed straight to the city's nautical heart, exploring the restored ships of the **Maritime Museum** and walking south along the waterfront. Victorian buildings—and plenty of other tourists—surround you on a stroll inland a few blocks to **Gaslamp Quarter,** where you can grab a happy-hour cocktail or mocktail before dining close to your hotel.

DAY 4: SEA WORLD, OLD TOWN, AND LA JOLLA

SeaWorld is 15 mins from Downtown; Old Town is 10 mins from SeaWorld; La Jolla is 20 mins from Old Town.

Two commercial and touristy sights are on the agenda, with a sunset cocktail the day's-end reward. With its walk-through shark tanks, **SeaWorld** delivers a ton of fun if you surrender to the experience. Also touristy, but with genuine historical significance, **Old Town** drips with Mexican and early Californian heritage. Soak it up in the plaza at **Old Town San Diego State Historic Park,** then browse the stalls and shops at **Fiesta de Reyes** and along San Diego Avenue. As the day winds down, make your way to **La Jolla Cove.** At the **Children's Pool,** look at, but don't go in the water, which is likely to be filled with barking seals. Have a sunset cocktail in La Jolla and dine there or Downtown.

DAY 5: SAN DIEGO ZOO

10 mins by car from Downtown San Diego.

Malayan tapirs in a faux-Asian rain forest, polar bears in an imitation Arctic, and pandas frolicking in the trees—the **San Diego Zoo** maintains a vast and varied collection of creatures in a world-renowned facility comprised of meticulously designed habitats. Come early, and wear comfy shoes. If you have time, explore a little of **Balboa Park,** which contains the zoo. Have dinner in the Hillcrest neighborhood near the park, or dine Downtown.

DAYS 6–7: DISNEYLAND

90 mins by car from San Diego to Disneyland.

As early as you can get moving, hop onto I–5 and drive north. By the time you reach San Clemente, you 'll be in **Orange County** (aka the O.C.). In less than an hour from there, you'll be in **Disneyland!** Skirt the lines at the box office with advance-purchased tickets in hand, and storm the gates of the Magic Kingdom. You can cram the highlights into a single day, but if you get a two-day ticket and stay the night, you can see the end-of-day parade and visit **Downtown Disney** before heading south. The **Grand Californian Hotel** is a top choice for lodging within the Disney Resort.

Hooray for Hollywood, 4 Days

If you are a movie fan, there's no better place to see it all than L.A. Always keep peeled: you never know when you might spot a celebrity.

DAY 1: LOS ANGELES

As soon as you land at LAX, make like a local, and hit the freeway. Even if L.A.'s top-notch art, history, and science museums don't tempt you, the mélange of art deco, Beaux Arts, and futuristic architecture begs at least a drive-by. Heading east from Santa Monica, Wilshire Boulevard cuts through a historical and cultural cross section of the city. Two stellar sights on its Miracle Mile are the encyclopedic **Los Angeles County Museum of Art** and the fossil-filled **La Brea Tar Pits.** Come evening, the open-air **Farmers Market** and its many eateries hum. Hotels in Beverly Hills or West Hollywood beckon, just a few minutes away.

DAY 2: HOLLYWOOD AND THE MOVIE STUDIOS

Avoid driving to the studios during rush hour. Studio tours vary in length—plan at least a half day for the excursion.

Every L.A. tourist should devote at least one day to the movies and take at least one studio tour in the San Fernando Valley. For fun, choose the special-effects theme park at **Universal Studios Hollywood**; for the nitty-gritty, choose **Warner Bros. Studios.** Nostalgic musts in Hollywood itself include the **Hollywood Walk of Fame** along **Hollywood Boulevard** and the celebrity footprints cast in concrete outside **Grauman's Chinese Theatre** (now known as the TCL Chinese Theater). When evening arrives, the Hollywood scene includes a bevy of trendy restaurants and nightclubs.

DAYS 3–4: BEVERLY HILLS AND SANTA MONICA

15–20 mins by car between destinations, but considerably longer in traffic.

The **Getty Center**'s pavilion architecture, hilltop gardens, and frame-worthy L.A. views make it a dazzling destination—and that's before you experience the extensive art collection. From the museum, descend to the sea via Santa Monica Boulevard for lunch along **Third Street Promenade,** followed by a ride on the historic carousel on the pier. The buff and the bizarre meet at Venice Beach's **Ocean Front Walk**—strap on some in-line skates if you want to join them. Over in Beverly Hills, the **Rodeo Drive** shopping district specializes in exhibitionism with a hefty price tag, but voyeurs are still welcome.

Splurge on breakfast or brunch at a posh café in the **Farmers Market,** then stroll through aisles and aisles of gorgeous produce and specialty food before you take a last look at the Pacific Ocean through the camera obscura at **Palisades Park** in Santa Monica.

Palm Springs and the Desert, 5 Days

Many visitors consider the Palm Springs area pure paradise, and not just for the opportunity to get a good tan or play golf on championship courses. Expect fabulous and funky spas, a dog-friendly atmosphere, and sparkling stars at night.

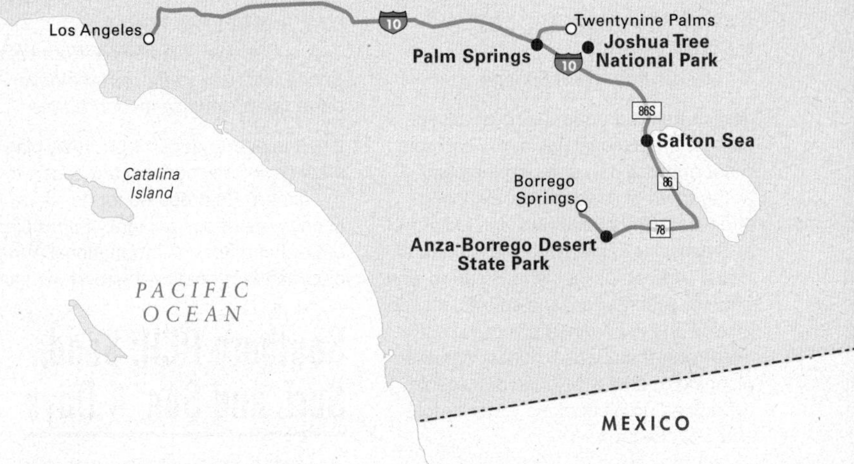

DAY 1: ARRIVE IN PALM SPRINGS

Just over 2 hrs by car from LAX, without traffic.

Somehow in harmony with the harsh environment, mid-century-modern homes and businesses with clean, low-slung lines define the **Palm Springs** style. Although the desert cities—Rancho Mirage, Palm Desert, Indian Wells, Indio, and La Quinta—comprise a trendy destination with sumptuous hotels, multicultural cuisine, abundant nightlife, and plenty of culture, a quiet atmosphere prevails. Fans of Palm Springs' legendary architecture won't want to miss the home tours, lectures, and other events at the annual Modernism Week held each February or the smaller fall preview event in October. If your visit doesn't coincide with these happenings, swing by the Palm Springs Visitor's Center for information on self-guided architecture tours.

The city seems far away when you hike in hushed **Tahquitz** or **Indian Canyon**; cliffs and palm trees shelter rock art, irrigation works, and other remnants of Agua Caliente culture. If your boots aren't made for walking, you can always practice your golf game or indulge in spa treatments at an area resort instead. Embrace the Palm Springs vibe, and park yourself at the modern-chic **Kimpton Rowan Palm Springs Hotel** or the legendary **Parker Palm Springs.** Alternatively, base yourself at the desert oasis, **La Quinta Resort,** about 40 minutes from downtown Palm Springs.

DAY 2: EXPLORE PALM SPRINGS

The Aerial Tram is 15 mins by car from central Palm Springs. Plan at least a half day for the excursion.

If riding a tram up an 8,516-foot mountain for a stroll or even a snowball fight above the desert sounds like fun, then show up at the **Palm Springs Aerial Tramway** before the first morning tram leaves (later, the line can get discouragingly long). Dress in layers, and wear decent footwear as it can be significantly colder at the top. Afterward, stroll through the **Palm Springs Art Museum,** with its shimmering display of contemporary studio glass, array of Native American baskets, and significant 20th-century sculptures by Henry Moore and others. After all that walking you may be ready for an early dinner. Nearly every restaurant in Palm Springs offers a happy hour, during which you can sip a cocktail and nosh on a light entrée, usually for half price.

DAY 3: JOSHUA TREE NATIONAL PARK

1 hr by car from Palm Springs.

Joshua Tree is among the most accessible of the national parks. You can see most of it in a day, entering the park at the town of Joshua Tree, exploring sites along **Park Boulevard,** and exiting at **Twentynine Palms.** With the signature trees, piles of rocks, glorious spring wildflowers, starlit skies, and colorful pioneer history, the experience is more like the Wild West than Sahara dunes. Whether planning to take a day hike or a scenic drive, load up on drinking water before entering the park.

DAY 4: ANZA-BORREGO DESERT STATE PARK AND THE SALTON SEA

About 2 hrs by car from Palm Springs.

The **Salton Sea,** about 60 miles southeast of Palm Springs via I–10 and Highway 86S, is one of the largest inland seas on Earth. Formed by the flooding of the Colorado River in 1905, it attracts thousands of migrating birds and bird-watchers every fall. **Anza-Borrego Desert State Park** to the west, California's largest state park, contains 600,000 acres of mostly untouched wilderness. The springtime wildflower displays here rank among the state's best. The park surrounds **Borrego Springs,** a tiny hamlet most notable for its 130 life-size bronze sculptures of animals that roamed this space millions of years ago. The desert is home to an archaeological site, where scientists continue to uncover remnants of prehistoric animals ranging from mastodons to horses. If you have four-wheel drive, a detour down the sandy track to **Font's Point** rewards the intrepid with unforgettable views of the Borrego badlands. However, do not take the challenging road conditions lightly—inquire with park rangers before setting out.

DAY 5: RETURN TO L.A.

LAX is just over 2 hrs by car from Palm Springs without traffic, but the drive often takes significantly more time.

If you intend to depart from LAX, plan for a full day of driving from the desert to the airport. Be prepared for heavy traffic at any time of day or night. If possible, fly out of Palm Springs International Airport or Ontario International Airport instead.

Southern PCH: Sand, Surf, and Sun, 4 Days

This tour along the southern section of the Pacific Coast Highway (PCH) is a beach vacation on wheels, taking in the highlights of the Southern California coast and its surfer-chic vibe. If at any point the drive feels like something out of a movie, that's because it likely is—this is the California of Hollywood legend. And this segment is only the warm-up: after you get to Santa Barbara you can just keep heading north as far up the coast as time permits. Roll the top down on the convertible and let the adventure begin.

DAY 1: LAGUNA BEACH TO NEWPORT BEACH

1 hr by car.

Easily accessed off I–5, the PCH begins near Dana Point, a town famous for its harbor and whale-watching excursions, but you can just as easily start 10 miles north in **Laguna Beach.** Browse the art galleries, and enjoy lunch in the charming downtown before or after walking along the Pacific. Then head north a few miles to **Crystal Cove State Park.** If the tide is low, this is a wonderful spot for tide pooling. Don't miss the historic beach cottages dating as far back as 1935.

From the park, continue north a few more miles to **Newport Beach.** The affluent coastal cities of Orange County (aka the O.C.) are familiar to many thanks to

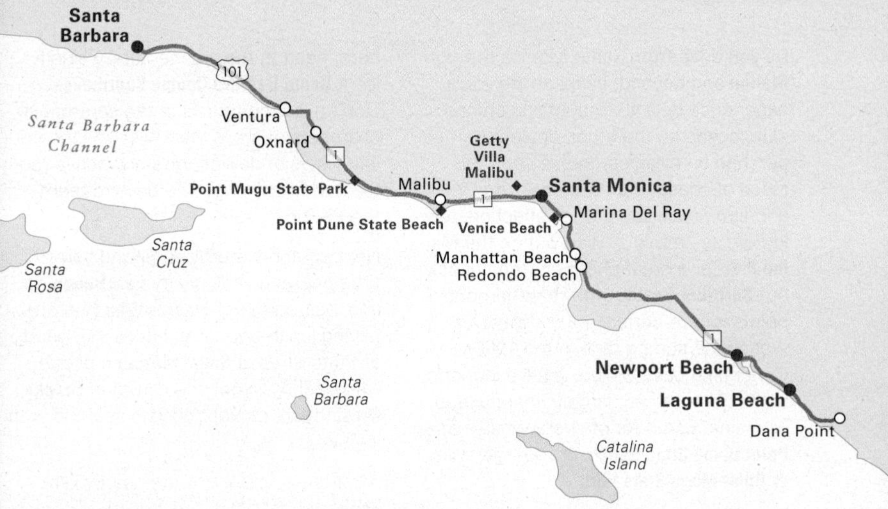

Arrested Development, The Real Wives of Orange County, and other TV shows, though the yachts and multimillion-dollar mansions of Newport Beach may still take you by surprise. **Balboa Island,** a quaint, if expensive, getaway, sits in the middle of Newport Harbor. Browse the boutiques along Marine Avenue before hopping in a Duffy (electric boat) for a harbor tour. Back on land, enjoy a Balboa Bar—the ice-cream treat is virtually mandatory for all Balboa Island visitors. Spend the night on Balboa Island or elsewhere in Newport Beach.

DAY 2: NEWPORT BEACH TO SANTA MONICA

About 2 hrs by car without traffic, but plan on it.

From Newport Beach, eschew Highway 1, driving north on Highway 55 to the 405 freeway also north. Exit at West 190st Street, following the signs to Redondo Beach, well-known, along with Hermosa and Manhattan beaches to the north, among beach-volleyball enthusiasts. If time permits, follow Highway 1 through Marina del Ray; otherwise skip this section of the PCH in favor of the 405 freeway. (As is always advisable near L.A., check current traffic reports before choosing your route.)

Get settled into a hotel near the **Santa Monica Pier,** then catch some of the action there before grabbing dinner along the **Third Street Promenade** or at Santa Monica Place.

DAY 3: SANTA MONICA TO SANTA BARBARA

About 2 hrs by car via Hwy. 1 and U.S. 101. When the weather's good, though, allow more time for beach stops.

Begin with a morning walk along **Santa Monica State Beach.** Check out of your hotel, but leave your bags there to pick up later. Rent beach cruiser bikes, and pedal south about 3 miles along the bike path to **Venice Beach.** When you've had your fill of skateboarders, bodybuilders, and street performers, head inland a few blocks to Abbott Kinney Boulevard for lunch at **Gjelina** and a browse in the local boutiques. Then head back to Santa Monica, drop off your bikes, and begin the drive north to Santa Barbara. If you plan to visit the **Getty Villa Malibu** and its impressive antiquities collection and jaw-dropping setting overlooking the Pacific, spend less time on the bike ride. And be sure to obtain free timed-entry tickets—the last admission is at 3 pm—online before your arrival.

As you drive from Santa Monica through **Malibu** and beyond, chances are you'll experience déjà vu: mountains on one side, ocean on the other, opulent homes perched on hillsides. You've seen this piece of coast countless times on TV and film. In Malibu proper, affectionately known as "the 'bu," walk out on the **Malibu Pier** for a great photo op, then check out **Surfrider Beach,** with three famous points where perfect waves ignited a worldwide surfing rage in the 1960s. Continuing past Malibu, you'll experience miles of protected, largely unpopulated coastline. Scout for offshore whales at **Point Dume State Beach,** or hike the trails at **Point Mugu State Park.**

On the north side of **Oxnard,** you'll trade Highway 1 for U.S. 101 (aka "the 101" and the Ventura Freeway) into **Ventura.** Approaching Ventura on a clear day, the Channel Islands are visible in the distance. If you haven't been held up in traffic too much, stretch your legs on the **Ventura Oceanfront** with a walk on **San Buenaventura State Beach** or around the picturesque **Ventura Harbor.** Otherwise, continue to **Santa Barbara,** and check into your hotel. Splurge on an overnight stay at the posh **Rosewood Miramar Beach** resort, or book a room at the **Santa Barbara Inn,** whose restaurant, **Convivo,** is a smart spot for dinner.

DAY 4: SANTA BARBARA

45 mins–1 hr by car.

Santa Barbara is a gem. Combining elegance with a laid-back coastal vibe, the city provides a tranquil escape from the congestion of Los Angeles and a dose of sophistication to the largely rural Central Coast.

Start your day at **Old Mission Santa Barbara,** known as the "Queen" of the 21 missions that comprise the California Mission Trail. Plan to spend some time here; if your visit doesn't coincide with one of the 60-minute docent-led tours, self-guided tours are also available. From here, head to the architecturally significant **Santa Barbara County Courthouse.** Don't miss the murals in the ceremonial chambers or, from the tower, the incredible views of downtown's distinctive red-tile-roofed buildings and beyond them the Pacific Ocean.

Next up: the waterfront. Spend some time enjoying vast, sandy **East Beach,** and walk a little of **Stearns Wharf** before having lunch two blocks from the wharf at State Street's **Santo Mezcal** (upscale Mexican) or across the harbor at **Brophy Bros.** (fresh, straightforward seafood with a view).

After lunch, peek into the nearby **Funk Zone**'s art galleries, and indulge in a wine tasting or two. Dine in this area, or head to tony **Montecito** for an elegant meal.

Santa Barbara Wine Country, 2 Days

It's been nearly two decades since the movie *Sideways* brought the Santa Barbara Wine Country to the world's attention, and interest in this area continues to grow. This itinerary, best done from Thursday through Monday when most of the wineries and restaurants are open, makes a perfect add-on to a trip to Los Angeles and for those touring farther north along the coast.

DAY 1: SANTA RITA HILLS, LOMPOC, AND LOS OLIVOS

Without stops, this route takes about 2 hrs by car. Plan to linger at—and detour down side roads to—the wineries.

Take the scenic drive along the coast on the 101 to Buellton, exiting west onto Highway 246. After ½ mile, turn south (left) on Industrial Way. Don't let the **Industrial Way** food-and-drink complex's warehouse setting deter you—the tasting rooms here include well-regarded producers, many of whose grapes

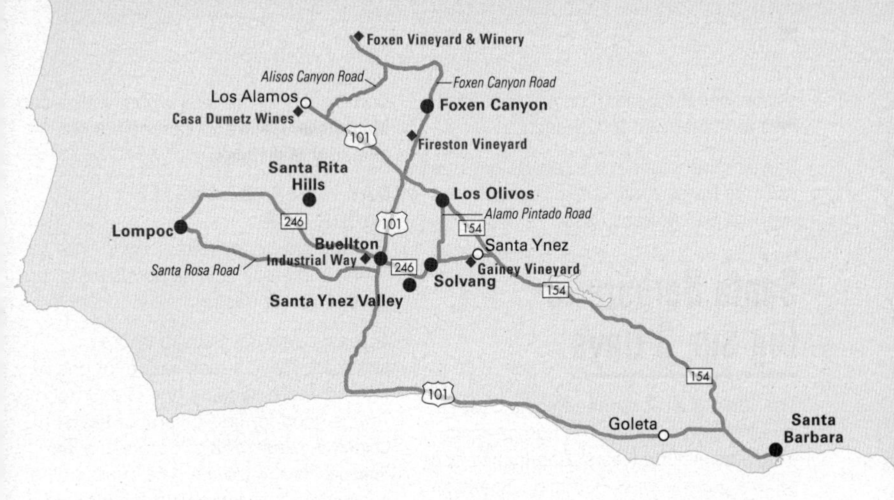

come from the Sta. Rita Hills AVA farther west a few miles. With its relatively cooler climate, the appellation excels at Chardonnay and Pinot Noir. **Alma Rosa Winery,** among the first noteworthy operations in these parts, is a good place to start. Consider also **Lafond Winery and Vineyards** and **McClain Cellars.** After or between tastings, walk to **Industrial Eats** for wood-fired pizzas and hearty salads and sandwiches.

Back on Highway 101, head north about 6 miles before exiting toward **Los Olivos,** where you can park the car and spend the rest of the day exploring on foot. Tasting rooms, galleries, boutiques, and restaurants have made this former stagecoach town quite wine-country chic. **Blair Fox Cellars** and **Coquelicot Estate Vineyard** are just two of the wineries with tasting rooms in town. If you're staying at **Fess Parker's Wine Country Inn and Spa** or just outside town at the **Ballard Inn,** dine at **Nella,** inside Fess Parker's. Alternatively, slip south a few miles to **Solvang,** check into the **Hotel Corque,** and have dinner in Buellton at the much-heralded **Tavern at Zaca Creek.**

DAY 2: SOLVANG, FOXEN CANYON, AND THE SANTA YNEZ VALLEY

About 1 hr of driving to wineries, plus 45 mins to return to Santa Barbara via Highway 154.

Start the day with pastries in the Danish town of **Solvang,** whose windmills and distinct half-timber architecture are charming, if touristy. Walk a little of Solvang before hitting the road.

Los Olivos, **Santa Ynez,** and Solvang are located just a few minutes apart, with wineries spread between them in an area known as the Santa Ynez Valley. A mile east of tiny Santa Ynez's commercial drag (4¼ miles east of Solvang) lies **Gainey Vineyard,** whose wines impress major critics. Past Los Olivos heading north, the Foxen Canyon Wine Trail (🌐 *www.foxencanyontrail.net* for info and a map) extends to Santa Maria. Expect some backtracking as you venture into the canyon. If it's being offered, the well-conceived tour at **Firestone Vineyard** is a must for those interested in wine making. Farther along, **Foxen Vineyard & Winery** earns plaudits for its Pinot Noirs. Before or after a tasting in **Los Alamos** at **Casa Dumetz** (Rhône-style reds), stop for lunch at **Bob's Well Bread Bakery** (sandwiches, salads, cheese boards) or, on weekends, **Pico** for its farm-to-fork brunch.

Stay another night in the region, or return to Santa Barbara via scenic Highway 154 over the San Marcos Pass

Santa Barbara to Big Sur, 3 Days

This drive is all about the Pacific Coast's jaw-dropping scenery. The human-made treasures include Hearst Castle, newspaper magnate William Randolph Hearst's opulent monument to his fabulousness. Book Big Sur lodgings weeks ahead, the castle at least several days ahead in summer.

DAY 1: SANTA BARBARA TO CAMBRIA

About 3 hrs by car, not counting stops.

Drive north from Santa Barbara on the combined Highway 1 and U.S. 101, exiting the latter when the former forks west (watch for signs to Lompoc and Vandenberg Air Force Base). For this stretch, Highway 1 is also signed as Cabrillo Highway. Stop for a spell at **Guadalupe-Nipomo Dunes Preserve,** where on a sunny day the enormous namesake dunes make for a fantastic photo op. Highway 1 rejoins U.S. 101 at **Pismo Beach.** If you're starving, detour for lunch, though downtown **San Luis Obispo** (aka SLO), 13 miles farther along, offers more variety. **Piadina** restaurant in the **Hotel San Luis Obispo** is a good choice, as are **Luna Red** and **Novo.**

After lunch, explore a little of SLO before, just north of downtown, picking up Highway 1 as it again separates west from the 101. **Morro Bay, Cayucos,** and tiny **Harmony** are among the fun potential stops en route to Cambria, where you'll spend the night at the **White Water Inn** or elsewhere in town (nearby Morro Bay and Cayucos also have affordable options).

End the day in Cambria with a walk along **Moonstone Beach** and a French-fusion dinner at **Madeline's.**

DAY 2: HEARST CASTLE TO BIG SUR

About 2 hrs by car. Allow ample time for hiking and stops at vista points and 2 hrs to tour Hearst Castle.

At least a few days ahead (more in summer), make a reservation for one of the mid-morning tours (the Grand Rooms Tour is good for first-timers) of **Hearst Castle,** 9 miles north of Cambria in **San Simeon.** Having traveled the surrounding coastline, you'll appreciate the bird's-eye perspective the castle provides. After the tour, have lunch down the hill at Hearst Ranch Winery, co-owned by one of William Randolph Hearst's great grandsons. On your way north out of San Simeon, don't miss the **Piedras Blancas Elephant Seal Rookery.**

The drive through coastal **Big Sur** is justifiably one of the world's most famous stretches of road. The curves, endless views, and scenic waypoints are the stuff of road-trip legend. Keep your camera handy, fill up the tank, and prepare to be wowed. Traffic can easily back up along the route, and you should be cautious while navigating the road's twists and turns. To fully experience the area, spend at least a night here. If room rates at the legendary **Post Ranch Inn** or **Ventana Big Sur** exceed your budget, seek out one of the more rustic options. If not dining at your lodging, do so at **Nepenthe,** which offers decent food and gorgeous views. Time your reservation (again, made well ahead) to witness the sunset.

DAY 3: BIG SUR

About 1 hr by car, not counting stops for hikes, beach exploration, and photo ops.

Start the morning off with a hike in southern Big Sur at **Julia Pfeiffer Burns State Park,** a draw for **McWay Falls,** which tumbles dramatically into the sea. There's no beach access due to trail erosion, but you can walk ½ mile to an overlook from a lot near the park's entrance. A pullout just to the north, near mile marker 36.2, also affords a view. Check the park's website for other trails open when you visit.

About 7½ miles north of the state park, watch for the odd-angled turnout for (the unmarked) Sycamore Canyon Road, which leads to **Pfeiffer Beach.** Following the road 2¼ miles toward the sea, you may question whether you are lost, but your perseverance will be rewarded when you reach the secluded beach and its signature rocky arch just offshore. Don't miss it!

If you're game for another hike, head into **Pfeiffer Big Sur State Park.** Near the Big Sur Lodge's restaurant are trailheads for a ¼-mile-loop, wheelchair-accessible **self-guided nature walk** and the **Valley View Trail,** a 2-mile moderate-to-strenuous loop past redwoods.

End your day 13 miles north of Big Sur Lodge (10 miles past the cluster of services known as Big Sur Village) at the extremely photogenic **Bixby Creek Bridge.** Pull over on the bridge's north side to get that perfect shot.

Most travelers continue north from here to Carmel-by-the-Sea or Monterey, either stopping there or returning to U.S. 101 via Highway 68 east from Monterey.

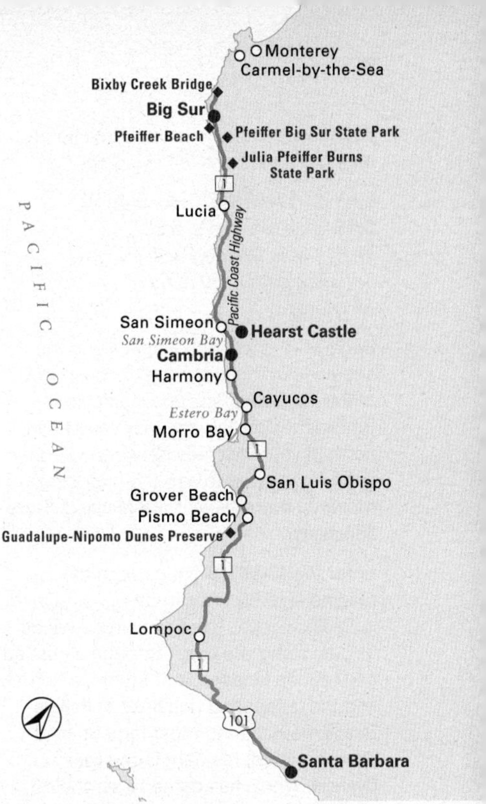

Monterey Bay to San Francisco, 4 Days

Another glorious section of Highway 1 stretches north from Monterey Bay to San Francisco. The drive to San Francisco only takes three hours, but there's enough history and scenery to fill three leisurely days. Book two nights at a Monterey or Carmel-by-the-Sea hotel or inn, arriving the evening before to maximize your time here. In the former, the tony **Monterey Plaza** is the gateway to Cannery Row, with the less-expensive **Casa Munras** winning bonus points for its tapas restaurant. Head to inland Carmel Valley to splurge at **Bernardus Lodge** or the **Quail Lodge & Golf Club;** Carmel's **Pine Inn** and **Tally Ho Inn** are less showy but well located.

DAY 1: MONTEREY

15 mins by car, less than an hour by foot.

Monterey is the perfect spot to kick off a coastal tour. Start with a visit to the enthralling **Monterey Bay Aquarium.** Exhibits such as the dramatic three-story kelp forest near the entrance give you a true sense of the local marine environment, much of it federally protected. For an even closer encounter, take to the water on a kayak or whale-watching tour. While undoubtedly touristy, the shops and galleries of **Cannery Row** still make for an interesting diversion, and it's fun to watch the colony of sea lions at **Fisherman's Wharf.** Enjoy a seafood dinner downtown and an evening stroll before hitting the road the following day.

DAY 2: 17-MILE DRIVE AND CARMEL-BY-THE-SEA

The 17-Mile Drive's Pacific Grove entrance gate is 20 mins by car from Monterey.

Begin your drive with a spin along the shoreline in the charming Victorian town of **Pacific Grove.** Pick up Ocean View Boulevard near the aquarium and head north. If your visit falls between October and March, stop to see the migrating monarch butterflies at the **Monarch Grove Sanctuary.**

Enter the **17-Mile Drive** through the tollgate ($10.50 per car) off Sunset Drive in Pacific Grove. This scenic road winds its way along the coast through a hushed and refined landscape of stunning homes and the celebrated golf links at **Pebble Beach.** Perhaps the most famous (and photographed) resident is the **Lone Cypress,** which has come to symbolize the coast's solitude and natural beauty. Even though the drive is only 17 miles, take your time. If you stop for lunch or souvenir shopping, inquire about a refund on the entry toll.

Upon exiting the drive, continue south to **Carmel-by-the-Sea.** Spend the afternoon browsing its boutiques and galleries before walking to **Carmel Beach** for sunset, followed by dinner at one of Carmel's many fine restaurants.

DAY 3: SANTA CRUZ

A little less than 1 hr by car from Monterey or Carmel-by-the-Sea.

Depart your hotel midmorning, and pick up Highway 1, following its curve around Monterey Bay north toward Santa Cruz. For a magical experience, book an excursion with the naturalists at **Elkhorn Slough Safari Nature Boat Tours** to see otters and other creatures up close. In Aptos, **Seacliff State Beach,** a strand known for its tall sandstone bluffs, is one of two beaches of note beyond **Moss Landing.** The visitor center at the other, Capitola's surfing spot **New Brighton State Beach,** has exhibits about the Chinese village that once existed here.

From the beaches, continue to Santa Cruz, and check into your hotel. If it fits your budget, the **Dream Inn Santa Cruz,** the city's only lodging directly on the beach, is the most convenient choice, with the **Hotel Paradox** another good option. Once settled in, stroll the **Santa Cruz Boardwalk,** and catch the sunset over cocktails, dinner, or both. If time permits, walk or drive a bit of **West Cliff Drive,** which winds around to a lighthouse.

DAY 4: SANTA CRUZ TO SAN FRANCISCO

90 mins by car in light traffic, not counting stops.

Highway 1 darts up the coast 77 miles to San Francisco, occasionally so close to the Pacific that a section collapses into the sea and must be rebuilt. Although not as dramatic as Big Sur to the south or Mendocino to the north, the landscape still is fetching.

Let your desire to arrive in San Francisco control your pace. As you drive north, you can stop to check out the art galleries in small **Davenport** or ogle the ocean from the cliffs above. Farther along, at **Año Neuvo State Park,** you can hike a short way to the dunes to observe the resident elephant seals.

If you're getting hungry, knotty-pine-paneled **Duarte's Tavern,** in business in **Pescadero** since 1894, delivers a blast from the past along with stick-to-your-ribs American standards like deep-fried calamari and pork chops with old-school applesauce. To reach the restaurant, head east 2 miles on Pescadero Creek Road. **Half Moon Bay,** 17 miles north, has more updated fare. Suburban encroachment becomes more evident as you approach San Francisco. If pressed for time, head east on Highway 92 to I–280 north to get to San Francisco more quickly.

San Francisco's Greatest Hits, 3 Days

DAY 1: UNION SQUARE, CHINATOWN, NORTH BEACH

30–45 mins on public transport.

Straight from the airport, drop your bags at the lighthearted **Hotel Zetta,** south of Market Street (SoMa). A walk north to **Union Square** packs a wallop of people-watching, window-shopping, and architecture viewing. **Chinatown**—chock-full of dim sum shops, storefront temples, and open-air markets—promises authentic bites for lunch. Catch a Powell Street **cable car** to the end of the line, and get off to see the bay views and the antique arcade games at **Musée Mécanique,** the hidden gem of otherwise mindless **Fisherman's Wharf.** No need to go any farther than cosmopolitan **North Beach** for cocktail hour, dinner, and live music.

DAY 2: GOLDEN GATE PARK

5 mins by car or taxi, 45 mins by public transport from Union Square.

In **Golden Gate Park,** linger amid the flora of the **Conservatory of Flowers** and the **San Francisco Botanical Garden at Strybing Arboretum,** soak up some art at the **de Young Museum,** and find serene refreshment at the **San Francisco Japanese Tea Garden.** The Pacific surf pounds the cliffs below the **Legion of Honor** art museum, which has an exquisite view of the **Golden Gate Bridge**—when the fog stays away. A late-afternoon cocktail at the **Beach Chalet** will whet your appetite for dinner back in SoMa.

DAY 3: ROAMIN' AROUND

About 1 hr of driving total, not counting traffic.

Begin the day with a dose of culture at the **San Francisco Museum of Modern Art,** visiting one or two of the other nearby downtown museums on a day when SFMOMA is closed. Walk, drive, rideshare, or hop on a public bus heading less than a mile east to the **Ferry Building,** browsing the bodegas and lunching here before walking some of the **Embarcadero.** Afterward, if you haven't ridden a cable car yet, catch one on California Street up to Nob Hill. If you've been driving, retrieve your vehicle, and proceed to **Japantown.** Otherwise, rideshare or switch to public transit (on Sacramento Street); if on the bus, alight at Webster Street and walk south a few blocks. From Japantown, head to the gay **Castro** before bidding the City by the Bay adieu at a downtown hotel's plush lounge or trendy bar.

Sierra Riches: Yosemite, Gold Country, and Tahoe, 7 Days

This tour of some of California's most inspiring terrain serves up gold-rush-era history and offers a chance to hike a trail or two. Particularly in summer, book a room within Yosemite National Park (the Ahwahnee Hotel and the Wawona Hotel being the two historic choices) well ahead of your visit. Gateway towns such as Oakhurst and Mariposa can be less expensive, but you'll have to drive more.

DAY 1: INTO THE HIGH SIERRA

4–5 hrs by car from San Francisco.

First thing in the morning, head for the hills. Arriving in **Yosemite National Park, Bridalveil Fall,** and **El Capitan,** the 350-story granite monolith, greet you on your way to **Yosemite Village.** Ditch the car, and pick up information and refreshment before hopping on the shuttle to explore. Justly famous sights cram Yosemite Valley: massive **Half Dome** and **Sentinel Dome,** thundering **Yosemite Falls,** and wispy **Ribbon Fall** and **Nevada Fall.** Invigorating short hikes off the shuttle route lead to numerous vantage points. Even if you're not staying at the **Ahwahnee Hotel,** celebrate your arrival with a cocktail at the bar here.

DAY 2: YOSEMITE NATIONAL PARK

Yosemite shuttles run every 10–30 mins.

Ardent hikers consider **John Muir Trail to Half Dome** a must-do, tackling the rigorous 12-hour round-trip to the top of Half Dome. Mere mortals hike downhill from Glacier Point on Four-Mile Trail or **Panorama Trail,** the latter an all-day trek past waterfalls. Less demanding still is a drive to Wawona to the **Mariposa Grove of Big Trees** followed by lunch at the 19th-century **Wawona Hotel Dining Room.** In bad weather, take shelter in the **Ansel Adams Gallery** and **Yosemite Museum.** If conditions permit, head to **Glacier Point** for a breathtaking sunset view.

Tip 

If possible, time your Sierras trip between late spring and early fall to avoid the summer crowds and road-closing winter snowfalls in Yosemite and around Lake Tahoe. Yosemite's waterfalls peak in spring and early summer, while autumn brings the grape harvest and farm-related festivals.

DAY 3: GOLD COUNTRY SOUTH

2½–3 hrs by car from Yosemite Valley to Plymouth.

Get an early start driving west from Yosemite to Highway 49, which traces the mother lode that yielded many fortunes in gold (and plenty of heartaches) in the 1800s. In the living-history town at **Columbia State Historic Park** you can ride a stagecoach and pan for riches. About 46 miles north, **Sutter Creek's** well-preserved downtown bursts with shopping opportunities, or you can explore history at the outdoor **Miner's Bend** park and **Knight Foundry.** Switch focus in the **Shenandoah Valley,** the heart of the Sierra Foothills Wine Country. Taste your way through Zinfandels at **Turley Wine Cellars,** that varietal plus Cabernets and Rhône-style wines at **Terra Rouge and Easton Wines,** or award-winning Barbera and much more at jolly **Jeff Renquist Wines.** Retire in modest boutique comfort at **Rest Hotel Plymouth,** whose owners also operate nearby **Taste** restaurant.

DAY 4: GOLD COUNTRY NORTH

1½–2 hrs by car from Plymouth to Nevada City, not counting stops.

From Plymouth, drive north on Highway 49. Once in El Dorado County,

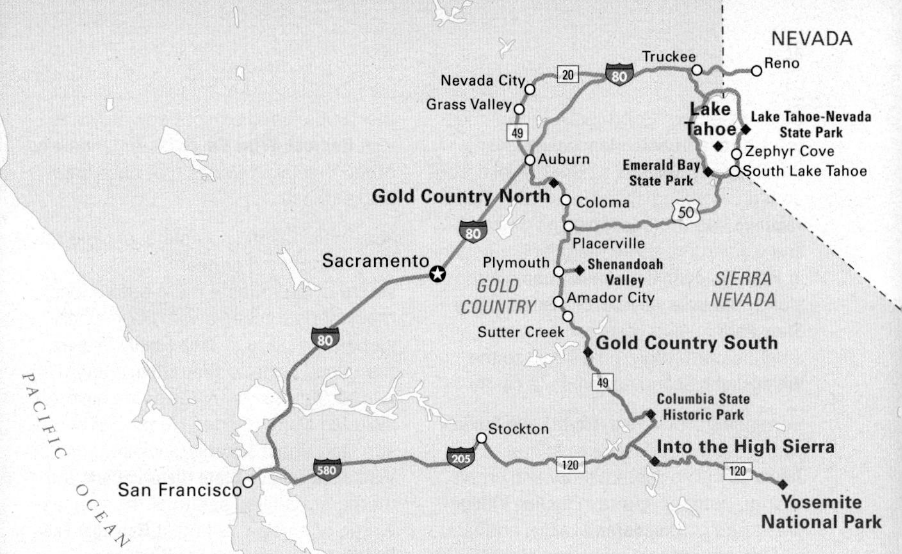

either detour east on U.S. 50 to learn about **Placerville**-area wines at **Starfield Vineyards** or **Lava Cap Winery,** or continue north on Highway 49 to **Marshall Gold Discovery State Historic Park.** Encompassing most of **Coloma,** the park preserves the spot where James Marshall's 1848 find set off the California gold rush.

If you went to the winery, backtrack to Highway 49, continuing north past Coloma, with the goal in all cases to stop in Old Town **Auburn** for lunch. The **Auburn Ale House** is open daily, but there are other choices in the historic district. After lunch, continue north to Grass Valley's **Empire Mine State Historic Park,** among the gold-rush's most productive mines. The park closes at 5 pm, so try to arrive by 3. The drive to the mine, which is off Highway 20, takes 35 minutes in light traffic.

The same company has transformed the mid-19th-century **Holbrooke Hotel** in Grass Valley and its Nevada City contemporary, the **National Exchange Hotel,** into boutique gems. Stay overnight at either lodging but have dinner at the latter's **Lola** restaurant. Grass Valley's more affordable **Gold Mine Inn** is also well-run.

DAYS 5–7: LAKE TAHOE

About 1 hr by car from Nevada City or Grass Valley.

If you didn't have time to stroll through Nevada City's historic district on Day 4, do so for an hour before heading east on Highway 20 and then I–80 toward Lake Tahoe. Stop in **Truckee** for lunch and a spin through its historic downtown. From there, continue south on Highway 89 to **Tahoe City,** on the northern shore of jewel-like **Lake Tahoe.**

Where you stay and the time of year will determine the order in which you explore the 72-mile shoreline of Lake Tahoe, bisected north–south by the California–Nevada border. No matter how much you plan, some backtracking is inevitable. Two lodgings worth considering in North Lake Tahoe are the **Sunnyside Steakhouse and Lodge** (Tahoe City, California side) and the **Hyatt Regency Incline Village** (Nevada side). **The Landing Tahoe Resort & Spa** and **Black Bear Lodge** are good South Lake Tahoe (California) choices; **The Lodge at Edgewood Tahoe** provides the classiest, albeit expensive, stay in Stateline (Nevada).

Clockwise from South Lake Tahoe, the top sights and activities include riding the **Heavenly Gondola** to see the lake from up high; hopping aboard a vintage **Tahoe Tastings** boat to (seasonally) sip wines; and visiting the three magnificent estates in **Pope-Baldwin Recreation Area.** Farther along, the lake views from **Emerald Bay State Park** inspire year-round; season and stamina permitting, hike down to the **Vikingsholm** Scandinavian-style castle.

Continuing clockwise, **North Lake Tahoe**'s pleasures include more boat rides from **Tahoe City** (also more history and ample dining); outdoor sports in **Incline Village** plus tours of **Thunderbird Lodge;** and Tahoe cruises aboard the stern-wheeler MS *Dixie II* departing from **Zephyr Cove.** Continue south to **Stateline,** to try your luck at the largest casinos, or head to the beaches and bays of **Lake Tahoe–Nevada State Park** to bask in the sun or go mountain biking.

Ultimate Napa and Sonoma Wine Trip, 4 Days

On this four-day loop north from San Francisco into the Wine Country, you'll taste well-known and under-the-radar wines, bed down in plush hotels, and dine at restaurants operated by celebrity chefs. Reservations are required for most tasting-room visits and recommended for dinner.

DAY 1: SOUTHERN SONOMA

About 90 mins total by car from San Francisco.

Head north from San Francisco to **Sonoma.** Less than an hour after crossing the Golden Gate Bridge, you'll be holding a glass of Chardonnay at **Sangiacomo Family Wines** (also known for Pinot Noir). The outdoor tasting areas here overlook land the Sangiacomos have farmed since 1927. For wines whose vines date from the 1800s, head straight downtown to visit **Bedrock Wine Co.** (with Zinfandel and other "heritage" wines that have great backstories).

Your initial tasting complete, explore the shops bordering or near Sonoma Plaza; if you're dying to taste more before lunch, many opportunities await. Have lunch just off the plaza at **Taub Family Outpost,** then head north to **Glen Ellen,** a town whose famous writer-residents have included M.F.K. Fisher, Hunter S. Thompson, and, most notably, Jack London. Visit **Jack London State Historic Park,** the memorabilia-filled estate of the famous writer, or enjoy a tasting at **Benziger Family Winery** or **Lasseter Family Winery.** Dine at **Glen Ellen Star,** and stay at the **Gaige House + Ryokan** or the **Olea Hotel.**

DAY 2: NORTHERN SONOMA

About 75 mins total by car.

From Glen Ellen, drive 40 minutes northwest on Highway 12 and north on U.S. 101 to **Healdsburg.** Start your tasting outside town amid rolling vineyards at **Ridge Vineyards** (Zinfandel, Cabernet, Petite Sirah) or **MacRostie Estate House** (Chardonnay and Pinot Noir). Have an informal lunch at **Dry Creek General Store,** in business since 1881.

After lunch, drive to the French-style château at **Jordan Vineyard & Winery** to taste Chardonnay and Cabernet Sauvignon. If you're staying at the luxurious, 250-acre **Montage Healdsburg** (with dinner at the resort's **Hazel Hill** restaurant), you're just minutes away. Two in-town lodgings, the **Harmon Guest House** and the **River Belle Inn,** are highly recommended. Have dinner at **Bravas Bar de Tapas** or **Valette,** both near the plaza. For a splurge, reserve a table (well ahead) at **SingleThread Farms Restaurant.**

DAY 3: NORTHERN NAPA VALLEY

About 75 mins total by car.

Head into the northern Napa Valley via Alexander Valley Road and Highway 128, which winds east to **Calistoga** through dairy pasture and the vineyards of the Knights Valley appellation. **Chateau Montelena** made history in the 1970s when its Chardonnay took top honors at a famous Paris tasting; the winery also makes Cabernet Sauvignon. After a tasting here or at nearby **Tamber Bey** (Cabernet and other Bordeaux-style reds), continue south 15 minutes on Highway 29 to St. Helena.

Much Napa Valley history unfolded at **Charles Krug Winery,** which began operations in 1861. Taste Cabernets and other Bordeaux-style reds here, then have lunch downtown at **Cook St. Helena** or **Market,**, afterward poking through Main Street shops before continuing south on Highway 29 to **Hall St. Helena** (high-scoring Cabernets, impressive art collection) or its homey neighbor **Prager Winery & Port Works.**

Backtrack to Calistoga to stay at **Embrace Calistoga,** a small inn known for superb hospitality, or **Solage,** a full-service, upscale-casual, luxury resort. The latter's **Solbar** restaurant ranks high among Calistoga restaurants, with **Evangeline** or **Sam's Social Club** two other fine options.

DAY 4: SOUTHERN NAPA VALLEY

45 mins driving in Napa Valley, 1 hr back to San Francisco

After breakfast at your lodging, head south on Highway 29 to Oakville, where sipping wine at **Nickel & Nickel** or **Silver Oak** makes clear why collectors covet Oakville Cabernet Sauvignons. Nickel & Nickel is on Highway 29; Silver Oak is east of it on Oakville Cross Road. After tasting, have lunch in **Yountville** at Thomas Keller's **Bouchon Bistro** or more casual **La Calenda.** Lunch completed, walk south on Washington Street, whose intriguing shops include **The Conservatory,** for "considered luxury," and **Montecristi Panama Hats. Heron House Yountville,** which pours the Cabernets of nine small producers, carries upscale fashion, art, and household items.

From Yountville, pop back on Highway 29, and head south to Highway 121. Turn west (right) to reach the Carneros District's **Domaine Carneros,** world-famous for its sparkling wines. There's hardly a more elegant way to bid a Wine Country adieu than on the vineyard-view terrace of this winery's splendid château.

If you can't tear yourself away from the Wine Country, extend your stay at the **Archer Hotel Napa** or the **Inn on First** in downtown Napa or the sprawling **Carneros Resort & Spa,** a few-minutes' drive east of Domaine Carneros.

Best of the Northern Coast, 5 Days

Hit coastal Northern California's highlights in one Highway 1 itinerary: scenic coastal drives, windswept towns, wine tasting, culinary delights, redwood forests. Make this route part of a longer trip north to the Oregon border, or loop back to San Francisco.

DAY 1: MARIN COUNTY AND POINT REYES NATIONAL SEASHORE

Without stops, Point Reyes National Seashore is about 1½ hrs by car from San Francisco on Hwy 1. Point Reyes Lighthouse is 45 mins by car from the visitor center.

As you head out of San Francisco on the Golden Gate Bridge, pull over at the **scenic lookout** on the north side, and take in the classic views of the city's skyline. If you haven't yet checked out the picturesque harbor community of **Sausalito,** just north of the bridge, now is your chance. It will be hard not to linger, but there is much to see today. Bidding San Francisco farewell, you will quickly find yourself immersed in the natural splendor of Marin County. Exit U.S. 101 onto Highway 1 at **Mill Valley** and head to **Muir Woods National Monument.** Walking among the tall coastal redwoods, you may forget that San Francisco lies less than a dozen miles away. However, the proximity to the city means that Muir Woods attracts throngs; accessing it can be difficult if you don't make a parking or shuttle reservation a day or two ahead (more in summer).

From Muir Woods, continue on Highway 1 past the laid-back beach towns of **Stinson Beach** and **Bolinas** to **Point Reyes National Seashore.** Spend the remainder of the day at the park tide pooling, kayaking, hiking one of the many trails, or exploring the **Point Reyes Lighthouse.** In the winter and early spring, be on the lookout for migrating gray whales.

Point Reyes Station offers a selection of shops and dining options, including **Tomales Bay Foods,** a foodies' favorite. Spend a quiet evening in town and stay overnight at one of the small inns nearby.

DAY 2: HEALDSBURG

Point Reyes Station to Healdsburg, via Jenner, is 2 hrs by car.

Continue north on Highway 1 past the town of **Bodega Bay,** which starred in the 1963 Alfred Hitchcock movie *The Birds.* At Jenner, known for its resident harbor seals, turn east on Highway 116 and follow the Russian River inland, taking time to stop at a winery or two along the way.

Not only is **Healdsburg** home to many acclaimed restaurants and luxurious hotels—making it an excellent place to stop for the night—but the town's compact layout and quality offerings also make it a favorite Wine Country destination. Ditch the car here, and stroll through the town's appealing square, with its many tasting rooms and boutiques.

DAYS 3–4: ANDERSON VALLEY AND MENDOCINO

Mendocino is 2 hrs by car from Healdsburg. Budget plenty of time for stops in Anderson Valley, and start early enough to ensure you end this scenic drive before sunset.

Driving north on U.S. 101 from Healdsburg, pick up Highway 128 at Cloverdale and head into the **Anderson Valley.** This wine region is famous for Pinot Noir and Chardonnay (also Gewürztraminer

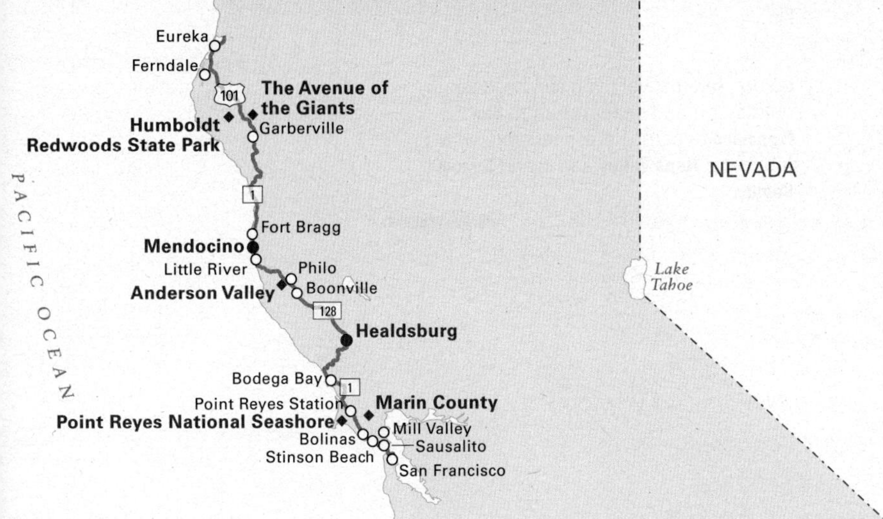

and other Alsace white varietals), and the laid-back atmosphere of its tasting rooms make them refreshing alternatives to those in Napa Valley. **Pennyroyal Farm, Roederer Estate,** and **Phillips Hill Winery** are all recommended. The small towns of **Boonville** and **Philo** have high-quality restaurants.

Highway 128 follows the Navarro River through several miles of dense and breathtaking redwood forest ending at the ocean. From here you meet up again with Highway 1 as it winds along a portion of the coast bestrewn with immense rock formations.

With their sophisticated restaurants and lodgings, the towns of **Mendocino** and **Little River,** just to the south, are great choices for your overnight stay, though Elk's **Harbor House Inn** wins the dining prize for its prix-fixe multicourse extravaganzas. **Fort Bragg** has reasonably priced motels and inns, some with full ocean views.

Spend the next day and a half exploring the area. Opportunities for stunning coastal walks abound, including the **Mendocino Headlands, Van Damme State Park,** and the **Fort Bragg Coastal Trail.** Save time to explore Mendocino itself with its New England–style architecture and art galleries and boutiques.

DAY 5: HUMBOLDT REDWOODS STATE PARK AND THE AVENUE OF THE GIANTS

Mendocino to Eureka via The Avenue of the Giants is 3 hrs by car.

Driving north on Highway 1, the road eventually curves inland and meets up with U.S. 101 near Leggett. Head north on U.S. 101 to reach the redwoods.

A drive through **The Avenue of the Giants** will take your breath away. The 32-mile stretch of road, also signed as Highway 254, runs alongside some of the planet's tallest trees as it weaves through a portion of **Humboldt Redwoods State Park.** Even if in a hurry, make time for a short hike through **Founders Grove** or **Rockefeller Forest.**

From here, you can continue your way up the coast through the **Redwood National and State Parks** and on to the Oregon border. Alternatively, you can head south on U.S. 101 and either return to **San Francisco** or combine this itinerary with a trip to the **Napa Valley** and inland **Sonoma County.**

Chapter 4

SAN DIEGO

Updated by
Claire Deeks van Der Lee, Marlise Kast-Myers,
Sabrina Medora, Kai Oliver-Kurtin, and Jeff Terich

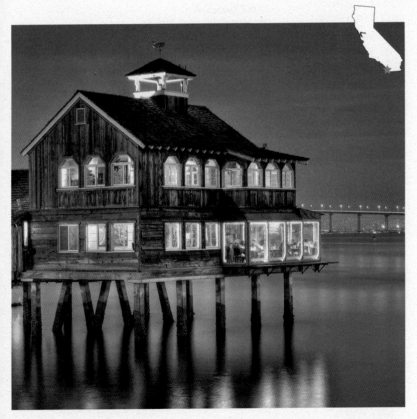

★★★★★

★★★★★

★★★★★

★★★★☆

★★★☆☆

WELCOME TO SAN DIEGO

TOP REASONS TO GO

★ **Sun and surf:** Legendary beaches and surfing in La Jolla, Coronado, and Point Loma.

★ **Good eats:** Brewpubs, a wide mix of ethnic cuisines, fresh seafood and produce, and modern cafés delight diners.

★ **Great golf:** A concentration of beautiful courses with sweeping ocean views and light breezes.

★ **Stellar shopping:** From hip boutiques and fine Mexican crafts to the upscale Fashion Valley Mall.

★ **Family time:** Fun for all ages at LEGOLAND, Balboa Park, the San Diego Zoo, and more.

★ **Outdoor sports:** A perfect climate for biking, hiking, sailing—anything—outdoors.

1 Downtown. This area is filled with walkable A-list attractions like the Gaslamp Quarter and the waterfront.

2 Balboa Park, Bankers Hill, and San Diego Zoo. San Diego's cultural heart is where you'll find most of the city's museums and its world-famous zoo.

3 Old Town and Uptown. California's first permanent European settlement is now preserved as a state historic park in Old Town. Uptown's neighborhoods offer a unique mix of historical charm and modern urbanity.

4 Mission Bay and the Beaches. With 27 miles of shoreline, this 4,600-acre aquatic park is a monument to sports and fitness.

5 La Jolla. This luxe, bluff-top enclave fittingly means "the jewel" in Spanish. Come here for fantastic upscale shopping and unspoiled stretches of coast.

6 Point Loma Peninsula. Visit the site of the first European landfall on Point Loma.

7 Coronado. Home to the Hotel Del, Coronado's island-like isthmus is a favorite celebrity haunt.

PACIFIC OCEAN

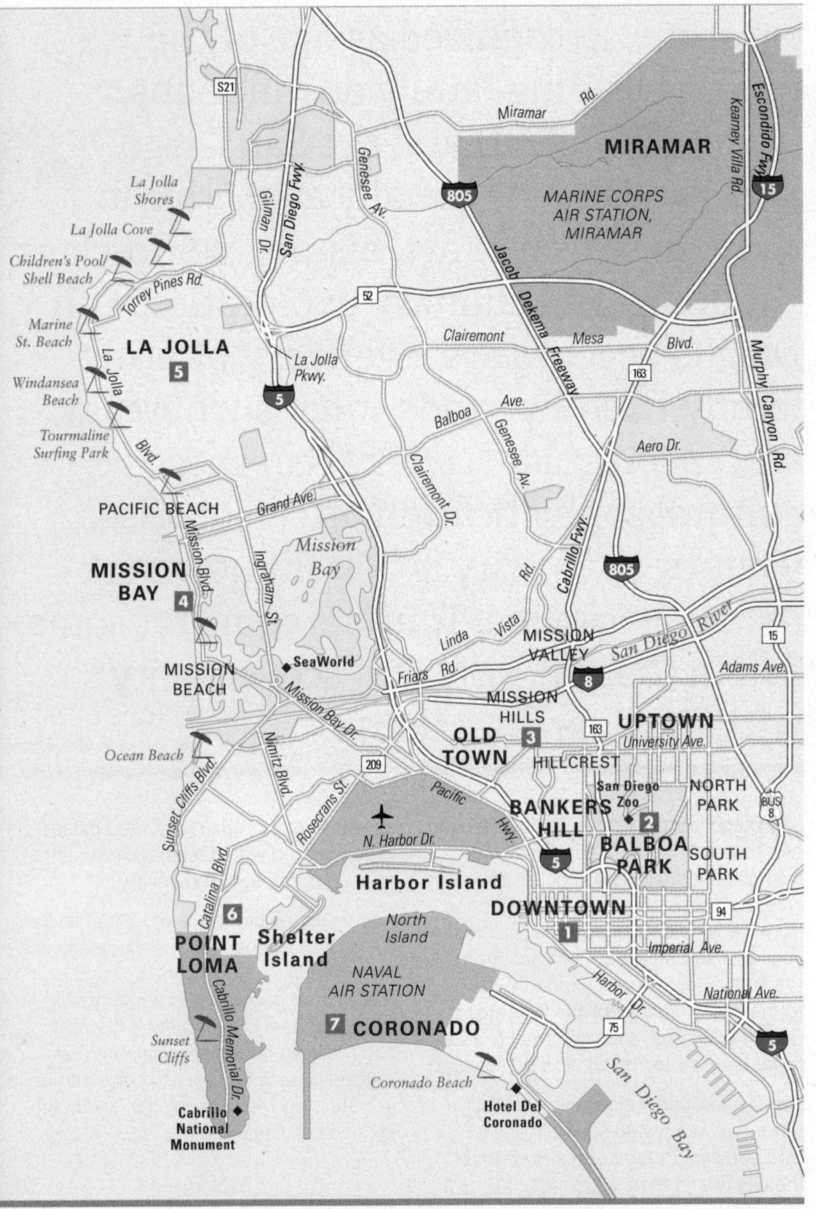
MIRAMAR
MARINE CORPS AIR STATION, MIRAMAR
Miramar Rd.
Escondido Fwy.
Kearney Villa Rd.
Genesee Av.
Gilman Dr.
San Diego Fwy.
La Jolla Shores
La Jolla Cove
Children's Pool/ Shell Beach
Torrey Pines Rd.
Marine St. Beach
LA JOLLA
La Jolla Blvd.
Windansea Beach
Tourmaline Surfing Park
La Jolla Pkwy.
Jacob Dekema Freeway
Clairemont Mesa Blvd.
Murphy Canyon Rd.
Balboa Ave.
Genesee Av.
Aero Dr.
Clairemont Dr.
PACIFIC BEACH
Grand Ave.
Mission Blvd.
Ingraham St.
Mission Bay
MISSION BAY
Cabrillo Fwy.
Linda Vista Rd.
MISSION VALLEY
San Diego River
Adams Ave.
SeaWorld
MISSION BEACH
Mission Bay Dr.
Friars Rd.
MISSION HILLS
OLD TOWN
UPTOWN
University Ave.
Ocean Beach
Sunset Cliffs Blvd.
Nimitz Blvd.
Rosecrans St.
Pacific Hwy.
HILLCREST
San Diego Zoo
NORTH PARK
BANKERS HILL
BALBOA PARK
SOUTH PARK
N. Harbor Dr.
Harbor Island
Catalina Blvd.
DOWNTOWN
North Island
POINT LOMA
Shelter Island
NAVAL AIR STATION
Imperial Ave.
Harbor Dr.
National Ave.
Cabrillo Memorial Dr.
CORONADO
Sunset Cliffs
Coronado Beach
San Diego Bay
Cabrillo National Monument
Hotel Del Coronado
S21
805
15
52
163
5
8
209
94
75
BUS 8
1
2
3
4
5
6
7

San Diego is a vacationer's paradise, complete with idyllic year-round temperatures and 70 miles of pristine coastline. Recognized as one of the nation's leading family destinations, with LEGOLAND and the San Diego Zoo, San Diego is equally attractive to those in search of art, history, world-class shopping, and culinary exploration. San Diego's beaches are legendary, offering family-friendly sands, killer surf breaks, and spectacular scenery. San Diego's cultural sophistication often surprises visitors, as the city is better known for its laid-back vibe. Tourists come for some fun in the sun, only to discover a city with much greater depth.

San Diego is a big California city—second only to Los Angeles in population—with a small-town feel. San Diego's many neighborhoods offer diverse adventures: from the tony boutiques in La Jolla to the yoga and surf shops of Encinitas; from the subtle sophistication of Little Italy to the flashy nightlife of the Downtown Gaslamp Quarter, each community adds flavor and flair to San Diego's personality.

San Diego County also covers a lot of territory, roughly 400 square miles of land and sea. To the north and south of the city are its famed beaches. Inland, a succession of chaparral-covered mesas is punctuated with deep-cut canyons that step up to forested mountains.

Known as the birthplace of California, San Diego was claimed for Spain by explorer Juan Rodríguez Cabrillo in 1542 and eventually came under Mexican rule. You'll find reminders of San Diego's Spanish and Mexican heritage throughout the region—in architecture and place-names, in distinctive Mexican cuisine, and in the historic buildings of Old Town.

In 1867 developer Alonzo Horton, who called the town's bay front "the prettiest place for a city I ever saw," began building a hotel, a plaza, and prefab homes on 960 Downtown acres. A remarkable number of these buildings are preserved in San Diego's historic Gaslamp Quarter today. The city's fate was sealed in the 1920s when the U.S. Navy, impressed by the city's excellent harbor and temperate climate, decided to build a destroyer base on San Diego Bay. Today, the military operates many bases and installations throughout the county (which, added together, form the largest military base in the world) and continues to be a major contributor to the local economy.

Planning

Getting Here and Around

AIR

The major airport is San Diego International Airport (SAN), formerly called Lindbergh Field. Most airlines depart and arrive at Terminal 2. Southwest, Frontier, and Alaska Airlines are reserved for Terminal 1. Free, color-coded shuttles loop the airport and match the parking lot they serve.

AIRPORT San Diego International Airport. ✉ *3225 N. Harbor Dr., off I–5* ☎ *619/400–2400* 🌐 *www.san.org.*

AIRPORT TRANSFERS San Diego Transit. ☎ *619/233–3004* 🌐 *www.511sd.com.* **SuperShuttle.** ☎ *800/258–3826* 🌐 *www.supershuttle.com.*

CAR

A car is necessary for getting around greater San Diego on the sprawling freeway system and for visiting the North County beaches, mountains, and desert. Driving around San Diego County is pretty simple: most major attractions are within a few miles of the Pacific Ocean. Interstate 5, which stretches north–south from Oregon to the Mexican border, bisects San Diego. Interstate 8 provides access from Yuma, Arizona, and points east. Drivers coming from the Los Angeles area, Nevada, and the mountain regions beyond can reach San Diego on Interstate 15. During rush hours there are jams on Interstate 5 and on Interstate 15 between Interstate 805 and Escondido.

There are a few border inspection stations along major highways in San Diego County, the largest just north of Oceanside on Interstate 5 near San Clemente. Travel with your driver's license, and passport if you're an international traveler.

PUBLIC TRANSPORTATION

Visit 🌐 *www.511sd.com*, which lists routes and timetables for the Metropolitan Transit System and North County Transit District. Local/urban bus fare is $2.50 one-way, or $6 for an unlimited day pass (exact change only; pay when you board). A one-way ride on the city's iconic red trolleys is $2.50; get your ticket at any trolley vending machine.

Under the umbrella of the Metropolitan Transit System, there are two major transit agencies in the area: San Diego Transit and North County Transit District (NCTD). You will need to buy a $2 compass card, available when you board for the first time, on which are loaded your destinations to use MTS. Day passes, available for 1 to 30 days and starting at $6, give unlimited rides on nonpremium regional buses and the San Diego Trolley. You can buy them from most trolley vending machines, at the Downtown Transit Store, and at Albertsons markets. A $12 Regional Plus Day Pass adds Coaster service and premium bus routes.

The bright-red trolleys of the San Diego Trolley light-rail system operate on three lines that serve Downtown San Diego, Mission Valley, Old Town, South Bay, the U.S. border, and East County. The trolleys operate seven days a week from about 5 am to midnight, depending on the station, at intervals of about 15 minutes. The trolley system connects with San Diego Transit bus routes—connections are posted at each trolley station. Bicycle lockers are available at most stations and bikes are allowed on buses and trolleys though space is limited. Trolleys can get crowded during morning and evening rush hours. Schedules are posted at each stop; on-time performance is excellent.

NCTD bus routes connect with Coaster commuter train routes between Oceanside and the Santa Fe Depot in San Diego. They serve points from Del Mar north to San Clemente, inland to Fallbrook, Pauma Valley, Valley Center, Ramona, and Escondido, with transfer points within the city of San Diego. The Sprinter light rail provides service between Oceanside and Escondido, with buses connecting to popular North County attractions.

San Diego Transit bus fares range from $2.50 to $5; North County Transit District bus fares are $2.50. You must have exact change in coins and/or bills. Pay upon boarding. Transfers are not included; the $6 day pass is the best option for most bus travel and can be purchased onboard.

San Diego Trolley tickets cost $2.50 and are good for two hours, but for one-way travel only. Round-trip tickets are double the one-way fare.

Tickets are dispensed from self-service machines at each stop; exact fare in coins is recommended, although some machines accept bills in $1, $5, $10, and $20 denominations and credit cards. Ticket vending machines will return up to $5 in change. For trips on multiple buses and trolleys, buy a day pass good for unlimited use all day.

FRED (FREE RIDE EVERYWHERE DOWNTOWN)

These open-air electric vehicles offer free rides throughout the Downtown area. Riders can make a pickup request through the FRED app, or simply flag one down. 🌐 *www.thefreeride.com*

CONTACTS North County Transit District. ☎ *760/966–6500* 🌐 *www.gonctd.com.* **San Diego Transit.** ☎ *619/233–3004* 🌐 *www.511sd.com.*

RIDE-SHARING

App-driven ride-sharing services such as Uber and Lyft are popular in San Diego. Drivers are readily available from most in-town destinations and also service the airport.

TRAIN

Amtrak serves Downtown San Diego's Santa Fe Depot with daily trains to and from Los Angeles, Santa Barbara, and San Luis Obispo. Amtrak trains stop in San Diego North County at Solana Beach and Oceanside. Coaster commuter trains, which run between Oceanside and San Diego Monday through Saturday, stop at the same stations as Amtrak as well as others. The frequency is about every half hour during the weekday rush hour, with four trains on Saturday. One-way fares are $5 to $6.50, depending on the distance traveled. The *Sprinter* runs between Oceanside and Escondido, with many stops along the way.

Metrolink operates high-speed rail service ($17) between the Oceanside Transit Center and Union Station in Los Angeles.

CONTACTS Coaster. ☎ *760/966–6500* 🌐 *www.gonctd.com/coaster.* **Metrolink.** ☎ *800/371–5465* 🌐 *www.metrolinktrains.com.*

Activities

San Diego offers bountiful opportunities for bikers, from casual boardwalk cruises to strenuous rides into the hills. The mild climate makes biking in San Diego a year-round delight. Bike culture is respected here, and visitors are often impressed with the miles of designated bike lanes running alongside city streets and coastal roads throughout the county.

If you're a beginner surfer, consider paddling in the waves off Mission Beach, Pacific Beach, Tourmaline Surfing Park, La Jolla Shores, Del Mar, or Oceanside. More experienced surfers usually head for Sunset Cliffs, La Jolla reef breaks, Black's Beach, or Swami's in Encinitas. All necessary equipment is included in the cost of all surfing schools. Beach-area Y's offer surf lessons and surf camp in the summer months and during spring break.

Beaches

San Diego's beaches have a different vibe from their northern counterparts in neighboring Orange County and glitzy Los Angeles farther up the coast. San Diego is more laid-back and less of a scene. Cyclists on cruiser bikes whiz by as surfers saunter toward the waves and sunbathers bronze under the sun, be it July or November.

Even at summer's hottest peak, San Diego's beaches are cool and breezy. Ocean waves are large, and the water will be colder than what you experience at tropical beaches—temperatures range from 55°F to 65°F from October through June, and 65°F to 73°F from July through September.

Finding a parking spot near the ocean can be hard in summer. Del Mar has a pay lot and metered street parking around the 15th Street Beach. La Jolla Shores has free street parking up to two hours. Mission Beach and other large beaches have unmetered parking lots, but space can be limited. Your best bet is to arrive early.

Pay attention to signs listing illegal activities; undercover police often patrol the beaches. Smoking and alcoholic beverages are completely banned on city beaches. Drinking in beach parking lots, on boardwalks, and in landscaped areas is also illegal. Glass containers are not permitted on beaches, cliffs, and walkways, or in park areas and adjacent parking lots. Littering is not tolerated, and skateboarding is prohibited at some beaches. Fires are allowed only in fire rings or elevated barbecue grills. Although it may be tempting to take a sea creature from a tide pool as a souvenir, it may upset the delicate ecological balance, and it's illegal, too.

Year-round, lifeguards are stationed at nine permanent stations from Sunset Cliffs to Black's Beach. All other beaches are covered by roving patrols in the winter, and seasonal towers in the summer. When swimming in the ocean be aware of rip currents, which are common in California shores. For a surf and weather report, call San Diego's Lifeguard Services at ☎ *619/221–8899*. Visit 🌐 *www.surfline.com* for live webcams on surf conditions and water temperature forecasts.

Dining

San Diego is an up-and-coming culinary destination, thanks to its stunning Pacific Ocean setting, proximity to Mexico, diverse population, and the area's extraordinary farming community. Increasingly the city's veteran top chefs are being joined by a new generation of talented chefs and restaurateurs who are adding stylish restaurants with innovative food and drink programs to the dining scene at a record pace. Yes, visitors still are drawn to the San Diego Zoo and miles of beaches, but now they come for memorable dining experiences as well.

The city's culinary scene got a significant boost when San Diego emerged as one of the world's top craft beer destinations, with artisan breweries and gastropubs now in almost every neighborhood. San Diego also was on the cutting edge of the farm-to-table, Slow Food movement. Local sourcing is possible for everything from seafood to just-picked produce from a host of nationally recognized producers like Chino Farms and Carlsbad Aquafarm. The city's ethnically diverse neighborhoods with their modest eateries offering affordable authentic international cuisines add spice to the dining mix.

San Diego's distinct neighborhoods have their own dining personalities with friendly restaurants and bistros catering to every craving in this sun-blessed city. The trendy Gaslamp Quarter delights visitors looking for a broad range of innovative and international dining and nightlife, while bustling Little Italy offers a mix of affordable Italian fare and posh new eateries. Modern restaurants and cafés thrive in East Village, amid the luxury condos near Petco Park.

The Uptown neighborhoods centered on Hillcrest—an urbane district with San Francisco flavor—are a mix of bars and independent restaurants, many of which specialize in ethnic cuisine. North Park, in particular, has a happening restaurant and craft beer scene, with just about every kind of cuisine you can think of, and laid-back prices to boot. And scenic La Jolla offers some of the best fine dining in the city with dramatic water views as an added bonus.

Restaurant reviews have been shortened. For full information, visit Fodors.com. Prices are the average cost of a main course at dinner, or if dinner is not served, at lunch.

What It Costs

	$	$$	$$$	$$$$
RESTAURANTS	under $18	$18–$27	$28–$35	over $35

Hotels

In San Diego, you could plan a luxurious vacation at the beach, staying at a resort with panoramic ocean views, private balconies, and a full-service spa. Or you could stay Downtown, steps from the bustling Gaslamp Quarter, in a modern hotel featuring lively rooftop pools, complimentary wine receptions, and high-tech entertainment systems. But with some flexibility—maybe opting for a partial-view room a quick drive from the action—it's possible to experience San Diego at half the price.

Sharing the city's postcard-perfect sunny skies are neighborhoods and coastal communities that offer great diversity; San Diego is no longer the sleepy beach town it once was. In action-packed Downtown, luxury hotels cater to solo business travelers and young couples with trendy restaurants and cabana-encircled pools. Budget-friendly options can be found in smaller neighborhoods just outside the Gaslamp Quarter such as Little Italy and Uptown (Hillcrest, Mission Hills, and North Park).

You'll need a car if you stay outside Downtown, but the beach communities are rich with lodging options. Across the bridge, Coronado's hotels and resorts offer access to a stretch of glistening white sand that's often recognized as one of the best beaches in the country. La Jolla offers many romantic, upscale ocean-view hotels and some of the area's best restaurants and specialty shopping. But it's easy to find a water view in any price range: surfers make themselves at home at the casual inns and budget stays of Pacific Beach and Mission Bay. If you're planning to fish, check out hotels located near the marinas in Shelter Island, Point Loma, or Coronado.

For families, Uptown, Mission Valley, and Old Town are close to SeaWorld and the San Diego Zoo, offering good-value accommodations with extras like sleeper sofas and video games. Mission Valley is ideal for business travelers; there are plenty of well-known chain hotels with conference space, modern business centers, and kitchenettes for extended stays.

When your work (or sightseeing) is done, join the trendsetters flocking to Downtown's Gaslamp Quarter for its eateries, lounges, and multilevel clubs that rival L.A.'s stylish scenes.

PRICES

Note that even in the most expensive areas, you can find affordable rooms. High season is summer, and rates are lowest in fall. If an ocean view is important, request it when booking, but it will cost you.

Hotel reviews have been shortened. For full information, visit Fodors.com. Prices are the lowest cost of a standard double room in high season.

What It Costs

$	$$	$$$	$$$$
HOTELS			
under $161	$161–$230	$231–$300	over $300

Nightlife

The San Diego nightlife scene is much more diverse and innovative than it was just a decade ago. Back then, options were limited to the pricey singles-heavy dance clubs Downtown, the party-hearty atmosphere of Pacific Beach, and a handful of charmingly musty neighborhood dive bars popular with locals. Today, options in San Diego have expanded dramatically, boasting more than 150 craft breweries throughout the county, not to mention several stylish cocktail lounges.

The Gaslamp Quarter is still one of the most popular areas to go for a night on the town. Named for actual gaslights that once provided illumination along its once-seedy streets (it housed a number of gambling halls and brothels), the neighborhood bears only a trace of its debauched roots. Between the Gaslamp and nearby East Village, Downtown San Diego mostly comprises chic nightclubs, tourist-heavy pubs, and a handful of live music venues. Even most of the hotels Downtown have a street-level or rooftop bar—so plan on making it a late night if that's where you intend to bunk. On weekends, parking can be tricky; most lots run about $20, and though there is metered parking (free after 6 pm and all day Sunday), motorists don't give up those coveted spots so easily. Some restaurants and clubs offer valet, though that can get pricey.

Hillcrest is a popular area for LGBTQ nightlife and culture, whereas just a little bit east of Hillcrest, ever-expanding North Park features a diverse range of bars and lounges that cater to a twenty- and thirtysomething crowd, bolstering its reputation as the city's hipster capital. Nearby Normal Heights is a slightly less pretentious alternative, though whichever of these neighborhoods strikes your fancy, a cab from Downtown will run about the same price: $15.

Nightlife along the beaches is more of a mixed bag. Where the scene in Pacific Beach might feel like every week is spring break, La Jolla veers toward being more cost-prohibitive. And although Point Loma is often seen as a sleepier neighborhood in terms of nightlife, it's coming into its own with some select destinations.

If your drink involves caffeine and not alcohol, there's no shortage of coffeehouses in San Diego, and some of the better ones in Hillcrest and North Park stay open past midnight. Many of them also serve beer and wine, if the caffeine buzz isn't enough.

Shopping

San Diego's retail landscape has changed radically in recent years with the opening of several new shopping centers—some in historic buildings—that are focused more on locally owned boutiques than national retailers. Where once the Gaslamp was the place to go for urban apparel and unique home decor, many independently owned boutiques have decided to set up shop in the charming neighborhoods east of Balboa Park known as North Park and South Park. Although Downtown is still thriving, any shopping trip to San Diego should include venturing out to the city's diverse and vibrant neighborhoods. Not far from Downtown, Little Italy is the place to find contemporary art, modern furniture, and home accessories.

Old Town is a must for pottery, ceramics, jewelry, and handcrafted baskets. Uptown is known for its mélange of funky bookstores, offbeat gift shops, and nostalgic collectibles and vintage stores. The beach towns offer the best swimwear and sandals. La Jolla's chic boutiques offer a more intimate shopping experience, along with some of the classiest clothes, jewelry, and shoes in the county. The new La Plaza La Jolla is an open-air shopping center with boutiques and galleries in a Spanish-style building overlooking the cove. Point Loma's Liberty Station shopping area in the former Naval Training Center has art galleries, restaurants, and home stores. Trendsetters will have no trouble finding must-have handbags and designer apparel at the world-class Fashion Valley mall in Mission Valley, a haven for luxury brands such as Hermès, Gucci, and Jimmy Choo.

Enjoy near-perfect weather year-round as you explore shops along the scenic waterfront. The Headquarters at Seaport is a new open-air shopping and dining center in the city's former Police Headquarters building. Here there are some big names, but mostly locally owned boutiques selling everything from gourmet cheese to coastal-inspired home accessories. Just next door, Seaport Village is still the place to go for trinkets and souvenirs. If you don't discover what you're looking for in the boutiques, head to Westfield Horton Plaza, the Downtown mall with more than 120 stores. The sprawling mall completed a major restoration project in 2016 to include a new public plaza, amphitheater, and fountains.

Most malls have free parking in a lot or garage, and parking is not usually a problem. Some of the shops in the Gaslamp Quarter offer validated parking or valet parking.

Tours

BOAT TOURS

Visitors to San Diego can get a great overview of the city from the water. Tour companies offer a range of harbor cruises, from one-hour jaunts to dinner and dancing cruises. In season, whale-watching voyages are another popular option.

Flagship Cruises and Events

BOAT TOURS | One- and two-hour tours of the San Diego Harbor loop north or south from the Broadway Pier throughout the day. Other offerings include dinner and dance cruises, brunch cruises, and winter whale-watching tours December–mid-April. ✉ *990 N. Harbor Dr., Embarcadero* ☎ *619/234–4111* 🌐 *www.flagshipsd.com* 🎫 *From $28.*

H&M Landing

BOAT TOURS | From mid-December to mid-March, this outfitter offers three-hour tours to spot migrating gray whales just off the San Diego coast. ✉ *2803 Emerson St.* ☎ *619/222–1144* 🌐 *www.hmlanding.com* 🎫 *From $55.*

Hornblower Cruises & Events

BOAT TOURS | Sixty- and 90-minute tours around San Diego Harbor depart from the Embarcadero several times a day and alternate between the northern and southern portion of the bay. If you're hoping to spot some sea lions, take the North Bay route. Dinner and brunch cruises are also offered, as well as whale-watching tours in winter. ✉ *970 N. Harbor Dr.* ☎ *619/686–8700, 888/467–6256* 🌐 *www.hornblower.com* 🎫 *From $30.*

San Diego SEAL Tours

BOAT TOURS | This amphibious tour drives along the Embarcadero before splashing into the San Diego Harbor for a cruise. The 90-minute tours depart daily from 10 am to 5 pm from Seaport Village and the Embarcadero. Call for daily departure times and locations. ✉ *500 Kettner Blvd., Embarcadero* ☎ *619/298–8687* 🌐 *www.sealtours.com* 🎫 *$42.*

Seaforth Boat Rentals

BOAT TOURS | For those seeking a private tour on the water, this company can provide a skipper along with your boat rental. Options include harbor cruises, whale-watching, and sunset sails. Seaforth has four locations and a diverse fleet of sail and motorboats to choose from. ✉ *1641 Quivira Rd., Mission Bay* ☎ *888/834–2628* 🌐 *www.seaforthboat-rental.com* 🎫 *From $160.*

BUS AND TROLLEY TOURS

For those looking to cover a lot of ground in a limited time, narrated trolley tours include everything from Balboa Park to Coronado. To venture farther afield, consider a coach tour to the desert, Los Angeles, or even Baja, Mexico.

DayTripper Tours

BUS TOURS | **FAMILY** | Single- and multiday trips throughout Southern California, the Southwest, and Baja depart from San Diego year-round. Popular day trips include the Getty Museum, and theater performances in Los Angeles. Call or check the website for pickup locations. ☎ *619/334–3394* 🌐 *www.daytripper.com* 🎫 *From $89.*

Five Star Tours

BUS TOURS | Private and group sightseeing bus tour options around San Diego and beyond include everything from the San Diego Zoo and brewery tours to city tours and trips to Baja, Mexico. ✉ *1050 Kettner Blvd.* ☎ *619/232–5040* 🌐 *www.fivestartours.com* 🎫 *From $50.*

Old Town Trolley Tours

GUIDED TOURS | **FAMILY** | Combining points of interest with local history, trivia, and fun anecdotes, this hop-on, hop-off trolley tour provides an entertaining overview of the city and offers easy access to all the highlights. The tour is narrated, and you can get on and off as you please. Stops include Old Town, Seaport Village, the Gaslamp Quarter, Coronado, Little Italy, and Balboa Park. The trolley leaves every 30 minutes, operates daily, and takes two hours to make a full loop. ✉ *San Diego* ☎ *866/754–0966* 🌐 *www.trolleytours.com/san-diego* 🎫 *From $42.*

WALKING TOURS

Several fine walking tours are available on weekdays or weekends; upcoming walks are usually listed in the *San Diego Reader.*

Balboa Park Walking Tours

GUIDED TOURS | On Tuesday and Sunday at 11 am, free, hour-long walks start from the Balboa Park Visitor Center. Tuesday tours are led by volunteers from the visitor center and Sunday tours are led by the park rangers. Reservations are not required, but no tours are scheduled between Thanksgiving and the New Year. Private, custom tours are also available for a fee, with proceeds going to the Balboa Park Conservancy. Contact the visitor center for details and to schedule. ✉ *Balboa Park Visitor Center, 1549 El Prado, Balboa Park* ☎ *619/239–0512* 🌐 *www.balboapark.org* 🎫 *Free.*

Coronado Walking Tours

WALKING TOURS | Departing from the Glorietta Bay Inn at 11 am Tuesday, Thursday, and Saturday, this 90-minute stroll through Coronado's historic district takes in the island's mansions, old Tent City, the Hotel del Coronado, and the castles and cottages that line the beautiful beach. Reservations are recommended. ✉ *1630 Glorietta Blvd.* ☎ *619/435–5993* 🌐 *www.coronadowalkingtour.com* 🎫 *$15* ☞ *Cash only.*

Gaslamp Quarter Historical Foundation

WALKING TOURS | Ninety-minute walking tours of the Downtown historic district depart from the William Heath Davis House at 1 pm on Thursday and 11 am on Saturday. ✉ *410 Island Ave.* ☎ *619/233–4692* 🌐 *gaslampfoundation.org* 🎫 *$20.*

Visitor Information

For general information and brochures before you go, contact the San Diego Tourism Authority, which publishes the helpful *San Diego Visitors Planning Guide.* When you arrive, stop by one of the local visitor centers for general information.

When to Go

San Diego's weather is so ideal that most locals shrug off the high cost of living and relatively lower wages as a "sunshine tax." Along the coast, average temperatures range from the mid-60s to the high 70s, with clear skies and low humidity. Annual rainfall is minimal, less than 10 inches per year.

The peak season for sun seekers is July through October. In July and August, the mercury spikes and everyone spills outside. From mid-December to mid-March, whale-watchers can glimpse migrating gray whales frolicking in the Pacific. In spring and early summer, a marine layer hugs the coastline for much or all of the day (locals call it "June Gloom"), which can be dreary and disappointing for those who were expecting to bask in Southern California sunshine.

Downtown

Nearly written off in the 1970s, today Downtown San Diego is a testament to conservation and urban renewal. Once derelict Victorian storefronts now house the hottest restaurants, and the *Star of India,* the world's oldest active sailing ship, almost lost to scrap, floats regally along the Embarcadero. Like many modern U.S. cities, Downtown San Diego's story is as much about its rebirth as its history. Although many consider Downtown to be the 16½-block Gaslamp Quarter, it's actually comprised of eight neighborhoods, including East Village, Little Italy, and Embarcadero.

Gaslamp Quarter

Considered the liveliest of the Downtown neighborhoods, the Gaslamp Quarter's 4th and 5th avenues are peppered with trendy nightclubs, swanky lounge bars, chic restaurants, and boisterous sports pubs. The Gaslamp has the largest collection of commercial Victorian-style buildings in the country. Despite this, when the move for Downtown redevelopment gained momentum in the 1970s, there was talk of bulldozing them and starting from scratch. In response, concerned history buffs, developers, architects, and artists formed the Gaslamp Quarter Council to clean up and preserve the quarter. The majority of the quarter's landmark buildings are on 4th and 5th avenues, between Island Avenue and Broadway.

Sights

Gaslamp Museum at the Davis-Horton House

HISTORIC SITE | The oldest wooden house in San Diego houses the Gaslamp Quarter Historical Foundation, the district's curator. Before developer Alonzo Horton came to town, Davis, a prominent San Franciscan, had made an unsuccessful attempt to develop the waterfront area. In 1850 he had this prefab saltbox-style house, built in Maine, shipped around Cape Horn and assembled in San Diego (it originally stood at State and Market Streets). Ninety-minute walking tours ($20) of the historic district leave from the house on Thursday at 1 pm (summer only) and Saturday at 11 am (year-round). If you can't time your visit with the tour, a self-guided tour map ($2) is available. *410 Island Ave., at 4th Ave., Gaslamp Quarter 619/233–4692 www.gaslampfoundation.org $5 self-guided, $10 with audio tour Closed Mon.*

Restaurants

Breakfast Republic

$ | AMERICAN | Just because it's the most important meal of the day doesn't mean it can't also be flashy or innovative. Breakfast Republic adds some hipster flair to typical brunch fare with a menu that combines hearty Southern staples (grits, jambalaya), Mexican food (chilaquiles, breakfast burritos), and over-the-top treats such as Oreo pancakes and s'mores French toast. Come hungry, but come early; the restaurant doesn't accept reservations and the wait can be a bit long. **Known for:** rich, gooey pancakes and French toast; kombucha flights; kitschy decor. *Average main: $12 707 G St., Gaslamp Quarter 619/501–8280 www.breakfastrepublic.com No dinner.*

Taka

$$ | JAPANESE | Pristine fish imported from around the world and presented creatively attracts crowds nightly to this intimate Gaslamp restaurant. Table service is available inside and outside where an *omakase* (tasting menu) or eight-piece rolls can be shared and savored; take a seat at the bar to watch one of the sushi chefs preparing appetizers. The restaurant is a favorite with Japanese visitors and conventioneers. **Known for:** uni sushi topped with wasabi; omakase tasting menu; upscale sake offerings. *Average main: $18 555 5th Ave., Gaslamp Quarter 619/338–0555 www.takasushi.com No lunch.*

Hotels

★ Hard Rock Hotel

$$$ | HOTEL | Self-billed as a hip playground for rock stars and people who want to party like them, the Hard Rock is near Petco Park overlooking glimmering San Diego Bay. The interior oozes laid-back sophistication, and guest rooms include branded Sleep Like a Rock beds and the option of renting a guitar. **Pros:** central location; energetic scene; luxurious rooms. **Cons:** pricey drinks; some attitude; party scene tends to be loud. *Rooms from: $249 207 5th Ave., Gaslamp Quarter 619/702–3000, 866/751–7625 www.hardrockhotelsd.com 420 rooms No meals.*

★ Pendry San Diego

$$$$ | HOTEL | Opened in early 2017, the Pendry San Diego is the Gaslamp's newest stunner. **Pros:** well situated in Gaslamp Quarter; excellent dining options; complimentary coffee in the mornings. **Cons:** pricey room rates; meals are expensive; not very family-friendly. *Rooms from: $480 550 J St., Gaslamp Quarter 619/738–7000 www.pendry.com 317 rooms No meals.*

★ The Sofia Hotel

$$$ | HOTEL | This stylish and centrally located boutique hotel may have small rooms, but it more than compensates with pampering extras like motion-sensor temperature controls, a Zen-like 24-hour yoga studio, an updated lobby, and a brand-new spa suite. **Pros:** upscale amenities; historic building; near shops and restaurants. **Cons:** busy area; small rooms; spotty Wi-Fi. *Rooms from: $259 ✉ 150 W. Broadway, Gaslamp Quarter ☎ 619/234–9200, 800/826–0009 🌐 www.thesofiahotel.com 211 rooms No meals.*

★ The U.S. Grant, a Luxury Collection Hotel

$$$$ | HOTEL | The U.S. Grant may be more than a hundred years old (it first opened in 1910) but thanks to a top-to-bottom renovation in 2017, this grand old dame is now one of the most glamorous hotels in Southern California. **Pros:** sophisticated rooms; great location; near shopping and restaurants. **Cons:** street noise can be heard from the guest rooms; no in-room minibars or coffeemakers; surrounded by many major construction projects Downtown. *Rooms from: $304 ✉ 326 Broadway, Gaslamp Quarter ☎ 619/232–3121, 800/325–3589 🌐 www.marriott.com 270 rooms No meals.*

Nightlife

★ The Grant Grill

BARS/PUBS | Though the Grant Grill—located on the ground floor of the historic U.S. Grant Hotel—is a full-service restaurant, it's built up a reputation in recent years for stepping up San Diego's craft cocktail game. The cocktail menu is updated seasonally with fresh ingredients and themes (one recently featured a mini "Voodoo" doll frozen inside of a large ice cube), all of which are both innovative and palate pleasant. The atmosphere is comfortable and elegant, even on its busiest nights. *✉ U.S. Grant Hotel, 326 Broadway, Gaslamp Quarter ☎ 619/744–2077 🌐 www.grantgrill.com.*

★ Vin de Syrah

WINE BARS—NIGHTLIFE | This "spirit and wine cellar" sends you down a rabbit hole (or at least down some stairs) to a whimsical spot straight out of Alice in Wonderland. Behind a hidden door (look for a handle in the grass wall), you'll find visual delights (grapevines suspended from the ceiling, vintage jars with flittering "fireflies," cozy chairs nestled around a faux fireplace and pastoral vista) that rival the culinary ones—the wine list is approachable and the charcuterie boards are exquisitely curated. **■ TIP→ More than just a wine bar, the cocktails are also worth a try.** *✉ 901 5th Ave., Gaslamp Quarter ☎ 619/234–4166 🌐 www.syrahwineparlor.com.*

★ Westgate Hotel Plaza Bar

PIANO BARS/LOUNGES | The old-money surroundings, including leather-upholstered seats, marble tabletops, and a grand piano, supply one of the most elegant and romantic settings for a drink in San Diego. *✉ 1055 2nd Ave., Gaslamp Quarter ☎ 619/238–1818 🌐 www.westgatehotel.com.*

Embarcadero

The Embarcadero cuts a scenic swath along the harbor front and connects today's Downtown San Diego to its maritime routes. The bustle of Embarcadero comes less these days from the activities of fishing folk than from the throngs of tourists, but this waterfront walkway, stretching from the convention center to the Maritime Museum, remains the nautical soul of the city. There are several seafood restaurants here, as well as sea vessels of every variety—cruise ships, ferries, tour boats, and navy destroyers.

A huge revitalization project is under way along the northern Embarcadero. The overhaul seeks to transform the area with large mixed-use development projects, inviting parks, walkways, and public art installations. The redevelopment will eventually head south along the waterfront, with plans under way for a major overhaul of the entire Central Embarcadero and Seaport Village.

Sights

★ Maritime Museum

MARINA | **FAMILY** | From sailing ships to submarines, the Maritime Museum is a must for anyone with an interest in nautical history. This collection of restored and replica ships affords a fascinating glimpse of San Diego during its heyday as a commercial seaport. The jewel of the collection, the *Star of India,* was built in 1863 and made 21 trips around the world in the late 1800s. Saved from the scrap yard and painstakingly restored, the windjammer is the oldest active iron sailing ship in the world. The newly constructed *San Salvador* is a detailed historic replica of the original ship first sailed into San Diego Bay by explorer Juan Rodriguez Cabrillo back in 1542, and the popular HMS *Surprise* is a replica of an 18th-century British Royal Navy frigate. The museum's headquarters are on the *Berkeley,* an 1898 steam-driven ferryboat, which served the Southern Pacific Railroad in San Francisco until 1958.

Numerous cruises of San Diego Bay are offered, including a daily 45-minute narrated tour aboard a 1914 pilot boat and three-hour weekend sails aboard the topsail schooner the *Californian,* the state's official tall ship, and 75-minute tours aboard a historic swift boat, which highlights the city's military connection. Partnering with the museum, the renowned yacht *America* also offers sails on the bay, and whale-watching excursions are available in winter. ✉ *1492 N. Harbor Dr., Embarcadero* ☎ *619/234–9153* 🌐 *www.sdmaritime.org* 🎟 *$18.*

★ Museum of Contemporary Art San Diego (MCASD)

MUSEUM | At the Downtown branch of the city's contemporary art museum, explore the works of international and regional artists in a modern, urban space. The Jacobs Building—formerly the baggage building at the historic Santa Fe Depot—features large gallery spaces, high ceilings, and natural lighting, giving artists the flexibility to create large-scale installations. MCASD's collection includes many pop art, minimalist, and conceptual works from the 1950s to the present. The museum showcases both established and emerging artists in temporary exhibitions, and has permanent, site-specific commissions by Jenny Holzer and Richard Serra. ✉ *1100 and 1001 Kettner Blvd., Downtown* ☎ *858/454–3541* 🌐 *www.mcasd.org* 🎟 *$10; free 3rd Thurs. of the month 5–7* ⏲ *Closed Wed.*

★ The New Children's Museum (NCM)

MUSEUM | **FAMILY** | The NCM blends contemporary art with unstructured play to create an environment that appeals to children as well as adults. The 50,000-square-foot structure was constructed from recycled building materials, operates on solar energy, and is convection-cooled by an elevator shaft. It also features a nutritious and eco-conscious café. Interactive exhibits include designated areas for toddlers and teens, as well as plenty of activities for the entire family. Several art workshops are offered each day, as well as hands-on studios where visitors are encouraged to create their own art. The studio projects change frequently and the entire museum changes exhibits every 18 to 24 months, so there is always something new to explore. The adjoining 1-acre park and playground is across from the convention center trolley stop. ✉ *200 W. Island Ave., Embarcadero* ☎ *619/233–8792* 🌐 *www.thinkplaycreate.org* 🎟 *$14* ⏲ *Closed Tues.*

Seaport Village

PEDESTRIAN MALL | FAMILY | You'll find some of the best views of the harbor at Seaport Village, three bustling shopping plazas designed to reflect the New England clapboard and Spanish Mission architectural styles of early California. On a prime stretch of waterfront the dining, shopping, and entertainment complex connects the harbor with hotel towers and the convention center. Specialty shops offer everything from a kite store and swing emporium to a shop devoted to hot sauces. You can dine at snack bars and restaurants, many with harbor views.

Live music can be heard daily from noon to 4 at the main food court. Additional free concerts take place every Sunday from 1 to 4 at the East Plaza Gazebo. The **Seaport Village Carousel** (rides $3) has 54 animals, hand-carved and hand-painted by Charles Looff in 1895. Across the street, the **Headquarters at Seaport Village** converted the historic police headquarters into several trendsetting shops and restaurants. ✉ *849 W. Harbor Dr., Downtown* ☎ *619/530–0704 office and events hotline* 🌐 *www.seaportvillage.com.*

★ **USS *Midway* Museum**

MILITARY SITE | FAMILY | After 47 years of worldwide service, the retired USS *Midway* began a new tour of duty on the south side of the Navy pier in 2004. Launched in 1945, the 1,001-foot-long ship was the largest in the world for the first 10 years of its existence. The most visible landmark on the north Embarcadero, it now serves as a floating interactive museum—an appropriate addition to the town that is home to one-third of the Pacific fleet and the birthplace of naval aviation. A free audio tour guides you through the massive ship while offering insight from former sailors. As you clamber through passageways and up and down ladder wells, you'll get a feel for how the *Midway*'s 4,500 crew members lived and worked on this "city at sea."

Though the entire tour is impressive, you'll really be wowed when you step out onto the 4-acre flight deck—not only the best place to get an idea of the ship's scale, but also one of the most interesting vantage points for bay and city skyline views. An F-14 Tomcat jet fighter is just one of many vintage aircraft on display. Free guided tours of the bridge and primary flight control, known as "the Island," depart every 10 minutes from the flight deck. Many of the docents stationed throughout the ship served in the Navy, some even on the *Midway*, and they are eager to answer questions or share stories. The museum also offers multiple flight simulators for an additional fee, climb-aboard cockpits, and interactive exhibits focusing on naval aviation. There is a gift shop and a café with pleasant outdoor seating. This is a wildly popular stop, with most visits lasting several hours. ⚠ **Despite efforts to provide accessibility throughout the ship, some areas can only be reached via fairly steep steps; a video tour of these areas is available on the hangar deck.** ✉ *910 N. Harbor Dr., Embarcadero* ☎ *619/544–9600* 🌐 *www.midway.org* 🎟 *$21.*

Restaurants

★ **Eddie V's Prime Seafood**

$$$ | SEAFOOD | Don't be put off by the name, or that it is part of a small chain. This fine-dining restaurant at the Headquarters at Seaport in Downtown has won a devoted following for classic seafood, casual but sophisticated settings, and nightly live jazz. Chilled oysters and other shellfish compete with Maine lobster tacos and kung pao–style calamari to start the meal. The polished staff helps with informed descriptions of almost two-dozen entrées starring fish flown in fresh daily and prime steaks. Sea bass in a savory soy broth and Parmesan-crusted sole are favorites, while the seafood chopped salad is light and sharable. Truffled mac and cheese and au gratin cheddar potatoes are not-to-be-missed sides. Nightly happy hours in the V Lounge offer $8 wines, cocktails, and appetizers. **Known for:** wallet-friendly happy hour deals; indulgent truffled mac and cheese. *Average main: $34 789 W. Harbor Dr., Embarcadero 619/615–0281 www.eddiev.com No lunch.*

★ Puesto

$ | **MEXICAN** | Bold graffiti graphics, chandeliers with tangled telephone wires, and beat-heavy music energize this Downtown eatery that celebrates Mexican street food with a modern twist. Settle into one of the interior rooms or the sunny patio under orange umbrellas to sip margaritas and other specialty cocktails, Baja wines, or fruity aguas frescas made daily. Guacamole, ceviche, seafood tostadas, and a festive stack of chili-and-salt-spiced mango whet appetites for tasty street tacos—nine varieties including lobster, mushroom, and striped bass that can be mixed and matched for plates of three. Deep-fried carnitas with a cactus leaf salad, grilled filet mignon, and octopus tacos round out the menu. The original (and smaller) Puesto is in downtown La Jolla. **Known for:** taco trio plates; unique Parmesan guacamole; fruit-infused margaritas made in-house. *Average main: $16 789 W. Harbor Dr., Downtown 619/233–8880 www.eatpuesto.com.*

Hotels

★ InterContinental San Diego

$$$ | **HOTEL** | A new addition to the waterfront skyline, InterContinental San Diego provides a more luxurious and stylish option for travelers in what's generally an area populated by more family-friendly lodging. **Pros:** stunning waterfront views; excellent dining options at Vistal and Garibaldi; close to both airport and attractions. **Cons:** a bit on the pricier side; pedestrian traffic can be hectic because of nearby shopping/boating areas; entrances and elevators are a bit confusing. *Rooms from: $269 901 Bayfront Ct., Embarcadero 619/501–9400 ihg.com 400 rooms No meals.*

Shopping

★ The Headquarters at Seaport

OUTDOOR/FLEA/GREEN MARKETS | This new upscale shopping and dining center is in the city's former police headquarters, a beautiful and historic Mission-style building featuring an open courtyard with fountains. Restaurants and shops, many locally owned, occupy former jail facilities and offices. Pop into **Urban Beach House** for coastal-inspired fashion from popular surf brands for men and women, including accessories and home decor. Swing by **Fair World** for ethically sourced fashion and handmade gifts. **Perfume Gallery** offers more than 1,000 different scents in its extensive collection. **Madison San Diego** offers a great selection of leather goods and accessories, from apparel and handbags to belts and travel accessories. *789 W. Harbor Dr., Downtown 619/235–4013 theheadquarters.com.*

East Village

The most ambitious of the Downtown projects is East Village, not far from the Gaslamp Quarter, and encompassing 130 blocks between the railroad tracks up to J Street, and from 6th Avenue east to around 10th Street. Sparking the rebirth of this former warehouse district was the 2004 construction of the San Diego Padres' baseball stadium, PETCO Park. The Urban Art Trail has added pizzazz to drab city thoroughfares by transforming such things as trash cans and traffic controller boxes into works of art. As the city's largest Downtown neighborhood, East Village is continually broadening its boundaries with its urban design of redbrick cafés, spacious galleries, rooftop bars, sleek hotels, and warehouse restaurants.

Downtown, Balboa Park, Bankers Hill, and San Diego Zoo
LITTLE ITALY
DOWNTOWN
GASLAMP QUARTER
EMBARCADERO
San Diego Harbor
Tuna Harbor
San Diego Cruise Terminal
B Street Pier
International Visitor Information Center
Coronado Ferry Terminal
Broadway Pier
Navy Pier
Tuna Harbor Park
Santa Fe Depot
County Center/ Little Italy
Firehouse Museum
Amici Park
American Plaza
Civic Center
City Park
Westfield Horton Plaza
Pantoja Park
Seaport Village
The Headquarters at Seaport District
Convention Center
San Diego Convention Center
PETCO Park
MTS Trolley
5th Ave
KEY
Exploring Sights
Restaurants
Hotels

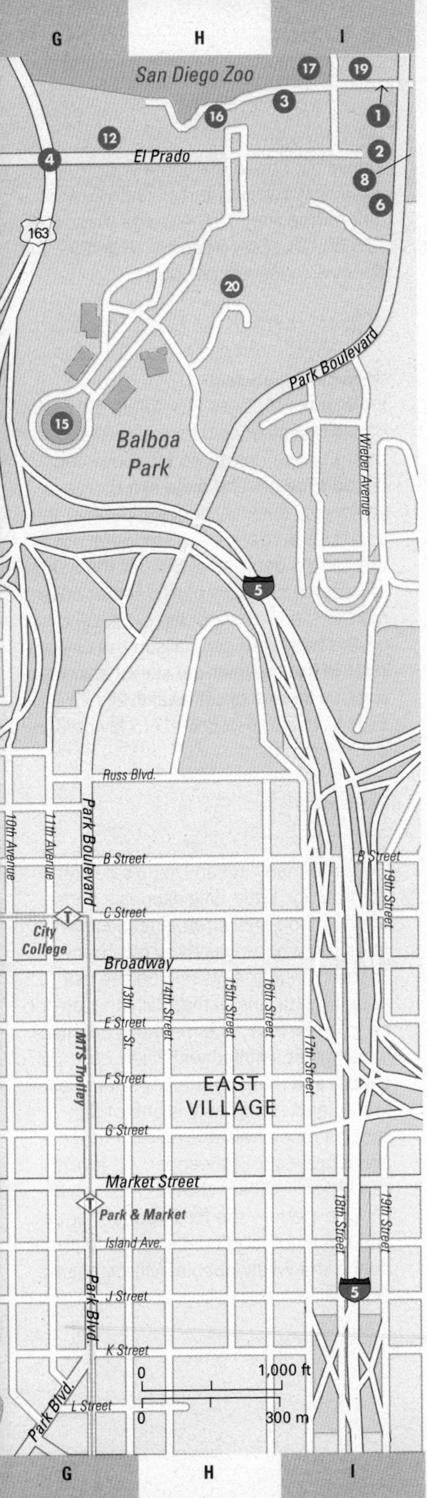

Sights

1 Balboa Park Carousel....I1
2 Bea Evenson Fountain...I1
3 Botanical Building........I1
4 Cabrillo Bridge.......... G1
5 Chicano Park............. E9
6 Fleet Science Center.....I1
7 Gaslamp Museum at the Davis-Horton House..... E8
8 Inez Grant Parker Memorial Rose Garden and Desert Garden.......I1
9 Little Italy Mercato C4
10 Maritime Museum...... A5
11 Museum of Contemporary Art San Diego (MCASD).... B6
12 The Museum of Us G1
13 The New Children's Museum (NCM)......... D8
14 Petco Park................ F9
15 San Diego Air & Space Museum G3
16 San Diego Museum of Art.......... H1
17 San Diego Zoo I1
18 Seaport Village.......... B9
19 Spanish Village Art Center.....................I1
20 Spreckels Organ Pavilion H2
21 USS *Midway* Museum A7

Restaurants

1 The Blind Burro.......... F9
2 Born and Raised.........C3
3 Breakfast Republic F8
4 Civico by The Park....... E1
5 The Crack Shack........ B2
6 Las Cuatro Milpas E9
7 Cucina Urbana........... E1
8 Eddie V's Prime Seafood.................. B8
9 Extraordinary Desserts................. D5
10 Herb & Wood........... B2
11 Little Italy Food Hall...... C4
12 Puesto.................... B8
13 ¡Salud!..................... E9
14 Taka E8

Hotels

1 Hard Rock Hotel E9
2 InterContinental San Diego............... B6
3 Pendry San Diego E8
4 The Sofia Hotel......... D6
5 The U.S. Grant, a Luxury Collection Hotel...................... E6

Sights

Petco Park

SPORTS VENUE | FAMILY | Petco Park is home to the city's major league baseball team, the San Diego Padres. The ballpark is strategically designed to give fans a view of San Diego Bay, the skyline, and Balboa Park. Reflecting San Diego's beauty, the stadium is clad in sandstone from India to evoke the area's cliffs and beaches; the 42,000 seats are dark blue, reminiscent of the ocean, and the exposed steel is painted white to reflect the sails of harbor boats on the bay. The family-friendly lawnlike berm, "Park at the Park," is a popular and affordable place for fans to view the game. The ballpark underwent a huge effort to improve dining in the park, and local food vendors and craft breweries now dominate the dining options. Behind-the-scenes guided tours of Petco, including the press box and the dugout, are offered throughout the year. ✉ *100 Park Blvd., East Village* ☎ *619/795–5011 tour hotline* 🌐 *sandiego.padres.mlb.com* 🎫 *$20 tour.*

Restaurants

The Blind Burro

$$ | MODERN MEXICAN | FAMILY | East Village families, baseball fans heading to or from Petco Park, and happy-hour-bound singles flock to this airy restaurant with Baja-inspired food and drink. Traditional margaritas get a fresh kick from fruit juices or jalapeño peppers; other libations include sangria and Mexican beers, all perfect pairings for house-made guacamole, ceviche, or salsas with chips. The menu doesn't include enchiladas or burritos, but the well-loved lobster and surf-and-turf tacos and extensive and innovative tortas like an Angus short rib topped with pico de gallo, and side dishes including Mexican-style corn dressed in cotija cheese as well as serrano-spiced pinto beans, more than make up for it. Save room for warm, cinnamon-sugar churros. **Known for:** house margarita with fruit infusions; surf-and-turf Baja-style tacos; gluten-free menu. 💲 *Average main: $18* ✉ *639 J St., East Village* ☎ *619/795–7880* 🌐 *www.theblindburro.com.*

Nightlife

★ Noble Experiment

PIANO BARS/LOUNGES | There are a handful of speakeasy-style bars in San Diego, though none deliver so far above and beyond the novelty quite like this cozy-yet-swank cocktail lounge hidden in the back of a burger restaurant. Seek out the hidden door (hint: look for the stack of kegs), tuck into a plush leather booth next to the wall of golden skulls, and sip on the best craft cocktails in the city. **■ TIP→ Reservations are almost always a must, so be sure to call ahead.** ✉ *777 G St., East Village* ☎ *619/888–4713* 🌐 *nobleexperimentsd.com.*

Little Italy

Home to many in San Diego's design community, Little Italy exudes a sense of urban cool while remaining authentic to its roots and marked by old-country charms: church bells ring on the half hour, and Italians gather daily to play bocce in Amici Park. The main thoroughfare, India Street, is filled with lively cafés, chic shops, and many of the city's trendiest restaurants. Little Italy is one of San Diego's most walkable neighborhoods, and a great spot to wander. Art lovers can browse gallery showrooms, while shoppers adore the Fir Street cottages. The neighborhood bustles each Saturday during the wildly popular Mercato farmers' market.

Sights

Little Italy Mercato

MARKET | Each Saturday tourists and residents alike flock to the Little Italy Mercato, one of the most popular farmers' markets in San Diego. More than 150 vendors line Date Street selling everything from paintings and pottery to flowers and farm-fresh eggs. Come hungry, as several booths and food trucks serve prepared foods. Alternatively, the neighborhood's many cafés and restaurants are just steps away. The Mercato is a great opportunity to experience one of San Diego's most exciting urban neighborhoods. ✉ *Date and India Sts., Little Italy* 🌐 *www.littleitalysd.com/events/mercato.*

Restaurants

★ Born and Raised

$$$$ | **STEAKHOUSE** | The name is cheeky if a little morbid; the title refers to the restaurant's speciality—steak. It's a twist on a classic steak house, with a menu full of aged, prime cuts of beef served with a number of sauces, or perhaps try the table-side-prepared steak Diane with flambéed jus. With its large gold doors, intimate booths, and stiff Manhattans, everything about the restaurant feels like old luxury, until you notice the portraits of famous rappers on the walls. **Known for:** table-side Caesar salad; aged New York steak; cheeky, glamorous decor. $ *Average main: $45* ✉ *1909 India St., Little Italy* ☎ *619/202–4577* 🌐 *www.bornandraisedsteak.com.*

★ The Crack Shack

$ | **AMERICAN** | **FAMILY** | Next to his successful fine-dining restaurant, Juniper and Ivy, celebrity chef Richard Blais has opened this more casual eatery complete with a walk-up counter, picnic-style tables, a boccie court, and a giant rooster—a nod to the egg- and chicken-theme menu. Ingredients are sourced from high-quality vendors and used for sandwiches, of which the fried chicken varieties shine, as well as salads and sides like fluffy minibiscuits with a miso-maple butter and a Mexican spin on poutine. The all-outdoor space feels like a cool playground for foodies, and there's even a slick bar that doles out craft cocktails. **Known for:** Señor Croque fried chicken sandwich with smoked pork belly; biscuits with miso-maple butter; all-outdoor seating with boccie court. $ *Average main: $12* ✉ *2266 Kettner Blvd., Little Italy* ☎ *619/795–3299* 🌐 *www.crackshack.com.*

★ Extraordinary Desserts

$ | **CAFÉ** | For Paris-perfect cakes and tarts embellished California-style with fresh flowers, head to this sleek, serene branch of Karen Krasne's pastry shop and café. The space with soaring ceilings hosts breakfasts, lunches, and light dinners, accompanied by a wide selection of teas, coffee, organic wines, and craft beers. For those who don't want to start with dessert, there are sandwiches, soups, salads, and artisanal cheeses, plus a kids' menu of grilled cheese or free-range turkey served on local bread. When it's time to satisfy your sweet tooth, try a slice of passion fruit ricotta cake, a mini-banana cream pie, or helping of croissant bread pudding. The original shop near Balboa Park, at 2929 5th Avenue, serves only desserts, coffees, and teas. **Known for:** blueberry coffee cake for breakfast; chocolate dulce de leche cake; house-made dips including onion dip and Parmesan pesto. $ *Average main: $14* ✉ *1430 Union St., Little Italy* ☎ *619/294–7001* 🌐 *www.extraordinarydesserts.com.*

★ Herb & Wood

$$ | **AMERICAN** | Design lovers will fall for celebrity chef Brian Malarkey's sprawling restaurant, a former art store that has been refashioned into four luxe spaces in one—an entryway lounge, outdoor lounge, fireplace-dotted patio, and the main dining room, which is flanked by beaded chandeliers, lush banquettes, and paintings in rich jewel tones. The menu is heavy on wood-roasted dishes, many of which are apt for sharing, like the roasted baby carrots or hiramasa with crispy quinoa. There are also larger options like an oxtail gnocchi and pizzas with toppings from mushrooms to bone marrow. Stop by the adjacent **Herb & Eatery** for coffee, pastries, prepared foods, and gift items. **Known for:** roasted baby carrots with cashew sesame dukkah; pillow-soft oxtail gnocchi; the secret menu Parker House rolls topped with Maldon sea salt. $ *Average main: $20* ✉ *2210 Kettner Blvd., Little Italy* ☎ *619/955–8495* 🌐 *www.herbandwood.com* 🕒 *No lunch.*

Little Italy Food Hall

$ | **FUSION** | **FAMILY** | A recently opened, chic update on the food court, Food Hall brings together a half dozen different innovative food counters to offer quick bites vastly more interesting than mall fare. Among its offerings are the seafood-centric Single Fin Kitchen and Wicked Maine Lobster, and an update on a local delicacy, Not Not Tacos. There's also a bar at the center, so every bite can be paired with a cold beer or cocktail. **Known for:** fusion tacos; bustling crowds of Mercato shoppers; beer/wine cart dispensing refreshments in the outdoor seating area. $ *Average main: $10* ✉ *550 W. Date St., Suite B, Little Italy* ☎ *619/269–7187* 🌐 *www.littleitalyfoodhall.com.*

Nightlife

★ Ballast Point Brewing Co.

BREWPUBS/BEER GARDENS | Until recently, you had to head to the Miramar/Scripps Ranch area for a tasting at Ballast Point, but now there's a spacious (and popular) local taproom in Little Italy. The Sculpin IPA is outstanding, as are the blue cheese duck nachos ✉ *2215 India St., Little Italy* ☎ *619/255–7213* 🌐 *www.ballastpoint.com.*

★ False Idol

BARS/PUBS | A walk-in refrigerator harbors the secret entrance to this tiki-theme speakeasy, which is attached to Craft & Commerce. Beneath fishing nets full of puffer-fish lights and elaborate tiki-head wall carvings, the knowledgeable staff serves up creative takes on tropical classics with the best selection of rums in town. **■ TIP→ The bar fills up quickly, especially on weekends. Make a reservation online a week or more in advance.** ✉ *675 W. Beech St., Little Italy* 🌐 *falseidoltiki.com.*

Karl Strauss' Brewing Company

BARS/PUBS | San Diego's first microbrewery now has multiple locations, but the original one remains a staple. This locale draws an after-work crowd for pints of Red Trolley Ale and later fills with beer connoisseurs from all walks of life to try Karl's latest concoctions. The German-inspired pub food is above average. ✉ *1157 Columbia St., Little Italy* ☎ *619/234–2739* 🌐 *www.karlstrauss.com.*

Barrio Logan

San Diego's Mexican-American community is centered in Barrio Logan, under the San Diego–Coronado Bay Bridge on the Downtown side. Chicano Park, spread along National Avenue from Dewey to Crosby streets, is the barrio's recreational hub. It's worth taking a short detour to see the huge murals of Mexican history painted on the bridge supports at National Avenue and Dewey Street; they're among the best examples of folk art in the city. Art enthusiasts will also enjoy the burgeoning gallery scene in the Barrio Logan neighborhood, rapidly becoming a hub for artists in San Diego.

GETTING HERE AND AROUND

Barrio Logan is located right off Interstate 5, at the Cesar E. Chavez Parkway exit. Driving is the easiest way to get there, especially coming from Downtown—in fact, it's only a mile from PETCO Park, and easily accessible via Imperial and Logan avenues. However, the Blue Line trolley also stops in Barrio Logan, and several bus lines also cross through the neighborhood, including the 9, 6, 20, 705, and 923.

When staying Downtown, Barrio Logan is also just a 15-minute walk, but with its somewhat isolated location under a bridge, visitors should exercise caution visiting the Chicano Park murals after dark.

Sights

★ Chicano Park

PUBLIC ART | FAMILY | The cultural center of the Barrio Logan neighborhood, Chicano Park—designated a National Historic Landmark in 2017—was born in 1970 from the activism of local residents who occupied the space after the state rescinded its promise to designate the land a park. Signed into law a year later, the park is now a protected area that brings together families and locals for both public and private events, a welcoming gathering space as well as an outdoor gallery featuring large murals documenting Mexican-American history and Chicano activism. Every year Chicano Park Day is held on April 21, filling the park with the sights and sounds of music, dancers, vintage cars, and food and clothing vendors. *✉ Logan Ave. and Cesar Chavez Pkwy., Barrio Logan 🌐 chicano-park.com; www.chicanoparksandiego.com.*

Restaurants

Las Cuatros Milpas

$ | MEXICAN | One of the oldest restaurants in San Diego, having opened in 1933, Las Cuatros Milpas feels like a closely held secret in Barrio Logan. Open daily until 3 pm, it almost inevitably attracts a big lunchtime rush, though the wait is worth it for the homemade tortillas, beans with chorizo, and rolled tacos. The menu is simple, though everything is delicious, and the interior—with checkered picnic tables—looks like it hasn't changed in 85 years. **Known for:** homemade tortillas; checkered picnic tables; chorizo con huevos. *[$] Average main: $5 ✉ 1857 Logan Ave., Barrio Logan ☎ 619/234–4460 🌐 www.las-cuatro-milpas.com ⏲ Closed Sun. ▭ No credit cards.*

★ ¡Salud!

$ | MEXICAN | The line that inevitably wraps around the building is indicative of the quality of the tacos and the large selection of local craft beers on tap. Indeed, these are some of the best tacos in all of San Diego, ranging from the classic carne asada and Baja fish tacos to fried-shell beef tacos and Califas, which features French fries inside the tortilla. Just remember—alcohol isn't allowed at the outdoor tables. **Known for:** Baja-style street tacos; Pruno de Piña (beer and fermented pineapple); churros and ice cream. *[$] Average main: $3 ✉ 2196 Logan Ave., Barrio Logan ☎ 619/255–3856 🌐 saludtacos.com.*

Balboa Park, Bankers Hill, and San Diego Zoo

Overlooking Downtown and the Pacific Ocean, 1,200-acre Balboa Park is the cultural heart of San Diego. Ranked as one of the world's best parks by the Project for Public Spaces, it's also where you can find most of the city's museums, art galleries, the Tony Award–winning Old Globe Theatre, and the world-famous San Diego Zoo. Often referred to as the "Smithsonian of the West" for its concentration of museums, Balboa Park is also a series of botanical gardens, performance spaces, and outdoor playrooms endeared to the hearts of residents and visitors alike.

In addition, the captivating architecture of Balboa's buildings, fountains, and courtyards gives the park an enchanted feel. Historic buildings dating from San Diego's

1915 Panama–California International Exposition are strung along the park's main east–west thoroughfare, El Prado, which leads from 6th Avenue eastward over the Cabrillo Bridge (formerly the Laurel Street Bridge), the park's official gateway. If you're a cinema fan, many of the buildings may be familiar—Orson Welles used exteriors of several Balboa Park buildings to represent the Xanadu estate of Charles Foster Kane in his 1941 classic, *Citizen Kane*. Prominent among them was the California Building, whose 200-foot tower, housing a 100-bell carillon that tolls the hour, is El Prado's tallest structure. Missing from the black-and-white film, however, was the magnificent blue of its tiled dome shining in the sun.

Bankers Hill is a small neighborhood west of Balboa Park, with gorgeous views ranging from Balboa Park's greenery in the east to the San Diego Bay in the west. It's become one of San Diego's hottest restaurant destinations.

Sights

★ Balboa Park Carousel

CAROUSEL | **FAMILY** | Suspended an arm's length away on this antique merry-go-round is the brass ring that could earn you an extra free ride (it's one of the few carousels in the world that continue this bonus tradition). Hand-carved in 1910, the carousel features colorful murals, big-band music, and bobbing animals including zebras, giraffes, and dragons; real horsehair was used for the tails. ✉ *1889 Zoo Pl., behind zoo parking lot, Balboa Park* ☎ *619/239–0512* 🌐 *www.balboapark.org* 🎫 *$3* 🕒 *Closed weekdays Labor Day–mid-June.*

Bea Evenson Fountain

FOUNTAIN | A favorite of barefoot children, this fountain shoots cool jets of water upwards of 50 feet. Built in 1972 between the Fleet Center and Natural History Museum, the fountain offers plenty of room to sit and watch the crowds go by. ✉ *Balboa Park* ✣ *East end of El Prado* 🌐 *www.balboapark.org.*

★ Botanical Building

GARDEN | The graceful redwood-lath structure, built for the 1915 Panama–California International Exposition, now houses more than 2,000 types of tropical and subtropical plants plus changing seasonal flower displays. Ceiling-high tree ferns shade fragile orchids and feathery bamboo. There are benches beside miniature waterfalls for resting in the shade. The rectangular pond outside, filled with lotuses and water lilies that bloom in spring and fall, is popular with photographers. ✉ *1549 El Prado, Balboa Park* ☎ *619/239–0512* 🌐 *www.balboapark.org* 🎫 *Free* 🕒 *Closed Thurs.*

Cabrillo Bridge

BRIDGE/TUNNEL | The official gateway into Balboa Park soars 120 feet above a canyon floor. Pedestrian-friendly, the 1,500-foot bridge provides inspiring views of the California Tower and El Prado beyond. **■ TIP→ This is a great spot for photo-capturing a classic image of the park.** ✉ *Balboa Park* ✣ *On El Prado, at 6th Ave. park entrance* 🌐 *www.balboapark.org.*

Fleet Science Center

MUSEUM | **FAMILY** | Interactive exhibits here are artfully educational and for all ages: older kids can get hands-on with inventive projects in Studio X, while the five-and-under set can be easily entertained with interactive play stations like the Ball Wall and Fire Truck in the center's Kid City. The IMAX Dome Theater, which screens exhilarating nature and science films, was the world's first, as was the Fleet's "NanoSeam" (seamless) dome ceiling that doubles as a planetarium. ✉ *1875 El Prado, Balboa Park* ☎ *619/238–1233* 🌐 *www.rhfleet.org* 🎫 *The Fleet experience includes gallery exhibits and 1 IMAX film $22; additional cost for special exhibits or add-on 2nd IMAX film or planetarium show.*

★ Inez Grant Parker Memorial Rose Garden and Desert Garden

GARDEN | These neighboring gardens sit just across the Park Boulevard pedestrian bridge and offer gorgeous views over Florida Canyon. The award-winning formal rose garden contains 1,600 roses representing nearly 130 varieties; peak bloom is usually in April and May but the garden remains beautiful and worthy of a visit year-round. The adjacent Desert Garden provides a striking contrast, with 2½ acres of succulents and desert plants seeming to blend into the landscape of the canyon below. ✉ *2525 Park Blvd., Balboa Park* 🌐 *www.balboapark.org.*

★ The Museum of Us

MUSEUM | **FAMILY** | Originally known as San Diego Museum of Man, the name was changed in efforts to reflect values of equity, inclusion, and decolonization. If the facade of this building—the landmark California Building—looks familiar, it's because filmmaker Orson Welles used it and its dramatic tower as the principal features of the Xanadu estate in his 1941 classic, *Citizen Kane.* Closed for 80 years, the tower was recently reopened for public tours. An additional timed ticket and a climb up 125 steps is required, but the effort will be rewarded with spectacular 360-degree views of the coast, Downtown, and the inland mountains. Back inside, exhibits at this highly respected anthropological museum focus on Southwestern, Mexican, and South American cultures. Carved monuments from the Mayan city of Quirigua in Guatemala, cast from the originals in 1914, are particularly impressive. Exhibits might include examples of intricate beadwork from across the Americas, the history of Egyptian mummies, or the lifestyles of the Kumeyaay peoples, American Indians who live in the San Diego area. ✉ *California Bldg., 1350 El Prado, Balboa Park* ☎ *619/239–2001* 🌐 *www.museumofman.org* 🎟 *$13; special exhibits and private tower tour cost extra* ☞ *Tower tours are timed-entry and can be booked in advance through website or on arrival at museum.*

★ San Diego Air & Space Museum

MUSEUM | **FAMILY** | By day, the streamlined edifice looks like any other structure in the park; at night, outlined in blue neon, the round building appears—appropriately enough—to be a landed UFO. Every available inch of space in the rotunda is filled with exhibits about aviation and aerospace pioneers, including examples of enemy planes from the World Wars. In all, there are more than 60 full-size aircraft on the floor and hanging from the rafters. In addition to exhibits from the dawn of flight to the jet age, the museum displays a growing number of space-age exhibits, including the actual *Apollo 9* command module. To test your own skills, you can ride in a two-seat Max Flight simulator or try out the Talon Racing simulator. Movies in the 3-D/4-D theater are included with admission. ✉ *2001 Pan American Pl., Balboa Park* ☎ *619/234–8291* 🌐 *www.sandiegoairandspace.org* 🎟 *$22; max flight simulator $8.*

★ San Diego Museum of Art

MUSEUM | Known for its Spanish baroque and Renaissance paintings, including works by El Greco, Goya, Rubens, and van Ruisdael, San Diego's most comprehensive art museum also has strong holdings of South Asian art, Indian miniatures, and contemporary California paintings. The museum's exhibits tend to have broad appeal, and if traveling shows from other cities come to town, you can expect to see them here. Free docent tours are offered throughout the day. An outdoor Sculpture Court and Garden exhibits both traditional and modern pieces. Enjoy the view over a craft beer and some locally sourced food in the adjacent Panama 66 courtyard restaurant. **■ TIP→ The museum hosts "Art After Hours" most Friday nights, with discounted admission 5–8 pm.** ✉ *1450 El Prado, Balboa Park* ☎ *619/232–7931* 🌐 *www.sdmart.org* 🎟 *$15; sculpture garden is free* ⏲ *Closed Wed.*

★ San Diego Zoo

ZOO | FAMILY | Balboa Park's—and perhaps the city's—most famous attraction is its 100-acre zoo. Nearly 4,000 animals of some 800 diverse species roam in hospitable, expertly crafted habitats that replicate natural environments as closely as possible. The flora in the zoo, including many rare species, is even more dear than the fauna. Walkways wind over bridges and past waterfalls ringed with tropical ferns; elephants in a sandy plateau roam so close you're tempted to pet them.

Exploring the zoo fully requires the stamina of a healthy hiker, but open-air double-decker buses that run throughout the day let you zip through three-quarters of the exhibits on a guided 35- to 40-minute, 3-mile tour. There are also express buses, used for quick transportation, that make five stops around the grounds and include some narration. The Skyfari Aerial Tram, which soars 170 feet above the ground, gives a good overview of the zoo's layout and, on clear days, a panorama of the park, Downtown San Diego, the bay, and the ocean, far beyond the San Diego–Coronado Bridge. **■TIP→ Unless you come early, expect to wait for the regular bus, and especially for the top tier—the line can take more than 45 minutes; if you come at midday on a weekend or school holiday, you'll be doing the in-line shuffle for a while.**

Don't forget the San Diego Safari Park, the zoo's 1,800-acre extension to the north at Escondido. ✉ *2920 Zoo Dr., Balboa Park* ☎ *619/234–3153* 🌐 *www.sandiegozoo.org* 🎫 *$62.*

★ Spanish Village Art Center

MUSEUM | More than 200 local artists, including glassblowers, enamel workers, wood-carvers, sculptors, painters, jewelers, and photographers work and give demonstrations of their craft on a rotating basis within and outside of these red tile–roof studio-galleries that were set up for the 1935–36 exposition in the style of an old Spanish village. The center is a great source for memorable gifts. ✉ *1770 Village Pl., Balboa Park* ☎ *619/233–9050* 🌐 *spanishvillageartcenter.com* 🎫 *Free.*

★ Spreckels Organ Pavilion

ARTS VENUE | The 2,400-bench-seat pavilion, dedicated in 1915 by sugar magnates John D. and Adolph B. Spreckels, holds the 4,518-pipe Spreckels Organ, the largest outdoor pipe organ in the world. You can hear this impressive instrument at one of the year-round, free, 2 pm Sunday concerts, regularly performed by the city's civic organist Raúl Prieto Ramírez and guest artists—a highlight of a visit to Balboa Park. On Monday evenings from late June to mid-August, internationally renowned organists play evening concerts. At Christmastime the park's Christmas tree and life-size Nativity display turn the pavilion into a seasonal wonderland. ✉ *2211 Pan American Rd., Balboa Park* ☎ *619/702–8138* 🌐 *spreckelsorgan.org.*

Restaurants

★ Civico by the Park

$ | ITALIAN | Dario and Pietro Gallo, the Italian brothers behind the Civico restaurants in Little Italy, have taken their concept into Banker's Hill, bringing with them authentic Italian dishes from the Calabria region of Southern Italy. The menu offers traditional and vegan options, as well as introducing a scratch pizza program in two distinct styles: Pinsa Romana (a healthier style of pizza derived from Ancient Rome) and Calabrian. The restaurant is beautifully done with notes of velvet and marble, and a towering bar standing as the central focus of the space showcases one of the city's largest collections of Amaro and Grappa. **Known for:** cocktails; vegan menu; Pinsa Romana and Calabrian pizza. Ⓢ *Average main: $14* ✉ *2550 5th Ave., Suite 120, Bankers Hill* ☎ *619/310–5669* 🌐 *www.civicobythepark.com.*

Continued on page 98

Polar bear, San Diego Zoo

LIONS AND TIGERS AND BEARS: The World-Famous San Diego Zoo

From diving polar bears and 6-ton elephants to swinging great apes, San Diego's most famous attraction has it all. Nearly 4,000 animals representing 800 species roam the 100-acre zoo in expertly crafted habitats that replicate the animals' natural environments. The pandas may have gone home (in 2019), but there are plenty of other cool creatures to see here, from teeny-tiny mantella frogs to two-story-tall giraffes. But it's not all just fun and games. Known for its exemplary conservation programs, the zoo educates visitors on how to go green and explains its efforts to protect endangered species.

SAN DIEGO ZOO TOP ATTRACTIONS

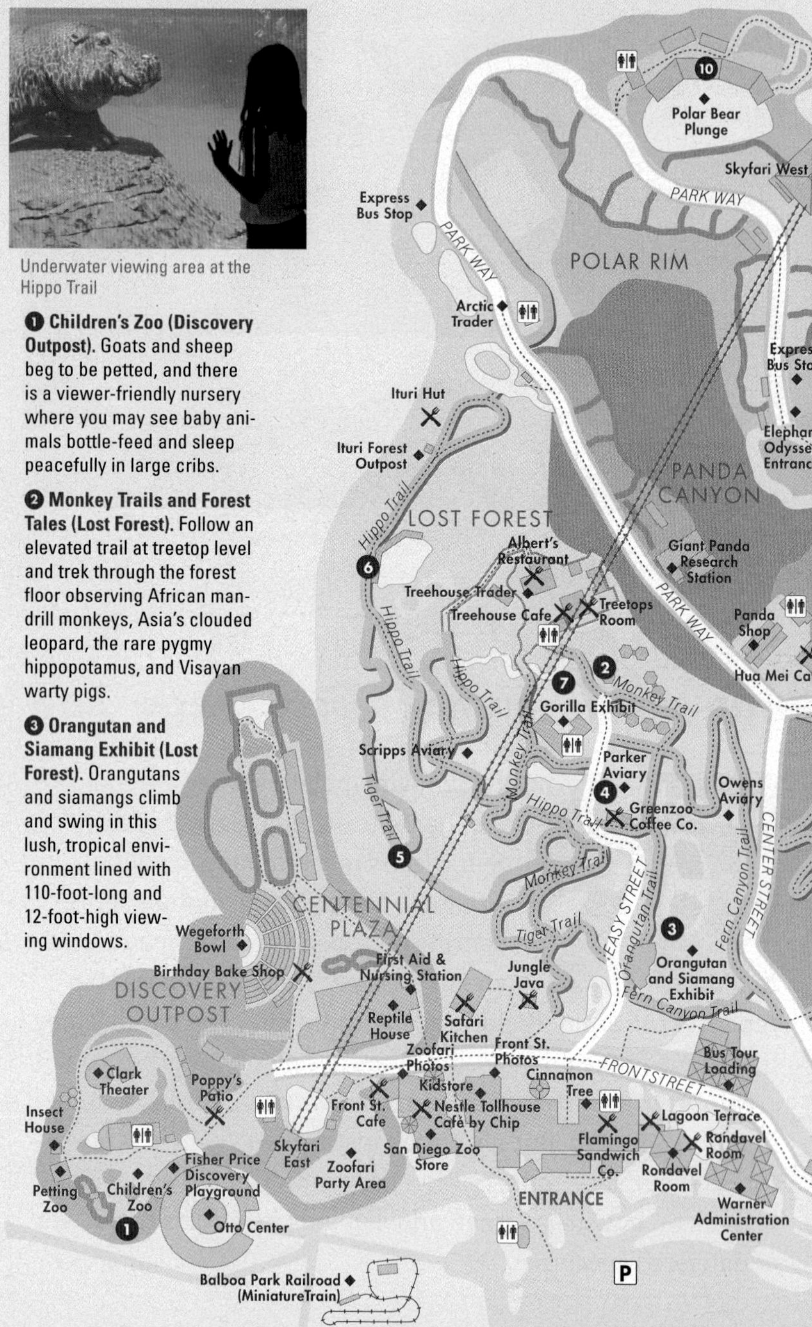

Underwater viewing area at the Hippo Trail

❶ **Children's Zoo (Discovery Outpost).** Goats and sheep beg to be petted, and there is a viewer-friendly nursery where you may see baby animals bottle-feed and sleep peacefully in large cribs.

❷ **Monkey Trails and Forest Tales (Lost Forest).** Follow an elevated trail at treetop level and trek through the forest floor observing African mandrill monkeys, Asia's clouded leopard, the rare pygmy hippopotamus, and Visayan warty pigs.

❸ **Orangutan and Siamang Exhibit (Lost Forest).** Orangutans and siamangs climb and swing in this lush, tropical environment lined with 110-foot-long and 12-foot-high viewing windows.

4 Scripps, Parker, and Owens Aviaries (Lost Forest). Wandering paths climb through the enclosed aviaries where brightly colored tropical birds swoop between branches inches from your face.

5 Tiger Trail (Lost Forest). The mist-shrouded trails of this simulated rainforest wind down a canyon. Tigers, Malayan tapirs, and Argus pheasants wander among the exotic trees and plants.

6 Hippo Trail (Lost Forest). Glimpse huge but surprisingly graceful hippos frolicking in the water through an underwater viewing window and buffalo cavorting with monkeys on dry land.

7 Gorilla Exhibit (Lost Forest). The gorillas live in one of the zoo's bioclimatic zone exhibits modeled on their native habitat with waterfalls, climbing areas, and an open meadow. The sounds of the tropical rain forest emerge from a 144-speaker sound system that plays CDs recorded in Africa.

8 Africa Rocks. This massive exhibit consists of six different rocky habitats designed to showcase the diversity of topography and species on the African continent. Penguins, meerkats, and a band of baboons are just a few of the animals that call this ambitious exhibit home.

Lories at Owen's Aviary

9 Sun Bear Forest (Asian Passage). Playful beasts claw apart the trees and shrubs that serve as a natural playground for climbing, jump¬ing, and general merrymaking.

10 Polar Bear Plunge (Polar Rim). Watch polar bears take a chilly dive from the underwater viewing room. There are also Siberian reindeer, white foxes, and other Arctic creatures here. Kids can learn about the Arctic and climate change through interactive exhibits.

11 Elephant Odyssey. Get a glimpse of the animals that roamed Southern California 12,000 years ago and meet their living counterparts. The 7.5-acre, multispecies habitat features elephants, California condors, jaguars, and more.

12 Koala Exhibit (Outback). The San Diego Zoo houses the largest number of koalas outside Australia. Walk through the exhibit for photo ops of these marsupials from Down-Under curled up on their perches or dining on eucalyptus branches.

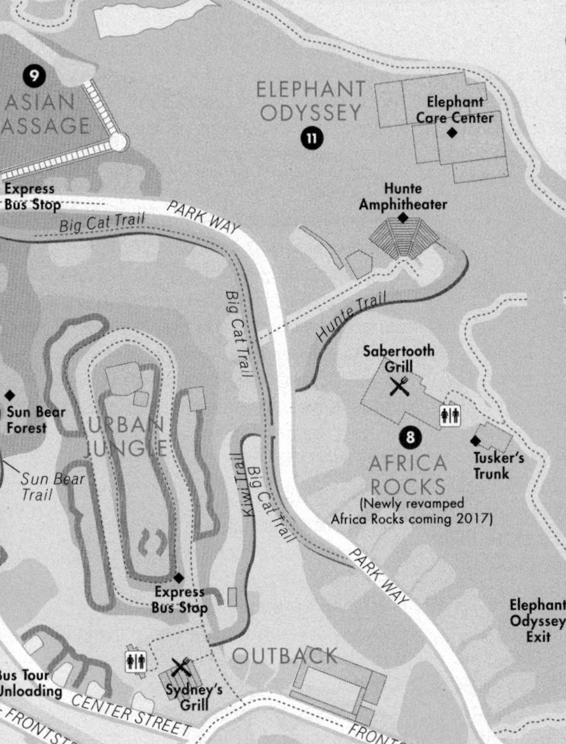

MUST-SEE ANIMALS

❶ GORILLA

This troop of primates engages visitors with their human-like expressions and behavior. The youngsters are sure to delight, especially when hitching a ride on mom's back. Up-close encounters might involve the gorillas using the glass partition as a backrest while peeling cabbage. By dusk the gorillas head inside to their sleeping quarters, so don't save this for your last stop.

❷ ELEPHANT

Asian and African elephants coexist at the San Diego Zoo. The larger African elephant is distinguished by its big flapping ears—shaped like the continent of Africa—which it uses to keep cool. An elephant's trunk has over 40,000 muscles in it—that's more than humans have in their whole body.

❸ ORANGUTAN

Bornean and Sumatran orangutans have been entertaining San Diego visitors since 1928. The exhibit has rope climbing structures, a man-made "termite mound" that's often filled with treats, rocky caves, and tall "sway poles" that allow the orangutans to swing like they would in trees. Don't be surprised if the orangutans come right up to the glass to observe the humans observing them!

❹ KOALA

While this collection of critters is one of the cutest in the zoo, don't expect a lot of activity from the koala habitat. These guys spend most of their day curled up asleep in the branches of the eucalyptus tree—they can sleep up to 20 hours a day. Although eucalyptus leaves are poisonous to most animals, bacteria in koalas' stomachs allow them to break down the toxins.

❺ POLAR BEAR

The trio of polar bears is one of the San Diego Zoo's star attractions, and their brand-new exhibit gets you up close and personal. Visitors sometimes worry about polar bears living in the warm San Diego climate, but there is no cause for concern. The San Diego-based bears eat a lean diet, thus reducing their layer of blubber and helping them keep cool.

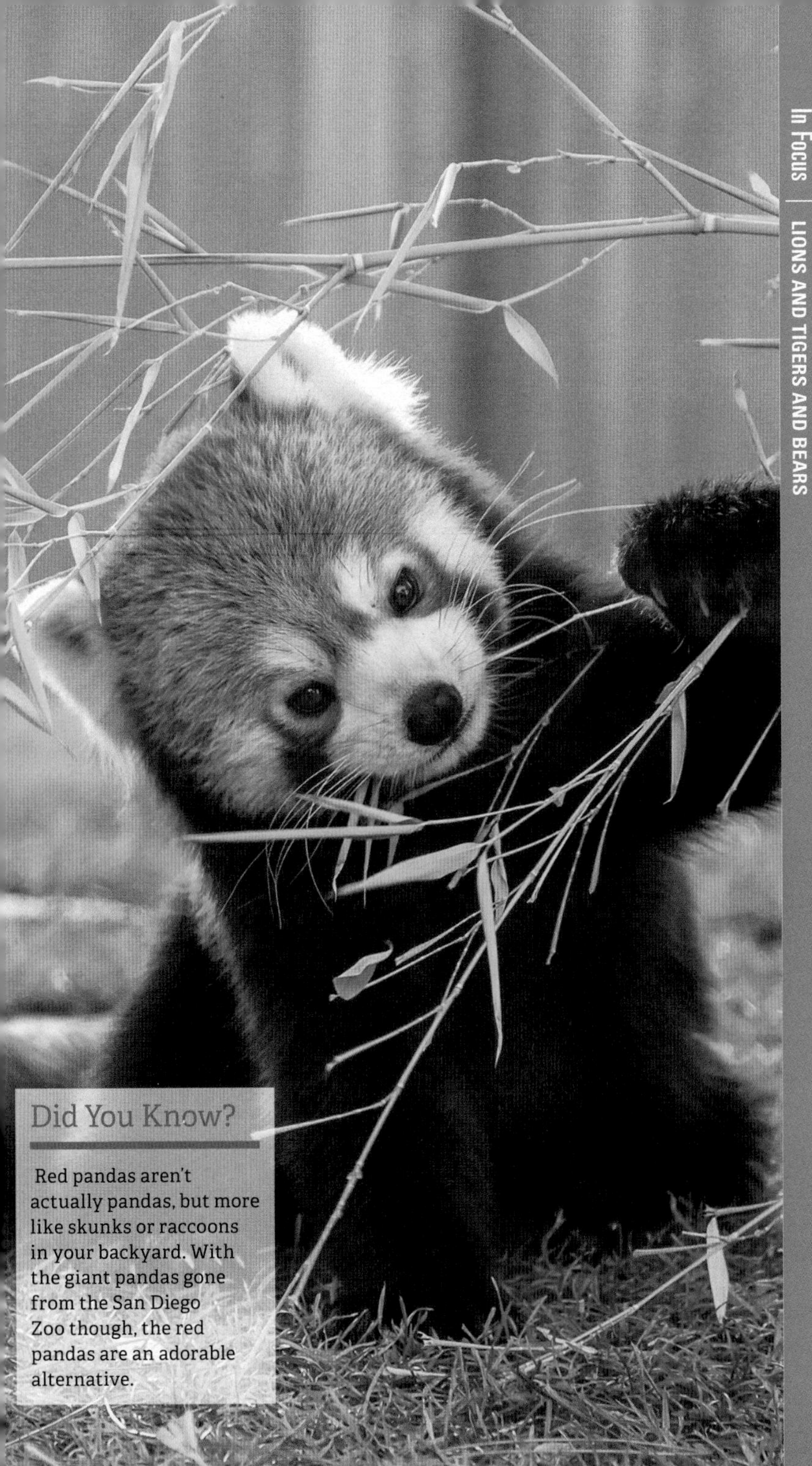

Did You Know?

Red pandas aren't actually pandas, but more like skunks or raccoons in your backyard. With the giant pandas gone from the San Diego Zoo though, the red pandas are an adorable alternative.

★ Cucina Urbana

$$ | **ITALIAN** | Twentysomethings mingle with boomers in this convivial Bankers Hill dining room and bar, one of the most popular restaurants in town. The open kitchen turns out innovative Italian food with a California sensibility including a selection of small plates and family-style pasta dishes alongside traditional entrées. Many dishes are under $20, including crowd-pleasing short-rib pappardelle, fried stuffed squash blossoms, creamy mascarpone polenta, and thin-crust pizzas. At the in-house wine shop, purchase reasonably priced bottles from California and Italy opened table-side for a $9 corkage fee. **Known for:** in-house wine shop with reasonably priced bottles and $9 corkage fee; seasonal polenta with ragu; ricotta-stuffed zucchini blossoms. *Average main: $21* ✉ *505 Laurel St., Bankers Hill* ☎ *619/239–2222* *www.cucinaurbana.com* *No lunch Sat.–Mon.*

Performing Arts

★ Globe Theatres

THEATER | This complex, comprised of the Sheryl and Harvey White Theatre, the Lowell Davies Festival Theatre, and the Old Globe Theatre, offers some of the finest theatrical productions in Southern California. Theater classics such as *Into the Woods* and *Dirty Rotten Scoundrels,* and more recent hits like *Bright Star* and *Meteor Shower*, premiered on these famed stages and went on to perform on Broadway. The Old Globe presents a renowned summer Shakespeare Festival with three to four plays in repertory. The theaters, done in a California version of Tudor style, sit between the sculpture garden of the San Diego Museum of Art and the California Tower. ✉ *1363 Old Globe Way, Balboa Park* ☎ *619/234–5623* *www.theoldglobe.org* *Box office closed Mon.*

Old Town and Uptown

San Diego's Spanish and Mexican roots are most evident in Old Town and the surrounding hillside of Presidio Park. Visitors can experience settlement life in San Diego from Spanish and Mexican rule to the early days of U.S. statehood. Nearby Uptown is composed of several smaller neighborhoods near Downtown and around Balboa Park: the vibrant neighborhoods of Hillcrest, Mission Hills, North Park, and South Park showcase their unique blend of historical charm and modern urban community.

Sights

★ Fiesta de Reyes

HISTORIC SITE | **FAMILY** | North of San Diego's Old Town Plaza lies the area's unofficial center, built to represent a colonial Mexican plaza. The collection of more than a dozen shops and restaurants around a central courtyard in blossom with magenta bougainvillea, scarlet hibiscus, and other flowers in season reflects what early California might have looked like from 1821 to 1872. Mariachi bands and folklorico dance groups frequently perform on the plaza stage—check the website for times and upcoming special events. **TIP→ Casa de Reyes is a great stop for a margarita and some chips and guacamole.** ✉ *4016 Wallace St., Old Town* ☎ *619/297–3100* *www.fiestadereyes.com.*

★ Old Town San Diego State Historic Park

HISTORIC SITE | **FAMILY** | The six square blocks on the site of San Diego's original pueblo are the heart of Old Town. Most of the 20 historic buildings preserved or re-created by the park cluster are around **Old Town Plaza,** bounded by Wallace Street on the west, Calhoun Street on the north, Mason Street on the east, and San Diego Avenue on the south. The plaza is a pleasant place to rest, plan your tour of the park, and watch passersby. San Diego Avenue is closed to vehicle traffic here.

Some of Old Town's buildings were destroyed in a fire in 1872, but after the site became a state historic park in 1968, reconstruction and restoration of the remaining structures began. Five of the original adobes are still intact.

Facing Old Town Plaza, the **Robinson-Rose House** was the original commercial center of Old San Diego, housing railroad offices, law offices, and the first newspaper press. The largest and most elaborate of the original adobe homes, the **Casa de Estudillo** was occupied by members of the Estudillo family until 1887 and later gained popularity for its billing as "Ramona's Marriage Place" based on a popular novel of the time. Albert Seeley, a stagecoach entrepreneur, opened the **Cosmopolitan Hotel** in 1869 as a way station for travelers on the daylong trip south from Los Angeles. Next door to the Cosmopolitan Hotel, the **Seeley Stable** served as San Diego's stagecoach stop in 1867 and was the transportation hub of Old Town until 1887, when trains became the favored mode of travel.

Several reconstructed buildings serve as restaurants or as shops purveying wares reminiscent of those that might have been available in the original Old Town. **Racine & Laramie**, a painstakingly reproduced version of San Diego's first cigar store in 1868, is especially interesting.

Pamphlets available at the Robinson-Rose House give details about all the historic houses on the plaza and in its vicinity. Free tours of the historic park are offered daily at 11:30 and 2; they depart from the Robinson-Rose House. **■ TIP→ The covered wagon located near the intersection of Mason and Calhoun Streets provides a great photo op.** ✉ *Visitor center (Robinson-Rose House), 4002 Wallace St., Old Town* ☎ *619/220–5422* 🌐 *www.parks.ca.gov* 🎫 *Free.*

The Whaley House Museum

HISTORIC SITE | A New York entrepreneur, Thomas Whaley came to California during the gold rush. He wanted to provide his East Coast wife with all the comforts of home, so in 1857 he had Southern California's first two-story brick structure built, making it the oldest double-story brick building on the West Coast. The house, which served as the county courthouse and government seat during the 1870s, stands in strong contrast to the Spanish-style adobe residences that surround the nearby historic plaza and marks an early stage of San Diego's "Americanization." A garden out back includes many varieties of prehybrid roses from before 1867. The place is perhaps most famed, however, for the ghosts that are said to inhabit it. You can tour on your own during the day, but must visit by guided tour after 4:30 pm. The evening tours are geared toward the supernatural aspects of the house. Tours start at 6 pm (5 pm on Saturday) and are offered every half hour, with the last tour departing at 9:30 pm. ✉ *2476 San Diego Ave., Old Town* ☎ *619/297–7511* 🌐 *www.whaleyhouse.org* 🎫 *From $10* ⏲ *Closed Sept.–May and Wed.*

Restaurants

El Agave

$$$ | **MEXICAN** | Not a typical San Diego taco shop, this Mexican eatery is upstairs in a shopping complex in the middle of a tequila museum with some 2,000 bottles dating from the 1930s. The owners are equally serious about food, calling their cuisine Hispanic-Mexican Gastronomy, which means meat and fish dishes with lots of unusual spicy chilies, herbs, spices, and moles. **Known for:** impressive tequila selection and tequila flights; variety of mole dishes; upscale option in generally casual Old Town. 💲 *Average main: $32* ✉ *2304 San Diego Ave., Old Town* ☎ *619/220–0692* 🌐 *www.elagave.com.*

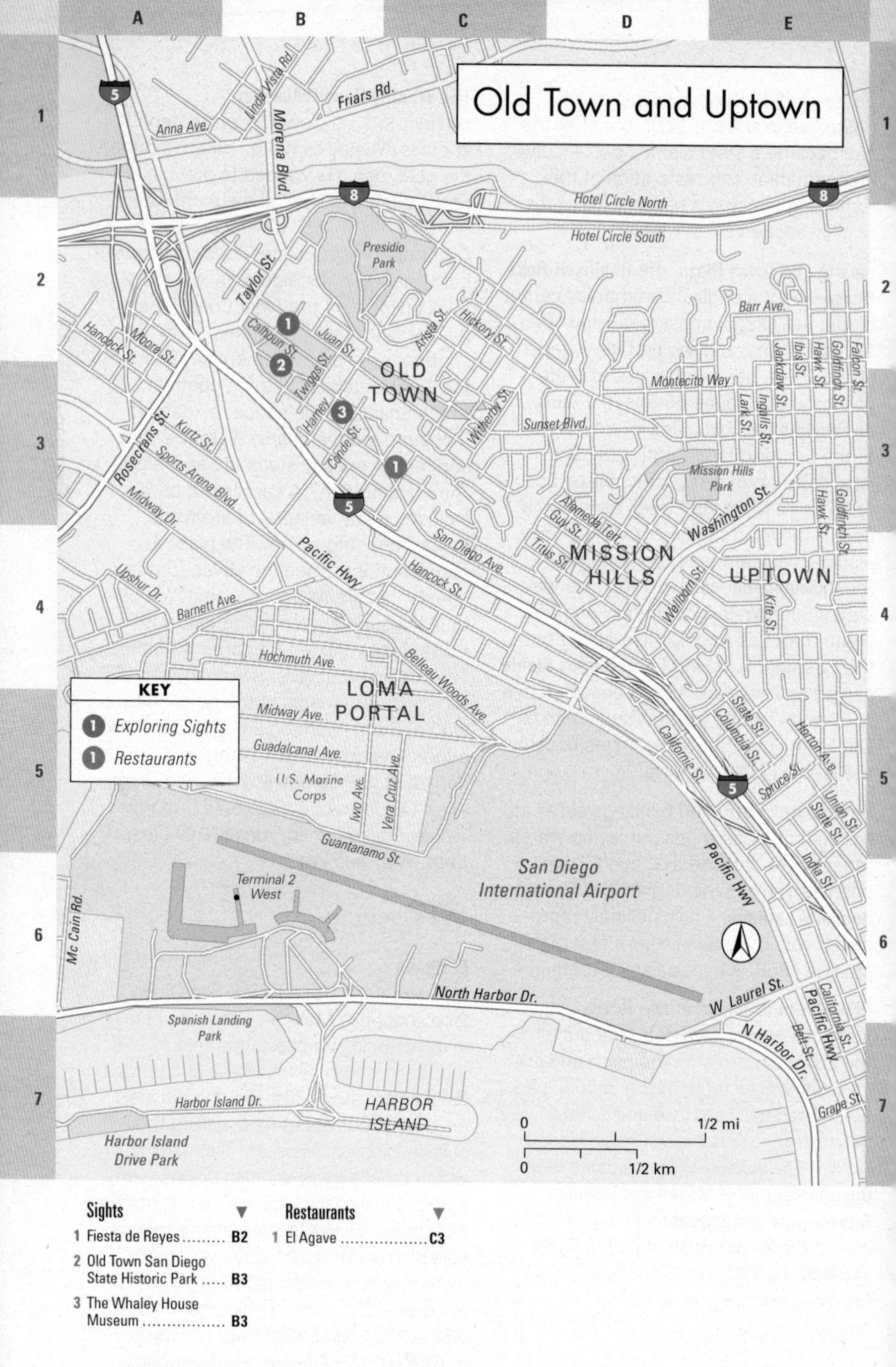

Sights ▼

1 Fiesta de Reyes **B2**

2 Old Town San Diego State Historic Park **B3**

3 The Whaley House Museum **B3**

Restaurants ▼

1 El Agave **C3**

Shopping

★ **Bazaar del Mundo Shops**

SHOPPING CENTERS/MALLS | With a Mexican villa theme, the Bazaar hosts riotously colorful gift shops such as **Ariana,** for ethnic and artsy women's fashions; **Artes de Mexico,** which sells handmade Latin American crafts and Guatemalan weavings; and **The Gallery,** which carries handmade jewelry, American Indian crafts, collectible glass, and original silk-screen prints. The **Laurel Burch Gallerita** carries the complete collection of its namesake artist's signature jewelry, accessories, and totes. ✉ *4133 Taylor St., at Juan St., Old Town* ☎ *619/296–3161* 🌐 *www.bazaardelmundo.com.*

Mission Bay and the Beaches

Mission Bay and the surrounding beaches are the aquatic playground of San Diego. The choice of activities available is astonishing, and the perfect weather makes you want to get out there and play. If you're craving downtime after all the activity, there are plenty of peaceful spots to relax and simply soak up the sunshine.

Mission Bay welcomes visitors with its protected waters and countless opportunities for fun. The 4,600-acre **Mission Bay Park** is the place for water sports like sailing, stand-up paddleboarding, and waterskiing. With 19 miles of beaches and grassy areas, it's also a great place for a picnic.

Mission Beach is a famous and lively fun zone for families and young people; if it isn't party time at the moment, it will be five minutes from now. The pathways in this area are lined with vacation homes, many for rent by the week or month.

North of Mission Beach is the college-packed party town of Pacific Beach, or "PB" as locals call it. The laid-back vibe of this surfer's mecca draws in free-spirited locals who roam the streets on skateboards and beach cruisers. The energy level peaks during happy hour, when PB's cluster of nightclubs, bars, and 150 restaurants open their doors to those ready to party.

Sights

★ **Belmont Park**

AMUSEMENT PARK/WATER PARK | **FAMILY** | The once-abandoned amusement park between the bay and Mission Beach boardwalk is now a shopping, dining, and recreation complex. Twinkling lights outline the **Giant Dipper,** an antique wooden roller coaster on which screaming thrill seekers ride more than 2,600 feet of track and 13 hills (riders must be at least 4 feet, 2 inches tall). Created in 1925 and listed on the National Register of Historic Places, this is one of the few old-time roller coasters left in the United States.

Other Belmont Park attractions include miniature golf, a laser maze, video arcade, bumper cars, a tilt-a-whirl, and an antique carousel. The zipline thrills as it soars over the crowds below, while the rock wall challenges both junior climbers and their elders. ✉ *3146 Mission Blvd., Mission Bay* ☎ *858/488–1549 for rides* 🌐 *www.belmontpark.com* 🎟 *Unlimited ride day package from $32.*

★ **Crystal Pier**

BEACH—SIGHT | Stretching out into the ocean from the end of Garnet Avenue, Crystal Pier is Pacific Beach's landmark. In the 1920s, it was a classic amusement park complete with ballroom. Today, it's mainly comprised of a series of quaint cottages that are all a part of the Crystal Pier Hotel. Guests have access to fishing, as well as the intersecting Mission Beach boardwalk. For those that aren't hotel guests, you may access the pier through a side gate from 8 am to sunset. ✉ *Pacific Beach* ✣ *At end of Garnet Ave.*

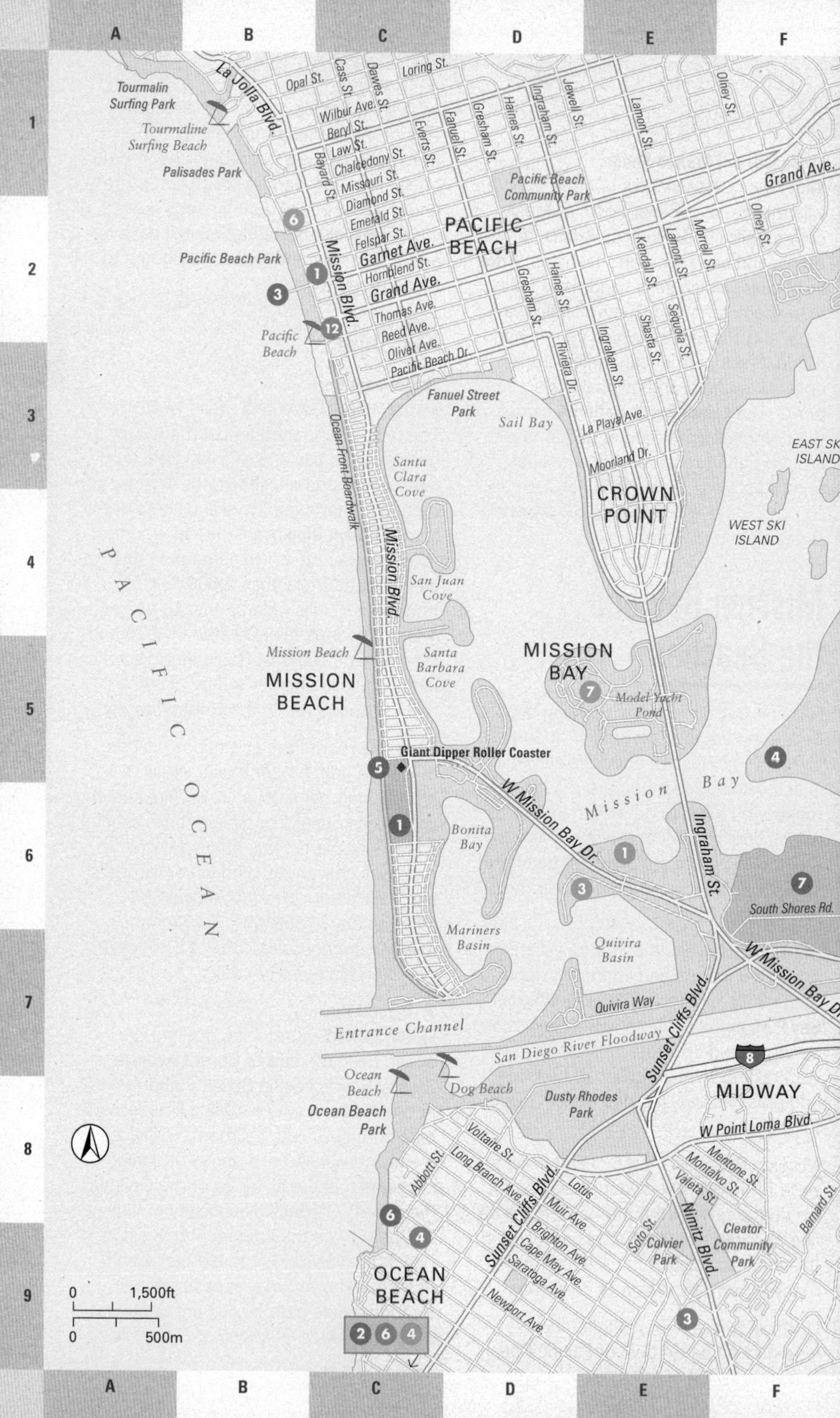

A
B
C
D
E
F
1
2
3
4
5
6
7
8
9
La Jolla Blvd.
Tourmalin Surfing Park
Tourmaline Surfing Beach
Palisades Park
Opal St.
Cass St.
Dawes St.
Loring St.
Wilbur Ave.
Beryl St.
Law St.
Bayard St.
Chalcedony St.
Missouri St.
Diamond St.
Emerald St.
Felspar St.
Garnet Ave.
Hornblend St.
Grand Ave.
Thomas Ave.
Reed Ave.
Oliver Ave.
Pacific Beach Dr.
Everts St.
Fanuel St.
Gresham St.
Haines St.
Ingraham St.
Jewell St.
Lamont St.
Olney St.
Grand Ave.
Pacific Beach Community Park
PACIFIC BEACH
Mission Blvd.
Pacific Beach Park
Pacific Beach
Kendall St.
Lamont St.
Morrell St.
Olney St.
Shasta St.
Sequoia St.
Riviera Dr.
Ingraham St.
Fanuel Street Park
Sail Bay
La Playa Ave.
Moorland Dr.
CROWN POINT
EAST SKI ISLAND
WEST SKI ISLAND
Ocean Front Boardwalk
Santa Clara Cove
San Juan Cove
Santa Barbara Cove
PACIFIC OCEAN
Mission Beach
MISSION BEACH
MISSION BAY
Model Yacht Pond
Giant Dipper Roller Coaster
W Mission Bay Dr.
Mission Bay
Bonita Bay
Ingraham St.
South Shores Rd.
Mariners Basin
Quivira Basin
W Mission Bay Dr.
Quivira Way
Entrance Channel
San Diego River Floodway
Sunset Cliffs Blvd.
8
MIDWAY
Ocean Beach
Dog Beach
Ocean Beach Park
Dusty Rhodes Park
W Point Loma Blvd.
Voltaire St.
Long Branch Ave.
Abbott St.
Sunset Cliffs Blvd.
Lotus
Muir Ave.
Brighton Ave.
Cape May Ave.
Saratoga Ave.
Newport Ave.
Mentone St.
Montalvo St.
Valeta St.
Nimitz Blvd.
Soto St.
Colvier Park
Cleator Community Park
Barnard St.
OCEAN BEACH
0
1,500ft
0
500m
1
2
3
4
5
6
7
12

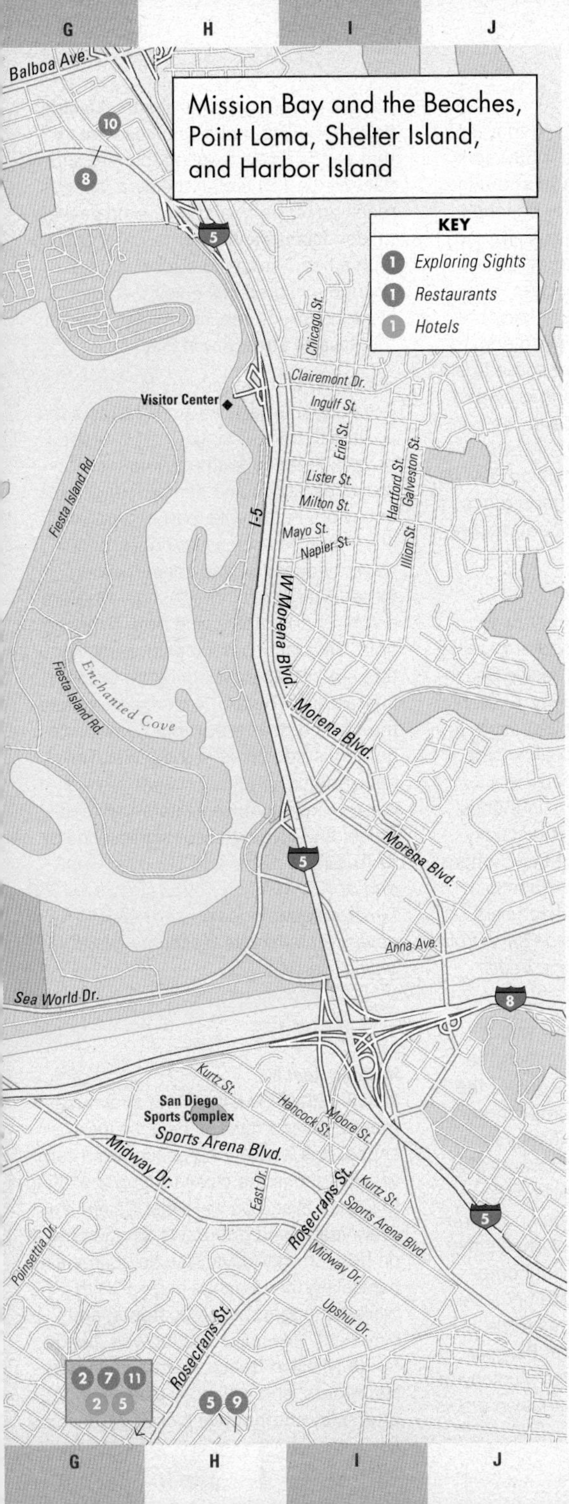

Mission Bay and the Beaches, Point Loma, Shelter Island, and Harbor Island

KEY

- 1 *Exploring Sights*
- 1 *Restaurants*
- 1 *Hotels*

Balboa Ave.
Visitor Center
Chicago St.
Clairemont Dr.
Ingulf St.
Erie St.
Lister St.
Milton St.
Mayo St.
Napier St.
Hartford St.
Galveston St.
Illion St.
I-5
W Morena Blvd.
Morena Blvd.
Fiesta Island Rd.
Enchanted Cove
Anna Ave.
Sea World Dr.
Kurtz St.
Hancock St.
Moore St.
San Diego Sports Complex
Sports Arena Blvd.
Midway Dr.
East Dr.
Rosecrans St.
Poinsettia Dr.
Upshur Dr.

Sights

1 Belmont Park........................C6
2 Cabrillo National Monument......C9
3 Crystal Pier......................... B2
4 Mission Bay Park...................F5
5 Mission Beach Boardwalk........C5
6 Ocean Beach Pier..................C8
7 SeaWorld San Diego..............F6

Restaurants

1 The Baked Bear.....................C2
2 Bali Hai.............................. G9
3 Cesarina E9
4 Hodad's C9
5 Liberty Public Market H9
6 The Little Lion Cafe C9
7 Point Loma Seafoods............. G9
8 Rubio's Coastal Grill G1
9 Stone Brewing World Bistro and Gardens............................ H9
10 Sushi Ota G1
11 Tom Ham's Lighthouse G9
12 Waterbar C2

Hotels

1 The Dana on Mission Bay E6
2 Homewood Suites San Diego Airport Liberty Station...................... G9
3 Hyatt Regency Mission Bay Spa and Marina.....................E6
4 Inn at Sunset Cliffs C9
5 Kona Kai Resort & Spa........... G9
6 Pacific Terrace Hotel............. B2
7 Paradise Point Resort & Spa......E5

★ Mission Bay Park

BEACH—SIGHT | San Diego's monument to sports and fitness, this 4,600-acre aquatic park has 27 miles of shoreline including 19 miles of sandy beaches. Playgrounds and picnic areas abound on the beaches and low, grassy hills. On weekday evenings, joggers, bikers, and skaters take over. In the daytime, swimmers, water-skiers, paddleboarders, anglers, and boaters—some in single-person kayaks, others in crowded powerboats—vie for space in the water. ✉ *2688 E. Mission Bay Dr., Mission Bay* ✣ *Off I–5 at Exit 22, E. Mission Bay Dr.* ☎ *858/581–7602 park ranger's office* 🌐 *www.sandiego.gov/park-and-recreation* 🎫 *Free.*

★ Mission Beach Boardwalk

BEACH—SIGHT | The cement pathway lining the sand from the southern end of Mission Beach north to Pacific Beach is always bustling with activity. Cyclists ping the bells on their beach cruisers to pass walkers out for a stroll alongside the oceanfront homes. Vacationers kick back on their patios, while friends play volleyball in the sand. The activity picks up alongside Belmont Park, where people stop to check out the action at the amusement park and beach bars. ✉ *Mission Beach* ✣ *Alongside sand from Mission Beach Park to Pacific Beach.*

SeaWorld San Diego

AMUSEMENT PARK/WATER PARK | **FAMILY** | Spread over 189 tropically landscaped bay-front acres, SeaWorld is one of the world's largest marine-life amusement parks. The majority of its exhibits are walk-through marine environments like **Shark Encounter,** where guests walk through a 57-foot acrylic tube and come face-to-face with a variety of sharks that call the 280,000-gallon habitat home. **Turtle Reef** offers an incredible up-close encounter with the green sea turtle, while the moving sidewalk at **Penguin Encounter** whisks you through a colony of nearly 300 penguins. The park also wows with its adventure rides like the **Electric Eel,** a shocking multilaunch coaster that sends riders twisting forward and backwards 150 feet in the air at speeds reaching 60 mph, and the comparatively milder **Journey to Atlantis,** a water coaster with a heart-stopping 60-foot plunge. Younger children will enjoy the rides, climbing structures, and splash pads at the **Sesame Street Bay of Play**.

SeaWorld is most famous for its large-arena entertainments, but this is an area in transition. The park's latest orca experience features a nature-inspired backdrop and demonstrates orca behaviors in the wild, part of SeaWorld's efforts to refocus its orca program toward education and conservation. Other live-entertainment shows feature dolphins, sea otters, and even household pets. Several upgraded animal encounters are available including the Dolphin Interaction Program, which gives guests the chance to interact with SeaWorld's bottlenose dolphins in the water. The hour-long program (20 minutes in the water), during which visitors can feed, touch, and give behavior signals, costs $215. ✉ *500 SeaWorld Dr., near west end of I–8, Mission Bay* ☎ *800/257–4268* 🌐 *www.seaworldparks.com* 🎫 *$92; advanced purchase discounts available online; parking $22.*

Beaches

Mission Beach

BEACH—SIGHT | **FAMILY** | With an amusement park and rows of eclectic local shops, this 2-mile-long beach has a carnival vibe and is the closest thing you'll find to Coney Island on the West Coast. It's lively year-round but draws a huge crowd on hot summer days. A wide boardwalk paralleling the beach is popular with walkers, joggers, skateboarders, and bicyclists. To escape the crowds, head to South Mission Beach. It attracts surfers, swimmers, and volleyball players, who often play competitive pickup games on the courts near the north jetty. The water near the Belmont Park roller coaster can be a bit rough but makes for good bodyboarding and bodysurfing. For free parking, you can try for a spot on the street, but your best bets are the two big lots at Belmont Park. **Amenities:** lifeguards; parking (no fee); showers; toilets. **Best for:** swimming; surfing; walking. ✉ *3000 Mission Blvd., Mission Bay* ✥ *Parking near roller coaster at West Mission Bay Dr.* 🌐 *www.sandiego.gov/lifeguards/beaches/mb.shtml.*

Pacific Beach/North Pacific Beach

BEACH—SIGHT | This beach, known for attracting a young college-age crowd and surfers, runs from the northern end of Mission Beach to Crystal Pier. The scene here is lively on weekends, with nearby restaurants, beach bars, and nightclubs providing a party atmosphere. In PB (as the locals call it) Sundays are known as "Sunday Funday," and pub crawls can last all day. Although drinking is no longer allowed on the beach, it's still likely you'll see people who have had one too many. The mood changes just north of the pier at North Pacific Beach, which attracts families and surfers. Although not quite pillowy, the sand at both beaches is nice and soft, which makes for great sunbathing and sandcastle building. **■TIP→ Kelp and flies can be a problem on this stretch, so choose your spot wisely.** Parking at Pacific Beach can also be a challenge. A few coveted free angle parking spaces are available along the boardwalk, but you'll most likely have to look for spots in the surrounding neighborhood. **Amenities:** food and drink; lifeguards; parking (no fee); showers, toilets. **Best for:** partiers; swimming; surfing. ✉ *4500 Ocean Blvd., Pacific Beach* 🌐 *www.sandiego.gov/lifeguards/beaches/pb.shtml.*

Tourmaline Surfing Park

BEACH—SIGHT | Offering slow waves and frequent winds, this is one of the most popular beaches for surfers. For windsurfing and kiteboarding, it's only sailable with northwest winds. The 175-space parking lot at the foot of Tourmaline Street normally fills to capacity by midday. Just like Pacific Beach, Tourmaline has soft, tawny-color sand, but when the tide is in the beach becomes quite narrow, making finding a good sunbathing spot a bit of a challenge. Parking will be difficult on evenings and weekends. **Amenities:** seasonal lifeguards; parking (no fee); showers; toilets. **Best for:** windsurfing; surfing. ✉ *600 Tourmaline St., Pacific Beach.*

Restaurants

★ The Baked Bear

$ | BAKERY | FAMILY | This build-your-own ice-cream-sandwich shop a block from Pacific Beach is a local favorite thanks to its homemade cookies and diverse array of ice-cream flavors, from birthday cake to peanut butter fudge. Don't miss out on their hot pressed ice-cream sandwiches! **Known for:** Bear Bowls made of cookies; doughnut ice-cream sandwiches; long lines on summer evenings. 💲 *Average main: $5* ✉ *4516 Mission Blvd., Suite C, Pacific Beach* ☎ *858/886–7433* 🌐 *www.thebakedbear.com.*

Rubio's Coastal Grill

$ | SEAFOOD | Credited with popularizing fish tacos in the United States, Ralph Rubio brought the Mexican staple to San Diego, opening his first restaurant in Pacific Beach where it still stands today. The original beer-battered fish tacos have fried pollock topped with white sauce, salsa, and cabbage atop a corn tortilla. **Known for:** the original fish taco; Taco Tuesday deal—fish taco and a beer for $5; $7 lunch specials. 💲 *Average main: $10* ✉ *4504 E. Mission Bay Dr., Pacific Beach* ☎ *858/272–2801* 🌐 *www.rubios.com.*

★ Sushi Ota

$$ | SUSHI | One fan called it "a notch above amazing"—an accolade not expected for a Japanese eatery wedged in a strip mall in Pacific Beach. But it's a destination for lovers of high-quality, superfresh raw fish from around San Diego and abroad; reservations strongly encouraged. **Known for:** velvety hamachi belly; sea urchin specials; chef's omakase tasting menu. *Average main: $25* *4529 Mission Bay Dr., Pacific Beach* *858/270–5670* *www.sushiota.com* *No lunch Sat.–Mon.*

★ Waterbar

$$ | SEAFOOD | Occupying a prime oceanfront lot just south of Crystal Pier, the views from the raised dining room are impressive. Throw in an excellent raw bar, a wide selection of shared plates, and a buzzy bar scene and you get Waterbar's "social seafood" concept. **Known for:** late-night "Boardwalk hour" oyster specials; boozy weekend brunch; ocean views. *Average main: $24* *4325 Ocean Blvd., Pacific Beach* *858/888–4343* *www.waterbarsd.com.*

Hotels

The Dana on Mission Bay

$$$ | RESORT | FAMILY | This waterfront resort, just down the road from SeaWorld, has an ideal location for active leisure travelers. **Pros:** water views; many outdoor activities; shuttle to SeaWorld. **Cons:** expensive resort fee; popular wedding venue; rooms vary in quality and view. *Rooms from: $289* *1710 W. Mission Bay Dr., Mission Bay* *619/222–6440, 800/445–3339* *www.thedana.com* *271 rooms* *No meals.*

Hyatt Regency Mission Bay Spa and Marina

$$$ | RESORT | FAMILY | This modern property has many desirable amenities, including balconies with excellent views of the garden, bay, ocean, or swimming pool courtyard. **Pros:** proximity to water sports; 120-foot waterslides in pools, plus kiddie slide; several suite configurations good for families. **Cons:** daily resort fee; not centrally located; some areas in need of updates. *Rooms from: $299* *1441 Quivira Rd., Mission Bay* *619/224–1234, 800/233–1234* *www.hyatt.com* *429 rooms* *No meals.*

Pacific Terrace Hotel

$$$$ | RESORT | Travelers love this terrific beachfront hotel and the ocean views from most rooms; it's a perfect place for watching sunsets over the Pacific. **Pros:** beach views; large rooms; friendly service. **Cons:** busy and sometimes noisy area; expensive in peak season; resort fee. *Rooms from: $569* *610 Diamond St., Pacific Beach* *858/581–3500, 800/344–3370* *www.pacificterrace.com* *73 rooms* *No meals.*

Paradise Point Resort & Spa

$$$ | RESORT | FAMILY | Minutes from SeaWorld but hidden in a quiet part of Mission Bay, the beautiful landscape of this 44-acre resort offers plenty of space for families to play and relax. **Pros:** water views; five pools; good service. **Cons:** not centrally located; motel-thin walls; parking and resort fees. *Rooms from: $296* *1404 Vacation Rd., Mission Bay* *858/274–4630, 800/344–2626* *www.paradisepoint.com* *462 rooms* *No meals.*

Nightlife

BARS

★ The Grass Skirt

BARS/PUBS | Accessed through a false freezer door inside Good Time Poke, this speakeasy-styled tiki bar serves a wide selection of rum-based tropical cocktails in delightfully kitsch surroundings. The Polynesian-inspired menu features shareable poke and pupus, but call ahead to reserve a table—this hidden gem is no secret! *910 Grand Ave., Pacific Beach* *858/412–5237* *www.thegrassskirt.com.*

JRDN

BARS/PUBS | This contemporary lounge (pronounced "Jordan") occupies the ground floor of Pacific Beach's chicest boutique hotel, Tower23, and offers a more sophisticated vibe in what is a very party-happy neighborhood. Sleek walls of windows and an expansive patio overlook the boardwalk. ✉ *723 Felspar St., Pacific Beach* ☎ *858/270–2323* 🌐 *www.t23hotel.com.*

 Activities

DIVING AND SNORKELING

The kelp forests and protected marine areas off the San Diego coast are easily accessible and offer divers ample opportunities to explore. Classes are available for beginners, while experienced divers will appreciate the challenges of local wreck and canyon dives. Water temperatures can be chilly, so check with a local outfitter for the appropriate gear before setting out.

The HMCS *Yukon,* a decommissioned Canadian warship, was intentionally sunk off Mission Beach to create the main diving destination in San Diego. A mishap caused the ship to settle on its side, creating a surreal, M.C. Escher–esque diving environment. This is a technical dive and should be attempted only by experienced divers; even diving instructors have become disoriented inside the wreck, and a few have even died trying to explore it.

SURFING

If you're a beginner, consider paddling in the waves off Mission Beach, Pacific Beach, and Tourmaline Surfing Park. Several outfitters offer year-round surf lessons as well as surf camp in the summer months and during spring break.

WATER SPORTS

Mission Bay Aquatic Center

BOATING | FAMILY | The world's largest instructional waterfront facility offers lessons in wakeboarding, sailing, surfing, waterskiing, rowing, kayaking, and windsurfing. Equipment rental is also available, but the emphasis is on instruction, and most rentals require a minimum two-hour orientation lesson before you can set out on your own. Reservations are recommended, particularly during the summer. Skippered keelboats and boats for waterskiing or wakeboarding can be hired with reservations. Free parking is available but keep an eye out for signage—not all the parking spots are free or overnight. ✉ *1001 Santa Clara Pl., Mission Beach* ☎ *858/488–1000* 🌐 *www.mbaquaticcenter.com.*

★ Seaforth Boat Rentals

BOATING | The Mission Bay outpost of this popular rental company offers a wide variety of motorized and nonmotorized craft. Jet Skis, SUPs, kayaks, and fishing skiffs are available alongside sailboats and powerboats of all sizes. For added relaxation, charter a skippered pontoon party boat, some with waterslides for added fun. ✉ *1641 Quivira Rd., Mission Bay* ☎ *888/834–2628* 🌐 *www.seaforthboatrental.com.*

La Jolla

La Jolla (pronounced La Hoya) means "the jewel" in Spanish and appropriately describes this small, affluent village and its beaches. Some beautiful coastline can be found here, as well as an elegant upscale atmosphere.

Sights

Birch Aquarium at Scripps

ZOO | FAMILY | Affiliated with the world-renowned Scripps Institution of Oceanography, this excellent aquarium sits at the end of a signposted drive leading off North Torrey Pines Road and has sweeping views of La Jolla coast below. More than 60 tanks are filled with colorful saltwater fish, and a 70,000-gallon tank simulates a La Jolla kelp forest. A special exhibit on sea horses features several examples of the species, plus mesmerizing sea dragons and a sea horse nursery. Besides the fish themselves, attractions include interactive educational exhibits based on the institution's ocean-related research and a variety of environmental issues. ✉ *2300 Expedition Way, La Jolla* ☎ *858/534–3474* 🌐 *www.aquarium.ucsd.edu* 🎟 *$17.*

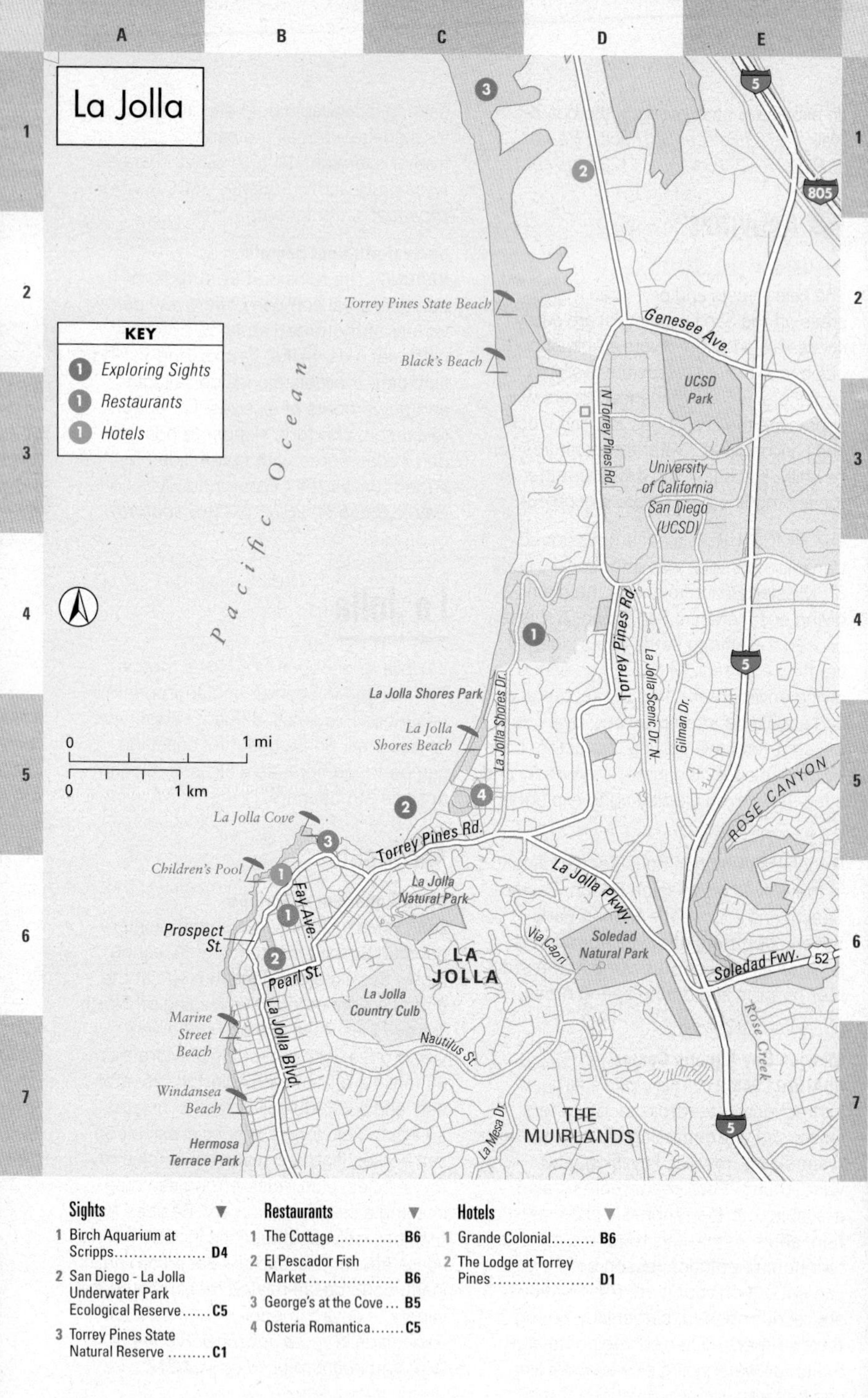

La Jolla
KEY
Exploring Sights
Restaurants
Hotels
Pacific Ocean
Torrey Pines State Beach
Black's Beach
Genesee Ave.
UCSD Park
N Torrey Pines Rd.
University of California San Diego (UCSD)
Torrey Pines Rd.
La Jolla Scenic Dr. N.
Gilman Dr.
La Jolla Shores Park
La Jolla Shores Beach
La Jolla Shores Dr.
ROSE CANYON
La Jolla Cove
Children's Pool
Fay Ave.
Prospect St.
Pearl St.
La Jolla Natural Park
La Jolla Pkwy.
Via Capri
Soledad Natural Park
Soledad Fwy.
LA JOLLA
La Jolla Country Culb
Rose Creek
Marine Street Beach
La Jolla Blvd.
Nautilus St.
Windansea Beach
Hermosa Terrace Park
La Mesa Dr.
THE MUIRLANDS
0
1 mi
0
1 km
5
805
52
A B C D E
1 2 3 4 5 6 7
Sights
1 Birch Aquarium at Scripps D4
2 San Diego - La Jolla Underwater Park Ecological Reserve C5
3 Torrey Pines State Natural Reserve C1
Restaurants
1 The Cottage B6
2 El Pescador Fish Market B6
3 George's at the Cove ... B5
4 Osteria Romantica....... C5
Hotels
1 Grande Colonial......... B6
2 The Lodge at Torrey Pines D1

San Diego-La Jolla Underwater Park Ecological Reserve

BODY OF WATER | Four habitats across 6,000 acres make up this underwater park and ecological reserve. When the water is clear, this is a diver's paradise with reefs, kelp beds, sand flats, and a submarine canyon. Plunge deeper to see guitarfish rays, perch, sea bass, anchovies, squid, and hammerhead sharks. Snorkelers, kayakers, and stand-up paddleboarders are likely to spot sea lions, seals, and leopard sharks. The Seven La Jolla Sea Caves, 75-million-year-old sandstone caves, are at the park's edge. ■ **TIP→ While the park can be explored on your own, the best way to view it is with a professional guide.** ✉ *La Jolla* ✣ *La Jolla Cove.*

★ **Torrey Pines State Natural Reserve**

NATIONAL/STATE PARK | *Pinus torreyana*, the rarest native pine tree in the United States, enjoys a 1,500-acre sanctuary at the northern edge of La Jolla. About 6,000 of these unusual trees, some as tall as 60 feet, grow on the cliffs here. The park is one of only two places in the world (the other is Santa Rosa Island, off Santa Barbara) where the Torrey pine grows naturally. The reserve has several hiking trails leading to the cliffs, 300 feet above the ocean; trail maps are available at the park station. Wildflowers grow profusely in spring, and the ocean panoramas are always spectacular. From December to March, whales can be spotted from the bluffs. When in this upper part of the park, respect the restrictions. Not permitted: picnicking, smoking, leaving the trails, dogs, alcohol, or collecting plant specimens.

You can unwrap your sandwiches, however, at Torrey Pines State Beach, just below the reserve. When the tide is out, it's possible to walk south all the way past the lifeguard towers to Black's Beach over rocky promontories carved by the waves (avoid the bluffs, however; they're unstable). **Los Peñasquitos Lagoon** at the north end of the reserve is one of the many natural estuaries that flow inland between Del Mar and Oceanside. It's a good place to watch shorebirds. Volunteers lead guided nature walks at 10 and 2 on most weekends and holidays. ✉ *12600 N. Torrey Pines Rd., La Jolla* ✣ *N. Torrey Pines Rd. exit off I–5 onto Carmel Valley Rd. going west, then turn left (south) on Coast Hwy. 101* ☎ *858/755–2063* 🌐 *www.torreypine.org* 🎫 *Parking from $20.*

Beaches

Black's Beach

BEACH—SIGHT | The powerful waves at this beach attract world-class surfers, and the strand's relative isolation appeals to nudist nature lovers (although by law nudity is prohibited) as well as gays and lesbians. Backed by 300-foot-tall cliffs whose colors change with the sun's angle, Black's can be accessed from Torrey Pines State Beach to the north, or by a narrow path descending the cliffs from Torrey Pines Glider Port. Be aware that the city has posted a "do not use" sign there because the cliff trails are unmaintained and highly dangerous, so use at your own risk. If you plan to access Black's from the beaches to the north or south, do so at low tide. High tide and waves can restrict access. Strong rip currents are common—only experienced swimmers should take the plunge. Lifeguards patrol the area only between spring break and mid-October. Also keep your eyes peeled for the hang gliders and paragliders who ascend from atop the cliffs. Parking is available at the Glider Port and Torrey Pines State Beach. **Amenities:** none. **Best for:** solitude; nudists; surfing. ✉ *Between Torrey Pines State Beach and La Jolla Shores, La Jolla* ✣ *2 miles south of Torrey Pines State Beach parking lot* 🌐 *www.sandiego.gov/lifeguards/beaches/blacks.shtml.*

A surfer prepares to head out before sunset at La Jolla's Torrey Pines State Beach and Reserve.

★ La Jolla Cove

BEACH—SIGHT | FAMILY | This shimmering blue-green inlet surrounded by cliffs is what first attracted everyone to La Jolla, from Native Americans to the glitterati. "The Cove," as locals refer to it, beyond where Girard Avenue dead-ends into Coast Boulevard, is marked by towering palms that line a promenade where people strolling in designer clothes are as common as Frisbee throwers. Ellen Browning Scripps Park sits atop cliffs formed by the incessant pounding of the waves and offers a great spot for picnics with a view. The Cove has beautiful white sand that is a bit coarse near the water's edge, but the beach is still a great place for sunbathing and lounging. At low tide, the pools and cliff caves are a destination for explorers. With visibility at 30-plus feet, this is the best place in San Diego for snorkeling, where bright-orange garibaldi fish and other marine life populate the waters of the **San Diego–La Jolla Underwater Park Ecological Reserve.** From above water, it's not uncommon to spot sea lions and birds basking on the rocks, or dolphin fins just offshore. The cove is also a favorite of rough-water swimmers, while the area just north is best for kayakers wanting to explore the Seven La Jolla Sea Caves. **Amenities:** lifeguards; showers; toilets. **Best for:** snorkeling; swimming; walking. ✉ *1100 Coast Blvd., east of Ellen Browning Scripps Park, La Jolla* 🌐 *www.sandiego.gov/lifeguards/beaches/cove.*

La Jolla Shores

BEACH—SIGHT | FAMILY | This is one of San Diego's most popular beaches due to its wide sandy shore, gentle waves, and incredible views of La Jolla Peninsula. There's also a large grassy park, and adjacent to La Jolla Shores lies the **San Diego–La Jolla Underwater Park Ecological Reserve**, 6,000 acres of protected ocean bottom and tide lands, bordered by the Seven La Jolla Sea Caves. The white powdery sand at La Jolla Sands is some of San Diego's best, and several surf and scuba schools teach here. Kayaks can also be rented nearby. A concrete boardwalk parallels the beach, and a boat launch for small vessels lies 300 yards south of the lifeguard station at Avenida de Playa. Arrive early to get a parking spot in the lot near Kellogg Park at the foot of Calle Frescota. Street parking is limited to one or two hours. **Amenities:** lifeguards; parking (no fee); showers; toilets. **Best for:** surfing; swimming; walking. ✉ *8200 Camino del Oro, in front of Kellogg Park, La Jolla* ✣ *2 miles north of downtown La Jolla* 🌐 *www.sandiego.gov/lifeguards/beaches/shores.shtml.*

★ Windansea Beach

BEACH—SIGHT | With its rocky shoreline and strong shore break, Windansea stands out among San Diego beaches for its dramatic natural beauty. It's one of the best surf spots in San Diego County. Professional surfers love the unusual A-frame waves the reef break here creates. Although the large sandstone rocks that dot the beach might sound like a hindrance, they actually serve as protective barriers from the wind, making this one of the best beaches in San Diego for sunbathing. The beach's palm-covered surf shack is a protected historical landmark, and a seat here at sunset may just be one of the most romantic spots on the West Coast. The name Windansea comes from a hotel that burned down in the late 1940s. You can usually find nearby street parking. **Amenities:** seasonal lifeguards; toilets. **Best for:** sunset; surfing; solitude. ✉ *Neptune Pl. at Nautilus St., La Jolla* 🌐 *www.sandiego.gov/lifeguards/beaches/windan.shtml.*

Restaurants

★ The Cottage

$ | **AMERICAN** | **FAMILY** | A cozy beach cottage sets the stage for American comfort food with a California twist at this La Jolla staple. The restaurant serves lunch and dinner, but it's the well-loved daily breakfast that has locals and visitors happily queuing—sometimes up to two hours on weekends. Egg dishes have unique fillings like soy chorizo and pork belly braised beef, and the sizable, shareable stuffed French toast is a can't-miss. Post-surf or hike, keep it healthy with the avocado smash and smoked salmon on rosemary bread. Lunch spans tuna melts and fish tacos, while dinner offers veggie fettuccine, peach BBQ-glazed ribs, and Vietnamese shrimp bowls. The drink menu, with Bloody Marys and hard kombucha, will have you justifying, "it's five o'clock somewhere." It's worth waiting for a patio seat that overlooks a charming stretch of downtown La Jolla. There's usually free coffee cake and coffee for those in line, or you can reserve a table with the "Yelp Waitlist" app. **Known for:** daily breakfast that people line up for; treats for those waiting in line; great patio seating. 💲 *Average main: $15* ✉ *7702 Fay Ave., La Jolla* ☎ *858/454–8409* 🌐 *www.cottagelajolla.com* ⏲ *No dinner Sun. and Mon.*

El Pescador Fish Market

$ | **SEAFOOD** | This bustling fish market and café in the heart of La Jolla Village has been popular with locals for its super-fresh fish for more than 30 years. Order the char-grilled, locally caught halibut, swordfish, or yellowtail on a toasted torta roll to enjoy in-house or to go for an oceanfront picnic at nearby La Jolla Cove. Other delicious choices include seafood cocktails, ceviche, Dungeness crab and shrimp salad, and fish and shrimp tacos. **Known for:** clam chowder; bustling on-site fish market; daily-caught cuts to go. 💲 *Average main: $15* ✉ *634 Pearl St., La Jolla* ☎ *858/456–2526* 🌐 *www.elpescadorfishmarket.com.*

George's at the Cove

$$$$ | **AMERICAN** | La Jolla's ocean-view destination restaurant includes three distinct levels: California Modern on the bottom floor, the Level2 bar in the middle, and Ocean Terrace on the roof. At the sleek main dining room, open only for dinner, give special consideration to the legendary "fish tacos" and the six-course chef's tasting menu; for a more casual and inexpensive lunch or dinner option, head to the outdoor-only Ocean Terrace for spectacular views; for unique craft cocktails, like the "La Jolla" chilled with seaweed-laced ice cubes, and a seasonal happy hour with small bites, cocktails, beer, and wine, it's the Level2 lounge. **Known for:** beef tartare with 67°F egg; excellent ocean views; attention to detail for special occasion dinners. *Average main: $37 ✉ 1250 Prospect St., La Jolla ☎ 858/454–4244 🌐 www.georgesatthe-cove.com.*

★ Osteria Romantica

$ | **ITALIAN** | Between music by Pavarotti, the checkered tablecloths, and the sight of homemade pasta and free-flowing vino, you'll swear you've died and gone to Italy. At this cozy La Jolla Shores eatery, northern and southwestern Italian flavors have fused into culinary magic—house-made breads, sauces, gnocchi, and pastas like pappardelle with braised lamb, and linguine with mussels—since 2004. The breaded veal and lobster ravioli are both exceptional. Pork osso buco in port wine sauce is a popular main course that can be enjoyed alfresco on warm summer nights on the dog-friendly patio. Despite its size, the tiramisu with espresso-dipped ladyfingers goes down way too easy. **Known for:** tender lamb pappardelle; cozy Italian vibe; homemade pasta, breads, and sauces. *Average main: $17 ✉ 2151 Av. de la Playa, La Jolla ☎ 858/551–1221 🌐 www.osteriaromantica.com.*

Hotels

★ Grande Colonial

$$$$ | **HOTEL** | This white-wedding-cake-style hotel in the heart of La Jolla Village has ocean views and charming European details that include chandeliers, mahogany railings, a wooden elevator, crystal doorknobs, and French doors. **Pros:** the Village's only four-diamond hotel; superb restaurant; hospitality extras included in rate. **Cons:** small pool; no fitness center; valet parking only. *Rooms from: $369 ✉ 910 Prospect St., La Jolla ☎ 888/828–5498 🌐 www.thegrandecolonial.com 93 rooms No meals.*

The Lodge at Torrey Pines

$$$$ | **RESORT** | Best known for its two 18-hole championship golf courses, this beautiful Craftsman-style lodge sits on a bluff between La Jolla and Del Mar with commanding coastal views, excellent service, a blissful spa, and the upscale A. R. Valentien restaurant, which serves farm-to-table California cuisine. **Pros:** spacious upscale rooms; remarkable service; adjacent to the famed Torrey Pines Golf Course; warm decor with Craftsman accents and hardwoods. **Cons:** not centrally located; expensive; $30 daily parking fee. *Rooms from: $452 ✉ 11480 N. Torrey Pines Rd., La Jolla ☎ 858/453–4420, 888/826–0224 🌐 www.lodgetorreypines.com Two 18-hole championship golf courses 170 rooms No meals.*

Activities

DIVING

Scuba San Diego

SCUBA DIVING | This center is well regarded for its top-notch instruction and certification programs, as well as for guided dive tours. Scuba Adventure classes for non-certified divers are held daily in Mission Bay, meeting near Mission Point. Trips for certified divers depart from La Jolla and include dives to kelp reefs in La Jolla Cove, and night diving at La Jolla Canyon. They also have snorkeling tours to La Jolla's Sea Caves. *✉ 8008 Girard St., La Jolla ☎ 619/260–1880 🌐 www.scubasandiego.com From $70 ☞ Scuba Adventure meeting point is 2615 Bayside La. in South Mission Bay, near Mission Point.*

GOLF

★ Torrey Pines Golf Course

GOLF | Due to its cliff-top location overlooking the Pacific and its classic championship holes, Torrey Pines is one of the best public golf courses in the United States. The course was the site of the 2008 and 2021 U.S. Open and has been the home of the Farmers Insurance Open since 1968. The par-72 South Course, redesigned by Rees Jones in 2001, receives rave reviews from touring pros; it is longer, more challenging, and more expensive than the North Course. Tee times may be booked from 4 to 90 days in advance (*858/552–1662*) and are subject to an advance booking fee ($45). ✉ *11480 N. Torrey Pines Rd., La Jolla* ☎ *858/452–3226, 800/985–4653* 🌐 *www.torreypinesgolfcourse.com* 🎫 *South: from $202. North: from $128; $40 for golf cart* ⛳ *South: 18 holes, 7707 yards, par 72. North: 18 holes, 7258 yards, par 72.*

HIKING

Los Peñasquitos Canyon Preserve

HIKING/WALKING | Twelve miles of trails at this inland park north of Mira Mesa accommodate equestrians, runners, walkers, and cyclists as well as leashed dogs. Look at maps for trails specific to bikes and horses. The trail parallels Los Peñasquitos and is marked by a small waterfall at the 3.5 mile marker. Hikers can cross the creek and loop back among large rock boulders—it's an unexpected oasis amid the arid valley landscape. ✉ *12020 Black Mountain Rd., Rancho Peñasquitos* ⊕ *From I–15, exit Mercy Rd., and head west to Black Mountain Rd.; turn right then left at first light; follow road to Ranch House parking lot* ☎ *858/484–7504* 🌐 *www.sdparks.org.*

Torrey Pines State Reserve

HIKING/WALKING | **FAMILY** | Hikers and runners will appreciate this park's many winning features: switchback trails that descend to the sea, an unparalleled view of the Pacific, and a chance to see the Torrey pine tree, one of the rarest pine breeds in the United States. The reserve hosts guided nature walks as well. Dogs and food are prohibited at the reserve. Parking is $20–$25, depending on day and season. ✉ *12600 N. Torrey Pines Rd., La Jolla* ⊕ *Exit I–5 at Carmel Valley Rd. and head west toward Coast Hwy. 101 until you reach N. Torrey Pines Rd.; turn left.* ☎ *858/755–2063* 🌐 *www.torreypine.org* 🎫 *Parking from $20.*

KAYAKING

Hike Bike Kayak Adventures

KAYAKING | This shop offers several kayak tours, from easy excursions in La Jolla Cove that are well suited to families and beginners to more advanced jaunts. Tours include kayaking the caves off La Jolla coast, and whale-watching (from a safe distance) December through March. Tours last 90 minutes to two hours and require a minimum of four people. ✉ *2222 Av. de la Playa, La Jolla* ☎ *858/551–9510* 🌐 *www.hikebikekayak.com* 🎫 *From $50.*

SURFING

★ Surf Diva Surf School

SURFING | Check out clinics, surf camps, and private lessons especially formulated for girls and women. Most clinics and trips are for women only, but there are some coed options. Guys can also book group or private lessons from the nationally recognized staff. Surf Diva is also home to a boutique that sells surf and stand-up paddleboard equipment. They also offer surf retreats in Costa Rica. ✉ *2160 Ave. de la Playa, La Jolla* ☎ *858/454–8273* 🌐 *www.surfdiva.com* 🎫 *Group lessons $69; private lessons $95.*

Point Loma

The hilly peninsula of Point Loma curves west and south into the Pacific and provides protection for San Diego Bay. Its high elevations and sandy cliffs provide incredible views, and make Point Loma a visible local landmark. Its maritime roots are evident, from its longtime ties to the U.S. Navy to its bustling sportfishing and sailing marinas. The funky community of Ocean Beach coexists alongside the stately homes of Sunset Cliffs and the honored graves at Fort Rosecrans National Cemetery.

Sights

★ Cabrillo National Monument

LIGHTHOUSE | FAMILY | This 166-acre preserve marks the site of the first European visit to San Diego, made by 16th-century Spanish explorer Juan Rodríguez Cabrillo when he landed at this spot on September 15, 1542. Today the site, with its rugged cliffs and shores and outstanding overlooks, is one of the most frequently visited of all the national monuments. There's a good visitor center and useful interpretive stations along the cliff-side walkways. Highlights include the moderately difficult Bayside Trail, the Old Point Loma Lighthouse, and the tide pools. There's also a sheltered viewing station where you can watch the gray whales' yearly migration from Baja California to Alaska (including high-powered telescopes). ✉ *1800 Cabrillo Memorial Dr., Point Loma* ☎ *619/ 523–4285* 🌐 *www.nps.gov/cabr* 🎫 *$20 per car, $10 per person on foot/bicycle, entry good for 7 days.*

Ocean Beach Pier

MARINA | This T-shape pier is a popular fishing spot and home to the Ocean Beach Pier Café and a small tackle shop. Constructed in 1966, it is the longest concrete pier on the West Coast and a perfect place to take in views of the harbor, ocean, and Point Loma Peninsula. Surfers flock to the waves that break just below. ✉ *1950 Abbott St., Ocean Beach.*

Sunset Cliffs

BEACH—SIGHT | As the name would suggest, this natural park near Point Loma Nazerene University is one of the best places in San Diego to watch the sunset thanks to its cliff-top location and expansive ocean views. Some limited beach access is accessible via an extremely steep stairway at the foot of Ladera Street. Beware of the treacherous cliff trails and pay attention to warning signs since the cliffs are very unstable. If you're going to make your way to the narrow beach below, it's best to go at low tide when the southern end, near Cabrillo Point, reveals tide pools teeming with small sea creatures. Farther north the waves lure surfers, and Osprey Point offers good fishing off the rocks. Keep your eyes peeled for migrating California gray whales during the winter months. Check WaveCast (🌐 *www.wavecast.com/tides*) for tide schedules. **Amenities:** parking (no fee). **Best for:** solitude; sunset; surfing. ✉ *Sunset Cliffs Blvd., between Ladera St. and Adair St., Point Loma* 🌐 *www.sunsetcliffs.info.*

★ Cesarina

$$ | ITALIAN | A wall of mason jars with pickled vegetables and brined olives transports you to an Italian market in Rome where the owner's mother perfected generations of recipes that have made their way into this Point Loma eatery. Since its 2019 opening, customers have lined up for homemade Italian staples including pasta, gnocchi, meatballs, sausage, bread, and decadent desserts. Portions are generous and flavors are as authentic as they get. The tagliere cutting board is piled high with prosciutto, burrata, green olives, artichoke hearts, and marinated vegetables beckoning a dunk of focaccia with every bite, while the risotto and tagliata are cooked to perfection and the spaghetti with mussels and clams will have you reenacting *Lady and the Tramp*. For the finale, bite into the chocolate cannoli and then be sure to check yourself in the mirror as the homemade cannoli shells are flaky. **Known for:** nearly everything made from scratch; authentic Italian cuisine; excellent vegan options. 💲 *Average main: $20* ✉ *4161 Voltaire St., Point Loma* ☎ *619/226–6222* 🌐 *www.cesarinarestaurant.com.*

★ Hodad's

$ | **BURGER** | **FAMILY** | Surfers with big appetites, and fans of Food Network's *Diners, Drive-ins and Dives,* chow down on huge, messy burgers, fries, onion rings, and shakes at this funky, hippie beach joint adorned with beat-up surfboards and license plates from almost every state. Don't be put off by lines out the door—they move quickly and the wait is worth it, especially now that they have their own microbrewery with six draft beers including a hazy IPA and a Mexican lager. A miniburger is a less-filling option, and there are veggie and chicken patty options for the red-meat averse. Newer outposts—as family-friendly as the original '60s joint—are Downtown and at Petco Park. **Known for:** legendary bacon cheeseburgers and thick-cut onion rings; surf-shack vibe; a little sass with your burger. *Average main: $10* ✉ *5010 Newport Ave., Ocean Beach* ☎ *619/224–4623* 🌐 *www.hodadies.com.*

★ Liberty Public Market

$ | **INTERNATIONAL** | **FAMILY** | The city's former Naval Training Center is home to more than 30 vendors so even the pickiest of diners will be pleased. Options include tacos and quesadillas at Cecilia's Taqueria; fried rice, pad Thai, and curries at Mama Made Thai; lavender lattes from Westbean Coffee Roasters; fried chicken and fries from Fluster Cluck; sweet and savory crepes from Ooh La La; more than a dozen Argentinean empanadas at Paraná; and croissants, éclairs, and macarons at Le Parfait Paris. There are a few communal tables indoors, but the best seating is the kid- and dog-friendly outdoor patio, outfitted with Adirondack chairs and market lights. **Known for:** cuisines from around the world; lively kid- and dog-friendly patio; the best regional foods under one roof. *Average main: $10* ✉ *2820 Historic Decatur Rd., Liberty Station* ☎ *619/487–9346* 🌐 *www.libertypublicmarket.com.*

★ The Little Lion Cafe

$$ | **MODERN AMERICAN** | Amid surf shacks and hippie beach bars, this restaurant perched on stunning Sunset Cliffs feels like a hidden European bistro. The sisters who run the show come from a long line of successful local restaurateurs and have brought their passed-down expertise to the simple, healthy menu and thoughtful service. Entrées include plant-based tacos, Baja shrimp in garlic butter, and grilled cheese with honey, Dijon, and Brie. Their morning menu features chia seed puddings and baked eggs, which are a welcome contrast to the typical indulgent brunch fare. **Known for:** eggs Benedict; cozy bistro setting; flash-fried cauliflower. *Average main: $20* ✉ *1424 Sunset Cliffs Blvd., Ocean Beach* ☎ *619/756–6921* 🌐 *www.thelittlelioncafe.com* *Closed Mon. No dinner Tues., Wed., and Sun.*

Point Loma Seafoods

$ | **SEAFOOD** | **FAMILY** | When fishing boats unload their catch on-site, a seafood restaurant and market earns the right to boast that they offer "the freshest thing in town." In the early 1960s, mostly sportfishermen came here, but word got out about the just-caught fried fish on San Francisco–style sourdough bread, and now locals and visitors come to enjoy bay views, sunshine, and a greatly expanded menu of seafood dishes. A friendly, efficient crew takes orders for food and drinks at the counter, keeping the wait down even on the busiest days. In addition to sandwiches, favorites include fish tacos, seafood cocktails, sushi, salads, and fried platters of fish, shrimp, and scallops. **Known for:** San Francisco–style seafood on sourdough; dockside bay views; hickory-wood smoked fish. *Average main: $15* ✉ *2805 Emerson St., Point Loma* ☎ *619/223–1109* 🌐 *www.pointlomaseafoods.com.*

Stone Brewing World Bistro and Gardens
$$ | **ECLECTIC** | **FAMILY** | This 50,000-square-foot monument to beer and good food is a crowd-pleaser, especially for fans of San Diego's nationally known craft beer scene. The global menu features dishes like the Bavarian pretzel and Brewmaster's Brisket Dip that pair perfectly with on-tap and bottled beers from around the world and Stone's famous IPAs. Dine indoors in high-ceiling rooms guarded by etched-metal gargoyles and lit by beer-bottle chandeliers. Or, relax outdoors where parents often unwind as their kids enjoy the patio. Before leaving, browse the company store for hip logo wear like hats, hoodies, and bomber jackets. **Known for:** massive outdoor patio; brew-friendly eats; artisanal burgers. *Average main: $22 2816 Historic Decatur Rd., Liberty Station 619/269–2100 www.stonelibertystation.com.*

Hotels

★ Homewood Suites San Diego Airport Liberty Station
$$$ | **HOTEL** | **FAMILY** | With amenities like kitchens and a business center, most guests stay at least five nights, turning this all-suites hotel into a home. **Pros:** outstanding central location near attractions; close to paths for joggers and bikers; complimentary airport shuttle. **Cons:** breakfast area can get crowded; far from nightlife. *Rooms from: $249 2576 Laning Rd., Point Loma 619/222–0500 www.homewoodsuites.com 150 suites Free breakfast.*

Inn at Sunset Cliffs
$$$$ | **HOTEL** | At this U-shape beachfront property, every room gets a glimpse of the ocean, meaning you can fall asleep to the sound of the crashing waves and wake up to the sight of surfers paddling at Pescadero break just in front of the hotel. **Pros:** midweek rates from $175; rooms remodeled in 2018; Rooms 201 and 214 have full ocean views. **Cons:** standard rooms are tiny; no elevator; thin walls. *Rooms from: $315 1370 Sunset Cliffs Blvd., Ocean Beach 619/222–7901, 866/786–2543 www.innatsunsetcliffs.com 28 rooms No meals.*

Activities

★ Bayside Trail at Cabrillo National Monument
HIKING/WALKING | Driving here is a treat in itself, as a vast view of the Pacific unfolds before you. The view is equally enjoyable on Bayside Trail (2 miles round-trip), which is home to the same coastal sagebrush that Juan Rodriguez Cabrillo saw when he first discovered the California coast in the 16th century. After the hike, you can explore nearby tide pools, the monument statue, and the Old Point Loma Lighthouse. Don't worry if you don't see everything on your first visit; your entrance receipt ($20 per car) is good for seven days. *1800 Cabrillo Memorial Dr., Point Loma From I–5, take Rosecrans exit and turn right on Canon St. then left on Catalina Blvd. (also known as Cabrillo Memorial Dr.); follow until end 619/523–4285 www.nps.gov/cabr Parking $20.*

Shelter Island

In 1950 San Diego's port director decided to raise the shoal that lay off the eastern shore of Point Loma above sea level with the sand and mud dredged up during the course of deepening a ship channel in the 1930s and '40s. The resulting peninsula, **Shelter Island,** became home to several marinas and resorts, many with Polynesian details that still exist today, giving them a retro flair. This reclaimed peninsula now supports towering palms and resorts, restaurants, and side-by-side marinas. A long sidewalk runs past boat brokerages to the hotels and marinas that line the inner shore, facing Point Loma. On the bay side, fishermen launch their boats and families relax at picnic tables along the grass, where there are fire rings and permanent barbeque grills.

Bali Hai

$$ | **HAWAIIAN** | For more than 50 years, generations of San Diegans and visitors have enjoyed this Polynesian-themed icon with its stunning bay and city skyline views. The menu is a fusion of Hawaiian and Asian cuisines with standouts like the Hawaiian tuna poke, Mongolian lamb with pad Thai, and wok-fried bass. **Known for:** potent Bali Hai mai tais; Sunday brunch buffet with a DIY sundae bar; Hawaiian and Asian-themed menu. *Average main: $25 2230 Shelter Island Dr., Shelter Island 619/222–1181 www.balihairestaurant.com No lunch Sun.*

★ **Kona Kai Resort & Spa**

$$$ | **RESORT** | A $30 million renovation took this Shelter Island resort up a notch, with remodeled rooms, a new pool, spa, gym, and lobby—making the marina view an added bonus rather than the main focus. **Pros:** private beach with firepits; near marina with water view; on-site sports rental equipment. **Cons:** not centrally located; resort fees; popular for business meetings and weddings. *Rooms from: $269 1551 Shelter Island Dr., Shelter Island 619/221–8000, 800/566–2524 www.resortkonakai.com 170 rooms No meals.*

Harbor Island

Following the successful creation of Shelter Island, in 1961 the U.S. Navy used the residue from digging berths deep enough to accommodate aircraft carriers to build **Harbor Island**. Restaurants and high-rise hotels dot the inner shore of this 1½-mile-long peninsula adjacent to the airport. Restaurants and high-rise hotels dot the inner shore while the bay's shore is lined with pathways, gardens, and scenic picnic spots. On the west point, the restaurant Tom Ham's Lighthouse has a U.S. Coast Guard–approved beacon shining from its tower and a sweeping view of San Diego's bay front.

Tom Ham's Lighthouse

$$$ | **SEAFOOD** | It's hard to top this long-time Harbor Island restaurant's incredible views across San Diego Bay to the Downtown skyline and Coronado Bridge. Now a new alfresco dining deck and a contemporary seafood-focused menu ensure the dining experience at this working lighthouse doesn't take a back seat to the scenery. Sample the iced shellfish platter before moving on to traditional lobster bouillabaisse and paella or grilled prawns with spicy grits. The family-owned institution also serves a popular Sunday brunch that stars crab legs, peel-and-eat shrimp, smoked salmon, and oysters along with bottomless orange or pineapple mimosas. Prefer beer? Choose from a long list of on-tap and bottled craft brews. **Known for:** bottomless mimosa Sunday brunch; alfresco dining deck with skyline and Coronado bridge views; fresh seafood and beer-battered cod. *Average main: $30 2150 Harbor Island Dr., Harbor Island 619/291–9110 www.tomhamslighthouse.com No lunch Sun.*

Coronado

As if freeze-framed in the 1950s, Coronado's quaint appeal is captured in its old-fashioned storefronts, well-manicured gardens, and charming **Ferry Landing Marketplace.** The streets of Coronado are wide, quiet, and friendly, and many of today's residents live in grand Victorian homes handed down for generations. Naval Air Station North Island was established in 1911 on Coronado's north end,

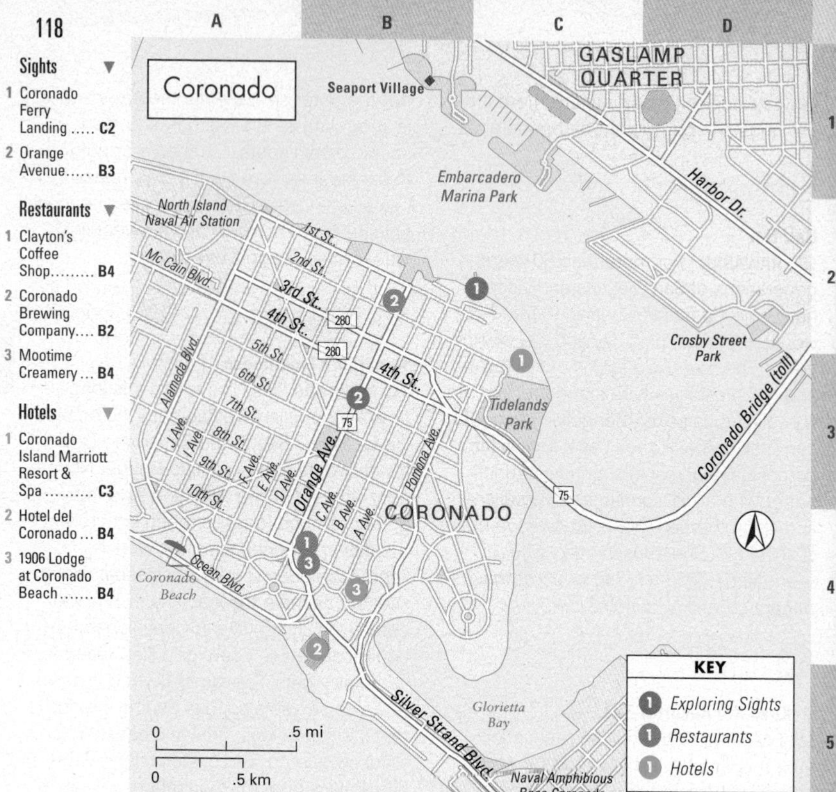

across from Point Loma, and was the site of Charles Lindbergh's departure on the transcontinental flight that preceded his famous solo flight across the Atlantic. Coronado's long relationship with the U.S. Navy and its desirable real estate have made it an enclave for military personnel; it's said to have more retired admirals per capita than anywhere else in the United States.

Coronado is accessible via the arching blue 2.2-mile-long San Diego–Coronado Bay Bridge, which offers breathtaking views of the harbor and Downtown. Alternatively, pedestrians and bikes can reach Coronado via the popular ferry service. Bus 904 meets the ferry and travels as far as Silver Strand State Beach. Bus 901 runs daily between the Gaslamp Quarter and Coronado.

Sights

Coronado Ferry Landing

STORE/MALL | **FAMILY** | This collection of shops at Ferry Landing is on a smaller scale than the Embarcadero's Seaport Village, but you do get a great view of the Downtown San Diego skyline. The little bay-side shops and restaurants resemble the gingerbread domes of the Hotel del Coronado. ✉ *1201 1st St., at B Ave., Coronado* 🌐 *www.coronadoferrylanding.com.*

★ Orange Avenue

NEIGHBORHOOD | Comprising Coronado's business district and its village-like heart, this avenue is surely one of the most charming spots in Southern California. Slow-paced and very "local" (the city fights against chain stores), it's a blast from the past, although entirely up-to-date in other respects. The military presence—Coronado is home to the U.S. Navy Sea, Air, and Land (SEAL) forces—is reflected in shops selling military gear and places like **McP's Irish Pub,** at No. 1107. A family-friendly stop for a good, all-American meal, it's the unofficial SEALs headquarters. Many clothing boutiques, home-furnishings stores, and upscale restaurants cater to visitors with deep pockets, but you can buy plumbing supplies, too, or get a genuine military haircut at **Crown Barber Shop,** at No. 947. If you need a break, stop for a latte at the sidewalk café of **Bay Books,** San Diego's largest independent bookstore, at No. 1029. ✉ *Orange Ave., near 9th St., Coronado.*

Beaches

★ Coronado Beach

BEACH—SIGHT | FAMILY | This wide beach is one of San Diego's most picturesque thanks to its soft white sand and sparkly blue water. The historic Hotel del Coronado serves as a backdrop, and it's perfect for sunbathing, people-watching, and Frisbee tossing. The beach has limited surf, but it's great for bodyboarding and swimming. Exercisers might include Navy SEAL teams or other military units that conduct training runs on beaches in and around Coronado. There are picnic tables, grills, and popular fire rings, but don't bring lacquered wood or pallets. Only natural wood is allowed for burning. There's also a dog beach on the north end. There's free parking along Ocean Boulevard, though it's often hard to snag a space. **Amenities:** food and drink; lifeguards; showers; toilets. **Best for:** walking; swimming. ✉ *Ocean Blvd., between S. O St. and Orange Ave., Coronado* ✣ *From San Diego–Coronado bridge, turn left on Orange Ave. and follow signs.*

Silver Strand State Beach

BEACH—SIGHT | FAMILY | This quiet beach on a narrow sand spit allows visitors a unique opportunity to experience both the Pacific Ocean and the San Diego Bay. The 2½ miles of ocean side is great for surfing and other water sports while the bay side, accessible via foot tunnel under Highway 75, has calmer, warmer water and great views of the San Diego skyline. Lifeguards and rangers are on duty year-round, and there are places for biking, volleyball, and fishing. Picnic tables, grills, and firepits are available in summer, and the Silver Strand Beach Cafe is open Memorial Day through Labor Day. The beach is close to Loews Coronado Bay Resort and the Coronado Cays, an exclusive community popular with yacht owners. You can reserve RV sites ($65 beach; $50 inland) online (🌐 *www.reserveamerica.com*). Three day-use parking lots provide room for 800 cars. **Amenities:** food and drink; lifeguards; parking (fee); showers; toilets. **Best for:** walking; swimming; surfing. ✉ *5000 Hwy. 75, Coronado* ✣ *4½ miles south of city of Coronado* ☎ *619/435–5184* 🌐 *www.parks.ca.gov/silverstrand* 🎫 *Parking $10, motor home $30.*

Restaurants

Clayton's Coffee Shop

$ | AMERICAN | FAMILY | A classic diner with bar seating in a circle, Clayton's is a great lunch or breakfast spot with a menu that ranges from classic American fare to Mexican-inspired dishes like the popular breakfast burrito. Just don't forget dessert! **Known for:** bottomless coffee; breakfast burrito; gooey cinnamon roll sundae. 💲 *Average main: $10* ✉ *979 Orange Ave., Coronado* ☎ *619/435–5425* 🌐 *www.claytonscoffeeshop.com.*

Coronado Brewing Company

$ | AMERICAN | FAMILY | Perfect for beer lovers with kids, this popular, laid-back Coronado brewpub offers a menu that features large portions of basic bar food like burgers, sandwiches, pizza, and salads. Enjoy a brew at a pair of sidewalk terraces or belly up to the bar and a new batch being made such as the Islander Pale Ale (IPA) or Mermaid's Red Ale. **Known for:** a good selection of house-crafted beers;

kids' menu; more strollers than bar stools. *Average main: $12* *170 Orange Ave., Coronado* *619/437–4452* *www.coronadobrewing.com.*

Mootime Creamery

$ | **CAFÉ** | **FAMILY** | For a deliciously sweet pick-me-up, check out the rich ice cream, frozen yogurt, and sorbet made fresh daily on the premises. Dessert nachos made from waffle-cone chips are an unusual addition to an extensive sundae menu. Just look for the statue of Elvis on the sidewalk in front. **Known for:** daily house-made ice cream, yogurt, and sorbet; dessert nachos; "moopies" sandwiches, with ice cream between two cereal bars. *Average main: $5* *1025 Orange Ave., Coronado* *619/435–2422* *www.mootime.com* *No credit cards.*

Hotels

★ Coronado Island Marriott Resort & Spa

$$$$ | **RESORT** | **FAMILY** | Near San Diego Bay, this snazzy hotel has rooms with great Downtown skyline views. **Pros:** spectacular views; on-site spa; close to water taxis. **Cons:** not in downtown Coronado; resort fee; expensive self-parking. *Rooms from: $329* *2000 2nd St., Coronado* *619/435–3000* *www.marriott.com/hotels/travel/sanci-coronado-island-marriott-resort-and-spa* *300 rooms* *No meals.*

★ Hotel del Coronado

$$$$ | **RESORT** | **FAMILY** | As much of a draw today as it was when it opened in 1888, the Victorian-style "Hotel Del" is always alive with activity, as guests—including U.S. presidents and celebrities—and tourists marvel at the fanciful architecture and ocean views. **Pros:** 17 on-site shops; on the beach; well-rounded spa. **Cons:** some rooms are small; expensive dining; hectic public areas. *Rooms from: $425* *1500 Orange Ave., Coronado* *800/468–3533, 619/435–6611* *www.hoteldel.com* *757 rooms* *No meals.*

★ 1906 Lodge at Coronado Beach

$$$$ | **B&B/INN** | Smaller but no less luxurious than the sprawling beach resorts of Coronado, this lodge—whose name alludes to the main building's former life as a boardinghouse built in 1906—welcomes couples for romantic retreats two blocks from the ocean. **Pros:** most suites feature Jacuzzi tubs, fireplaces, and porches; historic property; free underground parking. **Cons:** too quiet for families; no pool; limited on-site dining options. *Rooms from: $329* *1060 Adella Ave., Coronado* *619/437–1900, 866/435–1906* *www.1906lodge.com* *17 rooms* *Free breakfast.*

Activities

BIKING

Holland's Bicycles

BICYCLING | This is a great bike rental source on Coronado Island, so you can ride the Silver Strand Bike Path on an electric bike, beach cruiser, road bike, or tandem. *977 Orange Ave., Coronado* *619/435–3153* *www.hollandsbicycles.com* *From $8.*

Chapter 5

DISNEYLAND AND ORANGE COUNTY

WITH KNOTT'S BERRY FARM AND CATALINA ISLAND

Updated by
Jill Weinlein

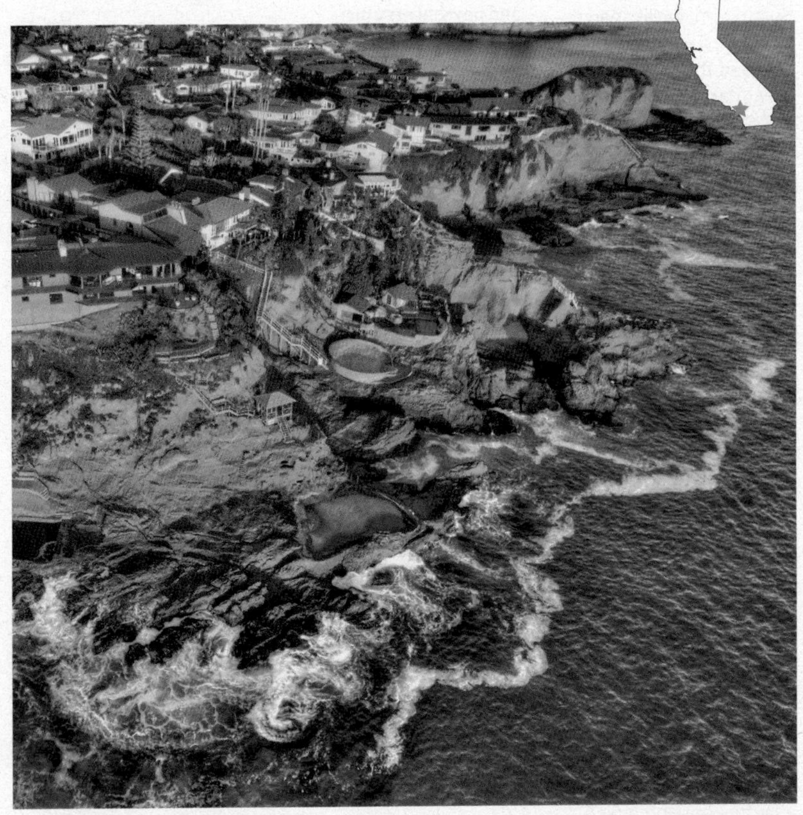

Sights	Restaurants	Hotels	Shopping	Nightlife
★★★★★	★★★★☆	★★★★★	★☆☆☆☆	★☆☆☆☆

WELCOME TO DISNEYLAND AND ORANGE COUNTY

TOP REASONS TO GO

★ **Disneyland:** Walking down Main Street, U.S.A., with Sleeping Beauty Castle straight ahead, you really will feel like you're in one of the happiest places on Earth.

★ **Beautiful beaches:** Surf, swim, kayak, paddleboard, or just relax on some of the state's most breathtaking stretches of coastline. Calm coves offer clear water for snorkeling and scuba diving.

★ **Santa Catalina Island:** Just 22 miles from the mainland, Santa Catalina Island is the only inhabited island of the Channel Islands chain. A fast and easy cruise away on a high-speed catamaran, once there you can explore the Mediterranean-inspired small town of Avalon, dive or snorkel through the state's first underwater park, or explore the unspoiled beauty of the island's wild interior.

★ **Family fun:** Ride roller coasters, eat ice cream and frozen chocolate-dipped bananas, bike on oceanfront paths, fish off ocean piers, or rent a Duffy boat and cruise around the calm harbors.

1 **Disneyland Resort.** Southern California's top draw is now a megaresort, with more attractions spilling over into Disney's California Adventure.

2 **Knott's Berry Farm.** Amusement park lovers will enjoy this Buena Park attraction, with thrill rides, the *Peanuts* gang, and lots of fried chicken and boysenberry pie.

3 **Huntington Beach.** This resort destination is often referred to as Surf City U.S.A.

4 **Newport Beach.** There's something for every taste here, from glamorous boutiques to simple snack huts.

5 **Corona del Mar.** No matter your preferred outdoor activity, you'll find it on one of the beaches here.

6 **Laguna Beach.** With 30 beaches and coves to explore, there's plenty to keep visitors busy.

7 **San Juan Capistrano.** Take a trip back in time among the historic missions.

8 **Catalina Island.** This island paradise—with its pocket-size town, Avalon, and large nature preserve—is just off the Orange County coast.

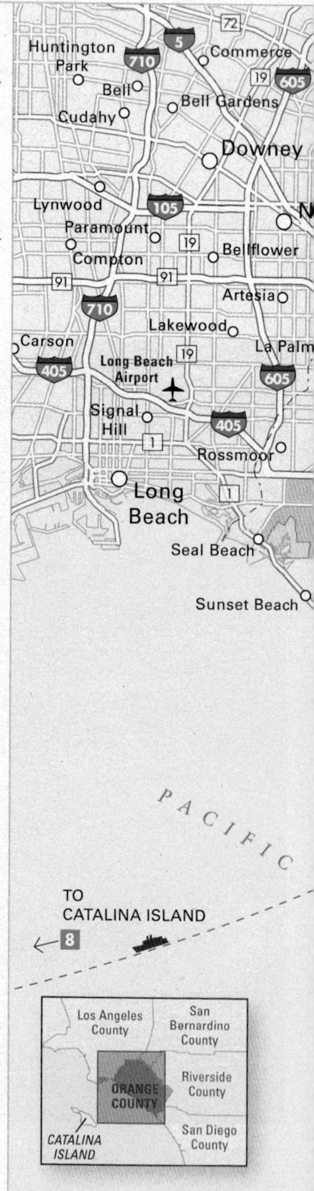

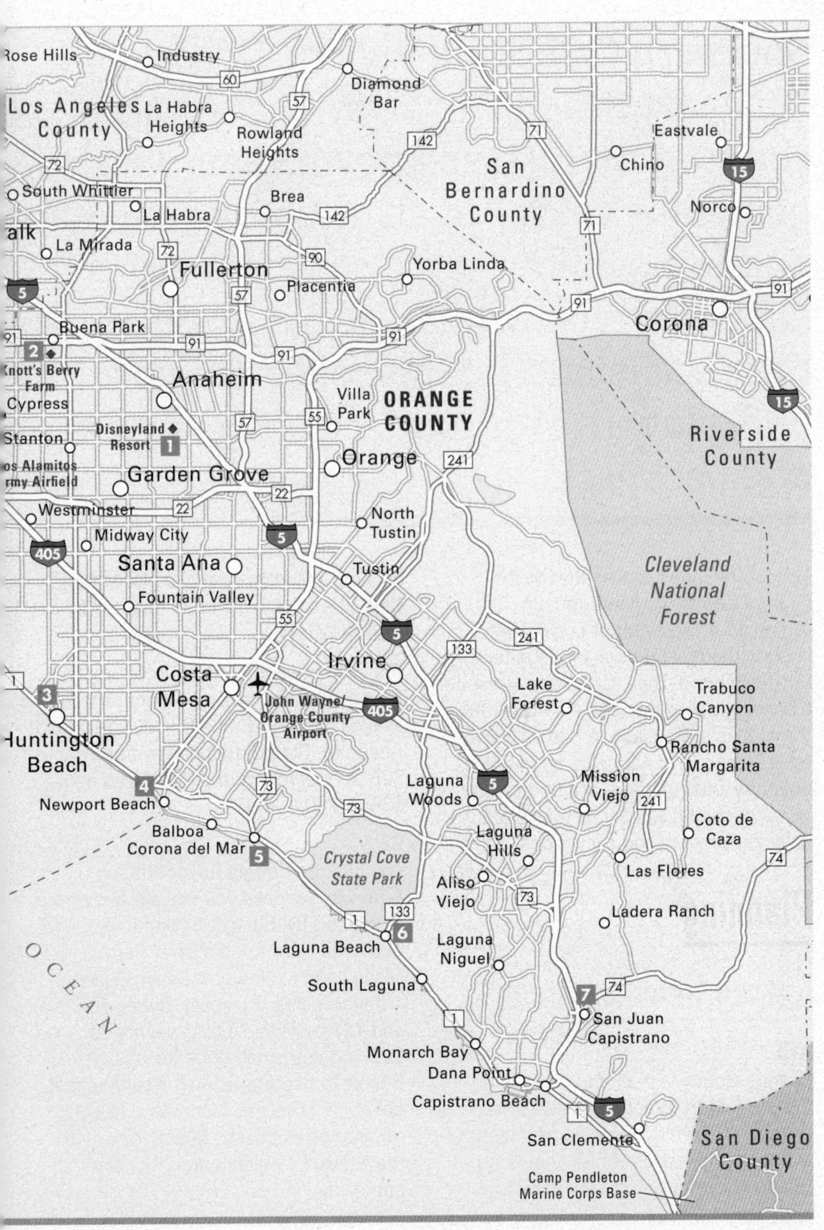

Rose Hills
Industry
Diamond Bar
Los Angeles County
La Habra Heights
Rowland Heights
San Bernardino County
Eastvale
Chino
Norco
South Whittier
La Habra
Brea
La Mirada
Fullerton
Placentia
Yorba Linda
Buena Park
Corona
Knott's Berry Farm
Anaheim
Cypress
Villa Park
ORANGE COUNTY
Disneyland Resort
Stanton
Orange
Riverside County
Los Alamitos Army Airfield
Garden Grove
Westminster
North Tustin
Midway City
Santa Ana
Tustin
Cleveland National Forest
Fountain Valley
Irvine
Costa Mesa
Lake Forest
Trabuco Canyon
John Wayne/ Orange County Airport
Huntington Beach
Rancho Santa Margarita
Laguna Woods
Mission Viejo
Newport Beach
Coto de Caza
Balboa
Corona del Mar
Laguna Hills
Crystal Cove State Park
Las Flores
Aliso Viejo
Ladera Ranch
Laguna Beach
Laguna Niguel
South Laguna
OCEAN
San Juan Capistrano
Monarch Bay
Dana Point
Capistrano Beach
San Clemente
San Diego County
Camp Pendleton Marine Corps Base

With its tropical flowers and palm trees, the stretch of coast between Seal Beach and San Clemente is often called the Southern California Riviera. Upscale Newport Beach and artsy Laguna are the stars, but lesser-known gems on the glistening coast—such as Corona del Mar and Dana Point—are also worth visiting. Offshore, meanwhile, lies picturesque Catalina Island, an unspoiled paradise and a favorite for tourists, boaters, divers, and backpacking campers alike.

Few of the citrus groves that gave Orange County its name remain. This region south and east of Los Angeles is now ruled by tourism and high-tech business rather than agriculture. Despite a building boom that began in the 1990s, the area is still a place to find wilderness trails, canyons, greenbelts, and natural environs. Just offshore is a deep-water wilderness that's possible to explore via daily whale-watching excursions.

Planning

Getting Here and Around

AIR

Orange County's main facility is John Wayne Airport Orange County (SNA), which is served by six major domestic airlines and one commuter line. Long Beach Airport (LGB) is served by four airlines, including its major player, JetBlue. It's roughly 20 to 30 minutes by car from Anaheim.

Super Shuttle and Prime Time Airport Shuttle provide transportation from John Wayne and LAX to the Disneyland area of Anaheim. Round-trip fares average about $28 per person from John Wayne and $34 to $80 from LAX.

BUS

The Orange County Transportation Authority will take you virtually anywhere in the county, but it will take time; OCTA buses go from Knott's Berry Farm and Disneyland to Newport Beach. Bus 1 travels along the coast; Buses 701 and 721 provide express service to Los Angeles. Anaheim offers Anaheim Resort Transportation (ART) service that connects hotels to Disneyland Resort, downtown Anaheim, Buena Park, and the Metrolink train center. Rides are $3 each way.

CONTACTS Anaheim Resort Transportation. ✉ *2099 S. State College Blvd., Suite 600, Anaheim* ☎ *714/563–5287* 🌐 *rideart.org.* **Orange County Transportation Authority.** ☎ *714/636–7433* 🌐 *www.octa.net.*

CAR

The San Diego Freeway (Interstate 405), the coastal route, and the Santa Ana Freeway (Interstate 5), the inland route, run north–south through Orange County. South of Laguna, Interstate 405 merges into Interstate 5 (called the San Diego Freeway south from this point). A toll road, Highway 73, runs 15 miles from Newport Beach to San Juan Capistrano; it costs $6.22–$8.48 (lower rates are for weekends and off-peak hours) and is usually less jammed than the regular freeways. Do your best to avoid all Orange County freeways during rush hours (6–9 am and 3:30–6:30 pm). Highway 55 leads to Newport Beach. The Pacific Coast Highway (Highway 1) allows easy access to beach communities and is the most scenic route but expect it to be crowded, especially on summer weekends and holidays.

FERRY

There are two ferries that service Catalina Island; Catalina Express runs multiple departures daily from San Pedro, Long Beach, and Dana Point. From each port, it takes about 90 minutes to reach the island. The Catalina Flyer runs from Newport Beach to Avalon in about 75 minutes. Reservations are strongly advised for summer months and weekends. During the winter months, ferry crossings are not as frequent.

TRAIN

Amtrak makes daily stops in Orange County at all major towns. Metrolink is a weekday commuter train that runs to and from Los Angeles and Orange County.

CONTACTS Metrolink. ✉ *800 N. Alameda St., Los Angeles* ☎ *800/371–5465* 🌐 *www.metrolinktrains.com.*

Restaurants

Guests dining at restaurants in Orange County generally wear beach casual, although at top resorts and fine dining venues, guests usually choose to dress up. Of course, there's also a swath of casual places along the beachfronts—seafood takeout, taquerias, burger joints—that won't mind if you wear shorts and flip-flops. Reservations are recommended for the nicest restaurants.

Many places don't serve past 11 pm, and locals tend to eat early. Remember that according to California law, smoking is prohibited in all enclosed areas.

Hotels

Along the coast there are remarkable luxury resorts; if you can't afford a stay, pop in for the view at Laguna Beach's Montage Mosiac Tile pool or the always welcoming Ritz-Carlton at Dana Point. For a taste of the O.C. glam life, the Resort at Pelican Hills is an idyllic place for lunch, brunch or dinner at its Coliseum Grill overlooking the world's largest circular pool and the ocean beyond. For a nautical experience, enjoy lunch or dinner next to multimillion-dollar yachts secured in Newport Bay at the Balboa Bay Resort.

As a rule, lodging prices tend to rise the closer the hotels are to the beach. If you're looking for value, consider a hotel that's inland along the Interstate 405 freeway corridor.

In most cases, you can take advantage of some of the facilities of the high-end resorts, such as restaurants and spas, even if you aren't an overnight guest.

Restaurant and hotel reviews have been shortened. For full information, visit Fodors.com. Prices in the restaurant reviews are the average cost of a main course at dinner or, if dinner is not served, at lunch. Prices in the hotel reviews are the lowest cost of a standard double room in high season.

What It Costs in U.S. Dollars			
$	$$	$$$	$$$$
RESTAURANTS			
under $20	$20–$30	$31–$40	over $40
HOTELS			
under $200	$200–$300	$301–$400	over $400

Visitor Information

Visit Anaheim is an excellent resource for both leisure and business travelers and can provide materials on many area attractions. Kiosks at the Anaheim Convention Center act as a digital concierge and allow visitors to plan itineraries and buy tickets to area attractions.

The Orange County Visitors Association's website is also a useful source of information.

CONTACTS Orange County Visitors Association. 🌐 *www.travelcostamesa.com/visittheoc* . **Visit Anaheim.** ✉ *2099 S. State College Blvd., Suite 600, Anaheim* ☎ *714/765–2800* 🌐 *www.visitanaheim.org.*

Disneyland Resort

26 miles southeast of Los Angeles, via I–5.

The snowcapped Matterhorn, the centerpiece of Disneyland, punctuates the skyline of Anaheim. Since 1955, when Walt Disney chose this once-quiet farming community for the site of his first amusement park, Disneyland has attracted more than 650 million visitors and tens of thousands of workers, and Anaheim has been their host. Today, there are more than 60 attractions and adventures in the park's nine themed lands: Fantasyland, Adventureland, Tomorrowland, Frontierland, Main Street U.S.A., New Orleans Square, Critter Country, Mickey's Toontown, and Star Wars: Galaxy's Edge.

The resort is a sprawling complex that includes Disney's two amusement parks (Disneyland and Disney's California Adventure); three hotels; and Downtown Disney, a shopping, dining, and entertainment promenade. Anaheim's tourist center includes Angel Stadium of Anaheim, home of baseball's Los Angeles Angels of Anaheim; the Honda Center (formerly the Arrowhead Pond), which hosts concerts and the Anaheim Ducks hockey team; and the enormous Anaheim Convention Center.

GETTING THERE

Disney is about a 30-mile drive from either LAX or Downtown. From LAX, follow Sepulveda Boulevard south to the Interstate 105 freeway and drive east 16 miles to the Interstate 605 north exit. Exit at the Santa Ana Freeway (Interstate 5) and continue south for 12 miles to the Disneyland Drive exit. Follow signs to the resort. From Downtown, follow Interstate 5 south 28 miles and exit at Disneyland Drive. **Disneyland Resort Express** (☎ *800/828–6699*) offers daily nonstop bus service between LAX, John Wayne Airport, and Anaheim. Reservations are not required. The cost is $30 one-way from LAX, and $20 from John Wayne Airport.

SAVING TIME AND MONEY

If you plan to visit for more than a day, you can save money by buying multiday Park Hopper tickets that grant same-day "hopping" privileges between Disneyland and Disney's California Adventure. You get a discount on the multiple-day passes if you buy online through the Disneyland website.

Single-day admission prices vary by date. A one-day Park Hopper pass costs $147–$185 for anyone 10 or older, $141–$177 for kids ages three to nine. Admission to either park (but not both) is $97–$135 for adults or $91–$127 for kids three to nine; kids two and under are free.

In addition to tickets, parking is $20–$35 (unless your hotel has a shuttle or is within walking distance), and meals in the parks and at Downtown Disney range from $15 to $75 per person.

Disneyland

★ Disneyland

AMUSEMENT PARK/WATER PARK | FAMILY | An imaginative original, Disneyland was an unproven concept when it opened in 1955, but Walt Disney himself could never have predicted the park's success and its beloved place in the hearts of Southern Californians. It is the only one of the parks to have been overseen by Walt himself, has a genuine historic feel, and occupies a unique place in the Disney legend. Expertly run, with perfectly maintained grounds and a helpful staff ("cast members" in the Disney lexicon), the park offers plenty of fun experiences that you won't find anywhere else: you can visit a galaxy far, far away in the *Star Wars* land; cruise to a world of pirates in search of Jack Sparrow from the *Pirates of the Caribbean* series; and take a ride to Storybook Land, with its miniature replicas of animated Disney scenes from classics such as *Frozen* and *Alice in Wonderland*. Beloved Disney characters appear for autographs and photos throughout the day; times and places are posted at the entrances and on the Disneyland mobile app. Live shows, parades, strolling musicians, fireworks (on weekends and during the summer and holidays), and endless creative snack choices add to the carnival atmosphere. You can also meet some of the animated icons at one of the character meals served at the three Disney hotels (open to the public, but reservations are needed). Belongings can be stored in lockers just off Main Street while stroller rentals, wheelchairs, and Electric Conveyance Vehicles (ECV) are at the entrance gate as convenient options for families with mobility challenges. The park's popularity means there are always crowds, especially during the holidays and summer months, so take advantage of the Disney FastPass Service to spend less time waiting in lines. Also be sure to make dining reservations at least three weeks before your visit to guarantee a table without a wait. ✉ *Disneyland Park, 1313 S. Disneyland Dr., between Ball Rd. and Katella Ave., Anaheim* ☎ *714/781–4636 guest information* 🌐 *disneyland.disney.go.com* 🎟 *From $97; parking $20.*

PARK NEIGHBORHOODS

Neighborhoods for Disneyland are arranged in geographic order.

MAIN STREET, U.S.A.

Walt's hometown of Marceline, Missouri, was the inspiration behind this romanticized image of small-town America, circa 1900. The sidewalks are lined with a penny arcade and shops that sell everything from tradeable pins to Disney-themed clothing, an endless supply of sugar confections, and a photo shop that offers souvenirs created via Disney's PhotoPass (on-site photographers capture memorable moments digitally—you can access them in person or online via the Disneyland app). Main Street opens half an hour before the rest of the park, so it's a good place to explore if you're getting an early start to beat the crowds (it's also open an hour after the other attractions close, so you may want to save your shopping for the end of the day).

Step into city hall to receive a complimentary button showcasing whatever you're celebrating (your first visit, a birthday, a marriage, or just Disney in general); throughout the day, Disney cast members will congratulate you with friendly smiles and well wishes. **Main Street Cinema** offers a cool respite from the crowds and six classic Disney

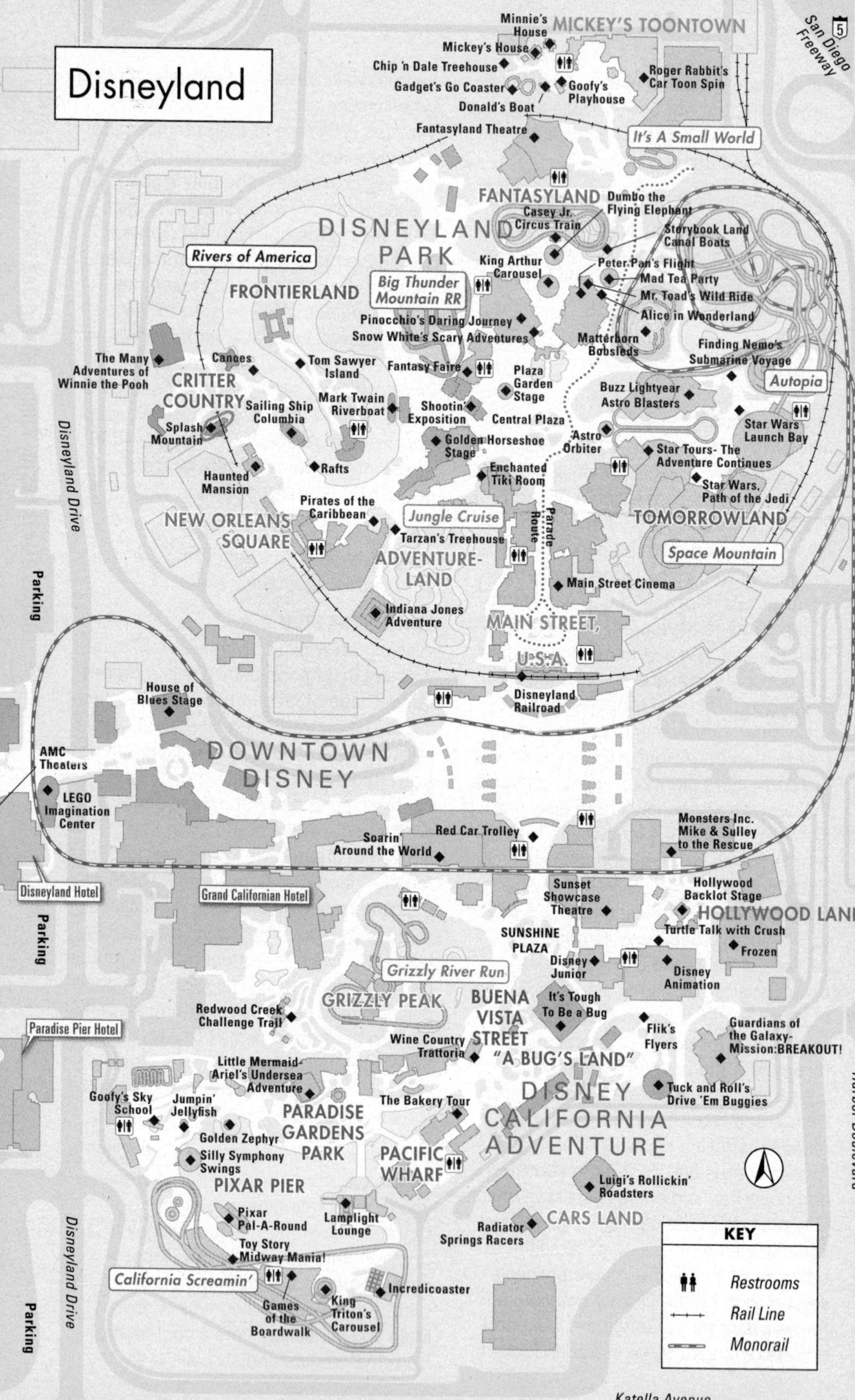
Disneyland
MICKEY'S TOONTOWN
Minnie's House
Mickey's House
Chip 'n Dale Treehouse
Gadget's Go Coaster
Goofy's Playhouse
Donald's Boat
Roger Rabbit's Car Toon Spin
San Diego Freeway
5
Fantasyland Theatre
It's A Small World
FANTASYLAND
Dumbo the Flying Elephant
Casey Jr. Circus Train
Storybook Land Canal Boats
DISNEYLAND PARK
King Arthur Carousel
Peter Pan's Flight
Mad Tea Party
Mr. Toad's Wild Ride
Alice in Wonderland
Rivers of America
FRONTIERLAND
Big Thunder Mountain RR
Pinocchio's Daring Journey
Snow White's Scary Adventures
Matterhorn Bobsleds
Finding Nemo's Submarine Voyage
Autopia
The Many Adventures of Winnie the Pooh
Canoes
Tom Sawyer Island
Fantasy Faire
Plaza Garden Stage
CRITTER COUNTRY
Sailing Ship Columbia
Mark Twain Riverboat
Shootin' Exposition
Buzz Lightyear Astro Blasters
Central Plaza
Star Wars Launch Bay
Splash Mountain
Golden Horseshoe Stage
Astro Orbiter
Star Tours- The Adventure Continues
Haunted Mansion
Rafts
Enchanted Tiki Room
Star Wars, Path of the Jedi
Disneyland Drive
Pirates of the Caribbean
Jungle Cruise
NEW ORLEANS SQUARE
Tarzan's Treehouse
Parade Route
TOMORROWLAND
ADVENTURE-LAND
Space Mountain
Main Street Cinema
Parking
Indiana Jones Adventure
MAIN STREET, U.S.A.
House of Blues Stage
Disneyland Railroad
DOWNTOWN DISNEY
AMC Theaters
LEGO Imagination Center
Red Car Trolley
Monsters Inc. Mike & Sulley to the Rescue
Soarin' Around the World
Disneyland Hotel
Grand Californian Hotel
Sunset Showcase Theatre
Hollywood Backlot Stage
Parking
HOLLYWOOD LAND
SUNSHINE PLAZA
Turtle Talk with Crush
Frozen
Disney Junior
Disney Animation
Grizzly River Run
GRIZZLY PEAK
BUENA VISTA STREET
It's Tough To Be a Bug
Redwood Creek Challenge Trail
Flik's Flyers
Guardians of the Galaxy- Mission:BREAKOUT!
Paradise Pier Hotel
Wine Country Trattoria
"A BUG'S LAND"
Little Mermaid- Ariel's Undersea Adventure
DISNEY CALIFORNIA ADVENTURE
Tuck and Roll's Drive 'Em Buggies
Harbor Boulevard
Goofy's Sky School
Jumpin' Jellyfish
The Bakery Tour
PARADISE GARDENS PARK
Golden Zephyr
Silly Symphony Swings
PACIFIC WHARF
PIXAR PIER
Luigi's Rollickin' Roadsters
Pixar Pal-A-Round
Lamplight Lounge
Radiator Springs Racers
CARS LAND
Disneyland Drive
Toy Story Midway Mania!
California Screamin'
Incredicoaster
Games of the Boardwalk
King Triton's Carousel
Parking
KEY
Restrooms
Rail Line
Monorail
Katella Avenue

animated shorts, including *Steamboat Willie*. There's rarely a wait to enter. Grab a cappuccino and fresh-made pastry at the Jolly Holiday bakery to jump-start your visit. Board the **Disneyland Railroad,** an authentic steam-powered train located at the entrance that makes stops in the park's different lands. Or the 18-minute scenic round-trip will also give you unique views of Star Wars: Galaxy's Edge, Autopia, Splash Mountain, the Grand Canyon, and Rivers of America.

NEW ORLEANS SQUARE

This minireplica of the French Quarter in New Orleans, with narrow streets, hidden courtyards, and live street performances, is home to two iconic attractions and the Cajun-inspired Blue Bayou restaurant. The **Pirates of the Caribbean** ride now features Jack Sparrow and the cursed Captain Barbossa of the blockbuster series, plus enhanced special effects and battle scenes (complete with cannonball explosions). Nearby **Haunted Mansion** continues to spook guests with its stretching walls and "doombuggy" rides (there's now an expanded storyline for the beating-heart bride). The *Nightmare Before Christmas* holiday overlay is an annual tradition that starts in the fall and extends throughout the holidays. This is a good area to eat; you can get a nonalcoholic mint julep and Mickey Mouse–shaped beignets; a Monte Cristo sandwich at Cafe Orleans; or corn chowder in a sourdough bread bowl, po-boy sandwiches, and jambalaya at the French Market Restaurant. Food carts offer everything from just-popped popcorn to churros and even fresh fruit.

FRONTIERLAND

Between Adventureland and Fantasyland, Frontierland transports you to the wild, wild West with its rustic buildings, shooting gallery, foot-stompin' dance hall, and singing birds in the Enchanted Tiki Room. The marquee attraction, **Big Thunder Mountain Railroad,** is a relatively tame roller coaster ride (no steep descents) that takes the form of a runaway mine car as it rumbles and turns through desert canyons and an old mining town. Tour the Rivers of America on the 19th-century **Mark Twain Riverboat,** which takes you on a 14-minute paddleboat cruise around Tom Sawyer Island, or the **Sailing Ship Columbia,** a full-scale replica of a merchant ship that once sailed the globe (usually limited to weekends). From here, you can also ride a motorized raft over to Pirate's Lair on **Tom Sawyer Island,** where you can explore pirate-themed caves, go on a treasure hunt, and climb a fort. Dine outside at the River Belle Terrace for Southern culinary favorites including Mickey Mouse pancakes for breakfast, barbecued ribs and fried chicken sandwich for lunch, and a healthier barbecued tofu for dinner. Or take a seat on the festive Mexican terrace at Rancho del Zocalo for a trio of street tacos, fire-grilled citrus-marinated chicken, and creamy flan for dessert.

CRITTER COUNTRY

Iconic Splash Mountain is the biggest draw to this down-home country-themed area, but you can also take a peek through Winnie the Pooh's Hundred-Acre Wood and paddle the Rivers of America on Davy Crockett's Explorer Canoes. The patio of the popular Hungry Bear Restaurant has great views of Tom Sawyer's Island, and beyond is a galaxy far, far away: the Star Wars: Galaxy's Edge section of the park.

STAR WARS: GALAXY'S EDGE

This 14-acre expansive land has guests step into the planet Batuu, designed from architectural locations in Morocco, Turkey, and Israel. At the ***Star Wars:* Rise of the Resistance** ride, you will accept a mission from the Resistance to fight against the First Order; to ride, guests need to obtain a timed boarding group on the Disneyland app or at the park's main entrance. You can also take a thrilling interactive ride on ***Millennium Falcon:* Smugglers Run,** where you will soar into hyperspace and be

Best Tips for Disneyland

Download the Disneyland mobile app. You can do a lot with this app so it's a no-brainer to download if you have a smartphone. It provides a ticket barcode to skip long ticket lines; you can view maps of both parks and get access to FastPass tickets via the digital MAXPASS; learn about shows and attraction wait times, character visits, and parade times; view restaurant menus and make dining reservations; preorder and pay for contactless pickup at both parks; and download and share Disney PhotoPass photos.

Buy entry tickets in advance. Lines at ticket booths can take more than an hour on busy days. Save time by buying in advance. Nearby hotels sell park admission tickets; you can also buy them through Disney's website and the Disneyland app. Seek out package deals offered through AAA and discount Disneyland Park Hopper tickets at Costco.

Come midweek. Weekends (especially during the summer, Halloween, and winter holidays) are often the busiest times to visit. A rainy winter weekday is often the least crowded time to check out the parks.

Plan your times to hit the most popular rides. Get to the park as early as possible, even before the gates open, and make a beeline for the top rides before the crowds reach a critical mass. Later in the evening the parks thin out and you can catch a special show or parade. Save the quieter attractions for midafternoon.

Use FastPass. These passes allow you to reserve your place in line at some of the most popular attractions (only one at a time). Distribution machines are posted near the entrances of each attraction. Show the barcode on your Disneyland app or feed in your park admission ticket, and you'll receive a pass with a printed time frame (up to one to four hours later) during which you can return to wait in a much shorter line or walk right onto the ride.

Avoid peak mealtime crowds. Outside food and beverages in nonglass containers are allowed inside the parks, but dining at one of the park's many theme restaurants can be an experience to remember. For any sit-down establishment, be sure to make dining reservations in advance or wait until after 2 pm to avoid a long wait. If you just need a quick recharge, Disney carts offer creative snacks including popcorn in souvenir buckets, Mickey Mouse–shaped pretzels, Rice Crispies treats, cake pops, and ice cream.

If you want to eat at the **Blue Bayou** in Disneyland's New Orleans Square or Carthay Circle at Disney California Adventure, you can make a reservation up to 60 days in advance of your visit online or via the Disneyland app. It's always a good idea to bring water, juice boxes, and snacks for little ones.

Check the daily events schedule online, on the Disneyland app, or at the park entrance. During parades, fireworks, and other special events, sections of the parks are filled with crowds. This distraction can work in your favor to take advantage of shorter lines at dining venues and rides. It also can work against you in maneuvering around a section of the park so plan ahead.

assigned to be a pilot, engineer, or gunner on a smuggling mission.

The Build-a-Droid Workshop is stocked with colorful parts, chips, and tech items. Starting at $99.99, you will receive a basket and blueprint to build your droid. Another treasure to purchase and take home is a hand-built lightsaber at Savi's Workshop.

For dining, popular Oga's Cantina is good for coffee, all-day light snacks, and unique cocktails for grown-ups. Galactic food and drink options can be found at the Milk Stand, where guests can sample Batuu's legendary blue and green beverages, similar to what Luke Skywalker drank in the movies.

ADVENTURELAND

Modeled after the lands of Africa, Polynesia, and Arabia, this tiny tropical paradise is worth braving the crowds that flock here for the ambience and better-than-average food. Sing along with the animatronic birds and tiki gods in the **Enchanted Tiki Room,** sail the rivers of the world with joke-cracking skippers on **Jungle Cruise,** and climb the *Disneyodendron semperflorens* (the always-blooming Disney tree) to **Tarzan's Treehouse,** where you can walk through scenes, some interactive, from the 1999 animated film. Cap off the visit with a wild jeep ride at **Indiana Jones Adventure,** where the special effects and decipherable hieroglyphics distract you while you're waiting in line. There's a single-rider option for a quicker ride. The skewers (some vegetarian options available) at Bengal Barbecue and pineapple whip at Tiki Juice Bar are some of the best fast-food options in the park.

FANTASYLAND

Sleeping Beauty Castle marks the entrance to Fantasyland, a visual wonderland of princesses, spinning teacups, flying elephants, and other classic storybook characters. Rides, and shops such as the princess-themed Bibbidi Bobbidi Boutique, take precedence over restaurants in this area of the park, but outdoor carts sell everything from churros to turkey legs. Tots love the **King Arthur Carousel, Casey Jr. Circus Train,** and **Storybook Land Canal Boats.** This is also home to **Mr. Toad's Wild Ride, Peter Pan's Flight, Snow White's Enchanted Wish,** and **Pinocchio's Daring Journey,** all classic movie-theater-dark rides that immerse riders in Disney fairy tales. Keep an eye out for the Abominable Snowman when he pops up on the **Matterhorn Bobsleds,** a roller coaster that twists and turns up and around on a made-to-scale model of the real Swiss mountain. Anchoring the east end of Fantasyland is **It's a Small World,** a smorgasbord of dancing animatronic dolls, cuckoo clock–covered walls, and variations of the song everyone knows, or soon *will* know, by heart. Beloved Disney characters like Ariel from *The Little Mermaid* are also part of the mix. Fantasy Faire is a fairy tale–style village that collects all the Disney princesses together. Each has her own reception nook in the Royal Hall. Condensed retellings of *Tangled* and *Beauty and the Beast* take place at the Royal Theatre.

MICKEY'S TOONTOWN

Geared toward small kids, this lopsided cartoonlike downtown, complete with cars and trolleys that invite interactive exploring, is where Mickey, Donald, Goofy, and other classic Disney characters hang their hats. One of the most popular attractions is **Roger Rabbit's Car Toon Spin,** a twisting, turning cab ride through the Toontown of *Who Framed Roger Rabbit?* You can also walk through **Mickey's House** to meet and be photographed with the famous mouse, take a low-key ride on **Gadget's Go Coaster,** or bounce around the fenced-in playground in front of **Goofy's Playhouse.** For food, you can enjoy pizza at Daisy's Diner, hot dogs at Pluto's Dog House, and sweet treats at Clarabelle's.

Did You Know?

The plain purple teacup in Disneyland's Mad Tea Party ride spins the fastest—though no one knows why.

TOMORROWLAND

This popular section of the park continues to tinker with its future, adding and enhancing rides regularly. *Star Wars*–themed attractions can't be missed, like the immersive, 3-D **Star Tours—The Adventures Continue,** where you can join the Rebellion in a galaxy far, far away. **Finding Nemo's Submarine Voyage** updates the old Submarine Voyage ride with the exploits of Nemo, Dory, Marlin, and other characters from the Disney-Pixar film. Try to visit this popular ride early in the day if you can, and be prepared for a wait. The interactive **Buzz Lightyear Astro Blasters** lets you zap your neighbors with laser beams and compete for the highest score. Hurtle through the cosmos on **Space Mountain** or check out mainstays like the futuristic **Astro Orbiter** rockets, ***Star Wars* Launch Bay,** which showcases costumes, models, and props from the franchise, and ***Star Wars,* Path of the Jedi,** which catches viewers up on all the movies with a quick 12-minute film. Put the pedal to the metal while driving a flashy coupe through winding roads at **Autotopia**, powered by Honda. Disneyland Monorail and Disneyland Railroad both have stations here. There's also a video arcade and dancing water fountain that makes a perfect playground for kids on hot summer days. The Jedi Training Academy spotlights future Luke Skywalkers in the crowd.

Besides the nine lands, the daily live-action shows and parades are always crowd pleasers. **■ TIP→ Arrive early to secure a good view; if there are two shows scheduled for the day, the second one tends to be less crowded. A fireworks display lights up weekends and most summer evenings.** Brochures with maps, available at the entrance, list show and parade times.

Disney California Adventure

★ Disney California Adventure

AMUSEMENT PARK/WATER PARK | FAMILY | The sprawling Disney California Adventure, adjacent to Disneyland (their entrances face each other), pays tribute to the Golden State with multiple theme areas that re-create vintage architectural styles and embrace several hit Pixar films via engaging attractions. Visitors enter through the art deco–style Buena Vista Street, past shops and a helpful information booth that advises wait times on attractions. The 12-acre Cars Land features Radiator Springs Racers, a speedy trip in six-passenger speedsters through scenes featured in the blockbuster hit. (FastPass tickets for the ride run out early most days, but there is a single rider line to experience the thrills quicker). Other popular attractions include the World of Color, a nighttime water-effects show and Toy Story Midway Mania!, an interactive adventure ride hosted by Woody and Buzz Lightyear. At night the park takes on neon hues as glowing signs light up Route 66 in Cars Land and Pixar Pal-A-Round, a giant Ferris wheel on the Pixar Pier. Cocktails, beer, and wine are available; craft beers and premium wines from California are poured. Live nightly entertainment also features a 1930s jazz troupe that arrives in a vintage jalopy. Some rides have a minimum height limit of 40 inches. Opened in 2021, the Avengers Campus is a land for a new generation of superheroes, focusing on the characters of the Marvel Cinemetic Universe. On Web-Slingers: A Spider-man Adventure, guests of all ages can help wrangle Spider-bots while wearing 3-D glasses; the free-falling Guardians of the Galaxy—Mission: BREAKOUT! is more for teens and adults. ✉ *1313 S. Disneyland Dr., between Ball Rd. and Katella Ave., Anaheim* ☎ *714/781–4636* 🌐 *disneyland.disney.go.com* 🎫 *From $97; parking $20.*

PARK NEIGHBORHOODS

BUENA VISTA STREET

California Adventure's grand entryway re-creates the lost 1920s Los Angeles that Walt Disney encountered when he moved to the Golden State. There's a **Red Car trolley** (modeled after Los Angeles's bygone streetcar line); hop on for the brief ride to Hollywood Land. Buena Vista Street is also home to a Starbucks outlet—within the Fiddler, Fifer and Practical Café—and the upscale Carthay Circle Restaurant and Lounge, which serves modern craft cocktails and beer. The comfy booths of the Carthay Circle restaurant on the second floor feel like a relaxing world away from the theme park outside. Keep an eye out for Officer Blue; he is known to give guests a citation to take home as a unique souvenir.

GRIZZLY PEAK

This woodsy land celebrates the great outdoors. Test your skills on the **Redwood Creek Challenge Trail,** a challenging trek across net ladders and suspension bridges. **Grizzly River Run** mimics the river rapids of the Sierra Nevadas; be prepared to get soaked.

Soarin' Around the World is a spectacular simulated hang-gliding ride over internationally known landmarks like Switzerland's Matterhorn and India's Taj Mahal.

HOLLYWOOD LAND

With a main street modeled after Hollywood Boulevard, a fake sky backdrop, and real soundstages, this area celebrates California's film industry. **Disney Animation** gives you an insider's look at how animators create characters. **Turtle Talk with Crush** lets kids have an unscripted chat with a computer-animated Crush, the sea turtle from *Finding Nemo.* The Hyperion Theater hosts **Frozen,** a 45-minute live performance from a Broadway-size cast with terrific visual effects. **■ TIP→ Plan on getting in line about half an hour in advance; the show is worth the wait.** On the film-inspired ride **Monsters, Inc. Mike & Sulley to the Rescue,** visitors climb into taxis and travel the streets of Monstropolis on a mission to safely return Boo to her bedroom.

CARS LAND

Amble down Route 66, the main thoroughfare of Cars Land, and discover a pitch-perfect re-creation of the vintage highway. Quick eats are found at the Cozy Cone Motel (in a teepee-shaped motor court) while Flo's V8 café serves hearty comfort food. Start your day at Radiator Springs Racers, the park's most popular attraction, where waits can be two hours or longer. Strap into a nifty sports car and meet the characters of Pixar's *Cars*; the ride ends in a speedy auto race through the red rocks and desert of Radiator Springs. **■ TIP→ To bypass the line, there's a single-rider option for Radiator Springs Racers.**

PACIFIC WHARF

In the midst of the California Adventure you'll find 10 different dining options, from light snacks to full-service restaurants. The Wine Country Trattoria is a great place for Italian specialties; relax outside on the restaurant's terrace for a casual bite while sipping a California-made craft beer or wine. Mexican cuisine and potent margaritas are available at the Cocina Cucamonga Mexican Grill and Rita's Baja Blenders, and Lucky Fortune Cookery serves Chinese stir-fry dishes.

PARADISE GARDENS PARK

The far corner of California Adventure is a mix of floating, zigzagging, and flying rides: soar via the **Silly Symphony Swings**; **Goofy's Sky School** rollicks and rolls through a cartoon-inspired landscape; and the sleek retro-style gondolas of the **Golden Zephyr** mimic 1920s movies and their sci-fi adventures. Journey through Ariel's colorful world on **The Little Mermaid—Ariel's Undersea Adventure.** The best views of the nighttime music, water, and light show, **World of Color,** are from the paths along Paradise Bay. FastPass tickets are available. Or for a guaranteed spot, book dinner at the Wine Country Trattoria that includes a ticket to a viewing area to catch all the show's stunning visuals.

PIXAR PIER

This section re-creates the glory days of California's seaside piers, themed with Pixar film characters. If you're looking for thrills, join The Incredibles family on the **Incredicoaster** as the fast-moving roller coaster takes its riders from 0 to 55 mph in about four seconds and proceeds through scream tunnels, steeply angled drops, and a 360-degree loop. **Pixar Pal-A-Round,** a giant Ferris wheel, provides a good view of the grounds, though some cars spin and sway for more kicks. There are also carnival games, an aquatic-themed carousel, and **Toy Story Midway Mania!,** an interactive ride where you can take aim at a series of cartoon targets. Soft-serve ice cream, turkey legs, hot dogs, and churros are readily available for quick snacking. At the **Lamplight Lounge** adults can chill out and overlook the action while sipping on craft cocktails.

OTHER ATTRACTIONS

Anaheim GardenWalk

PROMENADE | FAMILY | This popular dining, shopping, and entertainment outdoor complex offers 10 eateries, a bowling lounge, an escape room, and an Art on the Walk showcasing local artists and nonprofit organizations. Monthly and seasonal pop-up events are displayed on the website. ✉ *400 W. Disney Way, Anaheim* ☎ *562/695–1513* 🌐 *www.anaheimgardenwalk.com.*

Downtown Disney District

AMUSEMENT PARK/WATER PARK | FAMILY | The Downtown Disney District is a 20-acre promenade of dining, shopping, and entertainment that connects the resort's hotels and theme parks. Get refreshed at the bar or dining room at **Splitsville**, a mid-century modern–style bowling alley serving American comfort food. At **Ralph Brennan's Jazz Kitchen** you can dig into New Orleans–style food and music. Enjoy a cold beer at Ballast Point Brewery and gourmet burger at Black Tap Craft Burgers. Save room for sweets: **Salt and Straw** has gourmet ice cream while **Sprinkles** offers ultrarich cupcakes. Disney merchandise and artwork is showcased at the brightly lit **World of Disney** store. Deck your home and garden with Disney decorative items at **HOME;** they even have a Disney Tails & Pet Collection for your four-legged friends. At the megasize **LEGO Store** there are bigger than life LEGO creations, hands-on demonstrations and space to play with the latest LEGO creations. All visitors must pass through a security checkpoint and metal detectors before entering. ✉ *1580 Disneyland Dr., Anaheim* ☎ *714/781–4565* 🌐 *disneyland.disney.go.com/downtown-disney* 🎟 *Free.*

Restaurants

Anaheim White House

$$$$ | ITALIAN | FAMILY | Although a massive fire gutted the Anaheim White House in 2017, owner and executive chef Bruno Serato rebuilt and expanded the local landmark known for its specialty pastas. The 1909-built original mansion was the inspiration for the complete renovation, and Serato added olive trees and a courtyard outside and Italian frescoes and mosaics inside. **Known for:** classic Mediterranean cuisine; popular salmon chocolat (salmon with white chocolate mashed potatoes); friendly chef who is a pillar of the community. $ *Average main: $40* ✉ *887 S. Anaheim Blvd., Anaheim* ☎ *714/772–1381* 🌐 *www.anaheimwhitehouse.com* ⏲ *Closed Mon. and Tues.*

Catal Restaurant and Uva Bar and Cafe

$$ | MEDITERRANEAN | This relaxed bi-level Mediterranean spot offers more than 30 wines by the glass, craft beers, and craft cocktails that pair well with the Spanish-influenced dishes. Upstairs, Catal's menu has tapas, a variety of flavorful paellas, and charcuterie. **Known for:** gourmet burgers; good happy hour; outdoor terrace with Disneyland fireworks views. $ *Average main: $30* ✉ *Downtown*

Disney District, 1580 S. Disneyland Dr., Suite 103, Anaheim ☎ 714/774–4442 🌐 www.patinagroup.com.

Napa Rose

$$$$ | **AMERICAN** | Done up in a handsome Craftsman style, Napa Rose's rich seasonal cuisine is matched with an extensive wine list, with 1,500 labels and 80 available by the glass. For a look into the open kitchen, sit at the counter and watch the chefs as they whip up such signature dishes as grilled diver scallops and chanterelles, and lamb pot roast topped with a pomegranate mint glaze. **Known for:** excellent wine list; kid-friendly options; gorgeous dining room. *$ Average main: $50 ✉ Disney's Grand Californian Hotel, 1600 S. Disneyland Dr., Anaheim ☎ 714/300–7170, 714/781–3463 reservations 🌐 disneyland.disney.go.com/grand-californian-hotel/napa-rose.*

Hotels

Anaheim Fairfield Inn by Marriott

$$ | **HOTEL** | **FAMILY** | Attentive service and a great location just across the street from Disneyland's entrance makes this high-rise hotel a big draw for families. **Pros:** across the street from Disneyland; Disney-themed guest rooms; reasonable rates for the area. **Cons:** some rooms have just parking lot views; lack of green space; can be noisy when guests return from parks. *$ Rooms from: $225 ✉ 1460 S. Harbor Blvd., Anaheim ☎ 714/772–6777 🌐 www.marriott.com 467 rooms No meals.*

Anaheim Marriott

$ | **RESORT** | This busy two-tower hotel is well equipped for business travelers, and has nice amenities for vacationers. **Pros:** balconies in all rooms; large pool and deck area; offers shuttle to Disneyland. **Cons:** most rooms only have a shower; popular with conventioneers who often take over the place; no Disney-themed guest rooms. *$ Rooms from: $159 ✉ 700 W. Convention Way, Anaheim ☎ 714/750–8000, 888/236–2427 🌐 www.marriott.com 1030 rooms No meals.*

Desert Palms Hotel and Suites

$ | **HOTEL** | **FAMILY** | This hotel midway between Disneyland and the Anaheim Convention Center is a great value, with some one-bedroom suites that can accommodate groups of six or more. **Pros:** large lobby that welcomes with Disney decor; variety of special rates; free Wi-Fi. **Cons:** drab exterior fronts busy Katella Avenue; small pool gets limited sun; some noise issues. *$ Rooms from: $125 ✉ 631 W. Katella Ave., Anaheim ☎ 714/535–1133, 888/521–6420 🌐 www.desertpalmshotel.com 195 rooms No meals.*

★ Disney's Grand Californian Hotel and Spa

$$$$ | **RESORT** | **FAMILY** | The most opulent of Disneyland's three hotels, the Craftsman-style Grand Californian offers views of Disney California Adventure and Downtown Disney. **Pros:** gorgeous lobby; family-friendly with three beautiful pools; direct access to California Adventure. **Cons:** very expensive; standard rooms are on the small side; waits to dine at on-site restaurants. *$ Rooms from: $625 ✉ 1600 S. Disneyland Dr., Anaheim ☎ 714/635–2300 🌐 disneyland.disney.go.com/grand-californian-hotel 1019 rooms No meals.*

Doubletree Suites by Hilton Hotel Anaheim Resort-Convention Center

$ | **HOTEL** | This busy hotel near the Anaheim Convention Center and a 20-minute walk from Disneyland caters to business travelers and vacationers alike. **Pros:** huge suites; walking distance to a variety of restaurants; chocolate chip cookies at check-in. **Cons:** a bit far from Disneyland; pool area is small; daily parking fee. *$ Rooms from: $153 ✉ 2085 S. Harbor Blvd., Anaheim ☎ 714/750–3000, 800/215–7316 🌐 doubletreeanaheim.com 252 rooms No meals.*

Hilton Anaheim

$ | **HOTEL** | **FAMILY** | Next to the Anaheim Convention Center, this busy Hilton is the third-largest hotel in Southern California, with a restaurant and food court, hopping lobby lounge with communal tables, a full-service gym, and its own Starbucks. **Pros:** 15-minute walk to Disneyland; fast-casual dining options; some rooms have views of the park fireworks. **Cons:** huge size can be daunting; fee to use health club; megasize parking lot. *Rooms from: $159 777 Convention Way, Anaheim 714/750–4321, 800/445–8667 www.hiltonanaheimhotel.com 1572 rooms No meals.*

Hyatt Regency Orange County

$ | **HOTEL** | **FAMILY** | This Disney-friendly hotel sells park tickets in the lobby and offers a free shuttle to Disneyland. **Pros:** large suites for families; modern rooms in coastal colors; two pools, one kid-friendly and one with adult-only hours. **Cons:** North Tower rooms are dated in decor and furniture; parking is $28 a day; a little more than 1 mile from Disneyland Parks. *Rooms from: $199 11199 Harbor Blvd., Anaheim 714/750–1234 www.hyatt.com 653 rooms No meals.*

★ JW Marriott, Anaheim Resort

$$ | **RESORT** | **FAMILY** | The first luxury hotel in the area to open outside the Disneyland Resorts and the first JW Marriott in Orange County, this resort pays homage to the agricultural history of the region with unique architectural elements. **Pros:** gorgeous artwork throughout; great fireworks views; luxury amenities. **Cons:** popular event space for conventions and big gatherings; no Disneyland-themed rooms; valet parking only ($40 a day). *Rooms from: $225 1775 S. Clementine St., Anaheim 714/294–7800 www.marriott.com 468 rooms No meals.*

Majestic Garden Hotel

$ | **HOTEL** | **FAMILY** | If you're hoping to escape from the commercial atmosphere of the hotels near Disneyland and California Adventure, consider this sprawling replica of an English Tudor estate. **Pros:** large, attractive lobby; spacious rooms with comfortable beds; shuttle to the theme parks. **Cons:** confusing layout; hotel sits close to a busy freeway; small bathrooms. *Rooms from: $150 900 S. Disneyland Dr., Anaheim 714/778–1700, 844/227–8535 www.majesticgardenhotel.com 489 rooms No meals.*

Activities

Anaheim Ducks

HOCKEY | **FAMILY** | The National Hockey League's Anaheim Ducks, winners of the 2007 Stanley Cup, play at Honda Center. *Honda Center, 2695 E. Katella Ave., Anaheim 877/945–3946 nhl.com/ducks.*

Los Angeles Angels of Anaheim

BASEBALL/SOFTBALL | **FAMILY** | Professional baseball's Los Angeles Angels of Anaheim have called Anaheim and Angel Stadium home since 1966. An "Outfield Extravaganza" celebrates great plays on the field, with fireworks and a geyser exploding over a model evoking the California coast. *Angel Stadium, 2000 E. Gene Autry Way, Anaheim 714/426–4357 www.angels.com Metrolink Angels Express.*

Knott's Berry Farm

25 miles south of Los Angeles, via I–5, in Buena Park.

Once an actual farm, Knott's Berry Farm now offers a non-Disney theme park option for anyone with a love of roller coasters and boysenberries.

Knott's Berry Farm

AMUSEMENT PARK/WATER PARK | FAMILY | The land where the boysenberry was invented (by crossing raspberry, blackberry, and loganberry bushes) is now occupied by a popular amusement park. In 1934, Cordelia Knott began serving chicken dinners on her wedding china to supplement her family's income. The dinners and her boysenberry pies proved more profitable than her husband Walter's farm, so the two moved first into the restaurant business and then into the entertainment business. The park is now a 160-acre complex with close to 40 rides, dozens of restaurants and shops, arcade games, live shows, and a brick-by-brick replica of Philadelphia's Independence Hall. Take a step back into the 1880s while walking through Knott's Old West Ghost Town. Ride on a horse-drawn stagecoach or board a steam engine to start your journey into the park; just keep your valuables close to you, as bandits might enter your train car and put on quite a show. Camp Snoopy has plenty to keep small children occupied as they explore 15 kid-friendly attractions. The park is also known for its awesome thrill rides in the Boardwalk area, including the zooming HangTime that pauses dramatically then drops nearly 15 stories, and the Xcelerator that goes from zero to 80 mph in 2.3 seconds.

And, yes you can still get that boysenberry pie, as well as boysenberry soft serve ice cream, jam, juice, you name it. There's even a Boysenberry Food Festival once a year. In the fall, part of the park is turned into Knott's Scary Farm, a popular activity for teens and adults. Buy adult tickets online for a discount; FastLane wristbands give you quicker access to the most popular rides. Nearby Knott's Soak City is open during the summer for guests who want to float on the lazy river, go down waterslides, and swim in the wave pool. ✉ *8039 Beach Blvd., Buena Park* ✣ *Between La Palma Ave. and Crescent St., 2 blocks south of Hwy. 91* ☎ *714/220–5200* 🌐 *www.knotts.com* 🎫 *$82.*

Park Neighborhoods

THE BOARDWALK

Not-for-the-squeamish thrill rides and skill-based games dominate the scene at the **Boardwalk.** Roller coasters—Coast Rider, Surfside Glider, and Pacific Scrambler—surround a pond that keeps things cooler on hot days. **HangTime** towers 150 feet above the boardwalk as coaster cars hang, invert and drop the equivalent of 15 stories. The boardwalk is also home to a string of test-your-skill games that are fun to watch whether you're playing or not, and Johnny Rockets, the park's all-American diner.

CAMP SNOOPY

It can be gridlock on weekends, but kids love this miniature High Sierra wonderland where the *Peanuts* gang hangs out. Tykes can push and pump their own mini-mining cars on **Huff and Puff,** soar around via **Charlie Brown's Kite Flyer,** and hop aboard **Woodstock's Airmail,** a kids' version of the park's Supreme Scream ride. Most of the rides here are geared toward kids only, leaving parents to cheer them on from the sidelines. **Sierra Sidewinder,** a roller coaster near the entrance of Camp Snoopy, is aimed at older children, with spinning saucer-type vehicles that go a maximum speed of 37 mph.

FIESTA VILLAGE

Over in **Fiesta Village** are two more musts for adrenaline junkies: **Montezooma's Revenge,** a roller coaster that goes from 0 to 55 mph in less than five seconds, and **Jaguar!,** a three-minute long coaster, which simulates the motions of a cat stalking its prey, twisting, spiraling, and speeding up and slowing down as it takes you on its stomach-dropping course through a Mayan temple. There's also **Hat Dance,** a version of the spinning teacups but with sombreros, and a 100-year-old **Dentzel carousel,** complete with an antique organ and menagerie of hand-carved animals. In a nod to history, there are restored scale models of the California Missions at Fiesta Village's southern entrance.

GHOST TOWN

Clusters of authentic old buildings relocated from their original mining-town sites mark this section of the park. You can stroll down the street, stop and chat with a blacksmith, pan for gold (for a fee), crack open a geode, check out the chalkboard of a circa-1879 one-room schoolhouse, and ride an original Butterfield stagecoach. Looming over it all is **GhostRider,** Orange County's first wooden roller coaster. Traveling up to 56 mph and reaching 118 feet at its highest point, the park's biggest attraction is riddled with sudden dips and curves, subjecting riders to forces up to three times that of gravity. On the Western-themed **Silver Bullet,** riders are sent to a height of 146 feet and then back down 109 feet. Riders spiral, corkscrew, fly into a cobra roll, and experience overbanked curves. The **Calico Mine** ride descends into a replica of a working gold mine complete with 50 animatronic figures. The **Timber Mountain Log Ride** is a visitor favorite: the flume ride tours through pioneer scenes before splashing down. Also found here is the **Pony Express,** a roller coaster that lets riders saddle up on packs of "horses" tethered to platforms that take off on a series of hairpin turns and travel up to 38 mph. Take a step inside the **Western Trails Museum,** a dusty old gem full of Old West memorabilia and rural Americana, plus menus from the original chicken restaurant and an impressive antique button collection. **Calico Railroad** departs regularly from Ghost Town station for a round-trip tour of the park (bandit holdups notwithstanding). You can order a boysenberry soft-serve ice-cream cone nearby afterward.

This section is also home to **Big Foot Rapids,** a splash-fest of white-water river rafting over towering cliffs, cascading waterfalls, and wild rapids. Don't miss the visually stunning show at **Mystery Lodge,** which tells the story of Native Americans in the Pacific Northwest with lights, music, and special effects.

INDIAN TRAILS

Celebrate Native American traditions through interactive exhibits like tepees and daily dance and storytelling performances.

Knott's Soak City Waterpark is directly across from the main park on 13 acres next to Independence Hall. It has a dozen major water rides; **Pacific Spin** is an oversize waterslide that drops riders 75 feet into a catch pool. There's also a children's pool, a 750,000-gallon wave pool, and a fun house. Soak City's season runs mid-May to mid-September. It's open daily after Memorial Day, weekends only after Labor Day, and then closes for the season.

Restaurants

★ Mrs. Knott's Chicken Dinner Restaurant
$$ | AMERICAN | FAMILY | Cordelia Knott's fried chicken and boysenberry pies drew crowds so big that Knott's Berry Farm was built to keep the hungry customers occupied while they waited. The restaurant's current incarnation (outside the park's entrance) still serves crispy fried chicken, along with fluffy handmade biscuits, mashed potatoes, and Mrs. Knott's signature chilled cherry-rhubarb compote. **Known for:** famous fried chicken; long waits especially on weekends; pies and desserts. *Average main: $22* ✉ *Knott's Berry Farm Marketplace, 8039 Beach Blvd., Buena Park* ☎ *714/220–5200* 🌐 *www.knotts.com/california-marketplace/mrs-knott-s-chicken-dinner-restaurant.*

Hotels

Knott's Berry Farm Hotel
$ | HOTEL | FAMILY | This convenient low-rise hotel is run by the park and sits right on park grounds surrounded by graceful palm trees. **Pros:** easy access to Knott's Berry Farm; tennis court; decent on-site dining. **Cons:** lobby and hallways can be noisy; can hear the nearby roller coaster;

dated room decor. [$] *Rooms from: $129* ✉ *7675 Crescent Ave., Buena Park* ☎ *714/995–1111, 866/752–2444* 🌐 *www.knotts.com/knotts-berry-farm-hotel* *320 rooms* *No meals.*

Huntington Beach

40 miles southeast of Los Angeles.

Once a sleepy residential town with little more than a string of rugged surf shops, Huntington Beach has transformed itself into a resort destination,commonly referred to as Surf City U.S.A. The town's appeal is its broad white-sand beaches with often-towering waves, complemented by a lively pier, shops, and restaurants on Main Street, and a growing collection of resort hotels.

A draw for sports fans and partiers of all stripes is the U.S. Open professional surf competition, which brings a festive atmosphere to town annually in late July. There's even a Surfing Walk of Fame, with plaques set in the sidewalk around the intersection of PCH and Main Street.

ESSENTIALS

VISITOR INFORMATION Visit Huntington Beach. ✉ *301 Main St., Suite 212* ☎ *714/969–3492, 800/729–6232* 🌐 *www.surfcityusa.com.*

Sights

Bolsa Chica Ecological Reserve

NATURE PRESERVE | FAMILY | Wildlife lovers and bird-watchers flock to Bolsa Chica Ecological Reserve, which has a 1,445-acre salt marsh where 302 bird species—including great blue herons, snowy and great egrets, and brown pelicans—have been spotted. Throughout the reserve are trails for bird-watching, including a comfortable 1½-mile loop. There are two entrances off the Pacific Coast Highway: one close to the Interpretive Center and a second one 1 mile south on Warner Avenue, opposite Bolsa Chica State Beach. Each parking lot connects to 4 miles of walking and hiking trails with scenic overlooks. ✉ *Bolsa Chica Wetlands Interpretive Center, 3842 Warner Ave.* ☎ *714/846–1114* 🌐 *www.bolsachica.org* *Free.*

Bolsa Chica State Beach

BEACH—SIGHT | FAMILY | In the northern section of the city, Bolsa Chica State Beach is usually less crowded than its southern neighbors. The sand is somewhat gritty and not the cleanest, but swells make it a hot surfing spot. Picnic sites can be reserved in advance. Fire pits attract beachgoers most nights. **Amenities:** food and drink; lifeguards; parking; showers; toilets. **Best for:** sunset; surfing; swimming; walking; RV camping. ✉ *Pacific Coast Hwy., between Seapoint St. and Warner Ave.* ☎ *714/846–3460* 🌐 *www.parks.ca.gov* *$15 parking.*

Huntington Beach Pier

MARINA | FAMILY | This municipal pier stretches 1,856 feet out to sea, past the powerful waves that gave Huntington Beach the title of "Surf City U.S.A." Well above the waves, it's a prime vantage point to watch the dozens of surfers in the water below. On the pier you'll find a snack shop and a shop where you can buy fishing rod rentals, tackle, and bait to fish off the pier. ✉ *Pacific Coast Hwy.* 🌐 *www.surfcityusa.com.*

Huntington City Beach

BEACH—SIGHT | FAMILY | Stretching for 3½ miles from Bolsa Chica State Beach to Huntington State Beach, Huntington City Beach is most crowded around the pier; amateur and professional surfers brave the waves daily. Fire pits, numerous concession stands, an area for dogs, and well-raked white sand make this a popular beach come summertime. **Amenities:** food and drink; lifeguards; parking; showers; toilets. **Best for:** sunset; surfing; swimming; walking. ✉ *Pacific Coast Hwy., from Beach Blvd. to Seapoint St.* ☎ *714/536–5281, 714/536–9303 surf report* 🌐 *www.huntingtonbeachca.gov/residents/beach_info* *Parking from $15.*

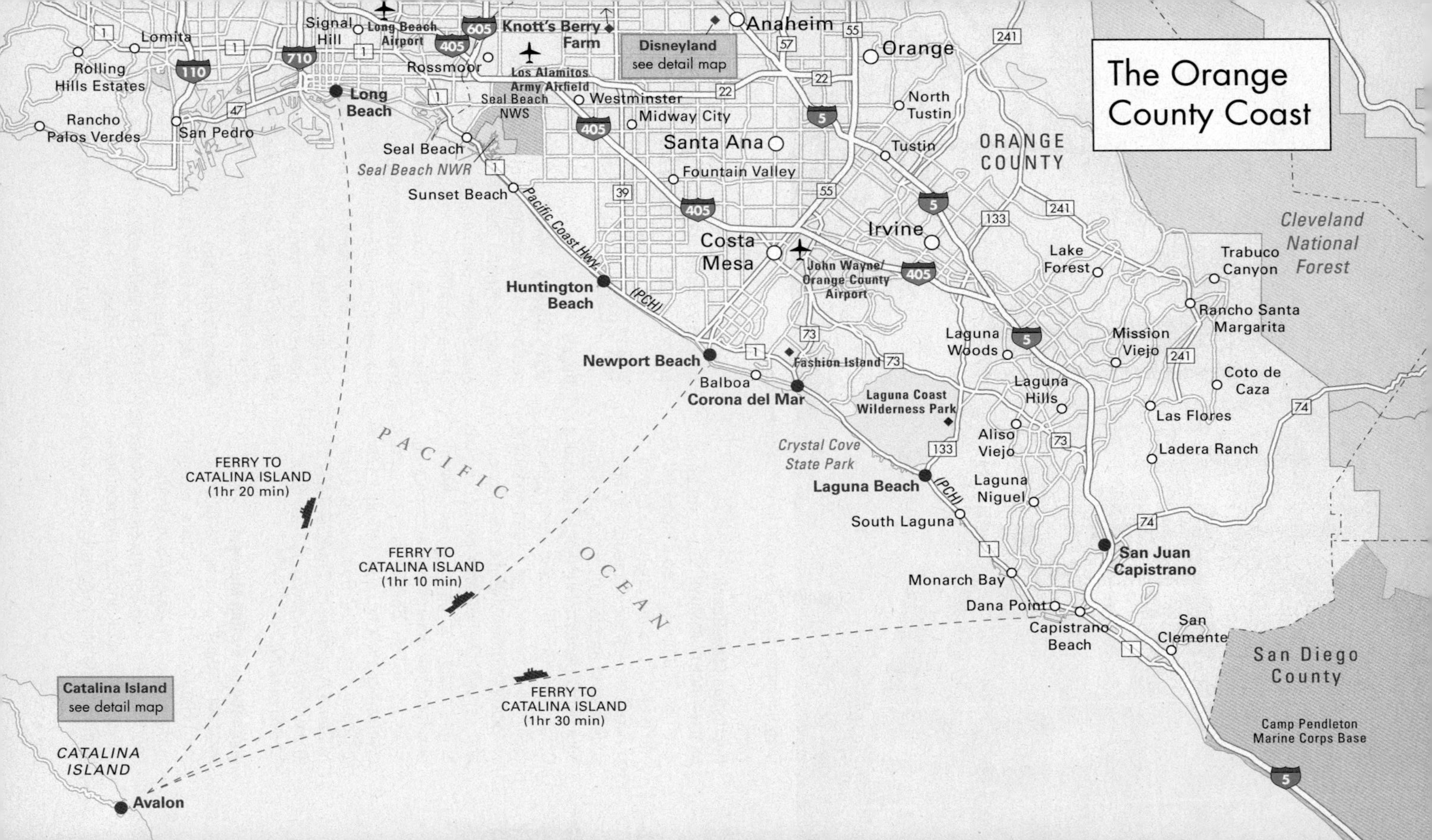

The Orange County Coast
Orange County
San Diego County
Cleveland National Forest
Pacific Ocean
Catalina Island
Catalina Island see detail map
Disneyland see detail map
Long Beach
Signal Hill
Long Beach Airport
Knott's Berry Farm
Anaheim
Orange
Rolling Hills Estates
Lomita
Rancho Palos Verdes
San Pedro
Rossmoor
Los Alamitos Army Airfield
Seal Beach NWS
Westminster
Midway City
Santa Ana
North Tustin
Tustin
Seal Beach
Seal Beach NWR
Sunset Beach
Pacific Coast Hwy. (PCH)
Fountain Valley
Costa Mesa
Irvine
John Wayne/Orange County Airport
Huntington Beach
Newport Beach
Balboa
Corona del Mar
Fashion Island
Laguna Coast Wilderness Park
Crystal Cove State Park
Laguna Beach
South Laguna
Laguna Woods
Laguna Hills
Aliso Viejo
Laguna Niguel
Monarch Bay
Dana Point
Capistrano Beach
San Clemente
San Juan Capistrano
Lake Forest
Mission Viejo
Trabuco Canyon
Rancho Santa Margarita
Coto de Caza
Las Flores
Ladera Ranch
Camp Pendleton Marine Corps Base
Ferry to Catalina Island (1hr 20 min)
Ferry to Catalina Island (1hr 10 min)
Ferry to Catalina Island (1hr 30 min)
Avalon

Lively Huntington Beach is a center for surfing on the coast.

Huntington State Beach

BEACH—SIGHT | **FAMILY** | This state beach also has 200 fire pits, so it's popular day and night. There are changing rooms, concession stands, lifeguards, Wi-Fi access, and ample parking. An 8.5-mile bike path connects Hunnington to Bolsa Chica State Beach. Picnic areas can be reserved in advance for a fee depending on location; otherwise it's first come, first served. On hot days, expect crowds at this broad, soft sandy beach. **Amenities:** food and drink; lifeguards; parking; showers; toilets. **Best for:** sunset; surfing; swimming; walking; surf fishing. ✉ *Pacific Coast Hwy., from Beach Blvd. south to Santa Ana River* ☎ *714/536–1454* 🌐 *www.parks.ca.gov/?page_id=643* 🎟 *$15 parking.*

International Surfing Museum

MUSEUM | **FAMILY** | Just up Main Street from Huntington Pier, the International Surfing Museum pays tribute to the sport's greats with an impressive collection of surfboards and related memorabilia. Exhibits are designed to encourage kids to study and to surf. ✉ *411 Olive Ave.* ☎ *714/465–4350* 🌐 *www.surfingmuseum.org* 🎟 *$3* 🕒 *Closed Mon.*

Restaurants

Duke's

$$$$ | **SEAFOOD** | **FAMILY** | Freshly caught seafood reigns supreme at this homage to surfing legend Duke Kahanamoku; it's also a prime people-watching spot right at the beginning of Huntington Beach Pier. Choose from several fish-of-the-day selections—many topped with Hawaiian ingredients—and shellfish like lobster, king crab, and shrimp. **Known for:** Hawaiian-style decor; gorgeous sunset views; mai tai cocktails. 💲 *Average main: $45* ✉ *317 Pacific Coast Hwy.* ☎ *714/374–6446* 🌐 *www.dukeshuntington.com.*

Wahoo's Fish Taco

$ | **MEXICAN FUSION** | **FAMILY** | Proximity to the ocean makes this eatery's seafood-filled tacos and burritos taste even better. The healthy fast-food chain—tagged with dozens of surf stickers—brought Baja's fish tacos north of the border to quick success. **Known for:** organic ingredients; Hawaiian onion ring burrito; casual beachy ambience. *Average main: $12* *120 Main St.* *714/536–2050* *www.wahoos.com.*

Hotels

Hyatt Regency Huntington Beach Resort and Spa

$$$ | **RESORT** | **FAMILY** | The Spanish design of this sprawling property incorporates arched courtyards, beautiful tiled fountains, and fire pits, all a nod to California's Mission period. **Pros:** close to beach; variety of pool areas; family-friendly vibe. **Cons:** some partial ocean-view rooms; resort and daily valet fees; some rooms can hear the traffic on PCH. *Rooms from: $360* *21500 Pacific Coast Hwy.* *714/698–1234* *www.hyatt.com* *517 rooms* *No meals.*

Kimpton Shorebreak Resort

$$ | **HOTEL** | **FAMILY** | This surfer-style Kimpton hotel is not only across the street from the beach, but it's the closest hotel to the Huntington Beach Pier and Main Street. **Pros:** proximity to beach and shops; free surfboard storage; quiet rooms despite central location. **Cons:** $35 valet parking fee; courtyard rooms have uninspiring alley views; additional resort fee to receive best perks. *Rooms from: $250* *500 Pacific Coast Hwy.* *714/861–4470, 877/212–8597* *www.shorebreakhotel.com* *157 rooms* *No meals.*

Pasea Hotel & Spa

$$$ | **RESORT** | **FAMILY** | Painted in shades of sea blue, the contemporary-styled Pasea is a rarity along the O.C. coast: at eight stories, almost every room has an ocean view and all have balconies to take in the fresh breezes. **Pros:** excellent ocean views; beach butlers to provide everything for a beach day; supercomfortable beds. **Cons:** pool can get crowded; $40 valet parking fee; noise issues from nearby bars at Pacific City. *Rooms from: $350* *21080 Pacific Coast Hwy.* *866/478–9702* *www.meritagecollection.com/pasea-hotel* *250 rooms* *No meals.*

The Waterfront Beach Resort, a Hilton Hotel

$$ | **RESORT** | **FAMILY** | This two-tower resort offers a variety of amenities for families, couples, and business travelers alike. **Pros:** quick walk to beach and pier; fun surf decor; oceanfront views from rooms. **Cons:** different towers have different vibes; valet parking only for $42; crowded pool and deck during summer. *Rooms from: $239* *21100 Pacific Coast Hwy.* *714/845–8000, 855/271–3617* *www.waterfrontresort.com* *437 rooms* *No meals.*

Shopping

HSS Main St

SPORTING GOODS | **FAMILY** | The largest surf-gear source in town is Huntington Surf and Sport, right across from Huntington Pier. Staffed by true surf enthusiasts, it's also one of the only surf shops with a coffee counter inside. Surfboard rentals are $15 an hour or $50 all day while soft top boards are $18 per hour or $30 a day. They also rent bodyboards and wetsuits. *300 Pacific Coast Hwy.* *714/841–4000* *www.hsssurf.com.*

Activities

SURFING

Corky Carroll's Surf School

SURFING | **FAMILY** | This surf school organizes lessons, weeklong workshops, and international surf camps at Bolsa Chica State Beach. They also provide hard and soft top boards and wetsuits to rent during your lesson. *Bolsa Chica State Beach, Lifeguard Tower 18* *714/969–3959* *www.surfschool.net.*

Dwight's Beach Concession

BICYCLING | FAMILY | You can rent surrey or cruiser bikes, wet suits, surfboards, bodyboards, umbrellas, and beach chairs at Dwight's, one block south of Huntington Pier. They also serve casual beach food, including their world-famous cheese strips. ✉ *201 Pacific Coast Hwy.* ☎ *714/536–8083* 🌐 *www.dwightsbeachconcession.com.*

Zack's HB

BICYCLING | FAMILY | This place offers beach equipment, surfing lessons and boards, wet suits, and bicycles. Food like hamburgers, corn dogs, fish-and-chips, grilled mahimahi, and Mexican favorites are sold here, too. ✉ *405 Pacific Coast Hwy., at Main St.* ☎ *714/536–0215* 🌐 *www.zackssurfcity.com.*

Newport Beach

6 miles south of Huntington Beach.

Newport Beach has evolved from a simple seaside village to an icon of chic coastal living. Its ritzy reputation comes from megayachts bobbing in the harbor, boutiques that rival those in Beverly Hills, and spectacular homes overlooking the ocean.

The city boasts some of the cleanest beaches in Southern California; inland Newport Beach's concentration of high-rise office buildings, shopping centers, and luxury hotels drives the economy. But on the city's Balboa Peninsula, you can still catch a glimpse of a more humble, down-to-earth town scattered with taco spots, tackle shops, and sailor bars.

VISITOR INFORMATION Visit Newport Beach Concierge. ✉ *Atrium Court at Fashion Island, 1600 Newport Center Dr.* ☎ *949/719–6100* 🌐 *www.newportbeachandco.com.*

Sights

★ Balboa Island

BEACH—SIGHT | FAMILY | This sliver of terra firma in Newport Harbor boasts quaint streets tightly packed with impossibly charming multimillion-dollar cottages. The island's main drag, Marine Avenue, is lined with equally picturesque cafés, frozen chocolate banana shops, and apparel stores. Rent a bike and pedal around on the car-free bike path and boardwalk encircling much of the island for an easy and scenic ramble. Be sure to visit the free Balboa Island Museum, too.

To get here, you can either park your car on the mainland side of the PCH in Newport Beach and walk or bike over the bridge onto Marine Avenue, or take the Balboa Island Ferry, the country's longest-running auto ferry. The one-way fare is $1.25 for an adult pedestrian; $1.50 for an adult with a bike; and $2.25 to take your car on board. ✉ *Marine Ave.* ☎ *949/719–6100* 🌐 *www.visitnewportbeach.com.*

Balboa Peninsula

BEACH—SIGHT | FAMILY | Newport's best beaches are on Balboa Peninsula, where many jetties pave the way to ideal swimming areas. The most intense spot for bodysurfing in Orange County, and arguably on the West Coast, known as the **Wedge,** is at the south end of the peninsula. It was created by accident in the 1930s when the Federal Works Progress Administration built a jetty to protect Newport Harbor. ⚠ **Rip currents and punishing waves mean it's strictly for the pros—but it sure is fun to watch an experienced local ride it.** ✉ *Newport Beach* 🌐 *www.visitnewportbeach.com/beaches-and-parks/the-wedge.*

Newport Beach Pier

BEACH—SIGHT | FAMILY | Jutting out into the ocean near 21st Street, Newport Pier is a popular fishing spot. Below is 5 miles of sandy beach for sunbathing, surfing, and walking along the beach. Street

Newport Beach is another popular place in the O.C. to catch waves.

parking is difficult, so grab the first space you find and be prepared to walk. Early on Wednesday–Sunday morning you're likely to encounter dory fishermen hawking their predawn catches, as they've done for generations. On weekends the area is alive with kids of all ages on in-line skates, skateboards, and bikes dodging pedestrians and whizzing past fast-food joints and classic dive bars. Skate, bike, and surfboard rental shops are nearby. ✉ *70 Newport Pier* ☎ *949/644–3309* 🌐 *www.visitnewportbeach.com.*

★ **Newport Harbor**

BEACH—SIGHT | **FAMILY** | Sheltering nearly 16,000 small boats, Newport Harbor may seduce even those who don't own a yacht. Spend an afternoon exploring the charming avenues and surrounding alleys or take California's longest-running auto ferry across to Balboa Island, popular with pedestrians, bicyclists, and automobiles. Several grassy areas on the primarily residential Lido Isle have views of the water. To truly experience the harbor, rent a kayak or an electric Duffy boat for a pleasant picnic cruise or try stand-up paddleboarding to explore the sheltered waters. ✉ *Pacific Coast Hwy.* 🌐 *www.balboaislandferry.com.*

Sculpture Exhibition in Civic Center Park

PUBLIC ART | **FAMILY** | This outdoor museum is a favorite walking spot for locals and visitors. Look for the array of meaningful and whimsical public art sculptures on a hillside looking out toward the Pacific Ocean. Families love "Bunnyhenge," a collection of 14 white bunny statues arranged in a circle. ✉ *1000 Avocado Ave.* ☎ *949/717–3802* 🌐 *www.newportbeachca.gov.*

Restaurants

Basilic Restaurant

$$$ | **BRASSERIE** | This intimate French-Swiss bistro adds a touch of old-world elegance to Balboa Island with its white linen and flower-topped tables. Chef Bernard Althaus grows the herbs used in his classic French dishes. **Known for:** French classics; fine wine; old-school ambience. 💲 *Average main: $32* ✉ *217 Marine Ave., Balboa*

Island ☎ *949/673–0570* 🌐 *www.basilicrestaurant.com* ⏲ *Closed Sun. and Mon.*

★ Bear Flag Fish Co.
$ | **SEAFOOD** | **FAMILY** | Expect long lines in summer at this indoor/outdoor dining spot serving up the freshest local fish (swordfish, sea bass, halibut, and tuna) and a wide range of creative seafood dishes (the Hawaiian-style *poke* salad with ahi tuna is a local favorite). Order at the counter, which doubles as a seafood market, and sit inside the airy dining room or outside on a grand patio. **Known for:** freshest seafood thanks to restaurant's own fishing boat; fish tacos with homemade hot sauce; craft beers. $ *Average main: $15* ✉ *Newport Peninsula, 3421 Via Lido* ☎ *949/673–3474* 🌐 *www.bearflagfishco.com.*

Bluewater Grill
$$$ | **SEAFOOD** | **FAMILY** | On the site of an old sportfishing dock, this popular spot offers a variety of seafood, from Idaho trout amandine and lemon pepper mahimahi to lobster, pan-seared scallops, and chipotle-blackened swordfish. There's a tranquil bay view from either the dining room, which is adorned with early-1900s fishing photos, or the waterfront patio. **Known for:** boat and harbor views; happy hour specials; daily-changing menu of fresh fish. $ *Average main: $35* ✉ *Lido Peninsula, 630 Lido Park Dr.* ☎ *949/675–3474* 🌐 *www.bluewatergrill.com.*

The Cannery
$$$ | **SEAFOOD** | This 1920s cannery building still teems with fish, but now they go into dishes on the eclectic Pacific Rim menu rather than being packed into crates. Settle in at the sushi bar, in the dining room, or on the patio before choosing between sashimi, freshly shucked oysters, or cilantro-marinated fish tacos. **Known for:** waterfront views; seafood specialties; craft cocktails. $ *Average main: $37* ✉ *3010 Lafayette Rd.* ☎ *949/566–0060* 🌐 *www.cannerynewport.com* ⏲ *Closed Mon. and Tues.*

Gulfstream
$$$ | **SEAFOOD** | **FAMILY** | Established in 1999, this on-trend restaurant has an open kitchen, comfortable booths, and outdoor seating. The patio is a fantastic place to hang out to enjoy a shrimp cocktail and glass of wine. **Known for:** oysters on the half shell; local hangout; outdoor patio. $ *Average main: $35* ✉ *850 Avocado Ave.* ☎ *949/718–0188* 🌐 *www.gulfstreamrestaurant.com.*

Hotels

Balboa Bay Resort
$$$ | **RESORT** | **FAMILY** | Sharing the same frontage as the private Balboa Bay Club that long ago hosted Humphrey Bogart, Lauren Bacall, and Ronald Reagan, this waterfront resort has one of the best bay views around, especially at its lively gastropub. **Pros:** exquisite bayfront views; comfortable beds; two popular restaurants for locals and visitors. **Cons:** swimming pool in the middle of the resort has no views; $35 nightly hospitality fee; some rooms don't face the bay. $ *Rooms from: $339* ✉ *1221 W. Coast Hwy.* ☎ *949/645–5000* 🌐 *www.balboabayresort.com* *159 rooms* 🍽 *No meals.*

Fashion Island Hotel
$$ | **RESORT** | **FAMILY** | Across a palm tree–lined boulevard from stylish Fashion Island, this 20-story tower caters to business types during the week and leisure travelers on weekends. **Pros:** lively lounge scene; large tropical heated pool; great location. **Cons:** steep valet parking prices; some rooms have views of mall parking; destination fee added to price. $ *Rooms from: $295* ✉ *690 Newport Center Dr.* ☎ *949/759–0808, 877/591–9145* 🌐 *www.fashionislandhotel.com* *295 rooms* 🍽 *No meals.*

Hyatt Regency Newport Beach
$$ | **RESORT** | **FAMILY** | The best aspect of this beloved resort-style Newport hotel is its lushly landscaped acres: 26 of them,

all overlooking the Back Bay. The casually elegant architecture, spread over the generous grounds, will appeal to travelers weary of high-rise hotels. **Pros:** high-quality linens; centrally located for shopping; numerous sport activities offered. **Cons:** $30 self-parking is far from main property; 10-minute drive to beach; $30 daily resort fee. *Rooms from: $235* *1107 Jamboree Rd.* *949/729–1234* *www.hyatt.com* *410 rooms* *No meals.*

★ Lido House, Autograph Collection

$$$ | **RESORT** | **FAMILY** | This Marriott Autograph Collection resort is located at the gateway of the exclusive Lido Island and three blocks from the beach. **Pros:** large hot tub and pool deck; lively hotel bar; free bikes to cruise the nearby boardwalk. **Cons:** pricey restaurant; $35 resort fee; $43 valet parking. *Rooms from: $325* *3300 Newport Blvd., Balboa Island* *949/524–8500* *www.lidohousehotel.com* *130 rooms, 5 cottages* *No meals.*

Newport Beach Hotel

$$$$ | **B&B/INN** | **FAMILY** | At this charming boutique hotel just steps from the beach and Newport Beach Pier, some of the coastal-themed guest rooms have ocean views, all have complimentary Wi-Fi, and most offer a whirlpool bathtub and shower. **Pros:** beach and oceanview guest rooms; in a lively area near restaurants; steps to the pier and beach. **Cons:** some rooms are small; not all rooms have views; parking is $25 a day. *Rooms from: $425* *2306 W. Oceanfront* *949/673–7030* *www.thenewportbeachhotel.com* *15 rooms* *Free breakfast.*

Newport Beach Marriott Hotel and Spa

$$ | **RESORT** | **FAMILY** | This centrally located property is across the street from the popular Fashion Island shopping and dining complex. **Pros:** million-dollar views of Orange County and beyond; large spa; central location across from Fashion Island. **Cons:** sprawling floor plan; smaller bathrooms; valet parking $36 a day. *Rooms from: $229* *900 Newport Center Dr.* *949/640–4000* *www.marriott.com* *523 rooms* *No meals.*

Shopping

★ Fashion Island

STORE/MALL | Shake the sand out of your shoes to head inland to the ritzy Fashion Island outdoor mall, a cluster of archways and courtyards complete with koi pond, fountains, and a mix of high-end shopping and chain dining. It has the luxe department stores Neiman Marcus, Nordstrom, and Bloomingdale's, plus expensive boutiques like Trina Turk, Kate Spade, and Michael Stars. *401 Newport Center Dr., between Jamboree and MacArthur Blvds., off PCH* *949/721–2000, 855/658–8527* *www.fashionisland.com.*

Activities

BOAT RENTALS

Balboa Boat Rentals

BOATING | **FAMILY** | You can tour the waterways surrounding Lido and Balboa isles on six-person power motorboats ($85 an hour), and electric Duffy boats ($95 to $115 an hour for 8 to 12 people) at Balboa Boat Rentals. *510 E. Edgewater Ave., Balboa Island* *855/690–0794* *www.boats4rent.com.*

BOAT TOURS

Catalina Flyer

TOUR—SPORTS | **FAMILY** | At Balboa Pavilion, the *Catalina Flyer* operates a 90-minute round-trip passage daily to Catalina Island for $70. Reservations are required; check the schedule for times, as crossings may be rescheduled due to weather or annual maintenance. All day parking is $27 a day in a nearby Newport Beach lot. Payment is made at self-serve pay stations. *400 Main St., Balboa Island* *949/673–5245* *www.catalinainfo.com.*

A whimbrel hunts for mussels at Crystal Cove State Park.

Hornblower Cruises and Events

TOUR—SPORTS | This operator books two-hour harbor cruises, Sunday brunch cruises, and three-hour weekend dinner cruises with dancing. The trips traverse the mostly placid and scenic waters of Newport Harbor. ✉ *2431 W. Coast Hwy.* ☎ *949/646–0155* 🌐 *www.hornblower.com.*

FISHING

Davey's Locker

FISHING | **FAMILY** | In addition to a complete tackle shop, Davey's Locker offers two-hour whale-watching cruises starting at $28, half-day sportfishing trips starting at $34; and overnight fishing excursions starting at $149. ✉ *Balboa Pavilion, 400 Main St., Balboa Island* ☎ *949/673–1434* 🌐 *www.daveyslocker.com.*

Corona del Mar

2 miles south of Newport Beach.

A small jewel on the Pacific Coast, Corona del Mar (known by locals as "CDM") has exceptional beaches that some say resemble their majestic Northern California counterparts. South of CDM is an area referred to as the Newport Coast or Crystal Cove—whatever you call it, it's another dazzling spot on the California Riviera.

Sights

Corona del Mar State Beach

BEACH—SIGHT | **FAMILY** | This beach is actually made up of two beaches, Little Corona and Big Corona, separated by a cliff. Both have soft, golden-hue sand. Facilities include fire pits and volleyball courts. Two colorful reefs (and the fact that it's off-limits to boats) make Corona del Mar great for snorkelers and beachcombers. Parking in the lot is pricey, but you can often find a spot on the street on weekdays. **Amenities:** lifeguards; parking; showers; toilets. **Best for:** snorkeling; sunset; swimming. ✉ *3100 Ocean Blvd., Corona del Mar* ☎ *949/644–3151* 🌐 *www.parks.ca.gov.*

★ Crystal Cove State Park

BEACH—SIGHT | FAMILY | Midway between Corona del Mar and Laguna, Crystal Cove State Park is a favorite of local beachgoers and wilderness trekkers. It encompasses a 3.2-mile stretch of unspoiled beach and has some of the best tide-pooling in Southern California. Here you can see starfish, crabs, and sea anemones near the rocks. The park's 2,400 acres of backcountry are ideal for hiking and mountain biking, but stay on the trails to preserve the beauty. The Moro Campground offers campsites with picnic tables, including spots designated for RVs and trailers. The Crystal Cove Historic District holds a collection of historic cottages (24 of which are available for overnight rental), decorated and furnished to reflect the 1935 to 1955 beach culture that flourished here. On the sand above the high tide line and on a bluff above the beach, the cottages offer a funky look at beach life in times past. ✉ *8471 N. Coast Hwy., Laguna Beach* ☎ *949/494–3539* 🌐 *www.crystalcovestatepark.org* 🎫 *$15 parking.*

Roger's Gardens

GARDEN | FAMILY | One of the largest retail gardens in Southern California, Roger's showcases some of the best holiday decorations during Halloween and Christmas. An on-site Farmhouse at Roger's Gardens restaurant is popular with visitors and locals, who enjoy the locally sourced menu items while overlooking the bucolic gardens. ✉ *2301 San Joaquin Hills Rd.* ☎ *949/640–5800* 🌐 *www.rogersgardens.com.*

Sherman Library and Gardens

GARDEN | FAMILY | This 2½-acre botanical garden and library specializes in the history of the Pacific Southwest. You can wander among cactus gardens, rose gardens, a cool fern garden, and a tropical conservatory. There's a good gift shop, too. Café Jardin serves lunch on weekdays and Sunday brunch. ✉ *2647 E. Pacific Coast Hwy.* ☎ *949/673–2261* 🌐 *www.thesherman.org* 🎫 *$5.*

Store

HISTORIC SITE | Located among the Crystal Cove Cottages in the area's Historic District, Store carries fine art works by local plein air artists, as well as seaglass and ocean-themed jewelry, children's toys, snacks, and beach apparel. ✉ *State Park Historic District, Newport Coast* ☎ *949/376–6200* 🌐 *www.crystalcove.org/visit/things-to-do/store-gallery.*

Restaurants

The Beachcomber Cafe at Crystal Cove

$$ | SEAFOOD | Beach culture flourishes in this Crystal Cove Historic District's restaurant, thanks to its umbrella-laden deck just a few steps above the white sand. This is where you can sip a really good mai tai at the Bootlegger Bar, while waiting for your chance to sample ahi tacos, Maine lobster pasta, or blue crab–stuffed salmon. **Known for:** beachside cocktails; fresh seafood; big crowds and long waits (try to make a reservation in advance). [$] *Average main: $25* ✉ *15 Crystal Cove* ☎ *949/376–6900* 🌐 *www.thebeachcombercafe.com.*

Shake Shack at Crystal Cove

$ | DINER | FAMILY | This Southern California landmark sitting on a bluff off the PCH is the perfect spot to get a quick breakfast or to sample a tasty Cove burger with a side of fries or cole slaw for lunch or dinner. The menu also includes a vegan Impossible burger, hot dogs, and fish-and-chips. **Known for:** over 30 different shake flavors; casual ocean-view dining;

small parking lot with 30 minute limit. *Average main: $15 7703 E. Coast Hwy., Newport Coast 949/464–0100 www.crystalcoveshakeshack.com.*

Hotels

The Resort at Pelican Hill

$$$$ | RESORT | FAMILY | Built on a protected coastal enclave across the PCH and Crystal Cove State Park, this upscale Italian Renaissance–style resort has a dramatic domed rotunda, antique olive jars, and Tuscan columns and pilasters in the lobby. **Pros:** ocean-view paradise for golfers; spectacular swimming pool (the largest of its kind in the world); great spa and dining options. **Cons:** one of the most expensive resorts in Orange County; swimming pool can get very crowded during the holidays; pricey resort fee. *Rooms from: $795 22701 Pelican Hill Rd. S, Newport Coast 949/612–0332, 888/507–6427 www.pelicanhill.com 204 rooms, 128 villas No meals.*

Shopping

Crystal Cove Promenade

STORE/MALL | FAMILY | Adding to Orange County's overwhelming supply of high-end shopping and dining is Crystal Cove Promenade, which might be described as the toniest strip mall in America. The mix of well-known storefronts, unique boutiques, and popular restaurants of this Mediterranean-inspired center are lined up across the street from Crystal Cove State Park, with the shimmering Pacific waters in plain view. *7845–8085 E. Coast Hwy., Newport Beach 949/494–1239 www.shopirvinecompany.com.*

Laguna Beach

10 miles south of Newport Beach on PCH, 60 miles south of Los Angeles, I–5 south to Hwy. 133, which turns into Laguna Canyon Rd.

Driving in along Laguna Canyon Road from the Interstate 405 freeway gives you the chance to cruise through a gorgeous coastal canyon, large stretches of which remain undeveloped, before arriving at a glistening wedge of ocean. There are 30 coves and beaches to visit, all with some of the cleanest water in Southern California. During the summer, there's a convenient and free trolley service through town that cruises from North Laguna to Main Beach and all the way to the Ritz Carlton Laguna Niguel.

Laguna's welcome mat is legendary. On the corner of Forest and Park avenues is a gate proclaiming, "This gate hangs well and hinders none, refresh and rest, then travel on." A gay community has long been established here; art galleries dot the village streets, and there's usually someone daubing up a plein air on the bluff in Heisler Park. Along the Pacific Coast Highway you'll find dozens of clothing boutiques, jewelry stores, and cafés.

VISITOR INFORMATION Visit Laguna Beach Visitors Center. *381 Forest Ave. 949/497–9229, 800/877–1115 www.visitlagunabeach.com.*

Sights

Festival of Arts and Pageant of the Masters

FESTIVAL | An outdoor amphitheater near the mouth of the canyon hosts the annual Pageant of the Masters, Laguna's signature event. Local participants arrange tableaux vivants, in which live models and carefully orchestrated backgrounds merge in striking mimicry of classical and contemporary paintings. The pageant is part of the **Festival of Arts,** held in July and August; tickets are in high demand, so plan ahead. ✉ *650 Laguna Canyon Rd.* ☎ *949/497–6582, 800/487–3378* 🌐 *www.foapom.com.*

Heisler Park

CITY PARK | **FAMILY** | One of the most picturesque parks in Laguna Beach, Heisler Park offers plenty of chances for fun and relaxation. Picnic Beach has picnic tables overlooking palm trees and panoramic ocean views while stairs lead down to Diver's Cove for snorkeling, scuba diving, and tidepool exploring. Take the paved walking path along the cliff all the way to Laguna's Main Beach. There are public restrooms and outdoor showers. This is also a popular area for plein-air artists to set up an easel and chair and paint for hours. ✉ *400 Cliff Dr.* 🌐 *www.visitlagunabeach.com.*

Laguna Art Museum

MUSEUM | This museum displays work by California artists from all time periods, representing scenery in Laguna, and life and history of the Golden State in general. Special exhibits change quarterly. ✉ *307 Cliff Dr.* ☎ *949/494–8971* 🌐 *www.lagunaartmuseum.org* 🎫 *$7* 🕒 *Closed Wed.*

Laguna Coast Wilderness Park

HIKING/WALKING | **FAMILY** | With easy, moderate, and difficult trails spread over 7,000 acres of canyon to coastal territory, Laguna Coast Wilderness Park is a hiker's paradise. The 40 miles of trails offer expansive views and are also popular with mountain bikers. Trails open daily at 7 am and stay open until sunset, weather permitting. No dogs are allowed in the park. ✉ *18751 Laguna Canyon Rd.* ☎ *949/923–2235* 🌐 *www.ocparks.com/parks/lagunac* 🎫 *$3 parking.*

Beaches

★ Main Beach Park

BEACH—SIGHT | **FAMILY** | Centrally located in the main town of Laguna Beach near multiple dining venues, art galleries, and shops, Main Beach Park has a fitting name. Walk along this soft-sand beach to Bird Rock and explore nearby tide pools or sit on one of the benches and watch people bodysurfing, playing beach volleyball, or scrambling around two half-basketball courts. The beach also has a children's play area with climbing equipment. Most of Laguna's hotels are within a short (but hilly) walk. **Amenities:** lifeguards; toilets; showers. **Best for:** sunrise, sunset; swimming. ✉ *Broadway at S. Coast Hwy.* 🌐 *www.visitlagunabeach.com.*

1,000 Steps Beach

BEACH—SIGHT | **FAMILY** | Off South Coast Highway at 9th Street, 1,000 Steps Beach isn't too hard to find and actually only has 207 steps. It's one of the many coves in Laguna Beach offering a long stretch of soft sand, waves, and dramatic rock formations. Sea caves and tide pools enhance the already beautiful natural spot. Walking back up to your car, you will feel like you got a good workout. **Amenities:** showers. **Best for:** snorkeling; surfing; swimming. ✉ *S. Coast Hwy., at 9th St.* 🌐 *www.visitlagunabeach.com.*

Wood's Cove

BEACH—SIGHT | **FAMILY** | Off South Coast Highway, Wood's Cove is especially quiet during the week. Big rock formations hide lurking crabs. This is a prime scuba-diving spot, and at high tide much of the beach is underwater. Climbing the steps to leave, you can see a Tudor-style mansion that was once home to Bette Davis. Street parking is free yet limited. **Amenities:** none. **Best for:** snorkeling; scuba diving; sunset. ✉ *Diamond St. and Ocean Way* 🌐 *www.visitlagunabeach.com.*

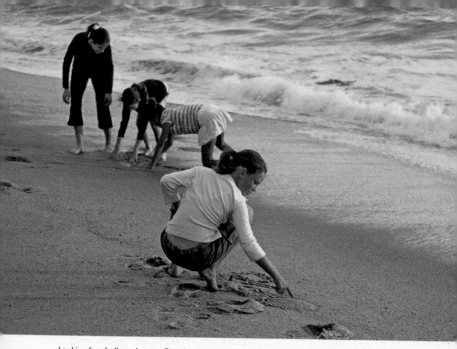

Looking for shells on Laguna Beach, one of the nicest stretches of sand in Southern California.

Restaurants

The Cliff

$$$ | SEAFOOD | FAMILY | Walk through the quaint Laguna Beach artist village to get to the Cliff and its 180-degree views of Main Beach and the Pacific coastline. The multilevel dining patios serve hearty breakfasts and coastal seafood for lunch and dinner. **Known for:** some of Laguna Beach's best ocean-view dining; reservations necessary; splurge-worthy seafood towers. *Average main: $35* *577 S. Coast Hwy.* *949/494–1956* *www.thecliffrestaurant.com.*

Gelato Paradiso

$ | EUROPEAN | Each morning this gelato shop makes fresh small batches of artisanal gelatos and dairy-free sorbettos in a variety of appealing flavors. Located in back of the charming Peppertree Lane shopping center, there is a small outdoor patio where people gather to enjoy the authentic Italian gelato after a day at the beach or to cap off an evening. **Known for:** authentic Italian gelato; fruit flavors; patio gathering spot. *Average main: $6* *Peppertree La. , 448 S. Coast Hwy.* *949/464–9255* *www.gelatoparadiso.com.*

★ Las Brisas

$$ | MEXICAN FUSION | FAMILY | Located in what used to be the Victor Hugo Inn, Las Brisas is now a Laguna Beach landmark restaurant. Sit on the expansive patio to take in the spectacular coastline views while enjoying signature margaritas and coastal Mexican cuisine with a California twist. **Known for:** fresh seafood; panoramic coastal views; reservations a must. *Average main: $30* *361 Cliff Dr.* *949/497–5434* *www.lasbrisaslagunabeach.com.*

The Rooftop Lounge

$$ | AMERICAN | Another popular sunset cocktail and light dinner venue in South Laguna for its views. Located at the top of La Casa del Camino, be sure to make a reservation to sit at a front row table to watch the sun lower behind Catalina Island. **Known for:** spectacular sunset views; craft cocktails; burgers, pasta, salads and sandwiches. *Average main:*

$30 ✉ *1289 S. Coast Hwy.* ☎ *949/497–2446* 🌐 *www.rooftoplagunabeach.com.*

Sapphire

$$ | **INTERNATIONAL** | **FAMILY** | This Laguna Beach establishment set in a historic Craftsman-style building is part gourmet pantry (a must-stop for your every picnic need) and part global dining adventure. Enjoy comfort cuisine from around the world paired with an eclectic wine and beer list. **Known for:** sapphire salad; weekend brunch; pet-friendly patio. $ *Average main: $30* ✉ *The Old Pottery Place, 1200 S. Coast Hwy.* ☎ *949/715–9888* 🌐 *www.sapphirelagunabeach.com.*

★ **Studio**

$$$$ | **MODERN AMERICAN** | In a nod to Laguna's art history, Studio has housemade specialties that entice the eye as well as the palate. The restaurant occupies its own Craftsman-style bungalow, atop a 50-foot bluff overlooking Treasure Island Park and the Pacific coastline. **Known for:** chef's creative tasting menu; great spot for special occasions; California coastal dishes with a French flair. $ *Average main: $75* ✉ *30801 S. Coast Hwy.* ☎ *949/715–6030* 🌐 *www.studiolagunabeach.com* ⏲ *No lunch.*

Taco Loco

$ | **MEXICAN** | **FAMILY** | This may look like a fast-food taco stand, and the hemp blackened burgers and brownies on the menu may make you think the kitchen's *really* laid-back, but the quality of the food here equals that in many higher-price restaurants. Some Mexican standards get a seafood twist, like swordfish, calamari, and shrimp tacos. **Known for:** vegetarian tacos; sidewalk seating; surfer clientele. $ *Average main: $16* ✉ *640 S. Coast Hwy.* ☎ *949/497–1635* 🌐 *www.lagunabeachmexicanfood.com.*

Urth Caffe

$$ | **BAKERY** | **FAMILY** | A local favorite for organic heirloom coffee and hand-blended fine organic teas, Urth is also the place to go for health-conscious breakfast dishes like an egg white and spinach breakfast panini. Sit outside on the charming garden patio looking out toward the Laguna Art Museum across the street. **Known for:** health-conscious cuisine; organic coffee and tea; long lines on the patio during peak hours and weekends. $ *Average main: $20* ✉ *308 N. Pacific Coast Hwy.* ☎ *949/376–8888* 🌐 *www.urthcaffe.com/laguna-beach.*

Zinc Café and Market

$ | **AMERICAN** | **FAMILY** | Families flock to this small Laguna Beach institution for reasonably priced breakfast and lunch options. Try the signature quiches or poached egg dishes in the morning, or swing by later in the day for healthy salads, homemade soups, quesadillas, or pizzettes. **Known for:** gourmet pastries, some gluten-free; avocado toast; busy outdoor patio. $ *Average main: $18* ✉ *350 Ocean Ave.* ☎ *949/494–6302* 🌐 *www.zinccafe.com* ⏲ *No dinner Nov.–Apr.*

Hotels

Inn at Laguna Beach

$$$ | **HOTEL** | **FAMILY** | This golden local landmark is stacked neatly on the hillside at the north end of Laguna's Main Beach and it's one of the few hotels in the area set almost on the sand. **Pros:** rooftop with fabulous ocean views; beach essentials provided; beachfront location. **Cons:** ocean-view rooms are pricey; tiny hot tub; some rooms are dark and small. $ *Rooms from: $379* ✉ *211 N. Coast Hwy.* ☎ *949/497–9722, 800/544–4479* 🌐 *www.innatlagunabeach.com* 🛏 *70 rooms* 🍽 *No meals.*

La Casa del Camino

$$ | **HOTEL** | The look is Old California at the 1929-built La Casa del Camino, with dark woods, arched doors, wrought iron, and a beautiful tiled fireplace in the lobby. **Pros:** breathtaking views from rooftop lounge; modern decor; steps to the beach. **Cons:** some rooms face

the highway; pipes can be noisy; some rooms are small. *Rooms from: $225* *1289 S. Coast Hwy.* *949/497–6029, 855/634–5736* *www.lacasadelcamino.com* *36 rooms* *Free breakfast.*

★ Montage Laguna Beach

$$$$ | RESORT | FAMILY | Built on a picturesque coastal bluff above the Pacific Ocean and Treasure Island Beach, this elegant Craftsmen-style resort features 30 acres of grassy lawns, soft sand beaches, and a marine sanctuary. **Pros:** picturesque coastal location; stunning tiled mosaic swimming pool; residential style villas with sweeping ocean views. **Cons:** one of the area's priciest resorts, especially during holidays or summer weekends; $60 valet parking; $42 daily resort fee. *Rooms from: $895* *30801 S. Coast Hwy.* *949/715–6000, 866/271–6953* *www.montagehotels.com/lagunabeach* *258 rooms* *No meals.*

★ Surf and Sand Resort

$$$$ | RESORT | FAMILY | One mile south of downtown, on an exquisite stretch of beach with thundering waves and gorgeous rocks, this is a getaway for those who want a boutique hotel experience without all the formalities. **Pros:** easy sandy beach access; intimate boutique resort; good restaurant with wonderful views. **Cons:** pricey valet parking; surf can be loud; no air-conditioning (but overhead fans help). *Rooms from: $450* *1555 S. Coast Hwy.* *877/741–5908* *www.surfandsandresort.com* *167 rooms* *No meals.*

Shopping

Coast Highway, Forest and Ocean avenues, and Glenneyre Street are full of art galleries, fine jewelry stores, souvenir shops, and clothing boutiques.

Adam Neeley Fine Art Jewelry

JEWELRY/ACCESSORIES | Be prepared to be dazzled at Adam Neeley Fine Art Jewelry, where artisan proprietor Adam Neeley creates one-of-a-kind modern pieces. *352 N. Coast Hwy.* *949/715–0953* *www.adamneeley.com.*

Art for the Soul

CRAFTS | A riot of color, Art for the Soul has hand-painted furniture, crafts, and unusual whimsical gifts. *272 Forest Ave.* *949/675–1791* *www.ra4ts.com.*

Candy Baron

FOOD/CANDY | FAMILY | Get your sugar fix at the time-warped Candy Baron, filled with old-fashioned goodies like gumdrops, licorice, bull's-eyes, sugar-free candies, and more than 50 flavors of saltwater taffy. *231 Forest Ave.* *949/497–7508* *www.thecandybaron.com.*

La Rue du Chocolat

FOOD/CANDY | Located off the PCH in the quaint Peppertree Lane boutique shopping center, this sophisticated chocolate and truffle shop sells handcrafted seasonal chocolates, chocolate-covered strawberries, and creative holiday treats. *Peppertree La., 448 S. Coast Hwy., Suite B* *949/494–2372* *www.laruedu-chocolat.com.*

San Juan Capistrano

5 miles north of Dana Point, 60 miles north of San Diego.

San Juan Capistrano is best known for its historic mission, where the swallows traditionally return each year, migrating from their winter haven in Argentina, but these days they are more likely to choose other local sites for nesting. St. Joseph's Day, March 19, launches a week of fowl festivities. Charming antiques stores, which range from pricey to cheap, line Camino Capistrano.

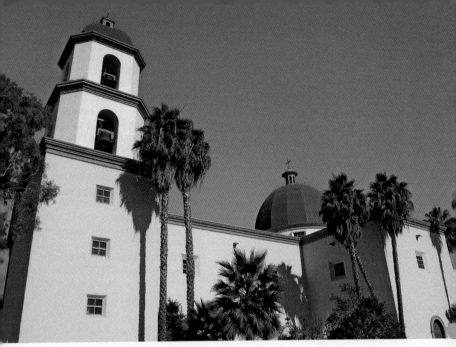

Mission San Juan Capistrano was founded in 1776.

GETTING HERE AND AROUND

If you arrive by train, which is far more romantic and restful than battling freeway traffic, you'll be dropped off across from the mission at the San Juan Capistrano depot. With its appealing brick café and preserved Santa Fe cars, the depot retains much of the magic of early American railroads. If driving, park near Ortega and Camino Capistrano, the city's main streets.

Sights

★ Los Rios Historic District

NEIGHBORHOOD | FAMILY | Take a walk back in time on the oldest residential street in Southern California, where houses date back to 1790. The Silvas Adobe is a typical example of the dozen or more one-room adobes in the area. Mission San Juan Capistrano was the first Californian mission to allow workers to live outside the mission grounds. On the street you'll also find the Historical Society Museum and the ZOOMARS petting zoo for families. Shopping and dining options abound. ✉ *31831 Los Rios St.* ☎ *949/493–8444* 🌐 *www.nps.gov.*

★ Mission San Juan Capistrano

RELIGIOUS SITE | FAMILY | Founded in 1776 by Father Junípero Serra (consecrated as St. Serra), Mission San Juan Capistrano was one of two Roman Catholic outposts between Los Angeles and San Diego. The Great Stone Church, begun in 1797, is the largest structure created by the Spanish in California. After extensive retrofitting, the golden-hued interiors are open to visitors who may feel they are touring among ruins in Italy rather than the O.C. Many of the mission's adobe buildings have been restored to illustrate mission life, with exhibits of an olive millstone, tallow ovens, tanning vats, metalworking furnaces, and the padres' living quarters. The beautiful gardens, with their fountains and koi pond, are a lovely spot in which to wander. The bougainvillea-covered Serra Chapel is believed to be the oldest church still standing in California and is the only building remaining in which St. Serra actually led Mass. Enter via a small gift shop in the gatehouse. ✉ 26801 Ortega Hwy. ☎ 949/234–1300 🌐 www.missionsjc.com 🎟 $14.

San Juan Capistrano Library

LIBRARY | **FAMILY** | Near Mission San Juan Capistrano is the San Juan Capistrano Library, a postmodern structure built in 1983. Architect Michael Graves combined classical and Mission styles to striking effect. Its courtyard has secluded places for reading. ✉ *31495 El Camino Real* ☎ *949/493–1752* 🌐 *ocpl.org/libloc/sjc* ⏲ *Closed Sun. and Mon.*

Restaurants

Cedar Creek Inn

$$ | **AMERICAN** | **FAMILY** | Just across the street from Mission San Juan Capistrano, this restaurant has a patio that's perfect for a late lunch or a romantic dinner. The menu is fairly straightforward, dishes are tasty, and portions are substantial—try the Cobb salad or a burger at lunch, or splurge on the prime rib for dinner. **Known for:** gluten-free and vegetarian options, rich desserts; comfortable seating. $ *Average main: $30* ✉ *26860 Ortega Hwy.* ☎ *949/240–2229* 🌐 *www.cedarcreekinn.com.*

L'Hirondelle

$$$ | **FRENCH** | Locals have romanced at cozy tables for decades at this delightful restaurant directly across from the San Juan Capistrano Mission. Such classic dishes as beef bourguignon and a New York strip in a black-peppercorn-and-brandy sauce are the hallmarks of this French and Belgian restaurant, whose name means "the little swallow." The extensive wine list is matched by an impressive selection of Belgian beers. **Known for:** popular Sunday brunch; traditional French and Belgian cuisine; good Belgian beer selection. $ *Average main: $39* ✉ *31631 Camino Capistrano* ☎ *949/661–0425* 🌐 *www.lhirondellesjc.com* ⏲ *Closed Mon.*

The Ramos House Cafe

$$$ | **AMERICAN** | It may be worth hopping the Amtrak to San Juan Capistrano just for the chance to have breakfast or lunch at one of Orange County's most beloved restaurants, located in a historic board-and-batten home dating back to 1881. This café sits practically on the railroad tracks across from the depot—nab a table on the patio and dig into a hearty breakfast featuring seasonal items, such as the smoked bacon scramble with wilted rocket and apple fried potatoes. **Known for:** Southern specialties; weekend brunch; historic setting. $ *Average main: $35* ✉ *31752 Los Rios St.* ☎ *949/443–1342* 🌐 *www.ramoshouse.com* ⏲ *Closed Wed. No dinner.*

Hotels

★ Inn at the Mission San Juan Capistrano

$$$ | **HOTEL** | **FAMILY** | This family-friendly hacienda-style boutique hotel is located across the street from the famed San Juan Capistrano Mission, and the property incorporates this history by featuring glass mission bell lighting fixtures and equestrian decor and art. **Pros:** great location next to the mission; terrific culinary program; luxury rooms and suites. **Cons:** guests may hear freeway noise; beach is just less than 3 miles away; expensive parking. $ *Rooms from: $350* ✉ *31692 El Camino Real* ☎ *949/503–5700* 🌐 *www.marriott.com* *135 rooms* *No meals.*

★ Ritz-Carlton, Laguna Niguel

$$$$ | **RESORT** | **FAMILY** | Combine the Ritz-Carlton's top-tier level of service with an unparalleled view of the Pacific, and you're in the lap of luxury at this resort. **Pros:** beautiful grounds and views; luxurious bedding; sophisticated service. **Cons:** some rooms are small for the price; in-house dining prices are high; $50 resort fee. $ *Rooms from: $685* ✉ *1 Ritz-Carlton Dr., Dana Point* ☎ *949/240–2000, 800/542–8680* 🌐 *www.ritzcarlton.com/en/hotels/california/laguna-niguel* *396 rooms* *No meals.*

Nightlife

Swallow's Inn

BARS/PUBS | Across the way from Mission San Juan Capistrano you may spot a line of Harleys in front of the down-home and downright funky Swallow's Inn. Despite a somewhat tough look, it attracts all kinds—bikers, surfers, modern-day cowboys, grandparents—for a drink, a casual bite, karaoke nights, and some rowdy live country music. ✉ *31786 Camino Capistrano* ☎ *949/493–3188* 🌐 *www.swallowsinn.com.*

Catalina Island

Just 22 miles out from the L.A. coastline, across from Newport Beach and Long Beach, Catalina has virtually unspoiled mountains, canyons, coves, and beaches; best of all, it gives you a glimpse of what undeveloped Southern California once looked like.

Water sports are a big draw, as divers and snorkelers come for the exceptionally clear water surrounding the island. Kayakers are attracted to the calm cove waters and thrill seekers book the eco-themed zipline that traverses a wooded canyon. The main town, Avalon, is a charming, old-fashioned beach community, where yachts and pleasure boats bob in the crescent bay. Wander beyond the main drag and find brightly painted little bungalows fronting the sidewalks; golf carts are the preferred mode of transport.

In 1919, William Wrigley Jr., the chewing-gum magnate, purchased a controlling interest in the company developing Catalina Island, whose most famous landmark, the Casino, was built in 1929 under his orders. Because he owned the Chicago Cubs baseball team, Wrigley made Catalina the team's spring training site, an arrangement that lasted until 1951.

In 1975, the Catalina Island Conservancy, a nonprofit foundation, acquired about 88% of the island to help preserve the area's natural flora and fauna, including the bald eagle and the Catalina Island fox. These days the conservancy is restoring the rugged interior country with plantings of native grasses and trees. The organization helps oversee the interior's 50 miles of bike trails and 165 miles of hiking trails and helps protect the island's 60 endemic species. Along the coast you might spot oddities like electric perch, saltwater goldfish, and flying fish.

GETTING HERE AND AROUND

FERRY TRAVEL

Two companies offer ferry service to Catalina Island. The boats have both indoor and outdoor seating and snack bars. Excessive baggage is not allowed, and there are extra fees for bicycles and surfboards. The waters around Catalina can get rough, so if you're prone to seasickness, come prepared. Winter, holiday, and weekend schedules vary, so reservations are strongly recommended.

Catalina Express makes an hour-long run from Long Beach or San Pedro to Avalon and a 90-minute run from Dana Point to Avalon with some stops at Two Harbors. Round-trip fares begin at $73.50, with discounts for seniors and kids. On busy days, a $15 upgrade to the Commodore Lounge, when available, is worth it. Service from Newport Beach to Avalon is available through the *Catalina Flyer.* The boat leaves from Balboa Pavilion at 9 am (in season), takes 75 minutes to reach the island, and costs $70 round-trip. The return boat leaves Catalina at 4:30 pm. Reservations are required for the *Catalina Flyer* and recommended for all weekend and summer trips. **■ TIP→ Keep an eye out for dolphins, which sometimes swim alongside the ferries.**

FERRY CONTACTS Catalina Express. ✉ *320 Golden Shore, Long Beach* ☎ *562/485–3200* 🌐 *www.catalinaexpress.com.* **Catalina Flyer.** ✉ *Balboa Pier, 400 Main St., Newport Beach* ☎ *949/673–5245* 🌐 *www.catalinainfo.com.*

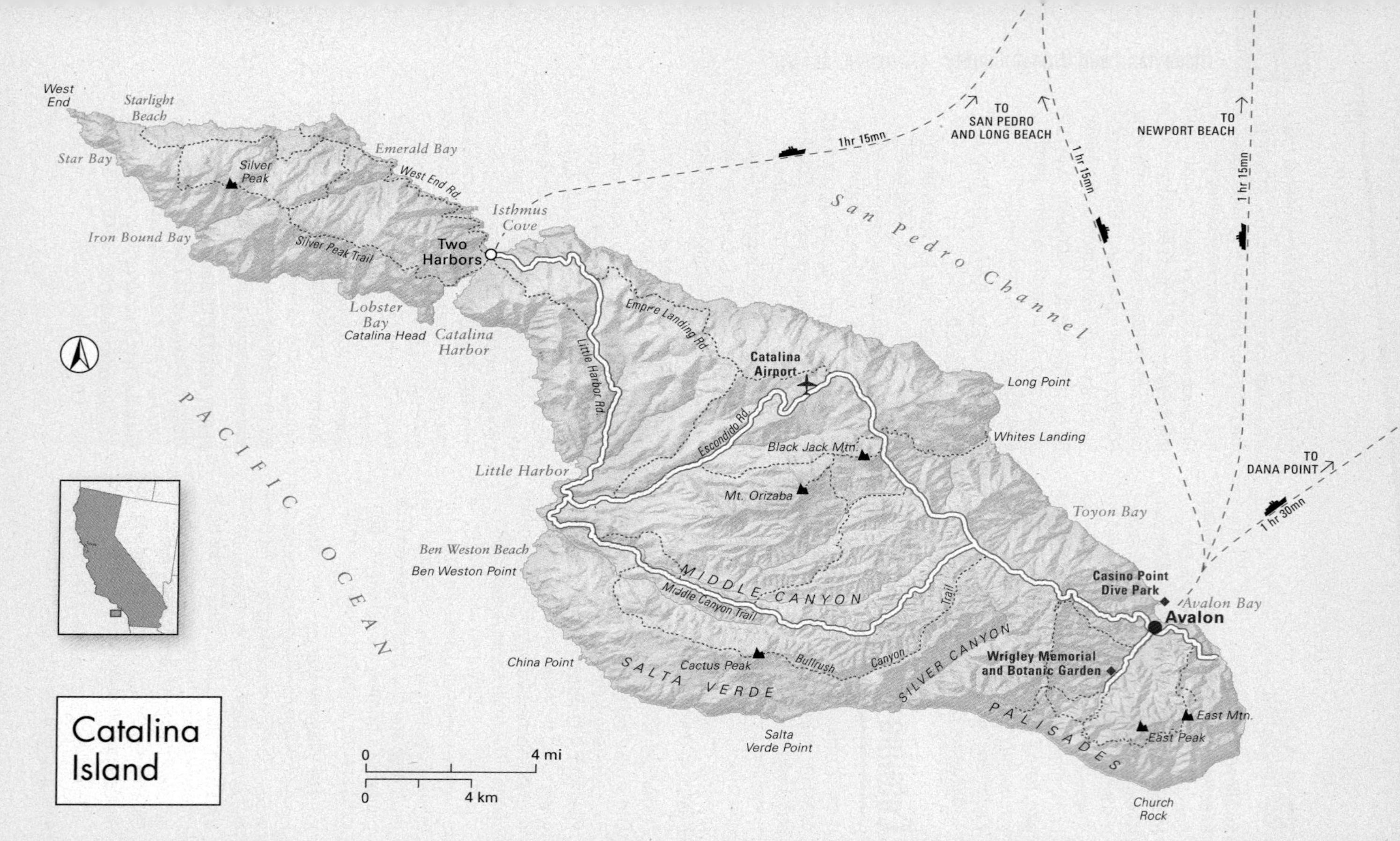
Catalina Island
West End
Starlight Beach
Star Bay
Silver Peak
Emerald Bay
West End Rd.
Iron Bound Bay
Silver Peak Trail
Isthmus Cove
Two Harbors
Lobster Bay
Catalina Head
Catalina Harbor
Empire Landing Rd.
Little Harbor Rd.
Catalina Airport
Long Point
Escondido Rd.
Black Jack Mtn.
Whites Landing
Mt. Orizaba
Little Harbor
Ben Weston Beach
Ben Weston Point
MIDDLE CANYON
Middle Canyon Trail
Trail
China Point
Cactus Peak
Bullrush
Canyon
SALTA VERDE
SILVER CANYON
Salta Verde Point
Toyon Bay
Casino Point Dive Park
Avalon Bay
Avalon
Wrigley Memorial and Botanic Garden
PALISADES
East Mtn.
East Peak
Church Rock
PACIFIC OCEAN
San Pedro Channel
TO SAN PEDRO AND LONG BEACH
1hr 15mn
1 hr 15mn
TO NEWPORT BEACH
1 hr 15mn
TO DANA POINT
1 hr 30mn
0
4 mi
0
4 km

GOLF CARTS

Golf carts constitute the island's main form of transportation for sightseeing in the area; however, some parts of town are off-limits, as is the island's interior. Drivers 21 and over with valid driver's license can rent them along Avalon's Crescent Avenue and Pebbly Beach Road for about $50 per hour with a $50 deposit, payable via cash only.

GOLF CART RENTALS Island Rentals. ✉ *125 Pebbly Beach Rd., Avalon* ☎ *310/510–1456* 🌐 *www.catalinagolfcartrentals.com.*

TIMING

Although Catalina can be seen in one thrilling day, several inviting hotels make it worth extending your stay for one or more nights. A short itinerary might include breakfast on the pier, a tour of the interior, a snorkeling excursion at Casino Point, or beach day at the Descanso Beach Club and a romantic waterfront dinner in Avalon.

After late October, rooms are much easier to find on short notice, rates drop dramatically, and many hotels offer packages that include transportation from the mainland and/or sightseeing tours. January to March you have a good chance of spotting migrating gray whales on the ferry crossing.

TOURS

Santa Catalina Island Company runs both land tours and ocean tours, including the *Flying Fish* boat trip (summer evenings only); a comprehensive inland motor tour; a tour of Skyline Drive; several Casino tours; a scenic tour of Avalon; a glass-bottom-boat tour; an undersea tour on a semisubmersible vessel; an eco-themed zipline tour that traverses a scenic canyon; a speedy Ocean Runner expedition that searches for all manner of sea creatures and a fast Cyclone boat tour that takes you to the less populated center of the island, Two Harbors. Reservations are highly recommended for the inland tours. Tours cost $22 to $130. There are ticket booths on the Green Pleasure Pier, in the plaza, and at the boat landing. Catalina Adventure Tours, which has booths at the boat landing and on the pier, also arranges excursions at comparable prices.

The Catalina Island Conservancy organizes custom ecotours and hikes of the interior. Naturalist guides drive open jeeps through some gorgeously untrammeled parts of the island. Tours start at $70 per person for a two-hour trip (two-person minimum). The tours run year-round.

CONTACTS Catalina Adventure Tours. ✉ *302 Pebbly Beach Rd., Avalon* ☎ *562/432–8828* 🌐 *www.catalinaadventuretours.com.* **Catalina Island Conservancy.** ✉ *708 Crescent Ave., Avalon* ☎ *310/510–2595* 🌐 *www.catalinaconservancy.org.* **Santa Catalina Island Company.** ☎ *877/778–8322* 🌐 *www.visitcatalinaisland.com.*

Avalon

A 1- to 2-hour ferry ride from Long Beach, Newport Beach, or San Pedro.

Avalon, Catalina's only real town, extends from the shore of its natural harbor to the surrounding hillsides. Its resident population is about 3,800, but it swells with tourists on summer weekends. Most of the city's activity, however, is centered on the pedestrian mall on Crescent Avenue, and most sights are easily reached on foot. Private cars are restricted and rental cars aren't allowed, but taxis, trams, and shuttles can take you anywhere you need to go. Bicycles, electric bikes, and golf carts can be rented from shops along Crescent Avenue.

Did You Know?

You can take a tour of Avalon's Scenic Drive for 7½ miles of panoramic views and a lesson in Catalina Island folklore.

Sights

★ Casino

BUILDING | Built in 1929, this circular white structure is one of the finest examples of art-deco architecture anywhere. Its Spanish-inspired floors and murals gleam with brilliant marine blue and sea foam green Catalina tiles. In this case, *casino,* the Italian word for "gathering place," has nothing to do with gambling. The circular ballroom once famously hosted 1940s big bands and is still used for gala events. The Santa Catalina Island Company leads two narrated walking tours of the Casino. ✉ *1 Casino Way* ☎ *310/510–0179* 🌐 *www.visitcatalinaisland.com.*

Casino Point Dive Park

BEACH—SIGHT | **FAMILY** | In front of the Casino are the crystal clear waters of the Casino Point Dive Park, a protected marine preserve where moray eels, bat rays, spiny lobsters, harbor seals, and the bright orange Garibaldi (California's state marine fish) cruise around kelp forests and along the sandy bottom. No need to don a wet suit: the brilliantly orange Garibaldi, can sometimes be viewed from the seawall. It's a terrific site for scuba diving, with some shallow areas suitable for snorkeling. Equipment can be rented on and near the pier. The shallow waters of Lover's Cove, east of the boat landing, are also good for snorkeling. ✉ *1 Casino Way* 🌐 *www.divingcatalina.com.*

Catalina Island Museum

MUSEUM | **FAMILY** | The exterior of the Catalina Island Museum is a nod to Catalina Island's developer William Wrigley Jr.—it's modeled after Wrigley Field in Chicago. Inside the interactive museum visitors can learn about the island's history from the native Chumash people to its role in Hollywood history and beyond. Two galleries host traveling exhibitions. The view from the outside terrace takes in lovely Avalon and its picturesque harbor. A small gift shop offers Catalina-themed souvenirs and reproductions of the island's signature colorful Catalina pottery tiles. ✉ *217 Metropole Ave.* ☎ *310/510–2414* 🌐 *www.catalinamuseum.org* 🎟 *$17* 🕒 *Closed Mon. and Tues.*

Catalina's Bison

Zane Grey, the writer who put the Western novel on the map, spent a lot of time on Catalina, and his influence is still evident in a peculiar way. As the story goes, when the movie version of Grey's book *The Vanishing American* was filmed here in 1924, American bison were ferried across from the mainland to give the land that western plains look. After the crew packed up and left, the buffalo stayed, and a small herd of about 150 still remains, grazing the interior.

Green Pleasure Pier

LOCAL INTEREST | **FAMILY** | Head to the Green Pleasure Pier for a good vantage point of Avalon. On the pier you can find the visitor information, snack stands, and scads of squawking seagulls. It's also the landing where visiting cruise-ship passengers catch tenders back out to their ship. ✉ *1 Green Pleasure Pier* 🌐 *www.lovecatalina.com.*

Wrigley Memorial and Botanic Garden

GARDEN | **FAMILY** | Two miles south of the bay is Wrigley Memorial and Botanic Garden, home to many plants native only to Southern California and the Channel Islands. Today there are five different sections where you can see Catalina ironwood, wild tomato, and rare Catalina mahogany. The Wrigley family commissioned the garden as well as the monument, which has a grand staircase and a Spanish-style mausoleum inlaid with colorful Catalina tile. Wrigley Jr. was once buried here but his remains were moved to Glendale, CA, during World War

II. ✉ *Avalon Canyon Rd.* ☎ *310/510–2897* 🌐 *www.catalinaconservancy.org* 🎫 *$8.*

Restaurants

Bluewater Grill

$$ | SEAFOOD | FAMILY | Overlooking the ferry landing and the entire harbor, the open-to-the-salt-air Bluewater Grill offers freshly caught fish, savory chowders, and all manner of shellfish. If they're on the menu, don't miss the swordfish steak, the lobster roll, or the sand dabs. **Known for:** fresh local fish; handcrafted cocktails; overwater harbor views. 💲 *Average main: $30* ✉ *306 Crescent Ave.* ☎ *310/510–3474* 🌐 *www.bluewatergrill.com.*

Descanso Beach Club

$ | AMERICAN | FAMILY | Set on an expansive deck overlooking the water, Descanso Beach Club serves a wide range of favorites: grilled burgers, street tacos, clam chowder, salads, and layered nachos are all part of the selection. Watch the harbor seals frolic just offshore while sipping the island's supersweet signature cocktail, the Buffalo Milk, a mix of fruit liqueurs, vodka, and whipped cream. **Known for:** tropical beach vibe; scenic views; chic cabana rentals. 💲 *Average main: $12* ✉ *Descanso Beach, 1 Descanso Ave.* ☎ *310/510–7410* 🌐 *www.visitcatalinaisland.com.*

★ Eric's on the Pier

$ | AMERICAN | This little snack bar has been an Avalon family–run institution since the 1920s. It's a good place to people-watch while drinking a draft beer and munching on a breakfast burrito, fish-and-chips, or signature buffalo burger. **Known for:** comfort foods; quick eats; beachside location. 💲 *Average main: $15* ✉ *2 Green Pier* ☎ *310/510–0894* 🌐 *www.lovecatalina.com/listing/erics-on-the-pier/23.*

The Lobster Trap

$$ | SEAFOOD | Seafood rules at the Lobster Trap—the restaurant's owner has his own boat and fishes for the catch of the day and, in season, spiny lobster. Ceviche is a great starter, always fresh and brightly flavored. **Known for:** locally caught seafood; convivial atmosphere; locals' hangout. 💲 *Average main: $25* ✉ *128 Catalina St.* ☎ *310/510–8585* 🌐 *catalinalobstertrap.com.*

Steve's Steakhouse and Seafood

$$$ | STEAKHOUSE | FAMILY | Within spitting distance of the bay, this second-floor restaurant keeps hungry diners happy with sizzling steaks and slow-cooked baby back ribs. There's also ample seafood, such as locally caught swordfish and shrimp. **Known for:** friendly staff; water views; steak and seafood dinners. 💲 *Average main: $32* ✉ *417 Crescent Ave.* ☎ *310/510–0333* 🌐 *www.stevessteakhouse.com.*

Hotels

Aurora Hotel

$$ | HOTEL | In a town dominated by historic properties, the Aurora is refreshingly contemporary, with a hip attitude and sleek furnishings. **Pros:** trendy design; quiet location off main drag; close to restaurants. **Cons:** standard rooms are small; no elevator; two-night minimum stay required. 💲 *Rooms from: $279* ✉ *137 Marilla Ave.* ☎ *310/510–0454* 🌐 *www.auroracatalina.com* 🛏 *18 rooms* 🍽 *Free breakfast.*

Bellanca Hotel

$$ | HOTEL | One of the closest boutique hotels to the Catalina Casino, this European-style hotel creates an intimate feel with brick courtyards and serene suites. **Pros:** romantic setting; close to beach; expansive sundeck with comfortable lounge furniture. **Cons:** ground-floor rooms can hear golf carts drive by; some rooms are on the small side; no elevator. 💲 *Rooms from: $299* ✉ *111 Crescent Ave.* ☎ *310/510–0555, 888/510–0555* 🌐 *www.bellancahotel.com* 🛏 *35 rooms* 🍽 *No meals.*

★ Hotel Atwater

$$ | **HOTEL** | **FAMILY** | Just one block from the beach in the center of Avalon, Hotel Atwater originally opened in 1920 and was recently redesigned to honor Helen Atwater's (daugher-in-law of famed local William Wrigley) impeccable sense of style and deep love for Catalina Island. **Pros:** unique and historical decor; central location; nice amenities. **Cons:** some rooms have street noise; certain rooms on the small side; not on the beach. *Rooms from: $269 125 Sumner Ave. 310/510–1789 www.visitcatalinaisland.com 95 rooms No meals.*

Hotel Mac Rae

$ | **HOTEL** | Family-owned for more than a century, the fourth generation now operates this boutique hotel right on Crescent Avenue, with a few rooms overlooking the beach and Avalon Bay. One of the best-priced hotels next to the beach, guests receive a complimentary continental breakfast; beach towels; Internet access; and after checkout luggage storage and shower facility to use after spending a day at the beach and before boarding a return boat home. **Pros:** great value for location; spectacular beachfront views; free breakfast. **Cons:** no elevator and hotel is on the second floor; basic rooms and furniture; restaurants and bars below can mean noise in the evening. *Rooms from: $150 409 Crescent Ave. 310/510–0246 www.HotelMacRae.com 26 rooms Free breakfast.*

Hotel Metropole and Market Place

$$ | **HOTEL** | **FAMILY** | Set over a bustling maze of shops, this hotel offers urban style in a quaint setting. **Pros:** family-friendly vibe; outdoor hot tub and sundeck; convenient location. **Cons:** some rooms on small side; soundproofing issues; no hotel shuttle to dock. *Rooms from: $250 205 Crescent Ave. 310/510–1884, 800/541–8528 www.hotel-metropole.com 53 rooms No meals.*

Hotel Vista del Mar

$$ | **HOTEL** | **FAMILY** | On the bay-facing Crescent Avenue, this third-floor property is steps from the beach, where complimentary towels, chairs, and umbrellas await guests. **Pros:** comfortable beds; central location; in-room fireplace. **Cons:** no restaurant or spa facilities; few rooms with ocean views; no elevator. *Rooms from: $235 417 Crescent Ave. 310/510–1452, 800/601–3836 www.hotel-vistadelmar.com 14 rooms Free breakfast.*

Mt. Ada

$$$$ | **B&B/INN** | If you stay in the 1921 mansion where Wrigley Jr. once lived, you can enjoy all the comforts of a millionaire's home—at a millionaire's prices. **Pros:** a step back in timeless charm; all-inclusive services, including complimentary shuttle from ferry dock; incredible canyon, bay, and ocean views. **Cons:** some rooms and bathrooms are small; a far walk into town; expensive. *Rooms from: $600 398 Wrigley Rd. 310/510–7330 www.visitcatalinaisland.com 6 rooms All-inclusive.*

Pavilion Hotel

$$ | **HOTEL** | **FAMILY** | This mid-century modern–style hotel is Avalon's most citified spot, though just a few steps from the sand. **Pros:** steps from the beach and harbor; plush bedding; chic decor. **Cons:** no pool; rooms near stairs can be noisy; no elevator. *Rooms from: $275 513 Crescent Ave. 310/510–1788 www.visitcatalinaisland.com 71 rooms No meals.*

★ Zane Grey Pueblo

$$$$ | **HOTEL** | The prolific best-selling Western novelist Zane Grey built his home as a retreat to take in the views of Avalon while writing over 100 books; his home was turned into this quaint boutique hotel in 1939. **Pros:** breathtaking views; complimentary continental breakfast; heated swimming pool with ocean views. **Cons:** three-story addition has no elevator; a hike up a hill from town; bell

tower chimes can be loud for some people. $ *Rooms from: $400* ✉ *199 Chimes Tower Rd.* ☎ *310/510–0966* 🌐 *www.zanegreyhotel.com* 🛏 *17 rooms* 🍴 *Free breakfast.*

Activities

BICYCLING

Brown's Bikes

BICYCLING | FAMILY | Look for rentals on Crescent Avenue and Pebbly Beach Road, where Brown's Bikes is located. Beach cruisers start at $25 per day, mountain bikes are $30 per day, and electric bikes are $50 for a day rental, and a good choice for Catalina's hills. ✉ *107 Pebbly Beach Rd.* ☎ *310/510–0986* 🌐 *www.catalinabiking.com.*

DIVING AND SNORKELING

The Casino Point Underwater Park, with its handful of wrecks and ample sea life, is best suited for diving. Lover's Cove is better for snorkeling (but you'll share the area with glass-bottom boats). Both are protected marine preserves.

Catalina Divers Supply

SCUBA DIVING | Head to Catalina Divers Supply to rent equipment, sign up for guided scuba and snorkel tours, and attend certification classes. It also has an outpost at the Dive Park at Casino Point and one on the Green Pleasure Pier. Both offer gear rental and tank air fills. ✉ *1 Casino Way* ☎ *310/510–0330* 🌐 *www.catalinadiverssupply.com.*

HIKING

Catalina Island Conservancy

HIKING/WALKING | FAMILY | Permits from the Catalina Island Conservancy are required for hiking into Santa Catalina Island's rugged interior, where there are more than 165 miles of trails of all levels to explore. If you plan to backpack overnight, you'll need a camping reservation. The interior is dry and desertlike; bring plenty of water, sunblock, a hat, and all necessary supplies. The permits are free or you can make a donation to the Conservancy. You don't need a permit for shorter hikes, such as the 20-minute one from Avalon to the Wrigley Botanical Garden. It's also possible to hike between Avalon and Two Harbors, starting at the Hogsback Gate, above Avalon, but the 28-mile journey has an elevation gain of 3,000 feet and is not for the weak. **■ TIP→ For a pleasant 4-mile hike out of Avalon, take Avalon Canyon Road to the Wrigley Botanical Garden and follow the trail to Lone Pine. At the top there's an amazing view of the Palisades cliffs and, beyond them, the sea.** ✉ *708 Crescent Ave.* ☎ *310/510–2595* 🌐 *www.catalinaconservancy.org.*

Chapter 6

LOS ANGELES

Updated by
Paul Feinstein, Michelle Rae Uy,
and Candice Yacono

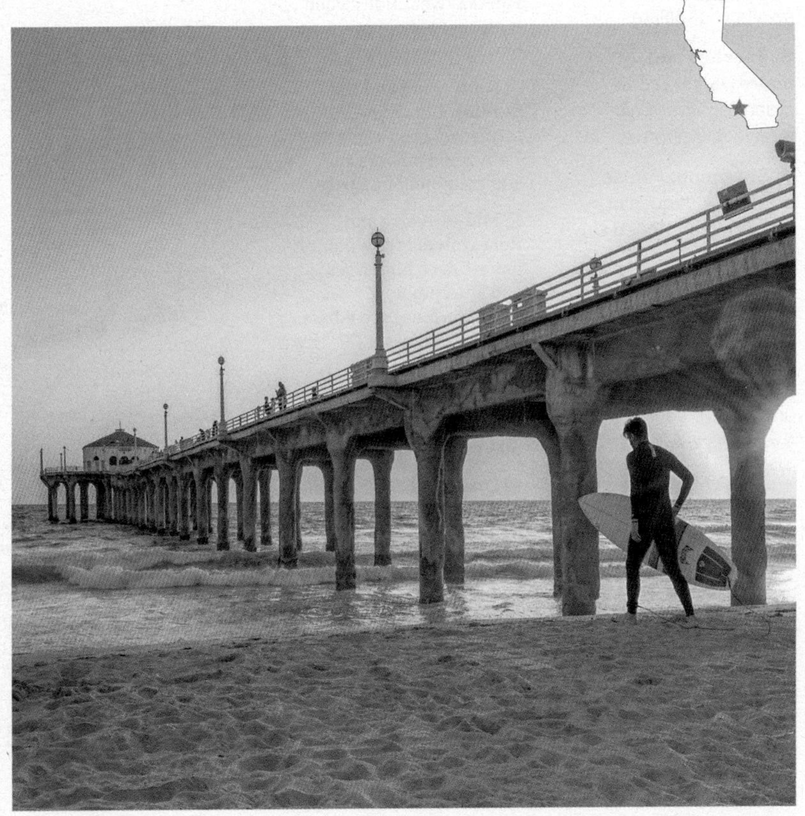

Sights ★★★★★

Restaurants ★★★★★

Hotels ★★★★★

Shopping ★★★★★

Nightlife ★★★★☆

WELCOME TO LOS ANGELES

TOP REASONS TO GO

★ **Seeing stars:** Both through the telescope atop Griffith Park and among the residents of Beverly Hills.

★ **Good eats:** From food trucks to fine dining, an unparalleled meal awaits your palate.

★ **Beaches and boardwalks:** The dream of '80s Venice is alive in California.

★ **Shopping:** Peruse eclectic boutiques or window-shop on Rodeo Drive.

★ **Architecture:** Art-deco wonders to Frank Gehry masterpieces abound.

★ **Scenic drives:** You haven't seen the sunset until you've seen it from a winding L.A. road.

1 **Santa Monica and Venice.** Expect a lively beach scene and a raffish mix of artists, beach punks, and yuppies.

2 **Beverly Hills.** The glamour here includes Rodeo Drive's excesses—both wretched and ravishing.

3 **West Hollywood and Fairfax.** West Hollywood is all about shopping, dining, and nightlife.

4 **Hollywood and the Studios.** Glitzy and tarnished, good and bad—Hollywood mirrors the entertainment business.

5 **Mid-Wilshire and Koreatown.** Mid-Wilshire has art-deco high-rises and Museum Row. Koreatown has great bars and restaurants.

6 **Downtown Los Angeles.** This older district shows off spectacular modern architecture.

7 **Los Feliz, Silver Lake, and the Eastside.** Head east for everything young, cool, and hip.

8 **Pasadena.** Arts and Crafts homes and two exceptional museums mark this genteel area.

9 **Malibu and the Beaches.** En route to chichi Malibu, stop at a white-sand beach to spy on sea lions or migrating whales.

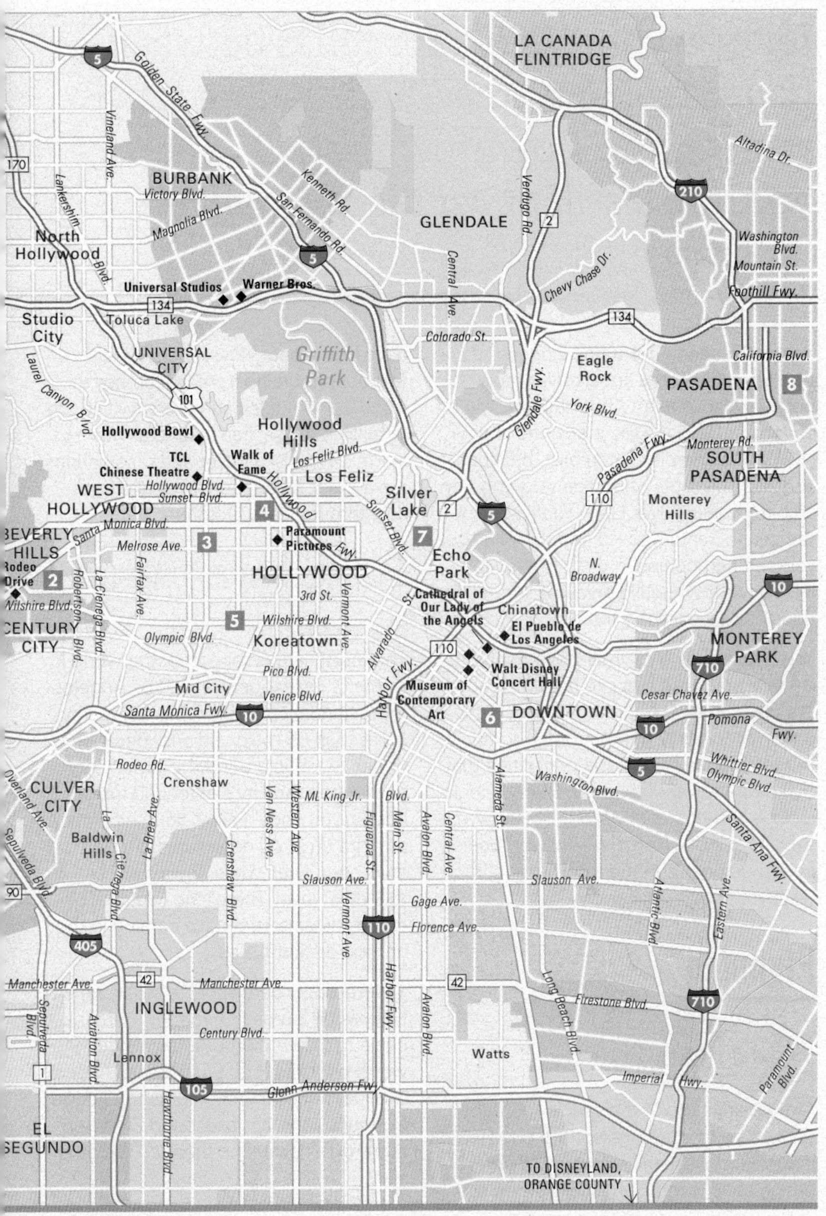
LA CANADA FLINTRIDGE
BURBANK
GLENDALE
North Hollywood
Studio City
Toluca Lake
UNIVERSAL CITY
Griffith Park
Hollywood Hills
Los Feliz
Silver Lake
Echo Park
Eagle Rock
PASADENA
SOUTH PASADENA
Monterey Hills
WEST HOLLYWOOD
BEVERLY HILLS
Rodeo Drive
HOLLYWOOD
CENTURY CITY
Koreatown
Mid City
Chinatown
MONTEREY PARK
DOWNTOWN
CULVER CITY
Baldwin Hills
Crenshaw
INGLEWOOD
Lennox
Watts
EL SEGUNDO
Universal Studios
Warner Bros.
Hollywood Bowl
TCL Chinese Theatre
Walk of Fame
Paramount Pictures
Cathedral of Our Lady of the Angels
El Pueblo de Los Angeles
Walt Disney Concert Hall
Museum of Contemporary Art
Golden State Fwy.
Kenneth Rd.
San Fernando Rd.
Vineland Ave.
Lankershim Blvd.
Victory Blvd.
Magnolia Blvd.
Verdugo Rd.
Central Ave.
Chevy Chase Dr.
Altadina Dr.
Washington Blvd.
Mountain St.
Foothill Fwy.
Colorado St.
California Blvd.
Glendale Fwy.
York Blvd.
Laurel Canyon Blvd.
Los Feliz Blvd.
Pasadena Fwy.
Monterey Rd.
Hollywood Blvd.
Sunset Blvd.
Hollywood Fwy.
Santa Monica Blvd.
Melrose Ave.
Fairfax Ave.
La Cienega Blvd.
Robertson Blvd.
Wilshire Blvd.
Olympic Blvd.
Vermont Ave.
3rd St.
Alvarado St.
N. Broadway
Pico Blvd.
Venice Blvd.
Harbor Fwy.
Santa Monica Fwy.
Cesar Chavez Ave.
Pomona Fwy.
Whittier Blvd.
Olympic Blvd.
Washington Blvd.
Santa Ana Fwy.
Rodeo Rd.
Overland Ave.
Sepulveda Blvd.
La Brea Ave.
Crenshaw Blvd.
Van Ness Ave.
Western Ave.
ML King Jr. Blvd.
Figueroa St.
Main St.
Avalon Blvd.
Central Ave.
Alameda St.
Slauson Ave.
Gage Ave.
Florence Ave.
Atlantic Blvd.
Eastern Ave.
Manchester Ave.
Long Beach Blvd.
Firestone Blvd.
Aviation Blvd.
Century Blvd.
Imperial Hwy.
Paramount Blvd.
Glenn Anderson Fwy.
Hawthorne Blvd.
TO DISNEYLAND, ORANGE COUNTY
5
170
134
101
2
210
110
10
710
90
405
42
105
1
2
3
4
5
6
7
8

Los Angeles is a polarizing place, but those who hate it just haven't found their niche—there's truly a corner of the city for everyone. Drive for miles between towering palm trees, bodega-lined streets, and Downtown's skyscrapers, and you'll still never discover all of L.A.'s hidden gems.

Yes, you'll encounter traffic-clogged freeways, but there are also walkable pockets like Venice's Abbot Kinney. You'll drive past Beverly Hills mansions and spy palaces perched atop hills, but you'll also see the roots of mid-century modern architecture in Silver Lake. You'll soak up the sun in Santa Monica and then find yourself barhopping in the city's revitalized Downtown while enjoying scrumptious fish tacos along the way.

You might think that you'll have to spend most of your visit in a car, but that's not the case. In fact, exploring by foot is the only way to really get to know the various fringe neighborhoods and mini-cities that make up the vast L.A. area. But no single locale—whether it's Malibu, Downtown, Beverly Hills, or Burbank—fully embodies Los Angeles. It's in the mix that you'll discover the city's character.

Planning

When to Go

Almost any time of the year is the right time to go to Los Angeles; the climate is mild and pleasant year-round. Winter brings crisp, sunny, unusually smogless days from about November to May (expect brief rains from December to April). Los Angeles summers, which are virtually rainless, can lead to air-quality alerts. Prices skyrocket and reservations are a must when tourism peaks from July through early October.

Getting Here and Around

AIR TRAVEL

The fourth-largest airport in the world in terms of passenger traffic, Los Angeles International Airport (LAX) is served by more than 65 major airlines. Because of heavy traffic around the airport (not to mention the city's extended rush hours), you should allow yourself plenty of extra time. All departures are from the upper level, while arrivals are on the lower level. There's no Metro in or out of the airport, but it's coming in the not-too-distant-future.

Several secondary airports serve the city. Hollywood Burbank Airport in Burbank is close to Downtown L.A., so it's definitely worth checking out. Long Beach Airport is equally convenient. Flights to Orange County's John Wayne Airport are often more expensive than those to the other secondary airports. Also check out L.A./ Ontario International Airport.

Driving times from LAX to different parts of the city vary considerably: it will take you 20 minutes to get to Santa Monica, 30 minutes to Beverly Hills, and at least 45 minutes to Downtown L.A. In heavy traffic it can take much longer. From Hollywood Burbank Airport, it's 30 minutes to Downtown. Plan on at least 45 minutes for the drive from Long Beach Airport, and an hour from John Wayne Airport or L.A./ Ontario International Airport.

AIRPORTS Hollywood Burbank Airport. (*BUR*) ✉ *2627 N. Hollywood Way, near I–5 and U.S. 101, Burbank* ☎ *818/840–8840* 🌐 *www.hollywoodburbankairport.com.* **John Wayne Airport.** (*SNA*) ✉ *18601 Airport Way, Santa Ana* ☎ *949/252–5200* 🌐 *www.ocair.com.* **L.A./Ontario International Airport.** (*ONT*) ✉ *2500 E. Airport Dr., off I–10, Ontario* ☎ *909/544–5300* 🌐 *www.flyontario.com.* **Long Beach Airport.** (*LGB*) ✉ *4100 Donald Douglas Dr., Long Beach* ☎ *562/570–2600* 🌐 *www.lgb.org.* **Los Angeles International Airport.** (*LAX*) ✉ *1 World Way, off Hwy. 1* ☎ *855/463–5252* 🌐 *www.flylax.com.*

SHUTTLES FlyAway. ☎ *714/507–1170* 🌐 *www.flylax.com/en/flyaway-bus.* **SuperShuttle.** ☎ *323/775–6600, 800/258–3826* 🌐 *www.supershuttle.com.*

BUS TRAVEL

Inadequate public transportation has plagued L.A. for decades. That said, many local trips can be made, with time and patience, by buses run by the Los Angeles County Metropolitan Transit Authority. In certain cases—visiting the Getty Center, for instance, or Universal Studios—buses may be your best option. There's a special Dodger Stadium Express that shuttles passengers between Union Station and the world-famous ballpark for home games. It's free if you have a ticket in hand and saves you parking-related stress.

Metro Buses cost $1.75, plus 50¢ for each transfer to another bus or to the subway. A one-day pass costs $7, and a weekly pass is $25 for unlimited travel on all buses and trains. Passes are valid from Sunday through Saturday. For the fastest service, look for the red-and-white Metro Rapid buses; these stop less frequently and are able to extend green lights. There are 25 Metro Rapid routes, including along Wilshire and Vermont boulevards.

Other bus services make it possible to explore the entire metropolitan area. DASH minibuses cover six different circular routes in Hollywood, Mid-Wilshire, and Downtown. You pay 50¢ every time you get on. The Santa Monica Municipal Bus Line, also known as the Big Blue Bus, is a pleasant and inexpensive way to move around the Westside. Trips cost $1.

You can pay your fare in cash on MTA, Santa Monica, and Culver City buses, but you must have exact change. You can buy MTA TAP cards at Metro Rail stations, customer centers throughout the city, and some convenience and grocery stores.

CONTACTS Culver CityBus. ☎ *310/253–6510* 🌐 *www.culvercitybus.com.* **DASH.** ☎ *310/808–2273* 🌐 *www.ladottransit.com.* **Los Angeles County Metropolitan Transit Authority.** ☎ *323/466–3876* 🌐 *www.metro.net.* **Santa Monica Municipal Bus Line.** ☎ *310/451–5444* 🌐 *www.bigbluebus.com.*

CAR TRAVEL

If you're used to urban driving, you shouldn't have too much trouble navigating the streets of Los Angeles. If not, L.A. can be unnerving. However, the city has evolved with drivers in mind. Streets are wide and parking garages abound, so it's more car-friendly than many older big cities.

If you get discombobulated while on the freeway, remember this rule of thumb: even-numbered freeways run east and west, odd-numbered freeways run north and south.

There are plenty of identical or similarly named streets in L.A. (Beverly Boulevard and Beverly Drive, for example), so be as specific as you can when asking directions or inputting into a map app. Expect sudden changes in addresses as streets pass through neighborhoods, then incorporated cities, then back into neighborhoods. This can be most bewildering on Robertson Boulevard, an otherwise useful north–south artery that, by crossing through L.A., West Hollywood, and Beverly Hills, dips in and out of several such numbering shifts in a matter of miles.

METRO/PUBLIC TRANSPORT

Metro Rail covers only a small part of L.A.'s vast expanse, but it's convenient, frequent, and inexpensive. Most popular with visitors is the underground Red Line, which runs from Downtown's Union Station through Mid-Wilshire, Hollywood, and Universal City on its way to North Hollywood, stopping at the most popular tourist destinations along the way.

The light-rail Green Line stretches from Redondo Beach to Norwalk, while the partially underground Blue Line travels from Downtown to the South Bay. The monorail-like Gold Line extends from Union Station to Pasadena and out to the deep San Gabriel Valley and Azusa. The Orange Line, a 14-mile bus corridor, connects the North Hollywood subway station with the western San Fernando Valley.

Most recently extended was the Expo Line, which connects Downtown to the Westside, and terminates in Santa Monica, two blocks from the Pacific Ocean.

Daily service is offered from about 4:30 am to 12:30 am, with departures every 5 to 15 minutes. On weekends trains run until 2 am. Buy tickets from station vending machines; fares are $1.75, or $7 for an all-day pass. Bicycles are allowed on Metro Rail trains at all times.

CONTACTS Los Angeles County Metropolitan Transit Authority. ☎ *323/466–3876* 🌐 *www.metro.net.*

RIDE-SHARING AND TAXI TRAVEL

Request a ride using apps like Lyft or Uber, and a driver will usually arrive within minutes. Fares increase during busy times, but it's often the most affordable option, especially for the convenience.

Instead of trying to hail a taxi on the street, phone one of the many taxi companies. The Curb Taxi app allows for online hailing of L.A. taxis. The metered rate is $2.70 per mile, plus a $2.85 per-fare charge and an additional $2 curb fee. Taxi rides from LAX have an additional $4 surcharge. Be aware that distances are greater than they might appear on the map so fares add up quickly.

CONTACTS Beverly Hills Cab Co. ☎ *800/273–6611* 🌐 *www.beverlyhillscab-co.com.* **Independent Cab Co.** ☎ *800/521–8294* 🌐 *www.lataxi.com/new.* **LA Checker Cab.** ☎ *800/300–5007* 🌐 *www.ineedtaxi.com.* **United Independent Taxi.** ☎ *800/822–8294, 323/653–5050 text to order taxi* 🌐 *www.unitedtaxi.com.* **Yellow Cab Los Angeles.** ☎ *424/222–2222* 🌐 *www.layellowcab.com.*

TRAIN TRAVEL

Downtown's Union Station is one of the great American railroad terminals. The interior includes comfortable seating, restaurants, and several bars. As the city's rail hub, it's the place to catch an Amtrak, Metrolink commuter train, or the Red, Gold, or Purple lines. Among Amtrak's Southern California routes are 11 daily trips to San Diego and 6 to Santa Barbara. Amtrak's luxury *Coast Starlight* travels along the spectacular coastline from Seattle to Los Angeles in just a day and a half (though it's often a little late). The *Sunset Limited* arrives from New Orleans, and the *Southwest Chief* comes from Chicago.

CONTACTS Metrolink. ☎ *800/371–5465* 🌐 *www.metrolinktrains.com.* **Union Station.** ✉ *800 N. Alameda St., Downtown* ☎ *213/683–6979* 🌐 *www.unionstationla.com* Ⓜ *Union Station.*

Restaurants

Los Angeles may be known for its beach living and celebrity-infused backdrop, but it was once a farm town. The hillsides were covered in citrus orchards and dairy farms, and agriculture was a major industry. Today, even as L.A. is urbanized, the city's culinary landscape has reembraced a local, sustainable, and seasonal philosophy at many levels—from fine dining to street snacks.

With a growing interest in farm-to-fork, the city's farmers' market scene has exploded, becoming popular at big-name restaurants and small eateries alike. In Hollywood and Santa Monica you can often find high-profile chefs scouring farm stands for fresh produce.

The status of the celebrity chef carries weight around this town. People follow the culinary zeitgeist with the same fervor as celebrity gossip. You can queue up with the hungry hordes at Nancy Silverton's **Mozza,** or try and snag a reservation at Ludo Lefebvre's ever-popular **Petit Trois** or David Chang's L.A. outpost, **Majordomo.**

International eats continue to be a backbone of the L.A. dining scene. People head to Koreatown for epic Korean cooking and late-night coffeehouses and to West L.A. for phenomenal sushi. Latin food is well represented in the city, making it tough to choose between Guatemalan eateries, Peruvian restaurants, nouveau Mexican bistros, and Tijuana-style taco trucks. With so many dining options, sometimes the best strategy is simply to drive and explore.

Hotels

When it comes to finding a place to stay, travelers have never been more spoiled for choice than in today's Los Angeles. From luxurious digs in Beverly Hills and along the coast to budget boutiques in Hollywood, hotels are stepping up service, upgrading amenities, and trying all-new concepts, like upscale hostels and retro-chic motels. Hotels in Los Angeles today are more than just a place to rest your head; they're a key part of the experience.

Restaurant and hotel reviews have been shortened. For full information, visit Fodors.com. Restaurant prices are the average cost of a main course at dinner or, if dinner is not served, at lunch. Hotel prices are for the lowest cost of a standard double room in high season.

What It Costs

$	$$	$$$	$$$$
RESTAURANTS			
under $14	$14–$22	$23–$31	over $31
HOTELS			
under $200	$200–$300	$301–$400	over $400

Nightlife

Los Angeles is not the city that never sleeps—instead it parties until 2 am (save for the secret after-hours parties at private clubs, Hollywood Hills mansions, and warehouses) and wakes up to imbibe green juices and breakfast burritos as hangover cures or to sweat it out in a yoga class. Whether you plan to test your limit at historic establishments Downtown or take advantage of a cheap happy hour at a Hollywood dive, this city's nightlife has something for you.

A night out in Los Angeles can simultaneously surprise and impress. Seeing an unscheduled set by an A-list comedian at a comedy club, being talked into singing karaoke at the diviest place you've ever seen, dancing at a bar with no dance floor because, well, the DJ is just too good at his job—going out isn't always what you expect, but it certainly is never boring.

The focus of nightlife once centered on the Sunset Strip, with its multitude of bars, rock clubs, and dance spots, but more neighborhoods are competing with each other and forcing the nightlife scene to evolve. Although the Strip can be a worthwhile trip, other areas of the city are catching people's attention. Downtown Los Angeles, for instance, is a destination in its own right. Other areas foster more of a neighborhood vibe. Silver Lake and Los Feliz have both cultivated a relaxed environment.

Performing Arts

The arts scene in Los Angeles extends beyond the screen and onto the stage. A place of artistic innovation and history, one can discover new and challenging theatrical works across L.A. stages, while the city still maintains a respect for tradition with its restored theaters and classic plays. See live music at impeccably designed amphitheaters like the Hollywood Bowl or listen in on captivating lectures by authors and directors at various intimate spaces. In homage to the city's roots as a filmmaking mecca, there are also retrospectives and rare screenings in movie theaters all over the city, often followed by Q&As with the cast.

Visitor Information

Discover Los Angeles, the official tourism site, has an annually updated general information packet that includes suggestions for entertainment, lodging, and dining and a list of special events. There are two visitor information centers, both accessible to Metro stops: the Hollywood & Highland Center and Union Station.

CONTACTS Discover Los Angeles. ☎ *213/624–7300* 🌐 *www.discoverlosangeles.com.*

Santa Monica and Venice

Santa Monica and Venice are two of the region's most iconic destinations, but while Santa Monica has its eyes firmly on the future, Venice enjoys indulging a bit in its past.

Silicon Beach, Southern California's tech hub, is centered on the Santa Monica area, which means employees from hundreds of companies like Activision, Hulu, and Snap (of Snapchat fame) flood the area and influence the flavor of its shops and restaurants. (Silicon Beach's influence also impacts many hotel amenity lists, to your benefit.) The Santa Monica Pier, with its Ferris wheel and roller coaster, is the scene of a thousand movie and television show filmings, from *Forrest Gump* to *Iron Man,* while Venice Beach has conjured images of greased-up bodybuilders, boho hippies, and boardwalk palm readers for generations.

Santa Monica

Sights

★ Santa Monica Pier

CAROUSEL | FAMILY | Souvenir shops, carnival games, arcades, eateries, an outdoor trapeze school, a small amusement park, and an aquarium all contribute to the festive atmosphere of this truncated pier at the foot of Colorado Boulevard below Palisades Park. The pier's trademark 46-horse Looff Carousel, built in 1922, has appeared in several films, including *The Sting.* The Soda Jerks ice-cream fountain (named for the motion the attendant makes when pulling the machine's

Santa Monica Pier's West Coaster and Pacific Wheel provide incredible ocean views.

arm) inside the carousel building is a pier staple. Free concerts are held on the pier in the summer. ✉ *Colorado Ave., Santa Monica* ☎ *310/458–8901* 🌐 *www.santamonicapier.org.*

Santa Monica State Beach

BEACH—SIGHT | The first beach you'll hit after the Santa Monica Freeway (Interstate 10) runs into the Pacific Coast Highway, wide and sandy Santa Monica is *the* place for sunning and socializing. The Strand, which runs across the beach and for 22 miles in total, is popular among walkers, joggers, and bicyclists. Be prepared for a mob scene on summer weekends, when parking becomes an expensive ordeal. Swimming is fine (with the usual poststorm-pollution caveat); for surfing, go elsewhere. For a memorable view, climb up the stairway over PCH to Palisades Park, at the top of the bluffs. Free summer concerts are held on the pier on Thursday evening. **Amenities:** parking; lifeguards; toilets; food and drink; showers; water sports. **Best for:** partiers; sunset; surfing; swimming; walking. ✉ *1642 Promenade, PCH at California Incline, Santa Monica* ☎ *310/458–8573* 🌐 *www.smgov.net/portals/beach* 🎫 *Parking from $7.*

★ Third Street Promenade and Santa Monica Place

COMMERCIAL CENTER | Stretch your legs along this pedestrian-only, three-block stretch of 3rd Street, close to the Pacific, lined with jacaranda trees, ivy-topiary dinosaur fountains, strings of lights, and branches of nearly every major U.S. retail chain; indeed, it always seems to house the most-coveted brands for each generation of teens. Outdoor cafés, street vendors, movie theaters, and a rich nightlife make this a main gathering spot for locals, visitors, street artists and musicians, and performance artists. Plan a night just to take it all in or take an afternoon for a long people-watching stroll. There's plenty of parking in city structures on the streets flanking the promenade. **Santa Monica Place,** at the south end of the promenade, is a sleek outdoor mall and foodie haven. Its three

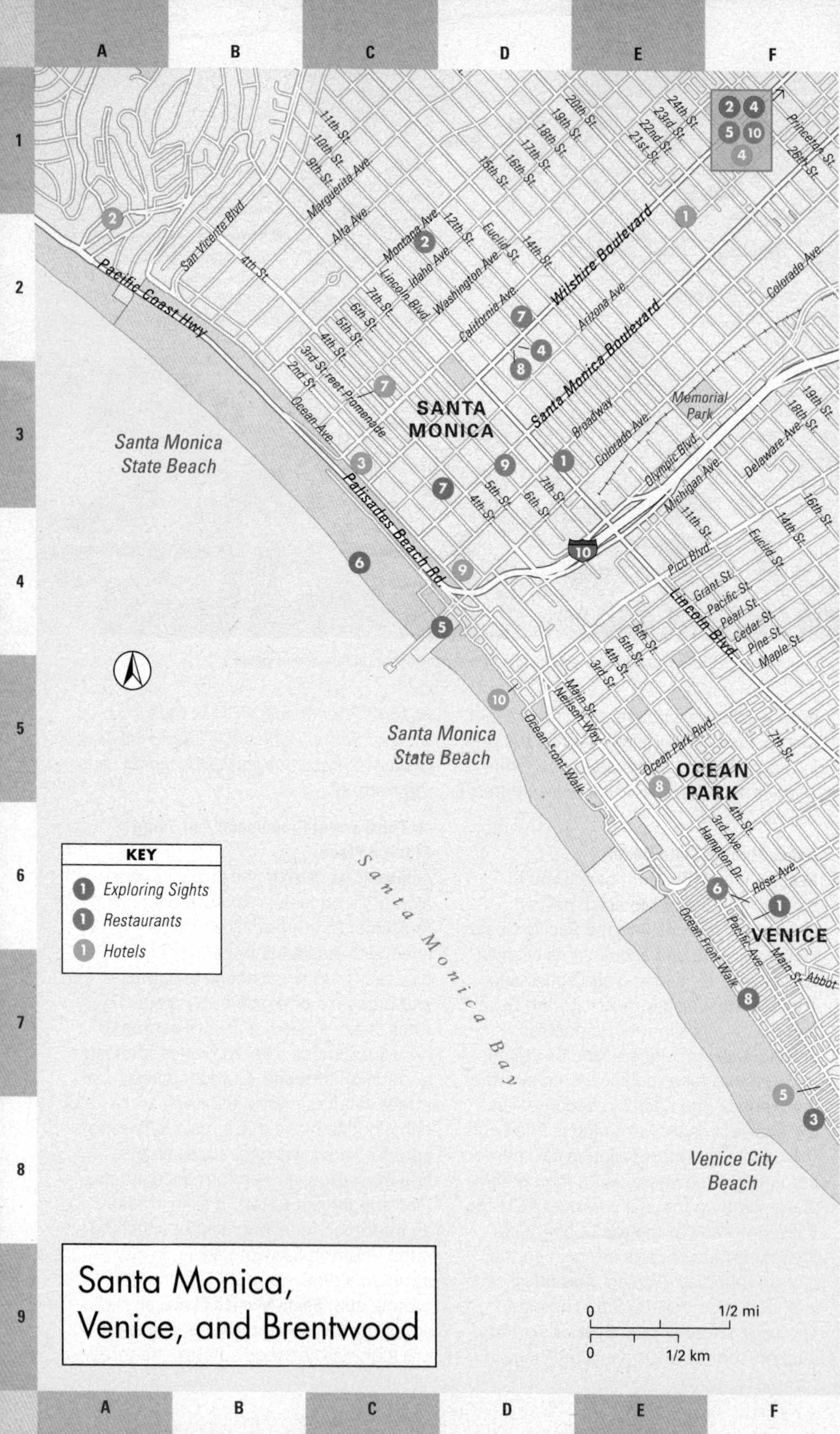

A B C D E F
1 2 3 4 5 6 7 8 9
Santa Monica, Venice, and Brentwood
KEY
Exploring Sights
Restaurants
Hotels
SANTA MONICA
OCEAN PARK
VENICE
Santa Monica State Beach
Santa Monica State Beach
Venice City Beach
Santa Monica Bay
Pacific Coast Hwy
Palisades Beach Rd.
Wilshire Boulevard
Santa Monica Boulevard
Lincoln Blvd.
Olympic Blvd.
Pico Blvd.
Ocean Park Blvd.
Ocean Front Walk
Main St.
Neilson Way
San Vicente Blvd.
Montana Ave.
Idaho Ave.
Washington Ave.
California Ave.
Arizona Ave.
Broadway
Colorado Ave.
Michigan Ave.
Delaware Ave.
Princeton St.
Marguerita Ave.
Alta Ave.
Euclid St.
3rd Street Promenade
Ocean Ave.
Grant St.
Pacific St.
Pearl St.
Cedar St.
Pine St.
Maple St.
Hampton Dr.
Rose Ave.
Pacific Ave.
Abbot
Memorial Park
10
0 1/2 mi
0 1/2 km

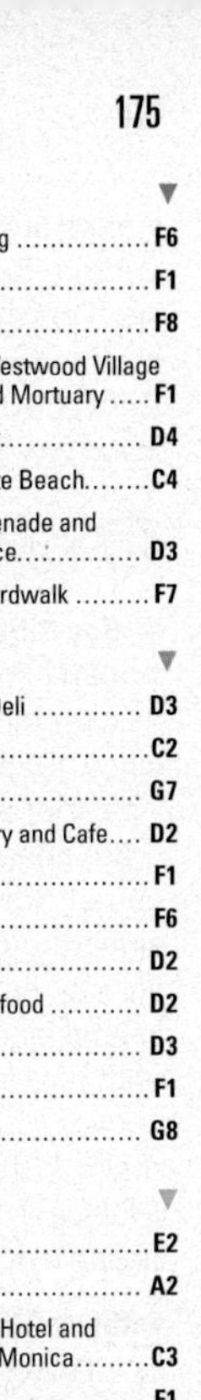

Sights

1 Binoculars Building F6
2 The Getty Center.................... F1
3 Muscle Beach F8
4 Pierce Brothers Westwood Village Memorial Park and Mortuary F1
5 Santa Monica Pier................. D4
6 Santa Monica State Beach........ C4
7 Third Street Promenade and Santa Monica Place............. D3
8 Venice Beach Boardwalk F7

Restaurants

1 Bay Cities Italian Deli D3
2 Father's Office C2
3 Gjelina.............................. G7
4 Huckleberry Bakery and Cafe.... D2
5 Lady Chocolatt....................... F1
6 Rose Cafe........................... F6
7 Rustic Canyon....................... D2
8 Santa Monica Seafood D2
9 Tar and Roses...................... D3
10 Toscana............................ F1
11 Venice Whaler G8

Hotels

1 The Ambrose........................ E2
2 Channel Road Inn.................. A2
3 Fairmont Miramar Hotel and Bungalows Santa Monica.........C3
4 Hotel Bel-Air F1
5 Hotel Erwin F7
6 The Kinney.......................... I7
7 Palihouse Santa Monica...........C3
8 Sea Shore Motel.................... E5
9 Shore Hotel......................... D4
10 Shutters on the Beach D5

stories are home to Nordstrom, Louis Vuitton, Coach, and other upscale retailers. Don't miss the ocean views from the rooftop food court. ✉ *3rd St., between Colorado and Wilshire Blvds., Santa Monica* 🌐 *www.downtownsm.com.*

 Restaurants

★ Bay Cities Italian Deli

$ | **DELI** | Part deli, part market, Bay Cities has been home to incredible Italian subs since 1925. This renowned counter-service spot is always crowded (best to order ahead), but monster subs run the gamut from the mighty meatball to the signature Godmother, made with prosciutto, ham, capicola, mortadella, Genoa salami, and provolone. **Known for:** market with rare imports; old-school, deli-style service; huge sandwiches. $ *Average main: $10* ✉ *1517 Lincoln Blvd., Santa Monica* ☎ *310/395–8279* 🌐 *www.baycitiesitaliandeli.com* ⊗ *Closed Mon.*

Father's Office

$$ | **AMERICAN** | Distinguished by its vintage neon sign, this gastropub is famous for handcrafted beers and a brilliant signature burger. Topped with Gruyère and Maytag blue cheeses, arugula, caramelized onions, and applewood-smoked bacon compote, the Office Burger is a guilty pleasure worth waiting in line for, which is usually required. **Known for:** addictive sweet potato fries; strict no-substitutions policy; 36 craft beers on tap. $ *Average main: $15* ✉ *1018 Montana Ave., Santa Monica* ☎ *310/736–2224* 🌐 *www.fathersoffice.com* ⊗ *No lunch weekdays.*

Huckleberry Bakery and Cafe

$$ | **AMERICANAMERICAN** | **FAMILY** | Founded by Santa Monica natives, Huckleberry brings together the best ingredients from local farmers and growers to craft diner-style comfort food with a chic twist. Everything is made on-site, even the hot sauce and almond milk. **Known for:** from-scratch diner-style breakfast options; delectable pastries; green eggs and Niman Ranch ham. $ *Average main: $14* ✉ *1014 Wilshire Blvd., Santa Monica* ☎ *310/451–2311* 🌐 *www.huckleberrycafe.com.*

★ Rustic Canyon

$$$$ | **MODERN AMERICAN** | A Santa Monica mainstay, the seasonally changing menu at this farm-to-table restaurant consistently upends norms and has even earned a Michelin star. The homey, minimalist space offers sweeping views of Wilshire Boulevard, and on any given night the menu of California cuisine may include Channel Island rockfish with shelling beans and Sun Gold tomatoes, or buttered ricotta dumplings with golden chanterelles and Coolea cheese. **Known for:** never-ending wine list; knowledgeable staff; everything is made in-house. $ *Average main: $35* ✉ *1119 Wilshire Blvd., Santa Monica* ☎ *310/393–7050* 🌐 *www.rusticcanyonrestaurant.com.*

Santa Monica Seafood

$$ | **SEAFOOD** | **FAMILY** | A Southern California favorite that seems like a tourist trap at first blush but decidedly isn't, this Italian seafood haven has been serving up fresh fish since 1939. This freshness comes from its pedigree as the largest seafood distributor in the Southwest. **Known for:** deliciously seasoned rainbow trout; oyster bar; historic fish market. $ *Average main: $20* ✉ *1000 Wilshire Blvd., Santa Monica* ☎ *310/393–5244* 🌐 *www.santamonicaseafood.com.*

★ Tar and Roses

$$$ | **MODERN AMERICAN** | This small and dimly lit romantic spot in Santa Monica is full of adventurous global options, like octopus skewers and venison loin. The new American cuisine, which is centered on the restaurant's wood-fired oven, also features standouts like braised lamb belly with minted apple chutney and drool-worthy strawberry ricotta crostata with honeycomb ice cream for dessert. **Known for:** phenomenal oxtail dumplings; delicious hanger steak; ever-changing

menu. $ *Average main: $30 ✉ 602 Santa Monica Blvd., Santa Monica ☎ 310/587–0700 🌐 www.tarandroses.com.*

 Hotels

The Ambrose

$$$ | **HOTEL** | Tranquillity pervades the airy, California Craftsman–style, four-story Ambrose, which blends right into its mostly residential Santa Monica neighborhood. **Pros:** "green" practices like nontoxic cleaners and recycling bins; partial ocean views; nice amenities (like car service and wine reception) for a $25 extra fee. **Cons:** quiet, residential area of Santa Monica; parking fee ($27); not walking distance to beach. $ *Rooms from: $359 ✉ 1255 20th St., Santa Monica ☎ 310/315–1555, 877/262–7673 🌐 www.ambrosehotel.com ⇆ 77 rooms 🍴 Free breakfast.*

★ Channel Road Inn

$$ | **B&B/INN** | A quaint surprise in Southern California, the Channel Road Inn is every bit the country retreat bed-and-breakfast lovers adore, with four-poster beds, fluffy duvets, and a cozy living room with a fireplace. **Pros:** free wine and cheese "minipicnic" each afternoon; home-cooked breakfast included; meditative rose garden on-site. **Cons:** no pool; need a car (or Uber) to get around; decidedly non-L.A. decor not for everyone. $ *Rooms from: $225 ✉ 219 W. Channel Rd., Santa Monica ☎ 310/459–1920 🌐 www.channelroadinn.com ⇆ 15 rooms 🍴 Free breakfast.*

Fairmont Miramar Hotel and Bungalows Santa Monica

$$$$ | **HOTEL** | A mammoth Moreton Bay fig tree dwarfs the main entrance of the 5-acre, beach-adjacent Santa Monica wellness retreat and lends its name to the inviting on-site Mediterranean-inspired restaurant, FIG, which focuses on local ingredients and frequently refreshes its menu. **Pros:** guests can play games on the heated patio; swanky open-air cocktail spot, the Bungalow, on-site; retrofitted '20s and '40s bungalows. **Cons:** all this luxury comes at a big price; standard rooms are on the small side; breakfast not included. $ *Rooms from: $599 ✉ 101 Wilshire Blvd., Santa Monica ☎ 310/576–7777, 866/540–4470 🌐 www.fairmont.com/santamonica ⇆ 334 rooms 🍴 No meals.*

Palihouse Santa Monica

$$$ | **HOTEL** | Tucked in a posh residential area three blocks from the sea and lively Third Street Promenade, Palihouse Santa Monica caters to design-minded world travelers, with spacious rooms and suites decked out in whimsical antiques. **Pros:** Apple TV in rooms; walking distance to Santa Monica attractions; fully equipped kitchens. **Cons:** no pool; decor might not appeal to more traditional travelers; parking fee ($45). $ *Rooms from: $355 ✉ 1001 3rd St., Santa Monica ☎ 310/394–1279 🌐 www.palihousesantamonica.com ⇆ 38 rooms 🍴 No meals.*

Sea Shore Motel

$ | **HOTEL** | On Santa Monica's busy Main Street, the Sea Shore (family-owned for almost 50 years) is a charming throwback to Route 66 and to '60s-style roadside motels in an ultratrendy neighborhood. **Pros:** close to beach and restaurants; free Wi-Fi, parking, and use of beach equipment; popular rooftop deck. **Cons:** street noise; motel-style decor and beds; not the Santa Monica style a lot of people are looking for. $ *Rooms from: $159 ✉ 2637 Main St., Santa Monica ☎ 310/392–2787 🌐 www.seashoremotel.com ⇆ 25 rooms 🍴 No meals.*

Shore Hotel

$$$$ | **HOTEL** | With views of the Santa Monica Pier, this hotel with a friendly staff offers eco-minded travelers stylish rooms with a modern design, just steps from the sand and sea. **Pros:** near beach and Third Street Promenade; rainfall showerheads; solar-heated pool and hot tub. **Cons:** expensive rooms and parking fees; fronting busy Ocean Avenue;

some sharing a room may be wary of the see-through shower. 💲 *Rooms from: $432* ✉ *1515 Ocean Ave., Santa Monica* ☎ *310/458–1515* 🌐 *shorehotel.com* 🛏 *164 rooms* 🍽 *No meals.*

★ Shutters on the Beach

$$$$ | **HOTEL** | **FAMILY** | Set right on the sand, this inn has become synonymous with staycations, with the beachfront location and show-house decor making it one of SoCal's most popular luxury hotels. **Pros:** built-in cabinets filled with art books and curios; rooms designed by Michael Smith; bathrooms come with whirlpool tubs. **Cons:** have to pay for extras like beach chairs; very expensive; breakfast not included. 💲 *Rooms from: $675* ✉ *1 Pico Blvd., Santa Monica* ☎ *310/458–0030, 800/334–9000* 🌐 *www.shuttersonthebeach.com* 🛏 *198 rooms* 🍽 *No meals.*

Nightlife

★ Chez Jay

BARS/PUBS | Around since 1959, this dive bar continues to be a well-loved place in Santa Monica. Everyone from the young to the old (including families) frequents this historical landmark. It's a charming place, from the well-worn booths with their red checkered tablecloths to the ship's wheel near the door. The backyard lounge is perfect for warm low-key days. ✉ *1657 Ocean Ave., Santa Monica* ☎ *310/395–1741* 🌐 *www.chezjays.com.*

The Galley

BARS/PUBS | Nostalgia reigns at this true neighborhood fixture, which has had the same owner for more than 30 years. As Santa Monica's oldest restaurant and bar, the Galley has a consistent nautical theme inside and out: the boatlike exterior features wavy blue neon lights and porthole windows; inside, fishing nets and anchors adorn the walls, and the whole place is aglow with colorful string lights. Most patrons tend to crowd the center bar, with the more dinner-oriented folks frequenting the booths. Prices are a good deal during "most hours" and a steal during "happy hours." And strangely enough, the secret-recipe salad dressing is justifiably famous. ✉ *2442 Main St., Santa Monica* ☎ *310/452–1934.*

Shopping

The Acorn Store

TOYS | **FAMILY** | Remember when toys didn't require computer programming? This old-fashioned shop (for ages 10 and under) sparks children's imaginations with dress-up clothes, picture books, and hand-painted wooden toys by brands like Poan and Haba. ✉ *1220 5th St., near Wilshire Blvd., Santa Monica* ☎ *310/451–5845* 🌐 *www.theacornstore.com.*

Limonaia

GIFTS/SOUVENIRS | This charming and cozy neighborhood boutique has something for every kind of gift recipient. Ben's Garden goods (pillows, coasters, trays, etc.) decorated with inspirational words, lovely cards for all occasions, beaded jewelry, cookbooks, and an extensive puzzle selection are just a few things shoppers can find here. ✉ *1325 Montana Ave., Santa Monica* ☎ *310/458–1858* 🌐 *www.shoplimonaia.com.*

Third Street Promenade

SHOPPING CENTERS/MALLS | There is no shortage of spots to shop everything from sporting goods to trendy fashions on this pedestrian-friendly strip. Outposts here are mainly of the chain variety, and in between splurging on books, clothing, sneakers, and more, shoppers can pop into one of the many eateries to stay satiated or even catch a movie at one of the theaters. Additionally, the chef-approved Farmers Market takes over twice a week, and with the beach just a few steps away, the destination is a quintessential California stop. ✉ *3rd St., between Broadway and Wilshire Blvd., Santa Monica.*

Venice

Sights

Binoculars Building

BUILDING | Frank Gehry is known around the world for his architectural masterpieces. In L.A. alone he's responsible for multiple houses and buildings like the Gehry Residence, Loyola Law School, and Walt Disney Hall. But one of his most interesting creations is the Binoculars Building, a quirky Venice spot that is exactly as advertised—a giant set of binoculars. The project was originally designed for the Chiat/Day advertising agency and today is home to one of Google's Silicon Beach offices. While you can't tour the building, you can take a clever Instagram shot out front. ✉ *340 Main St., Venice.*

Muscle Beach

LOCAL INTEREST | Bronzed young men bench-pressing five girls at once, weightlifters doing tricks on the sand—the Muscle Beach facility fired up the country's imagination from the get-go. There are actually two spots known as Muscle Beach. The original Muscle Beach, just south of the Santa Monica Pier, is where bodybuilders Jack LaLanne and Vic and Armand Tanny used to work out in the 1950s. When it was closed in 1959, the bodybuilders moved south along the beach to Venice, to a city-run facility known as "the Pen," and the Venice Beach spot inherited the Muscle Beach moniker. The spot is probably best known now as a place where a young Arnold Schwarzenegger first came to flex his muscles in the late '60s and began his rise to fame. The area now hosts a variety of sports and gymnastics events and the occasional "beach babe" beauty contests that always draw a crowd. But stop by any time during daylight for an eye-popping array of beefcakes (and would-be beefcakes). ✉ *1800 Ocean Front Walk, Venice* 🌐 *www.musclebeach.net.*

★ Venice Beach Boardwalk

PROMENADE | The surf and sand of Venice are fine, but the main attraction here is the boardwalk scene, which is a cosmos all its own. Go on weekend afternoons for the best people-watching experience. You can also swim, fish, surf, and skateboard, or play racquetball, handball, shuffleboard, and basketball (the boardwalk is the site of hotly contested pickup games). Or you can rent a bike or in-line skates and hit the Strand bike path, then pull up a seat at a sidewalk café and watch the action unfold. ✉ *1800 Ocean Front Walk, west of Pacific Ave., Venice* ☎ *310/392–4687* 🌐 *www.venicebeach.com.*

Restaurants

★ Gjelina

$$ | **AMERICAN** | This spot comes alive the moment you walk through the rustic wooden door and into a softly lit dining room with long communal tables. The menu is seasonal, with outstanding small plates, charcuterie, pastas, and pizza. **Known for:** lively crowd on the patio; late-night menu; Michelin-approved dishes like crispy duck leg confit. $ *Average main: $22* ✉ *1429 Abbot Kinney Blvd., Venice* ☎ *310/450–1429* 🌐 *www.gjelina.com.*

Rose Cafe

$$$ | **MODERN AMERICAN** | **FAMILY** | This indoor-outdoor restaurant has served Venice for decades but constantly reinvents itself, serving mouthwatering California cuisines with multiple patios, a full bar, and a bakery. Creative types loiter under the macramé chandeliers for the Wi-Fi and sip espressos, while young families gather out back to snack on smoked radiatore carbonara and crispy brussels sprouts. **Known for:** sophisticated but unpretentious vibe; location in the heart of Venice; lively patio seating. $ *Average main: $25* ✉ *220 Rose Ave., Venice* ☎ *310/399–0711* 🌐 *www.rosecafevenice.com.*

Venice Whaler
$$ | **AMERICAN** | This beachfront bar that's been the local watering hole for musicians like the Doors and the Beach Boys since 1944 boasts an amazing view and serves tasty California pub food like fish tacos, pulled-pork sliders, and avocado toast with a basic selection of beers. The Whaler Double Burger is an institution in itself. **Known for:** rock-n-roll history; great pub food; fun brunch. *Average main: $15* *10 W. Washington Blvd., Venice* *310/821–8737* *www.venicewhaler.com.*

Hotels

Hotel Erwin
$$$ | **HOTEL** | A boutique hotel a block off the Venice Beach Boardwalk, the Erwin will make you feel like a hipper version of yourself. **Pros:** dining emphasizing fresh ingredients; playful design in guest rooms; free Wi-Fi and use of hotel bikes. **Cons:** some rooms face a noisy alley; no pool; breakfast not included. *Rooms from: $369* *1697 Pacific Ave., Venice* *310/452–1111, 800/786–7789* *www.hotelerwin.com* *119 rooms* *No meals.*

★ **The Kinney**
$$ | **HOTEL** | Walking distance to Venice Beach and Abbot Kinney's artsy commercial strip, this playful hotel announces itself boldly with wall murals by Melissa Scrivner before you even enter the lobby. **Pros:** affordable, artistic rooms; Ping-Pong area; Jacuzzi bar. **Cons:** valet parking is a must ($15); hotel can get loud; some hipper-than-thou vibes. *Rooms from: $239* *737 Washington Blvd., Venice* *310/821–4455* *www.thekinneyvenicebeach.com* *68 rooms* *No meals.*

Nightlife

The Brig
BARS/PUBS | This charming bar has its pluses (interesting drinks, talented DJs) and minuses (ugh, parking) but is worth a look if you're in the area. There's always a food truck around, and the bar's fine with you bringing in outside food. *1515 Abbot Kinney Blvd., Venice* *310/399–7537* *www.thebrig.com.*

Shopping

General Store
GIFTS/SOUVENIRS | Right at home in the beachy, bohemian neighborhood, this well-curated shop is a decidedly contemporary take on the concept of general stores. The very definition of "California cool," General Store offers beauty and bath products loaded with organic natural ingredients, handmade ceramics, linen tea towels, and a spot-on selection of art books. Featuring an impressive number of local makers and designers, the boutique also sells modern, minimal clothing and has a kids' section that will wow even the hippest moms and dads. *1801 Lincoln Blvd., Venice* *310/751–6393* *www.shop-generalstore.com.*

Heist
CLOTHING | Owner Nilou Ghodsi has admitted that she stocks her Westside shop like an extension of her own closet, which in her case means keeping the focus on floaty, modern-yet-classic pieces as opposed to trendy ones. The airy boutique offers elegantly edgy separates from American designers like Nili Lotan and Ulla Johnson, as well as from hard-to-find French and Italian designers like Pas de Calais. *1100 Abbot Kinney Blvd., Venice* *310/450–6531* *www.shopheist.com.*

Strange Invisible Perfumes
PERFUME/COSMETICS | Finding your signature fragrance at this sleek Abbot Kinney boutique won't come cheap, but perfumer Alexandra Balahoutis takes creating her scents as seriously as a seasoned winemaker—and they're just as nuanced as a well-balanced glass of vino. Essences for the perfumes are organic, wild crafted, biodynamic, and bottled locally. Highlights from SI's core collection

include the cacao-spiked Dimanche and leathery Black Rosette. ✉ *1138 Abbot Kinney Blvd., Venice* ☎ *310/314–1505* 🌐 *www.siperfumes.com.*

Brentwood

Sights

★ The Getty Center

MUSEUM | FAMILY | Architect Richard Meier's Getty Center features stunning design, uncommon gardens, and fascinating art collections. The complex's rough-cut travertine marble skin seems to soak up the light on a sunny day. From the underground parking structure, walk or take a smooth, computer-driven tram up the steep slope, checking out the Bel Air estates across the 405 freeway. From the courtyard, plazas, and walkways, you can survey the city from the San Gabriel Mountains to the ocean. In a ravine separating the museum and the Getty Research Institute, artist Robert Irwin created the Central Garden in stark contrast to Meier's geometrical designs. Though the two sniped at each other during construction (Irwin stirred the pot with every loose twist his garden path took), the result is a refreshing garden walk whose focal point is an azalea maze—some insist the Mickey Mouse shape is on purpose—in a reflecting pool. Inside the pavilions are permanent collections of European paintings, drawings, sculpture, illuminated manuscripts, and decorative arts, as well as world-class temporary exhibitions and photographs gathered internationally. The collection of French furniture and decorative arts, especially from the early years of Louis XIV to the end of the reign of Louis XVI, is renowned for its quality and condition. You'll also find works by Rembrandt, Van Gogh, Monet, and James Ensor. The brochure in the entrance hall guides you to collection highlights, or you can opt for the instructive audio tour (free, but you have to leave your ID). The Getty also presents lectures, films, concerts, and programs for kids and families. Dining options include the upscale restaurant and the cafeteria with panoramic window views, plus outdoor coffee carts. **■ TIP→ On-site parking is subject to availability and can fill up by midday on holidays and in the summer, so try to come early in the day or after lunch.** A tram takes you from the street-level entrance to the top of the hill. Public buses (Metro Rapid Line 734) also serve the center and link to the Expo Rail extension. ✉ *1200 Getty Center Dr., Brentwood* ☎ *310/440–7300* 🌐 *www.getty.edu* 🎫 *Free; parking $15* ⏲ *Closed Mon.*

Pierce Brothers Westwood Village Memorial Park and Mortuary

CEMETERY | The who's who of the dearly departed can all be found at this peaceful, though unremarkable, cemetery. Notable residents include Marilyn Monroe and Joe DiMaggio; authors Truman Capote, Ray Bradbury, and Jackie Collins; actors Natalie Wood, Rodney Dangerfield, Farrah Fawcett, Jack Lemmon, and Dean Martin; and directors Billy Wilder and John Cassavetes. ✉ *1218 Glendon Ave., Westwood* ☎ *310/474–1579* 🌐 *www.dignitymemorial.com.*

Restaurants

Lady Chocolatt

$ | BELGIAN | The purveyor of the finest Belgian chocolate in all of Los Angeles, Lady Chocolatt is the perfect answer to the age-old question of what to gift on any special occasion. The ornate display case is filled with dark chocolate truffles, hazelnut pralines, Grand Marnier ganaches, and so much more. **Known for:** Belgian chocolate; Italian espresso; tasty sandwiches. $ *Average main: $5* ✉ *12008 Wilshire Blvd.* ☎ *310/442–2245* 🌐 *www.chocolatt.com.*

Toscana

$$$$ | ITALIAN | This rustic trattoria along San Vicente is a favorite celebrity haunt. Expect elevated sensory offerings, from its cozy atmosphere to its mouthwatering Tuscan fare and excellent wine list. **Known for:** excellent wine list; seasonal menu items like truffle sliders; great celeb-spotting. *Average main: $35* *11633 San Vicente Blvd., Brentwood* *310/820–2448* *www.toscanabrentwood.com.*

★ Hotel Bel-Air

$$$$ | HOTEL | This Spanish Mission–style icon has been a discreet hillside retreat for celebrities and society types since 1946 and was given a face-lift by star designers Alexandra Champalimaud and David Rockwell. **Pros:** shuttle available within 3 mile radius of hotel; perfect for the privacy minded; alfresco dining at Wolfgang Puck restaurant. **Cons:** not walking distance to restaurants or shops; hefty price tag; controversial ownership by the Sultan of Brunei. *Rooms from: $645* *701 Stone Canyon Rd., Bel Air* *310/472–1211* *www.dorchestercollection.com/en/los-angeles/hotel-bel-air* *103 rooms* *No meals.*

Beverly Hills

The rumors are true: Beverly Hills delivers on a dramatic, cinematic scale of wealth and excess. A known celebrity haunt, come here to daydream or to live like the rich and famous for a day. Window-shop or splurge at tony stores, and keep an eye out for filming locales; just walking around here will make you feel like you're on a movie set.

Museum of Tolerance

MUSEUM | FAMILY | A museum that unflinchingly confronts bigotry and racism, one of its most affecting sections covers the Holocaust, with film footage of deportations and concentration camps. Upon entering, you are issued a "passport" bearing the name of a child whose life was dramatically changed by the Nazis; as you go through the exhibit, you learn the fate of that child. Another exhibit called *Anne: The Life and Legacy of Anne Frank* brings her story to life through immersive environments, multimedia presentations, and interesting artifacts, while Simon Wiesenthal's Vienna office is set exactly as the famous "Nazi hunter" had it while conducting his research that brought more than 1,000 war criminals to justice.

Interactive exhibits include the Millennium Machine, which engages visitors in finding solutions to human rights abuses around the world; Globalhate.com, which examines hate on the Internet by exposing problematic sites via touch-screen computer terminals; and the Point of View Diner, a re-creation of a 1950s diner that "serves" a menu of controversial topics on video jukeboxes. **■ TIP→ Plan to spend at least three hours touring the museum; making a reservation is especially recommended for Friday, Sunday, and holiday visits.** *9786 W. Pico Blvd., south of Beverly Hills* *310/772–2505 for reservations* *www.museumoftolerance.com* *From $16* *Closed Sat.*

★ Rodeo Drive

NEIGHBORHOOD | The ultimate shopping indulgence, Rodeo Drive is one of L.A.'s bona fide tourist attractions. The art of window-shopping (and reenacting your *Pretty Woman* fantasies) is prime among the retail elite: Tiffany & Co., Gucci, Jimmy Choo, Valentino, Harry Winston, Prada—you get the picture. Near the southern end of Rodeo Drive is Via Rodeo, a curvy cobblestone street designed to resemble a European shopping area and the perfect backdrop to pose for your Instagram feed. To give your feet a rest, free trolley tours depart from the southeast corner of Rodeo Drive and Dayton Way from 11:30 to 4:30. They're a terrific way to get an overview of the neighborhood. ✉ *Rodeo Dr., Beverly Hills* 🌐 *www.rodeodrive-bh.com.*

★ Spadena House

BUILDING | Otherwise known as the Witch's House in Beverly Hills, the Spadena House has an interesting history. First built on the Willat Studios lot in 1920, the house was physically moved to its current ritzy location in 1924. The house is not open for tourists, but the fairy-tale-like appearance is viewable from the street for onlookers to snap pics. Movie buffs will also recognize it from a background shot in the film *Clueless.* ✉ *516 Walden Dr., Beverly Hills.*

Restaurants

Crustacean

$$$$ | **VIETNAMESE** | A Euro-Vietnamese fusion gem in the heart of Beverly Hills, Crustacean allows you to walk on water above exotic fish and see the kitchen preparing your perfect garlic noodles through a glass window. Standouts (besides the noodles) include Dungeness crab, A5 Wagyu beef, tuna cigars, and hearts-of-palm crab cakes. **Known for:** sake-simmered dishes; no-grease garlic noodles; unique cocktails like artichoke old-fashioneds. $ *Average main: $36* ✉ *468 N. Bedford Dr., Beverly Hills* ☎ *310/205–8990* 🌐 *crustaceanbh.com* ⏲ *Closed Mon.*

★ Gucci Osteria da Massimo Bottura

$$$$ | **ITALIAN** | Legendary Italian chef Massimo Bottura opened this spot, his first L.A. eatery, to loads of fanfare and celebrity sightings. The restaurant mirrors the Florence, Italy, location of the same name with a menu filled with favorites like a mouthwatering tortellini in brodo. **Known for:** excellent pastas; great people-watching; avant-garde design. $ *Average main: $80* ✉ *347 N. Rodeo Dr., Beverly Hills* ☎ *424/600–7490* 🌐 *www.gucci.com/us/en/st/capsule/gucci-osteria-beverly-hills.*

Nate 'n' Al's

$$ | **DELI** | A longtime refuge from California's lean cuisine, Nate 'n' Al's serves up steaming pastrami, matzo ball soup, and potato latkes. Big time media and entertainment insiders are often seen kibbitzing at this old-time East Coast–style establishment. **Known for:** matzo ball soup; killer pastrami; long waits. $ *Average main: $15* ✉ *414 N. Beverly Dr., Beverly Hills* ☎ *310/274–0101* 🌐 *www.natenals.com.*

Polo Lounge

$$$$ | **AMERICAN** | Nothing says Beverly Hills quite like the Polo Lounge inside the Beverly Hills Hotel. This classic, monied spot is home to Hollywood royalty and entertainment luminaries noshing on lobster Nicoise or the famed Wagyu burger during power lunches. **Known for:** celebrity sightings; mouthwatering Wagyu burgers; dress code of no ripped jeans or baseball caps. $ *Average main: $35* ✉ *The Beverly Hills Hotel, 9641 Sunset Blvd., Beverly Hills* ☎ *310/887–2777* 🌐 *www.dorchestercollection.com/en/los-angeles/the-beverly-hills-hotel/restaurants-bars/the-polo-lounge.*

★ Spago Beverly Hills

$$$$ | **MODERN AMERICAN** | Wolfgang Puck's flagship restaurant is a modern L.A. classic. Spago centers on a buzzing redbrick outdoor courtyard (with retractable roof) shaded by 100-year-old olive trees, and a daily-changing menu that offers dishes like smoked salmon pizza or off-menu schnitzel. **Known for:** great people-watching; off-menu schnitzel; sizzling smoked salmon pizza. $ *Average main: $35* ✉ *176 N. Canon Dr., Beverly Hills* ☎ *310/385–0880* 🌐 *www.wolfgangpuck.com* ⏲ *Closed Mon. and Tues.*

Hotels

Beverly Wilshire, a Four Seasons Hotel

$$$$ | **HOTEL** | Built in 1928, this Rodeo Drive–adjacent hotel is part Italian Renaissance (with elegant details like crystal chandeliers) and part contemporary. **Pros:** complimentary car service; Wolfgang Puck restaurant on-site; first-rate spa. **Cons:** small lobby; valet parking is expensive; might be too sceney for some. *Rooms from: $545* *9500 Wilshire Blvd., Beverly Hills* *310/275–5200, 800/427–4354* *www.fourseasons.com/beverlywilshire* *395 rooms* *No meals.*

The Crescent Beverly Hills

$$ | **HOTEL** | Built in 1927 as a dorm for silent-film actors, the Crescent is now a fanciful boutique hotel with a great location—within the Beverly Hills shopping triangle—and with an even better price (for the area). **Pros:** indoor/outdoor fireplace; lively on-site restaurant, Crescent Bar and Terrace; economic room available for $148. **Cons:** $30 resort fee is not optional; no elevator; rooms on the small side. *Rooms from: $245* *403 N. Crescent Dr., Beverly Hills* *310/247–0505* *www.crescentbh.com* *35 rooms* *Free breakfast.*

★ The Maybourne Beverly Hills

$$$$ | **HOTEL** | The nine-story, Mediterranean-style palazzo is dedicated to welcoming those who relish luxury, providing classic style and exemplary service. **Pros:** secret whiskey bar tucked upstairs; obliging, highly trained staff; lots of activities and amenities for kids. **Cons:** hefty tab for all this finery; not all rooms have balconies; pricey valet parking. *Rooms from: $550* *225 N. Canon Dr., Beverly Hills* *310/860–7800* *www.maybournebeverlyhills.com* *201 rooms* *No meals.*

★ Peninsula Beverly Hills

$$$$ | **HOTEL** | This French Riviera–style palace overflowing with antiques and art is a favorite of boldface names, but visitors consistently describe a stay here as near perfect. **Pros:** 24-hour check-in/check-out policy; sunny pool area with cabanas; complimentary Rolls-Royce takes you to nearby Beverly Hills. **Cons:** very expensive; room decor might feel too ornate for some; exclusive vibe can be intimidating. *Rooms from: $600* *9882 S. Santa Monica Blvd., Beverly Hills* *310/551–2888, 800/462–7899* *www.peninsula.com/en/beverly-hills/5-star-luxury-hotel-beverly-hills* *195 rooms* *No meals.*

SLS Hotel Beverly Hills

$$$ | **HOTEL** | From the sleek, Philippe Starck–designed lobby and lounge with fireplaces, hidden nooks, and a communal table to luxurious poolside cabanas, this hotel offers a cushy, dreamlike stay. **Pros:** great cocktails at lobby bar; complimentary house car for use within 3-mile radius; dreamy Ciel spa. **Cons:** standard rooms are compact; pricey dining and parking; on a busy intersection outside Beverly Hills. *Rooms from: $365* *465 S. La Cienega Blvd., Beverly Hills* *310/247–0400* *slshotels.com/beverlyhills* *297 rooms* *No meals.*

★ Viceroy L'Ermitage Beverly Hills

$$$$ | **HOTEL** | This all-suite hotel is the picture of luxury: French doors open to a mini-balcony with views of the Hollywood sign; inside the very large rooms you'll find soaking tubs and oversize bath towels. **Pros:** traditional French cuisine at Avec Nous on-site; free shuttle service within 2-mile radius; all rooms are large suites. **Cons:** small spa and pool; very expensive; a bit of a trek to Beverly Hills shopping. *Rooms from: $495* *9291 Burton Way, Beverly Hills* *310/278–3344* *www.viceroyhotelsandresorts.com/beverly-hills* *116 rooms* *No meals.*

Shopping

Cartier

JEWELRY/ACCESSORIES | Cartier has a bridal collection to sigh for in its chandeliered and respectfully hushed showroom, along with more playful pieces (chunky, diamond-encrusted panther cocktail rings, for example), watches, and accessories. The shop itself feels like the ultimate playground for A-list clientele, complete with a red-carpeted spiral staircase. ✉ *370 N. Rodeo Dr., Beverly Hills* ☎ *310/275–4272* 🌐 *www.cartier.com.*

Céline

CLOTHING | Under designer Hedi Slimane's creative direction, the Parisian brand has entered a new chapter. At the Beverly Hills brick-and-mortar, fashion lovers looking for French Cool Girl clothing will love the selection of the label's leather handbags, heels, and chic ready-to-wear clothing. ✉ *456 N. Rodeo Dr., Beverly Hills* ☎ *310/888–0120* 🌐 *www.celine.com.*

Gearys of Beverly Hills

GIFTS/SOUVENIRS | Since 1930, this has been the ultimate destination for those seeking the most exquisite fine china, crystal, silver, and jewelry, mostly from classic sources like Christofle, Baccarat, and Waterford. No wonder it's a favorite for registries of the rich and famous. ✉ *351 N. Beverly Dr., Beverly Hills* ☎ *310/273–4741* 🌐 *www.gearys.com.*

Harry Winston

JEWELRY/ACCESSORIES | Perhaps the most locally famous jeweler is Harry Winston, *the* source for Oscar-night jewelry. The three-level space, with a bronze sculptural facade, velvet-panel walls, private salons, and a rooftop patio, is as glamorous as the gems. ✉ *310 N. Rodeo Dr., Beverly Hills* ☎ *310/271–8554* 🌐 *www.harrywinston.com.*

Neiman Marcus

DEPARTMENT STORES | Luxury shopping at its finest, this couture salon frequently trots out designer trunk shows, and most locals go right for the shoe department, which features high-end footwear favorites like Giuseppe Zanotti and Christian Louboutin. A café on the third floor keeps your blood sugar high during multiple wardrobe changes, while a bar on the fourth is for celebrating those perfect finds with a glass of champagne. ✉ *9700 Wilshire Blvd., Beverly Hills* ☎ *310/550–5900* 🌐 *www.neimanmarcus.com.*

Taschen

BOOKS/STATIONERY | Philippe Starck designed the Taschen space to evoke a cool 1920s Parisian salon—a perfect showcase for the publisher's design-forward coffee-table books about architecture, travel, culture, and photography. A suspended glass cube gallery in back hosts art exhibits and features limited-edition books. ✉ *354 N. Beverly Dr., Beverly Hills* ☎ *310/274–4300* 🌐 *www.taschen.com.*

Tory Burch

CLOTHING | Preppy, stylish, and colorful clothes appropriate for a road trip to Palm Springs or a flight to Palm Beach fill this flagship boutique. ✉ *142 S. Robertson Blvd., Beverly Hills* ☎ *310/248–2612* 🌐 *www.toryburch.com.*

West Hollywood and Fairfax

West Hollywood is not a place to see things (like museums or movie studios) as much as it is a place to do things—like go to a nightclub, eat at a world-famous restaurant, or attend an art gallery opening. Since the end of Prohibition, the Sunset Strip has been Hollywood's nighttime playground, where stars headed to such glamorous nightclubs as the Trocadero, the Mocambo, and Ciro's.

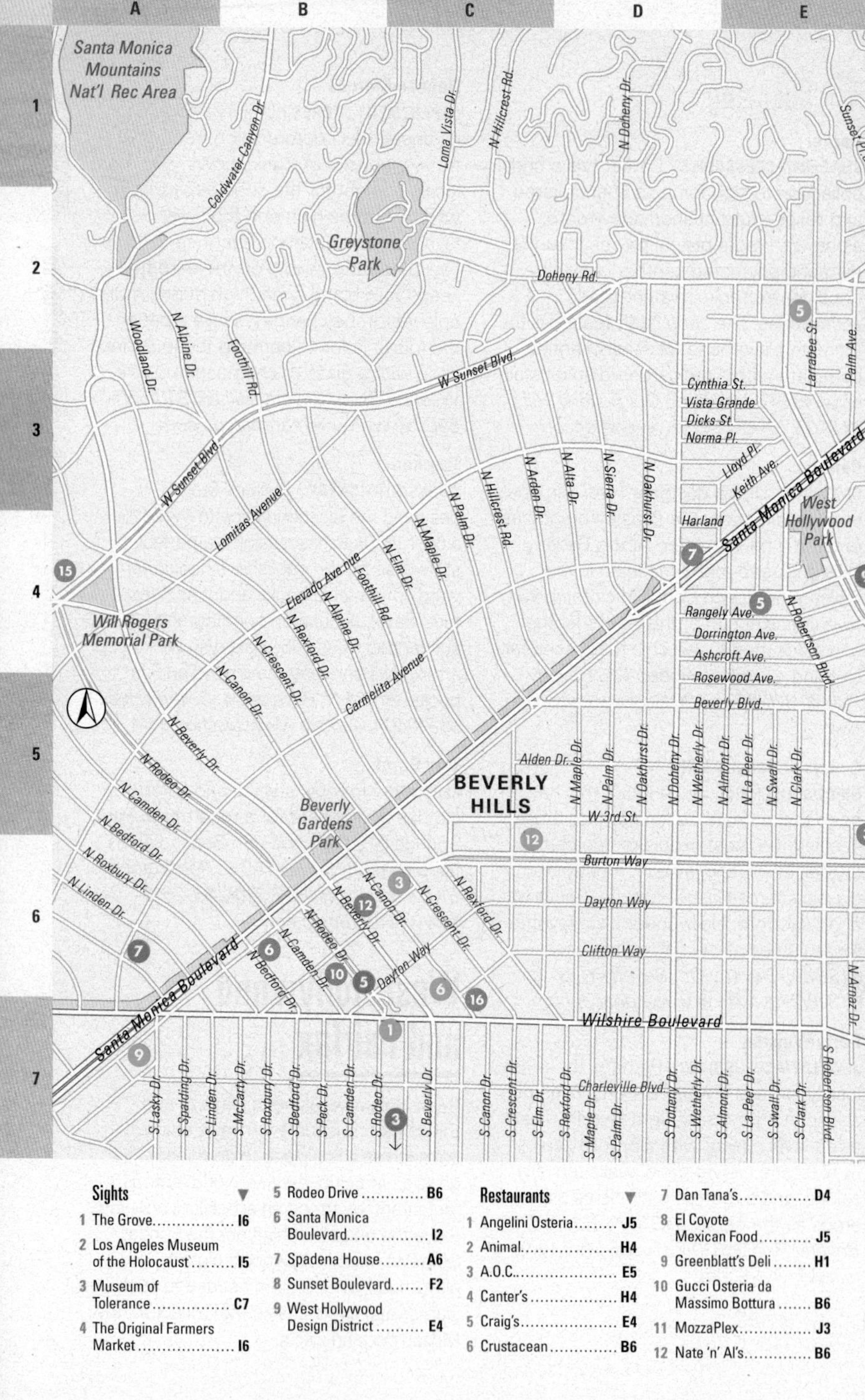

Sights

1 The Grove I6

2 Los Angeles Museum of the Holocaust I5

3 Museum of Tolerance C7

4 The Original Farmers Market I6

5 Rodeo Drive B6

6 Santa Monica Boulevard I2

7 Spadena House A6

8 Sunset Boulevard F2

9 West Hollywood Design District E4

Restaurants

1 Angelini Osteria J5

2 Animal H4

3 A.O.C. E5

4 Canter's H4

5 Craig's E4

6 Crustacean B6

7 Dan Tana's D4

8 El Coyote Mexican Food J5

9 Greenblatt's Deli H1

10 Gucci Osteria da Massimo Bottura B6

11 MozzaPlex J3

12 Nate 'n' Al's B6

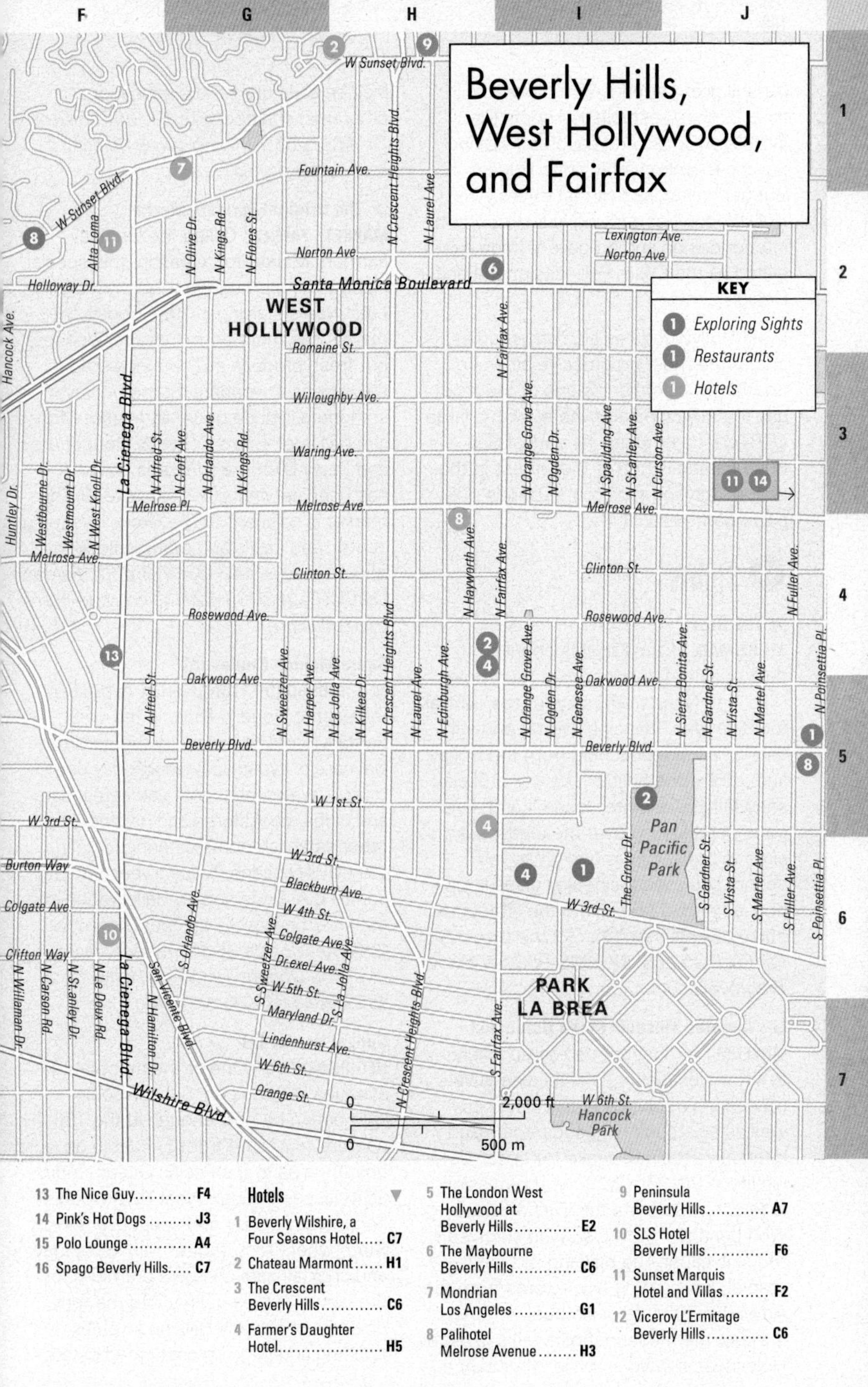

13 The Nice Guy **F4**
14 Pink's Hot Dogs **J3**
15 Polo Lounge **A4**
16 Spago Beverly Hills **C7**

Hotels

1 Beverly Wilshire, a Four Seasons Hotel **C7**
2 Chateau Marmont **H1**
3 The Crescent Beverly Hills **C6**
4 Farmer's Daughter Hotel **H5**
5 The London West Hollywood at Beverly Hills **E2**
6 The Maybourne Beverly Hills **C6**
7 Mondrian Los Angeles **G1**
8 Palihotel Melrose Avenue **H3**
9 Peninsula Beverly Hills **A7**
10 SLS Hotel Beverly Hills **F6**
11 Sunset Marquis Hotel and Villas **F2**
12 Viceroy L'Ermitage Beverly Hills **C6**

It's still going strong, with crowds still filing into well-established spots like Whisky A Go Go and paparazzi staking out the members-only Soho House. But hedonism isn't all that drives West Hollywood. Also thriving is an important interior design and art gallery trade exemplified by the Cesar Pelli–designed Pacific Design Center.

West Hollywood has also emerged as one of the most progressive cities in Southern California. It's one of the most gay-friendly cities anywhere, with a large LGBTQ+ community. Its annual Gay Pride Parade is one of the largest in the nation, drawing tens of thousands of participants each June.

Sights

★ The Grove

STORE/MALL | Come to this popular outdoor mall for familiar names like Apple, Nike, and Nordstrom; stay for the central fountain with "dancing" water and light shows, people-watching from the trolley, and, during the holiday season, artificial snowfall and a winter wonderland. Feel-good pop blasting over the loudspeakers aims to boost your mood while you spend, and a giant cineplex gives shoppers a needed break with the latest box office blockbusters. ✉ *189 The Grove Dr., Fairfax District* ☎ *323/900–8080* 🌐 *www.thegrovela.com.*

Los Angeles Museum of the Holocaust

MUSEUM | A museum dedicated solely to the Holocaust, it uses its extensive collections of photos and artifacts as well as award-winning audio tours and interactive tools to evoke European Jewish life in the 20th century. The mission is to commemorate the lives of those who perished and those who survived the Holocaust. The building is itself a marvel, having won two awards from the American Institute of Architects. Every Sunday, the museum hosts talks given by Holocaust survivors, while other events include a lecture series, educational programs, and concerts. ✉ *100 The Grove Dr.* ☎ *323/651–3704* 🌐 *www.holocaustmuseumla.org* 🎟 *Free.*

★ The Original Farmers Market

MARKET | FAMILY | Called the Original Farmers Market for a reason, this special piece of land brought out farmers to sell their wares starting in 1934. Today, the market has more permanent residences, but fresh produce still abounds among the dozens of vendors. Some purveyor standouts include gourmet market Monsieur Marcel, Bob's Coffee & Doughnuts, and Patsy D'Amore's Pizzeria, which has been serving slices since 1949. The market is adjacent to The Grove shopping center, and locals and tourists flock to both in droves. ✉ *6333 W. 3rd St., Fairfax District* ☎ *323/933–9211* 🌐 *www.farmersmarketla.com.*

Santa Monica Boulevard

NEIGHBORHOOD | From Fairfax Avenue in the east to Doheny Drive in the west, Santa Monica Boulevard is the commercial core of West Hollywood's gay community, with restaurants and cafés, bars and clubs, bookstores and galleries, and other establishments catering largely to the LGBTQ scene. Twice a year—during June's L.A. Pride and on Halloween—the boulevard becomes an open-air festival. ✉ *Santa Monica Blvd. between Fairfax Ave. and Doheny Dr., West Hollywood* ☎ *323/848-6400* 🌐 *weho.org.*

Sunset Boulevard

NEIGHBORHOOD | One of the most fabled avenues in the world, Sunset Boulevard began humbly enough in the 18th century as a route from El Pueblo de Los Angeles to the Pacific Ocean. Today, as it passes through West Hollywood, it becomes the sexy and seductive Sunset Strip, where rock and roll had its heyday and cocktail bars charge a premium for the views. It slips quietly into the tony environs of Beverly Hills and Bel-Air, twisting and winding past gated estates

From celebrity mansions to rock 'n' roll lore, Sunset Boulevard is a drive through Hollywood history.

and undulating vistas. ✉ *Sunset Blvd., West Hollywood* 🌐 *www.weho.org.*

West Hollywood Design District

STORE/MALL | More than 200 businesses—art galleries, antiques shops, fashion outlets (including Rag & Bone and James Perse), and interior design stores—are found in the design district. There are also about 30 restaurants, including the famous paparazzi magnet, the Ivy. All are clustered within walking distance of each other—rare for L.A. ✉ *Melrose Ave. and Robertson and Beverly Blvds., West Hollywood* ☎ *310/289–2534* 🌐 *westhollywooddesigndistrict.com.*

Restaurants

★ Angelini Osteria

$$$$ | **ITALIAN** | Despite its modest, rather congested dining room, this is one of L.A.'s most celebrated Italian restaurants. The keys are chef-owner Gino Angelini's consistently impressive dishes, like whole branzino, *tagliolini al limone,* veal chop *alla* Milanese, as well as lasagna oozing with *besciamella* (Italian béchamel sauce). **Known for:** large Italian wine selection; bold flavors; savory pastas. $ *Average main: $40* ✉ *7313 Beverly Blvd., Beverly–La Brea* ☎ *323/297–0070* 🌐 *www.angelinirestaurantgroup.com.*

Animal

$$$ | **AMERICAN** | Owned by Jon Shook and Vinny Dotolo of *Iron Chef* fame, this oft-packed James Beard Award–winning restaurant offers shareable plates with a focus on meat. Highlights include barbecue pork belly sandwiches, poutine with oxtail gravy, and braised rabbit legs with mushrooms. **Known for:** bacon-chocolate crunch bar for dessert; reputation as a must for foodies; menu that is carnivore heaven. $ *Average main: $30* ✉ *435 N. Fairfax Ave., Fairfax District* ☎ *323/782–9225* 🌐 *www.animalrestaurant.com* ⏲ *No lunch.*

A.O.C.

$$$ | MEDITERRANEAN | Not to be confused with the congresswoman from New York, the acronym here stands for Appellation d'Origine Contrôlée, the regulatory system that ensures the quality of local wines and cheeses in France. Fittingly, A.O.C. upholds this standard of excellence in its shared plates and perfect wine pairings in the stunning exposed-brick and vine-laden courtyard. **Known for:** amazing cocktail hour; quaint outdoor courtyard; charming indoor fireplaces. *Average main: $25 ✉ 8700 W. 3rd St., West Hollywood ☎ 310/859–9859 🌐 www.aocwinebar.com.*

Canter's

$ | DELI | FAMILY | This granddaddy of L.A. delicatessens (it opened in 1931) cures its own corned beef and pastrami and features delectable desserts from the in-house bakery. It's not the best (or friendliest) deli in town, but it's a classic. **Known for:** location adjacent to Kibitz Room bar; plenty of seating and short wait times; open 24 hours. *Average main: $12 ✉ 419 N. Fairfax Ave., Fairfax District ☎ 323/651–2030 🌐 www.cantersdeli.com.*

Craig's

$$$$ | AMERICAN | Behind the unremarkable facade is an übertrendy—yet decidedly old-school—den of American cuisine that doubles as a safe haven for the movie industry's most important names and well-known faces. Be aware that this joint is always busy so you might not even get a table and reservations are hard to come by. **Known for:** lots of celebrities; delicious chicken Parm; strong drinks. *Average main: $32 ✉ 8826 Melrose Ave., West Hollywood ☎ 310/276–1900 🌐 craigs.la.*

Dan Tana's

$$$$ | ITALIAN | If you're looking for an Italian vibe straight out of *Goodfellas,* your search ends here. Checkered tablecloths cover the tightly packed tables as Hollywood players dine on the city's best chicken and veal Parm, and down Scotches by the finger. **Known for:** elbow-room-only bar; lively atmosphere; celeb spotting. *Average main: $35 ✉ 9071 Santa Monica Blvd., West Hollywood ☎ 310/275–9444 🌐 www.dantanasrestaurant.com.*

★ El Coyote Mexican Food

$$ | MEXICAN | FAMILY | Open since 1931, this landmark spot is perfect for those on a budget or anyone after an authentic Mexican meal. The traditional fare is decadent and delicious while the margaritas are sweetened to perfection. **Known for:** affordable, quality cuisine; festive atmosphere; being an L.A. staple. *Average main: $14 ✉ 7312 Beverly Blvd., Beverly–La Brea ☎ 323/939–2255 🌐 www.elcoyotecafe.com ⊗ Closed Mon. and Tues.*

Greenblatt's Deli

$$ | DELI | In 1926, Herman Greenblatt opened his eponymous deli, which serves Jewish deli food, wine, and spirits. The restaurant claims to have the rarest roast beef in town—and they're probably right. **Known for:** matzo ball soup; pastrami sandwiches; old-school vibe. *Average main: $18 ✉ 8017 Sunset Blvd., West Hollywood ☎ 323/656–0606 🌐 www.greenblattsdeli.com.*

★ MozzaPlex

$$$ | ITALIAN | A trio of restaurants by star chef Nancy Silverton, MozzaPlex consists of Pizzeria Mozza, a casual pizza and wine spot; Osteria Mozza, an upscale Italian restaurant with incredible pastas; and chi SPACCA, an Italian steak house with succulent cuts of steak. The restaurant complex is one of the most beloved in the whole city and if you're craving any kind of Italian food, you'll want to get yourself inside. **Known for:** great pizzas; intimate atmosphere; the chi SPACCA burger. *Average main: $25 ✉ 641 N. Highland Ave., Beverly–La Brea ☎ 323/297–1130 🌐 www.mozzarestaurantgroup.com.*

The Nice Guy

$$$ | **ITALIAN** | This dark and brooding Italian restaurant sits discretely on La Cienega Boulevard and hides one of the cooler scenes in L.A. A favorite among privacy-minded celebs (there's a no-photo policy), the Nice Guy is known for its cavatelli *alla* vodka and mouthwatering chicken Parm. **Known for:** mouthwatering pastas; see-and-be-seen crowd; live piano music. *Average main: $25 ✉ 401 N. La Cienega Blvd., West Hollywood ☎ 310/360–9500 🌐 www.theniceguyla.com.*

★ Pink's Hot Dogs

$ | **HOT DOG** | **FAMILY** | Since 1939, Angelenos and tourists alike have been lining up at this roadside hot dog stand. But Pink's is more than just an institution, it's a beloved family-run joint that serves a damn good hot dog. **Known for:** the famous Brando Dog; late-night dining; chili fries. *Average main: $6 ✉ 709 N. La Brea Ave., Hollywood ☎ 323/931–4223 🌐 www.pinkshollywood.com.*

Hotels

Chateau Marmont

$$$$ | **HOTEL** | Built in 1929 as a luxury apartment complex, the Chateau is now one of the most unique see-and-be-seen hotel hot spots in all of L.A. A remarkably good-looking, young, and super-creative crowd of artists, writers, actors, and photographers roams about this historic haunt. **Pros:** private and exclusive vibe; famous history; beautiful pool. **Cons:** some may find it pretentious; service can be spotty; some of the rooms are underwhelming. *Rooms from: $450 ✉ 8221 Sunset Blvd., West Hollywood ☎ 323/656–1010 🌐 www.chateaumarmont.com ➡ 63 rooms 🍽 No meals.*

★ Farmer's Daughter Hotel

$$ | **HOTEL** | A favorite of *Price Is Right* and *Dancing with the Stars* hopefuls (both TV shows tape at the CBS studios nearby), this hotel has a tongue-in-cheek country style with a hopping Sunday brunch and a little pool accented by giant rubber duckies and a living wall. **Pros:** bikes for rent; fun brunch restaurant; book lending library. **Cons:** shaded pool; no bathtubs; restaurant food is just okay. *Rooms from: $200 ✉ 115 S. Fairfax Ave., Fairfax District ☎ 323/937–3930, 800/334–1658 🌐 www.farmersdaughterhotel.com ➡ 65 rooms 🍽 No meals.*

★ The London West Hollywood at Beverly Hills

$$$ | **HOTEL** | Cosmopolitan and chic, the London West Hollywood is known for its large suites, rooftop pool with citywide views, and luxury touches throughout. **Pros:** state-of-the-art fitness center; chef Anthony Keene oversees dining program; 110-seat screening room. **Cons:** too refined for kids to be comfortable; lower floors have mundane views; spa and restaurant are pricey. *Rooms from: $350 ✉ 1020 N. San Vicente Blvd., West Hollywood ☎ 310/854–1111 🌐 www.thelondonwesthollywood.com ➡ 226 suites 🍽 No meals.*

Mondrian Los Angeles

$$$ | **HOTEL** | The Mondrian has a city club feel; socializing begins in the lobby bar and lounge and extends from the restaurant to the scenic patio and pool, where you can listen to music underwater, and the lively Skybar. **Pros:** acclaimed Skybar on property; flirty social scene; double-paned windows keep out noise. **Cons:** pricy valet parking; late-night party scene not for everyone; Alice in Wonderland theme might be too much for some. *Rooms from: $300 ✉ 8440 Sunset Blvd., West Hollywood ☎ 323/650–8999, 800/606–6090 🌐 www.mondrianhotel.com ➡ 236 rooms 🍽 No meals.*

Palihotel Melrose Avenue

$$ | **HOTEL** | A mostly young and creative clientele flocks here, to one of the only boutique hotels on Melrose Avenue. **Pros:** great decor; walking distance to Melrose shops and restaurants; cheap bike rentals ($20/day). **Cons:** no gym, spa, or pool; neighborhood can be sketchy at night;

need to request alarm clocks and phones from front desk. *Rooms from: $200* *7950 Melrose Ave., West Hollywood* *323/272–4588* *www.pali-hotel.com* *33 rooms* *No meals.*

★ Sunset Marquis Hotel and Villas

$$$ | HOTEL | If you're in town to cut your new hit single, you'll appreciate this near-the-Strip hidden retreat in the heart of WeHo, with two on-site recording studios. **Pros:** favorite among rock stars; 53 villas with lavish extras like completely soundproof rooms; exclusive Bar 1200. **Cons:** rooms can feel dark; small balconies; vibe can feel too exclusive. *Rooms from: $365* *1200 N. Alta Loma Rd., West Hollywood* *310/657–1333, 800/858–9758* *www.sunsetmarquis.com* *152 rooms* *No meals.*

Nightlife

★ The Abbey

BARS/PUBS | The Abbey in West Hollywood is one of the most famous gay bars in the world. And rightfully so. Seven days a week, a mixed and very good-looking crowd comes to eat, drink, dance, and flirt. Creative cocktails are whipped up by buff bartenders with a bevy of theme nights and parties each day. *692 N. Robertson Blvd., West Hollywood* *310/289–8410* *www.theabbeyweho.com.*

Comedy Store

COMEDY CLUBS | Three stages give seasoned and unseasoned comedians a place to perform and try out new material, with big-name performers dropping by just for fun. The front bar along Sunset Boulevard is a popular hangout after or between shows, oftentimes with that night's comedians mingling with fans. *8433 Sunset Blvd., West Hollywood* *323/650–6268* *www.thecomedystore.com.*

Delilah

THEMED ENTERTAINMENT | Reservations are definitely required for this swanky, New York–style space in West Hollywood. Waiters in white coats serve a mix of upscale American cuisine, but the true reason to come happens a little later when live jazz and burlesque dancers turn the night into a sultry singles scene that's visited by the who's who of Hollywood celebrity royalty. *7969 Santa Monica Blvd., West Hollywood* *323/745–0600* *www.delilahla.com.*

Employees Only

BARS/PUBS | If you're looking for the best cocktail program in L.A., you'll find it at Employees Only. This very chic spot is a sister of the New York original and is consistently awarded worldwide for its delicious drinks. At this iteration, there are various themed nights with burlesque on Saturday and sporadic live music. In the back is a speakeasy called Harry's, which is a more intimate space where you can get up close and personal with the master barkeeps to tailor you the perfect drink. *7953 Santa Monica Blvd., West Hollywood* *323/536–9045* *www.employeesonlyla.com.*

Jones

BARS/PUBS | Italian food and serious cocktails are the mainstays at Jones. Whiskey is a popular choice for the classic cocktails, but the bartenders also do up martinis properly (read: strong). The Beggar's Banquet is their version of happy hour (10 pm to 2 am, Sunday through Thursday), with specials on drinks and pizza. *7205 Santa Monica Blvd., West Hollywood* *323/850–1726* *www.joneshollywood.com.*

Laugh Factory

COMEDY CLUBS | Top stand-up comics regularly appear at this Sunset Boulevard mainstay, often working out the kinks in new material in advance of national tours. Stars such as Tiffany Haddish and Kevin Nealon sometimes drop by unannounced, and theme nights like Midnight Madness and Chocolate Sundaes are extremely popular, with comics performing more daring sets. ✉ *8001 W. Sunset Blvd., West Hollywood* ☎ *323/656–1336* 🌐 *www.laughfactory.com.*

Rainbow Bar and Grill
BARS/PUBS | Its location next door to a long-running music venue, the Roxy, helped cement this bar and restaurant's status as a legendary watering hole for musicians (as well as their entourages and groupies). The Who, Guns N' Roses, Poison, Kiss, and many others have all passed through the doors. Expect a $5–$10 cover, but you'll get the money back in drink tickets or a food discount. ✉ *9015 W. Sunset Blvd., West Hollywood* ☎ *310/278–4232* 🌐 *www.rainbowbarandgrill.com.*

★ The Troubadour
MUSIC CLUBS | The intimate vibe of the Troubadour helps make this club a favorite with music fans. Around since 1957, this venue has a storied past where legends like Elton John and James Taylor have graced the stage. These days, the eclectic lineup is still attracting crowds, with the focus mostly on rock, indie, and folk music. Those looking for drinks can imbibe to their heart's content at the adjacent bar. ✉ *9081 Santa Monica Blvd., West Hollywood* 🌐 *www.troubadour.com.*

Whisky A Go Go
MUSIC CLUBS | The hard-core metal and rock scene is alive and well at the legendary Whisky A Go Go (the full name includes the prefix "World Famous"), where Janis Joplin, Led Zeppelin, Alice Cooper, Van Halen, the Doors (they were the house band for a short stint), and Frank Zappa have all played. On the Strip for more than five decades, the club books both underground acts and huge names in rock. ✉ *8901 W. Sunset Blvd., West Hollywood* ☎ *310/652–4202* 🌐 *www.whiskyagogo.com.*

Shopping

★ American Rag Cie
CLOTHING | Half the store features new clothing from established and emerging labels, while the other side is stocked with well-preserved vintage clothing organized by color and style. You'll also find plenty of shoes and accessories being picked over by the hippest of Angelenos. ✉ *150 S. La Brea Ave., West Hollywood* ☎ *323/935–3154* 🌐 *american-rag.com.*

Beverly Center
SHOPPING CENTERS/MALLS | This eight-level shopping center is home to luxury retailers like Gucci, Louis Vuitton, and Salvatore Ferragamo but also offers plenty of outposts for more affordable brands including Aldo, H&M, and Uniqlo. Don't miss the bevy of great dining options like Eggslut, an extraordinarily popular breakfast joint; Tocaya Organica, a modern Mexican concept with vegan, vegetarian, and gluten-free options; and Yardbird, a fried-chicken lovers' favorite, plus many, many more. ✉ *8500 Beverly Blvd., West Hollywood* ☎ *310/854–0070* 🌐 *www.beverlycenter.com.*

Book Soup
BOOKS/STATIONERY | One of the best independent bookstores in the country, Book Soup has been serving Angelenos since 1975. Given its Hollywood pedigree, it's especially deep in books about film, music, art, and photography. Fringe benefits include an international newsstand, a bargain-book section, and author readings several times a week. ✉ *8818 Sunset Blvd., West Hollywood* ☎ *310/659–3110* 🌐 *www.booksoup.com.*

★ Fred Segal
CLOTHING | One of the most well-known boutiques in all of Los Angeles, Fred Segal is a fashion design mecca that has been clothing the rich, famous, and their acolytes since the 1960s. Since moving from its original location on Melrose, the flagship store sits atop Sunset Boulevard

with more than 21,000 square feet of space that showcases innovative brands and high-end threads. Inside is also Fred Segal Café and Bakery, which offers fashionistas some fast casual fare as they peruse the merchandise. ✉ *8500 Sunset Blvd., West Hollywood* ☎ *310/432–0560* 🌐 *www.fredsegal.com.*

★ Maxfield

CLOTHING | This modern concrete structure is one of L.A.'s most desirable destinations for ultimate high fashion. The space is stocked with sleek offerings from Givenchy, Saint Laurent, Valentino, and Rick Owens, plus occasional pop-ups by fashion's labels-of-the-moment. For serious shoppers (or gawkers) only. ✉ *8825 Melrose Ave., West Hollywood* ☎ *310/274–8800* 🌐 *www.maxfieldla.com.*

★ Melrose Trading Post

OUTDOOR/FLEA/GREEN MARKETS | Hollywood denizens love this hip market, where you're likely to find recycled rock T-shirts or some vinyl to complete your collection in addition to antique furniture and quirky arts and crafts. Live music and fresh munchies entertain vintage hunters and collectors. The market is held 9 to 5 every Sunday—rain or shine—in Fairfax High School's parking lot and admission is $5. ✉ *Fairfax Ave. and Melrose Ave., Fairfax District* ☎ *323/655–7679* 🌐 *www.melrosetradingpost.org.*

Paul Smith

CLOTHING | You can't miss the massive, minimalist pink box that houses Paul Smith's fantastical collection of clothing, boots, hats, luggage, and objets d'art (seriously, there will be hordes of Instagrammers shooting selfies in front of the bright facade). Photos and art line the walls above shelves of books on pop culture, art, and Hollywood. As for the clothing here, expect the British brand's signature playfully preppy style, with vibrant colors and whimsical patterns mixed in with well-tailored closet staples. ✉ *8221 Melrose Ave., West Hollywood* ☎ *323/951–4800* 🌐 *www.paulsmith.com/uk.*

The Way We Wore

CLOTHING | Beyond the over-the-top vintage store furnishings, you'll find one of the city's best selections of well-cared-for and one-of-a-kind items, with a focus on sequins and beads. Upstairs, couture from Halston, Dior, and Chanel can cost up to $20,000. ✉ *334 S. La Brea Ave., Beverly–La Brea* ☎ *323/937–0878* 🌐 *www.thewaywewore.com.*

Hollywood and the Studios

The Tinseltown mythology of Los Angeles was born in Hollywood, still one of the city's largest and most vibrant neighborhoods. In the Hollywood Hills to the north of Franklin Avenue sit some of the most marvelous mansions the moguls ever built; in the flats below Sunset and Santa Monica boulevards are the classic Hollywood bungalows where studio workers once resided.

Reputation aside, though, it's mostly a workaday neighborhood without the glitz and glamour of places like Beverly Hills. The only major studio still located in Hollywood is Paramount; Warner Bros., Disney, and Universal Studios Hollywood are to the north in Burbank and Universal City.

Of course, the notion of Hollywood as a center of the entertainment industry can be expanded to include more than one neighborhood: to the north is Studio City, a thriving strip at the base of the Hollywood Hills, which is home to many smaller film companies; Universal City, where you'll find Universal Studios Hollywood; and Burbank, home to several major studios.

The San Fernando Valley is only a couple of miles north of the Hollywood Bowl, yet some say it's worlds away. Over the hill from the notably trendier areas of Downtown and Hollywood, "the Valley" gets a bad rap. But all snickering aside, this area is home to many of the places that have made Los Angeles famous: **Disney Studios, Warner Bros. Studios,** and **Universal Studios Hollywood.**

Hollywood

Sights

Dolby Theatre

ARTS VENUE | More than just a prominent fixture on Hollywood Boulevard, the Dolby Theatre has a few accolades under its belt as well, most notably as home to the Academy Awards. The theater is the blend of the traditional and the modern, where an exquisite classical design inspired by the grand opera houses of Europe meets a state-of-the-art sound and technical system for an immersive, theatrical experience. Watch a concert or a show here to experience it fully, but before you do, take a tour for an informative, behind-the-scenes look and to step into the VIP lounge where celebrities rub elbows on the big night. ✉ *6801 Hollywood Blvd., Hollywood* ☎ *323/308–6300* 🌐 *www.dolbytheatre.com* 🎫 *Tour $25.*

★Hollywood Bowl

ARTS VENUE | For those seeking a quintessential Los Angeles experience, a concert on a summer night at the Bowl, the city's iconic outdoor venue, is unsurpassed. The Bowl has presented world-class performers since it opened in 1920. The L.A. Philharmonic plays here from June to September; its performances and other events draw large crowds. Parking is limited near the venue, but there are additional remote parking locations serviced by shuttles. You can bring food and drink to any event, which Angelenos often do, though you can only bring alcohol when the L.A. Phil is performing. (Bars sell alcohol at all events, and there are dining options.) It's wise to bring a jacket even if daytime temperatures have been warm—the Bowl can get quite chilly at night. **TIP→Visitors can sometimes watch the L.A. Phil practice for free, usually on a weekday; call ahead for times.** ✉ *2301 Highland Ave., Hollywood* ☎ *323/850–2000* 🌐 *www.hollywoodbowl.com.*

★Hollywood Forever Cemetery

CEMETERY | One of the many things that makes this cemetery in the middle of Hollywood so fascinating is that it's the final resting place of many of the Hollywood greats, from directors like Cecil B. DeMille and actors like Douglas Fairbanks and Judy Garland to musicians like Johnny Ramone. Beyond its famous residents, however, the Hollywood Forever Cemetery is also frequented for its serene grounds peppered with intricately designed tombstones, not to mention by cinephiles in the summer and fall months for the outdoor movie screenings that take place under the stars on the Fairbanks Lawn. If you're looking for both tourist and local experiences while in town, this sight lets you tick off both in one visit. ✉ *6000 Santa Monica Blvd., Hollywood* ☎ *323/706–4826* 🌐 *www.hollywoodforever.com* 🎫 *Free; check online for film screenings.*

★Hollywood Museum

MUSEUM | Don't let its kitschy facade turn you off: the Hollywood Museum, nestled at the busy intersection of Hollywood and Highland, is worth it, especially for film aficionados. A museum deserving of its name, it boasts an impressive collection of exhibits from the moviemaking world, spanning several film genres and eras. Start in its pink, art deco lobby where the Max Factor exhibit pays tribute to the cosmetics company's pivotal role in Hollywood, make your way to the dark basement, where the industry's penchant for the macabre is on full display, and wrap up your visit by admiring Hollywood's most famous costumes and set props on the top floor. ✉ *1660 N. Highland Ave., at Hollywood Blvd., Hollywood* ☎ *323/464–7776* 🌐 *www.thehollywoodmuseum.com* 🎫 *$15* 🕒 *Closed Mon. and Tues.*

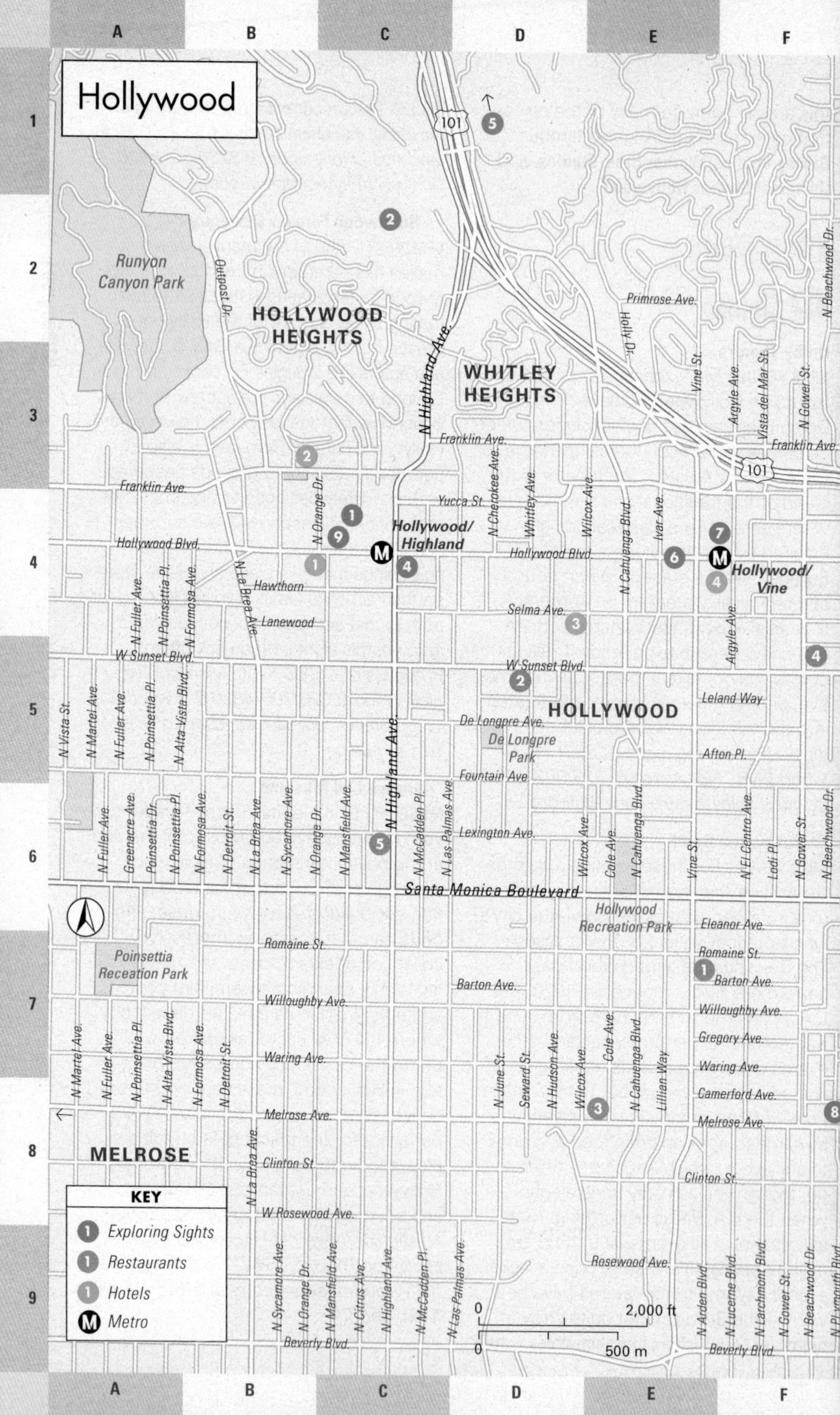
Hollywood
A
B
C
D
E
F
1
2
3
4
5
6
7
8
9
101
Runyon Canyon Park
Outpost Dr.
HOLLYWOOD HEIGHTS
N Highland Ave.
WHITLEY HEIGHTS
Primrose Ave.
Holly Dr.
Vine St.
Argyle Ave.
Vista del Mar St.
N Gower St.
N Beachwood Dr.
Franklin Ave.
Yucca St.
N Cherokee Ave.
Whitley Ave.
Wilcox Ave.
N Cahuenga Blvd.
Ivar Ave.
N Orange Dr.
Hollywood/ Highland
Hollywood Blvd.
Hollywood/ Vine
N Fuller Ave.
N Poinsettia Pl.
N Formosa Ave.
N La Brea Ave.
Hawthorn
Lanewood
Selma Ave.
W Sunset Blvd.
Leland Way
HOLLYWOOD
De Longpre Ave.
De Longpre Park
Afton Pl.
Fountain Ave.
N Vista St.
N Martel Ave.
N Alta Vista Blvd.
Greenacre Ave.
Poinsettia Dr.
N Detroit St.
N Sycamore Ave.
N Mansfield Ave.
N McCadden Pl.
N Las Palmas Ave.
Lexington Ave.
Cole Ave.
N El Centro Ave.
Lodi Pl.
Santa Monica Boulevard
Hollywood Recreation Park
Eleanor Ave.
Poinsettia Receation Park
Romaine St.
Barton Ave.
Willoughby Ave.
Gregory Ave.
Waring Ave.
N June St.
Seward St.
N Hudson Ave.
Lillian Way
Camerford Ave.
Melrose Ave.
MELROSE
Clinton St.
W Rosewood Ave.
Rosewood Ave.
N Citrus Ave.
N Arden Blvd.
N Lucerne Blvd.
N Larchmont Blvd.
N Plymouth Blvd.
Beverly Blvd.
KEY
Exploring Sights
Restaurants
Hotels
Metro
0
2,000 ft
500 m

Sights

1 Dolby Theatre C4
2 Hollywood Bowl C2
3 Hollywood Forever Cemetery G7
4 Hollywood Museum C4
5 Hollywood Sign D1
6 Hollywood Walk of Fame E4
7 Pantages Theatre F4
8 Paramount Pictures F8
9 TCL Chinese Theatre C4

Restaurants

1 Cactus Taquerias #1 .... E7
2 Gwen D5
3 Providence E8
4 Roscoe's House of Chicken & Waffles F5
5 Salt's Cure C6

Hotels

1 Hollywood Roosevelt Hotel C4
2 Magic Castle Hotel B3
3 Mama Shelter D4
4 W Hollywood E4

★ Hollywood Sign

LOCAL INTEREST | With letters 50 feet tall, Hollywood's trademark sign can be spotted from miles away. The icon, which originally read "Hollywoodland," was erected in the Hollywood Hills in 1923 to advertise a segregated housing development and was outfitted with 4,000 light bulbs. In 1949 the "land" portion of the sign was taken down. By 1973 the sign had earned landmark status, but because the letters were made of wood, its longevity came into question. A makeover project was launched and the letters were auctioned off (rocker Alice Cooper bought an "O" and singing cowboy Gene Autry sponsored an "L") to make way for a new sign made of sheet metal. Inevitably, the sign has drawn pranksters who have altered it over the years, albeit temporarily, to spell out "Hollyweed" (in the 1970s, to push for more lenient marijuana laws), "Go Navy" (before a Rose Bowl game), and "Perotwood" (during businessman Ross Perot's 1992 presidential bid). A fence and surveillance equipment have since been installed to deter intruders, but another vandal managed to pull the "Hollyweed" prank once again in 2017 after Californians voted to make recreational use of marijuana legal statewide. And while it's still very illegal to get anywhere near the sign, several area hikes will get you as close as possible for some photo ops; you can hike just over 6 miles up behind the sign via the Brush Canyon trail for epic views, especially at sunset. ⚠ **Use caution if driving up to the sign on residential streets; many cars speed around the blind corners.** ✉ *Griffith Park, Mt. Lee Dr., Hollywood* 🌐 *www.hollywoodsign.org.*

Hollywood Walk of Fame

LOCAL INTEREST | Along Hollywood Boulevard (and part of Vine Street) runs a trail of affirmations for entertainment-industry overachievers. On this mile-long stretch of sidewalk, inspired by the concrete handprints in front of TCL Chinese Theatre, names are embossed in brass, each at the center of a pink star embedded in dark gray terrazzo. They're not all screen deities; many stars commemorate people who worked in a technical field, such as sound or lighting. The first eight stars were unveiled in 1960 at the northwest corner of Highland Avenue and Hollywood Boulevard: Olive Borden, Ronald Colman, Louise Fazenda, Preston Foster, Burt Lancaster, Edward Sedgwick, Ernest Torrence, and Joanne Woodward (some of these names have stood the test of time better than others). Since then, more than 2,000 others have been immortalized, though that honor doesn't come cheap—upon selection by a special committee, the personality in question (or more likely his or her movie studio or record company) pays about $30,000 for the privilege. To aid you in spotting celebrities you're looking for, stars are identified by one of five icons: a motion-picture camera, a radio microphone, a television set, a record, or a theatrical mask. ✉ *Hollywood Blvd. and Vine St., Hollywood* 🌐 *www.walkoffame.com.*

Pantages Theatre

ARTS VENUE | Besides being home to the Academy Awards for a decade in the '50s, this stunning art deco–style theater near Hollywood and Vine has been playing host to many of the musical theater world's biggest and greatest productions, from the classics like *Cats, West Side Story*, and *Phantom of the Opera* to modern hits like *Hamilton* and *Wicked*. During your Los Angeles jaunt, see a show or two in order to really experience its splendor. While guided tours are not being offered to the public, an annual open house is available to season pass holders for an exclusive and informative tour of the theater and its history. ✉ *6233 Hollywood Blvd., Hollywood* ☎ *323/468–1770* 🌐 *www.broadwayinhollywood.com.*

★ Paramount Pictures

FILM STUDIO | With a history dating to the early 1920s, the Paramount lot was home to some of Hollywood's most luminous stars, including Mary Pickford, Rudolph Valentino, Mae West, Marlene Dietrich, and Bing Crosby. Director Cecil B. DeMille's base of operations for decades, Paramount offers probably the most authentic studio tour, giving you a real sense of the film industry's history. This is the only major studio from film's golden age left in Hollywood—all the others are now in Burbank, Universal City, or Culver City.

Memorable movies and TV shows with scenes shot here include *Sunset Boulevard, Forrest Gump,* and *Titanic.* Many of the *Star Trek* movies and TV series were shot entirely or in part here, and several seasons of *I Love Lucy* were shot on the portion of the lot Paramount acquired in 1967 from Lucille Ball. You can take a 2-hour studio tour or a 4½-hour VIP tour, led by guides who walk and trolley you around the back lots. As well as gleaning some gossipy history, you'll spot the sets of TV and film shoots in progress. Reserve ahead for tours, which are for those ages 10 and up. **■ TIP→ You can be part of the audience for live TV tapings (tickets are free), but you must book ahead.** ✉ *5515 Melrose Ave., Hollywood* ☎ *323/956–1777* 🌐 *www.paramountstudiotour.com* 🎫 *$60.*

TCL Chinese Theatre

ARTS VENUE | The stylized Chinese pagodas and temples of the former Grauman's Chinese Theatre have become a shrine both to stardom and the combination of glamour and flamboyance that inspire the phrase "only in Hollywood." Although you have to buy a movie ticket to appreciate the interior trappings, the courtyard is open to the public. The main theater itself is worth visiting, if only to see a film in the same setting as hundreds of celebrities who have attended big premieres here.

And then, of course, outside in front are the oh-so-famous cement hand- and footprints. This tradition is said to have begun at the theater's opening in 1927, with the premiere of Cecil B. DeMille's *King of Kings,* when actress Norma Talmadge just happened to step in wet cement. Now more than 160 celebrities have contributed imprints for posterity, including some oddball specimens, such as casts of Whoopi Goldberg's dreadlocks. ✉ *6925 Hollywood Blvd., Hollywood* ☎ *323/461–3331* 🌐 *www.tclchinesetheatres.com* 🎫 *Tour $20.*

Restaurants

Cactus Taqueria #1

$ | MEXICAN | FAMILY | A humble taco shack on the side of the road, Cactus offers up $3 tacos with all types of meat you could imagine, even beef tongue. They also have carne asada and chicken for the less adventurous. **Known for:** California burritos; delicious fries; excellent street-style tacos. [$] *Average main: $11* ✉ *950 Vine St., Hollywood* ☎ *323/464–5865* 🌐 *www.cactustaqueriainc.com.*

★ Gwen

$$$ | STEAKHOUSE | A heaven for upscale carnivores, this fine-dining restaurant serves impossibly exquisite dishes in a copper-and-marble setting. Cooking meat is more than an unceremonious, übermasculine endeavor here—it's an intricate, delicate art form. **Known for:** perfect steak; duck fat potatoes; strong cocktails. [$] *Average main: $25* ✉ *6600 Sunset Blvd., Hollywood* ☎ *323/946–7513* 🌐 *www.gwenla.com.*

★ Providence

$$$$ | SEAFOOD | This is widely considered one of the best seafood restaurants in the country, and chef-owner Michael Cimarusti elevates sustainably driven fine dining to an art form. The elegant space is the perfect spot to sample exquisite seafood with the chef's signature application of French technique, traditional American themes, and Asian accents. **Known for:** fresh seafood; superb chef tasting menu; exquisite dessert options. [$] *Average main: $150* ✉ *5955 Melrose Ave., Hollywood* ☎ *323/460–4170*

A concert at the Hollywood Bowl is a summertime tradition for Angelenos.

www.providencela.com *Closed Sun. and Mon. No lunch Tues.–Thurs. and Sat.*

★ Roscoe's House of Chicken and Waffles

$$ | SOUTHERN | FAMILY | Roscoe's is *the* place for down-home Southern cooking in Southern California. Just ask the patrons who drive from all over L.A. for bargain-priced fried chicken and waffles. The name of this casual eatery honors a late-night combo popularized in Harlem jazz clubs. **Known for:** simple yet famous chicken and waffles; classic soul food dishes; eggs with cheese and onions. *Average main: $15* *1514 N. Gower St., Hollywood* *323/466–7453* *www.roscoeschickenandwaffles.com.*

Salt's Cure

$$ | AMERICAN | FAMILY | Not only a part of the California gastronomy scene, Salt's Cure celebrates it by keeping all its ingredients locally sourced and homegrown. The former WeHo spot comes to Hollywood to prove that despite appearances, Californians love traditional meat-based staples just as much as they love their kale salads and smoothies. **Known for:** oatmeal griddle cakes; hearty sandwiches; all California-grown ingredients. *Average main: $15* *1155 N. Highland Ave., Hollywood* *323/465–7258* *www.saltscure.com* *Closed Mon. and Tues.*

Hotels

★ Hollywood Roosevelt Hotel

$$$$ | HOTEL | Poolside cabana rooms are adorned with cow-skin rugs and marble bathrooms, while rooms in the main building accentuate the property's history at this party-centric hotel in the heart of Hollywood. **Pros:** Spare Room bowling alley on-site; pool is a popular weekend hangout; great burgers at the on-site 25 Degrees restaurant. **Cons:** reports of noise and staff attitude; stiff parking fees ($45); decor is dated in places. *Rooms from: $419* *7000 Hollywood Blvd., Hollywood* *323/466–7000* *www.hollywoodroosevelt.com* *353 rooms* *No meals.*

Local Chains Worth Stopping For

It's said that the drive-in burger joint was invented in L.A., probably to meet the demands of an ever-mobile car culture. Burger aficionados line up at all hours outside **In-N-Out Burger** (⊕ *www.in-n-out.com, multiple locations*), still a family-owned operation whose terrific made-to-order burgers are revered by Angelenos. Visitors may recognize the chain as the infamous spot where Paris Hilton got nabbed for drunk driving, but locals are more concerned with getting their burger fix off the "secret" menu, with variations like "Animal Style" (mustard-grilled patty with grilled onions and extra spread), a "4 x 4" (four burger patties and four cheese slices, for big eaters) or the bun-less "Protein Style" that comes wrapped in a bib of lettuce. Go online for a list of every "secret" menu item.

Tommy's is best known for their delightfully sloppy chili burger. Visit their no-frills original location (✉ *2575 Beverly Blvd., Los Angeles* ☎ *213/389–9060*)—a culinary landmark. For rotisserie chicken that will make you forget the Colonel altogether, head to **Zankou Chicken** (✉ *5065 Sunset Blvd., Hollywood* ☎ *323/665–7845* ⊕ *www.zankouchicken.com*), a small chain noted for its golden crispy-skinned birds, potent garlic sauce, and Armenian specialties. One-of-a-kind-sausage lovers will appreciate **Wurstküche** (✉ *800 E. 3rd St., Downtown* ☎ *213/687–4444* ⊕ *www.jerrysfamousdeli.com*), where the menu includes items like rattlesnake and rabbit or pheasant with Herbs de Provence. With a lively bar scene, the occasional celebrity sighting, and a spot directly across from the beach, **BOA Steakhouse** (✉ *101 Santa Monica Blvd., Santa Monica* ☎ *310/899–4466* ⊕ *www.hillstone.com*) is a popular hangout, while **Lemonade** (✉ *9001 Beverly Blvd., West Hollywood* ☎ *310/247–2500* ⊕ *www.senorfish.net*) is known for its healthy seasonally driven menu, pulled straight from L.A.'s farmers' markets.

★ Magic Castle Hotel

$$ | HOTEL | FAMILY | Guests at the hotel can secure advance dinner reservations and attend magic shows at the Magic Castle, a private club in a 1908 mansion next door for magicians and their admirers. **Pros:** heated pool and lush patio; central location near Hollywood & Highland; access to fun Magic Castle shows. **Cons:** strict dress code; no elevator; highly trafficked street. *Rooms from: $250* ✉ *7025 Franklin Ave., Hollywood* ☎ *323/851–0800, 800/741–4915* ⊕ *magiccastlehotel.com* *43 rooms* *Free breakfast.*

★ Mama Shelter

$ | HOTEL | Even locals adore Mama Shelter, one of Hollywood's sexiest boutique hotels, thanks to the rooftop bar populated with beautiful people lounging on love seats, simple affordable rooms with quirky amenities like Bert and Ernie masks, and a down-home lobby restaurant that serves a mean Korean-style burrito. **Pros:** delicious food and cocktails on the property; affordable rooms that don't skimp on style; foosball in lobby. **Cons:** rooms on the small side; creaky elevators; bar and restaurant often get crowded. *Rooms from: $159* ✉ *6500 Selma Ave., Hollywood* ☎ *323/785–6600* ⊕ *www.mamashelter.com/en/los-angeles* *70 rooms* *No meals.*

W Hollywood

$$$$ | **HOTEL** | This centrally located, ultra-modernly lit location is outfitted for the wired traveler and features a rooftop pool deck and popular on-site bars, like the Station Hollywood and the mod Living Room lobby bar. **Pros:** Metro stop outside the front door; comes with in-room party necessities, from ice to cocktail glasses; comfy beds with petal-soft duvets. **Cons:** small pool; pricey dining and valet parking; location in noisy part of Hollywood. *Rooms from: $500 ✉ 6250 Hollywood Blvd., Hollywood ☎ 323/798–1300, 888/625–4955 🌐 www.whotels.com/hollywood 305 rooms No meals.*

Nightlife

Birds

BARS/PUBS | They call it your neighborhood bar, because even if you don't live in the neighborhood you'll feel at home at this Alfred Hitchcock–themed eatery. Located in Franklin Village, a block-long stretch of bars, cafés, and bookstores, come here for pub food or a cheap poultry-centric dinner. Weekend nights mean cheap beer and well drinks, crowds spilling onto the streets, and a few rounds of oversize Jenga. *✉ 5925 Franklin Ave., Hollywood ☎ 323/465–0175 🌐 www.birdshollywood.com.*

Burgundy Room

BARS/PUBS | Around since 1919, Burgundy Room attracts a fiercely loyal crowd of locals, as well as the occasional wandering tourist. The bar is supposedly haunted (check out the Ouija boards toward the back), but that just adds to its charm. Its rock-and-roll vibe, strong drinks, and people-watching opportunities make this a worthy detour on any night out on the town. *✉ 1621 N. Cahuenga Blvd., Hollywood ☎ 323/465–7530.*

★ **Dirty Laundry**

BARS/PUBS | Tucked away in a basement on the quiet Hudson Avenue, Dirty Laundry is a former speakeasy turned proper cocktail bar with live music and DJs spinning both fresh and throwback music. There's beer on hand, but here, cocktails are king. *✉ 1725 Hudson Ave., Hollywood ☎ 323/462–6531.*

★ **Good Times at Davey Wayne's**

BARS/PUBS | It's a fridge; it's a door; it's the entrance to Davey Wayne's, a bar and lounge that pulls out all the stops to transport you back in time to the '70s. The interior is your living room; the outside is an ongoing backyard barbecue with all your friends. Come early to beat the crowds or be prepared to get up close and personal with your neighbors. *✉ 1611 N. El Centro Ave., Hollywood ☎ 323/498–0859 🌐 www.goodtimesatdaveywaynes.com.*

Hotel Cafe

MUSIC CLUBS | This intimate venue caters to fans of folk, indie rock, and music on the softer side. With red velvet backdrops, hardwood furnishings, and the occasional celebrity surprise performance—notably John Mayer—music lovers will not only be very happy but will receive a respite from the ordinary Hollywood experience. *✉ 1623½ N. Cahuenga Blvd., Hollywood ☎ 323/461–2040 🌐 www.hotelcafe.com.*

★ **Musso and Frank Grill**

BARS/PUBS | **FAMILY** | The prim and proper vibe of this old-school steak house won't appeal to those looking for a raucous night out; instead, its appeal lies in its history and sturdy drinks. Established over a century ago, its dark wood decor, red tuxedo–clad waiters, and highly skilled bartenders can easily shuttle you back to its Hollywood heyday when Marilyn Monroe, F. Scott Fitzgerald, and Greta Garbo once hung around and sipped martinis. *✉ 6667 Hollywood Blvd.,*

Hollywood ☎ *323/467–7788* 🌐 *www.mussoandfrank.com.*

No Vacancy
BARS/PUBS | Though at first glance, No Vacancy might boast an air of exclusivity and pretentiousness, its relaxed interiors and welcoming staff will almost instantly make you feel like you're at a house party. You know, the kind with burlesque shows, tightrope performances, a speakeasy secret entrance, and mixologists who can pretty much whip up any drink your heart desires. ✉ *1727 N. Hudson Ave., Hollywood* ☎ *323/465–1902* 🌐 *www.novacancyla.com.*

Sassafras Saloon
BARS/PUBS | Put on your dancing shoes (or your cowboy boots) and step back in time. The Sassafras boasts not only an oddly cozy, Western atmosphere but plenty of opportunities to strut your moves on the dance floor. Indulge in exquisite craft mezcal, whiskey, and tequila cocktails for some liquid courage before you salsa the night away. ✉ *1233 N. Vine St., Hollywood* ☎ *323/467–2800* 🌐 *www.sassafrassaloon.com.*

Three Clubs
BARS/PUBS | Cocktail bars are a dime a dozen in Hollywood, but there's something about this Vine Street joint that makes patrons keep coming back for more. Maybe it's the down-to-earth attitude, delicious no-frills cocktails, and the fact that a taco stand serving greasy grub is right next door. Come to see one of the burlesque or comedy shows for a full experience. ✉ *1123 Vine St., Hollywood* ☎ *323/462–6441* 🌐 *www.threeclubs.com.*

Shopping

★ **Amoeba Records**
MUSIC STORES | Touted as the "World's Largest Independent Record Store," Amoeba is a playground for music lovers, with a knowledgeable staff and a focus on local artists. Catch free in-store appearances and signings by artists and bands that play sold-out shows at venues down the road. There's a massive and eclectic collection of vinyl records, CDs, and cassette tapes, not to mention VHS tapes, DVDs, and Blu-Ray discs. It's a paradise for both music and movie lovers. ✉ *6200 Hollywood Blvd., Hollywood* ☎ *323/245–6400* 🌐 *www.amoeba.com.*

Hollywood & Highland Center
SHOPPING CENTERS/MALLS | If you're on the hunt for unique boutiques, look elsewhere. However, if you prefer the biggest mall retail chains America has to offer, Hollywood & Highland is a great spot for a shopping spree. The design of the complex pays tribute to the city's film legacy, with a grand staircase leading up to a pair of three-story-tall stucco elephants, a nod to the 1916 movie *Intolerance*. Pause at the entrance arch, called Babylon Court, which frames a picture-perfect view of the Hollywood sign. This place is a huge tourist magnet, so don't expect to mingle with the locals. ✉ *6801 Hollywood Blvd., at Highland Ave., Hollywood* 🌐 *www.hollywoodandhighland.com.*

Larry Edmunds Bookshop
BOOKS/STATIONERY | Cinephiles have long descended upon this iconic 70-plus-year-old shop that in addition to stocking tons of texts about motion picture history offers film fans the opportunity to pick up scripts, posters, and photographs from Hollywood's golden era to the present. ✉ *6644 Hollywood Blvd., Hollywood* ☎ *323/463–3273* 🌐 *www.larryedmunds.com.*

The Record Parlour
MUSIC STORES | Vinyl records and music memorabilia abound in this hip yet modest record store–slash–music lover magnet that also touts vintage audio gear and retro jukeboxes. A visit here is usually a multihour affair, one that involves more than just browsing through display cases, digging through wooden carts of used vinyls, and playing your picks at the listening station. ✉ *6408 Selma Ave., Hollywood* ☎ *323/464–7757* 🌐 *therecordparlour.com.*

Activities

★ Runyon Canyon Trail and Park

HIKING/WALKING | Is Runyon Canyon the city's most famous trail? To the world, it just might be, what with so many A-listers frequenting it. Many folks visiting L.A. take the trail specifically for celebrity spotting. But, if that's not something you're into, this accessible trail right in the middle of Hollywood is also a good place to hike, run, see the Hollywood sign, photograph the city skyline, or simply get a bit of fresh air. If you just happen to run into a famous face, well that's just the cherry on the cake. ✉ *2000 N. Fuller Ave., Hollywood* ☎ *805/370–2301* 🌐 *www.nps.gov/samo/planyourvisit/runyoncanyon.htm.*

Studio City

Restaurants

Asanebo

$$$ | JAPANESE | One of L.A.'s finest sushi restaurants, Asanebo is an inviting, no-frills establishment serving top-quality sushi and a wealth of innovative dishes to an A-list clientele. The affable chefs will regale you with memorable specialties such as a caviar-topped lobster, succulent seared *toro* (tuna belly), or just simple morsels of pristine fish dusted with sea salt. **Known for:** omakase (chef's choice) dinners; halibut truffle; excellent sushi. [$] *Average main: $30* ✉ *11941 Ventura Blvd., Studio City* ☎ *818/760–3348* 🌐 *www.asanebo-restaurant.com/* ⏲ *Closed Mon. No lunch weekends.*

Good Neighbor Restaurant

$ | DINER | Its walls may be heavy with framed photographs of film and TV stars, and folks from the biz might regularly grace its tables, but this Studio City diner is every bit as down-to-earth as your next-door neighbor, even after 40-some years. It gets pretty busy, but a plateful of that home cooking is worth the wait; or if you're in a mad dash, grab a caffeine or fruit smoothie fix from the Neighbarista. **Known for:** craft-your-own omelet; cottage fries; excellent breakfast food. [$] *Average main: $13* ✉ *3701 Cahuenga Blvd., Studio City* ☎ *818/761–4627* 🌐 *goodneighborrestaurant.com.*

Hotels

Sportsmen's Lodge

$$ | HOTEL | FAMILY | This sprawling five-story hotel, a San Fernando Valley landmark just a short jaunt over the Hollywood Hills, has an updated contemporary look highlighted by the Olympic-size pool and summer patio with an outdoor bar. **Pros:** close to Ventura Boulevard restaurants; free shuttle to Universal Hollywood; quiet garden-view rooms worth asking for. **Cons:** pricey daily self-parking fee ($25); not centrally located to other Los Angeles sights; a bit pricey for the area. [$] *Rooms from: $249* ✉ *12825 Ventura Blvd., Studio City* ☎ *818/769–4700, 800/821–8511* 🌐 *www.sportsmenslodge.com* *190 rooms* *No meals.*

Nightlife

Baked Potato

MUSIC CLUBS | Baked Potato might be a strange name to give a world-famous jazz club that's been holding performances of well-known acts (Allan Holdsworth and Michael Landau) under its roof since the '70s, but it only takes a quick peek at the menu to understand. Twenty-four different types of baked potatoes dominate its otherwise short menu, each of which come with sour cream, butter, and salad to offset all that carb intake. ✉ *3787 Cahuenga Blvd., Studio City* ☎ *818/980–1615* 🌐 *www.thebakedpotato.com.*

★ Pinz Bowling Alley

BOWLING | "Bowl. Eat. Drink. Repeat" might be this bowling alley's motto, but thanks to its neon-slash-backlit lanes—each fully equipped with a touch-screen food and drink ordering system—and its very own arcade, Pinz is more than just your typical bowling experience. A few A-list names are among its loyal clientele, but you don't visit for celebrity sightings; all bells and whistles aside, it's a proper bowling alley and you come here to bowl. ✉ *12655 Ventura Blvd., Studio City* ☎ *818/769–7600* 🌐 *pinzla.com.*

Universal City

Sights

★ **Universal Studios Hollywood**
AMUSEMENT PARK/WATER PARK | FAMILY | A theme park with classic attractions like roller coasters and thrill rides, Universal Studios also provides a tour of some beloved television and movie sets. A favorite attraction is the tram tour, during which you can duck from King Kong; see the airplane wreckage of *War of the Worlds*; ride along with the cast of the *Fast and the Furious*; and get chills looking at the house from *Psycho*. **■TIP→ The tram ride is usually the best place to begin your visit, because the lines become longer as the day goes on.**

Most attractions are designed to give you a thrill in one form or another, including *Jurassic World*—The Ride and Revenge of the Mummy along with immersive rides like the 4D Simpsons Ride, where you can actually smell Maggie Simpson's baby powder. The Wizarding World of Harry Potter, however, is the crown jewel of the park, featuring magical rides, pints of frozen butterbeer, and enough merchandise to drain you wallet faster than you can shout "Expecto Patronum." If you're in town in October, stop by for Halloween Horror Nights, featuring mazes full of monsters, murderers, and jump scares.

Geared more toward adults, CityWalk is a separate venue run by Universal Studios, where you'll find shops, restaurants, nightclubs, and movie theaters. ✉ *100 Universal City Plaza, Universal City* ☎ *800/864–8377* 🌐 *www.universalstudioshollywood.com* 🎫 *$139.*

Restaurants

Café Sierra
$$$ | **SEAFOOD** | **FAMILY** | Don't let the fact that this airy Californian and pan-Asian spot is located inside a Hilton Hotel scare you; Café Sierra has a drool-worthy seafood and prime rib buffet. Lunching here can be a splurge, but it's worth every penny. **Known for:** champagne brunch; Alaskan king crab; live jazz music. $ *Average main: $30* ✉ *555 Universal Hollywood Dr., Universal City* ☎ *818/509–2030* 🌐 *www.cafesierrahilton.com.*

Dongpo
$$ | **SICHUAN** | **FAMILY** | Upmarket regional Chinese cuisine chain Meizhou Dongpo tries its hand at bringing its modern take on authentic Sichuanese cuisine to the area with Dongpo Kitchen, and it's exactly what the CityWalk needed to up its dining game. This bright, contemporary-meets-traditional Chinese restaurant serves delightful, affordable fare right in the middle of a sea of tourists. **Known for:** Dongpo roast duck; Sichuan dumplings; kung pao chicken. $ *Average main: $20* ✉ *1000 Universal Studios Blvd. V103, Universal City* ☎ *818/358–3272* 🌐 *www.citywalkhollywood.com.*

Hotels

Sheraton Universal
$$ | **HOTEL** | **FAMILY** | With large meeting spaces and a knowledgeable staff, this Sheraton buzzes year-round with business travelers and families, providing easy access to the free shuttle that takes guests to adjacent Universal Studios and CityWalk. **Pros:** pool area with cabanas and bar; oversize desks and office chairs in rooms; good for families and visitors to Universal Studios. **Cons:** average in-house restaurant; tourist crowd; chain hotel feel. $ *Rooms from: $250* ✉ *333 Universal Hollywood Dr., Universal City*

☎ *818/980–1212, 888/627–7184* 🌐 *www.sheratonuniversal.com* *461 rooms* *No meals.*

Burbank

Sights

★Warner Bros. Studios

FILM STUDIO | You don't need to be a big film nerd to appreciate a visit to the Warner Bros. Studios, where you can pretend to be your favorite TV or movie characters, whether at a working replica of Central Perk from *Friends* or via a Sorting Hat ceremony from the *Harry Potter*movies. You'll also visit backlots and soundstages to see how the magic is made.

If you're looking for an authentic behind-the-scenes look at how films and TV shows are made, head to this major studio center, one of the world's busiest. After a short film on the studio's movies and TV shows, hop aboard a tram for a ride through the sets and soundstages of such favorites as *Casablanca* and *Rebel Without a Cause*. You'll see the bungalows where Marlon Brando, Bette Davis, and other icons relaxed between shots, and the current production offices for Clint Eastwood and George Clooney. You might even spot a celeb or see a shoot in action—tours change from day to day depending on the productions taking place on the lot. ✉ *3400 W. Riverside Dr., Burbank* ☎ *818/977–8687* 🌐 *www.wbstudiotour.com* *From $69.*

Restaurants

Bea Bea's

$ | **DINER** | Just because Bea Bea's is a no-nonsense kind of place, it doesn't mean the food isn't special. This diner serves breakfast food that is about as close to extraordinary as the most important meal of the day can be. **Known for:** pancakes and French toast; friendly staff; classic diner grub. *Average main: $13* ✉ *353 N. Pass Ave., Burbank* ☎ *818/846–2327* 🌐 *www.beabeas.com.*

Centanni Trattoria

$$ | **ITALIAN** | In a city full of adventurous restaurants touting new takes on traditional dishes and swanking about with bells and whistles and stunning interiors, a run-of-the-mill-looking place like Centanni Trattoria might never make it onto the radar. But what this authentic Italian spot lacks in swagger, it more than makes up for in delicious home cooking. **Known for:** pappardelle with white truffle oil; risotto di funghi; great appetizers. *Average main: $20* ✉ *117 N. Victory Blvd., Burbank* ☎ *818/561–4643* 🌐 *www.centannila.com.*

Los Amigos

$$ | **MEXICAN** | **FAMILY** | If you're in the mood for good old-fashioned fun coupled with hearty Mexican fare and delicious margaritas, then you'll want to consider Los Amigos, whose legendary fruity margaritas alone are worth the drive. Pair those with something from the Platillos Mexicanos menu on karaoke night, and you're guaranteed a good time until the wee hours of the night. **Known for:** classic Mexican food; massive portions; casual dining. *Average main: $18* ✉ *2825 W. Olive Ave., Burbank* ☎ *818/842–3700* 🌐 *www.losamigosbarandgrill.com.*

Porto's Bakery

$ | **CUBAN** | **FAMILY** | Waiting in line at Porto's is as much a part of the experience as is indulging in one of its roasted pork sandwiches or chocolate-dipped croissants. This Cuban bakery and café has been an L.A. staple for more than 50 years, often drawing crowds during lunch. **Known for:** famous potato balls; must-try desserts; fast-moving counter service. *Average main: $8* ✉ *3614 W. Magnolia Blvd., Burbank* ☎ *818/846–9100* 🌐 *www.portosbakery.com.*

Hotels

Hotel Amarano Burbank

$$ | HOTEL | Close to Burbank's TV and movie studios, the smartly designed Amarano feels like a Beverly Hills boutique hotel, complete with 24-hour room service, a homey on-site restaurant and lounge, and lovely rooms. **Pros:** saltwater pool; complimentary bike rentals; comfortable beds. **Cons:** street noise; away from most of the city's action; breakfast not included. *Rooms from: $269 ✉ 322 N. Pass Ave., Burbank ☎ 818/842–8887, 888/956–1900 🌐 www.hotelamarano.com 132 rooms No meals.*

Nightlife

Flappers Comedy Club

COMEDY CLUBS | Even though this live comedy club doesn't exactly have as long a history as others in town (it opened in 2010), it's attracted an impressive list of big names like Jerry Seinfeld, Maria Bamford, and Adam Sandler thanks to its Celebrity Drop-In Tuesdays. The food and drinks are good though not great, but you're here for the laughs not the grub. ✉ *102 E. Magnolia Blvd., Burbank ☎ 818/845–9721 🌐 www.flapperscomedy.com.*

Shopping

Magnolia Park Vintage

SHOPPING NEIGHBORHOODS | Melrose Avenue might be Los Angeles's most well-known vintage shopping destination, but to many locals, especially those on the Eastside, Burbank's Magnolia Park is, in many ways, better. Spanning several blocks around Magnolia Avenue, this revitalized area blends vintage, thrift, and antique shopping opportunities with the laid-back small-town vibe that Melrose lacks. Great dining spots and modern coffee shops abound, as well as foot and nail spas for a bit of pampering. ✉ *W. Magnolia Blvd., between N. Niagara and N. Avon St., Burbank 🌐 www.visitmagnoliapark.com.*

Mid-Wilshire and Koreatown

While they're two distinctly different neighborhoods, Mid-Wilshire and Koreatown sit side by side and offer Angelenos some of the most interesting sights, sounds, and bites in the city.

Mid-Wilshire is broadly known for its wide variety of museums, but there's also a strip called Little Ethiopia, where you can find incredible cuisine. Koreatown, meanwhile, is a haven for Seoul food (pun intended) but also an area with multiethnic dining nuggets that hit the top of many restaurant lists. Once your stomach is sated, check out a Korean spa, where scrubbing and pampering can close out a perfectly long day.

Mid-Wilshire

Sights

★ Academy Museum of Motion Pictures

MUSEUM | FAMILY | The long-waited Academy Museum of Motion Pictures sits on the corner of Wilshire and Fairfax, and is highlighted by a giant spherical dome that features a 1,000-seat theater and stunning terrace with views of the Hollywood Hills. Inside, the museum has seven floors of exhibition space that delves into the history of cinema with interactive exhibits, features on award-winning story tellers, multiple theaters, and immersive experiences. Dedicated to the art and science of movies, the Academy Museum is the premier center that is a must-stop for film buffs and casual moviegoers alike. ✉ *6067 Wilshire Blvd., Mid-Wilshire ☎ 323/930–3000 🌐 www.academymuseum.org $25.*

La Brea Tar Pits Museum

ARCHAEOLOGICAL SITE | FAMILY | Show your kids where Ice Age fossils come from by taking them to the stickiest park in town. The area formed when deposits of oil rose to the earth's surface, collected in shallow pools, and coagulated into asphalt. In the early 20th century geologists discovered that all that goo contained the largest collection of Pleistocene (Ice Age) fossils ever found at one location: more than 600 species of birds, mammals, plants, reptiles, and insects. Roughly 100 tons of fossil bones have been removed in excavations during the last 100 years, making this one of the world's most famous fossil sites. You can see most of the pits through chain link fences, and the new Excavator Tour gets you as close as possible to the action.

Pit 91 and Project 23 are ongoing excavation projects; tours are offered, and you can volunteer to help with the excavations in the summer. Several pits are scattered around Hancock Park and the surrounding neighborhood; construction in the area has often had to accommodate them, and in nearby streets and along sidewalks, little bits of tar occasionally ooze up. The museum displays fossils from the tar pits and has a glass-walled laboratory that allows visitors to view paleontologists and volunteers as they work on specimens. **■TIP→ Museum admission is free for L.A. County residents weekdays 3–5 pm.** ✉ *5801 Wilshire Blvd., Miracle Mile* ☎ *323/934–7243* 🌐 *www.tarpits.org* 🎫 *$15; free 1st Tues. of every month (except July and Aug.) and every Tues. in Sept.*

★ Los Angeles County Museum of Art (LACMA)

MUSEUM | Los Angeles has a truly fabulous museum culture and everything that it stands for can be epitomized by the massive, eclectic, and ever-changing Los Angeles County Museum of Art. Opened at its current location in 1965, today the museum boasts the largest collection of art in the western United States with more than 135,000 pieces from 6,000 years of history across multiple buildings atop over 20 acres. Highlights include the *Urban Light* sculpture by Chris Burden (an Instagram favorite), *Levitated Mass* by Michael Heizer, and prominent works by Frida Kahlo, Wassily Kandinsky, Henri Matisse, and Claude Monet. With an illustrative permanent collection to go along with an ever-rotating array of temporary exhibits, film screenings, educational programs, and more, the museum is a beacon of culture that stands alone in the middle of the city. **■TIP→ Temporary exhibitions sometimes require tickets purchased in advance.** ✉ *5905 Wilshire Blvd., Miracle Mile* ☎ *323/857–6000* 🌐 *www.lacma.org* 🎫 *$20* 🕒 *Closed Wed.*

Petersen Automotive Museum

MUSEUM | **FAMILY** | L.A. is a mecca for car lovers, which explains the popularity of this museum with a collection of more than 300 automobiles and other motorized vehicles. But you don't have to be a gearhead to appreciate the Petersen; there's plenty of fascinating history here for all to enjoy. Learn how Los Angeles grew up around its freeways, how cars evolve from the design phase to the production line, and how automobiles have influenced film and television. To see how the vehicles, many of them quite rare, are preserved and maintained, take the 90-minute tour of the basement-level Vault (young kids aren't permitted in the Vault, but they'll find plenty to keep them occupied throughout the museum). ✉ *6060 Wilshire Blvd., Mid-Wilshire* ☎ *323/964–6331* 🌐 *www.petersen.org* 🎫 *From $17.*

Restaurants

★ Meals by Genet

$$ | **ETHIOPIAN** | In a tucked-away stretch along Fairfax Avenue is Little Ethiopia, where Angelenos of all stripes flock for the African country's signatures like *tibs*, *wat*, and *kitfo*. And while there is a plethora of Ethiopian options, no one does the cuisine justice quite like Meals by Genet. **Known for:** authentic Ethiopian cuisine; jovial atmosphere; unreal tibs.

Average main: $20 1053 S. Fairfax Ave., Mid-Wilshire 323/938–9304 www.mealsbygenetla.com Closed Mon.–Wed.

★ République

$$$$ | **FRENCH** | **FAMILY** | This stunning expansive space, originally built for Charlie Chaplin back in the 1920s, serves French delicacies for breakfast, lunch, and dinner every day of the week. The scent of homemade croissants wafts through the building in the morning; steak frites can be enjoyed at night. **Known for:** French classics like escargot; unbeatable pastries; nice bar menu. *Average main: $35 624 S. La Brea Ave., Beverly–La Brea 310/362–6115 www.republiquela.com.*

Sky's Gourmet Tacos

$ | **MEXICAN** | If you're searching for some of the spiciest and most succulent tacos in L.A., look no further than Sky's. This quaint taco joint offers up beef, chicken, turkey, seafood, and vegan options that will leave your mouth on fire and your belly full in all the best ways possible. **Known for:** amazing tacos with a variety of fillings (including breakfast tacos); lots of spices; jovial atmosphere. *Average main: $10 5303 W. Pico Blvd., Mid-Wilshire 833/759–8226 www.skysgourmettacos.com.*

Koreatown

Restaurants

The Boiling Crab

$$ | **SEAFOOD** | **FAMILY** | Put on your bib and prepare to get messy, because this crab shack is not for stodgy eaters. Choices of blue, Dungeness, snow, king, and southern king, are brought out in plastic bags where you can rip, tear, twist, and yank the meaty goodness out of their shells. **Known for:** giant crab legs; unfussy environment; long lines. *Average main: $20 3377 Wilshire Blvd., Suite 115, Koreatown 213/389–2722 www.theboilingcrab.com Wilshire/Normandie Station.*

Guelaguetza

$$ | **MEXICAN** | **FAMILY** | A classic L.A. Mexican eatery, Guelaguetza serves the complex but not overpoweringly spicy cooking of Oaxaca, one of Mexico's most renowned culinary capitals. Inside, you'll find a largely Spanish-speaking clientele bobbing their heads to nightly jazz and marimba while wolfing down the restaurant's specialty: the moles. **Known for:** salsa-covered chorizo; chili-marinated pork; family-owned restaurant. *Average main: $15 3014 W. Olympic Blvd., Koreatown 213/427–0608 www.ilovemole.com Closed Mon.*

★ Kobawoo House

$$ | **KOREAN** | **FAMILY** | Nestled into a dingy strip mall, this Korean powerhouse is given away by the lines of locals waiting outside. Once inside, scents of grilled meats and kimchi immediately fill your nostrils, and soon enough, your table will be littered with sides, *kalbi* beef, *dolsot* bibimbap, *wang bosam* (cabbage wraps with boiled pork), and tall bottles of Hite beer. **Known for:** perfect kalbi beef; long lines; cheap eats. *Average main: $17 698 S. Vermont Ave., Suite 109, Koreatown 213/389–7300 www.kobawoohouse.com Wilshire/Vermont.*

Hotels

Hotel Normandie

$ | **HOTEL** | Originally built in 1926, this Renaissance Revival gem has been renovated to today's standards and is now a hip and not-so-pricey spot to post up in the ever-booming center of Koreatown. **Pros:** Michelin-starred French restaurant; complimentary breakfast; cheap prices. **Cons:** feels dated; tiny bathrooms; restaurant is pricey. *Rooms from: $190 605 Normandie Ave., Koreatown 213/388–8138 www.hotelnormandiela.com 92 rooms Wilshire/Normandie.*

The Line

$$ | HOTEL | This boutique hotel pays homage to its Koreatown address with dynamic dining concepts and a hidden karaoke speakeasy. **Pros:** on-site bikes to explore the area; unique decor; fun bars on-site (ask about the speakeasy). **Cons:** expensive parking; lobby bar crowds public spaces; far from parts of the city you may want to explore. *Rooms from: $250* *3515 Wilshire Blvd., Koreatown* *213/381–7411* *www.thelinehotel.com* *384 rooms* *No meals* *Wilshire/Normandie Station.*

Nightlife

Dan Sung Sa

BARS/PUBS | Step through the curtained entrance and back in time to 1970s Korea at Dan Sung Sa, which gained wider popularity after Anthony Bourdain paid a visit. At this quirky time-capsule bar, woodblock menus feature roughly 100 small eats. You'll see much that looks familiar, but fortune favors the bold. Take a chance on corn cheese, or try the *makgeolli*: a boozy Korean rice drink you sip from a bowl. It pairs perfectly with good conversation and snacking all night long. *3317 W. 6th St., Koreatown* *213/487–9100* *Wilshire/Vermont.*

★ HMS Bounty

BARS/PUBS | This super-kitschy nautical-theme bar in the heart of Koreatown offers drink specials and food at prices that will make you swoon. Come for the wings, all-day breakfast specials, cheap drinks, and very eclectic crowds. *3357 Wilshire Blvd., Koreatown* *213/385–7275* *www.thehmsbounty.com* *Wilshire/Normandie.*

The Prince

BARS/PUBS | *Mad Men* and *New Girl* both had multiple scenes filmed in this Old Hollywood relic, which dates back to the early 1900s. The Prince is trimmed with vintage fabric wallpaper and bedecked with a stately mahogany bar; the grand piano waits in the wings. Squire lamps punctuate red-leather booths where you can enjoy Korean fare and standard cocktails, wine, and beer. Whatever you do, get the deep-fried chicken. *3198 W. 7th St., Koreatown* *213/389–1586* *Wilshire/Vermont Station.*

Activities

Aroma Spa & Sports

FITNESS/HEALTH CLUBS | It's not difficult to find amazing spa experiences throughout Koreatown. Most places will offer up standard scrubs, hot and cold baths, dry and wet saunas, and more. Aroma takes things to another level as the spa is just the centerpiece of an entire entertainment complex. Spa services include all the traditional treatments, but when you're done getting pampered, the rest of the facility includes a gym, a swimming pool, restaurants, and a state-of-the-art golf driving range. *3680 Wilshire Blvd., Koreatown* *213/387–2111* *www.aromaresort.com* *Wilshire/Western.*

Wi Spa

FITNESS/HEALTH CLUBS | Koreatown is filled with endless spa experiences, but there are a few that rise above the rest. Wi Spa is a 24/7 wonderland of treatments that includes hot and cold baths, unique sauna rooms, and floors for men, women, or co-ed family spa fun. Signature sauna rooms vary from intense 231-degree thermotherapy to salt-enriched stations and specialty clay imported from Korea. Just remember, Korean spas are not for the shy at heart—you will be nude, you will get scrubbed, and you will feel like a million bucks after. *2700 Wilshire Blvd., Koreatown* *213/487–2700* *www.wispausa.com* *Wilshire/Vermont.*

Downtown Los Angeles

If there's one thing Angelenos love, it's a makeover, and city planners have put the wheels in motion for a dramatic revitalization of this area in recent years. Downtown is both glamorous and gritty and is an example of Los Angeles's complexity as a whole. There's a dizzying variety of experiences not to be missed here if you're curious about the artistic, historic, ethnic, or sports-loving sides of L.A.

Downtown Los Angeles isn't just one neighborhood: it's a cluster of pedestrian-friendly enclaves where you can sample an eclectic mix of flavors, wander through world-class museums, and enjoy great live performances or sports events.

Sights

★Angels Flight Railway

TRANSPORTATION SITE (AIRPORT/BUS/FERRY/TRAIN) | The turn-of-the-20th-century funicular, dubbed "the shortest railway in the world," operated between 1901 and 1969, when it was dismantled to make room for an urban renewal project. Almost 30 years later, Angels Flight returned with its original orange-and-black wooden cable cars hauling travelers up a 298-foot incline from Hill Street to the fountain-filled Watercourt at California Plaza. Your reward is a stellar view of the neighborhood. Tickets are $1 each way, but you can buy a souvenir round-trip ticket for $2 if you want something to take home with you. ✉ *351 S. Hill St., between 3rd and 4th Sts., Downtown* ☎ *213/626–1901* 🌐 *www.angelsflight.org.*

Bradbury Building

BUILDING | Stunning wrought-iron railings, ornate plaster moldings, pink marble staircases, a birdcage elevator, and a skylighted atrium that rises almost 50 feet—it's easy to see why the Bradbury Building leaves visitors awestruck. Designed in 1893 by a novice architect who drew his inspiration from a science-fiction story and a conversation with his dead brother via a Ouija board, the office building was originally the site of turn-of-the-20th-century sweatshops, but now it houses a variety of businesses. Scenes from *Blade Runner*, *Chinatown*, and *500 Days of Summer* were filmed here, which means there's often a barrage of tourists snapping photos. Visits are limited to the lobby and the first-floor landing. **■TIP→Historic Downtown walking tours hosted by the L.A. Conservancy cost $15 and include the Bradbury Building.** ✉ *304 S. Broadway, Downtown* ☎ *213/626–1893* 🌐 *www.laconservancy.org/locations/bradbury-building* Ⓜ *Pershing Square Station.*

★The Broad Museum

MUSEUM | The talk of Los Angeles's art world when it opened in 2015, this museum in an intriguing, honeycomb-looking building was created by philanthropists Eli and Edythe Broad (rhymes with "road") to showcase their stunning private collection of contemporary art, amassed over five decades and still growing. With upward of 2,000 pieces by more than 200 artists, the collection has in-depth representations of the work of such prominent names as Jean Michel Basquiat, Jeff Koons, Ed Ruscha, Cindy Sherman, Cy Twombly, Kara Walker, and Christopher Wool. The "veil and vault" design of the main building integrates gallery space and storage space (visitors can glimpse the latter through a window in the stairwell): the veil refers to the fiberglass, concrete, and steel exterior; the vault is the concrete base. Temporary exhibits and works from the permanent collection are arranged in the small first-floor rooms and in the more expansive third floor of the museum, so you can explore everything in a few hours. Next door to the Broad is a small plaza with olive trees and seating, as well as the museum restaurant, Otium. Admission to the museum is free, but book timed tickets in advance to guarantee entry. ✉ *221 S. Grand Ave., Downtown* ☎ *213/232–6200* 🌐 *www.thebroad.org*

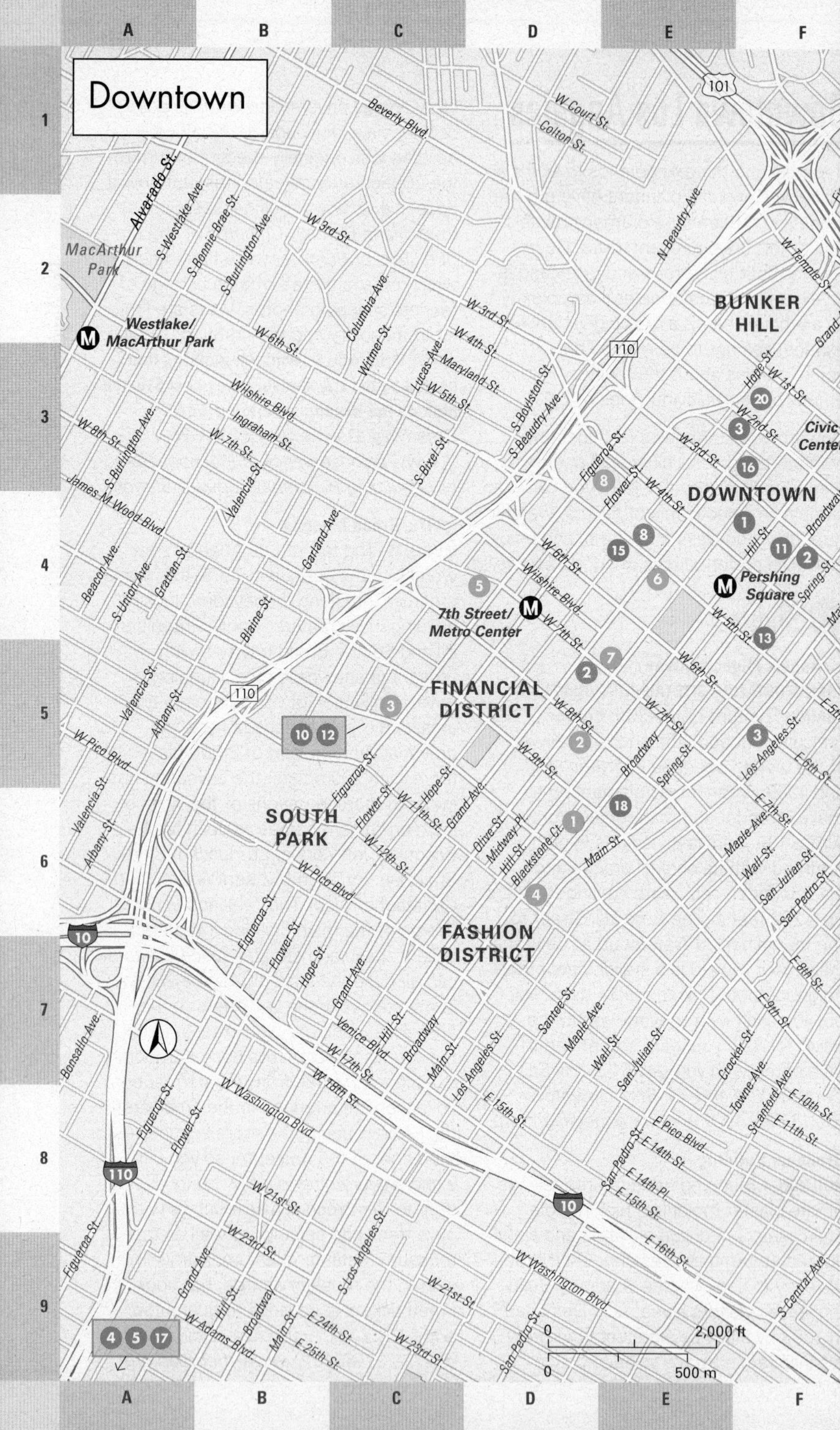
Downtown
A
B
C
D
E
F
1
2
3
4
5
6
7
8
9
MacArthur Park
Westlake/ MacArthur Park
BUNKER HILL
DOWNTOWN
Civic Center
Pershing Square
7th Street/ Metro Center
FINANCIAL DISTRICT
SOUTH PARK
FASHION DISTRICT
Alvarado St.
Beverly Blvd.
W Court St.
Colton St.
W 3rd St.
W 6th St.
Wilshire Blvd.
W 8th St.
James M Wood Blvd.
W Pico Blvd.
W Washington Blvd.
W 21st St.
W 23rd St.
W Adams Blvd.
E 24th St.
E 25th St.
Figueroa St.
Flower St.
Hope St.
Grand Ave.
Hill St.
Broadway
Main St.
Los Angeles St.
Spring St.
San Pedro St.
E Pico Blvd.
E 14th St.
E 15th St.
E 16th St.
S Central Ave.
0
2,000 ft
500 m

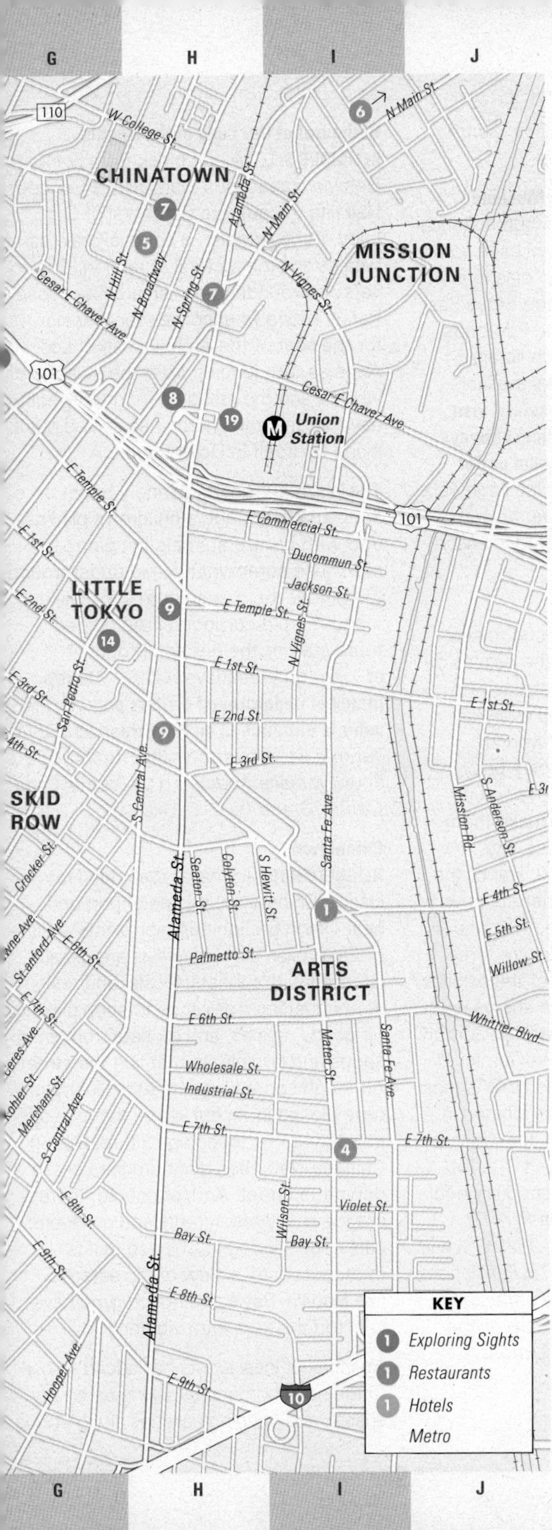

Sights

1 Angels Flight Railway F4
2 Bradbury Building F4
3 The Broad Museum F3
4 California African American Museum A9
5 California Science Center A9
6 Cathedral of Our Lady of the Angels G2
7 Chinatown H1
8 El Pueblo de Los Angeles H3
9 Geffen Contemporary at MOCA H4
10 GRAMMY Museum C5
11 Grand Central Market F4
12 L.A. Live C5
13 The Last Bookstore F4
14 Little Tokyo G4
15 Los Angeles Central Library E4
16 MOCA Grand Avenue F3
17 Natural History Museum of Los Angeles County A9
18 Orpheum Theatre E6
19 Union Station H3
20 Walt Disney Concert Hall F3

Restaurants

1 Bavel I6
2 Bottega Louie D5
3 Cole's French Dip F5
4 Guerrilla Tacos I7
5 Howlin' Ray's H2
6 Majordomo I1
7 Philippe the Original H2
8 71Above E4
9 Sushi Gen H5

Hotels

1 Ace Hotel Downtown Los Angeles D6
2 Freehand Los Angeles D5
3 Hotel Figueroa C5
4 The Hoxton D6
5 InterContinental Los Angeles Downtown D4
6 Millennium Biltmore Hotel E4
7 The NoMad Hotel E5
8 Westin Bonaventure Hotel and Suites E3

KEY
Exploring Sights
Restaurants
Hotels
Metro

Free *Closed Mon.* *Civic Center/ Grand Park Station.*

California African American Museum

MUSEUM | With more than 4,500 historical artifacts, this museum showcases contemporary art of the African diaspora. Artists represented here include Betye Saar, Charles Haywood, and June Edmonds. The museum has a research library with more than 6,000 books available for public use. **TIP→ If possible, visit on a Sunday, when there's almost always a diverse lineup of speakers and performances.** *600 State Dr., Exposition Park* *213/744–7432* *www.caamuseum.org* *Free; parking $12* *Closed Mon.* *Expo/Vermont Station.*

California Science Center

MUSEUM | **FAMILY** | You're bound to see excited kids running up to the dozens of interactive exhibits here that illustrate the prevalence of science in everyday life. Clustered in different "worlds," the center keeps young guests busy for hours. They can design their own buildings and learn how to make them earthquake-proof; watch Tess, the dramatic 50-foot animatronic star of the exhibit *Body Works*, demonstrate how the body's organs work together; and ride a bike across a trapeze wire three stories high in the air. One of the exhibits in the Air and Space section shows how astronauts Pete Conrad and Dick Gordon made it to outer space in the Gemini 11 capsule in 1966; also here is NASA's massive space shuttle *Endeavor*, located in the Samuel Oschin Pavilion, for which a timed ticket is needed to visit. The IMAX theater screens science-related large-format films. *700 Exposition Park Dr., Exposition Park* *323/724–3623* *www.californiasciencecenter.org* *Permanent exhibits free; fees for some attractions, special exhibits, and IMAX screenings vary; parking $12* *Expo/Vermont.*

Cathedral of Our Lady of the Angels

RELIGIOUS SITE | A half block from Frank Gehry's curvaceous Walt Disney Concert Hall sits the austere Cathedral of Our Lady of the Angels—a spiritual draw as well as an architectural attraction. Controversy surrounded Spanish architect José Rafael Moneo's unconventional design for the seat of the Archdiocese of Los Angeles. But judging from the swarms of visitors and the standing-room-only holiday masses, the church has carved out a niche for itself in Downtown L.A.

The plaza in front is glaringly bright on sunny days, though a children's play garden with bronze animals mitigates the starkness somewhat. Head underground to wander the mausoleum's mazelike white-marble corridors. Free guided tours start at the entrance fountain at 1 pm on weekdays. **TIP→ There's plenty of underground visitors parking; the vehicle entrance is on Hill Street.** *555 W. Temple St., Downtown* *213/680–5200* *www.olacathedral.org* *Free* *Civic Center/Grand Park.*

Chinatown

NEIGHBORHOOD | Smaller than San Francisco's Chinatown, this neighborhood near Union Station still represents a slice of East Asian life. Sidewalks are usually jammed with tourists, locals, and residents hustling from shop to shop picking up goods, spices, and trinkets from small shops and miniplazas that line the street. Although some longtime establishments have closed in recent years, the area still pulses with its founding culture. During Chinese New Year, giant dragons snake down the street. And, of course, there are the many restaurants and quick-bite cafés specializing in Chinese feasts. In recent years, a slew of hip eateries like Howlin' Ray's and Majordomo have injected the area with vibrancy.

An influx of local artists has added a spark to the neighborhood by taking up empty spaces and opening galleries along Chung

King Road, a faded pedestrian passage behind the West Plaza shopping center between Hill and Yale. Also look for galleries along a little side street called Gin Ling Way on the east side of Broadway. Chinatown has its main action on North Broadway. There are several garages available for parking here that range from $5 to $10 per day. ✉ *Bordered by the 110, 101, and 5 freeways, Downtown* 🌐 *chinatown-la.com* Ⓜ *Union Station.*

★ El Pueblo de Los Angeles

NEIGHBORHOOD | The oldest section of the city, known as El Pueblo de Los Angeles, represents the rich Mexican heritage of L.A. It had a close shave with disintegration in the early 20th century, but key buildings were preserved, and eventually **Olvera Street,** the district's heart, was transformed into a Mexican American marketplace. Today vendors still sell puppets, leather goods, sandals, and woolen shawls from stalls lining the narrow street. You can find everything from salt and pepper shakers shaped like donkeys to gorgeous glassware and pottery.

At the beginning of Olvera Street is the Plaza, a Mexican-style park with plenty of benches and walkways shaded by a huge Moreton Bay fig tree. On weekends, mariachi bands and folkloric dance groups perform. Nearby places worth investigating include the historic Avila Adobe, the Chinese American Museum, the Plaza Firehouse Museum, and the America Tropical Interpretive Center. Exhibits at the Italian American Museum of Los Angeles chronicle the area's formerly heavy Italian presence. ✉ *Avila Adobe/Olvera Street Visitors Center, 125 Paseo De La Plaza, Downtown* ☎ *213/485–6855* 🌐 *elpueblo.lacity.org* 🎟 *Free for Olvera St. and guided tours; fees at some museums.*

Geffen Contemporary at MOCA

MUSEUM | The Geffen Contemporary is one of architect Frank Gehry's boldest creations. One of three MOCA branches, the 40,000 square feet of exhibition space was once used as a police car warehouse. The museum's permanent collection includes works from artists like Willem de Kooning, Franz Kline, Jackson Pollock, Mark Rothko, and Cindy Sherman. ■ **TIP→ Present your TAP metro card to get two-for-one admission.** ✉ *152 N. Central Ave., Downtown* ☎ *213/626–6222* 🌐 *www.moca.org/visit/geffen-contemporary* 🎟 *Free; special exhibitions $18 or free every Thurs. 5–8; parking $9.*

GRAMMY Museum

MUSEUM | The GRAMMY Museum brings the music industry to life. Throughout four floors and 30,000 square feet of space, the museum showcases rare footage of GRAMMY performances, plus rotating and interactive exhibits on award-winning musicians and the history of music. A 200-seat theater is great for live events that include screenings, lectures, interviews, and intimate music performances. ✉ *800 W. Olympic Blvd., Downtown* ☎ *213/765–6800* 🌐 *www.grammymuseum.org* 🎟 *$15* 🕒 *Closed Tues.* Ⓜ *Pico.*

★ Grand Central Market

MARKET | With options that include handmade white-corn tamales, warm olive bread, dried figs, Mexican fruit drinks, and much more, this mouthwatering gathering place is the city's largest and most active food market. The spot bustles nonstop with locals and visitors surveying the butcher shop's display of everything from lambs' heads to pigs' tails. Produce stalls are piled high with locally grown avocados and heirloom tomatoes. Stop by **Chiles Secos** at stall C-12 for a remarkable selection of rare chilis and spices; **Ramen Hood** at C-2, for sumptuous vegan noodles and broth; or **Sticky Rice** at stall C-5, for fantastic Thai-style chicken. Even if you don't plan on buying anything, it's a great place to browse and people-watch. ✉ *317 S. Broadway, Downtown* ☎ *213/624–2378* 🌐 *www.grandcentralmarket.com* 🎟 *Free* Ⓜ *Pershing Square.*

L.A. Live

ARTS VENUE | The mammoth L.A. Live entertainment complex was opened in 2007 when there was little to do or see in this section of Downtown. Since its inception, this once creepy ghost town has become a major hub for sports, concerts, award shows, and more. The first things you'll notice as you emerge from the parking lot are the giant LED screens and sparkling lights, and the buzz of crowds as they head out to dinner before or after a Lakers game, movie, or live show at the Microsoft Theater. There are dozens of restaurants and eateries here, including Los Angeles favorite Katsuya, the spot for sizzling Kobe beef platters and excellent sushi (the crab rolls are not to be missed). **■ TIP→ Park for free on weekdays from 11 am to 2 pm if you eat at one of the dozen or so restaurants here.** ✉ *800 W. Olympic Blvd., Downtown* ☎ *213/763–5483* 🌐 *www.lalive.com* Ⓜ *Pico.*

★ The Last Bookstore

STORE/MALL | California's largest used and new book and record shop is a favorite for both book lovers and fans of a good photo op, thanks to elements like an archway created from curving towers of books, a peephole carved into the stacks, and an in-store vault devoted to horror texts. Aside from the awesome aesthetics, shoppers will love to get lost in the store's collection of affordable books, art, and music. ✉ *453 S. Spring St., ground fl., Downtown* ☎ *213/488–0599* 🌐 *www.lastbookstorela.com* Ⓜ *Pershing Square.*

★ Little Tokyo

NEIGHBORHOOD | One of three official Japantowns in the country—all of which are in California—Little Tokyo is blossoming again thanks to the next generation of Japanese Americans setting up small businesses. Besides dozens of sushi bars, tempura restaurants, and karaoke bars, there's a lovely garden at the Japanese American Cultural and Community Center and a renovated 1925 Buddhist temple with an ornate entrance at the Japanese American National Museum.

On 1st Street you'll find a strip of buildings from the early 1900s. Look down when you get near San Pedro Street to see the art installation called *Omoide no Shotokyo* ("Remembering Old Little Tokyo"). Embedded in the sidewalk are brass inscriptions naming the original businesses, quoted reminiscences from residents, and steel time lines of Japanese American history up to World War II. Nisei Week (a *nisei* is a second-generation Japanese American) is celebrated every August with traditional drums, dancing, a carnival, and a huge parade. **■ TIP→ Docent-led walking tours are available the last Saturday of every month starting at 10:15 am. The cost is $15 and includes entry to the Japanese American National Museum.** ✉ *Bounded by 1st and 3rd Sts., the 101 and 110 freeways, and LA River, Downtown* ☎ *213/880–6875* 🌐 *www.visitlittletokyo.com* Ⓜ *Civic Center/Grand Park Station.*

Los Angeles Central Library

LIBRARY | The nation's third-largest public library, the handsome Los Angeles Central Library was designed in 1926 by Bertram Goodhue. Restored to their pristine condition, a pyramid tower and a torch symbolizing the "light of learning" crown the building. The Cook rotunda on the second floor features murals by Dean Cornwell depicting the history of California, and the Tom Bradley Wing, named for a famed L.A. mayor, has a soaring eight-story atrium.

The library offers frequent special exhibits, plus a small café where you can refuel. Don't ignore the gift shop, which is loaded with unique items for readers and writers. Free docent walking tours are offered Monday through Friday at 12:30, Saturday at 11 and 2, and Sunday at 2. An Art-in-the-Garden tour is on Saturday at 12:30 pm. A self-guided tour map is also available on the library's website. ✉ *630 W. 5th St., Downtown* ☎ *213/228–7000* 🌐 *www.lapl.org* 🎫 *Free* Ⓜ *Pershing Square.*

MOCA Grand Avenue

MUSEUM | The main branch of the Museum of Contemporary Art, designed by Arata Isozaki, contains underground galleries and presents elegant exhibitions. A huge Nancy Rubins sculpture fashioned from used airplane parts graces the museum's front plaza. The museum gift shop offers apothecary items, modernist ceramics, and even toys and games for children to appease any art lover. **■ TIP→ Take advantage of the free audio tour.** ✉ *250 S. Grand Ave., Downtown* ☎ *213/626–6222* 🌐 *www.moca.org* 🎫 *General admission free; special exhibitions $18 or free Thurs. 5–8* ⏲ *Closed Tues.* Ⓜ *Civic Center/Grand Park.*

Natural History Museum of Los Angeles County

MUSEUM | **FAMILY** | The hot ticket at this beaux arts–style museum completed in 1913 is the Dinosaur Hall, whose more than 300 fossils include adult, juvenile, and baby skeletons of the fearsome *Tyrannosaurus rex.* The Discovery Center lets kids and curious grown-ups touch real animal pelts, and the Insect Zoo gets everyone up close and personal with the white-eyed assassin bug and other creepy crawlers. A massive hall displays dioramas of animals in their natural habitats. Also look for pre-Columbian artifacts and crafts from the South Pacific, or priceless stones in the Gem and Mineral Hall. Outdoors, the 3½-acre Nature Gardens shelter native plant and insect species and contain an expansive edible garden. **■ TIP→ Don't miss out on the Dino lab, where you can watch paleontologists unearth and clean real fossils.** ✉ *900 W. Exposition Blvd., Exposition Park* ☎ *213/763–3466* 🌐 *www.nhm.org* 🎫 *$15; free on 1st Tues. of month* Ⓜ *Expo/Vermont.*

Orpheum Theatre

ARTS VENUE | Opened in 1926, the opulent Orpheum Theatre played host to live attractions including classic comedians, burlesque dancers, jazz greats like Lena Horne, Ella Fitzgerald, and Duke Ellington, and later on rock-and-roll performers such as Little Richard. After extensive restorations, the Orpheum once again revealed a stunning white-marble lobby, majestic auditorium with fleur-de-lis panels, and two dazzling chandeliers. A thick red velvet and gold-trimmed curtain opens at showtime, and a white Wurlitzer pipe organ (one of the last remaining organs of its kind from the silent movie era) is at the ready. The original 1926 rooftop neon sign again shines brightly, signaling a new era for this theater. Today the theater plays host to live concerts, comedy shows, and movie screenings. ✉ *842 S. Broadway, Downtown* ☎ *877/677–4386* 🌐 *www.laorpheum.com/events.*

Union Station

HISTORIC SITE | Even if you don't plan on traveling by train anywhere, head here to soak up the ambience of a great rail station. Envisioned by John and Donald Parkinson, the architects who also designed the grand City Hall, the 1939 masterpiece combines Spanish Colonial Revival and art deco elements that have retained their classic warmth and quality. The waiting hall's commanding scale and enormous chandeliers have provided the backdrop for countless scenes in films, TV shows, and music videos. Recently added to the majesty are the Imperial Western Beer Company and the Streamliner, two bars that pay homage to the station's original architecture while serving homemade brews and inventive classic cocktails. **■ TIP→ Walking tours of Union Station are on Saturday at 10 and cost $15.** ✉ *800 N. Alameda St., Downtown* 🌐 *www.unionstationla.com* Ⓜ *Union Station.*

★ Walt Disney Concert Hall

CONCERTS | One of the architectural wonders of Los Angeles, the 2,265-seat hall is a sculptural monument of gleaming, curved steel designed by Frank Gehry. It's part of a complex that includes a public park, gardens, shops, and two outdoor amphitheaters, one of them atop the concert hall. The acoustically superlative venue is the home of the city's premier orchestra, the Los Angeles Philharmonic, whose music director, Gustavo Dudamel, is an international celebrity in his own right. The orchestra's season runs from late September to early June, before it heads to the Hollywood Bowl for the summer. **■ TIP→ Free 60-minute guided tours are offered on most days, and there are self-guided audio tours.** *111 S. Grand Ave., Downtown* *323/850–2000* *www.laphil.org* *Tours free* *Civic Center/Grand Park.*

Restaurants

★ Bavel

$$$$ | MIDDLE EASTERN | Fans of Bestia have been lining up for stellar Mediterranean cuisine at this Arts District hot spot, which is owned by the same restaurateurs. Rose gold stools give way to marble tabletops as the open kitchen bangs out hummus and baba ghanoush spreads, along with flatbreads and lamb-neck shawarma. **Known for:** delicious Mediterranean cuisine; sceney atmosphere; great vibes. *Average main: $40* *500 Mateo St., Downtown* *213/232–4966* *baveldtla.com.*

Bottega Louie

$$$ | ITALIAN | A Downtown dining staple, this lively Italian restaurant and gourmet market features open spaces, stark white walls, and majestic floor-to-ceiling windows. If the wait is too long at this no-reservations eatery, you can sip on Prosecco and nibble on pastries at the bar. **Known for:** mouthwatering chicken Parm; one-of-a-kind portobello fries; tartufo pizzas with black truffle mushrooms. *Average main: $25* *700 S. Grand Ave., Downtown* *213/802–1470* *www.bottegalouie.com* *7th Street/ Metro Center.*

★ Cole's French Dip

$ | AMERICAN | There's a fight in Los Angeles over who created the French dip sandwich. The first contender is Cole's, whose sign on the door says it's the originator of the salty, juicy, melt-in-your-mouth meats. **Known for:** historic L.A. dining; one of the top contenders for best French dip sandwich in the country; secret speakeasy in back. *Average main: $10* *118 E. 6th St., Downtown* *213/622–4090* *www.pouringwithheart.com/coles.*

★ Guerrilla Tacos

$ | MEXICAN FUSION | What started as a food truck serving gourmet tacos has turned into a brick-and-mortar space that also has an excellent (and cheap) bar. Chefs fire up some of the most inventive tacos in the city—think sweet potato with almond chili and feta or the Baja fried cod with chipotle crema. **Known for:** gourmet tacos; cheap drinks; long lines. *Average main: $11* *2000 E. 7th St., Downtown* *213/375–3300* *www.guerrillatacos.com.*

★ Howlin' Ray's

$$ | SOUTHERN | FAMILY | Don't let the hour-long waits deter you—if you want the best Nashville fried chicken in L.A., Howlin' Ray's is worth the effort. Right in the middle of Chinatown, this tiny chicken joint consists of a few bar seats, a few side tables, and a kitchen that sizzles as staff yell out "yes, chef" with each incoming order. **Known for:** spicy fried chicken; classic Southern sides; long waits. *Average main: $15* *727 N. Broadway, Suite 128, Downtown* *213/935–8399* *www.howlinrays.com* *Closed Sun. and Mon.* *Union Station.*

★ Majordomo

$$$$ | ECLECTIC | You would never just stumble upon this out-of-the-way spot in Chinatown, but world-famous celeb chef David Chang likes it that way. The beautifully designed minimal space with spacious patio, an exposed-duct ceiling, and elongated wood bar has a cuisine style that defies any singular category. **Known for:** chuck short rib with raclette; rice-based drinks; hard-to-get reservations (try to eat at the bar). *Average main: $40 1725 Naud St., Downtown 323/545–4880 www.majordomo.la Closed Mon. and Tues.*

★ Philippe the Original
$ | **AMERICAN** | **FAMILY** | First opened in 1908, Philippe's is one of L.A.'s oldest restaurants and claims to be the originator of the French dip sandwich. While the debate continues around the city, one thing is certain: the dips made with beef, pork, ham, lamb, or turkey on a freshly baked roll stand the test of time. **Known for:** 50¢ coffee; communal tables; post–Dodgers game eats. *Average main: $8 1001 N. Alameda St., Downtown 213/628–3781 www.philippes.com Union Station.*

71Above
$$$$ | **ECLECTIC** | As its name suggests, this sky-high dining den sits on the 71st floor, 950 feet above ground level. With that elevation comes the most stunning views of any restaurant in L.A., and the food is close to matching it. **Known for:** sky-high views; fine dining with a seafood focus; classy atmosphere and loosely enforced dress code (no shorts or flip-flops). *Average main: $39 633 W. 5th St., 71st fl., Downtown 213/712–2683 www.71above.com Pershing Square Station.*

Sushi Gen
$$ | **JAPANESE** | Consistently rated one of the top sushi spots in L.A., Sushi Gen continues to dole out the freshest and tastiest fish in town. Sit at the elongated bar and get to know the sushi masters while they prepare your lunch. **Known for:** chef-recommended sushi selections; limited seating; great lunch specials. *Average main: $20 422 E. 2nd St., Downtown 213/617–0552 www.sushigen-dtla.com Closed Sun. and Mon. No lunch Sat.*

Hotels

★ Ace Hotel Downtown Los Angeles
$$ | **HOTEL** | The L.A. edition of this bohemian-chic hipster haven is at once a hotel, theater, and poolside bar (called Upstairs), housed in the gorgeous Spanish Gothic–style United Artists building in the heart of Downtown. **Pros:** lively rooftop lounge/pool area; gorgeous building and views; location in the heart of Downtown. **Cons:** expensive parking rates compared to nightly rates ($36); some kinks in the service; compact rooms. *Rooms from: $239 929 S. Broadway, Downtown 213/623–3233 www.acehotel.com/losangeles 183 rooms No meals.*

★ Freehand Los Angeles
$ | **HOTEL** | Part hotel, part shared accommodation space, the Freehand is one of the newest hotels in Downtown Los Angeles and also one of the coolest. **Pros:** range of affordable rooms from lofts to bunk beds; active social scene; great rooftop pool and bar. **Cons:** sketchy area at night around the hotel; free lobby Wi-Fi attracts nonhotel guests; most affordable rooms are shared. *Rooms from: $100 416 W. 8th St., Downtown 213/612–0021 freehandhotels.com/los-angeles 59 shared rooms, 167 private rooms No meals Pershing Square.*

Hotel Figueroa
$$ | **HOTEL** | The 12-story Hotel Figueroa was originally built in 1926, and touches of that originality are still seen throughout with original skylights, wood beams, and tiles. **Pros:** a short walk to L.A. Live and the convention center; great poolside bar; in-room iPads and complimentary minibar snacks. **Cons:** the area can be sketchy at night; expensive parking ($40/night); smallish pool. *Rooms from: $200 939 S. Figueroa St., Downtown 866/734–6018 www.hotelfigueroa.com 268 rooms No meals Olympic/Figueroa.*

The Hoxton

$ | **HOTEL** | Now one of the chicest hotels in Downtown L.A., the Hoxton is an open-house hotel where the lobby is the hub of activity and thoughtful design touches permeate throughout. The historic building was once the headquarters of the L.A. Railway and now sits in an up-and-coming part of the city filled with restaurants and apartments. **Pros:** stellar restaurant; monthly event calendar; great rooftop pool. **Cons:** area can be dodgy at night; no gym; some rooms on the small side. *Rooms from: $160 1060 S. Broadway, Downtown 213/725–5900 www.thehoxton.com/downtown-la 174 rooms No meals.*

InterContinental Los Angeles Downtown

$$ | **HOTEL** | This five-star addition to the Downtown L.A. scene impresses with views, an enormous gym, dining, and an outdoor pool. **Pros:** best views in the city; incredible restaurants and bars; top-rate service. **Cons:** too big and impersonal; busy and tricky intersection; parking is $46/night. *Rooms from: $300 900 Wilshire Blvd., Downtown 213/688–7777 dtla.intercontinental.com 889 rooms No meals 7th Street/Metro Center.*

Millennium Biltmore Hotel

$ | **HOTEL** | As the local headquarters of John F. Kennedy's 1960 presidential campaign and the location of some of the earliest Academy Awards ceremonies, this Downtown treasure, with its gilded 1923 beaux arts design, exudes ambience and history. **Pros:** 24-hour business center; tiled indoor pool and steam room; impressive history. **Cons:** pricey valet parking; standard rooms are compact; some decor is dated. *Rooms from: $200 506 S. Grand Ave., Downtown 213/624–1011, 866/866–8086 www.millenniumhotels.com 683 rooms No meals Pershing Square.*

The NoMad Hotel

$$ | **HOTEL** | This stunningly refurbished property used to house the Bank of Italy and touches of the old bank can still be seen throughout—most notably in the lobby bathrooms that are cut out of the original vault. **Pros:** freestanding tubs; individually sourced artwork throughout; 24-hour gym. **Cons:** sketchy area at night; expensive parking ($48/night); some rooms are small. *Rooms from: $250 649 S. Olive St., Downtown 213/358–0000 www.thenomadhotel.com/los-angeles 241 rooms No meals 7th Street/Metro Center.*

Westin Bonaventure Hotel and Suites

$$ | **HOTEL** | **FAMILY** | Step inside the futuristic lobby of L.A.'s largest hotel to be greeted by fountains, an indoor lake and track, and 12 glass elevators leading up to the historic rooms of this 35-story property. Color-coded hotel floors help newcomers navigate the hotel, which takes up an entire city block. **Pros:** spa with shiatsu massage; revolving rooftop lounge; many on-site restaurants. **Cons:** massive hotel might feel too corporate; mazelike lobby and public areas; standard rooms are on the small side. *Rooms from: $250 404 S. Figueroa St., Downtown 213/624–1000 westin.marriott.com 1358 rooms No meals 7th Street/Metro Center.*

Nightlife

Broadway Bar

BARS/PUBS | This watering-hole-meets-dive sits in a flourishing section of Broadway (neighbors include the swank Ace Hotel). Bartenders mix creative cocktails while DJs spin tunes nightly. The two-story space includes a smoking balcony overlooking the street. The crowd is often dressed to impress. *830 S. Broadway, Downtown 213/614–9909 www.broadwaybarla.com.*

★ The Edison

BARS/PUBS | The glitz and glam of the Roaring '20s is alive and well in the Edison, where the decor serves as tribute to the power plant that once occupied these premises. Black-and-white silent films are projected onto the walls, and tasty nibbles and artisanal cocktails are served (in a private room, if you prefer). There's live entertainment many nights, from jazz bands to burlesque shows to magic. A dress code means no shorts, jerseys, hoodies, flip-flops, tennis shoes, or collarless shirts. ✉ *108 W. 2nd St., Downtown* ☎ *213/613–0000* 🌐 *www.theneverlands.com/edison.*

★ Golden Gopher

BARS/PUBS | Craft cocktails, beers on tap, an outdoor smoking patio, and retro video games—this bar in the heart of Downtown is not to be missed. With one of the oldest liquor licenses in Los Angeles (issued in 1905), the Golden Gopher is the only bar in Los Angeles with an on-site liquor store for to-go orders—just in case you want to buy another bottle before you head home. ✉ *417 W. 8th St., Downtown* ☎ *213/614–8001* 🌐 *www.pouringwithheart.com/golden-gopher* Ⓜ *7th Street/Metro Center.*

La Cita

BARS/PUBS | This dive bar may not look like much, but it more than makes up for it with an interesting mix of barflies, urban hipsters, and reasonable drink prices. Friday and Saturday night, DJs mix Top 40 hits and a tiny dance floor packs in the crowd. For those more interested in drinking and socializing, head to the back patio where a TV plays local sports. Every day has a differently themed happy hour—hip-hop happy hour on Wednesday or rockabilly happy hour on Thursday. Specials vary from $3 Tecates to free pizza. ✉ *336 S. Hill St., Downtown* ☎ *213/687–7111* 🌐 *www.lacitabar.com* Ⓜ *Pershing Square Station.*

The Love Song Bar

BARS/PUBS | Lovers of T. S. Eliot and vinyl will find themselves instantly at home inside this cozy establishment named after Eliot's "The Love Song of J. Alfred Prufrock." When not pouring drinks, bartenders often act as DJs, playing records (the best of the '60s through the '80s) in their entirety. As it's housed inside the Regent Theater, the cozy nature of the place can be disrupted when there's a concert scheduled. For those with an appetite, fantastic food can be ordered from the pizza parlor next door—naturally, it's called Prufrock's. ✉ *450 S. Main St., Downtown* ☎ *323/284–5728* 🌐 *www.spacelandpresents.com/events/the-love-song.*

Redwood Bar & Grill

BARS/PUBS | If you're looking for a place with potent drinks and a good burger, this kitschy bar fits the bill perfectly. Known today as the "pirate bar" because of its nautical decor, the place dates back to the 1940s, when it was rumored to attract mobsters, politicians, and journalists due to its proximity to city hall, the Hall of Justice, and the original location of the *Los Angeles Times*. There's nightly music from local rock bands, though it comes with a cover charge. ✉ *316 W. 2nd St., Downtown* ☎ *213/680–2600* 🌐 *www.theredwoodbar.com* Ⓜ *Civic Center/Grand Park.*

★ Resident

MUSIC CLUBS | Catch a lineup of indie tastemakers inside this converted industrial space, or hang outdoors in the beer garden while trying bites from on-site food truck KTCHN (on cooler evenings you can congregate around the fire pits). A wide variety of draft beers and a specially curated cocktail program are available inside at the bar or at the trailer bar outside. ✉ *428 S. Hewitt St., Downtown* ☎ *213/628–7503* 🌐 *www.residentdtla.com.*

★Seven Grand

BARS/PUBS | The hunting lodge vibe makes you feel like you need a whiskey in hand—luckily, this Downtown establishment stocks more than 700 of them. Attracting whiskey novices and connoisseurs, the bartenders here are more than willing to help you make a selection. Live jazz and blues bands play every night, so even if you're not a big drinker, there's still some appeal (although you're definitely missing out). For a more intimate setting, try the on-site **Bar Jackalope,** a bar within a bar, which has a "whiskey tasting library" specializing in Japanese varieties and seats only 18. ✉ *515 W. 7th St., 2nd fl., Downtown* ☎ *213/614–0736* 🌐 *www.sevengrandbars.com* Ⓜ *7th Street/Metro Center.*

The Varnish

BARS/PUBS | Beeline through the dining room of Cole's to find an unassuming door that leads to this small, dimly lit bar within a bar. Wooden booths line the walls, candles flicker, and live jazz is performed Sunday through Wednesday. The bartenders take their calling to heart and shake and stir some of the finest cocktails in the city. Those who don't have a drink of choice can list their wants ("gin-based and sweet," "strong whiskey and herbaceous") and be served a custom cocktail. Be warned: patrons requiring quick drinks will want to go elsewhere—perfection takes time. ✉ *118 E. 6th St., Downtown* ☎ *213/265–7089* 🌐 *www.pouringwithheart.com/the-varnish.*

Performing Arts

Ahmanson Theatre

THEATER | The largest of L.A.'s Center Group's three theaters, the 2,100-seat Ahmanson Theatre presents larger-scale classic revivals, dramas, musicals, and comedies like *Into the Woods,* which are either going to or coming from Broadway and the West End. The ambience is a theater lover's delight. ✉ *135 N. Grand Ave., Downtown* ☎ *213/972–7211* 🌐 *www.musiccenter.org/visit/Our-Venues/ahmanson-theatre* Ⓜ *Civic Center/Grand Park Station.*

★Dorothy Chandler Pavilion

CONCERTS | Though half a century old, this theater maintains the glamour of its early years, richly decorated with crystal chandeliers, classical theatrical drapes, and a 24-karat gold dome. Part of the Los Angeles Music Center, this pavilion is home to the L.A. Opera though a large portion of programming is made up of dance and ballet performances as well. Ticket holders can attend free talks that take place an hour before opera performances. **TIP→Reservations for the talks aren't required, but it's wise to arrive early, as space is limited.** ✉ *135 N. Grand Ave., Downtown* ☎ *213/972–0711* 🌐 *www.musiccenter.org/visit/Our-Venues/dorothy-chandler-pavilion* Ⓜ *Civic Center/Grand Park.*

Microsoft Theater

CONCERTS | The Microsoft Theater is host to a variety of concerts and big-name awards shows—the Emmys, American Music Awards, BET Awards, and the ESPYs. This theater and the surrounding L.A. Live complex are a draw for those looking for a fun night out. The building's emphasis on acoustics and versatile seating arrangements means that all 7,100 seats are good, whether you're at an intimate acoustic concert or the People's Choice Awards. Outside, the L.A. Live complex hosts restaurants and attractions, including the GRAMMY Museum, to keep patrons entertained before and after shows (though it's open whether or not there's a performance). ✉ *777 Chick Hearn Ct., Downtown* ☎ *213/763–6030* 🌐 *www.microsofttheater.com* Ⓜ *Pico.*

Shrine Auditorium

CONCERTS | Since opening in 1926, the auditorium has hosted nearly every major awards show at one point or another, including the Emmys and the GRAMMYs. Today, the venue and adjacent Expo Hall hosts concerts, film premieres, award shows, pageants, and special events. The Shrine's Moorish Revival–style architecture is a spectacle all its own. ✉ *665 W. Jefferson Blvd., Downtown* ☎ *213/748–5116* 🌐 *www.shrineauditorium.com.*

Los Feliz, Silver Lake, and the Eastside

The neighborhoods in L.A.'s Eastside are talked about with the same oh-my-god-it's-so-cool reverence by Angelenos as Brooklyn is by New Yorkers. These streets are dripping with trendiness—which will delight some and enrage others. Almost 20 years ago, Los Feliz was the first of these rediscovered, reinvented neighborhoods, then came Silver Lake, then Echo Park. As each one became more expensive, the cool kids relocated, leaving behind their style and influence. Now Highland Park is the center of the oh-so-hip universe. But, the epicenter is constantly shifting. No doubt, by the next edition of this guide, it'll be someplace else.

Los Feliz

Sights

Barnsdall Art Park

CITY PARK | FAMILY | The panoramic view of Hollywood alone is worth a trip to this hilltop cultural center. On the grounds you'll find the 1921 **Hollyhock House,** a masterpiece of modern design by architect Frank Lloyd Wright. It was commissioned by philanthropist Aline Barnsdall to be the centerpiece of an arts community. While Barnsdall's project didn't turn out the way she planned, the park now hosts the L.A. Municipal Art Gallery and Theatre, which provides exhibition space for visual and performance artists. Wright dubbed this style "California Romanza" (*romanza* is a musical term meaning "to make one's own form"). Stylized depictions of Barnsdall's favorite flower, the hollyhock, appear throughout the house in its cement columns, roof line, and furnishings. The leaded-glass windows are expertly placed to make the most of both the surrounding gardens and the city views. On summer weekends, there are wildly popular wine tastings and outdoor movie screenings. Self-guided tours are available Thursday through Sunday from 11 to 4. ✉ *4800 Hollywood Blvd., Los Feliz* ☎ *No phone* 🌐 *www.barnsdall.org* 🎫 *Free; house tours $7* ⏲ *House closed Mon.*

★ Griffith Observatory

OBSERVATORY | Most visitors barely skim the surface of this gorgeous spot in the Santa Monica Mountains, but those in the know will tell you there's more to the Griffith Observatory than its sweeping views and stunning Greek Revival architecture. To start, this free-to-the-public mountaintop observatory is home to the Samuel Oschin Planetarium, a state-of-the-art theater with an aluminum dome and a Zeiss star projector that plays a number of ticketed shows. Those spectacular shows are complemented by a couple of space-related exhibits, and several telescopes (naturally), as well as theater programs and events at the Leonard Nimoy Event Horizon Theater. For visitors who are looking to get up close and personal with the cosmos, monthly star-viewing parties with local amateur astronomers are also on hand. **■ TIP→ For a fantastic view, come at sunset to watch the sky turn fiery shades of red with the city's skyline silhouetted.** ✉ *2800 E. Observatory Ave., Los Feliz* ☎ *213/473–0800* 🌐 *www.griffithobservatory.org* ⏲ *Closed Mon.* ☞ *Observatory grounds and parking are open daily.*

★ Griffith Park

CITY PARK | FAMILY | The country's largest municipal park, the 4,310-acre Griffith Park is a must for nature lovers, the perfect spot for respite from the hustle and bustle of the surrounding urban areas. Plants and animals native to Southern California can be found within the park's borders, including deer, coyotes, and even a reclusive mountain lion. Bronson Canyon (where the Batcave from the 1960s *Batman* TV series is located) and Crystal Springs are favorite picnic spots.

The park is named after Colonel Griffith J. Griffith, a mining tycoon who donated 3,000 acres to the city in 1896. As you might expect, the park has been used as a film and television location for at least a century. Here you'll find the Griffith Observatory, the Los Angeles Zoo, the Greek Theater, two golf courses, hiking and bridle trails, a swimming pool, a merry-go-round, and an outdoor train museum. ✉ *4730 Crystal Springs Dr., Los Feliz* ☎ *323/644–2050* 🌐 *www.laparks.org/dos/parks/griffithpk* 🎫 *Free; attractions inside park have separate admission fees.*

Restaurants

★ The Best Fish Taco in Ensenada

$ | MEXICAN | FAMILY | In mirroring the taco stands of Ensenada, Mexico—simple, cheap, and unceremonious, with a selection of spicy homemade salsas—this little local treasure has achieved what many restaurants serving Baja tacos haven't: an authentic (and delicious) experience. **Known for:** fish-and-shrimp tacos; mango salsa; seafood shack atmosphere. $ *Average main: $6* ✉ *1650 Hillhurst Ave., Los Feliz* ☎ *323/466–5552* 🌐 *www.bestfishtacoinensenada.com.*

Kismet

$$ | MEDITERRANEAN | You may feel like you're about to walk into a sauna rather than a restaurant because of its minimalist light-color wood on white paint interior, but you'll find nothing but colorful gorgeous Middle Eastern dishes here at Kismet. This James Beard nominee perfectly blends comforting Middle Eastern and Israeli cuisine with Californian flavors and plant-based flair, all served in a modern space. **Known for:** Persian crispy rice; tasty lamb meatballs; Middle Eastern classics with a Cali twist. $ *Average main: $18* ✉ *4648 Hollywood Blvd., Los Feliz* ☎ *323/409–0404* 🌐 *www.kismetla.com.*

Little Dom's

$$ | ITALIAN | With a vintage bar and dapper barkeep who mixes up seasonally inspired retro cocktails, an attached Italian deli where you can pick up a pork-cheek sub, and an $18 Monday-night supper, it's not surprising that Little Dom's is a neighborhood gem. Cozy and inviting, with big leather booths you can sink into for the night, the restaurant puts a modern spin on classic Italian dishes such as *burrata* agnolotti and meatballs. **Known for:** ricotta cheese and fresh blueberry pancakes; excellent pizza margherita; fun weekend brunch. $ *Average main: $20* ✉ *2128 Hillhurst Ave., Los Feliz* ☎ *323/661–0055* 🌐 *www.littledoms.com.*

Nightlife

Covell

WINE BARS—NIGHTLIFE | This laid-back spot is the embodiment of what every unpretentious wine drinker wishes a wine bar should be. It's thankfully lacking in staff who might turn up their noses should you forget to swirl the glass. But what else would you expect from a spot with repurposed furnishings and a vintage motorcycle mounted to the wall? ✉ *4628 Hollywood Blvd., Los Feliz* ☎ *323/660–4400* 🌐 *www.barcovell.com.*

Dresden Room

PIANO BARS/LOUNGES | This bar's 1940s lounge decor makes it a favorite with folks in Los Angeles. The long-running house band, Marty and Elayne, has entertained patrons for more than three decades. (They found a new generation of fans, thanks to the film *Swingers*.) Other than the entertainment, perhaps the best reason to wander in is to sip on a Blood and Sand cocktail, self-proclaimed to be "the world's most tantalizing drink." ✉ *1760 N. Vermont Ave., Los Feliz* ☎ *323/665–4294* 🌐 *www.thedresden.com.*

Performing Arts

★ Greek Theatre

CONCERTS | With a robust lineup from May through November, acts such as Bruce Springsteen, John Legend, and Aretha Franklin (RIP) have all graced the stage at this scenic outdoor venue. Located at the base of Griffith Park, there's usually slow preshow traffic on concert nights, but that'll give you a chance to take in the beautiful park foliage and homes in the Hollywood Hills. Paid lots are available for parking, but wear comfortable shoes and expect to walk as some lots are fairly far from the theater. Or you can park and enjoy cocktails in trendy and chic Los Feliz before a show, then walk up to the venue. ✉ *2700 N. Vermont Ave., Los Feliz* ☎ *844/524–7335* 🌐 *www.lagreektheatre.com.*

Shopping

Skylight Books

BOOKS/STATIONERY | A neighborhood bookstore through and through, Skylight has excellent sections devoted to kids, fiction, travel, and food; it even has a live-in cat. The space also hosts book discussion groups, panels, and author readings with hip literati. Art lovers can peruse texts on design and photography, graphic novels, and indie magazines at Skylight's annex a few doors down. ✉ *1818 N. Vermont Ave., Los Feliz* ☎ *323/660–1175* 🌐 *www.skylightbooks.com.*

Soap Plant/Wacko

GIFTS/SOUVENIRS | This pop-culture supermarket offers a wide range of items, including rows of books on art and design. But it's the novelty stock that makes the biggest impression, with ant farms, X-ray specs, and anime figurines for sale. An adjacent gallery space, La Luz de Jesus, focuses on underground art. ✉ *4633 Hollywood Blvd., Los Feliz* ☎ *323/663–0122* 🌐 *www.soapplant.com.*

Vamp Shoes

CLOTHING | From well-known designers to up-and-coming handcrafters who make their shoes in small batches, boutique store Vamp Shoes has a solid collection of footwear for anyone who appreciates (and who's not afraid to invest in) gorgeous, excellent-quality soles. Inventory here also includes cool bags, hosiery, jewelry, and handcrafted ceramics. ✉ *1951 Hillhurst Ave., Los Feliz* ☎ *323/662–1150* 🌐 *www.vampshoeshop.com.*

Activities

Bronson Canyon

HIKING/WALKING | Bronson Canyon—or more popularly, Bronson Caves—is one of L.A.'s most famous filming locations, especially for western and sci-fi flicks. This section of Griffith Park, easily accessible through a trail that's less than half a mile, is a great place to visit whether you're a film buff or an exercise junkie. ✉ *3200 Canyon Dr., Hollywood.*

Silver Lake

Restaurants

★ Alimento

$$$ | **ITALIAN** | There's little surprise that chef Zach Pollack's soulful Italian masterpiece in Silver Lake features a lot of influences and inspirations that span the globe; the true-blue Angeleno, after all, grew up in a melting pot. Alimento's dishes are modern takes on traditional Italian cuisine, using locally sourced ingredients and varying in influences—from your classic American to Chinese and Mexican. **Known for:** chicken liver crostone; radiatori with braised pork sugo; surprising takes on Italian classics. *Average main: $25* *1710 Silver Lake Blvd., Silver Lake* *323/928–2888* *www.alimentola.com* *Closed Mon. No lunch.*

LaMill Coffee

$$ | **CAFÉ** | These folks take their coffee seriously, sourcing estate-grown beans that are prepared in a variety of ways (French press or Clover, to name but two) and offering an inventive list of espresso-based drinks. To go along with the requisite coffee is a breakfast-all-day menu, as well as a proper, if select, tea selection for those who take their leaves seriously. **Known for:** Japanese iced coffee; Varlhona mocha; breakfast items served all day. *Average main: $14* *1636 Silver Lake Blvd., Silver Lake* *323/663–4441* *www.lamillcoffee.com*

★ Night + Market Song

$$ | **THAI** | There are a lot of Thai restaurants in Los Angeles, but none have quite reached the level of cult status of Night + Market Song. Tucked between a free clinic, a small clothing store, and a tax office, this second rendition of chef Kris Yenbamroong's popular WeHo restaurant might be easy to miss, but keep an eye out, as its authentic (and properly spicy) Thai dishes are practically mandatory when you're in the neighborhood. **Known for:** startled pig; khao soi; long weekend lines. *Average main: $15* *3322 W. Sunset Blvd., Silver Lake* *323/665–5899* *www.nightmarketsong.com* *Closed Tues.*

Pine and Crane

$ | **TAIWANESE** | **FAMILY** | This is not the typical Chinese restaurant you might expect; it's a fast casual, often locally sourced Taiwanese restaurant housed in a modern setting. The menu changes based on season, the wine and beer list updates constantly, and the tea menu is carefully curated. **Known for:** dan dan noodles; traditional panfried omelet; friendly staff. *Average main: $12* *1521 Griffith Park Blvd., Silver Lake* *323/668–1128* *www.pineandcrane.com* *Closed Tues.*

Sawyer

$$$ | **SEAFOOD** | Simply put, Sawyer is a stunner with its restored brick walls, beautiful hardwood floor, and tiled patio, flourished with mid-century modern furniture; it's exactly the kind of bright and airy place you'd want to start off your day in. Yet most patrons come here less for the ambience and more for the food, with a menu that leans on the healthy side but isn't afraid to indulge in the hearty stuff, touting an assortment of traditional and modern American fare. **Known for:** seafood boil; lobster roll; weekend brunch. *Average main: $23* *3709 Sunset Blvd., Silver Lake* *323/641–3709* *No brunch weekdays.*

Silverlake Ramen

$$ | **RAMEN** | Now a franchise with several locations around Los Angeles (and a random one in Concord, NC), it's this original spot in the heart of the city's hipsterville that's still the best. The go-to ramen joint for Silverlake and Echo Park denizens is just the ticket if you're in dire need of some comfort food while also partaking in L.A.'s multicultural food scene. **Known for:** The Blaze, a spicy Tonkotsu ramen; crispy rice with spicy tuna; hearty Japanese fare. *Average main: $14* *2927 Sunset Blvd., Silver Lake* *323/660–8100* *www.silverlakeramen.com.*

Akbar

BARS/PUBS | This bar's welcoming feel is one of the reasons many people consider it their neighborhood bar, even if they don't live in the neighborhood. The crowd is friendly and inviting, and theme nights attract all sorts of folks, gay or straight.

The comedy nights are favorites, as are weekends, when DJs get everyone on the dance floor. ✉ *4356 W. Sunset Blvd., Silver Lake* ☎ *323/665–6810* 🌐 *www.akbarsilverlake.com.*

Cha Cha Lounge

BARS/PUBS | If chaos and the assortment of ill-matched furnishings and decor is something you can forgive—or revel in—then this import from Seattle is a Silver Lake staple you should check out. Grab your (cheap) poison then meander through the Mexican fiesta-theme bar. Foosball tables, a photo booth, and a vending machine will give you plenty to occupy your time. ✉ *2375 Glendale Blvd., Silver Lake* ☎ *323/660–7595* 🌐 *www.chachalounge.com.*

★ 4100

BARS/PUBS | With swaths of fabric draped from the ceiling, this low-lit bar with a bohemian vibe makes it perfect for dates. Groups of locals also come through for the night, making the crowd a plentiful mix of people. The bartenders know how to pour drinks that are both tasty and potent. There's plenty of seating at the tables and stools along the central bar, which gets crowded on the weekends. ✉ *1087 Manzanita St., Silver Lake* ☎ *323/666–4460* 🌐 *www.pouringwithheart.com/4100-bar.*

Silverlake Lounge

MUSIC CLUBS | Rock bands, burlesque performances, comedy sets, and even open-mike nights all have a home at the cross section of Sunset and Silver Lake at a little dive bar called the Silverlake Lounge. This small club with the yellow awning is a neighborhood spot—cash only, by the way—in the best way possible, with cheap drinks and local talent deserving of their time in the limelight. ✉ *2906 W. Sunset Blvd., Silver Lake* ☎ *323/663–9636* 🌐 *www.thesilverlakelounge.com.*

Thirsty Crow

BARS/PUBS | This whiskey bar serves up seasonal cocktails in a fun, rustic environment. Though small, it manages to find space for live musicians and an open-mike night on Saturday. Part of the same hospitality group as Bigfoot Lodge and Highland Park Bowl, it has a locals-only feel. As local L.A. musician Father John Misty once said, "nothing good ever happens at the goddamn Thirsty Crow," but we think you should go and see for yourself. ✉ *2939 W. Sunset Blvd., Silver Lake* ☎ *323/661–6007* 🌐 *www.thirstycrowbar.com.*

Shopping

Mohawk General Store

CLOTHING | Filled with a brilliant combination of indie and established designers, this upscale boutique is a mainstay for the modern minimalist. Pick up the wares of local favorites Cathy Callahan and Knotwork, as well as internationally loved labels like Acne Studios, Issey Miyake, and Levi's. The Sunset Boulevard store stocks goods for men and women as well as children, plus accessories and some home goods. ✉ *4011 W. Sunset Blvd., Silver Lake* ☎ *323/669–1601* 🌐 *www.mohawkgeneralstore.com.*

Secret Headquarters

BOOKS/STATIONERY | This could be the coolest comic-book store on the planet, with a selection to satisfy both the geekiest of collectors and those more interested in artistic and literary finds. Rich wood floors and a leather chair near the front window of this intimate space mark the sophisticated setting, which features wall displays neatly organized with new comics and filing cabinets marked DC and Marvel. ✉ *3817 W. Sunset Blvd., Silver Lake* ☎ *323/666–2228* 🌐 *www.thesecretheadquarters.com.*

Silver Lake Wine

WINE/SPIRITS | Boutique wineries from around the world provide this shop with the vintage bottles that fill the floor-to-ceiling racks. Looking relaxed and unassuming in jeans and T-shirts, the knowledgeable staff can steer you to the right wine or spirits for any occasion. Those who prefer to enjoy their wine in the privacy of their vacation rental or hotel will be pleased to know they also do deliveries around Silver Lake and the neighboring areas. ✉ *2395 Glendale Blvd., Silver Lake* ☎ *323/662–9024* 🌐 *www.silverlakewine.com.*

Echo Park

Sights

★ Dodger Stadium

SPORTS VENUE | **FAMILY** | Home of the Dodgers since 1962, Dodger Stadium is the third-oldest baseball stadium still in use and has had quite the history in baseball, including Sandy Koufax's perfect game in 1965 and Kirk Gibson's 1988 World Series home run. Not only has it played host to the Dodgers' ups and downs and World Series runs, it's also been the venue for some of the biggest performers in the world, including the Beatles, Madonna, and Beyoncé. The stadium can be tough to get into on game day, so consider getting dropped off in the park and walking up. Alternately, you can arrive early, as locals tend not to roll up until the third inning. If you have the opportunity to take in a Friday night game, make sure to stick around for the fireworks show that follows—if you're patient, you can even wait in line and watch it from the field. ✉ *1000 Vin Scully Ave., Echo Park* ☎ *866/363–4377* 🌐 *dodgers.mlb.com/la/ballpark.*

Elysian Park

HIKING/WALKING | **FAMILY** | Though not Los Angeles's biggest park—that honor belongs to Griffith Park—Elysian comes in second, and also has the honor of being the city's oldest. It's also home to one of L.A.'s busiest and most beloved attractions, Dodger Stadium, the home field to the Los Angeles Dodgers. For this reason, baseball fans flock to this 600-acre park for tailgate parties. The rest of the time, however, Elysian Park serves as the Echo Park residents' backyard, thanks to its network of hiking trails, picnic spaces, and public playgrounds. ✉ *929 Academy Rd., Echo Park* 🌐 *www.laparks.org/park/elysian.*

Restaurants

Masa of Echo Park

$$ | **PIZZA** | **FAMILY** | While Masa of Echo Park does do excellent "bistro pizzas," as the restaurant calls them, it's mostly known for the delectable deep-dish pies that may just be the best you'll find this side of Chicago. Be prepared though—it can take a while to get seated and up to 45 minutes to get that deep dish you ordered, so it might be best to call ahead. **Known for:** vegan menu options; family-style dining; Italian classics. $ *Average main: $20* ✉ *1800 W. Sunset Blvd., Echo Park* ☎ *213/989–1558* 🌐 *www.masaofechopark.com.*

Spoon and Pork

$$ | **PHILIPPINE** | In a city where food trucks can be successful enough to have their own brick-and-mortar spaces, and where Filipino food has quickly become a craze, it's no surprise that Spoon and Pork has found its rightful place in the neighborhood. With a name that cleverly plays on the traditional Filipino way of eating (using both spoon and fork), this modern Filipino food spot is the perfect introduction to the cuisine. **Known for:** adobo pork belly; lechon kawali; Filipino comfort food. $ *Average main: $14* ✉ *3131 W. Sunset Blvd., Echo Park* ☎ *323/922–6061* 🌐 *www.spoonandpork.com* ⏲ *Closed Mon.*

Nightlife

★ The Echo

MUSIC CLUBS | Echo Park is peppered with music venues, but if you want to be in the heart of the neighborhood's live music scene, you should head to the Echo. With a full bar and recurring theme nights, the spot hosts cutting-edge music from both up-and-coming local and touring acts as well as well-known bands. ✉ *1822 Sunset Blvd., Echoplex entrance at 1154 Glendale Blvd., Echo Park* ☎ *No phone* 🌐 *www.spacelandpresents.com.*

★ Mohawk Bend

BARS/PUBS | There are plenty of reasons to stop by Mohawk Bend: 72 craft beers on tap, a wide range of California-only liquor, a vegetarian and vegan-friendly menu that includes tailored-to-your-wants pizza, and a buffalo cauliflower that—rumor has it—started the whole trend. There might be a long line to get into this 100-year-old former theater in the evenings, but it's worth it. ✉ *2141 Sunset Blvd., Echo Park* ☎ *213/483–2337* 🌐 *mohawk.la.*

★ 1642

BARS/PUBS | This romantically lit hole-in-the-wall is easy to miss, but you should aim to check it out if you're a discerning wine connoisseur or looking to experience the best of California's microbreweries. Perfect for first dates, come here to experiment with craft beers or to warm up with wine while listening to some live old-time fiddle tunes. ✉ *1642 W. Temple St., Echo Park* ☎ *213/989–6836* 🌐 *www.1642bar.com.*

Shopping

Esqueleto

JEWELRY/ACCESSORIES | There's a touch of the macabre on display at Esqueleto, but what do you expect from a jewelry boutique with a name that means "skeleton" in Spanish? That doesn't mean the light, airy, contemporary shop is stereotypically Goth in style. Both its design and the inventory it stocks are perfectly polished and selected with a discerningly artistic eye. With a mix of excellent vintage finds and emerging designers, the shop has become a go-to destination for alternative brides' engagement rings and wedding bands. ✉ *1928 W. Sunset Blvd., Echo Park* ☎ *213/947–3508* 🌐 *www.shopesqueleto.com.*

Stories Books and Café

BOOKS/STATIONERY | With an off-the-beaten-path collection of new and used literature, a café catering to freelancers and free thinkers, and a back patio that showcases singer-songwriters, Stories Books and Café is an authentic reflection of Echo Park. Readings, signings, and other events are a regular occurrence. ✉ *1716 Sunset Blvd., Echo Park* ☎ *213/413–3733* 🌐 *www.storiesla.com.*

Time Travel Mart

SPECIALTY STORES | **FAMILY** | You probably won't find anything useful in the Time Travel Mart and that's exactly the point. From dinosaur eggs to robot milk, this is a store that touts the absurdly hilarious—all of which should bring back memories of your childhood and maybe a little bit of joy. That's because the store holds a secret: it's really a fundraiser for the nonprofit 826LA, which tutors neighborhood kids in the back section. So even when you're buying something unnecessary but absolutely wonderful, remember it's for a noble and worthy cause. ✉ *1714 W.*

Sunset Blvd., Echo Park ☎ 213/413–3388 🌐 826la.org/store.

Highland Park

Sights

Heritage Square Museum

MUSEUM | Looking like a prop street set up by a film studio, Heritage Square resembles a row of bright dollhouses in the modest Highland Park neighborhood. Five 19th-century residences, a train station, a church, a carriage barn, and a 1909 boxcar that was originally part of the Southern Pacific Railroad, all built between the Civil War and World War I, were moved to this small park from various locations in Southern California to save them from the wrecking ball. The latest addition, a re-creation of a World War I–era drugstore, has a vintage soda fountain and traditional products. Docents dressed in period costume lead visitors through the lavish homes, giving an informative picture of Los Angeles in the early 1900s. Don't miss the unique 1893 Octagon House, one of just a handful of its kind built in California. *✉ 3800 Homer St., Highland Park ☎ 323/225–2700 🌐 www.heritagesquare.org 🎫 $10 ⏲ Closed Tues.–Thurs. and federal holiday Mon.*

Restaurants

Cafe Birdie

$$ | **MEDITERRANEAN** | This spacious 1920s-style spot along a quickly revitalizing stretch of Figueroa has established itself as a neighborhood bistro frequented by Highland Park residents, as well as folks from nearby neighborhoods. The eclectic menu skillfully blends elements of European, Southern, and Japanese cuisines, tying them together with a fresh California flair and a gorgeous interior inspired by a fictional meeting-of-two-souls narrative. **Known for:** square pies; seasonal cocktails; modern, airy spot. *$ Average main: $19 ✉ 5631 N. Figueroa St., Highland Park ☎ 323/739–6928 🌐 www.cafebirdiela.com.*

★ Donut Friend

$ | **BAKERY** | When this music-influenced doughnut shop first opened on York Boulevard in the early days of Highland Park's renaissance, there wasn't much there, and its arrival helped shape the now bustling strip and its vegan inclinations. Donut Friend had evolved into a destination in its own right, touting both a signature and limited menu of purely vegan doughnuts—which also happen to be inspired by the pop punk and emo music scene. **Known for:** fun flavors like Green Teagan and Sara (with matcha tea glaze); all vegan ingredients; make-your-own doughnut option. *$ Average main: $4 ✉ 5107 York Blvd., Highland Park ☎ 213/908–2745 🌐 www.donutfriend.com.*

El Huarache Azteca

$ | **MEXICAN** | **FAMILY** | While you definitely should try the flat shoe-shaped dish El Huarache Azteca is named after—think somewhere between a flatbread and a tostada—you cannot go wrong with any of the other options at this family restaurant that's been a fixture in the area for the last couple of decades. Just be aware there's often a wait for the food to come out. **Known for:** no-frills Mexican dishes; agua fresca; super huarache. *$ Average main: $10 ✉ 5225 York Blvd., Highland Park ☎ 323/478–9572 🌐 elhuaracheaztecalive.com.*

★ Knowrealitypie

$ | **BAKERY** | The award-winning Knowrealitypie, hidden in a shop the size of a large walk-in closet, serves homemade pies every Friday through Saturday and only stays open until it sells out, which it often does. So hurry on down to partake in a rotating menu of seasonal savory and sweet pies, turnovers, and other pastries while supplies last. **Known for:** triple cherry Cabernet pie; caramel mango passion pie; small space that only stays open until they sell out. $ *Average main: $6* ✉ *5106 Townsend Ave., Highland Park* ☎ *916/799–5772* 🌐 *www.knowrealitypie.com* ⏲ *Closed Mon.–Thurs.*

Polka Polish Cuisine

$$ | POLISH | There's a coziness in Polka Polish Cuisine that can only be matched by a grandmother's living room. The food here, traditional Polish fare, also has that same comfort. **Known for:** hearty Polish comfort food; traditional pierogi and kielbasa; mom-and-pop ambience. $ *Average main: $20* ✉ *4112 Verdugo Rd., Highland Park* ☎ *323/255–7887* 🌐 *www.polkarestaurant.com* ⏲ *Closed Mon. and Tues.*

Nightlife

The Hermosillo

BARS/PUBS | This is the kind of laid-back pub every neighborhood should have, with an excellent selection of locally focused draft beer on tap, a rotating wine list, and mouthwatering food. To add to its allure, award-winning Highland Park Brewery got its start in the pub's back storage room and is still featured prominently on the menu. ✉ *5125 York Blvd., Highland Park* ☎ *323/739–6459* 🌐 *thehermosillo.com.*

★ Highland Park Bowl

BARS/PUBS | FAMILY | Once an ambitious restoration project, Highland Park Bowl now serves as a massive throwback to its Prohibition Era roots as an alcohol-prescribing doctor's office and drugstore with its own bowling alley. That bowling alley remains, complete with the original pin machine. The hooch-pushing doctor and druggist, however, are long gone. But now there's an Italian restaurant that serves excellent pizza made from scratch using a mother dough brought all the way from Italy. ✉ *5621 N. Figueroa St., Highland Park* ☎ *323/257–2695* 🌐 *www.highlandparkbowl.com.*

The York

BARS/PUBS | Since 2007, before Highland Park became trendy, the York has been holding its own as the ultimate neighborhood bar. It's not just that the aesthetic gives off that neighborhood vibe (think exposed brick and chalkboard menus), but the craft beers on tap are great, and the pub food is delicious—the cheddar burger and the fish-and-chips are favorites. ✉ *5018 York Blvd., Highland Park* ☎ *323/255–9675* 🌐 *www.theyorkonyork.com.*

Shopping

Galco's Soda Pop Stop

FOOD/CANDY | FAMILY | A local fixture in Highland Park for decades, Galco's is in some ways a trip down memory lane, carrying more than 600 sodas—most of which harken back to the days when soda was a regional affair—and options from all over the world. They also have a collection of retro candies, a soda creation station with more than 100 syrups to choose from, and a selection of alcohol that would put most liquor stores to shame. ✉ *5702 York Blvd., Highland Park* ☎ *323/255–7115* 🌐 *sodapopstop.com.*

Permanent Records

MUSIC STORES | Part of the vinyl resurgence since 2013, Permanent Records stocks new and used vinyl for every musical taste and does it without any snobbery. The record store, which often has in-store performances, also runs its own label that focuses on local bands, limited-edition runs, and reissues. ✉ *1906 Cypress Ave., Highland Park* ☎ *323/332–2312* 🌐 *www.permanentrecordsla.com.*

Pasadena

Although seemingly absorbed into the general Los Angeles sprawl, Pasadena is a separate and distinct city. It's best known for the Tournament of Roses, or more commonly, the Rose Bowl, seen around the world every New Year's Day. But the city has sites worth seeing year-round—from gorgeous Craftsman homes to exceptional museums, particularly the Norton Simon and the Huntington Library, Art Museum, and Botanical Gardens. Note that the Huntington and the Old Mill reside in San Marino, a well-heeled, 4-square-mile residential area just over the Pasadena line.

Sights

The Gamble House

HOUSE | Built by Charles and Henry Greene in 1908, this American Arts and Crafts bungalow illustrates the incredible craftsmanship that went into early L.A. architecture. The term "bungalow" can be misleading, since the Gamble House is a huge three-story home. To wealthy Easterners such as the Gambles (as in Procter & Gamble), this type of vacation home seemed informal compared with their mansions back home. Admirers swoon over the teak staircase and cabinetry, the Greene and Greene–designed furniture, and an Emil Lange glass door. The dark exterior has broad eaves, with sleeping porches on the second floor. An hour-long, docent-led tour of the Gamble's interior will draw your eye to the exquisite details. For those who want to see more of the Greene and Greene homes, there are guided walks around the historic Arroyo Terrace neighborhood. Advance tickets are highly recommended. ■ **TIP→ Film buffs might recognize this as Doc Brown's house from Back to the Future.** ✉ *4 Westmoreland Pl., Pasadena* ☎ *626/793–3334* 🌐 *gamblehouse.org* 🎟 *$15* 🕓 *Closed Mon.*

★ Huntington Library, Art Museum, and Botanical Gardens

MUSEUM | If you have time for just one stop in the Pasadena area, be sure to see this sprawling estate built for railroad tycoon Henry E. Huntington in the early 1900s. Henry and his wife, Arabella (who was also his aunt by marriage), voraciously collected rare books and manuscripts, botanical specimens, and 18th-century British art. The institution they established became one of the most extraordinary cultural complexes in the world.

The library contains more than 700,000 books and 4 million manuscripts, including one of the world's biggest history of science collections and a Gutenberg Bible.

Don't resist being lured outside into the 130-acre Botanical Gardens, which extend out from the main building. The 10-acre Desert Garden has one of the world's largest groups of mature cacti and other succulents (visit on a cool morning or late afternoon). The Shakespeare Garden, meanwhile, blooms with plants mentioned in Shakespeare's works. The Japanese Garden features an authentic ceremonial teahouse built in Kyoto in the 1960s. A waterfall flows from the teahouse to the ponds below. In the Rose Garden Tea Room, afternoon tea is served (reserve in advance). The Chinese Garden, which is among the largest outside China, sinews around waveless pools.

The Bing Children's Garden lets tiny tots explore the ancient elements of water, fire, air, and earth. A 1¼-hour guided tour of the Botanical Gardens is led by docents at posted times, and a free brochure with a map and property highlights is available in the entrance pavilion. Tickets for the monthly free admission day are snapped up within minutes, so plan carefully. ✉ *1151 Oxford Rd., San Marino* ☎ *626/405–2100* 🌐 *www.huntington.org* 🎟 *From $25; free admission 1st Thurs. of every month with advance ticket* 🕓 *Closed Tues.*

★ Norton Simon Museum

MUSEUM | As seen in the New Year's Day Tournament of Roses Parade, this low-profile brown building is one of the finest midsize museums anywhere, with a collection that spans more than 2,000 years of Western and Asian art. It all began in the 1950s when Norton Simon (Hunt-Wesson Foods, McCalls Corporation, and Canada Dry) started collecting works by Degas, Renoir, Gauguin, and Cézanne. His collection grew to include works by old masters and impressionists, modern works from Europe, and Indian and Southeast Asian art. Today the museum is richest in works by Rembrandt, Picasso, and, most of all, Degas.

Head down to the bottom floor to see temporary exhibits and phenomenal Southeast Asian and Indian sculptures and artifacts, where pieces like a Ban Chiang blackware vessel date back to well before 1000 BC. Don't miss a living artwork outdoors: the garden, conceived by noted Southern California landscape designer Nancy Goslee Power. The tranquil pond was inspired by Monet's gardens at Giverny. ✉ *411 W. Colorado Blvd., Pasadena* ☎ *626/449–6840* 🌐 *www.nortonsimon.org* 🎟 *$15; free 1st Fri. of month 5–8* ⏲ *Closed Tues.*

The Old Mill (El Molino Viejo)

BUILDING | Built in 1816 as a gristmill for the San Gabriel Mission, the mill is the state's oldest commercial building and one of the last remaining examples in Southern California of Spanish Mission architecture. The thick adobe walls and textured ceiling rafters give the interior a sense of quiet strength. Be sure to step into the back room, now a gallery with rotating quarterly exhibits. Outside, a chipped section of the mill's exterior reveals the layers of brick, ground seashell paste, and ox blood used to hold the structure together. The surrounding gardens are reason enough to visit, with a flower-decked arbor and old sycamores and oaks. In summer the Capitol Ensemble performs in the garden. ✉ *1120 Old Mill Rd., San Marino* ☎ *626/449–5458* 🌐 *www.old-mill.org* 🎟 *Free* ⏲ *Closed Mon.*

Old Town Pasadena

NEIGHBORHOOD | This 22-block historic district contains a vibrant mix of restored 19th-century brick buildings interspersed with contemporary architecture. Chain stores have muscled in, but there are still some homegrown shops, plenty of tempting cafés and restaurants, and a bustling beer scene. In recent years, a vibrant Asian food scene has popped up in the vicinity as well. In the evening and on weekends, the streets are packed with people. Old Town's main action takes place on Colorado Boulevard between Pasadena Avenue and Arroyo Parkway. ✉ *Pasadena* ☎ *626/356–9725* 🌐 *www.oldpasadena.org.*

★ Rose Bowl and Flea Market

MARKET | With an enormous rose on its exterior, this 90,000-plus-seat stadium is home to the UCLA Bruins and the annual Rose Bowl Game on New Year's Day, and also regularly sees performances from the biggest recording artists in the world. Set at the bottom of a wide arroyo in Brookside Park, the facility is closed except during games, concerts, and special events like its famed Flea Market, a Southern California institution. The massively popular and eclectic event, which happens the second Sunday of each month (rain or shine), deservedly draws crowds that come to find deals from more than 2,500 vendors on goods including mid-century and antique furniture, vintage clothing, pop culture collectibles, books, and music. Food and drink options are on hand to keep shoppers satiated, parking is free, and general admission is just $9, but VIP/early-bird options are available for a little extra. Crowds tend to peak mid-day. Bring cash to avoid an inevitable line at the ATM, and feel free to try your hand at haggling. ✉ *1001 Rose Bowl Dr., Pasadena* ☎ *626/577–3100* 🌐 *www.rosebowlstadium.com.*

Restaurants

Pie 'n Burger

$$ | **DINER** | Since 1963, this small and charming diner has done two things really well—pies and burgers. Most seats are counter-style, with a griddle searing up patties. **Known for:** simple burgers; enormous pie slices; retro-style decor. [$] *Average main: $14* ✉ *913 E. California Blvd., Pasadena* ☎ *626/795–1123* 🌐 *pienburger.com.*

The Raymond 1886

$$$ | **MODERN AMERICAN** | The coolest kid on the Pasadena block, the Raymond 1886 is carved out of an old cottage, and has an expansive patio with long wooden tables and hanging lights. Chefs dish out everything from a burrata-and-pear pairing to pork loin Milanese and tots with eel sauce. **Known for:** solid happy hour; great bar food; expansive patio. [$] *Average main: $30* ✉ *1250 S. Fair Oaks Ave., Pasadena* ☎ *626/441–3136* 🌐 *theraymond.com* 🕒 *Closed Mon.*

Shopping

Vroman's Bookstore

BOOKS/STATIONERY | Southern California's oldest and largest independent bookseller is justly famous for its great service. A newsstand, café, and stationery store add to the appeal, and it's a favorite with locals for its on-trend, eclectic gift selection. A regular rotation of events including trivia night, kids' story time, author meet-and-greets, crafting sessions, discussions, and more get the community actively involved. ✉ *695 E. Colorado Blvd., Pasadena* ☎ *626/449–5320* 🌐 *www.vromansbookstore.com.*

Malibu and the Beaches

The beaches and coastal areas of Los Angeles are an iconic symbol of the region's casual friendliness and endless optimism, and the local love for them is as much a trope as it is a reality. Angelenos are known for working hard and playing hard, and the coast is where they come to play. Getting some sand on the floor of your car is a rite of passage here. Like its most ardent fans, this stretch of the Pacific is best known for its beauty: cosmetically enhanced in some areas and ruggedly pristine in others. From the hillside mansions of Malibu, where even the air is rarified, to the cultural dynamism of Long Beach, the gently arching coastline tells an L.A. story all its own as it transitions from ultrarich to bohemian to working class. Through it all, the sand remains the center of the action.

Malibu

Sights

★ **Getty Villa Malibu**

HOUSE | Feeding off the cultures of ancient Rome, Greece, and Etruria, the villa exhibits astounding antiquities, though on a first visit even they take a backseat to their environment. This megamansion sits on some of the most valuable coastal property in the world. Modeled after the Villa dei Papiri in Herculaneum, a Roman estate owned by Julius Caesar's father-in-law that was covered in ash when Mt. Vesuvius erupted, the Getty Villa includes beautifully manicured gardens, reflecting pools, and statuary. The structures blend thoughtfully into the rolling terrain and significantly improve the public spaces, such as the outdoor amphitheater, gift store, café, and entry arcade. Talks, concerts, and educational programs are offered at an indoor theater. **■TIP→ An advance timed entry ticket is required for admission. Tickets are free and may be ordered from the museum's website or by phone.** ✉ *17985 Pacific Coast Hwy., Pacific Palisades* ☎ *310/440–7300* 🌐 *www.getty.edu* 🎫 *Free, tickets required; parking $20* ⏲ *Closed Tues.*

Malibu Lagoon State Beach

BEACH—SIGHT | Bird-watchers, take note: in this 5-acre marshy area near Malibu Beach Inn you can spot egrets, blue herons, avocets, and gulls. (You need to stay on the boardwalks so as not to disturb their habitats.) The path leads out to a rocky stretch of Surfrider Beach and makes for a pleasant stroll. The sand is soft, clean, and white, and you're also likely to spot a variety of marine life. Look for the signs to help identify these sometimes exotic-looking creatures. The lagoon is particularly enjoyable in the early morning and at sunset—and even more so now, thanks to a restoration effort that improved the lagoon's scent. The parking lot has limited hours, but street-side parking is usually available at off-peak times. An on-site museum reveals local history, and close by are shops and a theater. **Amenities:** parking (fee); lifeguards; toilets; showers. **Best for:** sunset; walking. ✉ *23200 Pacific Coast Hwy., Malibu* ☎ *310/457–8143* 🌐 *www.parks.ca.gov/?page_id=835* 🎫 *Parking $12.*

Malibu Pier

MARINA | **FAMILY** | This rustically chic 780-foot fishing dock is a great place to drink in the sunset, take in some coastal views, or watch local fishermen reel up a catch. Some tours also leave from here. A pier has jutted out on this spot since the early 1900s; storms destroyed the last one in 1995, and it was rebuilt in 2001. Over the years, private developers have worked with the state to refurbish the pier, which now yields a gift shop, water-sport rentals, a jeweler housed in a vintage Airstream trailer, and a wonderful farm-to-table restaurant with stunning views and locations at both ends of the pier. ✉ *Pacific Coast Hwy. at Cross Creek Rd., Malibu* 🌐 *www.malibupier.com.*

Westward Beach–Point Dume

BEACH—SIGHT | This famed promontory is a Malibu pilgrimage for any visitor to the area. Go tide pooling, fishing, snorkeling, or bird-watching (prime time is late winter to early spring). Hike to the top of the sandstone cliffs at Point Dume to whale-watch—their migrations can be seen between December and April—and take in dramatic coastal views. Westward is a favorite surfing beach, but the steep surf isn't for novices. The Sunset restaurant is between Westward and Point Dume (at 6800 Westward Beach Road). Otherwise, bring your own food, since the nearest concession is a long hike away. **Amenities:** parking (fee); lifeguards; toilets; food and drink; showers. **Best for:** surfing; walking. ✉ *71030 Westward Beach Rd., Malibu* ☎ *310/305–9503* 🎫 *Parking $14.*

Zuma Beach Park

BEACH—SIGHT | This 2-mile stretch of white sand, usually dotted with tanning teenagers, has it all, from fishing and kitesurfing to swings and volleyball courts. Beachgoers looking for quiet or privacy should head elsewhere. Stay alert in the water: the surf is rough and inconsistent and riptides can surprise even experienced swimmers. **Amenities:** parking; lifeguards; toilets; food and drink; showers. **Best for:** partiers; sunset; swimming; walking. ✉ *30000 Pacific Coast Hwy., Malibu* ☎ *310/305–9522* 🌐 *www.zuma-beach.com* 🎫 *Parking $10.*

Restaurants

Nobu Malibu

$$$$ | **JAPANESE** | At famous chef-restaurateur Nobu Matsuhisa's coastal outpost, super-chic clientele sails in for morsels of the world's finest fish. It's hard not to be seduced by the oceanfront property, and stellar sushi and ingenious specialties match the upscale setting. **Known for:** exotic fish; A-list celebrity chef; bento box Valrhona chocolate soufflé. *Average main: $35 22706 Pacific Coast Hwy., Malibu 310/317–9140 www.noburestaurants.com.*

Reel Inn

$$ | **SEAFOOD** | **FAMILY** | Escape the glitz and glamour at this decades-old, down-home Malibu institution. Long wooden tables and booths are often filled with fish-loving families chowing down on mahimahi sandwiches and freshly caught swordfish. **Known for:** easy-to-miss spot on the PCH; fresh catches; dog-friendly patio. *Average main: $17 18661 Pacific Coast Hwy., Malibu 310/456–8221 www.reelinnmalibu.com.*

Hotels

Malibu Beach Inn

$$$$ | **B&B/INN** | Set right on exclusive Carbon Beach in a stretch known as Billionaire's Beach, Malibu's hideaway for the super-rich remains the room to nab along the coast, with an ultrachic look thanks to designer Waldo Fernandez and an upscale restaurant and wine bar perched over the Pacific. **Pros:** views of the ocean from your private balcony; world-class chocolate chip cookies at reception; ultimate beachside luxury. **Cons:** millionaire's travel budget required; some in-room noise from PCH; no pool, gym, or hot tub. *Rooms from: $749 22878 Pacific Coast Hwy., Malibu 310/456–6444 www.malibubeachinn.com 47 rooms No meals.*

Nightlife

Duke's Barefoot Bar

BARS/PUBS | **FAMILY** | With a clear view of the horizon from almost everywhere, a sunset drink at Duke's Barefoot Bar is how many beachgoers like to end their day. The entertainment is in keeping with the bar's theme, with Hawaiian dancers as well as live music on Friday night by Hawaiian artists. The menu features island favorites like *poke* tacos, macadamia-crusted fish, and kalua pork and a Sunday brunch buffet from 10 to 2. Just don't expect beach-bum prices, unless you stop by the happy hour weekday events like Taco Tuesday (bargain-priced fish, kalua pork, or grilled chicken tacos and beers). *21150 Pacific Coast Hwy., Malibu 310/317–0777 www.dukesmalibu.com.*

Moonshadows

BARS/PUBS | This outdoor lounge attracts customers with its modern look and views of the ocean. Think dark woods, cabana-style draperies, and ambient lighting in the Blue Lounge, open late on weekends. DJs are constantly spinning lounge music in the background, and there's never a cover charge. Sunday afternoons perfectly blend the laid-back ambience with good vibes. Try a sunset dinner or the lobster roll and dessert lineup. *20356 Pacific Coast Hwy., Malibu 310/456–3010 www.moonshadowsmalibu.com.*

Shopping

★ Malibu Country Mart

SHOPPING CENTERS/MALLS | Stop by this outdoor outpost for the ultimate Malibu lifestyle experience, complete with browsing designer clothing (Rubin & Chapelle, Ron Herman, or Madison) and eclectic California housewares and gifts (Malibu Colony Company), picking up body-boosting wellness goodies at SunLife Organics, and finishing the day off with dinner at long-standing eatery

Tra di Noi, reputed to be a favorite of Barbra Streisand. If you can squeeze in a workout, there's a Pure Barre and a 5 Point Yoga to choose from, plus tarot readings at metaphysical outpost Malibu Shaman. Then reward yourself for your good health habits by stopping at K Chocolatier by Diane Krön for some of her famed truffles, derived from a Hungarian family recipe. ✉ *3835 Cross Creek Rd., Malibu* ☎ *310/456–7300* 🌐 *www.malibucountrymart.com.*

Manhattan Beach, Redondo Beach, and Long Beach

Sights

★ Aquarium of the Pacific

ZOO | FAMILY | Sea lions, zebra sharks, and penguins—this aquarium focuses on creatures of the Pacific Ocean and is home to more than 12,000 animals. The main exhibits include large tanks of sharks, stingrays, and ethereal sea dragons, which the aquarium has successfully bred in captivity. The museum's first major expansion in years, Pacific Visions, features a 29,000-square-foot multisensory experience in which attendees can immerse themselves in humankind's relationship with the natural world through video projections, soundscapes, tactile exhibits, a touchscreen wall, interactive game tables, rumbling theater seats, and more. For a nonaquatic experience, head to Lorikeet Forest, a walk-in aviary full of the friendliest parrots from Australia. Buy a cup of nectar and smile as you become a human bird perch.
If you're a true animal lover, book an up-close-and-personal Animal Encounters Tour (extra fee) to learn about and assist in the care and feeding of sharks, penguins, and other aquarium residents; or find out how the aquarium functions with the extensive Behind the Scenes Tour (extra fee). Certified divers can book a supervised dive in the aquarium's Tropical Reef Habitat (extra fee) and kids go wild for frequent overnight camp experiences in the aquarium. Twice-daily whale-watching trips on Harbor Breeze Cruises depart from the dock adjacent to the aquarium; summer sightings of blue whales are an unforgettable thrill. ✉ *100 Aquarium Way, Long Beach* ☎ *562/590–3100* 🌐 *www.aquariumofpacific.org* 🎟 *$30.*

Manhattan Beach

BEACH—SIGHT | A wide, sandy strip with good swimming and rows of volleyball courts, Manhattan Beach is the preferred destination of fit, tanned young professionals. There are also such amenities as a bike path, a playground, a bait shop, fishing equipment for rent, and a sizable fishing pier. It's also the perfect place to unwind during a long layover at LAX. **Amenities:** parking (fee); lifeguards; toilets; food and drink; showers. **Best for:** swimming; walking. ✉ *Manhattan Beach Blvd. at N. Ocean Dr., Manhattan Beach* ☎ *310/372–2166* 🌐 *beaches.lacounty.gov/manhattan-beach* 🎟 *Metered parking; long- and short-term lots.*

★ *Queen Mary*

HISTORIC SITE | FAMILY | Though berthed, the *Queen Mary* is an impressive example of 20th-century cruise ship opulence and sadly the last of its kind. The beautifully preserved art deco–style ocean liner was launched in 1936 and made 1,001 transatlantic crossings before finally berthing in Long Beach in 1967.

Take one of several daily themed tours such as the informative Glory Days historical walk, a traipse into the boiler rooms on the Steam and Steel Tour, or the downright spooky Haunted Encounters tour. (Spirits have reportedly been spotted in the pool and engine room.) You can add ongoing theatrical performances by illusionist Aiden Sinclair, a Winston Churchill exhibit, a 4-D documentary experience, a wine tasting room, and a daily British-style high tea. Holidays and special events are celebrated onboard as well, from a haunted Halloween experience to an annual Scottish festival. Stay for dinner at one of the ship's restaurants, listen to live jazz or order a cocktail in the Observation Bar (the sumptuous original first-class lounge), or even spend the night in one of the 347 wood-paneled cabins. The ship's neighbor, a geodesic dome originally built to house Howard Hughes's *Spruce Goose* aircraft, now serves as a terminal for Carnival Cruise Lines, making the *Queen Mary* the perfect pit stop before or after a cruise. Anchored next to the *Queen* is the *Scorpion*, a Russian submarine you can tour for a look at Cold War history. ✉ *1126 Queens Hwy., Long Beach* ☎ *877/342–0738* 🌐 *www.queenmary.com* ⊙ *Tours from $16.*

Redondo Beach

BEACH—SIGHT | The pier here marks the starting point of this wide, busy beach along a heavily developed shoreline community. Restaurants and shops flourish along the pier, excursion boats and privately owned crafts depart from launching ramps, and a reef formed by a sunken ship creates prime fishing and snorkeling conditions. If you're adventurous, you might try to kayak out to the buoys and hobnob with pelicans and sea lions. A series of free rock and jazz concerts takes place at the pier every summer. **Amenities:** parking; lifeguards; food and drink; toilets; showers; water sports. **Best for:** snorkeling; sunset; swimming; walking. ✉ *Torrance Blvd. at Catalina Ave., Redondo Beach* ☎ *310/372–2166* 🌐 *www.redondopier.com.*

Chapter 7

PALM SPRINGS

Updated by
Cheryl Crabtree

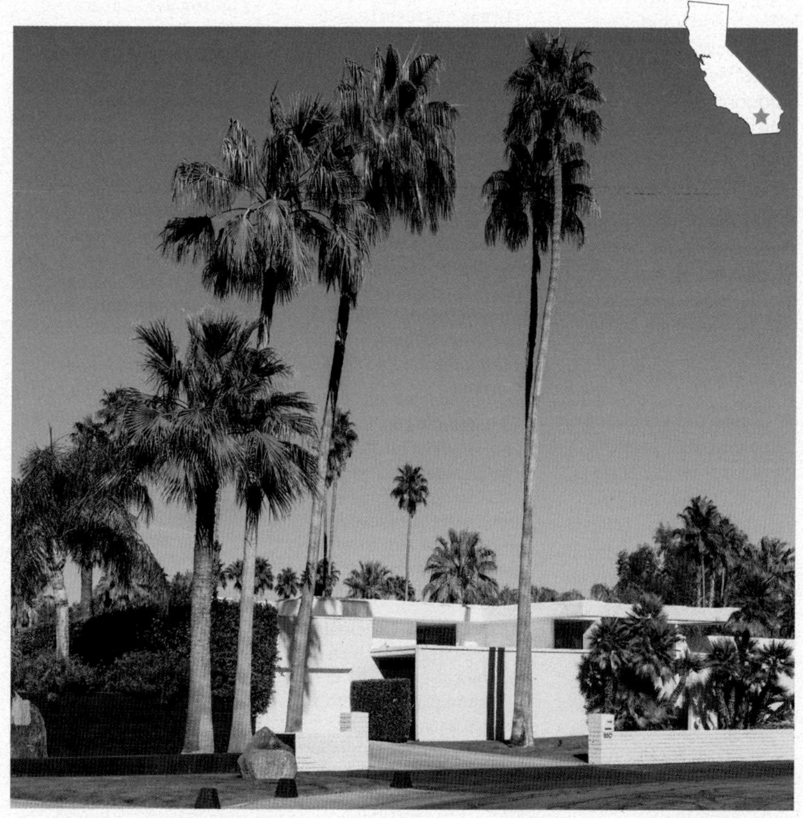

Sights ★★★★★ | Restaurants ★★★★☆ | Hotels ★★★★★ | Shopping ★★☆☆☆ | Nightlife ★★☆☆☆

WELCOME TO PALM SPRINGS

TOP REASONS TO GO

★ **Year-round sunshine:** The Palm Springs area has more than 300 days of sun each year, and the weather is usually ideal for playing one of the area's more than 100 golf courses.

★ **Spa under the stars:** Many resorts and small hotels now offer after-dark spa services, including outdoor soaks and treatments you can savor while sipping wine under the clear, starry sky.

★ **Personal pampering:** The resorts here have it all, beautifully appointed rooms packed with amenities, professional staffs, sublime spas, and delicious dining options.

★ **Divine desert scenery:** You'll probably spend a lot of time taking in the gorgeous 360-degree natural panorama, a flat desert floor surrounded by 10,000-foot mountains rising into a brilliant blue sky.

★ **The Hollywood connection:** The Palm Springs area has more celebrity ties than any other resort community. So keep your eyes open for your favorite star.

1 **Palm Springs.** A mid-century modern vibe and many restaurants, bars, and galleries line the avenues of Palm Springs. Hiking trails and an aerial tramway lead from the desert floor up to the San Jacinto mountain peaks.

2 **Rancho Mirage.** An elegant, upscale residential community, Rancho Mirage has resorts, golf courses and gated estates. A main draw here is Annenberg Retreat at Sunnylands, a grand garden estate open to the public for tours.

3 **Palm Desert.** The mile-long El Paseo shopping and restaurant district is the heart of Palm Desert, a peaceful community also known for its challenging golf courses and the Living Desert Zoo and Gardens.

4 **Indian Wells.** Exclusive Indian Wells hosts national tennis and pickleball championships at posh resorts, where spas and upscale restaurants pamper players and spectators alike.

5 **La Quinta.** Coachella Valley's first golf course opened at La Quinta in 1920 and morphed into a quaint town alongside a sprawling resort and club with multiple courses.

6 **Indio.** The date capital of the nation, Indio lures visitors with date shakes and date palm fields.

7 **Borrego Springs.** Superb wildflower viewing and numerous nature trails are among the draws at Borrego Springs within Anza-Borrego Desert State Park.

8 **Salton Sea.** Nature lovers retreat to the shores of the Salton Sea, a haven for birdwatching and lakefront activities.

9 **Desert Hot Springs.** To the north of Palm Springs, a concentrated network of hot springs flows through this community, where visitors come to soak in soothing mineral waters and rejuvenate mind and body.

10 **Yucca Valley.** A laid-back roadside city, Yucca Valley is a convenient stop on the way north to Joshua Tree National Park. In nearby Pioneertown, Pappy and Harriet's Pioneertown Palace serves classic Western food and big-name musical entertainment.

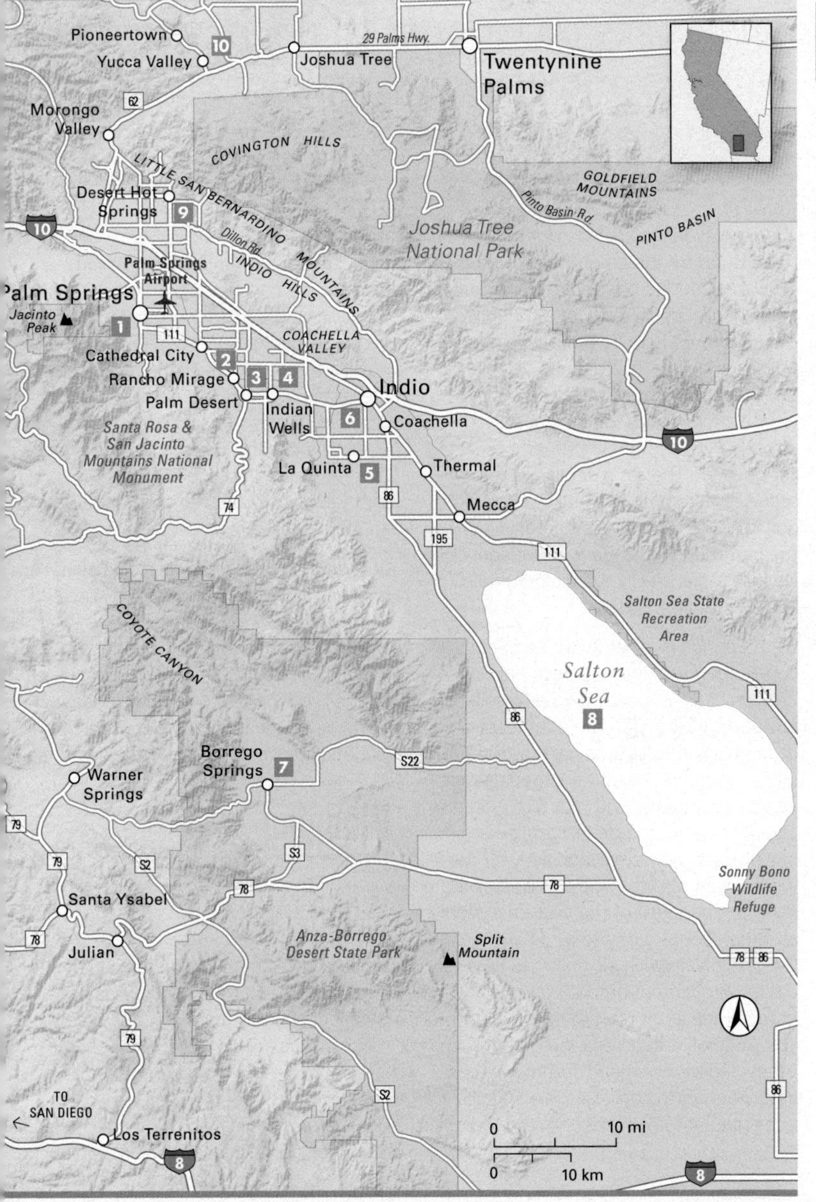

Pioneertown
Yucca Valley
Joshua Tree
29 Palms Hwy.
Twentynine Palms
Morongo Valley
COVINGTON HILLS
LITTLE SAN BERNARDINO MOUNTAINS
GOLDFIELD MOUNTAINS
Pinto Basin Rd.
PINTO BASIN
Desert Hot Springs
Joshua Tree National Park
Dillon Rd.
INDIO HILLS
Palm Springs Airport
Palm Springs
Jacinto Peak
COACHELLA VALLEY
Cathedral City
Rancho Mirage
Indio
Palm Desert
Indian Wells
Coachella
Santa Rosa & San Jacinto Mountains National Monument
La Quinta
Thermal
Mecca
Salton Sea State Recreation Area
COYOTE CANYON
Salton Sea
Borrego Springs
Warner Springs
Santa Ysabel
Sonny Bono Wildlife Refuge
Julian
Anza-Borrego Desert State Park
Split Mountain
TO SAN DIEGO
Los Terrenitos
0
10 mi
10 km

With the Palm Springs area's year-round sunshine, luxurious spas, chef-driven restaurants, and see-and-be-seen pool parties, it's no wonder that Hollywood A-listers and weekend warriors make the desert a getaway.

The Palm Springs area has long been a playground for the celebrity elite. In the 1920s Al Capone opened the Two Bunch Palms Hotel in Desert Hot Springs (with multiple tunnels to help him avoid the police); Marilyn Monroe was discovered poolside in the late 1940s at a downtown Palm Springs tennis club; Elvis and Priscilla Presley honeymooned here—the list goes on. There's a similar desert resort feel (replete with luxury lodgings, golf courses, and shopping enclaves) in the communities of Rancho Mirage, Palm Desert, Indian Wells, La Quinta, Indio, and Desert Hot Springs.

Palm Springs is laden with urban-chic contemporary artwork (check out Palm Canyon Drive in downtown or the Backstreet Arts District in the southeast end of town). Winter events celebrate the city's modernist design aesthetic as well as its connections with the film industry. Over the years, the desert arts scene has blossomed as spectacularly as the wildflowers of Anza-Borrego Desert State Park, to the south of the city. Each April, attention centers on Indio, where the Coachella Valley Music and Arts Festival, California's largest outdoor concert, attracts droves of rock music lovers from Los Angeles and across the globe. Yucca Valley and other artistic communities all have noteworthy galleries, art installations, and natural scenic views.

MAJOR REGIONS

Palm Springs and the Southern Desert Resorts. The city of Palm Springs is within the Colorado Desert, on the western edge of Coachella Valley and at the northwestern end of Highway 111. From there, the highway travels southeast, providing access to a string of desert resorts, including Rancho Mirage, Palm Desert, Indian Wells, La Quinta, and Indio. Farther south are the Salton Sea and Borrego Springs.

Desert Hot Springs to Twentynine Palms Highway. Northwest of Palm Springs, off I–10 and Scenic California Highway 62, is the resort of Desert Hot Springs, after which Highway 62 becomes Twentynine Palms Highway and travels northeast to Yucca Valley en route to Joshua Tree National Park and its gateway towns.

Planning

When to Go

January through April is the height of the visitor season: the desert weather is best during this time, and it's when major events such as the Palm Springs International Film Festival (mid-January), Modernism Week (mid-February), and Coachella (two weekends in April) are held. Big-time LGBTQ+ fests also happen during this time, including The Dinah (🌐 *thedinah.*

com), a rollicking lesbian party in late March, and White Party Palm Springs (🌐 *jeffreysanker.com*), a spring break extravaganza that draws tens of thousands of gay men from around the world.

The fall months are nearly as lovely, but less crowded and less expensive (although autumn draws many conventions). In summer, a popular time with European visitors, daytime temperatures may rise above 110°F, though evenings cool to the mid-70s. Some attractions and restaurants close or reduce their hours in this season, though.

FESTIVALS AND EVENTS

ANA Inspiration Championship. The best female golfers in the world compete in this late-March or early-April event held in Rancho Mirage. 🌐 *www.anainspiration.com*

BNP Paribas Open. Drawing 200 of the world's top players, this tennis tournament takes place at Indian Wells Tennis Garden for two weeks in March. 🌐 *www.bnpparibasopen.com*

La Quinta Arts Festival. More than 200 painters, sculptors, ceramacists, and other artists participate each March in a four-day juried show that's considered one of the best in the West. 🌐 *www.lqaf.com*

National Date Festival and Riverside County Fair. Indio celebrates its raison d'être in mid-February with exhibits of local dates, camel and ostrich races, a nightly musical pageant, a rodeo, a demolition derby, and monster truck shows. 🌐 *www.datefest.org*

Getting Here and Around

AIR TRAVEL

Palm Springs International Airport serves California's desert communities. Air Canada, Alaska, Allegiant, American, Delta, Flair, Frontier, JetBlue, Southwest, Sun Country, United, and WestJet all fly to Palm Springs, some only seasonally. Yellow Cab of the Desert and Desert City Cab serve the airport, which is about 3 miles from downtown. The fare is $4 to enter the cab and about $3.12 per mile.

AIRPORT INFORMATION Palm Springs International Airport. ✉ *3200 E. Tahquitz Canyon Way, Palm Springs* ☎ *760/318–3800 general information* 🌐 *www.palmspringsairport.com.*

AIRPORT TRANSFERS Desert City Cab. ✉ *3465 E. La Campana Way, Palm Springs* ☎ *760/328–3000* 🌐 *desertcitycab.com.* **Yellow Cab of the Desert.** ✉ *75150 St. Charles Pl., Palm Desert* ☎ *760/340–8294* 🌐 *www.yellowcabofthedesert.com.*

BUS

Greyhound provides service to Palm Springs from many cities. SunBus, operated by the SunLine Transit Agency, serves the entire Coachella Valley, from Desert Hot Springs to Mecca.

BUS CONTACTS SunLine Transit Agency. ☎ *760/343–3451* 🌐 *www.sunline.org.*

CAR

The desert resort communities occupy a 20-mile stretch between I–10 to the east and Palm Canyon Drive (Highway 111) to the west. The region is about a two-hour drive (up to a four-hour drive on spring and winter weekends when traffic is heavy) east of Los Angeles and a three-hour drive northeast of San Diego. From Los Angeles take the San Bernardino Freeway (I–10) east to Highway 111. From San Diego, I–15 north connects with the Pomona Freeway (Highway 60), leading to the San Bernardino Freeway east.

To reach Borrego Springs from Los Angeles, take I–10 east past the desert resorts area to Highway 86 south to the Borrego Salton Seaway (Highway S22) west. You can reach the Borrego area from San Diego via I–8 to Highway 79 through Cuyamaca State Park and to Highway 78 in Julian, which you follow east to Yaqui Pass Road (S3) into Borrego Springs.

TAXI

Yellow Cab of the Desert and Desert City Cab serve the entire Coachella Valley. The fare is $4 to enter a cab and about $3.12 per mile.

TRAIN

The Amtrak *Sunset Limited*, which runs between Florida and Los Angeles, and *Texas Eagle* (Chicago to Los Angeles) stop in Palm Springs. Amtrak buses also meet Pacific Surfliner trains in Fullerton to ferry passengers to the Palm Springs region.

Restaurants

The meat-and-potatoes crowd still has plenty of options, but an influx of talented chefs has also made it possible to find fresh, superbly prepared seafood, as well as contemporary Californian, Asian, Indian, and vegetarian cuisine. Mexican food abounds. Most restaurants have early-evening happy hours, with discounted drinks and small-plate menus. Although some restaurants close or offer limited service in July and August, those that remain open often discount deeply.

Hotels

In general, Palm Springs has the widest choice of lodgings, from tiny bed-and-breakfasts and chain motels to business and resort hotels. Massive resort properties predominate in down-valley communities, such as Palm Desert and Rancho Mirage. You can stay in the desert for as little as $100, or splurge for luxury digs at more than $1,000 a night. Rates vary widely by season and expected occupancy—a $200 room midweek can jump in price to $450 on Saturday.

Hotel and resort prices are frequently 50% cheaper in summer and fall than in winter and early spring. From January through May prices soar, and lodgings fill up far in advance. Book well ahead for stays during events such as Modernism Week or the Coachella music festival.

Most resort hotels charge a daily fee of up to $40 that is not included in the room rate; be sure to ask about extra fees when you book. Many hotels are pet-friendly and offer special services, though these also come with additional fees. Small boutique hotels and B&Bs have plenty of character and are popular with hipsters and artsy types; discounts are sometimes given for extended stays. Casino hotels often offer good deals on lodging. Take care, though, when considering budget lodgings; other than reliable chains, they may not be up to par.

Restaurant and hotel reviews have been shortened. For full information, visit Fodors.com. Restaurant prices are the average cost of a main course at dinner, or if dinner is not served, at lunch. Hotel prices are the lowest cost of a standard double room in high season.

What It Costs

$	$$	$$$	$$$$
RESTAURANTS			
under $17	$17–$26	$27–$36	over $36
HOTELS			
under $150	$150–$250	$251–$350	over $350

Tours

Best of the Best Tours

GUIDED TOURS | One of the valley's largest outfits leads tours into Andreas Canyon, along the celebrity circuit, or to view windmills up close. ☎ *760/320–1365* 🌐 *www.thebestofthebesttours.com* 💳 *From $45.*

Big Wheel Bike Tours

BICYCLING | This outfit delivers rental mountain, three-speed, and tandem bikes to area hotels. The company also conducts full- and half-day escorted on- and off-road bike tours, and also offers hiking and jeep tours to Joshua Tree National Park and the San Andreas Fault. Guides are first-rate. ✉ *Palm Springs* ☎ *760/779–1837 Palm Desert, 760/548–0500 Palm Springs* 🌐 *www.bwbtours.com* 🎫 *$119 per person.*

Desert Adventures

SPECIAL-INTEREST | This outfit's three- to six-hour jeep, SUV, or van tours explore Joshua Tree National Park, Indian Canyon, Mecca Hills Painted Canyons, and the San Andreas Fault. The groups are small and the guides are knowledgeable. Departures are from Palm Desert and/or Palm Springs; hotel pickups are available. ☎ *760/477–4290* 🌐 *www.red-jeep.com* 🎫 *From $135.*

Palm Springs

A tourist destination since the late 19th century, Palm Springs evolved into an ideal hideaway for early Hollywood celebrities who slipped into town to play tennis, lounge poolside, attend a party or two, and, unless things got out of hand, steer clear of gossip columnists. But the area blossomed in the 1930s, after actors Charlie Farrell and Ralph Bellamy bought 200 acres of land for $30 an acre and opened the Palm Springs Racquet Club, which soon listed Ginger Rogers, Humphrey Bogart, and Clark Gable among its members.

Today, Palm Springs is embracing its glory days. Owners of resorts, B&Bs, and galleries have renovated mid-century modern buildings, luring a new crop of celebs and high-powered executives. LGBTQ+ travelers, twentysomethings, and families also sojourn here. Pleasantly touristy Palm Canyon Drive is packed with alfresco restaurants, along with indoor cafés and semi-chic shops. Farther west is the Uptown Design District, the area's shopping and dining destination. Continuing east on Palm Canyon Drive, just outside downtown lie resorts and boutique hotels that host lively pool parties and house exclusive dining establishments and trendy bars.

GETTING HERE AND AROUND

Palm Springs is 90 miles southeast of Los Angeles on I–10. Most visitors arrive in the area by car from Los Angeles or San Diego area via this freeway, which intersects with Highway 111 north of Palm Springs. Tahquitz Canyon Way marks the division between north and south on major streets (e.g., North and South Palm Canyon Drive).

ESSENTIALS

VISITOR INFORMATION Greater Palm Springs Convention & Visitors Bureau. ✉ *Visitor Center, 70–100 Hwy. 111, at Via Florencia, Rancho Mirage* ☎ *760/770–9000, 800/967–3767* 🌐 *www.visitgreaterpalmsprings.com.* **Palm Springs Visitors Center.** ✉ *2901 N. Palm Canyon Dr.* ☎ *760/778–8418, 800/347–7746* 🌐 *www.visitpalmsprings.com.*

Sights

Backstreet Art District

MUSEUM | Galleries and live–work studios just off East Canyon Drive showcase the works of a number of highly acclaimed artists. Painter and ceramicist Linda Maxson, innovative digital photographer Taylor Mickle, and new and emerging artists at Galleria Marconi are among the stars here. ■ **TIP→ On the first Wednesday evening of the month, the galleries are open from 5 to 8.** ✉ *2600 S. Cherokee Way* 🌐 *www.backstreetartdistrict.com* 🎫 *Free* 🕐 *Most galleries closed Mon. and Tues.*

★ Indian Canyons

CANYON | **FAMILY** | The Indian Canyons are the ancestral home of the Agua Caliente, part of the Cahuilla people. You can see remnants of their ancient life, including rock art, house pits and foundations, irrigation ditches, bedrock mortars, pictographs, and stone houses and

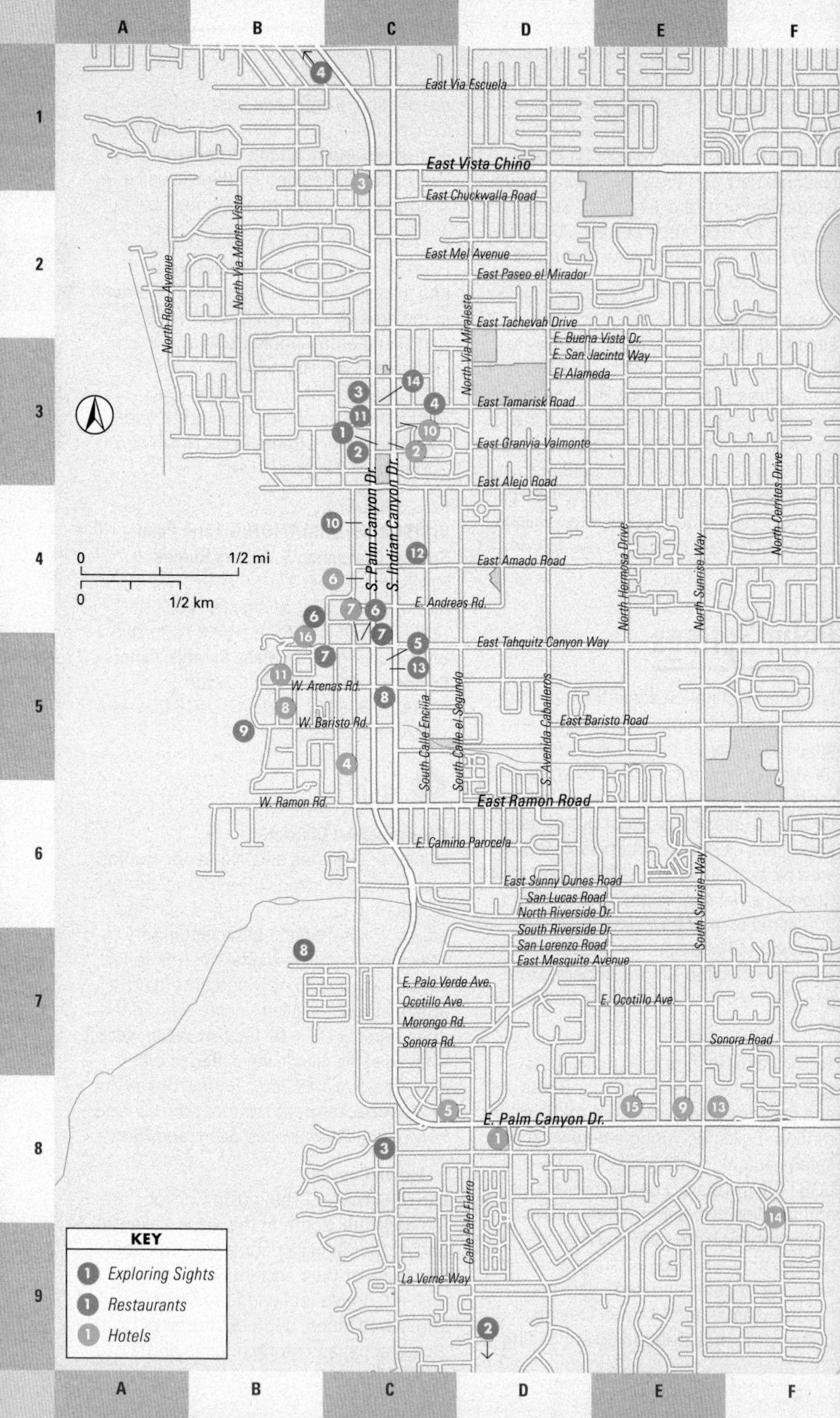

A
B
C
D
E
F
1
2
3
4
5
6
7
8
9
East Via Escuela
East Vista Chino
East Chuckwalla Road
East Mel Avenue
East Paseo el Mirador
East Tachevah Drive
E. Buena Vista Dr.
E. San Jacinto Way
El Alameda
East Tamarisk Road
East Granvia Valmonte
East Alejo Road
East Amado Road
E. Andreas Rd.
East Tahquitz Canyon Way
W. Arenas Rd.
W. Baristo Rd.
East Baristo Road
W. Ramon Rd.
East Ramon Road
E. Camino Parocela
East Sunny Dunes Road
San Lucas Road
North Riverside Dr.
South Riverside Dr.
San Lorenzo Road
East Mesquite Avenue
E. Palo Verde Ave.
Ocotillo Ave.
Morongo Rd.
Sonora Rd.
E. Ocotillo Ave.
Sonora Road
E. Palm Canyon Dr.
La Verne Way
North Rose Avenue
North Via Monte Vista
S. Palm Canyon Dr.
S. Indian Canyon Dr.
North Via Miraleste
South Calle Encilia
South Calle el Segundo
S. Avenida Caballeros
North Hermosa Drive
North Sunrise Way
South Sunrise Way
North Cerritos Drive
Calle Palo Fierro
0
1/2 mi
0
1/2 km
KEY
Exploring Sights
Restaurants
Hotels

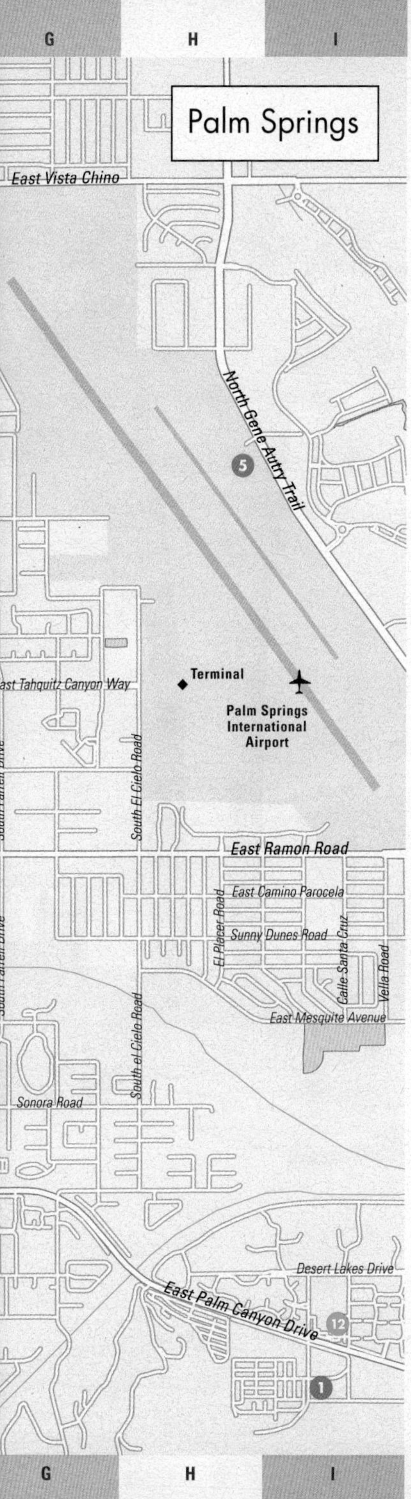

Sights

1 Backstreet Art District I9
2 Indian Canyons D9
3 Moorten Botanical Garden C8
4 Palm Springs Aerial Tramway B1
5 Palm Springs Air Museum H3
6 Palm Springs Art Museum B4
7 Palm Springs Walk of Stars C5
8 Tahquitz Canyon B7

Restaurants

1 Cheeky's C3
2 Copley's on Palm Canyon C3
3 EIGHT4NINE C3
4 El Mirasol at Los Arboles C3
5 Farm Palm Springs C5
6 4 Saints C5
7 Le Vallauris B5
8 LULU California Bistro C5
9 Spencer's Restaurant B5
10 Tac/Quila C4
11 Trio C3
12 The Tropicale C4
13 Tyler's Burgers C5
14 Workshop Kitchen + Bar C3

Hotels

1 Ace Hotel and Swim Club D8
2 Alcazar Palm Springs C3
3 ARRIVE C1
4 Avalon Hotel Palm Springs C5
5 Hotel California C8
6 The Hyatt Palm Springs C4
7 Kimpton Rowan Palm Springs Hotel C5
8 Korakia Pensione B5
9 La Maison E8
10 Movie Colony Hotel C3
11 Orbit In Hotel B5
12 The Parker Palm Springs I9
13 The Saguaro E8
14 Smoke Tree Ranch F8
15 Sparrows Lodge E8
16 Willows Historic Palm Springs Inn B5

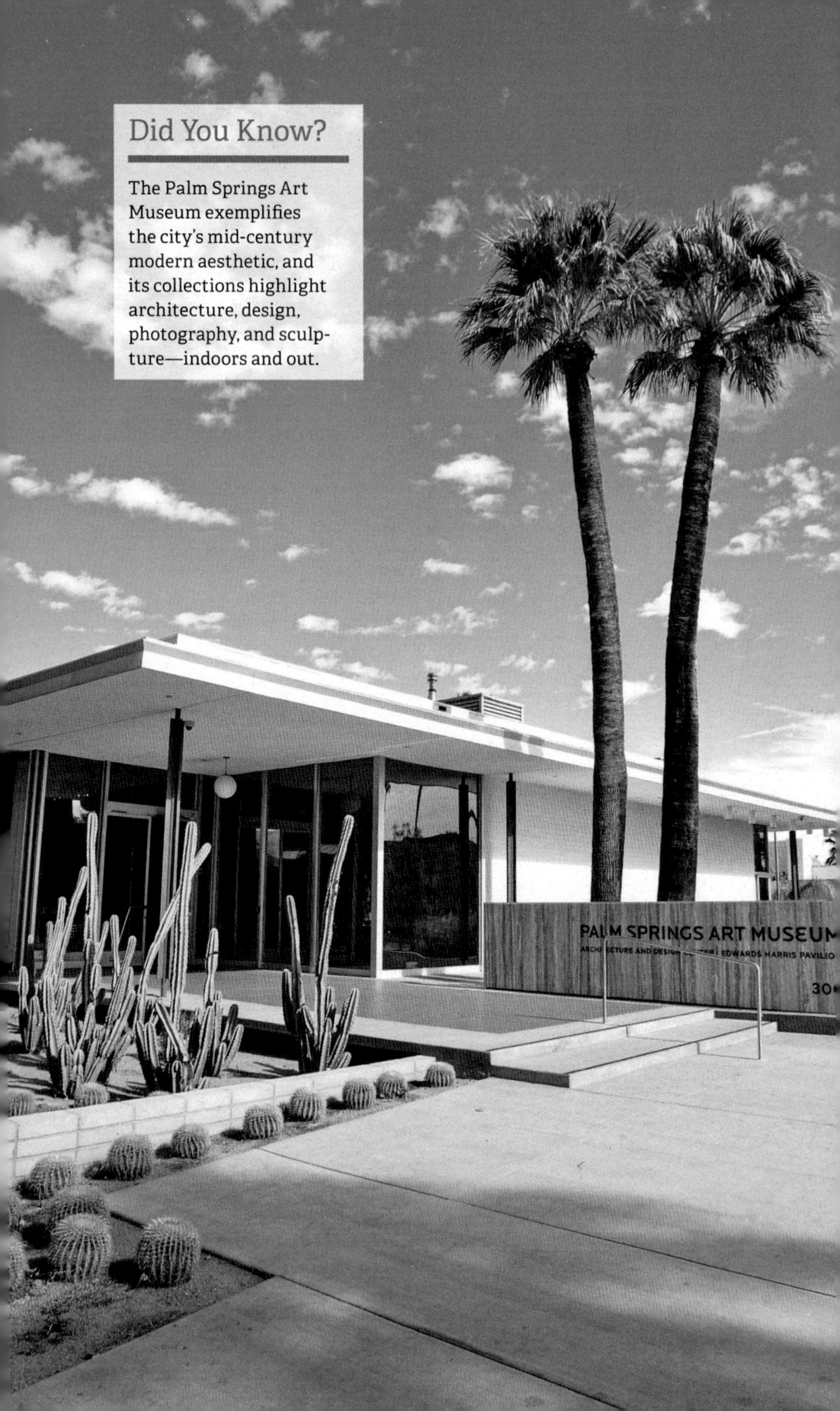

Did You Know?

The Palm Springs Art Museum exemplifies the city's mid-century modern aesthetic, and its collections highlight architecture, design, photography, and sculpture—indoors and out.

shelters atop cliff walls. Short easy walks through the canyons reveal palm oases, waterfalls, and, in spring, wildflowers. Tree-shaded picnic areas are abundant. The attraction includes three canyons open for touring: Palm Canyon, noted for its stand of Washingtonia palms; Murray Canyon, home of Peninsula bighorn sheep; and Andreas Canyon, where a stand of fan palms contrasts with sharp rock formations. Ranger-led hikes to Palm and Andreas canyons are offered Friday–Sunday for an additional charge (no dogs allowed). The trading post at the entrance to Palm Canyon has hiking maps and refreshments, as well as Native American art, jewelry, and weaving. ✉ *38520 S. Palm Canyon Dr., south of Acanto Dr.* ☎ *760/323–6018* 🌐 *www.indian-canyons.com* 🎟 *$9, ranger hikes $3* ⏲ *Closed Mon.–Thurs. July–Sept.*

Moorten Botanical Garden

GARDEN | In 1938, Chester "Cactus Slim" Moorten and his wife Patricia opened this showpiece for desert plants—now numbering in the thousands—that include an ocotillo, a massive elephant tree, a boojum tree, and vine cacti. Their son Clark now operates the garden. ■ **TIP→ Take a stroll through the Cactarium to spot rare finds such as the welwitschia, which originated in the Namib Desert in southwestern Africa.** ✉ *1701 S. Palm Canyon Dr.* ☎ *760/327–6555* 🌐 *www.moortengarden.com* 🎟 *$5* ⏲ *Closed Wed.*

★ **Palm Springs Aerial Tramway**

VIEWPOINT | **FAMILY** | A trip on the tramway provides a 360-degree view of the desert through the picture windows of rotating cars. The 2½-mile ascent through Chino Canyon, the steepest vertical cable ride in the United States, brings you to an elevation of 8,516 feet in less than 20 minutes. On clear days, which are common, the view stretches 75 miles—from the peak of Mt. San Gorgonio in the north to the Salton Sea in the southeast. Stepping out into the snow at the summit is a winter treat. At the top, a bit below the summit of Mt. San Jacinto, are several diversions. Mountain Station has an observation deck, two restaurants, a cocktail lounge, apparel and gift shops, picnic facilities, a small wildlife exhibit, and a theater that screens movies on the history of the tramway and the adjacent Mount San Jacinto State Park and Wilderness. Take advantage of free guided and self-guided nature walks through the state park, or if there's snow on the ground, rent skis, snowshoes, or snow tubes. The tramway generally closes for maintenance in mid-September. ■ **TIP→ Ride-and-dine packages are available in late afternoon. The tram is a popular attraction; to avoid a two-hour or longer wait, arrive before the first car leaves in the morning.** ✉ *1 Tramway Rd., off N. Palm Canyon Dr. (Hwy. 111)* ☎ *888/515–8726* 🌐 *www.pstramway.com* 🎟 *From $27* ⏲ *Closed 2 wks in Sept. for maintenance.*

★ **Palm Springs Air Museum**

MUSEUM | **FAMILY** | This museum's impressive collection of World War II, Vietnam, and Korea aircraft includes a B-17 Flying Fortress bomber, a Bell P-63 King Cobra, and a Grumman TBF Avenger. Among the cool exhibits are model warships, a Pearl Harbor diorama, and a Mohawk into which kids can crawl. Photos, artifacts, memorabilia, and uniforms are also on display; educational programs take place on Saturday; and flight demonstrations are scheduled regularly. Rides in vintage warbirds are also available, including a T-28 Trojan, PT-17 Stearman, T-33 Shooting Star Jet, and P-51D Mustang. ✉ *745 N. Gene Autry Trail* ☎ *760/778–6262* 🌐 *palmspringsairmuseum.org* 🎟 *$19.*

Palm Springs Art Museum

MUSEUM | This world-class art museum focuses on photography, modern architecture, and the traditional arts of the Americas. Outside, you're greeted by the 26-foot, 34,000-pound *Forever Marilyn*statue, designed by Seward Johnson, which depicts the actress in the iconic, billowing-skirt pose from her movie *The Seven Year Itch*. Inside the museum, bright, open galleries contain shimmering, permanent-collection works in glass by Dale Chihuly, Ginny Ruffner, and William Morris; handcrafted furniture by the late actor George Montgomery; mid-century modern architectural photos by Julius Shulman; enormous Native American baskets; and pieces by artists like Allen Houser, Arlo Namingha, and Fritz Scholder. Significant 20th-century sculptors whose works are displayed here include Henry Moore, Marino Marina, Deborah Butterfield, and Mark Di Suvero. The Annenberg Theater presents plays, concerts, lectures, operas, and other cultural events. The museum also has a separate Architecture and Design Center at 300 South Palm Canyon Drive. ✉ *101 Museum Dr., off W. Tahquitz Canyon Dr.* ☎ *760/322–4800* 🌐 *www.psmuseum.org* 🎟 *$14, free Thurs. 5–7 and 2nd Sun. each month* ⏲ *Closed Mon.–Wed.*

Palm Springs Walk of Stars

NEIGHBORHOOD | Along the walk, more than 300 bronze stars are embedded in the sidewalk (à la Hollywood Walk of Fame) to honor celebrities with a Palm Springs connection. Frank, Elvis, Marilyn, Dinah, Lucy, Ginger, Liz, and Liberace have all received their due. Those still around to walk the Walk and see their stars include Nancy Sinatra and Kathy Griffin. ✉ *Palm Canyon Dr., around Tahquitz Canyon Way, and Tahquitz Canyon Way, between Palm Canyon and Indian Canyon Drs.* ☎ *760/325–1577* 🌐 *www.palmsprings.com/walk-of-stars.*

Tahquitz Canyon

CANYON | On ranger-led tours of this secluded canyon on the Agua Caliente Reservation you can view a spectacular 60-foot waterfall, rock art, ancient irrigation systems, and native wildlife and plants. Tours are conducted several times daily; participants must be able to navigate 100 steep rock steps. (You can also take a self-guided tour of the 1.8-mile trail.) At the visitor center at the canyon entrance, watch a short video, look at artifacts, and pick up a map. ✉ *500 W. Mesquite Ave., west of S. Palm Canyon Dr.* ☎ *760/416–7044* 🌐 *www.tahquitzcanyon.com* 🎟 *$13* ⏲ *Closed Mon.–Thurs. July–Sept.*

 Restaurants

★ Cheeky's

$ | AMERICAN | The artisanal bacon bar and hangover-halting mimosas attract legions to this breakfast and lunch joint, but brioche French toast and other favorites also contribute to the epic wait on weekends (no reservations accepted). Huevos rancheros, a gem salad with green goddess dressing, and other farmcentric dishes entice the foodie crowd. **Known for:** homemade pastries and sausages; local organic ingredients; grass-fed burger topped with house bacon. 💲 *Average main: $13* ✉ *622 N. Palm Canyon Dr., at E. Granvia Valmonte* ☎ *760/327–7595* 🌐 *www.cheekysps.com* ⏲ *Closed Tues. No dinner.*

Copley's on Palm Canyon

$$$ | MODERN AMERICAN | Chef Manion Copley prepares innovative cuisine in a setting that's straight out of Hollywood—a hacienda once owned by Cary Grant. Dine in the clubby house or under the stars in the garden. **Known for:** romantic patio dining; fresh seafood and meats with innovative flavors; sweet and savory herb ice creams. 💲 *Average main: $34* ✉ *621 N. Palm Canyon Dr., at E. Granvia Valmonte* ☎ *760/327–9555* 🌐 *www.copleyspalmsprings.com* ⏲ *Closed July and Aug. No lunch.*

★ EIGHT4NINE

$$$ | AMERICAN | The dazzling interior design and eclectic Pacific Coast dishes made from scratch lure locals and visitors alike to this swank yet casual restaurant and lounge in the Uptown Design District. Sink into white patent leather chairs or comfy sofas in the lounge where you can gaze at historic celebrity photos, or choose a table in a grand corridor with a collection of private rooms, or in the outdoor patio with mountain views. **Known for:** nearly everything made from scratch; four-course chef's menu; all-day happy hour in lounge. *Average main: $28 849 N. Palm Canyon Dr. 760/325–8490 eight4nine.com.*

El Mirasol at Los Arboles

$$ | MODERN MEXICAN | Chef Felipe Castañeda owns two Mexican restaurants in Palm Springs—this one, part of Los Arboles Hotel, is outside on a charming patio set amid flower gardens and shaded by red umbrellas. Castañeda prepares classic combinations of tacos, tamales, and enchiladas, along with specialties such as double-cooked pork and *pollo en pipián* (chicken with a pre-Columbian sauce made of ground roasted pumpkin seeds and dry chilies). **Known for:** classic Mexican dishes; great vegetarian options; garden setting. *Average main: $22 266 Via Altamira, off N. Indian Canyon Dr. 760/459–3136 www.elmirasolrestaurants.com.*

★ Farm Palm Springs

$ | FRENCH | Farm-fresh, locally sourced ingredients and authentic, made-from-scratch, Provençal-style dishes elicit rave reviews of this cozy eatery in downtown's historic La Plaza. Feast on sweet and savory crepes, omelets, or brioche French toast for breakfast; a croque-monsieur or duck confit salad for lunch; and a five-course, seasonal, prix-fixe dinner in the evening. **Known for:** outdoor seating in a flower-filled courtyard; house-made jams, pressed coffee, loose-leaf teas; creative cocktails. *Average main: $16 6 La Plaza 760/322–2724 www.farmpalmsprings.com No dinner Wed. and Thurs. No reservations except for dinner.*

★ 4 Saints

$$$$ | CONTEMPORARY | Perched on the seventh-floor rooftop of the Kimpton Rowan Palm Springs, where stunning views unfold from nearly every table, 4 Saints serves inventive farm-to-table dishes in a slick, hipster dining room and outdoor patio. The eclectic, globally inspired menu focuses on small plates and main dishes made with locally sourced ingredients (e.g., seafood, duck, and short ribs) intended for sharing. **Known for:** creative and classic cocktails; lively social vibe; stellar seafood. *Average main: $43 100 W. Tahquitz Cyn. Way 760/392–2020 www.4saintspalmsprings.com.*

Le Vallauris

$$$ | FRENCH | A longtime favorite that occupies the historic Roberson House, Le Vallauris is popular with ladies who lunch, all of whom get a hug from the maître d'. The Belgian-French-inspired menu changes daily, and each day it's handwritten on a white board. **Known for:** prix-fixe menus for lunch and dinner; lovely tree-shaded garden; romantic setting. *Average main: $36 385 W. Tahquitz Canyon Way, west of Palm Canyon Dr. 760/325–5059 www.levallauris.com Closed July and Aug.*

LULU California Bistro

$$ | MODERN AMERICAN | LULU oozes hipness from morning to night, both within its spacious, mid-century modern dining room and outside on its well-situated terrace with prime Palm Canyon people-watching opportunities. The lengthy menu (the longest in Palm Springs) includes just about anything to please any type of palette, from an avocado-tuna tower to sandwiches, soups, and burgers to osso buco for two—there's even cotton candy. **Known for:** special all-day, vegetarian/vegan or treats-for-two menus; three-course, prix-fixe weekend brunch ($20); hip hangout at night. *Average main: $23 200 S. Palm Canyon Dr.*

☎ *760/327–5858* 🌐 *www.lulupalmsprings.com* ⏲ *No breakfast weekdays.*

Spencer's Restaurant

$$$ | **MODERN AMERICAN** | This swank dining space occupies a historic mid-century modern structure at the Palm Springs Tennis Club Resort. Crab cakes, kung pao calamari, and crispy flash-fried oysters are favorite starters. **Known for:** French–Pacific Rim influences; romantic patio; elegant dining room. Ⓢ *Average main: $35* ✉ *701 W. Baristo Rd.* ☎ *760/327–3446* 🌐 *www.spencersrestaurant.com.*

★ Tac/Quila

$$ | **MODERN MEXICAN** | From the lush, flower-laden, "living" walls and vibrant, mid-century modern, Mexico City furnishings to the extensive seafood-focused menu, Tac/Quila celebrates the culture and flavors of Mexico. Ingredients from the greater Palm Springs region help to give the ceviches, fajitas, street tacos, and tamales—made using traditional recipes from Jalisco and beyond—a fresh, California take. **Known for:** craft cocktails, more than 50 specialty tequilas and mezcals, beer and margarita flights; ceviche, taco, and other sampler platters; nightly live music. Ⓢ *Average main: $22* ✉ *415 N. Palm Canyon Dr.* ☎ *760/417–4471* 🌐 *www.tacquila.com.*

Trio

$$ | **MODERN AMERICAN** | The owners of this high-energy Uptown Design District restaurant claim that it's "where Palm Springs eats," and it certainly seems so on nights when the lines to get in run deep. The menu includes home-style staples such as Yankee pot roast, crawfish pie, and other dishes, along with veggie burgers and other vegetarian and gluten-free items. **Known for:** local artwork; inventive desserts; ample vegetarian and gluten-free options. Ⓢ *Average main: $22* ✉ *707 N. Palm Canyon Dr.* ☎ *760/864–8746* 🌐 *www.triopalmsprings.com.*

The Tropicale

$$$ | **INTERNATIONAL** | Tucked onto a side-street corner, the Tropicale is a mid-century-style watering hole with a contemporary vibe. The bar and main dining room hold cozy leather booths; flowers and water features brighten the outdoor area. **Known for:** globe-trotting menu; happy hour (all night on Wednesday); weekly specials. Ⓢ *Average main: $30* ✉ *330 E. Amado Rd., at N. Calle Encilia* ☎ *760/866–1952* 🌐 *www.thetropicale.com* ⏲ *No lunch.*

★ Tyler's Burgers

$ | **AMERICAN** | **FAMILY** | Families, singles, and couples head to Tyler's for simple lunch fare that appeals to carnivores and vegetarians alike. Expect mid-20th-century America's greatest hits: heaping burgers, stacks of fries, root-beer floats, milk shakes; on weekends, be prepared to wait with the masses. **Known for:** house-made cole slaw and potato salad; excellent burgers and fries; delicious shakes. Ⓢ *Average main: $12* ✉ *149 S. Indian Canyon Dr., at La Plaza* ☎ *760/325–2990* 🌐 *www.tylersburgers.com* ⏲ *Closed Sun. late May–mid-Feb. Closed mid-July–early Sept.*

Workshop Kitchen + Bar

$$$ | **AMERICAN** | Chef Michael Beckman's Uptown Design District hot spot pairs high-quality California cuisine with creative cocktails in a sleek, almost utilitarian setting. The outdoor patio lures the oversize sunglasses Sunday brunch crowd, who slurp cava mimosas and artisanal cocktails; inside, the sleek concrete booths are topped with black leather cushions. **Known for:** most ingredients sourced from within a 100-mile radius; artisanal cocktails; communal seating options. Ⓢ *Average main: $32* ✉ *800 N. Palm Canyon Dr., at E. Tamarisk Rd.* ☎ *760/459–3451* 🌐 *www.workshoppalmsprings.com* ⏲ *No lunch.*

Hotels

Ace Hotel and Swim Club
$$ | RESORT | With the hotel's vintage feel and hippie-chic decor, it would be no surprise to find guests gathered around cozy communal fire pits enjoying feel-good music. **Pros:** Amigo Room has late-night dining; poolside stargazing deck; weekend DJ scene at the pool. **Cons:** party atmosphere not for everyone; limited amenities; casual staff and service. *Rooms from: $189 ✉ 701 E. Palm Canyon Dr. ☎ 760/325–9900 🌐 www.acehotel.com/palmsprings 188 rooms No meals.*

Alcazar Palm Springs
$$ | HOTEL | Tucked at the border of the Uptown Design District and an area known as the Movie Colony, the hip, modern, and affordable Alcazar features ample, blazing-white guest rooms that wrap around a sparkling pool; some rooms have Jacuzzis, and many have private patios or fireplaces. **Pros:** walking distance of downtown; parking on-site; bikes available. **Cons:** limited service; wall air-conditioners; resort fee. *Rooms from: $180 ✉ 622 N. Indian Canyon Dr. ☎ 760/318–9850 🌐 www.alcazarpalmsprings.com 34 rooms No meals.*

★ ARRIVE
$$$ | HOTEL | By day, sip cocktails at the indoor–outdoor bar (which doubles as the reception desk), lounge in the pool on an inflatable seahorse, or dance to a live DJ; at night, relax in the outdoor hot tub, socialize around communal firepits (half of the rooms also have private patios and fireplaces), or cozy up in your king-size bed amid tasteful modern furnishings. **Pros:** private cabanas with misting systems; great restaurant, artisanal ice-cream shop, and local coffee shop on-site; easy access to Uptown Design District shops, restaurants, galleries. **Cons:** only king rooms available; shower offers little privacy; party scene may not suit everyone. *Rooms from: $329 ✉ 1551 N. Palm Canyon Dr. ☎ 760/507–1650 🌐 www.arrivehotels.com 32 rooms No meals.*

Avalon Hotel Palm Springs
$$$$ | RESORT | With three pools and a spa spread over 4 acres of gardens, the upscale Avalon Hotel Palm Springs calls back to 1960s swanky, with private bungalows, lush gardens, and an emphasis on style. **Pros:** poolside cabanas; complimentary fitness classes; luxurious on-site Estrella Spa and stylish restaurant Chi Chi. **Cons:** popular wedding site; some rooms and facilities need updating; noise travels through thin walls. *Rooms from: $400 ✉ 415 S. Belardo Rd. ☎ 760/318–3012 🌐 www.avalon-hotel.com/palm-springs 79 rooms No meals.*

★ Hotel California
$$ | HOTEL | Expect homey accommodations for all budgets at this delightful hotel that's decked out in rustic Mexican furniture. **Pros:** comfortable design; friendly hosts; free off-street parking. **Cons:** far from downtown; property needs updating; fronts a busy road. *Rooms from: $225 ✉ 424 E. Palm Canyon Dr. ☎ 760/322–8855 🌐 www.palmspringshotelcalifornia.com 14 rooms No meals.*

The Hyatt Palm Springs
$$ | HOTEL | The best-situated downtown hotel in Palm Springs, the Hyatt has spacious suites where you can watch the sun rise over the city, or set behind the mountains from your bedroom's balcony. **Pros:** underground parking; restaurant plus two outdoor bar-lounges; daily sunset hour with free wine, beer, and appetizers. **Cons:** lots of business travelers; some street noise; valet parking only. *Rooms from: $199 ✉ 285 N. Palm Canyon Dr. ☎ 760/322–9000 🌐 palmsprings.hyatt.com 197 suites No meals.*

★ Kimpton Rowan Palm Springs Hotel
$$$ | HOTEL | The Rowan Palm Springs dazzles locals and guests (especially the under-40 set) with stunning views from myriad picture windows and a rooftop deck, as well as an unpretentious vibe that puts people of any age at ease. **Pros:** friendly, attentive service; stunning mountain and valley views; in the heart of downtown. **Cons:** rooftop pool area can get crowded; valet parking only; $35 resort fee. *Ⓢ Rooms from: $259 ✉ 100 W. Tahquitz Canyon Way ☎ 760/904–5015, 800/532–7320 🌐 www.rowanpalmsprings.com ⇌ 153 rooms 🍴 No meals.*

★ Korakia Pensione
$$$$ | B&B/INN | The painter Gordon Coutts, best known for desert landscapes, constructed this Moroccan villa in 1924 as an artist's studio, and these days creative types gather in the main house and nearby Mediterranean-style villas, spread across 1½ acres on both sides of the street, to soak up the spirit of that era. **Pros:** two pools; lunch and dinner available on request (fee); yoga on weekends. **Cons:** might not appeal to those who prefer standard resorts; no TVs or phones in rooms; no children under 13. *Ⓢ Rooms from: $379 ✉ 257 S. Patencio Rd. ☎ 760/864–6411 🌐 www.korakia.com ⇌ 28 rooms 🍴 Free breakfast.*

La Maison
$$$ | B&B/INN | Offering all the comforts of home, this small B&B contains large rooms that surround the terra-cotta–tiled and very comfortable pool area, where you can spend quiet time soaking up the sun or taking a dip. **Pros:** restaurants nearby; quiet; genial hosts. **Cons:** on busy Highway 111; rooms open directly onto pool deck; some rooms on the small side. *Ⓢ Rooms from: $289 ✉ 1600 E. Palm Canyon Dr. ☎ 760/325–1600 🌐 www.lamaisonpalmsprings.com ⇌ 13 rooms 🍴 Free breakfast.*

Movie Colony Hotel
$$ | B&B/INN | Designed in 1935 by Albert Frey, this intimate hotel evokes a mid-century minimalist ambience throughout its gleaming-white, two-story buildings—flanked with balconies—and its SoCal desert–style rooms, which are elegantly appointed and have bright mid-century color accents. **Pros:** architectural icon; in the midtown Design District; property-wide remodel in 2019. **Cons:** close quarters; basic breakfast; staff not available 24 hours. *Ⓢ Rooms from: $169 ✉ 726 N. Indian Canyon Dr. ☎ 760/320–6340, 888/953–5700 🌐 www.moviecolonyhotel.com ⇌ 19 rooms 🍴 Free breakfast.*

★ Orbit In Hotel
$$ | B&B/INN | The exterior architectural style—nearly flat roofs, wide overhangs, glass everywhere—of this hip inn on a quiet backstreet dates from its 1955 opening, and the period feel continues inside. **Pros:** saltwater pool; Orbitini cocktail hour; free breakfast served poolside. **Cons:** best for couples; style not to everyone's taste; staff not available 24 hours. *Ⓢ Rooms from: $169 ✉ 562 W. Arenas Rd. ☎ 760/323–3585, 877/996–7248 🌐 www.orbitin.com ⇌ 9 rooms 🍴 Free breakfast.*

★ The Parker Palm Springs
$$$$ | RESORT | A cacophony of color and over-the-top contemporary art assembled by New York City–based designer Jonathan Adler mixes well with the brilliant desert garden, three pools (two outdoor), firepits, and expansive spa of this hip hotel that attracts a stylish, worldly clientele. **Pros:** celebrity clientele; on-site restaurants, bars, and spa; design-centric. **Cons:** pricey drinks and wine; a bit of a drive from downtown; resort fee ($35). *Ⓢ Rooms from: $399 ✉ 4200 E. Palm Canyon Dr. ☎ 760/770–5000, 800/543–4300 🌐 www.theparkerpalmsprings.com ⇌ 144 rooms 🍴 No meals.*

★ The Saguaro

$$ | HOTEL | A startling, rainbow-hued oasis—the brainchild of Manhattan-based architects Peter Stamberg and Paul Aferiat—the Saguaro caters to young, hip, pet-toting partygoers who appreciate its lively pool-party scene. **Pros:** lively pool scene with weekend DJ parties; daily yoga, on-site spa, 24-hour fitness center, beach cruisers; shuttle service to downtown. **Cons:** a few miles from downtown; pool area can be noisy and crowded; $33 resort fee. *Rooms from: $169 ✉ 1800 E. Palm Canyon Dr. ☎ 760/323–1711 🌐 thesaguaro.com 244 rooms No meals.*

Smoke Tree Ranch

$$$$ | RESORT | FAMILY | A laid-back genteel retreat since the mid-1930s for some of the world's foremost families, including Walt Disney's, the area's most under-the-radar resort complex occupies 385 pristine desert acres surrounded by mountains and unspoiled vistas, and still provides an experience reminiscent of the Old West. **Pros:** priceless privacy; simple luxury; recreational activities like horseback riding and more. **Cons:** no glitz; limited entertainment options; family atmosphere not for everyone. *Rooms from: $410 ✉ 1850 Smoke Tree La. ☎ 760/327–1221, 800/787–3922 🌐 www.smoketreeranch.com Closed Apr.–late Oct. 49 units All-inclusive.*

Sparrows Lodge

$$$$ | B&B/INN | Rustic earthiness meets haute design at the adult-centered Sparrows, just off Palm Springs's main drag. **Pros:** unique design; intimate property; private patios. **Cons:** not family-oriented, minimum age 21; daily resort fee; no TVs or phones in rooms. *Rooms from: $399 ✉ 1330 E. Palm Canyon Dr. ☎ 760/327–2300 🌐 www.sparrowshotel.com 20 rooms Free breakfast.*

★ Willows Historic Palm Springs Inn

$$$$ | B&B/INN | Set in two adjacent, opulent, Mediterranean-style mansions built in the 1920s to host the rich and famous, this luxurious hillside B&B has gleaming hardwood and slate floors, stone fireplaces, frescoed ceilings, hand-painted tiles, iron balconies, antiques throughout, and a 50-foot waterfall that splashes into a pool outside the dining room. **Pros:** short walk to art museum, restaurants, shops; pool; expansive breakfast and afternoon wine hour. **Cons:** closed from June to September; pricey; some rooms on the small side. *Rooms from: $425 ✉ 412 W. Tahquitz Canyon Way ☎ 760/320–0771 🌐 www.thewillowspalmsprings.com 17 rooms Free breakfast.*

Nightlife

BARS AND PUBS

Bootlegger Tiki

BARS/PUBS | Palm Springs tiki-drink traditions, especially during the two daily happy hours (4 to 6 pm and midnight to 2 am), draw loyal patrons to Bootlegger, which occupies the same space as Don the Beachcomber in the 1950s. *✉ 1101 N. Palm Canyon Dr. ☎ 760/318–4154 🌐 www.bootleggertiki.com.*

Tonga Hut

BARS/PUBS | The younger sibling of L.A.'s oldest tiki hut (opened in 1958 in North Hollywood), Tonga Hut Palm Springs transports guests to Polynesia with an authentic tiki vibe, pupu platters, and tropical drinks. It's on the second floor of a building in the heart of the downtown strip—try to nab a table on the lanai where you can experience the action from above. The bar and dining area are also fun and lively spaces; ask about the telephone booth that leads to a secret room, available for private parties. *✉ 254 N. Palm Canyon Dr. ☎ 760/322–4449 🌐 www.tongahut.com.*

Palm Springs Modernism

Some of the world's most forward-looking architects designed and constructed buildings around Palm Springs between 1940 and 1970. Described these days as mid-century modern—you'll also see the term "desert modernism" used—these structures, also popular elsewhere in California in the years after World War II, are ideal for desert living because they minimize the separation between indoors and outdoors. Houses with glass exterior walls are common, as are oversize flat roofs that provide shade from the sun. The style is also notable for elegant informality, simple landscaping, and clean lines that often mirror the shapes of surrounding topography.

Noteworthy examples include three buildings that are part of the Palm Springs Aerial Tramway complex, built in the 1960s. Albert Frey, a Swiss-born architect, designed the soaring A-frame Tramway Gas Station, visually echoing the pointed peaks behind it. Frey also created the glass-walled Valley Station, from which you get your initial view of the Coachella Valley before you board the tram to the Mountain Station, designed by E. Stewart Williams.

Frey, a Palm Springs resident for more than 60 years, also designed the indoor-outdoor City Hall, Fire Station No. 1, and numerous houses. His second home, atop stilts on a hill above the Palm Springs Art Museum, affords a sweeping Coachella Valley view through glass walls. The classy Movie Colony Hotel, one of Frey's first desert designs, might seem like a typical 1950s motel, with rooms surrounding a swimming pool, but when it was built in 1935, it was years ahead of its time.

Donald Wexler, who honed his vision with Los Angeles architect Richard Neutra, brought new ideas about the use of materials to the desert, where he teamed up with William Cody on projects such as the terminal at the Palm Springs Airport. Wexler also experimented with steel framing back in 1961, but the metal proved too expensive. Seven of his steel-frame houses can be seen in a neighborhood off Indian Canyon and Frances drives.

The Palm Springs Modern Committee website has lots of information and resources, including a downloadable app (🌐 *psmodcom.org/mid-century-modern-tour-app*) that guides you to the most interesting buildings. Note, too, that the desert communities celebrate the Palm Springs "look" during mid-February's Modernism Week (🌐 *modernismweek.com*), an 11-day event featuring lectures, films, and home and garden tours. A shorter preview week happens in October.

★ The Village

BARS/PUBS | With live entertainment, DJs, and friendly service, this popular bar caters to a young crowd. Happy hour is fantastic. On weekend days there is live music as well. ✉ *266 S. Palm Canyon Dr., at Baristo Rd.* ☎ *760/323–3265* 🌐 *thevillagepalmsprings.com.*

CASINOS

Casino Morongo

CASINOS | A 20-minute drive west of Palm Springs, this casino has 2,600 slot machines, video games, the Vibe nightclub, plus Vegas-style shows. ✉ *49500 Seminole Dr., off I–10, Cabazon*

☎ *800/252–4499, 951/849–3080* 🌐 *www.morongocasinoresort.com.*

Spa Resort Casino
CASINOS | This resort holds 1,000 slot machines, blackjack tables, a high-limit room, four restaurants, two bars, and the Cascade Lounge for entertainment. ✉ *401 E. Amado Rd., at N. Calle Encilia* ☎ *888/999–1995* 🌐 *www.sparesortcasino.com.*

GAY AND LESBIAN

Chill Bar Palm Springs
DANCE CLUBS | Dance, drink, and dine at this wildly popular nightclub in the heart of the gay-centric Arenas Road district. Socialize in the somewhat quieter front bar, where floor-to-ceiling windows let in scenes of the mountains, or the rowdier back bar, where DJs and other performers entice patrons to kick up their heels on the city's largest dance floor. ✉ *217 E. Arenas Rd.* ☎ *760/696–9493* 🌐 *www.chillbarpalmsprings.com.*

Hunter's Palm Springs
DANCE CLUBS | Drawing a young gay and straight crowd, Hunter's is a club-scene mainstay. ✉ *302 E. Arenas Rd., at Calle Encilia* ☎ *760/323–0700* 🌐 *hunterspalmsprings.com.*

Streetbar Palm Springs
BARS/PUBS | The first gay bar in town, laid-back Streetbar and its full slate of live performers (plus twice-weekly karaoke nights) continue to draw loyal patrons to casual digs in the heart of the Arenas neighborhood. ✉ *224 E. Arenas Rd.* ☎ *760/320–1266* 🌐 *www.psstreetbar.com.*

★ Toucans Tiki Lounge
BARS/PUBS | A friendly place with a tropical–rain forest setting, Toucans serves festive drinks and hosts live entertainment and theme nights. On Sunday it seems as though all of Palm Springs has turned out for drag night. ✉ *2100 N. Palm Canyon Dr., at W. Via Escuela* ☎ *760/416–7584* 🌐 *www.toucanstikilounge.com* ⏲ *Closed Tues.*

THEMED ENTERTAINMENT

★ Ace Hotel and Swim Club
THEMED ENTERTAINMENT | Events are held here nearly every night, including film screenings, full moon parties, live concerts, DJs, and dancing. Many are free, and some are family friendly. The poolside venue makes most events fun and casual. ✉ *701 E. Palm Canyon Dr., at Calle Palo Fierro* ☎ *760/325–9900* 🌐 *www.acehotel.com.*

Performing Arts

FILM

Palm Springs International Film Festival
FILM | In mid-January this 12-day festival brings stars and nearly 200 feature films from several dozen countries, plus panel discussions, short films, and documentaries, to various venues. The weeklong "Shortfest," celebrating more than 300 short films, takes place in June. ✉ *Palm Springs* ☎ *760/322–2930, 800/898–7256* 🌐 *www.psfilmfest.org.*

Shopping

Hadley's Fruit Orchards
FOOD/CANDY | At the Cabazon exit of Interstate 10, Hadley's sells dried fruit, nuts, wine, and their famous date shakes made with caramel-tasting Deglet Noor dates grown in California. The Hadleys developed the recipe for trail mix in the 1950s. In addition to the dried fruit, you can get candy and old-fashioned sodas here. There's also a snack bar. ✉ *47993 Morongo Trail, Cabazon* ☎ *951/849–5255* 🌐 *www.hadleyfruitorchards.com.*

BOUTIQUES

★ Just Fabulous
LOCAL SPECIALTIES | Find everything from original photography and art, coffee table books, greeting cards, designer home decor, candles, and many other eclectic items at this fun gift shop that celebrates the area's retro-modern lifestyle and desert dolce vita. ✉ *515 N. Palm Canyon Dr.* ☎ *760/864–1300* 🌐 *bjustfabulous.com.*

★ Trina Turk Boutique

CLOTHING | Celebrity designer Trina Turk's empire takes up a city block in the Uptown Design District. Turk, famous for men's and women's outdoor wear, reached out to another celebrity, interior designer Kelly Wearstler, to create adjoining clothing and residential boutiques. Lively fabrics brighten up the many chairs and couches for sale at the residential store, which also carries bowls, paintings, and other fun pieces to spiff up your home. ✉ *891 N. Palm Canyon Dr.* ☎ *760/416–2856* 🌐 *www.trinaturk.com.*

OUTLET MALLS

★ Desert Hills Premium Outlets

OUTLET/DISCOUNT STORES | About 20 miles west of Palm Springs lies one of California's largest outlet centers. The 180 brand-name discount fashion shops include Jimmy Choo, Neiman Marcus, Versace, Saint Laurent, J. Crew, Armani, Gucci, and Prada. ✉ *48400 Seminole Rd., off I–10, Cabazon* ☎ *951/849–5018* 🌐 *www.premiumoutlets.com.*

SHOPPING DISTRICTS

★ Uptown Design District

SHOPPING NEIGHBORHOODS | A loose-knit collection of consignment and secondhand shops, galleries, and lively restaurants extends north of Palm Springs's downtown. The theme here is decidedly retro. Many businesses sell mid-century modern furniture and decorator items, and others carry clothing and estate jewelry. One spot definitely worth a peek is **The Shag Store,** the gallery of fine art painter Josh Agle. If you dig the mid-mod aesthetic, breeze through the furnishings at **Towne Palm Springs.** ✉ *N. Palm Canyon Dr., between Amado Rd. and Vista Chino.*

Activities

GOLF

Indian Canyons Golf Resort

GOLF | Operated by the Aqua Caliente tribe, this spot at the base of the mountains includes two 18-hole courses open to the public. In the 1960s this was *the* place to play for celebrities visiting the desert, including presidents Dwight Eisenhower and Lyndon Johnson. The North Course, designed by William F. Bell, is adjacent to property once owned by Walt Disney and has six water hazards. The South Course, redesigned in 2004 by Casey O'Callaghan with input from the LPGA player Amy Alcott, has four ponds, hundreds of palm trees, and five par-5 holes. ✉ *1097 E. Murray Canyon Dr., at Kings Rd. E* ☎ *760/833–8724* 🌐 *www.indiancanyonsgolf.com* 🎫 *North Course, $99; South Course, $125* 🏌 *North Course: 18 holes, 6943 yards, par 72; South Course: 18 holes, 6582 yards, par 72.*

Tahquitz Creek Golf Resort

GOLF | Conveniently located in Palm Springs near Cathedral City, the resort has two popular courses open to the public. Golfers have been walking the Legend course for more than 50 years—the back nine here are challenging, particularly the greens. The newer Resort course, designed by Ted Robinson, offers sweeping mountain views and scenic waterscapes. ✉ *1885 Golf Club Dr., at 34th Ave.* ☎ *760/328–1005* 🌐 *www.tahquitzgolfresort.com* 🎫 *Legend Course, $69; Resort Course, $89* 🏌 *Legend Course: 18 holes, 6815 yards, par 71; Resort Course: 18 holes, 6705 yards, par 72.*

HORSEBACK RIDING

Smoke Tree Stables

HORSEBACK RIDING | At these stables you can explore desert canyons on horseback like the earliest pioneers. One-hour tours depart on the hour and take riders along the base of the Santa Rosa Mountains. Two-hour tours depart four times daily for trips that take in the Aqua Caliente Indian Reservation. ✉ *2500 S. Toledo Ave.* ☎ *760/327–1372* 🌐 *www.smoketreestables.com* 🎫 *From $80.*

Palm Springs is a golfer's paradise: the area is home to more than 125 courses.

SPAS

★ Estrella Spa at the Avalon Hotel Palm Springs

FITNESS/HEALTH CLUBS | This spa earns top honors each year for the indoor/outdoor experience it offers with a touch of Old Hollywood ambience. You can enjoy your massage in one of four outdoor treatment cabanas in a garden, experience a sugar or salt scrub, get a facial or pedicure fireside, or receive a full-body treatment with a honey-sugar blend. Whatever the treatment, you can use the spa's private pool, take a break for lunch, and order a drink from the hotel's bar. ✉ *Avalon Hotel Palm Springs, 415 S. Belardo Rd.* ☎ *760/318–3000* 🌐 *www.avalonpalmsprings.com* ☞ *Salon. Services: facials, specialty massages, prenatal massages, outdoor treatments, wellness classes. $175, 60-min massage or facial.*

Feel Good Spa at the Ace Hotel

FITNESS/HEALTH CLUBS | The Feel Good Spa within its own dedicated facility at the Ace Hotel has five treatment rooms. The estheticians use local clay, mud, sea algae, and other natural ingredients, which you can purchase at the on-site shop. ✉ *701 E. Palm Canyon Dr.* ☎ *760/866–6188* 🌐 *www.acehotel.com/palmsprings* ☞ *Fully equipped gym. Services: wraps and scrubs, massage, facials, in-room treatments, salon, wellness classes, yoga. $115, 60-min massage.*

Palm Springs Yacht Club

FITNESS/HEALTH CLUBS | It's all about fun at this nautical-theme spa with 15 treatment rooms on the grounds of the Parker estate. Guests receive a complimentary cucumber-infused cocktail while lounging in a poolside tent. Before spa treatments, you can choose music from a playlist and the staff will stream it to your room. Treatments might feature local clay or stones, or a Thai massage. ✉ *4200 E. Palm Canyon Dr.* ☎ *760/321–4606* 🌐 *www.theparkerpalmsprings.com/spa* ☞ *Sauna, steam room, indoor pool. Services: scrubs and wraps, massage, facials, manicures, pedicures, waxing, salon, fitness center with TechnoGym* *equipment, dining and cocktails. $195, 50-min massage.*

Rancho Mirage

12 miles southeast of Palm Springs.

The rich and famous of Rancho Mirage live in beautiful estates and patronize elegant resorts and expensive restaurants. Although many mansions here are concealed behind the walls of gated communities and country clubs, the grandest of them all, Sunnylands, the Annenberg residence, is open to the public. The city's golf courses host many high-profile tournaments. You'll also find some of the desert's fanciest resorts—as well as plenty of peace and quiet.

GETTING HERE AND AROUND

Rancho Mirage stretches from Ramon Road in the north to the hills south of Highway 111. The western border is Da Vall Drive, the eastern one Monterey Avenue. Major east–west cross streets are Frank Sinatra Drive and Country Club Drive. Most shopping and dining spots are on Highway 111.

Sights

Rancho Mirage Library and Observatory

OBSERVATORY | **FAMILY** | Gaze at planets, star clusters, and galaxies, and learn about extraterrestrial life at this city-owned observatory next to the public library. The complex includes five high-powered telescopes—four on the deck and a main telescope in the 360-degree observatory dome that's designed to look like a comet. Regular tours and stargazing parties are scheduled every month. *71–100 Hwy. 111 760/341–7323 www.ranchomiragelibrary.org Free Closed Sun. and Mon.*

★ Sunnylands Center & Gardens

HOUSE | The stunning, 25,000-square-foot winter home and retreat of the late Ambassador Walter H. Annenberg and his wife, Leonore, opened to the public in 2012. You can spend a whole day enjoying the 15 glorious acres of gardens, and there are guided walks, landscape tours, classes, and other programs. The history made here is as captivating as the surroundings, given that eight U.S. presidents—from Dwight Eisenhower to Barack Obama—and their First Ladies have visited Sunnylands. Britain's Queen Elizabeth and Prince Philip also relaxed here, as did Princess Grace of Monaco and Japanese Prime Minister Toshiki Kaifu. Photos, art, letters, journals, and mementos provide insight. *37–977 Bob Hope Dr., south of Gerald Ford Dr. 760/202–2222 www.sunnylands.org Historic walking tour $25; guided bird tour $39; open-air shuttle tour of grounds, $125 per shuttle (up to 6 persons); visitor center and gardens free Closed Mon. and Tues. Closed June–mid-Sept. and during retreats.*

Restaurants

Catalan

$$$ | **MEDITERRANEAN** | At this restaurant, known for its beautifully prepared Mediterranean cuisine, you can dine inside or under the stars in the atrium. The service here is attentive, and the menu roams Spain, Italy, California, and beyond. **Known for:** two-course, prix-fixe menu; delicious paella with clams; happy hour with inventive cocktails. *Average main: $28 70026 Hwy. 111 760/770–9508 www.catalanrestaurant.com Closed Mon.*

Las Casuelas Nuevas

$ | **MEXICAN** | **FAMILY** | Hundreds of artifacts from Guadalajara, Mexico, lend festive charm to this casual restaurant, which has an expansive garden patio. Tamales and shellfish dishes are among the specialties—expect more traditional Mexican fare, rather than California-influenced creations. **Known for:** vast tequila menu; weekend live entertainment; lively happy hour. $ *Average main: $16 ✉ 70–050 Hwy. 111 ☎ 760/328–8844 🌐 www.lascasuelasnuevas.com.*

Hotels

Agua Caliente Casino, Resort, Spa
$$ | RESORT | As in Las Vegas, the Agua Caliente casino is in the lobby, but once you get into the resort's spacious, beautifully appointed guest rooms, all of the cacophony at the entrance is forgotten. **Pros:** poolside cabanas outfitted with TV and Wi-Fi; package deals include access to Indian Canyons Golf Course; on-site Sunstone Spa. **Cons:** casino ambience; not appropriate for kids; some live performances draw huge crowds. $ *Rooms from: $250 ✉ 32–250 Bob Hope Dr. ☎ 888/999–1995 🌐 www.hotwatercasino.com ⇨ 366 rooms 🍽 No meals.*

Omni Rancho Las Palmas Resort & Spa
$$$ | RESORT | FAMILY | The desert's most family-friendly resort, this large venue holds Splashtopia, a huge water-play zone. **Pros:** rooms come with private balconies or patios; trails for hiking and jogging; nightly entertainment. **Cons:** second-floor rooms accessed by very steep stairs; golf course surrounds rooms; resort hosts conventions. $ *Rooms from: $299 ✉ 41-000 Bob Hope Dr. ☎ 760/568–2727 🌐 www.rancholaspalmas.com ⇨ 444 rooms 🍽 No meals.*

★ The Ritz Carlton, Rancho Mirage
$$$$ | RESORT | FAMILY | On a hilltop perch overlooking the Coachella Valley, this luxury resort spoils guests with exemplary service and comforts that include a trio of pools, access to the desert's finest spa, and private outdoor sitting areas for each room. **Pros:** firepit overlooking Coachella Valley; access to Mission Hills golf courses and tennis; spa that's a destination in itself. **Cons:** hefty rates; some airport noise; resort and parking fees ($40 each). $ *Rooms from: $430 ✉ 68900 Frank Sinatra Dr. ☎ 760/321–8282 🌐 www.ritz-carlton.com ⇨ 244 rooms 🍽 No meals.*

The Westin Mission Hills Golf Resort & Spa
$$$$ | RESORT | FAMILY | A sprawling resort on 360 acres, the Westin offers a slew of activities for all ages and is surrounded by fairways and putting greens, two family-friendly pools (one lagoon-style with a 75-foot waterslide) and an adults-only pool. **Pros:** gorgeous grounds; first-class golf facilities; daily activity programs for kids and adults. **Cons:** rooms are spread out; some buildings seem dated; far from town. $ *Rooms from: $369 ✉ 71333 Dinah Shore Dr. ☎ 760/328–5955, 877/253–0041 🌐 www.westinmission-hills.com ⇨ 552 rooms 🍽 No meals.*

Nightlife

Agua Caliente Casino
CASINOS | This elegant and surprisingly quiet casino contains 1,300 slot machines, 36 table games, an 18-table poker room, a high-limit room, a no-smoking area, and six restaurants. The Show, the resort's concert theater, presents acts such as The Moody Blues, Joe Bonamassa, Toni Braxton, and Theresa Caputo, as well as live sporting events. *✉ 32–250 Bob Hope Dr., at E. Ramon Rd. ☎ 888/999–1995 🌐 www.hotwatercasino.com.*

Shopping

MALL

The River at Rancho Mirage
SHOPPING CENTERS/MALLS | This shopping-dining-entertainment complex holds 20 high-end shops, all fronting a faux river with cascading waterfalls. Also here are a 12-screen cinema, an outdoor amphitheater, and many restaurants including Acqua (sister to the popular LULU in Palm Springs) and Babe's Bar-B-Que and Brewhouse. *✉ 71–800 Hwy. 111, at Bob Hope Dr. ☎ 760/341–2711 🌐 www.theriveratranchomirage.com.*

GOLF

★ Westin Mission Hills Resort Golf Club

GOLF | Golfers at the Westin Mission Hills have two courses to choose from, the Pete Dye and the Gary Player Signature. They're both great, with amazing mountain views and wide fairways, but if you've only got time to play one, choose the Dye. The club is a member of the Troon Golf Institute, and has several teaching facilities, including the Westin Mission Hills Resort Golf Academy and the *Golf Digest* Golf School. **■ TIP→ The resort's Best Available Rate program guarantees golfers (with a few conditions) the best Internet rate possible.** ✉ *71333 Dinah Shore Dr.* ☎ *760/328–3198* 🌐 *www.playmissionhills.com* *Gary Player, from $74; Pete Dye, from $114* *Pete Dye Resort: 18 holes, 5525 yards, par 72; Gary Player Signature: 18 holes, 5327 yards, par 70.*

SPAS

★ The Ritz Carlton Spa, Rancho Mirage

FITNESS/HEALTH CLUBS | Two hundred–plus suspended quartz crystals guard the entrance of the desert's premier spa. With private men's and women's areas, a co-ed outdoor soaking tub, food service, and some of the kindest spa technicians around, guests can expect pampering par excellence. The signature Spirit of the Mountains treatment, which starts with a full-body exfoliation, includes a massage, and ends with a body wrap and a scalp massage with lavender oil, is a blissful experience. The gym, equipped with state-of-the-art machines, is open 24/7. Private trainers are available to guide your workout; wellness classes are also available. ✉ *68900 Frank Sinatra Dr.* ☎ *760/202–6170* 🌐 *www.ritzcarlton.com* ☞ *Fully equipped gym. Salon. Services: body wraps, body scrubs, facials, mineral baths, specialty massages, outdoor treatments, waxing, wellness classes. $185, 50-min massage; $345, signature package.*

The Spa at Mission Hills

FITNESS/HEALTH CLUBS | The emphasis at this spa in a quiet corner of the Westin Mission Hills Resort is on comfort rather than glitz and glamour. Attentive therapists incorporate coconut lemon balm, thyme, lavender, hydrating honey, and other botanicals into their treatments. Yoga and other wellness classes are also available. ✉ *71333 Dinah Shore Dr.* ☎ *760/770–2180* 🌐 *www.spaatmissionhills.com* ☞ *Steam room. Gym with: machines, cardio, pool. Services: rubs and scrubs, massages, facials, nail services. $170, 50-min massage.*

Palm Desert

2 miles southeast of Rancho Mirage.

Palm Desert is a thriving retail and business community with popular restaurants, private and public golf courses, and premium shopping along its main commercial drag, El Paseo. Each October, the Palm Desert Golf Cart Parade launches "the season" with a procession of 80 golf carts decked out as floats buzzing up and down El Paseo. The town's stellar sight to see is the Living Desert complex.

GETTING HERE AND AROUND

Palm Desert stretches from north of I–10 to the hills south of Highway 111. West–east cross streets north to south are Frank Sinatra Drive, Country Club Drive (lined on both sides with gated golfing communities), and Fred Waring Drive. Monterey Avenue marks the western boundary, and Washington Street forms the eastern edge.

TOURS

Art in Public Places

SELF-GUIDED | Several self-guided tours cover the works in Palm Desert's 150-piece Art in Public Places collection. Each tour is walkable or drivable. Maps and information about guided tours (one Saturday each month) are available at the

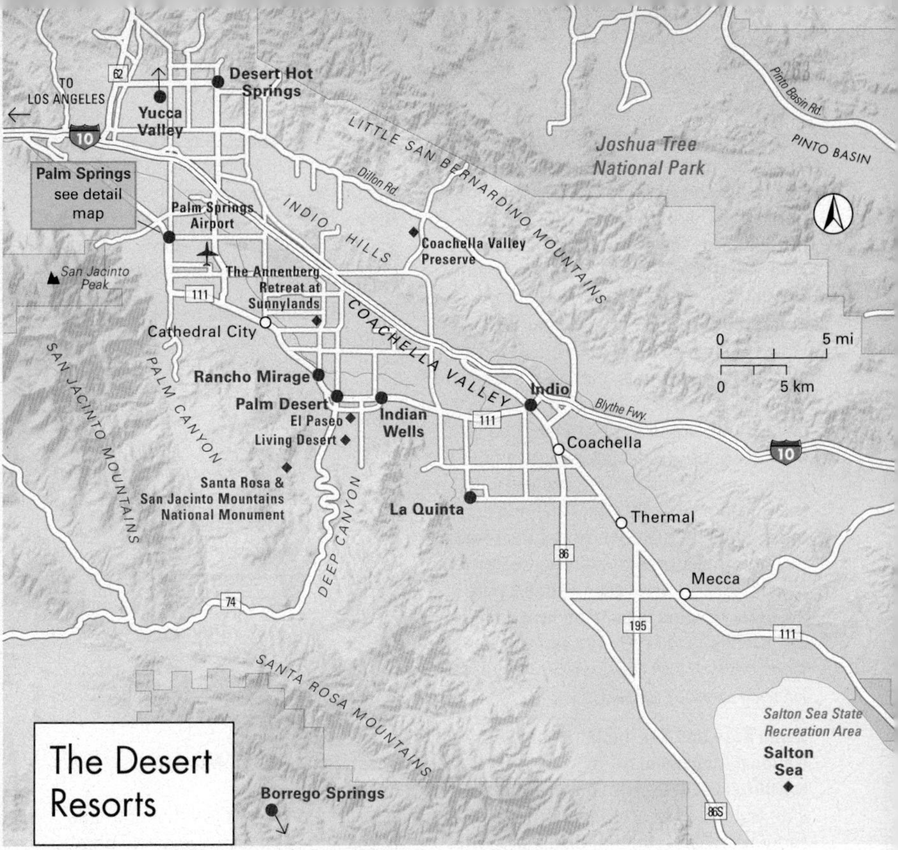

The Desert Resorts

city's visitor center and online. ✉ *Palm Desert Visitor Center, 73510 Fred Waring Dr.* ☎ *760/568–1441* 🌐 *www.palm-desert.org/arts-entertainment/public-art* 🎫 *Free.*

Sights

★ El Paseo

PEDESTRIAN MALL | West of and parallel to Highway 111, this mile-long, Mediterranean-style shopper's paradise is lined with fountains, courtyards, and upscale boutiques. You'll find shoe salons, jewelry stores, and children's shops, as well as two dozen restaurants and nearly as many art galleries. The strip is a pleasant place to stroll, window-shop, people-watch, and exercise your credit cards. **■ TIP→ In winter and spring, a free, bright-yellow shuttle ferries shoppers from store to store and back to their cars.** ✉ *Between Monterey and Portola Aves.* ☎ *760/674–9012* 🌐 *www.elpaseo.com.*

Faye Sarkowski Sculpture Garden

MUSEUM | This 4-acre desert garden at the west entrance to El Paseo holds 14 cutting-edge works by contemporary sculptors, including Donald Judd, Betty Gold, Yehiel Shemi, Felipe Castañeda, Jesús Bautista Moroles, Dan Namingha, Giò Pomodoro, and Dave McGary. ✉ *72–567 Hwy. 111* ☎ *760/346–5600* 🌐 *www.psmuseum.org/visit/faye-sarkowsky-sculpture-garden* 🎫 *Free.*

★ The Living Desert Zoo and Gardens

ZOO | **FAMILY** | Come eye-to-eye with wolves, coyotes, mountain lions, cheetahs, bighorn sheep, golden eagles, warthogs, and owls at the Living Desert, which showcases the flora and fauna of the world's arid landscapes. Easy to challenging scenic trails traverse terrain populated with plants of the Mojave, Colorado, and Sonoran deserts. In the 3-acre African WaTuTu village you'll find a traditional marketplace, as well as camels, leopards, hyenas, and other African animals. Children can pet domesticated African creatures, including Nigerian dwarf goats, in a "petting kraal." Gecko Gulch is a playground with crawl-through underground tunnels, climb-on snake sculptures, a carousel, and a Discovery Center that holds ancient Pleistocene animal bones. Wallabies, emus, and kookaburras interact with visitors in the immersive Australian Adventures experience, and a cool model train travels through miniatures of historic California towns. **■ TIP→ Time your visit to begin in the early morning to beat the heat and feed the giraffes.** ✉ *47900 Portola Ave., south from Hwy. 111* ☎ *760/346–5694* 🌐 *www.livingdesert.org* 🎟 *$25.*

Santa Rosa and San Jacinto Mountains National Monument

NATURE PRESERVE | Administered by the U.S. Bureau of Land Management, this monument protects Peninsula bighorn sheep and other wildlife on 280,000 acres of desert habitat. Stop by the visitor center for an introduction to the site and information about the natural history of the desert. A landscaped garden displays native plants and frames an impressive view. The well-informed staff can recommend hiking trails that show off the beauties of the desert. **■ TIP→ Free guided hikes are offered on Thursday and Saturday.** ✉ *51–500 Hwy. 74* ☎ *760/862–9984* 🌐 *www.blm.gov* 🎟 *Free.*

Restaurants

★ Bouchee Café & Deli

$ | **AMERICAN** | Devotees of this La Quinta favorite come here for farm-to-table Euro-style meals and deli items. Order the salads or gorgeous sandwiches—the salmon salad is to die for—at the counter, then retire to the French-inspired dining area or the shaded outdoor terrace. **Known for:** premade dinner to go; gourmet wine and cheese shop; locally sourced ingredients. Ⓢ *Average main: $15* ✉ *72–785 Hwy. 111* ✥ *Off Plaza Way near El Paseo* ☎ *442/666–3296* ⊗ *No dinner.*

Pacifica Seafood

$$$$ | **SEAFOOD** | Choice seafood and rooftop dining draw locals and visitors to this busy restaurant on the second floor of the Gardens of El Paseo. Seafood that arrives daily from San Diego shines in dishes such as twin lobster tails, grilled Pacific swordfish, and barbecued sugar-spiced salmon. **Known for:** inventive sauces and glazes; craft cocktails and bourbon; lower-price sunset menu from 3 to 5:30. Ⓢ *Average main: $38* ✉ *73505 El Paseo* ☎ *760/674–8666* 🌐 *www.pacificaseafoodrestaurant.com* ⊗ *No lunch June–Aug.*

Desert Springs J. W. Marriott Resort and Spa

$$$ | **RESORT** | **FAMILY** | With a dramatic U-shape design, this sprawling hotel, which attract business travelers, couples, and families alike, is set on 450 landscaped acres and wraps around the desert's largest private lake. **Pros:** gondola rides on the lake to restaurants; popular lobby bar; wonderful spa. **Cons:** crowded in-season; high resort fee; long walk from lobby to rooms. Ⓢ *Rooms from: $269* ✉ *74–855 Country Club Dr.* ☎ *760/341–2211, 888/538–9459* 🌐 *www.desertspringsresort.com* *884 rooms* *No meals.*

Hotel Paseo

$$$ | **HOTEL** | **FAMILY** | A half block from El Paseo, this hip luxury hotel, which is a member of Marriott's Autograph Collection, reflects the mid-century modern history and upscale, yet casual lifestyle of the desert. **Pros:** on-site restaurant; full-service spa; walk to El Paseo restaurants, shops, attractions. **Cons:** some rooms on the small side; pool area can seem small and crowded; street parking unless you pay for valet. *Rooms from: $289 45400 Larkspur La. 760/340–9001 www.hotelpaseo.com 149 rooms No meals.*

 Performing Arts

McCallum Theatre

THEATER | The principal cultural venue in the desert, this theater hosts productions from fall through spring. *The Phantom of the Opera* has played here; Lily Tomlin and Willie Nelson have performed; and Shen Yun dancers have twirled across the stage. *73–000 Fred Waring Dr. 760/340–2787 www.mccallumtheatre.com.*

 Activities

BALLOONING

Fantasy Balloon Flights

BALLOONING | Sunrise excursions over the southern end of the Coachella Valley lift off at 6 am and take from 60 to 90 minutes; a traditional champagne toast follows the landing. Afternoon excursions are timed to touch down at sunset. *Palm Desert 760/568–0997 www.fantasyballoonflight.com $195.*

GOLF

Desert Willow Golf Resort

GOLF | Praised for its environmentally smart design, this top-rated, public golf resort planted water-thrifty turf grasses and doesn't use pesticides. The Mountain View course has four configurations; Firecliff is tournament quality with five configurations. *38–995 Desert Willow Dr., off Country Club Dr. 760/346–0015 www.desertwillow.com Mountain View from $120, Firecliff from $120 Mountain View: 18 holes, 7079 yards, par 72; Firecliff: 18 holes, 7056 yards, par 72.*

Indian Wells

5 miles east of Palm Desert.

For the most part a quiet and exclusive residential enclave, Indian Wells hosts major tennis tournaments throughout the year, including the BNP Paribas Open. Three hotels share access to championship golf and tennis facilities, and there are several noteworthy resort spas and restaurants.

GETTING HERE AND AROUND

Indian Wells lies between Palm Desert and La Quinta, with most resorts, restaurants, and shopping set back from Highway 111.

 Restaurants

Vue Grille and Bar at the Indian Wells Golf Resort

$$$ | **AMERICAN** | This not-so-private restaurant at the Indian Wells Golf Resort offers a glimpse of how the country-club set lives. The service is impeccable, and the outdoor tables provide views of mountain peaks that seem close enough to touch. **Known for:** farm-to-table cuisine; grilled steaks and seafood; flatbreads and burgers. *Average main: $36 44–500 Indian Wells La. 760/834–3800 www.vuegrilleandbar.com.*

 Hotels

★ Hyatt Regency Indian Wells Resort & Spa

$$$$ | **RESORT** | **FAMILY** | This stark-white resort adjacent to the Golf Resort at Indian Wells is one of the grandest in the desert, with seven pools (one adults-only and several with slides in the HyTides waterpark), an outdoor game area and kids club, and a spa. **Pros:** excellent business services; butler service in some rooms; very pet-friendly. **Cons:** big and impersonal; spread out over 45 acres; noisy public areas. *Rooms from: $370 44–600 Indian Wells La. 760/776–1234 indianwells.regency.hyatt.com 520 rooms No meals.*

Miramonte Resort & Spa

$$$ | **RESORT** | Guest rooms at the most intimate of the Indian Wells hotels are in red-roof villas on 11 acres of bougainvillea-filled gardens against a backdrop of the Santa Rosa Mountains. **Pros:** three swimming pools (one adults-only); on-site farm-to-fork restaurant and lounge; one of the desert's best spas. **Cons:** extra resort fee; limited resort facilities on-site; long walk to lobby from some rooms. *Rooms from: $299 ✉ 45000 Indian Wells La. ☎ 760/341–2200 🌐 www.miramonteresort.com 215 rooms No meals.*

Renaissance Esmeralda Resort & Spa, Indian Wells

$$$ | **RESORT** | **FAMILY** | The centerpiece of this luxurious resort, adjacent to the Golf Resort at Indian Wells, is an eight-story atrium lobby, onto which most rooms open. **Pros:** adjacent to golf-tennis complex; kids club; bicycles available. **Cons:** higher noise level in rooms surrounding pool; somewhat impersonal ambience; service sometimes under par in off-season. *Rooms from: $289 ✉ 44–400 Indian Wells La. ☎ 760/773–4444 🌐 www.renaissancehotels.com 560 rooms No meals.*

Activities

GOLF

★ Indian Wells Golf Resort

GOLF | Adjacent to the Hyatt Regency Indian Wells, this complex includes the Celebrity Course, designed by Clive Clark and twice a host to the PGA's Skins game (lots of water here, including streams, lakes, and waterfalls), and the Players Course, designed by John Fought to incorporate views of the surrounding mountain ranges. Both courses consistently rank among the best public courses in California. **■ TIP→ It's a good idea to book tee times well in advance, up to 60 days.** *✉ 44–500 Indian Wells La. ☎ 760/346–4653 🌐 www.indianwellsgolfresort.com Both courses from $79 Celebrity Course: 18 holes, 7050 yards, par 72; Players Course: 18 holes, 7376 yards, par 72.*

SPAS

★ The Well Spa

FITNESS/HEALTH CLUBS | A luxurious, 12,000-square-foot facility, The Well draws on international treatments and ingredients to indulge the senses and relax the body. Hot-stone, Himalayan-salt, and full-body massages and table yoga are well worth the splurge. Sugar or salt exfoliating scrubs may well restore the soul in addition to the skin. *✉ Miramonte Resort, 45–000 Indian Wells La. ☎ 442/305–4505 🌐 www.miramonteresort.com Services: facials, nail care, solo and couple's massages, scrubs, and other body therapies. $175, 50-min massage.*

La Quinta

4 miles south of Indian Wells.

The desert became a Hollywood hideout in the 1920s, when La Quinta Hotel (now La Quinta Resort and Club) opened, introducing the Coachella Valley's first golf course. Old Town La Quinta is a draw, with eateries, shops, and galleries.

GETTING HERE AND AROUND

Most of La Quinta lies south of Highway 111. The main drag through town is Washington Street.

Restaurants

Arnold Palmer's

$$$ | **AMERICAN** | From the photos on the walls to the trophy-filled display cases, Arnie's essence infuses this restaurant. Families gather in the spacious dining room for birthdays and Sunday dinners, and the service is always attentive. **Known for:** homemade meat loaf, double-cut pork chops, mac and cheese; top-notch wine list; entertainment most nights. *Average main: $34 ✉ 78164 Ave. 52, near*

Desert Club Dr. ☎ 760/771–4653 🌐 www.arnoldpalmersrestaurant.com.

Cork & Fork

$$ | **MODERN AMERICAN** | A casual wine bar, restaurant, and popular local hangout in a cozy, contemporary, indoor–outdoor space near Lake La Quinta, Cork and Fork focuses on matching wines with an array of small and large dishes—all designed to share. The globe-trotting menu changes with the seasons, but you might feast on street tacos stuffed with filet mignon or tequila lime shrimp, Neapolitan-style pizzas, salads, or lobster penne in a creamy pink-vodka sauce. **Known for:** daily happy hour; eclectic list of affordable, food-friendly wines by the glass and bottle; special vegan menu (and much of the menu is gluten-free). *$ Average main: $17 ✉ 47875 Caleo Bay Dr., #A106 ☎ 760/777–7555 🌐 www.corkandforkwinebar.com ⏲ No lunch.*

★ Lavender Bistro

$$$$ | **BISTRO** | This romantic bistro with a spacious outdoor atrium decked out with flowers, fountains, and twinkling lights makes diners feel like they've been transported to southern France. Choices on the lengthy menu include crispy coastal calamari, a honey-brine pork chop, and lobster ravioli; for dessert, you can't go wrong with the baked apple tart or the warm chocolate lava cake. **Known for:** live music on the patio and in the fireside lounge; organic ingredients; extensive locavore menu. *$ Average main: $38 ✉ 78073 Calle Barcelona ☎ 760/564–5353 🌐 www.lavenderbistro.com ⏲ Closed June–Sept.*

Hotels

The Chateau at Lake La Quinta

$$ | **HOTEL** | Old-world French design, contemporary style, and luxe creature comforts make this lakeside inn a good choice for those who want intimate, upscale lodgings near La Quinta's main attractions. **Pros:** idyllic lakeside setting; on-site restaurant serves breakfast, lunch, and dinner; outdoor pool, deck with firepits. **Cons:** two-story building with no elevator; some rooms not as posh as others; adults-oriented, not ideal for families with children. *$ Rooms from: $189 ✉ 78–120 Caleo Bay Dr. ☎ 760/564–7332, 888/226–4546 🌐 www.thechateau.com 26 rooms 🍽 No meals.*

La Quinta Resort and Club

$$$ | **RESORT** | **FAMILY** | Opened in 1926 and now a member of the Waldorf-Astoria Collection, the desert's oldest resort is a 45-acre oasis with myriad rooms and villas, 23 tennis courts, and 41 pools. **Pros:** some rooms have private pools; gorgeous gardens; pet and family friendly. **Cons:** a party atmosphere sometimes prevails; spotty housekeeping/maintenance; swimming pools can be crowded. *$ Rooms from: $329 ✉ 49499 Eisenhower Dr. ☎ 760/564–4111 🌐 www.laquintaresort.com 796 units 🍽 No meals.*

Activities

GOLF

★ PGA West

GOLF | A world-class golf destination where Phil Mickelson and Jack Nicklaus play, this facility includes five resort courses and four private ones. Courses meander through indigenous desert landscapes, water features, and bunkers. The Norman, Nick Tournament, and TPC Stadium courses are "shot-makers" courses made for pros. TPC highlights include its two lakes, "San Andreas Fault" bunker, and island green called "Alcatraz." The Norman course has tight fairways and small greens. *✉ 49–499 Eisenhower Dr. ☎ 760/564–5729 for tee times 🌐 www.pgawest.com Mountain Course, from $159; Dunes, from $119; Greg Norman, from $159; TPC Stadium, from $189; Jack Nicklaus Tournament, from $159 Mountain Course: 18 holes, 6732 yards, par 72; Dunes: 18 holes, 6712 yards, par 72; Greg Norman: 18 holes, 7156 yards, par 72; TPC Stadium:*

18 holes, 7300 yards, par 72; Jack Nicklaus Tournament: 18 holes, 7204 yards, par 72.

SPAS

Spa La Quinta

FITNESS/HEALTH CLUBS | The gorgeous Spa La Quinta may be the grandest spa in the entire desert. At this huge standalone facility you'll find everything from massages to facials to salon services and classes, plus a beautiful garden setting with a large fountain, flowers galore, plenty of nooks where you can hide out and enjoy the sanctuary, and a Jacuzzi with a waterfall. ✉ *49499 Eisenhower Dr.* ☎ *760/777–4800* 🌐 *www.laquintaresort.com* ☞ *Fitness center with cardio. Services: aromatherapy, body wraps and scrubs, massage, skin care, salon services, water therapies. $170, 50-min massage; $295, 50-min HydraFacial.*

Indio

5 miles east of Indian Wells.

Indio is the home of the renowned date shake: an extremely thick and sweet milkshake made with dates. The city and surrounding countryside generate 95% of the dates grown and harvested in the United States. If you take a hot-air balloon ride, you will likely drift over the tops of date palm trees.

GETTING HERE AND AROUND

Indio is east of Indian Wells and north of La Quinta. Highway 111 runs right through Indio, and I–10 skirts it to the north.

Sights

Coachella Valley Preserve

NATURE PRESERVE | **FAMILY** | For a glimpse of how the desert appeared before development, head northeast from Palm Springs to this preserve. It has a system of sand dunes and several palm oases that were formed because the San Andreas Fault lines here allow water flowing underground to rise to the surface. A mile-long walk along Thousand Palms Oasis reveals pools supporting the tiny endangered desert pupfish and more than 183 bird species. Families like the relatively flat trail that is mostly shaded. The preserve has a visitor center, nature and equestrian trails, restrooms, and picnic facilities. Guided hikes are offered October–March. ■ **TIP→ Be aware that it's exceptionally hot in summer here.** ✉ *29200 Thousand Palms Canyon Rd., Thousand Palms* ☎ *760/343–1234* 🌐 *www.cnlm.org/portfolio_page/coachella-valley* 🎫 *Free* ⏲ *Visitor center closed May–Sept. Parking lot and hiking closed Aug.*

Shields Date Garden and Café

STORE/MALL | Sample, select, and take home some of Shields's locally grown dates. Ten varieties are available, including the giant supersweet royal medjools, along with specialty date products such as date crystals, stuffed dates, confections, and local honey. At the Shields Date Garden Café you can try an iconic date shake, dig into date pancakes, or go exotic with a date burger. Breakfast and lunch are served daily. ✉ *80–225 Hwy. 111* ☎ *760/347–0996* 🌐 *www.shieldsdategarden.com* ⏲ *No dinner.*

Restaurants

Ciro's Ristorante and Pizzeria

$ | **SICILIAN** | Serving pizza and pasta since the 1960s, this popular restaurant has a few unusual pies on the menu, including cashew with three cheeses. The decor is classic pizza joint, with checkered tablecloths and bentwood chairs. **Known for:** daily pasta specials; classic Italian dishes; house-made, hand-tossed pizza dough. 💲 *Average main: $16* ✉ *81–963 Hwy. 111* ☎ *760/347–6503* ⏲ *No lunch weekends.*

Performing Arts

MUSIC FESTIVALS

★ Coachella Valley Music and Arts Festival

FESTIVALS | Among Southern California's biggest parties, the festival draws hundreds of thousands of rock music fans to Indio each April for two weekends of live concerts. Headliners have included acts such as Lady Gaga, Childish Gambino, Ariana Grande, Tame Impala, Kendrick Lamar, Jack Johnson, and Radiohead. Many attendees camp on-site, but to give your ears a rest postconcert you might want to stay at a nearby hotel. **■ TIP→ The festival sells out before the lineup is announced, so expect to pay big bucks if you haven't purchased tickets by late fall.** ✉ *Empire Polo Club, 81–800 Ave. 51* 🌐 *www.coachella.com.*

Borrego Springs

66 miles southwest of Indio.

The permanent population of Borrego Springs, set squarely in the middle of Anza-Borrego Desert State Park, hovers around 2,500. From September through June, when temperatures stay in the '80s and '90s, you can engage in outdoor activities such as hiking, nature study, golfing, tennis, horseback riding, and mountain biking. If winter rains cooperate, Borrego Springs puts on some of the best wildflower displays in the low desert. In some years, the desert floor is carpeted with color: yellow dandelions and sunflowers, pink primrose, purple sand verbena, and blue wild heliotrope. The bloom generally lasts from late February through April. For current information on wildflowers around Borrego Springs, call Anza-Borrego Desert State Park's wildflower hotline (☎ *760/767–4684*).

GETTING HERE AND AROUND

You can access Anza Borrego by taking the Highway 86 exit from I–10, south of Indio. Highway 86 passes through Coachella and along the western shore of the Salton Sea. Turn west on Highway S22 at Salton City and follow it to Peg Leg Road, where you turn south until you reach Palm Canyon Drive. Turn west, and the road leads to the center of Borrego Springs, Christmas Circle, where most major roads come together. Well-marked roads radiating from the circle will take you to the most popular sites in the state park. If coming from the San Diego area, drive east on I–8 to the Cuyamaca Mountains, exit at Highway 79, and enjoy the lovely 23-mile drive through the mountains until you reach Julian; head east on Highway 78 and follow signs to Borrego Springs.

ESSENTIALS

VISITOR INFORMATION Borrego Springs Chamber of Commerce & Visitors Bureau. ✉ *786 Palm Canyon Dr.* ☎ *760/767–5555, 800/559–5524* 🌐 *www.borregospringschamber.com.*

Sights

★ Anza-Borrego Desert State Park

NATIONAL/STATE PARK | One of the richest living natural-history museums in the nation, this state park is a vast, nearly uninhabited wilderness where you can step through a field of wildflowers, cool off in a palm-shaded oasis, count zillions of stars in the black night sky, and listen to coyotes howl at dusk. The landscape, largely undisturbed by humans, reveals a rich natural history. There's evidence of a vast inland sea in the piles of oyster beds near Split Mountain and of the power of natural forces such as earthquakes and flash floods. In addition, recent scientific work has confirmed that the Borrego Badlands, with more than 6,000 meters of exposed fossil-bearing sediments, is likely the richest such deposit in North America, telling the story of 7 million years of climate change, upheaval, and prehistoric animals. Evidence has been unearthed of saber-toothed cats, flamingos, zebras, and the largest flying bird in the northern hemisphere beneath the now-parched sand.

Today the desert's most treasured inhabitants are the herds of elusive and endangered native bighorn sheep, or borrego, for which the park is named. Among the strange desert plants you may observe are the gnarly elephant trees. As these are endangered, rangers don't encourage visitors to seek out the secluded grove at Fish Creek, but there are a few examples at the visitor center garden. After a wet winter you can see a short-lived but stunning display of cacti, succulents, and desert wildflowers in bloom.

The park is unusually accessible to visitors. Admission to the park is free, and few areas are off-limits. There are two developed campgrounds, but you can camp anywhere; just follow the trails and pitch a tent wherever you like. There are more than 500 miles of dirt roads, two huge wilderness areas, and 110 miles of riding and hiking trails. Many sites can be seen from paved roads, but some require driving on dirt roads, for which rangers recommend you use a four-wheel-drive vehicle. When you do leave the pavement, carry the appropriate supplies: a cell phone (which may be unreliable in some areas), a shovel and other tools, flares, blankets, and plenty of water. The canyons are susceptible to flash flooding, so inquire about weather conditions (even on sunny days) before entering.

■ TIP→ Borrego resorts, restaurants, and the state park have Wi-Fi, but the service is spotty at best. If you need to talk to someone in the area, it's best to find a phone with a landline.

Stop by the **visitor center** to get oriented, to pick up a park map, and to learn about weather, road, and wildlife conditions. Designed to keep cool during the desert's blazing-hot summers, the center is built underground, beneath a demonstration desert garden containing examples of most of the native flora and a little pupfish pond. Displays inside the center illustrate the natural history of the area. Picnic tables are scattered throughout, making this a good place to linger and enjoy the view. ✉ *Visitor Center, 200 Palm Canyon Dr., Hwy. S22* ☎ *760/767–4205, 760/767–4684 wildflower hotline* 🌐 *www.parks.ca.gov* 🎫 *Free; day-use parking in campground areas $10* ☞ *Make a campground reservation at: reservecalifornia.com.*

★ Galleta Meadows

PUBLIC ART | FAMILY | At Galleta Meadows, camels, llamas, saber-toothed tigers, tortoises, and monumental gomphotherium (a sort of ancient elephant) appear to roam the Earth again. These life-size bronze figures are of prehistoric animals whose fossils can be found in the Borrego Badlands. The collection of more than 130 sculptures, created by Ricardo Breceda, was commissioned by the late Dennis Avery, who installed the works of art on property he owned for the entertainment of locals and visitors. Maps are available from Borrego Springs Chamber of Commerce. ✉ *Borrego Springs Rd., from Christmas Circle to Henderson Canyon* ☎ *760/767–5555* 🎫 *Free.*

Restaurants

The Arches

$$$ | MODERN AMERICAN | On the edge of the Borrego Springs Resort's golf course, set beneath a canopy of grapefruit trees, The Arches is a pleasant place to eat. For breakfast you'll find burritos alongside French toast, omelets, and eggs Benedict; lunch (best enjoyed on the patio) and dinner options include sandwiches and salads, as well as hearty pasta, seafood, grilled meats, and fish entrées. **Known for:** light fare; nightly specials; popular happy hour. 💲 *Average main: $27* ✉ *1112 Tilting T Dr.* ☎ *760/767–5700*

🌐 www.borregospringsresort.com/dining.asp ⏲ *Summer hrs vary; call ahead.*

Carlee's Place

$$ | **AMERICAN** | Sooner or later most visitors to Borrego Springs wind up at Carlee's Place for a drink and a bite to eat, drawn by an extra-long menu with everything from burgers, salads, and sandwiches to seafood dishes and prime rib. It's an all-American place, where your server might call you "honey" while setting a huge steak in front of you, and fellow diners might play pool and dance to jukebox music. **Known for:** down-home atmosphere; martinis and classic cocktails; everything made from scratch. *$ Average main: $25 ✉ 660 Palm Canyon Dr. ☎ 760/767–3262 🌐 www.carleesplace.com.*

Carmelita's Mexican Grill and Cantina

$ | **MEXICAN** | A friendly, family-run eatery tucked into a back corner of what is called "The Mall," Carmelita's draws diners all day, whether it's for a hearty breakfast, a cooked-to-order enchilada or burrito, or just a brew or margarita at the bar. The menu lists typical combination plates (enchiladas, burritos, tamales, and tacos). **Known for:** dog-friendly patio; house-made masa dough and salsas; full bar with sports TVs. *$ Average main: $15 ✉ 575 Palm Canyon Dr. ☎ 760/767–5666 🌐 www.facebook.com/carmelitasborrego.*

Coyote Steakhouse

$$$ | **MODERN AMERICAN** | This upscale restaurant at the Palms at Indian Head hotel caters to those who want a fancy dinner, particularly hunks of filet mignon or rack of lamb served at candlelit tables with white tablecloths overlooking the pool. Pet owners will appreciate the canine menu, whose treats include house-made peanut-butter dog cookies. **Known for:** romantic candlelit dining room; pork tenderloin and prime rib; classic mid-century setting. *$ Average main: $30 ✉ 2220 Hoberg Rd. ☎ 760/767–7788 🌐 www.thepalmsatindianhead.com ⏲ No breakfast or lunch.*

Los Jilberto's Taco Shop

$ | **MEXICAN** | A casual local favorite for affordable Mexican dishes, Jilberto's serves up big burritos and meaty enchiladas. **Known for:** authentic Mexican dishes cooked to order; all-day breakfast menu; reasonable prices. *$ Average main: $12 ✉ 655 Palm Canyon Dr. ☎ 760/767–1008 🌐 www.losjilbertostacoshop.com ▭ No credit cards.*

Hotels

Borrego Springs Resort & Spa

$$ | **RESORT** | The large rooms at this quiet resort are set around a swimming pool and come with either a shaded balcony or a patio with desert views. **Pros:** tennis courts and bikes available; good desert views from most rooms; close to sculpture gardens. **Cons:** rooms slightly dated; average service; breakfast not included. *$ Rooms from: $209 ✉ 1112 Tilting T Dr. ☎ 760/767–5700, 888/826–7734 🌐 www.borregospringsresort.com ⇨ 100 rooms 🍽 No meals.*

★ Borrego Valley Inn

$$$ | **B&B/INN** | Those looking for desert landscapes and some stargazing—guests must be 21 or older—may enjoy the adobe Southwestern-style buildings here that house spacious rooms, which boasts plenty of natural light, original art, pine beds, and corner fireplaces. **Pros:** swim under the stars in the clothing-optional pool; exquisite desert gardens; breakfast included. **Cons:** no kids and no pets; rooms could use sprucing up; service inconsistent. *$ Rooms from: $285 ✉ 405 Palm Canyon Dr. ☎ 760/767–0311, 800/333–5810 🌐 www.borregovalleyinn.com ⇨ 15 rooms 🍽 Free breakfast.*

★ La Casa Del Zorro

$$ | **RESORT** | **FAMILY** | The draws at this desert hideaway a short drive from Anza Borrego State Park include three guest-only pools, a hot tub, five night-lit

tennis courts and two pickleball courts, a yoga studio, a spa, a restaurant, and the lively Fox Den Bar. The 42-acre property pays tribute to its surroundings with a cactus garden, a firepit, and two tall, welded-metal animal sculptures by local artist Ricardo Breceda. **Pros:** private pool or hot tub in many casitas; 26 pools (including a 25-meter lap pool) and 14 water features; on-site spa, bar, and restaurant. **Cons:** service can be spotty; remote desert location; occasional strong desert winds sweep sand across the property. *Rooms from: $189* *3845 Yaqui Pass Rd.* *760/767–0100* *www.lacasadelzorro.com* *63 units* *No meals.*

Activities

GOLF

★ Rams Hill Golf Club

GOLF | Originally an exclusive, private course that fell into disrepair, the Tom Fazio–designed Rams Hill was resurrected and reopened in 2014. It's now consistently ranked as one of the top courses in California, with exceptional height variations, streams, waterfalls, and expansive views from its hilltop perch to the desert below. *1881 Rams Hill Rd.* *760/767–3500* *www.ramshill.com* *18 holes, 7232 yds, par 72* *From $120. Closed June–Oct.*

Shopping

Borrego Outfitters

CONVENIENCE/GENERAL STORES | This contemporary general store stocks high-end outdoor gear, hiking essentials, personal care items from Burt's Bees, footwear from Teva and Merrill, swimsuits, and tabletop items. You can browse through racks of clothing and piles of hats, all suited to the desert climate. *579 Palm Canyon Dr.* *760/767–3502* *www.borregooutfitters.com.*

Salton Sea

29 miles east of Borrego Springs; 30 miles southeast of Indio.

The Salton Sea, one of the largest inland seas on Earth, is the product of both natural and artificial forces. The sea occupies the Salton Basin, a remnant of prehistoric Lake Cahuilla. Over the centuries, the Colorado River flooded the basin, and the water drained into the Gulf of California. In 1905, a flood once again filled the Salton Basin, but the exit to the gulf was blocked by sediment. The floodwaters remained in the basin, creating a saline lake 228 feet below sea level and about 35 miles long and 15 miles wide, with a surface area of nearly 380 square miles. The sea, which lies along the Pacific Flyway, supports 400 species of birds. Fishing for tilapia, boating, camping, and bird-watching are popular activities year-round.

GETTING HERE AND AROUND

Salton Sea State Recreation Area includes about 14 miles of coastline on the northeastern shore of the sea, about 30 miles south of Indio via Highway 111. The Sonny Bono Salton Sea National Wildlife Refuge fills the southernmost tip of the sea's shore. To reach it from the recreation area, continue south about 60 miles to Niland; continue south to Sinclair Road, and turn west following the road to the Refuge Headquarters.

Sights

Salton Sea State Recreation Area

NATIONAL/STATE PARK | **FAMILY** | This huge recreation area on the sea's north shore draws thousands each year to its playgrounds, hiking trails, fishing spots, and boat launches. Ranger-guided bird walks take place on Saturday; you'll see migrating and native birds including Canada geese, pelicans, and shorebirds. *100–225 State Park Rd., North Shore*

760/393–3059, 760/393–3810 visitor center *www.parks.ca.gov* $7.

Sonny Bono Salton Sea National Wildlife Refuge

NATURE PRESERVE | The 2,200-acre wildlife refuge here, on the Pacific Flyway, is a wonderful spot for viewing migratory birds. There's an observation deck where you can watch Canada geese, and along the trails you might view eared grebes, burrowing owls, great blue herons, ospreys, and yellow-footed gulls. **⚠ Though the scenery is beautiful, the waters here give off an unpleasant odor, and the New River, which empties into the sea, is quite toxic.** *906 W. Sinclair Rd., Calipatria* *760/348–5278* *www.fws.gov/refuge/sonny_bono_salton_sea/* *Free* *Closed weekends Mar.–Oct.*

Desert Hot Springs

9 miles north of Palm Springs.

Desert Hot Springs's famous mineral waters, thought by some to have curative powers, bubble up at temperatures of 90°F to 148°F and flow into the wells of more than 40 hotel spas.

GETTING HERE AND AROUND

Desert Hot Springs lies due north of Palm Springs. Take Gene Autry Trail north to I–10, where the street name changes to Palm. Continue north to Pierson Boulevard, the town's center.

Cabot's Pueblo Museum

MUSEUM | Cabot Yerxa, the man who found the spring that made Desert Hot Springs famous, built a quirky, four-story, 35-room pueblo between 1939 and his death in 1965. Now a museum run by the city, the Hopi-inspired adobe structure is filled with memorabilia of Yerxa's time as a homesteader; his encounters with Hollywood celebrities at the nearby Bar-H Ranch; his expedition to the Alaskan gold rush; and many other events. The home, much of it crafted out of materials Yerxa recycled from the desert, can only be seen on hour-long tours. Outside, walk the grounds to a lookout with amazing desert views. *67–616 E. Desert View Ave., at Eliseo Rd.* *760/329–7610* *www.cabotsmuseum.org* *Grounds-only ticket $5, pueblo-tour ticket $13* *Closed Sun.–Wed.* *Tours every ½-hr 9–11:30 and 1:30–2:30.*

Two Bunch Palms

$$$ | RESORT | This adults-only hotel on a gorgeous, 72-acre property with stunning views of Mt. San Jacinto provides a luxurious and relaxing experience, with access to natural hot springs. **Pros:** on-site restaurant serves breakfast, lunch, and dinner; fresh juice bar open all day; full-service spa, popular since the 1940s. **Cons:** some rooms have no TV; no pets allowed; minimum age 18. *Rooms from: $349* *67425 Two Bunch Palms Trail* *760/676–5000* *twobunchpalms.com* *68 rooms* *No meals.*

Yucca Valley

21 miles northeast of Desert Hot Springs.

One of the high desert's fastest-growing cities, Yucca Valley is emerging as a bedroom community for people who work as far away as Ontario, 85 miles to the west. Here, you can shop for necessities, get your car serviced, grab coffee, purchase vintage furnishings, and chow down at fast-food outlets. Just up Pioneertown Road, you'll find the most-talked-about dining establishment in the desert: Pappy & Harriet's, the famed performance venue that hosts big-name talent.

GETTING HERE AND AROUND

The drive to Yucca Valley on Highway 62/Twentynine Palms Highway passes through the Painted Hills and drops down into a valley. Take Pioneertown Road north to the Old West outpost.

ESSENTIALS

VISITOR INFORMATION California Welcome Center Yucca Valley. ✉ *56711 Twentynine Palms Hwy.* ☎ *760/365–5464* 🌐 *www.californiawelcomecenter.com.* **Yucca Valley Chamber of Commerce.** ✉ *56711 Twentynine Palms Hwy.* ☎ *760/365–6323* 🌐 *www.yuccavalley.org.*

Sights

Hi-Desert Nature Museum

MUSEUM | **FAMILY** | Natural and cultural history of the Morongo Basis and High Desert are the focus here. A small live-animal display includes scorpions, snakes, lizards, and small mammals. You'll also find gems and minerals, fossils from the Paleozoic era, taxidermy, and Native American artifacts. There's also a children's area and art exhibits. ✉ *Yucca Valley Community Center, 57090 Twentynine Palms Hwy.* ☎ *760/369–7212* 🌐 *hidesertnaturemuseum.org* 🎟 *Free* ⏲ *Closed Sun.–Tues.*

Pioneertown

TOWN | In 1946, Roy Rogers, Gene Autry, the Sons of the Pioneers (the music group for which the town is named), and Russ Hayden built Pioneertown, an 1880s-style Wild West movie set complete with hitching posts, a saloon, and an OK Corral. You can stroll past wooden and adobe storefronts and feel like you're back in the Old West. Pappy & Harriet's Pioneertown Palace, now the town's top draw, has evolved into a hip venue for indie and mainstream performers such as Dengue Fever, Neko Case, and Robert Plant. ✉ *53688 Pioneertown Rd., Pioneertown* ✣ *4 miles north of Yucca Valley* 🌐 *pappyandharriets.com.*

Restaurants

Frontier Café

$ | **CAFÉ** | A cozy coffeehouse with a counterculture vibe, Frontier is a good place to stop before heading into the park or up to Pioneertown. Fill up on a breakfast bagel or fresh-baked muffin paired with a coffee drink, and pick up a salad, hot or cold sandwich, and dessert for lunch. **Known for:** fresh bakery items; vegan, veggie, and gluten-free options; daily specials. [$] *Average main: $12* ✉ *55844 Twentynine Palms Hwy.* ☎ *760/820–1360* 🌐 *www.cafefrontier.com* ⏲ *No dinner.*

★ **Pappy & Harriet's Pioneertown Palace**

$$ | **AMERICAN** | **FAMILY** | Smack in the middle of what looks like the set of a Western is this cozy saloon where you can have dinner, relax over a drink at the bar, and catch some great indie bands or legendary artists—Leon Russell, Lorde, Paul McCartney, and Robert Plant have all played here. Pappy & Harriet's may be in the middle of nowhere, but you'll need reservations for dinner on weekends. **Known for:** live music several days/nights a week; Tex-Mex, Santa Maria–style barbecue; fun and lively atmosphere. [$] *Average main: $25* ✉ *53688 Pioneertown Rd., Pioneertown* ☎ *760/365–5956* 🌐 *www.pappyandharriets.com* ⏲ *Closed Tues. and Wed.*

Hotels

Pioneertown Motel

$$ | **HOTEL** | Built in 1946 as a bunkhouse for Western film stars shooting in Pioneertown, this motel sticks close to its roots: its clean rooms are rustic and modern, with Western-style accents and exposed-wood-beam ceilings. **Pros:** Western movie time warp; great stargazing; surrounded by mesas and protected land. **Cons:** no frills; small rooms; hot in summer. [$] *Rooms from: $180* ✉ *5040 Curtis Rd., Pioneertown* ☎ *760/365–7001* 🌐 *www.pioneertown-motel.com* 🛏 *19 rooms* 🍽 *No meals.*

Chapter 8

JOSHUA TREE NATIONAL PARK

Updated by
Cheryl Crabtree

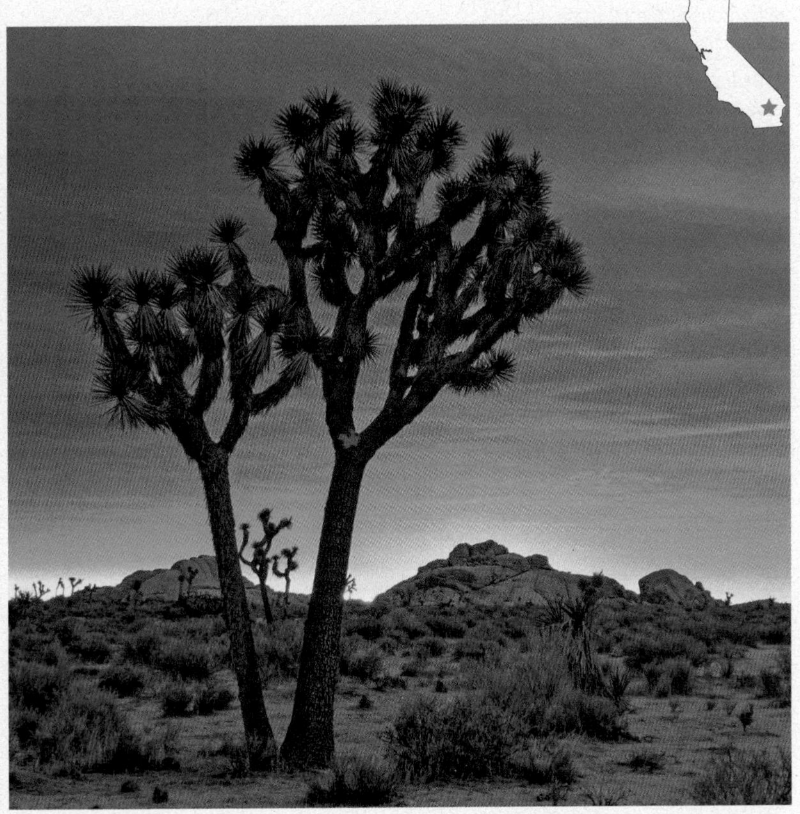

Camping	Hotels	Activities	Scenery	Crowds
★★★★★	★★★★☆	★★★★★	★★★★★	★★★★☆

WELCOME TO JOSHUA TREE NATIONAL PARK

TOP REASONS TO GO

★ **Rock climbing:** Joshua Tree is a world-class site with challenges for climbers of just about every skill level.

★ **Peace and quiet:** Roughly two hours from Los Angeles, this great wilderness is the ultimate escape from technology.

★ **Stargazing:** You'll be mesmerized by the Milky Way flowing across the summer sky. For spectacular natural fireworks, visit in mid-August during the Perseid meteor shower and watch shooting stars streak overhead.

★ **Wildflowers:** In spring, the hillsides explode in a patchwork of yellow, blue, pink, and white.

★ **Sunsets:** Twilight is a magical time here, especially during the winter, when the setting sun casts a golden glow on the mountains.

1 **Park Boulevard.** Drive the paved loop road between the west and north entrances to explore many of the park's main sights. Crawl between the big rocks at Hidden Valley, and you'll understand why this boulder-strewn area near the park's west entrance was once a cattle rustlers' hideout.

2 **Keys View Road.** Keys View is the park's most dramatic overlook—on clear days you can see Signal Mountain in Mexico.

3 **Highway 62.** Spot wildlife at Black Rock and Indian Cove (you might spy a desert tortoise). Near the park's north entrance, walk the nature trail around Oasis of Mara, which the first settlers, the Serrano, dubbed "the place of little springs and much grass."

4 **Pinto Basin Road.** Pull out binoculars at Cottonwood Spring, one of the best birding spots in the park. Come to Cholla Cactus Garden in the late afternoon, when the spiky stalks of the bigelow (jumping) cholla cactus are backlit against an intense blue sky.

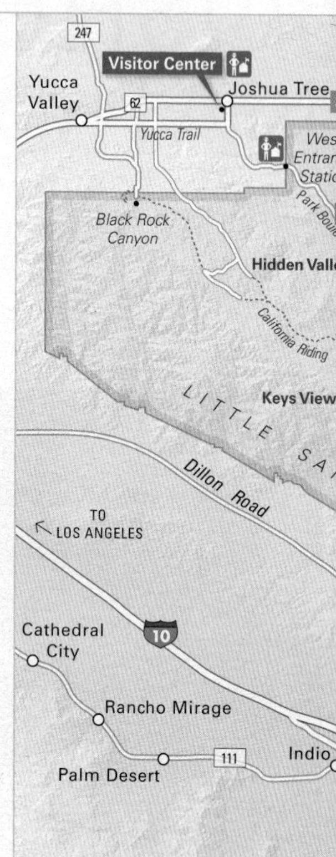

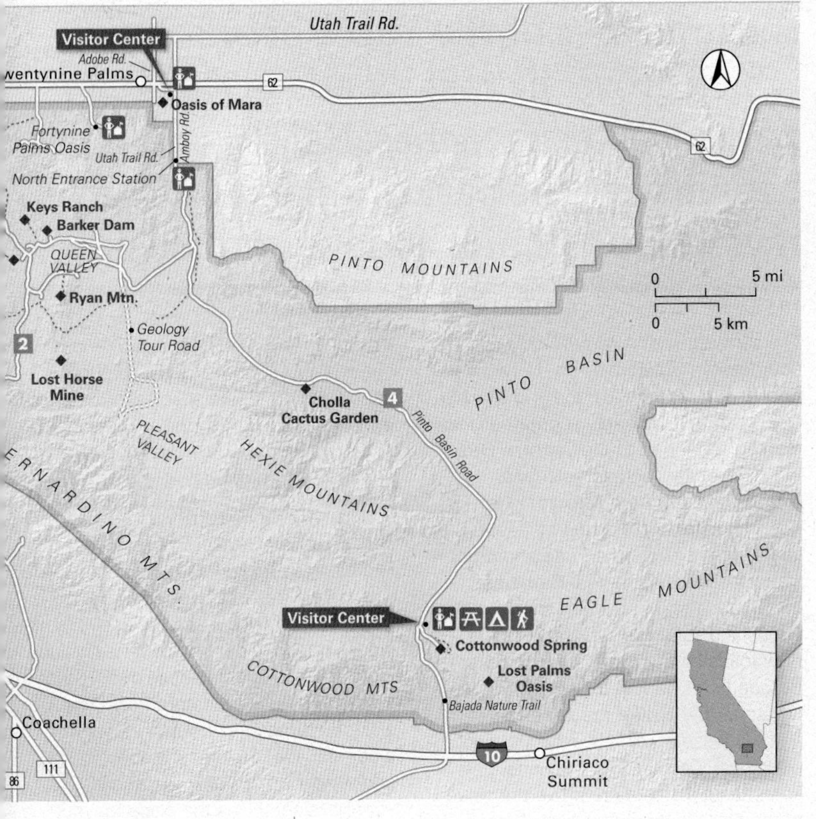
Utah Trail Rd.
Visitor Center
Adobe Rd.
wentynine Palms
62
Oasis of Mara
Fortynine Palms Oasis
Amboy Rd.
Utah Trail Rd.
North Entrance Station
Keys Ranch
Barker Dam
QUEEN VALLEY
Ryan Mtn.
Geology Tour Road
2
Lost Horse Mine
PINTO MOUNTAINS
62
0
5 mi
0
5 km
PINTO BASIN
Cholla Cactus Garden
4
Pinto Basin Road
PLEASANT VALLEY
HEXIE MOUNTAINS
ERNARDINO MTS.
EAGLE MOUNTAINS
Visitor Center
Cottonwood Spring
COTTONWOOD MTS
Lost Palms Oasis
Bajada Nature Trail
Coachella
111
86
10
Chiriaco Summit

Joshua Tree teems with fascinating landscapes and life-forms, including its namesake trees. Dagger-like tufts grace the branches of the Yucca brevifolia, which grows in vast stands in the park's western reaches. Nearly 3 million people visit the park annually, but it's mysteriously quiet at dawn and dusk.

The park occupies a remote area in southeastern California, where two distinct ecosystems meet: the arid Mojave Desert and the sparsely vegetated Colorado Desert—part of the Sonoran Desert, which stretches across California, Arizona, and northern Mexico. Humans have inhabited the area for at least 5,000 years, starting with the Pinto and other Native American cultures. Cattlemen, miners, and homesteaders arrived in the 1800s and early 1900s. By the 1920s, new roads lured developers and others. Pasadena resident and plant enthusiast Minerva Hoyt visited the desert often and witnessed reckless poaching and pillaging of cacti and other plants. She spearheaded studies to prove the value of regional plants and wildlife. Thanks to her dedicated efforts, Joshua Tree National Monument (825,000 acres) was established in 1936.

The 29 Palms Corporation deeded part of the historic Oasis of Mara to the National Park Service in 1950, and the monument became an official national park on October 31, 1994. Today the park encompasses about 800,000 acres (nearly 600,000 is designated wilderness). Elevation ranges from 536 feet to the peak of 5,814-foot Quail Mountain. The diverse habitats within the park protect more than 800 plant, 250 bird, and 57 mammal species, including the desert bighorn sheep and 46 reptile species, such as the endangered desert tortoise. The park also preserves numerous archaeological sites and historic structures.

You can experience Joshua Tree National Park on several levels. Even on a short excursion along Park Boulevard between the Joshua Tree entrance station and Oasis of Mara, you'll see the essence of North American desert scenery—including a staggering abundance of flora along a dozen self-guided nature trails. You'll also see remnants of homesteads from a century ago, now mostly abandoned and wind-worn. If rock climbing is your passion, this is the place for you: boulder-strewn mountaintops and slopes beckon. Nightfall brings opportunities for stellar stargazing—Joshua Tree was designated an official International Dark Sky Park in 2017. Though trails are closed after sunset, you can park at any of the road pullouts and check out the sparkling shows above. Joshua Tree National Park is a pristine wilderness where you can enjoy a solitary stroll along a trail and commune with nature. Be sure to take some time to explore on your own and enjoy the peace and quiet.

AVERAGE HIGH/LOW TEMPERATURES					
JAN.	FEB.	MAR.	APR.	MAY	JUNE
62/32	65/37	72/40	80/50	90/55	100/65
JULY	AUG.	SEPT.	OCT.	NOV.	DEC.
105/70	101/78	96/62	85/55	72/40	62/31

Planning

When to Go

October through May, when the desert is cooler, is when most visitors arrive. Daytime temperatures range from the mid-70s in December and January to mid-90s in October and May. Lows can dip to near freezing in midwinter, and you may even encounter snow at the higher elevations. Summers can be torrid, with daytime temperatures reaching 110°F.

Getting Here and Around

AIR

Palm Springs International Airport is the closest major air gateway to Joshua Tree National Park. It's about 45 miles from the park. The drive from Los Angeles International Airport to Joshua Tree takes about two to three hours.

CAR

An isolated island of pristine wilderness—a rarity these days—Joshua Tree National Park is within a short drive of 11 million Southern California residents. Most visitors, in fact, make the two- to three-hour drive from the Los Angeles area to enjoy a weekend of solitude in 792,726 acres of untouched desert. The urban sprawl of Palm Springs (home to the nearest airport) is 45 miles away, but gateway towns Joshua Tree, Yucca Valley, and Twentynine Palms are just north of the park. If you're staying in the Palm Springs area, you can enjoy the highlights of the park in one day, including a stop for a picnic at a scenic spot. Within the park, passenger cars are fine for paved areas, but you'll need four-wheel drive for many of the rugged backcountry roadways. At the park's most popular sites, parking is limited. Joshua Tree does not have public transportation.

■ TIP→ **If you'd prefer not to drive, most Palm Springs area hotels can arrange a half- or full-day tour that hits the highlights of Joshua Tree National Park.** But you'll need to spend two or three days camping here to truly experience the quiet beauty of the desert.

Park Essentials

ACCESSIBILITY

Black Rock Canyon and Jumbo Rocks campgrounds have one accessible campsite each. Nature trails at Oasis of Mara, Bajada, Keys View, and Cap Rock are accessible. Some trails at roadside viewpoints can be negotiated by those with limited mobility.

PARK FEES AND PERMITS

Park admission is $30 per car; $15 per person on foot, bicycle, or horse; and $25 per person by motorcycle. The Joshua Tree Pass, good for one year, is $55.

PARK HOURS

The park is open every day, around the clock, but visitor centers are staffed from approximately 8 am to 5 pm. The park is in the Pacific time one.

CELL PHONE RECEPTION

Cell phones don't work in most areas of the park, and there are no telephones in its interior.

Joshua Tree in One Day

After stocking up on water, snacks, and lunch in Yucca Valley or Joshua Tree (you won't find any supplies inside the park), begin your visit at the **Joshua Tree Visitor Center,** where you can pick up maps and peruse exhibits to get acquainted with what awaits you. Enter the park itself at the nearby **West Entrance Station,** and continue driving along the highly scenic and well-maintained **Park Boulevard.** Stop first at **Hidden Valley** to relax at the picnic area or hike the easy, mile-long loop trail. After a few more miles, turn left onto the spur road to the trailhead for the **Barker Dam Nature Trail**. Walk the easy 1.1-mile loop to view a water tank ranchers built to quench their cattle's thirst; along the way, you'll spot birds and a handful of cactus varieties. Return to Park Boulevard and head south; you'll soon leave the main road again for the drive to **Keys View**. The easy loop trail here is only ¼ mile, but the views extend for miles in every direction—look for the San Andreas Fault, the Salton Sea, and nearby mountains. Return to Park Boulevard, where you'll find **Cap Rock,** another short loop trail winding amid rock formations and Joshua trees.

Continuing along Park Boulevard, the start of the 18-mile self-guided **Geology Tour Road** will soon appear on your right. A brochure outlining its 16 stops is available at visitor centers; note that the round-trip will take about two hours, and high-clearance, four-wheel-drive vehicles are recommended after stop 9. ■ TIP→ **Do not attempt if it has recently rained.** Back on Park Boulevard, you'll soon arrive at the aptly named **Skull Rock**. This downright spooky formation is next to the parking lot; a nearby trailhead marks the beginning of a 1.7-mile nature trail. End your day with a stop at the **Visitor Center** in Twentynine Palms, where you can stroll through the historic **Oasis of Mara,** popular with area settlers. ■ TIP→ **Reverse the itinerary to avoid long lines of cars at the Joshua Tree entrance on weekends and anytime during high season.** The 29 Palms entrance is just 15 miles east, and is usually less crowded, so precious parking spots are more likely to be available.

Hotels

Area lodging choices are limited to a few motels, chain hotels, vacation rentals, and several upscale establishments in the gateway towns. In general, most offer few amenities and are modestly priced. For a more extensive range of lodging options, you'll need to head to Palm Springs and the surrounding desert resort communities. Book ahead for the spring wildflower season—reservations may be difficult to obtain then.

Restaurants

Dining options in the gateway towns around the park are extremely limited—you'll mostly find fast-food outlets and a few casual eateries in Yucca Valley and Twentynine Palms. The exception is the restaurant at 29 Palms Inn, which has an interesting California-cuisine menu that features lots of veggies. For the most part, though, plan on traveling to the Palm Springs desert resort area for a fine-dining experience.

Hotel and restaurant reviews have been shortened. For full information visit Fodors.com. Hotel prices are the lowest cost of a standard double room in high season. Restaurant prices are the average cost of a main course at dinner, or if dinner is not served, at lunch.

What It Costs

$	$$	$$$	$$$$
RESTAURANTS			
under $17	$17–$26	$27–$36	over $36
HOTELS			
under $150	$150–$250	$251–$350	over $350

Tours

Big Wheel Tours

EXCURSIONS | Based in Palm Desert, Big Wheel Tours offers van excursions, jeep tours, and hiking trips through the park. Bicycle tours (road and mountain bike) are available outside the park boundary. Pickups are available at Palm Springs area hotels. ✉ *41625 Eclectic St., Suite O-1, Palm Desert* ☎ *760/779–1837* 🌐 *www.bwbtours.com* *From $169.*

Joshua Tree Adventures

GUIDED TOURS | A local family operates this well-respected tour company, which offers a range of customized private outings, from hikes and scenic tours to full- and multiday hike-and-climb combinations. ✉ *61622 El Cajon Dr., Joshua Tree* ☎ *802/673–4385* 🌐 *jtreeadventures.com* *From $70.*

★ Keys Ranch Tour

GUIDED TOURS | A guide takes you through the former home of a family that homesteaded here for 60 years. In addition to the ranch, a workshop, store, and schoolhouse are still standing, and the grounds are strewn with vehicles and mining equipment. The 90-minute tour, which begins at the Keys Ranch gate, tells the history of the family that built the ranch. Tickets are $10, and reservations are required. ✉ *Keys Ranch gate* ☎ *760/367–5522* 🌐 *www.nps.gov/jotr.*

Mojave Guides

SPECIAL-INTEREST | Led by resident and certified climbing instructor Seth Pettit, a team of expert guides provides customized half-, full-, and multiday technical rock-climbing courses for everyone from beginners to experts. ✉ *Joshua Tree* ☎ *760/820–2806* 🌐 *www.mojaveguides.com* *From $100.*

Twentynine Palms Astronomy Club

SPECIAL-INTEREST | Book a private night sky experience for 2 to 10 people led by astrophotographer Steve Caron and others who have a passion for sharing the night sky. They bring high-powered telescopes and other equipment to a location of your choice in the Morongo Basin—from Morongo Valley in the west to Wonder Valley in the east, plus Pioneertown and Landers. ✉ *Twentynine Palms* ☎ *760/401–3004* 🌐 *www.29palmsastronomy.org* *From $250 for a 2-hr session.*

Visitor Information

CONTACTS Joshua Tree National Park. ✉ *74485 National Park Dr., Twentynine Palms* ☎ *760/367–5522* 🌐 *www.nps.gov/jotr.*

Park Boulevard

Well-paved Park Boulevard—the park's main artery—loops between the west entrance near the town of Joshua Tree and the north entrance just south of Twentynine Palms. If you have time only for a short visit, driving Park Boulevard is your best choice. It traverses the most scenic portions of Joshua Tree in the park's high-desert section. Along with some sweeping desert views, you'll see jumbles of splendid boulder formations, stands of Joshua trees, and Hidden Valley and Barker Dam, remnants of the area's wild and woolly past. From the Oasis Visitor Center, drive south. After about 5 miles, the road forks; turn right and head west toward Jumbo Rocks (clearly marked with a road sign).

Sights

HISTORIC SIGHTS

Hidden Valley

NATURE SITE | **FAMILY** | This legendary cattle-rustlers' hideout is set among big boulders along a 1-mile loop trail. Kids love to scramble on and around the rocks. There are shaded picnic tables here. ✉ *Park Blvd.* ✣ *14 miles south of west entrance.*

★ Keys Ranch

HOUSE | This 150-acre ranch, which once belonged to William and Frances Keys and is now on the National Historic Register, illustrates one of the area's most successful attempts at homesteading. The couple raised five children under extreme desert conditions. Most of the original buildings, including the house, school, store, and workshop, have been restored to the way they were when William died in 1969. The only way to see the ranch is on one of the 90-minute walking tours, usually offered Friday–Sunday, October–May and weekends in summer; reservations are required. ✉ *Joshua Tree National Park* ✣ *2 miles north of Barker Dam Rd.* ☎ *877/444–6777* 🌐 *www.nps.gov/jotr/planyourvisit/ranch-tour.htm* 🎟 *$10, reservations through recreation.gov.*

SCENIC STOPS

Barker Dam

DAM | Built around 1900 by ranchers and miners to hold water for cattle and mining operations, the dam now collects rainwater and is a good place to spot wildlife such as the elusive bighorn sheep. ✉ *Barker Dam Rd.* ✣ *Off Park Blvd., 10 miles south of west entrance.*

TRAILS

Hidden Valley Trail

TRAIL | **FAMILY** | Crawl through the rocks surrounding Hidden Valley to see where cattle rustlers supposedly hung out on this 1-mile loop. *Easy.* ✉ *Joshua Tree National Park* ✣ *Trailhead: At Hidden Valley Picnic Area.*

★ Ryan Mountain Trail

TRAIL | The payoff for hiking to the top of 5,461-foot Ryan Mountain is one of the best panoramic views of Joshua Tree. From here, you can see Mt. San Jacinto, Mt. San Gorgonio, Lost Horse Valley, and the Pinto Basin. You'll need two to three hours to complete the 3-mile round-trip with 1,000-plus feet of elevation gain. *Moderate.* ✉ *Joshua Tree National Park* ✣ *Trailhead: At Ryan Mountain parking area, 13 miles southeast of park's west entrance, or Sheep Pass, 16 miles southwest of Oasis Visitor Center.*

Skull Rock Trail

TRAIL | The 1.7-mile loop guides hikers through boulder piles, desert washes, and a rocky alley. It's named for what is perhaps the park's most famous rock formation, which resembles the eye sockets and nasal cavity of a human skull. Access the trail from within Jumbo Rocks Campground or from a small parking area on the highway just east of the campground. *Easy.* ✉ *Joshua Tree National Park* ✣ *Trailhead: At Jumbo Rocks Campground.*

Split Rock Loop Trail

TRAIL | Experience rocks, trees, and geological wonders along this 2½-mile loop trail (including a short spur to Face Rock) through boulder fields and oak and pine woodlands up to Joshua tree stands. *Moderate.* ✉ *Joshua Tree National Park* ✣ *Trailhead: Along dirt road off main Park Blvd. (signs point the way).*

VISITOR CENTERS

Joshua Tree Visitor Center

INFO CENTER | This visitor center has maps and interesting exhibits illustrating park geology, cultural and historic sites, and hiking and rock-climbing activities. There's also a small bookstore and café. Restrooms with flush toilets are on the premises. ✉ *6554 Park Blvd., Joshua Tree* ☎ *760/366–1855* 🌐 *www.nps.gov/jotr.*

Keys View Road

Keys View Road travels south from Park Boulevard from Cap Rock up to Keys View, the best vista point in the park. If you plan to hike up to historic Lost Horse Mine, you'll find the trailhead along the way.

HISTORIC SIGHTS

Lost Horse Mine

MINE | This historic mine, which produced 10,000 ounces of gold and 16,000 ounces of silver between 1894 and 1931, was among Southern California's most productive mines. The 10-stamp mill is considered one of the best preserved of its type in the park system. The site is accessed via a fairly strenuous, 4-mile, round-trip hike. Mind the park warnings, and don't enter any mine in Joshua Tree. ✉ *Keys View Rd.* ✥ *About 15 miles south of west entrance.*

SCENIC STOPS

★ Keys View

VIEWPOINT | At 5,185 feet, this point affords a sweeping view of the Santa Rosa Mountains and Coachella Valley, the San Andreas Fault, the peak of 11,500-foot Mt. San Gorgonio, the shimmering surface of Salton Sea, and—on a rare clear day—Signal Mountain in Mexico. Sunrise and sunset are magical times, when the light throws rocks and trees into high relief before bathing the hills in brilliant shades of red, orange, and gold. ✉ *Keys View Rd.* ✥ *16 miles south of park's west entrance.*

TRAILS

Cap Rock

TRAIL | This ½-mile, wheelchair-accessible loop—named after a boulder that sits atop a huge rock formation like a cap—winds through other fascinating rock formations and has signs that explain the geology of the Mojave Desert. *Easy.* ✉ *Joshua Tree National Park* ✥ *Trailhead: Keys View Rd. near junction with Park Blvd.*

Highway 62

Highway 62 stretches along the northern border of the park, from Yucca Valley in the West and Twentynine Palms in the east. Visitors can access the Black Rock, Indian Cove, Fortynine Palms, and Oasis of Mara sections of the park off this road, as well as the main visitor centers and park entrances in Joshua Tree and Twentynine Palms.

SCENIC STOPS

Fortynine Palms Oasis

NATIVE SITE | A short drive off Highway 62, this site is a bit of a preview of what the park's interior has to offer: stands of fan palms, interesting petroglyphs, and evidence of fires built by early Native Americans. Because animals frequent this area, you may spot a coyote, bobcat, or roadrunner. ✉ *End of Canyon Rd.* ✥ *4 miles west of Twentynine Palms.*

Indian Cove

RESTAURANT—SIGHT | The view from here is of rock formations that draw thousands of climbers to the park each year. This isolated area is reached via Twentynine Palms Highway. ✉ *End of Indian Cove Rd.*

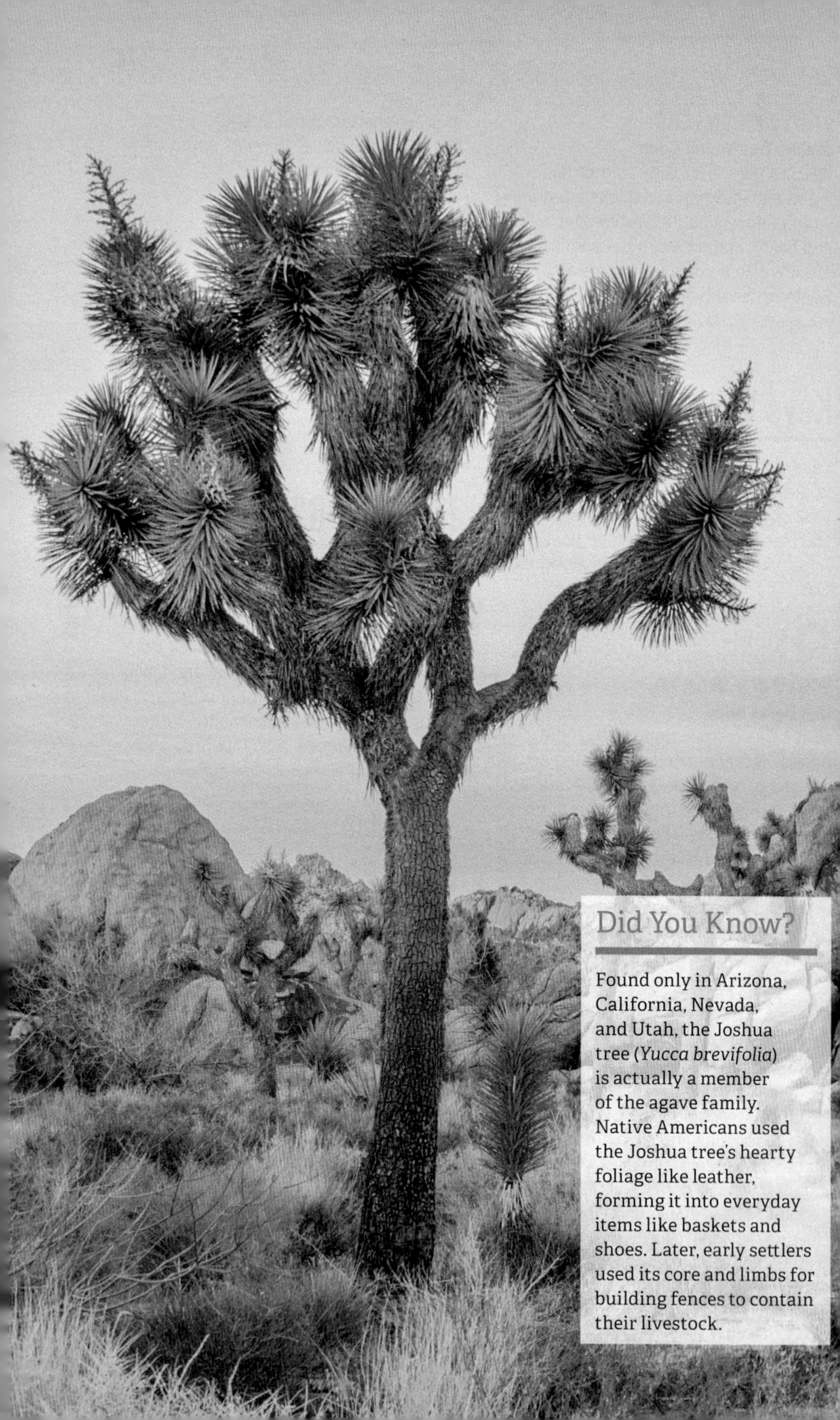

Did You Know?

Found only in Arizona, California, Nevada, and Utah, the Joshua tree (*Yucca brevifolia*) is actually a member of the agave family. Native Americans used the Joshua tree's hearty foliage like leather, forming it into everyday items like baskets and shoes. Later, early settlers used its core and limbs for building fences to contain their livestock.

TRAILS

Hi-View Nature Trail

TRAIL | This 1.3-mile loop climbs nearly to the top of 4,500-foot Summit Peak. The views of nearby Mt. San Gorgonio (snow-capped in winter) make the moderately steep journey worth the effort. You can pick up a pamphlet describing the vegetation you'll see along the way at any visitor center. *Moderate.* ✉ *Joshua Tree National Park* ✣ *Trailhead: ½ mile west of Black Rock Canyon Campground.*

Indian Cove Trail

TRAIL | Look for lizards and roadrunners along this ½-mile loop that follows a desert wash. A walk along this well-signed trail reveals signs of Native American habitation, animals, and flora such as desert willow and yucca. *Easy.* ✉ *Joshua Tree National Park* ✣ *Trailhead: At west end of Indian Cove Campground.*

Oasis of Mara Trail

TRAIL | A stroll along this short, wheelchair-accessible trail, located just outside the visitor center, reveals how early settlers took advantage of this oasis, which was first settled by the Serrano tribe. *Mara* means "place of little springs and much grass" in their language. The Serrano, who farmed the oasis until the mid-1850s, planted one palm tree for each male baby born during the first year of the settlement. *Easy.* ✉ *Joshua Tree National Park* ✣ *Trailhead: At Oasis Visitor Center.*

VISITOR CENTERS

Oasis Visitor Center

INFO CENTER | Exhibits here illustrate how Joshua Tree was formed, reveal the differences between the park's two types of desert, and demonstrate how plants and animals eke out an existence in this arid climate. Take the ½-mile nature walk through the nearby Oasis of Mara, which is alive with palm trees and mesquite shrubs. Facilities include picnic tables, restrooms, and a bookstore. ✉ *74485 National Park Dr., Twentynine Palms* ☎ *760/367–5500* 🌐 *www.nps.gov/jotr.*

Pinto Basin Road

This paved road takes you from high Mojave desert to low Colorado desert. A long, slow drive, the route runs from the main part of the park to Interstate 10; it can add as much as an hour to and from Palm Springs (round-trip), but the views and roadside exhibits make it worth the extra time. From the Oasis Visitor Center, drive south. After about 5 miles, the road forks; take a left, and continue another 9 miles to the Cholla Cactus Garden, where the sun fills the cactus needles with light. Past that is the Ocotillo Patch, filled with spindly plants bearing razor-sharp thorns and, after a rain, bright green leaves and brilliant red flowers. Side trips from this route require a 4X4.

SCENIC DRIVES

Geology Tour Road

SCENIC DRIVE | Some of the park's most fascinating landscapes can be observed from this 18-mile dirt road. Parts of the journey are rough; a 4X4 vehicle is required after mile marker 9. Sights to see include a 100-year-old stone dam called Squaw Tank, defunct mines, and a large plain with an abundance of Joshua trees. There are 16 stops along the way, so give yourself about two hours to complete the round-trip trek. ✉ *South of Park Blvd., west of Jumbo Rocks.*

SCENIC STOPS

Cholla Cactus Garden

GARDEN | This stand of bigelow cholla (sometimes called jumping cholla, because its hooked spines seem to jump at you) is best seen and photographed in late afternoon, when the backlit spiky stalks stand out against a colorful sky. ✉ *Pinto Basin Rd.* ✣ *20 miles north of Cottonwood Visitor Center.*

Cottonwood Spring

NATIVE SITE | Home to the native Cahuilla people for centuries, this spring provided water for travelers and early prospectors. The area, which supports a large stand of fan palms and cottonwood trees, is one of the best stops for bird-watching, as migrating birds (and bighorn sheep) rely on the water as well. A number of gold mines were located here, and the area still has some remains, including concrete pillars. ✉ *Cottonwood Visitor Center.*

Lost Palms Oasis

TRAIL | More than 100 fan palms comprise the largest group of the exotic plants in the park. A spring bubbles from between the rocks but disappears into the sandy, boulder-strewn canyon. The 7½-mile, round-trip hike is not for everyone, and not recommended during summer months. Bring plenty of water! ✉ *Cottonwood Visitor Center.*

Ocotillo Patch

GARDEN | Stop here for a roadside exhibit on the dramatic display made by the red-tipped succulent after even the shortest rain shower. ✉ *Pinto Basin Rd.* ✣ *About 3 miles east of Cholla Cactus Gardens.*

TRAILS

Bajada

TRAIL | Learn all about what plants do to survive in the Colorado Desert on this ¼-mile loop. *Easy.* ✉ *Joshua Tree National Park* ✣ *Trailhead: South of Cottonwood Visitor Center, ½ mile from park entrance.*

Mastodon Peak Trail

TRAIL | Some boulder scrambling is optional on this 3-mile hike that loops up to the 3,371-foot Mastodon Peak, and the journey rewards you with stunning views of the Salton Sea. The trail passes through a region where gold was mined from 1919 to 1932, so be on the lookout for open mines. The peak draws its name from a large rock formation that early miners believed looked like the head of a prehistoric behemoth. *Moderate.* ✉ *Joshua Tree National Park* ✣ *Trailhead: At Cottonwood Spring Oasis.*

VISITOR CENTERS

Cottonwood Visitor Center

INFO CENTER | The south entrance is the closest to Interstate 10, the east–west highway from Los Angeles to Phoenix. Exhibits in this small center, staffed by rangers and volunteers, illustrate the region's natural history. The center also has restrooms with flush toilets. ✉ *Cottonwood Spring, Pinto Basin Rd.* 🌐 *www.nps.gov/jotr.*

Activities

BIKING

Covington Flats

BICYCLING | This 4-mile route takes you past impressive Joshua trees as well as pinyon pines, junipers, and areas of lush desert vegetation. It's tough going toward the end, but once you reach 5,518-foot Eureka Peak you'll have great views of Palm Springs, the Morongo Basin, and the surrounding mountains. ✉ *Joshua Tree National Park* ✣ *Trailhead: At Covington Flats picnic area, La Contenta Rd., 10 miles south of Rte. 62.*

Pinkham Canyon and Thermal Canyon Roads

BICYCLING | This challenging 20-mile route begins at the Cottonwood Visitor Center and loops through the Cottonwood Mountains. The unpaved trail follows Smoke Tree Wash through Pinkham Canyon, rounds Thermal Canyon, and loops back to the beginning. Rough and narrow in places, the road travels through soft sand and rocky floodplains. ✉ *Joshua Tree National Park* ✣ *Trailhead: At Cottonwood Visitor Center.*

Queen Valley

BICYCLING | This 13.4-mile network of mostly level roads winds through one of the park's most impressive groves of Joshua trees. You can also leave your bike at one of the racks placed in the area and explore on foot. ✉ *Joshua Tree National Park* ✣ *Trailhead: At Hidden Valley*

Campground, and accessible opposite Geology Tour Rd. at Big Horn Pass.

BIRD-WATCHING

Joshua Tree, located on the inland portion of the Pacific Flyway, hosts about 250 species of birds, and the park is a popular seasonal location for bird-watching. During the fall migration, which runs mid-September through mid-October, there are several reliable sighting areas. At Barker Dam you might spot white-throated swifts, several types of swallows, or red-tailed hawks. Lucy's warblers, flycatchers, and Anna's hummingbirds cruise around Cottonwood Spring, a serene palm-shaded setting; occasional ducks, herons, and egrets, as well as migrating rufous and calliope hummingbirds, wintering prairie falcons, and a resident barn owl could show up. Black Rock Canyon sees pinyon jays, while Covington Flats reliably gets mountain quail, and you may see La Conte's thrashers, ruby-crowned kinglets, and warbling vireos at either locale. Rufous hummingbirds, Pacific slope flycatchers, and various warblers are frequent visitors to Indian Cove. Lists of birds found in the park, as well as information on recent sightings, are available at visitor centers.

CAMPING

Park campgrounds, set at elevations from 3,000 to 4,500 feet, have only primitive facilities; few have drinking water. Most accept reservations up to six months in advance but only for October through Memorial Day. Campsites at Belle, Hidden Valley, and White Tank are first-come, first-served. Belle and White Tank campgrounds, and parts of Black Rock Canyon, Cottonwood, and Indian Cove campgrounds, are closed from the day after Memorial Day to September. ■ **TIP→ Campgrounds fill quickly, so reserve well in advance. Also, the park may soon require reservations at all campgrounds.**

Belle Campground. This small campground is popular with families as there are a number of boulders kids can scramble over and around. ✉ *9 miles south of Oasis of Mara* ☎ *760/367–5500* 🌐 *www.nps.gov/jotr.*

Black Rock Canyon Campground. Set among juniper bushes, cholla cacti, and other desert shrubs, Black Rock Canyon is one of the park's prettiest campgrounds. ✉ *Joshua La., south of Hwy. 62 and Hwy. 247* ☎ *877/444–6777* 🌐 *www.recreation.gov.*

Cottonwood Campground. In spring, this campground, the southernmost one in the park (and therefore often the last to fill up), is surrounded by some of the desert's finest wildflowers and is a great spot to watch the night sky. ✉ *Pinto Basin Rd., 32 miles south of North Entrance Station* ☎ *877/444–6777* 🌐 *www.nps.gov/jotr.*

Hidden Valley Campground. This campground is a favorite with rock climbers, who make their way up valley formations that have names like the Blob, Old Woman, and Chimney Rock. ✉ *Off Park Blvd., 20 miles southwest of Oasis of Mara* ☎ *760/367–5500* 🌐 *www.nps.gov/jotr.*

Indian Cove Campground. This is a sought-after spot for rock climbers, primarily because it lies among the 50 square miles of rugged terrain at the Wonderland of Rocks. ✉ *Indian Cove Rd., south of Hwy. 62* ☎ *877/444–6777* 🌐 *www.nps.gov/jotr.*

Jumbo Rocks. Each campsite at this well-regarded campground tucked among giant boulders has a bit of privacy. It's a good home base for visiting many of Joshua Tree's attractions. ✉ *Park Blvd., 11 miles from Oasis of Mara* ☎ *877/444–6777* 🌐 *www.nps.gov/jotr.*

Learn about the park's flora and fauna by attending the ranger programs.

White Tank. This small, quiet campground is popular with families because a nearby trail leads to a natural arch. ✉ *Pinto Basin Rd., 11 miles south of Oasis of Mara* ☎ *760/367–5500* 🌐 *www.nps.gov/jotr.*

EDUCATIONAL PROGRAMS

The Desert Institute at Joshua Tree National Park

COLLEGE | The nonprofit educational partner of the park offers a full schedule of lectures, classes, and hikes. Class topics include basket making, painting, and photography, while field trips include workshops on cultural history, natural science, and how to survive in the desert. ✉ *74485 National Park Dr., Twentynine Palms* ☎ *760/367–5535* 🌐 *www.joshuatree.org.*

Stargazing

COLLEGE | At Joshua Tree National Park, designated an International Dark Sky Park in 2017, you can tour the Milky Way on summer evenings using binoculars. Rangers also offer programs on some evenings when the moon isn't visible. Browse the schedule online. The park also partners with Sky's the Limit Observatory on the Utah Trail in Twentynine Palms (🌐 *www.skysthelimit29.org*); check the website for current offerings. ✉ *Cottonwood Campground Amphitheater, Oasis Visitor Center, Sky's the Limit Observatory* 🌐 *www.nps.gov/jotr/planyourvisit/calendar.htm.*

RANGER PROGRAMS

Evening Programs

TOUR—SIGHT | Rangers present 45-minute-long programs, often on Friday or Saturday evening, at Cottonwood Amphitheater, Indian Cove Amphitheater, and Jumbo Rocks Campground. Topics range from natural history to local lore. As times and days for such offerings aren't fixed, it's best to check the online schedule. ✉ *Joshua Tree National Park* 🎟 *Free.*

HIKING

There are more than 190 miles of hiking trails in Joshua Tree, ranging from ¼-mile nature trails to 35-mile treks. Some connect with each other, so you can design your own desert maze. Remember that drinking water is hard to come by—you won't find it in the park except at the entrances. Bring along at least a gallon per person for all but the shortest hikes, more if the weather is hot.

Before striking out on a hike or apparent nature trail, check out the signage. Roadside signage identifies hiking- and rock-climbing routes.

ROCK CLIMBING

With an abundance of weathered igneous boulder outcroppings, Joshua Tree is one of the nation's top winter-climbing destinations. There are more than 4,500 established routes offering a full menu of climbing experiences—from bouldering for beginners in the Wonderland of Rocks to multiple-pitch climbs at Echo Rock and Saddle Rock. The best-known climb in the park is Hidden Valley's Sports Challenge Rock. A map inside the *Joshua Tree Guide* shows locations of selected wilderness and nonwilderness climbs.

Joshua Tree Rock Climbing School

CLIMBING/MOUNTAINEERING | The school offers several programs, from one-day introductory classes to multiday programs for experienced climbers, and provides all needed equipment. Beginning classes, offered year-round on most weekends, are limited to six people age eight or older. ✉ *Joshua Tree National Park* ☎ *760/366–4745* 🌐 *www.joshuatreerockclimbing.com* 🎫 *From $195.*

Vertical Adventures Rock Climbing School

CLIMBING/MOUNTAINEERING | About 1,000 climbers each year learn the sport in Joshua Tree National Park through this school. Classes, offered September–May, meet at a designated location in the park, and all equipment is provided. ✉ *Joshua Tree National Park* ☎ *800/514–8785 office, 949/322–6108 mobile/text* 🌐 *www.vertical-adventures.com* 🎫 *From $165.*

What's Nearby

Joshua Tree

12 miles east of Yucca Valley.

Artists and renegades have long found solace in the small upcountry desert town of Joshua Tree, home to artsy vintage shops, cafés, and B&Bs and a gateway to Joshua Tree National Park. Those who zip through town might wonder what all the hype is about, but if you slow down and spend time chatting with the folks in this funky community, you'll find much to love.

GETTING HERE AND AROUND

Highway 62 is the main route to and through Joshua Tree. Most businesses are here or along Park Boulevard as it heads toward the park.

Sights

★ Noah Purifoy Desert Art Museum of Assemblage Art

ARTS VENUE | This vast, 10-acre art installation full of "assemblage art" on a sandy tract of land in the town of Joshua Tree honors the work of artist Noah Purifoy. The sculptures blend with the spare desert in an almost postapocalyptic way. Purifoy lived most of his life in this desert until his death is 2004. He used found materials to make commentary on social issues. His art has been showcased at LACMA, J. Paul Getty Museum, MOCA, and many more. ✉ *63030 Blair La.* 🌐 *www.noahpurifoy.com* 🎫 *Free* 🕓 *Closes at sunset.*

Restaurants

Crossroads Cafe

$$ | **AMERICAN** | Mexican breakfasts, chicken-cilantro soup, and hearty sandwiches are among the draws at this Joshua Tree institution for prehike breakfasts, birthday lunches, and early dinners. Taxidermied animals and beer-can lights hint at the

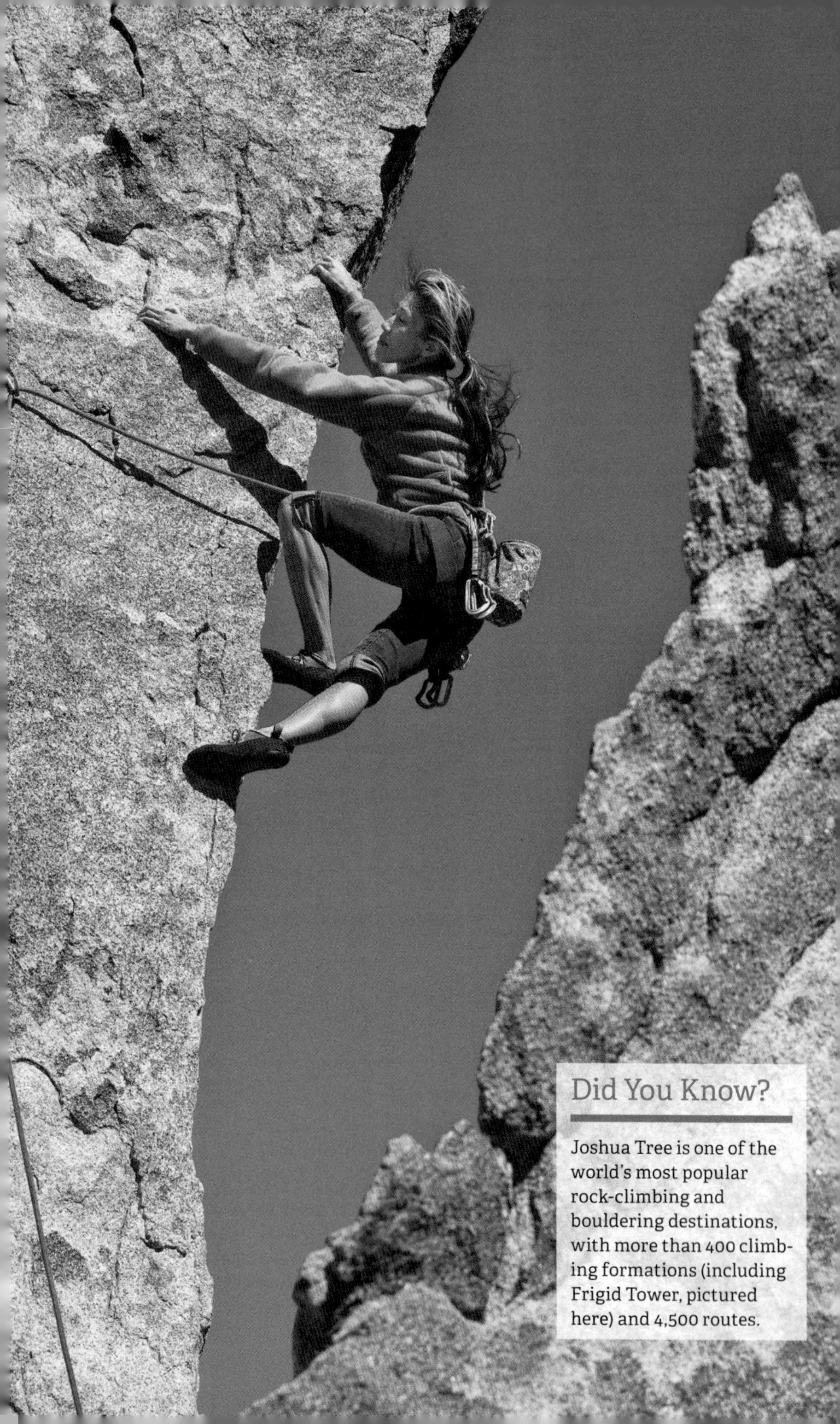

Did You Know?

Joshua Tree is one of the world's most popular rock-climbing and bouldering destinations, with more than 400 climbing formations (including Frigid Tower, pictured here) and 4,500 routes.

community's consciousness, while the tattooed waitresses and slew of veggie options make it clear that the Crossroads is unlike anywhere else in San Bernardino County. **Known for:** rustic wooden interior and bar; hearty and affordable meals; vegetarian and vegan dishes. $ *Average main: $12 ✉ 61715 Twentynine Palms Hwy. ☎ 760/366–5414 🌐 crossroadscafe-jtree.com.*

Twentynine Palms

12 miles east of Joshua Tree.

The main gateway town to Joshua Tree National Park, Twentynine Palms is also the location of the U.S. Marine Air Ground Task Force Training Center. You can find services, supplies, and lodging in town.

GETTING HERE AND AROUND

Highway 62 is the main route to and through Twentynine Palms. Most businesses here center on Highway 62 and Utah Trail, 3 miles north of Joshua Tree's entrance.

ESSENTIALS

VISITOR INFORMATION Twentynine Palms Visitor Center and Gallery. *✉ 73484 Twentynine Palms Hwy. 🌐 www.visit29.org.*

Sights

Oasis of Murals

PUBLIC ART | Twenty-six murals painted on the sides of buildings depict the history, wildlife, and landscape of Twentynine Palms. You can't miss the art on a drive around town, but you can also pick up a free map from the visitor center. *✉ Twentynine Palms 🌐 www.action29palmsmurals.com.*

Sky's the Limit Observatory & Nature Center

OBSERVATORY | Run by a dedicated, local nonprofit, this 15-acre park near the northern entrance to Joshua Tree National Park educates visitors on the region's celestial and terrestial attributes. It has an observatory dome with a 14-inch telescope, nature trails that feature desert plants, a meditation garden, and an orrery (a scaled rendition of what's happening in the night sky). The public is invited to free star parties every Saturday night (except when the moon is full) and to join classes, clinics, and special programs. *✉ 9697 Utah Trail ☎ 760/490–9561 🌐 www.skysthelimit29.org.*

29 Palms Art Gallery

MUSEUM | This gallery features work by local painters, sculptors, and jewelry makers inspired by the desert landscape. If you find yourself inspired as well, sign up for one of the day-long art workshops. *✉ 74055 Cottonwood Dr. ☎ 760/367–7819 🌐 www.29palmsartgallery.com ⏲ Closed Mon.–Wed. Also closed Thurs. in summer.*

Restaurants

Campbell Hill Bakery

$ | **BAKERY** | Prepare to wait in line to order from the counter at this tiny but exceedingly popular eatery, owned and operated by professionals in the bakery business who escaped from New York City to the California high desert. Delectable loaves of bread, scones, muffins, and other sweet and savory treats take center stage, but you can also pick up sandwiches and various entrées—from beef pot pie and flatbreads to pizza and lasagna. **Known for:** hefty Cubano, Philly cheesesteak, and Italian subs; daily specials; good place to pick up food before touring the park. $ *Average main: $12 ✉ 73491 Twentynine Palms Hwy. ☎ 760/401–8284 🌐 campbellhillbakery.com ⏲ No dinner. Closed Sun.*

Kitchen in the Desert

$ | **AMERICAN** | This popular spot in a renovated courtyard complex with murals and mining artifacts serves comfort food with a Caribbean flair. The chef, who hails from Trinidad, creates artful dishes derived from family recipes with dashes of American and global influences—for example, Trinidadian doubles (curried chickpeas with dahl bread, cucumbers, and tamarind sauce), Dan Dan noodles (cumin-spiced pork and soba noodles with tahini), bacon burgers, and fried Oreos and donuts for dessert. **Known for:** convenient location near the junction of Highway 62 and National Park Drive; meats grilled or smoked outdoors over a mesquite fire; vegetarian and gluten-free dishes. *Average main: $15 6427 Mesquite Ave. 760/865–0245 kitcheninthedesert.com No lunch.*

Hotels

Campbell House

$$ | **B&B/INN** | To the wealthy pioneer who erected the stone mansion now occupied by this bed-and-breakfast, expense was no object, which is evident in the 50-foot-long, planked-maple floor in the great room, the intricate carpentry, and the huge stone fireplaces that warm the house on the rare cold night. **Pros:** elegant rooms and public spaces; access to amenities at sister property, 29 Palms Inn; great horned owls on property. **Cons:** somewhat isolated location; three-story main building doesn't have an elevator; no TVs or refrigerators in some rooms. *Rooms from: $165 74744 Joe Davis Dr. 760/367–3238 www.campbellhouse29palms.com 12 units Free breakfast.*

Harmony Motel

$ | **HOTEL** | In 1987, the rock band U2 stayed at the roadside Harmony Motel—set on two acres of natural desert with onubstructed views of the mountains of Joshua Tree National Park—while posing for images to adorn their legendary album *U2: The Joshua Tree*. **Pros:** cactus gardens and nature trail; outdoor pool and hot tub; close to Fortynine Palms Oasis and Indian Cove. **Cons:** small property that books quickly; not close to restaurants or entertainment; on a busy highway. *Rooms from: $95 71161 Twentynine Palms Hwy. 760/367–3351 www.harmonymotel.com 11 units No meals.*

Sunnyvale Garden Suites

$ | **HOTEL** | Bay Area retirees transformed this former 1990s condominium complex into an all-suite hotel with paths that meander through carefully tended desert gardens that have sitting areas. **Pros:** outdoor hot tub, game room, community patio with fire pit, exercise room; close to national park entrance and military base; personal attention from owners and staff. **Cons:** noise can travel through thin walls and ceilings; no breakfast included; 3 miles to nearest grocery store. *Rooms from: $111 73843 Sunnyvale Dr. 760/361–3939 sunnyvalesuites.com 21 suites No meals.*

★ 29 Palms Inn

$$ | **B&B/INN** | **FAMILY** | The closest lodging to the entrance to Joshua Tree National Park, the funky 29 Palms Inn scatters a collection of adobe and wood-frame cottages, some dating back to the 1920s and 1930s, over 70 acres of grounds that include the ancient Oasis of Mara, a popular destination for birds and bird-watchers year-round. **Pros:** gracious hospitality; exceptional bird-watching; art gallery, pool, and on-site restaurant. **Cons:** rustic accommodations; limited amenities; no in-room Wi-Fi. *Rooms from: $140 73950 Inn Ave. 760/367–3505 www.29palmsinn.com 24 units Free breakfast.*

Chapter 9

MOJAVE DESERT

Updated by
Cheryl Crabtree

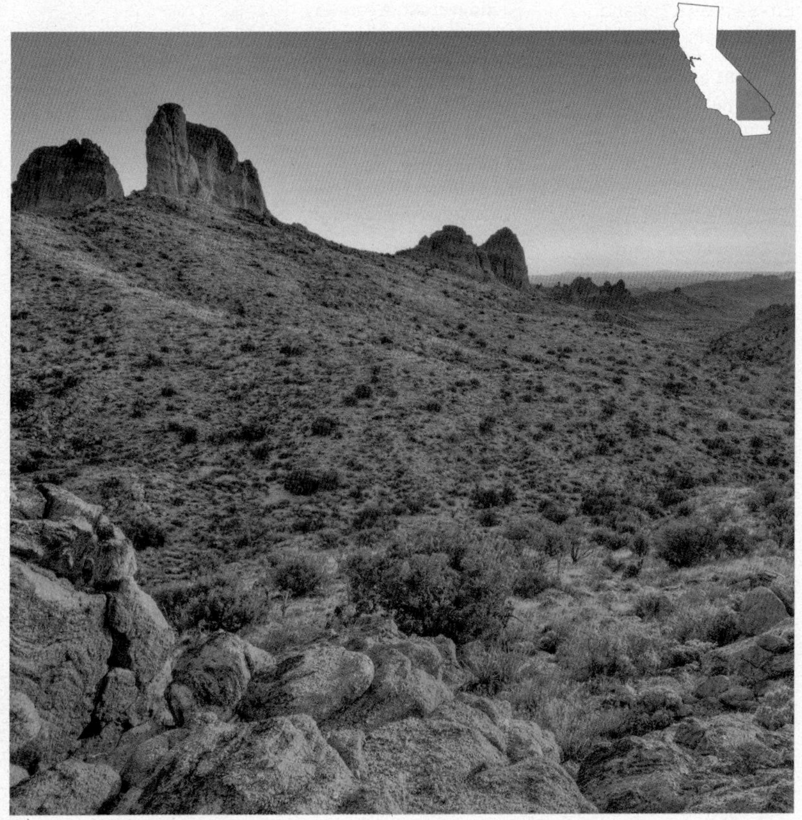

Sights ★★★★★
Restaurants ★★☆☆☆
Hotels ★☆☆☆☆
Shopping ★☆☆☆☆
Nightlife ★☆☆☆☆

WELCOME TO MOJAVE DESERT

TOP REASONS TO GO

★ **Nostalgia:** Old neon signs, historic motels, and restored (or neglected but still striking) rail stations abound across this desert landscape. Don't miss the classic eateries along the way, including Emma Jean's Holland Burger Cafe in Victorville.

★ **Great ghost towns:** California's gold rush brought miners to the Mojave, and the towns they left behind have their own unique charms.

★ **Desert flora and fauna:** Explore the Mojave National Preserve to view Joshua trees, volcanic cinder cones, huge sand dunes, desert tortoises, and other natural wonders. Combine a visit to the Mojave with one to Death Valley to experience still more of the region's unique desert terrain.

★ **Explore ancient history:** The Mojave Desert is replete with rare petroglyphs, some dating back almost 16,000 years.

1 Lancaster. Poppies and aerospace tech (including Edwards Air Force Base) thrive in and near this western Mojave hub.

2 Red Rock Canyon State Park. Colorful formations, Native American heritage, and mining history converge in an eerily gorgeous setting.

3 Ridgecrest. A gateway to Death Valley, the northern Mojave's largest town is a welcome oasis near Trona Pinnacles and Petroglyph Canyons.

4 Randsburg. Wander the well-preserved streets of a historic mining town.

5 Victorville. Experience the Mother Road at the California Route 66 Museum.

6 Barstow. Visit the Mojave's "capital" to explore museums (many in the restored Harvey House depot) and Calico Ghost town.

7 Mojave National Preserve. Ancient lava beds, rare plants and animals, and towering dunes are among this 1.6-million-acre sanctuary's sights.

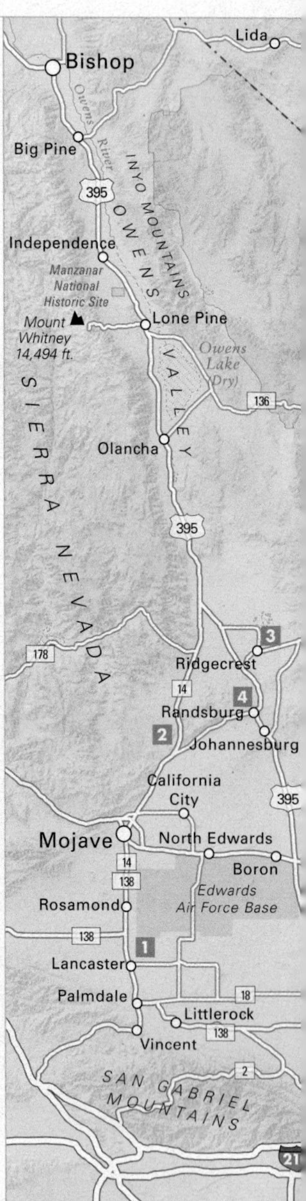

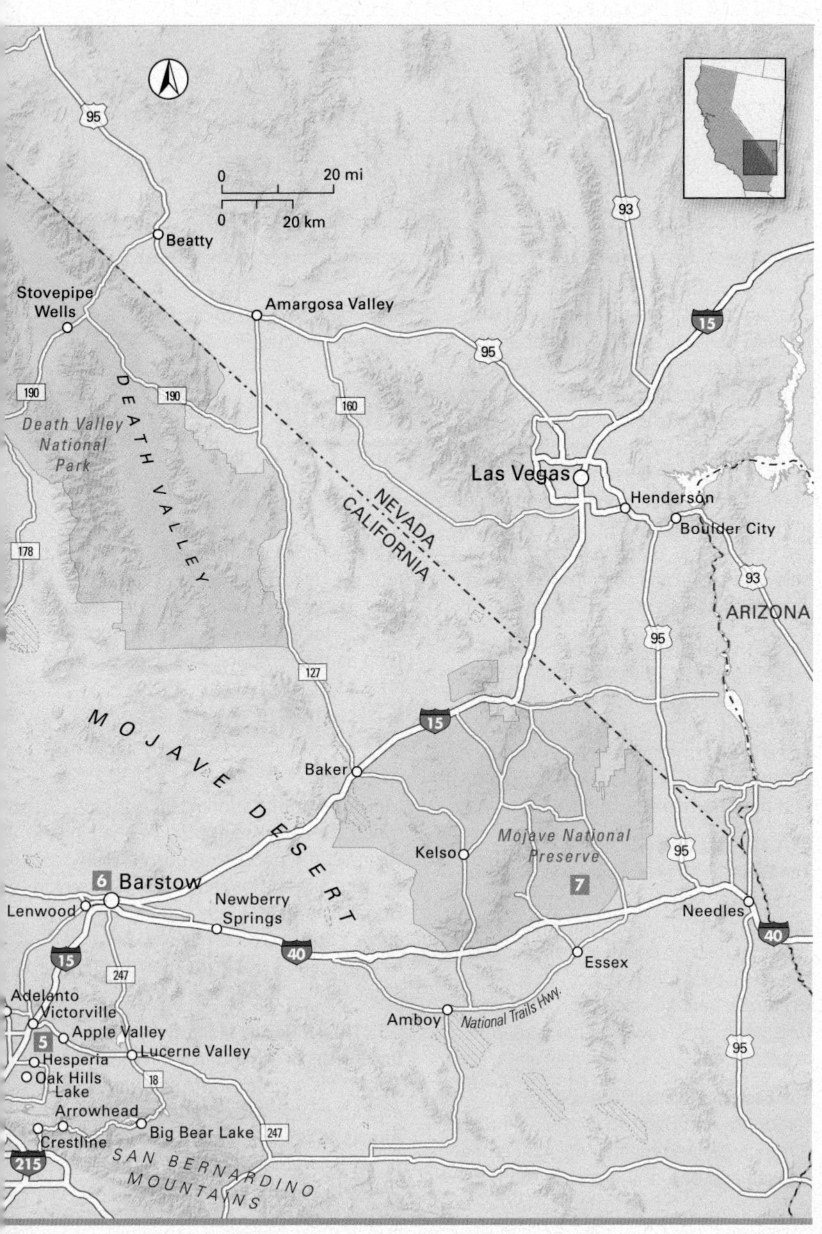
0 20 mi
0 20 km
Beatty
Stovepipe Wells
Amargosa Valley
Death Valley National Park
DEATH VALLEY
NEVADA
CALIFORNIA
Las Vegas
Henderson
Boulder City
ARIZONA
MOJAVE DESERT
Baker
Kelso
Mojave National Preserve
7
6 Barstow
Lenwood
Newberry Springs
Needles
Essex
Amboy
National Trails Hwy.
Adelanto
Victorville
5
Apple Valley
Hesperia
Oak Hills
Lucerne Valley
Lake Arrowhead
Crestline
Big Bear Lake
SAN BERNARDINO MOUNTAINS
95
93
15
190
160
178
127
40
247
18
215

Dust and desolation, tumbleweeds and rattlesnakes, barren landscapes and failed dreams—these are the bleak images that come to mind when most people hear the word *desert*. Yet the remote regions east of the Sierra Nevada possess a singular beauty.

The vast spaces here are peppered with creosite bushes, spiky Joshua trees and cacti, undulating sand dunes, faulted mountains, and dramatic rock formations. The topography is extreme: the Mojave Desert, once part of an ancient inland sea, is one of the largest swaths of open land in Southern California, with elevations ranging from 3,000 to 5,000 feet, while Death Valley, to the north, drops to almost 300 feet below sea level and contains the lowest (and hottest) spot in North America.

Access to the Mojave is via I–40 and I–15, Highways 14 and 95, and U.S. 395. As abandoned homesteads can attest, the area is not heavily populated, with just a few communities separated by expanses in which visitors can both lose and find themselves.

MAJOR REGIONS

The Western Mojave. Lancaster, Red Rock Canyon State Park, Ridgecrest, and Randsburg are all in this vast area, where wildflowers bloom in spring and snow caps the mountain peaks year-round. The scenery is especially beautiful along U.S. 395, which runs north up to towns at the western edge of Death Valley National Park.

The Eastern Mojave. Here you'll find Victorville and Barstow, the main hubs of a region defined by majestic, wide-open spaces and one of the state's most rewarding but demanding destinations: Mojave National Preserve.

Planning

When to Go

Spring and fall are the best seasons to tour the desert. Winters are generally mild, but summers can be cruel. If you're on a budget, be aware that room rates drop as the temperatures rise.

Getting Here and Around

AIR

McCarran International (slated to be renamed Harry Reid International) in Las Vegas is the nearest airport to many eastern Mojave destinations. Hollywood Burbank is the largest and closest airport to the western Mojave region. Barstow and Inyokern airports serve small, private planes.

CONTACTS County of San Bernardino Department of Airports. ✉ *For Needles and Barstow-Daggett* 🌐 *cms.sbcounty.gov/airports/Home.aspx*. **Hollywood Burbank Airport.** ✉ *2627 N. Hollywood Way, Burbank* ☎ *818/840–8840* 🌐 *hollywoodburbankairport.com*. **Inyokern Airport.** ✉ *1669*

Airport Rd., off Hwy. 178, 9 miles west of Ridgecrest, Inyokern ☎ *760/377–5844* 🌐 *www.inyokernairport.com.* **McCarran International Airport.** ✉ *5757 Wayne Newton Blvd., Las Vegas* ☎ *702/261–5211* 🌐 *www.mccarran.com.*

BUS

Greyhound provides bus service to Barstow and Victorville; check with the chambers of commerce about local bus service, which is generally more useful to residents than to tourists.

CAR

The major north–south route through the western Mojave is U.S. 395, which intersects with I–15 between Cajon Pass and Victorville. Farther west, Highway 14 runs north–south between Inyokern (near Ridgecrest) and Lancaster. Two major east–west routes travel through the Mojave: to the north, I–15 to Las Vegas, Nevada; to the south, I–40 to the Mojave National Preserve. At the intersection of the two interstates, in Barstow, I–15 veers south toward Victorville and Los Angeles, and I–40 gives way to Highway 58 west toward Bakersfield.

■ **TIP→ For the latest Mojave traffic and weather, tune in to the Highway Stations (98.1 FM near Barstow, 98.9 FM near Essex, and 99.7 FM near Baker).** Traffic can be especially troublesome Friday through Sunday, when thousands of Angelenos head to Las Vegas for a bit of R&R.

TRAIN

Amtrak trains traveling east and west stop in Victorville and Barstow, but the stations aren't staffed, so you'll have to purchase tickets in advance and handle your own baggage. The Barstow station is served daily by Amtrak California motor coaches that stop in Los Angeles, Bakersfield, Las Vegas, and elsewhere. Amtrak buses also stop in Lancaster and Mojave. Metrolink's Antelope Valley line travels from Los Angeles Union Station north to Burbank Airport, Palmdale, and Lancaster.

CONTACTS Metrolink. ☎ *800/371–5465* 🌐 *metrolinktrains.com.*

Restaurants

Throughout the desert, dining is a fairly simple affair. There are chain establishments in Ridgecrest, Lancaster, Victorville, and Barstow, as well as some ethnic eateries.

Hotels

Chain hotel properties and roadside motels are the desert's primary lodging options. The tourist season runs from late May through September. Reservations are rarely a problem, but it's still wise to make them.

Restaurant and hotel reviews have been shortened. For full information, visit Fodors.com. Restaurant prices are the average cost of a main course at dinner, or if dinner is not served, at lunch. Hotel prices are the lowest cost of a standard double room in high season.

What it Costs

	$	$$	$$$	$$$$
RESTAURANTS	under $17	$17–$26	$27–$36	over $36
HOTELS	under $150	$150–$250	$251–$350	over $350

Tours

Sierra Club

SPECIAL-INTEREST | The San Gorgonio Chapter of the Sierra Club and the chapter's Mojave Group conduct interesting field trips and desert excursions. Activities are often volunteer-run and free, but participants are sometimes required to cover parking and other expenses.

951/684–6203 sangorgonio2.sierraclub.org Some free; fee tour prices vary.

Visitor Information

CONTACTS Bureau of Land Management. *California Desert District Office, 22835 Calle San Juan De Los Lagos, Moreno Valley 951/697–5200, 760/833–7100 www.blm.gov/office/california-desert-district-office.* **California Welcome Center Barstow.** *2796 Tanger Way, Suite 100, Barstow off Lenwood Rd. 760/253–4782 www.visitcalifornia.com/experience/california-welcome-center-barstow/.*

Lancaster

70 miles north of Los Angeles.

Points of interest around Lancaster include a state poppy reserve that bursts to life in the spring and Edwards Air Force Base, which many consider the birthplace of supersonic flight. Lancaster was founded in 1876, when the Southern Pacific Railroad arrived. Before that, several Native American tribes, some of whose descendants still live in the surrounding mountains, inhabited it. The adjacent town of Palmdale (often included with Lancaster as part of the Antelope Valley region) evolved from a sleepy agricultural community into an aerospace and defense capital when Edwards Air Force Base and U.S. Air Force Plant 42 were established after World War II.

GETTING HERE AND AROUND

From the Los Angeles basin, take Highway 14, which proceeds north to Mojave and Highway 58, a link between Bakersfield and Barstow. Regional Metrolink trains serve Lancaster from the Los Angeles area. Local transit exists, but a car is the best way to experience this area.

ESSENTIALS

VISITOR INFORMATION Antelope Valley Chambers of Commerce. *554 W. Lancaster Blvd. 661/948–4518 www.avchambers.org.* **Destination Lancaster.** *554 W. Lancaster Blvd. 661/400–0342 www.destinationlancasterca.org.*

Sights

Antelope Valley California Poppy Reserve
NATIONAL/STATE PARK | The California poppy, the state flower, can be spotted throughout the state, but this quiet park holds the densest concentration. Eight miles of trails wind through 1,745 acres of hills carpeted with poppies and other wildflowers, including a paved section that allows wheelchair access. Keep in mind that poppy flowers will curl up their petals if it's too windy or cold, so plan accordingly. Heed the rules and stay on the official trails when taking photos. **TIP→ Blooming season is usually March through May.** On a clear day at any time of year, you'll be treated to sweeping views of Antelope Valley. Visit the website or call the wildflower hotline for the current bloom status. *15101 Lancaster Rd., west off Hwy. 14, Ave. I Exit 661/724–1180 wildflower hotline, 661/946–6092 administration www.parks.ca.gov/poppyreserve $10 per vehicle Visitor center closed mid-May–Feb.*

Antelope Valley Indian Museum
MUSEUM | **FAMILY** | This museum got its start as a private collection of American Indian antiquities gathered in the 1920s by artist and amateur naturalist Howard Arden Edwards. Today, his Swiss chalet–style home is a state museum known for one-of-a-kind artifacts from California, Southwest, and Great Basin native cultures, including ancient tools, artwork, basketry, and rugs. To get here, exit north off Highway 138 at 165th Street East and follow the signs, or take the Avenue K exit off Highway 14. *15701 E. Ave. M 661/946–3055 www.avim.parks.ca.gov $3 Closed weekdays.*

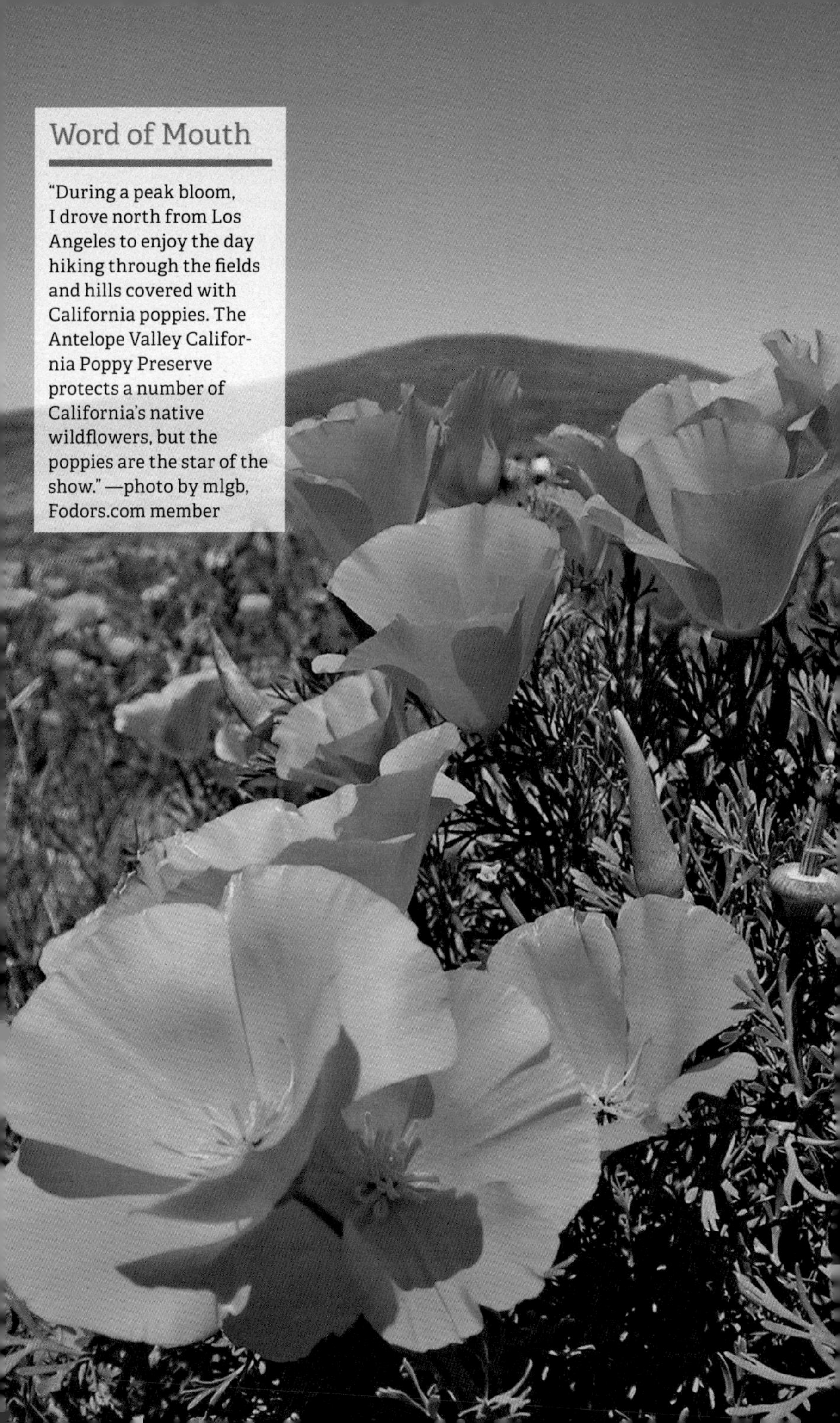

Word of Mouth

"During a peak bloom, I drove north from Los Angeles to enjoy the day hiking through the fields and hills covered with California poppies. The Antelope Valley California Poppy Preserve protects a number of California's native wildflowers, but the poppies are the star of the show." —photo by mlgb, Fodors.com member

Antelope Valley Winery/Donato Family Vineyard

STORE/MALL | Cyndee and Frank Donato purchased the Los Angeles–based McLester Winery in 1990 and moved it to Lancaster, where the high-desert sun and nighttime chill work their magic on wine grapes such as Merlot, Zinfandel, and Sangiovese. In addition to tastings, the winery hosts a Saturday farmers' market (from May through November between 9 and noon) and sells grass-fed buffalo and other game and exotic meats such as venison, pheasant, and wild boar. ✉ *42041 20th St. W, at Ave. M* ☎ *661/722–0145, 888/282–8332* 🌐 *www.avwinery.com* 🎫 *Winery free, tastings from $12* 🕒 *Closed Mon. and Tues.*

The BLVD

ARTS VENUE | Lancaster's downtown arts and culture district and social hub, The BLVD, stretches for nine blocks along West Lancaster Boulevard from 10th Street West to Sierra Highway. Boeing Plaza anchors the east end and marks the start of the Aerospace Walk of Honor—a series of murals and monuments lauding 100 legendary figures, including Neil Armstrong and Chuck Yaeger. The district is also home to the Lancaster Performing Arts Center, the Lancaster Museum of Art & History, galleries, restaurants, boutiques, coffee and tea shops, craft breweries, and entertainment venues. ✉ *W. Lancaster Blvd.* ✥ *10th St. W to Sierra Hwy. and Jackman to Milling Sts.* ☎ *661/723–6078* 🌐 *www.theblvdlancaster.com.*

Exotic Feline Breeding Compound's Feline Conservation Center

ZOO | About two dozen species of wild cats, from the unusual, weasel-size jaguarundi to leopards, tigers, and jaguars, inhabit this small, orderly facility. You can see the cats up close (behind barrier fences) in the parklike public zoo and research center, and docents are available to answer questions. ✉ *Rhyolite Ave. off Mojave-Tropico Rd., Rosamond* ☎ *661/256–3793* 🌐 *www.wildcatzoo.org* 🎫 *$10* 🕒 *Closed Wed. and Sun.*

St. Andrew's Abbeys

RELIGIOUS SITE | Nestled in the foothills of the Antelope Valley, this peaceful enclave is both Benedictine monastery and restful retreat for those wanting to get away from the bustle of everyday life. Day visitors can walk the lush tree-lined grounds, including a large, shaded pond teeming with ducks and red-eared turtles, or browse the well-stocked gift shop for religious keepsakes. An extensive collection of ceramic tiles in the image of saints and angels by Father Maur van Doorslaer, a Belgian monk whose work U.S. and Canadian collectors favor, are among the items sold here to help sustain the monastery and its good works. ✉ *31001 N. Valyermo Rd., south of Hwy. 138, Valyermo* ☎ *661/944–2178 ceramics studio* 🌐 *www.saintandrewsabbey.com* 🎫 *Free.*

Red Rock Canyon State Park

48 miles north of Lancaster.

On the stretch of Highway 14 that slices through Red Rock Canyon State Park, it's easy to become caught up in the momentum of rushing to your "real" destination. But it would be a shame not to stop for this deeply beautiful canyon, with its rich, layered colors and Native American heritage.

GETTING HERE AND AROUND

The only practical way to get here is by car, taking Highway 14 north from the Palmdale-Lancaster area or south from Ridgecrest.

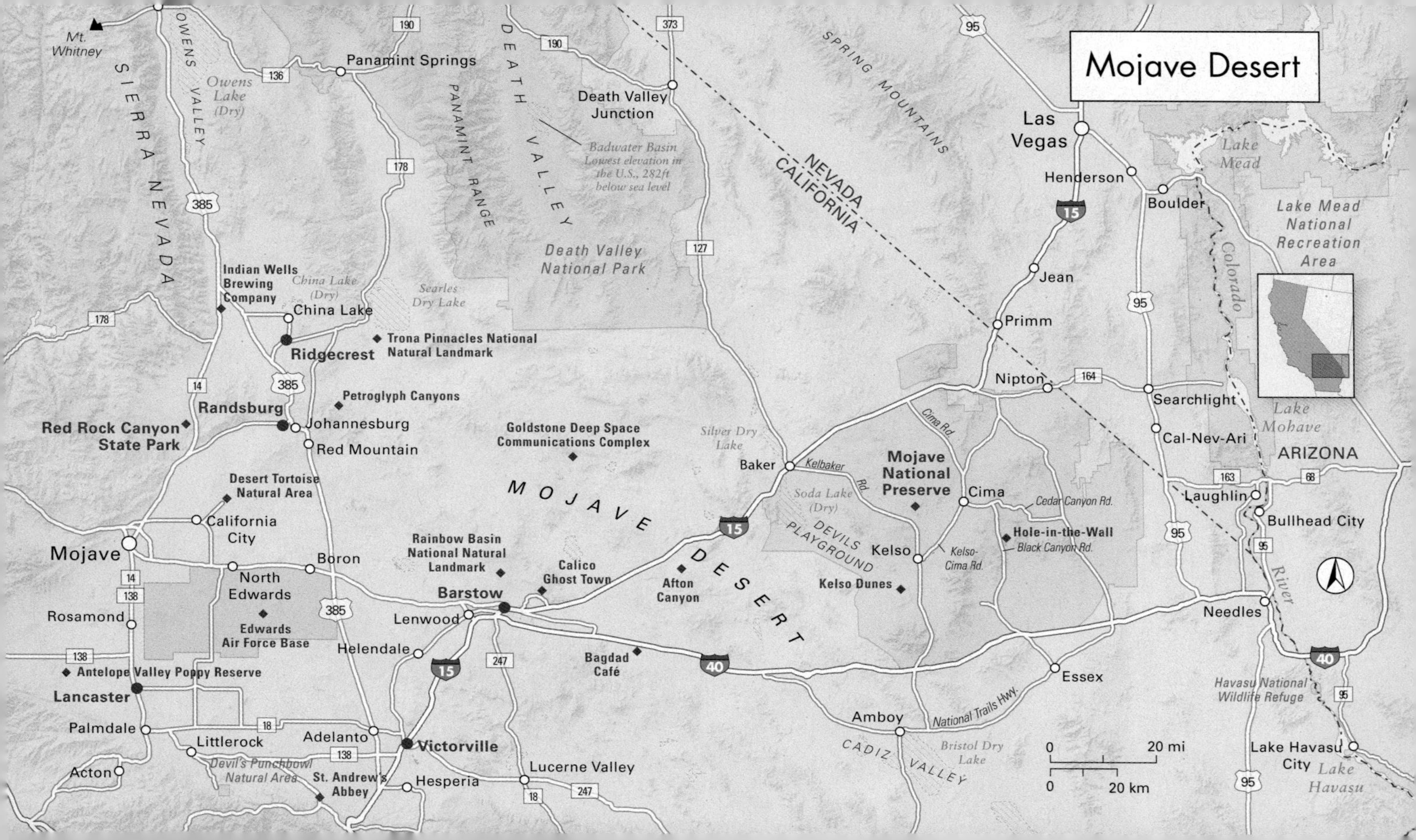
Mojave Desert
Las Vegas
Henderson
Boulder
Lake Mead
Lake Mead National Recreation Area
Colorado River
Jean
Primm
NEVADA
CALIFORNIA
SPRING MOUNTAINS
Nipton
Searchlight
Cal-Nev-Ari
Lake Mohave
ARIZONA
Laughlin
Bullhead City
Needles
Havasu National Wildlife Refuge
Lake Havasu City
Lake Havasu
Essex
Amboy
National Trails Hwy.
Bristol Dry Lake
CADIZ VALLEY
0 20 mi
0 20 km
Mojave National Preserve
Cima
Cima Rd.
Cedar Canyon Rd.
Hole-in-the-Wall
Black Canyon Rd.
Kelso
Kelso-Cima Rd.
Kelso Dunes
Kelbaker Rd.
Baker
Soda Lake (Dry)
DEVILS PLAYGROUND
Silver Dry Lake
MOJAVE DESERT
Afton Canyon
Calico Ghost Town
Barstow
Bagdad Café
Rainbow Basin National Natural Landmark
Goldstone Deep Space Communications Complex
Lenwood
Helendale
Victorville
Hesperia
Lucerne Valley
Adelanto
St. Andrew's Abbey
Devil's Punchbowl Natural Area
Littlerock
Palmdale
Acton
Lancaster
Antelope Valley Poppy Reserve
Rosamond
Mojave
Edwards Air Force Base
North Edwards
Boron
California City
Desert Tortoise Natural Area
Red Rock Canyon State Park
Randsburg
Johannesburg
Red Mountain
Petroglyph Canyons
Ridgecrest
China Lake
China Lake (Dry)
Indian Wells Brewing Company
Trona Pinnacles National Natural Landmark
Searles Dry Lake
Death Valley National Park
DEATH VALLEY
PANAMINT RANGE
Badwater Basin Lowest elevation in the U.S., 282ft below sea level
Death Valley Junction
Panamint Springs
Owens Lake (Dry)
OWENS VALLEY
SIERRA NEVADA
Mt. Whitney
15
40
95
385
14
138
18
247
127
373
190
178
136
164
163
68

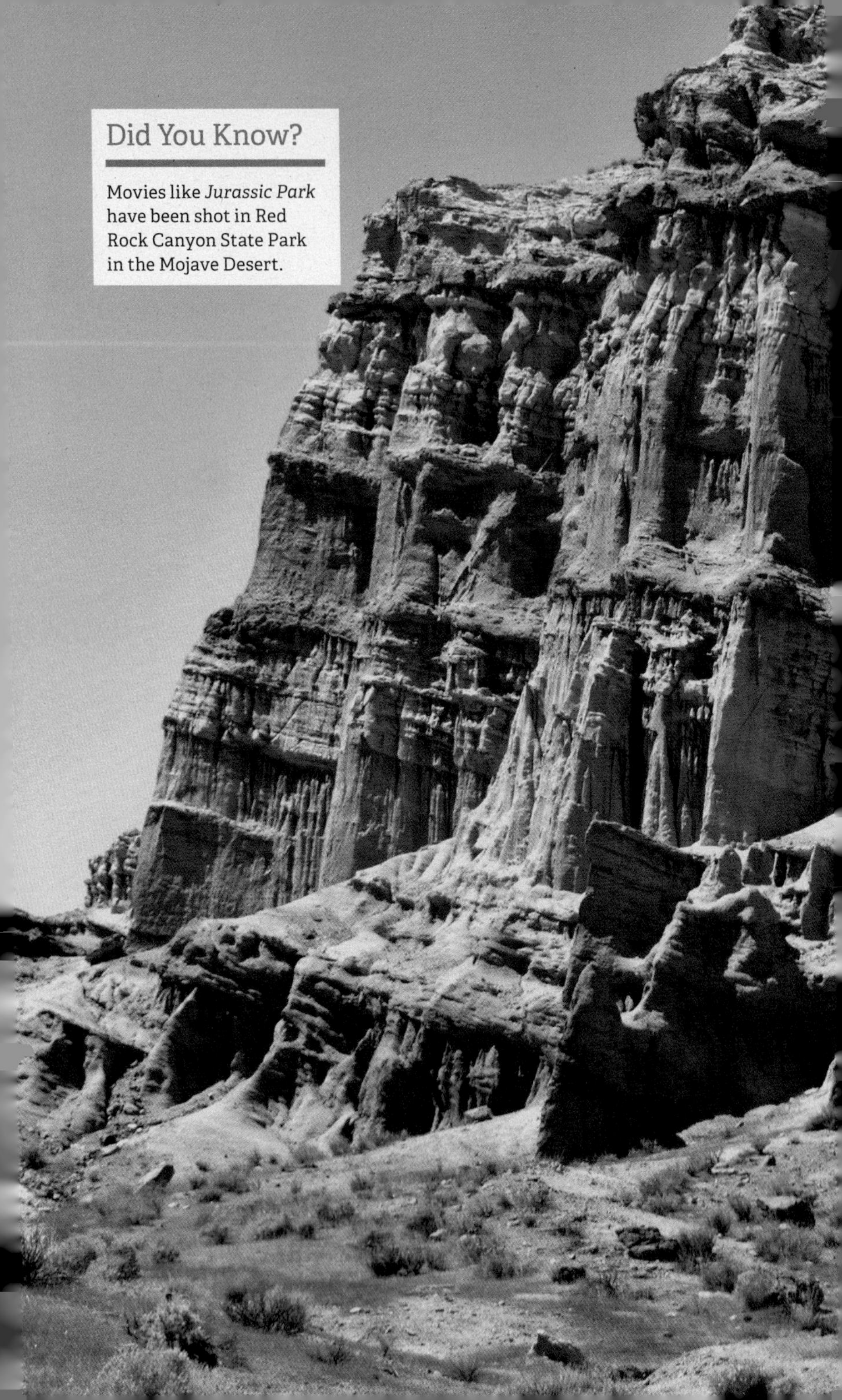

Did You Know?

Movies like *Jurassic Park* have been shot in Red Rock Canyon State Park in the Mojave Desert.

Sights

Red Rock Canyon State Park

NATIONAL/STATE PARK | A geological feast for the eyes with its layers of pink, white, red, and brown rock, this remote canyon is also a region of fascinating biological diversity—the ecosystems of the Sierra Nevada, the Mojave Desert, and the Basin Range all converge here. Native Americans known as the Kawaiisu lived here some 20,000 years ago; later, Mojave Indians roamed the land for centuries. You can still see remains of gold mining operations in the park, and movies such as *Jurassic Park* have been shot here. For a quiet nature trail a little off the beaten path try the 0.75-mile loop at Red Cliffs Natural Preserve on Highway 14, across from the entrance to the Ricardo Campground. ✉ *Visitor Center, 37749 Abbott Dr., off Hwy. 14, Cantil* ☎ *661/946–6092* 🌐 *www.parks.ca.gov* 🎫 *$6 per vehicle.*

Ridgecrest

28 miles northeast of Red Rock Canyon State Park, 77 miles south of Lone Pine.

A military town that serves the U.S. Naval Weapons Center to its north, Ridgecrest has scores of stores, restaurants, and hotels. With about 29,000 residents, it's the last city of any significant size you'll encounter as you head northeast toward Death Valley National Park. It's a good base for visiting regional attractions such as the Trona Pinnacles and Petroglyph Canyons.

GETTING HERE AND AROUND

Arrive here by car via U.S. 395 or, from the Los Angeles area, Highway 14.

ESSENTIALS

TRANSPORTATION CONTACTS

VISITOR INFORMATION Ridgecrest Area Convention and Visitors Bureau. ✉ *643 N. China Lake Blvd.* ☎ *760/375–8202, 800/847–4830* 🌐 *goridgecrest.com.*

Sights

Indian Wells Brewing Company

WINERY/DISTILLERY | After driving through the hot desert, you'll surely appreciate a cold one at Indian Wells Brewing Company, where master brewer Rick Lovett lovingly crafts his Lobotomy Bock, Amnesia I.P.A., and Lunatic Lemonade, among others. If you have the kids along, grab a six-pack of his specialty root beer, black cherry, orange, or cream soda. ✉ *2565 N. Hwy. 14, 2 miles west of U.S. 395, Inyokern* ☎ *760/377–5989* 🌐 *www.mojavered.com.*

Maturango Museum

CANYON | FAMILY | The museum contains interesting exhibits that survey the Upper Mojave Desert area's art, history, and geology, and sponsors tours of the amazing rock drawings in Petroglyph Canyons. ✉ *100 E. Las Flores Ave., at Hwy. 178* ☎ *760/375–6900* 🌐 *www.maturango.org* 🎫 *$5.*

★ **Petroglyph Canyons**

CANYON | FAMILY | Thousands of well-preserved images of animals and humans are scratched or pecked into dark basaltic rocks at Big Petroglyph and Little Petroglyph canyons in the Coso Mountain range, the largest concentration of ancient rock art in the Northern Hemisphere. The canyons lie within the million-acre U.S. Naval Weapons Center at China Lake. Only the drawings of Little Petroglyph can be visited, and only on a guided tour arranged in advance through the Maturango Museum. Tour participants must be U.S. citizens over 10 years of age, and fill out an online application to obtain security clearance. Detailed information about the spring and fall tours, which fill up fast, is provided on the museum's website. ✉ *100 E. Las Flores Ave.* ☎ *760/375–6900* 🌐 *www.maturango.org* 🎫 *$60* 🕒 *Closed Dec.–Feb. and June–mid-Sept.*

Trona Pinnacles National Natural Landmark
ARCHAEOLOGICAL SITE | Fantastic-looking formations of calcium carbonate, known as tufa, were formed underwater along fault lines in the bed of what is now Searles Dry Lake. Some of the more than 500 spires stand as tall as 140 feet, creating a landscape so surreal that it doubled for outer-space terrain in the film *Star Trek V.* An easy-to-walk ½-mile trail allows you to see the tufa up close, but wear sturdy shoes—tufa cuts like coral. The best road to the area can be impassable after a rainstorm. ✉ *Pinnacle Rd.* ✣ *5 miles south of Hwy. 178, 18 miles east of Ridgecrest* ☎ *760/384–5400 Ridgecrest BLM office* 🌐 *www.blm.gov/visit/trona-pinnacles.*

Hotels

Hampton Inn & Suites Ridgecrest
$$ | HOTEL | Clean and reliable, the Hampton has a well-equipped exercise room, pool, spotless Internet service, and complimentary breakfast. **Pros:** attentive, friendly service; good breakfast; big rooms. **Cons:** a rather strong chain vibe; thin walls; basic breakfast. $ *Rooms from: $159* ✉ *104 E. Sydnor Ave.* ☎ *760/446–1968* 🌐 *hamptoninn3.hilton.com* *93 rooms* *Free breakfast.*

Randsburg

21 miles south of Ridgecrest, 26 miles east of Red Rock Canyon State Park.

Randsburg and nearby Red Mountain and Johannesburg make up the Rand Mining District, which first boomed with the discovery of gold in the Rand Mountains in 1895. Rich tungsten ore, used in World War I to make steel alloy, was discovered in 1907, and silver was found in 1919. The boom has gone bust, but the area still has some residents, a few antiques shops, and plenty of character. Butte Avenue is the main drag in Randsburg, whose tiny city jail, just off Butte, is among the original buildings still standing. An archetypal Old West cemetery perched on a hillside looms over Johannesburg.

GETTING HERE AND AROUND

Arriving by car is the best transportation option. From Red Rock Canyon, drive east on Redrock Randsburg Road. From Ridgecrest, drive south on South China Lake Road and U.S. 395.

Sights

Desert Tortoise Natural Area
NATURE PRESERVE | It may not always be easy to spot the elusive desert tortoise in this peaceful protected habitat but the approximately 40-square-mile area often blazes with wildflowers in the spring and early summer. It is also a great spot to see desert kit fox, red-tailed hawks, cactus wrens, and Mojave rattlesnakes; walking paths and a small interpretive center are part of the experience. ✉ *8 miles northeast of California City via Randsburg Mojave Rd.* ☎ *442/294–4258* 🌐 *www.tortoise-tracks.org* *Free.*

General Store
RESTAURANT—SIGHT | Built as Randsburg's Drug Store in 1896, the General Store is one of the area's few surviving ghost-town buildings with an original tin ceiling, light fixtures, and 1904-era marble-and-stained-glass soda fountain. You can still enjoy a phosphate soda from that same fountain, or a lunch of burgers, hot dogs, and chili. ✉ *35 Butte Ave.* ☎ *760/374–2143* 🌐 *www.randsburggeneralstore.com* ⏲ *Closed Tues. and Wed.*

Victorville

87 miles south of Ridgecrest.

At the southwest corner of the Mojave is sprawling Victorville, a town with a rich Route 66 heritage and a museum dedicated to the Mother Road. Victorville was named for Santa Fe Railroad pioneer

Jacob Nash Victor, who drove the first locomotive through the Cajon Pass here in 1885. Once home to Native Americans, the town later became a rest stop for Mormons and missionaries. In 1941, George Air Force Base, now an airport and storage area, brought scores of military families to the area, many of which have stayed on to raise families of their own.

GETTING HERE AND AROUND

Drive here on I–15 from Los Angeles or Las Vegas, or from the north via U.S. 395. Amtrak and Greyhound also serve the town. There are local buses, but touring by car is more practical.

Sights

California Route 66 Museum

MUSEUM | Visitors from around the world still think of Historic Route 66 as one of the best ways to see the real America and this 4,500-square-foot museum is chock-full of memorabilia such as maps and postcards, photographs, paintings, and nostalgic displays that bring the iconic highway's history to life. Friendly museum volunteers are more than happy to answer questions and take your picture inside the flower-painted VW Love Bus. ✉ *16825 S. D St., between 5th and 6th Sts.* ☎ *760/951–0436* 🌐 *califrt66museum.org* *Free* *Closed Tues. and Wed.*

Mojave Narrows Regional Park

CITY PARK | **FAMILY** | This 840-acre park is one of the few spots where the Mojave River flows aboveground, and the result is open pastures, wetlands, and two lakes surrounded by cottonwoods and cattails. Amenities include camping, fishing, equestrian/walking trails, and a large playground with water park. ✉ *18000 Yates Rd., north on Ridgecrest Rd. off Bear Valley Rd.* ☎ *760/245–2226* 🌐 *cms.sbcounty.gov/parks* *From $8* *Closed Tues. and Wed.*

Restaurants

Emma Jean's Holland Burger Cafe

$ | **DINER** | The short-order cook and his grill are literally center stage in this tiny, family-owned restaurant along Historic Route 66, which has changed little since it first opened in 1947. It's the peach cobbler, Brian burger, and fried chicken that keep locals lining up at the door, but anyone wanting a glimpse of 20th-century Americana can get their kicks here, too. **Known for:** Route 66 memorabilia; historical diner; hearty breakfasts. *Average main: $12* ✉ *17143 N. D St., at Water Power Housing Dr.* ☎ *760/243–9938* 🌐 *www.hollandburger.com* *No credit cards* *Closed Sun. No dinner.*

Molly Brown's Country Cafe

$ | **AMERICAN** | **FAMILY** | There's no mystery why this place is a locals' favorite—the cozy eatery offers a mouthwatering breakfast menu that includes everything from chicken fried steak to a sizzling garden skillet brimming with fresh vegetables. Lunch includes sandwiches, salads, and hot plates such as meat loaf with potatoes, veggies, and corn bread. **Known for:** hearty breakfasts; locals' favorite; homemade breads. *Average main: $13* ✉ *15775 Mojave Dr.* ☎ *760/241–4900* 🌐 *www.mollybrownscountrycafe.com.*

Hotels

Courtyard Marriott Victorville Hesperia

$$ | **HOTEL** | **FAMILY** | Rooms are spacious and contemporary, and there is both an indoor pool and large outdoor patio and pool area ideal for large groups. **Pros:** convenient location off I–15; some rooms with desert views; two pools. **Cons:** breakfast only with certain room rates; bistro menu options limited; some rooms close to freeway noise. *Rooms from: $168* ✉ *9619 Mariposa Rd., Hesperia* ☎ *760/956–3876* 🌐 *www.marriott.com* *131 rooms* *No meals.*

Many of the buildings in the popular Calico Ghost Town are authentic.

Barstow

32 miles northeast of Victorville.

Barstow was born in 1886, when a subsidiary of the Atchison, Topeka, and Santa Fe Railway began construction of a Harvey House depot and hotel here. The depot has been restored and includes two free museums; the family-friendly Calico Ghost Town is just north of town, and there are well-known chain motels and restaurants right off I–15 if you need a rest and refuel before the next stop.

GETTING HERE AND AROUND

Driving here on I–15 from Los Angeles or Las Vegas is the best option, although you can reach Barstow via Amtrak or Greyhound. The local bus service is helpful for sights downtown.

ESSENTIALS

TRANSPORTATION INFORMATION
Barstow Area Transit/Victor Valley Transit. ☎ *760/948–3030* 🌐 *vvta.org.*

VISITOR INFORMATION Barstow Area Chamber of Commerce and Visitors Bureau. ✉ *229 E. Main St.* ☎ *760/256–8617* 🌐 *www.barstowchamber.com.* **California Welcome Center Barstow.** ✉ *2796 Tanger Way, Suite 100, off Lenwood Rd.* ☎ *760/253–4782* 🌐 *www.visitcalifornia.com/experience/california-welcome-center-barstow.* **Mojave National Preserve Headquarters.** ✉ *2701 Barstow Rd.* ☎ *760/252–6100* 🌐 *www.nps.gov/moja/planyourvisit/visitorcenters.htm.*

Sights

Afton Canyon

CANYON | Because of its colorful, steep walls, Afton Canyon is often called the Grand Canyon of the Mojave. It was carved over thousands of years by the rushing waters of the Mojave River, which makes one of its few aboveground appearances here. The dirt road that leads to the canyon is ungraded in spots, so it is best to explore it in an all-terrain vehicle. ✉ *Off Afton Rd., 36 miles northeast of Barstow via I–15* 🌐 *www.recreation.gov.*

Bagdad Café

RESTAURANT—SIGHT | Tourists from all over the world flock to this Route 66 eatery, built in the 1940s and where the 1987 film of the same name was shot. The divey café's walls are crammed with memorabilia donated by visitors famous and otherwise. The very limited bill of fare includes the Bagdad omelet and a buffalo burger with fries, but this place is really about soaking up the Route 66-Americana vibe. ✉ *46548 National Trails Hwy., at Nopal La., Newberry Springs* ☎ *760/257–3101*.

★ **Calico Ghost Town**

GHOST TOWN | **FAMILY** | This former silver-mining boom town was founded in 1881, and, within a few years, it boasted 500 mines and 22 saloons. Its reconstruction by Walter Knott of Knott's Berry Farm makes it more about G-rated family entertainment than the town's gritty past, but that doesn't seem to take away from the fun of panning for (fool's) gold, touring the original tunnels of Maggie Mine, or taking a leisurely ride on the Calico Odessa Railroad. Five of the original buildings are still standing, such as the impressive Lane's General Store, and its setting among the stark beauty of the Calico Hills can make a stroll along this once-bustling Main Street downright peaceful. ■ **TIP→ Calico also has ghost tours and regular events such as the yearly bluegrass festival on Mother's Day weekend.** ✉ *36600 Ghost Town Rd., off I–15, Yermo* ☎ *760/254–1123* 🌐 *parks.sbcounty.gov/park/calico-ghost-town-regional-park* 🎫 *$8*.

Casa Del Desierto Harvey House

HISTORIC SITE | This historic train depot was built around 1911 (the original 1885 structure was destroyed by fire) and was one of the original Harvey Houses, providing dining and lodging for weary travelers along the rail lines. Waitresses at the depots were popularized in movies such as *The Harvey Girls* with Judy Garland. It now houses offices and two museums: the Western American Railroad and Route 66 Mother Road, but you can still walk along the porticos of the impressive Spanish Renaissance Classical building, or stroll into the restored lobby where you'll find the original staircase, terrazzo floor, and copper chandeliers. ✉ *681 N. 1st Ave., near Riverside Dr.* ☎ *760/818–4400* 🌐 *www.barstowharveyhouse.com* 🎫 *Free* ⏲ *Closed Sun*.

Desert Discovery Center

MUSEUM | **FAMILY** | The center's main attraction is Old Woman Meteorite, the second-largest such celestial object ever found in the United States. It was discovered in 1976 about 50 miles from Barstow. The center also has exhibits of fossils, plants, and local animals. Environmental education, history, and the arts are among the topics of workshops and presentations the center hosts. Follow the outdoor desert nature trail with interpretive signs on desert plants and early man's relationship with native plants for shelter, medicine, clothing, food, and weaponry. ■ **TIP→ Reserve a spot in advance for the Stone Age to Space Age tour, offered the first Saturday of the month at 10 am (about 1½ hours, donations appreciated). It begins with a Route 66 history presentation at the Desert Discovery Center, followed by visits to the Main Street Murals and the NASA Goldstone Visitor Center.** ✉ *831 Barstow Rd.* ☎ *760/252–6060* 🌐 *www.desertdiscoverycenter.com* 🎫 *Free* ⏲ *Closed Sun. and Mon*.

★ **Goldstone Deep Space Communications Complex**

MUSEUM | **FAMILY** | Friendly and enthusiastic staffers conduct guided tours of this 53-square-mile complex at Fort Irwin Military Base, 35 miles north of Barstow. Tours start at the Goldstone Museum, where exhibits detail past and present space missions and Deep Space Network history. From there, you'll drive out to see the massive concave antennas, starting with those used for early manned space flights and culminating with the 24-story-tall "listening" device. This is one of only three complexes in the world that make up the Deep Space Network, tracking and communicating with spacecraft throughout our solar system. Appointments are required; contact the complex to reserve a slot. ✉ *NASA Goldstone Visitor Center, 681 N. 1st Ave.* ☎ *760/255–8688* 🌐 *www.gdscc.nasa.gov* 🎫 *Free* 🕑 *Closed Sun.*

Main Street Murals

PUBLIC ART | FAMILY | More than two dozen hand-painted murals in downtown Barstow depict the town's history, from prehistoric times and early explorers to pioneer caravans, mining eras, and Route 66. Walking tour guides are available at the Barstow Chamber of Commerce and the public library. Contact the Desert Discovery Center for more details on the murals and monthly guided tours. ✉ *E. Main St.* ✥ *Between 1st and 7th Sts.* ☎ *760/252–6060* 🌐 *www.mainstreetmurals.com.*

Mojave River Valley Museum

MUSEUM | FAMILY | The floor-to-ceiling collection of local history, both quirky and conventional, includes Ice Age fossils such as a giant mammoth tusk dug up in 2006, Native American artifacts, 19th-century handmade quilts, and displays on early settlers. Entrance is free and there's a little gift shop with a nice collection of books about the area. **■ TIP→ The story about Possum Trot and its population of folk-art dolls is not to be missed.** ✉ *270 E. Virginia Way, at Barstow Rd.* ☎ *760/256–5452* 🌐 *www.mojaverivervalleymuseum.org* 🎫 *Free.*

Rainbow Basin National Natural Landmark

NATIONAL/STATE PARK | Many science-fiction movies set on Mars have been filmed at this landmark 8 miles north of Barstow. Huge slabs of red, orange, white, and green stone tilt at crazy angles like ships about to capsize and traces of ancient beasts such as mastodons and bear-dogs, which roamed the basin up to 16 million years ago have been discovered in its fossil beds. The dirt road around the basin is narrow and bumpy so vehicles with higher clearance are recommended and rain can quickly turn the road to mud; at times, only four-wheel-drive vehicles are permitted. ✉ *Fossil Bed Rd., 3 miles west of Fort Irwin Rd. (head north from I–15)* ☎ *760/252–6000* 🌐 *www.blm.gov/visit/rainbow-basin-natural-area.*

Skyline Drive-In Theatre

ARTS VENUE | Check out a bit of surviving Americana at this dusty drive-in, where you can watch the latest Hollywood flicks among the Joshua trees and starry night sky. Keep in mind the old-time speakers are no more; sound is tuned in via car radio. ✉ *31175 Old Hwy. 58* ☎ *760/256–3333* 🎫 *$10 per person* 🕑 *Closed early Dec.–early Mar.*

Western America Railroad Museum

MUSEUM | FAMILY | You can almost hear the murmur of passengers and rhythmic, metal-on-metal clatter as you stroll past the old cabooses, railcars and engines, such as Sante Fe number 95, that are on display outside the historic Barstow station where this museum is located. The next stop is the indoor portion of the collection, including a train simulator, rail equipment, model railroad display, and other memorabilia. A handful of artifacts from the depot's Harvey House days are on display, as well as period dining-car china from railways around the country. ✉ *Casa Del Desierto, 685 N. 1st Ave., near Riverside Dr.* ☎ *760/256–9276* 🌐 *barstowharveyhouse.com* 🎫 *Free* 🕑 *Closed Mon.–Thurs.*

Restaurants

Peggy Sue's 50s Diner

$ | **AMERICAN** | **FAMILY** | Checkerboard floors and life-size versions of Elvis and Marilyn Monroe greet you at this funky '50s coffee shop and pizza parlor in the middle of the Mojave. The fare is basic American—fries, onion rings, burgers, pork chops—with some fun surprises such as pineapple pie and deep-fried dill pickles. **Known for:** movie, TV memorabilia; over-the-top '50s vibe; gift shop, jukebox, soda fountain, duck pond. *Average main: $14 35654 W. Yermo Rd., at Daggett-Yermo Rd., Yermo 760/254-3370 www.peggysuesdiner.com.*

Hotels

Ayres Hotel Barstow

$ | **HOTEL** | **FAMILY** | In a sea of chain hotels this one has a few homespun touches up its sleeves, such as fresh-baked cookies in the cozy lobby lounge every evening. **Pros:** clean rooms, engaged management; entirely nonsmoking; Tesla charging stations. **Cons:** pricey for Barstow; near freeway; shared parking lot with other businesses. *Rooms from: $139 2812 Lenwood Rd. 760/307-3121 www.ayreshotels.com/ayres-hotel-barstow 92 rooms Free breakfast.*

Mojave National Preserve

Visitor center 118 miles east of Barstow, 58 miles west of Needles.

The 1.6 million acres of the Mojave National Preserve hold a surprising abundance of plant and animal life—especially considering their elevation (nearly 8,000 feet in some areas). There are traces of human history here as well, including abandoned army posts and vestiges of mining and ranching towns. The Cinder Cone Lava Beds area holds 75 inactive volcanoes; the youngest is 11,500 years old. North Cima Road passes a significant Joshua tree forest. Mojave National Preserve rangers also oversee the adjacent 20,920-acre Castle Mountains National Monument, created in 2016.

GETTING HERE AND AROUND

A car is the best way to access the preserve, which lies between I–15 and I–40. Kelbaker Road bisects the park from north to south; northbound from I–40, Essex Road gets you to Hole-in-the-Wall on pavement but is graveled beyond there.

Sights

Hole-in-the-Wall

NATURE SITE | Created millions of years ago by volcanic activity, Hole-in-the-Wall formed when gases were trapped between layers of deposited ash, rock, and lava; the gas bubbles left holes in the solidified material. You will encounter one of California's most distinctive hiking experiences here. Proceeding clockwise from a small visitor center, you walk gently down and around a craggy hill, past cacti and fading petroglyphs to Banshee Canyon, whose pockmarked walls resemble Swiss cheese. From there you head back out of the canyon, supporting yourself with widely spaced iron rings (some of which wiggle precariously from their rock moorings) as you ascend a 50-foot incline that deposits you back near the visitor center. The one-hour adventure can be challenging but wholly entertaining. **TIP→ There are no services (gas or food) nearby; be sure to fill your tank and pack some snacks before heading out here.** *Mojave National Preserve 760/252-6104 www.nps.gov/moja Free.*

★ Kelso Dunes

NATURE SITE | As you enter the preserve from the south, you'll pass miles of open scrub brush, Joshua trees, and beautiful red-black cinder cones before encountering the Kelso Dunes. These golden, fine-sand slopes cover 70 square miles, reaching heights of 600 feet. You can reach them via a short walk from the main parking area, but be prepared for a serious workout. When you reach the top of a dune, kick a little bit of sand down the lee side and listen to the sand "sing." North of the dunes, in the town of Kelso, is the Mission revival–style **Kelso Depot Visitor Center.** The striking building, which dates from 1923, contains several rooms of desert- and train-theme exhibits. ✉ *For Kelso Depot Visitor Center, take Kelbaker Rd. exit from I–15 (head south 34 miles) or I–40 (head north 22 miles)* ☎ *760/252–6100, 760/252–6108* 🌐 *www.nps.gov/moja* 🎫 *Free* 🕓 *Kelso Depot visitor center closed Tues. and Wed.*

Chapter 10

DEATH VALLEY NATIONAL PARK

Updated by
Cheryl Crabtree

Camping
★★★☆☆

Hotels
★★★★☆

Activities
★★★☆☆

Scenery
★★★★★

Crowds
★★☆☆☆

WELCOME TO DEATH VALLEY NATIONAL PARK

TOP REASONS TO GO

★ **Roving rocks:** Death Valley's Racetrack is home to moving boulders, a rare phenomenon that until recently had scientists baffled.

★ **Lowest spot on the continent:** Stand on the lowest spot on the continent at Badwater, 282 feet below sea level.

★ **Wildflower explosion:** In spring, this desert landscape is ablaze with greenery and colorful flowers, especially between Badwater and Ashford Mill.

★ **Ghost towns:** Death Valley is renowned for its Wild West heritage and is home to dozens of crumbling settlements including Chloride City, Greenwater, Harrisburg, Keeler, Leadfield, Panamint City, and Skidoo, as well as nearby Ballarat and Rhyolite.

★ **Naturally amazing:** From canyons to sand dunes to salt flats and dry lake beds, Death Valley serves up plenty of geological treasures.

1 Central Death Valley. Furnace Creek sits in the heart of Death Valley—if you have only a short time in the park, head here. You can visit gorgeous Golden Canyon, Zabriskie Point, the Salt Creek Interpretive Trail, and Artists Drive, among other popular points of interest.

2 Northern Death Valley. This region is uphill from Furnace Creek, which means marginally cooler temperatures. Be sure to stop by Rhyolite Ghost Town on Highway 374 before entering the park and exploring colorful Titus Canyon and jaw-dropping Ubehebe Crater.

3 Southern Death Valley. This is a desolate area, but there are plenty of sights that help convey Death Valley's rich history. Don't miss the Dublin Gulch Caves.

4 Western Death Valley. Panamint Springs Resort is a nice place to grab a meal and get your bearings before moving on to quaint Darwin Falls, smooth rolling sand dunes, beehive-shape Wildrose Charcoal Kilns, and historic Stovepipe Wells Village.

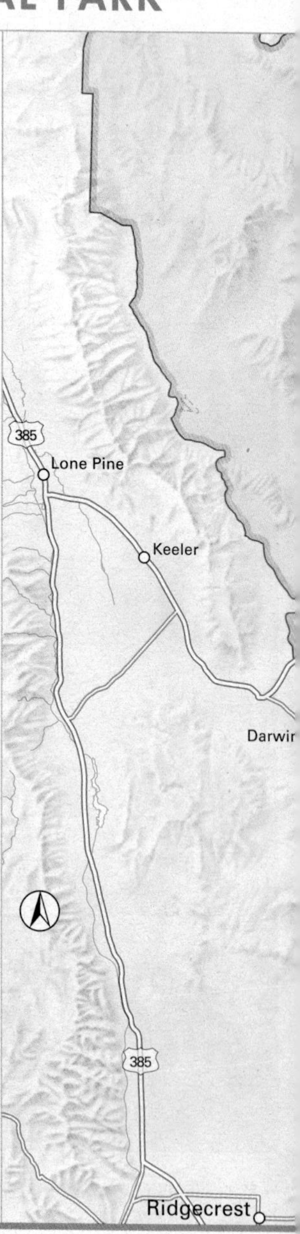

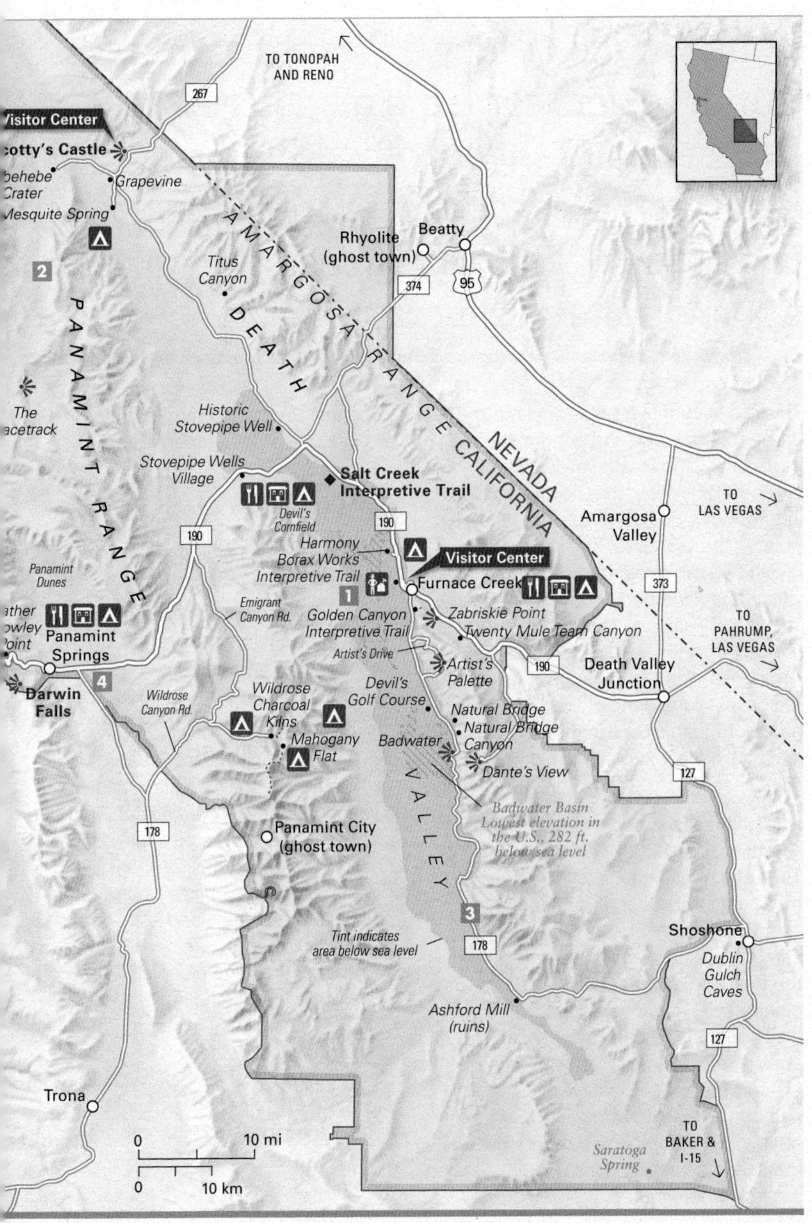
TO TONOPAH AND RENO
267
Visitor Center
Scotty's Castle
Ubehebe Crater
Grapevine
Mesquite Spring
2
PANAMINT RANGE
AMARGOSA RANGE
DEATH
Titus Canyon
Rhyolite (ghost town)
Beatty
374
95
The Racetrack
Historic Stovepipe Well
Stovepipe Wells Village
Salt Creek Interpretive Trail
NEVADA
CALIFORNIA
Devil's Cornfield
190
Harmony Borax Works Interpretive Trail
Visitor Center
Furnace Creek
1
Panamint Dunes
Emigrant Canyon Rd.
Golden Canyon Interpretive Trail
Zabriskie Point
Twenty Mule Team Canyon
Father Crowley Point
Panamint Springs
Artist's Drive
Artist's Palette
4
Darwin Falls
Wildrose Canyon Rd.
Wildrose Charcoal Kilns
Devil's Golf Course
Natural Bridge
Natural Bridge Canyon
Mahogany Flat
Badwater
Dante's View
VALLEY
Badwater Basin Lowest elevation in the U.S., 282 ft. below sea level
178
Panamint City (ghost town)
3
Tint indicates area below sea level
Ashford Mill (ruins)
TO LAS VEGAS
Amargosa Valley
373
TO PAHRUMP, LAS VEGAS
Death Valley Junction
127
Shoshone
Dublin Gulch Caves
Trona
0
10 mi
10 km
Saratoga Spring
TO BAKER & I-15

The natural riches of Death Valley—the largest national park outside Alaska—are overwhelming: rolling waves of sand dunes, black cinder cones thrusting up hundreds of feet from a blistered desert floor, riotous sheets of wildflowers, bizarrely shaped Joshua trees basking in the orange glow of a sunset, tiny pupfish, and a dramatic silence.

This is a land of extremes of climate (hottest and driest) and geography. The park centers on Death Valley, which extends 156 miles from north to south and includes Badwater Basin, the lowest point in the USA (282 feet below sea level). Two mountain ranges border the valley: the Panamint on the west, where Telescope Peak juts more than 11,000 feet up from the valley floor, and the Amargosa in the east. Salt basins, spring-fed oases, sand dunes, deep canyons, and more than a thousand miles of paved and dirt roads punctuate the barren landscapes.

Humans first roamed this once-lush region around 10,000 years ago. The Timbisha Shoshone have lived here for more than a thousand years, originally along the shores of a 30-foot-deep lake. They called the area Timbisha for the red-hued rocks in the hillsides. Gold-rush pioneers looking for a shortcut to California traversed the barren expanse in 1849; some met their demise in the harsh environment, and those who survived named the place Death Valley. Silver and borax mining companies soon arrived on the scene. They didn't last long (most had stopped operations by 1910), but they left ghost towns and ramshackle mines as evidence of their dreams.

In 1933, President Herbert Hoover proclaimed the area a national monument to protect both its natural beauty and its scientific importance. In 1994, Congress passed the California Desert Protection Act, adding 1.3 million acres and designating the region a national park. Today, Death Valley National Park encompasses nearly 3.5 million acres, 93% of which is designated wilderness.

Despite its moniker, Death Valley teems with life. More than a million visitors a year come here to view plants and animals that reveal remarkable adaptations to the desert environment, hike through deep canyons and up mountain trails, gaze at planets and stars in a vast night sky, and follow in the footsteps of ancient cultures and pioneers. They come to explore an outstanding, exceptionally diverse outdoor natural history museum, filled with excellent examples of the planet's geological history. Most of all, they come to experience peace, quiet, and solitude in a stark, surreal landscape found nowhere else on Earth.

Death Valley in One Day

If you begin the day in Furnace Creek, you can see several sights without doing much driving. Bring plenty of water with you and some food, too. Rise early and drive the 20 miles on Badwater Road to **Badwater,** which looks out on the lowest point in the Western Hemisphere and is a dramatic place to watch the sunrise. Returning north, stop at **Natural Bridge,** a medium-size conglomerate rock formation that has been hollowed at its base to form a span across the canyon, and then at the **Devil's Golf Course,** so named because of the large pinnacles of salt present here. Detour to the right onto **Artists Drive,** a 9-mile one-way, northbound route that passes **Artists Palette.** The reds, yellows, oranges, and greens come from minerals in the rocks and the earth. Four miles north of Artists Drive is the **Golden Canyon Interpretive Trail,** a 2-mile round-trip that winds through a canyon with colorful rock walls. Just before Furnace Creek, take Highway 190 3 miles east to **Zabriskie Point,** overlooking dramatic, furrowed red-brown hills and the **Twenty Mule Team Canyon.** Return to Furnace Creek, where you can grab a meal and visit the museum at the Furnace Creek Visitor Center. Heading north from Furnace Creek, pull off the highway and take a look at the historic **Harmony Borax Works.**

AVERAGE HIGH/LOW TEMPERATURES

JAN.	FEB.	MAR.	APR.	MAY	JUNE
65/39	72/46	80/53	90/62	99/71	109/80
JULY	**AUG.**	**SEPT.**	**OCT.**	**NOV.**	**DEC.**
115/88	113/85	106/75	92/62	76/48	65/39

Planning

When to Go

Most of the park's 1.7 million annual visitors come between late fall and early spring, taking advantage of moderate temperatures and the lack of rainfall. During these cooler months, you will need to book a room in advance, but don't worry: the park never feels crowded. If you visit in summer, believe everything you've ever heard about desert heat—it can be brutal, with temperatures often topping 120°F. The dry air wicks moisture from the body without causing a sweat, so drink plenty of water. Bring sunglasses, a hat, and sufficient clothing to block the sun's rays and the wind. Flash floods are fairly common; sections of roadway can be flooded or washed away, as they were after a major flood in 2015. The wettest month is February, when the park receives an average of 0.3 inch of rain.

Getting Here and Around

AIR

The closest airport to the park with commercial service, Las Vegas McCarran (slated to be renamed Harry Reid) International Airport, is 130 miles away, so you'll still need to drive a couple of hours to reach the park. Roughly 160 miles to the west, Burbank's Bob Hope Airport is the second-closest airport.

CAR

It can take more than three hours to cross from one side of the park to another, so it's important to choose an entrance point that makes sense for what you want to see. If you're driving from Los Angeles, enter through the western portion along Highway 395; from Las Vegas, enter from the north at Beatty, Nevada, or via the central entrance at Death Valley Junction. Travelers from Orange County, San Diego, and the Inland Empire should access the park via Interstate 15 North at Baker.

Distances can be deceiving: what seems close can be very far away. Much of the park can be viewed on regularly scheduled bus tours, but these often don't allow time for hikes to sites not seen from the road, such as Salt Creek, Golden Canyon, and Natural Bridge. The best option is to drive to a number of the sites, get out of the car, and walk.

When driving in Death Valley, reliable maps are important, as signage is often limited or, in a few places, nonexistent. Bring a phone, but don't rely on cell coverage exclusively in every remote area, and pack plenty of food and water (3 gallons per person per day is recommended). Cars, especially in summer, should be prepared for the hot, dry weather, too. Some of the park's most spectacular canyons are accessible only via four-wheel-drive vehicles, but make sure the trip is well planned and use a backcountry map. Be aware of possible winter closures or driving restrictions because of snow. The National Park Service's website (🌐 *nps.gov/deva*) stays up-to-date on road closures during the wet (and popular) months. ⚠ **One of the park's signature landmarks, Scotty's Castle, and the 8-mile road connecting it to the park border may be closed until 2022 due to damage from a 2015 flood.**

CONTACTS California Highway Patrol. ☎ *800/427–7623 recorded info from CalTrans, 760/872–5900 live dispatcher at Bishop Communications Center* 🌐 *www.chp.ca.gov.* **California State Department of Transportation Hotline** ☎ *800/427–7623* 🌐 *www.dot.ca.gov.*

Park Essentials

ACCESSIBILITY

All of Death Valley's visitor centers, contact stations, and museums are accessible to all visitors. The campgrounds at Furnace Creek, Sunset, and Stovepipe Wells have wheelchair-accessible sites. Highway 190, Badwater Road, and paved roads to Dante's View and Wildrose provide access to the major scenic viewpoints and historic points of interest.

PARK FEES AND PERMITS

The entrance fee is $30 per vehicle, $25 for motorcycles, and $15 for those entering on foot or bike. The payment, valid for seven consecutive days, is collected at the park's ranger stations, self-serve fee stations, and the visitor center at Furnace Creek. Annual park passes, valid only at Death Valley, are $55.

A permit is not required for groups of 14 or fewer, but if you're planning an overnight visit to the backcountry, complete a registration form at the Furnace Creek Visitor Center. Backcountry camping is allowed in areas that are at least 2 miles from maintained campgrounds and the main paved or unpaved roads and ¼ mile from water sources. Most abandoned mining areas are restricted to day use.

PARK HOURS

The park is open day or night year-round. Most facilities operate daily 8–6.

CELL PHONE RECEPTION
Results vary, but in general you should be able to get fairly good reception on the valley floor. In the surrounding mountains, however, don't count on it.

Hotels

It's difficult to find lodging anywhere in Death Valley that doesn't have breathtaking views of the park and surrounding mountains. Most accommodations, aside from the Inn at Death Valley, are homey and rustic. Rooms fill up quickly during the fall and spring seasons, and reservations are required about three months in advance for the prime weekends.

Restaurants

Inside the park, if you're looking for a special evening out, head to the Inn at Death Valley Dining Room, which is also a great spot to start the day with a hearty gourmet breakfast. Most other eateries within the park are mom-and-pop-type places with basic American fare.

Hotel and restaurant reviews have been shortened. For full information visit Fodors.com. Hotel prices are the lowest cost of a standard double room in high season. Restaurant prices are the average cost of a main course at dinner, or if dinner is not served, at lunch.

What It Costs

$	$$	$$$	$$$$
RESTAURANTS			
under $17	$17–$26	$27–$36	over $36
HOTELS			
under $150	$150–$250	$251–$350	over $350

Tours

Furnace Creek Visitor Center programs
GUIDED TOURS | This center has many programs, including ranger-led hikes that explore natural wonders such as Golden Canyon, nighttime stargazing parties with telescopes, and evening ranger talks. ✉ *Furnace Creek Visitor Center, Rte. 190, 30 miles northwest of Death Valley Junction, Death Valley* ☎ *760/786–2331* 🌐 *www.nps.gov/deva/planyourvisit/tours.htm* 🎫 *Free.*

Visitor Information

CONTACTS Death Valley National Park. ☎ *760/786–3200* 🌐 *www.nps.gov/deva.*

Central Death Valley

12 miles west of the Death Valley National Park Highway 190 entrance.

Furnace Creek village (194 feet below sea level) was once the center of mining operations for the Pacific Coast Borax Company. Today, it's the hub of Death Valley National Park, home to park headquarters and visitor center; the Timbisha Indian Village; and the Oasis at Death Valley hotels, golf course, restaurants, and market. Many major park sites are a short drive from here, including Artists Drive, Badwater Basin, Dante's View, and Zabriskie Point. Stovepipe Wells Village (where you will want to fill up at the gas station) lies 25 miles northwest of Furnace Creek.

Sights

HISTORIC SIGHTS

Harmony Borax Works
HISTORIC SITE | Death Valley's mule teams hauled borax from here to the railroad town of Mojave, 165 miles away. The teams plied the route until 1889, when the railroad finally arrived in Zabriskie.

Constructed in 1883, one of the oldest buildings in Death Valley houses the Borax Museum, 2 miles south of the borax works at the Ranch at the Oasis at Death Valley (between the restaurants and the post office). Originally a miners' bunkhouse, the building once stood in Twenty Mule Team Canyon. Now it displays mining machinery and historical exhibits. The adjacent structure is the original mule-team barn. ✉ *Harmony Borax Works Rd., west of Hwy. 190 at Ranch at Death Valley* 🌐 *www.nps.gov/deva/historyculture/harmony.htm.*

SCENIC DRIVE

Artists Drive

SCENIC DRIVE | This 9-mile, one-way route skirts the foothills of the Black Mountains and provides intimate views of the changing landscape. Once inside the palette, the valley's expanses are replaced by the small-scale natural beauty of pigments created by volcanic deposits or sedimentary layers. It's a quiet, lonely drive, and shouldn't be rushed. Reach Artists Palette by heading south on Badwater Road from its intersection with Route 190. ✉ *Death Valley National Park.*

SCENIC STOPS

Artists Palette

NATURE SITE | So called for the contrasting colors of its volcanic deposits and sedimentary layers, this is one of the signature sights of Death Valley. Artists Drive, the approach to the area, is one-way heading north off Badwater Road, so if you're visiting Badwater from Furnace Creek, come here on the way back. The drive winds through foothills of sedimentary and volcanic rocks. About 4 miles along, a short side road veers right to a parking lot that's a few hundred feet before the "palette," whose natural colors include shades of green, gold, and pink. ✉ *Off Badwater Rd., Death Valley* ✣ *11 miles south of Furnace Creek.*

Badwater Basin

NATURE SITE | At 282 feet below sea level, Badwater is the lowest spot of land in North America—and also one of the hottest. Stairs and wheelchair ramps descend from the parking lot to a wooden platform that overlooks a sodium chloride pool, a small but remarkably persistent reminder that the valley floor used to contain a lake. You can continue past the platform on a broad, white path that peters out after a ½ mile or so. Badwater is one of the most popular and easily accessible sites within the park. From this lowest point, be sure to look across to Telescope Peak, which towers more than 2 miles above the valley floor. ✉ *Badwater Rd., Death Valley* ✣ *19 miles south of Furnace Creek.*

Devil's Golf Course

NATURE SITE | Thousands of miniature salt pinnacles carved into surreal shapes by the desert wind dot this wildly varied landscape. The salt was pushed up to the surface by pressure created as underground salt- and water-bearing gravel crystallized. Get out of your vehicle and take a closer look; you may see perfectly round holes descending into the ground. ✉ *Badwater Rd., Death Valley* ✣ *13 miles south of Furnace Creek. Turn right onto dirt road and drive 1 mile.*

Golden Canyon

NATURE SITE | Just south of Furnace Creek, these glimmering mountains are perhaps best known for their role in the original *Star Wars*. The canyon is also a fine hiking spot, with gorgeous views of the Panamint Mountains, ancient dry lake beds, and alluvial fans. ✉ *Hwy. 178, Death Valley* ✣ *From Furnace Creek Visitor Center, drive 2 miles south on Hwy. 190, then 2 miles south on Hwy. 178 to parking area; the lot has kiosk with trail guides.*

The Mesquite Flat Sand Dunes

Mesquite Flat Sand Dunes

NATURE SITE | These dunes, made up of minute pieces of quartz and other rock, are ever-changing products of the wind-rippled hills, with curving crests and a sun-bleached hue. The dunes are the most photographed destination in the park, and you can see them at their best at sunrise and sunset. Keep your eyes open for animal tracks—you may even spot a coyote or fox. Bring plenty of water, and note where you parked your car: it's easy to become disoriented in this ocean of sand. If you lose your bearings, climb to the top of a dune, and scan the horizon for the parking lot. ✉ *Death Valley* ✥ *19 miles north of Hwy. 190, northeast of Stovepipe Wells Village.*

Zabriskie Point

VIEWPOINT | Although only about 710 feet in elevation, this is one of the park's most scenic spots, overlooking a striking panorama of wrinkled, multicolor hills. It's a great place to watch the sunrise, but it can be bustling any time of day. Pair it with a drive out to magnificent Dante's View. ✉ *Hwy. 190, Death Valley* ✥ *5 miles south of Furnace Creek.*

TRAILS

Keane Wonder Mine Trail

TRAIL | This fascinating relic of Death Valley's gold-mining past, built in 1907, reopened in November 2017 after nine years of repair work. Its most unique feature is the mile-long tramway that descends 1,000 vertical feet, which once carried gold ore and still has the original cables attached. From here, a network of trails leads to other old mines. A climb to the uppermost tramway terminal is rewarded by expansive views of the valley. ✉ *Access road off Beatty Cutoff Rd., 17½ miles north of Furnace Creek, Death Valley.*

Mosaic Canyon Trail

TRAIL | FAMILY | A gradual uphill trail (4 miles round-trip) winds through the smoothly polished, marbleized limestone walls of this narrow canyon. There are dry falls to climb at the upper end. *Moderate.* ✉ *Death Valley* ✥ *Trailhead: Access road off Hwy. 190, ½ mile west of Stovepipe Wells Village.*

Natural Bridge Canyon Trail

TRAIL | A rough 2-mile access road from Badwater Road leads to a trailhead. From there, set off to see interesting geological features in addition to the bridge, which is a ½ mile away. The one-way trail continues for a few hundred yards, but scenic returns diminish quickly, and eventually you're confronted with climbing boulders. *Easy.* ✉ *Death Valley* ✣ *Trailhead: Access road off Badwater Rd., 15 miles south of Furnace Creek.*

Salt Creek Interpretive Trail

TRAIL | **FAMILY** | This trail, a ½-mile boardwalk circuit, loops through a spring-fed wash. The nearby hills are brown and gray, but the floor of the wash is alive with aquatic plants such as pickleweed and salt grass. The stream and ponds here are among the few places in the park to see the rare pupfish, the only native fish species in Death Valley. They're most easily seen during their spawning season in February and March. Animals such as bobcats, foxes, coyotes, and snakes visit the spring, and you may also see ravens, common snipes, killdeer, and great blue herons. *Easy.* ✉ *Death Valley* ✣ *Trailhead: Off Hwy. 190, 14 miles north of Furnace Creek.*

VISITOR CENTERS

Furnace Creek Visitor Center and Museum

INFO CENTER | The exhibits and artifacts here provide a broad overview of how Death Valley formed; you can pick up maps at the bookstore run by the Death Valley Natural History Association. This is also the place to find out about ranger programs (available November through April) or check out a live presentation about the valley's cultural and natural history. The helpful center offers regular showings of a 20-minute film about the park, and this is the place for children to get their free Junior Ranger booklet, packed with games and information about the park and its critters. ✉ *Hwy. 190, Death Valley* ✣ *30 miles northwest of Death Valley Junction* ☎ *760/786–3200* 🌐 *www.nps.gov/deva.*

Restaurants

★ **Inn at the Oasis at Death Valley Dining Room**

$$$$ | **AMERICAN** | Fireplaces, beamed ceilings, and spectacular views provide a visual feast to match this fine-dining restaurant's ambitious menu. Dinner entrées include salmon, free-range chicken, and filet mignon, and there's a seasonal menu of vegetarian dishes. **Known for:** views of surrounding desert; old-school charm; can be pricey. Ⓢ *Average main: $42* ✉ *Inn at the Oasis at Death Valley, Hwy. 190, Furnace Creek* ☎ *760/786–3385* 🌐 *www.oasisatdeathvalley.com.*

Last Kind Words Saloon

$$$ | **AMERICAN** | Swing through wooden doors into a spacious dining room that re-creates an authentic Old West saloon, decked out with a wooden bar and furniture, mounted animal heads, fugitive wanted fliers, film posters, and other memorabilia. The traditional steak house menu also includes crab cakes and other seafood, along with pastas, flatbreads, and vegan and gluten-free options. **Known for:** hefty steaks, ribs, and seasonal game dishes; extensive drinks menu, from local craft beer to whiskeys and wines; outdoor patio with fireplace. Ⓢ *Average main: $29* ✉ *The Ranch at the Oasis at Death Valley, Hwy. 190, Furnace Creek* ☎ *760/786–3335* 🌐 *www.oasisatdeathvalley.com/dine/last-kind-words-saloon.*

Hotels

★ **The Inn at the Oasis at Death Valley**

$$$$ | **HOTEL** | Built in 1927, this adobe-brick-and-stone lodge in one of the park's greenest oases reopened in 2018 after a $100 million renovation, offering Death Valley's most luxurious accommodations, including 22 brand-new one- and two-bedroom casitas. **Pros:** refined; comfortable; great views. **Cons:** services reduced during low season (July and August); expensive; resort fee. Ⓢ *Rooms* *from: $499* ✉ *Furnace Creek Village, near intersection of Hwy. 190 and Badwater Rd., Death Valley* ☎ *760/786–2345* 🌐 *www.oasisatdeathvalley.com* 🛏 *88 rooms* 🍽 *No meals.*

The Ranch at the Oasis at Death Valley
$$$ | **RESORT** | **FAMILY** | Originally the crew headquarters for the Pacific Coast Borax Company, the four buildings here have motel-style rooms that are a great option for families. **Pros:** good family atmosphere; central location; walk to the golf course. **Cons:** rooms can get hot in summer despite a/c; resort fee; thin walls and ceilings in some rooms. 💲 *Rooms from: $279* ✉ *Hwy. 190, Furnace Creek* ☎ *760/786–2345* 🌐 *www.oasisatdeathvalley.com* 🛏 *224 rooms* 🍽 *No meals.*

Stovepipe Wells Village Hotel
$ | **HOTEL** | If you prefer quiet nights and an unfettered view of the night sky and nearby Mesquite Flat Sand Dunes and Mosaic Canyon, this property is for you. **Pros:** intimate, relaxed; no big-time partying; authentic desert-community ambience. **Cons:** isolated; cheapest patio rooms very small; limited Wi-Fi access. 💲 *Rooms from: $144* ✉ *51880 Hwy. 190, Stovepipe Wells* ☎ *760/786–7090* 🌐 *www.deathvalleyhotels.com* 🛏 *83 rooms* 🍽 *No meals.*

Northern Death Valley

6 miles west of Beatty, Nevada, via Nevada Hwy. 374, and 54 miles north of Furnace Creek via Hwy. 190 and Scotty's Castle Rd.

Venture into the remote northern region of the park to travel along the 27-mile Titus Canyon scenic drive, visit Racetrack and Ubehebe Crater, and hike along Fall Canyon and Titus Canyon Trails. Scotty's Castle, one of the park's main sights, and the 8-mile road that connects it to the park border, is currently closed to repair damage from a 2015 flood; it's expected to reopen in 2022. Check the park website for updates before you visit.

Sights

SCENIC DRIVES

Titus Canyon
SCENIC DRIVE | This popular, one-way, 27-mile drive starts at Nevada Highway 374 (Daylight Pass Road), 2 miles from the park's boundary. Highlights include the Leadville Ghost Town and the spectacular limestone and dolomite narrows. Toward the end, a two-way section of gravel road leads you into the mouth of the canyon from Scotty's Castle Road (closed until at least 2022). This drive is steep, bumpy, and narrow. High-clearance vehicles are strongly recommended. ✉ *Death Valley National Park* ✥ *Access road off Nevada Hwy. 374, 6 miles west of Beatty, NV.*

SCENIC STOPS

Racetrack
NATURE SITE | Getting here involves a 28-mile journey over a washboard dirt road, but the reward is well worth the trip. Where else in the world do rocks move on their own? This mysterious phenomenon, which baffled scientists for years, now appears to have been "settled." Research has shown that the movement merely involves a rare confluence of conditions: rain and then cold to create a layer of ice that becomes a sail, thus enabling gusty winds to readily push the rocks along—sometimes for several hundred yards. When the mud dries, a telltale trail remains. The trek to the Racetrack can be made in a truck or SUV with thick tires (including spares) and high clearance; other types of vehicles aren't recommended as sharp rocks can slash tires. ✉ *Death Valley* ✥ *27 miles west of Ubehebe Crater via rough dirt road.*

Ubehebe Crater
VOLCANO | At 500 feet deep and ½ mile across, this crater resulted from underground steam and gas explosions, some as recently as 300 years ago. Volcanic ash spreads out over most of the area, and the cinders lie as deep as 150 feet near

the crater's rim. Trek down to the crater's floor or walk around it on a fairly level path. Either way, you need about an hour and will be treated to fantastic views. The hike from the floor can be strenuous. ⊠ *N. Death Valley Hwy., Death Valley* ✣ *8 miles northwest of Scotty's Castle.*

TRAILS

Fall Canyon Trail

TRAIL | This is a 3-mile, one-way hike from the Titus canyon parking area. First, walk ½ mile north along the base of the mountains to a large wash, then go 2½ miles up the canyon to a 35-foot dry fall. You can continue by climbing around to the falls on the south side. *Moderate.* ⊠ *Death Valley National Park* ✣ *Trailhead: Access road off Scotty's Castle Rd., 33 miles northwest of Furnace Creek.*

Titus Canyon Trail

TRAIL | The narrow floor of Titus Canyon is made of hard-packed gravel and dirt, and it's a constant, moderate, uphill walk (3-mile round-trip is the trail's most popular tack). Klare Spring and some petroglyphs are 5½ miles from the western mouth of the canyon, but you can get a feeling for the area on a shorter walk. *Easy.* ⊠ *Death Valley National Park.*

Southern Death Valley

Entrance on Hwy. 178, 1 mile west of Shoshone and 73 miles southeast of Furnace Creek.

Highway 178 traverses Death Valley from its southern border near Shoshone, through Badwater Basin, and up to Furnace Creek.

Sights

SCENIC STOPS

★ Dante's View

VIEWPOINT | This lookout is 5,450 feet above sea level in the Black Mountains. In the dry desert air you can see across most of 160-mile-long Death Valley. The view is astounding. Take a 10-minute, mildly strenuous walk from the parking lot toward a series of rocky overlooks, where, with binoculars, you can spot some signature sites. A few interpretive signs point out the highlights below in the valley and across in the Sierra. Getting here from Furnace Creek takes about an hour—time well invested. ⊠ *Dante's View Rd., Death Valley* ✣ *Off Hwy. 190, 35 miles from Badwater, 20 miles south of Twenty Mule Team Canyon.*

Western Death Valley

Panamint Springs is on Hwy. 190, 30 miles southwest of Stovepipe Wells and 50 miles east of Lone Pine and Hwy. 395.

Panamint Springs, a tiny burg with a rustic resort, market, and gas station, anchors the western portion of the park and is a good base for hiking several trails. Pull over at Father Crowley Vista Point for exceptional views of the Panamint Valley and the high Sierra on Highway 190 if you're traveling between Lone Pine and Panamint Springs.

Sights

SCENIC STOPS

Father Crowley Vista Point

VIEWPOINT | Pull off Highway 190 in Western Death Valley into the vista point parking lot to gaze at the remnants of eerie volcanic flows down to Rainbow Canyon. Stroll a short distance to catch a sweeping overview of northern Panamint Valley. This is also an excellent site for stargazing. ⊠ *Death Valley National Park.*

TRAILS

★ Darwin Falls

TRAIL | **FAMILY** | This lovely, 2-mile round-trip hike rewards you with a refreshing year-round waterfall surrounded by thick vegetation and a rocky gorge. No swimming or bathing is allowed, but it's a beautiful place for a picnic. Adventurous hikers can scramble higher toward more rewarding views of the falls. ⚠ **Some sections of the trail are not passable for those with mobility issues.** *Easy.* ✉ *Death Valley National Park* ✣ *Trailhead: Access the 2-mile graded dirt road and parking area off Hwy. 190, 1 mile west of Panamint Springs Resort.*

★ Telescope Peak Trail

TRAIL | The 14-mile round-trip (with 3,000 feet of elevation gain) trail begins at Mahogany Flat Campground, which is accessible by a rough dirt road. The steep and at some points treacherous trail winds through pinyon, juniper, and bristlecone pines, with excellent views of Death Valley and Panamint Valley. Ice axes and crampons may be necessary in winter—check at the Furnace Creek Visitor Center. It takes a minimum of six grueling hours to hike to the top of the 11,049-foot peak and then return. *Difficult.* ✉ *Death Valley* ✣ *Trailhead: Off Wildrose Rd., south of Charcoal Kilns.*

Restaurants

Panamint Springs Resort Restaurant

$ | **AMERICAN** | This is a great place for steak and a beer—choose from more than 150 different beers and ales—or pasta and a salad. In summer, evening meals are served outdoors on the porch, which has spectacular views of Panamint Valley. **Known for:** good burgers; extensive beer selection; great views from the porch. $ *Average main: $15* ✉ *Hwy. 190, Death Valley* ✣ *31 miles west of Stovepipe Wells* ☎ *775/482–7680* 🌐 *www.panamintsprings.com/services/dining-bar.*

Activities

BIKING

Mountain biking is permitted on any of the back roads and roadways open to the public (bikes aren't permitted on hiking trails). Visit 🌐 *www.nps.gov/deva/planyourvisit/bikingandmtbiking.htm* for a list of suggested routes for all levels of ability.

Escape Adventures

BICYCLING | Ride into the heart of Death Valley on the Death Valley & Red Rock Mountain Bike Tour, a five-day trip through the national park. A customizable two-day journey (on single-track trails and jeep roads) includes accommodations (both camping and inns). Bikes, tents, and other gear may be rented for an additional price. Tours are available February–April and October only. ✉ *Death Valley National Park* ☎ *800/596–2953, 702/596–2953* 🌐 *www.escapeadventures.com* 🎫 *From $1950.*

BIRD-WATCHING

Approximately 350 bird species have been identified in Death Valley. You can download a complete park bird checklist, divided by season, at 🌐 *www.nps.gov/deva/learn/nature/upload/death-valley-bird-checklist.pdf.* Rangers at Furnace Creek Visitor Center often lead birding walks through various locations between November and March.

CAMPING

Camping is prohibited in historic sites and day-use spots. You'll need a high-clearance or 4X4 vehicle to reach campgrounds. For backcountry camping information, visit 🌐 *www.nps.gov/deva/planyourvisit/camping.htm.*

Fires are permitted only in metal grates and may be restricted in summer. Wood gathering is prohibited at all campgrounds, and it's best to bring your own. Firewood is expensive and limited in supply at general stores in Furnace Creek and Stovepipe Wells.

Furnace Creek. This campground, 196 feet below sea level, has some shaded tent sites and is open all year. ✉ *Hwy. 190, Furnace Creek* ☎ *760/786–2441.*

Mahogany Flat. If you have a four-wheel-drive vehicle and want to scale Telescope Peak, the park's highest mountain, you might want to sleep at one of the few shaded spots in Death Valley, at a cool 8,133 feet. ✉ *Off Wildrose Rd., south of Charcoal Kilns* ☎ *No phone.*

Panamint Springs Resort. Part of a complex that includes a motel and cabin, this campground is surrounded by cottonwoods. The daily fee includes use of the showers and restrooms. ✉ *Hwy. 190, 28 miles west of Stovepipe Wells* ☎ *775/482–7680.*

Sunset Campground. This first-come, first-served campground is a gravel-and-asphalt RV city. Closed mid-April to mid-October. ✉ *Sunset Campground Rd., 1 mile north of Furnace Creek* ☎ *800/365–2267.*

Texas Spring. This campsite south of the Furnace Creek Visitor Center has good views and facilities and is a few dollars cheaper than Furnace Creek. It's closed mid-May to mid-October. ✉ *Off Badwater Rd., south of Furnace Creek Visitor Center* ☎ *800/365–2267.*

EDUCATIONAL PROGRAMS

Junior Ranger Program

TOUR—SIGHT | FAMILY | Children can pick up a workbook and complete activities to earn a souvenir badge. ✉ *Death Valley National Park.*

FOUR-WHEELING

Butte Valley

TOUR—SPORTS | A high-clearance, four-wheel-drive vehicle and nerves of steel are required to tackle this 21-mile road in the southwest part of the park. It climbs from 200 feet below sea level to an elevation of 4,700 feet, and the geological formations along the way reveal the development of Death Valley. It also travels through Butte Valley, passing the Warm Springs talc mine, to Geologist's Cabin, a charming and cheery little structure where you can spend the night, if nobody else beats you to it. The cabin, which sits under a cottonwood tree, has a fireplace, table and chairs, and a sink. Farther up the road, Stella's Cabin and Russell Camp are also open for public use. Keep the historic cabins clean, and restock any items that you use. The road is even rougher if you continue over Mengel Pass. Check road conditions before heading out. ✉ *Trailhead on Warm Spring Canyon Rd., Death Valley* ✣ *50 miles south of Furnace Creek Visitor Center.*

GOLF

Furnace Creek Golf Course at the Oasis at Death Valley

GOLF | Golfers rave about how their drives carry at altitude, so what happens on the lowest golf course in the world (214 feet below sea level)? Its improbably green fairways are lined with date palms and tamarisk trees, and its level of difficulty is rated surprisingly high. You can rent clubs and carts, and there are golf packages available for resort guests. In fall and winter, reservations are essential. ✉ *Hwy. 190, Furnace Creek* ☎ *760/786–3373* 🌐 *www.oasisatdeathvalley.com* 💵 *From $48* 🏌 *18 holes, 6215 yards, par 70.*

HIKING

Plan to hike before or after midday in the spring, summer, or fall, unless you're in the mood for a masochistic baking. Carry plenty of water, wear protective clothing, and keep an eye out for black widows, scorpions, snakes, and other potentially dangerous creatures.

HORSEBACK AND CARRIAGE RIDES

Furnace Creek Stables

HORSEBACK RIDING | FAMILY | Set off on a one- or two-hour guided horseback, carriage, or hay wagon ride from Furnace Creek Stables. The rides traverse trails with views of the surrounding mountains, where multicolor volcanic rock and alluvial fans form a background for date palms and other vegetation. Evening carriage rides take passengers around the golf course and the Ranch at Death Valley. The stables are open October–May only. ✉ *Hwy. 190, Furnace Creek* ☎ *760/614–1018* 🌐 *www.oasisatdeathvalley.com/plan/horseback-wagon-rides* 💵 *From $60.*

What's Nearby

Beatty

7 miles east of Death Valley National Park Devil's Gate entrance.

The tiny Old West town of Beatty, a northeastern gateway to Death Valley National Park, has a well-preserved historic downtown district that's worth exploring. It's also a good place to relax and refresh thanks to its cluster of hotels, restaurants, and other services. Hundreds of hiking, biking, and off-highway vehicle roads stretch out from here in all directions. Beatty is also home to the Death Valley Nut and Candy Company, Nevada's largest candy store, and the Rhyolite Ghost Town is just 5 miles west of downtown.

ESSENTIALS

VISITOR INFORMATION Beatty Chamber of Commerce. ✉ *119 E. Main St., Beatty* ☎ *775/553–2424* 🌐 *www.beattynevada.org.*

Sights

Rhyolite

GHOST TOWN | FAMILY | Though it's not within the boundary of Death Valley National Park, this Nevada ghost town, named for the silica volcanic rock nearby, is still a big draw. Around 1904, Rhyolite's Montgomery Shoshone Mine caused a financial boom, and fancy buildings sprung up all over town. Today you can still explore many of the crumbling edifices. The Bottle House, built by miner Tom Kelly out of almost 50,000 Adolphus Busch beer bottles, is a must-see. ✉ *Hwy. 374* ✣ *35 miles north of Furnace Creek Visitor Center and 5 miles west of Beatty* 🌐 *www.nps.gov/deva/learn/historyculture/rhyolite-ghost-town.htm.*

Restaurants

Smokin J's BBQ

$$ | BARBECUE | A local favorite, this central Texas–style barbecue joint slow cooks brisket, pulled pork, ribs, and chicken on an oak-fired grill and serves them in baskets heaping with fries, onion rings, and other sides. Pick up meats by the pound to feast on at your lodgings later on. **Known for:** smoked-meat sandwiches; brisket chili bowls; great-value combo plates and meals. $ *Average main: $17* ✉ *107 W. Main St., Beatty* ☎ *775/553–5160* 🌐 *www.facebook.com/Smokinjsbarbecue.*

Shoshone

1 mile from Death Valley National Park's Badwater entrance.

A prospector founded this tiny burg in 1910, hoping to build businesses around a new rail stop. He and his family eventually developed the town, and his descendents still run Shoshone Village, which encompasses a hotel, general store, gas station, museum, spring-fed swimming pool, restaurant, campground, and RV park. Nearby nature trails wind through wetlands, pupfish ponds, and bird and endangered-species habitats.

ESSENTIALS

VISITOR INFORMATION Shoshone Museum Visitor Center. ✉ *Rte. 127, Shoshone* ☎ *760/852–4524* 🌐 *shoshonevillage.com/shoshone-museum.html.*

Sights

Dublin Gulch

CAVE | FAMILY | A series of caves, carved into the caliche soil by miners during the 1920s, is a great spot for exploring and is a hit with kids. Among its more famous residents were Shorty Harris and Death Valley Scotty, who spent many nights weaving tales of strikes and adventures to entertain fellow miners. You aren't allowed to walk inside, but you can view the cells—with their stone walls, sleeping platforms, and metal chimneys—from the exterior. *Shoshone* *0.3 miles southwest of Shoshone Village off Hwy. 127* *www.shoshonevillage.com/explore-shoshone.*

Marta Becket's Amargosa Opera House
An artist and dancer from New York, Marta Becket first visited the former railway town of Death Valley Junction while on tour in 1967. Later that year, she returned to town and leased a boarded-up social hall that sat amid a group of rundown mock Spanish–colonial buildings. The nonprofit she formed in the early 1970s eventually purchased the property, where she performed for nearly 50 years. To compensate for the sparse audiences in the early days, Becket painted a Renaissance-era Spanish crowd on the walls and ceiling, turning the theater into a trompe-l'oeil masterpiece. A hotel and café still operate on-site, and the opera house presents performances from October to May. Guided tours are available year-round for a suggested $5 donation per person. *Rte. 127, Death Valley Junction* *27 miles north of Shoshone* *760/852–4441* *www.amargosaoperahouse.org* *Varies.*

Shoshone Museum
MUSEUM | This museum chronicles the local history of Death Valley and houses a unique collection of period items and minerals and rocks from the area. *Rte. 127, Shoshone* *760/852–4524* *www.shoshonevillage.com/shoshone-museum.html* *Free.*

Restaurants

Crowbar Café and Saloon
$ | AMERICAN | FAMILY | In an old wooden building where antique photos adorn the walls and mining equipment stands in the corners, the Crowbar serves enormous helpings of regional dishes such as steak and taco salads. Home-baked fruit pies make fine desserts, and frosty beers are surefire thirst quenchers. **Known for:** home-baked fruit pies; rattlesnake chili; great breakfast spot. *Average main: $15* *Rte. 127, Shoshone* *760/852–4123* *www.shoshonevillage.com/shoshone-crowbar-cafe-saloon.html.*

Hotels

Shoshone Inn
$ | HOTEL | Built in 1956, the rustic Shoshone Inn has simple, cozy rooms surrounding a motor court and a warm spring-fed swimming pool built into the foothills. **Pros:** walk to market, restaurant, museum; courtyard with firepit; peaceful retreat. **Cons:** an hour's drive to main park sights; certain rooms and beds too small for some; no room phones, spotty cell service. *Rooms from: $135* *Hwy. 127, Shoshone* *760/852–4335* *www.shoshonevillage.com/death-valley-lodging-shoshone-inn* *18 units* *No meals.*

Chapter 11

THE CENTRAL COAST

FROM VENTURA TO BIG SUR WITH CHANNEL ISLANDS NATIONAL PARK

Updated by
Cheryl Crabtree

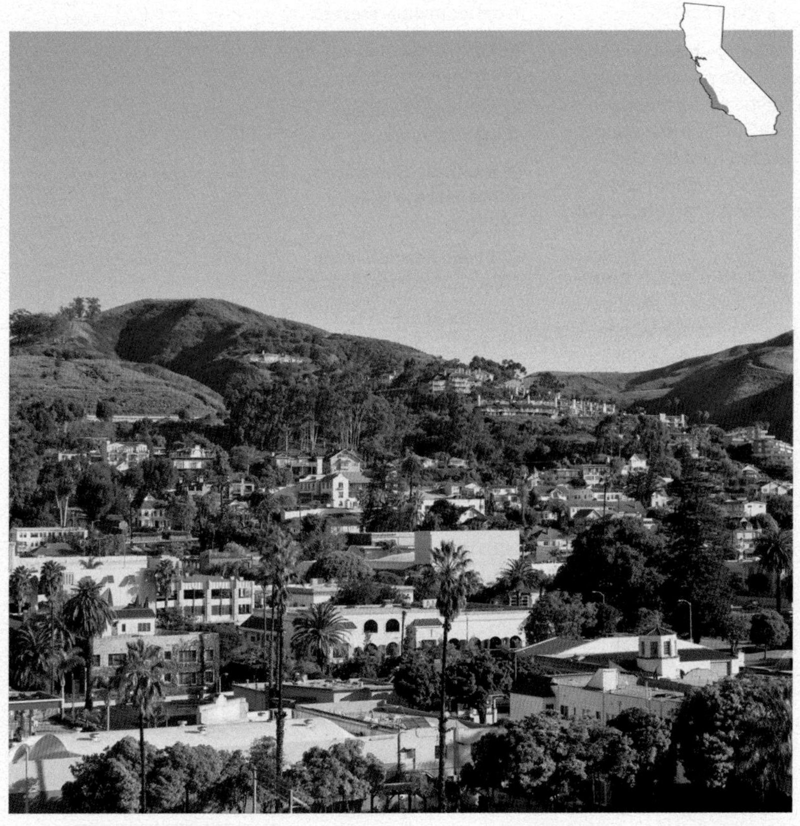

Sights	Restaurants	Hotels	Shopping	Nightlife
★★★★★	★★★★☆	★★★★★	★★☆☆☆	★☆☆☆☆

WELCOME TO THE CENTRAL COAST

TOP REASONS TO GO

★ **Incredible nature:** The wild and wonderful Central Coast is home to Channel Islands National Park, two national marine sanctuaries, state parks and beaches, and the rugged Los Padres National Forest.

★ **Edible bounty:** Land and sea provide enough fresh regional foods to satisfy the most sophisticated foodies. Get your fill at countless farmers' markets, wineries, and restaurants.

★ **Outdoor activities:** Kick back and revel in the California lifestyle. Surf, golf, kayak, hike, play tennis—or just hang out and enjoy the gorgeous scenery.

★ **Small-town charm, big-city culture:** With all the amazing cultural opportunities—museums, theater, music, and festivals—you might start thinking you're in L.A. or San Francisco.

★ **Wine tasting:** Central Coast wines earn high critical praise. Sample them in urban tasting rooms, dusty crossroads towns, and at high- and low-tech rural wineries.

1 **Ventura.** A walkable city with miles of beaches.

2 **Channel Islands National Park.** North America's Galapagos.

3 **Ojai.** Lush site of the film *Lost Horizon.*

4 **Santa Barbara.** The American Riviera.

5 **Santa Ynez.** An 1880s frontier town preserved.

6 **Los Olivos.** Has tasting rooms galore.

7 **Solvang.** America's "Little Denmark."

8 **Buellton.** Gateway to Santa Barbara wine country.

9 **Pismo Beach.** Classic California coastal city.

10 **Avila Beach.** A tiny village in a sunny cove.

11 **San Luis Obispo.** A busy university town.

12 **Paso Robles.** A small city amid a booming wine region.

13 **Morro Bay.** Outdoor activities reign here.

14 **Cambria.** A historic village with scenic shores and towering pines.

15 **San Simeon.** Home to Hearst Castle.

16 **Big Sur Coast.** A bucket-list road trip.

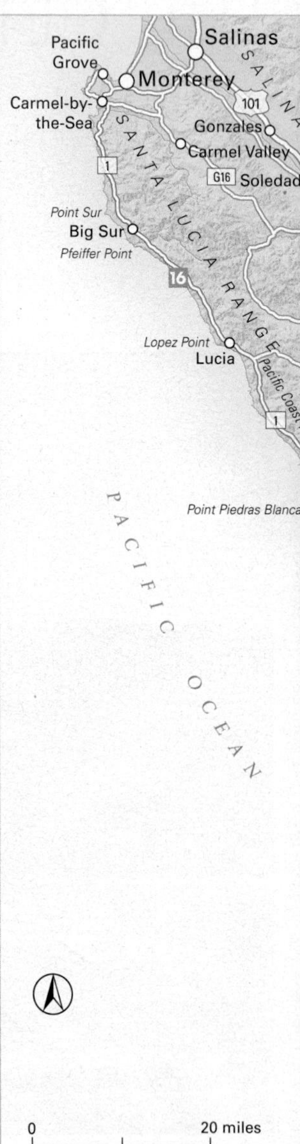

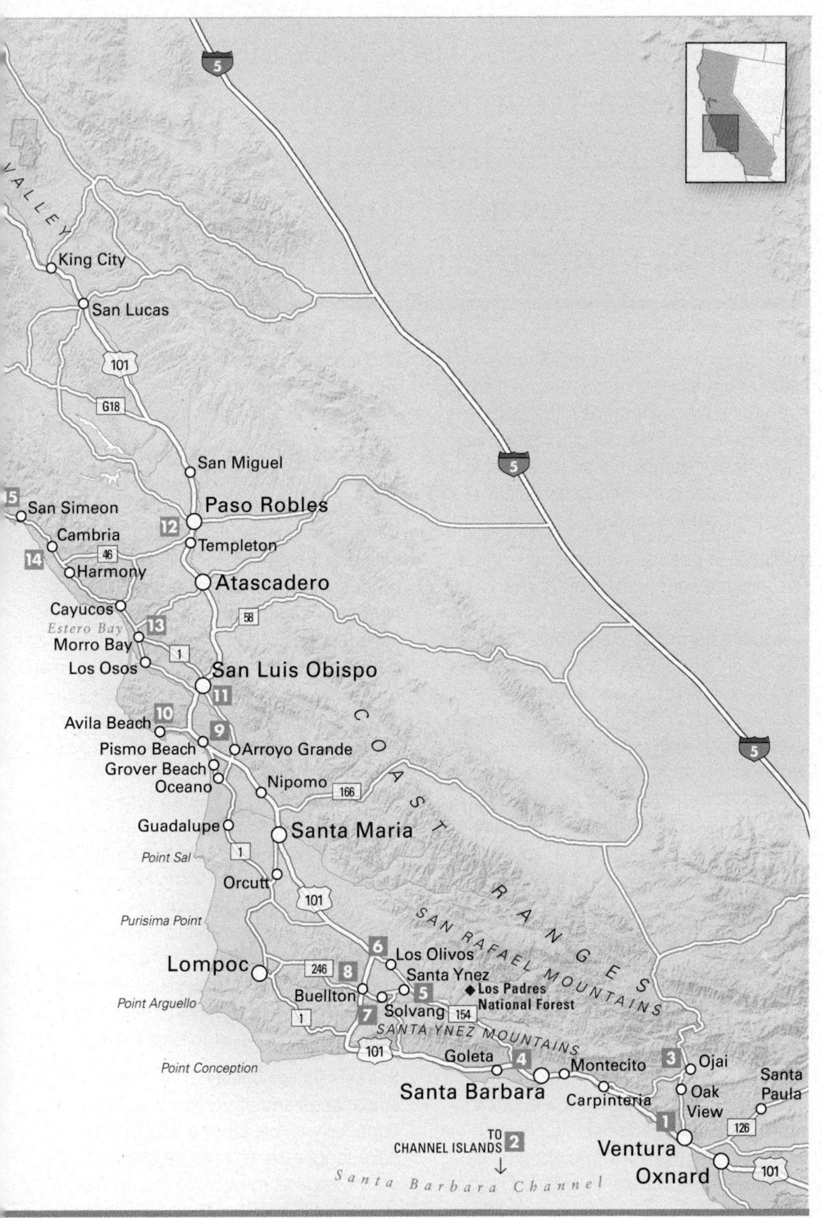

VALLEY
King City
San Lucas
101
G18
San Miguel
Paso Robles
San Simeon
Cambria
Templeton
46
Harmony
Atascadero
Cayucos
58
Estero Bay
Morro Bay
1
Los Osos
San Luis Obispo
Avila Beach
Pismo Beach
Arroyo Grande
Grover Beach
Oceano
Nipomo
166
Guadalupe
Santa Maria
Point Sal
1
Orcutt
101
Purisima Point
COAST RANGES
SAN RAFAEL MOUNTAINS
Los Olivos
Lompoc
246
Santa Ynez
Los Padres National Forest
Point Arguello
Buellton
Solvang
154
1
SANTA YNEZ MOUNTAINS
101
Goleta
Point Conception
Montecito
Ojai
Santa Barbara
Carpinteria
Oak View
Santa Paula
126
TO CHANNEL ISLANDS
Ventura
Oxnard
101
Santa Barbara Channel
5

Balmy weather, glorious beaches, crystal-clear air, and serene landscapes have lured people to the Central Coast since prehistoric times. Today it's also known for its farm-fresh bounty, from grapes vintners crafted into world-class wines, to strawberries and other produce used by chefs in distinctive cuisine.

The scenic variety along the Pacific coast is equally impressive—you'll see everything from dramatic cliffs and grass-tufted bluffs to wildlife estuaries and miles of dunes. It's an ideal place to relax, slow down, and appreciate the abundant natural beauty.

Offshore, a pristine national park and a vast marine sanctuary protect the wild, wonderful underwater resources of this incredible corner of the planet. But not all of the Central Coast's top attractions are natural: Ventura, Santa Barbara, and San Luis Obispo are filled with sparkling examples of Spanish-Mediterranean architecture, bustling shopping districts, and first-rate restaurants showcasing regional foods and wines.

MAJOR REGIONS

Ventura County. Ventura County was first settled by the Chumash Indians. Spanish missionaries were the first Europeans to arrive, followed by Americans and other Europeans, who established towns, transportation networks, and farms. Since the 1920s, agriculture has been steadily replaced as the area's main industry—first by the oil business and more recently by tourism. Accessible via boat or plane from Ventura (as well as Santa Barbara), Channel Islands National Park consists of five protected islands just 11 miles offshore where hiking, kayaking, and wildlife viewing abound.

Santa Barbara County. The Santa Ynez Mountains divide the county geographically; U.S. 101 passes through a mountain tunnel leading inland. The South Coast includes the city of Santa Barbara and other coastal towns and small cities. Northern Santa Barbara County, which includes the communities of Buellton, Solvang, Santa Ynez, and Los Olivos, used to be known for sprawling ranches and strawberry and broccoli fields. Today, its nearly 300 wineries and 15,000 acres of vineyards stretch from the Santa Ynez Valley in the south to Santa Maria in the north. More than 70 grape varietals grow here, but over half the vineyards are planted with Chardonnay, Pinot Noir, and Syrah. Two-lane Highway 154 over San Marcos Pass is the shortest and most scenic route from Santa Barbara into the Santa Ynez Valley. Alternatively, U.S. 101 travels north 43 miles to Buellton, then 7 miles east through Solvang to Santa Ynez.

San Luis Obispo County. The area's pristine landscapes and abundant wildlife areas, especially those around Morro Bay, have long attracted nature lovers. In the south, coastal towns like Pismo Beach have great sand and surf. An inland wine region stretches from the Edna, Arroyo Grande, and Avila valleys and Nipomo in the south to Paso Robles in the north. A good way to explore the county is to follow the 101-mile Highway 1 Discovery Route (*highway1discoveryroute.com*), which travels off the beaten track through 10 small communities, from to Oceano/Nipomo, Arroyo Grande, Avila Beach, and Edna Valley in the south to Los Osos/Baywood Park, Cayucos, Cambria, San Simeon, and Ragged Point in the north.

Big Sur Coast. Long a retreat of artists and writers, Big Sur is a place of ancient forests and rugged shores that stretch 90 miles from San Simeon to Carmel. Residents have protected it from overdevelopment, and much of the region lies within state parks and the more than 165,000-acre Ventana Wilderness, itself part of the Los Padres National Forest.

Planning

When to Go

The Central Coast climate is mild year-round. If you like to swim in warmer (if still nippy) ocean waters, July and August are the best months to visit. Be aware that this is also high season. Fog often rolls in along the coastal areas in early summer; you'll need a jacket, especially after sunset, close to the shore. It usually rains from December through March. From April to early June and early fall the weather is almost as fine as in high season, and the pace is less hectic.

FESTIVALS AND EVENTS

Old Spanish Days Fiesta. Santa Barbara celebrates its Spanish, Mexican, and Chumash heritage in early August with music, dancing, an all-equestrian parade, a carnival, and a rodeo. *www.sbfiesta.org.*

Paso Robles Wine Festival. Most local wineries pour at this mid-May outdoor festival with winery open houses, winemaker dinners, live bands, and food vendors. *pasowine.com.*

Santa Barbara International Film Festival. The 11-day festival in February or early March attracts film enthusiasts and major stars to downtown venues for screenings, panels, and tributes. *sbiff.org.*

Summer Solstice Celebration. More than 100,000 revelers celebrate the arts at this mid-June Santa Barbara event featuring a parade of costumed participants who dance, drum, and ride people-powered floats up State Street. *www.solsticeparade.com.*

Getting Here and Around

AIR

Alaska Air, American, Contour, Delta, Frontier, Southwest, and United fly to Santa Barbara Airport (SBA), 9 miles from downtown. United, Alaska, and American provide service to San Luis Obispo County Regional Airport (SBP), 3 miles from downtown San Luis Obispo.

Santa Barbara Airbus shuttles travelers between Santa Barbara and Los Angeles for $60 one-way and $110 round-trip. The Santa Barbara Metropolitan Transit District Bus 11 ($1.75) runs every 30 minutes from the airport to the downtown transit center. A taxi between the airport and the hotel districts costs between $22 and $40.

AIRPORT CONTACTS San Luis Obispo County Regional Airport. *(SBP) 901 Airport Dr., off Hwy. 227, San Luis Obispo 805/781–5205 sloairport.com.* **Santa Barbara Airbus.** *805/964–7759, 800/423–1618 www.sbairbus.com.* **Santa Barbara Airport.** *(SBA) 500 Fowler Rd., off U.S. 101 Exit 104B, Santa Barbara 805/683–4011 www.flysba.santabarbaraca.gov.*

BUS

Greyhound provides service from Los Angeles and San Francisco to San Luis Obispo, Ventura, and Santa Barbara. In addition to serving these three cities, several local transit companies provide regional service, including Gold Coast Transit (Ventura and Ojai); Santa Barbara Metropolitan Transit District (the city and the county's south coast, from Goleta in the west to Carpinteria in the east); Santa Ynez Valley Transit (Santa Ynez, Los Olivos, Ballard, Solvang, and Buellton); and San Luis Obispo Regional Transit Authority (SLORTA; San Luis Obispo, Paso Robles, and Pismo Beach and other coastal towns).

BUS CONTACTS Gold Coast Transit. ☎ *805/487–4222* 🌐 *goldcoasttransit.org.* **San Luis Obispo Regional Transit Authority.** ☎ *805/541–2228* 🌐 *www.slorta.org.* **Santa Barbara Metropolitan Transit District.** ☎ *805/963–3366* 🌐 *sbmtd.gov.* **Santa Ynez Valley Transit.** ☎ *805/688–5452* 🌐 *www.syvt.com.*

CAR

Driving is the easiest way to experience the Central Coast. The main north–south routes to and through the Central Coast from Los Angeles and San Francisco are U.S. 101, which travels inland, and highly scenic Highway 1, which hugs the coast. ■ **TIP→ A great way to see the region is by following the Highway 1 Discovery Route, a 101-mile designated road trip that takes you off the beaten track through 10 small towns and cities.** Note that, between Ventura County and northern Santa Barbara County, U.S. 101 and Highway 1 are the same road. Highway 1 separates from U.S. 101 north of Gaviota, rejoining it again at Pismo Beach. Along any stretch where these two highways are separate, U.S. 101 is the quicker route.

The most dramatic section of the Central Coast is the 70 miles between San Simeon and Big Sur. The road is narrow and twisting, with a single lane in each direction. In fog or rain the drive can be downright nerve-racking; in wet seasons mudslides can close portions of the road. Other routes into the Central Coast include Highway 46 and Highway 33, which head, respectively, west and south from I–5 near Bakersfield.

CONTACTS California Highway 1 Discovery Route. 🌐 *highway1discoveryroute.com.*

TRAIN

The Amtrak *Coast Starlight,* which runs between Los Angeles and Seattle via Oakland, stops in Paso Robles, San Luis Obispo, Santa Barbara, and Oxnard. Amtrak also runs several *Pacific Surfliner* trains and buses daily between San Luis Obispo, Santa Barbara, Los Angeles, and San Diego. Metrolink Regional Rail Service trains connect Ventura and Oxnard with Los Angeles and points between.

TRAIN CONTACTS Metrolink. ☎ *800/371–5465* 🌐 *metrolinktrains.com.*

Restaurants

The cuisine in Ventura and Santa Barbara is every bit as eclectic as it is in California's bigger cities; fresh seafood is a standout. A foodie renaissance has overtaken the entire region from Ventura to Paso Robles, spawning dozens of restaurants touting locavore cuisine made with fresh organic produce and meats. Dining attire on the Central Coast is generally casual, though slightly dressy casual wear is the custom at pricier restaurants.

Hotels

Expect to pay top dollar for rooms along the shore, especially in summer. Moderately priced hotels and motels do exist—most just a short drive inland from their higher-price counterparts. Make your reservations as early as possible, and take advantage of midweek specials to get the best rates. It's common for lodgings to require two-day minimum stays on holidays and some weekends, especially in summer, and to double rates during festivals and other events.

Restaurant and hotel reviews have been shortened. For full information, visit Fodors.com. Restaurant prices are the average cost of a main course at dinner, or if dinner is not served, at lunch. Hotel prices are the lowest cost of a standard double room in high season.

What It Costs			
$	**$$**	**$$$**	**$$$$**
RESTAURANTS			
under $17	$17–$26	$27–$36	over $36
HOTELS			
under $150	$150–$250	$251–$350	over $350

Tours

Many tour companies will pick you up at your hotel or central locations; ask about this when booking.

Central Coast Food Tours
SPECIAL-INTEREST | Food and wine destinations are the focus of this outfit's walking tours of shops, restaurants, wineries, and other spots in San Luis Obispo, Paso Robles, and elsewhere. ☎ *844/337–1686* 🌐 *centralcoastfoodtours.com* 🎫 *From $94.*

Cloud Climbers Jeep and Wine Tours
SPECIAL-INTEREST | This outfit conducts trips in open-air, six-passenger jeeps to the Santa Barbara/Santa Ynez mountains and Wine Country. Tour options include wine tasting, mountain, sunset, and a discovery adventure for families. The company also offers a four-hour All Around Ojai Tour and arranges horseback riding and trap-shooting tours. ☎ *805/646–3200* 🌐 *ccjeeps.com* 🎫 *From $400 for exclusive jeep tour w/ driver guide.*

Grapeline Wine Tours
SPECIAL-INTEREST | Wine and vineyard picnic tours in Paso Robles and the Santa Ynez Valley are Grapeline's specialty. ☎ *951/693–5755* 🌐 *gogrape.com* 🎫 *From $139.*

Santa Barbara Adventure Company
SPECIAL-INTEREST | This outfit provides coastal kayak tours, bike tours, and surf and SUP lessons. Sister company Santa Barbara Wine Country Tours shuttles guests on tasting adventures in the Santa Ynez Valley. ✉ *32 E. Haley St., Santa Barbara* ☎ *805/824–9283* 🌐 *www.sbadventureco.com.*

Santa Barbara Wine Country Cycling Tours
BICYCLE TOURS | The company leads half- and full-day tours of the Santa Ynez wine region, conducts hiking and cycling tours, and rents bicycles and e-bikes. ☎ *888/557–8687, 805/686–9490* 🌐 *winecountrycycling.com* 🎫 *From $125.*

Stagecoach Co. Wine Tours
SPECIAL-INTEREST | Locally owned and operated, Stagecoach runs daily wine-tasting excursions and group and private tours to smaller boutique wineries through the Santa Ynez Valley in Sprinter vans or a minicoach. ✉ *Solvang* ☎ *805/686–8347* 🌐 *winetourssantaynez.com* 🎫 *From $183.*

Sustainable Vine Wine Tours
SPECIAL-INTEREST | This green-minded company specializes in eco-friendly Santa Ynez Valley wine tours in luxury vans and Tesla SUVs. Trips include tastings at limited-production wineries committed to sustainable practices. An organic picnic lunch is served. ☎ *805/698–3911* 🌐 *sustainablevine.com* 🎫 *From $185.*

TOAST Tours
SPECIAL-INTEREST | Owned and operated by a sommelier couple with extensive guiding experience in Europe, Napa and Sonoma before relocating to Paso Robles, TOAST leads small-group tours to Central Coast wineries tasting rooms and Hearst Castle. They also offer three-day

tours from either Los Angeles or San Francisco to Central Coast wineries and Hearst Castle, as well as private tours, charters, and transportation. ☎ *805/400–3141* 🌐 *www.toasttours.com* *From $139.*

Visitor Information

CONTACTS Central Coast Tourism Council. 🌐 *centralcoast-tourism.com.* **Santa Barbara Vintners.** ☎ *805/688–0881* 🌐 *www.sbcountywines.com.* **SLO Coast Wine.** ☎ *805/550–2506* 🌐 *slocoastwine.com.* **Visit Santa Barbara.** 🌐 *www.santabarbaraca.com.* **Visit the Santa Ynez Valley.** 🌐 *www.visitsyv.com.* **Visit SLO CAL.** ☎ *805/541–8000* 🌐 *slocal.com.*

Ventura

60 miles north of Los Angeles.

Ventura Harbor is home to myriad fishing boats, restaurants, and water-activity centers where you can rent boats and take harbor cruises. The city is also very walkable. If you drive here, park your car in one of the city's free 24-hour parking lots, and explore on foot.

The most popular outdoor activities in Ventura are beach-going and whale-watching. California gray whales migrate offshore through the Santa Barbara Channel from late December through March; giant blue and humpback whales feed here from mid-June through September. The channel teems with marine life year-round, so tours, which depart from Ventura Harbor, include more than just whale sightings. The harbor is also home to the Channel Islands National Park visitor center and to Island Packers, which transports visitors to the park's islands.

GETTING HERE AND AROUND

U.S. 101 is the north–south main route into town, but for a scenic drive, take Highway 1 north from Santa Monica. The highway merges with U.S. 101 just south of Ventura. **■ TIP→ Traveling north to Ventura from Los Angeles on weekdays, it's best to depart before 6 am, between 10 and 2, or after 7 pm, or you'll get caught in the extended rush-hour traffic. Coming south from Santa Barbara, depart before 1 or after 6 pm.** On weekends, traffic is generally fine except southbound on U.S. 101 between Santa Barbara and Ventura on Sunday late afternoon and early evening.

ESSENTIALS

VISITOR INFORMATION Ventura Visitors and Convention Bureau. ✉ *Downtown Visitor Center, 101 S. California St.* ☎ *805/641–1400* 🌐 *visitventuraca.com.*

Sights

Mission San Buenaventura

HISTORIC SITE | The ninth of the 21 California missions, Mission San Buenaventura was established in 1782, and the current church was rebuilt and rededicated in 1809. A self-guided tour takes you through a small museum, a quiet courtyard, and a chapel with 250-year-old paintings. ✉ *211 E. Main St., at Figueroa St.* ☎ *805/648–4496 gift shop* 🌐 *www.sanbuenaventuramission.org* *$5.*

Museum of Ventura County

MUSEUM | Exhibits in a contemporary complex of galleries and a sunny courtyard plaza tell the story of Ventura County from prehistoric times to the present. A highlight is the gallery that contains Ojai artist George Stuart's historical figures, dressed in exceptionally detailed, custom-made clothing reflecting their particular eras. In the courtyard, eight panels made with 45,000 pieces of cut glass form a history time line. ✉ *100 E. Main St., at S. Ventura Ave.* ☎ *805/653–0323* 🌐 *www.venturamuseum.org* *$5* ⏲ *Closed Mon.–Wed.*

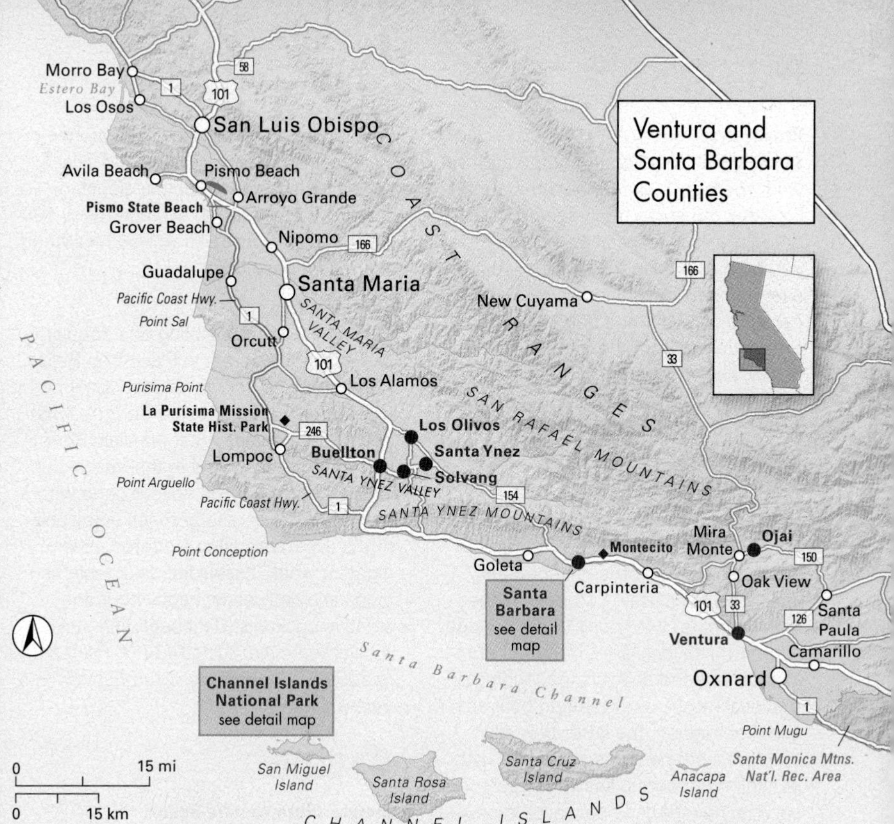

★ Ventura Oceanfront

PROMENADE | Four miles of gorgeous coastline stretch from the county fairgrounds at the northern border of the city of San Buenaventura, through San Buenaventura State Beach, down to Ventura Harbor Village in the south. The main attraction here is the San Buenaventura City Pier, a landmark built in 1872 and restored in 1993. Surfers rip the waves just north of the pier, and sunbathers relax on white-sand beaches on either side. The mile-long promenade and the Omer Rains Bike Trail north of the pier attract scores of joggers, surrey cyclers, and bikers throughout the year. ✉ *California St., at ocean's edge.*

Restaurants

Andria's Seafood

$$ | **SEAFOOD** | The specialties at this casual, family-oriented restaurant in Ventura Harbor Village are fresh fish-and-chips and homemade clam chowder. After placing your order at the counter, you can sit outside on the patio and enjoy the view of the harbor and marina. **Known for:** harbor views; plates with locally caught grilled fish; wide-ranging menu of salads, burgers, chicken, and sides. *$ Average main: $18* ✉ *1449 Spinnaker Dr., Suite A* ☎ *805/654–0546* 🌐 *andriasseafood.com.*

Brophy Bros

$$ | **SEAFOOD** | The Ventura outpost of the wildly popular Santa Barbara restaurant provides the same fresh seafood-oriented meals in a spacious second-story setting overlooking the harbor. Feast on everything from fish-and-chips and crab cakes to chowder and delectable fish—often straight from the boats moored below. **Known for:** lively atmosphere; harbor views; killer clam bar. *Average main: $26* ✉ *1559 Spinnaker Dr., in Ventura Harbor Village* ☎ *805/639–0865* 🌐 *brophybros.com.*

★ Café Zack

$$$ | **AMERICAN** | A local favorite for anniversaries and other celebrations, Zack's serves classic European dishes in an intimate, two-room 1930s cottage adorned with local art. Entrées of note include seafood specials (depending on the local catch), slow-roasted boar shank, and filet mignon, the latter typically crusted in peppercorns or topped with porcini mushrooms. **Known for:** personal service; house-made desserts; excellent California wines. *Average main: $32* ✉ *1095 E. Thompson Blvd., at S. Ann St.* ☎ *805/643–9445* 🌐 *cafezack.com* ⏲ *Closed Sun. No lunch Sat.*

Harbor Cove Café

$ | **CAFÉ** | Waterfront views (from beside the Channel Islands National Park Robert J. Lagomarsino Visitor Center), hearty, cooked-to-order meals, and boxed picnic lunches make this casual dockside eatery a popular spot for island travelers and beachgoers. **Known for:** hearty breakfasts; harbor views; seafood tacos. *Average main: $15* ✉ *1867 Spinnaker Dr.* ☎ *805/658–1639* ⏲ *No dinner.*

Lure Fish House

$$ | **SEAFOOD** | Fresh, sustainably caught seafood charbroiled over a mesquite grill, a well-stocked oyster bar, specialty cocktails, and a wine list heavy on local vintages lure diners into this slick, nautical-theme space downtown. The menu, which emphasizes the use of organic vegetables alongside the local catches, includes tacos, sandwiches, and salads. **Known for:** shrimp-and-chips; cioppino; charbroiled oysters. *Average main: $25* ✉ *60 S. California St.* ☎ *805/567–4400* 🌐 *lurefishhouse.com.*

Rumfish y Vino

$$ | **CARIBBEAN** | The sibling of a popular namesake restaurant in Placencia, Belize, Rumfish y Vino serves up zesty Caribbean fare with a California Wine Country twist in a courtyard venue just off Main Street near the mission. Dine in the beach-chic dining room or on the heated patio with a roaring fireplace, and perhaps enjoy one of the live music shows offered several nights a week. **Known for:** delectable fish tacos and flatbreads; happy hour and creative cocktails; Caribbean fish stew. *Average main: $26* ✉ *434 N. Palm St.* ☎ *805/667–9288* 🌐 *www.rumfishyvino-ventura.com.*

Hotels

Crowne Plaza Ventura Beach

$$ | **HOTEL** | A 12-story hotel with an enviable location on the beach and next to a historic pier, the Crowne Plaza is within walking distance of downtown restaurants and nightlife. **Pros:** on the beach; near downtown; steps from waterfront. **Cons:** early-morning train noise; waterfront crowded in summer; self parking is in an adjacent public lot. *Rooms from: $200* ✉ *450 E. Harbor Blvd.* ☎ *800/842–0800, 805/648–2100* 🌐 *cpventura.com* *235 rooms* *No meals.*

Four Points by Sheraton Ventura Harbor Resort

$$ | **RESORT** | An on-site restaurant, spacious rooms, and a slew of amenities make this 17-acre property—which includes sister hotel Holiday Inn Express—a popular and practical choice for Channel Islands visitors. **Pros:** close to island transportation; quiet location; short drive to historic downtown. **Cons:** not in the heart of downtown; noisy seagulls

sometimes congregate nearby; service can be spotty. *Rooms from: $199* *1050 Schooner Dr.* *805/658–1212, 800/368–7764* *fourpoints.com/ventura* *106 rooms* *No meals.*

Holiday Inn Express Ventura Harbor
$$ | **HOTEL** | A favorite among Channel Islands visitors, this quiet, comfortable, lodge-inspired property sits right at the Ventura Harbor entrance. **Pros:** quiet at night; easy access to harbor restaurants and activities; five-minute drive to downtown. **Cons:** busy area on weekends; complaints of erratic service; fee for parking. *Rooms from: $189* *1080 Navigator Dr.* *805/856–9533, 888/233–9450* *hiexpress.com* *109 rooms* *Free breakfast.*

Ventura Beach Marriott
$$ | **HOTEL** | Spacious, contemporary rooms, a peaceful location just steps from San Buenaventura State Beach, and easy access to downtown arts and culture make the Marriott a popular choice. **Pros:** walk to beach, biking/jogging trails, and restaurants; a block from historic pier; great value for location. **Cons:** close to highway; near busy intersection; special event noise some evenings. *Rooms from: $239* *2055 E. Harbor Blvd.* *805/643–6000, 888/236–2427* *marriottventurabeach.com* *285 rooms* *No meals.*

Waypoint Ventura
$$ | **HOTEL** | Stay in a meticulousy restored vintage Airstream or Spartan trailer in a landscaped park on a bluff overlooking Ventura State Beach. **Pros:** a block from Ventura Pier and a short walk to downtown; free access to fire pits, barbecues, lawn games, and house bikes; walk to craft brewery (sister business). **Cons:** near the train tracks; can be difficult to find; near several ongoing construction sites. *Rooms from: $209* *398 S. Ash St., Unit E* *805/888–5750* *www.waypointventura.com* *19 vintage trailers* *No meals.*

Channel Islands National Park

Via boat, Santa Cruz Island is 32 miles southwest of Ventura Harbor and 28 miles south of Santa Barbara.

On crystal-clear days the craggy peaks of the Channel Islands are easy to see from the mainland, jutting from the Pacific in such sharp detail it seems you could reach out and touch them. The islands are not too far away—a high-speed boat will whisk you to the closest ones in less than an hour—yet very few people ever visit them. Those who do venture out to the islands will experience one of the most splendid land-and-sea wilderness areas on the planet. Camping is your only lodging choice on the islands, but it's a fantastic way to experience the natural beauty and isolation of the park. Campsites are primitive, with no water (except on Santa Rosa and Santa Cruz) or electricity. Campsites are $15 per night; you must arrange your transportation before you reserve your site (*877/444–6777*) or online (*www.recreation.gov*) up to five months in advance.

Channel Islands National Park includes five of the eight Channel Islands and the one nautical mile of ocean that surrounds them. Six nautical miles of surrounding channel waters are designated a National Marine Sanctuary and are teeming with life, including giant kelp forests, 345 fish species, dolphins, whales, seals, sea lions, and seabirds. To maintain the integrity of their habitats, pets are not allowed in the park.

GETTING HERE AND AROUND

Most visitors access the Channel Islands via an Island Packers boat from Ventura Harbor. To reach the harbor by car, exit U.S. 101 in Ventura at Seaward Boulevard or Victoria Avenue and follow the signs to Ventura Harbor/Spinnaker Drive. An Island Packers boat heads to Anacapa

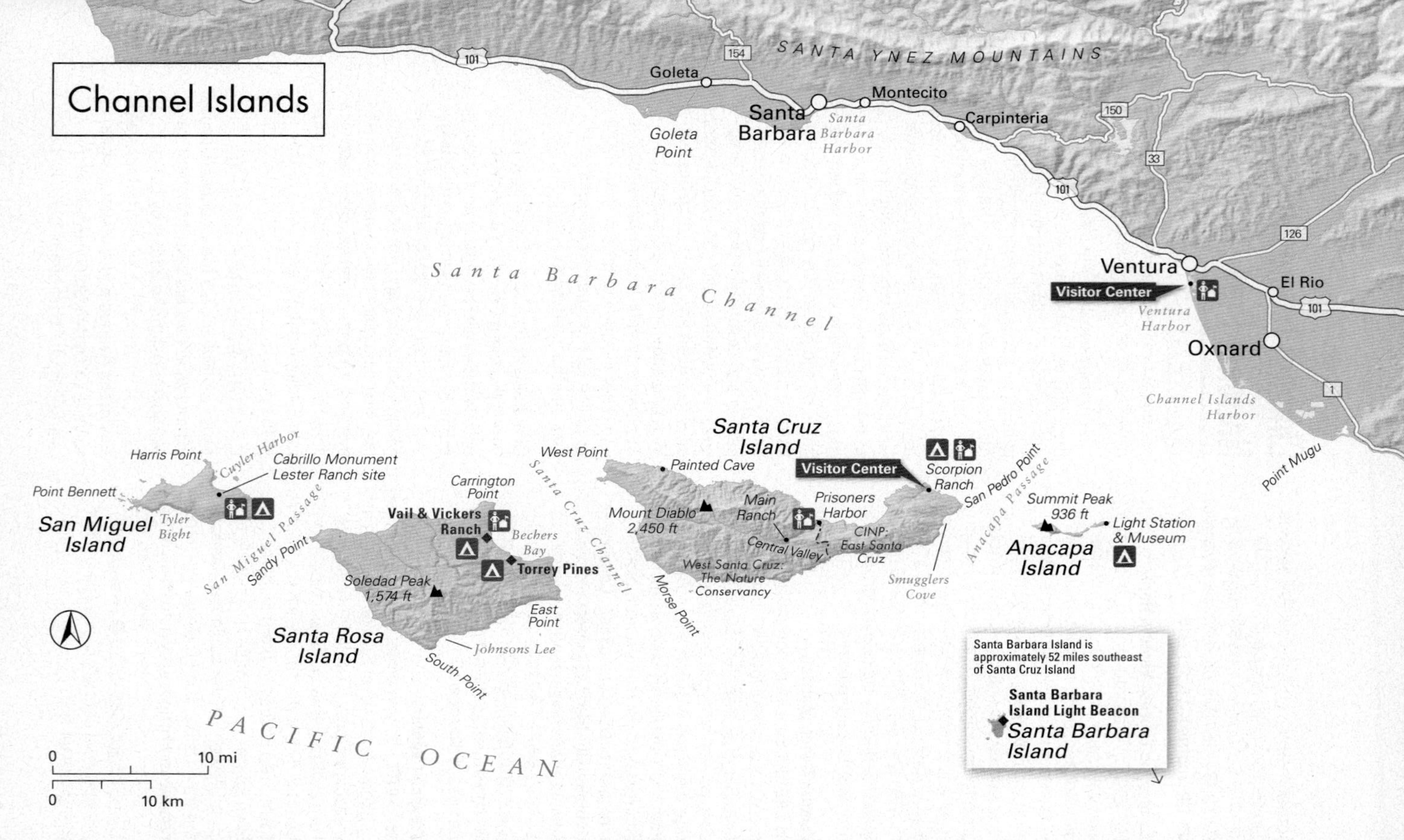
Channel Islands
SANTA YNEZ MOUNTAINS
101
154
Goleta
Goleta Point
Santa Barbara
Santa Barbara Harbor
Montecito
Carpinteria
150
33
101
126
Ventura
Visitor Center
Ventura Harbor
El Rio
101
Oxnard
1
Channel Islands Harbor
Point Mugu
Santa Barbara Channel
Santa Cruz Island
West Point
Painted Cave
Mount Diablo 2,450 ft
Main Ranch
Central Valley
Visitor Center
Prisoners Harbor
CINP: East Santa Cruz
West Santa Cruz: The Nature Conservancy
Morse Point
Scorpion Ranch
San Pedro Point
Smugglers Cove
Anacapa Passage
Summit Peak 936 ft
Light Station & Museum
Anacapa Island
Harris Point
Cuyler Harbor
Cabrillo Monument Lester Ranch site
Point Bennett
San Miguel Island
Tyler Bight
San Miguel Passage
Sandy Point
Carrington Point
Vail & Vickers Ranch
Bechers Bay
Torrey Pines
Santa Cruz Channel
Soledad Peak 1,574 ft
East Point
Santa Rosa Island
Johnsons Lee
South Point
PACIFIC OCEAN
0
10 mi
0
10 km
Santa Barbara Island is approximately 52 miles southeast of Santa Cruz Island
Santa Barbara Island Light Beacon
Santa Barbara Island

Island from Oxnard's Channel Islands Harbor, which you can reach from Ventura Harbor by following Harbor Boulevard south about 6 miles and continuing south on Victoria Avenue. Private vehicles are not permitted on the islands.

BOAT TOURS

Channel Islands Expeditions

EXCURSIONS | Channel Islands Expeditions runs kayaking, paddleboarding, hiking, snorkeling, and scuba excursions to the National Marine Sanctuary and Channel Islands National Park. Boats depart from Santa Barbara Harbor and Channel Islands Harbor in Oxnard, south of Ventura. ✉ *Santa Barbara Harbor* ☎ *805/899–4925* 🌐 *explorechannelislands.com.*

Island Packers

BOAT TOURS | **FAMILY** | Sailing on high-speed catamarans from Ventura or a monohull vessel from Oxnard, Island Packers goes to Santa Cruz Island daily most of the year, weather permitting. The boats also go to Anacapa several days a week and to the outer islands from April through November. They also cruise along Anacapa's north shore on three-hour wildlife tours (no disembarking) several times a week. Rates start at $40 for whale-watching and wildlife cruises; other types of trips start at $63. ✉ *1691 Spinnaker Dr., Ventura* ☎ *805/642–1393* 🌐 *islandpackers.com.*

Sights

Anacapa Island

ISLAND | Most people think of Anacapa as an island, but it's actually comprised of three narrow islets. Although the tips of these volcanic formations nearly touch, the islets are inaccessible from one another except by boat. All three have towering cliffs, isolated sea caves, and natural bridges; Arch Rock, on East Anacapa, is one of the best-known symbols of Channel Islands National Park.

Wildlife viewing is the main activity on East Anacapa, particularly in summer when seagull chicks are newly hatched and sea lions and seals lounge on the beaches. Exhibits at East Anacapa's compact **museum** include the original lead-crystal Fresnel lens from the 1932 lighthouse.

On West Anacapa, depending on the season and the number of desirable species lurking about here, boats travel to **Frenchy's Cove.** On a voyage here you might see anemones, limpets, barnacles, mussel beds, and colorful marine algae in the pristine tide pools. The rest of West Anacapa is closed to protect nesting brown pelicans. ✉ *Channel Islands National Park.*

Channel Islands National Park Robert J. Lagomarsino Visitor Center

INFO CENTER | The park's visitor center has a three-story observation tower with telescopes, a bookstore, and a museum. A 24-minute film, *Treasure in the Sea,* provides an engaging overview of the islands, and, in the marine life exhibit, sea stars cling to rocks, and a brilliant orange Garibaldi darts around. Also on display are full-size reproductions of a male northern elephant seal and the pygmy mammoth skeleton unearthed on Santa Rosa Island in 1994.

On weekends and holidays at 11 am and 3 pm, rangers lead various free public programs describing park resources, and, from Wednesday through Saturday in summer, the center screens live ranger broadcasts of hikes and dives on Anacapa Island. Webcam images of bald eagles and other land and sea creatures are also shown at the center and on the park's website. ✉ *1901 Spinnaker Dr., Ventura* ☎ *805/658–5730* 🌐 *www.nps.gov/chis.*

San Miguel Island

ISLAND | The westernmost of the Channel Islands, San Miguel Island is frequently battered by storms sweeping across the North Pacific. The 15-square-mile island's wild windswept landscape is lush with vegetation. Point Bennett, at the western tip, offers one of the world's most spectacular wildlife displays when more than 30,000 pinnipeds hit its beach. Explorer Juan Rodríguez Cabrillo was the first European to visit this island; he claimed it for Spain in 1542. Legend holds that Cabrillo died on one of the Channel Islands—no one knows where he's buried, but there's a memorial to him on a bluff above Cuyler Harbor. ✉ *Channel Islands National Park.*

Santa Barbara Island

ISLAND | At about 1 square mile, Santa Barbara Island is the smallest of the Channel Islands and nearly 35 miles south of the others. Triangular in shape, Santa Barbara's steep cliffs—which offer a perfect nesting spot for the Scripps's murrelet, a rare seabird—are topped by twin peaks. In spring you can enjoy a brilliant display of yellow coreopsis. Learn about the wildlife on and around the islands at the island's small museum. ✉ *Channel Islands National Park.*

★ Santa Cruz Island

ISLAND | Five miles west of Anacapa, 96-square-mile Santa Cruz Island is the largest of the Channel Islands. The National Park Service manages the easternmost 24% of the island; the rest is owned by the Nature Conservancy, which requires a permit to land. When your boat drops you off on a portion of the 70 miles of craggy coastline, you see two rugged mountain ranges with peaks soaring to 2,500 feet and deep canyons traversed by streams. This landscape is the habitat of a remarkable variety of flora and fauna—more than 600 types of plants, 140 kinds of land birds, 11 mammal species, five varieties of reptiles, and three amphibian species live here. Bird-watchers may want to look for the endemic island scrub jay, which is found nowhere else in the world.

One of the largest and deepest sea caves in the world, **Painted Cave** lies along the northwest coast of Santa Cruz. Named for the colorful lichen and algae that cover its walls, Painted Cave is nearly ¼ mile long and 100 feet wide. In spring a waterfall cascades over the entrance. Kayakers may encounter seals or sea lions cruising alongside their boats inside the cave. The Channel Islands hold some of the richest archaeological resources in North America; all artifacts are protected within the park. Remnants of a dozen Chumash villages can be seen on the island. The largest of these villages, at the eastern end, occupied the area now called **Scorpion Ranch.** The Chumash mined extensive chert deposits on the island for tools to produce shell-bead money, which they traded with people on the mainland. You can learn about Chumash history and view artifacts, tools, and exhibits on native plant and wildlife at the interpretive visitor center near the landing dock. Visitors can also explore remnants of the early-1900s ranching era in the restored historic adobe and outbuildings. ✉ *Channel Islands National Park.*

Santa Rosa Island

ISLAND | Between Santa Cruz and San Miguel, Santa Rosa is the second largest of the Channel Islands. The terrain along the coast varies from broad, sandy beaches to sheer cliffs—a central mountain range, rising to 1,589 feet, breaks the island's relatively low profile. Santa Rosa is home to about 500 species of plants, including the rare Torrey pine, and three unusual mammals, the island fox, the spotted skunk, and the deer mouse. They hardly compare, though, to their predecessors: a nearly complete skeleton of a 6-foot-tall pygmy mammoth was unearthed in 1994.

From 1901 to 1998, cattle were raised at the island's **Vail & Vickers Ranch.** The route from Santa Rosa's landing dock to the campground passes by the historic ranch buildings, barns, equipment, and the wooden pier where cattle were brought onto the island. ✉ *Channel Islands National Park.*

Activities

Channel Islands Adventure Company leads guided sea cave kayak and snorkel tours at Scorpion Anchorage in Channel Islands National Park. Snorkel equipment is also available for rent on the island. Various concessionaires at Ventura Harbor Village (☎ *805–477–0470* 🌐 *www.venturaharborvillage.com*) arrange diving, paddling, kayaking, and other Channel Islands excursions out of Ventura. Island Packers provides public transportation to the islands and conducts whale-watching and wildlife cruises.

DIVING

Some of the best snorkeling and diving in the world can be found in the cool waters surrounding the Channel Islands. In the relatively warm water around Anacapa and eastern Santa Cruz, photographers can get great shots of rarely seen giant black bass swimming among the kelp forests. Here you also find a reef covered with red brittle starfish. If you're an experienced diver, you might swim among five species of seals and sea lions, or try your hand at spearing rockfish or halibut near San Miguel and Santa Rosa. The best time to scuba dive is in summer and fall, when the water is often clear up to a 100-foot depth.

KAYAKING

The most remote parts of the Channel Islands are accessible only by a sea kayak. Some of the best kayaking in the park can be found on Anacapa, Santa Barbara, and the eastern tip of Santa Cruz. It's too far to kayak from the mainland out to the islands, but outfitters have tours that take you to the islands. Tours are offered year-round, but high seas may cause trip cancellations between December and March. ⚠ **Channel waters can be unpredictable and challenging. Guided trips are highly recommended.**

WHALE-WATCHING

About a third of the world's cetacean species (27 to be exact) can be seen in the Santa Barbara Channel. In July and August, humpback and blue whales feed off the north shore of Santa Rosa. From late December through March, up to 10,000 gray whales pass through the Santa Barbara Channel on their way from Alaska to Mexico and back again; if you go on a whale-watching trip during this time frame you're likely to spot one or more of them. Other types of whales, but fewer in number, swim the channel from June through August.

Ojai

15 miles north of Ventura.

The Ojai Valley, which director Frank Capra used as a backdrop for his 1936 film *Lost Horizon*, sizzles in the summer when temperatures routinely reach 90°F. The acres of orange and avocado groves here evoke postcard images of long-ago agricultural Southern California. Many artists and celebrities have sought refuge from life in the fast lane in lush Ojai.

GETTING HERE AND AROUND

From northern Ventura, Highway 33 veers east from U.S. 101 and climbs inland to Ojai. From Santa Barbara, exit U.S. 101 at Highway 150 in Carpinteria, then travel east 20 miles on a twisting, two-lane road that is not recommended at night or during poor weather. You can also access Ojai by heading west from I–5 on Highway 126. Exit at Santa Paula and follow Highway 150 north for 16 miles to Ojai.

Ojai can be easily explored on foot; you can also hop on the Ojai Trolley ($1.50, or $4 day pass), which, until about 5 pm, follows two routes around Ojai and neighboring Miramonte on weekdays and one route on weekends. Tell the driver you're visiting, and you'll get an informal guided tour.

ESSENTIALS

BUS CONTACTS Ojai Trolley. *805/646–5581 ojaitrolley.com.*

VISITOR INFORMATION Ojai Visitors Bureau. *ojaivisitors.com.*

Sights

Ojai Art Center

ARTS VENUE | California's oldest nonprofit, multipurpose arts center exhibits visual art from various disciplines and presents theater, dance, and other performances. *113 S. Montgomery St., near E. Ojai Ave. 805/646–0117 www.ojaiart-center.org Closed Mon.*

Ojai Avenue

NEIGHBORHOOD | The work of local artists is displayed in the Spanish-style shopping arcade along the avenue downtown. On Sunday between 9 and 1, organic and specialty growers sell their produce at the outdoor market behind the arcade.

Ojai Valley Museum

MUSEUM | **FAMILY** | The museum collects, preserves, and presents exhibits about the art, history, and culture of Ojai and Ojai Valley. Walking tours of Ojai depart from here. *130 W. Ojai Ave. 805/640–1390 ojaivalleymuseum.org Museum $5, walking tours from $7 Closed Mon.–Thurs.*

Ojai Valley Trail

TRAIL | The 18-mile trail is open to pedestrians, joggers, equestrians, bikers, and others on nonmotorized vehicles. You can access it anywhere along its route. *Parallel to Hwy. 33 from Soule Park in Ojai to ocean in Ventura 888/652–4669 ojaivisitors.com.*

Restaurants

Boccali's

$ | **ITALIAN** | Edging a ranch, citrus groves, and a seasonal garden that provides produce for menu items, the modest but cheery Boccali's attracts many loyal fans. When it's warm, you can dine alfresco in the oak-shaded patio and lawn area and sometimes listen to live music. **Known for:** family-run operation; hand-rolled pizzas and home-style pastas; seasonal strawberry shortcake. *Average main: $16 3277 Ojai Ave., about 2 miles east of downtown 805/646–6116 bocca-lis.com No lunch Mon. and Tues.*

Farmer and the Cook

$ | **AMERICAN** | An organic farmer and his chef-wife run this funky café/bakery/market in Meiners Oaks, just a few miles west of downtown Ojai. Fill up at the soup and salad bar, order a wood-fired pizza, bento box, sandwich, or a daily special, then grab a table indoors or out on the patio. **Known for:** many veggie, vegan, and gluten-free options; grab-and-go meals; Mexican-focused menu. *Average main: $16 339 W. El Roblar 805/640–9608 www.farmerandcook.com.*

★ Nocciola

$$$ | **ITALIAN** | Authentic northern Italian dishes with a California twist, a cozy fire-place dining room in a century-old Crafts-man-style house, and a covered patio amid the oaks draw locals and visitors alike to this popular eatery, owned by an Italian chef and his American wife (the family lives upstairs). The menu changes seasonally, but regular stars include seared sea scallops with Parmesan fondue and truffle shavings, homemade pastas made with organic egg yolks, and *pappardelle* with slow-roasted wild boar. **Known for:** great wild fish and game; Moment Pink signature cocktail; five-course tasting menu. *Average main:*

$35 ✉ *314 El Paseo Rd.* ☎ *805/640–1648* 🌐 *nocciolaojai.com* ⏲ *No lunch.*

Hotels

The Iguana Inns of Ojai

$$ | **B&B/INN** | Artists own and operate these two bohemian-chic inns: The Blue Iguana, a cozy Southwestern-style hotel about 2 miles west of downtown, and the Emerald Iguana, which has art nouveau rooms, suites, and cottages in a secluded residential setting near downtown Ojai. **Pros:** colorful art everywhere; secluded; pet-friendly (Blue Iguana). **Cons:** 2 miles from downtown; on a highway; no children under 14 (or pets) at Emerald Iguana. *Rooms from: $189* ✉ *11794 N. Ventura Ave.* ☎ *805/646–5277* 🌐 *iguanainnsofojai.com* *20 units* *Free breakfast.*

Ojai Rancho Inn

$$ | **HOTEL** | A collection of one-story buildings and cottages tucked between Ojai Avenue and the bike trail, this ranch-style motel attracts hipsters and those who appreciate a rustic getaway with modern comforts and a laid-back vintage vibe. **Pros:** free loaner cruiser bikes; small on-site bar; nice pool area with lounge chairs. **Cons:** not fancy or luxurious; rooms could use soundproofing; some road noise in rooms close to the road. *Rooms from: $209* ✉ *615 W. Ojai Ave.* ☎ *805/646–1434* 🌐 *ojairanchoinn.com* *17 rooms* *No meals.*

★ Ojai Valley Inn & Spa

$$$$ | **RESORT** | This outdoorsy, golf-oriented resort and spa is set on 220 beautifully landscaped, oak-studded acres, with hillside views in nearly all directions. **Pros:** championship golf course, separate family and adult swimming pools, exceptional outdoor activities; on-site spa with 24 treatment rooms and two pools; multiple on-site restaurants serving regional cuisine. **Cons:** high room rates for the region; areas near restaurants can be noisy; not near downtown Ojai or Ventura. *Rooms from: $500* ✉ *905 Country Club Rd.* ☎ *855/697–8780* 🌐 *ojairesort.com* *303 rooms* *No meals.*

Su Nido Inn

$$ | **B&B/INN** | A short walk from downtown Ojai sights and restaurants, this posh Mission Revival–style inn sits in a quiet neighborhood a few blocks from Libbey Park. **Pros:** walking distance from downtown; homey feel; soaking tubs and private patios or balconies in some rooms. **Cons:** no pool (and can get hot in summer); too quiet for some; 2-night minimum stay on weekends. *Rooms from: $229* ✉ *301 N. Montgomery St.* ☎ *805/754–3513, 866/646–7080* 🌐 *www.sunidoinn.com* *12 rooms* *No meals.*

Santa Barbara

27 miles northwest of Ventura and 29 miles west of Ojai.

Santa Barbara has long been an oasis for Los Angelenos seeking respite from big-city life. The attractions begin at the ocean and end in the foothills of the Santa Ynez Mountains. The waterfront here is beautiful, with palm-studded promenades and plenty of sand.

In the few miles between the beaches and the hills are downtown, Mission Santa Barbara, and the Santa Barbara Botanic Garden. For spectacular views of the city and the Santa Barbara Channel, drive along Alameda Padre Serra, a hillside road that begins near the mission and continues to Montecito.

GETTING HERE AND AROUND

U.S. 101 is the main route into Santa Barbara. If you're staying in town, a car is handy but not essential; the beaches and downtown are easily explored by bicycle or on foot. Visit the Santa Barbara Car Free website for bike-route and walking-tour maps, suggestions for car-free vacations, and transportation discounts.

Santa Barbara Metropolitan Transit District's Line 22 bus serves major tourist sights. Several bus lines connect with the very convenient electric shuttles that cruise the waterfront every 10 to 15 minutes (50¢ each way, $1 day pass).

CONTACTS Santa Barbara Car Free. ☎ *805/696–1100* 🌐 *santabarbaracarfree.org.*

TOURS

Land and Sea Tours

SPECIAL-INTEREST | This outfit conducts 90-minute narrated tours in an amphibious 49-passenger vehicle nicknamed the Land Shark. The adventure begins with a drive through the city, followed by a plunge into the harbor for a cruise along the coast. ✉ *10 E. Cabrillo Blvd., at Stearns Wharf* ☎ *805/683–7600* 🌐 *out2seesb.com* 🎫 *From $40.*

Santa Barbara Trolley Company

SPECIAL-INTEREST | Loop past major hotels, shopping areas, and attractions on a 90-minute tour ($25) aboard a motorized, San Francisco–style cable car. The company sometimes offers a hop-on-hop-off option, but days when this option is offered vary, so check ahead. ☎ *805/965–0353* 🌐 *www.sbtrolley.com.*

ESSENTIALS

VISITOR INFORMATION Garden Street Visitor Center. ✉ *1 Garden St., at Cabrillo Blvd.* ☎ *805/965–3021* 🌐 *www.sbchamber.org.* **State Street Visitor Center.** ✉ *120 State St.* ☎ *805/869–2632* 🌐 *sbchamber.org.*

Sights

Andree Clark Bird Refuge

NATURE PRESERVE | This peaceful lagoon and its gardens sit north of East Beach. Bike trails and footpaths, punctuated by signs identifying native and migratory birds, skirt the lagoon. ✉ *1400 E. Cabrillo Blvd., near the zoo* 🎫 *Free.*

Carriage and Western Art Museum

MUSEUM | **FAMILY** | The country's largest collection of old horse-drawn vehicles—painstakingly restored—is exhibited here, everything from polished hearses to police buggies to old stagecoaches and circus vehicles. In August the Old Spanish Days Fiesta borrows many of the vehicles for a jaunt around town. Docents lead free tours from 1 to 4 pm the third Sunday of the month. ✉ *Pershing Park, 129 Castillo St.* ☎ *805/962–2353* 🌐 *carriagemuseum.org* 🎫 *Free* ⊗ *Closed weekends.*

El Presidio State Historic Park

MILITARY SITE | **FAMILY** | Founded in 1782, El Presidio was one of four military strongholds established by the Spanish along the coast of California. The park encompasses much of the original site in the heart of downtown. El Cuartel, the adobe guardhouse, is the oldest building in Santa Barbara and the second oldest in California. ✉ *123 E. Canon Perdido St., at Anacapa St.* ☎ *805/965–0093* 🌐 *www.sbthp.org* 🎫 *$5.*

Funk Zone

NEIGHBORHOOD | A formerly run-down industrial neighborhood near the waterfront and train station, the Funk Zone has evolved into a hip hangout filled with wine-tasting rooms, arts-and-crafts studios, murals, breweries, distilleries, restaurants, and small shops. It's fun to poke around the three-square-block district. **■ TIP→ Street parking is limited, so leave your car in a nearby city lot and cruise up and down the alleys on foot.** ✉ *Between State and Garden Sts. and Cabrillo Blvd. and U.S. 101* 🌐 *funkzone.net.*

★ Lotusland

GARDEN | **FAMILY** | The 37-acre estate called Lotusland—often ranked among the world's 10 best gardens—once belonged to the Polish opera singer Ganna Walska, who purchased it in 1941 and lived here until her death in 1984. Many of the exotic trees and other subtropical flora were planted in 1882 by horticulturist R. Kinton Stevens. On the self-guided tour—the only option for visiting unless you're a member (reserve well ahead in summer)—you'll see an outdoor theater, a topiary garden, a lotus pond, and a huge collection of rare cycads, an unusual plant genus that has been around since the time of the dinosaurs. ✉ *695 Ashley Rd., off Sycamore Canyon Rd. (Hwy. 192), Montecito* ✣ *Visitor entrance gate is on Cold Spring Rd., at Sycamore Canyon Rd.* ☎ *805/969–9990* 🌐 *lotusland.org* 🎫 *$50* ⏲ *Closed mid-Nov.–mid-Feb. No tours Sun.–Tues., except every 3rd Sun. of month.*

Montecito

TOWN | Since the late 1800s, the tree-studded hills and valleys of this town have attracted the rich and famous: Hollywood icons, business tycoons, tech moguls, and old-money families who installed themselves years ago. Shady roads wind through the community, which consists mostly of gated estates. Swank boutiques line **Coast Village Road,** where well-heeled residents such as Oprah Winfrey, Katy Perry, and Prince Harry and Meghan Markle find peaceful refuge from the paparazzi. Residents also hang out in the Upper Village, a chic shopping area with restaurants and cafés at the intersection of San Ysidro and East Valley roads.

★ MOXI–The Wolf Museum of Exploration and Innovation

MUSEUM | **FAMILY** | It took more than two decades of unrelenting community advocacy to develop this exceptional science hub, which opened in early 2017 in a three-story, Spanish-Mediterranean building next to the train station and a block from Stearns Wharf and the beach. The 70-plus interactive exhibits—devoted to science, technology, engineering, arts, and mathematics (STEAM)—are integrated so curious visitors of all ages can explore seven themed areas (called tracks). In the Speed Track, build a model car and race it against two others on a test track—then use the collected data to reconfigure your car for improved performance. In the Fantastic Forces space, construct a contraption to send on a test flight in a wind column. Other sections include the Light, Tech, and Sound Tracks, plus the Innovation Workshop maker space and the Interactive Media Track, which hosts temporary exhibits. On the rooftop Sky Garden, which has terrific downtown panoramas, make music with wind- and solar-powered instruments, splash around in the interactive Whitewater feature, and peer down through glass floor windows to view the happy faces of explorers below. ✉ *125 State St.* ☎ *805/770–5000* 🌐 *moxi.org* 🎫 *$16.*

★ Old Mission Santa Barbara

RELIGIOUS SITE | **FAMILY** | Dating from 1786 and widely referred to as the "Queen of Missions," this is one of the most beautiful and frequently photographed buildings in coastal California. The architecture evolved from adobe-brick buildings with thatch roofs to more permanent edifices as the mission's population burgeoned. An 1812 earthquake destroyed the third church built on the site. Its replacement, the present structure, is still a functioning Catholic church. Old Mission Santa Barbara has a splendid Spanish/Mexican colonial art collection, as well as Chumash sculptures and the only Native American–made altar and tabernacle left in the California missions. ✉ *2201 Laguna St., at E. Los Olivos St.* ☎ *805/682–4149 gift shop, 805/682–4713 tours* 🌐 *www.santabarbaramission.org* 🎫 *$15 self-guided tour.*

Santa Barbara Botanic Garden

GARDEN | **FAMILY** | Five miles of scenic trails meander through the garden's 78 acres of native plants. The Mission Dam, built in 1806, stands just beyond the redwood grove and above the restored aqueduct that once carried water to the Old Mission Santa Barbara. More than a thousand plant species thrive in various themed sections, including mountains, deserts, meadows, redwoods, and

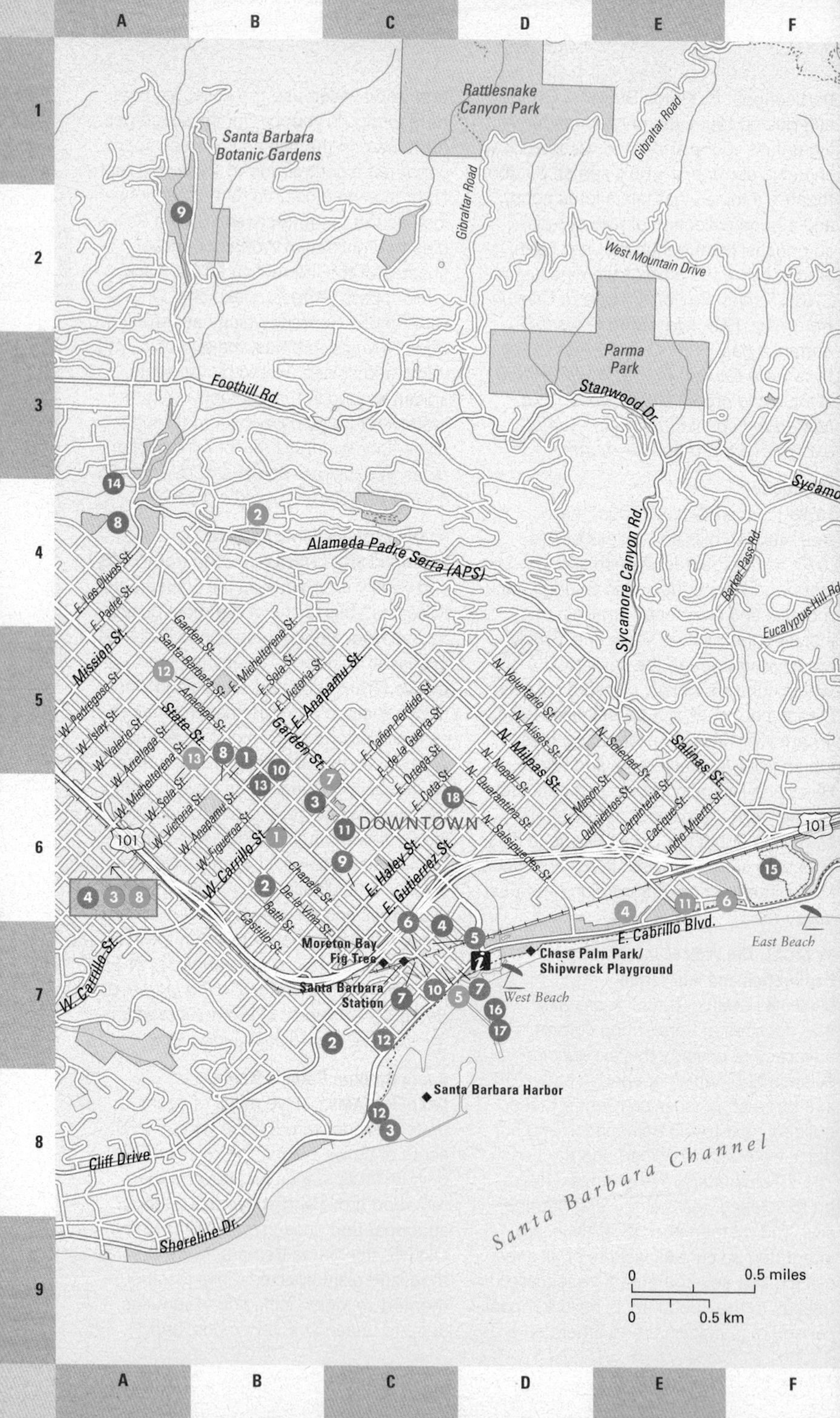
A
B
C
D
E
F
1
2
3
4
5
6
7
8
9
Rattlesnake Canyon Park
Santa Barbara Botanic Gardens
Gibraltar Road
West Mountain Drive
Parma Park
Foothill Rd.
Stanwood Dr.
Sycamore Canyon Rd.
Alameda Padre Serra (APS)
Barker Pass Rd.
Eucalyptus Hill Rd.
E. Los Olivos St.
E. Padre St.
Mission St.
Garden St.
Santa Barbara St.
E. Micheltorena St.
E. Sola St.
E. Victoria St.
E. Anapamu St.
Anacapa St.
State St.
W. Pedregosa St.
W. Islay St.
W. Valerio St.
W. Arrellaga St.
W. Micheltorena St.
W. Sola St.
W. Victoria St.
W. Anapamu St.
W. Figueroa St.
W. Carrillo St.
E. Cañon Perdido St.
E. de la Guerra St.
E. Ortega St.
E. Cota St.
N. Voluntario St.
N. Alisos St.
N. Milpas St.
N. Nopal St.
N. Quarantina St.
N. Salsipuedes St.
N. Soledad St.
Salinas St.
E. Mason St.
Quinientos St.
Carpinteria St.
Cacique St.
Indio Muerto St.
DOWNTOWN
101
Chapala St.
De la Vina St.
Bath St.
Castillo St.
E. Haley St.
E. Gutierrez St.
E. Cabrillo Blvd.
Moreton Bay Fig Tree
Santa Barbara Station
Chase Palm Park/ Shipwreck Playground
West Beach
East Beach
Santa Barbara Harbor
Cliff Drive
Shoreline Dr.
Santa Barbara Channel
0
0.5 miles
0
0.5 km

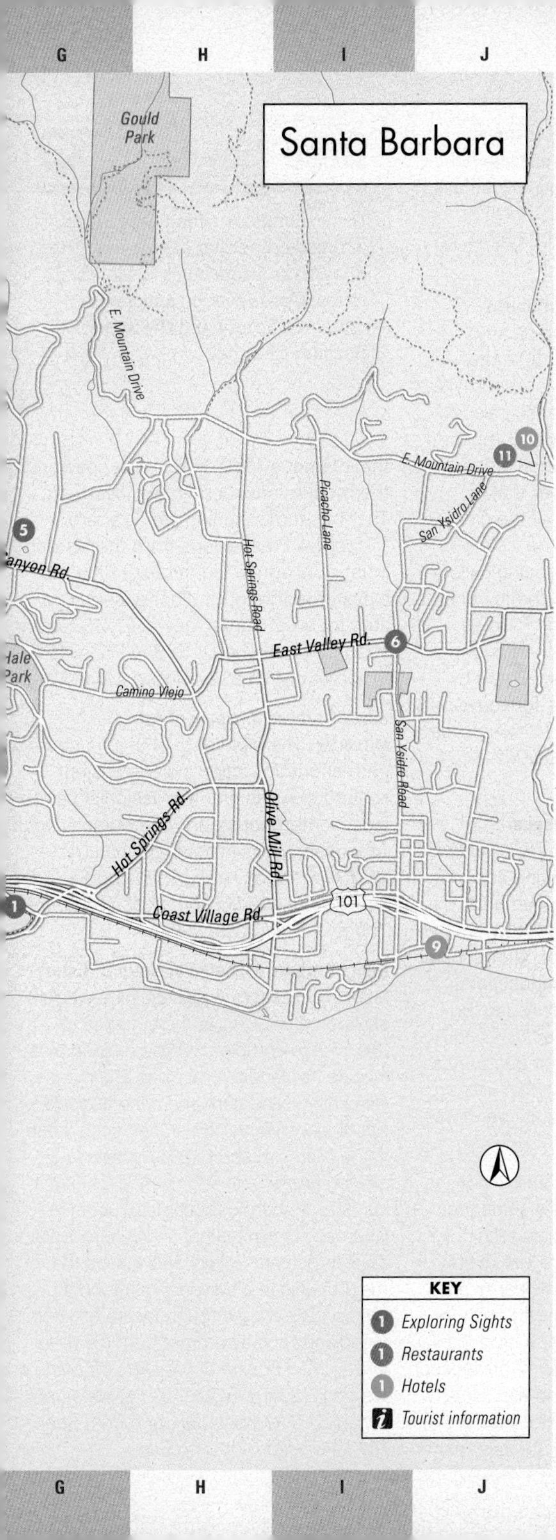

Santa Barbara

Sights

1 Andree Clark Bird Refuge **G6**
2 Carriage and Western Art Museum **C7**
3 El Presidio State Historic Park ... **B6**
4 Funk Zone **C7**
5 Lotusland **G3**
6 Montecito **I4**
7 MOXI--The Wolf Museum of Exploration and Innovation **C7**
8 Old Mission Santa Barbara **A4**
9 Santa Barbara Botanic Garden **A2**
10 Santa Barbara County Courthouse **B6**
11 Santa Barbara Historical Museum **C6**
12 Santa Barbara Maritime Museum **C8**
13 Santa Barbara Museum of Art **B6**
14 Santa Barbara Museum of Natural History **A3**
15 Santa Barbara Zoo **F6**
16 Sea Center **D7**
17 Stearns Wharf **D7**
18 Urban Wine Trail **D6**

Restaurants

1 Arigato Sushi **B6**
2 Barbareño **B6**
3 Brophy Bros. **C8**
4 Jeannine's **A6**
5 The Lark **C7**
6 Loquita **C7**
7 Oku **D7**
8 Olio e Limone **B6**
9 Palace Grill **C6**
10 Santo Mezcal **C7**
11 The Stonehouse **J3**
12 Toma **C7**

Hotels

1 Canary Hotel **B6**
2 El Encanto, a Belmond Hotel **B4**
3 The Goodland **A6**
4 Hilton Santa Barbara Beachfront Resort **E6**
5 Hotel Californian **C7**
6 Mar Monte Hotel **F6**
7 Palihouse Santa Barbara **C6**
8 The Ritz-Carlton Bacara, Santa Barbara **A6**
9 Rosewood Miramar Beach **J6**
10 San Ysidro Ranch **J3**
11 Santa Barbara Inn **E6**
12 Simpson House Inn **B5**
13 The Upham **B5**

KEY

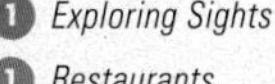

Exploring Sights
Restaurants
Hotels
Tourist information

Channel Islands. ■ **TIP→ A conservation center dedicated to rare and endangered plant species presents rotating exhibitions.** ✉ *1212 Mission Canyon Rd., north of Foothill Rd. (Hwy. 192)* ☎ *805/682–4726* 🌐 *www.sbbg.org* 🎫 *$16.*

★ Santa Barbara County Courthouse

GOVERNMENT BUILDING | Hand-painted tiles and a spiral staircase infuse the courthouse, a national historic landmark, with the grandeur of a Moorish palace. This magnificent building was completed in 1929. An elevator rises to an arched observation area in the tower that provides a panoramic view of the city. Before or after you take in the view, you can (if it's open) visit an engaging gallery devoted to the workings of the tower's original, still operational Seth Thomas clock. The murals in the second-floor ceremonial chambers were painted by an artist who did backdrops for some of Cecil B. DeMille's films. ✉ *1100 Anacapa St., at E. Anapamu St.* ☎ *805/962–6464* 🌐 *sbcourthouse.org.*

Santa Barbara Historical Museum

MUSEUM | The historical society's museum exhibits decorative and fine arts, furniture, costumes, and documents from the town's past. Adjacent to it is the Gledhill Library, a collection of books, photographs, maps, and manuscripts. Tours are by appointment only. Admission is free for anyone under 18. ✉ *136 E. De La Guerra St., at Santa Barbara St.* ☎ *805/966–1601* 🌐 *www.sbhistorical.org* 🎫 *Museum $7; library from $2 per hr for research* ⏲ *Closed Mon.*

Santa Barbara Maritime Museum

MUSEUM | **FAMILY** | California's seafaring history is the focus here. High-tech, hands-on exhibits, such as a virtual sportfishing activity that lets participants haul in a "big one" and a local surfing history retrospective, make this a fun stop for families. In 2018, the museum introduced a fascinating History of Oil in the Santa Barbara Channel exhibit that traces the Chumash Indians' use of natural seeps to the infamous 1969 oil spill that spawned the modern environmental movement. The museum's shining star is a rare, 17-foot-tall Fresnel lens from the historic Point Conception Lighthouse. Ride the elevator to the fourth-floor observation area for great harbor views. ✉ *113 Harbor Way, off Shoreline Dr.* ☎ *805/962–8404* 🌐 *sbmm.org* 🎫 *$8* ⏲ *Closed Mon.–Wed.*

Best Views

Drive along Alameda Padre Serra, a hillside road that begins near the mission and continues to Montecito, to feast your eyes on spectacular views of the city and the Santa Barbara Channel.

Santa Barbara Museum of Art

MUSEUM | The highlights of this museum's permanent collection include ancient sculpture, Asian art, impressionist paintings, contemporary art, photography, and American works in several mediums. ✉ *1130 State St., at E. Anapamu St.* ☎ *805/963–4364* 🌐 *sbma.net* 🎫 *$10, free Thurs. 5–8* ⏲ *Closed Mon.*

Santa Barbara Museum of Natural History

MUSEUM | **FAMILY** | A gigantic blue whale skeleton greets you at the entrance to this 17-acre complex, whose major draws include its planetarium, paleo and marine life exhibits, and gem and mineral displays. Startlingly alive-looking stuffed specimens in the Mammal and Bird Halls include a smiling grizzly bear and nesting California condors. A room of dioramas illustrates Chumash Indian history and culture while a Santa Barbara Gallery showcases the region's unique biodiversity. Outdoors, nature trails wind through the serene oak woodlands and a summer butterfly pavilion. ✉ *2559 Puesta del Sol Rd., off Mission Canyon Rd.* ☎ *805/682–4711* 🌐 *sbnature.org* 🎫 *$17; free one Sun. of month Sept.–Apr.* ⏲ *Closed Mon. and Tues.*

California's Missions

California history changed forever in the 18th century when Spanish explorers founded a series of missions along the Pacific coast. Believing they were following God's will, they wanted to spread the gospel and convert as many natives as possible. The process produced a collision between the Hispanic and California Indian cultures, resulting in one of the most striking legacies of Old California: the Spanish mission churches. Rising like mirages in the middle of desert plains and rolling hills, these historic sites transport you back to the days of the Spanish colonial period.

Father of the Missions

Father Junípero Serra is an icon of the Spanish colonial period. At the behest of the Spanish government, the diminutive padre—then well into his fifties, and despite a chronic leg infection—started out on foot from Baja California to search for suitable mission sites, with a goal of reaching Monterey. In 1769 he helped establish Alta California's first mission in San Diego and continued his travels until his death in 1784, by which time he had founded eight more missions.

El Camino Real

The system ended about a decade after the Mexican government took control of Alta California in the early 1820s and began to secularize the missions. In 1848, the Americans assumed control of the territory, and California became part of the United States. Today, all 21 of these missions stand as extraordinary monuments to their colorful past. Many are found on or near the "King's Road"—El Camino Real—which linked these mission outposts. At the height of the mission system the trail was approximately 600 miles long, eventually extending from San Diego to Sonoma. Today the road is commemorated on portions of Routes 101 and 82 in the form of roadside bell markers erected by CalTrans every 1 to 2 miles between San Diego and San Francisco.

Mission Architecture

Mission architecture reflects a gorgeous blend of European and New World influences. While naves followed the simple forms of Franciscan Gothic, cloisters (with beautiful arcades) adopted aspects of the Romanesque style, and ornamental touches of the Spanish Renaissance—including red-tiled roofs and wrought-iron grilles—added even more elegance. In the 20th century, the Mission Revival Style had a huge impact on architecture and design in California, as seen in examples ranging from San Diego's Union Station to Stanford University's main quadrangle. For information on California's missions, see 🌐 *californiamissionsfoundation.org.*

Santa Barbara Zoo

ZOO | **FAMILY** | This compact zoo's gorgeous grounds shelter elephants, gorillas, Australian wildlife, exotic birds, and big cats, and has many exhibits that educate visitors on conservation efforts to save endangered species like the California condor and the red-legged frog. For small children, there's a scenic railroad and barnyard area where they can feed domestic sheep. Three high-tech dinosaurs and an 8-foot-tall grizzly bear puppet perform in live stage shows (free with admission), daily in summer and on weekends the rest of the year. Kids especially love feeding the giraffes from a view deck overlooking the beach. ■ **TIP→ The palm-studded lawns on a hilltop overlooking the beach are perfect spots for family picnics.** ✉ *500 Niños Dr., off El Cabrillo Blvd.* ☎ *805/962–5339 main line, 805/962–6310 info line* 🌐 *santabarbarazoo.org* 🎫 *Zoo $20, parking $11.*

Sea Center

ZOO | **FAMILY** | A branch of the Santa Barbara Museum of Natural History, the center specializes in Santa Barbara Channel marine life and conservation. Though small compared to aquariums in Monterey and Long Beach, this is a fascinating, hands-on marine science laboratory that lets you participate in experiments, projects, and exhibits, including touch pools. The two-story glass walls here open to stunning ocean, mountain, and city views. ✉ *211 Stearns Wharf* ☎ *805/962–2526* 🌐 *sbnature.org* 🎫 *$10.*

Stearns Wharf

MARINA | Built in 1872, Stearns Wharf is Santa Barbara's most visited landmark. Expansive views of the mountains, cityscape, and harbor unfold from every vantage point on the three-block-long pier. Although it's a nice walk from the Cabrillo Boulevard parking areas, you can also park on the pier and then wander through the shops or stop for a meal at one of the wharf's restaurants. ✉ *Cabrillo Blvd. and State St.* 🌐 *stearnswharf.org.*

Urban Wine Trail

WINERY/DISTILLERY | More than 30 winery tasting rooms in six neighborhoods form the Urban Wine Trail. Most are within walking distance of the waterfront and the lower State Street shopping and restaurant district. **Santa Barbara Winery** (202 Anacapa St.), **The Valley Project** (116 E. Yanonali St.), and **Grassini Family Vineyards** (813 Anacapa St.) are good places to start your oenological trek. ✉ *Santa Barbara* 🌐 *urbanwinetrailsb.com.*

Santa Barbara Style

After a 1925 earthquake demolished many buildings, the city seized a golden opportunity to assume a Spanish-Mediterranean style. It established an architectural board of review, which, along with city commissions, created strict building codes for the downtown district: red-tile roofs, earth-tone facades, arches, wrought-iron embellishments, and height restrictions (about four stories).

Beaches

Arroyo Burro Beach

BEACH—SIGHT | **FAMILY** | The beach's usually gentle surf makes it ideal for families with young children. It's a local favorite because you can walk for miles in both directions when tides are low. Leashed dogs are allowed on the main stretch of beach and westward; they are allowed to romp off-leash east of the slough at the beach entrance. The parking lots fill early on weekends and throughout the summer, but the park is relatively quiet at other times. Walk along the beach just a few hundreds yards away from the main steps at the entrance to escape crowds on warm-weather days. Surfers, swimmers, stand-up paddlers, and boogie boarders regularly ply the waves, and photographers come often to catch the vivid sunsets. **Amenities:** food and drink; lifeguard in summer; parking; showers; toilets. **Best for:** sunset; surfing; swimming; walking. ✉ *Cliff Dr. and Las Positas Rd.* 🌐 *countyofsb.org/parks.*

★ **East Beach**

BEACH—SIGHT | **FAMILY** | The wide swath of sand at the east end of Cabrillo Boulevard is a great spot for people-watching. East Beach has sand volleyball courts,

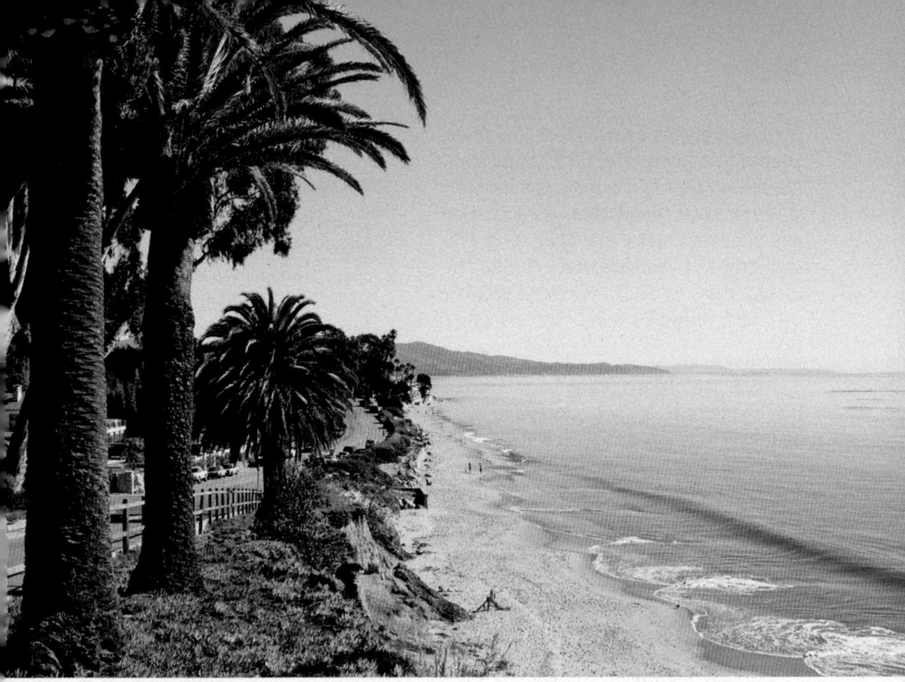

Be sure to visit Santa Barbara's beautiful—and usually uncrowded—beaches.

summertime lifeguard and sports competitions, and arts-and-crafts shows on Sundays and holidays. You can use showers, a weight room, and lockers (bring your own towel) and rent umbrellas and boogie boards at the Cabrillo Bathhouse. Next door, there's an elaborate jungle-gym play area for kids. Hotels line the boulevard across from the beach. **Amenities:** food and drink; lifeguards in summer; parking (fee); showers; toilets; water sports. **Best for:** walking; swimming; surfing. *1118 Cabrillo Blvd., at Ninos Dr. 805/897–2680.*

Restaurants

Arigato Sushi

$$$ | **JAPANESE** | You might have to wait for a table at this two-story restaurant and sushi bar—locals line up early for the wildly creative combination rolls and other delectables (first come, first served). Fans of authentic Japanese food sometimes disagree about the quality of the seafood, but all dishes are fresh and artfully presented. **Known for:** innovative creations; lively atmosphere; patio and second-floor balcony seating. *Average main: $30 1225 State St., near W. Victoria St. 805/965–6074 www.arigatosb.com No lunch.*

Barbareño

$$$ | **MODERN AMERICAN** | Determined to push the boundaries of farm-to-table, college friends who worked at the same Los Angeles eatery banded together in 2014 to launch Barbareño. They churn their own butter, bake their own breads, make condiments from scratch, and forage mushrooms, eucalyptus leaves, and other ingredients from the wild. **Known for:** youthful, sophisticated vibe; chef's sampler plate; monthly seasonal menu. *Average main: $31 205 W. Canon Perdido St., at De La Vina St. 805/963–9591 barbareno.com Closed Mon. and Tues. No lunch.*

Brophy Bros

$$ | **SEAFOOD** | The outdoor tables at this casual harborside restaurant have perfect views of the marina and mountains. Staffers serve enormous, exceptionally

fresh fish dishes and will text you when your table's ready so you can stroll along the breakwater and explore the harbor while you wait. **Known for:** seafood salad and chowder; stellar clam bar; long wait times. *Average main: $26 119 Harbor Way, off Shoreline Dr. 805/966–4418 brophybros.com.*

Jeannine's

$ | **AMERICAN** | Take a break from waterfront and State Street explorations at Jeannine's, revered locally for its wholesome sandwiches, salads, and baked goods, made from scratch with organic and natural ingredients. Dine in the expansive dining room or patio, or pick up a turkey cranberry or chicken pesto sandwich to go, and picnic on the beach or nearby Chase Palm Park. Jeannine's also has outlets in Montecito, Uptown, and Goleta. **Known for:** fantastic pastries; hearty, healthful breakfasts; turkey roasted or smoked in-house. *Average main: $16 1 State St., at Cabrillo Blvd. 805/687–8701 jeannines.com No dinner.*

★ **The Lark**

$$$ | **MODERN AMERICAN** | Shared dining—small plates and larger—and a seasonal menu showcasing local ingredients are the focus at this urban-chic restaurant named for an overnight all-Pullman train that chugged into the nearby railroad station for six decades. Sit at the 24-seat communal table set atop vintage radiators, or at tables and booths crafted from antique Spanish church pews and other repurposed or recycled materials. **Known for:** social environment; wines curated by a master sommelier; handcrafted locavore cocktails. *Average main: $35 131 Anacapa St., at E. Yanonali St. 805/284–0370 www.thelarksb.com No lunch.*

Loquita

$$$ | **SPANISH** | In a cozy space on a prime corner at the gateway to the Funk Zone near Stearns Wharf, Loquita honors Santa Barbara's Spanish heritage by serving up authentic Spanish dishes, wines, and cocktails made with fresh, sustainably sourced local ingredients. The menu covers all bases, from tapas to wood-fired seafood and grilled meats to Spanish wines, vermouth, gin and tonics, and sangria. **Known for:** multiple types of paella; counter and takeaway items; great gin and tonic. *Average main: $31 202 State St. 805/880–3380 www.loquitasb.com.*

Take the Kids

Two fun playgrounds provide welcome interludes for the young set. Children love tooling around **Kids' World** (*Garden and Micheltorena Sts.*), a public playground with a castle-shaped maze of climbing structures, slides, and tunnels. At **Shipwreck Playground** (*Chase Palm Park, E. Cabrillo Blvd., east of Garden St.*), parents take as much pleasure in the waterfront views as the kids do in the nautical-theme diversions.

Oku

$$$ | **MODERN ASIAN** | Locals and visitors alike flock to this sleek, Asian-inspired restaurant across from Stearns Wharf and East Beach (reserve a second-story table for killer views). The eclectic menu focuses mostly on small plates meant for sharing and includes classic dishes like sushi, sashimi, yakisoba, ramen soup with pork belly, and black garlic filet mignon, but also creative surprises like the halibut-crab-avocado "lollipop" and lobster-tempura-wagyu beef roll. **Known for:** two cocktail bars and a sushi bar; crispy Korean cauliflower with yuzu-shiso aioli, kalbi-style short ribs; craft cocktails, extensive wine and sake list. *Average main: $28 29 E. Cabrillo Blvd. 805/690–1650 www.okurestaurant.com.*

Olio e Limone

$$$ | **ITALIAN** | Sophisticated Italian cuisine with an emphasis on Sicily is served at this restaurant near the Arlington. The juicy veal chop is popular, but surprises abound here; be sure to try unusual dishes such as ribbon pasta with quail and sausage in a mushroom ragout, or the duck ravioli. **Known for:** grilled veal and lamb chops; cozy white-tablecloth dining room; adjacent raw bar and casual pizzeria. *Average main: $32 17 W. Victoria St., at State St. 805/899–2699 www.olioelimone.com No lunch Sun.*

Palace Grill

$$$ | **SOUTHERN** | Mardi Gras energy, team-style service, lively music, and great Cajun, creole, and Caribbean food have made the Palace a Santa Barbara icon. Be prepared to wait for a table on Friday and Saturday nights, though the live entertainment and free appetizers, sent out front when the line is long, will whet your appetite for the feast to come. **Known for:** blackened fish and meats; Louisiana bread pudding soufflé; Cajun martini served in a mason jar. *Average main: $32 8 E. Cota St., at State St. 805/963–5000 palacegrill.com.*

Santo Mezcal

$$$ | **MODERN MEXICAN** | Authentic flavors of coastal Mexico and fresh local ingredients make for packed indoor and outdoor tables at this popular eatery a block from the train station. For breakfast, fill up on huevos rancheros or chilaquiles; for lunch or dinner feast on seafood ceviches, grilled chicken breast with authentic mole poblano, or Mexican shrimp in a creamy mezcal sauce. **Known for:** weekday happy hour; fresh crab enchiladas and quesadillas, grilled rib-eye tacos; good selection of tequila, mezcal, cocktails. *Average main: $28 119 State St. 805/883–3593 www.santomezcalsb.com.*

★ The Stonehouse

$$$$ | **AMERICAN** | The elegant Stonehouse—consistently lauded as one of the nation's top restaurants—is inside a century-old granite former farmhouse at the San Ysidro Ranch resort. The menu changes constantly, but might include pan-seared abalone or classic steak Diane flambéed table-side. **Known for:** ingredients from on-site garden; heated ocean-view deck with fireplace; elegant dining room. *Average main: $63 900 San Ysidro La., off San Ysidro Rd., Montecito 805/565–1720 www.sanysidroranch.com.*

★ Toma

$$$ | **ITALIAN** | Seasonal, locally sourced ingredients and softly lit muted-yellow walls evoke the flavors and charms of Tuscany and the Mediterranean at this rustic-romantic restaurant across from the harbor and West Beach. Ahi sashimi tucked in a crisp sesame cone is a popular appetizer, after which you can proceed to a house-made pasta dish or rock shrimp gnocchi. **Known for:** house-made pastas and gnocchi; wines from Italy and California's Central Coast; romantic waterfront setting. *Average main: $34 324 W. Cabrillo Blvd., near Castillo St. 805/962–0777 www.tomarestaurant.com No lunch.*

Hotels

Canary Hotel

$$$$ | **HOTEL** | A full-service hotel in the heart of downtown, this Kimpton property blends a casual, beach-getaway feel with contemporary California style. **Pros:** upscale local cuisine at on-site Finch & Fork restaurant; rooms come with candles, yoga mats, and binoculars (for touring); adjacent fitness center. **Cons:** across from transit center; a mile from the beach; some rooms on the small side. *Rooms from: $515 31 W. Carrillo St. 805/884–0300, 855/546–7866 www.canarysantabarbara.com 97 rooms No meals.*

★ El Encanto, a Belmond Hotel
$$$$ | **HOTEL** | Built in 1915 and following more than a $100 million of extensive renovations a century later, this Santa Barbara icon lives on to thrill a new generation of guests with its relaxed-luxe bungalow rooms, lush gardens, and personalized service. **Pros:** dining terrace with panoramic city and ocean views; stellar spa facility; infinity pool with ocean views. **Cons:** long walk to downtown; pricey; guests staying for more than a few days may find the restaurant menus limited. *Rooms from: $990* *800 Alvarado Pl.* *805/845–5800, 800/393–5315* *www.belmond.com* *92 rooms* *No meals.*

The Goodland
$$$ | **HOTEL** | A vintage Woody car, a silver Airstream trailer, and a lobby record shop are among the elements that bring 1960s California surf culture to life at this Kimpton hotel in Goleta. **Pros:** cool and casual vibe; live music or DJs several evenings a week; complimentary wine-and-beer social hour and s'mores by the fireside. **Cons:** not close to downtown Santa Barbara; some rooms on the small side; thin walls allow for noise transfer from neighboring rooms. *Rooms from: $284* *5650 Calle Real, Goleta* *877/480–1465, 805/964–6241* *www.thegoodland.com* *158 rooms* *No meals.*

Hilton Santa Barbara Beachfront Resort
$$$$ | **RESORT** | A full-scale resort with seven buildings spread over 24 landscaped acres across from East Beach, this hotel was founded by the late TV actor Fess Parker, best known for playing Davy Crockett and Daniel Boone. **Pros:** numerous amenities; right across from the beach; free shuttle to train station and airport. **Cons:** train noise filters into some rooms; too spread out for some; pricey. *Rooms from: $475* *633 E. Cabrillo Blvd.* *800/879–2929, 805/564–4333* *www.hiltonsantabarbarabeachfrontresort.com* *360 rooms* *No meals.*

★ Hotel Californian
$$$$ | **HOTEL** | A sprawling collection of Spanish-Moorish buildings that opened in 2017 at the site of the historic 1925 Hotel Californian, this sophisticated hotel with a hip youthful vibe occupies nearly three full blocks just steps from Stearns Wharf and the harbor. **Pros:** steps from the waterfront, Funk Zone, MOXI, and beaches; resort-style amenities; on-site parking. **Cons:** area gets crowded in summer and holiday weekends; must walk or bike to downtown attractions; train whistle noise in rooms close to station. *Rooms from: $699* *36 State St.* *805/882–0100* *www.thehotelcalifornian.com* *121 rooms* *No meals.*

Mar Monte Hotel
$$$$ | **HOTEL** | A complex of five buildings on 3 landscaped acres across from East Beach, the historic Mar Monte, part of the Hyatt family of properties, completed a $27 million renovation in 2020 and is an appealing lodging option. **Pros:** steps from the beach; many room types and rates; on-site restaurant, pool, bar/café. **Cons:** not in the heart of downtown; busy area in summer; no on-site self-parking, only valet service (fee). *Rooms from: $429* *1111 E. Cabrillo Blvd.* *805/882–1234, 800/643–1994* *www.hyatt.com* *174 rooms* *No meals.*

Palihouse Santa Barbara
$$$$ | **HOTEL** | A ½ block from the Presidio in the heart of downtown, this secluded retreat celebrates Santa Barbara style and design, from the Spanish-Mediterranean exterior with wrought-iron balconies to the interior's Palisociety signature hipster interpretation of local character (e.g., bright colors throughout, a custom playlist that sets an upbeat mood, a bowl of bright yellow tennis balls in the lobby lounge). **Pros:** walk to downtown shops, restaurants, sights; indoor parking beneath the hotel; spacious rooms. **Cons:** resort fee (includes parking); not on the waterfront; too small and serene for those who prefer a lively setting.

Rooms from: $475 ⊠ 915 Garden St. ☎ 805/564–4700 🌐 www.palisociety.com/hotels/santa-barbara ⇨ 24 rooms 🍽 No meals.

★ The Ritz-Carlton Bacara, Santa Barbara

$$$$ | RESORT | A luxury resort with four restaurants and a 42,000-square-foot spa and fitness center with 36 treatment rooms, the Ritz-Carlton Bacara provides a gorgeous setting for relaxing retreats. **Pros:** many diversions including hiking and stargazing; three zero-edge pools; three golf courses nearby. **Cons:** pricey; not close to downtown; sand on beach not pristine enough for some. *Rooms from: $499 ⊠ 8301 Hollister Ave., Goleta ☎ 805/968–0100 🌐 www.ritzcarlton.com/en/hotels/california/santa-barbara ⇨ 358 rooms 🍽 Free breakfast.*

★ Rosewood Miramar Beach

$$$$ | RESORT | This luxury resort, opened in 2019, sprawls across 16 lush acres on one of the area's most scenic and exclusive beaches. **Pros:** two cabana-lined pools; six restaurants and bars; steps to the beach. **Cons:** too expensive for some; next to a busy freeway and train tracks; popular weekend wedding site with lively partiers. *Rooms from: $1650 ⊠ 1759 S. Jameson La., Montecito ☎ 805/900–8388 🌐 www.rosewoodhotels.com/en/miramar-beach-montecito ⇨ 160 rooms 🍽 No meals.*

★ Santa Barbara Inn

$$$$ | HOTEL | This full-service, family-owned, Spanish-Mediterranean hotel occupies a prime waterfront corner across from East Beach. **Pros:** many rooms have ocean views; suites come with whirlpool tubs; delicious on-site restaurant Convivo. **Cons:** on a busy boulevard; limited street parking; not within easy walking distance of downtown. *Rooms from: $399 ⊠ 901 E. Cabrillo Blvd. ✣ At Milpas St. ☎ 800/231–0431, 805/966–2285 🌐 www.santabarbarainn.com ⇨ 70 rooms 🍽 No meals.*

★ San Ysidro Ranch

$$$$ | RESORT | At this romantic hideaway on a historic property in the Montecito foothills—where John and Jackie Kennedy spent their honeymoon and Oprah sends her out-of-town visitors—guest cottages are scattered among groves of orange trees and flower beds. **Pros:** rooms come with private outdoor spas; 17 miles of hiking trails nearby; Plow & Angel Bistro and Stonehouse restaurants on-site are Santa Barbara institutions. **Cons:** very expensive; too remote for some; noise from nearby bridal parties travels to some suites. *Rooms from: $1895 ⊠ 900 San Ysidro La., Montecito ☎ 805/565–1700 🌐 www.sanysidroranch.com ⇨ 38 units 🍽 All-inclusive ☞ 2-day minimum stay on weekends, 3 days on holiday weekends.*

★ Simpson House Inn

$$$ | B&B/INN | If you're a fan of traditional bed-and-breakfast inns, this property, with its beautifully appointed Victorian main house and acre of lush gardens, is for you. **Pros:** elegant furnishings; impeccable landscaping; within walking distance of downtown. **Cons:** some rooms in main building are small; two-night minimum stay on weekends May–October; no pets allowed. *Rooms from: $339 ⊠ 121 E. Arrellaga St. ☎ 805/963–7067 🌐 www.simpsonhouseinn.com ⇨ 15 rooms 🍽 Free breakfast.*

The Upham

$$$ | B&B/INN | Built in 1871, this Victorian in the downtown arts and culture district has been restored as a full-service hotel. **Pros:** 1-acre garden; easy walk to theaters; excellent on-site restaurant. **Cons:** some rooms are small; not near beach or waterfront; no in-room safes. *Rooms from: $285 ⊠ 1404 De la Vina St. ☎ 805/962–0058 🌐 www.uphamhotel.com ⇨ 50 rooms 🍽 No meals ☞ 2-night minimum stay on weekends.*

Nightlife

The bar, club, and live music scene centers on lower State Street, between the 300 and 800 blocks.

Draughtsmen Aleworks
BREWPUBS/BEER GARDENS | A low-key taproom with board and card games for entertainment, Draughtsmen pours its own craft beer, wine, cider, and hop tea. At the main taproom in Goleta, you can view the brewing facilities and sometimes take a tour. ✉ *1131 State St., in Mosaic Locale* ☎ *805/259–4356* 🌐 *www.draughtsmenaleworks.com.*

The Good Lion
BARS/PUBS | The cocktail menu at this intimate neighborhood bar near The Granada Theatre changes weekly, depending on the fresh organic bounty available at the markets. All juices are organic and squeezed fresh daily, and all syrups are made in house with organic produce and sweeteners. ✉ *1212 State St.* ☎ *805/845–8754* 🌐 *www.goodlion-cocktails.com.*

Joe's Cafe
BARS/PUBS | Steins of beer and stiff cocktails accompany hearty bar food at Joe's. It's a fun, if occasionally rowdy, collegiate scene. ✉ *536 State St., at E. Cota St.* ☎ *805/966–4638* 🌐 *joescafesb.com.*

Lucky's
BARS/PUBS | A slick sports bar attached to an upscale steak house owned by the maker of Lucky Brand dungarees, this place attracts hip patrons hoping to see and be seen. ✉ *1279 Coast Village Rd., near Olive Mill Rd., Montecito* ☎ *805/565–7540* 🌐 *luckys-steakhouse.com.*

M. Special Brewing Company
BREWPUBS/BEER GARDENS | A favorite stop on the local beer trail, this lively taproom has more than a dozen craft beers and live music on weekends. A second taproom (and the main brewery) is in Goleta, near UCSB. ✉ *634 State St.* ☎ *805/968–6500* 🌐 *www.mspecialbrewco.com.*

Milk & Honey
BARS/PUBS | Artfully prepared tapas, mango mojitos, and exotic cocktails lure trendy crowds to swank M&H, despite high prices and a reputation for inattentive service. ✉ *30 W. Anapamu St., at State St.* ☎ *805/275–4232* 🌐 *www.milknhoneytapas.com.*

SOhO
MUSIC CLUBS | A lively restaurant, bar, and music venue, SOhO books all kinds of musical acts, from jazz to blues to rock. ✉ *1221 State St., at W. Victoria St.* ☎ *805/962–7776* 🌐 *www.sohosb.com.*

Performing Arts

The arts district, with theaters, restaurants, and cafés, starts around the 900 block of State and continues north to the 1300 block. To see what's scheduled around town, pick up the free weekly *Santa Barbara Independent* newspaper or visit its website, 🌐 *www.independent.com.*

Arlington Theatre
ARTS CENTERS | This Moorish-style auditorium presents touring performers and films throughout the year. ✉ *1317 State St., at Arlington Ave.* ☎ *805/963–4408* 🌐 *thearlingtontheatre.com.*

Center Stage Theatre
ARTS CENTERS | This venue hosts plays, music, dance, and readings. ✉ *Paseo Nuevo Center, Chapala and De la Guerra Sts., 2nd fl.* ☎ *805/963–0408* 🌐 *www.centerstagetheater.org.*

Ensemble Theatre Company (ETC)
THEATER | The company stages classic and contemporary comedies, musicals, and dramas. ✉ *33 W. Victoria St., at Chapala St.* ☎ *805/965–5400* 🌐 *www.etcsb.org.*

The Granada Theatre
THEATER | A restored, modernized landmark that dates from 1924, the Granada hosts Broadway touring shows and dance, music, and other cultural events.

✉ *1214 State St., at E. Anapamu St.* ☎ *805/899–2222* 🌐 *granadasb.org.*

Lobero Theatre

THEATER | A state landmark, the Lobero hosts community theater groups and touring professionals. ✉ *33 E. Canon Perdido St., at Anacapa St.* ☎ *805/963–0761* 🌐 *www.lobero.com.*

Shopping

BOOKS

Book Den

BOOKS/STATIONERY | Bibliophiles have browsed for new, used, and out-of-print books at this independent shop since 1933. ✉ *15 E. Anapamu St., at State St.* ☎ *805/962–3321* 🌐 *bookden.com.*

Chaucer's Bookstore

BOOKS/STATIONERY | This well-stocked independent shop is a favorite of many locals. ✉ *Loreto Plaza, 3321 State St., at Los Positas Rd.* ☎ *805/682–6787* 🌐 *www.chaucersbooks.com.*

CLOTHING

Channel Islands Surfboards

CLOTHING | Come here for top-of-the-line surfboards and the latest in California beachwear, sandals, and accessories. ✉ *36 Anacapa St., at E. Mason St.* ☎ *805/966–7213* 🌐 *www.cisurfboards.com.*

DIANI

CLOTHING | This upscale, European-style women's boutique dresses clients in designer clothing from around the world. Sibling shoe and home-and-garden shops are nearby. ✉ *1324 State St., at Arlington Ave.* ☎ *805/966–3114, 805/966–7175 shoe shop* 🌐 *dianiboutique.com.*

SeaVees

SHOES/LUGGAGE/LEATHER GOODS | Santa Barbara–based SeaVees makes and sells casual, comfortable, '60s-style California sneakers that have a classy, dressed-up flair. ✉ *24 E. Mason St.* ☎ *805/774–1964* ⏲ *Closed Tues.*

Surf N Wear's Beach House

CLOTHING | This shop carries surf clothing, gear, and collectibles; it's also the home of Santa Barbara Surf Shop and the exclusive local dealer of Surfboards by Yater. ✉ *10 State St., at Cabrillo Blvd.* ☎ *805/963–1281* 🌐 *www.surfnwear.com.*

Wendy Foster

CLOTHING | This store sells casual-chic women's fashions at its flagship store downtown and four other outlets around the county. ✉ *1220 State St., at E. Victoria St.* ☎ *805/966–2276* 🌐 *wendyfoster.com.*

FOOD AND WINE

Santa Barbara Public Market

FOOD/CANDY | A dozen food and beverage vendors occupy this spacious arts district galleria. Stock up on gourmet goodies; sip on handcrafted wines and beers while watching sports events; and nosh on noodle bowls, sushi, artisanal ice cream, and savory street tacos. ✉ *38 W. Victoria St., at Chapala St.* ☎ *805/770–7702* 🌐 *sbpublicmarket.com.*

SHOPPING AREAS

★ El Paseo

SHOPPING NEIGHBORHOODS | Wine-tasting rooms, shops, art galleries, and studios share the courtyard and gardens of this historic arcade. ✉ *Canon Perdido St., between State and Anacapa Sts.*

★ State Street

SHOPPING NEIGHBORHOODS | Between Cabrillo Boulevard and Sola Street, State Street is a shopper's paradise. Chic malls, quirky storefronts, antiques emporia, elegant boutiques, and funky thrift shops abound. Numerous community activities take place at **Paseo Nuevo,** an open-air mall in the 700 block. Shops, restaurants, galleries, and fountains line the tiled walkways of **La Arcada,** a small complex of landscaped courtyards in the 1100 block designed by architect Myron Hunt in 1926.

Summerland

SHOPPING NEIGHBORHOODS | Serious antiques hunters head southeast of Santa Barbara to Summerland, which is full of shops and markets. Several good ones are along Lillie Avenue and Ortega Hill Road. ✉ *Summerland.*

Activities

BIKING

Cabrillo Bike Path

BICYCLING | The level, two-lane, 3-mile Cabrillo Bike Path passes the Santa Barbara Zoo, the Andree Clark Bird Refuge, beaches, and the harbor. Stop for a meal at one of the restaurants along the way, or for a picnic along the palm-lined path looking out on the Pacific.

Mad Dogs & Englishmen

BICYCLING | Tucked in a storefront near Butterfly Beach, Andree Clark Bird Refuge, and miles of bike lanes, Mad Dogs & Englishmen rents and sells premium e-bikes and custom sidecars (great for kids and pets). It also provides self-guided, private, and guided cycling tours in Santa Barbara and at sister shops in downtown Carmel, Monterey, and Mill Valley. ✉ *1080 Coast Village Rd.* ☎ *805/837–0033* 🌐 *maddogsenglishmen.com.*

Wheel Fun Rentals

BICYCLING | You can rent bikes (electric, cruiser, and regular), quadricycles, electric vehicles, and skates here. ✉ *24 E. Mason St.* ☎ *805/966–2282* 🌐 *wheelfunrentalssb.com.*

BOATS AND CHARTERS

★ ***Condor Express***

BOATING | From SEA Landing, the *Condor Express,* a 75-foot, high-speed catamaran, whisks up to 149 passengers toward the Channel Islands on whale-watching excursions and sunset and dinner cruises. ✉ *301 W. Cabrillo Blvd.* ☎ *805/882–0088, 888/779–4253* 🌐 *condorexpress.com.*

Earth Day

In 1969, 200,000 gallons of crude oil spilled into the Santa Barbara Channel, causing an immediate outcry from residents. The day after the spill, Get Oil Out (GOO) was established; the group helped lead the successful fight for legislation to limit and regulate offshore drilling in California. The Santa Barbara spill also spawned Earth Day, which is still celebrated across the nation today.

Paddle Sports Center

WATER SPORTS | This full-service center in the harbor rents kayaks, stand-up paddleboards, surfboards, boogie boards, and water-sports gear. ✉ *117 B Harbor Way, off Shoreline Dr.* ☎ *805/617–3425 rentals* 🌐 *www.paddlesportsca.com.*

Santa Barbara Sailing Center

BOATING | The center offers sailing instruction, rents and charters sailboats, kayaks, and stand-up paddleboards, and organizes dinner and sunset champagne cruises, island excursions, and whale-watching trips. ✉ *Santa Barbara Harbor launching ramp* ☎ *805/962–2826* 🌐 *sbsail.com.*

Santa Barbara Water Taxi

BOATING | **FAMILY** | Children beg to ride *Lil' Toot,* a cheery yellow water taxi that cruises from the harbor to Stearns Wharf and back again. The fare for kids is $2 each way. ✉ *Santa Barbara Harbor and Stearns Wharf* ☎ *805/465–6676* 🌐 *www.celebrationsantabarbara.com/* 🎫 *$5 one-way.*

SEA Landing

BOATING | This outfit operates surface and deep-sea fishing charters year-round. ✉ *Cabrillo Blvd., at Bath St., and breakwater in Santa Barbara Harbor* ☎ *805/963–3564* 🌐 *sealanding.net.*

TENNIS

City of Santa Barbara Parks and Recreation Department

TENNIS | The City of Santa Barbara Parks and Recreation Department oversees the Municipal Tennis Center, which has hard courts (9 tennis and 12 pickleball) in an enclosed stadium. The department also operates public outdoor courts throughout town with lighted play until 9 pm weekdays. You can purchase day permits ($5) at the courts or by calling the rec department. ☎ *805/564–5573* 🌐 *santabarbaraca.gov/tennis.*

Santa Ynez

31 miles northeast of Santa Barbara.

Founded in 1882, the tiny town of Santa Ynez still has many of its original frontier buildings. You can walk through its three-block downtown in a few minutes, shop for antiques, and hang around the old-time saloon. At some of the Santa Ynez Valley's best restaurants, you just might bump into one of the celebrities who own nearby ranches.

GETTING HERE AND AROUND

Take Highway 154 over San Marcos Pass or U.S. 101 north 43 miles to Buellton, then 7 miles east.

Gainey Vineyard

WINERY/DISTILLERY | The 1,800-acre Gainey Ranch, straddling the banks of the Santa Ynez River, includes about 100 acres of organic vineyards: Sauvignon Blanc, Merlot, Cabernet Sauvignon, and Cabernet Franc. The winery also makes wines from Chardonnay, Pinot Noir, and Syrah grapes from the Santa Rita Hills. You can taste the latest releases—the estate Pinot Noir is especially good—in a Spanish-style hacienda overlooking the ranch. ✉ *3950 E. Hwy. 246* ☎ *805/688–0558* 🌐 *www.gaineyvineyard.com* *Tastings from $20, jeep tour and barn tasting $25.*

S.Y. Kitchen

$$$ | **ITALIAN** | The owners of Toscana, a popular eatery in L.A.'s Brentwood neighborhood, run this rustic-chic restaurant with an Italy–meets–California Wine Country vibe. Chef and co-owner Luca Crestanelli, a native of Verona, Italy, typically offers multiple seasonal daily specials. **Known for:** wood-fired pizzas and oak-grilled entrées; creative craft cocktails; gelatos and "not-so-classic" tiramisu. *Average main: $28* ✉ *1110 Faraday St., at Sagunto St.* ☎ *805/691–9794* 🌐 *www.sykitchen.com.*

ForFriends Inn

$$ | **B&B/INN** | Close friends own and operate this luxury B&B, designed as a social place where friends gather to enjoy good wine, food, and music in a casual backyard setting. **Pros:** three-course breakfast, evening wine and appetizers included; friendly innkeepers; "Friendship Pass" provides perks and savings at restaurants and wineries. **Cons:** not suitable for children; no pets allowed; must climb stairs to second-floor rooms. *Rooms from: $245* ✉ *1121 Edison St.* ☎ *805/693–0303* 🌐 *www.forfriendsinn.com* *7 units* *Free breakfast.*

Cloud Nine Glider Rides

FLYING/SKYDIVING/SOARING | The outfit's scenic glider rides last from 10 to 50 minutes. Tour options include the Santa Ynez Valley, coastal mountains and the Channel Islands, and celebrity homes. ✉ *Santa Ynez Airport, 900 Airport Rd.* ☎ *805/602–6620* 🌐 *cloud9gliderrides.com* *From $185.*

Los Olivos

4 miles north of Santa Ynez.

This pretty village was once on Spanish-built El Camino Real (Royal Road) and later a stop on major stagecoach and rail routes. Tasting rooms, art galleries, antiques stores, and country markets line Grand Avenue and intersecting streets for several blocks.

GETTING HERE AND AROUND

From U.S. 101 north or south, exit at Highway 154 and drive east about 8 miles. From Santa Barbara, travel 30 miles northwest on Highway 154.

Sights

Blair Fox Cellars

WINERY/DISTILLERY | Blair Fox, a Santa Barbara native, crafts small-lot Rhône-style wines made from organic grapes. The bar in his rustic Los Olivos tasting room, where you can sample exceptional vineyard-designated Syrahs and other wines, was hewn from Australian white oak reclaimed from an old Tasmanian schoolhouse. *2477 Alamo Pintado Ave. 805/691–1678 www.blairfoxcellars.com Tastings $15 Closed Tues. and Wed.*

Coquelicot Estate Vineyard

WINERY/DISTILLERY | Named for the vivid red poppy flowers that blanket the French countryside and appear on all its labels, this limited-production winery focuses on handcrafted Bordeaux wines made from grapes at its certified organic 58-acre Santa Ynez Valley vineyard. Don't miss samples of the flagship wines: Sixer (a Syrah and Viogner blend), Mon Amour (a Bordeaux blend), and the estate Sauvignon Blanc and Rosé. *2884 Grand Ave. 805/688–1500 www.coquelicotwines.com Tastings from $18.*

Firestone Vineyard

WINERY/DISTILLERY | Heirs to the Firestone tire fortune developed (but no longer own) this winery known for Chardonnay, Gewürztraminer, Cabernet Sauvignon, and Syrah—and for the fantastic valley views from its tasting room (reservations required) and picnic area. The walking tour here is highly informative. *5017 Zaca Station Rd., off U.S. 101 805/688–3940 www.firestonewine.com Tastings from $20, tour $25.*

Restaurants

Los Olivos Wine Merchant Cafe

$$ | **AMERICAN** | Part wine store and part social hub, this café focuses on wine-friendly fish, pasta, and meat dishes, plus salads, pizzas, and burgers. Don't miss the brie baked in cinnamon puff pastry or the homemade focaccia bread and dipping oil. **Known for:** nearly everything made in-house; ingredients from own organic café farm; wines from own estate winery. *Average main: $24 2879 Grand Ave. 805/688–7265 www.winemerchantcafe.com No breakfast.*

Hotels

★ Ballard Inn & The Gathering Table

$$$ | **B&B/INN** | Set among orchards and vineyards in the tiny town of Ballard, 2 miles south of Los Olivos, this inn makes an elegant Wine Country escape. **Pros:** exceptional food; attentive staff; secluded setting. **Cons:** some baths could use updating; restaurant noise sometimes travels upstairs; no in-room phones or TVs. *Rooms from: $329 2436 Baseline Ave., Ballard 805/688–7770, 800/638–2466 ballardinn.com 15 rooms Free breakfast.*

Fess Parker's Wine Country Inn

$$$$ | **B&B/INN** | This luxury inn includes an elegant, tree-shaded French country–style main building and an equally attractive annex across the street with a pool and day spa. **Pros:** convenient wine-touring base; walking distance from restaurants and galleries; Nella restaurant on-site. **Cons:** pricey for the area; not pet-friendly; thin walls between some rooms. $ *Rooms from: $395* ✉ *2860 Grand Ave.* ☎ *805/688–7788, 800/446–2455* 🌐 *www.fessparkerinn.com* *19 rooms* *Free breakfast.*

Solvang

5 miles south of Los Olivos.

You'll know you've reached the town of Solvang when the architecture suddenly changes to half-timber buildings and windmills. Danish educators settled the town in 1911—the flatlands and rolling green hills reminded them of home. Solvang has attracted tourists for decades, but it's lately become more sophisticated, with smorgasbords giving way to galleries, upscale restaurants, and wine-tasting rooms by day and wine bars by night.

GETTING HERE AND AROUND

Highway 246 West (Mission Drive) traverses Solvang, connecting with U.S. 101 to the west and Highway 154 to the east. Alamo Pintado Road connects Solvang with Ballard and Los Olivos to the north. Park your car in one of the free public lots and stroll the town. Or take the bus: Santa Ynez Valley Transit shuttles run between Solvang and nearby towns.

ESSENTIALS

VISITOR INFORMATION Solvang Visitors Center. ✉ *1639 Copenhagen Dr., at 2nd St.* ☎ *805/688–6144* 🌐 *www.solvangusa.com.*

Sights

Buttonwood Farm Winery & Vineyard

WINERY/DISTILLERY | Winemaker Karen Steinwachs transforms Bordeaux and Rhône varietals grown on Buttonwood Farm's 42-acre, sustainably farmed estate vineyard into delicious, value-laden wines. The flagship wines—Sauvignon Blanc, Cabernet Franc, and Cabernet Sauvignon—are distributed regionally, but many are small-lot specialty wines and blends available only at the winery. Steinwachs also crafts Chardonnay and Pinot Noir wines with grapes from a vineyard in the cool-climate Sta. Rita Hills AVA 25 miles to the west. Sign up in advance for the hour-long Vineyard Walk (daily at 10 am) followed by a reserve tasting. ✉ *1500 Alamo Pintado Rd.* ☎ *805/688–3032* 🌐 *www.buttonwoodwinery.com* *Tasting $15, walk and reserve tasting $35.*

Mission Santa Inés

RELIGIOUS SITE | The mission holds an impressive collection of paintings, statuary, vestments, and Chumash and Spanish artifacts in a serene bluff-top setting. You can tour the museum, sanctuary, and gardens. ✉ *1760 Mission Dr., at Alisal Rd.* ☎ *805/688–4815* 🌐 *missionsantaines.org* *$6.*

Restaurants

★ First & Oak

$$$$ | **AMERICAN** | Create your own custom tasting menu by choosing among five different groups of eclectic California–French dishes paired with local wines at this elegant farm-to-table restaurant inside the Mirabelle Inn. The seasonal menu changes constantly, but regulars include smoked sweet-and-spicy duck wings, truffle-roasted cauliflower, local spot prawns, short rib bourguignonne, and pears poached in red wine from the sommelier-owner's organic Coceliquot Estate Vineyard. **Known for:** intimate fine-dining setting; sommelier-owner selected wine list; complex dishes and presentation. $ *Average main: $37* ✉ *409 1st St.* *At Oak St.* ☎ *805/688–1703* 🌐 *www.firstandoak.com.*

peasants FEAST

$$ | **MODERN AMERICAN** | **FAMILY** | This low-key, family-friendly eatery in the heart of town serves up fresh-as-it-gets, made-from-scratch dishes that showcase seasonal local bounty sourced from trusted fishers and farmers. Feast on soups, beef-and-cheese smash burgers, and various salads and sandwiches in the casual interior or in the cozy brick patio. **Known for:** tacos with rockfish, gourmet mushrooms, or slow-cooked pork; house-cured and smoked bacon, pickled organic veggies, pastrami-smoked salmon; house-made ice cream and desserts. *Average main: $17 487 Atterdag Rd. 805/686–4555 www.peasantsfeast.com Closed Mon. and Tues.*

★ Sear Steakhouse

$$$$ | **STEAKHOUSE** | This true farm-to-table restaurant (most ingredients come from the owners' organic farm, planted with more than 100 varieties of fruits, veggies, and herbs) serves classic steak house dishes that have a regional flair. Steaks come from high-end purveyors in Colorado and local ranches; seafood from regional waters; and other dishes like watermelon gazpacho, creamed spinach, and sauteed mushrooms showcase seasonal bounty. **Known for:** lively bar scene with dining until 2 am; classic and modern cocktails; culinary feasts on the farm (check website for schedule). *Average main: $43 478 4th Place 805/245–9564 www.searsteakhouse.com Closed Mon. No lunch.*

Succulent Café

$$$ | **AMERICAN** | Locals flock to this cozy café for its comfort cuisine and regional wines and craft beers. Order at the counter, and staffers will deliver your meal to the interior dining areas or the sunny outdoor patio. **Known for:** artisanal charcuterie plates; pet-friendly patio; homemade biscuits and gravy, house-roasted turkey. *Average main: $28 1555 Mission Dr., at 4th Pl. 805/691–9444 succulentcafe.com Closed Tues.*

Hotels

★ Alisal Guest Ranch and Resort

$$$$ | **RESORT** | Since 1946 celebrities and plain folk alike have come to this 10,000-acre ranch to join in a slew of activities, including horseback riding, tennis, golf, archery, boating, and fishing. **Pros:** Old West atmosphere; breakfast and dinner included in the rate; free Wi-Fi. **Cons:** no in-room phones or TVs; not close to downtown; jacket required for dinner. *Rooms from: $735 1054 Alisal Rd. 805/688–6411, 800/425–4725 alisal.com 73 rooms All-inclusive.*

★ Hotel Corque

$$ | **HOTEL** | Owned by the Santa Ynez Band of Chumash Indians, the stunning three-story "Corque" provides a full slate of upscale amenities. **Pros:** friendly, professional staff; short walk to shops, tasting rooms and restaurants; free Wi-Fi. **Cons:** no kitchenettes or laundry facilities; some rooms need updating; not pet-friendly. *Rooms from: $239 400 Alisal Rd. 805/688–8000 hotel-corque.com 132 rooms No meals.*

The Landsby

$$$ | **B&B/INN** | New owners remodeled the former old-world-style Petersen Village Inn and transformed it into a cozy, contemporary Scandinavian retreat that feels like a residence in downtown Copenhagen. **Pros:** in the heart of Solvang; easy parking; courtyard with fire pits. **Cons:** on highway; unusual hallway configuration can be confusing; thin walls in some rooms. *Rooms from: $279 1576 Mission Dr. 805/688–3121 thelandsby.com 51 rooms No meals.*

★ Mirabelle Inn

$$$ | **B&B/INN** | French, Danish, and American flags at the entrance and crystal chandeliers, soaring ceilings, and skylights in the lobby set the tone from the get-go in this elegant four-story inn a few blocks from the main tourist hub. **Pros:** excellent farm-to-table restaurant (dinner only); on-site concierge and sommelier; away from noisy crowds. **Cons:** some rooms on the small side; not in the heart of town; restaurant noise travels to nearby rooms. *Rooms from: $260 409 1st St. At Oak St. 805/688–1703, 800/786–7925 mirabelleinn.com 12 rooms No meals.*

Performing Arts

Solvang Festival Theater

THEATER | Pacific Conservatory of the Performing Arts presents crowd-pleasing musicals like *A Gentleman's Guide to Love and Murder* and *Million Dollar Quartet*, as well as Oscar Wilde's *The Importance of Being Earnest*, and contemporary plays at this 700-seat outdoor amphitheater. ✉ *420 2nd St., at Molle Way* ☎ *805/922–8313* 🌐 *pcpa.org* ☞ *Performances June–Oct.*

Buellton

3 miles west of Solvang.

A crossroads town at the intersection of U.S. 101 and Highway 246, Buellton has evolved from a sleepy gas and coffee stop into an enclave of wine-tasting rooms, beer gardens, and restaurants. It's also a gateway to the Santa Rita Hills Wine Trail to the west and to Solvang, Santa Ynez, and Los Olivos to the east.

GETTING HERE AND AROUND

Driving is the easiest way to get to Buellton. From Santa Barbara, follow U.S. 101 north to the Highway 246 exit. Santa Ynez Valley Transit serves Buellton with shuttle buses from Solvang and nearby towns.

ESSENTIALS

VISITOR INFORMATION Discover Buellton. ✉ *597 Ave. of the Flags, No. 101* ☎ *805/688–7829* 🌐 *discoverbuellton.com.* **Santa Rita Hills Wine Trail.** 🌐 *santaritahillswinetrail.com.*

Sights

Alma Rosa Winery

WINERY/DISTILLERY | Winemaker Richard Sanford helped put Santa Barbara County on the international wine map with a 1989 Pinot Noir. For Alma Rosa, started in 2005, he crafts wines from grapes grown on 100-plus acres of certified organic vineyards in the Santa Rita Hills. The Pinot Noirs and Chardonnays are exceptional. Vineyard tours and tastings are available by appointment. ✉ *181 C Industrial Way, off Hwy. 246, west of U.S. 101* ☎ *805/688–9090* 🌐 *almarosawinery.com* 🎟 *Tastings $20.*

Industrial Way

NEIGHBORHOOD | A half mile west of U.S. 101, head south from Highway 246 on Industrial Way to explore a hip and happening collection of food and drink destinations. Top stops include **Industrial Eats** (a craft butcher shop and restaurant), **Figueroa Mountain Brewing Kitchen,** the **Alma Rosa Winery** tasting room, and **McClain Cellars.** ✉ *Industrial Way, off Hwy. 246* 🌐 *www.industrialwaysbc.com.*

Lafond Winery and Vineyards

WINERY/DISTILLERY | A rich, concentrated Pinot Noir is the main attention-getter at this winery that also produces noteworthy Chardonnays and Syrahs. Bottles with Lafond's SRH (Santa Rita Hills) label are an especially good value. The winery also has a tasting room at 111 East Yanonali Street in Santa Barbara's Funk Zone. ✉ *6855 Santa Rosa Rd., west off U.S. 101 Exit 139* ☎ *805/688–7921* 🌐 *lafondwinery.com* 🎟 *Tastings $15.*

La Purísima Mission State Historic Park

RELIGIOUS SITE | **FAMILY** | The state's most fully restored mission, founded in 1787, stands in a stark and still remote location that powerfully evokes the lives and isolation of California's Spanish settlers. Docents lead tours Wednesday to Sunday (daily June to August), and vivid displays illustrate the secular and religious activities that formed mission life. ✉ *2295 Purisima Rd., off Hwy. 246, 14 miles west of Buellton, Lompoc* ☎ *805/733–3713* 🌐 *www.lapurisimamission.org* 🎟 *$6 per vehicle.*

Los Alamos

HISTORIC SITE | A tiny stagecoach town founded in 1876, Los Alamos is a fun, Old West stopover when driving along Highway 101. Many of its original structures, including the 1880 Union Hotel, still line several blocks of Bell Street, the main drag. In recent years Los Alamos has evolved into a hip food-and-wine destination with first-rate tasting rooms and restaurants within the western-style buildings. Standouts include **Pico Los Alamos, Bob's Well Bread,** and **Casa Dumetz Wines.** ✉ *On Hwy. 101, 15 miles north of Buellton* 🌐 *www.visitsyv.com/discover-syv/los-alamos.*

Restaurants

The Hitching Post II

$$$$ | **AMERICAN** | You'll find everything from grilled artichokes to quail at this casual eatery, but most people come for the smoky Santa Maria–style barbecue. Be sure to try a glass of owner-chef-winemaker Frank Ostini's signature Highliner Pinot Noir, a star in the film *Sideways.* **Known for:** entrées grilled over local red oak; chef-owner makes his own wines; classic cocktails. $ *Average main: $38* ✉ *406 E. Hwy. 246, off U.S. 101* ☎ *805/688–0676* 🌐 *www.hitchingpost2.com* ⏲ *No lunch.*

Hotels

Inn at Zaca Creek

$$$$ | **HOTEL** | Originally built by descendants of Buellton's founding family and reinvented as a rustic luxury resort after decades of dormancy, this elegant collection of suites, a restaurant, and secluded, multitiered spaces on 3 tree-studded acres pays homage to the land's historic roots and pastoral setting. **Pros:** on-site fine-dining restaurant and bar; secluded site near ranches and a residential area; attentive and personal service and hospitality. **Cons:** next to Highway 101; popular wedding venue with lively guests; not in the heart of town. $ *Rooms from: $360* ✉ *1297 Jonata Park Rd.* ☎ *805/688–2412* 🌐 *zaca-creek.com* *6 suites* 🍽 *No meals.*

Volcanoes?

Those eye-catching sawed-off peaks along the drive from Pismo Beach to Morro Bay are called the Nine Sisters—a series of ancient volcanic plugs. Morro Rock, the northernmost sibling and a state historic monument, is the most famous and photographed of the clan.

Pismo Beach

51 miles northwest of Buellton.

About 20 miles of sandy shoreline—nicknamed the Bakersfield Riviera for the throngs of vacationers who come here from the Central Valley—begins at the town of Pismo Beach. The southern end of town runs along sand dunes, some of which are open to cars and off-road vehicles. Sheltered by the dunes, a grove of eucalyptus trees attracts thousands of migrating monarch butterflies from November through February. A long, broad beach fronts the center of town, where a municipal pier extends into the sea at the foot of shop-lined Pomeroy Street. To the north, hotels and homes perch atop chalky oceanfront cliffs. Fewer than 10,000 people live in this quintessential surfer haven, but Pismo Beach has a slew of hotels and restaurants with great views of the Pacific Ocean.

GETTING HERE AND AROUND

Pismo Beach straddles both sides of U.S. 101. If you're coming from the south and have time for a scenic drive, exit U.S. 101 in Santa Maria and take Highway 166 west for 8 miles to Guadalupe and follow Highway 1 north 16 miles to

Pismo Beach. South County Area Transit (SCAT; ⊕ *www.slorta.org*) buses run throughout San Luis Obispo and connect the city with nearby towns. On summer weekends, the free Avila Trolley extends service to Pismo Beach.

ESSENTIALS

VISITOR INFORMATION California Welcome Center. ✉ *333 5 Cities Dr.* ☎ *805/688–7354* ⊕ *www.visitcalifornia.com/experience/california-welcome-center-pismo-beach/.* **Pismo Beach Visitor Information Center.** ✉ *Dolliver St./Hwy. 1 , at Hinds Ave.* ☎ *800/443–7778, 805/556–7397* ⊕ *classiccalifornia.com.*

Beaches

★ Oceano Dunes State Vehicular Recreation Area

BEACH—SIGHT | Part of the spectacular Guadalupe-Nipomo Dunes, this 3,600-acre coastal playground is one of the few places in California where you can drive or ride off-highway vehicles on the beach and sand dunes. Hike, ride horses, kiteboard, join a Hummer tour, or rent an ATV or a dune buggy and cruise up the white-sand peaks for spectacular views. At **Oso Flaco Lake Nature Area**—3 miles west of Highway 1 on Oso Flaco Road—a 1½-mile boardwalk over the lake leads to a platform with views up and down the coast. Leashed dogs are allowed in much of the park except Oso Flaco and Pismo Dunes Natural Reserve. **Amenities:** food and drink; lifeguards (seasonal); parking (fee); showers; toilets; water sports. **Best for:** sunset; surfing; swimming; walking. ✉ *West end of Pier Ave., off Hwy. 1, Oceano* ☎ *805/773–7170* ⊕ *www.parks.ca.gov* *$5 per vehicle.*

Pismo State Beach

BEACH—SIGHT | Hike, surf, ride horses, swim, fish in a lagoon or off the pier, and dig for Pismo clams at this busy state beach. One of the day-use parking areas is off Highway 1 near the **Monarch Butterfly Grove,** where from November through February monarch butterflies nest in eucalyptus and Monterey pines. The other parking area is about 1½ miles south at Pier Avenue. **Amenities:** food and drink; lifeguards (seasonal); parking (fee); showers; toilets; water sports. **Best for:** sunset; surfing; swimming; walking. ✉ *555 Pier Ave., off Hwy. 1, 3 miles south of downtown Pismo Beach, Oceano* ☎ *805/473–7220* ⊕ *www.parks.ca.gov* *Day-use $10 per vehicle if parking at beach.*

Restaurants

Cracked Crab

$$$ | **SEAFOOD** | This traditional New England–style crab shack imports fresh seafood daily from Australia, Alaska, and the East Coast. Fish is line-caught, much of the produce is organic, and everything is made from scratch. **Known for:** shellfish meals in a bucket, dumped on the table; casual setting; menu changes daily. $ *Average main: $32* ✉ *751 Price St., near Main St.* ☎ *805/773–2722* ⊕ *www.crackedcrab.com.*

★ Ember

$$$ | **MODERN AMERICAN** | A barn-style restaurant with high ceilings and an open kitchen, Ember enjoys a red-hot reputation for Italian-inflected dishes prepared in an authentic Tuscan fireplace or a wood-burning oven. Chef-owner Brian Collins, a native of Arroyo Grande, the town bordering Pismo Beach, honed his culinary skills at Berkeley's legendary Chez Panisse Restaurant. **Known for:** seasonal menu changes monthly; wood-fired flatbread pizzas; long lines during prime time (no reservations). $ *Average main: $34* ✉ *1200 E. Grand Ave., at Brisco Rd., Arroyo Grande* ☎ *805/474–7700* ⊕ *www.emberwoodfire.com* ⏱ *Closed Mon. and Tues. No lunch.*

Giuseppe's Cucina Italiana

$$$ | **ITALIAN** | The classic flavors of southern Italy are highlighted at this lively downtown spot. Most recipes originate from Bari, a seaport on the Adriatic; the menu includes breads and pizzas baked in the wood-burning oven, hearty dishes such as dry-aged steak and rack of lamb, and homemade pastas. **Known for:** lively family-style atmosphere; daily specials; most fruits and veggies come from owner's 12-acre farm. *Average main: $28 891 Price St., at Pismo Ave. 805/773–2870 giuseppesrestaurant.com No lunch weekdays.*

Splash Café

$ | **SEAFOOD** | Folks stand in line down the block for clam chowder served in a sourdough bread bowl at this wildly popular seafood stand. You can also order beach food such as fresh steamed clams, burgers, and fried calamari at the counter (no table service) here and at Splash's second location in San Luis Obispo, which has an on-site bakery and additional menu items. **Known for:** famous clam chowder; sourdough bread bowls baked in-house; cheery hole-in-the-wall. *Average main: $12 197 Pomeroy St., at Cypress St. 805/773–4653 splashcafe.com.*

The Spoon Trade

$$ | **AMERICAN** | A silver spoon display at the entrance reflects this casual eatery's mission to "spoon food and trade stories" with diners who indulge in traditional American comfort food with a modern twist. Perennial menu faves include tri-tip tartare, deviled eggs, meat loaf Stroganoff, and fried chicken with sourdough waffles; save room for a root beer float or brown sugar pot de creme for dessert. **Known for:** pet-friendly patio; house-made pastas; lively dining room with open kitchen. *Average main: $25 295 W. Grand Ave. 805/904–6773 www.thespoontrade.com Closed Mon. and Tues. No lunch weekdays.*

Ventana Grill

$$$ | **FUSION** | Perched on a bluff at the northern edge of Pismo Beach, Ventana Grill offers ocean views from nearly every table, unusual seafood-centered Latin American–California fusion dishes, and more than 50 tequilas plus craft cocktails at the bar. Reservations are essential—this place is almost always packed, especially during the weekday happy hour. **Known for:** happy hour with sunset views; salsas and sauces made from scratch; more than 50 tequila selections. *Average main: $28 2575 Price St. 805/773–0000 ventanagrill.com.*

Hotels

The Cliffs Hotel & Spa

$$ | **RESORT** | Lawns and palm trees surround this full-service resort that perches dramatically on an oceanfront cliff. **Pros:** beach access via short downhill path; oceanfront restaurant and lounge; bluff-top walking trail. **Cons:** not close to downtown; rooms near service areas and elevator can be noisy; resort fee. *Rooms from: $239 2757 Shell Beach Rd. 805/773–5000, 800/826–7827 www.cliffsresort.com 160 rooms No meals.*

Dolphin Bay Resort & Spa

$$$$ | **RESORT** | On grass-covered bluffs overlooking Shell Beach, this luxury resort looks and feels like an exclusive community of villas; choose among sprawling one- or two-bedroom suites, each with a gourmet kitchen, laundry room with washer and dryer, and contemporary furnishings. **Pros:** lavish apartment units; Lido farm-to-table restaurant; many suites have ocean views. **Cons:** hefty price tag; vibe too upper-crust for some; not close to downtown. *Rooms from: $489 2727 Shell Beach Rd. 805/773–4300, 800/516–0112 reservations, 805/773–8900 restaurant www.thedolphinbay.com 60 suites No meals.*

Inn at the Pier

$$$$ | **HOTEL** | The luxe Inn at the Pier opened in winter 2017, covering a prime city block just steps from the sand and across from the pier. **Pros:** walk to downtown restaurants, sights, shops; fitness

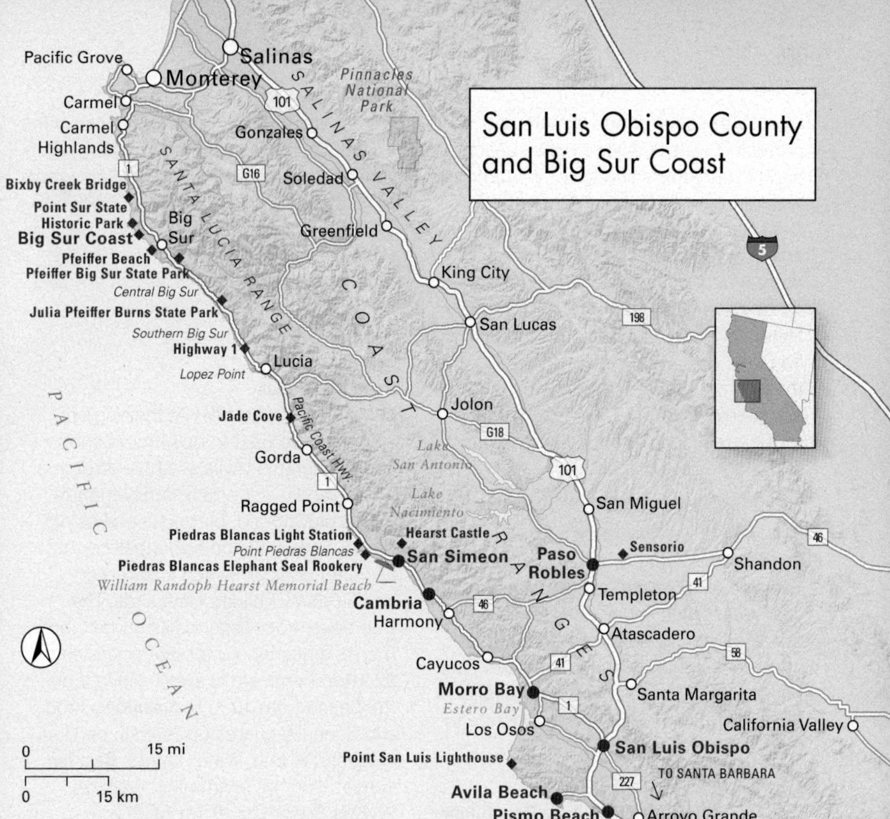

center and cruiser bike rentals; new building. **Cons:** daily resort fee; valet parking only; bar noise travels to some rooms. *Rooms from: $359 601 Cypress St. 805/295–5565 www.theinnatthepier.com 104 rooms No meals.*

Pismo Lighthouse Suites

$$$ | **HOTEL** | Each of the well-appointed two-room, two-bath suites at this oceanfront resort has a private balcony or patio. **Pros:** sport court features life-size chess game; nautical-style furnishings; nice pool area. **Cons:** not easy to walk to main attractions; some units are next to busy road; first-floor units can hear footsteps from suites above. *Rooms from: $269 2411 Price St. 805/773–2411, 800/245–2411 www.pismolighthousesuites.com 70 suites Free breakfast.*

SeaVenture Beach Hotel & Restaurant

$$$ | **HOTEL** | The bright, homey rooms at this hotel all have fireplaces and featherbeds; most have balconies with private hot tubs, and some have beautiful ocean views. **Pros:** on the beach; excellent food; romantic rooms. **Cons:** touristy area; some rooms and facilities dated; dark hallways. *Rooms from: $279 100 Ocean View Ave. 805/773–4994 www.seaventure.com 50 rooms No meals.*

Avila Beach

4 miles north of Pismo Beach.

Because the village of Avila Beach and the sandy, cove-front shoreline for which it's named face south into the Pacific Ocean, they get more sun and less fog than any other stretch of coast in the area. With its fortuitous climate and protected waters, Avila's public beach draws sunbathers and families; summer weekends are very busy. Downtown Avila Beach has a lively seaside promenade and some shops and hotels, but for real local color, head to the far end of the cove and watch the commercial fishers off-load their catch on the old Port San Luis wharf. On Friday from mid-April through mid-September, a fish and farmers' market livens up the beach area with music, fresh local produce and seafood, and children's activities.

GETTING HERE AND AROUND

Exit U.S. 101 at Avila Beach Drive and head 3 miles west to reach the beach. The free Avila Trolley operates weekends year-round, plus Friday afternoon and evening from April to September. The minibuses connect Avila Beach and Port San Luis to Shell Beach, with multiple stops along the way. Service extends to Pismo Beach in summer.

ESSENTIALS

VISITOR INFORMATION Avila Beach Tourism Alliance. *visitavilabeach.com.*

Sights

Avila Valley Barn

RESTAURANT—SIGHT | FAMILY | An old-fashioned, family-friendly country store jam-packed with local fruits and vegetables, prepared foods, and gifts, Avila Valley Barn also gives visitors a chance to experience rural American traditions. You can pet farm animals and savor homemade ice cream and pies daily, and on weekends ride a hay wagon out to the fields to pick your own produce. *560 Avila Beach Dr., San Luis Obispo 805/595–2816 www.avilavalleybarn.com Closed Tues. and Wed. Jan.–Mar.*

Point San Luis Lighthouse

LIGHTHOUSE | FAMILY | Docents lead hikes along scenic Pecho Coast Trail (3½ miles round-trip) to see the historic 1890 lighthouse and its rare Fresnel lens. **■ TIP→ If you'd prefer a lift out to the lighthouse, join a shuttle tour. Hikes and tours require reservations.** *Point San Luis, 1¾ miles west of Harford Pier, Port San Luis 805/540–5771 www.pointsanluislighthouse.org Shuttle tours $25; hikes free ($10 to enter lighthouse).*

Beaches

Avila City Beach

BEACH—SIGHT | FAMILY | At the edge of a sunny cove next to downtown shops and restaurants, Avila's ½-mile stretch of white sand is especially family-friendly, with a playground, barbecue and picnic tables, volleyball and basketball courts, and lifeguards on watch in summer and on many holiday weekends. The free beachfront parking fills up fast, but there's a nearby pay lot ($6 for the day, $2 after 4 pm). Dogs aren't allowed on the beach from 10 to 5. **Amenities:** food and drink; lifeguards (seasonal); parking; showers; toilets; water sports. **Best for:** sunset; surfing; swimming; walking. *Avila Beach Dr., at 1st St. www.visitavilabeach.com Free.*

Restaurants

Mersea's

$ | SEAFOOD | Walk down the pier to this casual crab shack where you can order at the counter, grab a drink at the bar, and find a seat on the deck or in the casual indoor dining area to gaze at spectacular Avila Bay views while you dine. The menu includes chowder bowls, burgers, sandwiches, seafood, and salads, plus bowls of fish, shrimp, or chicken served over rice pilaf and veggies. **Known for:** clam chowder in sourdough bread bowls; fish tacos; fresh local ingredients. *Average main: $16 3985 Port San Luis Pier At Port San Luis 805/548–2290 www.merseas.com.*

Ocean Grill

$$$ | SEAFOOD | Across from the promenade, beach, and pier, Ocean Grill serves up fresh seafood to diners who typically arrive before sunset to enjoy the views. Boats anchored in the bay provide much of the seafood, which pairs well with the mostly regional wines on the list. **Known for:** fantastic ocean views; wood-fired pizzas; gluten-free and vegetarian options. *Average main: $29* *268 Front St.* *805/595–4050* *www.oceangrillavila.com* *No lunch Mon.–Thurs.*

Hotels

Avila La Fonda
$$$ | **HOTEL** | Modeled after a village in early California's Mexican period, Avila La Fonda surrounds guests with rich jewel tones, fountains, and upscale comfort; its facade replicates eight different casitas, including several famous historic homes in Mexico. **Pros:** one-of-a-kind theme and artwork; flexible room combinations; a block from the beach. **Cons:** pricey for the area; most rooms don't have an ocean view; spotty Wi-Fi. *Rooms from: $329* *101 San Miguel St.* *805/595–1700* *www.avilalafondahotel.com* *28 rooms* *No meals.*

Avila Lighthouse Suites
$$$$ | **HOTEL** | Families, honeymooners, and business travelers all find respite at this two-story, all-suites luxury hotel. **Pros:** directly across from beach; easy walk to restaurants and shops; free underground parking. **Cons:** noise from passersby can be heard in room; some ocean-view rooms have limited vistas; basic breakfast. *Rooms from: $359* *550 Front St.* *805/627–1900, 800/372–8452* *www.avilalighthousesuites.com* *54 suites* *Free breakfast.*

Sycamore Mineral Springs Resort & Spa
$$$ | **RESORT** | This wellness resort's hot mineral springs bubble up into private outdoor tubs on an oak-and-sycamore-forest hillside. **Pros:** great place to rejuvenate; nice hiking nearby; incredible spa with yoga classes, integrative healing arts, and many treatments. **Cons:** rooms vary in quality; 2½ miles from the beach; road noise can travel to certain areas of property. *Rooms from: $259* *1215 Avila Beach Dr., San Luis Obispo* *805/595–7302* *www.sycamoresprings.com* *72 rooms* *No meals.*

San Luis Obispo

8 miles north of Avila Beach.

About halfway between San Francisco and Los Angeles, San Luis Obispo spreads out below gentle hills and rocky extinct volcanoes. Its main appeal lies in its architecturally diverse, pedestrian-friendly downtown, which bustles with shoppers, restaurant goers, and students from California Polytechnic State University, known as Cal Poly. On Thursday evening from 6 to 9 the city's famed farmers' market fills Higuera Street with local produce, entertainment, and food stalls.

San Luis Obispo is the commercial center of a wine region whose appellations (Edna Valley, Arroyo Grande Valley) stretch west toward the coast and east toward the inland mountains. Many of the nearly 30 wineries here line Highway 227 and connecting roads. The region is known for Chardonnay and Pinot Noir, although many wineries experiment with other varietals and blends. Wine-touring maps are available around San Luis Obispo. Many wineries charge a small tasting fee; most tasting rooms close at 5.

GETTING HERE AND AROUND

U.S. 101/Highway 1 traverses the city for several miles. From the north, Highway 1 merges with U.S. 101 when it reaches the city limits. The wineries of the Edna Valley and Arroyo Grande Valley wine regions lie south of town off Highway 227, the parallel (to the east) Orcutt Road, and connecting roads.

SLO City Transit buses operate daily. The Downtown Trolley provides evening service to the city's hub every Thursday, on Friday from June to early September, and Saturday from April through October.

ESSENTIALS

VISITOR INFORMATION San Luis Obispo Chamber of Commerce. ✉ *895 Monterey St.* ☎ *805/781–2777* 🌐 *slochamber.org.* **San Luis Obispo City Visitor Information.** ☎ *877/756–8696* 🌐 *visitslo.com.*

Sights

Biddle Ranch Vineyard

WINERY/DISTILLERY | Glass doors and walls in a converted dairy barn fill the Biddle Ranch Vineyard tasting room with light and sweeping valley, mountain, and vineyard views. The small-production winery focuses on estate Chardonnay (the adjacent 17-acre vineyard is planted exclusively to the grape), plus Pinot Noir and various red blends. ✉ *2050 Biddle Ranch Rd.* ✣ *At Hwy. 227* ☎ *805/543–2399* 🌐 *www.biddleranch.com* 🎫 *Tastings $25 (reservations required)* ⏲ *Closed Tues. and Wed.*

Claiborne & Churchill

WINERY/DISTILLERY | An eco-friendly winery built from straw bales, C&C makes small lots of aromatic Alsatian-style wines such as dry Riesling and Gewürztraminer, plus Pinot Noir blends, Syrah, and Chardonnay. ✉ *2649 Carpenter Canyon Rd., at Price Canyon Rd.* ☎ *805/544–4066* 🌐 *www.clairbornechurchill.com* 🎫 *Tastings $22.*

Mission San Luis Obispo de Tolosa

RELIGIOUS SITE | Sun-dappled Mission Plaza fronts the fifth mission established in 1772 by Franciscan friars. A small museum exhibits artifacts of the Chumash Indians and early Spanish settlers. ✉ *751 Palm St., at Chorro St.* ☎ *805/543–6850* 🌐 *www.missionsanluisobispo.org* 🎫 *$3.*

Old Edna

TOWN | This peaceful, 2-acre site once *was* the town of Edna. Nowadays you can peek at the vintage 1897 and 1908 farmhouse cottages, taste Sextant wines, pick up sandwiches at the gourmet deli, and stroll along Old Edna Lane. ✉ *1653 Old Maxwellton Rd., at Hwy. 227* ☎ *805/710–3701 Old Edna Townsite, 805/542–0133 tasting room and deli* 🌐 *oldedna.com.*

San Luis Obispo Children's Museum

MUSEUM | **FAMILY** | Activities at this facility geared to kids under age 10 include an "imagination-powered" elevator that transports visitors to a series of underground caverns. Elsewhere, simulated lava and steam sputter from an active volcano. Kids can pick rubber fruit at a farmers' market and race in a fire engine to fight a fire. ✉ *1010 Nipomo St., at Monterey St.* ☎ *805/544–5437* 🌐 *www.slocm.org* 🎫 *$8* ⏲ *Closed Tues. Closed nonholiday Mon. Sept.–Apr.*

Talley Vineyards

WINERY/DISTILLERY | Acres of Chardonnay and Pinot Noir, plus smaller parcels of Sauvignon Blanc, Syrah, and other varietals blanket Talley's mountain-ringed dell in the Arroyo Grande Valley. Enjoy stunning estate views in the sleek interior and on the adjacent patio, where all tastings are seated (no tasting bar) and require an appointment. Standout wines include the single-vineyard Rosemary's Pinot Noir and Chardonnay. ✉ *3031 Lopez Dr., off Orcutt Rd., Arroyo Grande* ☎ *805/489–0446* 🌐 *www.talleyvineyards.com* 🎫 *Tastings from $30.*

Deep Roots

Way back in the 1700s, the Spanish padres who accompanied Father Junípero Serra planted grapevines from Mexico along California's Central Coast and began using European wine-making techniques to turn the grapes into delectable vintages.

Wolff Vineyards

WINERY/DISTILLERY | Syrah, Petite Sirah, and Riesling join the expected Pinot Noir and Chardonnay as the stars at this family-run winery 6 miles south of downtown. The pourers are friendly, and you'll often meet one of the owners or their children in the tasting room. With its hillside views, the outdoor patio is a great place to enjoy an afternoon picnic. *6238 Orcutt Rd., near Biddle Ranch Rd.* *805/781–0448* *www.wolffvineyards.com* *Tastings $15.*

Restaurants

Big Sky Café

$$ | **ECLECTIC** | Family-friendly Big Sky turns local and organically grown ingredients into global dishes, starting with breakfast. Just pick your continent: braised Argentinian lamb shanks, Southeast Asian noodle bowls, Middle Eastern lamb burger, Maryland crab cakes. **Known for:** artsy, creative vibe; ample choices for vegetarians; locavore pioneer. *Average main: $21* *1121 Broad St., at Higuera St.* *805/545–5401* *bigskycafe.com.*

★ Giuseppe's Cucina Rustica

$$$ | **ITALIAN** | The younger sibling of the hugely popular Guiseppe's restaurant in Pismo Beach, this lively downtown eatery serves up authentic southern Italian fare in the historic Sinsheimer Bros. building, originally constructed in 1884. Dine in the spacious main restaurant amid high ceilings, fireplaces, and bar, or in the courtyard beneath strings of twinkling lights. **Known for:** bread, sauce, pasta, gelato and other desserts made in-house; organic ingredients from the owner's 12-acre farm or sourced from local purveyors; historic ambience. *Average main: $27* *849 Monterey St.* *805/541–9922* *www.giuseppesrestaurant.com.*

Luna Red

$$$ | **INTERNATIONAL** | A spacious, contemporary space with a festive outdoor patio, this restaurant near Mission Plaza serves creative tapas and cocktails. The small plates include birria-braised beef tacos, avocado-tuna ceviche, and empanadas stuffed with squash and goat cheese. **Known for:** excellent traditional Valencian paellas; craft cocktails; lively music scene. *Average main: $27* *1023 Chorro St., at Monterey St.* *805/540–5243* *www.lunaredslo.com.*

Mo's Smokehouse BBQ

$ | **SOUTHERN** | Barbecue joints abound on the Central Coast, but this one excels. Various Southern-style sauces season tender hickory-smoked ribs and shredded-meat sandwiches, and sides such as baked beans, coleslaw, homemade potato chips, and garlic bread extend the pleasure. **Known for:** barbecue sampler with ribs, pork, and chicken; barbecue chicken and other fresh salads; house-made potato chips, garlic fries, and other sides. *Average main: $16* *1005 Monterey St., at Osos St.* *805/544–6193* *smokinmosbbq.com.*

Novo Restaurant & Lounge

$$ | **ECLECTIC** | In the colorful dining room or on the large creek-side deck, this animated downtown eatery will take you on a culinary world tour. The salads, small plates, and entrées come from nearly every continent. **Known for:** value-laden happy hour from 3 to 6; savory curry and noodle dishes; local farmers' market ingredients. *Average main: $25* *726 Higuera St., at Broad St.* *805/543–3986* *www.novorestaurant.com.*

SLO Provisions

$ | **AMERICAN** | Stop at this casual café/market in the Upper Monterey neighborhood for a sit-down or take-away meal all day. Apart from full meals, order specialty sandwiches, farm-fresh salads, and baked goods, or hang out and taste wine or beer at the casual tasting bar. **Known for:** house-roasted rotisserie meats; family-style dinners; daily specials. *Average main: $16* *1255 Monterey St.* *805/439–4298* *www.sloprovisions.com* *Closed Sun.*

Hotels

Garden Street Inn

$$ | **B&B/INN** | From this restored 1887 Italianate Queen Anne downtown, you can walk to many restaurants and attractions; uniquely decorated rooms, each with private bath, are filled with antiques, and some rooms have stained-glass windows, fireplaces, and decks. **Pros:** lavish homemade breakfast; convenient location; complementary wine-and-cheese reception. **Cons:** city noise filters into some rooms; not great for families; no elevator. *Rooms from: $249 1212 Garden St. 805/545–9802 www.gardenstreetinn.com 13 rooms Free breakfast.*

Granada Hotel & Bistro

$$$ | **HOTEL** | Built in 1922 in the heart of downtown and sparkling again after 2012 renovations, the two-story Granada is a vintage-style retreat with hardwood floors, redbrick walls, and antique rugs. **Pros:** one of a few full-service hotels in the heart of downtown; easy walk to restaurants, shops, and sights; farm-to-table Granada Bistro and Nightcap cocktail bar, and grab-and-go restaurant on-site. **Cons:** some rooms are tiny; sometimes noisy near restaurant kitchen; late-night bar noise travels to some rooms. *Rooms from: $279 1126 Morro St. 805/544–9100 www.granadahotelandbistro.com 17 rooms No meals.*

★ Hotel Cerro

$$$ | **HOTEL** | San Luis Obispo's Chumash, mission, and 19th-century industrial eras blend with urban sophistication in this eco-friendly, four-story complex, which opened in summer 2019. **Pros:** on-site restaurant, café, and lobby lounge; tree-lined outdoor terrace; designed and built to meet LEED Silver status. **Cons:** in the heart of the downtown bar scene; limited on-site valet parking only; room designs not ideal for families with small children. *Rooms from: $275 1125 Garden St. 805/548–1000 www.hotelcerro.com 65 rooms No meals.*

Hotel San Luis Obispo

$$$$ | **HOTEL** | Completed in 2019, the sleek, three-story Hotel San Luis Obispo offers a full range of services and upscale amenities, just a block from the mission and steps from restaurants, shops, and nightlife. **Pros:** in the heart of the downtown historic district; park the car and walk to most attractions; new building. **Cons:** valet parking only; some rooms overlook a parking garage; too pet-friendly for some guests. *Rooms from: $459 877 Palm St. 805/235–0700 hotel-slo.com 78 rooms No meals.*

The Kinney San Luis Obispo

$$ | **HOTEL** | The Kinney celebrates nearby Cal Poly's culture and history in fun, hipster fashion, with local photos, college sports equipment displays, and hanging wicker swings and vintage games and books in the lobby lounge. **Pros:** close to Cal Poly campus; heated pool and sundeck; free parking and Wi-Fi. **Cons:** a/c less than adequate in some rooms; tiny fitness center; motel vibe. *Rooms from: $175 1800 Monterey St. 805/544–8600 www.thekinneyslo.com 100 rooms Free breakfast.*

★ Madonna Inn

$$ | **HOTEL** | From its rococo bathrooms to its pink-on-pink froufrou steak house, the Madonna Inn is fabulous or tacky, depending on your taste. **Pros:** fun, one-of-a-kind experience; infinity pool, exercise room, and day spa; each room has its own distinct identity, for example, Safari Room. **Cons:** rooms vary widely; must appreciate kitsch; no elevator. *Rooms from: $229 100 Madonna Rd. 805/543–3000, 800/543–9666 www.madonnainn.com 110 rooms No meals.*

Petit Soleil

$$ | **B&B/INN** | A cobblestone courtyard, country-French custom furnishings, and Gallic music piped through the halls evoke a Provençal mood at this cheery inn. **Pros:** includes wine and appetizers at cocktail hour; includes scrumptious

breakfasts; cozy rooms with luxury touches. **Cons:** sits on a busy avenue; cramped parking; some rooms are tiny. *Rooms from: $189 1473 Monterey St. 805/549–0321, 800/676–1588 www.psslo.com 16 rooms Free breakfast.*

Nightlife

SLO's club scene is centered on Higuera Street, off Monterey Street.

Koberl at Blue
BARS/PUBS | A trendy crowd hangs out at this upscale restaurant's slick bar to sip on exotic martinis and the many local and imported beers and wines. *998 Monterey St., at Osos St. 805/783–1135 www.epkoberl.com.*

The Libertine Brewing Company
BREWPUBS/BEER GARDENS | Come to Libertine to savor 76 craft beers and wines on tap, house-made brews of kombucha and cold brew coffee, and pub food infused with the brewery's own wild ales. *1234 Broad St. 805/548–2337 www.libertinebrewing.com/san-luis-obispo.*

Nightcap
BARS/PUBS | Indulge in craft and vintage cocktails at the Granada Hotel's artsy cocktail lounge, decked out in pink- and rose-colored velvet, mirrored ceilings, and marble tables and countertops. *1130 Morro St. 805/544–9100.*

Performing Arts

Performing Arts Center, San Luis Obispo
ARTS CENTERS | A truly great performance space, the center hosts live theater, dance, and music. *Cal Poly, 1 Grand Ave., off U.S. 101 805/756–4849 www.calpolyarts.org.*

San Luis Obispo Repertory Theatre
THEATER | SLO County's only nonprofit, fully professional theater group presents dramas, musicals, readings, and other performances year-round. *888 Morro St. 805/786–2440 box office www.slolittletheatre.org.*

Shopping

Higuera Street
SHOPPING NEIGHBORHOODS | Many of San Luis Obispo's locally owned and operated shops cluster around downtown's Higuera Street in the blocks east of the mission. Also head up Monterey Street just north of the mission to find more small stores with one-of-a-kind treasures. *San Luis Obispo.*

Paso Robles

30 miles north of San Luis Obispo, 25 miles northwest of Morro Bay.

In the 1860s, tourists began flocking to this ranching outpost to "take the cure" in a bathhouse fed by underground mineral hot springs. An Old West town emerged, and grand Victorian homes went up, followed in the 20th century by Craftsman bungalows. These days, the wooded hills of Paso Robles west of U.S. 101 and the flatter, more open land to the freeway's east hold more than 250 wineries, many with tasting rooms. Hot summer days, cool nights, and varied soils and microclimates allow growers to cultivate an impressive array of Bordeaux, Rhône, and other grape types.

Cabernet Sauvignon grows well in the Paso Robles AVA—40,000 of its 600,000-plus acres are planted to grapes—as do Petit Verdot, Grenache, Syrah, Viognier, and Zinfandel. In recognition of the diverse growing conditions, the AVA was divided into 11 subappellations in 2014. Pick up a wine-touring map at lodgings, wineries, and attractions around town. The fee at most tasting rooms is between $10 and $25; many lodgings pass out discount coupons.

Upmarket restaurants, bars, antiques stores, and little shops fill the streets around oak-shaded City Park, where special events of all kinds—custom car shows, an olive festival, Friday-night summer concerts—take place on many weekends. Despite its increasing sophistication, Paso (as the locals call it) retains a small-town vibe. The city celebrates its cowboy roots in late July and early August with the two-week California Mid-State Fair, complete with livestock auctions, carnival rides, and corn dogs.

GETTING HERE AND AROUND

U.S. 101 runs north–south through Paso Robles. Highway 46 West links Paso Robles to Highway 1 and Cambria on the coast. Highway 46 East connects Paso Robles with I–5 and the San Joaquin Valley. Public transit is not convenient for wine touring and sightseeing.

ESSENTIALS

VISITOR INFORMATION Paso Robles CAB Collective. ☎ *805/543–2288* 🌐 *pasoroblescab.com.* **Paso Robles Wine Country Alliance.** ☎ *805/239–8463* 🌐 *pasowine.com.* **Paso Robles Visitor Center.** ✉ *1225 Park St., near 12th St.* ☎ *805/238–0506* 🌐 *travelpaso.com.* **Rhone Rangers/Paso Robles.** 🌐 *www.rhonerangers.org.*

Brecon Estate

WINERY/DISTILLERY | Small-batch super-premium wines sold exclusively in the tasting room are the main focus of this much-lauded, 40-acre, Westside estate winery. Specialties include Albariño, Cabernet Franc, and Rhone blends. Brecon also crafts Bordeaux varietals, including the reserve Old Vine Cabernet Sauvignon, with estate grapes from one of the oldest vines in Paso Robles. Taste wines within the urban-chic cedar barn, which combines Scandinavian and Australian design elements, or at tables on the shady patio. ✉ *7450 Vineyard Dr.* ☎ *805/239–2200* 🌐 *breconestate.com* 🎟 *Tastings $20.*

★ Calcareous Vineyard

WINERY/DISTILLERY | Elegant wines, a stylish tasting room, and knockout hilltop views make for a winning experience at this winery along winding Peachy Canyon Road. Cabernet Sauvignon, Syrah, and Zinfandel grapes thrive in the summer heat and limestone soils of the two vineyards near the tasting room; and a third vineyard on cooler York Mountain produces Pinot Noir, Chardonnay, and a Cabernet with a completely different character from the Peachy Canyon edition. ■ **TIP→ The picnic area's expansive eastward views invite lingering.** ✉ *3430 Peachy Canyon Rd.* ☎ *805/239–0289* 🌐 *calcareous.com* 🎟 *Tastings $20; tour and tasting (reservations required) from $35.*

Denner Vineyards

WINERY/DISTILLERY | The sloping roof of this winery's tasting room and production facility mimics the gently rolling, limestone-laden landscape it occupies. The respect for the terrain that the architecture exhibits repeats itself in the farming and cellar techniques used to create Denner's mostly Rhône-style wines, which—along with Zinfandel, Cabernet Sauvignon, and a few other reds—routinely receive mid-90s scores from major critics. Appointment-only tastings indoors or out take advantage of hilltop views of Willow Creek District trees, vines, and pastures. ✉ *5414 Vineyard Dr.* ☎ *805/239–4287* 🌐 *www.dennervineyards.com* 🎟 *Tastings $25.*

Eberle Winery

WINERY/DISTILLERY | Even if you don't drink wine, stop here for a tour (reservations essential) of the huge wine caves beneath the vineyards. Eberle produces wines from Bordeaux, Rhône, and Italian varietals and makes intriguing blends including Côte-du-Rôbles Blanc and Rouge and Cabernet Sauvignon–Syrah. ✉ *3810 Hwy. 46 E, 3½ miles east of U.S. 101* ☎ *805/238–9607* 🌐 *www.eberlewinery.com* 🎟 *Basic tasting free ($10 reservation fee for up to 6 people),* *private tour and tasting (up to 6 people) $50 by appointment.*

Firestone Walker Brewing Company

WINERY/DISTILLERY | At this working craft brewery you can sample medal-winners such as the Double Barrel Ale and learn about the beer-making process on 45-minute guided tours of the brewhouse and cellar. ✉ *1400 Ramada Dr., east side of U.S. 101; exit at Hwy. 46 W/ Cambria, but head east* ☎ *805/296–7454 visitor center* 🌐 *www.firestonebeer.com* 🎫 *Tastings from $2 per sample, tour $12 (includes 4 samples).*

Halter Ranch Vineyard

WINERY/DISTILLERY | A good place to learn about contemporary Paso Robles wine making, this ultramodern operation produces high-quality wines from estate-grown Bordeaux and Rhône grapes grown in sustainably farmed vineyards. The gravity-flow winery, which you can view on tours, is a marvel of efficiency. Ancestor, the flagship wine, a potent Bordeaux-style blend of Cabernet Sauvignon, Petit Verdot, and Malbec, is named for the ranch's huge centuries-old coast oak tree. ✉ *8910 Adelaida Rd., at Vineyard Dr.* ☎ *888/367–9977* 🌐 *www.halterranch.com* 🎫 *Tastings from $35.*

JUSTIN Vineyards & Winery

WINERY/DISTILLERY | This suave winery built its reputation on Isosceles, a hearty Bordeaux blend, usually of Cabernet Sauvignon, Cabernet Franc, and Merlot. JUSTIN's Cabernet Sauvignon is also well regarded, as is the Right Angle blend of Cab and three other varietals. Tastings here take place in an expansive room whose equally expansive windows provide views of the hillside vineyards. ✉ *11680 Chimney Rock Rd., 15 miles west of U.S. 101's Hwy 46 E exit; take 24th St. west and follow road (name changes along the way) to Chimney Rock Rd.* ☎ *805/238–6932* 🌐 *justinwine.com* 🎫 *Tastings $40, tour and tasting $65* ☞ *Tours 10 and 2:30 (reservations recommended).*

★ **Niner Wine Estate**

WINERY/DISTILLERY | A family-owned winery in the Willow Creek district, Niner is known equally for its range of estate wines (especially powerful reds) and its farm-fresh lunches designed to complement wine tasting flights. For a special treat, sign up for the Fog Catcher flight, which focuses on components of its Bordeaux blend. The option to order lunch is available with tasting reservations, which are required. ✉ *2400 Hwy. 46 W* ☎ *805/239–2233* 🌐 *www.ninerwine.com* 🎫 *Tastings $30, Fog Catcher flight $50.*

Opolo

WINERY/DISTILLERY | Opolo means "fun" in Greek, an apt name for a crowd-pleasing winery that effectively combines casual food, accessible wines, and peppy service—plus regular events that often inspire spontaneous singing and dancing. Wine-tasting flights at the westside vineyard include Opolo's flagship wine, Mountain Zinfandel, and specialty single varietals. The on-site Willow Creek Distillery produces nearly a dozen types of brandies and whiskeys; the $10 tasting flight is a good introduction to spirits. ✉ *7110 Vineyard Dr.* ☎ *805/238–9593.*

Paso Robles Market Walk

MARKET | Taste wine and craft beer, feast on ramen bowls, burgers, and sweet treats, and shop for one-of-a-kind gifts in this upscale public market in a residential area six blocks north of City Park. The eclectic collection of purveyors showcases the products of local chefs, vintners, and makers—all committed to sustainable business practices. ■ **TIP→ Book a room in one of the six luxury lofts on the market's second floor for convenient dining and shopping before or after wine touring.** ✉ *1803 Spring St.* ☎ *805/720–1255* 🌐 *www.pasomarketwalk.com.*

★ **Pasolivo**

WINERY/DISTILLERY | While touring the idyllic west side of Paso Robles, take a break from wine tasting by stopping at Pasolivo. Find out how the artisans here make their Tuscan-style olive oils on a high-tech Italian press, and test the acclaimed results. If you're in downtown Paso Robles, stop by Pasolivo's urban tasting room at 1229 Park Street. ✉ *8530 Vineyard Dr., west off U.S. 101 (Exit 224) or Hwy. 46 W (Exit 228)* ☎ *805/227–0186* 🌐 *www.pasolivo.com* 🎫 *Tastings $5.*

Re:Find Handcrafted Spirits

WINERY/DISTILLERY | The owners of Villacana Winery in west Paso Robles launched the first local distillery in 2011, aiming to repurpose the saignee (free-run juice) that's typically tossed out during the wine-making process. They ferment and distill the leftover high-quality juices into premium spirits, thus reclaiming about 60 acres of premium wine grapes. Taste vodka, gin, whiskey, bourbon, limoncello, and kumquat liqueurs in the tiny barrel-room tasting space or outdoors under the oaks. ✉ *2725 Adelaida Rd.* ☎ *805/239–9456* 🌐 *refinddistillery.com* 🎫 *Tastings $20* ⏲ *Closed Mon. and Tues.*

River Oaks Hot Springs & Spa

SPA—SIGHT | The lakeside spa, on 240 hilly acres near the intersection of U.S. 101 and Highway 46 East, is a great place to relax after wine tasting or festival-going. Soak in a private indoor or outdoor hot tub fed by natural mineral springs, or indulge in a massage or facial. ✉ *800 Clubhouse Dr., off River Oaks Dr., just north of River Oaks Golf Course* ☎ *805/238–4600* 🌐 *riveroakshotsprings.com* 🎫 *From $16 per hr.*

★ Sensorio

PUBLIC ART | This 386-acre interactive garden engages the senses; honors the natural topography; and offers a wide range of amusing, mystical, and kinetic experiences. It launched in 2019 with internationally renowned artist Bruce Munro's solar-powered, 15-acre, walk-through installation, *Field of Light,* an array of 58,800 fiber-optic illuminated stemmed spheres that subtly morph into undulating colors. In 2021, Sensorio added *Light Towers,* a stunning collection of 69 colorful, fiber-optic-lit towers composed of more than 17,000 wine bottles that ripple to a custom musical score. A visit begins in the pre-dusk hours to capture the changing light of the landscape and the installation as darkness descends. A hospitality area offers live entertainment by local musicians, snacks, meals, beer, and wine. Sign up for the VIP Experience to gain exclusive access to an Airstream bar, private tables, and firepits on a terrace overlooking *Field of Light.* Reserve your timed-entry space well in advance: Sensorio is phenomenally popular. ✉ *4380 E. Hwy. 46* ☎ *805/226–4287* 🌐 *sensoriopaso.com* 🎫 *General admission $32, VIP Experience $81* ⏲ *Closed Mon.–Wed.*

★ Sixmilebridge Vineyards

WINERY/DISTILLERY | In a cutting-edge facility on a 95-acre Westside estate, Sixmilebridge (named for the owner's ancestral home in Ireland), produces limited-production Cabernet Sauvignon and Bordeaux blends crafted mostly from organically grown estate fruit. A spacious terrace surrounding a 150-year-old coastal oak tree is reserved for those who purchase a glass or bottle of wine (picnics welcome). ✉ *5120 Peachy Canyon Rd.* ☎ *805/239–5844* 🌐 *sixmilebridge.com* 🎫 *Tastings from $30.*

SummerWood Winery

WINERY/DISTILLERY | Rhône varietals do well in the Paso Robles AVA, where many wineries, including this one, produce "GSM" (Grenache, Syrah, Mourvèdre) red blends, along with whites such as Viognier, Marsanne, and Grenache Blanc. Winemaker Mauricio Marchant displays a subtle touch with Rhône whites and reds, as well as Sentio, a Petit Verdot–heavy Bordeaux red blend. Tastings here are relaxed and informal, and there's a patio from which you can enjoy the vineyard views. ✉ *2175 Arbor Rd., off Hwy. 46W* ☎ *805/227–1365* 🌐 *summerwoodwine.com* 🎫 *Tastings $20, reserve $40.*

Tabias Creek Vineyard

WINERY/DISTILLERY | Tucked in the western hills of Paso Robles, Tablas Creek is known for its blends of certified biodynamically grown, hand-harvested Rhône varietals. Roussanne and Viognier are the standout whites; the Mourvèdre-heavy blend called Panoplie (it also includes Grenache and Syrah) has received high praise in recent years. ■ **TIP→ There's a fine picnic area here.** ✉ *9339 Adelaida Rd., west of Vineyard Dr.* ☎ *805/237–1231* 🌐 *www.tablascreek.com* 🎫 *Tastings from $20 (reserve $45 by appointment), tour free.*

★ **Tin City**

WINERY/DISTILLERY | This industrial park on the southern border of Paso Robles houses a collection of wineries, craft breweries, distilleries, and specialty shops where you can pick up sheep's milk ice cream, fresh pasta, and other local wares. Good places to start your explorations include Giornata Winery, Levo Winery, and TinCity Cider Co. Dine casually at McPhee's Canteen restaurant or upscale (dinner only) at Six Test Kitchen. ✉ *Limestone Way* ✣ *East of Ramada Dr. via Marquita Ave.* 🌐 *www.tincitypaso.com.*

Restaurants

BL Brasserie

$$$ | **FRENCH** | Owner-chef Laurent Grangien's handsome, welcoming French bistro occupies an 1890s brick building across from City Park. He focuses on traditional dishes such as duck confit, rack of lamb, and onion soup, but always prepares a few au courant daily specials as well. **Known for:** classic French dishes made with local ingredients; good selection of local and international wines; four-tasting menu Thurs. $ *Average main: $34* ✉ *1202 Pine St., at 12th St.* ☎ *805/226–8191* 🌐 *www.blbrasserie.com* ⏲ *Closed Mon. No lunch Sun.*

SIP Certification

Many wineries in Paso Robles take pride in being SIP (Sustainability in Practice) Certified, for which they undergo a rigorous third-party audit of their entire operations. Water and energy conservation practices are reviewed, along with pest management and other aspects of farming. Also considered are the wages, benefits, and working conditions of the employees, and the steps taken to mitigate the impact of grape growing and wine production on area habitats.

The Hatch

$$ | **AMERICAN** | A wood-fired rotisserie in an open kitchen, simple but tasty comfort foods and a lively bar scene attract locals and visitors alike to this cozy, casual space in an historic brick building a block north from the main square. Fuel up body and soul with menu favorites like meat loaf, shrimp and grits, bacon burgers, pies, cakes, and sundaes. **Known for:** house-made sauces, house-pickled fruits and veggies, house-cured ham; craft cocktails and small-batch whiskies; daily rotisserie specials: chicken, ribs, lamb, tri-tip. $ *Average main: $22* ✉ *835 13th St.* ☎ *805/221–5727* 🌐 *hatchpasorobles.com* ⏲ *No lunch.*

Il Cortile

$$$$ | **MODERN ITALIAN** | One of two Paso establishments owned by chef Santos MacDonal and his wife, Carole, this Italian restaurant entices diners with complex flavors and a contemporary space with art-deco overtones. Consistent crowd-pleasers often on the menu include beef carpaccio with white truffle cream sauce and shaved black truffles and pappardelle with wild boar ragu. **Known for:** house-made pastas; excellent wine pairings; ingredients from chef's garden. *Average main: $38 ✉ 608 12th St., near Spring St. ☎ 805/226–0300 🌐 www.ilcortileristorante.com ⏲ Closed Mon. and Tues. No lunch.*

Jeffry's Wine Country BBQ

$ | AMERICAN | Award-winning local chef Jeff Wiesinger and his wife Kathleen opened this casual eatery, tucked in a hidden courtyard a block from downtown City Park. Feast indoors or out on made-to-order sandwiches, hearty mac-and-cheese bowls, house-made potato chips, fresh salads, craft beer, and local wines while listening to throwback soundtracks from the '60s and '70s. **Known for:** delectable mac-and-cheese dishes; smoked tri-tip and other meats; savory paella. *Average main: $16 ✉ 819 12th St., Suite B ⊕ In alley between 12th and 13th Sts. ☎ 805/ 369–2132 🌐 jeffryswinecountrybbq.com ⏲ Closed Wed.*

La Cosecha

$$$ | SOUTH AMERICAN | At barlike, tin-ceilinged La Cosecha (Spanish for "the harvest"), Honduran-born chef Santos MacDonal faithfully re-creates dishes from Spain and South America. Noteworthy starters include *pastelitos catracho,* Honduran-style empanadas in a light tomato sauce served with *queso fresco* (fresh cheese) and micro cilantro. **Known for:** fusion of Latin spices and fresh local fare; daily paella special; artisanal cocktails. *Average main: $34 ✉ 835 12th St., near Pine St. ☎ 805/237–0019 🌐 www.lacosechabr.com ⏲ Closed Mon. Closed Tues. Jan. and Feb.*

McPhee's Grill

$$$$ | AMERICAN | Just south of Paso Robles in tiny Templeton, this casual chophouse in an 1860s wood-frame storefront serves sophisticated, contemporary versions of traditional Western fare such as oak-grilled filet mignon and fresh seafood tostadas. The house-label wines, made especially for the restaurant, are quite good. **Known for:** meats grilled over red oak; local seasonal menu; excellent wine selections. *Average main: $39 ✉ 416 S. Main St., at 5th St., Templeton ☎ 805/434–3204 🌐 mcpheesgrill.com ⏲ Closed Mon. and Tues. No lunch.*

Hotels

★ Allegretto

$$$ | RESORT | This swank, 20-acre Tuscan-style resort amid estate vineyards is also a private museum where owner Douglas Ayres displays hundreds of artworks and artifacts collected on his world travels: ancient Indian river stones and statues; a massive cross section from a giant sequoia; Russian and California impressionist paintings; mandalas; and more (nonguests are welcome to walk around). **Pros:** yoga in medieval abbey; full-service restaurant Cello and spa; bocce ball, firepit, and other diversions. **Cons:** not close to downtown square; pricey; some rooms close to courtyard music. *Rooms from: $349 ✉ 2700 Buena Vista Dr. ☎ 805/369–2500 🌐 www.allegrettoresort.com 171 rooms No meals.*

★ Hotel Cheval

$$$$ | HOTEL | Equestrian themes surface throughout this intimate European-style boutique hotel a half block from the main square and near some of Paso's best restaurants. **Pros:** most rooms have fireplaces; sip wine and champagne at the on-site Pony Club and zinc bar; extremely personalized service. **Cons:** views aren't great; no pool or hot tub; no elevator. *Rooms from: $410 ✉ 1021 Pine St. ☎ 805/226–9995, 866/522–6999 🌐 www.hotelcheval.com 16 rooms Free breakfast.*

JUST Inn

$$$$ | B&B/INN | Fine wines, a destination restaurant, and a vineyard's-edge setting make a stay at Justin winery's on-site inn an exercise in sophisticated seclusion. **Pros:** amazing night skies; vineyard views; destination restaurant. **Cons:** half-hour drive to town; location may be too secluded for some; spotty cell service.

$ Rooms from: $620 ✉ 11680 Chimney Rock Rd. ☎ 805/238–6932, 800/726–0049 ⊕ www.justinwine.com 4 suites 🍴 Free breakfast.

La Quinta Inn & Suites

$$ | **HOTEL** | A good value for Paso Robles, this three-story chain property attracts heavy repeat business with its upbeat staff and slew of perks. **Pros:** apartment-style suites in separate building; free happy hour with local wines and appetizers; good for leisure or business travelers. **Cons:** conventional decor; not downtown; basic breakfast. $ *Rooms from: $189 ✉ 2615 Buena Vista Dr. ☎ 805/239–3004, 800/753–3757 ⊕ www.laquintapasorobles.com 101 rooms 🍴 Free breakfast.*

Paso Robles Inn

$$ | **HOTEL** | On the site of an old spa hotel of the same name, the various buildings at this historic inn cluster around a lush, shaded garden with a pool. **Pros:** private hot tubs in many rooms; special touches like unique photography in each room; across from town square. **Cons:** fronts a busy street; rooms vary in size and amenities; some areas could use an upgrade. $ *Rooms from: $189 ✉ 1103 Spring St. ☎ 805/238–2660, 800/676–1713 ⊕ www.pasoroblesinn.com 122 rooms 🍴 No meals.*

★ SummerWood Inn

$$$ | **B&B/INN** | Easygoing hospitality, vineyard-view rooms, and elaborate breakfasts make this inn a mile west of U.S. 101 worth seeking out. **Pros:** convenient wine-touring base; elaborate breakfasts; complimentary tastings at associated winery. **Cons:** some noise from nearby highway during the day; no elevator; not close to downtown restaurants. $ *Rooms from: $340 ✉ 2130 Arbor Rd., 1 mile west of U.S. 101, at Hwy. 46W ☎ 805/227–1111 ⊕ www.summerwoodwine.com/inn 9 rooms 🍴 Free breakfast.*

Nightlife

1122 Speakeasy

BARS/PUBS | Press the doorbell and request permission to enter this elegant, 1930s-era cocktail lounge and speakeasy on the back patio of Pappy McGregor's Pub on the main square. It has just 28 seats, so be prepared to wait in line on weekend nights. *✉ 1122 Pine St. ↔ Entrance on Railroad St. or walk through pub ☎ 805/238–4141 ⊕ www.eleven-twentytwo.com ☞ Closed Mon. and Tues.*

Performing Arts

Vina Robles Amphitheatre

CONCERTS | At this 3,300-seat, Mission-style venue with good food, wine, and sight lines, you can enjoy acclaimed musicians in concert. *✉ Vina Robles winery, 3800 Mill Rd., off Hwy. 46 ☎ 805/286–3680 ⊕ www.vinarobles-amphitheatre.com ☞ Performances Apr.–Nov.*

Morro Bay

30 miles southwest of Paso Robles, 14 miles north of San Luis Obispo.

Commercial fishermen slog around Morro Bay in galoshes, and beat-up fishing boats bob in the bay's protected waters. Nature-oriented activities take center stage here: kayaking, hiking, biking, fishing, and wildlife-watching around the bay and national marine estuary and along the state beach.

GETTING HERE AND AROUND

From U.S. 101 south or north, exit at Highway 1 in San Luis Obispo and head west. Scenic Highway 1 passes through the eastern edge of town. From Atascadero, two-lane Highway 41 West treks over the mountains to Morro Bay. San Luis Obispo RTA Route 12 buses travel year-round between Morro Bay, San Luis

Obispo, Cayucos, Cambria, San Simeon, and Hearst Castle. The Morro Bay Shuttle picks up riders throughout the town from Friday through Monday in summer ($1.25 one-way, $3 day pass).

ESSENTIALS

VISITOR INFORMATION Morro Bay Tourism. ✉ *695 Harbor St., at Napa Ave.* 🌐 *www.morrobay.org.*

Sights

Embarcadero

NEIGHBORHOOD | The center of Morro Bay action on land is the Embarcadero, where vacationers pour in and out of souvenir shops and seafood restaurants and stroll or bike along the scenic half-mile Harborwalk to Morro Rock. From here, you can get out on the bay in a kayak or tour boat. ✉ *On waterfront from Beach St. to Tidelands Park.*

Montaña de Oro State Park

NATIONAL/STATE PARK | West of San Luis Obispo, Los Osos Valley Road winds past farms and ranches to this state park whose miles of nature trails traverse rocky shoreline, wild beaches, and hills overlooking dramatic scenery. Check out the tide pools, watch the waves roll into the bluffs, and picnic in the eucalyptus groves. From Montaña de Oro you can reach Morro Bay by following the coastline along South Bay Boulevard 8 miles through the quaint residential villages of Los Osos and Baywood Park. ✉ *West about 13 miles from downtown San Luis Obispo on Madonna Rd., to Los Osos Valley Rd., to Pecho Valley Rd.; to continue on to Morro Bay, backtrack east to Los Osos Valley Rd., then head north on S. Bay Blvd., and west on State Park Rd., San Luis Obispo* ☎ *805/772–6101* 🌐 *www.parks.ca.gov.*

Morro Bay State Park Museum of Natural History

MUSEUM | **FAMILY** | The museum's entertaining interactive exhibits explain the natural environment and how to preserve it—in the bay and estuary and on the rest of the planet. **■ TIP→ Kids age 16 and under are admitted free.** ✉ *20 State Park Rd., south of downtown* ☎ *805/772–2694* 🌐 *centralcoastparks.org* *$3.*

Morro Rock

NATURE PRESERVE | At the mouth of Morro Bay stands 576-foot-high Morro Rock, one of nine small volcanic peaks, or morros, in the area. A short walk leads to a breakwater, with the harbor on one side and crashing ocean waves on the other. You may not climb the rock, where endangered falcons and other birds nest. Sea lions and otters often play in the water below the rock. ✉ *Northern end of Embarcadero.*

Restaurants

Dorn's Original Breakers Cafe

$$ | **SEAFOOD** | This restaurant overlooking the harbor has satisfied local appetites since 1942 and serves straight-ahead dishes such as cod or shrimp fish-and-chips or calamari tubes sautéed in butter and wine. **Known for:** sweeping views of Morro Rock and the bay; fresh local seafood; friendly, efficient service. [$] *Average main: $23* ✉ *801 Market Ave., at Morro Bay Blvd.* ☎ *805/772–4415* 🌐 *www.dornscafe.com.*

Taco Temple

$ | **SOUTHWESTERN** | This family-run diner serves some of the freshest food around. The seafood-heavy menu includes salmon burritos, superb fish tacos with mango salsa, and other dishes hailing from somewhere between California and Mexico. **Known for:** fresh seafood and salsa bar; hefty portions; daily specials. [$] *Average main: $16* ✉ *2680 Main St., at Elena St.,* *just north of Hwy. 1/Hwy. 41 junction* ☎ *805/772–4965* 🌐 *tacotemple.com.*

★ Tognazzini's Dockside

$$ | **SEAFOOD** | Captain Mark Tognazzini catches seasonal seafood and delivers the bounty to his family's collection of down-home, no-frills enterprises in the harbor: a fish market with patio dining and up-close views of Morro Rock (Dockside Too), and the original Dockside restaurant. Local musicians play live music nearly every day at the outdoor patio at Dockside Too. **Known for:** fresh-as-it-gets local seafood; live music nearly every day year-round; front-row seats to Morro Rock views. *Average main: $20* ✉ *1245 Embarcadero* ☎ *805/772–8100 restaurant, 805/772–8120 fish market and patio dining* 🌐 *www.morrobaydockside.com.*

Windows on the Water

$$$$ | **SEAFOOD** | Diners at this second-floor restaurant view the sunset through giant picture windows. Meanwhile, fresh fish and other dishes based on local ingredients emerge from the wood-fired oven in the open kitchen, and oysters on the half shell beckon from the raw bar. **Known for:** sustainably sourced seafood; 20-plus wines by the glass; menu changes nightly. *Average main: $39* ✉ *699 Embarcadero, at Pacific St.* ☎ *805/772–0677* 🌐 *www.windowsmb.com* ⏲ *Closed Sun. and Mon. No lunch.*

Hotels

★ Anderson Inn

$$$ | **B&B/INN** | Friendly, personalized service and an oceanfront setting keep loyal patrons returning to this Embarcadero inn, which features well-appointed rooms with state-of-the-art tiled bathrooms and cozy comforters atop king beds. **Pros:** walk to restaurants and sights; spacious rooms; oceanfront rooms have fireplaces and private balconies. **Cons:** not low-budget; waterfront area can get crowded; need to book well in advance—fills quickly. *Rooms from: $285* ✉ *897 Embarcadero* ☎ *805/772–3434, 866/950–3434 toll-free reservations* 🌐 *andersoninnmorrobay.com* *8 rooms* *No meals.*

The Inn at Morro Bay

$$ | **RESORT** | Surrounded by eucalyptus trees, this inn abuts a heron rookery and Morro Bay State Park. **Pros:** great for wildlife lovers; stellar views from restaurant and some rooms; nearby golf course, wellness center on-site. **Cons:** some rooms on the small side; birds and seals can wake you early; remote location, not close to the Embarcadero. *Rooms from: $189* ✉ *60 State Park Rd.* ☎ *805/772–5651* 🌐 *innatmorrobay.com* *98 rooms* *No meals.*

Activities

Lost Isle Adventures

BOATING | Offerings include 45-minute jaunts around Morro Bay ($20) or adults-only sunset cruises ($25) aboard a tiki-themed boat. A faster adventure boat is used for 90-minute whale-watching excursions ($85). ✉ *Giovanni's Fish Market, 1001 Front St., on the Embarcadero* ☎ *805/440–8170* 🌐 *morrobaytikiboat.com.*

Sub-Sea Tours & Kayaks

BOATING | You can view sea life aboard this outfit's glass-bottom boat, watch whales from its catamaran, or rent a kayak, canoe, or stand-up paddleboard. ✉ *699 Embarcadero* ☎ *805/772–9463* 🌐 *subseatours.com.*

Virg's Landing

FISHING | Virg's conducts deep-sea-fishing and whale-watching trips. ✉ *1169 Market Ave.* ☎ *805/772–1222* 🌐 *virgslanding.com.*

Cambria

28 miles west of Paso Robles, 20 miles north of Morro Bay.

Cambria, set on piney hills above the sea, was settled by Welsh miners in the 1890s. In the 1970s the isolated setting attracted artists and other independent types; the town now caters to tourists, but it still bears the imprint of its bohemian past. Both of Cambria's downtowns, the original East Village and the newer West Village, are packed with art and crafts galleries, antiques shops, cafés, restaurants, and B&Bs.

Two diverting detours lie between Morro Bay and Cambria. In the laid-back beach town of Cayucos, 4 miles north of Morro Bay, you can stroll the long pier, feast on chowder (at Duckie's), and sample the namesake delicacies of the Brown Butter Cookie Co. Over in Harmony, a quaint former dairy town 7 miles south of Cambria (population 18), you can take in the glassworks, pottery, and other artsy enterprises.

GETTING HERE AND AROUND

Highway 1 leads to Cambria from the north and south. Highway 246 West curves from U.S. 101 through the mountains to Cambria. San Luis Obispo RTA Route 12 buses stop in Cambria (and Hearst Castle).

ESSENTIALS

VISITOR INFORMATION Cambria Chamber of Commerce. ✉ *767 Main St.* ☎ *805/927–3624* 🌐 *www.cambriachamber.org.*

Sights

Covell Ranch Clydesdale Horses

NATURE PRESERVE | Come to the 2,000-acre Covell Ranch to see one of the world's largest private stands of endangered Monterey pines and witness herds of gentle Clydesdales roaming the range. Much of the ranch is in a conservation easement that will never be developed. The 1½-hour guided vehicle tours take you through pastures and historic pine groves to the barn. The ranch also offers trail rides. ✉ *5694 Bridge St.* ☎ *805/975–7332* 🌐 *www.covellsclydesdaleranch.com* 🎫 *Tours $200 for up to 5 persons* ⏲ *Tours and trail rides by appointment only.*

Fiscalini Ranch Preserve

NATURE PRESERVE | Walk down a mile-long coastal bluff trail to spot migrating whales, otters, and shorebirds at this 450-acre public space. Miles of additional scenic trails crisscross the protected habitats of rare and endangered species of flora and fauna, including a Monterey pine forest, western pond turtles, monarch butterflies, and burrowing owls. Dogs are permitted on-leash everywhere and off-leash on all trails except the bluff. ✉ *Hwy. 1, between Cambria Rd. and Main St. to the north, and Burton Dr. and Warren Rd. to the south; access either end of bluff trail off Windsor Blvd.* ☎ *805/927–2856* 🌐 *www.fiscaliniranch-preserve.org.*

Leffingwell Landing

CITY PARK | A state picnic ground, the landing is a good place for examining tidal pools and watching otters as they frolic in the surf. ✉ *North end of Moonstone Beach Dr.* ☎ *805/927–2070.*

Moonstone Beach Drive

SCENIC DRIVE | The drive runs along a bluff above the ocean, paralleled by a 3-mile boardwalk that winds along the beach. On this photogenic walk you might glimpse sea lions and sea otters, and perhaps a gray whale during winter and spring. Year-round, birds fly about, and tiny creatures scurry amid the tidepools. ✉ *Off Hwy. 1.*

★ Stolo Family Vineyards

WINERY/DISTILLERY | Just 3 miles from the ocean and a short drive from Cambria's East Village, the 52-acre Stolo estate produces about 4,000 cases of premium wine each year. The estate Syrahs consistently win top awards; sample these and other estate wines, including Pinot Noir, dry Gewurztraminer, Sauvignon Blanc, and Chardonnays, in the hilltop tasting room on the site of a former dairy farm. If the weather's nice, sit out on the sprawling lawn near a 1920s barn and 1895 farmhouse. ✉ *3776 Santa Rosa Creek Rd.* ☎ *805/924–3131* 🌐 *stolofamilyvineyards.com.*

Restaurants

Linn's Restaurant

$$ | **AMERICAN** | **FAMILY** | Homemade olallieberry pies, soups, potpies, and other farmhouse comfort foods share the menu at this spacious East Village restaurant with fancier farm-to-table dishes such as organic, free-range chicken topped with raspberry-orange-cranberry sauce. Also on-site are a bakery, a café serving more casual fare (take-out available), and a gift shop that sells gourmet foods. **Known for:** olallieberry pie; numerous gluten-free and vegan options; family-owned and-operated for decades. *$ Average main: $25* ✉ *2277 Main St., at Wall St.* ☎ *805/927–0371* 🌐 *www.linnsfruitbin.com.*

★ Madeline's

$$$ | **FRENCH FUSION** | Dine on stellar French-American delights at a romantic, candlit table in this tiny restaurant within a tasting room and wineshop in Cambria's West Village. The menu changes seasonally, but you might start with diver scallops or stuffed quail, then move on to Louisiana seafood gumbo or Long Island duck breast, and bananas foster or crème brûlée for dessert. **Known for:** lamb osso buco, octopus, and other unusual dishes; excellent selection of local wines; bread pudding and other house-made desserts. *$ Average main: $33* ✉ *788 Main St.* ☎ *805/927–4175* 🌐 *www.madelinescambria.com.*

Robin's

$$$ | **ECLECTIC** | An international, vegetarian-friendly dining experience awaits you at this cozy East Village cottage. Dinner choices include chicken enchiladas, grilled Skuna Bay salmon, lamb curry, and short ribs. **Known for:** savory curries; top-notch salmon bisque; secluded (heated) garden patio. *$ Average main: $28* ✉ *4095 Burton Dr., at Center St.* ☎ *805/927–5007* 🌐 *robinsrestaurant.com.*

★ Sea Chest Oyster Bar and Restaurant

$$$ | **SEAFOOD** | Cambria's best place for seafood fills up soon after it opens at 5:30 (no reservations taken). Those in the know grab seats at the oyster bar and take in spectacular sunsets while watching the chefs broil fresh halibut, steam garlicky clams, and fry crispy calamari steaks; if you arrive to a wait, play cribbage or checkers in the game room. **Known for:** New England chowder house vibe; savory cioppino; waiting areas in wine bar, game room, and patio with firepit. *$ Average main: $35* ✉ *6216 Moonstone Beach Dr., near Weymouth St.* ☎ *805/927–4514* 🌐 *seachestoysterbar.com* ▭ *No credit cards* ⏲ *Closed Tues. mid-Sept.–May. No lunch.*

Hotels

Cambria Pines Lodge

$$ | **RESORT** | This 25-acre retreat up the hill from the East Village is a good choice for families; accommodations range from basic fireplace cabins to motel-style standard rooms to large fireplace suites and deluxe suites with spa tubs. **Pros:** short walk from downtown; live music nightly in the lounge; verdant gardens. **Cons:** service and housekeeping not always top-quality; some units need updating; thin walls in some units. *$ Rooms from: $169* ✉ *2905 Burton Dr.* ☎ *805/927–4200, 800/966–6490* 🌐 *www.cambriapineslodge.com* *152 rooms* *Free breakfast.*

Moonstone Landing
$$ | **HOTEL** | This up-to-date motel's amenities, reasonable rates, and accommodating staff make it a Moonstone Beach winner. **Pros:** sleek furnishings; across from the beach; cheery lounge. **Cons:** narrow property; some rooms overlook a parking lot; noise occasionally travels from next-door restaurant machinery. *Rooms from: $189 ✉ 6240 Moonstone Beach Dr. ☎ 805/927–0012, 800/830–4540 ⊕ www.moonstonelanding.com 29 rooms Free breakfast.*

★ **Olallieberry Inn**
$$ | **B&B/INN** | The second-oldest home in Cambria (built in 1875) and a national historic monument, this painstakingly restored B&B inn offers luxurious creature comforts in a pristine English garden setting on the banks of Santa Rosa Creek. **Pros:** gourmet three-course breakfast; wine hour with homemade appetizers; walk to East Village restaurants and shops. **Cons:** no elevator; no children under 12; some rooms front busy road. *Rooms from: $225 ✉ 2476 Main St. ☎ 805/927–3222 ⊕ www.olallieberry.com 9 rooms Free breakfast.*

★ **White Water Cambria**
$$$$ | **HOTEL** | A fascinating design that blends beach-boho 1970s California with Scandinavian modern elements (clean lines, light woods, natural accents), an inviting lobby lounge with sweeping ocean views, and cozy rooms that evoke unfussy luxury make White Water stand out among Moonstone Beach lodgings. **Pros:** lobby lounge with small bites and shared plates, cocktails, wine, and craft beer; steps to the beach and walking trails; fleet of complimentary Linus bikes. **Cons:** not in downtown Cambria; some rooms on the small side; fog sometimes obscures ocean views. *Rooms from: $399 ✉ 6736 Moonstone Beach Dr. ☎ 805/927–1066 ⊕ whitewatercambria.com 25 rooms Free breakfast.*

San Simeon

9 miles north of Cambria, 65 miles south of Big Sur.

Whalers founded San Simeon in the 1850s, but had virtually abandoned it by 1865, when Senator George Hearst began purchasing most of the surrounding ranch land. Hearst turned San Simeon into a bustling port, and his son, William Randolph Hearst, further developed the area while erecting Hearst Castle (one of the many remarkable stops you'll encounter when driving along Highway 1). Today San Simeon is basically a strip of unremarkable gift shops and so-so motels that straddle Highway 1 about 4 miles south of the castle's entrance, but Old San Simeon, right across from the entrance, is worth a peek. Julia Morgan, William Randolph Hearst's architect, designed some of the village's Mission Revival–style buildings.

GETTING HERE AND AROUND

Highway 1 is the only way to reach San Simeon. Connect with the highway off U.S. 101 directly or via rural routes such as Highway 41 West (Atascadero to Morro Bay) and Highway 46 West (Paso Robles to Cambria).

ESSENTIALS

VISITOR INFORMATION San Simeon Chamber of Commerce Visitor Center. *✉ 250 San Simeon Ave. ☎ 805/927–3500 ⊕ www.visitsansimeonca.com.*

Sights

★ **Hearst Castle**
CASTLE/PALACE | Officially known as "Hearst San Simeon State Historical Monument," Hearst Castle sits in solitary splendor atop La Cuesta Encantada (the Enchanted Hill). Its buildings and gardens spread over 127 acres that were the heart of newspaper magnate William Randolph Hearst's 250,000-acre ranch. Hearst commissioned renowned

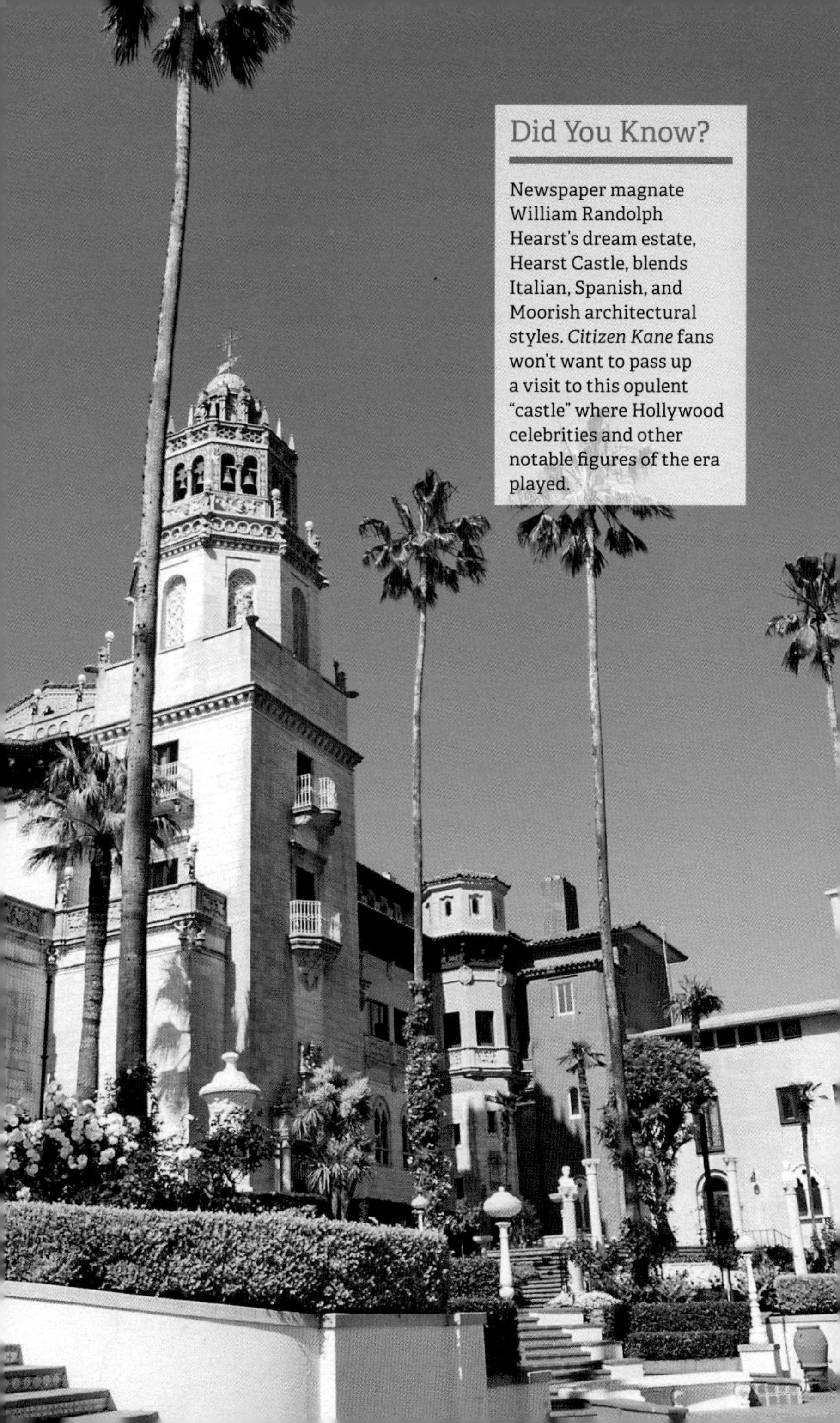

Did You Know?

Newspaper magnate William Randolph Hearst's dream estate, Hearst Castle, blends Italian, Spanish, and Moorish architectural styles. *Citizen Kane* fans won't want to pass up a visit to this opulent "castle" where Hollywood celebrities and other notable figures of the era played.

California architect Julia Morgan to design the estate, but he was very much involved with the final product, a blend of Italian, Spanish, and Moorish styles. The 115-room main structure and three huge "cottages" are connected by terraces and staircases and surrounded by pools, gardens, and statuary. In its heyday the castle, whose buildings hold about 22,000 works of fine and decorative art, was a playground for Hearst and his guests—Hollywood celebrities, political leaders, scientists, and other well-known figures. Construction began in 1919 and was never officially completed. Work was halted in 1947 when Hearst had to leave San Simeon because of failing health. The Hearst Corporation donated the property to the State of California in 1958, and it is now part of the state park system.

Access to the castle is through the visitor center at the foot of the hill, where you can view educational exhibits and a 40-minute film about Hearst's life and the castle's construction. Buses from the center zigzag up to the hilltop estate, where guides conduct four daytime tours, each with a different focus: Grand Rooms, Upstairs Suites, Designing the Dream, and Cottages and Kitchen. These tours take about three hours and include a movie screening, and time at the end to explore the castle's exterior and gardens. In spring and fall, docents in period costume portray Hearst's guests and staff for the Evening Tour, which begins around sunset. Reservations are recommended for all tours, which include a ½-mile walk and between 150 and 400 stairs. *Be sure to check the website in advance of your visit for any updates and to make tour reservations.* ✉ *San Simeon State Park, 750 Hearst Castle Rd.* ☏ *800/444–4445, 518/218–5078 international reservations* 🌐 *www.hearstcastle.org* 🎫 *Daytime tours from $25, evening tours $36.*

Hearst Ranch Winery

WINERY/DISTILLERY | Old whaling equipment and Hearst Ranch and Hearst Castle memorabilia decorate this winery's casual Old San Simeon outpost. The tasting room occupies a historic warehouse building with a gift shop, deli, and an outdoor deck and umbrella-shaded tables overlooking San Simeon Cove. The flagship wines include a Bordeaux-style red blend with Petite Sirah added to round out the flavor, and Rhône-style white and red blends. Malbec and Tempranillo are two other strong suits. ✉ *442 SLO San Simeon Rd., off Hwy. 1* ☏ *805/927–4100* 🌐 *www.hearstranchwinery.com* 🎫 *Tastings from $25.*

Piedras Blancas Elephant Seal Rookery

NATURE PRESERVE | **FAMILY** | A large colony of elephant seals (at last count 25,000) gathers every year at Piedras Blancas Elephant Seal Rookery, on the beaches near Piedras Blancas Lighthouse. The huge males with their pendulous, trunklike noses typically start appearing on shore in late November, and the females begin to arrive in December to give birth—most babies are born in the last two weeks of January. The newborn pups spend about four weeks nursing before their mothers head out to sea, leaving them on their own; the "weaners" leave the rookery when they are about 3½ months old. The seals return in the spring and summer months to molt or rest, but not en masse as in winter. You can watch them from a boardwalk along the bluffs just a few feet above the beach; do not attempt to approach them as they are wild animals. The nonprofit Friends of the Elephant Seal runs a small visitor center and gift shop (*250 San Simeon Ave.*) in San Simeon. ✉ *Off Hwy. 1, 4½ miles north of Hearst Castle, just south of Piedras Blancas Lighthouse* ☏ *805/924–1628* 🌐 *www.elephantseal.org.*

Piedras Blancas Light Station

TOUR—SIGHT | If you think traversing craggy, twisting Highway 1 is tough, imagine trying to navigate a boat up the rocky coastline (*piedras blancas* means "white rocks" in Spanish) near San Simeon before lighthouses were built. Captains must have cheered wildly when the beam began to shine here in 1875. Try to time a visit to include the 9:45 am tour held on Tuesday, Thursday, and Saturday year-round, as well as on Monday and Friday in summer. ■ **TIP→ Do not meet your guide at the gate to the lighthouse—you'll miss the tour. Meet instead at the former Piedras Blancas Motel, 1½ miles north of the light station.** ✉ *San Simeon* ☎ *877/444–6777* 🌐 *www.piedrasblancas.org* 🎫 *$10, advance reservations and online ticket purchase required* ☞ *No pets allowed.*

Beaches

William Randolph Hearst Memorial Beach

BEACH—SIGHT | This wide, sandy beach edges a protected cove on both sides of San Simeon Pier. Fish from the pier or from a charter boat, picnic and barbecue on the bluffs, or boogie board or bodysurf the relatively gentle waves. In summer you can rent a kayak and paddle out into the bay for close encounters with marine life and sea caves. The NOAA Coastal Discovery Center, next to the parking lot, has interactive exhibits and hosts educational activities and events. **Amenities:** food and drink; parking; toilets; water sports. **Best for:** sunset; swimming; walking. ✉ *750 Hearst Castle Rd., off Hwy. 1, west of Hearst Castle entrance* ☎ *805/927–2035* 🌐 *www.parks.ca.gov/?page_id=589* 🎫 *Free.*

Big Sur Coast

76 miles north along Hwy. 1 from San Simeon to Bixby Creek Bridge.

The countercultural spirit of Big Sur—a loose string of coast-hugging properties along Highway 1—is alive and well. Its few residents include the very wealthy, the enthusiastically outdoorsy, and the utterly evolved: since the 1960s, the Esalen Institute, a center for alternative education and East–West philosophical study, has attracted seekers of higher consciousness and devotees of the property's hot springs. Today, posh and rustic resorts amid the redwoods cater to visitors drawn by the scenery and the serenity. Southern Big Sur, the 52-mile stretch between San Simeon and Julia Pfeiffer Burns State Park, is especially rugged—a rocky world of mountains, cliffs, and beaches.

GETTING HERE AND AROUND

To explore Southern Big Sur from the south, access Highway 1 from U.S. 101 in San Luis Obispo; from the north, take rural route Highway 46 West (Paso Robles to Cambria) or Highway 41 West (Atascadero to Morro Bay). Nacimiento-Fergusson Road snakes through mountains and forest from U.S. 101 at Jolon about 25 miles to Highway 1 at Kirk Creek, about 4 miles south of Lucia; this curving, sometimes precipitous road is a motorcyclist favorite, not recommended for the faint of heart or during inclement weather.

To reach Central Big Sur, head north from Julia Pfeiffer Burns State Park on Highway 1 or follow Highway 1 south out of Carmel. Monterey-Salinas Transit runs the Line 22 Big Sur bus from Monterey and Carmel to Central Big Sur (last stop is Nepenthe) daily from late May to early September and on weekends the rest of the year.

BUS CONTACT Monterey-Salinas Transit. ☎ *888/678–2871* 🌐 *www.mst.org.*

ESSENTIALS

Stop by Big Sur Station to talk to staff, get information on activities and road conditions, and take advantage of public restrooms and fairly reliable cell service.

VISITOR INFORMATION Big Sur Chamber of Commerce. ☎ *831/667–2100* 🌐 *bigsurcalifornia.org.* **Big Sur Station.** ✉ *47555 California Hwy. 1, ¼ mile south of Pfeiffer Big Sur State Park entrance, Big Sur* ☎ *831/667–2315.*

Did You Know?

McWay Cove at Julia Pfeiffer Burns State Park is a renowned spot on the Big Sur Coast.

Sights

Bixby Creek Bridge

BRIDGE/TUNNEL | The graceful arc of Bixby Creek Bridge is a photographer's dream. Built in 1932, the bridge spans a deep canyon, more than 100 feet wide at the bottom. From the north-side parking area you can admire the view or walk the 550-foot structure. ✉ *Hwy. 1, 6 miles north of Point Sur State Historic Park, 13 miles south of Carmel, Big Sur.*

★ Highway 1

SCENIC DRIVE | One of California's most spectacular drives snakes up the coast north of San Simeon. Numerous pullouts offer tremendous views and photo ops. On some beaches, huge elephant seals lounge nonchalantly, seemingly oblivious to the attention of rubberneckers. Heavy rain can cause mudslides that block the highway north and south of Big Sur. ⚠ **Sections of Highway 1 are sometimes closed for general maintenance or repairs. Before traveling, visit bigsurcalifornia.org and click on the Highway 1 Conditions and Information link.** 🌐 *www.dot.ca.gov.*

Julia Pfeiffer Burns State Park

NATIONAL/STATE PARK | The park provides fine hiking, from an easy ½-mile stroll with marvelous coastal views to a strenuous 6-mile trek through redwoods. The big draw here, an 80-foot waterfall that drops into the ocean, gets crowded in summer; still, it's an astounding place to contemplate nature. Migrating whales, harbor seals, and sea lions can sometimes be spotted just offshore. *Trails east of Highway 1 and beach access to McWay Falls were closed in 2021 due to fire and slide damage; check website for current status.* ✉ *Hwy. 1, 15 miles north of Lucia* ☎ *831/667–1112* 🌐 *www.parks.ca.gov* 🎫 *$10.*

Pfeiffer Big Sur State Park

NATIONAL/STATE PARK | Among the many hiking trails at Pfeiffer Big Sur, a short route through a redwood-filled valley leads to a waterfall. You can double back or continue on the more difficult trail along the valley wall for views over miles of treetops to the sea. ✉ *47231 Hwy. 1, Big Sur* ☎ *831/667–2315* 🌐 *www.parks.ca.gov* 🎫 *$10 per vehicle.*

★ Pfeiffer Canyon Bridge

BRIDGE/TUNNEL | In February 2017, heavy winter rains caused an old concrete bridge built in 1968 to crack and slip downhill at Pfeiffer Canyon, in the heart of Big Sur. Engineers deemed the old bridge irreparable, and auto and pedestrian access to Highway 1 south of the bridge was cut off indefinitely. CalTrans quickly made plans to construct a new, $24-million bridge to span the deep canyon. Normally, such a massive project would take at least seven years, but CalTrans accelerated the project and completed it in less than a year. The new bridge—a 21st-century engineering marvel—stretches 310 feet across the ravine without the need for column support. It's made of 15 steel girders, each weighing 62 tons and connected by steel plates holding 14,000 bolts. ✉ *Hwy. 1, Big Sur* ✣ *0.7 mile south of Big Sur Station.*

Point Sur State Historic Park

NATIONAL/STATE PARK | An 1889 lighthouse at this state park still stands watch from atop a large volcanic rock. Four lighthouse keepers lived here with their families until 1974, when the light station became automated. Their homes and working spaces are open to the public only on three-hour ranger-led tours. Considerable walking, including up two stairways, is involved. Strollers are not allowed. ✉ *Hwy. 1, 7 miles north of Pfeiffer Big Sur State Park, Big Sur* ☎ *831/625–4419* 🌐 *www.pointsur.org* 🎫 *$15* ☞ *Call or visit website for current tour schedule.*

Beaches

Pfeiffer Beach

BEACH—SIGHT | Through a hole in one of the gigantic boulders at secluded Pfeiffer Beach, you can watch the waves break first on the seaside and then on the beach side. Keep a sharp eye out for the unsigned, nongated road to the beach: it branches west of Highway 1 between the post office and Pfeiffer Big Sur State Park. The 2-mile, one-lane road descends sharply. **Amenities:** parking (fee); toilets. **Best for:** solitude; sunset. ✉ *Off Hwy. 1, 1 mile south of Pfeiffer Big Sur State Park, Big Sur* 🎫 *$12 per vehicle.*

Restaurants

★ Deetjen's Big Sur Inn

$$$ | **AMERICAN** | The candle-lighted, creaky-floor restaurant in the main house at the historic inn of the same name is a Big Sur institution. It serves spicy seafood paella, grass-fed filet mignon, and rack of lamb for dinner and flavorful eggs Benedict for breakfast. **Known for:** rustic, romantic setting; ingredients from sustainable purveyors; stellar weekend breakfast. $ *Average main: $32* ✉ *Hwy. 1, 3½ miles south of Pfeiffer Big Sur State Park, Big Sur* ☎ *831/667–2378* 🌐 *www.deetjens.com* 🕑 *Closed Weds. and Thurs. No lunch.*

★ Nepenthe

$$$$ | **AMERICAN** | It may be that no other restaurant between San Francisco and Los Angeles has a better coastal view than Nepenthe, named for an opiate mentioned in Greek literature that would induce a state of "no sorrow." For the real show, settle on the terraced deck in the late afternoon, order a glass from the extensive wine list, and watch the sun slip into the Pacific Ocean. **Known for:** ambrosia burger, fresh fish, hormone-free steaks; multiple view decks; brunch and lunch at casual outdoor Café Kevah. $ *Average main: $39* ✉ *48510 Hwy. 1, 2½ miles south of Big Sur Station, Big Sur* ☎ *831/667–2345* 🌐 *nepenthebigsur.com.*

★ Sierra Mar

$$$$ | **AMERICAN** | At cliff's edge 1,200 feet above the Pacific at the ultrachic Post Ranch Inn, Sierra Mar serves cutting-edge American cuisine made from mostly organic, seasonal ingredients, some from the on-site chef's garden. The four-course prix-fixe option always shines. **Known for:** stunning panoramic ocean views; one of the nation's most extensive wine lists; iconic Big Sur farm-to-table experience. $ *Average main: $145* ✉ *Hwy. 1, 1½ miles south of Pfeiffer Big Sur State Park, Big Sur* ☎ *831/667–2800* 🌐 *www.postranchinn.com/dining.*

Hotels

Big Sur Lodge

$$$ | **HOTEL** | The lodge's modern, motel-style cottages with Mission-style furnishings and vaulted ceilings sit in a meadow surrounded by redwood trees and flowering shrubbery. **Pros:** secluded setting near trailheads; good camping alternative; rates include state parks pass. **Cons:** basic rooms; walk to main lodge; thin common walls in some units. $ *Rooms from: $279* ✉ *Pfeiffer Big Sur State Park, 47225 Hwy. 1, Big Sur* ☎ *855/238–6950 reservations* 🌐 *www.bigsurlodge.com* *62 rooms* *No meals.*

Big Sur River Inn

$$$ | **B&B/INN** | During summer at this rustic property you can sip drinks beside—or in—the Big Sur River fronted by the inn's wooded grounds; if you're here on a Sunday afternoon between May and September you can enjoy live music on the restaurant's deck. **Pros:** riverside setting complete with outdoor pool; next to a restaurant and small market; recently renovated baths. **Cons:** standard motel rooms across the road; no phone in rooms; fronts busy road. $ *Rooms from: $295* ✉ *Hwy. 1, 2 miles north of Pfeiffer Big Sur State Park, Big Sur* ☎ *831/667–2700, 831/667–2743, 800/548–3610* 🌐 *www.bigsurriverinn.com* *22 rooms* *No meals.*

Deetjen's Big Sur Inn

$$$ | **B&B/INN** | This historic 1930s Norwegian-style property is endearingly rustic, with its village of cabins nestled in the redwoods; many of the very individual rooms have their own fireplaces. **Pros:** tons of character; wooded grounds; excellent food and wine in on-site restaurant. **Cons:** thin walls; some rooms don't have private baths; no TVs or Wi-Fi, limited cell service. *Rooms from: $250 Hwy. 1, 3½ miles south of Pfeiffer Big Sur State Park, Big Sur 831/667–2377 www.deetjens.com 20 rooms, 15 with bath No meals 2-night minimum stay on weekends.*

Glen Oaks Big Sur

$$$ | **HOTEL** | At this rustic-modern cluster of adobe-and-redwood buildings, you can choose between motel-style rooms, cabins, and cottages in the woods. **Pros:** in the heart of town; natural river-rock radiant-heated tiles; restaurant across the street. **Cons:** near busy road and parking lot; no TVs; some cabins tiny. *Rooms from: $320 Hwy. 1, 1 mile north of Pfeiffer Big Sur State Park, Big Sur 831/667–2105 www.glenoaksbigsur.com 29 units No meals.*

★ Post Ranch Inn

$$$$ | **RESORT** | This luxurious retreat is perfect for getaways; the redwood guesthouses, all of which have views of the sea or the mountains, blend almost invisibly into a wooded cliff 1,200 feet above the ocean. **Pros:** units come with fireplaces and private decks; on-site activities like yoga and stargazing; gorgeous property with hiking trails and spectacular views. **Cons:** expensive; austere design; not a good choice if you're afraid of heights. *Rooms from: $1425 Hwy. 1, 1½ miles south of Pfeiffer Big Sur State Park, Big Sur 831/667–2200, 800/527–2200 www.postranchinn.com 41 units Free breakfast.*

Ragged Point Inn

$$ | **HOTEL** | At this cliff-top resort—the only inn and restaurant for miles around—glass walls in most rooms open to awesome ocean views. **Pros:** on the cliffs; good burgers and locally made ice cream; idyllic views. **Cons:** busy road stop during the day; often booked for weekend weddings; spotty cell phone service. *Rooms from: $239 19019 Hwy. 1, 15 miles north of San Simeon, Ragged Point 805/927–4502, 805/927–5708 restaurant, 888/584–6374 www.raggedpointinn.com 39 rooms No meals.*

Treebones Resort

$$$$ | **RESORT** | Perched on a hilltop surrounded by national forest and stunning, unobstructed ocean views, this yurt resort provides a stellar back-to-nature experience along with creature comforts. **Pros:** luxury yurts with cozy beds; lodge with fireplace and games; local food at Wild Coast Restaurant and decked sushi bar. **Cons:** steep paths; no private bathrooms; not good for families with young children. *Rooms from: $390 71895 Hwy. 1, Willow Creek Rd., 32 miles north of San Simeon, 1 mile north of Gorda 805/927–2390, 877/424–4787 www.treebonesresort.com 23 camping options Free breakfast 2-night minimum.*

★ Ventana Big Sur

$$$$ | **HOTEL** | Hundreds of celebrities have escaped to Ventana Big Sur, a romantic resort on 160 tranquil acres 1,200 feet above the Pacific. **Pros:** secluded; nature trails everywhere; rates include daily guided hike, yoga, wine and cheese hour. **Cons:** expensive; some rooms lack an ocean view; not family-friendly. *Rooms from: $1500 Hwy. 1, almost 1 mile south of Pfeiffer Big Sur State Park, Big Sur 831/667–2331, 800/628–6500 www.ventanabigsur.com 74 units All-inclusive.*

Chapter 12

MONTEREY BAY AREA

FROM CARMEL TO SANTA CRUZ

Updated by
Cheryl Crabtree

Sights ★★★★★
Restaurants ★★★★☆
Hotels ★★★★★
Shopping ★★☆☆☆
Nightlife ★☆☆☆☆

WELCOME TO MONTEREY BAY AREA

TOP REASONS TO GO

★ **Marine life:** Monterey Bay is the location of the world's third-largest marine sanctuary, home to whales, otters, and other underwater creatures.

★ **Getaway central:** For more than a century, urbanites have come to the Monterey Bay area to unwind, relax, and have fun. It's a great place to browse unique shops and galleries, ride a giant roller coaster, or play a round of golf on a world-class course.

★ **Nature preserves:** More than the sea is protected here: the region boasts nearly 30 state parks, beaches, and preserves—fantastic places for walking, jogging, hiking, and biking.

★ **Wine and dine:** The area's rich agricultural bounty translates into abundant fresh produce, great wines, and fabulous dining. It's no wonder more than 300 culinary events take place here every year.

★ **Small-town vibes:** Even the cities here are friendly, walkable places where you'll feel like a local.

1 **Carmel-by-the-Sea.** Galleries and cobblestone streets are among its charms.

2 **Carmel Valley.** An esteemed wine region marks this celebrity enclave.

3 **Pebble Beach.** This world-class golf destination also has the stunning 17-Mile Drive.

4 **Pacific Grove.** A picturesque city known for its migrating butterflies.

5 **Monterey.** The state's first capital is rich in history and marine life.

6 **Salinas.** The heart of Steinbeck country is also known for its fruits and veggies.

7 **Pinnacles National Park.** A volcano with jagged spires and caves.

8 **Moss Landing.** This tiny fishing port is near marine preserves.

9 **Aptos.** A charming village that edges redwood forests and stellar beaches.

10 **Capitola and Soquel.** Seaside gateways to mountain wine country.

11 **Santa Cruz.** World-famous surf and a university are among its draws.

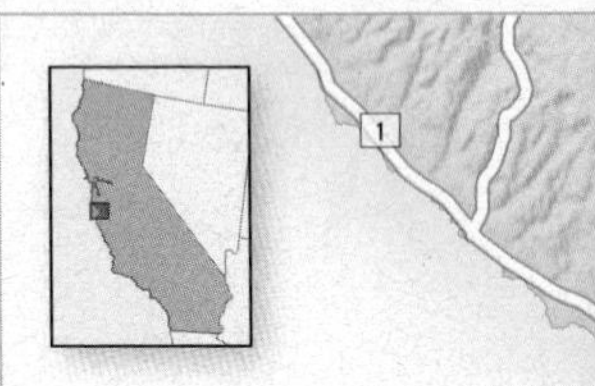

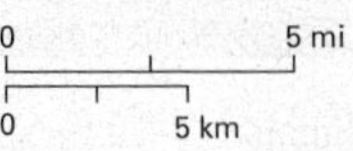

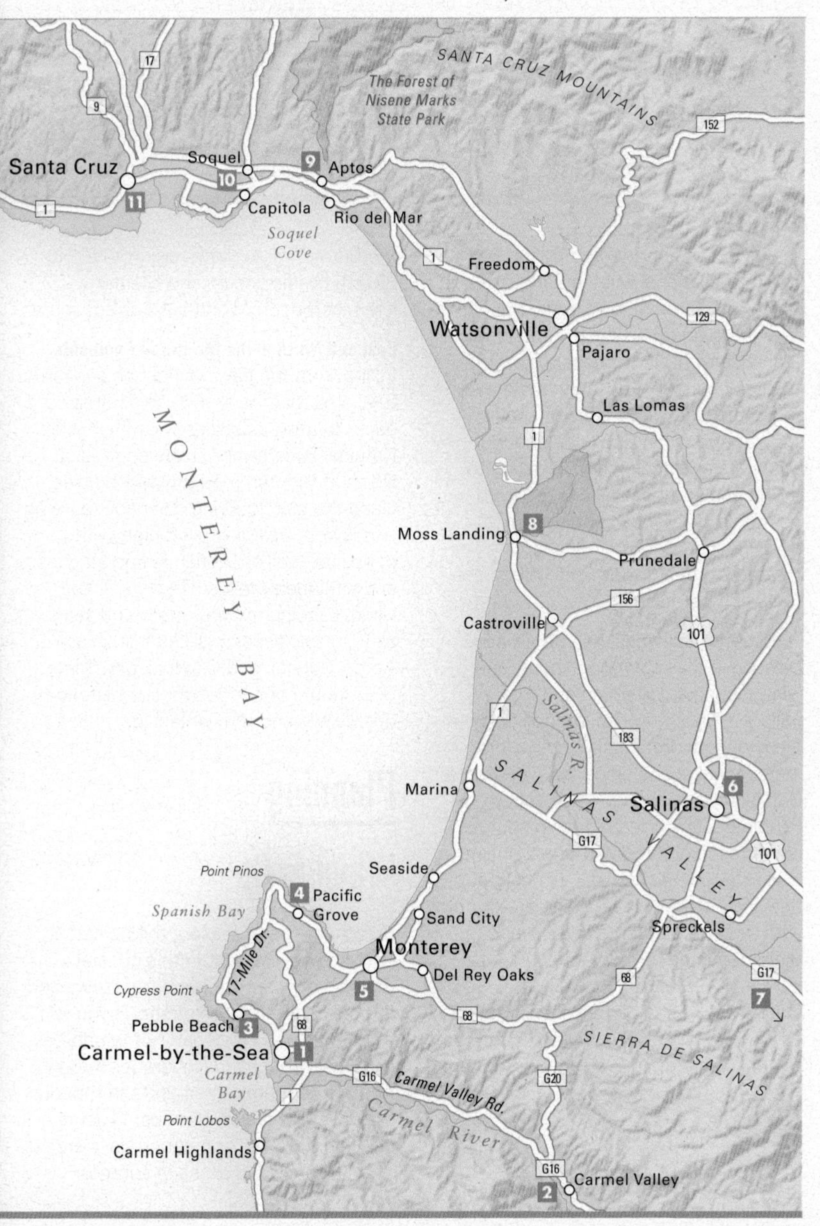
SANTA CRUZ MOUNTAINS
The Forest of Nisene Marks State Park
Santa Cruz
Soquel
Aptos
Capitola
Rio del Mar
Soquel Cove
Freedom
Watsonville
Pajaro
Las Lomas
MONTEREY BAY
Moss Landing
Prunedale
Castroville
Salinas R.
SALINAS VALLEY
Marina
Salinas
Seaside
Point Pinos
Pacific Grove
Spanish Bay
Sand City
Spreckels
Monterey
Del Rey Oaks
17-Mile Dr.
Cypress Point
Pebble Beach
Carmel-by-the-Sea
Carmel Bay
SIERRA DE SALINAS
Carmel Valley Rd.
Carmel River
Point Lobos
Carmel Highlands
Carmel Valley
1
2
3
4
5
6
7
8
9
10
11
17
9
152
129
156
101
183
G17
68
G16
G20

North of Big Sur, the coastline softens into lower bluffs, windswept dunes, pristine estuaries, and long, sandy beaches bordering one of the world's most amazing marine environments—Monterey Bay.

The bay itself is protected by the Monterey Bay National Marine Sanctuary, which holds the nation's largest undersea canyon—bigger and deeper than the Grand Canyon. Sunny coastal communities such as Aptos, Capitola, Soquel, and Santa Cruz offer miles of sand and surf. On-the-water activities abound, from whale-watching and kayaking to sailing and surfing. Bay cruises from Monterey and Moss Landing almost always encounter other enchanting sea creatures, among them sea otters, sea lions, and porpoises.

Land-based activities include hiking, ziplining in the redwood canopy, and wine tasting along urban and rural trails. Golf has been an integral part of the Monterey Peninsula's social and recreational scene since the Del Monte Golf Course opened in 1897. Today, Pebble Beach's championship courses host prestigious tournaments. Quaint, walkable towns such as Carmel-by-the-Sea and Carmel Valley Village are dotted with smart restaurants and galleries that encourage culinary and cultural immersion. Monterey's well-preserved waterfront invites historical exploration. Of course, whatever activity you pursue, natural splendor appears at every turn.

MAJOR REGIONS

The Monterey Peninsula. On the peninsula at the bay's southern end are Carmel-by-the-Sea—a good jumping-off point for the Carmel Valley wine region—Pebble Beach, Pacific Grove, and Monterey itself, home to a world-famous aquarium.

East and North of the Monterey Peninsula. Inland from the bay, amid a rich agricultural area that many refer to as Steinbeck Country, is Salinas, with Pinnacles National Park farther to the southeast. North of Monterey, Highway 1 cruises along the bay's curving coastline, passing windswept beaches piled high with dunes, as well as wetlands and artichoke and strawberry fields. Here you'll find Moss Landing, where otters and seals play; classic seaside villages such as Aptos, Soquel, and Capitola; and Santa Cruz, home of surf legends, a historic boardwalk, and UC Santa Cruz.

Planning

When to Go

Summer is peak season; mild weather brings in big crowds. In this coastal region a cool breeze generally blows and fog often rolls in from offshore; you will frequently need a sweater or windbreaker. Off-season, from November through April, fewer people visit and the mood is mellower. Rainfall is heaviest in January and February. Fall and spring days are often clearer than those in summer.

FESTIVALS AND EVENTS

Carmel Bach Festival. This three-week, mid-July festival has presented the works of Johann Sebastian Bach and his contemporaries since 1935. 🌐 *bachfestival.org*

Jazz Bash by the Bay. Bands play early jazz, big band, swing, ragtime, blues, zydeco, and gypsy jazz at waterfront venues during this festival, held on the first full weekend of March. 🌐 *jazzbashmonterey.com.*

Monterey International Blues Festival. This event on the last weekend in June draws blues fans to the Monterey Fairgrounds. 🌐 *montereyinternationalbluesfestival.com.*

Monterey Jazz Festival. The world's oldest jazz festival, held the third full weekend in September, attracts top-name performers and their fans to the Monterey Fairgrounds. 🌐 *montereyjazzfestival.org.*

Getting Here and Around

AIR

Monterey Regional Airport, 3 miles east of downtown Monterey off Highway 68, is served by Alaska, Allegiant, American, Avelo, JSX, and United. Taxi service costs from $14 to $16 to downtown, and from $23 to $25 to Carmel. Monterey Airbus service between the region and the San Jose and San Francisco airports starts at $42; the Early Bird Airport Shuttle costs from $100 to $235 ($250 from Oakland).

AIRPORT CONTACTS Monterey Regional Airport. *(MRY)* ✉ *200 Fred Kane Dr., at Olmsted Rd., off Hwy. 68, Monterey* ☎ *831/648–7000* 🌐 *www.montereyairport.com.*

GROUND TRANSPORTATION Central Coast Cab Company. ☎ *831/626–3333* 🌐 *www.centralcoastcabcompany.com.* **Early Bird Airport Shuttle.** ☎ *831/462–3933* 🌐 *www.earlybirdairportshuttle.com.* **Monterey Airbus.** ☎ *831/373–7777* 🌐 *www.montereyairbus.com.* **Yellow Cab.** ☎ *831/333–1234* 🌐 *www.yellowcab1234.com.*

BUS

Greyhound serves Santa Cruz and Salinas from San Francisco (3 hours) and San Jose (4½ hours). Monterey-Salinas Transit (MST) provides frequent service in Monterey County (from $2.50 to $3.50; day pass $10), and Santa Cruz METRO ($2; day pass from $6 to $14) buses operate throughout Santa Cruz County. You can switch between the lines in Watsonville.

BUS CONTACTS Monterey-Salinas Transit. ☎ *888/678–2871* 🌐 *mst.org.* **Santa Cruz METRO.** ☎ *831/425–8600* 🌐 *scmtd.com.*

CAR

Highway 1 runs south–north along the coast, linking the towns of Carmel-by-the-Sea, Monterey, and Santa Cruz; some sections have only two lanes. The freeway, U.S. 101, lies to the east, roughly parallel to Highway 1. The two roads are connected by Highway 68 from Pacific Grove to Salinas; Highway 156 from Castroville to Prunedale; Highway 152 from Watsonville to Gilroy; and Highway 17 from Santa Cruz to San Jose. **■ TIP→ Traffic near Santa Cruz can crawl to a standstill during commuter hours. Avoid traveling between 7 and 9 am and between 4 and 7 pm.**

The drive south from San Francisco to Monterey can be made comfortably in three hours or less. The most scenic way is to follow Highway 1 down the coast. A generally faster route is I–280 south to Highway 85 to Highway 17 to Highway 1. The drive from the Los Angeles area takes five or six hours. Take U.S. 101 to Salinas, and head west on Highway 68. You can also follow Highway 1 up the coast.

TRAIN

Amtrak's *Coast Starlight* runs between Los Angeles, Oakland, and Seattle. You can also take the *Pacific Surfliner* to San Luis Obispo and connect to Amtrak buses to Salinas or San Jose. From the train station in Salinas you can connect with buses serving Carmel and Monterey, and from the train station in San Jose with buses to Santa Cruz.

Restaurants

The Monterey Bay area is a culinary paradise. The surrounding waters are full of fish, wild game roams the foothills, and the inland valleys are some of the most fertile in the country—local chefs draw on this bounty for their fresh, truly Californian cuisine. Except at beachside stands and inexpensive eateries, where anything goes, casual but neat dress is the norm.

Hotels

Accommodations in the Monterey area range from no-frills motels to luxurious hotels. Pacific Grove, amply endowed with ornate Victorian houses, is the region's bed-and-breakfast capital; Carmel also has charming inns. Lavish resorts cluster in exclusive Pebble Beach and pastoral Carmel Valley.

High season runs from May through October. Rates in winter, especially at the larger hotels, may drop by 50% or more, and smaller inns often offer midweek specials. Whatever the month, some properties require a two-night stay on weekends. **■ TIP→ Many of the fancier accommodations aren't suitable for children; if you're traveling with kids, ask before you book.**

Restaurant and hotel reviews have been shortened. For full information, visit Fodors.com. Restaurant prices are the average cost of a main course at dinner, or if dinner is not served, at lunch. Hotel prices are the lowest cost of a standard double room in high season

What It Costs

$	$$	$$$	$$$$
RESTAURANTS			
under $17	$17–$26	$27–$36	over $36
HOTELS			
under $150	$150–$250	$251–$350	over $350

Tours

Ag Venture Tours & Consulting
GUIDED TOURS | Crowd-pleasing half- and full-day wine tasting, sightseeing, walking, and agricultural tours are Ag Venture's specialty. Tastings are at Monterey and Santa Cruz Mountains wineries; sightseeing opportunities include the Monterey Peninsula, Big Sur, and Santa Cruz; and the agricultural forays take in the Salinas and Pajaro valleys. Customized itineraries can be arranged. ☎ *831/761–8463* 🌐 *agventuretours.com* 🎫 *From $55 (half-day) and $110 (full day).*

Monterey Guided Wine Tours
SPECIAL-INTEREST | The company's guides lead customized wine tours in Monterey, Carmel, and Carmel Valley, along with the Santa Lucia Highlands, the Santa Cruz Mountains, and the Paso Robles area. Tours, which typically last from four to six hours, take place in a town car, a stretch limo, or a party bus. ☎ *831/920–2792* 🌐 *montereyguidedwinetours.com* 🎫 *From $175.*

Visitor Information

CONTACTS Monterey County Convention & Visitors Bureau. ☎ *888/221–1010* 🌐 *www.seemonterey.com.* **Monterey Wine Country.** ☎ *831/375–9400* 🌐 *www.montereywines.org.* **Santa Cruz Mountains Winegrowers Association.** ✉ *335 Spreckels Dr., #B, Aptos* ☎ *831/685–8463* 🌐 *winesofthesantacruzmountains.com.* **Visit Santa Cruz County.** ✉ *303 Water St.,*

No. 100, Santa Cruz ☎ *831/425–1234, 800/833–3494* 🌐 *visitsantacruz.org.*

Carmel-by-the-Sea

26 miles north of Big Sur.

Even when its population quadruples with tourists on weekends and in summer, Carmel-by-the-Sea, commonly referred to as Carmel, retains its identity as a quaint village. Self-consciously charming, the town is populated by many celebrities, major and minor, and has its share of quirky ordinances. For instance, women wearing high heels do not have the right to pursue legal action if they trip and fall on the cobblestone streets, and drivers who hit a tree and leave the scene are charged with hit-and-run.

Buildings have no street numbers—street names are written on discreet white posts—and consequently no mail delivery. One way to commune with the locals: head to the post office. Artists started this community, and their legacy is evident in the numerous galleries.

GETTING HERE AND AROUND

From north or south follow Highway 1 to Carmel. Head west at Ocean Avenue to reach the main village hub.

TOURS

Carmel Food Tours

WALKING TOURS | Taste your way through Carmel-by-the-Sea culinary delights on this guided walking tour to restaurants and shops that serve small portions of standout offerings, from empanadas and ribs to honey and chocolate. Along the way, guides share colorful tales about local culture, history, and architecture. The Classic Tour (which departs from the Sunset Cultural Center) includes seven tasting stops and lasts three hours. The five-hour Bikes, Bites, & Bevs Tour combines a morning e-bike tour through Carmel to Point Lobos with four food and wine/cocktail destinations in the afternoon. Tickets must be purchased in advance. ✉ *Sunset Cultural Center, 9th Ave. at San Carlos St., Carmel* ☎ *831/256–3007, 831/216–8533 tickets* 🌐 *www.carmelfoodtour.com* 🎟 *From $94.*

Carmel Walks

WALKING TOURS | For insight into Carmel's history and culture, join one of these guided two-hour ambles through hidden courtyards, gardens, and pathways. Tours depart from the Pine Inn courtyard, on Lincoln Street. Call to reserve a spot. ✉ *Lincoln St. at 6th Ave., Carmel* ☎ *831/223–4399* 🌐 *carmelwalks.com* 🎟 *From $30.*

ESSENTIALS

VISITOR INFORMATION Carmel Chamber of Commerce. ✉ *Visitor center, in Carmel Plaza, Ocean Ave. between Junipero and Mission Sts., Carmel* ☎ *831/624–2522, 800/550–4333* 🌐 *carmelchamber.org.*

Sights

Carmel Mission

RELIGIOUS SITE | Long before it became a shopping and browsing destination, Carmel was an important religious center during the establishment of Spanish California. That heritage is preserved in the Mission San Carlos Borroméo del Rio Carmelo, more commonly known as the Carmel Mission. Founded in 1771, it served as headquarters for the mission system in California under Father Junípero Serra. Adjoining the stone church is a tranquil garden planted with California poppies. Museum rooms at the mission include an early kitchen, Serra's spartan sleeping quarters and burial shrine, and the first college library in California. ✉ *3080 Rio Rd., at Lasuen Dr., Carmel* ☎ *831/624–1271* 🌐 *carmelmission.org* 🎟 *$10* ⏲ *Closed Mon. and Tues.*

★ Ocean Avenue

NEIGHBORHOOD | Downtown Carmel's chief lure is shopping, especially along its main street, Ocean Avenue, between

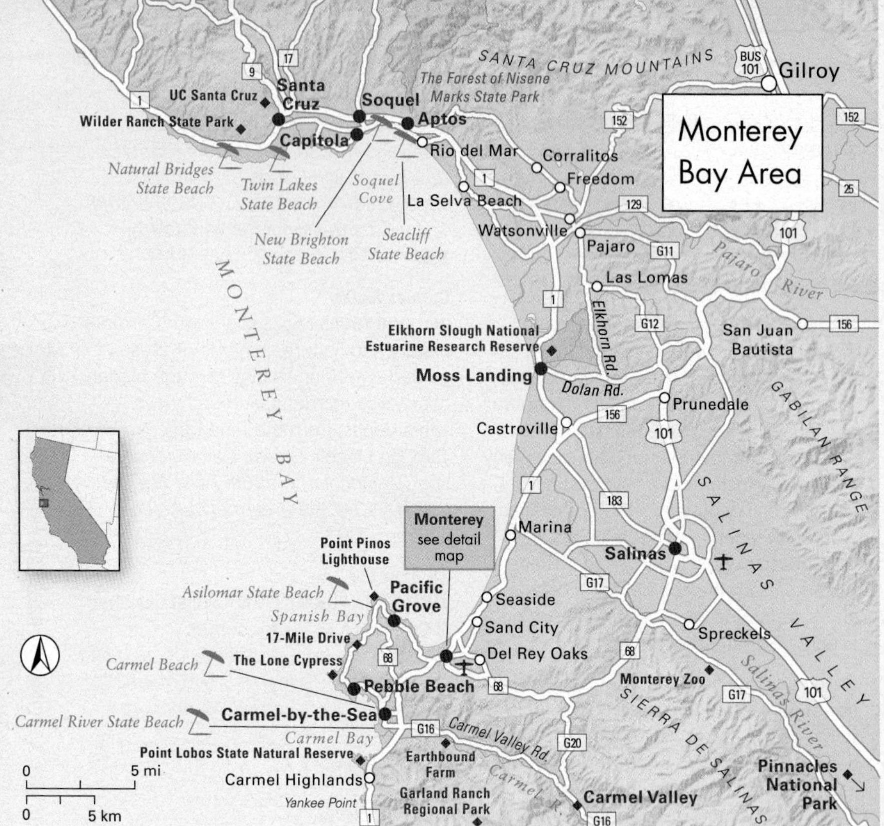

Junipero Avenue and Camino Real. The architecture here is a mishmash of ersatz Tudor, Mediterranean, and other styles. ✉ *Carmel.*

★ Point Lobos State Natural Reserve

NATIONAL/STATE PARK | A 350-acre headland harboring a wealth of marine life, the reserve lies a few miles south of Carmel. The best way to explore here is to walk along one of the many trails. The Cypress Grove Trail leads through a forest of Monterey cypress (one of only two natural groves remaining) that clings to the rocks above an emerald-green cove. Sea Lion Point Trail is a good place to view sea lions. From those and other trails, you might also spot otters, harbor seals, and (in winter and spring) migrating whales. An additional 750 acres of the reserve is an undersea marine park open to qualified scuba divers. No pets are allowed. **■ TIP→ Arrive early (or in late afternoon) to avoid crowds; the parking lots fill up.** ✉ *Hwy. 1, Carmel* ☎ *831/624–4909* 🌐 *www.pointlobos.org* *$10 per vehicle.*

Tor House

HOUSE | Scattered throughout the pines of Carmel-by-the-Sea are houses and cottages originally built for the writers, artists, and photographers who discovered the area decades ago. Among the most impressive dwellings is Tor House, a stone cottage built in 1919 by poet Robinson Jeffers on a craggy knoll overlooking the sea. Portraits, books, and unusual art objects fill the low-ceilinged rooms. The highlight of the small estate is Hawk Tower, a detached edifice set with stones from the Carmel coastline—as well as one from the Great Wall of China. The docents who lead tours (six people maximum) are well informed about the poet's work and life. Reservations are required. Call the reservation line or click on the reservation link on the website. ✉ *26304 Ocean View Ave., Carmel* ☎ *831/624–1813 direct docent office line, Mon., Tues., and Thurs. only* 🌐 *www.torhouse.org* 🎫 *$12* ☞ *No children under 12.*

Beaches

Carmel Beach

BEACH—SIGHT | Carmel-by-the-Sea's greatest attraction is its rugged coastline, with pine and cypress forests and countless inlets. Carmel Beach, an easy walk from downtown shops, has sparkling white sands and magnificent sunsets. **■ TIP→ Dogs are allowed to romp off-leash here.** **Amenities:** parking (no fee); toilets. **Best for:** sunset; surfing; walking. ✉ *End of Ocean Ave., Carmel.*

Carmel River State Beach

NATURE PRESERVE | This sugar-white beach, stretching 106 acres along Carmel Bay, is adjacent to a bird sanctuary, where you might spot pelicans, kingfishers, hawks, and sandpipers. Dogs are allowed on leash. **Amenities:** parking (no fee); toilets. **Best for:** sunrise; sunset; walking. ✉ *Off Scenic Rd., south of Carmel Beach, Carmel* ☎ *831/649–2836* 🌐 *www.parks.ca.gov* 🎫 *Free.*

Restaurants

Anton and Michel

$$$ | **AMERICAN** | Carefully prepared California cuisine is the draw at this airy restaurant. The rack of lamb is carved at the table, the grilled halloumi cheese and tomatoes are meticulously stacked and served with basil and Kalamata olive tapenade, and the desserts are set aflame before your eyes. **Known for:** romantic courtyard with fountain; elegant interior with fireplace lounge; flambé desserts. 💲 *Average main: $35* ✉ *Mission St. and 7th Ave., Carmel* ☎ *831/624–2406* 🌐 *antonandmichel.com.*

★ Aubergine

$$$$ | **AMERICAN** | To eat and sleep at luxe L'Auberge Carmel is an experience in itself, but even those staying elsewhere can splurge at the inn's intimate restaurant, which was awarded a Michelin star in 2019. Chef Justin Cogley's nine-course prix-fixe tasting menu (your only option at dinner, $205 per person) is a gastronomical experience unrivaled in the region. **Known for:** exceptional chef's choice tasting menu; expert wine pairings; intimate nine-table dining room. 💲 *Average main: $185* ✉ *Monte Verde at 7th Ave., Carmel* ☎ *831/624–8578* 🌐 *auberginecarmel.com* ⏲ *No lunch.*

★ Basil

$$ | **MODERN AMERICAN** | Eco-friendly Basil was Monterey County's first restaurant to achieve a green-dining certification, recognition of its commitment to using organic, sustainably cultivated ingredients in creative dishes such as black squid linguine with sea urchin sauce, charred octopus, and smoked venison and other house-made charcuterie. **Known for:** organic ingredients; creative cocktails; year-round patio dining. 💲 *Average main: $25* ✉ *Paseo Square, San Carlos St., between Ocean Ave. and 7th Ave., Carmel* ☎ *831/626–8226* 🌐 *basilcarmel.com.*

Casanova

$$$ | **MEDITERRANEAN** | This restaurant inspires European-style celebration and romance in an intimate French-country setting. Feast on authentic dishes from southern France and northern Italy—think beef tartare and escargot. **Known for:** house-made pastas and gnocchi; private dining at antique Van Gogh's table; romantic candlelight dining room and outdoor patio. 💲 *Average main: $34* ✉ *5th Ave., between San Carlos and Mission Sts., Carmel* ☎ *831/625–0501* 🌐 *www.casanovacarmel.com.*

The Cottage Restaurant

$$ | **AMERICAN** | This family-friendly spot serves sandwiches, pizzas, and homemade soups at lunch, but the best meal

Point Lobos State Natural Reserve offers stunning vistas of sea and sky.

is breakfast (good thing it's served all day). The menu offers six variations on eggs Benedict and all kinds of sweet and savory crepes. **Known for:** artichoke soup; eggs Benedict and crepes; daily specials. *Average main: $17 Lincoln St. between Ocean and 7th Aves., Carmel 831/625–6260 cottagerestaurant.com No dinner.*

Flying Fish Grill

$$$ | **SEAFOOD** | Simple in appearance yet bold with its flavors, this Japanese–California seafood restaurant is one of Carmel's most inventive eateries. The warm, wood-lined dining room is broken up into very private booths. **Known for:** almond-crusted sea bass served with Chinese cabbage and rock shrimp stir-fry; clay pot dinners for two cooked at the table; authentic Asian decor. *Average main: $30 Carmel Plaza, Mission St. between Ocean and 7th Aves., Carmel 831/625–1962 flyingfishgrill.com No lunch.*

Grasing's Coastal Cuisine

$$$$ | **AMERICAN** | Chef Kurt Grasing draws from fresh Carmel Coast and Central Valley ingredients to whip up contemporary adaptations of European-provincial and American dishes. Longtime menu favorites include duck with fresh cherries in a red wine sauce, a savory sausage and seafood paella, and grilled steaks and chops. **Known for:** artichoke-heart lasagna; grilled steaks; bar, patio lounge, and rooftop deck. *Average main: $39 6th Ave. and Mission St., Carmel 831/624–6562 grasings.com.*

L'Escargot

$$$ | **FRENCH** | Chef-owner Kericos Loutas personally sees to each plate of food served at this romantic, unpretentious French restaurant. Order the pan-roasted duck breast or the veal medallions with wild mushrooms or white wine sauce; or, if you can't decide, choose the three-course prix-fixe dinner. **Known for:** authentic French-country dishes; prix-fixe dinner option; locally sourced ingredients. *Average main: $36 Mission*

and 4th Ave., Carmel ☎ 831/620–1942 ⊕ escargot-carmel.com ⊙ Closed Mon. and Tues.

★ The Pocket

$$ | **MODERN ITALIAN** | In surf lingo, "the pocket" is a perfect riding spot within a barrel-shape wave, and this Italian–Californian restaurant is likewise a perfect (casual and unfussy) gathering spot for those who seek first-rate food, wine, and cocktails. The co-owners—a chef and sommelier with years of experience running restaurants in Pebble Beach and around the world—craft seasonal menus that focus on seafood, fresh pastas, curries, steaks, and braised meats. **Known for:** sleek marble, wood, and slate dining room and bar, spacious garden seating; full bar, extensive list of more than 400 wines; lively atmosphere, especially during the daily happy hour. *Average main: $32 ✉ Lincoln St., between 5th and 6th Ave., Carmel ☎ 831/626–8000 ⊕ www.thepocketcarmel.com.*

Vesuvio

$$$ | **ITALIAN** | Chef and restaurateur Rich Pèpe heats up the night with this lively trattoria downstairs and swinging rooftop terrace, the Starlight Lounge 65°. Pèpe's elegant take on traditional Italian cuisine yields dishes such as wild-boar Bolognese pappardelle, lobster ravioli, and velvety limoncello mousse cake. **Known for:** traditional cuisine of Campania, Italy; two bars with pizzas and small plates; live music on rooftop terrace in summer. *Average main: $30 ✉ 6th and Junipero Aves., Carmel ☎ 831/625–1766 ⊕ vesuviocarmel.com ⊙ No lunch.*

Hotels

Cypress Inn

$$$ | **B&B/INN** | This luxurious inn has a fresh, Mediterranean ambience with Moroccan touches. **Pros:** luxury without snobbery; popular lounge and restaurant; British-style afternoon tea on Saturdays. **Cons:** not for the pet-phobic; some rooms and baths are tiny; basic amenities. *Rooms from: $279 ✉ Lincoln St. and 7th Ave., Carmel ☎ 831/624–3871, 800/443–7443 ⊕ cypress-inn.com 44 rooms Free breakfast.*

The Hideaway

$$$ | **HOTEL** | On a quiet street with a residential vibe, The Hideaway is a peaceful haven for those seeking stylish comfort in the heart of town. **Pros:** easy walk to shops, restaurants, galleries; short walk to Carmel Beach; pet-friendly amenities. **Cons:** street parking only; no pool or hot tub; some rooms are tiny. *Rooms from: $295 ✉ Junipero St. at 8th Ave., Carmel ☎ 888/565–1420 ⊕ hideawaycarmel.com 24 rooms Free breakfast.*

Hyatt Carmel Highlands

$$$$ | **HOTEL** | High on a hill overlooking the Pacific, this place has superb views and accommodations that include king rooms with fireplaces, suites with personal Jacuzzis, and full town houses with many perks. **Pros:** killer views; romantic getaway; great food. **Cons:** thin walls; must drive to the center of town; some rooms and buildings need update. *Rooms from: $499 ✉ 120 Highlands Dr., Carmel ☎ 831/620–1234 ⊕ www.hyatt.com 48 rooms No meals.*

La Playa Carmel

$$$$ | **HOTEL** | A historic complex of lush gardens and Mediterranean-style buildings, La Playa has light and airy interiors done in Carmel Bay beach-cottage style. **Pros:** historic restaurant and bar; manicured gardens; two blocks from the beach. **Cons:** four stories (no elevator); busy lobby; some rooms are on the small side. *Rooms from: $449 ✉ Camino Real at 8th Ave., Carmel ☎ 800/582–8900, 831/293–6100 ⊕ laplayahotel.com 75 rooms Free breakfast.*

★ L'Auberge Carmel

$$$$ | **B&B/INN** | Stepping through the doors of this elegant inn is like being transported to a little European village. **Pros:** in town but off the main drag; four

blocks from the beach; full-service luxury. **Cons:** touristy area; not a good choice for families; no a/c. $ *Rooms from: $485 ✉ Monte Verde at 7th Ave., Carmel ☎ 831/624–8578 ⊕ www.laubergecarmel.com ⇨ 20 rooms ¶◯¶ Free breakfast.*

Mission Ranch

$$ | **HOTEL** | Movie star Clint Eastwood owns this sprawling property whose accommodations include rooms in a converted barn, and several cottages, some with fireplaces. **Pros:** farm setting; pastoral views; great for tennis buffs. **Cons:** busy parking lot; must drive to the heart of town; old buildings. $ *Rooms from: $175 ✉ 26270 Dolores St., Carmel ☎ 831/624–6436, 800/538–8221, 831/625–9040 restaurant ⊕ www.missionranchcarmel.com ⇨ 31 rooms ¶◯¶ Free breakfast.*

Pine Inn

$$ | **HOTEL** | A favorite with generations of visitors, the Pine Inn is four blocks from the beach and has Victorian-style furnishings, complete with a grandfather clock, padded fabric wall panels, antique tapestries, and marble tabletops. **Pros:** elegant; close to shopping and dining; full breakfast included weekdays. **Cons:** on the town's busiest street; public areas a bit dark; limited parking. $ *Rooms from: $189 ✉ Ocean Ave. and Monte Verde St., Carmel ☎ 831/624–3851, 800/228–3851 ⊕ pineinn.com ⇨ 49 rooms ¶◯¶ Free breakfast.*

Tally Ho Inn

$$ | **B&B/INN** | This inn is nearly all suites, many of which have fireplaces and floor-to-ceiling glass walls that open onto ocean-view patios. **Pros:** within walking distance of shops, restaurants, beach; free parking; spacious rooms. **Cons:** small property; busy area; basic breakfast. $ *Rooms from: $229 ✉ Monte Verde St. and 6th Ave., Carmel ☎ 831/624–2232, 800/652–2632 ⊕ tallyho-inn.com ⇨ 12 rooms ¶◯¶ Free breakfast.*

Tickle Pink Inn

$$$$ | **B&B/INN** | Atop a towering cliff, this inn has views of the Big Sur coastline, which you can contemplate from your private balcony. **Pros:** close to great hiking; intimate; dramatic views. **Cons:** close to a big hotel; lots of traffic during the day; basic breakfast. $ *Rooms from: $389 ✉ 155 Highland Dr., Carmel ☎ 831/624–1244, 800/635–4774 ⊕ ticklepink.com ⇨ 34 units ¶◯¶ Free breakfast.*

Nightlife

BARS AND PUBS

Barmel

BARS/PUBS | Al Capone and other Prohibition-era legends once sidled up to this hip nightspot's carved wooden bar. Rock to DJ music and sit indoors, or head out to the pet-friendly patio. Some menu items pay homage to California's early days, and you can order Baja-style dishes from the adjacent Pescadero restaurant, which is under the same ownership. *✉ San Carlos St., between Ocean and 7th Aves., Carmel ☎ 831/626–2095 ⊕ www.facebook.com/BarmelByTheSea.*

Mulligan Public House

BARS/PUBS | A sports bar with seven TV screens, 12 beers on tap, and extensive menu packed with hearty American pub food, Mulligan usually stays open until midnight. *✉ 5 Dolores St., at Ocean ☎ 831/250–5910 ⊕ mulliganspublichouse.com.*

Shopping

ART GALLERIES

Carmel Art Association

ART GALLERIES | Carmel's oldest gallery, established in 1927, exhibits original paintings and sculptures by local artists. *✉ Dolores St., between 5th and 6th Aves., Carmel ☎ 831/624–6176 ⊕ carmelart.org ⊙ Closed Tues. and Wed.*

Dawson Cole Fine Art

ART GALLERIES | Amazing images of dancers, athletes, and other humans in motion come to life in this gallery that is devoted to the artworks of Monterey Bay resident Richard MacDonald, one of the most famed figurative sculptors of our time. ✉ *Lincoln St., at 6th Ave., Carmel* ☎ *831/624–8200* 🌐 *dawsoncolefineart.com* 🎟 *Free.*

Galerie Plein Aire

ART GALLERIES | The gallery showcases the oil paintings (mostly large-format seascapes and landscapes) of local artists Cyndra Bradford and Jeff Daniel Smith. ✉ *3663 The Barnyard, Carmel* ☎ *831/277–6165* 🌐 *galeriepleinaire.com* ⏲ *Closed Tues. and Wed.*

Gallery Sur

ART GALLERIES | Fine art photography of the Big Sur Coast and the Monterey Peninsula, including scenic shots and golf images, is the focus here. ✉ *6th Ave., between Dolores and Lincoln Sts., Carmel* ☎ *831/626–2615* 🌐 *gallerysur.com.*

★ **Weston Gallery**

ART GALLERIES | Run by the family of the late Edward Weston, this is hands down the best photography gallery around, with contemporary color photography and classic black-and-whites. ✉ *6th Ave., between Dolores and Lincoln Sts., Carmel* ☎ *831/624–4453* 🌐 *westongallery.com.*

MALLS

Carmel Plaza

SHOPPING CENTERS/MALLS | Tiffany & Co. and Anthropologie are among the name brands doing business at this mall on Carmel's east side, but what makes it worth a stop are homegrown enterprises such as Carmel Honey Company for local honey; Madrigal for women's fashion; and J. Lawrence Khaki's for debonair menswear. Flying Fish Grill and several other restaurants are here, along with the Wrath Wines tasting room (Chardonnay and Pinot Noir). The Carmel Chamber of Commerce Visitor Center (open daily) is on the second floor. ✉ *Ocean Ave. and Mission St., Carmel* ☎ *831/624–1385* 🌐 *carmelplaza.com.*

SPECIALTY SHOPS

Bittner

SPECIALTY STORES | The shop carries collectible and vintage pens from around the world. ✉ *Ocean Ave., between Mission and San Carlos Sts., Carmel* ☎ *831/626–8828* 🌐 *bittner.com.*

elizabethW

GIFTS/SOUVENIRS | Named after the designer and owner's pioneering great-grandmother, elizabethW handcrafts fragrances, essential oils, candles, silk eye pillows, and other soul-soothing goods for bath, body, and home. ✉ *Ocean Ave., between Monte Verde and Lincoln, Carmel* ☎ *831/626–3892* 🌐 *elizabethw.com.*

Foxy Couture

CLOTHING | Shop for one-of-a-kind treasures at this curated collection of gently used luxury couture and vintage clothes and accessories—think Chanel, Hermes, and Gucci—without paying a hefty price tag. ✉ *San Carlos St., in Vanervort Court, between Ocean and 7th Aves., Carmel* ☎ *831/625–9995* 🌐 *foxycouturecarmel.com* ⏲ *Closed Tues. and Wed.*

Intima

SPECIALTY STORES | The European lingerie ranges from lacy to racy. ✉ *San Carlos St., between Ocean and 6th Aves., Carmel* ☎ *831/625–0599* 🌐 *www.intimacarmel.com.*

Jan de Luz

SPECIALTY STORES | This shop monograms and embroiders fine linens (including bathrobes) while you wait. ✉ *Dolores St., at 6th Ave. NE, Carmel* ☎ *831/622–7621* 🌐 *jandeluzlinens.com.*

Carmel Valley

10 miles east of Carmel.

Carmel Valley Road, which heads inland from Highway 1 south of Carmel, is the main thoroughfare through this valley, a secluded enclave of horse ranchers and other well-heeled residents who prefer the area's sunny climate to coastal fog and wind. Once thick with dairy farms, the valley has evolved into an esteemed wine appellation. Carmel Valley Village has crafts shops, art galleries, and the tasting rooms of numerous local wineries.

GETTING HERE AND AROUND

From U.S. 101 north or south, exit at Highway 68 and head west toward the coast. Scenic, two-lane Laureles Grade winds west over the mountains to Carmel Valley Road north of the village.

TOURS

Carmel Valley Grapevine Express

BUS TOURS | An incredible bargain, the express—aka MST's Bus 24—travels between downtown Monterey and Carmel Valley Village, with stops near wineries, restaurants, and shopping centers. ☎ *888/678–2871* 🌐 *mst.org* 🎫 *$10 all-day pass.*

Sights

Bernardus Tasting Room

WINERY/DISTILLERY | At the tasting room of Bernardus, known for its Bordeaux-style red blend, called Marinus, and Chardonnays, you can sample current releases and library and reserve wines. ✉ *5 W. Carmel Valley Rd., at El Caminito Rd.* ☎ *831/298–8021, 800/223–2533* 🌐 *bernardus.com* 🎫 *Tastings from $15.*

Cowgirl Winery

WINERY/DISTILLERY | Cowgirl chic prevails in the main tasting building here, and it's just plain rustic at the outdoor tables, set amid chickens, a tractor, and a flatbed truck. The wines include Chardonnay, Cabernet Sauvignon, Malbec, Pinot Noir, Rosé, and some blends. ✉ *25 Pilot Rd., off W. Carmel Valley Rd.* ☎ *831/298–7030* 🌐 *cowgirlwinery.com* 🎫 *Tastings from $20.*

Earthbound Farm

FARM/RANCH | **FAMILY** | Pick up fresh vegetables, ready-to-eat meals, gourmet groceries, flowers, and gifts at Earthbound Farm, the world's largest grower of organic produce. You can also take a romp in the kids' garden, cut your own herbs, and stroll through the chamomile aromatherapy labyrinth. Special events, on Saturday from April through December, include bug walks and garlic-braiding workshops. ✉ *7250 Carmel Valley Rd., Carmel* ☎ *831/625–6219* 🌐 *www.ebfarm.com* 🎫 *Free.*

★ Folktale Winery & Vineyards

WINERY/DISTILLERY | The expansive winery on a 15-acre estate (formerly Chateau Julienne) offers daily tastings, live music on weekends (plus Friday in summer and fall), and special events and programs such as Saturday yoga in the vineyard. Best-known wines include the estate Pinot Noir, Sparkling Rosé, and Le Mistral Joseph's Blend. Chefs in the on-site restaurant cook up small plates with wine pairing suggestions. Tours of the winery and organically farmed vineyards are available by appointment. ✉ *8940 Carmel Valley Rd.* ✣ *At Schetter Rd.* ☎ *831/293–7500* 🌐 *folktalewinery.com* 🎫 *Tastings from $20; tours $40 (includes tasting)* ⏲ *Closed Mon.–Wed.*

Garland Ranch Regional Park

NATIONAL/STATE PARK | Hiking trails stretch across much of this park's 4,500 acres of meadows, forested hillsides, and creeks. ✉ *700 W. Carmel Valley Rd., 9 miles east of Carmel-by-the-Sea* ☎ *831/372–3196* 🌐 *www.mprpd.org.*

★ Holman Ranch Vineyards Tasting Room

WINERY/DISTILLERY | Estate-grown Chardonnay and Pinot Noir are among the standout wines made by Holman Ranch, which pours samples in its chic tasting room and on two patios in the historic Will's Fargo tavern building. The 15-acre ranch itself is just up the road, set amid rolling hills that were once part of the Carmel mission's land grant. You can book winery and vineyard tours by appointment ✉ *18 W. Carmel Valley Rd.* ☎ *831/601–8761* 🌐 *holmanranch.com* 🎫 *Tastings from $35* ⏲ *Closed Tues. and Wed.*

Restaurants

Café Rustica

$$ | EUROPEAN | European country cooking is the focus at this lively roadhouse, where specialties include roasted meats, seafood, pastas, and thin-crust pizzas from the wood-fired oven. It can get noisy inside; for a quieter meal, request a table outside. **Known for:** Tuscan-flavored dishes from Alsace; open kitchen with wood-fired oven; outdoor patio seating. $ *Average main: $26* ✉ *10 Delfino Pl., at Pilot Rd., off Carmel Valley Rd.* ☎ *831/659–4444* 🌐 *caferusticavillage.com* ⏲ *Closed Mon. No lunch Tues. and Wed.*

Corkscrew Café

$$ | MODERN AMERICAN | Farm-fresh food is the specialty of this casual, Old Monterey–style bistro. Herbs and seasonal produce come from the Corkscrew's own organic gardens, the catch of the day comes from local waters, and the meats are hormone-free. **Known for:** wood-fired pizzas; fantastic regional wine list; garden patio. $ *Average main: $22* ✉ *55 W. Carmel Valley Rd.* ☎ *831/659–8888* 🌐 *www.corkscrewcafe.com* ⏲ *Closed Jan.*

Roux

$$$ | MODERN FRENCH | Chef Fabrice Roux, who hails from France, worked at lauded Parisian restaurants for more than a decade before coming to Carmel Valley to wow diners with his contemporary takes on traditional French-Mediterranean cuisine. The eclectic menu, with mostly small and large plates meant for sharing, focuses on local ingredients procured that week: perhaps crispy duck leg confit, tuna tartare, or braised wild-boar bourguignon. **Known for:** expert food and wine pairings; European-style cottage with private room for dining and tastings; extensive wine list with more than 400 labels. $ *Average main: $33* ✉ *6 Pilot Rd.* ☎ *831/659–5020* 🌐 *rouxcarmel.com* ⏲ *Closed Tues. No lunch Wed. and Thurs.* 💳 *No credit cards.*

Wagon Wheel Coffee Shop

$ | AMERICAN | This local hangout—decorated with wagon wheels, cowboy hats, and lassos—serves terrific hearty breakfasts, including oatmeal and banana pancakes, eggs Benedict, and biscuits and gravy. The lunch menu includes a dozen different burgers and other sandwiches. **Known for:** traditional American breakfast; cowboy-theme setting; lively local clientele. $ *Average main: $15* ✉ *Valley Hill Center, 7156 Carmel Valley Rd., next to Quail Lodge, Carmel* ☎ *831/624–8878* 💳 *No credit cards* ⏲ *No dinner.*

Hotels

★ Bernardus Lodge & Spa

$$$$ | RESORT | The spacious guest rooms at this luxury spa resort have vaulted ceilings, French oak floors, featherbeds, fireplaces, patios, and bathrooms with heated-tile floors and soaking tubs for two. **Pros:** exceptional personal service; outstanding food and wine; serene, cushy full-service spa. **Cons:** hefty rates; can feel a little snooty; resort fee. $ *Rooms from: $445* ✉ *415 W. Carmel Valley Rd.* ☎ *831/658–3400* 🌐 *www.bernarduslodge.com* *73 rooms* 🍽 *No meals.*

★ Carmel Valley Ranch

$$$$ | RESORT | The activity options at this luxury ranch are so varied that the resort provides a program director to guide you through them. **Pros:** stunning natural setting; tons of activities; River Ranch center with a pool, splash zone, boccie courts, and fitness center. **Cons:** must drive several miles to shops and nightlife; high rates; footsteps from neighboring rooms easy to hear in some buildings. *Rooms from: $699 1 Old Ranch Rd., Carmel 831/625–9500, 855/687–7262 toll-free reservations carmelvalleyranch.com 181 suites No meals.*

Quail Lodge & Golf Club

$$$$ | **HOTEL** | **FAMILY** | A sprawling collection of ranch-style buildings on 850 acres of meadows, fairways, and lakes, Quail Lodge offers luxury rooms and outdoor activities at surprisingly affordable rates. **Pros:** on the golf course; on-site restaurant; spacious rooms. **Cons:** service sometimes spotty; 5 miles from the beach and Carmel Valley Village; basic amenities. *Rooms from: $395 8205 Valley Greens Dr., Carmel 866/675–1101 reservations, 831/624–2888 www.quaillodge.com 93 rooms No meals.*

★ Stonepine Estate

$$$$ | **RESORT** | Set on 330 pastoral acres, the former estate of the Crocker banking family has been converted to a luxurious inn. **Pros:** supremely exclusive; close to Carmel Valley Village; attentive, personalized service. **Cons:** difficult to get a reservation; far from the coast; expensive rates. *Rooms from: $500 150 E. Carmel Valley Rd. 831/659–2245 www.stonepineestate.com 13 units No meals.*

Activities

GOLF

Quail Lodge & Golf Club

GOLF | Robert Muir Graves designed this championship semiprivate 18-hole course next to Quail Lodge that provides challenging play for golfers of all skill levels. The scenic course, which incorporates five lakes and edges the Carmel River, was completely renovated in 2015 by golf architect Todd Eckenrode to add extra challenge to the golf experience, white sand bunkers, and other enhancements. For the most part flat, the walkable course is well maintained, with stunning views, lush fairways, and ultrasmooth greens. *8000 Valley Greens Dr., Carmel 831/620–8808 golf shop, 831/620–8866 club concierge www.quaillodge.com $196 18 holes, 6500 yards, par 71.*

SPAS

★ Refuge

FITNESS/HEALTH CLUBS | At this co-ed, European-style center on 2 serene acres you can recharge without breaking the bank. Heat up in the eucalyptus steam room or cedar sauna, plunge into cold pools, and relax indoors in zero-gravity chairs or outdoors in Adirondack chairs around firepits. Repeat the cycle a few times, then lounge around the thermal waterfall pools. Talk is not allowed, and bathing suits are required. *27300 Rancho San Carlos Rd., south off Carmel Valley Rd., Carmel 831/620–7360 refuge.com $44 $52 admission; $155 50-min massage (includes Refuge admission), $12 robe rental, hot tubs (outdoor), sauna, steam room. Services: aromatherapy, hydrotherapy, massage.*

Pebble Beach

Off North San Antonio Ave. in Carmel-by-the-Sea or off Sunset Dr. in Pacific Grove.

In 1919 the Pacific Improvement Company acquired 18,000 acres of prime land on the Monterey Peninsula, including the entire Pebble Beach coastal region and much of Pacific Grove. Pebble Beach Golf Links and The Lodge at Pebble Beach opened the same year, and the private enclave evolved into a world-class golf destination with three posh lodges, five golf courses, hiking and riding trails, and some of the West Coast's ritziest homes. Pebble Beach has hosted major international golf tournaments, including the U.S. Open in 2019. The annual Pebble Beach Food & Wine, a four-day event in late April with 100 celebrity chefs, is one of the West Coast's premier culinary festivals.

GETTING HERE AND AROUND

If you drive south from Monterey on Highway 1, exit at 17-Mile Drive/Sunset Drive in Pacific Grove to find the northern entrance gate. Coming from Carmel, exit at Ocean Avenue and follow the road almost to the beach; turn right on North San Antonio Avenue to the Carmel Gate. You can also enter through the Highway 1 Gate off Highway 68. Monterey–Salinas Transit buses provide regular service in and around Pebble Beach.

Sights

★ The Lone Cypress

FOREST | The most-photographed tree along 17-Mile Drive is the weather-sculpted Lone Cypress, which grows out of a precipitous outcropping above the waves about 1½ miles up the road from Pebble Beach Golf Links. You can't walk out to the tree, but you can stop for a view of it at a small parking area off the road.

★ 17-Mile Drive

SCENIC DRIVE | Primordial nature resides in quiet harmony with palatial, mostly Spanish Mission–style estates along 17-Mile Drive, which winds through an 8,400-acre microcosm of the Pebble Beach coastal landscape. Dotting the drive are rare Monterey cypresses, trees so gnarled and twisted that Robert Louis Stevenson described them as "ghosts fleeing before the wind." The most famous of these is the **Lone Cypress**. Other highlights include **Bird Rock** and **Seal Rock,** home to harbor seals, sea lions, cormorants, and pelicans and other sea creatures and birds, and the **Crocker Marble Palace,** inspired by a Byzantine castle and easily identifiable by its dozens of marble arches.

■ TIP→ If you spend $35 or more on dining in Pebble Beach and show a receipt upon exiting, you'll receive a refund off the drive's $10.75 per-car fee. ✉ *Hwy. 1 Gate, 17-Mile Dr., at Hwy. 68* *$11 per car, free for bicyclists.*

Hotels

★ Casa Palmero

$$$$ | **RESORT** | This exclusive boutique hotel evokes a stately Mediterranean villa. **Pros:** ultimate in pampering; sumptuous decor; more private than sister resorts. **Cons:** rates out of reach for most visitors; not the best views compared to sister lodges; some showers on the small side. *Rooms from: $1150* ✉ *1518 Cypress Dr.* ☎ *831/622–6650, 800/877–0597 reservations* *www.pebblebeach.com* *24 rooms* *Free breakfast.*

The Inn at Spanish Bay

$$$$ | **RESORT** | This resort sprawls along a breathtaking stretch of shoreline and has plush, 600-square-foot rooms. **Pros:** attentive service; many amenities; spectacular views. **Cons:** huge hotel; 4 miles from other Pebble Beach Resorts facilities; atmosphere too snobbish for some. *Rooms from: $870* ✉ *2700 17-Mile Dr.* ☎ *831/647–7500, 800/877–0597* *www.pebblebeach.com* *269 rooms* *No meals.*

The Lodge at Pebble Beach

$$$$ | **RESORT** | Most rooms have wood-burning fireplaces and many have wonderful ocean views at this circa-1919 resort, which was expanded to include the 38-room Fairway One complex in 2017. **Pros:** world-class golf; borders the ocean and fairways; fabulous facilities. **Cons:** some rooms are on the small side; very pricey; not many activities if you don't golf. *Rooms from: $990* ✉ *1700 17-Mile Dr.* ☎ *831/624–3811, 800/877–0597* *www.pebblebeach.com* *199 rooms* *No meals.*

Activities

GOLF

The Hay

GOLF | The only 9-hole, par-3 course on the Monterey Peninsula open to the public, Peter Hay attracts golfers of all skill levels. It's an ideal place for warm-ups, practicing short games, and for those

Did You Know?

The Lone Cypress has stood on this rock for more than 250 years. The tree is the official symbol of the Pebble Beach Company.

who don't have time to play 18 holes. ✉ *17-Mile Dr. and Portola Rd.* ☎ *800/877–0597* 🌐 *www.pebblebeach.com* 🎫 *$65* ⛳ *9 holes, 725 yards, par 27.*

Links at Spanish Bay

GOLF | This course, which hugs a choice stretch of shoreline, was designed by Robert Trent Jones Jr., Tom Watson, and Sandy Tatum in the rugged manner of traditional Scottish links, with sand dunes and coastal marshes interspersed among the greens. A bagpiper signals the course's closing each day. **■ TIP→ Nonguests of the Pebble Beach Resorts can reserve tee times up to two months in advance.** ✉ *17-Mile Dr., north end* ☎ *800/877–0597* 🌐 *www.pebblebeach.com* 🎫 *$295* ⛳ *18 holes, 6821 yards, par 72.*

★ Pebble Beach Golf Links

GOLF | Each February, show-business celebrities and golf pros team up at this course, the main site of the glamorous AT&T Pebble Beach National Pro-Am tournament. On most days the rest of the year, tee times are available to guests of the Pebble Beach Resorts who book a minimum two-night stay. Nonguests can reserve a tee time only one day in advance on a space-available basis; resort guests can reserve up to 18 months in advance. ✉ *17-Mile Dr., near The Lodge at Pebble Beach* ☎ *800/877–0597* 🌐 *www.pebblebeach.com* 🎫 *$575* ⛳ *18 holes, 6828 yards, par 72.*

Poppy Hills

GOLF | An 18-hole course designed in 1986 by Robert Trent Jones Jr., Poppy Hills reopened in 2014 after a yearlong renovation that Jones supervised. Each hole has been restored to its natural elevation along the forest floor, and all 18 greens have been rebuilt with bent grass. Individuals may reserve up to a month in advance. **■ TIP→ Poppy Hills, owned by a golfing nonprofit, represents good value for this area.** ✉ *3200 Lopez Rd., at 17-Mile Dr.* ☎ *831/622–8239* 🌐 *poppyhillsgolf.com* 🎫 *$250* ⛳ *18 holes, 7002 yards, par 73.5.*

Spyglass Hill

GOLF | With three holes rated among the toughest on the PGA tour, Spyglass Hill, designed by Robert Trent Jones Sr. and Jr., challenges golfers with its varied terrain but rewards them with glorious views. The first 5 holes border the Pacific, and the other 13 reach deep into the Del Monte Forest. Reservations are essential and may be made up to one month in advance (18 months for resort guests). ✉ *Stevenson Dr. and Spyglass Hill Rd.* ☎ *800/877–0597* 🌐 *www.pebblebeach.com* 🎫 *$415* ⛳ *18 holes, 6960 yards, par 72.*

Pacific Grove

3 miles north of Carmel-by-the-Sea.

This picturesque town, which began as a summer retreat for church groups more than a century ago, recalls its prim and proper Victorian heritage in its host of tiny board-and-batten cottages and stately mansions. However, long before the church groups flocked here the area received thousands of annual pilgrims—in the form of bright orange-and-black monarch butterflies. They still come, migrating south from Canada and the Pacific Northwest to take residence in pine and eucalyptus groves from October through March. In Butterfly Town USA, as Pacific Grove is known, the sight of a mass of butterflies hanging from the branches like a long, fluttering veil is unforgettable.

A prime way to enjoy Pacific Grove is to walk or bicycle the 3 miles of city-owned shoreline along Ocean View Boulevard, a cliff-top area landscaped with native plants and dotted with benches meant for sitting and gazing at the sea. You can spot many types of birds here, including the web-footed cormorants that crowd the massive rocks rising out of the surf. Two Victorians of note along Ocean View are the Queen Anne–style Green Gables, at No. 301—erected in 1888, it's now an inn—and the 1909 Pryor House, at No. 429, a massive, shingled, private residence with a leaded- and beveled-glass doorway.

GETTING HERE AND AROUND

Reach Pacific Grove via Highway 68 off Highway 1, just south of Monterey. From Cannery Row in Monterey, head north until the road merges with Ocean Boulevard and follow it along the coast. MST buses travel within Pacific Grove and surrounding towns.

Sights

Lovers Point Park

CITY PARK | **FAMILY** | The coastal views are gorgeous from this waterfront park whose sheltered beach has a children's pool and a picnic area. The main lawn has a volleyball court and a snack bar. ✉ *Ocean View Blvd. northwest of Forest Ave.* 🌐 *www.cityofpacificgrove.org/living/recreation/parks/lovers-point-park.*

Monarch Grove Sanctuary

NATURE PRESERVE | **FAMILY** | The sanctuary is a reliable spot for viewing monarch butterflies between November and February. **■ TIP→ The best time to visit is between noon and 3 pm.** ✉ *250 Ridge Rd., off Lighthouse Ave.* 🌐 *www.pgmuseum.org/monarch-viewing.*

Pacific Grove Museum of Natural History

MUSEUM | The museum, a good source for the latest information about monarch butterflies, has permanent exhibitions about the butterflies, birds of Monterey County, biodiversity, and plants. There's a native plant garden, and a display documents life in Pacific Grove's 19th-century Chinese fishing village. ✉ *165 Forest Ave., at Central Ave.* ☎ *831/648–5716* 🌐 *pgmuseum.org* 🎫 *$9* 🕓 *Closed Mon.*

Point Pinos Lighthouse

LIGHTHOUSE | **FAMILY** | At this 1855 structure, the West Coast's oldest continuously operating lighthouse, you can learn about the lighting and foghorn operations and wander through a small museum containing U.S. Coast Guard memorabilia. ✉ *Asilomar Ave., between Lighthouse Ave. and Del Monte Blvd.* ☎ *831/648–5722* 🌐 *cityofpg.org/lighthouse* 🎫 *$5* 🕓 *Closed weekdays some months; visit website for current schedule.*

Beaches

Asilomar State Beach

BEACH—SIGHT | A beautiful coastal area, Asilomar State Beach stretches between Point Pinos and the Del Monte Forest. The 100 acres of dunes, tidal pools, and pocket-size beaches form one of the region's richest areas for marine life—including surfers, who migrate here most winter mornings. Leashed dogs are allowed on the beach. **Amenities:** none. **Best for:** sunrise; sunset; surfing; walking. ✉ *Sunset Dr. and Asilomar Ave.* ☎ *831/646–6440* 🌐 *www.parks.ca.gov.*

Restaurants

Beach House

$$$ | **MODERN AMERICAN** | Patrons of this bluff-top perch sip classic cocktails, sample California fare, and watch the otters frolic on Lovers Point Beach below. The sunset discounts between 4 and 5:30 (reservations recommended) are a great value. **Known for:** sweeping bluff-top views; heated patio; seafood and organic pastas. [$] *Average main: $28* ✉ *620 Ocean View Blvd.* ☎ *831/375–2345* 🌐 *beachhousepg.com* 🕓 *No lunch.*

★ Fandango

$$$ | **MEDITERRANEAN** | The menu here is mostly Mediterranean and southern French, with such dishes as osso buco and paella. The decor follows suit: stone walls and country furniture lend the restaurant the earthy feel of a European farmhouse. **Known for:** wood-fire-grilled rack of lamb, seafood, and beef; convivial residential vibe; traditional European flavors. [$] *Average main: $36* ✉ *223 17th*

St., south of Lighthouse Ave. ☎ 831/372–3456 🌐 fandangorestaurant.com.

Fishwife

$$ | **SEAFOOD** | Fresh fish with a Latin accent makes this a favorite of locals for lunch or a casual dinner. Standards are the sea garden salads—topped with your choice of fish—and the fried seafood plates. **Known for:** fisherman's bowls with fresh local seafood; house-made desserts; crab cakes and New Zealand mussels. *Average main: $22 ✉ 1996½ Sunset Dr., at Asilomar Blvd. ☎ 831/375–7107 🌐 fishwife.com.*

Jennini Kitchen + Wine Bar

$$ | **MEDITERRANEAN** | Sommelier Thamin Saleh, who named his lively restaurant and wine bar after his hometown in Palestine, designed a seasonally changing menu of small plates and entrées that showcases the cuisine of the eastern Mediterranean and southern Spain. Dishes might include chicken and merguez tagine, crispy lamb shanks, hummus and baba ghanoush, and filone bread with goat butter. **Known for:** Sunday night paella (order 24 hours in advance other nights); eclectic, value-driven wine list with 180 selections; creative twists on classic dishes. *Average main: $25 ✉ 542 Lighthouse Ave. ☎ 831/920–2662 🌐 www.jeninni.com ⏲ No lunch. Closed Tues. and Wed.*

★ Passionfish

$$$ | **MODERN AMERICAN** | South American artwork and artifacts decorate Passionfish, and Latin and Asian flavors infuse the dishes. The chef shops at local farmers' markets several times a week to find the best produce, fish, and meat available, then pairs it with creative sauces like a caper, raisin, and walnut relish. **Known for:** sustainably sourced seafood and organic ingredients; reasonably priced wine list that supports small producers; slow-cooked meats. *Average main: $28 ✉ 701 Lighthouse Ave. ☎ 831/655–3311 🌐 www.passionfish.net ⏲ No lunch.*

Peppers Mexicali Cafe

$$ | **MEXICAN** | This cheerful, white-walled storefront serves traditional dishes from Mexico and Latin America, with an emphasis on fresh seafood. Excellent red and green salsas are made throughout the day, and there's a large selection of beers, along with fresh lime margaritas. **Known for:** traditional Latin American dishes; fresh lime margaritas; daily specials. *Average main: $20 ✉ 170 Forest Ave., between Lighthouse and Central Aves. ☎ 831/373–6892 🌐 peppersmexicalicafe.com ⏲ Closed Tues. No lunch Sun.*

Red House Café

$$ | **AMERICAN** | When it's nice out, sun pours through the big windows of this cozy restaurant and across tables on the porch; when fog rolls in, the fireplace is lit. The American menu changes with the seasons, but grilled lamb chops atop mashed potatoes are often on offer for dinner, and a grilled calamari steak might be served for lunch, either in a salad or as part of a sandwich. **Known for:** cozy homelike dining areas; comfort food; stellar breakfast and brunch. *Average main: $22 ✉ 662 Lighthouse Ave., at 19th St. ☎ 831/643–1060 🌐 redhousecafe.com ⏲ No dinner Mon.*

Hotels

Gosby House Inn

$$ | **B&B/INN** | Though in the town center, this turreted butter-yellow Queen Anne Victorian has an informal feel. **Pros:** peaceful; homey; within walking distance of shops and restaurants. **Cons:** too frilly for some; area is busy during the day; limited parking. *Rooms from: $165 ✉ 643 Lighthouse Ave. ☎ 831/375–1287 🌐 gosbyhouseinn.com 22 rooms 🍽 Free breakfast.*

★ Green Gables Inn

$$ | **B&B/INN** | Stained-glass windows and ornate interior details compete with spectacular ocean views at this Queen Anne–style mansion. **Pros:** exceptional

views; impeccable attention to historic detail; afternoon wine and cheese served in the parlor. **Cons:** some rooms are small; thin walls; breakfast room can be crowded. $ *Rooms from: $179* ✉ *301 Ocean View Blvd.* ☎ *831/375–2095* 🌐 *www.greengablesinnpg.com* 🛏 *11 rooms* 🍽 *Free breakfast.*

Martine Inn

$$$ | **B&B/INN** | The glassed-in parlor and many guest rooms at this 1899 Mediterranean-style villa have stunning ocean views. **Pros:** romantic; exquisite antiques; ocean views. **Cons:** not child-friendly; sits on a busy thoroughfare; inconvenient parking. $ *Rooms from: $259* ✉ *255 Ocean View Blvd.* ☎ *831/373–3388* 🌐 *martineinn.com* 🛏 *25 rooms* 🍽 *Free breakfast.*

Monterey

2 miles southeast of Pacific Grove, 2 miles north of Carmel.

Monterey is a scenic city filled with early California history: adobe buildings from the 1700s, Colton Hall, where California's first constitution was drafted in 1849, and Cannery Row, made famous by author John Steinbeck. Thousands of visitors come each year to mingle with otters and other sea creatures at the world-famous Monterey Bay Aquarium and in the protected waters of the national marine sanctuary that hugs the shoreline.

GETTING HERE AND AROUND

From San Jose or San Francisco, take U.S. 101 south to Highway 156 West at Prunedale. Head west about 8 miles to Highway 1 and follow it about 15 miles south. From San Luis Obispo, take U.S. 101 north to Salinas and drive west on Highway 68 about 20 miles.

Many MST bus lines connect at the Monterey Transit Center, at Pearl Street and Munras Avenue. In summer (daily from 10 until at least 7) and on weekends and holidays the rest of the year, the free MST Monterey Trolley travels from downtown Monterey along Cannery Row to the Aquarium and back.

TOURS

Old Monterey Walking Tour

WALKING TOURS | Learn all about Monterey's storied past by joining a guided walking tour through the historic district. Tours begin at the Custom House in Custom House Plaza, across from Fisherman's Wharf and are typically offered Thursday through Sunday at 11, 1, and 3. ■ **TIP→ Tours are free for everyone on the last Sunday of the month.** ✉ *Monterey* 🌐 *www.parks.ca.gov/?page_id=951* 🎟 *Tours $10.*

The Original Monterey Walking Tours

WALKING TOURS | Learn more about Monterey's past, primarily the Mexican period until California statehood, on a guided tour through downtown Monterey. You can also join a guided walking tour of Cannery Row in the morning. Tours last 1½ to 2 hours and are offered Thursday–Sunday at 10 am and 2. Reservations are essential. ✉ *Monterey* ☎ *831/521–4884* 🌐 *www.walkmonterey.com* 🎟 *From $25.*

ESSENTIALS

VISITOR INFORMATION Visit Monterey. ✉ *401 Camino El Estero* ☎ *888/221–1010* 🌐 *www.seemonterey.com.*

Sights

A Taste of Monterey

WINERY/DISTILLERY | Without driving the back roads, you can taste the wines of nearly 100 area vintners (craft beers, too) while taking in fantastic bay views. Bottles are available for purchase, and food is served from 11:30 until closing. ✉ *700 Cannery Row, Suite KK* ☎ *831/646–5446* 🌐 *atasteofmonterey.com* 🎟 *Tastings $20.*

Cannery Row

NEIGHBORHOOD | When John Steinbeck published the novel *Cannery Row* in 1945, he immortalized a place of rough-edged working people. The waterfront street, edging a mile of gorgeous coastline, once was crowded with sardine canneries processing, at their peak, nearly 200,000 tons of the smelly silver fish a year. During the mid-1940s, however, the sardines disappeared from the bay, causing the canneries to close. Through the years the old tin-roof canneries have been converted into restaurants, art galleries, and malls with shops selling T-shirts, fudge, and plastic sea otters. Recent tourist development along the row has been more tasteful, however, and includes stylish inns and hotels, wine tasting rooms, and upscale specialty shops. ✉ *Cannery Row, between Reeside and David Aves.* 🌐 *canneryrow.com.*

Colton Hall

MUSEUM | A convention of delegates met here in 1849 to draft the first state constitution. The stone building, which has served as a school, a courthouse, and the county seat, is a city-run museum furnished as it was during the constitutional convention. The extensive grounds outside the hall surround the Old Monterey Jail. ✉ *570 Pacific St., between Madison and Jefferson Sts.* ☎ *831/646–3933* 🌐 *www.monterey.org/museums* 🎫 *Free.*

Fisherman's Wharf

PEDESTRIAN MALL | FAMILY | The mournful barking of sea lions provides a steady soundtrack all along Monterey's waterfront, but the best way to actually view the whiskered marine mammals is to walk along one of the two piers across from Custom House Plaza. Lined with souvenir shops, the wharf is undeniably touristy, but it's lively and entertaining. At Wharf No. 2, a working municipal pier, you can see the day's catch being unloaded from fishing boats on one side and fishermen casting their lines into the water on the other. The pier has a couple of low-key restaurants, from whose seats lucky customers might spot otters and harbor seals. ✉ *At end of Calle Principal* 🌐 *www.montereywharf.com.*

Fort Ord National Monument

NATIONAL/STATE PARK | Scenic beauty, biodiversity, and miles of trails make this former U.S. Army training grounds a haven for nature lovers and outdoor enthusiasts. The 7,200-acre park, which stretches east over the hills between Monterey and Salinas, is also protected habitat for 35 species of rare and endangered plants and animals. There are 86 miles of single-track, dirt, and paved trails for hiking, biking, and horseback riding. The main trailheads are the Creekside, off Creekside Terrace near Portola Road, and Badger Hills, off Highway 68 in Salinas. Maps are available at the various trail-access points and on the park's website. **■ TIP→ Dogs are permitted on trails, but should be leashed when other people are nearby.** ✉ *Bordered by Hwy. 68 and Gen. Jim Moore and Reservation Rds.* ☎ *831/582–2200* 🌐 *www.blm.gov/programs/national-conservation-lands/california/fort-ord-national-monument* 🎫 *Free.*

★ Monterey Bay Aquarium

ZOO | FAMILY | Playful otters and other sea creatures surround you the minute you enter this extraordinary facility, where all the exhibits convey what it's like to be in the water with the animals. Leopard sharks swim in a three-story, sunlit kelp forest exhibit; sardines swim around your head in a circular tank; and jellyfish drift in and out of view in dramatically lighted spaces that suggest the ocean depths. A petting pool puts you literally in touch with bat rays, and the million-gallon Open Seas exhibit illustrates the variety of creatures—from hammerhead sharks to placid-looking turtles—that live in the eastern Pacific. Splash Zone's 45, interactive, bilingual exhibits let kids commune with African penguins, clownfish, and other marine life. The only drawback to the aquarium experience is that it must be shared with the throngs that congregate

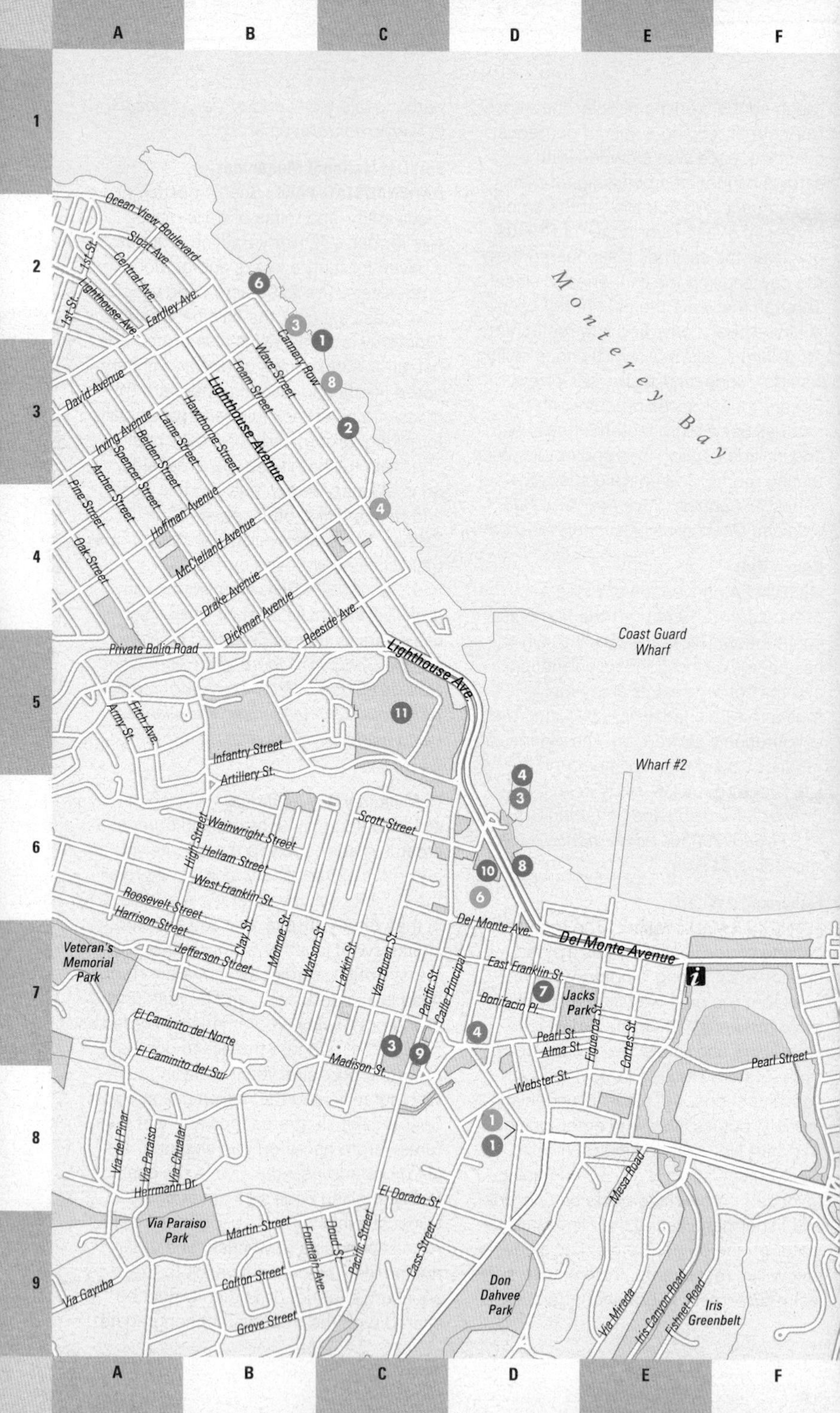

A
B
C
D
E
F
1
2
3
4
5
6
7
8
9
Monterey Bay
Ocean View Boulevard
Sloat Ave.
Central Ave.
1st St.
Lighthouse Ave.
Eardley Ave.
Cannery Row
Wave Street
Foam Street
Lighthouse Avenue
David Avenue
Irving Avenue
Belden Street
Laine Street
Hawthorne Street
Spencer Street
Archer Street
Pine Street
Hoffman Avenue
McClelland Avenue
Oak Street
Drake Avenue
Dickman Avenue
Reeside Ave.
Private Bolio Road
Lighthouse Ave.
Coast Guard Wharf
Army St.
Fitch Ave.
Infantry Street
Artillery St.
Wharf #2
Scott Street
High Street
Wainwright Street
Hellam Street
West Franklin St.
Roosevelt Street
Harrison Street
Del Monte Ave.
Del Monte Avenue
Veteran's Memorial Park
Jefferson Street
Clay St.
Monroe St.
Watson St.
Larkin St.
Van Buren St.
Pacific St.
Calle Principal
East Franklin St.
Bonifacio Pl.
Jacks Park
Figueroa St.
Cortes St.
Pearl St.
Alma St.
Pearl Street
El Caminito del Norte
El Caminito del Sur
Madison St.
Webster St.
Via del Pinar
Via Paraiso
Via Chualar
Herrmann Dr.
Mesa Road
El Dorado St.
Via Paraiso Park
Martin Street
Fountain Ave.
Doud St.
Pacific Street
Cass Street
Colton Street
Via Gayuba
Grove Street
Don Dahvee Park
Via Mirada
Iris Canyon Road
Fishnet Road
Iris Greenbelt

Monterey

KEY

1 *Exploring Sights*
1 *Restaurants*
1 *Hotels*
i *Tourist information*

Sights

Restaurants

Hotels

daily, but most visitors think it's worth it. ✉ *886 Cannery Row* ☎ *831/648–4800 info, 866/963–9645 for advance tickets* 🌐 *www.montereybayaquarium.org* 🎫 *$50.*

Monterey County Youth Museum (*MY Museum*)
MUSEUM | FAMILY | Monterey Bay comes to life from a child's perspective in this fun-filled, interactive indoor exploration center. The seven exhibit galleries showcase the science and nature of the Big Sur coast, theater arts, Pebble Beach golf, and beaches. Also here are a live performance theater, a creation station, a hospital emergency room, and an agriculture corner where kids follow artichokes, strawberries, and other fruits and veggies on their evolution from sprout to harvest to farmers' markets. ✉ *425 Washington St., between E. Franklin St. and Bonifacio Pl.* ☎ *831/649–6444* 🌐 *mymuseum.org* 🎫 *$8* ⏲ *Closed Mon.*

Monterey History and Art Association Salvador Dali Exposition
MUSEUM | Whether you're a fan of surrealist art or not, come to The Dali Expo to gain rare insight into the life and work of famed Spanish artist Salvador Dali, who lived in Monterey in the 1940s. The permanent exhibition houses nearly 600 artworks in various media, including 400 Dali originals. The museum's name reflects Dali's ties to nearby 17-Mile Drive, where he lived, worked, and hosted parties that included Andy Warhol, Walt Disney, Bob Hope, and other celebrities. ✉ *5 Custom House Plaza* ☎ *831/372–2608* 🌐 *www.mhaadali.com* 🎫 *$20.*

Monterey Museum of Art at Pacific Street
MUSEUM | Photographs by Ansel Adams and Edward Weston and works by other artists who have spent time on the peninsula are on display here, along with international folk art, from Kentucky hearth brooms to Tibetan prayer wheels. ✉ *559 Pacific St., across from Colton Hall* ☎ *831/372–5477* 🌐 *montereyart.org* 🎫 *$15* ⏲ *Closed Sun.–Wed.*

Steinbeck's Cannery Row

"Cannery Row in Monterey in California is a poem, a stink, a grating noise, a quality of light, a tone, a habit, a nostalgia, a dream. Cannery Row is the gathered and scattered, tin and iron and rust and splintered wood, chipped pavement and weedy lots and junk heaps, sardine canneries of corrugated iron, honky tonks, restaurants and whore houses, and little crowded groceries, and laboratories and flophouses." —John Steinbeck, *Cannery Row*

★ **Monterey State Historic Park**
NATIONAL/STATE PARK | You can glimpse Monterey's early history in several well-preserved adobe buildings in Custom House Plaza and the downtown area. Although most are only open via guided tours (check ahead for details), some also have beautiful gardens to explore. Set in what was once a hotel and saloon, the **Pacific House Museum** now houses a visitor center and exhibits of gold-rush relics; photographs of old Monterey; and Native American baskets, pottery, and other artifacts. The adjacent **Custom House,** built by the Mexican government in 1827 and now California's oldest standing public building, was the first stop for sea traders whose goods were subject to duties. (In 1846 Commodore John Sloat raised the American flag over this adobe structure and claimed California for the United States.)

Exhibits at **Casa Soberanes** (1842), once a customs-house guard's residence, survey Monterey life from Mexican rule to the present. A veranda encircles the second

California sea lions are intelligent, social animals that live (and sleep) close together in groups.

floor of **Larkin House** (1835), whose namesake, an early California statesman, brought many of the antique furnishings inside from New Hampshire. **Stevenson House** was named in honor of author Robert Louis Stevenson, who boarded here briefly in a tiny upstairs room that's now furnished with items from his family's estate. Other rooms include a gallery of memorabilia and a children's nursery with Victorian toys. **■TIP→ If the buildings are closed, you can access a cell-phone tour 24/7 (831/998–9458) or download an app.** ✉ *Pacific House Museum visitor center, 10 Custom House Plaza* ☎ *831/649–2907* 🌐 *www.parks.ca.gov/mshp* 🎫 *Free–$5, 1-hr history walk $10.*

Presidio of Monterey Museum

MUSEUM | This spot has been significant for centuries. Its first incarnation was as a Native American village for the Rumsien tribe. The Spanish explorer Sebastián Vizcaíno landed here in 1602, and Father Junípero Serra arrived in 1770. Notable battles fought here include the 1818 skirmish in which the corsair Hipólito Bruchard conquered the Spanish garrison that stood on this site and claimed part of California for Argentina. The indoor museum tells the stories; plaques mark the outdoor sites. ✉ *Presidio of Monterey, Corporal Ewing Rd., off Lighthouse Ave.* ☎ *831/646–3456* 🌐 *www.monterey.org/museums* 🎫 *Free* 🕓 *Closed Tues. and Wed.*

Restaurants

Estéban Restaurant

$$$ | **SPANISH** | In a festive fireplace dining room at Casa Munras hotel, Estéban serves modern and classic versions of Spanish cuisine: empanadas, Moorish chickpea stew, and three types of paella. Midweek specials abound: on Tuesday nights, feast on a four-course prix-fixe paella dinner ($38 per person), bottles of wine are half off on Monday, and Wednesday wine flights are just $16 for three tastes. **Known for:** daily tapas happy hour from 4:30 to 6; patio with firepit; special menus for kids and pups. *$ Average main: $30* ✉ *700 Munras Ave.*

☎ *831/375–0176* 🌐 *www.estebanrestaurant.com* ⏲ *No lunch.*

Monterey's Fish House
$$ | **SEAFOOD** | Casual yet stylish and always packed, this seafood restaurant is removed from the hubbub of the wharf. The bartenders and waitstaff will gladly advise you on the perfect wine to go with your poached, blackened, or oak-grilled seafood. **Known for:** seafood, steaks, house-made pasta; festive atmosphere; oyster bar. $ *Average main: $22* ✉ *2114 Del Monte Ave., at Dela Vina Ave.* ☎ *831/373–4647* 🌐 *montereyfishhouse.com* ⏲ *No lunch weekends.*

Old Fisherman's Grotto
$$$ | **SEAFOOD** | Otters and seals frolic in the water just below this nautical-theme Fisherman's Wharf restaurant famous for its creamy clam chowder. Seafood paella, sand dabs, filet mignon, teriyaki chicken, and several pastas are among the many entrée options. **Known for:** Monterey-style clam chowder and calamari; bay views; full bar and carefully curated wine list. $ *Average main: $29* ✉ *39 Fisherman's Wharf* ☎ *831/375–4604* 🌐 *oldfishermansgrotto.com.*

Old Monterey Café
$ | **AMERICAN** | Breakfast here gets constant local raves—its fame rests on familiar favorites: a dozen kinds of omelets, and pancakes from blueberry to cinnamon-raisin-pecan. For lunch are good soups, salads, and sandwiches. **Known for:** seven types of eggs Benedict; upbeat, team-style service; all meals cooked to order. $ *Average main: $15* ✉ *489 Alvarado St., at Munras Ave.* ☎ *831/646–1021* 🌐 *oldmontereycafeca.com* ⏲ *No dinner.*

Tarpy's Roadhouse
$$$ | **AMERICAN** | Fun, dressed-up American favorites—a little something for everyone—are served in this renovated early-1900s stone farmhouse several miles east of town. The kitchen cranks out everything from Cajun-spiced prawns to meat loaf with marsala–mushroom gravy to grilled ribs and steaks. **Known for:** American comfort food with a California twist; rustic dining: indoor fireplace or garden courtyard; generous portions. $ *Average main: $29* ✉ *2999 Monterey–Salinas Hwy., Hwy. 68* ☎ *831/647–1444* 🌐 *tarpys.com.*

Hotels

Casa Munras Garden Hotel & Spa
$$ | **HOTEL** | **FAMILY** | A cluster of Spanish-themed buildings in the heart of downtown, Casa Munras pays homage to Monterey's roots and the legacy of Spanish diplomat Don Estéban Munras, who built a residence on the site in 1824. **Pros:** full-service spa, heated swimming pool, hot tub, and fitness room; excellent on-site tapas restaurant; walk to downtown sights and restaurants. **Cons:** $15 parking fee; pool area can get noisy; thin walls. $ *Rooms from: $199* ✉ *700 Munras Ave.* ☎ *831/375–2411, 800/222–2446* 🌐 *www.hotelcasamunras.com* *163 rooms* *No meals.*

Hyatt Regency Monterey
$$ | **RESORT** | **FAMILY** | A 22-acre resort amid cypress forests on the Del Monte Golf Course, the Hyatt Regency Monterey is a good choice for business travelers and families (especially those with pets) seeking relatively affordable lodgings with numerous on-site services. **Pros:** half the rooms overlook the golf course; six tennis courts, firepits, two pools and hot tubs, hammocks, swings on property; on-site restaurant with live weekend entertainment. **Cons:** not in heart of downtown; sprawling resort that can seem packed during busy seasons; not ideal for pet-phobic guests. $ *Rooms from: $179* ✉ *1 Old Golf Course Rd.* ☎ *831/372–1234* 🌐 *www.hyatt.com* *560 rooms* *No meals.*

InterContinental the Clement Monterey
$$$ | **HOTEL** | **FAMILY** | Spectacular bay views, upscale amenities, assiduous service, and a superb location next to the

The Monterey Bay National Marine Sanctuary 

Although Monterey's coastal landscapes are stunning, their beauty is more than equaled by the wonders that lie offshore. The Monterey Bay National Marine Sanctuary—which stretches 276 miles, from north of San Francisco almost down to Santa Barbara—teems with abundant life, and has topography as diverse as that aboveground.

The preserve's 5,322 square miles include vast submarine canyons, which reach down 10,663 feet at their deepest point. They also encompass dense forests of giant kelp—a kind of seaweed that can grow more than a hundred feet from its roots on the ocean floor. These kelp forests are especially robust off Monterey.

The sanctuary was established in 1992 to protect the habitat of the many species that thrive in the bay. Some animals can be seen quite easily from land. In summer and winter you might glimpse the offshore spray of gray whales as they migrate between their summer feeding grounds in Alaska and their breeding grounds in Baja. Clouds of marine birds—including white-faced ibis, three types of albatross, and more than 15 types of gull—skim the waves, or roost in the rock islands along 17-Mile Drive. Sea otters dart and gambol in the calmer waters of the bay; and of course, you can watch the sea lions—and hear their round-the-clock barking—on the wharves in Santa Cruz and Monterey.

The sanctuary supports many other creatures, however, that remain unseen by most on-land visitors. Some of these are enormous, such as the giant blue whales that arrive to feed on plankton in summer; others, like the more than 22 species of red algae in these waters, are microscopic. So whether you choose to visit the Monterey Bay Aquarium, take a whale-watch trip, or look out to sea with your binoculars, remember you're seeing just a small part of a vibrant underwater kingdom.

aquarium propelled this luxury hotel to immediate stardom. **Pros:** a block from the aquarium; fantastic waterfront views from some rooms; great for families. **Cons:** a tad formal; not budget; Cannery Row crowds everywhere on busy weekends and holidays. *Rooms from: $305 750 Cannery Row 831/375–4500 www.ictheclementmonterey.com 208 rooms No meals.*

Monterey Plaza Hotel & Spa
$$$ | **HOTEL** | Guests at this Cannery Row hotel can see frolicking sea otters from its wide outdoor patio and many room balconies. **Pros:** on the ocean; many amenities; attentive service. **Cons:** touristy area; heavy traffic; resort fee. *Rooms from: $306 400 Cannery Row 831/920–6710 www.montereyplaza-hotel.com 290 rooms No meals.*

Monterey Tides
$$ | **RESORT** | One of the area's best values, this hotel has a great waterfront location—2 miles north of Monterey, with views of the bay and the city skyline—and offers a surprising array of amenities. **Pros:** on the beach; great value; family-friendly. **Cons:** several miles from major attractions; big-box mall neighborhood; most rooms on the small side. *Rooms from: $206 2600 Sand Dunes Dr. 831/394–3321, 800/242–8627 montereytides.com 196 rooms No meals.*

Portola Hotel & Spa at Monterey Bay
$$$ | **HOTEL** | One of Monterey's largest hotels, and locally owned and operated for more than 40 years, the coastal-themed Portola anchors a prime city block between Custom House Plaza and the Monterey Conference Center. **Pros:** walk to sights and downtown restaurants and shops; three on-site restaurants and coffee shop; pet- and family-friendly. **Cons:** crowded when conferences convene; no limit on dog size; parking fee. *Rooms from: $269* *2 Portola Plaza* *831/649–4511, 888/222–5851* *www.portolahotel.com* *379 rooms* *No meals.*

The Sanctuary Beach Resort
$$$$ | **HOTEL** | **FAMILY** | Walk to the sand from spacious, luxurious bungalows furnished in contemporary, ocean-themed style at this 19-acre, wellness-centered resort next to Marina Dunes Preserve and a secluded stretch of Marina State Beach. **Pros:** easy access to hiking and biking trails; heated pool, on-site spa services; each bungalow has two rooms that can combine for families and groups. **Cons:** not in the heart of town; parking lot relatively far from rooms; area weather is often cooler than other parts of the bay. *Rooms from: $399* *3295 Dunes Dr., Seaside* *855/693–6583* *www.thesanctuarybeachresort.com* *60 rooms* *No meals.*

Spindrift Inn
$$$ | **HOTEL** | This boutique hotel on Cannery Row has beach access and a rooftop garden that overlooks the water. **Pros:** close to aquarium; steps from the beach; friendly staff. **Cons:** throngs of visitors outside; can be noisy; not good for families. *Rooms from: $279* *652 Cannery Row* *831/646–8900, 800/841–1879* *www.spindriftinn.com* *45 rooms* *Free breakfast.*

Former Capital of California

In 1602 Spanish explorer Sebastián Vizcaíno stepped ashore on a remote California peninsula. He named it after the viceroy of New Spain—Count de Monte Rey. Soon the Spanish built a military outpost, and the site was the capital of California until the state came under American rule.

Nightlife

BARS

Alvarado Street Brewery & Grill
BREWPUBS/BEER GARDENS | Housed in an historic Beaux Arts building that dates back to 1916, this craft brewery lures locals and visitors alike with a full bar and 20 craft beers on tap, decent gastropub menu, beer garden, and shaded sidewalk patio. The company also has a brewery, bistro, and wine bar in Carmel Plaza in Carmel-by-the-Sea. *426 Alvarado St.* *831/655–2337* *www.alvaradostreetbrewery.com.*

Cibo
MUSIC CLUBS | An Italian restaurant and event venue with a big bar area, Cibo brings live jazz and other music to downtown from Tuesday through Sunday. *301 Alvarado St., at Del Monte Ave.* *831/649–8151* *cibo.com.*

Crown & Anchor
BARS/PUBS | An authentic British pub, downtown Crown & Anchor has 20 beers on tap, classic cocktails, and a full menu, including 18 daily specials available in the restaurant and heated patio until midnight. *150 W. Franklin St.* *831/649–6496* *crownandanchor.net.*

Peter B's Brewpub

BREWPUBS/BEER GARDENS | House-made beers, 18 HDTVs, a decent pub menu, and a pet-friendly patio ensure lively crowds at this craft brewery in back of the Portola Hotel & Spa. ✉ *2 Portola Plaza* ☎ *831/649–2699* 🌐 *www.peterbsbrewpub.com.*

Turn 12 Bar & Grill

BARS/PUBS | The motorcycles and vintage photographs at this downtown watering hole pay homage to nearby 11-turn Laguna Seca Raceway. The large-screen TVs, heated outdoor patio, happy-hour specials, and live entertainment keep the place jumpin' into the wee hours. ✉ *400 Tyler St., at E. Franklin St.* ☎ *831/372–8876* 🌐 *turn12barandgrill.com.*

Shopping

Alvarado and nearby downtown streets are good places to start a Monterey shopping spree, especially if you're interested in antiques and collectibles.

Cannery Row Antique Mall

ANTIQUES/COLLECTIBLES | Bargain hunters can sometimes find little treasures at the mall, which houses more than 100 local vendors under one roof. ✉ *471 Wave St.* ☎ *831/655–0264* 🌐 *canneryrowantiquemall.com.*

The Custom House Gift Shop

SPECIALTY STORES | This store sells 1800s-theme items such as toys, as well as books related to Monterey and California heritage. ✉ *Custom House Plaza, in the Custom House bldg.* ☎ *831/649–7111.*

Old Monterey Book Co.

BOOKS/STATIONERY | Antiquarian books and prints are this shop's specialties. ✉ *136 Bonifacio Pl., off Alvarado St.* ☎ *831/372–3111* ⏲ *Closed Mon.*

Activities

Monterey Bay waters never warm to the temperatures of their Southern California counterparts—the warmest they get is the low 60s. That's one reason why the marine life here is so diverse, which in turn brings out the fishers, kayakers, and whale-watchers. During the rainy winter, the waves grow larger, and surfers flock to the water. On land pretty much year-round, bikers find opportunities to ride, and walkers have plenty of waterfront to stroll.

BIKING

Adventures by the Sea

BICYCLING | You can rent surreys plus tandem, standard, and electric bicycles from this outfit that also conducts bike and kayak tours, and rents kayaks and stand-up paddleboards. There are multiple locations along Cannery Row and Custom House Plaza as well as branches at Lovers Point in Pacific Grove and 17-Mile Drive in Pebble Beach. ✉ *299 Cannery Row* ☎ *831/372–1807, 800/979–3370 reservations* 🌐 *adventuresbythesea.com.*

FISHING

J&M Sport Fishing

FISHING | This outfit takes beginning and experienced fishers out to sea to catch rock cod, ling cod, sand dabs, mackerel, halibut, salmon (in season), albacore, squid, Dungeness crab, and other species. ✉ *66 Fisherman's Wharf* ☎ *831/372–7440* 🌐 *jmsportfishing.com.*

HIKING

Monterey Bay Coastal Recreation Trail

HIKING/WALKING | From Custom House Plaza, you can walk along the coast in either direction on this 29-mile-long trail and take in spectacular views of the sea. The trail runs from north of Monterey in Castroville south to Pacific Grove, with sections continuing around Pebble Beach. Much of the path follows an old Southern Pacific Railroad route. ☎ *888/221–1010* 🌐 *seemonterey.com/things-to-do/parks/coastal-trail.*

KAYAKING

★ Monterey Bay Kayaks
KAYAKING | For many visitors the best way to see the bay is by kayak. This company rents equipment and conducts classes and natural-history tours. ✉ *693 Del Monte Ave.* ☎ *831/373–5357* 🌐 *www.montereybaykayaks.com.*

WHALE-WATCHING

Thousands of gray whales pass close by the Monterey Coast on their annual migration between the Bering Sea and Baja California, and a whale-watching cruise is the best way to see these magnificent mammals close up. The migration south takes place from December through March; January is prime viewing time. The whales migrate north from March through June. Blue whales and humpbacks also pass the coast; they're most easily spotted in late summer and early fall.

Fast Raft Ocean Safaris
TOUR—SPORTS | Naturalists lead whale-watching and sightseeing tours of Monterey Bay aboard the 33-foot *Ranger*, a six-passenger, rigid-hull, inflatable boat. The speedy craft slips into coves inaccessible to larger vessels, and its quiet engines enable intimate marine experiences without disturbing wildlife. Children ages eight and older are welcome to participate. From April to November, the boat departs from Moss Landing Harbor North Boat Launching Ramp. ✉ *32 Cannery Row, Suite F2* ☎ *408/659–3900* 🌐 *www.fastraft.com* 🎫 *From $185.*

Monterey Bay Whale Watch
WHALE-WATCHING | The marine biologists here lead three- to five-hour whale-watching tours. ✉ *84 Fisherman's Wharf* ☎ *831/375–4658* 🌐 *montereybaywhalewatch.com.*

Princess Monterey Whale Watching
WHALE-WATCHING | Tours are offered daily on a 100-passenger high-speed cruiser and a large 100-foot boat. ✉ *96 Fisherman's Wharf* ☎ *831/372–2203* 🌐 *montereywhalewatching.com.*

Salinas

17 miles east of Monterey on Hwy. 68.

Salinas, a hardworking city surrounded by vineyards and fruit and vegetable fields, honors the memory and literary legacy of John Steinbeck, its most famous native, with the National Steinbeck Center. The facility is in Old Town Salinas, where renovated turn-of-the-20th-century stone buildings house shops and restaurants.

ESSENTIALS

VISITOR INFORMATION California Welcome Center. ✉ *1213 N. Davis Rd.* ☎ *831/757–8687* 🌐 *www.visitcalifornia.com.*

Sights

Monterey Zoo
ZOO | FAMILY | Exotic animals, many of them retired from film, television, and live production work or rescued from less-than-ideal environments, find sanctuary here. The zoo offers daily tours (1 pm and 3 pm June–August, 1 pm September–May), but for an in-depth experience, stay in a safari bungalow on-site at Vision Quest Safari B&B, where guests can join the elephants in their enclosures for breakfast. The inn's room rate includes a complimentary zoo tour. ✉ *400 River Rd.* ☎ *831/455–1901* 🌐 *www.montereyzoo.com* 🎫 *$35.*

★ National Steinbeck Center
MUSEUM | The center's exhibits document the life of Pulitzer- and Nobel-prize winner John Steinbeck and the history of the nearby communities that inspired novels such as *East of Eden*. Highlights include reproductions of the green pickup-camper from *Travels with Charley* and the bunk room from *Of Mice and Men*. **Steinbeck House,** the author's Victorian birthplace, at 132 Central Avenue, is two blocks from the center. Now a popular (lunch-only) restaurant and gift shop with docent-led tours, it displays memorabilia.

✉ 1 Main St. ☎ 831/775–4721 ⊕ www.steinbeck.org 🎫 $15.

San Juan Bautista State Historic Park
HISTORIC SITE | With the low-slung, colonnaded **Mission San Juan Bautista** as its drawing card, this park 20 miles northeast of Salinas is about as close to early-19th-century California as you can get. Historic buildings ring the wide green plaza, among them an adobe home furnished with Spanish-colonial antiques, a hotel frozen in the 1860s, a blacksmith shop, a pioneer cabin, and a jailhouse. The mission's cemetery contains the unmarked graves of more than 4,300 Native American converts. **■TIP→ On the first Saturday of the month, costumed volunteers engage in quilting bees, tortilla making, and other frontier activities, and sarsaparilla and other nonalcoholic drinks are served in the saloon.** *✉ 19 Franklin St., San Juan Bautista ☎ 831/623–4881 ⊕ www.parks.ca.gov 🎫 $3 park, $4 mission.*

Pinnacles National Park

38 miles southeast of Salinas.

It was Teddy Roosevelt who recognized the uniqueness of this ancient volcano—its jagged spires and monoliths thrusting upward from chaparral-covered mountains—when he made it a national monument in 1908. Though only about two hours from the bustling Bay Area, the outside world seems to recede even before you reach the park's gates.

GETTING HERE AND AROUND

One of the first things you need to decide when visiting Pinnacles is which entrance—east or west—you'll use, because there's no road connecting the two rugged peaks separating them. Entering from Highway 25 on the east is straightforward. The gate is only a mile or so from the turnoff. From the west, once you head east out of Soledad on Highway 146, the road quickly becomes narrow and hilly, with many blind curves. Drive slowly and cautiously along the 10 miles or so before you reach the west entrance.

ESSENTIALS

Pinnacles Visitor Center
INFO CENTER | At the park's main visitor center, near the eastern entrance, you'll find a helpful selection of maps, books, and gifts. The adjacent campground store sells light snacks. *✉ 5000 Hwy. 146, Paicines ☎ 831/389–4485 ⊕ www.nps.gov/pinn.*

West Pinnacles Visitor Contact Station
INFO CENTER | This small ranger station is just past the park's western entrance, about 10 miles east of Soledad. Here you can get maps and information, watch a 13-minute film about Pinnacles, and view interpretive exhibits. No food or drink is available here. *✉ Hwy. 146, Soledad ☎ 831/389–4427 ⊕ www.nps.gov/pinn.*

Sights

Pinnacles National Park
NATIONAL/STATE PARK | FAMILY | The many attractions at Pinnacles include talus caves, 30 miles of hiking trails, and hundreds of rock-climbing routes. A mosaic of diverse habitats supports an amazing variety of wildlife species: 160 birds, 48 mammals, 70 butterflies, and nearly 400 bees. The park is also home to some of the world's remaining few hundred condors in captivity and release areas. Fourteen of California's 25 bat species live in caves and other habitats in the park. President Theodore Roosevelt declared this remarkable 26,000-acre geologic and wildlife preserve a national monument in 1908. President Barack Obama officially designated it a national park in 2013.

The pinnacles are believed to have been created when two major tectonic plates collided and pushed a smaller plate down beneath the earth's crust, spawning volcanoes in what's now called the Gabilan Mountains, southeast of Salinas and

Monterey. After the eruptions ceased, the San Andreas Fault split the volcanic field in two, carrying part of it northward to what is now Pinnacles National Park. Millions of years of erosion left a rugged landscape of rocky spires and crags, or pinnacles. Boulders fell into canyons and valleys, creating talus caves and a paradise for modern-day rock climbers. Spring is the most popular time to visit, when colorful wildflowers blanket the meadows; the light and scenery can be striking in fall and winter; the summer heat is often brutal. The park has two entrances—east and west—but they are not connected. The Pinnacles Visitor Center, Bear Gulch Nature Center, Park Headquarters, the Pinnacles Campground, and the Bear Gulch Cave and Reservoir are on the east side. The Chaparral Parking Area is on the west side, where you can feast on fantastic views of the Pinnacles High Peaks from the parking area. Dogs are not allowed on hiking trails. **TIP→ The east entrance is 32 miles southeast of Hollister via Highway 25. The west entrance is about 12 miles east of Soledad via Highway 146.** ✉ *5000 Hwy. 146, Paicines* ☎ *831/389–4486* 🌐 *www.nps.gov/pinn* 🎫 *$30 per vehicle, $15 per visitor if biking or walking.*

Activities

HIKING

Hiking is the most popular activity at Pinnacles, with more than 30 miles of trails for every interest and level of fitness. Because there isn't a road through the park, hiking is also the only way to experience its interior, including the High Peaks, the talus caves, and the reservoir.

★ Balconies Cliffs–Cave Loop

TRAIL | FAMILY | Grab your flashlight before heading out from the Chaparral Trailhead parking lot for this 2.4-mile loop that takes you through the Balconies Caves. This trail is especially beautiful in spring, when wildflowers carpet the canyon floor. About 0.6 mile from the start of the trail, turn left to begin ascending the Balconies Cliffs Trail, where you'll be rewarded with close-up views of Machete Ridge and other steep, vertical formations; you may run across rock climbers testing their skills before rounding the loop and descending back through the cave. *Easy–Moderate.* ✉ *Pinnacles National Park* ✣ *Trailhead: Chaparral Parking Area.*

★ Bear Gulch Cave–Moses Spring–Rim Trail Loop

TRAIL | FAMILY | Perhaps the most popular hike at Pinnacles, this relatively short (2.2-mile) loop trail is fun for kids and adults. It leads to the Bear Gulch cave system, and if your timing is right, you'll pass by several seasonal waterfalls inside the caves (flashlights are required). If it's been raining, check with a ranger, as the caves can flood. The upper side of the cave is usually closed in spring and early summer to protect the Townsend's big-ear bats and their pups. *Easy.* ✣ *Trailhead: Bear Gulch Day Use Area.*

Moss Landing

12 miles north of Salinas.

Moss Landing is not much more than a couple of blocks of cafés and restaurants, art galleries, and studios, plus a busy fishing port, but therein lies its charm. It's a fine place to overnight or stop for a meal and get a dose of nature.

GETTING HERE AND AROUND

From Highway 1 north or south, exit at Moss Landing Road on the ocean side. MST buses serve Moss Landing.

TOURS

Elkhorn Slough Safari Nature Boat Tours

This outfit's naturalists lead two-hour tours of Elkhorn Sough aboard a 27-foot pontoon boat. Reservations are required. ✉ *Moss Landing Harbor* ☎ *831/633–5555* 🌐 *elkhornslough.com* 🎫 *$43.*

ESSENTIALS

VISITOR INFORMATION Moss Landing Chamber of Commerce. ☎ *831/633–4501* 🌐 *mosslandingchamber.com.*

Sights

Elkhorn Slough National Estuarine Research Reserve

NATURE PRESERVE | The reserve's 1,700 acres of tidal flats and salt marshes form a complex environment that supports some 300 species of birds. A walk along the meandering waterways and wetlands can reveal hawks, white-tailed kites, owls, herons, and egrets. Also living or visiting here are sea otters, sharks, rays, and many other animals. ✉ *1700 Elkhorn Rd., Watsonville* ☎ *831/728–2822* 🌐 *elkhornslough.org* ⏲ *Closed Mon. and Tues.*

Restaurants

Haute Enchilada

$$ | SOUTH AMERICAN | Part of a complex that includes art galleries and an events venue, the Haute adds bohemian character to the seafaring village of Moss Landing. The inventive Latin American–inspired dishes include shrimp and black corn enchiladas topped with a citrus cilantro cream sauce, and roasted *pasilla* chilies stuffed with mashed plantains and caramelized onions. **Known for:** extensive cocktail and wine list; many vegan and gluten-free options; artsy atmosphere. $ *Average main: $26* ✉ *7902 Moss Landing Rd.* ☎ *831/633–5843* 🌐 *hauteenchilada.com* ⏲ *Closed Tues. and Wed.*

Phil's Fish Market & Eatery

$$ | SEAFOOD | Exquisitely fresh, simply prepared seafood (try the cioppino) is on the menu at this warehouselike restaurant on the harbor; all kinds of glistening fish are for sale at the market in the front. **Known for:** cioppino; clam chowder; myriad artichoke dishes. $ *Average main: $22* ✉ *7600 Sandholdt Rd.* ☎ *831/633–2152* 🌐 *philsfishmarket.com.*

Hotels

Captain's Inn

$$ | B&B/INN | Commune with nature and pamper yourself with upscale creature comforts at this green-certified complex in the heart of town. **Pros:** walk to restaurants and shops; tranquil natural setting; closest Monterey Bay hotel to Pinnacles National Park. **Cons:** rooms in historic building don't have water views; far from urban amenities; not appropriate for young children. $ *Rooms from: $189* ✉ *8122 Moss Landing Rd.* ☎ *831/633–5550* 🌐 *www.captainsinn.com* *10 rooms* 🍽 *Free breakfast.*

Activities

KAYAKING

Monterey Bay Kayaks

KAYAKING | Rent a kayak to paddle out into Elkhorn Slough for up-close wildlife encounters. ✉ *2390 Hwy. 1, at North Harbor* ☎ *831/373–5357* 🌐 *montereybaykayaks.com.*

Aptos

17 miles north of Moss Landing.

Backed by a redwood forest and facing the sea, downtown Aptos—known as Aptos Village—is a place of wooden walkways and false-fronted shops. Antiques dealers cluster along Trout Gulch Road, off Soquel Drive east of Highway 1.

GETTING HERE AND AROUND

Use Highway 1 to reach Aptos from Santa Cruz or Monterey. Exit at State Park Drive to reach the main shopping hub and Aptos Village. You can also exit at Freedom Boulevard or Rio del Mar. Soquel Drive is the main artery through town.

ESSENTIALS

VISITOR INFORMATION Aptos Chamber of Commerce. ✉ *7605–A Old Dominion Ct.* ☎ *831/688–1467* 🌐 *aptoschamber.com.*

★ **Seacliff State Beach**
BEACH—SIGHT | FAMILY | Sandstone bluffs tower above this popular beach with a long fishing pier. The 1.5-mile walk north to adjacent New Brighton State Beach in Capitola is one of the nicest on the bay. Leashed dogs are allowed on the beach. **Amenities:** food and drink; lifeguards; parking (fee); showers; toilets. **Best for:** sunset; swimming; walking. ✉ *201 State Park Dr.* ☎ *831/685–6500* 🌐 *www.parks.ca.gov* *$10 per vehicle.*

Bittersweet Bistro
$$$ | **MEDITERRANEAN** | A large old tavern with cathedral ceilings houses this popular bistro, where the Mediterranean–California menu changes seasonally, but regular highlights include paella, seafood puttanesca, and pepper-crusted rib-eye steak with Cabernet demi-glace. **Known for:** value-laden happy hour; seafood specials; house-made desserts. *Average main: $29* ✉ *787 Rio Del Mar Blvd., off Hwy. 1* ☎ *831/662–9799* 🌐 *www.bittersweetbistro.com* *Closed Mon. and Tues.*

Seascape Beach Resort
$$$$ | **RESORT** | **FAMILY** | It's easy to unwind at this full-fledged resort on a bluff overlooking Monterey Bay. The spacious suites sleep from two to eight people. **Pros:** time share–style apartments; access to miles of beachfront; superb views. **Cons:** far from city life; most bathrooms are small; some rooms need updating. *Rooms from: $387* ✉ *1 Seascape Resort Dr.* ☎ *831/662–7171, 866/867–0976* 🌐 *seascaperesort.com* *285 suites* *No meals.*

Capitola and Soquel

4 miles northwest of Aptos.

On the National Register of Historic places as California's first seaside resort town, the village of Capitola has been in a holiday mood since the late 1800s. Casual eateries, surf shops, and ice cream parlors pack its walkable downtown. Inland, across Highway 1, antiques shops line Soquel Drive in the town of Soquel. Wineries dot the Santa Cruz Mountains beyond.

GETTING HERE AND AROUND

From Santa Cruz or Monterey, follow Highway 1 to the Capitola/Soquel (Bay Avenue) exit about 7 miles south of Santa Cruz and head west to reach Capitola and east to access Soquel Village. On summer weekends, park for free in the lot behind the Crossroads Center, a block west of the freeway, and hop aboard the free Capitola Shuttle to the village.

ESSENTIALS

VISITOR INFORMATION Capitola-Soquel Chamber of Commerce. ✉ *716-G Capitola Ave., Capitola* ☎ *831/475–6522* 🌐 *capitolachamber.com.*

★ **New Brighton State Beach**
BEACH—SIGHT | FAMILY | Once the site of a Chinese fishing village, New Brighton is now a popular surfing and camping spot. Its Pacific Migrations Visitor Center traces the history of the Chinese and other peoples who settled around Monterey Bay. It also documents the migratory patterns of the area's wildlife, such as monarch butterflies and gray whales. Leashed dogs are allowed in the park. New Brighton connects with Seacliff Beach, and at low tide you can walk or run along this scenic stretch of sand for nearly 16 miles south (though you might have to wade through a few creeks). ■ **TIP→ The 1½-mile stroll from**

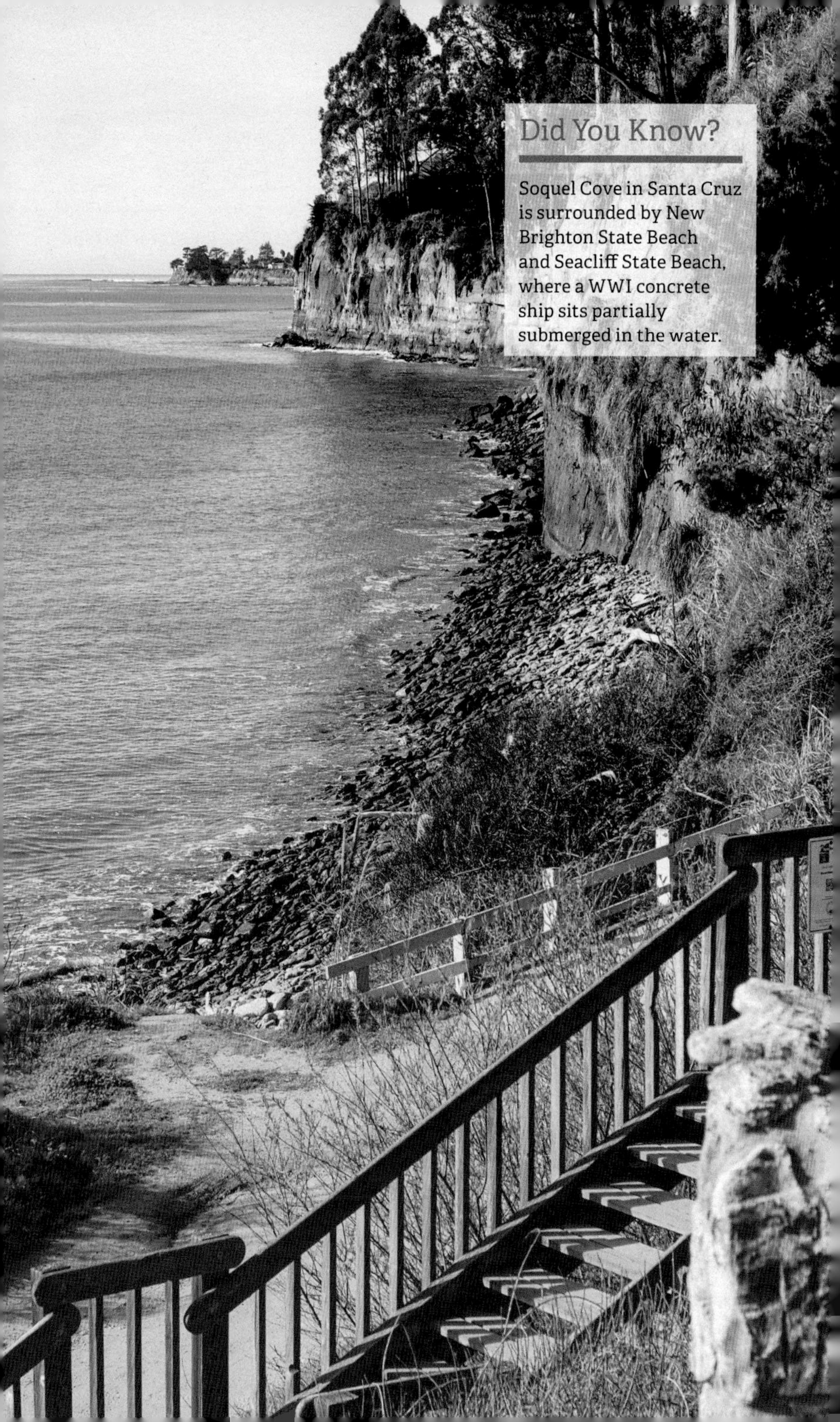

Did You Know?

Soquel Cove in Santa Cruz is surrounded by New Brighton State Beach and Seacliff State Beach, where a WWI concrete ship sits partially submerged in the water.

New Brighton to Seacliff's concrete ship is a local favorite. Amenities: parking (fee); showers; toilets. **Best for:** sunset; swimming; walking. ✉ *1500 State Park Dr., off Hwy. 1, Capitola* ☎ *831/464–6329* 🌐 *www.parks.ca.gov* 🎟 *$10 per vehicle.*

Restaurants

Carpo's

$ | **SEAFOOD** | **FAMILY** | Locals love this casual counter where seafood predominates, but you can also order burgers, salads, and steaks. Baskets of battered snapper are among the favorites, along with calamari, prawns, seafood kebabs, fish-and-chips, and homemade olallieberry pie. **Known for:** large portions of healthy comfort food; lots of options under $12; soup and salad bar. [$] *Average main: $14* ✉ *2400 Porter St., at Hwy. 1, Soquel* ☎ *831/476–6260* 🌐 *carposrestaurant.com.*

Gayle's Bakery & Rosticceria

$$ | **CAFÉ** | **FAMILY** | Whether you're in the mood for an orange-olallieberry muffin, a wild rice and chicken salad, or tri-tip on garlic toast, this bakery-deli's varied menu is likely to satisfy. Munch on your lemon meringue tartlet or chocolate brownie on the shady patio, or dig into the daily blue-plate dinner—teriyaki grilled skirt steak with edamame–shiitake sticky rice, perhaps, or roast turkey breast with Chardonnay gravy—amid the whirl of activity inside. **Known for:** prepared meals to go; on-site bakery and rosticceria; deli and espresso bar. [$] *Average main: $17* ✉ *504 Bay Ave., Capitola* ☎ *831/462–1200* 🌐 *www.gaylesbakery.com.*

Shadowbrook

$$$$ | **EUROPEAN** | To get to this romantic spot overlooking Soquel Creek, you can take a cable car or walk the stairs down a steep, fern-lined bank beside a running waterfall. Dining room options include the rooftop Redwood Room, the wood-paneled Wine Cellar, the creek-side, glass-enclosed Greenhouse, the Fireplace Room, and the airy Garden Room. **Known for:** romantic creek-side setting; prime rib and grilled seafood; local special-occasion favorite for nearly 70 years. [$] *Average main: $36* ✉ *1750 Wharf Rd., at Lincoln Ave., Capitola* ☎ *831/475–1511* 🌐 *www.shadowbrook-capitola.com.*

California's Oldest Resort Town

As far as anyone knows for certain, Capitola is the Pacific coast's oldest seaside resort town. In 1856, a pioneer acquired Soquel Landing, the picturesque lagoon and beach where Soquel Creek empties into the bay, and built a wharf. Another man opened a campground along the shore, and his daughter named it Capitola after a heroine in a novel series. After the train came to town in the 1870s, thousands of vacationers began arriving to bask in the sun on the glorious beach.

Hotels

Inn at Depot Hill

$$$ | **B&B/INN** | This inventively designed B&B in a former rail depot views itself as a link to the era of luxury train travel. **Pros:** short walk to beach and village; historic charm; excellent service. **Cons:** fills quickly; hot-tub conversation audible in some rooms; rooms need updating. [$] *Rooms from: $309* ✉ *250 Monterey Ave., Capitola* ☎ *831/462–3376, 800/572–2632* 🌐 *www.innatdepothill.com* 🛏 *13 rooms* 🍽 *Free breakfast.*

Santa Cruz

5 miles west of Capitola, 48 miles north of Monterey.

The big city on this stretch of the California coast, Santa Cruz (pop. 63,364) is less manicured than Carmel or Monterey. Long known for its surfing and its amusement-filled beach boardwalk, the town is an eclectic mix of grand Victorian-era homes, beachside inns, and multimillion dollar compounds owned by tech gurus. The opening of the University of California campus in the 1960s swung the town sharply to the left politically, and the counterculture more or less lives on here. At the same time, a revitalized downtown and an insane real-estate market reflect the city's proximity to Silicon Valley, which is just a 30-minute drive to the north, and to a growing wine region in the surrounding mountains.

Amble around downtown's Santa Cruz Farmers' Market (Wednesday afternoons year-round) to experience the local culture, which derives much of its character from close connections to food and farming. The market covers a city block and includes not just the expected organic produce, but also live music and booths with local crafts and prepared food.

GETTING HERE AND AROUND

From the San Francisco Bay area, take Highway 17 south over the mountains to Santa Cruz, where it merges with Highway 1. Use Highway 1 to get around the area. The Santa Cruz Transit Center is at 920 Pacific Avenue, at Front Street, a short walk from the wharf and boardwalk, with connections to public transit throughout the Monterey Bay and San Francisco Bay areas. You can purchase day passes for Santa Cruz METRO buses here.

ESSENTIALS

VISITOR INFORMATION Visit Santa Cruz County. ✉ *303 Water St., Suite 100* ☎ *831/425–1234, 800/833–3494* 🌐 *www.visitsantacruz.org.*

Sights

Monterey Bay National Marine Sanctuary Exploration Center

INFO CENTER | FAMILY | The interactive and multimedia exhibits at this fascinating interpretive center reveal and explain the treasures of the nation's largest marine sanctuary. The two-story building, across from the main beach and municipal wharf, has films and exhibits about migratory species, watersheds, underwater canyons, kelp forests, and intertidal zones. The second-floor deck has stellar ocean views and an interactive station that provides real-time weather, surf, and buoy reports. ✉ *35 Pacific Ave., near Beach St.* ☎ *831/421–9993* 🌐 *montereybay.noaa.gov/vc/sec* *Free* *Closed Mon. and Tues.*

Mystery Spot

LOCAL INTEREST | Hokey tourist trap or genuine scientific enigma? Since 1940, curious throngs baffled by the Mystery Spot have made it one of the most visited attractions in Santa Cruz. The laws of gravity and physics don't appear to apply in this tiny patch of redwood forest, where balls roll uphill and people stand on a slant. **TIP→ On weekends and holidays, it's wise to purchase tickets online in advance.** ✉ *465 Mystery Spot Rd., off Branciforte Dr. (north off Hwy. 1)* ☎ *831/423–8897* 🌐 *mysteryspot.com* *$8, parking $5.*

Pacific Avenue

NEIGHBORHOOD | When you've had your fill of the city's beaches and waters, take a stroll in downtown Santa Cruz, especially on Pacific Avenue between Laurel and Water streets. Vintage boutiques and mountain-sports stores, sushi bars, and Mexican restaurants, day spas, and nightclubs keep the main drag and the surrounding streets hopping from midmorning until late evening.

★ Santa Cruz Beach Boardwalk

CAROUSEL | FAMILY | Santa Cruz has been a seaside resort since the mid-19th century. Along one end of the broad, south-facing beach, the boardwalk has entertained holidaymakers for more than a century. Its Looff carousel and classic wooden Giant Dipper roller coaster, both dating from the early 1900s, are surrounded by high-tech thrill rides and easygoing kiddie rides with ocean views. Video and arcade games, a minigolf course, and a laser-tag arena pack one gigantic building, which is open daily even if the rides aren't running. You have to pay to play, but you can wander the entire boardwalk for free while sampling carnival fare such as corn dogs and garlic fries. ✉ *Along Beach St.* ☎ *831/423–5590 info line* 🌐 *beachboardwalk.com* 🎫 *$40 day pass for unlimited rides, or pay per ride* ⏲ *Some rides closed Sept.–May.*

Santa Cruz Municipal Wharf

MARINA | FAMILY | Jutting half a mile into the ocean near one end of the boardwalk, the century-old Municipal Wharf is lined with seafood restaurants, a wine bar, souvenir shops, and outfitters offering bay cruises, fishing trips, and boat rentals. A salty soundtrack drifts up from under the wharf, where barking sea lions lounge in heaps on the crossbeams. ✉ *Beach St. and Pacific Ave.* ☎ *831/459–3800* 🌐 *www.santacruzwharf.com.*

Santa Cruz Surfing Museum

MUSEUM | This museum inside the Mark Abbott Memorial Lighthouse chronicles local surfing history. Photographs show old-time surfers, and a display of boards includes rarities such as a heavy redwood plank predating the fiberglass era and the remains of a modern board chomped by a great white shark. Surfer docents reminisce about the good old days. ✉ *Lighthouse Point Park, 701 W. Cliff Dr. near Pelton Ave.* ☎ *831/420–6289* 🎫 *$2 suggested donation* ⏲ *Closed Tues. and Wed. except open Tues. July–early Sept.*

Seymour Marine Discovery Center

ZOO | FAMILY | Part of the Long Marine Laboratory at the University of California Santa Cruz's Institute of Marine Sciences, the center looks more like a research facility than a slick aquarium. Interactive exhibits demonstrate how scientists study the ocean, and the aquarium displays creatures of interest to marine biologists. The 87-foot blue whale skeleton is one of the world's largest. **■ TIP→ General tours take place in the afternoon, and there's an abbreviated tour at 11 am for families with small children.** ✉ *100 Shaffer Rd., end of Delaware Ave., west of Natural Bridges State Beach* ☎ *831/459–3800* 🌐 *seymourcenter.ucsc.edu* 🎫 *$10* ⏲ *Closed Mon.*

Surf City Vintners

WINERY/DISTILLERY | A dozen tasting rooms of limited-production wineries occupy renovated warehouse spaces west of the beach. MJA, Sones Cellars, Santa Cruz Mountain Vineyard, and Equinox are good places to start. Also here are the Santa Cruz Mountain Brewing Company and El Salchichero, popular for its homemade sausages, jams, and pickled and candied vegetables. ✉ *Swift Street Courtyard, 334 Ingalls St., at Swift St., off Hwy. 1 (Mission St.)* 🌐 *surfcityvintners.com.*

UC Santa Cruz

COLLEGE | The 2,000-acre University of California Santa Cruz campus nestles in the forested hills above town. Its sylvan setting, ocean vistas, and redwood architecture make the university worth a visit, as does its **arboretum** ($5, open daily from 9 to 5), whose walking path leads through areas dedicated to the plants of California, Australia, New Zealand, and South Africa. **■ TIP→ Free shuttles help students and visitors get around campus, and you can join a guided tour (online reservation required).** ✉ *Main entrance at Bay and High Sts. (turn left on High for arboretum)* ☎ *831/459–0111* 🌐 *www.ucsc.edu/visit.*

★ West Cliff Drive

SCENIC DRIVE | The road that winds along an oceanfront bluff from the municipal wharf to Natural Bridges State Beach makes for a spectacular drive, but it's even more fun to walk or bike the paved path that parallels the road. Surfers bob and swoosh in Monterey Bay at several points near the foot of the bluff, especially at a break known as **Steamer Lane.** Named for a surfer who died here in 1965, the nearby Mark Abbott Memorial Lighthouse stands at Point Santa Cruz, the cliff's major promontory. From here you can watch pinnipeds hang out, sunbathe, and frolic on Seal Rock. ✉ *Santa Cruz.*

Wilder Ranch State Park

NATIONAL/STATE PARK | In this park's Cultural Preserve you can visit the homes, barns, workshops, and bunkhouse of a 19th-century dairy farm. Nature has reclaimed most of the ranch land, and native plants and wildlife have returned to the 7,000 acres of forest, grassland, canyons, estuaries, and beaches. Hike, bike, or ride horseback on miles of ocean-view trails. Dogs aren't allowed at Wilder Ranch. ✉ *Hwy. 1, 1 mile north of Santa Cruz* ☎ *831/426–0505 Interpretive Center, 831/423–9703 trail information* 🌐 *www.parks.ca.gov* 🎟 *$10 per car* ⏲ *Interpretive center closed Mon.–Wed.*

Beaches

Natural Bridges State Beach

BEACH—SIGHT | **FAMILY** | At the end of West Cliff Drive lies this stretch of soft sand edged with tide pools and sea-sculpted rock bridges. ■ **TIP→ From September to early January a colony of monarch butterflies roosts in the eucalyptus grove.** **Amenities:** lifeguards; parking (fee); toilets. **Best for:** sunrise; sunset; surfing; swimming. ✉ *2531 W. Cliff Dr.* ☎ *831/423–4609* 🌐 *www.parks.ca.gov* 🎟 *Beach free, parking $10.*

Twin Lakes State Beach

BEACH—SIGHT | **FAMILY** | Stretching a half mile along the coast on both sides of the small-craft jetties, Twin Lakes is one of Monterey Bay's sunniest beaches. It encompasses Seabright State Beach (with access in a residential neighborhood on the upcoast side) and Black's Beach on the downcoast side. Families often come here to sunbathe, picnic, and hike the nature trail around adjacent Schwann Lake. Parking is tricky from May through September—you need to pay for an $8 day-use permit at a kiosk and the lot fills quickly—but you can park all day in the harbor pay lot and walk here. Leashed dogs are allowed. **Amenities:** food and drink; lifeguards (seasonal); parking; showers; toilets; water sports (seasonal). **Best for:** sunset; surfing; swimming; walking. ✉ *7th Ave., at East Cliff Dr.* ☎ *831/427–4868* 🌐 *www.parks.ca.gov.*

Restaurants

Crow's Nest

$$$ | **SEAFOOD** | **FAMILY** | Vintage surfboards and local surf photography line the walls and nearly every table overlooks sand and surf at this restaurant on the Santa Cruz Harbor. For sweeping ocean views and fish tacos, burgers, and other casual fare, head upstairs to the Breakwater Bar & Grill. **Known for:** house-smoked salmon and calamari apps; crab-cake eggs Benedict and olallieberry pancakes; on-site market with pizzas, sandwiches, soups, and salads. 💲 *Average main: $27* ✉ *2218 E. Cliff Dr., west of 7th Ave.* ☎ *831/476–4560* 🌐 *crowsnest-santacruz.com.*

★ Laili Restaurant

$$ | **MEDITERRANEAN** | Exotic Mediterranean flavors with an Afghan twist take center stage at this artsy, stylish space with soaring ceilings. In the evening, locals come to relax over wine and soft jazz at the blue-concrete bar, on the heated patio with twinkly lights, or at a communal table near the open kitchen.

Known for: house-made pastas and numerous vegetarian and vegan options; fresh naan, chutneys, and dips with every meal; traditional dishes like pomegranate eggplant and maushawa soup. *Average main: $24* *101–B Cooper St., near Pacific Ave.* *831/423–4545* *lailirestaurant.com.*

La Posta Via

$$ | **ITALIAN** | Authentic Italian fare made with fresh local produce lures diners into cozy, modern-rustic La Posta. Nearly everything is made in-house, from the pizzas and breads baked in the brick oven to the pasta and the vanilla-bean gelato. **Known for:** seasonal wild-nettle lasagna; braised lamb shank; in the heart of the Seabright neighborhood. *Average main: $24* *538 Seabright Ave., at Logan St.* *831/457–2782* *lapostarestaurant.com* *Closed Mon. No lunch.*

Oswald

$$$$ | **EUROPEAN** | Sophisticated yet unpretentious European-inspired California cooking is the order of the day at this intimate and stylish bistro with a seasonal menu, which might include such items as seafood risotto or crispy duck breast in a pomegranate reduction sauce. The creative concoctions poured at the slick marble bar include whiskey mixed with apple and lemon juice, and tequila with celery juice and lime. **Known for:** house-made pork sausage; craft cocktails; local art displays that change monthly. *Average main: $34* *121 Soquel Ave., at Front St.* *831/423–7427* *oswaldrestaurant.com* *Closed Sun.–Tues.*

★ Soif

$$$ | **MEDITERRANEAN** | Wine reigns at this sleek bistro and wineshop that takes its name from the French word for thirst—the selections come from near and far, and you can order many of them by the taste or glass. Mediterranean-inspired small plates and entrées are served at the copper-top bar, the big communal table, and private tables. **Known for:** Mediterranean-style dishes; diverse, interesting wine selection; jazz combo or solo pianist plays on some evenings. *Average main: $27* *105 Walnut Ave.* *831/423–2020* *www.soifwine.com* *Closed Mon. and Tues. No lunch.*

Zachary's

$ | **AMERICAN** | This noisy café filled with students and families defines the funky essence of Santa Cruz. It also dishes up great breakfasts: stay simple with sourdough pancakes, or go for Mike's Mess—eggs scrambled with bacon, mushrooms, and home fries, then topped with sour cream, melted cheese, and fresh tomatoes. **Known for:** nearly everything made in-house; "Mike's Mess" egg dishes; local organic ingredients. *Average main: $15* *819 Pacific Ave.* *831/427–0646* *www.zacharyssantacruz.com* *Closed Mon. No dinner.*

Hotels

Babbling Brook Inn

$$$ | **B&B/INN** | Though it's in the middle of Santa Cruz, this B&B has lush gardens, a running stream, and tall trees that make you feel like you're in a secluded wood. **Pros:** close to UCSC; within walking distance of downtown shops; woodsy feel. **Cons:** near a high school; some rooms close to a busy street; many stairs and no elevator. *Rooms from: $280* *1025 Laurel St.* *831/427–2437, 800/866–1131* *babblingbrookinn.com* *13 rooms* *Free breakfast.*

Carousel Beach Inn

$$ | **HOTEL** | This basic but comfy motel, decorated in bold, retro, seaside style and across the street from the boardwalk, is ideal for travelers who want easy access to the sand and the amusement park rides without spending a fortune. **Pros:** steps from Santa Cruz Main Beach; affordable lodging rates and ride packages; free parking and Wi-Fi. **Cons:** no pool or spa; no exercise room; not pet-friendly. *Rooms from: $159* *110 Riverside Ave.* *831/425–7090*

carousel-beach-inn.com 34 rooms Free breakfast.

★ Chaminade Resort & Spa

$$$ | RESORT | FAMILY | Secluded on 300 hilltop acres of redwood and eucalyptus forest laced with hiking trails, this Mission-style complex also features a lovely terrace restaurant with expansive views of Monterey Bay. Guest rooms are furnished in an eclectic, bohemian style that pays homage to the artsy local community and the city's industrial past. **Pros:** peaceful, verdant setting; full-service spa and large pool; ideal spot for romance and rejuvenation. **Cons:** not within walking distance of downtown; not near the ocean; resort fee. *Rooms from: $279 1 Chaminade La. 800/283–6569, 831/475–5600 www.chaminade.com 156 rooms No meals.*

Dream Inn Santa Cruz

$$$$ | HOTEL | A short stroll from the boardwalk and wharf, this full-service luxury hotel is the only lodging in Santa Cruz directly on the beach, and its rooms all have private balconies or patios overlooking Monterey Bay. Accommodations have contemporary furnishings, bold colors, and upscale linens, but the main draw here is having the ocean at your doorstep. **Pros:** restaurant with sweeping views of Monterey Bay; cool mid-century modern design; walk to boardwalk and downtown. **Cons:** expensive; area gets congested on summer weekends; pool area and hallways can be noisy. *Rooms from: $324 175 W. Cliff Dr. 831/740–8069 www.dreaminnsantacruz.com 165 rooms No meals.*

Hotel Paradox

$$$ | HOTEL | About a mile from the ocean and two blocks from Pacific Avenue, this stylish, forest-theme complex (part of the Marriott Autograph Collection) is among the few full-service hotels in town. **Pros:** close to downtown and main beach; spacious pool area with cabanas, firepits, hot tub, and dining and cocktail service; on-site farm-to-table restaurant. **Cons:** pool area can get crowded on warm-weather days; some rooms on the small side; thin walls. *Rooms from: $279 611 Ocean St. 831/425–7100, 855/425–7200 hotelparadox.com 172 rooms No meals.*

Hyatt Place Santa Cruz

$$ | HOTEL | Vintage surfboards and local art grace the walls of the spacious, ocean-theme lobby at this downtown hotel. **Pros:** close to restaurants and shops; outdoor pool and hot tub and 24-hour fitness center; on-site restaurant and bar. **Cons:** not on the beach; valet parking only; fronts busy road. *Rooms from: $219 407 Broadway 831/226–2304 hyattplace.com 106 rooms No meals.*

Pacific Blue Inn

$$ | B&B/INN | Green themes predominate in this three-story, eco-friendly inn on a sliver of prime downtown real estate. **Pros:** free parking; free bicycles; downtown location. **Cons:** tiny property; not suitable for children; parking lot is a block away. *Rooms from: $189 636 Pacific Ave. 831/600–8880 pacificblueinn.com 9 rooms No meals.*

Sea & Sand Inn

$$ | HOTEL | Location is the main appeal of this motel atop a waterfront bluff, where all rooms have an ocean view and the boardwalk is just down the street. **Pros:** beach is steps away; friendly staff; tidy landscaping. **Cons:** tight parking lot; fronts a busy road; can be noisy. *Rooms from: $249 201 W. Cliff Dr. 831/427–3400 seaandsandinn.com 22 units Free breakfast.*

★ West Cliff Inn

$$$ | B&B/INN | On bluffs across from Cowell Beach, this three-story, Italianate property, built in 1877, exudes classic California beach style. **Pros:** killer bay and boardwalk views; walking distance of the beach; close to downtown. **Cons:** boardwalk noise; street traffic. *Rooms from: $299 174 West Cliff Dr.*

☎ *831/457–2200* 🌐 *www.westcliffinn.com* *9 units* *Free breakfast.*

Catalyst
DANCE CLUBS | This huge, grimy, and fun club books rock, indie rock, punk, death-metal, reggae, and other acts. ✉ *1011 Pacific Ave.* ☎ *877/987–6487* 🌐 *catalystclub.com.*

Kuumbwa Jazz Center
MUSIC CLUBS | The center draws top performers such as Lee Ritenour, Chris Potter, and the Dave Holland Trio. A café serves meals an hour before most shows. ✉ *320–2 Cedar St.* ☎ *831/427–2227* 🌐 *kuumbwajazz.org.*

Moe's Alley
MUSIC CLUBS | Blues, salsa, reggae, funk: delightfully casual Moe's presents it all (and more). ✉ *1535 Commercial Way* ☎ *831/479–1854* 🌐 *moesalley.com* ⏲ *Closed Mon.*

Tannery Arts Center
ARTS CENTERS | The former Salz Tannery now contains nearly 30 studios and live-work spaces for artists whose disciplines range from ceramics and glass to film and digital media; most have public hours of operation. Performances also take place at the on-site Colligan Theater, and the center hosts assorted arts events on weekends and, occasionally, on weekdays. ✉ *1060 River St., at intersection of Hwys. 1 and 9* 🌐 *tanneryartscenter.org.*

Bookshop Santa Cruz
BOOKS/STATIONERY | In 2021, the town's best and most beloved independent bookstore celebrated its 55th anniversary of selling new, used, and remaindered titles. The children's section is especially comprehensive, and the shop's special events calendar is packed with readings, social mixers, book signings, and discussions. ✉ *1520 Pacific Ave.* ☎ *831/423–0900* 🌐 *bookshopsantacruz.com.*

O'Neill Surf Shop
SPORTING GOODS | Local surfers get their wetties (wet suits) and other gear at this O'Neill store or the one in Capitola, at 1115 41st Avenue. There's also a satellite shop on the Santa Cruz Boardwalk. ✉ *110 Cooper St.* ☎ *831/469–4377* 🌐 *www.oneill.com.*

Santa Cruz Downtown Farmers' Market
OUTDOOR/FLEA/GREEN MARKETS | **FAMILY** | Santa Cruz is famous for its long tradition of organic growing and sustainable living, and its downtown market (one of five countywide) reflects the incredible diversity and quality of local agriculture and the synergistic daily life of community-minded residents. The busy market, which always has live music, happens every Wednesday from 1 to 6, rain or shine. The stalls cover much of an entire city block near Pacific Avenue and include fresh produce plus everything from oysters, beer, bread, and charcuterie to arts and crafts to prepared foods made from ingredients sourced from on-site vendors. ✉ *Cedar St. at Lincoln St.* ☎ *831/454–0566* 🌐 *www.santacruzfarmersmarket.org.*

BICYCLING

Another Bike Shop
BICYCLING | Mountain bikers should head here for tips on the best area trails and to browse cutting-edge gear made and tested locally. ✉ *2361 Mission St., at King St.* ☎ *831/427–2232* 🌐 *www.anotherbikeshop.com.*

BOATS AND CHARTERS

***Chardonnay II* Sailing Charters**
BOATING | The 70-foot *Chardonnay II* departs year-round from Santa Cruz yacht harbor on whale-watching, sunset, and other cruises around Monterey Bay. Most

O'Neill: A Santa Cruz Icon

O'Neill wet suits and beachwear weren't exactly born in Santa Cruz, but as far as most of the world is concerned, the O'Neill brand is synonymous with Santa Cruz and surfing legend.

The O'Neill wet-suit story began in 1952, when Jack O'Neill and his brother, Robert, opened their first surf shop in a garage across from San Francisco's Ocean Beach. While shaping balsa surfboards and selling accessories, the O'Neills experimented with solutions to a common surfer problem: frigid waters. Tired of being forced back to shore, blue-lipped and shivering after just 20 or 30 minutes riding the waves, they played with various materials and eventually designed a neoprene vest.

In 1959, Jack moved his shop 90 miles south to Cowell's Beach in Santa Cruz. It quickly became a popular surf hangout, and O'Neill's new wet suits began to sell like hotcakes. In the early 1960s, the company opened a warehouse for manufacturing on a larger scale. Santa Cruz soon became a major surf city, attracting wave riders to prime breaks at Steamer Lane, Pleasure Point, and the Hook. In 1965, O'Neill pioneered the first wet-suit boots, and, in 1971, Jack's son invented the surf leash. By 1980, O'Neill stood at the top of the world wet-suit market. On June 2, 2017, Jack O'Neill passed away at the age of 94, in his longtime Pleasure Point residence overlooking the surf.

regularly scheduled excursions cost $70; food and drink are served on many of them. Reservations are essential. ✉ *Santa Cruz West Harbor, 790 Mariner Park Way* ☎ *831/423–1213* 🌐 *chardonnay.com.*

Stagnaro Sport Fishing, Charters & Whale Watching Cruises

BOATING | Stagnaro (aka Santa Cruz Whale Watching) offers salmon, albacore, and rock-cod fishing expeditions (fees include bait) as well as whale-watching, dolphin, and sea-life cruises year-round. ✉ *1718 Brommer St., near Santa Cruz Harbor* ☎ *831/427–0230* 🌐 *stagnaros.com* 🎫 *From $61.*

GOLF

DeLaveaga Golf Course

GOLF | Woodsy DeLaveaga, a public course set in a hilly park, overlooks Santa Cruz and the bay. With its canyons, tree-lined fairways, and notoriously difficult par-5, dogleg 10th hole, the course challenges novices and seasoned golfers. ✉ *401 Upper Park Rd.* ☎ *831/423–7214* 🌐 *www.delaveagagolf.com* 🎫 *$60 weekdays, $80 weekends/holidays* 🏌 *18 holes, 5700 yards, par 70.*

Pasatiempo Golf Club

GOLF | Designed by famed golf architect Dr. Alister MacKenzie in 1929, this semiprivate course, set amid undulating hills just above the city, is among the nation's top championship courses. Golfers rave about the spectacular views and challenging terrain. According to the club, MacKenzie, who designed Pebble Beach's exclusive Cypress Point course and Augusta National in Georgia, the home of the Masters Golf Tournament, declared this his favorite layout. ✉ *20 Clubhouse Rd.* ☎ *831/459–9155* 🌐 *www.pasatiempo.com* 🎫 *From $325* 🏌 *18 holes, 6125 yards, par 72.*

KAYAKING

Kayak Connection

KAYAKING | From March through May, participants in this outfit's tours mingle with gray whales and their calves on their northward journey to Alaska. Throughout the year, the company rents kayaks and paddleboards and conducts tours of Natural Bridges State Beach, Capitola, and Elkhorn Slough. ✉ *Santa Cruz Harbor, 413 Lake Ave., No. 3* ☎ *831/479–1121* 🌐 *kayakconnection.com* 🎫 *From $65 for scheduled tours.*

Venture Quest Kayaking

KAYAKING | Explore hidden coves and kelp forests on guided two-hour kayak tours that depart from Santa Cruz Wharf. The tours include a kayaking lesson. Venture Quest also rents kayaks (and wet suits and gear), and arranges tours at other Monterey Bay destinations, including Elkhorn Slough. ✉ *2 Santa Cruz Wharf* ☎ *831/427–2267 kayak hotline, 831/425–8445 rental office* 🌐 *kayaksantacruz.com* 🎫 *From $35 for rentals, $60 for tours.*

SURFING

Club-Ed Surf School and Camps

SURFING | Find out what all the fun is about at Club-Ed. Your first private or group lesson ($100 and up) includes all equipment. ✉ *Cowell's Beach, at Dream Inn Santa Cruz* ☎ *831/464–0177* 🌐 *club-ed.com.*

Cowell's Surf Shop

SURFING | This shop sells gear, clothing, and swimwear; rents surfboards, stand-up paddleboards, and wet suits; and offers lessons. ✉ *30 Front St.* ☎ *831/427–2355* 🌐 *www.facebook.com/cowellssurfshop.*

Richard Schmidt Surf School

SURFING | Since 1978, Richard Schmidt has shared the stoke of surfing and the importance of ocean awareness and conservation with legions of students of all ages. Today, the outfit offers surfing and stand-up paddleboard lessons (equipment provided) as well as marine adventure tours in Santa Cruz and elsewhere on the bay. Locations depend on where the waves are breaking or the wind's a'blowing, but outings typically convene at Cowell's Beach or Pleasure Point. ✉ *Santa Cruz* ☎ *831/423–0928* 🌐 *www.richardschmidt.com* 🎫 *From $100.*

ZIPLINING

Mount Hermon Adventures

TOUR—SPORTS | Zipline through the redwoods at this adventure center in the Santa Cruz Mountains. On some summer weekends there's an aerial adventure course with obstacles and challenges in the redwoods. ■ **TIP→ To participate (reservations essential), you must be at least 10 years old and at least 54 inches tall, and weigh between 75 and 250 pounds.** ✉ *17 Conference Dr., 9 miles north of downtown Santa Cruz near Felton, Mount Hermon* ☎ *831/430–4357* 🌐 *mounthermonadventures.com* 🎫 *From $79.*

Chapter 13

SEQUOIA AND KINGS CANYON NATIONAL PARKS

Updated by Cheryl Crabtree

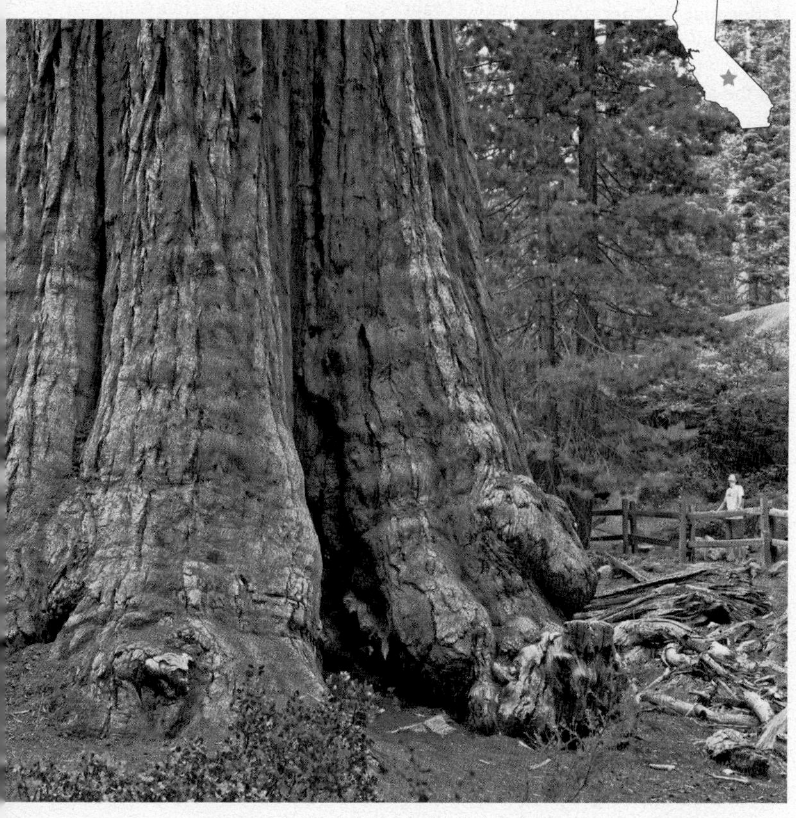

Camping ★★★★☆ | Hotels ★★★★☆ | Activities ★★★★☆ | Scenery ★★★★★ | Crowds ★★★☆☆

WELCOME TO SEQUOIA AND KINGS CANYON NATIONAL PARKS

TOP REASONS TO GO

★ **Gentle giants:** You'll feel small—in a good way—walking among some of the world's largest living things in Sequoia's Giant Forest and Kings Canyon's Grant Grove.

★ **Because it's there:** You can't even glimpse it from the main part of Sequoia, but the sight of majestic Mt. Whitney is worth the trip to the eastern face of the High Sierra.

★ **Underground exploration:** Far older even than the giant sequoias, the gleaming limestone formations in Crystal Cave will draw you along dark, marble passages.

★ **A grander-than-Grand Canyon:** Drive the twisting Kings Canyon Scenic Byway down into the jagged, granite Kings River canyon, deeper in parts than the Grand Canyon.

★ **Regal solitude:** To spend a day or two hiking in a subalpine world of your own, pick one of the many trailheads at Mineral King.

1 **Giant Forest–Lodgepole Village.** One of Sequoia's most visited areas has major sights such as Giant Forest, General Sherman Tree, Crystal Cave, and Moro Rock.

2 **Grant Grove Village–Redwood Canyon.** The "thumb" of Kings Canyon is its busiest section, where Grant Grove, General Grant Tree, Panoramic Point, and Big Stump are the main draws.

3 **Cedar Grove.** The drive through the high-country of Kings Canyon to Cedar Grove Village, on the canyon floor, reveals magnificent granite formations of varied hues. Rock meets river in breathtaking fashion at Zumwalt Meadow.

4 **Mineral King.** In Sequoia's southeast section, the highest road-accessible part of the park is a good place to hike, camp, and soak up the grandeur of the Sierra Nevada.

5 **Mt. Whitney.** The highest peak in the Lower 48 stands on the eastern edge of Sequoia; to get there from Giant Forest you must either backpack eight days through the mountains or drive nearly 300 miles around the park to its other side.

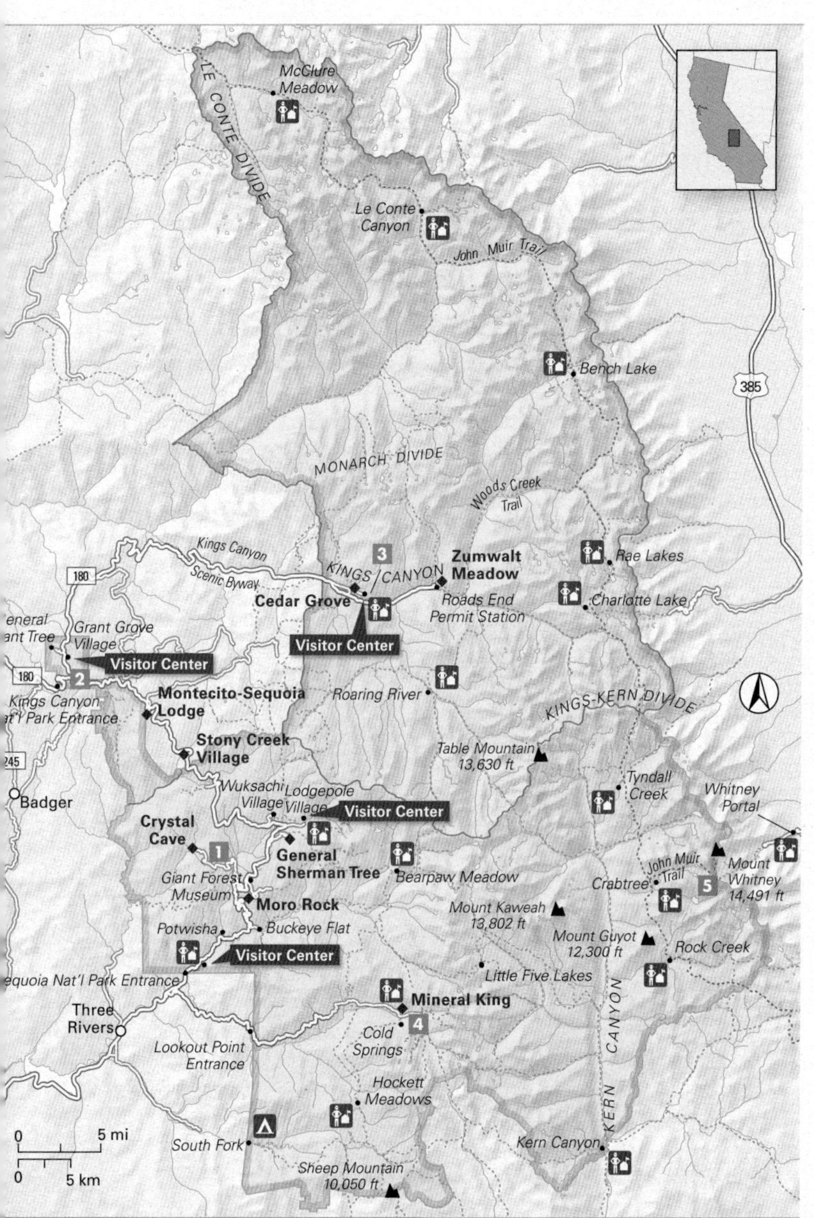
LE CONTE DIVIDE
McClure Meadow
Le Conte Canyon
John Muir Trail
Bench Lake
385
MONARCH DIVIDE
Woods Creek Trail
Kings Canyon Scenic Byway
180
3
KINGS CANYON
Zumwalt Meadow
Cedar Grove
Roads End Permit Station
Rae Lakes
Charlotte Lake
Visitor Center
Grant Grove Village
Visitor Center
180
2
Kings Canyon Nat'l Park Entrance
Montecito-Sequoia Lodge
Roaring River
KINGS-KERN DIVIDE
Stony Creek Village
Table Mountain 13,630 ft
245
Badger
Wuksachi Village
Lodgepole Village
Visitor Center
Crystal Cave
1
General Sherman Tree
Tyndall Creek
Whitney Portal
Mount Whitney 14,491 ft
John Muir Trail
Crabtree
5
Bearpaw Meadow
Giant Forest Museum
Moro Rock
Mount Kaweah 13,802 ft
Potwisha
Buckeye Flat
Mount Guyot 12,300 ft
Rock Creek
Visitor Center
Sequoia Nat'l Park Entrance
Little Five Lakes
Mineral King
Three Rivers
4
Cold Springs
KERN CANYON
Lookout Point Entrance
Hockett Meadows
0
5 mi
0
5 km
South Fork
Kern Canyon
Sheep Mountain 10,050 ft

The word "exceptional" best describes these two parks, which offer some of the nation's greatest escapes. Drives along their byways deliver stunning vistas at nearly every turn. Varied ecosystems provide opportunities for repeat adventures, among them hikes to groves of giant sequoias—some of the planet's largest, and oldest, living organisms.

This rare species of tree grows only at certain elevations and in particular environments on the Central Sierra's western slopes. Their monstrously thick trunks and branches, remarkably shallow root systems, and neck-craning heights really are almost impossible to believe, as is the fact they can live for more than 2,500 years. Several Native American groups lived among these magnificent trees for thousands of years before modern visitors arrived. By the late 1800s, word of the giant sequoias (*Sequoiadendron giganteum*) had spread, attracting logging enterprises and mobilizing those who wanted to protect these living treasures.

Sequoia National Park—the nation's second oldest after Yellowstone—was established in 1890, officially preserving the world's largest sequoia groves in the Giant Forest and other areas of the park. At first, visitors traveled along a pack road to view the towering marvels. In 1903, a road into the Giant Forest allowed access by wagon. It wasn't until 1926, with the opening of the General's Highway, that autos could chug up the mountain. Kings Canyon National Park, which included the General Grant National Park formed a week after Sequoia, was established in 1940.

Today, the two parks, which share a boundary and have been administered jointly since World War II, encompass 865,964 wild and scenic acres between the foothills of California's Central Valley and its eastern borders along the craggy ridgeline of the Sierra's highest peaks. Next to or a few miles off the 46-mile Generals Highway are most of Sequoia National Park's main attractions, as well as Grant Grove Village, the orientation hub for Kings Canyon National Park.

Sequoia includes Mt. Whitney, the highest point in the lower 48 states (although it is impossible to see from the western part of the park and is a chore to ascend from either side). Kings Canyon has two portions: the smaller is shaped like a bent finger and encompasses Grant Grove Village and Redwood Mountain Grove (both with many sequoias), and the larger is home to stunning Kings River Canyon, where unspoiled peaks and valleys are a backpacker's dream.

AVERAGE HIGH/LOW TEMPERATURES (MID-LEVEL ELEVATIONS)					
JAN.	**FEB.**	**MAR.**	**APR.**	**MAY**	**JUNE**
42/24	44/25	46/26	51/30	58/36	68/44
JULY	**AUG.**	**SEPT.**	**OCT.**	**NOV.**	**DEC.**
76/51	76/50	71/45	61/38	50/31	44/27

Planning

When to Go

The best times to visit are spring and fall, when temperatures are moderate and crowds thin. Summertime can draw hordes of tourists to see the giant sequoias, and the few, narrow roads mean congestion at peak holiday times. If you must visit in summer, go during the week. By contrast, in wintertime you may feel as though you have the parks all to yourself. But because of heavy snows, sections of the main park roads can be closed without warning, and low-hanging clouds can move in and obscure mountains and valleys for days. From early October to late April, check road and weather conditions before venturing out. **■TIP→ Even in summer, you can escape hordes of people just walking ¼ to ½ mile off the beaten path on a less-used trail.**

Getting Here and Around

AIR

The closest airport to Sequoia and Kings Canyon national parks is Fresno Yosemite International Airport (FAT).

AIRPORT CONTACTS Fresno Yosemite International Airport. *(FAT) ✉ 5175 E. Clinton Way, Fresno ☎ 800/244–2359 automated info, 559/621–4500 🌐 www.flyfresno.com.*

CAR

Sequoia is 36 miles east of Visalia on Route 198; Grant Grove Village in Kings Canyon is 56 miles east of Fresno on Route 180. There is no automobile entrance on the eastern side of the Sierra. Routes 198 and 180 are connected by Generals Highway, a paved two-lane road (also signed as Highway 198) that sometimes sees delays at peak times due to ongoing improvements. The road is extremely narrow and steep from Route 198 to Giant Forest, so keep an eye on your engine temperature gauge, as the incline and congestion can cause vehicles to overheat; to avoid overheated brakes, use low gears on downgrades.

If you are traveling in an RV or with a trailer, study the restrictions on these vehicles. Do not travel beyond Potwisha Campground on Generals Highway (Route 198) with an RV longer than 22 feet; take straighter, easier Route 180 through the Kings Canyon park entrance instead. Maximum vehicle length on Generals Highway is 40 feet, or 50 feet combined length for vehicles with trailers. For current road and weather conditions, call ☎ *559/565–3341* or visit the park website: 🌐 *www.nps.gov/seki.*

Park Essentials

ACCESSIBILITY

All the visitor centers, the Giant Forest Museum, and Big Trees Trail are wheelchair accessible, as are some short ranger-led walks and talks. General Sherman Tree can be reached via a paved, level trail near a parking area. None of the caves is accessible, and wilderness areas must be reached by horseback or on foot. Some picnic tables are extended to accommodate wheelchairs. Many of the major sites are in the 6,000-foot

Seeing the Parks in One Day

Sequoia National Park in One Day

After overnighting in Visalia or Three Rivers, take off early on Route 198 to the **Sequoia National Park entrance.** Pull over at the **Hospital Rock** picnic area to gaze up at the imposing granite Moro Rock, which you later will climb. Heed signs that advise "10 mph" around tight turns as you climb 3,500 feet on **Generals Highway** to the **Giant Forest Museum.** Spend a half hour here, then examine trees firsthand by circling the lovely **Round Meadow** on the **Big Trees Trail,** to which you must walk from the museum or its parking lot across the road.

Get back in your car, and continue a few miles north on Generals Highway to see the jaw-dropping **General Sherman Tree.** Then set off on the **Congress Trail** so that you can be further awed by the Senate and House big-tree clusters. Buy lunch at the **Lodgepole** complex, 2 miles to the north, and eat at the nearby **Pinewood** picnic area. Now you're ready to climb **Moro Rock.**

You can drive there or, if it is summer, park at the museum lot and take the free shuttle. Count on spending at least an hour for the 350-step ascent and descent, with a pause on top to appreciate the 360-degree view. Next, proceed past the **Tunnel Log** to **Crescent Meadow.** Spend a relaxing hour or two strolling on the trails that pass by, among other things, **Tharp's Log.** By now you've probably renewed your appetite; head to **Lodgepole Grill & Market** or the restaurant at **Wuksachi Lodge.**

Kings Canyon National Park in One Day

Enter the park via the **Kings Canyon Scenic Byway** (Route 180), having spent the night in Fresno or Visalia. Or wake up already in **Grant Grove Village**, perhaps in the **John Muir Lodge.** Stock up for a picnic with takeout from the **Grant Grove Restaurant** or with food from the nearby market. Drive east a mile to see the **General Grant Tree** and compact **Grant Grove's** other sequoias. If it's no later than mid-morning, walk up the short trail at **Panoramic Point,** for a view of Hume Lake and the High Sierra. Either way, return to Route 180, and continue east. Stop at Junction View to take in several peaks towering over Kings Canyon. From here, visit **Boyden Cavern** or continue to **Cedar Grove Village**, pausing along the way at **Grizzly Falls.** Eat at a table by the **South Fork of the Kings River** or on the Cedar Grove Snack Bar's deck. Now you are ready for the day's highlight: strolling **Zumwalt Meadow,** which lies a few miles past the village.

After you have enjoyed that short trail and its views of **Grand Sentinel** and **North Dome**, head to **Roads End**, where backpackers embark for the High Sierra wilderness. Make the return trip—with a stop at **Roaring River Falls**—past Grant Grove and briefly onto southbound **Generals Highway.** Stop at **Redwood Mountain Overlook**, and use binoculars to look down upon the world's largest sequoia grove. Drive another couple of miles to the **Kings Canyon Overlook** to survey some of what you have done today. Make reservations for a late dinner at **Wuksachi Lodge.**

range, and thin air at high elevations can cause respiratory distress for people with breathing difficulties. Carry oxygen if necessary. Contact the park's main number for more information.

PARK FEES AND PERMITS

The admission fee is $35 per vehicle, $30 per motorcycle, and $20 per person for those who enter by bus, on foot, bicycle, horse, or any other mode of transportation; it is valid for seven days in both parks. U.S. residents over the age of 62 pay $80 for a lifetime pass, and permanently disabled U.S. residents are admitted free.

If you plan to camp in the backcountry, you need a permit, which costs $15 for hikers or $30 for stock users (e.g., horseback riders). One permit covers the group. Availability of permits depends upon trailhead quotas. Reservations are accepted by mail or email for a $15 processing fee, beginning March 1, and must be made at least 14 days in advance (☎ *559/565–3766*). Without a reservation, you may still get a permit on a first-come, first-served basis starting at 1 pm the day before you plan to hike. For more information on backcountry camping or travel with pack animals (horses, mules, burros, or llamas), contact the Wilderness Permit Office (☎ *530/565–3766*).

PARK HOURS

The parks are open 24/7 year-round. They are in the Pacific time zone.

CELL PHONE RECEPTION

Cell phone reception is poor to nonexistent in the higher elevations and spotty even on portions of Generals Highway, where you can (on rare clear days) see the Central Valley. Public telephones may be found at the visitor centers, ranger stations, some trailheads, and at all restaurants and lodging facilities in the park.

Hotels

Hotel accommodations in Sequoia and Kings Canyon are limited, and, although they are clean and comfortable, they tend to lack much in-room character. Keep in mind, however, that the extra money you spend on lodging here is offset by the time you'll save by being inside the parks. You won't be faced with a 60- to 90-minute commute from the less-expensive motels in Three Rivers (by far the most charming option), Visalia, or Fresno. Reserve as far in advance as you can, especially for summertime stays.

Restaurants

In Sequoia and Kings Canyon national parks, you can treat yourself (and the family) to a high-quality meal in a wonderful setting in the Peaks restaurant at Wuksachi Lodge, but otherwise you should keep your expectations modest. You can grab bread, spreads, drinks, and fresh produce at one of several small grocery stores for a picnic, or get takeout food from the Grant Grove Restaurant, the Cedar Grove Grill, or one of the two small Lodgepole eateries.

Hotel and restaurant reviews have been shortened. For full information visit Fodors.com. Hotel prices are the lowest cost of a standard double room in high season. Restaurant prices are the average cost of a main course at dinner, or if dinner is not served, at lunch.

What It Costs

	$	$$	$$$	$$$$
RESTAURANTS				
	under $17	$17–$26	$27–$36	over $36
HOTELS				
	under $150	$150–$250	$251–$350	over $350

Tours

★ Sequoia Parks Conservancy Field Institute

SPECIAL-INTEREST | The Sequoia Parks Conservancy's highly regarded educational division conducts half-, single-, and multiday tours that include backpacking hikes, natural-history walks, astronomy programs, snowshoe treks, and custom adventures. ✉ *47050 Generals Hwy., Unit 10, Three Rivers* ☎ *559/565–4251* 🌐 *www.sequoiaparksconservancy.org* 🎫 *From $150 for 2-hr guided tour.*

Sequoia Sightseeing Tours

GUIDED TOURS | This locally owned operator's friendly, knowledgeable guides conduct daily interpretive sightseeing tours in Sequoia and Kings Canyon. Reservations are essential. The company also offers private tours. ✉ *Three Rivers* ☎ *559/561–4189* 🌐 *www.sequoiatours.com* 🎫 *From $79 tour of Sequoia; from $169 tour of Kings Canyon.*

Visitor Information

NATIONAL PARK SERVICE Foothills Visitor Center. ✉ *47050 Generals Hwy., Rte. 198, 1 mile north of Ash Mountain entrance, Sequoia National Park* ☎ *559/565–3341.*
Sequoia and Kings Canyon National Parks. ✉ *47050 Generals Hwy. (Rte. 198), Three Rivers* ☎ *559/565–3341* 🌐 *nps.gov/seki.*

Sequoia National Park

Sequoia National Park is all about the trees, and to understand the scale of these giants you must walk among them. If you do nothing else, get out of the car for a short stroll through one of the groves. But there is much more to the park than the trees. Try to access one of the vista points that provide a panoramic view over the forested mountains. Generals Highway (which connects Routes 198 and 180) will be your route to most of the park's sights. A few short spur roads lead from the highway to some sights, and Mineral King Road branches off Route 198 to enter the park at Lookout Point, winding east from there to the park's southernmost section.

Giant Forest—Lodgepole Village

Giant Forest is 16 miles from the Sequoia National Park Visitor Center.

The Sequoia National Park entrance at Ash Mountain is the main gateway to the Giant Forest and many of the park's major sights. From there, the narrow, twisty General's Highway snakes up the mountain from a 1,700-foot elevation through the Giant Forest (a 45-minute drive from the entrance) up to 6,720 feet at Lodgepole Village.

Sights

HISTORIC SIGHTS

Giant Forest Museum

MUSEUM | Well-imagined and interactive displays at this worthwhile stop provide the basics about sequoias, of which there are 2,161 with diameters exceeding 10 feet in the approximately 2,000-acre Giant Forest. ✉ *Sequoia National Park* ✣ *Generals Hwy., 4 miles south of Lodgepole Visitor Center* ☎ *559/565–4436* 🎫 *Free* ☞ *Shuttle: Giant Forest or Moro Rock–Crescent Meadow.*

SCENIC DRIVES

★ Generals Highway

SCENIC DRIVE | One of California's most scenic drives, this 46-mile road (also signed as Route 198) is the main asphalt artery between Sequoia and Kings Canyon national parks. Named after the landmark Grant and Sherman trees that leave so many visitors awestruck, Generals Highway runs from Sequoia's Foothills Visitor Center north to Kings Canyon's Grant Grove Village. Along the way, it passes the turnoff to Crystal Cave, the Giant Forest Museum, Lodgepole Village, and other popular attractions. The lower portion, from Hospital Rock to the Giant Forest, is especially steep and winding. If your vehicle is 22 feet or longer, avoid that stretch by entering the parks via Route 180 (from Fresno) rather than Route 198 (from Visalia or Three Rivers). Take your time on this road—there's a lot to see, and wildlife can scamper across at any time. ✉ *Sequoia National Park.*

SCENIC STOPS

Auto Log

FOREST | Before its wood showed signs of severe rot, cars drove right on top of this giant fallen sequoia. Now it's a great place to pose for pictures or shoot a video. ✉ *Sequoia National Park* ✣ *Moro Rock–Crescent Meadow Rd., 1 mile south of Giant Forest.*

Crescent Meadow

TRAIL | A sea of ferns signals your arrival at what John Muir called the "gem of the Sierra." Walk around for an hour or two, and you might decide that the Scotland-born naturalist was exaggerating a bit, but the verdant meadow is quite pleasant, and you just might see a bear. Wildflowers bloom here throughout the summer. ✉ *Sequoia National Park* ✣ *End of Moro Rock–Crescent Meadow Rd., 2.6 miles east off Generals Hwy.* ☞ *Shuttle: Moro Rock–Crescent Meadow.*

★ Crystal Cave

CAVE | One of more than 200 caves in Sequoia and Kings Canyon, Crystal Cave is composed largely of marble, the result of limestone being hardened under heat and pressure. It contains several eye-popping formations. There used to be more, but some were damaged or obliterated by early-20th-century dynamite blasting. You can see the cave only on a tour. The Daily Tour ($17), a great overview, takes about 50 minutes. To immerse yourself in the cave experience—at times you'll be crawling on your belly—book the exhilarating Wild Cave Tour ($140). Availability is limited—reserve tickets at least 48 hours in advance at 🌐 *www.recreation.gov* or stop by either the Foothills or Lodgepole visitor center first thing in the morning to try to nab a same-day ticket; they're not sold at the cave itself. ✉ *Crystal Cave Rd., off Generals Hwy.* ☎ *877/444–6777* 🌐 *www.sequoiaparksconservancy.org/crystalcave.html* 🎫 *$17* ⏲ *Closed Oct.–late May.*

★ General Sherman Tree

LOCAL INTEREST | The 274.9-foot-tall General Sherman is one of the world's tallest and oldest sequoias, and it ranks No. 1 in volume, adding the equivalent of a 60-foot-tall tree every year to its approximately 52,500 cubic feet of mass. The tree doesn't grow taller, though—it's dead at the top. A short, wheelchair-accessible trail leads to the tree from Generals Highway, but the main trail (½ mile) winds down from a parking lot off Wolverton Road. The walk back up the main trail is steep, but benches along the way provide rest for the short of breath. ✉ *Sequoia National Park* ✣ *Main trail Wolverton Rd. off Generals Hwy. (Rte. 198)* ☞ *Shuttle: Giant Forest or Wolverton–Sherman Tree.*

★ Moro Rock

NATURE SITE | This sight offers panoramic views to those fit and determined enough to mount its 350 or so steps. In a case where the journey rivals the destination, Moro's stone stairway is so impressive in its twisty inventiveness that it's on the National Register of Historic Places. The rock's 6,725-foot summit overlooks the Middle Fork Canyon, sculpted by the Kaweah River and approaching the depth of Arizona's Grand Canyon, although smoggy, hazy air often compromises the view. ✉ *Sequoia National Park* ✣ *Moro Rock–Crescent Meadow Rd., 2 miles east off Generals Hwy. (Rte. 198) to parking area* ☞ *Shuttle: Moro Rock–Crescent Meadow.*

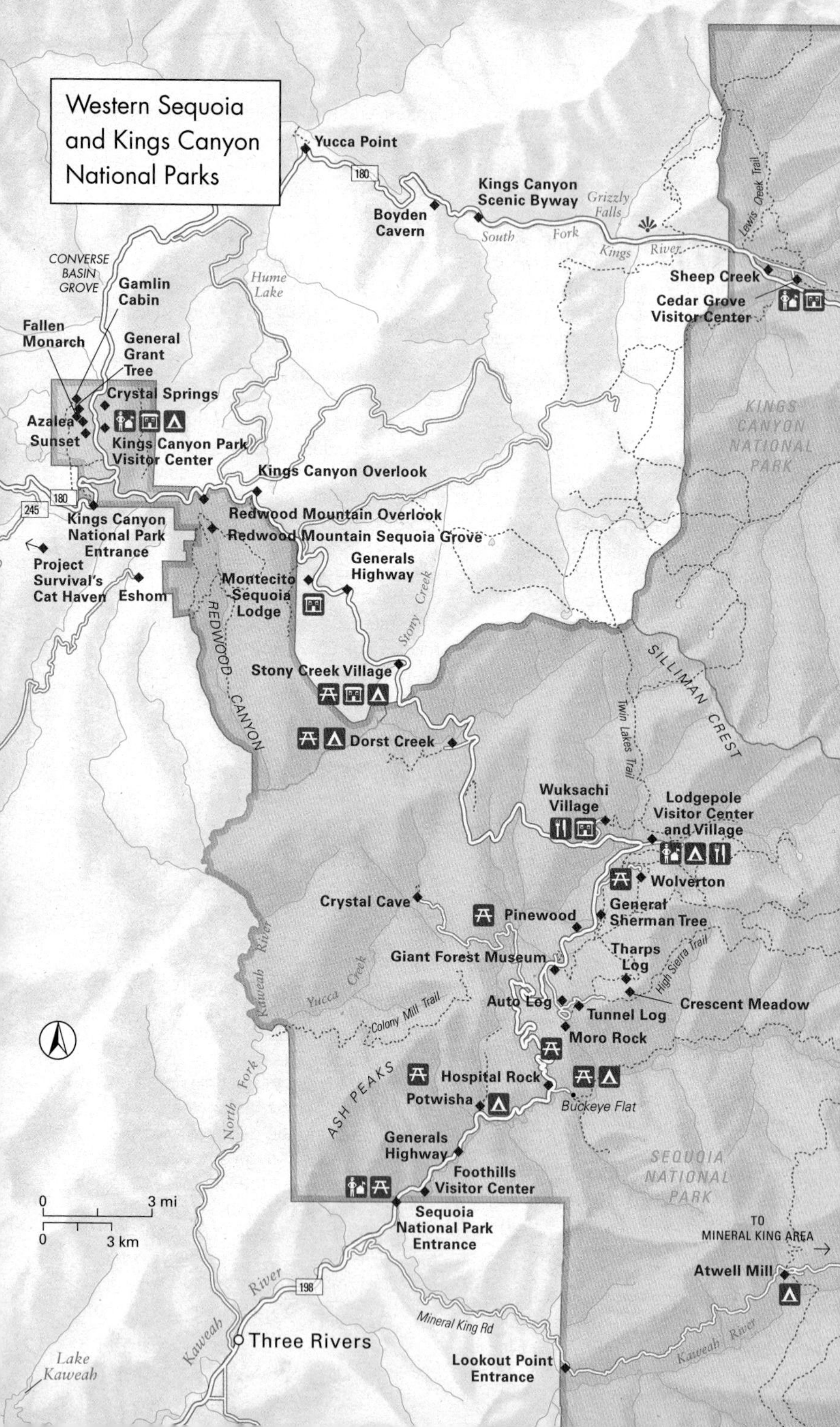
Western Sequoia and Kings Canyon National Parks
Yucca Point
180
Boyden Cavern
Kings Canyon Scenic Byway
Grizzly Falls
South Fork Kings River
Lewis Creek Trail
Sheep Creek
Cedar Grove Visitor Center
CONVERSE BASIN GROVE
Gamlin Cabin
Hume Lake
Fallen Monarch
General Grant Tree
Crystal Springs
Azalea
Sunset
Kings Canyon Park Visitor Center
KINGS CANYON NATIONAL PARK
Kings Canyon Overlook
180
245
Kings Canyon National Park Entrance
Redwood Mountain Overlook
Redwood Mountain Sequoia Grove
Project Survival's Cat Haven
Eshom
Montecito Sequoia Lodge
Generals Highway
Stony Creek
REDWOOD CANYON
Stony Creek Village
SILLIMAN CREST
Twin Lakes Trail
Dorst Creek
Wuksachi Village
Lodgepole Visitor Center and Village
Wolverton
Crystal Cave
Pinewood
General Sherman Tree
Giant Forest Museum
Tharps Log
High Sierra Trail
Kaweah River
Yucca Creek
Colony Mill Trail
Auto Log
Tunnel Log
Crescent Meadow
Moro Rock
ASH PEAKS
Hospital Rock
Potwisha
Buckeye Flat
North Fork
Generals Highway
Foothills Visitor Center
SEQUOIA NATIONAL PARK
0
3 mi
0
3 km
Sequoia National Park Entrance
TO MINERAL KING AREA
Atwell Mill
River
198
Mineral King Rd
Kaweah River
Three Rivers
Kaweah
Lake Kaweah
Lookout Point Entrance

Tunnel Log

LOCAL INTEREST | This 275-foot tree fell in 1937, and soon a 17-foot-wide, 8-foot-high hole was cut through it for vehicular passage (not to mention the irresistible photograph) that continues today. Large vehicles take the nearby bypass. ✉ *Sequoia National Park* ✥ *Moro Rock–Crescent Meadow Rd., 2 miles east of Generals Hwy. (Rte. 198)* ☞ *Shuttle: Moro Rock–Crescent Meadow.*

TRAILS

★ Big Trees Trail

TRAIL | The 0.7-mile, wheelchair-accessible portion of this path is a must, as it does not take long, and the setting is spectacular: beautiful Round Meadow, surrounded by many mature sequoias. Well-thought-out interpretive signs along the way explain the ecology on display. Parking at the trailhead lot off Generals Highway is for cars with handicap placards only. The full, round-trip loop from the Giant Forest Museum is about a mile long. *Easy.* ✉ *Sequoia National Park* ✥ *Trailhead: Off Generals Hwy. (Rte. 198), near the Giant Forest Museum* ☞ *Shuttle: Giant Forest.*

★ Congress Trail

TRAIL | This 2-mile trail, arguably the best hike in the parks in terms of natural beauty, is a paved loop that begins near General Sherman Tree. You'll get close-up views of more big trees here than on any other Sequoia hike. Watch for the clusters known as the House and Senate. The President Tree, also on the trail, supplanted the General Grant Tree in 2012 as the world's second largest in volume (behind the General Sherman). An offshoot of the Congress Trail leads to Crescent Meadow, where, in summer, you can catch a free shuttle back to the Sherman parking lot. *Easy.* ✉ *Sequoia National Park* ✥ *Trailhead: Off Generals Hwy. (Rte. 198), 2 miles north of Giant Forest* ☞ *Shuttle: Giant Forest.*

Crescent Meadow Trails

TRAIL | A 1-mile trail loops around lush Crescent Meadow to Tharp's Log, a cabin built from a fire-hollowed sequoia. From there you can embark on a 60-mile trek to Mt. Whitney, if you're prepared and have the time. Brilliant wildflowers bloom here in midsummer. *Easy.* ✉ *Sequoia National Park* ✥ *Trailhead: The end of Moro Rock–Crescent Meadow Rd., 2.6 miles east off Generals Hwy. (Rte. 198)* ☞ *Shuttle: Moro Rock–Crescent Meadow.*

Little Baldy Trail

TRAIL | Climbing 700 vertical feet in 1¾ miles of switchbacking, this trail ends at a granite dome with a great view of the peaks of the Mineral King area and the Great Western Divide. The walk to the summit and back takes about four hours. *Moderate.* ✉ *Sequoia National Park* ✥ *Trailhead: Little Baldy Saddle, Generals Hwy. (Rte. 198), 9 miles north of General Sherman Tree* ☞ *Shuttle: Lodgepole-Wuksachi-Dorst.*

Marble Falls Trail

TRAIL | The 3.7-mile trail to Marble Falls crosses through the rugged foothills before reaching the cascading water. Plan on three to four hours one-way. *Moderate.* ✉ *Sequoia National Park* ✥ *Trailhead: Off dirt road across from concrete ditch near site 17 at Potwisha Campground, off Generals Hwy. (Rte. 198).*

Muir Grove Trail

TRAIL | You will attain solitude and possibly see a bear or two on this unheralded gem of a hike, a 4-mile round-trip from the Dorst Creek Campground. The remote grove is small but lovely, its soundtrack provided solely by nature. The trailhead is subtly marked. In summer, park in the amphitheater lot and walk down toward the group campsite area. *Easy.* ✉ *Sequoia National Park* ✥ *Trailhead: Dorst Creek Campground, Generals Hwy. (Rte. 198), 8 miles north of Lodgepole Visitor Center* ☞ *Shuttle: Lodgepole-Wuksachi-Dorst.*

Tokopah Falls Trail

TRAIL | This trail with a 500-foot elevation gain follows the Marble Fork of the Kaweah River for 1¾ miles one-way and dead-ends below the impressive granite cliffs and cascading waterfall of Tokopah Canyon. The trail passes through a mixed-conifer forest. It takes 2½ to 4 hours to make the round-trip journey. *Moderate.* ✉ *Sequoia National Park* ✥ *Trailhead: Off Generals Hwy. (Rte. 198), ¼ mile north of Lodgepole Campground* ☞ *Shuttle: Lodgepole-Wuksachi-Dorst.*

VISITOR CENTERS

Lodgepole Visitor Center

INFO CENTER | Along with exhibits on the area's history, geology, and wildlife, the center screens an outstanding 22-minute film about bears. You can buy books, maps, wilderness permits, and tickets to cave tours here. ✉ *Sequoia National Park* ✥ *Generals Hwy. (Rte. 198), 21 miles north of Ash Mountain entrance* ☎ *559/565–3341* ⏲ *Closed Oct.–Apr.* ☞ *Shuttle: Giant Forest or Wuksachi-Lodgepole-Dorst.*

Restaurants

Lodgepole Market and Café

$ | CAFÉ | The choices here run the gamut from simple to very simple, with several counters only a few strides apart in a central eating complex. The café also sells fresh and prepackaged salads, sandwiches, and wraps. **Known for:** quick and convenient dining; many healthful options; grab-and-go items for picnics. [$] *Average main: $12* ✉ *Next to Lodgepole Visitor Center* ☎ *559/565–3301* 🌐 *www.visitsequoia.com/dine/lodgepole-dining.*

The Peaks

$$$ | MODERN AMERICAN | Huge windows run the length of the Wuksachi Lodge's high-ceilinged dining room, and a large fireplace on the far wall warms both body and soul. The diverse dinner menu—by far the best at both parks—reflects a commitment to locally sourced and sustainable products. **Known for:** seasonal menus with fresh local ingredients; great views of sequoia grove; box lunches. [$] *Average main: $28* ✉ *Wuksachi Lodge, 64740 Wuksachi Way, Wuksachi Village* ☎ *559/625–7700* 🌐 *www.visitsequoia.com/dine/the-peaks-restaurant.*

Hotels

★ **Wuksachi Lodge**

$$ | HOTEL | The striking cedar-and-stone main building is a fine example of how a structure can blend effectively with lovely mountain scenery. **Pros:** best place to stay in the parks; lots of wildlife; easy access to hiking and snowshoe/ski trails. **Cons:** rooms can be small; main lodge is a few-minutes' walk from guest rooms; slow Wi-Fi. [$] *Rooms from: $229* ✉ *64740 Wuksachi Way, Wuksachi Village* ☎ *559/625–7700, 888/252–5757 reservations* 🌐 *www.visitsequoia.com/lodging/wuksachi-lodge* 🛏 *102 rooms* 🍽 *No meals.*

Mineral King

25 miles east of Generals Hwy. (Rte. 198) via Mineral King Rd.

A subalpine valley of fir, pine, and sequoia trees with myriad lakes and hiking trails, Mineral King sits at 7,500 feet at the end of a steep, winding road. This is the highest point to which you can drive in the park. It is open only from Memorial Day through late October.

Sights

SCENIC DRIVES

Mineral King Road

SCENIC DRIVE | Vehicles longer than 22 feet are prohibited on this side road into southern Sequoia National Park, and for good reason: it's smaller than a regular two-lane road, some sections are unpaved, and it contains 589 twists and turns. Anticipating an average speed of 20 mph is optimistic. The scenery is splendid as you climb nearly 6,000 feet from Three Rivers to the Mineral King Area. In addition to maneuvering the blind curves and narrow stretches, you might find yourself sharing the pavement with bears, rattlesnakes, and even softball-size spiders. Allow 90 minutes each way. ✉ *Sequoia National Forest* ✥ *East off Sierra Dr. (Rte. 198), 3 ½ miles northeast of Three Rivers* ⏲ *Road typically closed Nov.–late May.*

TRAILS

Mineral King Trails

TRAIL | Many trails to the high country begin at Mineral King. Two popular day hikes are Eagle Lake (6.8 miles round-trip) and Timber Gap (4.4 miles round-trip). At the Mineral King Ranger Station (☎ *559/565–3768*) you can pick up maps and check about conditions from late May to late September. *Difficult.* ✉ *Sequoia National Park* ✥ *Trailheads: At end of Mineral King Rd., 25 miles east of Generals Hwy. (Rte. 198).*

VISITOR CENTERS

Mineral King Ranger Station

INFO CENTER | The station's small visitor center has exhibits on area history. Wilderness permits and some books and maps are available. ✉ *Sequoia National Park* ✥ *Mineral King Rd., 24 miles east of Rte. 198* ☎ *559/565–3341* ☞ *Typically closed mid-Sept.–mid-May.*

Hotels

Silver City Mountain Resort

$$$ | **RESORT** | High on Mineral King Road, this privately owned resort has rustic cabins and deluxe chalets—all with a stove, refrigerator, and sink—plus three hotel rooms with private baths. **Pros:** rustic setting; friendly staff; great location for hikers. **Cons:** long, winding road is not for everybody; not much entertainment except hiking; some units have shared baths. $ *Rooms from: $170* ✉ *Sequoia National Park* ✥ *Mineral King Rd., 21 miles southeast of Rte. 198* ☎ *559/242–3510, 559/561–1322 reservations* 🌐 *www.silvercityresort.com* ⏲ *Closed Nov.–late May* 🛏 *16 units* 🍽 *No meals.*

Mt. Whitney

276 miles by car from Sequoia National Park/Foothills Visitor Center (looping around the Sierra Nevada) on U.S. 395, 60 miles on foot (an 8-day trek) along Mt. Whitney Trail.

At 14,494 feet, Mt. Whitney is the highest point in the contiguous United States and the crown jewel of Sequoia National Park's wild eastern side. The peak looms high above the tiny, high-mountain desert community of Lone Pine, where numerous Hollywood Westerns have been filmed. The high mountain ranges, arid landscape, and scrubby brush of the eastern Sierra are beautiful in their vastness and austerity.

Despite the mountain's scale, you can't see it from the more traveled west side of the park because it is hidden behind the Great Western Divide. The only way to access Mt. Whitney from the main part of the park is to circumnavigate the Sierra Nevada via a 10-hour, nearly 400-mile drive outside the park. No road ascends the peak; the best vantage point from which to catch a glimpse of the mountain is at the end of Whitney Portal Road. The 13 miles of winding road leads from U.S. 395 at Lone Pine to the trailhead for the hiking route to the top of the mountain. Whitney Portal Road is closed in winter.

Sights

TRAILS

Mt. Whitney Trail

TRAIL | The most popular route to the summit, the Mt. Whitney Trail can be conquered by very fit and experienced hikers. If there's snow on the mountain, this is a challenge for expert mountaineers only. All overnighters must have a permit, as must day hikers on the trail beyond Lone Pine Lake, about 2½ miles from the trailhead. From May through October, permits are distributed via a lottery run each February by 🌐 *recreation.gov*. The Eastern Sierra Interagency Visitor Center (☎ *760/876–6200*), on Route 136 at U.S. 395 about a mile south of Lone Pine, is a good resource for information about permits and hiking. ⊠ *Kings Canyon National Park* ☎ *760/873–2483 trail reservations* 🌐 *www.fs.usda.gov/inyo*.

Activities

BIRD-WATCHING

More than 200 species of birds inhabit Sequoia and Kings Canyon national parks. Not seen in most parts of the United States, the white-headed woodpecker and the pileated woodpecker are common in most mid-elevation areas here. There are also many hawks and owls, including the renowned spotted owl. Due to the changes in elevation, both parks have diverse species ranging from warblers, kingbirds, thrushes, and sparrows in the foothills to goshawk, blue grouse, red-breasted nuthatch, and brown creeper at the highest elevations. The Sequoia Parks Conservancy (☎ *559/565–4251* 🌐 *www.sequoiaparksconservancy.org*) has information about bird-watching in the southern Sierra.

CAMPING

Some campgrounds are open year-round, others only seasonally. Except for Bearpaw (around $350 a night including meals), fees at the campgrounds range from $22 to $45, depending on location and size. There are no RV hookups at any of the campgrounds. Expect a table and a fire ring with a grill at standard sites. You can make reservations (book as far ahead as possible) at Bearpaw, Dorst Creek, Lodgepole, and Potwisha. The rest are first-come, first-served. The Lodgepole and Dorst Creek campgrounds can be quite busy in the summer and are popular with families. Black bears are prevalent in these areas; carefully follow all posted instructions about food storage. Bear-proof metal containers are provided at many campgrounds.

Atwell Mill Campground. At 6,650 feet, this peaceful, tent-only campground is just south of the Western Divide. ⊠ *Mineral King Rd., 20 miles east of Rte. 198* ☎ *559/565–3341*.

Bearpaw High Sierra Camp. Classy camping is the order of the day at this tent hotel and restaurant. Make reservations starting on January 2. ⊠ *High Sierra Trail, 11.5 miles from Lodgepole Village* ☎ *866/807–3598* 🌐 *www.visitsequoia.com*.

Buckeye Flat Campground. This tents-only campground at the southern end of Sequoia National Park is smaller—and consequently quieter—than campgrounds elsewhere in the park. Because of its low elevation (2,800 feet), it's hot in summer. ⊠ *Generals Hwy., 6 miles north of Foothills Visitor Center* ☎ *559/784–1500*.

Dorst Creek Campground. Wildlife sightings are common at this large campground at elevation 6,700 feet. ⊠ *Generals Hwy., 8 miles north of Lodgepole Visitor Center* ☎ *559/565–3341, 877/444–6777*.

Lodgepole Campground. The largest Lodgepole-area campground is also the noisiest, though things quiet down at night. ⊠ *Off Generals Hwy. beyond Lodgepole Village* ☎ *559/565–3341, 877/444–6777*.

Potwisha Campground. On the Marble Fork of the Kaweah River, this midsize, year-round campground at an elevation of 2,100 feet gets no snow in winter and can be hot in summer. ✉ *Generals Hwy., 4 miles north of Foothills Visitor Center* ☎ *559/565–3341, 877/444–6777.*

CROSS-COUNTRY SKIING

Alta Market and Ski Shop

SKIING/SNOWBOARDING | Rent cross-country skis and snowshoes here. Depending on snowfall amounts, instruction may also be available. Reservations are recommended. Marked trails cut through Giant Forest, about 5 miles south of Wuksachi Lodge. ✉ *Sequoia National Park* ✥ *At Lodgepole, off Generals Hwy. (Rte. 198)* ☎ *559/565–3301* ☞ *Shuttle: Wuksachi-Lodgepole-Dorst.*

EDUCATIONAL PROGRAMS

Free Nature Programs

WILDLIFE-WATCHING | Almost any summer day, ½-hour to 1½-hour ranger talks and walks explore subjects such as the life of the sequoia, the geology of the park, and the habits of bears. Giant Forest Museum, Lodgepole Visitor Center, and Wuksachi Village are frequent starting points. Look for less frequent tours in the winter from Grant Grove. Check bulletin boards throughout the park for the week's offerings. 🌐 *www.sequoiaparks-conservancy.org.*

Junior Ranger Program

HIKING/WALKING | **FAMILY** | Children over age five can earn a patch upon completion of a fun set of age-appropriate tasks outlined in the Junior Ranger booklet. Pick one up at any visitor center. ☎ *559/565–3341.*

Sequoia Parks Conservancy Evening Programs

HIKING/WALKING | The Sequoia Parks Conservancy offers hikes and evening lectures during the summer and winter. The popular Wonders of the Night Sky programs celebrate the often stunning views of the heavens experienced at both parks year-round. ✉ *Sequoia National Park* ☎ *559/565–4251* 🌐 *www.sequoiaparksconservancy.org.*

Sequoia Parks Conservancy Seminars

WILDLIFE-WATCHING | Expert naturalists lead seminars on a range of topics, including birds, wildflowers, geology, botany, photography, park history, backpacking, and pathfinding. Reservations are required. Information about times and prices is available at the visitor centers or through the Sequoia Parks Conservancy. ✉ *Sequoia National Park* ☎ *559/565–4251* 🌐 *www.sequoiaparksconservancy.org.*

FISHING

There's limited trout fishing in the creeks and rivers from late April to mid-November. The Kaweah River is a popular spot; check at visitor centers for open and closed waters. Some of the park's secluded backcountry lakes have good fishing. A California fishing license, required for persons 16 and older, costs about $16 for one day, $24 for two days, and $48 for 10 days (discounts are available for state residents and others). For park regulations, closures, and restrictions, call the parks at ☎ *559/565–3341* or stop at a visitor center. Licenses and fishing tackle are usually available at Hume Lake.

California Department of Fish and Game

FISHING | The department supplies fishing licenses and provides a full listing of regulations. ☎ *916/928–5805* 🌐 *www.wildlife.ca.gov.*

HORSEBACK RIDING

Grant Grove Stables

HORSEBACK RIDING | Grant Grove Stables isn't too far from parts of Sequoia National Park and is perfect for short rides from June to September. Reservations are recommended. ☎ *559/335–9292 summer* 🌐 *www.nps.gov/seki/planyourvisit/horseride.htm* 💵 *From $50.*

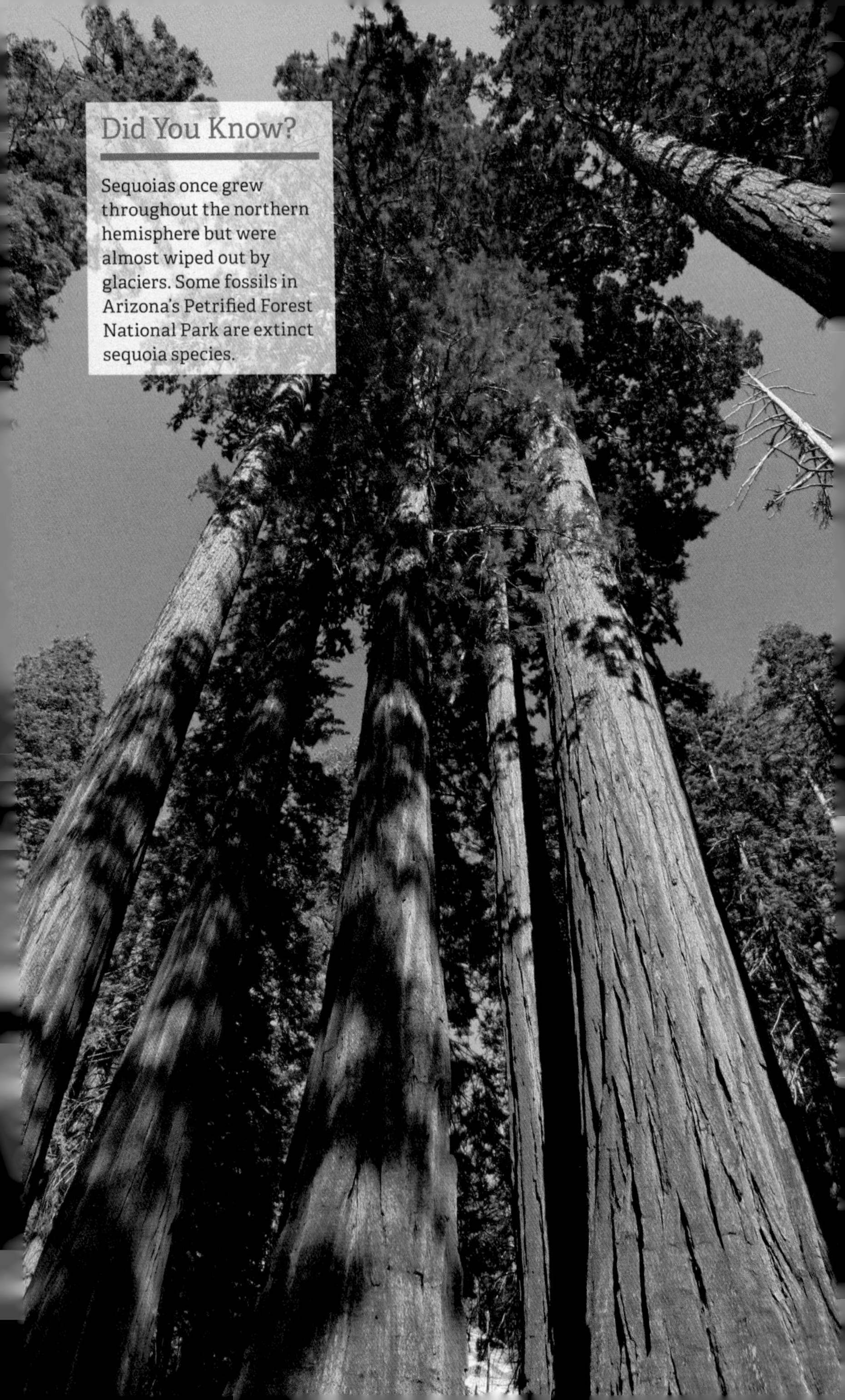
Did You Know?
Sequoias once grew throughout the northern hemisphere but were almost wiped out by glaciers. Some fossils in Arizona's Petrified Forest National Park are extinct sequoia species.

Horse Corral Packers

HORSEBACK RIDING | One- and two-hour trips through Sequoia are available for beginning and advanced riders. ✉ *Big Meadow Rd., 12 miles east of Generals Hwy. (Rte. 198) between Sequoia and Kings Canyon national parks* ☎ *559/565–3404 summer, 559/565–6429 off-season,* 🌐 *hcpacker.com* 🎫 *From $50.*

Kings Canyon National Park

Kings Canyon National Park consists of two sections that adjoin the northern boundary of Sequoia National Park. The western portion, covered with sequoia and pine forest, contains the park's most visited sights, such as Grant Grove. The vast eastern portion is remote high country, slashed across half its southern breadth by the deep, rugged Kings River canyon. Separating the two is Sequoia National Forest, which encompasses Giant Sequoia National Monument. The Kings Canyon Scenic Byway (Route 180) links the major sights within and between the park's two sections.

Grant Grove Village—Redwood Canyon

56 miles east of Fresno on Rte. 180, 26 miles north of Lodgepole Village in Sequoia National Park.

Grant Grove Village, home to the Kings Canyon Visitor Center, Grant Grove Cabins, John Muir Lodge, a market, and two restaurants, anchors the northwestern section of the park. Nearby attractions include the General Grant Tree and Redwood Canyon sequia grove. The Kings Canyon Scenic Byway begins here and travels 30 miles down to the Kings River Canyon and Cedar Grove.

Sights

HISTORIC SIGHTS

Fallen Monarch

TOUR—SIGHT | This toppled sequoia's hollow base was used in the second half of the 19th century as a home for settlers, a saloon, and even a U.S. Cavalry stable. As you walk through it (assuming entry is permitted, which is not always the case), notice how little the wood has decayed, and imagine yourself tucked safely inside, sheltered from a storm or protected from the searing heat. ✉ *Kings Canyon National Park* ✣ *Grant Grove Trail, 1 mile north of Kings Canyon Park Visitor Center.*

Gamlin Cabin

BUILDING | Despite being listed on the National Register of Historic Places, this replica of a modest 1872 pioneer cabin is only borderline historical. The structure, which was moved and rebuilt several times over the years, once served as U.S. Cavalry storage space and, in the early 20th century, a ranger station. ✉ *Grant Grove Trail.*

SCENIC DRIVES

★ Kings Canyon Scenic Byway

SCENIC DRIVE | The 30-mile stretch of Route 180 between Grant Grove Village and Zumwalt Meadow delivers eye-popping scenery—granite cliffs, a roaring river, waterfalls, and Kings River canyon itself—much of which you can experience at vista points or on easy walks. The canyon comes into view about 10 miles east of the village at **Junction View.** Five miles beyond, at **Yucca Point,** the canyon is thousands of feet deeper than the more famous Grand Canyon. **Canyon View,** a special spot 1 mile east of the Cedar Grove Village turnoff, showcases evidence of the area's glacial history. Here, perhaps more than anywhere else, you'll understand why John Muir compared Kings Canyon vistas with those in Yosemite. ■ **TIP→ Note that this byway is a dead-end road—you have to turn around and head back the way you came.**

The drive takes about an hour each way without stops. ✉ *Kings Canyon National Park ✣ Rte. 180 north and east of Grant Grove village.*

SCENIC STOPS

Boyden Cavern

NATURE SITE | The Kings River has carved out hundreds of caverns, including Boyden, which brims with stalagmite, stalactite, drapery, flowstone, and other formations. In summer, the Bat Grotto shelters a slew of bats. If you can't make it to Crystal Cave in Sequoia, Boyden is a reasonable substitute. Regular tours take about 45 minutes and start with a steep walk uphill. ✉ *Sequoia National Forest, 74101 E. Kings Canyon Rd. (Rte. 180), between Grant Grove and Cedar Grove* ☎ *888/965–8243* 🌐 *boydencavern.com* 🎫 *$16.*

General Grant Tree

LOCAL INTEREST | President Coolidge proclaimed this to be the "nation's Christmas tree," and, 30 years later, President Eisenhower designated it as a living shrine to all Americans who have died in wars. Bigger at its base than the General Sherman Tree, it tapers more quickly. It's estimated to be the world's third-largest sequoia by volume. A spur trail winds behind the tree, where scars from a long-ago fire remain visible. ✉ *Kings Canyon National Park ✣ Trailhead: 1 mile north of Grant Grove Visitor Center.*

Project Survival's Cat Haven

ZOO | Take the rare opportunity to glimpse a Siberian lynx, a clouded leopard, a Bengal tiger, and other endangered wild cats at this conservation facility that shelters more than 30 big cats. A guided hour-long tour along a ¼-mile walkway leads to fenced habitat areas shaded by trees and overlooking the Central Valley. ✉ *38257 E. Kings Canyon Rd. (Rte. 180), 15 miles west of Kings Canyon National Park, Dunlap* ☎ *559/338–3216* 🌐 *cathaven.com* 🎫 *$15* ⏲ *Closed Tues. May–Sept. Closed Tues. and Wed. Oct.–Apr.*

Redwood Mountain Sequoia Grove

FOREST | One of the world's largest sequoia groves, Redwood contains within its 2,078 acres nearly 2,200 specimens whose diameters exceed 10 feet. You can view the grove from afar at an overlook or hike 6 to 10 miles via moderate loop trails down into the richest regions, which include two of the world's 25 heaviest trees. ✉ *Kings Canyon National Park ✣ Drive 6 miles south of Grant Grove on Generals Hwy. (Rte. 198), then turn right at Quail Flat; follow it 2 miles to the Redwood Canyon trailhead.*

TRAILS

Big Baldy Trail

TRAIL | This hike climbs 600 feet and 2 miles up to the 8,209-foot summit of Big Baldy. Your reward is the view of Redwood Canyon. Round-trip, the hike is 4 miles. *Moderate.* ✉ *Kings Canyon National Park ✣ Trailhead: 8 miles south of Grant Grove on Generals Hwy. (Rte. 198).*

Big Stump Trail

TRAIL | From 1883 until 1890, logging was done here, complete with a mill. The 1-mile loop trail, whose unmarked beginning is a few yards west of the Big Stump entrance, passes by many enormous stumps. *Easy.* ✉ *Kings Canyon National Park ✣ Trailhead: Near Big Stump Entrance, Generals Hwy. (Rte. 180).*

★ Grant Grove Trail

TRAIL | Grant Grove is only 128 acres, but it's a big deal. More than 120 sequoias here have a base diameter that exceeds 10 feet, and the **General Grant Tree** is the world's third-largest sequoia by volume. Nearby, the Confederacy is represented by the **Robert E. Lee Tree,** recognized as the world's 11th-largest sequoia. Also along the easy-to-walk trail are the **Fallen Monarch** and the **Gamlin Cabin,** built by 19th-century pioneers. *Easy.* ✉ *Kings Canyon National Park ✣ Trailhead: Off Generals Hwy. (Rte. 180), 1 mile north of Kings Canyon Park Visitor Center.*

Panoramic Point Trail

TRAIL | You'll get a nice view of whale-shape Hume Lake from the top of this Grant Grove path, which is paved and only 300 feet long. It's fairly steep—strollers might work here, but not wheelchairs. Trailers and RVs are not permitted on the steep and narrow road that leads to the trailhead parking lot. *Moderate.* ✉ *Kings Canyon National Park* ✥ *Trailhead: At end of Panoramic Point Rd., 2.3 miles from Grant Grove Village.*

Redwood Canyon Trails

TRAIL | Two main trails lead into Redwood Canyon grove, the world's largest sequoia grove. The 6.5-mile **Hart Tree and Fallen Goliath Loop** passes by a 19th-century logging site, pristine Hart Meadow, and the hollowed-out Tunnel Tree before accessing a side trail to the grove's largest sequoia, the 277.9-foot-tall Hart Tree. The 6.4-mile **Sugar Bowl Loop** provides views of Redwood Mountain and Big Baldy before winding down into its namesake, a thick grove of mature and young sequoias. *Moderate.* ✉ *Kings Canyon National Park* ✥ *Trailhead: Off Quail Flat. Drive 5 miles south of Grant Grove on Generals Hwy. (Rte. 198), turn right at Quail Flat and proceed 1½ miles to trailhead.*

VISITOR CENTERS

Kings Canyon Visitor Center

INFO CENTER | The center's 15-minute film and various exhibits provide an overview of the park's canyon, sequoias, and human history. Books, maps, and weather advice are dispensed here, as are (if available) $15 wilderness permits. ✉ *Kings Canyon National Park* ✥ *Grant Grove Village, Generals Hwy. (Rte. 198), 3 miles northeast of Rte. 180, Kings Canyon National Park entrance at Big Stump* ☎ *559/565–3341.*

Restaurants

Grant Grove Restaurant

$ | **AMERICAN** | Gaze at giant sequoias and a verdant meadow while enjoying a meal in this eco-friendly restaurant's spacious dining room with a fireplace or on its expansive deck. The menu centers around locally sourced natural and organic ingredients and offers standard American fare. **Known for:** takeout service year-round; walk-up window for pizza, sandwiches, coffee, ice cream; picnic tables on outdoor deck. $ *Average main: $16* ✉ *Grant Grove Village* ☎ *559/335–5500.*

Hotels

Grant Grove Cabins

$ | **HOTEL** | Some of the wood-panel cabins here have heaters, electric lights, and private baths, but most have woodstoves, battery lamps, and shared baths. **Pros:** warm, woodsy feel; clean; walk to Grant Grove Restaurant. **Cons:** can be difficult to walk up to if you're not in decent physical shape; costly for what you get; only basic amenities. $ *Rooms from: $135* ✉ *Kings Canyon Scenic Byway in Grant Grove Village* ☎ *866/807–3598* 🌐 *www.visitsequoia.com/Grant-Grove-Cabins.aspx* ⇌ *50 units* 🍽 *No meals.*

John Muir Lodge

$$ | **HOTEL** | In a wooded area in the hills above Grant Grove Village, this modern, timber-sided lodge has rooms and suites with queen- or king-size beds and private baths. **Pros:** open year-round; common room stays warm; quiet. **Cons:** check-in is down in the village; spotty Wi-Fi; remote location. $ *Rooms from: $210* ✉ *Kings Canyon Scenic Byway, ¼ mile north of Grant Grove Village, 86728 Hwy. 180* ☎ *866/807–3598* 🌐 *www.visitsequoia.com/john-muir-lodge.aspx* ⇌ *36 rooms* 🍽 *No meals.*

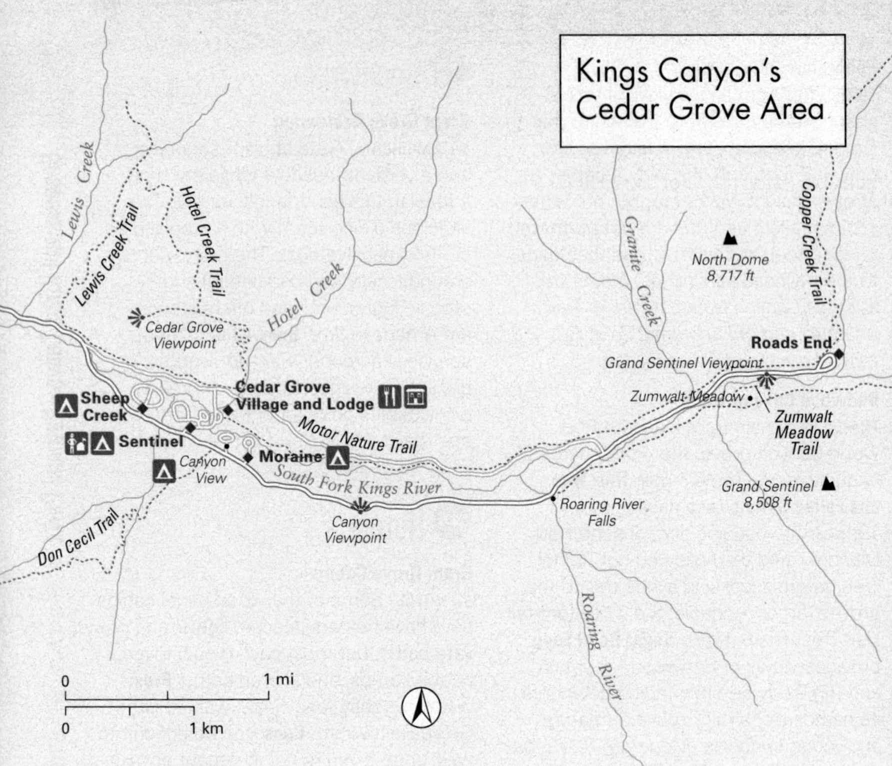

Montecito-Sequoia Lodge
$$ | **HOTEL** | **FAMILY** | Outdoor activities are what this year-round family resort is all about, including many that are geared toward teenagers and small children. **Pros:** friendly staff; great for kids; lots of fresh air and planned activities. **Cons:** can be noisy with all the activity; no TVs or phones in rooms; not within national park. *Rooms from: $229* *63410 Generals Hwy., 11 miles south of Grant Grove, Sequoia National Forest* *559/565–3388, 800/227–9900* *www.mslodge.com* *Closed 1st 2 wks of Dec.* *52 rooms* *All meals.*

Cedar Grove

35 miles east of Grant Grove Village.

The Cedar Grove section of Kings Canyon National Park bears many similarities to Yosemite Valley: a mighty river flowing through a verdant valley, ringed by massive glacier-hewn granite cliffs that loom several thousand feet above. Drive along the Kings Canyon Scenic Byway to access this relatively uncrowded wonderland, where you can hike excellent backcountry trails, stroll around lush Zumwalt Meadows, and take a break in Cedar Grove Village.

Sights

HISTORIC SIGHTS

Knapp's Cabin

BUILDING | Stop here not so much for the cabin itself, but as an excuse to ogle the scenery. George Knapp, a Santa Barbara businessman, stored gear in this small wooden structure when he commissioned fishing trips into the canyon in the 1920s. ✉ *Kings Canyon National Park* ✣ *Kings Canyon Scenic Byway, 2 miles east of Cedar Grove Village turnoff.*

TRAILS

Don Cecil Trail

TRAIL | This trail climbs 4,000 feet up the cool north-facing slope of the Kings River canyon, passing Sheep Creek Cascade and providing several fine glimpses of the canyon and the 11,000-foot Monarch Divide. The trail leads to Lookout Peak, which affords a panorama of the park's backcountry. This strenuous, all-day hike covers 13 miles round-trip. *Difficult.* ✉ *Kings Canyon National Park* ✣ *Trailhead: At Sentinel Campground, Cedar Grove Village.*

Hotel Creek Trail

TRAIL | For gorgeous canyon views, take this trail from Cedar Grove up a series of switchbacks until it splits. Follow the route left through chaparral to the forested ridge and rocky outcrop known as Cedar Grove Overlook, where you can see the Kings River canyon stretching below. This strenuous, 5-mile round-trip hike gains 1,200 feet and takes three to four hours to complete. *Difficult.* ✉ *Kings Canyon National Park* ✣ *Trailhead: At Cedar Grove Pack Station, 1 mile east of Cedar Grove Village.*

Mist Falls Trail

TRAIL | This sandy trail follows the glaciated South Fork Canyon through forest and chaparral, past several rapids and cascades, to one of the largest waterfalls in the two parks. Nine miles round-trip, the hike is relatively flat, but climbs 600 feet in the last 2 miles. It takes from four to five hours to complete. *Moderate.* ✉ *Kings Canyon National Park* ✣ *Trailhead: At end of Kings Canyon Scenic Byway, 5½ miles east of Cedar Grove Village.*

Roaring River Falls Walk

TRAIL | Take a shady five-minute walk to this forceful waterfall that rushes through a narrow granite chute. The trail is paved and mostly accessible. *Easy.* ✉ *Kings Canyon National Park* ✣ *Trailhead: 3 miles east of Cedar Grove Village turnoff from Kings Canyon Scenic Byway.*

★ Zumwalt Meadow Trail

TRAIL | Rangers say this is the best (and most popular) day hike in the Cedar Grove area. Just 1½ miles long, it offers three visual treats: the South Fork of the Kings River, the lush meadow, and the high granite walls above, including those of Grand Sentinel and North Dome. *Easy.* ✉ *Kings Canyon National Park* ✣ *Trailhead: 4½ miles east of Cedar Grove Village turnoff from Kings Canyon Scenic Byway.*

VISITOR CENTERS

Cedar Grove Visitor Center

INFO CENTER | Off the main road and behind the Sentinel Campground, this small ranger station has books and maps, plus information about hikes and other activities. ✉ *Kings Canyon National Park* ✣ *Kings Canyon Scenic Byway, 30 miles east of Rte. 180/198 junction* ☎ *559/565–3341* ⏲ *Closed mid-Sept.–mid-May.*

Restaurants

Cedar Grove Grill

$ | **AMERICAN** | The menu here is surprisingly extensive, with dinner entrées such as pasta, pork chops, trout, and steak. For breakfast, try the egg burrito, French toast, or pancakes; sandwiches, wraps, burgers (including vegetarian patties) and hot dogs dominate the lunch choices. **Known for:** scenic river views; extensive options; alfresco dining on balcony overlooking the Kings River. $ *Average main:*

$16 ✉ Cedar Grove Village ☎ 886/807–3598 🌐 www.visitsequoia.com/dine/cedar-grove-grill ⏲ Closed Oct.–May.

Hotels

Cedar Grove Lodge
$ | **HOTEL** | Backpackers like to stay here on the eve of long treks into the High Sierra wilderness, so bedtimes tend to be early. **Pros:** a definite step up from camping in terms of comfort; great base camp for outdoor adventures; on-site snack bar. **Cons:** impersonal; not everybody agrees it's clean enough; remote location. *$ Rooms from: $147 ✉ Kings Canyon Scenic Byway ☎ 866/807–3598 🌐 www.visitsequoia.com/lodging/cedar-grove-lodge ⏲ Closed mid-Oct.–mid-May ⇨ 21 rooms 🍽 No meals.*

Activities

CAMPING

Azalea Campground. Of the three campgrounds in the Grant Grove area, Azalea is the only one open year-round. It sits at 6,500 feet amid giant sequoias. *✉ Kings Canyon Scenic Byway, ¼ mile north of Grant Grove Village ☎ 559/565–3341.*

Canyon View Campground. The smallest and most primitive of four campgrounds near Cedar Grove, this one is near the start of the Don Cecil Trail, which leads to Lookout Point. The elevation of the camp is 4,600 feet along the Kings River. There are no wheelchair-accessible sites. *✉ Off Kings Canyon Scenic Byway, ½-mile east of Cedar Grove Village ☎ No phone.*

Crystal Springs Campground. Near the Grant Grove Village and the towering sequoias, this camp is at 6,500 feet. There are accessible sites here. *✉ Off Generals Hwy. (Rte. 198), ¼ mile north of Grant Grove Visitor Center ☎ No phone.*

Sentinel Campground. At 4,600 feet and within walking distance of Cedar Grove Village, Sentinel fills up fast in summer. *✉ Kings Canyon Scenic Byway, ¼ mile west of Cedar Grove Village ☎ 559/565–3341.*

Sheep Creek Campground. Of the overflow campgrounds, this is one of the prettiest. *✉ Off Kings Canyon Scenic Byway, 1 mile west of Cedar Grove Village ☎ No phone.*

Sunset Campground. Many of the easiest trails through Grant Grove are adjacent to this large camp, near the giant sequoias at 6,500 feet. *✉ Off Generals Hwy., near Grant Grove Visitor Center ☎ No phone.*

CROSS-COUNTRY SKIING

Grant Grove Ski Touring Center
SKIING/SNOWBOARDING | The Grant Grove Market doubles as the ski-touring center, where you can rent cross-country skis or snowshoes in winter. This is a good starting point for a number of marked trails, including the Panoramic Point Trail and the General Grant Tree Trail. *✉ Grant Grove Market, Generals Hwy. (Rte. 198), 3 miles northeast of Rte. 180, Big Stump entrance ☎ 559/335–5500 🌐 www.visitsequoia.com/cross-country-skiing.aspx 🎟 From $15.*

FISHING

There is limited trout fishing in the park from late April to mid-November, and catches are minor. Still, Kings River is a popular spot. Some of the park's secluded backcountry lakes have good fishing. Licenses are available, along with fishing tackle, in Grant Grove and Cedar Grove. *See Activities, in Sequoia National Park for more information about licenses.*

HIKING

Roads End Permit Station
INFO CENTER | You can obtain wilderness permits, maps, and information about the backcountry at this station, where bear canisters, a must for campers, can be rented or purchased. When the station is closed (typically October–mid-May), complete a self-service permit form. *✉ Kings Canyon National Park ✣ Eastern end of Kings Canyon Scenic Byway, 6 miles east of Cedar Grove Visitor Center.*

HORSEBACK RIDING

Cedar Grove Pack Station

HORSEBACK RIDING | Take a day ride or plan a multiday adventure along the Kings River canyon with Cedar Grove Pack Station. Popular routes include the Rae Lakes Loop and Monarch Divide. Closed early September–late May. ✉ *Kings Canyon National Park* ✣ *Kings Canyon Scenic Byway, 1 mile east of Cedar Grove Village* ☎ *559/565–3464 summer, 559/337–2413 off-season* 🌐 *www.nps.gov/seki/planyourvisit/horseride.htm* 🎫 *From $50 per hr or $90 per day.*

Grant Grove Stables

HORSEBACK RIDING | A one- or two-hour trip through Grant Grove leaving from the stables provides a taste of horseback riding in Kings Canyon. The stables are closed October–early June. ✉ *Kings Canyon National Park* ✣ *Rte. 180, ½ mile north of Grant Grove Visitor Center* ☎ *559/335–9292* 🌐 *www.nps.gov/seki/planyourvisit/horseride.htm* 🎫 *From $50 per hr, $90 for 2 hrs.*

What's Nearby

Three Rivers

7 miles south of Sequoia National Park's Foothills Visitor Center.

Three Rivers is a good spot to find a room when park lodgings are full. Either because residents here appreciate their idyllic setting or because they know that tourists are their bread and butter, you'll find them eager to share tips about the best spots for "Sierra surfing" the Kaweah's smooth, moss-covered rocks or where to find the best cell reception (it's off to the cemetery for Verizon customers).

GETTING HERE AND AROUND

Driving is the easiest way to get to and around Three Rivers, which straddles a stretch of Highway 198. In summer, the Sequoia Shuttle connects Three Rivers to Visalia and Sequoia National Park.

CONTACTS Sequoia Shuttle. ☎ *877/287–4453* 🌐 *www.sequoiashuttle.com.*

Sights

Sequoia National Forest and Giant Sequoia National Monument

FOREST | Delicate spring wildflowers, cool summer campgrounds, and varied winter-sports opportunities—not to mention more than half of the world's giant sequoia groves—draw outdoorsy types year-round to this sprawling district surrounding the national parks. Together, the forest and monument cover nearly 1,700 square miles, south from the Kings River and east from the foothills along the San Joaquin Valley. The monument's groves are both north and south of Sequoia National Park. One of the most popular is the **Converse Basin Grove,** home of the Boole Tree, the forest's largest sequoia. The grove is accessible by car on an unpaved road.

The Hume Lake Forest Service District Office, at 35860 Kings Canyon Scenic Byway (Route 180), has information about the groves, along with details about recreational activities. In springtime, diversions include hiking among the wildflowers that brighten the foothills. The floral display rises with the heat as the mountain elevations warm up in summer, when hikers, campers, and picnickers become more plentiful. The abundant trout supply attracts anglers to area waters, including 87-acre **Hume Lake,** which is also ideal for swimming and nonmotorized boating. By fall, the turning leaves provide the visual delights, particularly in the Western Divide, Indian Basin, and the Kern Plateau. Winter activities include downhill and cross-country skiing, snowshoeing, and snowmobiling. ✉ *Sequoia National Park* ✣ *Northern Entrances: Generals Hwy. (Rte. 198), 7* *miles southeast of Grant Grove; Hume Lake Rd. between Generals Hwy. (Rte. 198) and Kings Canyon Scenic Byway (Rte. 180); Kings Canyon Scenic Byway (Rte. 180) between Grant Grove and Cedar Grove. Southern Entrances: Rte. 190 east of Springville; Rte. 178 east of Bakersfield ☎ 559/784–1500 forest and monument, 559/338–2251 Hume Lake 🌐 www.fs.usda.gov/sequoia.*

Restaurants

Gateway Restaurant and Lodge
$$$ | **AMERICAN** | The view's the draw at this roadhouse that overlooks the Kaweah River as it plunges out of the high country. The Gateway serves everything from osso buco and steaks to shrimp in Thai chili sauce; dinner reservations are essential on summer weekends. **Known for:** scenic riverside setting; fine dining in otherwise casual town; popular bar. $ *Average main: $30* ✉ *45978 Sierra Dr.* ☎ *559/561–4133* 🌐 *www.gateway-sequoia.com.*

Sierra Subs and Salads
$ | **AMERICAN** | This well-run sandwich joint satisfies carnivores and vegetarians alike with crispy-fresh ingredients prepared with panache. Depending on your preference, the centerpiece of the Bull's Eye sandwich, for instance, will be roast beef or a portobello mushroom; whichever you choose, the accompanying flavors—of ciabatta bread, horseradish-and-garlic mayonnaise, roasted red peppers, Havarti cheese, and spinach—will delight your palate. **Known for:** many vegetarian, vegan, and gluten-free options; weekly specials; Wi-Fi. $ *Average main: $12* ✉ *41651 Sierra Dr.* ☎ *559/561–4810* 🌐 *www.sierrasubsandsalads.com* ⏲ *Closed Sun. and Mon. No dinner.*

Hotels

Buckeye Tree Lodge
$$ | **B&B/INN** | Every room at this two-story motel has a patio facing a sun-dappled grassy lawn, right on the banks of the Kaweah River; individually decorated cottages and cabins across the river have private outdoor spaces with barbecue grills. **Pros:** near the park entrance; fantastic river views; kitchenette in some rooms. **Cons:** can fill up quickly in the summer; could use a little updating; some rooms are tiny. $ *Rooms from: $200* ✉ *46000 Sierra Dr., Hwy. 198* ☎ *559/561–5900* 🌐 *www.buckeyetree.com* *22 units* 🍽 *Free breakfast* ☞ *2-night minimum on summer weekends.*

Lazy J Ranch Motel
$$ | **B&B/INN** | Surrounded by 12 acres of green lawns and a split-rail fence, the Lazy J is a modest compound of one-story motel buildings and freestanding cottages near the banks of the Kaweah River. **Pros:** pleasant landscaping; quiet rooms; friendly staff. **Cons:** on the far edge of town; can't see the river from most rooms; dated style and fixtures. $ *Rooms from: $150* ✉ *39625 Sierra Dr., Hwy. 198* ☎ *559/561–4449* 🌐 *www.lazyjranchmotel.com* *18 units* 🍽 *Free breakfast.*

★ **Rio Sierra Riverhouse**
$$$ | **B&B/INN** | Guests at Rio Sierra come for the river views, the sandy beach, and the proximity to Sequoia National Park (6 miles away), but invariably end up raving equally about the warm, laid-back hospitality of proprietress Mars Roberts. **Pros:** seductive beach; river views from all rooms; contemporary ambience. **Cons:** books up quickly in summer; some road noise audible in rooms; long walk or drive to restaurants. $ *Rooms from: $275* ✉ *41997 Sierra Dr., Hwy. 198* ☎ *559/561–4720* 🌐 *www.rio-sierra.com* *3 rooms* 🍽 *No meals* ☞ *2-night min stay on summer weekends. Closed Jan.–mid-Mar.*

Activities

HORSEBACK RIDING

Wood 'n' Horse Training Stables

HORSEBACK RIDING | For hourly horseback rides, riding lessons, or trail rides in the foothills, contact this outfit. Rates start at $50 for lessons and $70 for trail rides. *42846 N. Fork Dr.* *559/561–4268* *www.wdnhorse.com.*

RAFTING

Kaweah White Water Adventures

BOATING | Kaweah's trips include a two-hour excursion (good for families) through Class III rapids, a longer paddle through Class IV rapids, and an extended trip (typically Class IV and V rapids). *40443 Sierra Dr.* *559/740–8251* *www.kaweah-whitewater.com* *From $50 per person.*

Visalia

35 miles west of the Sequoia National Park entrance.

Visalia's combination of a reliable agricultural economy and civic pride has produced the Central Valley's most vibrant downtown, with numerous restaurants, craft breweries, and cafés. If you're into history, drop by the visitor center and pick up a free map of a self-guided historic downtown walking tour. A clear day's view of the Sierra from Main Street is spectacular, and even Sunday night can find the streets bustling with pedestrians. Visalia provides easy access to grand Sequoia National Park and the serene Kaweah Oaks Preserve.

GETTING HERE AND AROUND

Highway 198, just east of its exit from Highway 99, cuts through town (and proceeds up the hill to Sequoia National Park). Greyhound stops here, but not Amtrak. KART buses serve the locals, and, in summer, the Sequoia Shuttle ($20) travels among Visalia, Three Rivers, and Sequoia National Park with a stop in Three Rivers.

VISITOR INFORMATION

CONTACTS Visalia Convention & Visitors Bureau (Visit Visalia). *112 E. Main St.* *559/334–0141, 800/524–0303* *www.visitvisalia.com.*

Bravo Farms Traver

FACTORY | FAMILY | For one-stop truck-stop entertainment, pull off the highway in Traver, where at Bravo Farms you can try your luck at an arcade shooting gallery, watch cheese being made, munch on barbecue and ice cream, play a round of mini golf, peruse funky antiques, buy produce, visit a petting zoo, and climb a multistory tree house. Taste a few "squeekers" (fresh cheese curds, so named because chewing them makes your teeth squeak), and then be on your way. *36005 Hwy. 99, 9 miles north of Hwy. 198 and Visalia, Traver* *559/897–5762* *www.bravofarms.com* *Free.*

★ Colonel Allensworth State Historic Park

HISTORIC SITE | It's worth the slight detour off Highway 99 to learn about and pay homage to the dream of Allen Allensworth and other Black pioneers who in 1908 founded Allensworth, the only California town settled, governed, and financed by African Americans. At its height, the town prospered as a key railroad transfer point, but after cars and trucks reduced railroad traffic and water was diverted for Central Valley agriculture, the town declined and was eventually deserted. Today, the restored and rebuilt schoolhouse, library, and other structures commemorate Allensworth's heyday, as do festivities that take place each October. *4129 Palmer Ave., 48 miles south of Visalia, Allensworth* *From Visalia, take Hwy. 99 south to Earlimart, and then turn west toward Allensworth* *661/849–3433* *www.parks.ca.gov* *$6 per car.*

Exeter Murals

PUBLIC ART | More than two dozen murals in the Central Valley city of Exeter's cute-as-a-button downtown make it worth a quick detour if you're traveling on Route 198. Several of the murals, which depict the area's agricultural and social history, are quite good. All adorn buildings within a few blocks of the intersection of Pine and E streets. If you're hungry, the **Wildflower Cafe,** at 121 South E Street, serves inventive salads and sandwiches. Shortly after entering Exeter, head west on Pine Street (it's just before the water tower) to reach downtown. ✉ *204 E. Pine St., Exeter* ✣ *Rte. 65, 2 miles south of Rte. 198, about 11 miles east of Visalia* 🌐 *cityofexeter.com/galleries/exeter-murals.*

Kaweah Oaks Preserve

NATURE PRESERVE | Trails at this 344-acre wildlife sanctuary off the main road to Sequoia National Park lead past majestic valley oak, sycamore, cottonwood, and willow trees. Among the 134 bird species you might spot are hawks, hummingbirds, and great blue herons. Bobcats, lizards, coyotes, and cottontails also live here. The Sycamore Trail has digital signage with QR codes you can scan with your smartphone to access plant and animal information. ✉ *Follow Hwy. 198 for 7 miles east of Visalia, turn north on Rd. 182, and proceed ½ mile to gate on left side* ☎ *559/738–0211* 🌐 *www.sequoiariverlands.org* 🎫 *Free.*

Lake Kaweah

BODY OF WATER | The Kaweah River rushes out of the Sierra from high above Mineral King in Sequoia National Park. When it reaches the hills above the Central Valley, the water collects in Lake Kaweah, a reservoir operated by the Army Corps of Engineers. You can swim, sail, kayak, water ski, hike, camp, fish, and picnic here. The visitor center at Lemon Hill has interesting exhibits about the dam that created the lake. ✉ *34443 Sierra Dr. (Rte. 198), about 20 miles east of Visalia* ☎ *559/597–2301, 877/444–6777 campground reservations, 559/597–2005 Lemon Hill visitor center* 🎫 *$5 day use.*

★ McKellar Family Farms

FARM/RANCH | **FAMILY** | Taste, touch, and feel your way through orange and mandarin groves on a guided tour of this 180-acre working citrus farm. Tours last 60 minutes; tractor-pulled wagon tours are also available. Kids and adults love the challenge of navigating the nation's only orange-grove maze, answering questions at a series of checkpoints to earn a prize at the end. ✉ *32985 Rd. 164, north of Hwy. 216, Ivanhoe* ☎ *559/731–7925* 🌐 *www.mckellarfamilyfarms.com* 🎫 *Tour $100 for up to 2 persons, $10 for each additional person.*

 Restaurants

Fugazzi's Bistro

$$ | **ITALIAN** | An upscale restaurant in Visalia's downtown hub, Fugazzi's serves up Italian-American and international-fusion dishes in a slick, contemporary space with leather booths and shiny metal tables. The extensive lunch and dinner menus feature everything from quinoa-and-kale salad and Thai chicken wraps to traditional Italian dishes and filet mignon. **Known for:** full bar with classic and creative cocktails; house-made sauces; upscale yet casual vibe. 💲 *Average main: $19* ✉ *127 W. Main St.* ☎ *559/625–0496* 🌐 *www.fugazzisbistro.com.*

Pita Kabob Gastropub

$ | **MEDITERRANEAN** | A large and ever-changing selection of craft beers, a lively dining garden, and authentic Mediterranean and fusion dishes—from kebabs, shawarma, hummus, and gyros to rice bowls and burgers—lure locals and visitors to this popular downtown eatery. Pack in multiple flavors by ordering a combination or sampler plate. **Known for:** daily specials; 31 beers on tap; veggie and vegan options. 💲 *Average main: $12* ✉ *227 N. Court St.* ☎ *559/627–2337* 🌐 *pitakabob.com* 🕒 *Closed Mon.*

★ The Vintage Press

$$$ | **EUROPEAN** | Established in 1966, this is one of the best restaurants in the Central Valley. The California–continental cuisine includes dishes such as crispy veal sweetbreads with a port-wine sauce and filet mignon with a cognac-mustard sauce. **Known for:** wine list with more than 900 selections; chocolate Grand Marnier cake and other house-made desserts; sophisticated vibe. *Average main: $32* *216 N. Willis St.* *559/733–3033* *www.thevintagepress.com.*

Hotels

★ The Darling Hotel

$$ | **HOTEL** | Developers meticulously restored a dilapidated, three-story, 1930s building to create this hotel, where rooms have a modern take on art-deco style, with plush furnishings, 12-foot ceilings, and spacious bathrooms with period accents. **Pros:** in the heart of downtown; outdoor pool; rooftop lounge and restaurant with panoramic mountain and city views. **Cons:** some rooms on the small side; fronts a busy street; vintage single-pane glass windows don't block urban noise. *Rooms from: $179* *210 N. Court St.* *559/713–2113* *thedarlingvisalia.com* *32 rooms* *No meals.*

Lamp Liter Inn

$ | **HOTEL** | **FAMILY** | A classic, 1960s, roadside motel, Lamp Liter Inn has basic but comfy rooms in several two-story buildings that surround tree-studded gardens and a spacious outdoor pool and terrace. **Pros:** family-owned and operated, personal service; on-site restaurant with full bar; convenient lodging for Sequoia National Park visitors. **Cons:** rooms could use updating; not near downtown; outdoor noise travels through thin walls in some rooms. *Rooms from: $96* *3300 W. Mineral King Ave.* *559/732–4511, 800/662–6692* *www.lampliter.net* *100 rooms* *No meals.*

Fresno

44 miles north of Visalia.

Fresno, with half a million people, is the center of the richest agricultural county in the United States. Cotton, grapes, and tomatoes are among the major crops; poultry and milk are also important. About 75 ethnic groups, including Armenians, Laotians, and Indians, live here. The city has a relatively vibrant arts scene, several public parks, and many low-price restaurants. The **Tower District**—with its restaurants, coffeehouses, and performance venues—is the town's arts and nightlife nexus. It's the closest large city to Sequoia National Park, though at some 78 miles away it's not that close, so it's an option if there's nothing available in the park itself, Three Rivers, or Visalia.

GETTING HERE AND AROUND

Highway 99 is the biggest road through Fresno. Highways 41 and 180 also bisect the city. Amtrak trains stop here daily (and often).

VISITOR INFORMATION Fresno / Clovis Convention & Visitors Bureau. *1180 E. Shaw Ave.* *559/981–5500, 800/788–0836* *playfresno.org.*

Sights

★ Forestiere Underground Gardens

GARDEN | **FAMILY** | Sicilian immigrant Baldassare Forestiere spent four decades (1906–46) carving out an odd, subterranean realm of rooms, tunnels, grottoes, alcoves, and arched passageways that once extended for more than 10 acres between Highway 99 and busy, mall-pocked Shaw Avenue. Though not an engineer, Forestiere called on his memories of the ancient Roman structures he saw as a youth and on techniques he learned digging subways in New York and Boston. Only a fraction of his prodigious output is on view, but you can tour his underground living quarters, including bedrooms (one with a fireplace), the kitchen, living room, and bath, as well as a fishpond and auto tunnel. Skylights allow exotic full-grown fruit trees to flourish more than 20 feet belowground. *5021 W. Shaw Ave., 2 blocks east of Hwy. 99* *559/271–0734* *www.undergroundgardens.com* *$19* *Closed Dec.–Mar.*

Fresno Art Museum

MUSEUM | The museum's key permanent collections include pre-Columbian Mesoamerican art, Andean pre-Columbian textiles and artifacts, Japanese prints, Berkeley School abstract expressionist paintings, and contemporary sculpture. Temporary exhibits include important traveling shows. *Radio Park, 2233 N. 1st St., at E. Yale Ave.* *559/441–4221* *www.fresnoartmuseum.org* *$10* *Closed Mon.–Wed.*

Restaurants

School House Restaurant & Tavern

$$$ | **MODERN AMERICAN** | A Wine Country–style establishment that sources ingredients from the on-site gardens and surrounding farms and orchards, this popular restaurant occupies a redbrick 1921 schoolhouse in the town of Sanger. Chef Ryan Jackson, who grew up on local fruit farms, creates seasonal menus from the bounty of familiar backyards, mostly filled with classic American dishes with a contemporary twist. **Known for:** fresh ingredients from neighboring farms and orchards; historic country setting; convenient stop between Kings Canyon and Fresno. *Average main: $29* *1018 S. Frankwood Ave., at Hwy. 180 (King's Canyon Rd.), 20 miles east of Fresno, Sanger* *559/787–3271* *schoolhousesanger.com* *Closed Mon. and Tues.*

Hotels

Best Western Plus Fresno Inn

$ | **HOTEL** | With a location near Highway 41 (the main route to Yosemite), Fresno State, and a big mall, this well-run hotel is popular with families, businesspeople, and parents with offspring at the university. **Pros:** convenient location; attentive staff; 24-hour business center. **Cons:** mildly sterile feel; on a busy street; small pool. *Rooms from: $130* *480 E. Shaw Ave.* *559/229–5811* *bestwestern.com* *55 rooms* *Free breakfast.*

Hotel Piccadilly

$ | **HOTEL** | This two-story property has 7½ attractively landscaped acres and a big swimming pool. **Pros:** big rooms; nice pool; on-site restaurant/pub. **Cons:** some rooms show mild wear; neighborhood is somewhat sketchy; no elevator. *Rooms from: $119* *2305 W. Shaw Ave.* *559/348–5520* *hotel-piccadilly.com* *187 rooms* *Free breakfast.*

Activities

WHITE-WATER RAFTING

Kings River Expeditions

TOUR—SPORTS | This outfit arranges one- and two-day white-water rafting trips on the Kings River. The office is in Clovis, but all trips depart from Twin Pines Camp, 60 miles east of Fresno. *Twin Pines Camp, Clovis* *559/233–4881, 800/846–3674* *www.kingsriver.com* *From $145.*

Chapter 14

YOSEMITE NATIONAL PARK

Updated by
Cheryl Crabtree

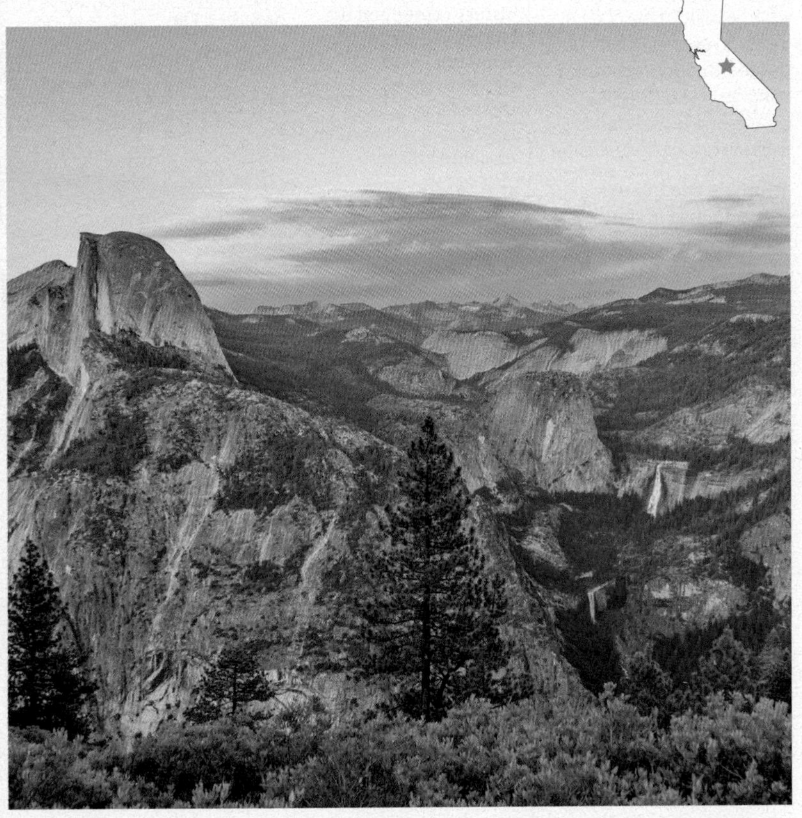

Camping ★★★★★

Hotels ★★★★☆

Activities ★★★★★

Scenery ★★★★★

Crowds ★★★★☆

WELCOME TO YOSEMITE NATIONAL PARK

TOP REASONS TO GO

★ **Scenic falls:** An easy stroll brings you to the base of Lower Yosemite Fall, where roaring springtime waters make for misty lens caps and lasting memories.

★ **Tunnel vision:** Approaching Yosemite Valley, Wawona Road passes through a mountainside and emerges before one of the park's most heart-stopping vistas.

★ **Inhale the beauty:** Pause to take in the light, pristine air as you travel about the High Sierra's Tioga Pass and Tuolumne Meadows, where 10,000-foot granite peaks just might take your breath away.

★ **Walk away:** Leave the crowds behind—but do bring along a buddy—and take a hike somewhere along Yosemite's 800 miles of trails.

★ **Winter wonder:** Observe the snowflakes and stillness of winter in the park.

1 Yosemite Valley. At an elevation of 4,000 feet, in roughly the center of the park, beats Yosemite's heart. This is where you'll find the park's most famous sights and biggest crowds.

2 Wawona. The park's southern tip holds Wawona, with its grand old hotel and pioneer history center, and the Mariposa Grove of Giant Sequoias. These are closest to the south entrance, 35 miles (a one-hour drive) south of Yosemite Village.

3 Tuolumne Meadows. The highlight of east-central Yosemite is this wildflower-strewn valley that's laced with hiking trails and nestled among sharp, rocky peaks. It's a 1½-hour drive northeast of Yosemite Valley along Tioga Road (closed mid-October–late May).

4 Hetch Hetchy. The most remote, least visited part of Yosemite accessible by automobile, this glacial valley is dominated by a reservoir and veined with wilderness trails. It's near the park's western boundary, about a half-hour drive north of the Big Oak Flat entrance.

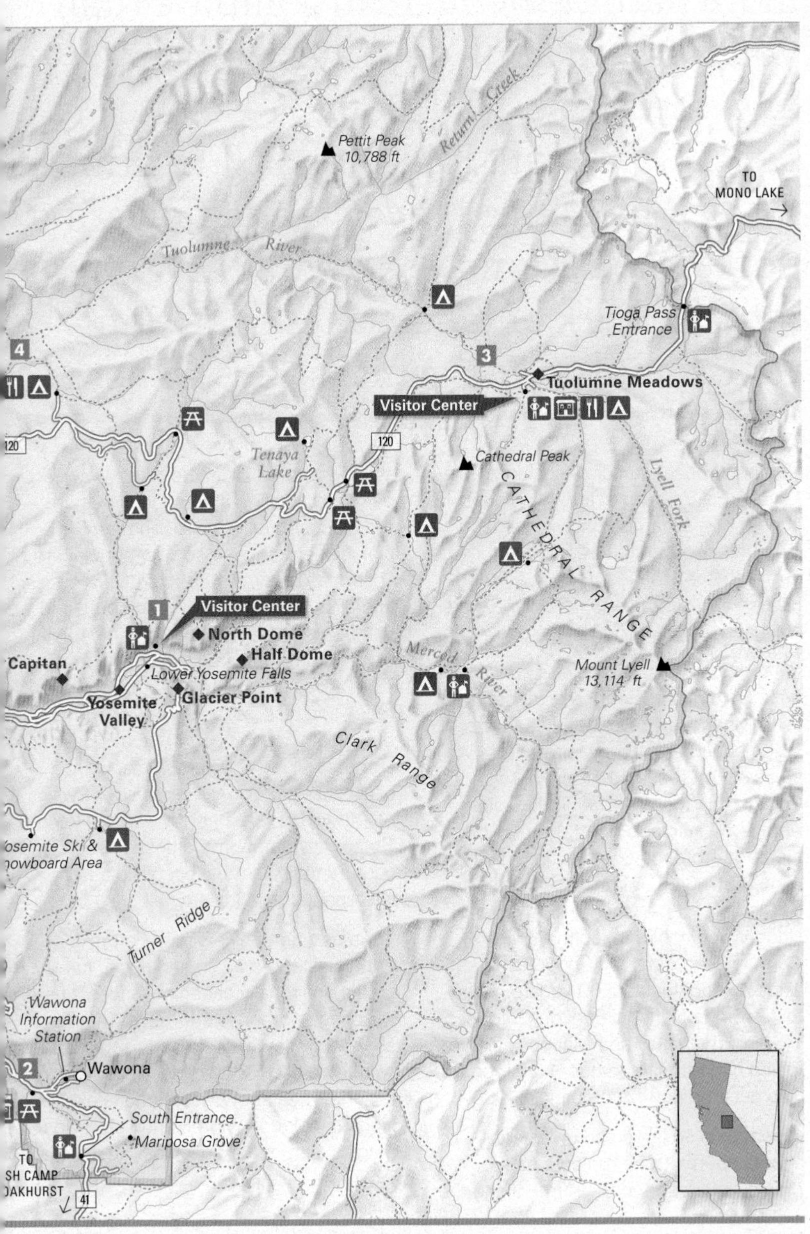
Pettit Peak
10,788 ft
Return Creek
Tuolumne River
TO
MONO LAKE
Tioga Pass
Entrance
Tuolumne Meadows
Visitor Center
120
Tenaya
Lake
Cathedral Peak
CATHEDRAL RANGE
Lyell Fork
Visitor Center
North Dome
Half Dome
Capitan
Lower Yosemite Falls
Yosemite
Valley
Glacier Point
Merced River
Mount Lyell
13,114 ft
Clark Range
osemite Ski &
owboard Area
Turner Ridge
Wawona
Information
Station
Wawona
South Entrance
Mariposa Grove
TO
SH CAMP
AKHURST
41

By merely standing in Yosemite Valley and turning in a circle, you can see more natural wonders in a minute than you could in a full day pretty much anywhere else. Half Dome, Yosemite Falls, El Capitan, Bridalveil Fall, Sentinel Dome, the Merced River, white-flowering dogwood trees, maybe even bears ripping into the bark of fallen trees or sticking their snouts into beehives—it's all here.

Native American nations—including the Miwok, Paiute, Mono, and Ahwahneechee tribes—roamed this wonderland long before other cultures. Indeed, some of the footpaths used by Native Americans to cross mountains and valleys are still used as park hiking trails today.

In the mid-1800s, the valley's special geologic qualities and the giant sequoias of Mariposa Grove 30 miles to the south began attracting visitors. The two areas so impressed a group of influential Californians that they lobbied President Abraham Lincoln to grant them to the state for protection, which he did on June 30, 1864. Further lobbying efforts by naturalist John Muir and Robert Underwood Johnson, editor of *The Century Magazine*, led Congress to set aside an additional 1,500 square miles for Yosemite National Park on October 1, 1890. The valley and Mariposa Grove, which had remained under state control, also became part of the park in 1906.

Yosemite is so large and diverse, it almost seems to be multiple parks. Many visitors spend their time along the southwestern border, between Wawona, which is open all year and is where the giant sequoias stand, and the Big Oak Flat entrance. Also very popular are Yosemite Valley, famous for its waterfalls and cliffs and also open year-round, and the Badger Pass Ski Area, a winter-only destination. The seasonal, east–west Tioga Road spans the park north of the valley and bisects Tuolumne Meadows, the subalpine high country that's open for summer hiking and camping; in winter, it's accessible only via cross-country skis or snowshoes. The northwestern Hetch Hetchy district, home of less-used backcountry trails, is most accessible from late spring through early fall.

Photographers, hikers, and nature enthusiasts visit again and again, lured by the seasonally changing landscapes. In spring, waterfalls are robust thanks to abundant snowmelt. In early summer, wildflowers blanket alpine meadows. In fall, the trees showcase glorious explosions of color. In winter, snows provide a magical setting for activities like ice skating in the valley or cross-country skiing to Glacier Point.

AVERAGE HIGH/LOW TEMPERATURES					
JAN.	FEB.	MAR.	APR.	MAY	JUNE
48/29	53/30	55/32	61/36	69/43	78/49
JULY	AUG.	SEPT.	OCT.	NOV.	DEC.
85/55	84/55	79/49	70/42	56/34	47/29

Planning

When to Go

During extremely busy periods—such as weekends and holidays throughout the year—you will experience delays at the entrance gates. For smaller crowds, visit midweek. Or come January through March, when the park is a bit less busy, and the days usually are sunny and clear.

Summer rainfall is rare. In winter, heavy snows occasionally cause road closures, and tire chains or four-wheel drive may be required on the routes that remain open. The road to Glacier Point beyond the turnoff for the Badger Pass Ski Area is closed after the first major snowfall. Tioga Road is closed from late October through May or mid-June. Mariposa Grove Road is typically closed for a shorter period in winter.

Getting Here and Around

AIR

The closest airport to the south and west entrances is Fresno Yosemite International Airport (FAT). Mammoth Yosemite Airport (MMH) is closest to the east entrance. Sacramento International Airport (SMF) is also close to the north and west entrances.

BUS AND TRAIN

Amtrak's daily *San Joaquins* train stops in Merced and connects with YARTS buses that travel to Yosemite Valley along Highway 140 from there. Seasonal YARTS buses (typically mid-May to late September) also travel along Highway 41 from Fresno, Highway 120 from Sonora, and Highway 395 and Tioga Road from Mammoth Lakes with scheduled stops at towns along the way. Once you're in Yosemite Valley, you can take advantage of the free shuttle buses, which operate on low emissions, have 21 stops, and run from 7 am to 10 pm year-round. Buses run about every 10 minutes in summer, a bit less frequently in winter. A separate (but also free) summer-only shuttle runs out to El Capitan. Also in summer, you can pay to take the "hikers' bus" from Yosemite Valley to Tuolumne or to ride a tour bus up to Glacier Point. During the snow season, buses run regularly between Yosemite Valley and Badger Pass Ski Area.

CAR

Roughly 200 miles from San Francisco, 300 miles from Los Angeles, and 500 miles from Las Vegas, Yosemite takes a while to reach—and its many sites and attractions merit much more time than what rangers say is the average visit: four hours.

Of the park's four entrances, Arch Rock is the closest to Yosemite Valley. The road that goes through it, Route 140 from Merced and Mariposa, is a scenic western approach that snakes alongside the boulder-packed Merced River. Route 41, through Wawona, is the way to come from Los Angeles (or Fresno, if you've flown in and rented a car). Route 120, through Crane Flat, is the most direct route from San Francisco. The only way in from the east is Tioga Road, which may be the best route in terms of scenery—though due to snow accumulation it's open for a frustratingly short amount of time each year (typically early June through mid-October). Once you enter Yosemite Valley, park your car in one of the two main day-parking areas, at Yosemite Village and Yosemite Falls, then visit the sights via the free shuttle bus system. Or walk or bike along the valley's 12 miles of paved paths.

There are few gas stations within Yosemite (Crane Flat and Wawona, none in the valley), so fuel up before you reach the park. From late fall until early spring, the weather is especially unpredictable, and driving can be treacherous. You should carry chains during this period as they are required when roads are icy and when it snows.

Park Essentials

ACCESSIBILITY

Yosemite's facilities are continually being upgraded to make them more accessible. Many of the valley floor trails—particularly at Lower Yosemite Fall, Bridalveil Fall, and Mirror Lake—are wheelchair accessible, though some assistance may be required. The Valley Visitor Center is fully accessible, as are the park shuttle buses. A sign-language interpreter is available for ranger programs. Visitors with respiratory difficulties should take note of the park's high elevations—the valley floor is approximately 4,000 feet above sea level, but Tuolumne Meadows and parts of the high country hover around 10,000 feet.

PARK FEES AND PERMITS

The admission fee, valid for seven days, is $35 per vehicle, $30 per motorcycle, or $20 per individual.

If you plan to camp in the backcountry or climb Half Dome, you must have a wilderness permit. Availability of permits depends upon trailhead quotas. It's best to make a reservation, especially if you will be visiting May through September. You can reserve two days to 24 weeks in advance by phone, mail, or fax (preferred method) (✉ *Box 545, Yosemite, CA* ☎ *209/372–0826*); you'll pay $5 per person plus $5 per reservation if and when your reservations are confirmed. You can apply online via the park website (🌐 *www.nps.gov/yose/planyourvisit/backpacking.htm*). Without a reservation, you may still get a free permit on a first-come, first-served basis at wilderness permit offices at Big Oak Flat, Hetch Hetchy, Tuolumne Meadows, Wawona, the Wilderness Center in Yosemite Village, and Yosemite Valley in summer. From fall to spring, visit the Valley Visitor Center.

PARK HOURS

The park is open 24/7 year-round. All entrances are open at all hours, except for the Hetch Hetchy entrance, which is open roughly dawn to dusk. Yosemite is in the Pacific Time Zone.

CELL PHONE RECEPTION

Cell phone reception can be hit or miss everywhere in the park. There are public telephones at entrance stations, visitor centers, all park restaurants and lodging facilities, gas stations, and in Yosemite Village.

Hotels

Indoor lodging options inside the park appear more expensive than initially seems warranted, but that premium pays off big-time in terms of the time you'll save—unless you are bunking within a few miles of a Yosemite entrance, you will face long commutes to the park when you stay outside its borders (though the Yosemite View Lodge, on Route 140, is within a reasonable half-hour's drive of Yosemite Valley).

Because of the park's immense popularity—not just with tourists from around the world but with Northern Californians who make weekend trips here—reservations are all but mandatory. Book up to one year ahead. ■ **TIP➔ If you're not set**

on a specific hotel or camp but just want to stay somewhere inside the park, call the main reservation number to check for availability and reserve (888/413–8869 or 602/278–8888 international). Park lodgings have a seven-day cancellation policy, so you may be able to snag last-minute reservations.

Restaurants

Yosemite National Park has a couple of moderately priced restaurants in lovely (which almost goes without saying) settings: the Mountain Room at Yosemite Valley Lodge and the dining room at the Wawona Hotel. The Ahwahnee hotel provides one of the finest dining experiences in the country.

Otherwise, food service is geared toward satisfying the masses as efficiently as possible. Yosemite Valley Lodge's Base Camp Eatery is the valley's best lower-cost, hot-food option, with Italian, classic American, and world-cuisine counter options. In Curry Village, the offerings at Seven Tents are overpriced and usually fairly bland, but you can get decent pizzas on the adjacent outdoor deck. In Yosemite Valley Village, the Village Grill whips up burgers and fries, Degnan's Kitchen has made-to-order sandwiches, and The Loft at Degnan's has an open, chaletlike dining area in which to enjoy barbecue meals and appetizers.

The White Wolf Lodge and Tuolumne Meadows Lodge—both off Tioga Road and therefore guaranteed open only from early June through September—have small restaurants where meals are competently prepared. Tuolumne Meadows also has a grill, and the gift shop at Glacier Point sells premade sandwiches, snacks, and hot dogs. During ski season, you'll also find one at the Badger Pass Ski Area, off Glacier Point Road.

Hotel and restaurant reviews have been shortened. For full information, visit Fodors.com. Hotel prices are the lowest cost of a standard double room in high season. Restaurant prices are the average cost of a main course at dinner, or if dinner is not served, at lunch.

What It Costs

	$	$$	$$$	$$$$
RESTAURANTS	under $17	$17–$26	$27–$36	over $36
HOTELS	under $150	$150–$250	$251–$350	over $350

Tours

★ Ansel Adams Camera Walks

SPECIAL-INTEREST | Photography enthusiasts shouldn't miss these guided, 90-minute walks offered four mornings (Monday, Tuesday, Thursday, and Saturday) each week by professional photographers. All are free, but participation is limited to 15 people so reservations are essential. Meeting points vary. ✉ *Yosemite National Park* ☎ *209/372–4413* 🌐 *www.anseladams.com* 🎟 *Free.*

Discover Yosemite

GUIDED TOURS | This outfit operates daily tours to Yosemite Valley, Mariposa Grove, and Glacier Point in 14- and 29-passenger vehicles. The tour travels along Highway 41 with stops in Bass Lake, Oakhurst, and Fish Camp; rates include lunch. Sunset tours to Sentinel Dome are additional summer options. ☎ *559/642–4400* 🌐 *discoveryosemite.com* 🎟 *From $158.*

Glacier Point Tour

GUIDED TOURS | This four-hour trip takes you from Yosemite Valley to the Glacier Point vista, 3,214 feet above the valley floor. Some people buy a $29 one-way ticket and hike down. Shuttles depart from the Yosemite Valley Lodge three times a day. ✉ *Yosemite National Park* ☎ *888/413–8869* 🌐 *www.travelyosemite.*

com 🎫 *From $57* ⏲ *Closed Nov.–late May* ✍ *Reservations essential.*

Grand Tour

GUIDED TOURS | For a full-day tour of Yosemite Valley, the Mariposa Grove of Giant Sequoias, and Glacier Point, try the Grand Tour, which departs from the Yosemite Valley Lodge in the valley. The tour stops for a picnic lunch (included) at the historic Wawona Hotel. ✉ *Yosemite National Park* ☎ *209/372–1240* 🌐 *www.travelyosemite.com* 🎫 *$110* ✍ *Reservations essential.*

Moonlight Tour

GUIDED TOURS | This after-dark version of the Valley Floor Tour takes place on moonlit nights from June through September, depending on weather conditions. ✉ *Yosemite National Park* ☎ *209/372–4386* 🌐 *www.travelyosemite.com* 🎫 *$38.*

Tuolumne Meadows Hikers Bus

BUS TOURS | For a full day's outing to the high country, opt for this ride up Tioga Road to Tuolumne Meadows. You'll stop at several overlooks, and you can connect with another shuttle at Tuolumne Lodge. This service is mostly for hikers and backpackers who want to reach high-country trailheads, but everyone is welcome. ✉ *Yosemite National Park* ☎ *209/372–1240* 🌐 *www.travelyosemite.com* 🎫 *$15 one-way, $23 round-trip* ⏲ *Closed Labor Day–mid-June* ✍ *Reservations essential.*

Valley Floor Tour

GUIDED TOURS | Take a two-hour tour of Yosemite Valley's highlights, complete with narration on the area's history, geology, and flora and fauna. Tours (offered year round) are either in trams or enclosed motor coaches, depending on weather conditions. ✉ *Yosemite National Park* ☎ *209/372–1240, 888/413–8869 reservations* 🌐 *www.travelyosemite.com* 🎫 *From $38.*

Visitor Information

PARK CONTACT INFORMATION Yosemite National Park. ☎ *209/372–0200* 🌐 *www.nps.gov/yose.*

Yosemite Valley

Yosemite Valley Visitor Center is 11.5 miles from the Arch Rock entrance and 15 miles east of El Portal.

The glacier-carved Yosemite Valley stretches nearly 8 miles along the Merced River. It holds many of the park's major sights, including El Capitan, Half Dome, Glacier Point, and famous waterfalls. The valley is accessible year-round. Park your car at Yosemite Village (home of the visitor center, museum, market, and other services), Curry Village, or near Yosemite Falls. Free shuttle buses loop through the eastern and western sections of the valley.

Sights

HISTORIC SITES

The Ahwahnee

HOTEL—SIGHT | Gilbert Stanley Underwood, architect of the Grand Canyon Lodge, also designed The Ahwahnee hotel. Opened in 1927, it is generally considered his best work. You can stay here (for about $500 a night), or simply explore the first-floor shops and perhaps have breakfast or lunch in the bustling and beautiful Dining Room or more casual bar. The Great Lounge, 77 feet long with magnificent 24-foot-high ceilings and all manner of artwork on display, beckons with big, comfortable chairs and relative calm. ✉ *Yosemite Valley, Ahwahnee Rd., Yosemite Village* ✣ *About ¾ mile east of Yosemite Valley Visitor Center* ☎ *209/372–1489* 🌐 *www.travelyosemite.com/lodging/the-ahwahnee.*

Yosemite's Valley Floor

KEY
Ranger Station
Campground
Picnic Area
Restaurant
Lodge
Trailhead
Restrooms
Scenic Viewpoint
Walking/Hiking Trails
John Muir Trail
Bicycle Path
Valley Floor
Yosemite Falls
Indian Village of Ahwahnee
YOSEMITE VILLAGE
Yosemite Museum
Wilderness Office
P.O.
Valley Visitor Center
Yosemite Valley Lodge
Merced River
Chapel
bicycle path
Road open only to bicycles and shuttlebuses
Housekeeping Camp
Yosemite Conservation Heritage Center
The Ahwahnee
Royal Arch Cascade
Royal Arches
Washington Column
Mirror Lake
Half Dome
North Pines
Lower Pines
Clarks Bridge
Upper Pines
Curry Village Store
Curry Village
Moran Point
Staircase Falls
Union Point
Four Mile Trail
Glacier Point
Glacier Point Road
Pohono Trail
Panorama Trail
Sentinel Rock
Sentinel Fall
Sentinel Dome
Happy Isles Bridge
Happy Isles Art & Nature Center
Grizzly Peak
Sierra Point
John Muir Trail
Illilouette Gorge
Vernal Fall
Emerald Pools
Mist Trail
Liberty Cap
Footbridge
Clark Point
Nevada Fall
Panorama Cliff
0
1/2 mi
0
1/2 km

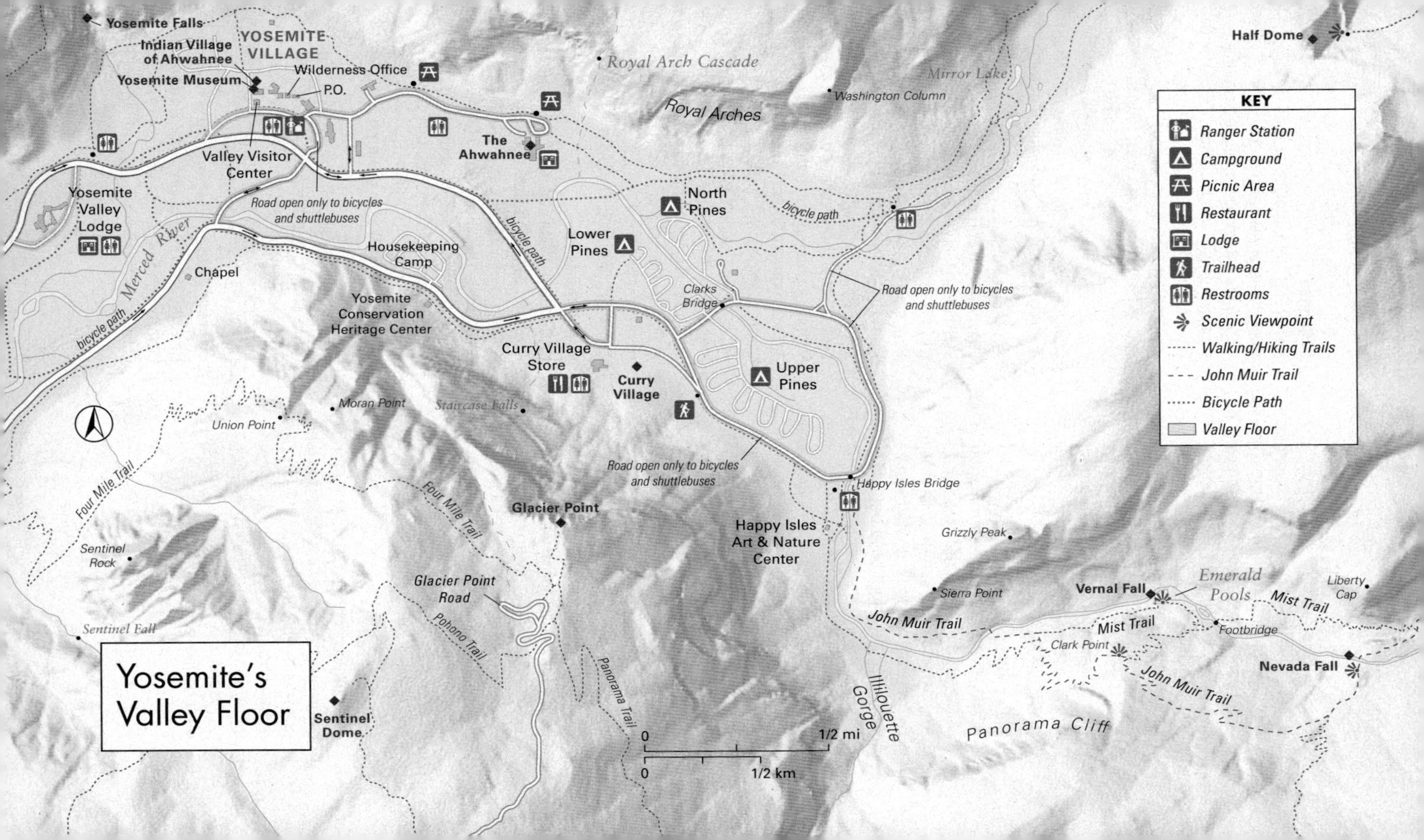

Curry Village

HOTEL—SIGHT | A couple of schoolteachers from Indiana founded Camp Curry in 1899 as a low-cost option for staying in the valley, which it remains today. Curry Village's 400-plus lodging options, many of them tent cabins, are spread over a large chunk of the valley's southeastern side. This is one family-friendly place, but it's more functional than attractive. ✉ *Southside Dr.* ✣ *About ½ mile east of Yosemite Village.*

Indian Village of Ahwahnee

MUSEUM VILLAGE | This solemn smattering of structures, accessed by a short loop trail behind the Yosemite Valley Visitor Center, offers a look at what Native American life might have been like in the 1870s. One interpretive sign points out that the Miwok people referred to the 19th-century newcomers as "Yohemite" or "Yohometuk," which have been translated as meaning "some of them are killers." ✉ *Northside Dr., Yosemite Village* 🎟 *Free.*

Yosemite Museum

MUSEUM | This small museum consists of a permanent exhibit that focuses on the history of the area and the people who once lived here. An adjacent gallery promotes contemporary and historic Yosemite art in revolving gallery exhibits. A docent demonstrates traditional Native American basket-weaving techniques a few days a week. ✉ *Yosemite Village* ☎ *209/372–0299* 🎟 *Free.*

SCENIC STOPS

Bridalveil Fall

BODY OF WATER | This 620-foot waterfall is often diverted dozens of feet one way or the other by the breeze. It is the first marvelous site you will see up close when you drive into Yosemite Valley. ✉ *Yosemite Valley, access from parking area off Wawona Rd.*

El Capitan

NATURE SITE | Rising 3,593 feet—more than 350 stories—above the valley, El Capitan is the largest exposed-granite monolith in the world. Since 1958, people have been climbing its entire face, including the famous "nose." You can spot adventurers with your binoculars by scanning the smooth and nearly vertical cliff for specks of color. ✉ *Yosemite National Park* ✣ *Off Northside Dr., about 4 miles west of Valley Visitor Center.*

★ Glacier Point

VIEWPOINT | If you lack the time, desire, or stamina to hike more than 3,200 feet up to Glacier Point from the Yosemite Valley floor, you can drive here—or take a bus from the valley—for a bird's-eye view. You are likely to encounter a lot of day-trippers on the short, paved trail that leads from the parking lot to the main overlook. Take a moment to veer off a few yards to the Geology Hut, which succinctly explains and illustrates what the valley looked like 10 million, 3 million, and 20,000 years ago. ✉ *Yosemite National Park* ✣ *Glacier Point Rd., 16 miles northeast of Rte. 41* ☎ *209/372–0200* ⏲ *Closed late Oct.–mid-May.*

★ Half Dome

NATURE SITE | Visitors' eyes are continually drawn to this remarkable granite formation that tops out at more than 4,700 feet above the valley floor. Despite its name, the dome is actually about three-quarters intact. You can hike to the top of it on an 8½-mile (one-way) trail whose last 400 feet must be ascended while holding onto a steel cable. Permits, available only by lottery, are required and are checked on the trail. Call ☎ *877/444–6777* or visit 🌐 *www.recreation.gov* well in advance of your trip for details. Back down in the valley, see Half Dome reflected in the Merced River by heading to Sentinel Bridge just before sundown. The brilliant orange light on Half Dome is a stunning sight.

✉ *Yosemite National Park* 🌐 *www.nps.gov/yose/planyourvisit/halfdome.htm.*

Nevada Fall

BODY OF WATER | Climb Mist Trail from Happy Isles for an up-close view of this 594-foot cascading beauty. If you don't want to hike (the trail's final approach is quite taxing), you can see it—albeit distantly—from Glacier Point. Stay safely on the trail, as there have been fatalities in recent years after visitors have fallen and been swept away by the water. ✉ *Yosemite Valley, access via Mist Trail from Nature Center at Happy Isles.*

Ribbon Fall

BODY OF WATER | At 1,612 feet, this is the highest single fall in North America. It's also the first waterfall to dry up in summer; the rainwater and melted snow that create the slender fall evaporate quickly at this height. Look just west of El Capitan for the best view of the fall from the base of Bridalveil Fall. ✉ *Yosemite Valley, west of El Capitan Meadow.*

Sentinel Dome

VIEWPOINT | The view from here is similar to that from Glacier Point, except you can't see the valley floor. A moderately steep, 1.1-mile path climbs to the viewpoint from the parking lot. Topping out at an elevation of 8,122 feet, Sentinel is more than 900 feet higher than Glacier Point. ✉ *Glacier Point Rd., off Rte. 41.*

Vernal Fall

BODY OF WATER | Fern-covered black rocks frame this 317-foot fall, and rainbows play in the spray at its base. You can get a distant view from Glacier Point, or hike to see it close up. You'll get wet, but the view is worth it. ✉ *Yosemite Valley, access via Mist Trail from Nature Center at Happy Isles.*

★ Yosemite Falls

BODY OF WATER | Actually three falls, they together constitute the highest combined waterfall in North America and the fifth highest in the world. The water from the top descends a total of 2,425 feet, and when the falls run hard, you can hear them thunder across the valley. If they dry up—that sometimes happens in late summer—the valley seems naked without the wavering tower of spray. If you hike the mile-long loop trail (partially paved) to the base of the Lower Fall in spring, prepare to get wet. You can get a good full-length view of the falls from the lawn of Yosemite Chapel, off Southside Drive. ✉ *Yosemite Valley, access from Yosemite Valley Lodge or trail parking area.*

TRAILS

Cook's Meadow Loop

TRAIL | **FAMILY** | Take this 1-mile, wheelchair-accessible, looped path around Cook's Meadow to see and learn the basics about Yosemite Valley's past, present, and future. A trail guide (available at a kiosk just outside the entrance) explains how to tell oaks, cedars, and pines apart; how fires help keep the forest floor healthy; and how pollution poses significant challenges to the park's inhabitants. *Easy.* ✉ *Yosemite National Park* ✢ *Trailhead: Across from Valley Visitor Center.*

Four-Mile Trail

TRAIL | If you decide to hike up Four-Mile Trail and back down again, allow about six hours for the challenging, 9½-mile round-trip. (The original 4-mile-long trail, Yosemite's first, has been lengthened to make it less steep.) The trailhead is on Southside Drive near Sentinel Beach, and the elevation change is 3,220 feet. For a considerably less strenuous experience, you can take a morning tour bus up to Glacier Point and enjoy a one-way downhill hike. *Difficult.* ✉ *Yosemite National Park* ✢ *Trailheads: At Glacier Point and on Southside Dr.*

★ John Muir Trail to Half Dome

TRAIL | Ardent and courageous trekkers continue on from Nevada Fall to the top of Half Dome. Some hikers attempt this entire 10- to 12-hour, 16¾-mile round-trip trek in one day; if you're planning to do this, remember that the 4,800-foot elevation gain and the 8,842-foot altitude will cause shortness of breath. Another option is to hike to a campground in Little Yosemite Valley near the top of Nevada Fall the first day, then climb to the top of Half Dome and hike out the next day. Get your wilderness permit (required for a one-day hike to Half Dome, too) at least a month in advance. Be sure to wear hiking boots and bring gloves. The last pitch up the back of Half Dome is very steep—the only way to climb this sheer rock face is to pull yourself up using the steel cable handrails, which are in place only from late spring to early fall. Those who brave the ascent will be rewarded with an unbeatable view of Yosemite Valley below and the high country beyond. Only 300 hikers per day are allowed atop Half Dome, and they all must have permits, which are distributed by lottery, one in the spring before the season starts and another two days before the climb. Contact 🌐 *www.recreation.gov* for details. *Difficult.* ✉ *Yosemite National Park* ✥ *Trailhead: At Happy Isles* 🌐 *www.nps.gov/yose/planyourvisit/halfdome.htm.*

Mirror Lake Trail

TRAIL | FAMILY | Along this trail, you'll look up at Half Dome directly from its base and also take in Tenaya Canyon, Mt. Watkins, and Washington Column. The way is paved for a mile to Mirror Lake itself (total of 2 miles out and back). The trail that loops around the lake continues from there (for a total of 5 miles). Interpretive exhibits provide insight on the area's natural and cultural history. *Easy–Moderate.* ✉ *Yosemite Village* ✥ *Trailhead: Shuttle bus stop #17 on the Happy Isles Loop.*

Mist Trail

TRAIL | Except for Lower Yosemite Fall, more visitors take this trail (or portions of it) than any other in the park. The trek up to and back from Vernal Fall is 3 miles. Add another 4 miles total by continuing up to 594-foot Nevada Fall; the trail becomes quite steep and slippery in its final stages. The elevation gain to Vernal Fall is 1,000 feet, and to Nevada Fall an additional 1,000 feet. The Merced River tumbles down both falls on its way to a tranquil flow through the valley. *Moderate.* ✉ *Yosemite National Park* ✥ *Trailhead: At Happy Isles.*

★ Panorama Trail

TRAIL | Few hikes come with the visual punch that this 8½-mile trail provides. It starts from Glacier Point and descends to Yosemite Valley. The star attraction is Half Dome, visible from many intriguing angles, but you also see three waterfalls up close and walk through a manzanita grove. *Moderate.* ✉ *Yosemite National Park* ✥ *Trailhead: At Glacier Point.*

★ Yosemite Falls Trail

TRAIL | Yosemite Falls is the highest waterfall in North America. The upper fall (1,430 feet), the middle cascades (675 feet), and the lower fall (320 feet) combine for a total of 2,425 feet, and when viewed from the valley appear as a single waterfall. The ¼-mile trail leads from the parking lot to the base of the falls. Upper Yosemite Fall Trail, a strenuous 7.2-mile round-trip climb rising 2,700 feet, takes you above the top of the falls. Lower trail: *Easy.* Upper trail: *Difficult.* ✉ *Yosemite National Park* ✥ *Trailhead: Off Camp 4, north of Northside Dr.*

VISITOR CENTERS

Valley Visitor Center

INFO CENTER | Learn about Yosemite Valley's geology, vegetation, and human inhabitants at this visitor center, which is also staffed with helpful rangers and contains a bookstore with a wide selection of books and maps. Two films, including one by Ken Burns, alternate on the half hour in the theater behind the visitor center. ✉ *Yosemite Village* ☎ *209/372–0200* 🌐 *www.nps.gov/yose.*

Yosemite Conservation Heritage Center

INFO CENTER | This small but striking National Historic Landmark (formerly Le Conte Memorial Lodge), with its granite walls and steeply pitched shingle roof, is Yosemite's first permanent public information center. Step inside to see the cathedral-like interior, which contains a library and environmental exhibits. To find out about evening programs, check the kiosk out front. ✉ *Southside Dr., about ½ mile west of Half Dome Village* 🌐 *sierraclub.org/yosemite-heritage-center* ⏲ *Closed Mon., Tues., and Oct.–Apr.*

Restaurants

★ The Ahwahnee Dining Room

$$$$ | **EUROPEAN** | Rave reviews about The Ahwahnee hotel's dining room's appearance are fully justified—it features towering windows, a 34-foot-high ceiling with interlaced sugar-pine beams, and massive chandeliers. Reservations are always advised, and the attire is "resort casual." **Known for:** lavish $56 Sunday brunch; finest dining in the park; bar menu with lighter lunch and dinner fare at more affordable prices. $ *Average main: $39* ✉ *The Ahwahnee, Ahwahnee Rd., about ¾ mile east of Yosemite Valley Visitor Center, Yosemite Village* ☎ *209/372–1489* 🌐 *www.travelyosemite.com.*

Base Camp Eatery

$ | **AMERICAN** | The design of this modern food court, open for breakfast, lunch, and dinner, honors the history of rock climbing in Yosemite. Choose from a wide range of menu options, from hamburgers, salads, and pizzas, to rice and noodle bowls. **Known for:** grab-and-go selections; best casual dining venue in the park; automated ordering kiosks to speed up service. $ *Average main: $12* ✉ *Yosemite Valley Lodge, about ¾ mile west of visitor center, Yosemite Village* ☎ *209/372–1265* 🌐 *www.travelyosemite.com.*

Curry Village Seven Tents

$$ | **AMERICAN** | Formerly Curry Village Pavilion, this cafeteria-style eatery serves everything from roasted meats and salads to pastas, burritos, and beyond. Alternatively, order a pizza from the stand on the deck, and take in the views of the valley's granite walls. **Known for:** convenient eats; cocktails at Bar 1899; additional venues (Meadow Grill, Pizza Patio, Coffee Corner). $ *Average main: $18* ✉ *Curry Village* ☎ *209/372–8303* ⏲ *Closed mid-Oct.–mid-Apr. No lunch.*

★ Mountain Room

$$$ | **AMERICAN** | Gaze at Yosemite Falls through this dining room's wall of windows—almost every table has a view—as you nosh on steaks, seafood, and classic California salads and desserts. The Mountain Room Lounge, a few steps away in the Yosemite Valley Lodge complex, has about 10 beers on tap. **Known for:** locally sourced, organic ingredients; usually there is a wait for a table (no reservations); vegetarian and vegan options. $ *Average main: $29* ✉ *Yosemite Valley Lodge, Northside Dr., about ¾ mile west of visitor center, Yosemite Village* ☎ *209/372–1403* 🌐 *www.travelyosemite.com* ⏲ *No lunch except Sun. brunch.*

Village Grill Deck

$ | **FAST FOOD** | If a burger joint is what you've been missing, head to this bustling eatery in Yosemite Village that serves veggie, salmon, and a few other burger varieties in addition to the usual beef patties. Order at the counter, then take your tray out to the deck, and enjoy your meal under the trees. **Known for:** burgers, sandwiches, and hot dogs; crowds; outdoor seating on expansive deck. $ *Average main: $12* ✉ *Yosemite Village* ✣ *100 yards east of Yosemite Valley Visitor Center* ☎ *209/372–1207* 🌐 *www.travelyosemite.com* ⏲ *Closed Oct.–Apr. No dinner.*

Hotels

★ The Ahwahnee

$$$$ | **HOTEL** | This National Historic Landmark is constructed of sugar-pine logs and features Native American design motifs; public spaces are enlivened with art-deco flourishes, Persian rugs, and

elaborate iron- and woodwork. **Pros:** best lodge in Yosemite; helpful concierge; in the historic heart of the valley. **Cons:** expensive rates; some reports that service has slipped in recent years; slow or nonexistent Wi-Fi in some hotel areas. *$ Rooms from: $581 ✉ Ahwahnee Rd., about ¾ mile east of Yosemite Valley Visitor Center, Yosemite Village ☎ 801/559–4884 🌐 www.travelyosemite.com 125 rooms No meals.*

Curry Village
$ | HOTEL | Opened in 1899 as a place for budget-conscious travelers, Curry Village has plain accommodations: standard motel rooms, simple cabins with either private or shared baths, and tent cabins with shared baths. **Pros:** close to many activities; family-friendly atmosphere; surrounded by iconic valley views. **Cons:** community bathrooms need updating; can be crowded; sometimes a bit noisy. *$ Rooms from: $143 ✉ South side of Southside Dr. ☎ 888/413–8869, 602/278–8888 international 🌐 www.travelyosemite.com 583 units No meals.*

Yosemite Valley Lodge
$$$ | HOTEL | This 1915 lodge near Yosemite Falls is a collection of numerous two-story, glass-and-wood structures tucked beneath the trees. **Pros:** centrally located; dependably clean rooms; lots of tours leave from out front. **Cons:** can feel impersonal; high prices; no in-room a/c. *$ Rooms from: $260 ✉ 9006 Yosemite Valley Lodge Dr., Yosemite Village ☎ 888/413–8869 🌐 www.travelyosemite.com 245 rooms No meals.*

Shopping

Ansel Adams Gallery
ART GALLERIES | Framed prints of the famed nature photographer's best works are on sale here, as are affordable posters. New works by contemporary artists are also available, along with Native American jewelry and handicrafts. The elegant camera shop conducts photography workshops, from free camera walks a few mornings a week to five-day courses. *✉ Northside Dr., Yosemite Village ☎ 209/372–4413 🌐 anseladams.com.*

Curry Village Gift & Grocery
CONVENIENCE/GENERAL STORES | You can pick up groceries and supplies at this bustling shop at the east end of the valley. *✉ Curry Village ☎ 209/372–8391.*

Housekeeping Camp General Store
You'll find the basics here for picnics, campfires, and other outdoor activities. *✉ Southside Dr., ½ mile west of Half Dome Village ☎ 209/372–8353.*

Village Store
CONVENIENCE/GENERAL STORES | The Yosemite Valley's largest store has an extensive selection of groceries (including many organic items), household products, and personal-care items. It also has an extensive gift and souvenir shop. *✉ Yosemite Village ☎ 209/372–1253.*

Yosemite Bookstore
BOOKS/STATIONERY | An extensive selection of maps and books is available at this store in the Valley Visitor Center. *✉ Valley Visitor Center, Yosemite Village ☎ 209/372–0299 🌐 shop.yosemite.org.*

Yosemite Museum Shop
CRAFTS | In addition to books on California's Native Americans, this tiny shop sells traditional arts and crafts. *✉ Yosemite Village ☎ 209/372–0295.*

Wawona

27 miles from Yosemite Valley Visitor Center, 7½ miles north of Fish Camp.

Wawona is a small village (elevation 4,000 feet) about an hours' drive south of Yosemite Valley. It's rich in pioneer history (visit the Pioneer Yosemite History Center to learn more) and is home to the Victorian-era Wawona Hotel. The park's famous Mariposa Grove of Giant Sequoias is a few miles down the road.

Sights

HISTORIC SIGHTS

Pioneer Yosemite History Center

MUSEUM | FAMILY | These historic buildings reflect different eras of Yosemite's history, from the 1850s through the early 1900s. They were moved to Wawona (the largest stage stop in Yosemite in the late 1800s) from various areas of Yosemite in the '50s and '60s. There is a self-guided-tour pamphlet available for 50 cents. Weekends and some weekdays in the summer, costumed docents conduct free blacksmithing and "wet-plate" photography demonstrations, and for a small fee you can take a stagecoach ride. ✉ *Rte. 41, Wawona* ☎ *209/375–9531* 🌐 *www.nps.gov/yose/planyourvisit/waw.htm* 🎫 *Free* ⏲ *Closed Mon., Tues., and mid-Sept.–early June.*

Wawona Hotel

HOTEL—SIGHT | Imagine a white-bearded Mark Twain relaxing in a rocking chair on one of the broad verandas of one of the park's first lodges, a whitewashed series of two-story buildings from the Victorian era. Plop down in one of the dozens of white Adirondack chairs on the sprawling lawn, and look across the road at the area's only golf course, one of the few links in the world that does not employ fertilizers or other chemicals. ✉ *Rte. 41, Wawona* ☎ *209/375–1425* 🌐 *www.travelyosemite.com/lodging/wawona-hotel* ⏲ *Closed Dec.–Mar. except 2 wks around Christmas and New Year's.*

SCENIC DRIVES

Route 41

SCENIC DRIVE | Entering Yosemite National Park via this road, which follows an ultimately curvy course 55 miles from Fresno through the Yosemite gateway towns of Oakhurst and Fish Camp, presents you with an immediate, important choice: turn right to visit the Mariposa Grove of Giant Sequoias 4 miles to the east, or turn left to travel via Wawona to Yosemite Valley, 31 miles away. Try to do both. (You can get by with an hour in Mariposa Grove if you're really pressed for time.) As you approach the valley, you will want to pull into the Tunnel View parking lot (it's on the east side of the mile-long tunnel) and marvel at what lies ahead: from left to right, El Capitan, Half Dome, and Bridalveil Fall. From here, the valley is another 5 miles. The drive time on Wawona Road alone is about an hour. Make a full day of it by adding Glacier Point to the itinerary; get there via a 16-mile seasonal road that shoots east from Route 41 and passes the Badger Pass Ski Area. ✉ *Yosemite National Park.*

SCENIC STOPS

Mariposa Grove of Giant Sequoias

FOREST | Of Yosemite's three sequoia groves—the others being Merced and Tuolumne, both near Crane Flat and Hetch Hetchy well to the north—Mariposa is by far the largest and easiest to walk around. Grizzly Giant, whose base measures 96 feet around, has been estimated to be one of the world's largest. Perhaps more astoundingly, it's about 1,800 years old. Park at the grove's welcome plaza, and ride the free shuttle (required most of the year). Summer weekends are crowded. ✉ *Yosemite National Park* ✣ *Rte. 41, 2 miles north of south entrance station* 🌐 *www.nps.gov/yose/planyourvisit/mg.htm.*

TRAILS

Chilnualna Falls Trail

TRAIL | This Wawona-area trail runs 4 miles one-way to the top of the falls, then leads into the backcountry, connecting with other trails. This is one of the park's most inspiring and secluded—albeit strenuous—trails. Past the tumbling cascade, and up through forests, you'll emerge before a panorama at the top. *Difficult.* ✉ *Wawona* ✣ *Trailhead: At Chilnualna Falls Rd., off Rte. 41.*

Did You Know?
In mid- to late February, when the conditions are right in the evenings (clear sky, flowing falls), Horsetail Fall, on the eastern edge of El Capitan, experiences Firefall—it looks like the falls are on fire.

Restaurants

Wawona Hotel Dining Room

$$$ | AMERICAN | Watch deer graze in the meadow while you dine in the romantic, candlelit dining room of the whitewashed Wawona Hotel, which dates from the late 1800s. The American-style cuisine favors fresh ingredients and flavors; trout and flatiron steaks are menu staples. **Known for:** Saturday-night barbecues on the lawn; historic ambience; Mother's Day and other Sunday holiday brunches. *Average main: $28 ✉ 8308 Wawona Rd., Wawona ☎ 209/375–1425 ⏲ Closed most of Dec., Jan., Feb., and Mar.*

Hotels

Redwoods in Yosemite

$$$ | RENTAL | This collection of more than 125 homes in the Wawona area is a great alternative to the overcrowded valley. **Pros:** sense of privacy; peaceful setting; full kitchens. **Cons:** 45-minute drive from the valley; some units have no a/c; cell phone service can be spotty. *Rooms from: $260 ✉ 8038 Chilnualna Falls Rd., off Rte. 41, Wawona ☎ 209/375–6666 international, 844/355–0039 🌐 www.redwoodsinyosemite.com 125 units No meals.*

Wawona Hotel

$$ | HOTEL | This 1879 National Historic Landmark at Yosemite's southern end is a Victorian-era mountain resort, with whitewashed buildings, wraparound verandas, and pleasant, no-frills rooms decorated with period pieces. **Pros:** lovely building; peaceful atmosphere; historic photos in public areas. **Cons:** few modern amenities, such as phones and TVs; an hour's drive from Yosemite Valley; shared bathrooms in half the rooms. *Rooms from: $157 ✉ 8308 Wawona Rd., Wawona ☎ 888/413–8869 🌐 www.travelyosemite.com ⏲ Closed Dec.–Mar., except mid-Dec.–Jan. 2 104 rooms, 50 with bath Free breakfast.*

Shopping

Wawona Store

The Wawona area's only market carries essentials (for some, that means ice cream) in its grocery section. There's also a gift shop. *✉ Rte. 41 at Forest Dr., Wawona ☎ 209/375–6574.*

Tuolumne Meadows

56 miles from Yosemite Valley, 21 miles west of Lee Vining via Tioga Rd.

The largest subalpine meadow in the Sierra (at 8,600 feet) is a popular way station for backpack trips along the Pacific Crest and John Muir trails. The setting is not as dramatic as Yosemite Valley, 56 miles away, but the almost perfectly flat basin, about 2½ miles long, is intriguing, and in July it's resplendent with wildflowers. The most popular day hike is to Lembert Dome, atop which you'll have breathtaking views of the basin below. Note that Tioga Road rarely opens before June and usually closes by November.

Sights

SCENIC DRIVES

Tioga Road

SCENIC DRIVE | Few mountain drives can compare with this 59-mile road, especially its eastern half between Lee Vining and Olmstead Point. As you climb 3,200 feet to the 9,945-foot summit of Tioga Pass (Yosemite's sole eastern entrance for cars), you'll encounter broad vistas of the granite-splotched High Sierra and its craggy but hearty trees and shrubs. Past the bustling scene at Tuolumne Meadows, you'll see picturesque Tenaya Lake and then Olmsted Point, where you'll get your first peek at Half Dome. Driving Tioga Road one way takes approximately 1½ hours. Wildflowers bloom here in July and August. By November, the high-altitude road closes for the winter;

it sometimes doesn't reopen until early June. ✉ *Yosemite National Park.*

SCENIC STOPS

High Country

NATURE PRESERVE | The high-alpine region east of the valley—a land of alpenglow and top-of-the-world vistas—is often missed by crowds who come to gawk at the more publicized splendors. Summer wildflowers, which pop up mid-July through August, carpet the meadows and mountainsides with pink, purple, blue, red, yellow, and orange. On foot or on horseback are the only ways to get here. For information on trails and backcountry permits, check with the visitor center. ✉ *Yosemite National Park.*

Restaurants

Tuolumne Meadows Grill

$ | FAST FOOD | Serving throughout the day until 5 or 6 pm, this fast-food eatery cooks up basic breakfast, lunch, and snacks. It's possible that ice cream tastes better at this altitude. **Known for:** soft-serve ice cream; crowds; fresh local ingredients. *$ Average main: $8 ✉ Tioga Rd. (Rte. 120), 1½ miles east of Tuolumne Meadows Visitor Center ☎ 209/372–8426 🌐 www.travelyosemite.com ⏲ Closed Oct.–Memorial Day. No dinner.*

Tuolumne Meadows Lodge Restaurant

$$ | AMERICAN | In a central dining tent beside the Tuolumne River, this restaurant serves a menu of hearty American fare at breakfast and dinner. The red-and-white-checkered tablecloths and a handful of communal tables give it the feeling of an old-fashioned summer camp. **Known for:** box lunches; communal tables; small menu. *$ Average main: $24 ✉ Tioga Rd. (Rte. 120) ☎ 209/372–8413 🌐 www.travelyosemite.com ⏲ Closed late Sept.–mid-June. No lunch.*

White Wolf Lodge Restaurant

$$ | AMERICAN | Those fueling up for a day on the trail or famished after a high-country hike will appreciate the all-you-can-eat, family-style breakfasts and dinners in this tiny dining room. Mashed potatoes, big pots of curried vegetables, and heaps of pasta often grace the tables in this cozy out-of-the-way place. **Known for:** all you can eat; box lunches available; rustic vibe. *$ Average main: $24 ✉ Yosemite National Park ✣ Tioga Rd. (Rte. 120), 25 miles west of Tuolumne Meadows and 15 miles east of Crane Flat ☎ 209/372–8416 🌐 www.travelyosemite.com ⏲ Closed mid-Sept.–mid-June. No lunch.*

Hotels

White Wolf Lodge

$ | HOTEL | Set in a subalpine meadow, the White Wolf Lodge has rustic accommodations and makes an excellent base camp for hiking the backcountry. **Pros:** quiet location; near some of Yosemite's most beautiful, less crowded hikes; good restaurant. **Cons:** far from the valley; tent cabins share bathhouse; remote setting. *$ Rooms from: $138 ✉ Yosemite National Park ✣ Off Tioga Rd. (Rte. 120), 25 miles west of Tuolumne Meadows and 15 miles east of Crane Flat ☎ 801/559–4884 ⏲ Closed mid-Sept.–mid-June 28 cabins No meals.*

Shopping

Tuolumne Meadows Store

CONVENIENCE/GENERAL STORES | The only retailer in the high country carries backpacking and camping supplies, climbing gear, trail maps and guides, food and beverages, and fishing licenses. ✉ *Yosemite National Park ✣ Tioga Rd. Rte. 120, 1½ miles east of Tuolumne Meadows Visitor Center ☎ 209/372–8096 ⏲ Closed Oct.–early June.*

Hetch Hetchy

18 miles from the Big Oak Flat entrance station, 43 miles north of El Portal via Hwy. 120 and Evergreen Rd.

This glacier-carved valley (now filled with water) and surrounding peaks anchor the northwestern section of the park. Drive about 2 miles west of the Big Oak Flat entrance station and turn right on Evergreen Road, which leads down to the Hetch Hetchy entrance and trails along the dam and into the mountains. Two groves of giant sequoia trees—Merced and Tuolumne—grow near Crane Flat, a tiny collection of services south of Big Oak Flat at the intersection of Highway 120 and Tioga Road.

Sights

SCENIC STOPS

Hetch Hetchy Reservoir

BODY OF WATER | When Congress approved the O'Shaughnessy Dam in 1913, pragmatism triumphed over aestheticism. Some 2.5 million residents of the San Francisco Bay Area continue to get their water from this 117-billion-gallon reservoir. Although spirited efforts are being made to restore the Hetch Hetchy Valley to its former, pristine glory, three-quarters of San Francisco voters in 2012 ultimately opposed a measure to even consider draining the reservoir. Eight miles long, the reservoir is Yosemite's largest body of water, and one that can be seen up close from several trails. ✉ *Hetch Hetchy Rd., about 15 miles north of Big Oak Flat entrance station.*

Tuolomne Grove of Giant Sequoias

FOREST | About two dozen mature giant sequoias stand in Tuolumne Grove in the park's northwestern region, just east of Crane Flat and south of the Big Oak Flat entrance. Park at the trailhead and walk about a mile to see them. The trail descends about 500 feet down to the grove, so it's a relatively steep hike back up. Be sure to bring plenty of drinking water. ✉ *On Tioga Rd., just east of Crane Flat, about a 45-minute drive from Yosemite Valley.*

TRAILS

Merced Grove of Giant Sequoias

FOREST | Hike 1½ miles (3 miles round-trip, 500-foot elevation drop and gain) to the small and scenic Merced Grove and its approximately two dozen mature giant sequoias. The setting here is typically uncrowded and serene. Note that you can also park here and hike about 2 miles round-trip to the Tuolumne Grove. Bring plenty of water for either outing. *Moderate.* ✉ *Big Oak Flat Rd.* ✣ *East of the Big Oak Flat entrance, about 6 miles west of Crane Flat and a 45-minute drive from Yosemite Valley.*

Hotels

Evergreen Lodge at Yosemite

$$$ | **RESORT** | **FAMILY** | Amid the trees near Yosemite National Park's Hetch Hetchy entrance, this sprawling property is perfect for families. **Pros:** cabin complex includes amphitheater, pool, and more; guided tours available; great roadhouse-style restaurant. **Cons:** no in-room TVs; long, winding access road; spotty cell service. 💲 *Rooms from: $280* ✉ *33160 Evergreen Rd., 30 miles east of town of Groveland, Groveland* ☎ *209/379–2606* 🌐 *www.evergreen-lodge.com* 🛏 *88 cabins* 🍽 *No meals.*

★ Rush Creek Lodge

$$$$ | **RESORT** | **FAMILY** | Occupying 20 acres on a wooded hillside, this sleek, nature-inspired complex has a saltwater pool and hot tubs, a restaurant and tavern with indoor and outdoor seating, a guided recreation program, a spa and wellness program, a general store, nature trails, and outdoor play areas that include a zip line and a giant slide. **Pros:** close to Yosemite's Big Oak Flat entrance; YARTS bus stops here and connects with Yosemite Valley and Sonora

Half Dome at sunset

spring–fall; year-round evening s'mores. **Cons:** no in-room TVs; pricey in high season; spotty cell service. *Rooms from: $410 34001 Hwy. 120, Groveland 25 miles east of Groveland, 23 miles north of Yosemite Valley 209/379–2373 www.rushcreeklodge.com 143 rooms No meals.*

Shopping

Crane Flat Store

CONVENIENCE/GENERAL STORES | This small store is a convenient place to get gas and pick up snacks and camping supplies if you're arriving via Route 120. The store is closed November–March. *Yosemite National Park Intersection of Big Oak Flat Rd. and Tioga Rd., 7 miles east of Big Oak Flat entrance 209/379–2742 Closed Dec.–Mar.*

Activities

BIKING

One enjoyable way to see Yosemite Valley is to ride a bike beneath its lofty granite monoliths. The eastern valley has 12 miles of paved, flat bicycle paths across meadows and through woods, with bike racks at convenient stopping points. For a greater challenge, you can ride on 196 miles of paved park roads elsewhere. Note, though, that bicycles are not allowed on hiking trails or in the backcountry, and kids under 18 must wear a helmet.

Yosemite bike rentals

BICYCLING | You can arrange rentals ($12 per hour or $36 per day) at Yosemite Valley Lodge and Curry Village bike stands. Bikes with child trailers, baby-jogger strollers, and wheelchairs are also available. *Yosemite Valley Lodge or Curry Village 209/372–4386 www.travelyosemite.com.*

BIRD-WATCHING

More than 250 bird species have been spotted in the park, including the sage sparrow, pygmy owl, blue grouse, and mountain bluebird. Park rangers lead free bird-watching walks in Yosemite Valley a few days each week in summer; check at a visitor center or information station for times and locations. Binoculars sometimes are available for loan.

Birding seminars

BIRD WATCHING | The Yosemite Conservancy organizes day- and weekend-long seminars for beginner and intermediate birders, as well as bird walks a few times a week. They can also arrange private naturalist-led walks any time of year. ✉ *Yosemite National Park* 🌐 *www.yosemite.org* 🎫 *From $99.*

CAMPING

If you are going to concentrate solely on valley sites and activities, you should endeavor to stay in one of the "Pines" campgrounds, which are clustered near Curry Village and within an easy stroll from that busy complex's many facilities. For a more primitive and quiet experience, and to be near many backcountry hikes, try one of the Tioga Road campgrounds.

RESERVATIONS

National Park Service Reservations Office

Reservations are required at many of Yosemite's campgrounds. You can book a site up to five months in advance, starting on the 15th of the month. Unless otherwise noted, book your site through the central National Park Service Reservations Office. If you don't have reservations when you arrive, many sites, especially those outside Yosemite Valley, are available on a first-come, first-served basis. ☎ *877/444–6777 reservations, 518/885–3639 international, 888/448–1474 customer service* 🌐 *www.recreation.gov.*

RECOMMENDED CAMPGROUNDS YOSEMITE VALLEY

Camp 4. Formerly known as Sunnyside Walk-In, this is the only valley campground available on a walk-in basis—and the only one west of Yosemite Lodge. Open year-round, it's favored by rock climbers and solo campers. From mid-September to mid-May, the camp operates on a first-come, first-served basis; it typically fills early in the morning except in winter. From mid-May to mid-September, campsites are available only by daily lottery (one day in advance via Recreation.gov from midnight to 4 pm Pacific Time) for up to 12 people per application, 6 people per campsite. This is a tents-only campground with 36 sites. ✉ *Base of Yosemite Falls Trail, just west of Yosemite Valley Lodge on Northside Dr., Yosemite Village.*

Housekeeping Camp. Each of the 266 units here consists of three walls (usually concrete) that are covered with two layers of canvas; the open-air side can be closed off with a heavy, white-canvas curtain. Inside, typically, are bunk beds and a full-size bed (dirty mattresses included); outside is a covered patio, fire ring, picnic table, and bear box. You rent "bedpacks," consisting of blankets, sheets, and other comforts in the main building, which also has a small grocery. Lots of guests take advantage of the adjacent Merced River. ✉ *Southside Dr., ½ mile west of Curry Village.*

Lower Pines. This moderate-size campground with 60 small tent/RV sites sits directly along the Merced River; it's a short walk to the trailheads for the Mirror Lake and Mist trails. Expect lots of people. ✉ *At east end of valley.*

Upper Pines. One of the valley's largest campgrounds, with 238 tent and RV sites, is also the closest one to the trailheads. Expect large crowds in the summer—and little privacy. ✉ *At east end of valley, near Curry Village.*

CRANE FLAT

Crane Flat. This 166-site camp for tents and RVs is on Yosemite's western boundary, south of Hodgdon Meadow and just 17 miles from the valley but far from its bustle. A small grove of sequoias is nearby. ✉ *From Big Oak Flat entrance on Rte. 120, drive 10 miles east to campground entrance on right.*

WAWONA

Bridalveil Creek. This campground sits among lodgepole pines at 7,200 feet, above the valley on Glacier Point Road. From here, you can easily drive to Glacier Point's magnificent valley views. Fall evenings can be cold. The 74 sites can accommodate tents and RVs. ✉ *From Rte. 41 in Wawona, go north to Glacier Point Rd. and turn right; entrance to campground is 25 miles ahead on right side.*

Wawona. Near the Mariposa Grove, just downstream from a popular fishing spot, this year-round campground's 93 sites for tents and RVs are larger and less densely packed than those at campgrounds in Yosemite Valley. The downside? It's an hour's drive to the valley's attractions. ✉ *Rte. 41, 1 mile north of Wawona.*

TUOLUMNE MEADOWS

Porcupine Flat. Sixteen miles west of Tuolumne Meadows, this campground sits at 8,100 feet. Sites are close together, but if you want to be in the high country and Tuolumne Meadows is full, this is a good bet. There is no water available. The campground's 52 sites for tents and RVs can't accommodate rigs of 35 feet or longer. ✉ *Rte. 120, 16 miles west of Tuolumne Meadows.*

Tuolumne Meadows. In a wooded area at 8,600 feet, just south of its namesake meadow, this is one of the most spectacular and sought-after campgrounds in Yosemite. Hot showers can be used at the Tuolumne Meadows Lodge—though only at certain times. Half the 314 tent and RV sites are first-come, first-served, so arrive early, or make reservations. The campground is open July–September. ✉ *Rte. 120, 46 miles east of Big Oak Flat entrance station.*

White Wolf. Set in the beautiful high country at 8,000 feet, this is a prime spot for hikers from early July to mid-September. There are 87 tent and RV sites; rigs of up to 27 feet long are permitted. ✉ *Tioga Rd., 15 miles east of Big Oak Flat entrance.*

EDUCATIONAL OFFERINGS

CLASSES AND SEMINARS

Art Classes

LOCAL SPORTS | Professional artists conduct workshops in watercolor, etching, drawing, and other media. Bring your own materials, or purchase the basics at the Happy Isles Art and Nature Center. Children under 12 must be accompanied by an adult. The center also offers beginner art workshops and children's art and family craft programs ($20–$40 per person). ✉ *Happy Isles Art and Nature Center* 🌐 *www.yosemite.org* 🎫 *$20* 🕒 *No classes Sun. Closed Dec.–Feb.*

Happy Isles Art and Nature Center

LOCAL SPORTS | **FAMILY** | This family-focused center has a rotating selection of kid-friendly activities and hands-on exhibits that teach tykes and their parents about the park's ecosystem. Books, toys, and T-shirts are stocked in the small gift shop. ✉ *Yosemite National Park* ✣ *Off Southside Dr., about ¾ mile east of Curry Village* 🎫 *Free* 🕒 *Closed Oct.–Apr.*

Yosemite Outdoor Adventures

LOCAL SPORTS | Naturalists, scientists, and park rangers lead multihour to multiday outings on topics from woodpeckers to fire management to day hikes and bird-watching. Most sessions take place spring through fall with just a few in winter. ✉ *Yosemite National Park* 🌐 *www.yosemite.org* 🎫 *From $99.*

RANGER PROGRAMS

Junior Ranger Program

LOCAL SPORTS | FAMILY | Children ages 3 to 13 can participate in the informal, self-guided Junior Ranger program. Park activity handbooks ($3.50 for ages 7 to 13 and $3 for Junior Cubs ages 3 to 6) are available at the Valley Visitor Center, the Happy Isles Art and Nature Center, the Tuolumne Visitor Center, and the Wawona Visitor Center. Once kids complete the book, rangers present them with a badge and, in some cases, a certificate. ✉ *Valley Visitor Center or the Happy Isles Art & Nature Center* ☎ *209/372–0299.*

Ranger-Led Programs

LOCAL SPORTS | Rangers lead entertaining walks and give informative talks several times a day from spring to fall. The schedule is more limited in winter, but most days you can find a program somewhere in the park. In the evenings at Yosemite Valley Lodge and Curry Village, lectures, slide shows, and documentary films present unique perspectives on Yosemite. On summer weekends, campgrounds at Curry Village and Tuolumne Meadows host sing-along campfire programs. Schedules and locations are posted on bulletin boards throughout the park as well as in the indispensable *Yosemite Guide,* which is distributed to visitors as they arrive at the park. ✉ *Yosemite National Park* 🌐 *nps.gov/yose.*

Wee Wild Ones

LOCAL SPORTS | FAMILY | Designed for kids under 10, this 45-minute program includes naturalist-led games, songs, stories, and crafts about Yosemite wildlife, plants, and geology. The event is held outdoors before the regular Yosemite Valley Lodge evening programs in summer and fall. All children must be accompanied by an adult. ✉ *Yosemite National Park* ☎ *209/372–1153* 🌐 *www.travelyosemite.com* 🎟 *Free.*

FISHING

The waters in Yosemite are not stocked; trout, mostly brown and rainbow, live here but are not plentiful. Yosemite's fishing season begins on the last Saturday in April and ends on November 15. Some waterways are off-limits at certain times; be sure to inquire at the visitor center about regulations.

A California fishing license is required; licenses cost around $17 for one day, $26.50 for two days, and $53 for 10 days. Full-season licenses cost $53 for state residents and $142 for nonresidents (costs fluctuate year to year). Buy your license in season at **Yosemite Mountain Shop in Curry Village** (☎ *209/372–1286*) or at the **Wawona Store** (☎ *209/375–6574*).

GOLF

The Wawona Golf Course is one of the country's few organic golf courses; it's also an Audubon Cooperative sanctuary for birds. You can play a round or take a lesson from the pro here.

Wawona Golf Course

GOLF | This organic (one of only a handful in the United States), 9-hole course has two sets of tee positions per hole to provide an 18-hole course. ✉ *Rte. 41, Wawona* ☎ *209/375–4386* 🌐 *www.travelyosemite.com* 🎟 *$24 for 9 holes; $39 for 18 holes* 🏌 *9 holes, 3011 yards, par 35* ☞ *Closed Nov.–early May.*

HIKING

Wilderness Center

HIKING/WALKING | This facility provides free wilderness permits, which are required for overnight camping (advance reservations are available for $5 per person plus $5 per reservation and are highly recommended for popular trailheads in summer and on weekends). The staff here also provides maps and advice to hikers heading into the backcountry. If you don't have your own bear-resistant canisters, which are required, you can buy or rent them here. ✉ *Between Ansel*

Adams Gallery and post office, Yosemite Village ☎ *209/372–0308.*

Yosemite Mountaineering School and Guide Service

HIKING/WALKING | From April to November, you can rent gear, hire a guide, or join a two-hour to full-day trek with Yosemite Mountaineering School. They also lead backpacking and overnight excursions. Reservations are recommended. In winter, cross-country ski programs are available at Badger Pass Ski Area. ✉ *Yosemite Mountain Shop, Curry Village* ☎ *209/372–8344* 🌐 *yosemitemountaineering.com.*

HORSEBACK RIDING

Reservations for guided trail rides must be made in advance at hotel tour desks or by phone. Scenic trail rides range from two hours to a half day. Four- and six-day High Sierra saddle trips are also available.

Wawona Stable

HORSEBACK RIDING | Two-hour rides at this stable start at $70, and a challenging full-day ride to the Mariposa Grove of Giant Sequoias (for experienced riders in good physical condition only) costs $144. Reservations are recommended. ✉ *Rte. 41, Wawona* ☎ *209/375–6502* 🌐 *www.travelyosemite.com/things-to-do/horseback-mule-riding.*

ICE-SKATING

Curry Village Ice Skating Rink

ICE SKATING | Winter visitors have skated at this outdoor rink for decades, and there's no mystery why: it's a kick to glide across the ice while soaking up views of Half Dome and Glacier Point. ✉ *South side of Southside Dr., Curry Village* ☎ *209/372–8319* 🌐 *www.travelyosemite.com* 🎫 *$11 per session, $5 skate rental.*

RAFTING

Rafting is permitted only on designated areas of the Middle and South forks of the Merced River. Check with the Valley Visitor Center for closures and other restrictions.

Curry Village Recreation Center

WHITE-WATER RAFTING | The per-person rental fee at Curry Village Recreation Center covers the four- to six-person raft, two paddles, and life jackets, plus a return shuttle after your trip. ✉ *South side of Southside Dr., Curry Village* ☎ *209/372–4386* 🌐 *www.travelyosemite.com/things-to-do/rafting* 🎫 *From $33.*

ROCK CLIMBING

The granite canyon walls of Yosemite Valley are world renowned for rock climbing. El Capitan, with its 3,593-foot vertical face, is the most famous, but there are many other options here for all skill levels.

Yosemite Mountain Shop

SPECIALTY STORES | A comprehensive selection of camping, hiking, backpacking, and climbing equipment, along with experts who can answer all your questions, make this store a valuable resource for outdoors enthusiasts. This is the best place to ask about climbing conditions and restrictions around the park, as well as purchase almost any kind of climbing gear. ✉ *Curry Village* ☎ *209/372–8436.*

Yosemite Mountaineering School and Guide Service

CLIMBING/MOUNTAINEERING | The one-day basic lesson offered by this outfit includes some bouldering and rappelling and three or four 60-foot climbs. Climbers must be at least 10 years old and in reasonably good physical condition. Intermediate and advanced classes include instruction in first aid; anchor building; and multipitch, summer-snow, and big-wall climbing. There's a Nordic program in the winter. ✉ *Yosemite Mountain Shop, Curry Village* ☎ *209/372–8444* 🌐 *www.travelyosemite.com* 🎫 *From $172.*

SKIING AND SNOWSHOEING

The beauty of Yosemite under a blanket of snow has long inspired poets and artists, as well as ordinary folks. Skiing and snowshoeing activities in the park center on Badger Pass Ski Area, California's

Ansel Adams's Black-and-White Yosemite 

What John Muir did for Yosemite with words, Ansel Adams did with photographs. His photographs have inspired millions of people to visit the park, and his persistent activism helped to ensure its conservation.

Born in 1902, Adams first came to the valley when he was 14, photographing it with a Box Brownie camera. He later said his first visit "was a culmination of experience so intense as to be almost painful. From that day in 1916 my life has been colored and modulated by the great earth gesture of the Sierra." By 1919, he was working in the valley, as custodian of LeConte Memorial Lodge (now called Yosemite Conservation Heritage Center), the Sierra Club headquarters in Yosemite National Park.

Adams had harbored dreams of a career as a concert pianist, but the park sealed his fate as a photographer in 1928, the day he shot *Monolith: The Face of Half Dome*, which remains one of his most famous works. That same year, Adams also married Virginia Best in her father's valley studio (now the Ansel Adams Gallery).

As the photographer's career took off, Yosemite began to sear itself into the American consciousness. David Brower, first executive director of the Sierra Club, later said of Adams's impact, "That Ansel Adams came to be recognized as one of the great photographers of this century is a tribute to the places that informed him."

In 1934, Adams was elected to the Sierra Club's board of directors; he would serve until 1971. As a representative of the conservation group, he combined his work with the club's mission, showing his photographs of the Sierra to influential officials such as Secretary of the Interior Harold L. Ickes, who showed them to President Franklin Delano Roosevelt. The images were a key factor in the establishment of Kings Canyon National Park.

In 1968, the Department of the Interior granted Adams its highest honor, the Conservation Service Award, and, in 1980, he received the Presidential Medal of Freedom in recognition of his conservation work. Until his death in 1984, Adams continued not only to record Yosemite's majesty on film but to urge the federal government and park managers to do right by the park.

In one of his many public pleas on behalf of Yosemite, Adams said, "Yosemite Valley itself is one of the great shrines of the world and—belonging to all our people—must be both protected and appropriately accessible." As an artist and an activist, Adams never gave up on his dream of keeping Yosemite wild yet within reach of every visitor who wants to experience it.

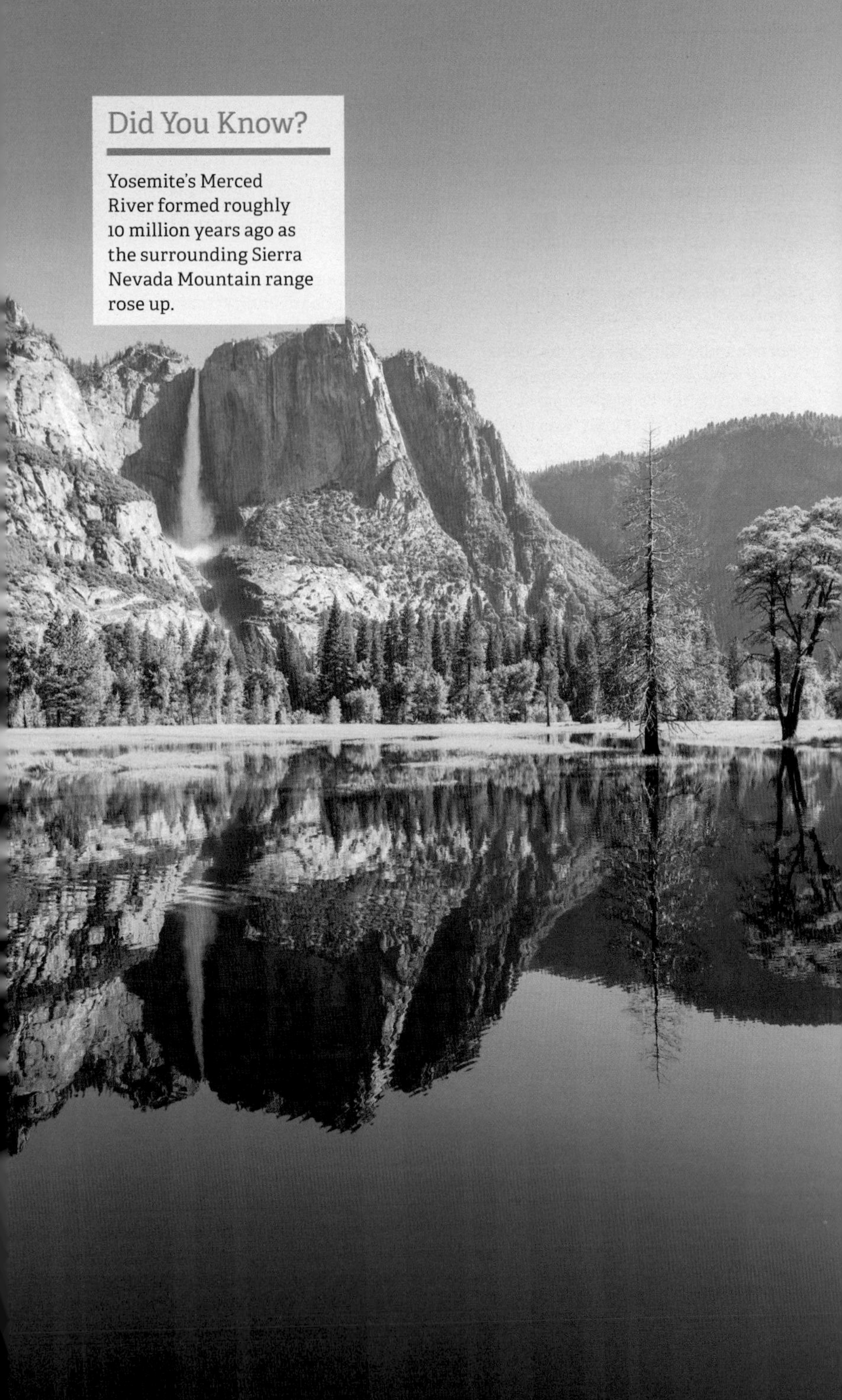

Did You Know?

Yosemite's Merced River formed roughly 10 million years ago as the surrounding Sierra Nevada Mountain range rose up.

oldest snow-sports resort, which is about 40 minutes away from the valley on Glacier Point Road. Here you can rent equipment, take a lesson, have lunch, and join a guided excursion.

Badger Pass Ski Area

SKIING/SNOWBOARDING | California's first ski resort has 10 downhill runs and 90 miles of groomed cross-country trails. Lessons, backcountry guiding, and cross-country and snowshoeing tours are also available. You can rent downhill, telemark, and cross-country skis, as well as snowshoes and snowboards. Note that shuttle buses run twice daily between the valley and the ski area. **Facilities:** 10 trails; 90 acres; 800-foot vertical drop; 5 lifts. ✉ *Yosemite National Park* ✥ *Badger Pass Rd., off Glacier Point Rd., 18 miles from Yosemite Valley* ☎ *209/372–8430* 🌐 *www.travelyosemite.com/winter/badger-pass-ski-area* 🎫 *Lift ticket: from $62.*

Badger Pass Ski Area School

SKIING/SNOWBOARDING | The gentle slopes of Badger Pass Ski Area make the ski school an ideal spot for children and beginners to learn downhill skiing or snowboarding for as little as $75 for a group lesson. ☎ *209/372–8430* 🌐 *www.travelyosemite.com.*

Badger Pass Ski Area Sport Shop

SKIING/SNOWBOARDING | Stop here to gear (and bundle!) up for downhill and cross-country skiing, snowboarding, and snowshoeing adventures. ✉ *Yosemite National Park* ✥ *Yosemite Ski & Snowboard Area, Badger Pass Rd., off Glacier Point Rd., 18 miles from Yosemite Valley* ☎ *209/372–8444* 🌐 *www.travelyosemite.com/winter/badger-pass-ski-area.*

Yosemite Cross-Country Ski School

SKIING/SNOWBOARDING | The highlight of Yosemite's cross-country skiing center is a 21-mile loop from Badger Pass Ski Area to Glacier Point. You can rent cross-country skis for $28 per day at the Cross-Country Ski School, which also rents snowshoes ($26.50 per day) and telemarking equipment ($36). ☎ *209/372–8444* 🌐 *www.travelyosemite.com.*

Yosemite Mountaineering School

SKIING/SNOWBOARDING | This branch of the Yosemite Mountaineering School, open at the Badger Pass Ski Area during ski season only, conducts snowshoeing, cross-country skiing, telemarking, and skate-skiing classes starting at $44. ✉ *Badger Pass Ski Area* ☎ *209/372–8444* 🌐 *www.travelyosemite.com.*

What's Nearby

Mariposa

43 miles west of Yosemite's Arch Rock Entrance.

Mariposa marks the southern end of the Mother Lode. Much of the land in this area was part of a 44,000-acre land grant Colonel John C. Fremont acquired from Mexico before gold was discovered and California became a state. Many people stop here on the way to Yosemite National Park, about an hour's drive east on Highway 140.

GETTING HERE AND AROUND

If driving, take Highway 49 or Highway 140. YARTS (🌐 *www.yarts.com*), the regional transit system, can get you to Mariposa from the Central Valley town of Merced (where you can also transfer from Amtrak) or from Yosemite Valley. Otherwise, you'll need a car.

Sights

California State Mining and Mineral Museum

MUSEUM | **FAMILY** | A California state park, the museum has displays on gold-rush history including a replica hard-rock mine shaft to walk through, a miniature stamp mill, and a 13-pound chunk of crystallized gold. ✉ *5005 Fairground Rd., off Hwy. 49* ☎ *209/742–7625* 🌐 *www.parks.*

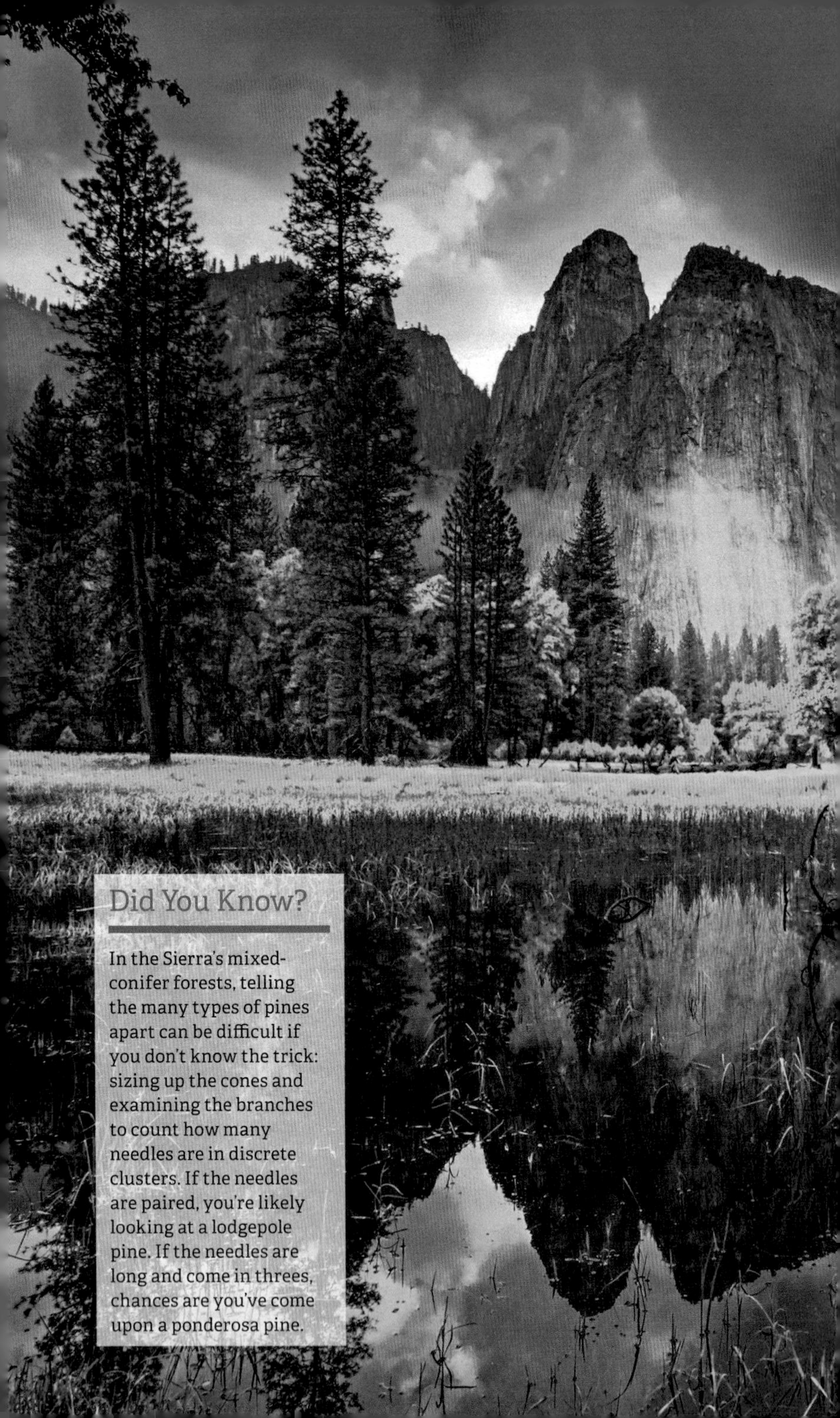

Did You Know?

In the Sierra's mixed-conifer forests, telling the many types of pines apart can be difficult if you don't know the trick: sizing up the cones and examining the branches to count how many needles are in discrete clusters. If the needles are paired, you're likely looking at a lodgepole pine. If the needles are long and come in threes, chances are you've come upon a ponderosa pine.

ca.gov/miningandmineralmuseum *$4* *Closed Mon.–Wed.*

Mariposa Museum and History Center
MUSEUM VILLAGE | You'll leave this small museum feeling like you just found your own gold nugget. Detailed exhibits, both indoors and out, tell the history of Mariposa County. Visit a replica of a typical miner's cabin; see a working stamp mill; tour the blacksmith shop. Artifacts, photographs, and maps, along with the knowledgeable staff, will capture your imagination and transport you back to 1849. *5119 Jessie St.* *209/966–2924* *www.mariposamuseum.com* *$5.*

Restaurants

Charles Street Dinner House
$$$ | **AMERICAN** | Centrally located Charles Street, its rustic decor heavy on the wood and Old West adornments, at once evokes gold-rush days and the 1980s, when it opened. The extensive straightforward menu includes hand-cut steaks, honey-barbecue baby back ribs, several pasta dishes, chicken, pork loin, lamb, a few well-adorned burgers, and some vegetarian options. **Known for:** excellent steaks; cheesecake, sundae, crème brûlée for dessert; local feel. *Average main: $27* *Hwy. 140 and 7th St.* *209/966–2366* *www.charlesstreetdinnerhouse.net* *Closed Sun. and Mon. No lunch.*

1850 Restaurant & Brewery
$$$ | **AMERICAN** | The name, decor, and menu at this lively brewpub pay homage to California's Gold Rush era and the year the state and county were officially established. Many of the craft beers on tap come from the owners' 1850 Brewing Company, and dishes include everything from traditional Bavarian pretzels and hearty steak-and-ale pie to ahi nachos and salmon cakes. **Known for:** brine-marinated fried chicken; nearly a dozen types of burgers; rotating local seasonal beers on tap. *Average main: $22* *5114 Hwy. 140* *209/966–2229* *www.1850restaurant.com* *Closed Mon.*

Savoury's
$$ | **AMERICAN** | Seafood, pasta, and portobello mushrooms are some of the savory treats that draw high praise from locals at the kind of refined space you'd expect in an urban environment, not in mellow Mariposa. Contemporary paintings and photography set aglow by track lighting create a gallerylike atmosphere. **Known for:** well-prepared steak and seafood; full bar; vegetarian and vegan options. *Average main: $20* *5034 Hwy. 140* *209/966–7677* *Closed Tues. and Wed. No lunch.*

El Portal

29 miles northwest of Mariposa, 15 miles west of Yosemite's Arch Rock Entrance on Hwy. 140.

The market in town is a good place to pick up provisions before you get to Yosemite. You'll find a post office and a gas station, but not much else.

GETTING HERE AND AROUND

The drive here on Highway 140 from Mariposa and, farther west, Merced, is the prettiest and gentlest route to Yosemite National Park. Much of the road follows the Merced River in a rugged canyon. The Yosemite Area Regional Transportation System (YARTS *www.yarts.com*) is a cheap and dependable way to go between Merced and Yosemite Valley; all buses stop in El Portal, where many park employees reside.

Hotels

Yosemite View Lodge
$$ | **HOTEL** | Two miles outside Yosemite's Arch Rock entrance, this modern property is the most convenient place to spend the night if you are unable to secure lodgings in the valley. **Pros:** great location;

good views; lots of on-site amenities. **Cons:** somewhat pricey; it can be a challenge to get the dates you want; rooms could use an update. *Rooms from: $239 11136 Hwy. 140 209/379–2681, 888/742–4371 www.yosemiteresorts.com/yosemite-view-lodge 335 rooms No meals.*

Oakhurst

23 miles south of Yosemite's South Entrance.

Motels, restaurants, gas stations, and small businesses line Highway 41 in Oakhurst, the last sizable community before Yosemite National Park and a good spot to find provisions.

GETTING HERE AND AROUND

At the junction of highways 41 and 49, Oakhurst is about an hour's drive north of Fresno. It's the southern gateway to Yosemite, so many people fly into Fresno and rent a car to get here and beyond.

Restaurants

★ South Gate Brewing Company

$$ | **AMERICAN** | Locals pack this family-friendly, industrial-chic restaurant to socialize and savor small-lot beers, crafted on-site, along with tasty meals. The creative pub fare runs a wide gamut, from thin-crust brick-oven pizzas to fish tacos, fish-and-chips, and vegan black-bean burgers. **Known for:** craft beer; house-made desserts; live-music calendar. *Average main: $18 40233 Enterprise Dr., off Hwy. 49, north of Von's shopping center 559/692–2739 southgatebrewco.com.*

Hotels

Best Western Plus Yosemite Gateway Inn

$$ | **HOTEL** | **FAMILY** | Perched on 11 hillside acres, Oakhurst's best motel has carefully tended landscaping and rooms with stylish contemporary furnishings and hand-painted murals of Yosemite. **Pros:** on-site restaurant; indoor and outdoor swimming pools; frequent deer and wildlife sightings. **Cons:** some rooms on the small side; Internet connection can be slow; some rooms need updating. *Rooms from: $249 40530 Hwy. 41 559/683–2378 www.yosemitegatewayinn.com 149 rooms No meals.*

Homestead Cottages

$$ | **B&B/INN** | Set on 160 acres of rolling hills that once held a Miwok village, these cottages (the largest sleeps six) have gas fireplaces, fully equipped kitchens, and queen-size beds. **Pros:** remote location; quiet setting; friendly owners. **Cons:** might be too quiet for some; breakfasts on the simple side; 7 miles from center of Oakhurst. *Rooms from: $189 41110 Rd. 600, 2½ miles off Hwy. 49, Ahwahnee 559/683–0495 www.homesteadcottages.com 7 cottages Free breakfast.*

Sierra Sky Ranch

$$ | **HOTEL** | Off Highway 41 just 10 miles south of the Yosemite National Park, this 19th-century cattle ranch near a hidden grove of giant sequoia trees provides a restful, rustic retreat. **Pros:** peaceful setting; historic property; short drive to giant sequoias. **Cons:** some rooms on the small side; not in town; basic breakfast. *Rooms from: $249 50552 Rd. 632 559/683–8040 www.sierraskyranch.com 26 rooms Free breakfast.*

Bass Lake

7 miles northwest of Oakhurst via Hwy. 41 to Bass Lake Road 222.

Almost surrounded by the Sierra National Forest, Bass Lake is a reservoir whose waters can reach 80°F in summer. Created by a dam on a tributary of the San Joaquin River, the lake is owned by Pacific Gas and Electric Company and is used to generate electricity as well as for recreation.

Restaurants

Ducey's on the Lake/Ducey's Bar & Grill
$$$ | **AMERICAN** | With elaborate chandeliers sculpted from deer antlers, the lodge-style restaurant at Ducey's attracts boaters, locals, and tourists with its lake views and standard lamb, beef, seafood, and pasta dishes. It's also open for breakfast: try the Bass Lake seafood omelet, huevos rancheros, or the Rice Krispies–crusted French toast. **Known for:** steaks and fresh fish; lake views; upstairs bar and grill with more affordable eats. *Average main: $32 ✉ Pines Resort, 54432 Rd. 432 ☎ 559/642–3131 🌐 www.basslake.com.*

Activities

BOATING

Bass Lake Boat Rental & Water Sports
BOATING | This outfit on Bass Lake Reservoir, 3 miles north and 6 miles east of Oakhurst, rents ski boats, patio boats, fishing boats, canoes, tubes, and other things that float. The folks here also conduct guided fishing and scenic tours. In summer the noisy reservoir is packed shortly after it opens at 8 am (off-season hours are from 9 to 5). There's also a shop with snacks and gifts. *✉ 54406 Marina Dr. ☎ 559/642–3200 🌐 basslake-boatrentals.com.*

Fish Camp

14 miles north of Oakhurst.

As you climb in elevation along Highway 41 northbound, you see nothing but trees until you get to Fish Camp, where there's a post office and general store. (For gas, head 7 miles north to Wawona, in Yosemite, or 14 miles south to Oakhurst.)

GETTING HERE AND AROUND

Highway 41 is the main drag. YARTS transit stops in Fish Camp on its route between Fresno and Yosemite Valley.

Sights

Yosemite Mountain Sugar Pine Railroad
TRANSPORTATION SITE (AIRPORT/BUS/FERRY/TRAIN) | **FAMILY** | Travel back to a time when powerful steam locomotives hauled massive log trains through the Sierra. This 4-mile, narrow-gauge railroad excursion takes you near Yosemite's south gate. There's a moonlight special ($63), with dinner and entertainment, and you can visit the free museum. *✉ 56001 Hwy. 41, 8 miles south of Yosemite ☎ 559/683–7273 🌐 www.ymsprr.com $28 Closed Nov.–Mar. Closed some weekdays Apr. and Oct.*

Hotels

Narrow Gauge Inn
$$ | **HOTEL** | Rooms at this family-owned property have balconies with views of the surrounding woods and mountains. **Pros:** close to Yosemite's south entrance; nicely appointed rooms; wonderful balconies. **Cons:** rooms can be a bit dark; dining options are limited, especially for vegetarians; housekeeping service can be spotty. *Rooms from: $229 ✉ 48571 Hwy. 41 ☎ 559/683–7720 🌐 www.narrowgaugeinn.com 27 rooms No meals.*

★ Tenaya Lodge
$$$$ | **RESORT** | **FAMILY** | One of the region's largest hotels is ideal for people who enjoy wilderness treks by day but prefer creature comforts at night. **Pros:** close to Yosemite and Mariposa Grove of Giant Sequoias; exceptional spa and exercise facility, 36 miles of mountain bike trails; activities for all ages. **Cons:** so big it can seem impersonal; pricey during summer; daily resort fee. *Rooms from: $379 ✉ 1122 Hwy. 41 ☎ 559/683–6555, 888/514–2167 🌐 www.tenayalodge.com 352 rooms No meals.*

Lee Vining

13 miles northeast of Yosemite's Tioga Pass Entrance (near Tuolumne Meadows).

Tiny Lee Vining is known primarily as the eastern gateway to Yosemite National Park (summer only) and the location of vast and desolate Mono Lake. Pick up supplies at the general store year-round, or stop here for lunch or dinner before or after a drive through the high country. In winter, the town is all but deserted, except for the ice climbers who come to scale frozen waterfalls.

Most people enter Yosemite National Park from the west, having driven out from the Bay Area or Los Angeles. The eastern entrance on Tioga Pass Road (Highway 120 off Highway 395), however, provides stunning, sweeping views of the High Sierra. Gray rocks shine in the bright sun, with scattered, small vegetation sprinkled about the mountainside.

To drive from Lee Vining to Tuolumne Meadows is an unforgettable experience, but keep in mind that the road is closed for at least seven months of the year.

GETTING HERE AND AROUND

Lee Vining is on U.S. 395, north of the road's intersection with Highway 120 and on the south side of Mono Lake. In summer YARTS public transit (*yarts.com*) can get you here from Yosemite Valley, but you'll need a car to explore the area.

VISITOR INFORMATION Lee Vining Chamber of Commerce. *760/647–6629 www.leevining.com.* **Mono Basin National Forest Scenic Area Visitor Center.** *Visitor Center Dr., off U.S. 395, 1 mile north of Hwy. 120 760/647–6595 www.fs.usda.gov/recarea/inyo/recarea/?recid=20620.*

Sights

June Lake Loop

SCENIC DRIVE | Heading south, U.S. 395 intersects the June Lake Loop. This gorgeous 17-mile drive follows an old glacial canyon past Grant, June, Gull, and Silver lakes before reconnecting with U.S. 395 on its way to Mammoth Lakes. **■ TIP→ The loop is especially colorful in fall.** *Hwy. 158 W.*

★ Mono Lake

BODY OF WATER | Since the 1940s, Los Angeles has diverted water from this lake, exposing striking towers of tufa, or calcium carbonate. Court victories by environmentalists have meant fewer diversions, and the lake is rising again. Although to see the lake from U.S. 395 is stunning, make time to visit South Tufa, whose parking lot is 5 miles east of U.S. 395 off Highway 120. There, in summer, you can join the naturalist-guided **South Tufa Walk,** which lasts about 90 minutes. The **Scenic Area Visitor Center,** off U.S. 395, is a sensational stop for its interactive exhibits and sweeping Mono Lake views (closed in winter). In town, at U.S. 395 and 3rd Street, the **Mono Lake Committee Information Center & Bookstore**, open from 9 to 5 daily (extended hours in summer), has more information about this beautiful area. *Hwy. 120, east of Lee Vining 760/647–3044 visitor center, 760/647–6595 info center www.monolake.org Free.*

Restaurants

Epic Cafe

$ | **AMERICAN** | **FAMILY** | Hungry travelers and locals feast on fresh, healthy, cooked-to-order comfort food at this casual café at Lakeview Lodge, near the Tioga Road and Highway 395 junction. The menu changes daily, but you can count on items like waffles and fritattas for breakfast; paninis, sandwiches, salads, rice bowls, and soups for lunch; and three special dinner entrées, perhaps locally caught fish, chicken potpie, or braised short ribs. **Known for:** local and organic food sources; cozy indoor dining room and garden patio; fresh-baked scones, muffins, desserts, and other goodies. *Average main: $15* *349 Lee Vining Ave.* *760/965–6282* *epiccafesierra.com* *Closed Nov.–early May. Closed Sun.*

Mono Cone

$ | **AMERICAN** | Get soft-serve ice cream, burgers, and fries at this hopping shack in the middle of Lee Vining, but be prepared to wait in line. There's some indoor seating, but unless the clouds are leaking, take your food to nearby (and quiet) Hess Park, whose views of Mono Lake make it one of the best picnic spots in eastern California. *Average main: $9* *51508 U.S. 395* *760/647–6606* *No credit cards* *Closed in winter.*

Tioga Gas Mart & Whoa Nelli Deli

$$ | **AMERICAN** | This might be the only gas station in the United States serving craft beers and lobster taquitos, but its appeal goes beyond novelty. Order at the counter and grab a seat inside, or sit at one of the picnic tables on the lawn outside and take in the distant view of Mono Lake. **Known for:** fish tacos and barbecued ribs; regular live music; convenient location. *Average main: $16* *Hwy. 120 and U.S. 395* *760/647–1088* *www.whoanelliedeli.com* *Closed early Nov.–late Apr.*

Lake View Lodge

$ | **B&B/INN** | Cottages, enormous rooms, and landscaping that includes several shaded sitting areas set this motel apart from its competitors in town. **Pros:** convenient access to Yosemite, Mono Lake, Bodie State Historic Park; peaceful setting; on-site restaurant. **Cons:** could use updating; slow Wi-Fi in some areas; no views from some rooms. *Rooms from: $143* *51285 U.S. 395* *760/647–6543, 800/990–6614* *www.lakeviewlodgeyosemite.com* *88 units* *No meals.*

Bodie State Historic Park

31 miles northeast of Lee Vining.

Bodie State Historic Park's scenery is spectacular, with craggy, snowcapped peaks looming over vast prairies. The town of Bridgeport is the gateway to the park, and the only supply center for miles around. Bridgeport's claims to fame include a courthouse that's been in continuous use since 1880 and excellent fishing—the California state record brown trout, at 26 pounds 12 ounces, was caught in Bridgeport's Twin Lakes. In winter, much of Bridgeport shuts down.

GETTING HERE AND AROUND

A car is the best way to reach this area. Bodie is on Highway 270 about 13 miles east of U.S. 395.

★ Bodie Ghost Town

GHOST TOWN | The mining village of Rattlesnake Gulch, abandoned mine shafts, and the remains of a small Chinatown are among the sights at this fascinating ghost town. The town boomed from about 1878 to 1881; by the late 1940s, though, all its residents had departed. A state park was established here in 1962, with a mandate to preserve everything in a state of "arrested decay." Evidence of Bodie's wild past survives at an excellent museum, and you can tour an old stamp mill where ore was crushed into fine powder to extract gold and silver. Bodie lies 13 miles east of U.S. 395 off Highway 270. The last 3 miles are unpaved, and snow may close the highway from late fall through early spring. No food, drink, or lodging is available in Bodie. *Bodie Rd., off Hwy. 270, Bodie* *760/616–5040* *www.parks.ca.gov/bodie* *$8.*

Chapter 15

EASTERN SIERRA

Updated by
Cheryl Crabtree

Sights	Restaurants	Hotels	Shopping	Nightlife
★★★★★	★★★★☆	★★★★★	★☆☆☆☆	★☆☆☆☆

WELCOME TO EASTERN SIERRA

TOP REASONS TO GO

★ **Hiking:** Whether you walk the paved loops in the national parks or head off the beaten path into the backcountry, a hike through groves and meadows or alongside streams and waterfalls will allow you to see, smell, and feel nature up close.

★ **Winter fun:** Famous for its incredible snowpack—some of the deepest in the North American continent—the Sierra Nevada has something for every winter-sports fan.

★ **Live it up:** Mammoth Lakes is eastern California's most exciting resort area.

★ **Road trip heaven:** Legendary Highway 395 is one of California's most scenic byways, traveling to Independence, Lone Pine, Bishop, and beyond, for a glimpse of Old West history.

★ **Go with the flow:** Fish, float, raft, and row in the abundant lakes, hot springs, creeks, and rivers.

1 **Lone Pine.** Mount Whitney and the Alabama Hills in Lone Pine have provided authentic backdrops for hundreds of films and TV shows for nearly a century, as evidenced in the town's Museum of Western Film History.

2 **Independence.** The moving Manzanar National Historic Site, where 11,000 Japanese-Americans were interned during World War II, lies 6 miles south of Independence, a tiny Old West town.

3 **Bishop.** One of the largest towns along Highway 395, Bishop is an excellent road stop and base camp for exploration in the surrounding mountains.

4 **Mammoth Lakes.** Easy access to year-round outdoor adventures has made Mammoth Lakes one of the Sierra Nevada's most popular destinations. The bustling town's many attractions include sprawling Mammoth Mountain Ski and Bike Area and nearby Mammoth Lakes Basin and Devil's Postpile National Monument.

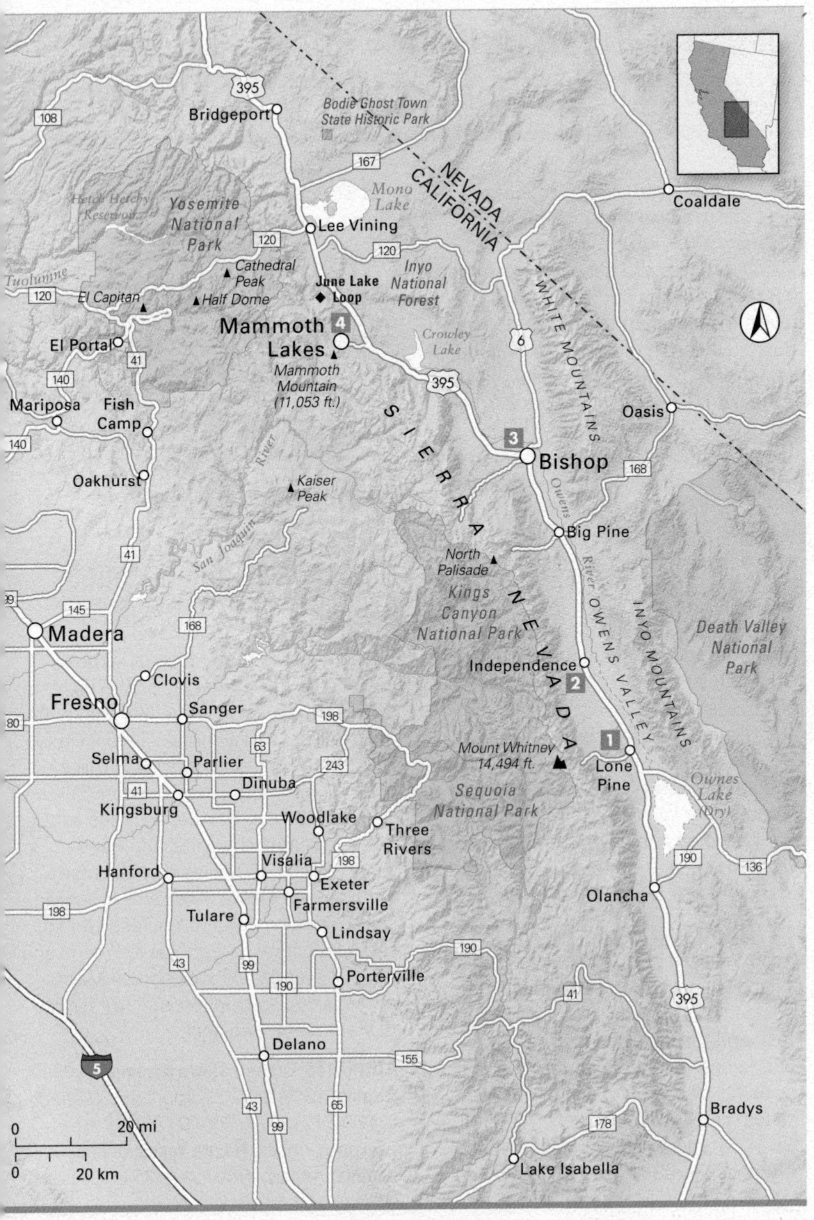
Bridgeport
Bodie Ghost Town State Historic Park
NEVADA
CALIFORNIA
Mono Lake
Hetch Hetchy Reservoir
Yosemite National Park
Lee Vining
Coaldale
Tuolumne
Cathedral Peak
Half Dome
El Capitan
June Lake Loop
Inyo National Forest
WHITE MOUNTAINS
Mammoth Lakes
Crowley Lake
El Portal
Mammoth Mountain (11,053 ft.)
Mariposa
Fish Camp
Oasis
SIERRA NEVADA
Bishop
Oakhurst
Kaiser Peak
River
San Joaquin
Owens River
Big Pine
North Palisade
Kings Canyon National Park
OWENS VALLEY
INYO MOUNTAINS
Death Valley National Park
Madera
Independence
Clovis
Fresno
Sanger
Mount Whitney 14,494 ft.
Selma
Parlier
Lone Pine
Dinuba
Owens Lake (Dry)
Kingsburg
Sequoia National Park
Woodlake
Three Rivers
Visalia
Hanford
Exeter
Farmersville
Olancha
Tulare
Lindsay
Porterville
Delano
Bradys
Lake Isabella
0 20 mi
0 20 km
395
108
167
120
6
41
140
168
145
198
63
243
190
136
43
99
155
65
178
5
1
2
3
4

The granite peaks and ancient pines of the Eastern Sierra bedazzle heart and soul so completely that, for many visitors, the experience surpasses that at more famous urban attractions.

This rugged region offers some of the most dramatic sightseeing in California. Highway 395, one of the state's most beautiful routes and generally open year-round, is the main north–south road. It travels the length of the region, from the Mojave Desert in the south to Bridgeport in the north, and along the eastern side of the Sierra Nevada, at the western edge of the Great Basin. Main towns along the route include Lone Pine, Independence, Bishop, and Mammoth Lakes, as well as Lee Vining, a small town at the eastern endpoint of Tioga Road (open only seasonally) into Yosemite National Park.

Pristine lakes and rolling hills outside the parks offer year-round opportunities for rest and relaxation. Or not. In winter, the thrill of Mammoth Lakes slopes—and their relative isolation compared to busy Lake Tahoe—draws a hearty breed of outdoor enthusiasts. From late spring through early fall, a hike through groves and meadows or alongside streams and waterfalls allows you to see, smell, and feel nature up close.

MAJOR REGIONS

Owens Valley. In this undervisited region, the snowcapped Sierra Nevada range rises abruptly and majestically to the west, and the high desert whistles to the east. In between are a series of roadside towns full of character, history, and outfits that cater to adventurers. Along U.S. 395 in this region are Lone Pine, Independence, and Bishop, with Lone Pine and Bishop having the best selection of dining and lodging options.

Mammoth Lakes. North of Owens Valley, en route to the gateway towns east of Yosemite National Park, is the megaresort of Mammoth Lakes, which lures skiers and snowboarders in winter and hikers and mountain bikers in warmer months.

Planning

Getting Here and Around

AIR

Fresno Yosemite International Airport (FAT) is the main gateway on the western side of the Eastern Sierra. Airports to the region's east and along U.S. 395 include Mammoth–Yosemite (MMH), 6 miles east of Mammoth Lakes; Eastern Sierra Regional (BIH) in Bishop, 45 miles southeast of Mammoth Lakes; and Reno–Tahoe (RNO), 130 miles north of Mammoth Lakes. Alaska, Allegiant, American, Delta, Frontier, JSX, Southwest, United, and a few other carriers serve Fresno and Reno. Advanced Airlines serves Mammoth Lakes, and United and JSX fly into Eastern Sierra Regional.

AIRPORTS Eastern Sierra Regional Airport. (*BIH*) ✉ *703 Airport Rd., Bishop* ☎ *760/872–2971, 760/ 937–4017 after business hours.* **Fresno Yosemite International Airport.** (*FAT*) ✉ *5175 E. Clinton*

Ave., Fresno ☎ *800/244–2359 automated information, 559/454–2052 terminal info desk* 🌐 *www.flyfresno.com.* **Mammoth–Yosemite Airport.** *(MMH)* ✉ *1200 Airport Rd., Mammoth Lakes* ☎ *760/934–2712, 888/466–2666* 🌐 *www.visitmammoth.com/getting-mammoth-lakes.* **Reno–Tahoe International Airport.** *(RNO)* ✉ *2001 E. Plumb La., Reno* ☎ *775/328–6400* 🌐 *www.renoairport.com.*

BUS

Eastern Sierra Transit Authority buses serve Mammoth Lakes, Bishop, and other Eastern Sierra towns along Highway 395, from Reno in the north to Lancaster in the south. In summer, YARTS (Yosemite Area Regional Transportation System) connects Yosemite National Park with Mammoth Lakes, June Lake, and Lee Vining, as well as Central Valley cities and towns in the west, including Fresno and Merced. This is a good option during summer, when parking in Yosemite Valley and elsewhere in the park can be difficult.

BUS CONTACTS Eastern Sierra Transit Authority. ☎ *760/872–1901 general, 800/922–1930 toll-free, 760/924–3184 Mammoth Lakes* 🌐 *www.estransit.com.* **YARTS.** ☎ *877/989–2787* 🌐 *www.yarts.com.*

CAR

Interstate 5 and Highway 99 travel north–south along the western side of the Sierra Nevada. U.S. 395 follows a roughly parallel route on the eastern side. In summer, Tioga Pass Road in Yosemite National Park opens to car and bus travel, intersecting with U.S. 395 at Lee Vining.

From San Francisco: Head east on I–80 to Sacramento, then continue on I–80 to U.S. 395, east of Lake Tahoe's north shore, or take U.S. 50 to Lake Tahoe's south shore and continue on 207E to U.S. 395, then head south.

From Los Angeles: Head north on I–5, exiting and continuing north onto Highway 14 and later onto U.S. 395.

■ TIP→ Gas stations are few and far between in the Sierra, so fill your tank when you can. Between October and May, heavy snow may cover mountain roads. Always check conditions before driving. Carry tire chains, and know how to install them. On I–80 and U.S. 50, and at the Mammoth Lakes exit off U.S. 395, chain installers assist travelers (for $40), but elsewhere you're on your own.

TRAIN

Amtrak's daily *San Joaquin* train stops in Fresno and Merced, where you can connect to YARTS for travel to Yosemite National Park and, in summer, to Mammoth Lakes, June Lake, and the Yosemite gateway town of Lee Vining.

Restaurants

Most small towns in the Sierra Nevada have at least one restaurant. Standard American fare is the norm, but you'll also find sophisticated cuisine. With few exceptions, dress is casual. Local grocery stores and delis stock picnic fixings, good to have on hand should the opportunity for an impromptu meal under giant trees emerge.

Hotels

The lodgings in Mammoth Lakes and nearest Yosemite National Park generally fill up the quickest; book hotels everywhere in the Eastern Sierra well in advance in summer.

Restaurant and hotel reviews have been shortened. For full information, visit Fodors.com. Restaurant prices are the average cost of a main course at dinner, or if dinner is not served, at lunch. Hotel prices are the lowest cost of a standard double room in high season.

What It Costs

$	$$	$$$	$$$$
RESTAURANTS			
under $17	$17–$26	$27–$36	over $36
HOTELS			
under $150	$150–$250	$251–$350	over $350

Tours

MAWS Transportation

BUS TOURS | This outfit (aka Mammoth All Weather Shuttle) operates summer tours from Mammoth Lakes to Yosemite; north to June Lake, Mono Lake, and Bodie Ghost Town; and around the lakes region. The company also transfers passengers from the Bishop and Mammoth–Yosemite airports into Mammoth Lakes, drops off and picks up hikers at trailheads, and runs charters to Los Angeles, Reno, and Las Vegas airports—useful when inclement weather causes flight cancellations at Mammoth's airport. ✉ *Mammoth Lakes* ☎ *760/709–2927* 🌐 *www.mawshuttle.com* 🎫 *From $60.*

Visitor Information

CONTACTS Eastern Sierra Visitor Center. ✥ *2 miles south of Lone Pine, at junctions of U.S. Hwy. 395 and CA Hwy. 136* ☎ *760/876–6200* 🌐 *www.fs.usda.gov/recarea/inyo/recarea/?recid=20698.* **Mammoth Lakes Tourism.** ☎ *760/934–2712, 888/466–2666* 🌐 *www.visitmammoth.com.* **Mono County Tourism.** ☎ *800/845–7922* 🌐 *monocounty.org.*

Lone Pine

100 miles southeast of Mammoth Lakes.

Mt. Whitney towers majestically over this tiny community, which supplied nearby gold- and silver-mining outposts in the 1860s, and for the past century the town has been touched by Hollywood glamour: several hundred movies, TV episodes, and commercials have been filmed here.

GETTING HERE AND AROUND

Arrive via U.S. 395 from the north or south. (If you're heading from Death Valley National Park, you can also take Highway 190 or Highway 138.) Eastern Sierra Transit buses connect Lone Pine to Reno in the north and Lancaster in the south.

ESSENTIALS

VISITOR INFORMATION Lone Pine Chamber of Commerce & Visitor Center. ✉ *120 S. Main St., at Whitney Portal Rd.* ☎ *760/876–4444* 🌐 *www.lonepinechamber.org.*

Sights

Alabama Hills

MOUNTAIN—SIGHT | Drop by the Lone Pine Visitor Center for a map of the Alabama Hills, and drive up Whitney Portal Road (turn west at the light) to this wonderland of granite boulders. Erosion has worn the rocks smooth; some have been chiseled into arches and other formations. The hills have become a popular location for rock climbing. Tuttle Creek Campground sits among the rocks, with a nearby stream for fishing. The area has served as a scenic backdrop for hundreds of films; ask about the self-guided tour of the various movie locations at the Museum of Western Film History. ✉ *Whitney Portal Rd., 4½ miles west of Lone Pine.*

Highway 395

SCENIC DRIVE | For a gorgeous view of the eastern Sierra, travel north of Death Valley along Highway 395 where you'll discover wandering elk herds, trout hatcheries, and breathtaking views of Mt. Whitney, the highest mountain (14,496 feet) in the continental United States. Drive south on Highway 395, between Olancha and Big Pine, and you'll notice the massive salt-crusted Owens Lake, which was drained between 1900 and

1920 as water from the Sierra was diverted to Los Angeles. Today, up to one-fourth of the water flow is being reintroduced to the lake. If you drive to the northwest end of the lake, near the abandoned Pittsburg Plate Glass Soda Ash Plant, you can see brilliant red salt flats, caused by billions of microscopic halobacteria that survive there. Revered by the National Audubon Society, the lake is home to more than 240 migrating birds, including the snowy plover, American white pelican, golden eagle, and countless grebes, bitterns, blue herons, and cranes. ✉ *Death Valley.*

Mt. Whitney

MOUNTAIN—SIGHT | Straddling the border of Sequoia National Park and Inyo National Forest–John Muir Wilderness, Mt. Whitney (14,496 feet) is the highest mountain in the contiguous United States. A favorite game for travelers passing through Lone Pine is trying to guess which peak is Mt. Whitney. Almost no one gets it right, because Mt. Whitney is hidden behind other mountains. There is no road that ascends the peak, but you can catch a glimpse of the mountain by driving curvy Whitney Portal Road west from Lone Pine into the mountains. The pavement ends at the trailhead to the top of the mountain, which is also the start of the 211-mile John Muir Trail from Mt. Whitney to Yosemite National Park. Day and overnight permits are required to ascend Mt. Whitney. The highly competitive lottery for these permits opens on February 1st. At the portal, a restaurant (known for its pancakes) and a small store cater to hikers and campers staying at Whitney Portal Campground. You can see a waterfall from the parking lot and go fishing in a small trout pond. The portal area is closed from mid-October to early May; the road closes when snow conditions require. ✉ *Whitney Portal Rd., west of Lone Pine* 🌐 *www.fs.usda.gov/attmain/inyo.*

Museum of Western Film History

MUSEUM | Hopalong Cassidy, Barbara Stanwyck, Roy Rogers, John Wayne—even Robert Downey Jr.—are among the celebrities who have starred in Westerns and other films shot in the Alabama Hills and surrounding dusty terrain. The marquee-embellished museum relates this Hollywood-in-the-desert tale via exhibits and a rollicking 20-minute documentary. ✉ *701 S. Main St., U.S. 395* ☎ *760/876–9909* 🌐 *www.museumofwesternfilmhistory.org* 🎫 *$5* ⏲ *Closed Tues. and Wed.*

Restaurants

Alabama Hills Café & Bakery

$ | **AMERICAN** | The extensive breakfast and lunch menus at this eatery just off the main drag include many vegetarian items. Sandwiches are served on homemade bread; choose from up to six varieties baked fresh daily, and get a homemade pie, cake, or loaf to go. **Known for:** house-roasted turkey and beef; huge portions; on-site bakery. $ *Average main: $14* ✉ *111 W. Post St., at S. Main St.* ☎ *760/876–4675* 🌐 *alabamahills-cafe.com.*

The Grill

$$ | **AMERICAN** | **FAMILY** | Open for three meals a day, this small restaurant next to the Dow Villa Motel is a convenient place to stop for a break while driving along Highway 395. The extensive menu includes an array of options, from omelets and French toast for breakfast and sandwiches and burgers for lunch to grilled steaks and fish for dinner. **Known for:** hearty meals with large portions; friendly service; house-made desserts. $ *Average main: $21* ✉ *446 S. Main St.* ☎ *760/876–4240.*

Mt. Whitney Restaurant

$ | **AMERICAN** | A boisterous family-friendly restaurant with four flat-screen televisions, this place serves the best burgers in town. In addition to the usual beef variety, you can choose from ostrich, elk, venison, and buffalo burgers. **Known for:** burgers; John Wayne memorabilia; convenient fuel-up stop on Highway 395. *Average main: $13 ✉ 227 S. Main St. ☎ 760/876–5751.*

Seasons Restaurant

$$$ | AMERICAN | This inviting, country-style diner serves all kinds of traditional American fare. For a special treat, try the medallions of Cervena elk, smothered in port wine, dried cranberries, and toasted walnuts; finish with the Baileys Irish Cream cheesecake or the Grand Marnier crème brûlée for dessert. **Known for:** high-end dining in remote area; steaks and wild game; children's menu. *Average main: $27 ✉ 206 S. Main St. ☎ 760/876–8927 ⊕ seasonslonepine.club ⊗ Closed Mon. Nov.–Mar. No lunch.*

Hotels

Dow Villa Motel and Dow Hotel

$ | HOTEL | Built in 1923 to cater to the film industry, the Dow Villa Motel and the historic Dow Hotel sit in the center of Lone Pine. **Pros:** clean rooms; great mountain views; in-room whirlpool tubs in some motel rooms. **Cons:** some rooms in hotel share bathrooms; sinks in some rooms are in the bedroom, not the bath; on busy highway. *Rooms from: $119 ✉ 310 S. Main St. ☎ 760/876–5521, 800/824–9317 ⊕ www.dowvillamotel.com 92 rooms No meals.*

Independence

17 miles north of Lone Pine.

Named for a military outpost that was established near here in 1862, sleepy Independence has some wonderful historic buildings and is worth a stop for another reason: 6 miles south of the small downtown lies the Manzanar National Historic Site, one of 10 camps in the west where people of Japanese descent were confined during World War II.

GETTING HERE AND AROUND

Eastern Sierra Transit buses pass through town, but most travelers arrive by car on U.S. 395.

Sights

Ancient Bristlecone Pine Forest

FOREST | FAMILY | About an hour's drive from Independence or Bishop you can view some of the oldest living trees on Earth, a few of which date back more than 40 centuries. The world's largest bristlecone pine can be found in Patriarch Grove, while the world's oldest known living tree is along Methusula Trail in Schulman Grove. Getting to Patriarch Grove is slow going along the narrow dirt road, especially for sedans with low clearance, but once there you'll find picnic tables, restrooms, and interpretive trails. *✉ Schulman Grove Visitor Center, White Mountain Rd., Bishop ✣ From U.S. 395, turn east onto Hwy. 168 and follow signs for 23 miles ⊕ www.fs.usda.gov/main/inyo/home $3.*

★ Manzanar National Historic Site

HISTORIC SITE | A reminder of an ugly episode in U.S. history, the former Manzanar War Relocation Center is where more than 11,000 Japanese-Americans were confined behind barbed-wire fences between 1942 and 1945. A visit here is both deeply moving and inspiring—the former because it's hard to comprehend that the United States was capable of confining its citizens in such a way, the latter because those imprisoned here showed great pluck and perseverance in making the best of a bad situation. Most of the buildings from the 1940s are gone, but two sentry posts, the auditorium, and numerous Japanese rock gardens remain. One of eight guard towers, two barracks, and a women's latrine have been reconstructed, and a mess hall has been restored. Interactive exhibits inside the barracks include audio and video clips from people who were incarcerated in Manzanar during WWII. You can drive the one-way road on a self-guided tour past various ruins to a small cemetery, where a monument stands. Signs mark where the barracks, a hospital, a school, and the fire station once stood. An outstanding 8,000-square-foot interpretive center has exhibits and documentary photographs and screens a short film. ✉ *Independence* ✥ *West side of U.S. 395 between Independence and Lone Pine* ☎ *760/878–2194* 🌐 *www.nps.gov/manz* 🎟 *Free.*

Mt. Whitney Fish Hatchery

FISH HATCHERY | **FAMILY** | A delightful place for a family picnic, the hatchery was one of California's first trout farms. The Tudor Revival–style structure, completed in 1917, is an architectural stunner, its walls nearly 3 feet thick with locally quarried granite. Fish production ceased in 2007 after a fire and subsequent mudslide, but dedicated volunteers staff the facility and raise trout for display purposes in a large pond out front. Bring change for the fish-food machines. ✉ *1 Golden Trout Circle, 2 miles north of town* ☎ *760/279–1592* 🌐 *www.mtwhitneyfishhatchery.org* 🎟 *Free (donations welcome)* ⏲ *Closed mid-Dec.–mid-Apr. Closed Tues. and Wed.*

Bishop

43 miles north of Independence.

One of the biggest towns along U.S. 395, bustling Bishop has views of the Sierra Nevada and the White and Inyo mountains. First settled by the Northern Paiute people, the area was named in 1861 for cattle rancher Samuel Bishop, who established a camp here. Paiute and Shoshone people reside on four reservations in the area. Bishop kicks off the summer season with its Mule Days Celebration. Held over Memorial Day weekend, the five-day event includes mule races, a rodeo, an arts-and-crafts show, and country-music concerts.

GETTING HERE AND AROUND

To fully enjoy the many surrounding attractions, you should get here by car. Arrive and depart via U.S. 395 or, from Nevada, U.S. 6. Local transit provides limited service to nearby tourist sites.

ESSENTIALS

VISITOR INFORMATION Bishop Chamber of Commerce. ✉ *690 N. Main St., at Park St.* ☎ *760/873–8405* 🌐 *www.bishopvisitor.com.*

Sights

Laws Railroad Museum

MUSEUM | **FAMILY** | The laid-back and wholly nostalgic railroad museum celebrates the Carson and Colorado Railroad Company, which set up a narrow-gauge railroad yard here in 1883. Among the exhibits are a self-propelled car from the Death Valley Railroad, a stamp mill from an area mine, and a full village of rescued buildings, including a post office, the original 1883 train depot, and a restored 1900 ranch house. Many of the buildings are full of "modern amenities" of days gone by. ✉ *200 Silver Canyon Rd., off U.S. 6, 4.5 miles north of town* ☎ *760/873–5950* 🌐 *www.lawsmuseum.org* 🎟 *$5 suggested donation.*

Restaurants

Erick Schat's Bakkerÿ

$ | **BAKERY** | A bustling stop for motorists traveling to and from Mammoth Lakes, this shop is crammed with delicious pastries, cookies, rolls, and other baked goods. The biggest draw, though, is the sheepherder bread, a hand-shaped and stone hearth–baked sourdough that was introduced during the gold rush by immigrant Basque sheepherders in 1907. **Known for:** sheepherder bread and pastries; convenient place to stock up; hefty sandwiches. 💲 *Average main: $12* ✉ *763 N. Main St., near Park St.* ☎ *760/873–7156* 🌐 *www.erickschatsbakery.com.*

Great Basin Bakery

$ | **AMERICAN** | Stop at this small, old-world-style community bakery for fresh and healthy salads, sandwiches (made all day), bagels, artisan breads, cookies, pies, and pastries. Savor your goodies indoors and listen to local banter (it's a favorite gathering spot), or take them along to eat at a picnic spot while adventuring nearby. **Known for:** sandwiches on fresh-baked, house-made bread; all items made and packaged by hand; stellar pies and other desserts. *Average main: $14* *275 S. Main St.* *760/873–9828* *greatbasinbakerybishop.com.*

Hotels

Bishop Creekside Inn

$$ | **B&B/INN** | The nicest spot to stay in Bishop, this clean and comfortable mountain-style hotel is a good base from which to explore the town or go skiing and trout fishing nearby. **Pros:** nice pool; spacious and modern rooms; on-site restaurant. **Cons:** pets not allowed; hotel fronts busy road; basic breakfast. *Rooms from: $180* *725 N. Main St.* *760/872–3044, 800/273–3550* *www.bishopcreeksideinn.com* *89 rooms* *Free breakfast.*

Activities

The Owens Valley is trout country; its glistening alpine lakes and streams are brimming with feisty rainbow, brown, brook, and golden trout. Good spots include Owens River, the Owens River gorge, and Pleasant Valley Reservoir. Although you can fish year-round here, some fishing is catch-and-release. Bishop is the site of fishing derbies throughout the year, including the Blake Jones Blind Bogey Trout Derby in March. Rock-climbing, mountain biking, and hiking are also popular Owens Valley outdoor activities.

FISHING

Reagan's Sporting Goods

FISHING | Stop at Reagan's to pick up bait, tackle, and fishing licenses and to find out where the fish are biting. They can also recommend guides. *963 N. Main St.* *760/872–3000* *www.facebook.com/ReaganSportingGoods.*

HORSE PACKING

Rock Creek Pack Station

HORSEBACK RIDING | The Rock Creek Pack Station outfit runs 3- to 10-day horse-packing trips in the High Sierra, including Mt. Whitney, Yosemite National Park, and other parts of the John Muir Wilderness. One expedition tracks wild mustangs through Inyo National Forest; another is an old-fashioned horse drive between the Owens Valley and the High Sierra. Shorter day rides are also available. Season is mid-June through September. *Bishop* *760/872–8331* *www.rockcreekpackstation.com.*

TOURS

Sierra Mountain Center

TOUR—SPORTS | The guided experiences Sierra Mountain offers include hiking, skiing, snowshoeing, rock-climbing, and mountain-biking trips for all levels of expertise. *200 S. Main St.* *760/873–8526* *www.sierramountaincenter.com* *From $150.*

Sierra Mountain Guides

TOUR—SPORTS | Join expert guides on custom and scheduled alpine adventures, from backcountry skiing and mountaineering to backpacking and mountain running. Programs range from half-day forays to treks that last several weeks. *312 N. Main St.* *760/648–1122* *www.sierramtnguides.com* *From $170.*

Twin Lakes, in the Mammoth Lakes region, is a great place to unwind.

Mammoth Lakes

43 miles northwest of Bishop; 30 miles south of the eastern edge of Yosemite National Park.

International real-estate developers joined forces with Mammoth Mountain Ski Area to transform the once sleepy town of Mammoth Lakes (elevation 7,800 feet) into an upscale ski destination. Relatively sophisticated dining and lodging options can be found at the Village at Mammoth complex, and multimillion-dollar renovations to tired motels and restaurants have revived the "downtown" area of Old Mammoth Road. Also here is the hoppin' Mammoth Rock 'n' Bowl, a two-story activity, dining, and entertainment complex. Winter is high season at Mammoth; in summer, the room rates drop.

GETTING HERE AND AROUND

The best way to get to Mammoth Lakes is by car. The town is about 2 miles west of U.S. 395 on Highway 203, signed as Main Street in Mammoth Lakes and Minaret Road west of town. In summer and early fall (until the first big snow), you can drive to Mammoth Lakes east through Yosemite National Park on scenic Tioga Pass Road. Signed as Highway 120 outside the park, this road connects to U.S. 395 north of Mammoth. In summer, YARTS provides once-a-day public-transit service between Mammoth Lakes and Yosemite Valley. The shuttle buses of Eastern Sierra Transit Authority serve Mammoth Lakes and nearby tourist sites.

ESSENTIALS

HOTEL CONTACTS Mammoth Reservations. ☎ *800/223–3032* 🌐 *www.mammothreservations.com.*

VISITOR INFORMATION Mammoth Lakes Visitor Center. ✉ *Welcome Center, 2510 Main St., near Sawmill Cutoff Rd.* ☎ *760/934–2712, 888/466–2666* 🌐 *www.visitmammoth.com.*

Sights

★ Devils Postpile National Monument

NATURE SITE | Volcanic and glacial forces sculpted this formation of smooth, vertical basalt columns. For a bird's-eye view, take the short, steep trail to the top of a 60-foot cliff. To see the monument's second scenic wonder, **Rainbow Falls,** hike 2 miles past Devils Postpile. A branch of the San Joaquin River plunges more than 100 feet over a lava ledge here. When the water hits the pool below, sunlight turns the resulting mist into a spray of color. From mid-June to early September, day-use visitors must ride the shuttle bus from the Mammoth Mountain Ski Area to the monument. ✉ *Mammoth Lakes ✢ 13 miles southwest of Mammoth Lakes off Minaret Rd. (Hwy. 203)* ☎ *760/934–2289, 760/872–1901 shuttle* 🌐 *www.nps.gov/depo* 🎫 *$10 per vehicle (allowed when the shuttle isn't running, usually early Sept.–mid-Oct.), $15 per person shuttle.*

Hot Creek Geological Site

NATURE SITE | Forged by an ancient volcanic eruption, the geological site is a landscape of boiling hot springs, fumaroles, and occasional geysers. Swimming is prohibited—the water can go from warm to boiling in a short time—but you can look down from the parking area into the canyon to view the steaming volcanic features, a very cool sight indeed. You can also hike the foot path along the creek shores. Fly-fishing for trout is popular upstream from the springs. ✉ *Hot Creek Hatchery Rd., off U.S. 395 (airport exit), about 10 miles southeast of Mammoth Lakes* ☎ *760/873–2400* 🌐 *www.fs.usda.gov/inyo* 🎫 *Free.*

Hot Creek Trout Hatchery

FISH HATCHERY | **FAMILY** | This outdoor fish hatchery has the breeding ponds for many of the fish—typically from 3 to 5 million annually—with which the state stocks Eastern Sierra lakes and rivers. In recent years budget cuts have reduced these numbers, but locals have formed foundations to keep the hatchery going. For more details, take the worthwhile self-guided tour. ■ **TIP→ Kids enjoy feeding the fish here.** ✉ *121 Hot Creek Hatchery Rd., off U.S. 395 (airport exit), about 10 miles southeast of Mammoth Lakes* ☎ *760/934–2664* 🌐 *wildlife.ca.gov/Fishing/Hatcheries/Hot-Creek* 🎫 *Free.*

June Lake Loop

SCENIC DRIVE | Heading south, U.S. 395 intersects the June Lake Loop. This gorgeous 17-mile drive follows an old glacial canyon past Grant, June, Gull, and Silver lakes before reconnecting with U.S. 395 on its way to Mammoth Lakes. ■ **TIP→ The loop is especially colorful in fall.** ✉ *Hwy. 158 W, Lee Vining.*

★ Mammoth Lakes Basin

BODY OF WATER | Mammoth's seven main lakes are popular for fishing and boating in summer, and a network of multiuse paths connects them to the North Village. First comes Twin Lakes, at the far end of which is Twin Falls, where water cascades 300 feet over a shelf of volcanic rock. Also popular are Lake Mary, the largest lake in the basin; Lake Mamie; and Lake George. ■ **TIP→ Horseshoe Lake is the only lake in which you can swim.** ✉ *Lake Mary Rd., off Hwy. 203, southwest of town.*

Mammoth Rock 'n' Bowl

RESTAURANT—SIGHT | **FAMILY** | A sprawling complex with sweeping views of the Sherwin Mountains, Mammoth Rock 'n' Bowl supplies one-stop recreation, entertainment, and dining. Downstairs are 12 bowling lanes, lounge areas, Ping-Pong and foosball tables, dartboards, and a casual bar-restaurant ($$) serving burgers, pizzas, and small plates. The upstairs floor has three golf simulators, a pro shop, and Mammoth Rock Brasserie ($$$), an upscale dining room and lounge. ■ **TIP→ If the weather's nice, sit on the outdoor patio or the upstairs deck and enjoy the unobstructed vistas.** ✉ *3029 Chateau Rd., off Old Mammoth Rd.*

☎ *760/934–4200* ⊕ *mammothrocknbowl.com* 🎫 *Bowling: from $20.*

Minaret Vista

NATURE SITE | The glacier-carved sawtooth spires of the Minarets, the remains of an ancient lava flow, are best viewed from the Minaret Vista. Pull off the road, park your car in the visitors' viewing area, and walk along the path, which has interpretive signs explaining the spectacular peaks, ridges, and valleys beyond. ✉ *Off Hwy. 203, 1¼ mile west of Mammoth Mountain Ski Area.*

★ Panorama Gondola

MOUNTAIN—SIGHT | FAMILY | Even if you don't ski, ride the gondola to see Mammoth Mountain, the aptly named dormant volcano that gives Mammoth Lakes its name. Gondolas serve skiers in winter and mountain bikers and sightseers in summer. The high-speed, eight-passenger gondolas whisk you from the chalet to the summit, where you can learn about the area's volcanic history in the interpretive center, have lunch in the café, and take in top-of-the-world views. Standing high above the tree line, you can look west 150 miles across the state to the Coastal Range; to the east are the highest peaks of Nevada and the Great Basin beyond. You won't find a better view of the Sierra High Country without climbing. ⚠ **The air is thin at the 11,053-foot summit; carry water, and don't overexert yourself.** ✉ *Boarding area at Main Lodge, off Minaret Rd. (Hwy. 203), west of village center* ☎ *760/934–0745, 800/626–6684* ⊕ *www.mammothmountain.com* 🎫 *From $40.*

Village at Mammoth

TOWN | This huge complex of shops, restaurants, and luxury accommodations is the town's tourist center, and the venue for many special events—check the website for the weekly schedule. The complex is also the transfer hub for the free public transit system, with fixed routes throughout the Mammoth Lakes area. The free village gondola starts here and travels up the mountain to Canyon Lodge and back. ■ **TIP➔ Unless you're staying in the village and have access to the on-site lots, parking can be very difficult here.** ✉ *100 Canyon Blvd.* ⊕ *villageatmammoth.com.*

Restaurants

Black Velvet

$ | CAFÉ | Start your day the way scores of locals do—with a stop at the slick Black Velvet espresso bar for Belgian waffles, baked treats, and coffee drinks made from small batches of beans roasted on-site. Then return in the afternoon or evening to hang out with friends in the upstairs wine bar (open 4 to 9). **Known for:** small-batch coffee roasting; small-lot wines by the glass; Belgian waffles. 💲 *Average main: $16* ✉ *3343 Main St., Suite F* ⊕ *www.blackvelvetcoffee.com.*

Bleu Handcrafted Foods

$$ | MODERN AMERICAN | Handcrafted artisanal cheeses and meats, wine and beer tastings, bread baked on-site, and specialty meats and seafood draw patrons to Bleu, a combination market, restaurant (lunch and dinner), and wine bar. Bleu also cooks up savory pub fare at The Eatery at Mammoth Brewing Company. **Known for:** organic, locally sourced ingredients; bar and lounge with cocktails and wine or craft beer tastings; on-site deli, butchery, bakery, and market. 💲 *Average main: $20* ✉ *106 Old Mammoth Rd.* ☎ *760/914–2538* ⊕ *www.bleufoods.com.*

Burgers

$$ | AMERICAN | Don't even think about coming to this bustling restaurant unless you're hungry. Burgers is known, appropriately enough, for its burgers and sandwiches, and everything comes in mountainous portions. **Known for:** great service; hefty portions; burgers and seasoned fries. 💲 *Average main: $17* ✉ *6118 Minaret Rd., across from the Village* ☎ *760/934–6622* ⊕ *www.*

burgersrestaurant.com ⏲ *Closed 2 wks in May and 4–6 wks in Oct. and Nov.*

Mammoth Brewing Company

$$ | **AMERICAN** | Steps from the Village gondola and main bus transfer hub, this brewery lures hungry patrons with about a dozen craft beers on tap, tasty grub from the on-site restaurant, tasting flights, a contemporary vibe at two spacious bar areas, and a beer garden. The dining menu changes constantly, but reflects a locals' twist on pub food, for example, wild game sausages, peach-and-goat-cheese flatbread, or house-made sweet-potato tots. **Known for:** craft beer made on-site; upscale pub food; popular après-ski hangout. [$] *Average main: $17* ✉ *18 Lake Mary Rd.* ✥ *At intersection of Main St. and Minaret Rd.* ☎ *760/934–7141* 🌐 *mammothbrewingco.com.*

The Mogul

$$$ | **STEAKHOUSE** | **FAMILY** | Come here for straightforward steaks—top sirloin, New York, filet mignon, and T-bone. The only catch is that the waiters cook them, and the results vary depending on their skill level; but generally things go well, and kids love the experience. **Known for:** traditional alpine atmosphere; servers custom-grill your order; all-you-can-eat salad bar. [$] *Average main: $30* ✉ *1528 Tavern Rd., off Old Mammoth Rd.* ☎ *760/934–3039* 🌐 *www.themogul.com* ⏲ *No lunch.*

Petra's Bistro & Wine Bar

$$$ | **AMERICAN** | The ambience at Petra's—quiet, dark, and warm (there's a great fireplace)—complements its seductive meat and seafood entrées and smart selection of wines from California and around the world. With its pub grub, whiskies, and craft beers and ales, the downstairs Clocktower Cellar bar provides a lively, if sometimes rowdy, alternative. **Known for:** romantic atmosphere; top-notch service; lively downstairs bar. [$] *Average main: $30* ✉ *Alpenhof Lodge, 6080 Minaret Rd.* ☎ *760/934–3500* 🌐 *www.petrasbistro.com* ⏲ *Closed Mon. No lunch.*

★ **Restaurant at Convict Lake**

$$$ | **AMERICAN** | The lake is one of the most spectacular spots in the Eastern Sierra, and the food here lives up to the view. The woodsy room has a vaulted knotty-pine ceiling and a copper-chimney fireplace; natural light abounds in the daytime, but if it's summer, opt for a table outdoors under the white-barked aspens. **Known for:** beef Wellington, rack of lamb, and pan-seared local trout; exceptional service; extensive wine list with reasonably priced European and California bottlings. [$] *Average main: $36* ✉ *Convict Lake Rd. off U.S. 395, 4 miles south of Mammoth Lakes* ☎ *760/934–3800* 🌐 *www.convictlake.com* ⏲ *No lunch early Sept.–mid-June.*

Toomey's

$$ | **MODERN AMERICAN** | **FAMILY** | A passionate baseball fan, chef Matt Toomey designed this casual space near the Village Gondola to resemble a dugout, and decorated it with baseball memorabilia. Fill up on buffalo meat loaf, seafood jambalaya, or a New Zealand elk rack chop after an outdoor adventure. **Known for:** lobster taquitos and fish tacos; curbside take-out delivery to your car; homemade organic and gluten-free desserts. [$] *Average main: $20* ✉ *6085 Minaret Rd., at the Village* ☎ *760/924–4408* 🌐 *toomeysmammoth.com.*

★ **The Warming Hut**

$$ | **AMERICAN** | **FAMILY** | Warm up by a crackling fire in the stone fireplace while fueling up on healthy, made-from-scratch breakfast, lunch, and dinner dishes at this ski-lodge-style eatery. The flexible menu allows for lots of choice, including a DIY breakfast with more than 20 mix-and-match items, five types of hash, keto selections, grab-and-go sandwiches, salads, burgers, and soups. **Known for:** nearly everything made in-house, including ketchup; build-your-own pancake stack (batters, mix-ins, toppings); family-owned and operated. [$] *Average main: $20* ✉ *343*

Old Mammoth Rd. ☎ *760/965–0549* 🌐 *www.thewarminghutmammoth.com.*

Hotels

Alpenhof Lodge

$$ | HOTEL | Across from the Village at Mammoth, this mom-and-pop motel (with rooms and a couple of cabins) offers basic comforts and a few niceties such as attractive pine furniture. **Pros:** convenient for skiers; reasonable rates; excellent dinner at on-site restaurant, Petra's. **Cons:** some bathrooms are small; rooms above pub can be noisy; no elevator. *$ Rooms from: $159 ✉ 6080 Minaret Rd., Box 1157 ☎ 760/934–6330, 800/828–0371 🌐 www.alpenhof-lodge.com ⇨ 57 units 🍴 Free breakfast.*

★ Convict Lake Resort

$$ | RESORT | The cabins at this resort a 10-minute drive south from Mammoth Lakes range from rustic to modern and come with fully equipped kitchens, including coffeemakers and premium coffee. **Pros:** great views; tranquil atmosphere; wildlife galore. **Cons:** the smallest quarters feel cramped; spotty Wi-Fi and cell service; too remote for some. *$ Rooms from: $219 ✉ Convict Rd., 2 miles off U.S. 395 ☎ 760/934–3800 🌐 www.convictlake.com ⇨ 31 units 🍴 No meals.*

★ Double Eagle Resort and Spa

$$ | RESORT | Lofty pines tower over this June Lake Loop spa retreat with rooms in four buildings overlooking a pond, as well as a three-bedroom house and knotty-pine two-bedroom cabins—all with fully equipped kitchens. **Pros:** pretty setting; spectacular indoor pool; 1½ miles from June Mountain Ski Area. **Cons:** expensive; remote; no in-room a/c. *$ Rooms from: $249 ✉ 5587 Hwy. 158, Box 736, June Lake ☎ 760/648–7004 🌐 www.doubleeagle.com ⇨ 34 units 🍴 No meals.*

Holiday Haus

$$ | HOTEL | A short walk from the Village, Holiday Haus is a collection of reasonably priced, contemporary, mountain-activity-theme rooms and suites, many with full kitchens, as well as a separate hostel-style building with private and bunk rooms (rates start at $42 and include bedding and linens). **Pros:** free parking and Wi-Fi; good option for groups and families; walk to the Village. **Cons:** showers, no tubs in most rooms; no 24-hour desk; basic breakfast. *$ Rooms from: $159 ✉ 3905 Main St. ☎ 760/934–2414 🌐 holidayhausmotelandhostel.com ⇨ 51 units 🍴 No meals.*

Juniper Springs Resort

$$ | RESORT | Tops for slope-side comfort, these condominium-style units have full kitchens and ski-in ski-out access to the mountain. **Pros:** bargain during summer; direct access to the slopes in winter; free shuttle to town in winter. **Cons:** no nightlife within walking distance; no air-conditioning; property needs updating. *$ Rooms from: $199 ✉ 4000 Meridian Blvd. ☎ 760/924–1102, 800/626–6684 🌐 www.mammothmountain.com ⇨ 184 units 🍴 No meals.*

Mammoth Mountain Inn

$$ | RESORT | If you want to be within walking distance of the Mammoth Mountain Main Lodge, this is the place. **Pros:** great location; big rooms; a traditional place to stay. **Cons:** can be crowded in ski season; needs updating; not in the heart of town. *$ Rooms from: $199 ✉ 1 Minaret Rd. ☎ 760/934–2581, 800/626–6684 🌐 www.mammothmountain.com ⇨ 266 units 🍴 No meals.*

Sierra Nevada Resort & Spa

$$ | RESORT | This full-service resort has it all: Old Mammoth rustic elegance, three restaurants, four bars, a spa facility, on-site ski and snowboard rentals, a seasonal pool and Jacuzzi, seasonal miniature golf, and room and suite options in three buildings. **Pros:** kids' club on weekends from 4 to 9; walk to restaurants on property or downtown; complimentary shuttle service. **Cons:** must drive or ride a bus or shuttle to the slopes; thin walls in older rooms; resort fee. *Rooms from: $199* *164 Old Mammoth Rd.* *760/934–2515, 800/824–5132* *thesierranevadaresort.com* *149 units* *No meals.*

★ Tamarack Lodge Resort & Lakefront Restaurant

$$ | RESORT | On the edge of the John Muir Wilderness Area, where cross-country ski trails lace the woods, this 1924 lodge looks like something out of a snow globe. **Pros:** rustic; eco-sensitive; many nearby outdoor activities. **Cons:** high price tag; shared bathrooms for some main lodge rooms; spartan furnishings in lodge rooms. *Rooms from: $239* *Lake Mary Rd., off Hwy. 203* *760/934–2442, 800/626–6684* *www.tamaracklodge.com* *46 units* *No meals.*

The Village Lodge

$$ | RESORT | With their exposed timbers and peaked roofs, these four-story condo buildings at the epicenter of Mammoth's dining and nightlife scene pay homage to Alpine style. **Pros:** central location; big rooms; good restaurants nearby. **Cons:** pricey; can be noisy outside; somewhat sterile decor. *Rooms from: $239* *1111 Forest Trail* *760/934–1982, 800/626–6684* *www.mammothmountain.com* *277 units* *No meals.*

★ Westin Monache Resort

$$$$ | RESORT | On a hill just steps from the Village at Mammoth, the Westin provides full-service comfort and amenities close to restaurants, entertainment, and free public transportation. **Pros:** full bar, pool, 24-fitness center; prime location; free gondola to the slopes is across the street. **Cons:** long, steep stairway down to village; added resort fee; large property with confusing layout. *Rooms from: $359* *50 Hillside Dr.* *760/934–0400, 760/934–4686* *www.marriott.com/mmhwi* *230 rooms* *No meals.*

NIGHTLIFE

The Village at Mammoth hosts events and has several rockin' bars and clubs.

Clocktower Cellar

BARS/PUBS | Nearly 30 beers on tap and more than 50 by the bottle—plus 160 whiskeys and an extensive, Bavarian-themed pub menu—ensure plenty of variety at this lively gathering spot across from the Village Gondola. *6080 Minaret Rd.* *760/934–2725* *www.clocktowercellar.com.*

Lakanuki

BARS/PUBS | Sip mai tais at the tiki bar at Lakanuki, which is in the Village near the gondola. *6201 Minaret Rd.* *760/934–7447* *lakanuki.net.*

Rafters

BARS/PUBS | Most nights, the upscale lounge in Rafter's Restaurant at the Sierra Nevada Resort has live entertainment. *202 Old Mammoth Rd.* *760/934–2515* *raftersmammoth.com.*

Activities

BIKING

★ Mammoth Bike Park

BICYCLING | The park opens when the snow melts, usually by July, and has 80 miles of single-track trails—from mellow to super-challenging. Chairlifts and shuttles provide trail access, and rentals are available. *Mammoth Mountain Ski Area* *760/934–0677, 800/626-6684* *www.mammothmountain.com* *$55 day pass.*

CLIMBING

Via Ferrata

CLIMBING/MOUNTAINEERING | In Europe, a Via Ferrata is a protected climbing network that allows people to experience the thrills of rock climbing and mountaineering without as much risk. Mammoth's version has six different routes of varying ability, with steel cables, iron rungs, and a suspended bridge, all permanently affixed to the rock. The fully guided tour begins with a gondola ride up the mountain. Clip yourself into a cable and climb

Camping in the Eastern Sierra

Camping in the Sierra Nevada means gazing up at awe-inspiring constellations and awakening to the sights of nearby meadows and streams and the unforgettable landscape of giant granite. More than a hundred campgrounds, from remote, tents-only areas to full-service facilities with RV hookups close to the main attractions, operate in the Eastern Sierra. Be aware that Yosemite National Park's most accessible campgrounds can be jam-packed and claustrophobic in the summer. Luckily, there are many options to the east, including calm and beautiful sites such as Lake Mary Campground in the Mammoth Lakes area. The following campsites are recommended. Reserve sites at *www.recreation.gov.*

Convict Lake Campground. A 10-minute drive south of Mammoth, this campground near the Convict Lake Resort is run by the U.S. Forest Service. *Convict Lake Rd., 2 miles off U.S. 395 760/924–5500 88 campsites.*

Lake Mary Campground. There are few sites as beautiful as this lakeside campground at 8,900 feet, open from June to September. *Lake Mary Loop Dr., off Hwy. 203 760/924–5500 No credit cards 48 sites (tent or RV) No meals.*

securely to sweeping views of the Sierra Nevada range. If time and group ability allow, you can follow multiple routes during a session. No climbing experience is required. *Mammoth Mountain, 10001 Minaret Rd. 800/626–6684 www.mammothmountain.com From $199.*

FISHING

The main fishing season runs from the last Saturday in April until November 15; there are opportunities for catch-and-release fishing in winter. Crowley Lake is the top trout-fishing spot in the area; Convict Lake, June Lake, and the lakes of the Mammoth Basin are other prime spots. One of the best trout rivers is the super-scenic Upper Owens River, near the east side of Crowley Lake. Hot Creek, a designated Wild Trout Stream, is renowned for fly-fishing (catch-and-release only).

Kittredge Sports

FISHING | This outfit rents rods and reels and conducts guided trips. *3218 Main St., at Forest Trail 760/934–7566 kittredgesports.com.*

Sierra Drifters Guide Service

FISHING | To maximize your time on the water, get tips from local anglers, or better yet, book a guided fishing trip, contact Sierra Drifters. *Mammoth Lakes 760/935–4250 www.sierradrifters.com.*

HIKING

Hiking in Mammoth is stellar, especially along the trails that wind through alpine scenery around the Lakes Basin. Carry lots of water; and remember, the air is thin at 8,000-plus feet.

You can pick up trail map and permits for backpacking in wilderness areas at the Mammoth Lakes Visitor Center just east of town. For descriptions of more than 300 miles of trails—as well as maps and a wealth of information on recreation in Mammoth Lakes and the Inyo National Forest in all seasons—visit the Mammoth Lakes Trail System website (*www.mammothtrails.org*).

Convict Lake Loop

HIKING/WALKING | This 2.8-mile trail loops gently around deep blue Convict Lake, a popular site for anglers. Feast your eyes on stunning views of tall peaks, glistening water, and aspen and cottonwood groves while you hike. *Easy.* ✉ *Trailhead: At Convict Lake, 9 miles south of Mammoth Lakes.*

Duck Lake

HIKING/WALKING | This popular and busy trail (11 miles round-trip) heads up Coldwater Canyon along Mammoth Creek, past a series of spectacular lakes and wildflower meadows over 10,797-foot Duck Pass to dramatic Duck Lake, which eventually links up with the John Muir Trail. *Difficult.* ✉ *Trailhead: Coldwater Campground.*

Emerald Lake and Sky Meadows

HIKING/WALKING | The first part of this trail travels through shady pine forest along Coldwater Creek to bright-green Emerald Lake (1.8 miles round-trip). Extend the hike by climbing up a trail along an inlet stream up to Gentian Meadow and Sky Meadows (4 miles round-trip), especially beautiful in July and August when various alpine wildflowers, fed by snowmelt, are at their peak splendor. *Moderate.* ✉ *Trailhead: Coldwater Campground.*

Minaret Falls

HIKING/WALKING | **FAMILY** | Hike along portions of both the Pacific Crest and John Muir trails on this scenic trail (3 miles round-trip), which leads to Devil's Postpile, Minaret Falls, and natural volcanic springs. This is a good family hike, especially in late summer when the water has receded a bit and kids can climb boulders and splash around. *Easy.* ✉ *Trailhead: At Devil's Postpile National Monument.*

HORSEBACK RIDING

Stables around Mammoth are typically open from June through September.

Mammoth Lakes Pack Outfit

HORSEBACK RIDING | This company runs day and overnight horseback and mule trips and will shuttle you to the high country. ✉ *Lake Mary Rd., between Twin Lakes and Lake Mary* ☎ *760/934–2434* 🌐 *www.mammothpack.com.*

McGee Creek Pack Station

HORSEBACK RIDING | These folks customize pack trips or will shuttle you to camp alone. ✉ *2990 McGee Creek Rd., Crowley Lake* ☎ *760/935–4324 summer, 760/874–8314 winter* 🌐 *www.mcgeecreekpackstation.com.*

SKIING

In winter, call the Snow Report (☎ *760/934–7669 or 888/766–9778*) for information about Mammoth weather conditions.

June Mountain Ski Area

SKIING/SNOWBOARDING | **FAMILY** | Snowboarders especially dig June Mountain, a compact, low-key resort north of Mammoth Mountain. Several beginner-to-intermediate terrain areas—including the Surprise Fun Zone and Buckey's Playground—are for both skiers and boarders. There's rarely a line for the lifts here: if you must ski on a weekend and want to avoid the crowds, this is the place to come, and in a storm it's better protected from wind and blowing snow than Mammoth is. (If it starts to storm, you can use your Mammoth ticket at June.) The services include a rental-and-repair shop, a ski school, and a sports shop. There's food, but the options are better at Mammoth. **■ TIP→ Kids 12 and under ski and ride free.** ✉ *3819 Hwy. 158/June Lake Loop, off U.S. 395, 22 miles northwest of Mammoth, June Lake* ☎ *760/648–7733, 888/586–3686* 🌐 *www.junemountain.com* 🎫 *From $120* ☞ *35 trails on 1,400 acres, rated 35% beginner, 45% intermediate, 20% advanced. Longest run 2 miles, base 7,545 feet, summit 10,190 feet. Lifts: 7.*

★ **Mammoth Mountain Ski Area**

SKIING/SNOWBOARDING | One of the West's largest and best ski areas, Mammoth has more than 3,500 acres of skiable terrain and a 3,100-foot vertical drop. The

Why Is There So Much Snow?

The Sierra Nevada receives some of the deepest snow anywhere in North America. In winter, houses literally get buried, and homeowners have to build tunnels to their front doors (though many install enclosed wooden walkways). In the high country, it's not uncommon for a single big storm to bring 10 feet of snow and for 30 feet of snow to accumulate at the height of the season. In the enormous bowls of Mammoth Mountain, you might ski past a tiny pine that looks like a miniature Christmas tree—until you remember that more than 30 feet of tree is under the snow.

To understand the weather, you have to understand the terrain. The Sierra Nevada are marked by a gentle western rise from sea level to the Sierra crest, which tops out at a whopping 14,494 feet at Sequoia National Park's Mt. Whitney, the highest point in the continental United States. On the eastern side of the crest, at the escarpment, the mountains drop sharply—as much as 5,000 feet—giving way to the Great Basin and the high-mountain deserts of Nevada and Utah.

When winter storms blow in off the Pacific, carrying vast stores of water with them, they race across the relatively flat, 100-mile-wide Central Valley. As they ascend the wall of mountains, though, the decrease in temperature and the increase in pressure on the clouds force them to release their water. Between October and April, that means snow—lots of it. Storms can get hung up on the peaks for days, dumping foot after foot of the stuff. By the time they finally cross over the range and into the Great Basin, there isn't much moisture left for the lower elevations on the eastern side. This is why, if you cross the Sierra eastward on your way to U.S. 395, you'll notice that brightly colored wildflowers and forest-green trees give way to pale-green sagebrush and brown sand as you drop out of the mountains.

The coastal cities and farmlands of the rest of the state depend heavily on the water from the Sierra snowpack. Most of the spring and summer runoff from the melting snows is caught in reservoirs in the foothills and routed to farmlands and cities throughout the state via a complex system of levees and aqueducts, which you'll no doubt see in the foothills and Central Valley, to the west of the range. But much of the water remains in the mountains, forming lakes, most notably giant Lake Tahoe to the north, Mono Lake to the east, and the thousands of little lakes along the Sierra Crest. The lakes are an essential part of the ecosystem, providing water for birds, fish, and plant life.

views from the 11,053-foot summit are some of the most stunning in the Sierra. Below, you'll find a 6½-mile-wide swath of groomed boulevards and canyons, as well as pockets of tree-skiing and a dozen vast bowls. Snowboarders are everywhere on the slopes; there are seven outstanding freestyle terrain parks of varying difficulty, with jumps, rails, tabletops, and giant super pipes—this is the location of several international snowboarding competitions, and, in summer, mountain-bike meets. Mammoth's season begins in November and often lingers into July. Lessons and equipment are available, and there's a children's ski and snowboard school. Mammoth runs free shuttle-bus routes around town and to the ski area, and the Village Gondola runs from the Village complex to Canyon Lodge. However, only overnight guests are allowed to park at the Village for more than a few hours. **Facilities:** 155 trails; 3,500 acres; 3,100-foot vertical drop; 25 lifts. ✉ *Minaret Rd., west of Mammoth Lakes, Rte. 203, off U.S. 395* ☎ *760/934–2571, 800/626–6684, 760/934–0687 shuttle* 🌐 *www.mammothmountain.com* 🎫 *From $109.*

Tamarack Cross Country Ski Center

SKIING/SNOWBOARDING | Trails at the center, adjacent to Tamarack Lodge, meander around several lakes. Rentals are available. ✉ *Lake Mary Rd., off Hwy. 203* ☎ *760/934–5293, 760/934–2442* 🌐 *tamaracklodge.com* 🎫 *$68 all-inclusive day rate.*

SKI RENTALS

★ Black Tie Ski Rentals

SKIING/SNOWBOARDING | Skiers and snowboarders love this rental outfit whose staffers will deliver and custom-fit equipment for free. They also offer slope-side assistance. ✉ *501 Old Mammoth Rd.* ☎ *760/934–7009* 🌐 *mammoth.blacktieskis.com.*

Footloose

SKIING/SNOWBOARDING | When the U.S. Ski Team visits Mammoth and needs boot adjustments, everyone heads to Footloose, the best place in town—and possibly all California—for ski-boot rentals and sales, as well as custom insoles. ✉ *3043 Main St., at Mammoth Rd.* ☎ *760/934–2400* 🌐 *www.footloosesports.com.*

Kittredge Sports

SKIING/SNOWBOARDING | Advanced skiers should consider this outfit, which has been around since the 1960s. ✉ *3218 Main St.* ☎ *760/934–7566* 🌐 *kittredgesports.com.*

Woolly's Tube Park & Snow Play

SNOW SPORTS | **FAMILY** | Ride a lift to the top of the hill and whoosh down in a high-speed snow tube as often as you like during a 1¼-hour session. The park has six lanes, a heated deck, and snack shop. Discounts available for a second session if you're not ready to stop riding. Little ones can hang out in the snow play area with sleds and saucers. ✉ *9000 Minaret Rd.* ☎ *800/626–6684 reservations, 760/934–7533 direct line* 🌐 *www.mammothmountain.com* 🎫 *From $45, play area $25.*

SNOWMOBILING

Mammoth Snowmobile Adventures

SNOW SPORTS | Mammoth Snowmobile Adventures conducts guided tours along wooded trails. ✉ *Mammoth Mountain Main Lodge* ☎ *760/934–9645, 800/626–6684* 🌐 *www.mammothmountain.com* 🎫 *From $160.*

ZIP LINING

Mammoth Mega Zip

ZIP LINING | Mammoth Mountain's zipline tour has the tallest vertical drop (2,100 feet) in North America. Ride the Panoramic Gondola up to the summit of Mammoth Mountain, then descend side by side on parallel cables that run more than a mile back down to the base, at speeds of up to 60 mph (minimum weight 75 lbs). ✉ *Mammoth Adventure Center, 10001 Minaret Rd.* ☎ *800/626–6684* 🌐 *www.mammothmountain.com.*

Chapter 16

SACRAMENTO AND THE GOLD COUNTRY

Updated by
Daniel Mangin

Sights ★★★★☆ | Restaurants ★★★★☆ | Hotels ★★★★☆ | Shopping ★★★☆☆ | Nightlife ★★★☆☆

WELCOME TO SACRAMENTO AND THE GOLD COUNTRY

TOP REASONS TO GO

★ **Gold rush:** Marshall Gold Discovery State Park is where it all started—it's a must-see—but there are historic and modern gems all along California Highway 49 from Nevada City to Jamestown.

★ **State capital:** Easygoing Sacramento offers sights like the Capitol and historic Old Sacramento.

★ **Bon appétit:** Sacramento has emerged as a foodie destination, but its celebrations of food, drink, and culture date back to the gold-rush parade of immigrants.

★ **Wine tasting:** With bucolic scenery and friendly tasting rooms, El Dorado County and the Shenandoah Valley are winning acclaim for their diverse offerings.

★ **Rivers, sequoias, and caverns:** Natural beauty here is rich (stream beds are still lined with gold), high (sequoias in Calaveras Big Trees State Park), and deep (the main chamber at Moaning Caverns could hold the Statue of Liberty).

The Gold Country is a sizable rural destination popular with those seeking a reasonably priced escape from Southern California and the Bay Area. Sacramento, Davis, Winters, and Lodi are in enormous valleys just west of the Sierra Nevada range. Foothills communities along Highway 49 tell the gold-rush story, support the nascent wine-growing scene, or serve as gateways to Yosemite or Lake Tahoe. A few function as all three.

1 **Sacramento.** The capital also serves as a regional hub.

2 **Davis.** Agriculture meets academics in this university town.

3 **Winters.** A foodie haven perfect for a day trip.

4 **Lodi.** "Zinfandel Capital of the World" excels at many other wines.

5 **Nevada City.** "Queen of the Northern Mines" is a real beauty.

6 **Grass Valley.** Here, the Empire Mine thrived for years.

7 **Auburn.** Old Town charms with steep hills, cobblestone streets.

8 **Coloma.** The gold rush started here.

9 **Placerville.** Over a million people visit Apple Hill each year.

10 **Plymouth.** Vines date from 1869 in nearby Shenandoah Valley.

11 **Amador City.** Shops hold this former mining town's treasures these days.

12 **Sutter Creek.** Much gold-rush history unfolded here.

13 **Volcano.** Explorable caverns lie just outside town.

14 **Jackson.** Two mines produced $70 million in gold in these parts.

15 **Mokelumne Hill.** Rowdy miners once called "Moke Hill" home.

16 **Angels Camp.** Mark Twain wrote about this town's famous frog-jumping contest.

17 **Murphys.** Main Street's vibe is upscale but unpretentious; redwoods and caverns await nearby.

18 **Columbia.** Experience gold-rush living history in this throwback village.

19 **Jamestown.** Hollywood often films in or around Railtown 1897.

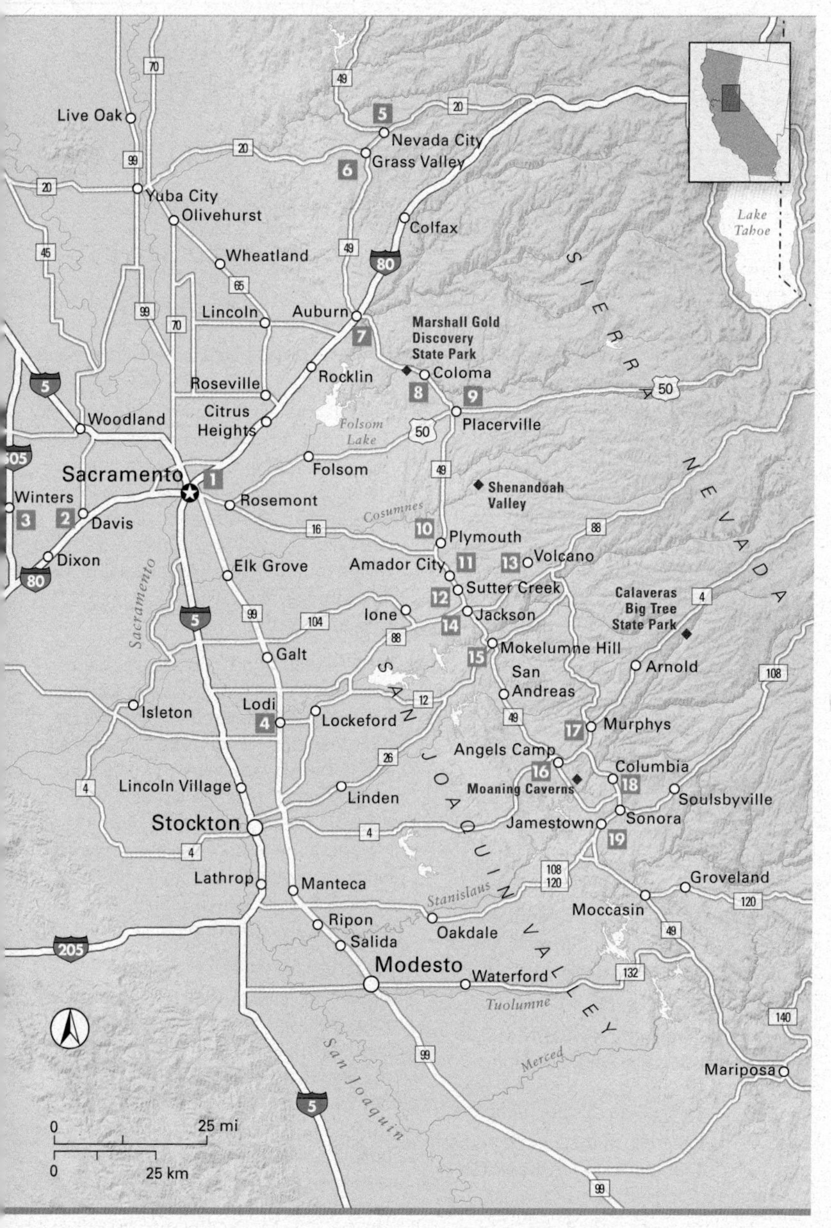
Live Oak
Nevada City
Grass Valley
Yuba City
Olivehurst
Colfax
Wheatland
Lincoln
Auburn
Marshall Gold Discovery State Park
Coloma
Rocklin
Roseville
Citrus Heights
Woodland
Folsom Lake
Placerville
Sacramento
Folsom
Shenandoah Valley
Winters
Rosemont
Davis
Cosumnes
Plymouth
Dixon
Volcano
Elk Grove
Amador City
Sutter Creek
Sacramento
Ione
Jackson
Calaveras Big Tree State Park
Mokelumne Hill
Galt
San Andreas
Arnold
Isleton
Lodi
Lockeford
Murphys
Angels Camp
Columbia
Moaning Caverns
Soulsbyville
Lincoln Village
Linden
Sonora
Stockton
Jamestown
Lathrop
Manteca
Groveland
Stanislaus
Moccasin
Ripon
Oakdale
Salida
Modesto
Waterford
Tuolumne
Merced
San Joaquin
Mariposa
SIERRA NEVADA
SAN JOAQUIN VALLEY
Lake Tahoe
0 25 mi
0 25 km

The Gold Country is one of California's less expensive yet still sublime destinations, a region of the Sierra Nevada foothills filled with natural and cultural pleasures. Visitors come for the boomtowns and ghost towns, art galleries and antiques shops, "farm-to-fork" cuisine and delicious wines, and atmospheric inns and historic hotels.

Spring brings wildflowers, and in fall the hills are colored by bright red berries and changing leaves. Because it offers plenty of outdoor diversions, the Gold Country is a great place to take kids. Sacramento is an ethnically diverse city, with significant Mexican, Hmong, and Ukrainian populations, among many others. Many present-day immigrants are relatively recent arrivals, but the capital city has absorbed several waves of newcomers since 1848, when James Marshall turned up a gold nugget in the American River. At the time, Mexico and the United States were still wrestling for ownership of what would become the Golden State. Marshall's discovery provided the incentive for the United States to tighten its grip on the region, and prospectors from all over the world soon came to seek their fortunes in the Mother Lode, a vein of gold-bearing quartz that stretched 150 miles across the foothills.

As gold fever seized the nation, California's population of 15,000 swelled to 265,000 within three years. The mostly young, male adventurers who arrived in search of gold—the '49ers—became part of a culture that discarded many of the button-down conventions of the eastern states. It was also a violent time. Yankee prospectors chased Mexican miners off their claims, and California's leaders initiated a plan to exterminate the local Native American population. Bounties were paid, and private militias were hired to wipe out the Native Americans or sell them into slavery. California was to be dominated by the Anglo.

The gold-rush boom lasted scarcely 20 years, but it changed California forever, producing 546 mining towns, of which fewer than 250 remain. The hills of the Gold Country were alive, not only with prospecting and mining but also with business, the arts, gambling, and a fair share of crime. Opera houses went up alongside brothels, and the California State Capitol, in Sacramento, was built partly with the gold dug out of the hills.

MAJOR REGIONS

Sacramento and Ag Country. The gateway to the Gold Country, the seat of state government, and a key "ag" (agricultural) hub, Sacramento plays many contemporary roles. Nearly 2½ million people live in the metropolitan area, whose sunshine, mild climate, and fertile soil are responsible for the region's current riches: fresh and bountiful food and high-quality wines. There's a growing local craft-beer scene, too. Visits to Sacramento and nearby towns like Davis and Winters provide the broad agricultural perspective, Lodi the wine-making one. Wineries here earn national recognition, yet they're without the high prices of Napa and Sonoma.

Highway 49. Sacramento's museums provide an excellent introduction to the Gold Country's illustrious history, but the region's heart lies along Highway 49, which winds the approximately 300-mile north–south length of the famed Mother Lode mining area past or near the following towns: Nevada City, Grass Valley, Auburn, Coloma, Placerville, Plymouth, Amador City, Sutter Creek, Jackson, Mokelumne Hill, Angels Camp, Murphys, Columbia, and Jamestown. Some can be explored as easy day trips from Sacramento, but to immerse yourself in this storied setting, consider staying overnight at least a day or two, especially if you'll be stopping at the many wineries of the Sierra Foothills appellation. On days when it's not too hot or cold, the highway—a hilly, often twisting two-lane road—begs for a convertible with the top down.

Planning

When to Go

The Gold Country is most pleasant in spring, when the wildflowers are in bloom, and in fall. Summers can be hot in the valley (temperatures of 100°F are fairly common), so head for the hills. Sacramento winters tend to be cool, with occasionally foggy or rainy days. Throughout the year, Gold Country towns stage community and cultural celebrations. In December, many towns are decked out for the holidays.

Getting Here and Around

AIR

Sacramento International Airport (SMF) is served by airlines that include Aeromexico, Air Canada, Alaska/Horizon, American, Delta, Frontier, Hawaiian, JetBlue, Southwest, and United. A taxi from the airport to Downtown Sacramento costs about $40; services like Lyft and Uber often cost less. Public buses are also an option.

CONTACTS Sacramento International Airport. ✉ *6900 Airport Blvd., Sacramento* ✢ *12 miles northwest of Downtown off I–5* ☎ *916/929–5411* 🌐 *www.sacramento.aero/smf.*

BUS AND LIGHT-RAIL

Greyhound serves Sacramento from San Francisco and Los Angeles. Sacramento Regional Transit serves the capital area with buses and light-rail vehicles. Yolobus public transit connects SMF airport and Downtown Sacramento, West Sacramento, and Davis.

CONTACTS Sacramento Regional Transit. ☎ *916/321–2877* 🌐 *www.sacrt.com.* **Yolobus.** ☎ *530/666–2877, 916/371–2877* 🌐 *www.yolobus.com.*

CAR

Interstate 5 (north–south) and I–80 (east–west) are the two main routes into and out of Sacramento. From there, three highways fan out toward the east, all intersecting with historic Highway 49: I–80 heads northeast 34 miles to Auburn; U.S. 50 goes east 40 miles to Placerville; and Highway 16 angles southeast 45 miles to Plymouth. Two-lane Highway 49 winds and climbs through foothills and valleys, linking the principal Gold Country towns. Traveling by car is the only practical way to explore the region.

TRAIN

Amtrak serves Sacramento and Davis from the Bay Area and beyond.

Restaurants

Sacramento's dining scene has experienced a recent changing of the guard. Longtime favorites have closed their doors, and a new generation of chefs has begun capitalizing on inland California's agricultural bounty. American, Italian, Chinese, and Mexican restaurants remain common, but Gold Country chefs also prepare ambitious international and contemporary regional cuisine. Grass Valley's meat- and vegetable-stuffed *pasties,* introduced by 19th-century gold miners from Cornwall, England, are one of the area's more unusual treats.

Hotels

Downtown Sacramento contains boutique and full-service hotels as well as a few small inns. Chain motels predominate in the larger towns—among them Auburn, Grass Valley, and Jackson—along Highway 49, but you'll also find restored historic hotels and luxurious bed-and-breakfasts throughout the Gold Country. Although some 19th-century properties could use sprucing up, they're still appealing for their legacies and lower rates.

Restaurant and hotel reviews have been shortened. For full information, visit Fodors.com. Restaurant prices are the average cost of a main course at dinner, or if dinner is not served, at lunch. Hotel prices are the lowest cost of a standard double room in high season.

What It Costs

	$	$$	$$$	$$$$
RESTAURANTS	under $17	$17–$26	$27–$36	over $36
HOTELS	under $150	$150–$250	$251–$350	over $350

Visitor Information

EVENTS AND ENTERTAINMENT Sacramento 365. 🌐 *www.sacramento365.com.*

TOURISM AGENCIES Greater Grass Valley Chamber of Commerce. ✉ *128 E. Main St., Grass Valley* ☎ *530/273–4667* 🌐 *www.grassvalleychamber.com.* **Tuolumne County Visitors Bureau.** ✉ *193 S. Washington St., Sonora* ☎ *209/533–4420, 800/446–1333* 🌐 *www.yosemitegoldcountry.com.* **Visit Amador.** ☎ *209/267–9249* 🌐 *www.visitamador.com.* **Visit El Dorado.** ✉ *542 Main St., Placerville* ☎ *530/621–5885* 🌐 *visit-eldorado.com.*

Sacramento

87 miles northeast of San Francisco, 384 miles north of Los Angeles.

All around the Golden State's seat of government you'll experience echoes of the gold-rush days, most notably in Old Sacramento, whose wooden sidewalks and horse-drawn carriages on cobblestone streets lend the waterfront district a 19th-century feel. The California State Railroad Museum and other venues hold artifacts of state and national significance, and historic buildings house shops and restaurants. River cruises and train rides are fun family diversions.

Due east of Old Sacramento is Downtown, where landmarks include the Capitol building and the surrounding Capitol Park. Golden 1 Center, a sports and concert venue, is part of DOCO, short for Downtown Commons, which also includes shops, restaurants, hotels, and grassy and concrete gathering spaces.

Farther east, starting at about 15th Street, lies Midtown, a mix of Victorian edifices, ultramodern lofts, and innovative restaurants and cozy wine bars. A few intersections are jumping most evenings when the weather's good; they include the corner of 20th and L streets in what's known as Lavender Heights, the center of the city's gay and lesbian community.

GETTING HERE AND AROUND

Most people drive to Sacramento and get around by car. Lyft and Uber tend to work out better than the cab options.

Sacramento Regional Transit buses and light-rail vehicles serve the area. Bus 30 links Old Sacramento, Midtown, and Sutter's Fort.

Assuming that traffic is not a factor (though it often is), Sacramento is a 90-minute drive from San Francisco and a seven-hour drive from Los Angeles. Parking garages serve Old Sacramento and other tourist spots; on-street parking in Downtown can be difficult to find.

TRANSPORTATION CONTACTS Sacramento Regional Transit. ☎ *916/321–2877* 🌐 *www.sacrt.com.*

ESSENTIALS

VISITOR INFORMATION Sacramento Visitor Center. ✉ *1002 2nd St.* ☎ *916/442–7644* 🌐 *www.oldsacramento.com.* **Visit Sacramento.** ✉ *1608 I St.* ☎ *916/808–7777* 🌐 *www.visitsacramento.com.*

Sights

California Automobile Museum

MUSEUM | More than 120 automobiles—from Model Ts, Hudsons, and Studebakers to modern-day electric-powered ones—are on display at this museum that pays tribute to automotive history and car culture. Check out a replica of Henry Ford's 1896 Quadricycle and a 1920s roadside café and garage exhibit. The docents are ready to explain everything you see. The museum is south of Downtown and Old Sacramento, with ample free parking. ✉ *2200 Front St., Downtown* ☎ *916/442–6802* 🌐 *www.calautomuseum.org* *$10* *Closed Tues.*

★ **California State Railroad Museum**

MUSEUM | FAMILY | Sprawling over three floors and taking up the equivalent of 2½ acres of space, this museum celebrates the history of trains from their 19th-century English origins to the pre–jet age glory days of rail travel and the high-speed trains of today's Europe and Asia. A permanent exhibit that debuted in 2019 for the 150th anniversary of the transcontinental railroad's completion (Sacramento was the western terminus) details the contributions of Chinese laborers. Another section contains a cast gold "Last Spike," one of several spikes issued to commemorate the joining in Utah of the west-to-east Central Pacific and east-to-west Union Pacific lines. Twenty-two of the museum's railroad cars and engines—among them Pullman-style cars and steam locomotives—are on display at any one time, and there are interactive displays and a play area for kids. The exhibits of toy trains delight youngsters and adults. ✉ *125 I St., at 2nd St., Old Sacramento* ☎ *916/323–9280* 🌐 *www.csrmf.org* *$12.*

★ **Capitol**

GOVERNMENT BUILDING | Built in 1869 and topped by a 128-foot gilded dome, the Capitol functions as both a working museum and the active seat of California's government. When the building is open, you can wander freely by reproductions of century-old state offices and into legislative chambers (in session from January to September) decorated in the style of the 1890s. Look for the abstract portrait of Edmund G. "Jerry" Brown, alongside those of fellow former

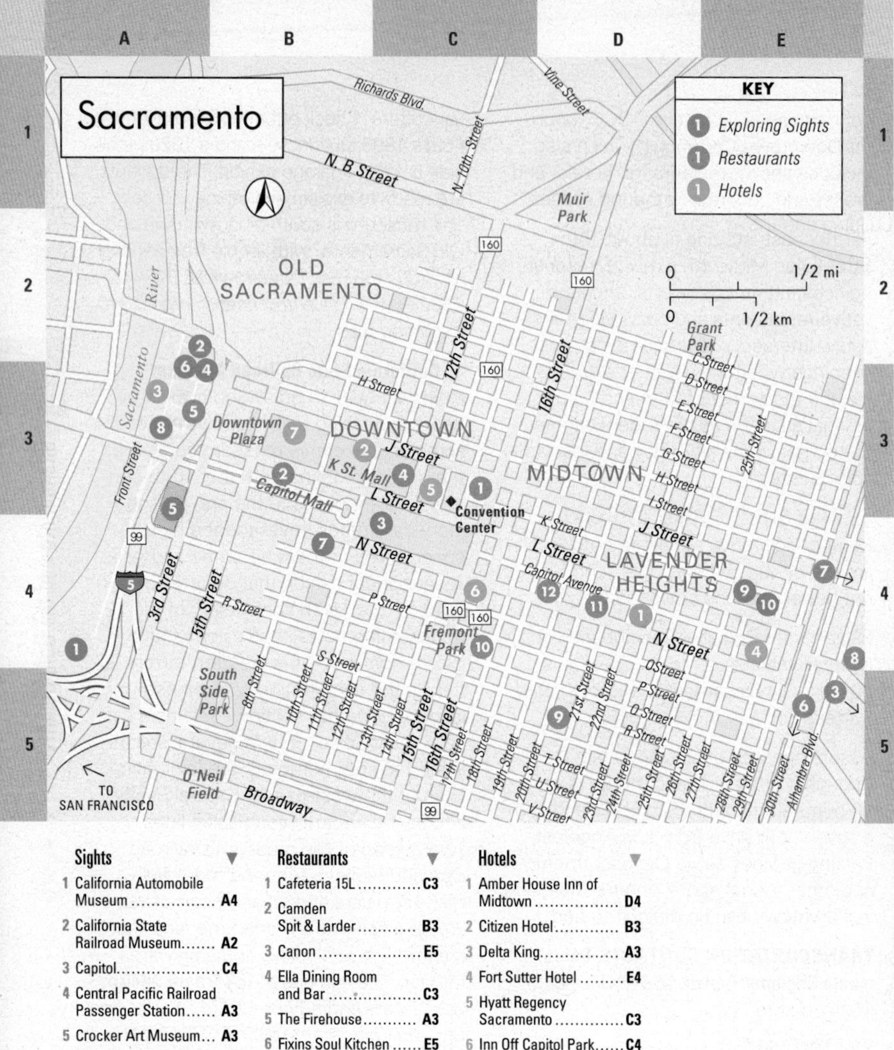

Sights

1 California Automobile Museum **A4**
2 California State Railroad Museum....... **A2**
3 Capitol........................ **C4**
4 Central Pacific Railroad Passenger Station...... **A3**
5 Crocker Art Museum... **A3**
6 Hunting, Hopkins & Co. Hardware Store......... **A3**
7 Leland Stanford Mansion State Historic Park **B4**
8 Old Sacramento Schoolhouse Museum **A3**
9 State Indian Museum ... **E4**
10 Sutter's Fort.............. **E4**

Restaurants

1 Cafeteria 15L............ **C3**
2 Camden Spit & Larder........... **B3**
3 Canon **E5**
4 Ella Dining Room and Bar **C3**
5 The Firehouse........... **A3**
6 Fixins Soul Kitchen **E5**
7 The Kitchen............... **E4**
8 Kru.......................... **E4**
9 Localis **D5**
10 Magpie Cafe.............. **C4**
11 The Waterboy........... **D4**
12 Zócalo Midtown **D4**

Hotels

1 Amber House Inn of Midtown **D4**
2 Citizen Hotel............ **B3**
3 Delta King................ **A3**
4 Fort Sutter Hotel **E4**
5 Hyatt Regency Sacramento **C3**
6 Inn Off Capitol Park...... **C4**
7 Kimpton Sawyer Hotel..................... **B3**

governors Ronald Reagan (who succeeded Brown's father, Edmund G. "Pat" Brown) and Arnold Schwarzenegger. On most days, guides conduct tours of the building and the 40-acre Capitol Park, which contains a rose garden, a fragrant display of camellias (Sacramento's city flower), and California Veterans Memorials. ■ TIP→ **The Capitol's diverse trees include more than 1,000 types from around the world.** ✉ *10th St. and L St., Downtown* ☎ *916/324–0333* 🌐 *capitolmuseum.ca.gov* 🎫 *Free.*

Central Pacific Railroad Passenger Station
TRANSPORTATION SITE (AIRPORT/BUS/FERRY/TRAIN) | **FAMILY** | At this reconstructed 1876 depot there's rolling stock to admire and a typical waiting room. On summer weekends and a few other times, a train departs from the freight depot, south of the passenger station, making a 45-minute out-and-back trip that starts along the banks of the Sacramento River. ■ TIP→ **Cookies and hot chocolate are served aboard sellout Polar Express rides between Thanksgiving and Christmas that include appearances by characters from the famous story.** ✉ *930 Front St., at J St., Old Sacramento* ☎ *916/445–5995* 🌐 *www.csrmf.org/events/train-rides* 🎫 *Train rides from $15* ⏲ *Hrs vary.*

★ **Crocker Art Museum**
MUSEUM | Established in 1885, Sacramento's premier fine-arts museum specializes in California art, European master drawings, and international ceramics. A highlight is the magnificent *Great Canyon of the Sierra, Yosemite* (1871) by Thomas Hill. Some works are displayed in two architecturally significant 19th-century structures: the original Italianate Crocker residence and a villa-like gallery. A contemporary, 125,000-square-foot space hosts outstanding traveling exhibitions. ✉ *216 O St., at 3rd St., Downtown* ☎ *916/808–7000* 🌐 *www.crockerartmuseum.org* 🎫 *$12* ⏲ *Closed Mon.–Wed. (but check).*

Huntington, Hopkins & Co. Hardware Store
MUSEUM | Picks, shovels, and other paraphernalia used by gold-rush miners are on display at this re-creation of a 19th-century hardware store that also displays tools and accessories for households, farms, and machine shops. Though it's named for two of the Big Four railroad barons, their store was far more elaborate. ✉ *113 I St., at Front St., Old Sacramento* ☎ *916/323–7234* 🌐 *www.csrmf.org/visit/outside-the-museum* 🎫 *Free* ⏲ *Closed Mon.–Wed.*

★ **Leland Stanford Mansion State Historic Park**
HOUSE | In 1856, this structure's original owner built a modest two-story row house purchased a few years later by Leland Stanford, a railroad baron, California governor, and U.S. senator who expanded it into a 19,000-square-foot mansion. The opulent space is open for touring except on days when California's governor hosts official events. Before Stanford's wife and heir, Jane, died, she donated the mansion to Sacramento's Roman Catholic diocese, whose nuns ran it first as an orphanage and later a home for teenage girls. Luckily for the restoration efforts, which began in 1986 after the state acquired the property, the nuns had stashed many original furnishings and fixtures in the attic, and the renowned photographer Eadweard Muybridge had shot images in the 1870s that made clear what rooms looked like and where things belonged. ■ TIP→ **Guided tours of small groups depart hourly from 10 to 4.** ✉ *800 N St., at 8th St., Downtown* ☎ *916/324–0575 recorded info, 916/324–9266 visitor center* 🌐 *www.parks.ca.gov/stanfordmansion* 🎫 *Free.*

Old Sacramento Schoolhouse Museum
MUSEUM | **FAMILY** | A kid-friendly attraction that shows what one-room schoolhouses were like in central California and the Sierra foothills in the late 1800s, this replica built in 1976 is a fun, quick stop a block from the waterfront. ✉ *1200 Front St., at*

L St., Old Sacramento *www.oldsac-schoolhouse.org* Free Closed Sun.

State Indian Museum

MUSEUM | Adjacent to Sutter's Fort, this small but engaging museum explores the lives and history of California's native peoples. Arts-and-crafts displays, a demonstration village, and other exhibits offer a fascinating portrait of the state's earliest inhabitants. *2618 K St., at 26th St., Midtown 916/324–0971 www.parks.ca.gov/indianmuseum $5.*

Sutter's Fort

MUSEUM VILLAGE | **FAMILY** | German-born Swiss immigrant John Augustus Sutter founded Sacramento's earliest Euro-American settlement in 1839. A self-guided tour includes a blacksmith's shop, bakery, prison, living quarters, and livestock areas. Costumed docents sometimes reenact fort life, demonstrating crafts, food preparation, and firearms maintenance. *2701 L St., at 27th St., Midtown 916/445–4422 www.suttersfort.org From $5.*

Restaurants

Cafeteria 15L

$$ | **AMERICAN** | The exposed brick, reclaimed wood, mismatched chairs, and natural light streaming through large-paned windows of this easygoing comfort-food hangout make a great first impression and a lasting one on the many repeat customers. Favorites like tater tots (in truffle oil) and chicken and waffles (with pecan butter, maple syrup, Tabasco-and-black-pepper pork, and gravy) prove simultaneously familiar and intriguing. **Known for:** two outdoor patios; nostalgic food with a modern twist; weekend brunch with bottomless mimosas. *Average main: $20 1116 15th St., at L St., Downtown 916/492–1960 www.cafeteria15l.com.*

Camden Spit & Larder

$$$ | **MODERN AMERICAN** | Upscale London haberdasheries reportedly inspired the aesthetic of this impeccably designed, pressed-metal-ceilinged paean to spit-roasted, Brit-influenced meat dishes. Near Golden 1 Center and Downtown Commons, it's a place to share small offerings like sausage rolls, steak tartare, and local caviar and crumpets (Sacramento is a center of caviar production) before proceeding to Loch Duart salmon, spit-roasted chicken, or the house specialty, roast rib of beef with roasted bone marrow, horseradish, and Bordelaise. **Known for:** beef-fat hash browns with sour-cream horseradish; wine, beer, and cider selection; craft cocktails incorporating seasonal fruits, herbs, and vegetables. *Average main: $34 555 Capitol Mall, at 6th St., Downtown 916/619–8897 www.camdenspitandlarder.com Closed Sun. and Mon. No lunch Sat.*

★ Canon

$$$ | **MODERN AMERICAN** | Farmhouse meets semi-industrial open-kitchen chic at this light-filled restaurant whose executive chef found success in the Midwest and the Napa Valley before returning to Sacramento, where his culinary career began. Carefully chosen produce and proteins go into small and large plates, meant to be shared, that might range from crispy shrimp heads, caviar, and smoked-cheddar biscuits to a broccoli Caesar salad, fondant potatoes, and roasted duck. **Known for:** alfresco patio dining in good weather; seasonal cocktails with fresh herbs and fruit; vegan, vegetarian, and gluten-free options. *Average main: $29 1719 34th St. 916/469–2433 canoneastsac.com Closed Mon. and Tues. No lunch.*

★ Ella Dining Room and Bar

$$$$ | **MODERN AMERICAN** | This swank restaurant and bar near the Capitol is artfully designed and thoroughly modern. The California–French, farm-to-table cuisine changes seasonally, but typical dishes include oysters on the half shell and a popular steak tartare with garlic popovers as appetizers, the house Caesar, and entrées like wood-fired steaks and pork chops and poached or pan-roasted fish of the day. **Known for:** fresh, seasonal local ingredients; waitstaff's attention to detail; cocktail and wine selection. *Average main: $43* ✉ *1131 K St., at 12th St., Downtown* ☎ *916/443–3772* 🌐 *www.elladiningroomandbar.com* ⏲ *Closed Sun. and Mon. No lunch Sat.*

The Firehouse

$$$$ | **AMERICAN** | Sacramento's rich and famous, including California governors going back to Ronald Reagan, settle into the elegant spaces within the city's restored first brick firehouse to dine on award-winning contemporary cuisine. The creative fare ranges from carpaccio, seasonal oysters, and braised pork belly to delicately spiced, seared sea bass and herb-crusted rack of lamb, rib eye (with black garlic butter), and other specialty meat cuts. **Known for:** steaks and seafood; happy-hour menu weekdays 4–6; courtyard patio. *Average main: $41* ✉ *1112 2nd St., at L St., Old Sacramento* ☎ *916/442–4772* 🌐 *www.firehouseoldsac.com* ⏲ *No lunch (check on weekdays).*

Fixins Soul Kitchen

$ | **AMERICAN** | A cheery, sometimes boisterous vibe prevails at this ode to Black cuisine and culture that former NBA star and past Sacramento mayor Kevin Johnson and his wife, Michelle, founded in a high-ceilinged, quasi-industrial space 3½ miles southeast of the Capitol. Expect heapin' helpings of soul food's greatest hits—gumbo, shrimp and grits, oxtails, and fried chicken, catfish, and pork chops among them—that you can pair with sides that include hush puppies, black-eyed peas, candied yams, collard greens (with turkey necks). **Known for:** art on the walls, sports on bar TVs; Kool-Aid for kids and (with alcohol) for adults; banana pudding for dessert. *Average main: $16* ✉ *3428 3rd Ave., at Broadway* ✥ *From Downtown or Midtown take X St. southeast to 34th St. and turn south (right)* ☎ *916/999–7685* 🌐 *fixinssoulkitchen.com.*

★ The Kitchen

$$$$ | **MODERN AMERICAN** | The chefs and front-of-house staff at this perennial favorite with a prix-fixe menu pull out all the stops to deliver a multisensory gustatory experience. The flamboyant presentation of courses as a series of "Acts"—not to mention the dramatically lit, flower-bestrewn dining room's intentionally buoyant atmosphere—might distract from the modern American cuisine were it not so well conceived and prepared with such panache and precision. **Known for:** one seating each evening (plan on 3½–4 hours); optional wine pairing; impeccably sourced ingredients. *Average main: $155* ✉ *2225 Hurley Way* ✥ *6 miles east of Downtown off Hwy. 160 to Exposition Blvd.* ☎ *916/568–7171* 🌐 *thekitchenrestaurant.com* ⏲ *Closed Mon. and Tues.*

Kru

$$$ | **JAPANESE** | It's worth the drive a little past Sutter's Fort to this mod-Japanese restaurant whose owner-chef fashions fresh, wildly creative sushi for patrons seated at blond-wood tables, a counter, or an open-air patio. Order a sunshine roll—spicy tuna, escolar, and shrimp tempura enlivened by the tart contribution of green apples and lemon—perhaps pairing it with cooked fare like smoked duck *kushiyaki* with plum-wine katsu sauce or hot or cold ramen, including pork belly, poached shrimp, and mushroom broth. **Known for:** smart decor; nearly two dozen rolls; impressive sake, wine, and whiskeys. *Average main: $30* ✉ *3135 Folsom Blvd., at Seville Way* ☎ *916/551–1559* 🌐 *www.krurestaurant.com* ⏲ *No lunch.*

★ Localis

$$$$ | **MODERN AMERICAN** | Exquisite plating and compelling, at times piquant, flavor combinations are the trademarks of this restaurant whose chef-sommelier owner, Chris Barnum-Dann, won the debut (2021) season of the culinary-competition TV show *The Globe*. The open-kitchen choreography of Barnum-Dann and his team deftly preparing one intricate dish after another (7–12 courses, prix-fixe $155–$197) lends the proceedings a balletic air. **Known for:** fresh ingredients from top purveyors creatively combined and presented; thoughtful menu notes; global, well-chosen wines. *Average main: $155 ✉ 2031 S St., at 21st St., Midtown ☎ 916/737–7699 🌐 www.localissacramento.com ⏱ Closed Sun.–Tues. (but check). No lunch.*

★ Magpie Cafe

$$ | **AMERICAN** | This Midtown eatery with a vaguely industrial look and a casual vibe takes its food seriously: nearly all the produce is sourced locally, and the chefs prepare only sustainable seafood. Banh mi sandwiches and grass-fed beef burgers (including a plant-based option) are among the staples, as are steak and fries and pan-roasted fish with seasonal vegetables. **Known for:** outdoor park-view patio; beer, cider, wine, and cocktail lineup; homemade ice-cream sandwiches. *Average main: $23 ✉ 1601 16th St., Midtown ☎ 916/452–7594 🌐 www.magpiecafe.com ⏱ Closed Mon.–Wed. (but check).*

★ The Waterboy

$$$ | **EUROPEAN** | Rural French cooking with locally sourced, seasonal, high-quality, often organic ingredients is the hallmark of this upscale, white-tablecloth, corner storefront restaurant that's as appealing for a casual meal with friends as it is for a drawn-out romantic dinner for two. Among the mains, try the steak, duck breast, or seasonal seafood, and save room for one of the palate-cleansing desserts. **Known for:** exceptional French cooking; quality local ingredients; global wine list. *Average main: $32 ✉ 2000 Capitol Ave., at 20th St., Midtown ☎ 916/498–9891 🌐 www.waterboyrestaurant.com ⏱ Closed Sun.–Tues. (but check). No lunch Sat.*

Zócalo Midtown

$$ | **MEXICAN** | Inside a glamorously renovated Hudson Motor Car showroom from the 1920s that looks out of a movie set, Zócalo puts an upscale spin on Mexican classics. Pair the house margarita or its blackberry variation with a guac or ceviche starter before moving on to a burrito; enchiladas; or a bowl with chicken, salmon, carne asada, or vegetarian ingredients. **Known for:** festive setting; outdoor patio; happy hour daily 3–6 pm. *Average main: $18 ✉ 1801 Capitol Ave., at 18th St., Midtown ☎ 916/441–0303 🌐 experiencezocalo.com.*

Hotels

Amber House Inn of Midtown

$$ | **B&B/INN** | Veer from the beaten path of traditional lodging at Amber House Inn's two historic homes—one a 1905 Craftsman, the other an 1895 Dutch colonial–revival—just 1 mile from the Capitol. **Pros:** Midtown location; attentive service; full breakfast served in-room if desired. **Cons:** older buildings and style; B&B regimen not for everyone; lacks spa, fitness center, and other big-hotel amenities. *Rooms from: $179 ✉ 1315 22nd St., Midtown ☎ 916/444–8085 🌐 www.amberhouse.com 10 rooms Free breakfast.*

Citizen Hotel

$$ | **HOTEL** | This boutique hotel within the historic 1926 Cal Western Life building is dapper and refined, with marble stairs, striped wallpaper, and plush velvet chairs, lending the place a Roaring '20s charm. **Pros:** sophisticated decor; smooth service; restaurant and bar. **Cons:** rooms near elevator can be noisy; rates vary widely depending on conventions, legislature,

season; expensive parking. *Rooms from: $170* *926 J St., Downtown* *916/447–2700* *www.thecitizenhotel.com* *198 rooms* *No meals.*

Delta King

$$ | **HOTEL** | Wake up to the sound of geese taking flight along the river when you book a stay in one of Sacramento's most unusual and historic relics, a carefully restored riverboat hotel permanently moored on Old Sacramento's waterfront. **Pros:** unique lodgings; steps from Old Sacramento shopping and dining; period feel. **Cons:** slanted floors can feel a bit jarring; rooms are cramped; some noise issues. *Rooms from: $159* *1000 Front St., Old Sacramento* *At end of K St.* *916/444–5464, 800/825–5464* *www.deltaking.com* *44 rooms* *Free breakfast.*

★ Fort Sutter Hotel

$$ | **HOTEL** | Two local restaurateurs are behind this six-story, boutique, Hilton Tapestry Collection whose guest rooms win points for their expansive windows, contemporary style, smartly designed bathrooms, and works by local artists. **Pros:** above-average food for a hotel restaurant; near Midtown dining, entertainment, and shopping; Capitol views from upper floors facing west. **Cons:** diagonally across from a hospital; rooms lack refrigerators and microwaves; more than a mile walk to Downtown. *Rooms from: $179* *1308 28th St, Midtown* *916/603–2301* *www.fortsutterhotel.com* *105 rooms* *No meals.*

Hyatt Regency Sacramento

$$ | **HOTEL** | With a marble-and-glass lobby and luxurious rooms, this multitiered, glass-dominated hotel across from the Capitol and adjacent to the convention center has a striking Mediterranean design. **Pros:** best rooms have Capitol Park views; some rooms have small balconies; excellent service. **Cons:** nearby streets can feel dodgy at night; somewhat impersonal; many corporate events. *Rooms from: $189* *1209 L St., Downtown* *916/443–1234* *sacramento.regency.hyatt.com* *505 rooms* *No meals.*

Inn Off Capitol Park

$$ | **HOTEL** | Business and leisure travelers seeking a touch of style along with comfort and value appreciate the amenities at this Ascend Collection property near the Capitol. **Pros:** convenient location; good value; well run. **Cons:** many rooms are small (220 or 260 square feet); no tub in some rooms; insufficient on-site parking spaces when hotel is full. *Rooms from: $154* *1530 N St., Downtown* *916/447–8100* *www.choicehotels.com* *37 rooms* *Free breakfast.*

★ Kimpton Sawyer Hotel

$$ | **HOTEL** | Soft shades of brown and gray and furniture milled from California oak lend an haute-rustic feel to the spacious rooms and suites of this full-service hotel amid Sacramento's Downtown Commons (DOCO) shopping and entertainment complex. **Pros:** pool deck and Revival bar; "living room" lobby; convenient to Downtown and Old Sacramento. **Cons:** pricey in-season; no tubs in many rooms; may be too high-style for some guests. *Rooms from: $219* *500 J St., Downtown* *916/545–7100 front desk, 877/678–6255 reservations* *www.sawyerhotel.com* *285 rooms* *No meals.*

Nightlife

Drakes: The Barn

BREWPUBS/BEER GARDENS | Drake's Brewing serves up beer, food, and musical and other events at and around a dramatically curving, cedar-shingled pavilion on 2 acres along the Sacramento River. Chefs prepare pizzas, and there are food trucks. The Barn is closed on Monday. *985 Riverfront St., at Garden St., West Sacramento* *Across Sacramento River from Downtown near Sutter Health Park* *510/568–2739* *drinkdrakes.com/barn.*

Harlow's

MUSIC CLUBS | Blues, rock, and other musicians take to the stage of this restaurant's art-deco bar–nightclub. Repair to the patio when you need to cool off. ✉ *2708 J St., at 27th St., Midtown* ☎ *916/441–4693* 🌐 *www.harlows.com.*

★ Midtown BierGarten

BREWPUBS/BEER GARDENS | The neighborhood feel and selection of beers, ales, porters, stouts, sours, and ciders make a trip to this boisterous beer garden a fun occasion, with the garlic fries, fresh pretzels with mustard, old-fashioned hot dogs, and other small bites a definite bonus. A 40-foot cargo container holds the bar, and a 20-footer contains the bathrooms, with the rest of the setting alfresco. ✉ *2332 K St., at 24th St.* ☎ *916/346–4572* 🌐 *beergardensacramento.com.*

★ Midtown's Cantina Alley

BARS/PUBS | Flavorful, colorful, fruity cocktails, some served in hollowed-out pineapples or watermelons, are the specialty of this bar and restaurant whose equally rich-hued decor and corrugated-metal ceiling intentionally evoke spots throughout Mexico. While sipping sangria, a cerveza, or the house margarita in several flavors, you can nibble on street tacos, posole, *elote* (corn on a stick, rolled in mayonnaise and topped with cheese and spices), and other small plates. Closed on Monday, the cantina opens for lunch on Friday and weekends. ✉ *2320 Jazz Alley, Midtown* ✥ *Off 24th St. between J and K Sts.* ☎ *833/232–0639* 🌐 *www.cantinaalley.com.*

Punch Bowl Social

BARS/PUBS | This restaurant and entertainment complex offers bowling, billiards, karaoke, Giant Jenga, virtual reality, pinball, and Skee-Ball. After you've worked up an appetite, dine on updated pub grub and sip well-chosen craft beers, wine, specialty cocktails, or boozeless beverages. ✉ *500 J St., Downtown* ✥ *At 5th St.* ☎ *916/925–5610* 🌐 *www.punchbowlsocial.com/sacramento.*

Tiger

BARS/PUBS | Concrete walls and black-metal beams and railings reinforce the post-industrial mood at this two-level bar, which draws a youngish crowd for craft cocktails based on Sacramento produce, zesty small bites and larger plates, and often live music. ✉ *722 K St., at 8th St., Downtown* ☎ *916/382–9610* 🌐 *www.tiger700block.com.*

Performing Arts

Broadway Sacramento

THEATER | This group presents Broadway shows at two Downtown venues. Past shows include *Hamilton* and *The Wiz.* ✉ *SAFE Credit Union Performing Arts Center, 1301 L St., at 13th St., Downtown* ☎ *916/557–1999* 🌐 *www.broadwaysacramento.com.*

Crest Theatre

ARTS CENTERS | It's worth peeking inside the Crest even if you don't catch a show, just to see the swirling art-deco design in the foyer, or to dine at the Empress Tavern restaurant within. It's a beloved venue for classic and art-house films, along with concerts and other cultural events. ✉ *1013 K St., at 10th St., Downtown* ☎ *916/476–3356* 🌐 *www.crestsacramento.com.*

★ The Sofia

ARTS CENTERS | The long-running B Street Theatre—known for well-staged comedies, dramas, the occasional farce, and productions for children—is the resident company at this industrial-suave performing arts center. The two theaters, plus three rehearsal spaces sometimes used for workshop productions, also present musicians, solo acts, and speakers. ✉ *2700 Capitol Ave., at 27th St.* ☎ *916/443–5300* 🌐 *bstreettheatre.org.*

Shopping

Downtown Commons (*DOCO*)
SHOPPING CENTERS/MALLS | As its name implies, this multiblock complex adjoining the Golden 1 Center aspires to be a gathering spot for locals and tourists as much as a place to shop, dine, catch a movie, or sip a cocktail. ✉ *660 J St., Downtown* ✣ *Between 5th and 7th Sts., J and L Sts.* ☎ *916/273–8124.*

★ **Kulture**
GIFTS/SOUVENIRS | This vibrant shop sells Mexican art, jewelry, and gifts, along with the pithy Keepin It Paisa line of T-shirts, hoodies, and ball caps. The owners and other vendors sell furniture, clothing, and other items in an adjacent space. ✉ *2331 K St., Midtown* ✣ *At 24th St.* ☎ *916/442–2728* 🌐 *kulturedc.wixsite.com/kulture* ⏲ *Closed Mon.*

American River Bicycle Trail
BICYCLING | The Jedediah Smith Memorial Trail, as it's formally called, runs for 32 miles from Old Sacramento to Beals Point in Folsom. Walk or ride a bit of it and you'll see why local cyclists and pedestrians adore its scenic lanes. Enjoy great views of the American River and the bluffs overlooking it. ■ **TIP→ Bring lunch or a snack. Parks and picnic areas dot the trail.** ✉ *Old Sacramento* 🌐 *www.americanriverbiketrail.com.*

Davis

10 miles west of Sacramento.

Davis began as a rich agricultural area and remains one, but it doesn't feel like a cow town. It's home to the University of California at Davis, whose 40,000 or so students hang at downtown cafés, galleries, and bookstores (most of the action takes place between Second and Fourth and B and E streets), lending the city a decidedly college-town feel.

GETTING HERE AND AROUND

Most people arrive by car via I–80, though Yolobus serves the area from Sacramento, and downtown is walkable. Touring by bicycle is also a popular option—Davis is very flat.

California Agriculture Museum
MUSEUM | FAMILY | This gigantic space in the nearby community of Woodland provides a thorough historical overview of motorized agricultural vehicles through dozens and dozens of threshers, harvesters, combines, tractors, and other contraptions. A separate wing surveys the evolution of the truck, with an emphasis on those used for farm work. ✉ *1958 Hays La., south off Douglas La. from East Main St., Woodland* ✣ *From Davis, take 5th St. east to Polehill Rd./County Rd. 102 north 10 miles; from Sacramento, take I–5 for 18 miles northwest to Exit 536* ☎ *530/666–9700* 🌐 *www.californiaagmuseum.org* 💵 *$10* ⏲ *Closed Mon. and Tues.*

University of California, Davis
COLLEGE | A top research university, UC Davis educates many of the Wine Country's vintners and grape growers, in addition to farmers, veterinarians, and brewmasters. When offered, campus tours depart from Buehler Alumni and Visitors Center. On a tour or not, worthy stops include the **Arboretum,** the **Manetti Shrem Museum of Art,** and the **Mondavi Center,** a striking modern glass structure that presents top-tier performing artists. ✉ *Visitor Center, 550 Alumni La.* ☎ *530/752–8111 for tour information* 🌐 *visit.ucdavis.edu.*

Restaurants

Mustard Seed

$$$ | **AMERICAN** | Many patrons at this restaurant serving eclectic seasonal California cuisine are attending performing-arts events at the Mondavi Center a short walk away or visiting their kids at UC Davis. With hardwood floors and tables topped with white linen, the dining room is cozy and romantic, but when the weather's fine, the tree-shaded patio out back is the best place to enjoy dishes like tomato bisque topped with a puff pastry and herb-crusted rack of lamb. **Known for:** lunchtime salads and sandwiches; desserts aren't an afterthought; reasonably priced California wines. *Average main: $35 ✉ 222 D St., Suite 11 ☎ 530/758–5750 🌐 www.mustardseedofdavis.com ⏲ No lunch Sat.–Mon.*

Hotels

Best Western Plus Palm Court Hotel

$$ | **HOTEL** | Rich accents of gold and cobalt blue add boutique flair to the spacious rooms of this dependable choice for business and leisure travelers. **Pros:** off-campus but nearby; on-site Cafe Bernardo for comfort food; some rooms sleep up to 6 people. **Cons:** pricey during major UC Davis events; no pool; chain's usual free breakfast not offered. *Rooms from: $155 ✉ 234 D St. ☎ 530/753–7100 🌐 bestwestern.com 27 rooms No meals.*

Hyatt Place UC Davis

$$ | **HOTEL** | A full-service hotel right on campus, the Hyatt distinguishes itself with an enthusiastic staff and clean, well-designed rooms and suites. **Pros:** generous breakfasts; pool, fitness room, café, and bar; convenient to university and downtown restaurants and shopping. **Cons:** only rooms with queen beds have tubs; noise from campus and nearby train tracks (when booking, ask for a quieter room); only suites have microwaves. *Rooms from: $159 ✉ 173 Old Davis Rd. Extension ☎ 530/756–9500, 855/516–1090 🌐 hyatt.com 127 rooms Free breakfast.*

Winters

14 miles west of Davis.

Almonds, walnuts, and fruit are the main crops grown in this rural Yolo County town (population 7,300), whose several-block historic district's wine-tasting opportunities and nationally recognized restaurant scene lure tourists and Bay Area and Sacramento Valley day-trippers. The district's Main Street bustles on weekends, especially when music and other events close part of it.

GETTING HERE AND AROUND

It's easiest to drive to Winters, whose main drag, Grant Avenue, doubles as Highway 128 in town. From Davis, follow Russell Boulevard west until it becomes Grant Avenue, from which Railroad Avenue leads south to the historic district. Yolobus serves Winters from Davis.

Sights

Berryessa Gap Vineyards Tasting Room

WINERY/DISTILLERY | Nicole Salengo, the longtime winemaker of this operation whose origins date to the late 1960s, displays a light but knowing touch with even the heaviest reds. A case in point is Berryessa Gap's singular Petite Sirah, whose aromatics and acidity are more pronounced than in most of the wine's California peers. The several rosés poured here make the tasting room a magnet for "drink pink" aficionados. *✉ 15 E. Main St., near Railroad Ave. ☎ 539/795–3201 🌐 berryessagap.com Tastings from $15.*

Turkovich Family Wines Tasting Room

WINERY/DISTILLERY | Third-generation farmer Chris Turkovich and his wife, Luciana, whose parents back in her native Argentina are both involved in the wine business, founded this winery known for bold, balanced reds. The two craft many of their wines from Spanish varietals, though Petite Sirah dominates the flagship blend The Boss. Albariño and rosé of Grenache are among the noteworthy lighter wines. The storefront tasting room's sidewalk seating is good for people-watching, the patio in back is good for quieter sipping. *304 Railroad Ave., near Main St. 530/795–3842 turkovichwines.com Tastings from $8.*

Restaurants

Ficelle

$$ | ECLECTIC | If you're in Winters on a day this self-proclaimed "delightfully random place to eat" is open, try to score a seat (no reservations) to enjoy internationally inspired small plates that might include chicken tostadas, marinated lamb, empanadas, or baked eggplant. With a few tables indoors, plus counter seating on stools and more tables outside on a wooden deck, Ficelle, run on the whim of its European owners, lives up to its motto. **Known for:** festive ambience; alfresco dining; fanciful flavors. *Average main: $25 5C E. Main St., east of Railroad Ave. Behind Steady Eddy's 530/795–9593 www.ficelle-restaurant.com Closed Sun.–Wed. No lunch.*

Preserve

$$ | MODERN AMERICAN | The seasonal produce of nearby purveyors figures in nearly every dish at Preserve, which pairs elevated gastropub fare with artisanal beers, wines, and cocktails. Chicken-fried oysters, grilled sturgeon, slow-roasted pork belly, pizzas, elaborate burgers, fried chicken, and shrimp and grits with aged cheddar are typical menu items, served in the brick-walled, rustic-industrial, semi-chic bar or the plant-laden outdoor patio. **Known for:** fine-dining menu (pricey) some nights; craft cocktails; upscale-casual feel. *Average main: $24 200 Railroad Ave., near Russell St. 530/795–9963 www.preservewinters.com Closed Mon. and Tues. No lunch Wed. and Thurs. No dinner Sun.*

Putah Creek Cafe

$$ | AMERICAN | The wood-fired pizza oven blazing away on the sidewalk turns out this café's handmade pies, but the lunch and dinner fare extends well beyond them to tacos, cauliflower buffalo wings, pastrami sandwiches, fish in béarnaise sauce, and fresh salads with ingredients from a local farm. The brick-walled dining room has been a farmers' hangout for breakfast (you name it) for decades. **Known for:** signature corn pie (cornmeal, cheddar, and jack) with roasted tomato sauce; alfresco patio dining; sister restaurant Buckhorn Steakhouse, a Winters culinary anchor, across the street. *Average main: $22 1 Main St., at Railroad Ave. 530/795–2682 www.putahcreekcafe.com.*

Hotels

Hotel Winters

$$ | HOTEL | Art by regional artists adorns the hallways of this dapper, three-story, downtown historic district boutique property that opened in 2019 and became an instant favorite of business folk, leisure travelers, and local brides. **Pros:** fresh look; spacious rooms with 10-foot ceilings; town and mountain views from rooftop bar. **Cons:** some street-side noise (ask for a room toward the back); shallow "water lounge" has a mesmerizing water feature, but there's no legit pool; irregular hours at rooftop bar. *Rooms from: $170 12 Abbey St. 530/505–9123, 877/514–3870 www.hotelwinters.com 78 rooms No meals.*

Lodi

34 miles south of Sacramento.

With with more than 100,000 acres of mostly alluvial soils planted to more than 125 grape varietals—more types than in any other California viticultural area—Lodi is a major grape-growing hub. Eighty-five or so wineries do business in Lodi, the self-proclaimed Zinfandel Capital of the World, and neighboring towns. (Although plenty of Zin grows here, these days farmers devote nearly the same amount of land to Cabernet Sauvignon.) Founded on agriculture, Lodi was once the country's watermelon capital. Today it's surrounded by fields of asparagus, pumpkins, beans, safflowers, sunflowers, melons, squashes, peaches, and cherries. Lodi retains an old rural charm. You can stroll downtown or visit a wildlife refuge, all the while benefiting from a Sacramento River delta breeze that keeps this microclimate cooler in summer than anyplace else in the area.

GETTING HERE AND AROUND

Most of Lodi lies west of Highway 99 and east of Interstate 5. Amtrak trains stop here frequently. GrapeLine (☎ *209/333–6806*) buses pass by many wineries, but touring by car is more efficient.

ESSENTIALS

VISITOR INFORMATION Visit Lodi. ✉ *25 N. School St.* ☎ *209/365–1195, 800/798–1810* 🌐 *www.visitlodi.com.*

Sights

Acquiesce Winery

WINERY/DISTILLERY | Expect no heavy reds at this boutique operation specializing in Rhône-style whites. The enthusiastic owners, who sourced their grapes' vines from Château de Beaucastel in France's Châteauneuf du Pape appellation, produce Viognier, Roussanne, and Grenache Blanc but also spotlight lower-profile varietals like Bourboulenc and Clairette Blanche. (There's also a Grenache rosé.) Tastings, by appointment only, take place in a 100-year-old barn or just outside it, in either case with vineyard views. ✉ *22353 N. Tretheway Rd., Acampo* ✣ *From downtown Lodi take Hwy. 12 east, Bruella Rd. north, and E. Peltier Rd. east* ☎ *209/333–6102* 🌐 *www.acquiescevineyards.com* 🎫 *Tastings $20.*

Berghold Estate Winery

WINERY/DISTILLERY | The appointment-only tasting room at Berghold recalls an earlier wine era with its vintage Victorian interior, including restored, salvaged mantlepieces, leaded glass, and a 26-foot-long bar. The wines—among them Viognier, Cabernet Sauvignon, Syrah, and Zinfandel—pay homage to French wine-making styles. ✉ *17343 Cherry Rd., off E. Victor Rd./Hwy. 12* ☎ *209/333–9291* 🌐 *bergholdvineyards.com* 🎫 *Tastings $10* 🕓 *Closed Mon.–Wed.*

★ Bokisch Vineyards

WINERY/DISTILLERY | This operation 11 miles outside of downtown comes highly recommended for its excellent Spanish varietals and warm hospitality. The Albariño white and Tempranillo and Graciano reds often receive favorable critical notice, but everything is well made, including the non-Spanish Petit Verdot and old-vine Carignane. **■ TIP→ Bokisch welcomes picnickers; pick up fixings in town and enjoy vineyard views while you dine.** ✉ *18921 Atkins Rd.* ✣ *From Hwy. 99 head east on Hwy. 12, north on Hwy. 88, and east on Brandt Rd.* ☎ *209/642–8880* 🌐 *www.bokischvineyards.com* 🎫 *Tastings from $15* 🕓 *Closed Tues. and Wed.*

Harney Lane Winery

WINERY/DISTILLERY | The Harney family has grown grapes in Lodi since the 1900s dawned but only started a winery in 2006. Three Zinfandels star in a lineup that includes Albariño, Chardonnay, two rosés, Cabernet Sauvignon, Petite Sirah, Primitivo, Tempranillo, and an old-vine Zinfandel port-style dessert wine. Extend your tasting with a glass in the "forest" garden, where three-century-old cedars supply the shade. **■TIP→ When offered, the Grape to Glass tour is a great way to learn about both the family and Lodi.** ✉ *9010 E. Harney La.* ✣ *About 6½ miles south of downtown, Hwy. 99 to E. Harney La. exit* ☎ *209/365–1900* 🌐 *www.harneylane.com* 🎫 *Tastings $10, tour $25.*

Jeremy Wine Co.

WINERY/DISTILLERY | Originally a bank, the downtown tasting room of owner-winemaker Jeremy Trettevik has the feel of a spiffed-up old-time saloon, though in good weather everyone sips under the bright-red umbrellas shading the patio out back. Creative red blends, most from well-sourced Lodi appellation grapes, are the specialty here, with sweet yet clean-on-the-palate wines like the Orange Muscat and the Bluebonnet Albariño–Orange Muscat blend among the lighter options. There's also a chocolate port-style dessert wine. ✉ *6 W. Pine St. , at S. Sacramento St.* ☎ *209/367–3773* 🌐 *jeremywineco.com* 🎫 *Tastings from $10.*

★ Klinker Brick Winery

WINERY/DISTILLERY | The old-vine Zinfandels of this winery named for the bricks used to construct Lodi buildings of days past score well in wine competitions for their smooth tannins and complex flavors. Like the Cabernet Sauvignon (among Lodi's best), they're reasonably priced considering the quality. Lighter offerings include sparkling wines, Albariño, Grenache Blanc, and the Vorgänger blend of three white grapes. If the weather's good, taste outside and enjoy garden and vineyard views. **■TIP→ Request a reserve tasting ($15) to sample the top-of-the-line reds.** ✉ *15887 N. Alpine Rd.* ☎ *209/333–1845* 🌐 *klinkerbrickwinery.com* 🎫 *Tastings from $5.*

Lodi Wine & Visitor Center

WINERY/DISTILLERY | A fine place to sample Lodi wines, the center has a tasting bar and viticultural exhibits. You can also buy wine and pick up a free winery map. ✉ *2545 W. Turner Rd., at Woodhaven La.* ☎ *209/365–0621* 🌐 *www.lodiwine.com* 🎫 *Tastings $12* 🕒 *Closed Mon.–Wed. (but check).*

Lucas Winery

WINERY/DISTILLERY | David Lucas was one of the first local producers to start making serious wine, and today the Zinfandels he and his wife, Heather Pyle-Lucas, make are among Lodi's most sought-after vintages. The Lucases, who previously worked at the Robert Mondavi Winery (she also made wine at Opus One), also craft a Chardonnay with subtle oaky flavors and a 100% Zinfandel rosé. Tastings, by appointment only, often take place on a patio with a vineyard view. ✉ *18196 N. Davis Rd., at W. Turner Rd.* ☎ *209/368–2006* 🌐 *www.lucaswinery.com* 🎫 *Tastings from $20* 🕒 *Closed Mon. and Tues.*

★ M2 Wines

WINERY/DISTILLERY | With its translucent polycarbonate panels, concrete floor, and metal framing, this winery's high-ceilinged tasting room strikes an iconoclastic, industrial-sleek pose along an otherwise rural lane north of Lodi. The Soucie Vineyard old-vine Zinfandel and the Trio and Duality red blends are three to seek out, but all the wines here are good. ✉ *2900 E. Peltier Rd., Acampo* ✣ *Take Hwy. 99 north from downtown to Peltier Rd. exit and head west* ☎ *209/339–1071* 🌐 *www.m2wines.com* 🎫 *Tastings from $10* 🕒 *Closed Tues.–Thurs. (but check).*

★ McCay Cellars

WINERY/DISTILLERY | Wine critics applaud owner-winemaker Michael McCay's pursuit of balance and restraint with his flagship TruLux Zinfandel and Faith Lot 13 Zin from century-old vines. A longtime grower who started his namesake label in 2007, McCay also makes several rosés and whites, plus Cabernet Franc, Cinsaut, Petite Sirah, Tempranillo, and other reds. He's often on-site at his winery's tasting room. ✉ *18817 E. Hwy. 88* ✣ *From downtown Lodi, take E. Victor*

Rd./Hwy. 12 east to Hwy. 88 north (turn left) ☎ *209/368–9463* 🌐 *www.mccaycellars.com* 🎫 *Tastings $15* ⏲ *Closed Tues. and Wed.*

Michael David Winery

WINERY/DISTILLERY | *Wine Enthusiast* magazine anointed Adam Mettler of Michael David its winemaker of the year in 2018 in recognition of his skill in developing smooth but characterful red blends like Petite Petit (Petite Sirah and Petit Verdot) and Freakshow Zinfandel. Taste these and other wines at the sprawling roadside **Phillips Farms Fruit Stand,** where fifth-generation farmers turned winery owners Michael and David Philips also sell their family's gorgeous produce. **■ TIP→ Breakfast or lunch at the stand's café is a treat.** ✉ *4580 W. Hwy. 12, at N. Ray Rd.* ☎ *209/368–7384* 🌐 *www.michaeldavidwinery.com* 🎫 *Tastings from $10.*

Micke Grove Regional Park

AMUSEMENT PARK/WATER PARK | FAMILY | This 258-acre, oak-shaded park has a Japanese tea garden, picnic tables, children's play areas, an agricultural museum, a zoo, a golf course, and a water-play feature. **Fun Town at Micke Grove,** a family-oriented amusement park, is geared toward younger children. ✉ *11793 N. Micke Grove Rd.* ✣ *Off Hwy. 99 Armstrong Rd. exit* ☎ *209/953–8800 park info* 🎫 *From $5.*

Restaurants

The Dancing Fox Winery and Bakery

$ | AMERICAN | A good downtown stop especially for lunch, the Dancing Fox also has a tasting room for its eponymous wines. The restaurant, whose decor shimmers with fairy-tale whimsy, serves sandwiches, salads, pizzas, burgers, and wraps and has more than a dozen beers on tap. **Known for:** Sunday brunch; wine tasting; historic downtown setting. [$] *Average main: $15* ✉ *203 S. School St.* ☎ *203/366–2634* 🌐 *www.dancingfoxlodi.com* ⏲ *Closed Mon. No dinner Sun.*

Pietro's Trattoria

$$ | ITALIAN | Lodi's go-to spot for Italian American classics wins fans for its quality ingredients, Tuscan-courtyard ambience, and plant-filled outdoor patio (reservations essential on weekends). Expect straightforward, well-executed renditions of chicken piccata and pork Milanese, filling lasagna and seasonal risotto, pizzas, and the like, all delivered with informal good cheer by the cadre of servers. **Known for:** Italian-American classics; meatball and chicken pesto with cheese sandwiches for lunch; Lodi and Italian wines. [$] *Average main: $22* ✉ *317 E. Kettleman La.* ☎ *209/368–0613* 🌐 *www.pietroslodi.com* ⏲ *Closed Sun.*

★ Towne House Restaurant

$$$$ | MODERN AMERICAN | Special-occasion dinners often take place in the distinguished rooms of this former residence behind, and part of, the Wine & Roses hotel. Painted in rich, textured hues offset by wide white molding, the rooms exude a subtle sophistication matched by seasonal dishes that might include porcini-dusted lamb chops or fish atop risotto. **Known for:** fresh seasonal local ingredients; weekend brunch with varied offerings; Town Corner Café & Market for breakfast and lunch daily. [$] *Average main: $39* ✉ *2505 W. Turner Rd., at Woodhaven La.* ☎ *209/371–6160* 🌐 *winerose.com/the-restaurant* ⏲ *No lunch.*

Hotels

Wine & Roses Hotel

$$$ | HOTEL | Set on 7 acres amid a tapestry of informal gardens, this hotel has cultivated a sense of refinement that's typically associated with Napa or Carmel. **Pros:** luxurious setting; popular restaurant; spa treatments. **Cons:** expensive for the area; some guests mention that walls are thin; many events. [$] *Rooms from: $299* ✉ *2505 W. Turner Rd.* ☎ *209/334–6988* 🌐 *www.winerose.com* 🛏 *66 rooms* 🍽 *No meals.*

Nevada City

61 miles northeast of Sacramento.

Nevada City, once known as the Queen City of the Northern Mines, is the most appealing of the northern Mother Lode towns. The iron-shutter brick buildings that line downtown streets contain antiques shops, galleries, boutiques, B&Bs, restaurants, a winery, and some tasting rooms. Gas street lamps and historic structures like the distinctive 1861 Firehouse No. 1, at 241 Main Street, and the still active 1865 Nevada Theatre, at 401 Broad Street, add to the romance. At one point in the 1850s, Nevada City had a population of nearly 10,000—enough to support much cultural activity. Today, about 3,000 people live here, but the visual and performing-arts scenes remain vibrant.

GETTING HERE AND AROUND

You'll need a car to get here. From Sacramento take I–80 east to Highway 49 north; from Reno take I–80 and Highway 20 west. Nevada County Connects (☎ *530/477–0103*) provides public transit.

ESSENTIALS

VISITOR INFORMATION Nevada City Chamber of Commerce. ✉ *132 Main St.* ☎ *530/265–2692* 🌐 *www.nevadacitychamber.com.*

Sights

Nevada City Winery

WINERY/DISTILLERY | The area's oldest operating winery, established in 1980, pours its wines, many from Sierra Foothills grapes, in a tasting room whose back patio perches over the wine-making facility. Chardonnay is a best seller, with Cabernet Sauvignon and Rhône and Italian reds among the other specialties. ✉ *321 Spring St., at Bridge St.* ☎ *530/265–9463* 🌐 *www.ncwinery.com* 🎫 *Tastings from $16.*

Szabo Vineyards

WINERY/DISTILLERY | Taste for yourself what makes Sierra Foothills wines unique at the brick-walled sipping salon of owner-winemaker Sándor "Alex" Szabo. In addition to growing the grapes 7 miles west of his downtown tasting room and making the wines, Alex is often the one pouring them. His Zinfandel, Petite Sirah, Grenache, Syrah, and other wines impress with their soft tannins, ample acidity, and long finish. ✉ *316 Broad St., at York St.* ☎ *530/265–8792* 🌐 *www.szabovineyards.com* 🎫 *Tastings $10* 🕑 *Closed Mon.–Thurs.*

Restaurants

★ Lola

$$$ | MODERN AMERICAN | Riffing off the calculated flamboyance of its namesake, the gold-rush-era celebrity Lola Montez, the National Exchange Hotel's restaurant flirts with excess yet retains its composure decorated as it is with Persian rugs, long turquoise banquette benches, and brushed-bronze shepherd's-hook lighting fixtures. The chefs show a similar knack for incorporating unexpected elements, as with a recent entrée of honey-garlic buttermilk fried chicken whose sides—heirloom grits and dinosaur kale with candied kumquats—enlivened the dish but didn't undermine it. **Known for:** Tarantula Dance tequila-mescal specialty-cocktail homage to Lola's stage act; atypical small plates and salads; most ingredients "organic, ethically raised, and locally sourced". $ *Average main: $30* ✉ *211 Broad St., at Spring St.* ☎ *530/362–7605* 🌐 *thenationalexchangehotel.com/dining* 🕑 *No lunch.*

Sushi in the Raw

$$$ | JAPANESE | Landlocked Nevada City might seem like an odd place for a sushi haven, but this brick-walled restaurant with an open kitchen consistently ranks at the top of local "best-of" lists for Japanese cuisine. Owners Susan and Kaoru "Ru" Suzuki (he's the executive

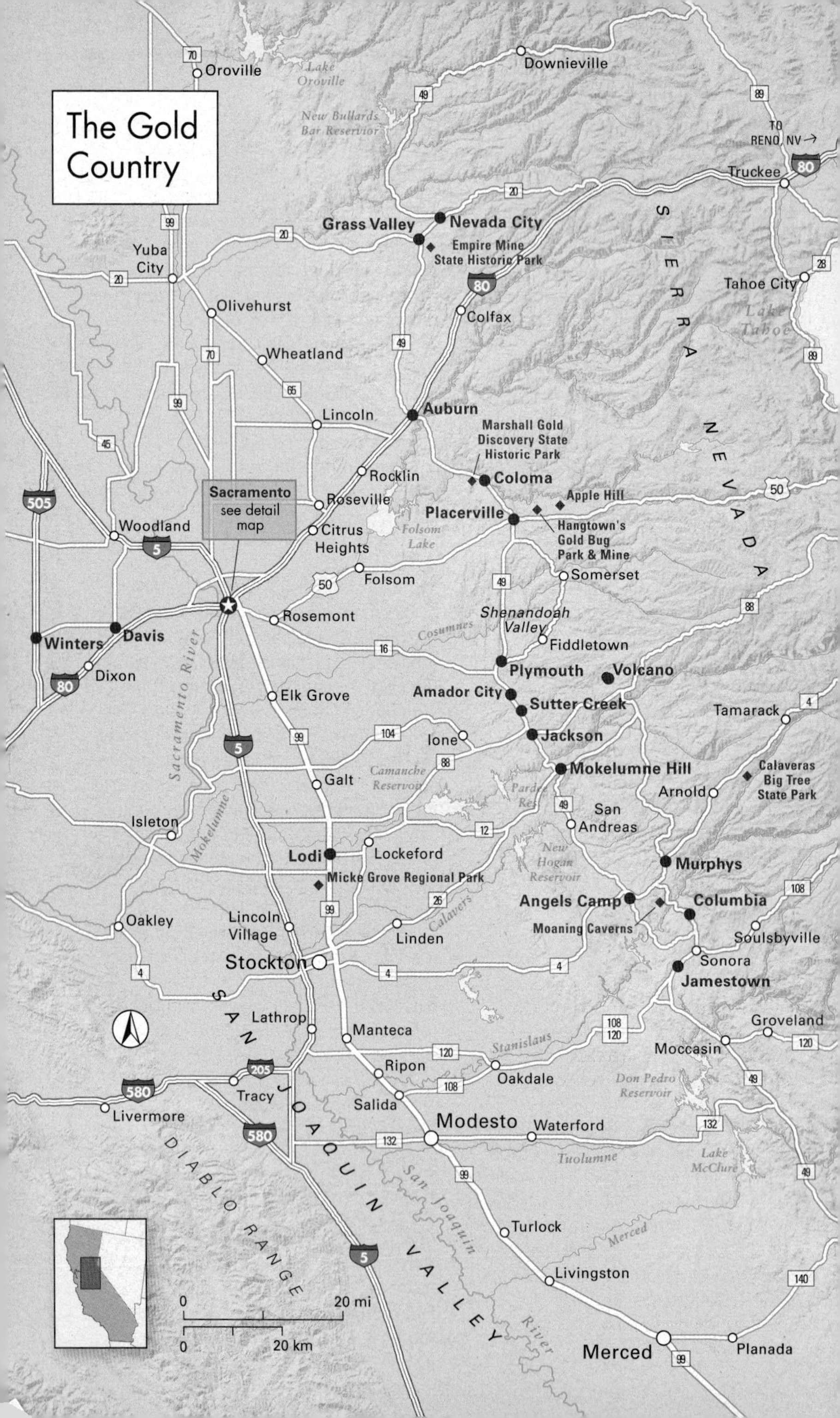

The Gold Country
Oroville
Lake Oroville
New Bullards Bar Reservoir
Downieville
TO RENO, NV →
Truckee
Grass Valley
Nevada City
Empire Mine State Historic Park
SIERRA NEVADA
Yuba City
Olivehurst
Colfax
Tahoe City
Lake Tahoe
Wheatland
Lincoln
Auburn
Marshall Gold Discovery State Historic Park
Rocklin
Coloma
Apple Hill
Roseville
Placerville
Hangtown's Gold Bug Park & Mine
Sacramento see detail map
Woodland
Citrus Heights
Folsom Lake
Folsom
Somerset
Rosemont
Shenandoah Valley
Cosumnes
Winters
Davis
Fiddletown
Dixon
Plymouth
Volcano
Sacramento River
Elk Grove
Amador City
Sutter Creek
Tamarack
Ione
Jackson
Camanche Reservoir
Galt
Mokelumne Hill
Calaveras Big Tree State Park
Pardee Res
Arnold
San Andreas
Isleton
Mokelumne
New Hogan Reservoir
Lodi
Lockeford
Murphys
Micke Grove Regional Park
Angels Camp
Columbia
Moaning Caverns
Oakley
Lincoln Village
Linden
Calaveras
Soulsbyville
Stockton
Sonora
Jamestown
SAN JOAQUIN VALLEY
Lathrop
Manteca
Groveland
Moccasin
Stanislaus
Ripon
Oakdale
Tracy
Don Pedro Reservoir
Livermore
Salida
Modesto
Waterford
DIABLO RANGE
Tuolumne
Lake McClure
San Joaquin
Turlock
Merced
Livingston
River
Merced
Planada
0
20 mi
0
20 km

chef and creative whiz), emphasize old-school techniques and ultrafresh ingredients, enlivening the proceedings with offbeat items like truffle sashimi and the signature trout, salmon, and other "shooters" in shot glasses or quail eggs. **Known for:** cooked fish heads in soy marinade; baked and vegetarian items for the non-sushi crowd; gluten-free menu. *Average main: $30* *315 Spring St., near Pine St.* *530/478–9503* *sushiintheraw.net* *Closed Sun. and Mon. No lunch.*

Three Forks Bakery & Brewing Co.

$ | **AMERICAN** | Baked goods, wood-fired pizzas, excellent coffee (teas and kombucha, too), and microbrews made on-site draw locals and tourists to this redbrick spot with a high, heavy-beamed open ceiling. The food's ingredients come from nearby organic sources; the beers on tap range from blonde and pale ales to triple IPAs and several porters. **Known for:** lunch and dinner menu changes with the seasons; breads, muffins, scones, cookies, and cakes; soups and salads. *Average main: $14* *211 Commercial St.* *530/470–8333* *www.threeforksnc.com* *Closed Tues.*

Hotels

Madison House Bed & Breakfast

$$ | **B&B/INN** | A convenient downtown location, filling breakfasts showcasing local organic products, and welcoming hosts who exceed expectations make for a winning combination at this northern Gold Country B&B inside a romantic Victorian house. **Pros:** landscaped garden and sun porch; homemade baked goods; historic, romantic atmosphere. **Cons:** no elevator to upper-floor rooms; some noise and sun in front rooms; weekend minimum-stay requirement. *Rooms from: $205* *427 Broad St.* *530/470–6127* *www.themadisonhouse.net* *5 rooms* *Free breakfast.*

★ **The National Exchange Hotel**

$$ | **HOTEL** | Once more proudly anchoring the southern portion of Nevada City's historic district, this three-story boutique property, whose structure dates from 1856, reopened in 2021 following a period-sensitive multiyear makeover. **Pros:** contemporary, boutique-hotel style yet evokes the past; near shops, tasting rooms, and restaurants; as in the 1800s, a swank bar. **Cons:** smaller rooms have full or queen beds and sleep only two; no elevator to third-floor rooms; expensive on summer weekends. *Rooms from: $184* *211 Broad St.* *530/362–7605* *www.thenationalexchangehotel.com* *38 rooms* *No meals.*

Outside Inn

$ | **HOTEL** | **FAMILY** | It looks like a typical one-story motel, but the Outside Inn offers a variety of unique accommodations inspired by nature or activities in nature (there's a climbing wall in the rock-climbing suite), in an ideal location to enjoy Northern California's four seasons. **Pros:** fun reinvention of a motel; convenient to trails and hikes; affiliated Inn Town Campground for camping and glamping. **Cons:** rooms are on the small side; might be too funky for some guests; ½-mile walk to downtown. *Rooms from: $99* *575 E. Broad St.* *530/265–2233* *www.outsideinn.com* *15 rooms* *No meals.*

Performing Arts

Miners Foundry

ARTS CENTERS | The foundry, erected in 1856, produced machines for gold mining and logging. The Pelton Water Wheel, a power source for the mines credited with jump-starting the hydroelectric power industry, was invented here. The building is now used to stage art, dance, music, and film events, and there's a combination bar and café. *325 Spring St.* *530/265–5040* *www.minersfoundry.org.*

Grass Valley

4 miles south of Nevada City.

More than half of California's total gold production was extracted from mines around Grass Valley, including the Empire Mine, among the Gold Country's most fascinating attractions. The mine and the North Star Mining Museum, also worth a stop, are a few miles from the downtown historic district, which though walkable isn't as quaint as nearby Nevada City's.

GETTING HERE AND AROUND

You'll need a car to get here. Highway 49 is the north–south route into town, Highway 20 the east–west one. Nevada County Connects (*530/477–0103*) provides public transit.

Sights

★ Empire Mine State Historic Park

NATIONAL/STATE PARK | **FAMILY** | Starting with the "secret map" that mine management hid from miners, you can relive the days of gold, grit, and glory, when this mine was one of the biggest and most prosperous hard-rock gold mines in North America. Empire Mine yielded an estimated 5.8 million ounces of gold from 367 miles of underground passages. You can walk into a mine shaft and peer into dark, deep recesses and almost imagine what it felt like to work this vast operation. On some days, you might see tradesfolk in action at the blacksmith shop. The grounds have the Bourn Cottage (exquisite redwood interior; call for tour times), picnic tables, and gentle trails—perfect for a family outing. *10791 E. Empire St.* *530/273–8522* *www.parks.ca.gov* *$7.*

North Star Mining Museum

MUSEUM | **FAMILY** | Inside a former powerhouse, the museum displays a 32-foot-high Pelton Water Wheel said to be the largest ever built. The wheel, used to power mining operations, was a forerunner of modern turbines that generate hydroelectricity. Other exhibits, some geared to children, document life in the mines and the environmental effects mining had on the area. You can picnic nearby. *10933 Allison Ranch Rd.* *Head south from Main St. on Mill St.* *530/264–7569* *www.nevadacounty-history.org* *Donation requested.*

Restaurants

Cirino's at Main Street

$$ | **ITALIAN** | **FAMILY** | A family-owned spot with exposed brick walls, a tall ceiling, and a well-worn bar and floor, Cirino's serves up a vast menu of hefty Italian American favorites like Corsican rosemary chicken, steak à la Gorgonzola, and pork chop Milanese. The bar crew, which slings the signature Bloody Mary and other specialty cocktails, is as friendly as the rest of the team. **Known for:** old-school recipes presented with flair; homemade soups and sauces; family-friendly attitude. *Average main: $24* *213 W. Main St.* *530/477–6000* *www.cirinosatmainstreet.com* *Closed Mon.–Wed. (but check).*

Grass Valley Pasty Co.

$ | **BRITISH** | Eat like a 19th-century Cornish miner at this modest restaurant serving home-baked pasties, flaky on the outside with moist and flavorful meat, vegetable, and other fillings. Jammed with skirt steak, potatoes, and turnips, the Cousin Jack, named for a long-time shop on this site, hews closer to tradition, with the vegetarian, barbecued pulled pork, and a recent offering of turkey, pesto, sun-dried tomatoes, and cheese typical of the equally satisfying updates. **Known for:** at least one vegetarian option; family-run business; closes early evening. *Average main: $10* *100 S. Auburn St., at W. Main St.* *530/802–5202* *Closed Mon.*

Dancing Her Way to Fame

One of the most colorful personalities of the gold-rush era was Lola Montez (1821–61), a dancer, singer, courtesan, and gender rebel who earned international notoriety for her suggestive "spider dance." By contemporary accounts, her contortions, though not universally admired, were known to inspire approving miners to toss gold nuggets onto the stage.

Countess, Mistress, Possible Witch

Born Eliza Rosanna Gilbert in Ireland, Montez recast herself in young adulthood as a Spanish countess, performing in Europe, where her lovers included the composer Franz Liszt and the ill-fated King Ludwig of Bavaria. Famous, in part, for being famous, the entertainer cooled her heels in the Gold Country not long after her calls for Bavarian democracy contributed to Ludwig's overthrow and her banishment as a witch. Or so one version goes.

Lola Lives On

For a spell, Montez resided in Grass Valley, where a reproduction of her house downtown still stands at 248 Mill Street. Now a family-counseling center, the house isn't accessible, but Lola's memory lives on throughout the Gold Country, where rooms and suites in a few lodgings are named in her honor. Lola, the stylish restaurant in Nevada City's National Exchange Hotel, replicates the opulence of its namesake's glory years.

South Pine Cafe

$ | **AMERICAN** | Locals flock to this always-busy diner on a Victorian's ground floor for lobster Benedict, a spiced-up Mexican chicken scramble, and other dishes that are anything but your ordinary eggs and pancakes (though you can order those, too, and vegetarian versions of several items). Imaginative burritos, wraps, burgers, and more lobster in the form of a melt sandwich appear for lunch. **Known for:** homemade muffins; vegan and gluten-free options; many ingredients sourced from local family farms. *Average main: $14 ✉ 102 Richardson St., at N. Auburn St. ☎ 707/274–0261 🌐 www.southpinecafe.com ⏲ No dinner.*

Hotels

Gold Miners Inn

$$ | **HOTEL** | Just off Highway 49 and superbly run, this Ascend Collection property provides a comfortable experience, with art and artifacts reflecting the area's mining heritage gracing public areas and guest rooms. **Pros:** clean downtown hotel; art and artifacts reflecting the area's mining heritage; complimentary hot breakfast. **Cons:** no pool; despite stylish touches has a chain-like feel; some light sleepers find highway-side rooms noisy (ask for courtyard accommodations). *Rooms from: $155 ✉ 121 Bank St. ☎ 530/477–1700 🌐 www.goldminersinngrassvalley.com 81 rooms Free breakfast.*

Holbrooke Hotel

$$$ | **HOTEL** | A Main Street icon from the mid-1800s—when the A-list guest list included entertainer Lola Montez, writer Mark Twain, and Ulysses S. Grant—this two-story, historic-district hotel received a down-to-the-studs (in some cases bricks) makeover and reopened in 2020 as a boutique property. **Pros:** convenient to shops and restaurants; mix of antique, reproduction, and contemporary furnishings; ground-floor saloon is reportedly the West's oldest continuously

operating bar. **Cons:** expensive pet fee; street-side rooms pick up traffic noise; books up well ahead on many weekends. *Rooms from: $255 ✉ 212 W. Main St. ☎ 530/460–3078 🌐 www.holbrooke.com 28 rooms No meals.*

Nightlife

The Pour House

BARS/PUBS | The owners of this downtown bar aim to please lovers of beer and wine with a dozen-plus pours of each, many from local and regional craft breweries and boutique wineries. Across from the Holbrooke Hotel, the storefront space (closed on Sunday and Monday) serves soups, dips, soft pretzels, and other comfort bites. There's live music some nights. *✉ 217 W. Main St., at Church St. ☎ 530/802–5414 🌐 www.thepourhousegv.com.*

Auburn

24 miles south of Grass Valley, 34 miles northeast of Sacramento.

Halfway between San Francisco and Reno, Auburn is convenient to gold-rush sites, outdoor recreation opportunities, and wineries. The self-proclaimed "endurance capital of the world" is abuzz almost every summer weekend with running, cycling, rafting, kayaking, and equestrian events. Old Town Auburn has its own gold-rush charm, with narrow climbing streets, cobblestone lanes, wooden sidewalks, and many original buildings.

GETTING HERE AND AROUND

Amtrak serves Auburn, though most visitors arrive by car on Highway 49 or I–80. Once downtown, you can tour on foot.

Sights

Placer County Museum

MUSEUM | Visible from the highway, Auburn's standout structure is the Placer County Courthouse. The classic bronze-domed building houses the Placer County Museum, which documents the area's history—Native American, railroad, agricultural, and mining—from the early 1700s to 1900. Look for the gold nuggets valued at more than $338,000 today, and don't miss the women's cell under the Maple Street staircase. **■ TIP→ Ask about other nearby county-run history museums.** *✉ 101 Maple St. ☎ 530/889–6500 🌐 www.placer.ca.gov/2489/museums Free.*

Restaurants

Auburn Alehouse

$ | **AMERICAN** | **FAMILY** | Inside the historic American Block building, which dates to 1856, you can see this craft operation's beers being made through glass walls behind the dining room, which serves burgers, nachos, salads, wraps, and other decent gastropub fare. Gold Country Pilsner, Old Town Brown, and Gold Digger IPA are all Great American Beer Festival award winners. **Known for:** chicken, pork, and fish tacos; herb-brined buttermilk fried chicken; kids menu. *Average main: $16 ✉ 289 Washington St. ☎ 530/885–2537 🌐 www.auburnalehouse.com.*

Awful Annie's

$ | **AMERICAN** | **FAMILY** | One of Auburn's favorite old-time breakfast and lunch spots entices patrons with waffles, pancakes, Monte Cristo French toast, and a slew of egg dishes you can wash down with an award-winning Bloody Mary or two. Feast on burgers, sandwiches, and more Bloody Marys for lunch. **Known for:** heartiest breakfast in the foothills; Grandma's bread pudding with brandy sauce; town-hangout feel. *Average main: $13*

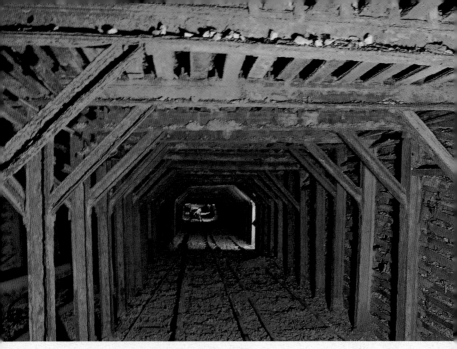

Almost 6 million ounces of gold were extracted from the Empire Mine.

✉ *13460 Lincoln Way* ☎ *530/888–9857* 🌐 *www.awfulannies.com* 🕒 *No dinner.*

Carpe Vino Marketplace & Lounge

$$$ | **MODERN AMERICAN** | What started as a boutique wine retailer inside a restored 19th-century saloon evolved into a must-visit bistro serving imaginative cuisine. By 2022, reboots of both the space and the menu, with the focus reportedly shifting to cocktails and small plates, should be complete. **Known for:** varied wine list; historic setting; imaginative fare. *Average main: $27* ✉ *1568 Lincoln Way* ☎ *530/823–0320* 🌐 *www.carpevinoauburn.com* 🕒 *No lunch (but check).*

The Pour Choice

$ | **AMERICAN** | Black subway tiles, contemporary bistro furniture, and a gray-marble counter lit by orb-shape Edison bulbs lend urban flair to this fine spot for a craft coffee or one of more than two dozen local, national, and international brews on tap. In a space once occupied by a drugstore, the Pour Choice, which bills itself as Auburn's living room, serves light fare that might include a grilled gourmet-cheese sandwich on ciabatta with bacon. **Known for:** upbeat vibe; talented baristas; outdoor terrace in good weather. *Average main: $11* ✉ *177 Sacramento St.* ☎ *530/820–3451* 🌐 *thepourchoice.com.*

Hotels

Holiday Inn Auburn Hotel

$$ | **HOTEL** | **FAMILY** | Above the freeway across from Old Town, this hotel has a welcoming lobby and chain-standard but well-organized rooms with refrigerators, microwaves, and work areas. **Pros:** some rooms sleep four people; suitable base for Gold Country exploring; on-site restaurant. **Cons:** lacks style; some traffic noise; can't walk to Old Town restaurants and shops. *Rooms from: $153* ✉ *120 Grass Valley Hwy.* ☎ *530/887–8787, 800/814–8787* 🌐 *www.auburnhi.com* *96 rooms* *No meals.*

Coloma

18 miles southeast of Auburn.

The California gold rush started in Coloma when James W. Marshall discovered flecks of metal in the bottom of a ditch. "Boys, I believe I've found a gold mine!" he exclaimed in January 1848 to colleagues at John Sutter's mill here. In short order, California's coastal communities began to empty as prospectors flocked to the hills, getting a jump on East Coasters, who didn't hear about the boom until mid-August.

GETTING HERE AND AROUND

A car is the only practical way to get to Coloma, via Highway 49. Once parked, you can walk to all the worthwhile sights.

Sights

★ Marshall Gold Discovery State Historic Park

NATIONAL/STATE PARK | **FAMILY** | The American River's south fork slices through this park commemorating California's mining history. Trails lead from the parking lot to a statue of James Marshall with sublime views; beyond it to the north stands a working reproduction of an 1840s mill erected near where he first spotted gold. Most of Coloma lies within the park. Though crowded with tourists in summer, the town hardly resembles the mob scene it was in 1849, when 2,000 prospectors staked out claims along the streambed. Coloma's population grew to 4,000, supporting seven hotels, three banks, and many stores and other businesses. But when reserves of the precious metal dwindled, the prospectors left as quickly as they had come. **■ TIP→ For $8 per person, rangers give gold-panning lessons on the hour, year-round.** ✉ *310 Back St., off Hwy. 49* ☎ *530/622–3470* 🌐 *www.parks.ca.gov/marshallgold* 🎫 *$8 per vehicle.*

Placerville

9 miles south of Coloma, 44 miles east of Sacramento.

It's hard to imagine now, but in 1849 about 4,000 miners staked out every gully and hillside in Placerville, turning the town into a rip-roaring camp of log cabins, tents, and clapboard houses. The area was then known as Hangtown, a graphic allusion to the nature of frontier justice. It took on the name Placerville in 1854 and became an important supply center for the miners.

Many of the always hoppin' downtown historic district's restaurants, indie shops, coffeehouses, and wine bars occupy rehabbed 19th-century buildings. A defining characteristic of nearby El Dorado AVA wineries (🌐 *eldoradowines.org*) is their vineyards' high elevation, from 1,200 to 3,500 feet.

GETTING HERE AND AROUND

You'll need a car to get to and around Placerville. It's a 45-minute drive from Sacramento via U.S. 50.

Sights

Apple Hill

FARM/RANCH | **FAMILY** | From July to late December, Apple Hill Growers Association members open their orchards and vineyards for apple and berry picking; picnicking; and wine, cider, pressed-juice, and other tastings. Treasure hunts, pond fishing, pie making, and other activities attract families. The Apple Hill website has a map and an events calendar, or download the Official Apple Hill Growers app. **■ TIP→ On autumn weekends, take U.S. 50's Camino exit to avoid some of the traffic congestion.** ✉ *Placerville* ✣ *Starting 2 miles east of Hwy. 49, Exits 48–57 off U.S. 50* ☎ *530/644–7692* 🌐 *www.applehill.com.*

Boeger Winery

WINERY/DISTILLERY | In 1972, Greg Boeger revived a gold rush–era farm that once supported fruit and nut orchards, a winery, and a distillery. These days Boeger produces estate wines from 30 varietals grown on two parcels totaling 100 acres, with Sauvignon Blanc and Barbera the best sellers and Zinfandel and Primitivo also worth seeking out. Visits are by appointment (same-day often possible). ■ TIP→ **The creek-side picnic area fronting the tasting room hosts bands and food vendors on Friday evenings in summer (reserve space well ahead).** ✉ *1709 Carson Rd.* ✣ *Head north from U.S. 50, Exit 48, then northeast (right) on Carson Rd.* ☎ *530/622–8094* 🌐 *www.boegerwinery.com* 🎫 *Tastings from $10.*

★ **Delfino Farms—Edio Vineyards**

WINERY/DISTILLERY | Apple growers since 1964, the Delfino family occupies one of El Dorado County's most idyllic sites. The clan gained early notice for Joan Delfino's apple pies and the fun farm events here. In the 2010s, her grandchildren started a winery named for her husband, local agricultural icon Edio Delfino. They pour their superb whites and reds in a gleaming-silver contemporary space whose patio perches over apple trees surrounded by grapevines ringed by a forest. ■ TIP→ **Wine tasting takes place year-round; bakery visits and apple events occur seasonally.** ✉ *3205 N. Canyon Rd., off Carson Rd.* ☎ *530/622–0184* 🌐 *delfinofarms.com* 🎫 *Tastings from $10* ⊙ *Tasting room closed Tues. and Wed.*

Element 79 Vineyards

WINERY/DISTILLERY | This winery's owner envisioned his sleek hospitality space as "a country club" for experiencing wines by the glass or flight, with or without the charcuterie and cheese sold on-site. The glass back wall and adjoining patio edge the 32-acre estate vineyard, which guests can hike on their own (there's a map) or on occasional tours. Winemaker Scott Johnson's red blends and Cabernets stand out, as does the unconventional, canned, dry-hopped Viognier sparkler (Johnson also brews beer). ✉ *7350 Fairplay Rd., southeast 1½ miles off Mt. Aukum Rd., Fair Play* ☎ *530/497–0750* 🌐 *element79vineyards.com* 🎫 *Tastings from $5.*

Hangtown's Gold Bug Park & Mine

MINE | FAMILY | Take a self-guided tour of this fully lighted mine shaft within a park owned by the City of Placerville. The worthwhile audio tour (included) makes clear what you're seeing. ■ TIP→ **A shaded stream runs through the park, and there are picnic facilities.** ✉ *2635 Goldbug La., Exit U.S. 50 at Bedford Ave. and follow signs* ☎ *530/642–5207* 🌐 *www.goldbugpark.org* 🎫 *Park free; mine tour $10* ⊙ *Closed weekdays late fall–early spring except for a few holidays.*

★ **Holly's Hill Vineyards**

WINERY/DISTILLERY | The founders of this woodsy hilltop winery 7 miles south of Apple Hill tasted Châteauneuf-du-Pape on their honeymoon, sparking a lifetime passion for Rhône wines made in classic French style. Mourvèdre is a specialty, by itself and in blends with Grenache, Syrah, or both. Carignane, Counoise, and other lower-profile Rhône reds are also made, along with whites that include the Roussanne-dominant Patriarche Blanc blend. By appointment only (same-day usually okay), taste these estate wines in a space with views that extend 75 miles on a clear day. ✉ *3680 Leisure La., off Pleasant Valley Rd.* ✣ *From U.S. 50, Exit 49, follow Broadway east to Newtown Rd. and Pleasant Valley Rd. southeast* ☎ *530/344–0227* 🌐 *www.hollyshill.com* 🎫 *Tastings $10.*

★ **Lava Cap Winery**

WINERY/DISTILLERY | Nineteenth-century miners knew if they found the type of volcanic rocks visible everywhere on this winery's property that gold was nearby. These days, the rocky soils and vineyard elevations as high as 2,800 feet play pivotal roles in creating Lava Cap's fruit-forward yet elegant wines. Zinfandel, Grenache, Cabernet Franc, and Petite Sirah star among the reds, Chardonnay and Viognier among the whites. ■ **TIP→ After a tasting you can picnic on the patio and enjoy Sierra foothills vistas.** *2221 Fruitridge Rd. 530/621–0175 www.lavacap.com Tastings from $15.*

★ Starfield Vineyards

WINERY/DISTILLERY | Its many microclimates inspired owner-winemaker Tom Sinton to purchase a 67-acre hillside property he transformed into a magnificent showcase for wines from mostly Rhône and Italian varietals. With a nature trail, a 300-foot-long rose arbor, an amphitheater for events, a lakeside pavilion, and an upper patio with views of trees near and far, the wines could have taken a back seat, but Sinton crafts them with such grace and precision that they more than match the setting and hospitality. *2750 Jacquier Rd. 3 miles northeast of downtown Placerville. 530/748–3085 www.starfieldvineyards.com Tastings from $10.*

Restaurants

★ Allez

$$ | FRENCH | The tale of how the couple running this spot for to-go or dine-in French food came to be husband and wife says all one needs to know about their passion for beautifully crafted cuisine: he won her heart with his escargot sauce. In a casual space with ocher walls, six utilitarian stools at the wine bar, and a few tables inside and out, the two serve baguette sandwiches, salads, crepes, stews, and entrées like coq au vin, cassoulet, and pork tenderloin. **Known for:** all-day prix-fixe menu (a deal), plus à la carte; sandwich, salad, and dessert lunch boxes; many vegetarian and gluten-free items. *Average main: $22 4242 Fowler La., Diamond Springs Off Hwy. 49, 3 miles south of downtown Placerville 530/621–1160 www.allezeldorado.com Closed Sun. and Mon.*

★ Creekside Cork & Brew

$$ | AMERICAN | At shift's end, workers from Fair Play wineries gather with neighbors at this nouveau rustic roadside watering hole whose chefs prepare elevated farm-to-table comfort cuisine—from soups, salads, and sandwiches to fish, meat, and pasta entrées. Among the crowd-pleasing burgers—served at high-top and regular tables, at the bar, or on the patio outside—is the one with bacon, Brie, and fig, though the prize for decadence goes to the weekend-brunch mash-up with candied maple bacon, a fried egg, and hollandaise. **Known for:** local wines and beers; patio dining; live music on many Fridays and Sundays. *Average main: $19 7915 Fairplay Rd., at Perry Creek Rd. 530/503–0044 creeksidecorkandbrew.com Closed Tues. and Wed.*

Heyday Cafe

$$ | AMERICAN | Inside an exposed-brick 1857 former assay office where miners exchanged gold nuggets for the coin of the realm, the Heyday is a happy haven for salads, panini, and thin-crust pizzas at lunch and dinner entrées like seared salmon, baby back ribs, and risotto. The mood is casual, but the food is prepared with style. **Known for:** local to international wine list; molasses gingerbread cake; sister restaurant, The Independent, at 629 Main. *Average main: $24 325 Main St. 530/626–9700 www.heydaycafe.com Closed Mon. (but check).*

★ Smith Flat House

$$$ | MODERN AMERICAN | Carefully sourced ingredients from local purveyors, meticulous execution, and a historic setting at a former mine site 3 miles east of downtown have made this restaurant a hit among locals, Gold Country tourists, and travelers heading to or from Tahoe. The seasonally changing menu might include a wild-mushroom Bordelaise appetizer, jambalaya risotto, and the Black and White entrée of filet mignon and perfectly grilled prawns. **Known for:** waffle Benedict at

Sunday brunch; salads, pizzas, burgers for lunch; outdoor dining area. *Average main: $29 2021 Smith Flat Rd. From U.S. 50, Exit 49, head north on Point View Dr. and Jacquier Rd. and east on Smith Flat Rd. 530/621–1003 www.smithflathouse.com Closed Mon. and Tues. No lunch Wed. and Thurs.*

Solid Ground Brewing

$ | ECLECTIC | The chef at this brewpub with a no-nonsense industrial decor (high ceilings, concrete floor, huge garage doors) tailors the cuisine to the namesake beers produced by two Sierra foothills natives, one with an enology degree, the other with extensive experience in European beer making. Carnitas tacos, a buttermilk fried-chicken sandwich, and a burger with the cheese of your choice are among the gastropub options. **Known for:** seasonal ciders and spritzers; wine blended into some beers, others aged in wine barrels; good stop for lunch on a hot day. *Average main: $13 553 Pleasant Valley Rd., Diamond Springs Off Hwy. 49, 3 miles south of downtown Placerville 530/344–7442 solidgroundbrewing.com.*

That Little Italian Place

$$ | ITALIAN | The chef-owner of this order-at-the-counter restaurant also known as The Place describes the menu's influences as his East Coast grandmother's multicourse Sunday family suppers, his later culinary explorations, and his zeal about creating "fresh and original" Italian cuisine. The country-road setting, butcher-block tables, and open kitchen dominated by a copper-clad, wood-fired oven accentuate the "just like home" feeling, as do the calzones, pizzas, and pasta dishes. **Known for:** antipasti, salads, panini, and "grind-ahs" (submarine sandwiches); vegetarian and gluten-free items; live music on the patio some nights. *Average main: $19 2530 Pleasant Valley Rd., at Bucks Bar Rd. From Main St., take Cedar Ravine Rd. southeast 5¾ miles and turn left (east) 530/621–1680 thatlittleitalianplace.com/placerville Closed Mon. and Tues.*

Totem Coffee

$ | CAFÉ | The best spot in the historic district to relax over coffee and espresso drinks—or sip tea, kombucha, and sometimes hot chocolate—sources its beans from ethical producers worldwide. Enjoy your beverage inside the informal contemporary-rustic space or on a tree-shaded outdoor patio to the sounds of a large fountain. **Known for:** superb cappuccinos and lattes; pastries, muffins, doughnuts for breakfast; light lunch fare. *Average main: $8 312 Main St., Suite 104 530/903–3280 www.totemcoffeeroasters.com Closed Tues.*

Hotels

★ Eden Vale Inn

$$$ | B&B/INN | FAMILY | This lavish but rustic B&B occupies a converted turn-of-the-20th-century hay barn, the centerpiece of which is a 27-foot slate fireplace that rises to a sloping ceiling of timber beams. **Pros:** exceptionally plush rooms; stunning patio and grounds; romantic setting. **Cons:** expensive for the area; summer weekends book up far ahead; weekend minimum-stay requirement. *Rooms from: $309 1780 Springvale Rd. 530/621–0901 www.edenvaleinn.com 7 rooms Free breakfast.*

★ Lucinda's Country Inn

$$ | B&B/INN | Effusive but not intrusive hospitality is the trademark of this contemporary inn between Placerville and Plymouth whose spacious light-filled suites have views of the oaks, firs, and other trees surrounding the property. **Pros:** romantic setting; convenient for wine touring; filling breakfast and catered dinner option. **Cons:** some rooms sleep only two; long drive to Placerville or Plymouth restaurants; lacks amenities of larger properties. *Rooms from: $180 6701 Perry Creek Rd., Fair Play 530/409–4169* *www.lucindascountryinn.com 5 rooms Free breakfast.*

Plymouth

20 miles south of Placerville.

The most concentrated Gold Country wine-touring area lies in the hills of the Shenandoah Valley, east of Plymouth—you could easily spend two or three days just hitting the highlights. Zinfandel is the primary grape grown here, but area vineyards produce many other varietals, from Rhônes like Syrah and Mourvèdre to Spanish Tempranillo and Italian Barbera and Sangiovese. Most wineries are open for tastings at least on Friday and weekends, and some of the top ones are open daily; many welcome picnickers.

GETTING HERE AND AROUND

A car is necessary to explore the Shenandoah Valley. Highway 49 runs north–south through Plymouth. To reach the valley from the highway, head east and then north on Shenandoah Road (also signed as E16).

Sights

Amador Cellars

WINERY/DISTILLERY | Larry and Linda Long made wine out of their home in Truckee for 15 years before opening their down-home Amador County winery. Their son Michael is head winemaker, daughter Ashley his assistant. Estate-grown Zinfandel is the biggest seller, but this small operation also does well with Syrah, Barbera, Tempranillo, and the Portuguese varietal Touriga (one of the Port grapes), and there's a GSM (Grenache, Syrah, and Mourvèdre) Rhône-style blend. Tastings, by appointment, take place in a barn surrounded by grapevines or just outside. *11093 Shenandoah Rd., Plymouth 209/245–6150 amadorcellars.com Closed Tues. and Wed.*

Helwig Winery

WINERY/DISTILLERY | Splashier than many of its neighbors and a draw as much for its restaurant and seasonal live music as its wines, family-operated Helwig occupies a hilltop steel, wood, and glass tasting space with knockout views. The winery specializes in fruit-forward reds, most notably Barbera, Graciano, and Tempranillo; the sparkling rosé of Sangiovese shines among the lighter wines. **TIP→ If the weather's good, it's worth the small extra fee to sip alfresco on the deck.** *11555 Shenandoah Rd., Plymouth 209/245–5200 www.helwigwinery.com Tastings from $10.*

★ Jeff Runquist Wines

WINERY/DISTILLERY | Judges at the 2018 San Francisco International Wine Competition bestowed Winery of the Year honors on this operation whose tasting room ranks among the Shenandoah Valley's jolliest. Known for elegant, fruit-forward wines with velvety tannins, Jeff Runquist specializes in Barbera, Zinfandel, and Petite Sirah but makes several other reds and Muscat Canelli, Verdelho, and Viognier whites. *10776 Shenandoah Rd., Plymouth 209/245–6282 www.jeffrunquistwines.com Free.*

Rombauer Sierra Foothills

WINERY/DISTILLERY | For years Rombauer, famous for its Napa Valley Chardonnays, farmed foothills Zinfandel vineyards, so it wasn't a total surprise when the winery acquired an existing facility here. Inside the brightly lit tasting room or at umbrella-shaded tables you can sample the Classic flight—Sauvignon Blanc, Chardonnay, Cabernet Sauvignon, Merlot, and Sierra Foothills Zinfandel—or sip these or other wines by the glass or bottle. **TIP→ The winery sells charcuterie and cheeses but also allows outside food.** *12225 Steiner Rd., Plymouth 866/280–2582 www.rombauer.com Tastings from $13 glass, $20 flight.*

Scott Harvey Wines

WINERY/DISTILLERY | Founder Scott Harvey helped elevate the profile of Amador County wines in the 1970s, later developing two wine programs in the Napa Valley. Harvey describes the foothills as similar to Italy's Piemonte region, where Barbera originated, but with one additional benefit: it's sunnier here, which this grape loves. Barbera, Zinfandel (one from vines planted in 1869), and Syrah are the focus, but you'll also find Cabernet Sauvignon and other reds along with Sauvignon Blanc, Riesling, and sparkling and ice-style wines. ✉ *10861 Shenandoah Rd., Plymouth* ☎ *209/245–3670* 🌐 *www.scottharvey-wines.com* 🎟 *Tastings from $15.*

Sobon Estate

WINERY/DISTILLERY | You can sip fruity, robust Zinfandels—old vine and new—and learn about wine making and Shenandoah Valley pioneer life at the museum here. This winery was established in 1856 and has been run since 1989 by the owners of nearby Shenandoah Vineyards, which is open daily. ■ **TIP→ To sample the best Zins, pay the modest fee for the reserve tasting.** ✉ *14430 Shenandoah Rd., Plymouth* ☎ *209/245–4455* 🌐 *www.sobon-wine.com* 🎟 *Tastings from $5* ⏲ *Closed Mon.–Thurs. (but check).*

★ Terre Rouge and Easton Wines

WINERY/DISTILLERY | The winery of Bill Easton and Jane O'Riordan achieves success with two separate labels. Terre Rouge, which focuses on Rhône-style wines, makes some of California's best Syrahs. The Easton label specializes in high-scoring Zinfandels from old and new vines and does well with Sauvignon Blanc and Cabernet Sauvignon. ■ **TIP→ You can picnic on the lawn here.** ✉ *10801 Dickson Rd., Plymouth* ☎ *209/245–4277* 🌐 *www.terrerougewines.com* 🎟 *Tastings from $10* ⏲ *Closed Tues. and Wed.*

★ Turley Wine Cellars

WINERY/DISTILLERY | Zinfandel fans won't want to miss Turley, which makes a dozen and a half single-vineyard wines (collectors love them) from old-vine grapes grown all over California. Some of the wines, including a few from Amador County, are available only in the tasting room. Petite Sirah and Cabernet Sauvignon are two other emphases. All visits are by appointment only. ✉ *10851 Shenandoah Rd., Plymouth* ☎ *209/245–3938* 🌐 *www.turleywinecellars.com/amador* 🎟 *Tastings $25* ⏲ *Closed Mon.–Wed. (but check).*

Vino Noceto

WINERY/DISTILLERY | Owners Suzy and Jim Gullett draw raves for their Sangioveses, which range from light and fruity to rich and heavy. They also produce Rosato di Sangiovese (aka rosé), old-vine Zinfandel, and a few other varietals. Most tastings take place in the red barn where the couple began operations in the 1980s or on a nearby patio. ✉ *11011 Shenandoah Rd., at Dickson Rd., Plymouth* ☎ *209/245–6556* 🌐 *www.noceto.com* 🎟 *Tastings from $10, tour $18.*

Restaurants

Amador Vintage Market

$ | AMERICAN | Area caterer Beth Sogaard spiffed up Plymouth's original general store, transforming its handsome red- and sand-color brick building into a dandy stop for gourmet sandwiches and deli specialties like Dijon potato salad and house-smoked salmon. A recent Reuben with pepper Jack cheese, pickled onions, and grain mustard on house-made rosemary focaccia is typical of Sogaard's reimagining of comfort-food staples you can enjoy on-site, at nearby wineries, or in the park next door. **Known for:** homemade truffle potato chips; French dip sandwiches; selection of local wines. [$] *Average main: $11* ✉ *9393 Main St., Plymouth* ☎ *209/245–3663* 🌐 *beth-sogaard.com* ⏲ *Closed Mon.–Thurs. (but check). No dinner.*

★ **Taste**

$$$$ | **MODERN AMERICAN** | A serendipitous find in downtown Plymouth, Taste serves eclectic modern dishes made from fresh local fare. The signature mushroom "cigars"—sautéed shiitake, crimini, and oyster mushrooms rolled with goat cheese in phyllo dough and served with porcini sauce and white truffle oil—are a small-plate staple, and sturgeon, rack of lamb, and duck confit are examples of the sustainably sourced, creative entrées. **Known for:** superb beer and wine list; knowledgeable sommeliers; seasonal cocktails. *Average main: $39 9402 Main St., Plymouth 209/245–3463 www.restauranttaste.com Closed Tues.–Thurs. No lunch (check for updates).*

Hotels

★ **Grand Reserve Inn**

$$$$ | **B&B/INN** | Guests typically leave this B&B gushing over just about everything—the Tuscan-villa atmosphere, the expansive vineyard vistas, the sublime hospitality, the elaborate breakfasts, the luxurious accommodations, even the ultrasoft sheets. **Pros:** idyllic setting; gracious well-trained staff; marvelous special-occasion splurge. **Cons:** pricey for the area; maximum room occupancy two people except for two-bedroom Vineyard House; per website "no children or pets permitted." *Rooms from: $449 19890 Shenandoah School Rd., Plymouth 209/245–5466 www.grandreserveinn.com 6 suites Free breakfast.*

★ **Rest Hotel Plymouth**

$$ | **B&B/INN** | The team behind Plymouth's Taste restaurant converted two adjacent run-down buildings into this boutique hotel whose individually decorated rooms rank among the area's finest. **Pros:** attention to detail; continental breakfast's baked goods; evening wine hour. **Cons:** minimum stay requirement some weekends; lacks big-city hotel amenities; some noise in street-side rooms. *Rooms from: $165 9372 Main St., Plymouth 209/245–6315 www.hotel-rest.net 16 rooms Free breakfast.*

Amador City

6 miles south of Plymouth.

The history of tiny Amador City (population less than 200) mirrors the boom-bust-boom cycle of many Gold Country towns. With an output of $42 million in gold, its Keystone Mine was one of the most productive in the Mother Lode. After all the gold was extracted, the miners cleared out, and the area suffered. Amador City now derives its wealth from tourists browsing through its antiques and specialty shops.

GETTING HERE AND AROUND

Park where you can along Old Highway 49 (off Highway 49), and walk around.

Hotels

Imperial Hotel, Saloon & Restaurant

$ | **B&B/INN** | An 1879 hotel on the bend in this one-block town, the redbrick Imperial charms its guests with six second-floor rooms (two at the front have balconies) whose antique furnishings include iron-and-brass beds, gingerbread flourishes, and, in one instance, art-deco appointments. **Pros:** history-evoking stay; good restaurant and bar; two rooms with balconies. **Cons:** no phones or TVs in rooms; rooms and hotel could use a refresh; noise issues in street-side rooms. *Rooms from: $130 14202 Old Hwy. 49 209/267–9172 www.imperialamador.com 9 rooms Free breakfast.*

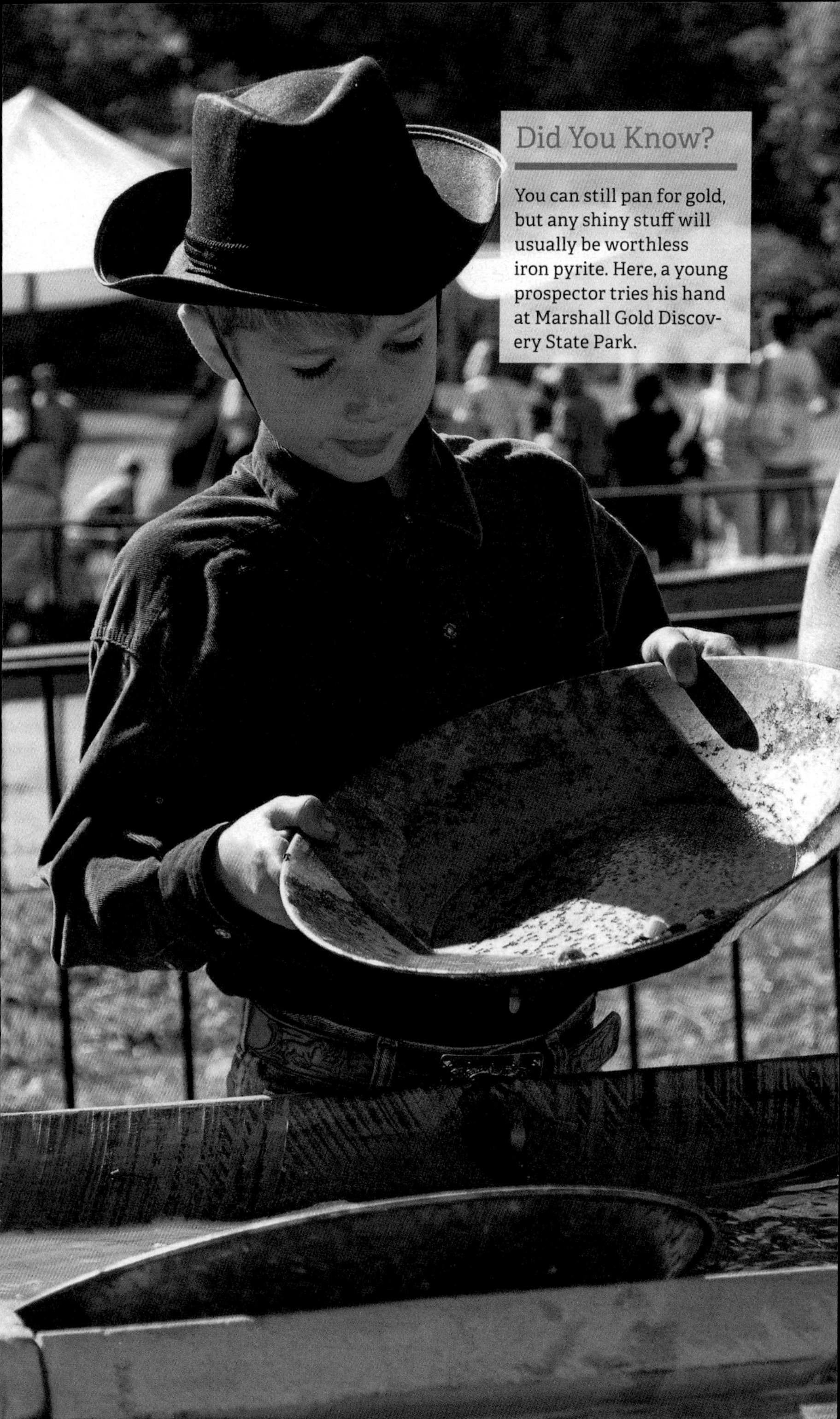

Did You Know?

You can still pan for gold, but any shiny stuff will usually be worthless iron pyrite. Here, a young prospector tries his hand at Marshall Gold Discovery State Park.

Sutter Creek

2 miles south of Amador City.

Sutter Creek is a charming conglomeration of balconied buildings, Victorian homes, and neo–New England structures. At any time of year Main Street (formerly part of Highway 49) is worth a stroll for its shops selling antiques and works by local artists and craftspeople. Tasting rooms of note include Bella Grace, Feist, and Scott Harvey.

GETTING HERE AND AROUND

Arrive here by car on Highway 49. There's no public transit, but downtown is walkable. The visitor center organizes walking tours.

ESSENTIALS

VISITOR INFORMATION Sutter Creek Visitor Center. ✉ *71A Main St.* ☎ *209/267–5647* 🌐 *www.suttercreek.org.*

Sights

Knight Foundry

FACTORY | Pivotal accomplishments in engineering history occurred at the nation's last functioning water-powered foundry and machine shop, established in 1873 and these days run by volunteers. Namesake Samuel Knight's innovations included a revolutionary system for casting iron and the one-piece Knight Water Wheel for generating power. On the second Saturday of the month or on work days (usually Wednesdays), you can take a tour. **■ TIP→ Plaques and outdoor exhibits accessible at all hours convey some of this facility's fascinating story.** ✉ *81 Eureka St., 2 blocks east of Main St.* ☎ *209/560–6160* 🌐 *www.knightfoundry.com* 🎫 *Tour $15, outdoor exhibits free.*

Miners' Bend Historic Gold Mining Park

CITY PARK | Volunteers converted a parking lot into a compact open-air tribute to the area's mining legacy. Signs along the path describe 19th-century mining operations and the 16 pieces of equipment on display used to extract or process ore. ✉ *29 Old Hwy. 49* ☎ *209/560–6880* 🌐 *suttercreekfoundation.org* 🎫 *Free.*

Restaurants

Gold Dust Pizza

$$ | PIZZA | Zesty pies like the Miner Moe's BBQ Chicken, with red onions, pineapple, bacon, and cheese, make this casual spot a few steps off Main Street an excellent choice, particularly for lunch or a mid-afternoon snack. You can also build your own pizza or order a sandwich; there's some indoor seating, but when the weather's good most folks eat outside on the front patio or the creekside one out back. **Known for:** ultracrispy crust; chicken wings and calzone; combo meals. 💲 *Average main: $17* ✉ *20 Eureka St., off Main St., Davis* ☎ *209/267–1900* 🌐 *www.golddustpizza.org.*

Sina's Backroads Cafe

$ | AMERICAN | Homemade lunches and breakfasts served with warmth and good cheer are the trademarks of this restaurant and coffee shop in Sutter Creek's historic district. Egg scrambles, pancakes, bagel sandwiches, French toast, and biscuits and gravy headline at breakfast, with soups, salads, sandwiches, and wraps on the menu for lunch. **Known for:** quiches and specials; good stop for coffee; cookies, muffins, and pastries. 💲 *Average main: $9* ✉ *74 Main St.* ☎ *209/267–0440* 🌐 *sinasbackroadscafe.com* 🕒 *Closed Wed. and Thurs. No dinner.*

Hotels

The Foxie

$$ | B&B/INN | A yellow-clapboard house that dates from the mid-1800s contains four of the rooms at this boutique-style historic-district property formerly called the Foxes Inn; a carriage house built more than a century later holds the other three. **Pros:** convenient to shops and tasting rooms; English-style gardens;

private-dinner option. **Cons:** two-night minimum stay requirement; five rooms have queen beds (kings in other two); per website "most suitable" for children over age 12. *Rooms from: $209 ✉ 77 Main St. ☎ 209/267–5882 🌐 www.thefoxie.com 7 rooms Free breakfast.*

Inn at 161

$$ | B&B/INN | For many years known as the Grey Gables Inn, this property at the northern end of Sutter Creek's historic downtown received a boutique-style makeover following an early-2021 change of ownership. **Pros:** gas-log fireplaces in all rooms; some rooms have a soaking or Jacuzzi tub; landscaped grounds. **Cons:** along town's busy main drag; minimum weekend-stay requirement; some bathrooms could use updating. *Rooms from: $159 ✉ 161 Hanford St. ☎ 209/267–1039 🌐 www.innat161.com 11 rooms Free breakfast.*

Volcano

13 miles east of Sutter Creek.

Many roads, all of them winding, all of them scenic, lead to Volcano, an off-the-beaten-path former mining town of about 120 people, the entirety of which is a California Historical Landmark. Black Chasm Cavern is the main attraction.

GETTING HERE AND AROUND

A car is the practical way to get to Volcano. From Sutter Creek or Jackson, pick up Highway 88 heading east. GPS can be sketchy here, so plot and save your route when you have good coverage.

Black Chasm Cavern National Natural Landmark

CAVE | FAMILY | Guided 50-minute tours take you past stalactites, stalagmites, and rare formations of delicate helictites in three underground chambers, one of which also contains a lake. Black Chasm isn't the largest cave in the Gold Country, but its crystals dazzle both eye and camera—the Landmark Chamber, the tour's third stop, inspired a scene in the 2003 film *The Matrix Reloaded.*Outside is an area where kids can "pan" for crystals. **■ TIP→ The same outfit also conducts tours of California Cavern State Historic Landmark, 32 miles south of Volcano, though the days open are less regular.** *✉ 15701 Pioneer Volcano Rd., Volcano ✣ ¾ mile south of Volcano off Pine Grove–Volcano Rd. ☎ 209/296–5007 🌐 blackchasmcavern.com $19 Closed Mon.–Thurs. in Jan.*

Volcano Pub + Inn

$ | B&B/INN | The folks behind Plymouth's Taste restaurant and Rest hotel operate this four-room second-floor inn whose first incarnation, from the 1880s into the 1920s, was as a saloon and boardinghouse for miners and other mostly long-term guests. **Pros:** daily specials at pub; simple but pleasing decor; homemade full breakfast with egg dish, fresh fruit, and baked goods. **Cons:** per website "not suited for small children"; two rooms have a shower but no tub; lacks big-city hotel amenities. *Rooms from: $127 ✉ 21375 Consolation St., Volcano ☎ 209/296–7711 🌐 www.volcanounion.com 4 rooms Free breakfast.*

Jackson

8 miles south of Sutter Creek.

Jackson wasn't the Gold Country's rowdiest town, but the party lasted longer here than most anywhere else: "girls' dormitories" (aka brothels) and nickel slot machines flourished until the mid-1950s. Jackson also had the world's deepest and richest gold mines, the Kennedy and the Argonaut, which together produced $70 million in gold. Most of the miners who worked the lode were of Serbian or Italian origin, and they gave the town a European character that persists to this day. A walking-tour map of historic sites, downloadable from the city's website (🌐 *ci.jackson.ca.us; click on "Visit Jackson" and then "Things to Do"*), includes the town's steeply terraced Serbian cemetery.

GETTING HERE AND AROUND

Arrive by car on Highway 49. You can walk downtown but otherwise will need a car.

Sights

Kennedy Gold Mine

HISTORIC SITE | On weekends and some major holidays half the year, docents offer guided 90-minute surface tours of one of the most prolific mines of the gold-rush era and one of the deepest gold mines in the world. Exhibits inside the remaining buildings illustrate how gold flakes were melted for shipment to San Francisco and how "skips" were used to lower miners and materials into the mile-long shaft and carry ore to the surface. ✉ *Kennedy Mine Rd., at Argonaut La.* ✣ *½ mile east of Hwy. 49* ☎ *209/223–9542* 🌐 *www.kennedygoldmine.com* 🎫 *Free; guided tour $12* ⏲ *Closed most weekdays year-round, all weekends Nov.–Mar.*

Preston Castle

HISTORIC SITE | History buffs and ghost hunters regularly make the trip to this fantastically creepy, 156-room, Romanesque Revival structure erected in 1894 to house troubled youth. Having fallen into disrepair, the building is slowly undergoing a full restoration. On tours, which take place on many Saturdays between April and August, you'll hear all sorts of spine-tingling tales. ✉ *909 Palm Dr., Ione* ✣ *12 miles west of Jackson via Hwys. 88 and 104* ☎ *209/256–3623* 🌐 *www.prestoncastle.org* 🎫 *From $35 for 1–2 guests* ⏲ *Closed Sept.–Mar.*

Restaurants

Mel and Faye's Diner

$ | AMERICAN | FAMILY | Since 1956, the Gillman family has been serving up its famous "Moo Burger" with two patties and special sauce—so big it still makes cow sounds, presumably. The vibe is convivial at this homey diner. **Known for:** hearty breakfasts served until 11 am; milkshakes and floats; freshly baked pies. 💲 *Average main: $15* ✉ *31 Hwy. 88* ☎ *209/223–0853* 🌐 *melandfayes.homestead.com.*

Teresa's Place

$$ | ITALIAN | Ease back in time at this rustic roadside favorite of Gold Country residents and regulars that dates back to 1921, when its namesake, an Italian immigrant, opened a boardinghouse for local miners. Run by her descendants, the restaurant serves unfussy renditions of Italian-American classics—pastas, wood-fired pizzas, veal and chicken dishes, and steak and seafood. **Known for:** full bar; local wines and microbrews; minestrone from family recipe. 💲 *Average main: $26* ✉ *1235 Jackson Gate Rd.* ✣ *From downtown head north 1¼ miles on N. Main St.; from Hwy. 49 north of town take Jackson Gate Rd. east 1½ miles* ☎ *209/223–1786* ⏲ *Closed Wed. and Thurs. No lunch Sat.–Tues.*

Mokelumne Hill

7 miles south of Jackson.

At first glance you'd never guess that in its 1850s heyday Mokelumne Hill—pronounced *muh-KOHL-ah-mee,* though residents say Moke Hill)—was a whirlwind of mining activity. So rich were the veins of gold in the surrounding countryside that the town's population soared to 15,000. These days, fewer than 700 reside here, but the few-block historic district's galleries and shops and the Hotel Léger's saloon make Moke Hill worth a peek. On

Fridays and weekends, sip a free flight at nearby Renegade Winery's tasting room, which hosts live music some days.

GETTING HERE AND AROUND

Arrive by car on Highway 49. The historic area is walkable.

Hotels

Hotel Léger

$ | HOTEL | A rowdy gold-rush miners' haunt, this hotel anchoring Moke Hill's historic downtown contains rooms and suites decorated with a mishmash of Victorian antiques and utilitarian pieces. **Pros:** rich in history, including a 2013 "Hotel Impossible" makeover; individually decorated rooms; restaurant and 19th-century saloon. **Cons:** some rooms share a bathroom or bathroom is in hallway; rooms above the saloon can be noisy; some rooms feel cramped. *Rooms from: $110* *8304 Main St., Mokelumme Hill* *209/286–1401* *www.hotelleger.com* *14 rooms* *No meals.*

Angels Camp

20 miles south of Jackson.

Angels Camp is famous chiefly for its May jumping-frog contest, based on Mark Twain's short story "The Celebrated Jumping Frog of Calaveras County." The writer reputedly heard the story of the jumping frog from Ross Coon, proprietor of Angels Hotel, which opened in 1856. Sidewalk plaques downtown à la the Hollywood Walk of Fame celebrate the winning frogs in the continuing competition. Either training's gotten way better, or something else is in play—the 1929 victor jumped only 4 feet, but for the last three decades most of the leaps have been from 18- to 20-plus feet. In addition to the contests, Angels Camp's draws include its explorable subterranean caverns and river and lake fishing spots for salmon, trout, and bass.

GETTING HERE AND AROUND

Angels Camp is at the intersection of Highway 49 and Highway 4. You'll need a car to get here and around.

Sights

★ Angels Camp Museum

HISTORIC SITE | FAMILY | Learn a little bit about Mark Twain's "The Celebrated Jumping Frog of Calaveras County"—and Angels Camp's celebrated frog-jumping contests—at this museum's street-side facility, then head to the 3-acre spread behind it for a fascinating survey of gold rush–era mining history. The grounds include a carriage house with pre-automotive farming and passenger coaches and wagons and a large building with mining equipment. Outside, in its original mountings, stands the 27-foot-diameter water wheel that powered machinery at the area's Angels Quartz Mine. *753 S. Main St.* *209/736–2963* *angelscamp.gov/museum* *$15.*

★ Moaning Caverns Adventure Park

CAVE | FAMILY | For a different sort of underground jewel, wander into an ancient limestone cave, where stalactites and stalagmites, not gold and silver, await. Take the 235-step Spiral Tour down a staircase built in 1922 into the vast main cavern, or descend farther on the Expedition Tour caving adventure. Outside are ziplines and a climbing tower. *5350 Moaning Cave Rd., off Parrotts Ferry Rd./E18, Vallecito* *Take Hwy. 4 northeast from Angels Camp (7 miles) or south from Murphys (6 miles) and follow signs* *209/736–2708* *www.moaningcaverns.com* *Tours from $22, zipline $50* *Closed Tues. and Wed. (sometimes varies).*

Murphys

10 miles northeast of Angels Camp.

A well-preserved hamlet of white-picket fences and Victorian houses, compact Murphys has an upscale yet unpretentious vibe. Shops and restaurants line several blocks of Main Street, punctuated by wine-tasting rooms, some open only on Fridays and weekends much of the year. The Calaveras Wine Alliance's staff and volunteers excel at pairing wine lovers with the right winery, in some cases providing discount passes. Horatio Alger, Ulysses S. Grant, and other celebs passed through Murphys when they and other 19th-century tourists came to investigate the giant sequoia groves in nearby Calaveras Big Trees State Park.

GETTING HERE AND AROUND

Murphys is 10 miles northeast of Highway 49 on Highway 4. You'll need to drive here. Parking can be difficult on summer weekends.

CONTACTS Calaveras Wine Alliance. ✉ *202 Main St., at Big Trees Rd.* ☎ *209/728–9467* 🌐 *calaveraswines.org.*

Sights

★ Calaveras Big Trees State Park

NATIONAL/STATE PARK | FAMILY | The park protects hundreds of the largest and rarest living things on the planet—magnificent giant sequoia redwood trees. Some are 3,000 years old, 90 feet around at the base, and 250 feet tall. There are campgrounds, cabin rentals, and picnic areas; swimming, wading, fishing, and sunbathing on the Stanislaus River are popular in summer. Enjoy the "three senses" trail, designated for the blind, with interpretive signs in braille that guide visitors to touch the bark and encourage children to slow down and enjoy the forest in a more sensory way. ✉ *1170 E. Hwy. 4, Arnold* ✣ *15 miles northeast of Murphys, 4 miles northeast of Arnold* ☎ *209/795–2334* 🌐 *www.parks.ca.gov/calaverasbigtrees* 🎟 *$10 per vehicle.*

Ironstone Vineyards

WINERY/DISTILLERY | The spectacular, impeccably maintained gardens at 1,150-acre Ironstone—not to mention the 44-pound specimen of crystalline gold on display—make a visit here enjoyable even if you don't drink wine. The winery, known for Lodi and Sierra Foothills Merlot, Cabernet Sauvignon, Cabernet Franc, and old-vine Zinfandel, hosts concerts and other events. Its deli has picnic items. **■ TIP→ The history-oriented estate tour, conducted on Friday and Saturday, takes in the gardens and wine caverns.** ✉ *1894 6 Mile Rd.* ✣ *From Main St. in town, head south on Scott St.* ☎ *209/728–1251* 🌐 *www.ironstonevineyards.com* 🎟 *Tastings $6, estate tour (no tasting) $10* ⊗ *Closed Mon.–Wed. (but check).*

Mercer Caverns

CAVE | Light-hearted, well-informed guides lead 45-minute tours (208 steps down, 232 steps up) into caverns a prospector named Walter J. Mercer discovered in 1885. Millions of years in the making, the sheer, draperylike formations and aragonite crystals that resemble snowflakes enthrall visitors. **■ TIP→ Dress in layers (even in summer) and wear nonskid closed-toe shoes for this mildly strenuous adventure.** ✉ *1665 Sheep Ranch Rd.* ✣ *Head north 1¼ miles from 400 block of Main St.* ☎ *209/728–2101* 🌐 *mercercaverns.net* 🎟 *$19.*

Newsome Harlow Wines

WINERY/DISTILLERY | Single-vineyard Sierra Foothills Zinfandels are the passion of Newsome Harlow's owner-winemaker Scott Klann. The ebullient Klann also makes Petite Sirah, Syrah, Carignane, and the Meritage blend of Cabernet Sauvignon and other Bordeaux varietals—whites include a Sauvignon Blanc on several local restaurants' wine lists. The lively in-town tasting room benefits from its upbeat staff, playful atmosphere, and indoor and outdoor tasting spaces. ✉ *403 Main St.* ☎ *209/728–9817* 🌐 *nhvino.com* 🎫 *Tastings $15.*

Villa Vallecito Vineyards Tasting Room
WINERY/DISTILLERY | Winery CEO Ghee Sanchez-Hagedorn's first vineyard memories involve playing amid the Sonoma County grapevines that her migrant-farmer parents tended. After successful Silicon Valley careers, she and her husband began growing Calaveras grapes, later establishing Villa Vallecito, whose Syrah-Grenache Payaso blend often scores high in statewide competitions. The Barbera Reserve and Grenache are two other stars, with Chardonnay and Viognier among the whites. The downtown tasting room's Mexican style honors Sanchez-Hagedorn's heritage. **■ TIP→ Call or check the website about visiting the winery.** ✉ *263 Main St., Suite C* ☎ *209/890–3157* 🌐 *www.villavallecitovineyards.com* 🎫 *Tastings from $15* ⏲ *Closed Mon.–Thurs.*

★ Vina Moda
WINERY/DISTILLERY | The downtown tasting room of owner-winemaker Nathan Vader's boutique winery occupies a restored 1891 structure made of volcanic rock. Top Sierra Foothills vineyards supply grapes for his primarily reds lineup, led by best sellers Barbera and the Primitivo-based Phoenix blend. Grenache, Syrah, and Mourvèdre, alone or with each other, rank among the other stars, served inside or on the shaded rear patio. ✉ *147 Main St.* ☎ *209/743–6226* 🌐 *vinamoda.com* ⏲ *Closed Tues. and Wed. year-round, closed Mon. and Thurs. early fall–late spring.*

Restaurants

Alchemy Cafe
$$ | AMERICAN | A casual spot on the eastern edge of town, Alchemy serves sturdy comfort food like braised lamb shank over couscous, seared mahimahi, and meat loaf. Pork belly, fried calamari with roasted jalapeños, and mussels with crusty bread are among the starters that pair well with a bourbon rosemary sour specialty cocktail or an Alchemy Bloody Mary, hopped up with a splash of Firestone Pivo Pilsner. **Known for:** Calaveras County wines well represented; omelets, waffles, French toast for breakfast; mildly pricey but reliable. 💲 *Average main: $26* ✉ *191 Main St.* ☎ *209/728–0700* 🌐 *alchemymurphys.com* ⏲ *Closed Tues. and Wed. No lunch Thurs. and Mon. (but check).*

Aria Bakery & Espresso Cafe
$ | BAKERY | For a place as small as it is, this bakery-café produces a staggering array of sweet and savory pastries, sandwiches, salads, and desserts you can enjoy with a well-brewed (if not always swiftly made) coffee, espresso drink, or tea. The croissants are golden and flaky, the quiches moist and filling, and the scones large and flavorful; the breads for lunchtime sandwiches include sourdough, focaccia, and polenta wheat. **Known for:** limited seating inside and out; blueberry muffins, savory croissants, and other baked goods; vegetarian, vegan, gluten-free options. 💲 *Average main: $12* ✉ *458 Main St., Suite B* ☎ *209/728–9250* ⏲ *Closed Mon.–Wed. (but check). No dinner.*

★ Grounds
$$ | AMERICAN | From potato pancakes for breakfast to grilled rib eye for dinner, this bustling bistro with a series of wainscoted rooms and an outdoor back patio has something for all palates. Lighter grilled vegetables, chicken, sandwiches, salads, and homemade soups always shine here, as does heartier fare that might include elk medallions and prawns, forager-mushroom risotto, and cioppino with a relatively delicate yet full-flavored broth. **Known for:** full bar; wines by local producers; attentive service. 💲 *Average main: $26* ✉ *402 Main St.* ☎ *209/728–8663* 🌐 *www.groundsrestaurant.com* ⏲ *Closed Mon. and Tues. No dinner Sun.*

★ JoMa's Artisan Ice Cream

$ | **AMERICAN** | The smell of waffle cones will direct you to this town treasure whose Portuguese-Swiss namesake has been making ice cream since she was a young lass. Handcrafted flavors include Chill'n Cherry Chip (cherries and dark chocolate) and Wake Up Murphys (coffee, cocoa, and fudge). **Known for:** fruity sorbets; cookies and ice-cream cakes; vegan and gluten-free flavors. *Average main: $7 ✉ 386 Main St. ☎ 209/728–8655 🌐 www.jomasicecream.com.*

Rob's Place

$$ | **AMERICAN** | Comfort food crafted with care and served by solicitous staffers makes a trip to this low-slung restaurant on downtown's edge a pleasure whether you dine inside on linen-topped tables or the dog-friendly street-facing patio. Several burgers, one vegetarian, another named for a local winemaker, entice the regulars, but don't overlook dinner entrées that might include shrimp curry, lamb and grits, or grilled Indian-spice tofu with pistachios and Sriracha. **Known for:** clever appetizers; only local wines; plentiful vegetarian, vegan, and gluten-free options. *Average main: $23 ✉ 140 Main St. ☎ 209/813–7003 🌐 robsplacerestaurant.com ⏲ Closed Tues. and Wed.*

Hotels

★ Dunbar House Inn

$$ | **B&B/INN** | The oversize rooms in this elaborate Italianate-style home have brass beds, down comforters, gas-burning stoves, and claw-foot tubs. **Pros:** great breakfasts; colorful gardens; accommodating staff. **Cons:** expensive in-season; not kid-friendly; minimum-stay requirement on weekends and some holidays. *Rooms from: $196 ✉ 271 Jones St. ☎ 209/728–2897 🌐 www.dunbarhouse.com ⇨ 6 rooms 🍴 Free breakfast.*

Murphys Inn Motel

$ | **HOTEL** | Reasonably well run if steadfastly nondescript, this two-story motel built in the late 1990s has three things going for it: a convenient location on the edge of downtown, a pool for hot Gold Country days, and bargain rates most of the year. **Pros:** clean rooms; bargain rates; convenient location. **Cons:** thin walls; some road noise; lacks style and big-hotel amenities. *Rooms from: $89 ✉ 76 Main St. ☎ 209/728–1818, 888/796–1800 reservations 🌐 www.murphysinnmotel.com ⇨ 37 rooms 🍴 No meals.*

The Victoria Inn

$$ | **B&B/INN** | Decorated with contemporary furnishings with 19th-century accents, this inn, whose owners also manage 10 area vacation rentals, benefits from a prime Main Street location within walking distance of restaurants, shops, and wine-tasting rooms. **Pros:** convenient location; romantic feel; four spacious rooms with king beds. **Cons:** no TVs in rooms; minimum weekend-stay requirement; noise issues in some rooms. *Rooms from: $161 ✉ 420 Main St. ☎ 209/728–8933 🌐 www.victoriainn-murphys.com ⇨ 13 rooms 🍴 No meals.*

Columbia

14 miles south of Angels Camp.

Columbia is the gateway for Columbia State Historic Park, one of the Gold Country's most visited sites. It's a great place for families to participate in living-history activities, like candle dipping and soap making on weekends. There are several inviting spots for a picnic in the area.

GETTING HERE AND AROUND

The only way to get here is by car, via either Highway 4 (the northern route) or Highway 49 (the southern) from Angels Camp.

Sights

★ Columbia State Historic Park

NATIONAL/STATE PARK | FAMILY | Columbia, whose mines yielded $87 million in gold, is both a functioning community and a historically preserved town. Usually you can ride a stagecoach, pan for gold, and watch a blacksmith working at an anvil. Street musicians perform in summer. Restored or reconstructed buildings include a Wells Fargo Express office, a Masonic temple, an old-fashioned candy store, saloons, a firehouse, churches, a school, and a newspaper office. At times, all are staffed to simulate a working 1850s town. Also in the park is the **Fallon House Theater,** a gorgeous Victorian structure that sometimes hosts plays and live music. The town's two reasonably priced, historic lodgings, the Fallon Hotel and City Hotel, perch you in the past; reserve a room or cottage at *www.reserve-california.com.* ✉ *11255 Jackson St.* ☎ *209/588–9128* *www.parks.ca.gov/columbia* *Free.*

Restaurants

Diamondback Grill and Wine Bar

$ | AMERICAN | The bright decor and refined atmosphere suggest more ambitious fare, but massive half-pound burgers and sandwiches like the Ultimate Grilled Cheese with smoked bacon and tomato between three thick slices of sourdough bread are what this place inside a late-19th-century stone-walled building is about. Locals crowd the tables, especially after 6 pm, for the ground-meat patties, beer-battered onion rings, veggie burgers, and fine wines. **Known for:** garlic fries; wine bar and wine club; homemade desserts. *Average main: $14* ✉ *93 S. Washington St., Sonora* ☎ *209/532–6661* *diamondback-grillsonora.com.*

Activities

Zephyr Whitewater Expeditions

WHITE-WATER RAFTING | Challenging rapids and awe-inspiring scenery make white-water rafting trips along the Tuolumne River near Yosemite National Park among California's most popular runs. This well-regarded outfit conducts trips here and on a few other Gold Country rivers. Prices start at $109 for a half day. ✉ *Headquarters (trips leave from elsewhere), 22517 Parrotts Ferry Rd.* ☎ *209/532–6249, 800/431–3636* *zrafting.com.*

Jamestown

7 miles south of Columbia.

Jamestown supplies a touristy view of life during the two gold rushes in these parts. The first took place in the 1850s, the second in the 1880s. Shops in brightly colored buildings along Main Street sell antiques and gift items. You can try your hand at panning for gold in Jamestown or explore a bit of railroad history.

GETTING HERE AND AROUND

Jamestown lies at the intersection of north–south Highway 49 and east–west Highway 108. You'll need a car to tour.

Sights

Gold Prospecting Adventures

TOUR—SIGHT | FAMILY | You'll get a real feel (sort of) for the life of a prospector on the three-hour gold-panning excursions (reservations recommended) led by this outfit's congenial tour guides. You might even strike gold at the Jimtown Mine. Even if you're not panning, it's fun to look at the gold-rush artifacts on display here. ✉ *18170 Main St.* ☎ *209/984–4653* *www.goldprospecting.com* *Call for prices.*

★ Railtown 1897 State Historic Park

NATIONAL/STATE PARK | FAMILY | A must for rail enthusiasts and families with kids, this is one of the most intact early roundhouses (maintenance facilities) in North America. You can hop aboard a steam train for a 40-minute journey—bring along the family dog if you'd like. The docents entertain guests with tales about the history of locomotion. Listen to the original rotor and pulleys in the engine house and take in the smell of axle grease. Walk through a genteel passenger car with dusty-green velvet seats and ornate metalwork, where Grace Kelly and Gary Cooper filmed a scene in *High Noon*. **TIP→ When offered, Polar Express excursions at Christmastime sell out quickly.** *18115 5th Ave.* *209/984–3953* *www.railtown1897.org* *Park $5, rides from $15 (includes park fee).*

Restaurants

Service Station

$$ | AMERICAN | Exposed brick walls and a pressed-metal ceiling lend an air of nostalgia that's heightened by this restaurant's theme, the golden age of road trips and automobile service stations. Half-pounder burgers and pulled-pork, tri-tip, and other sandwiches and wraps count among the menu's highlights, along with small plates like nacho fries and fried calamari and entrées that might include chicken, grilled salmon, or steak. **Known for:** outdoor beer garden; local wines, craft beers on tap; salads and vegetarian wraps and burgers for noncarnivores. *Average main: $21* *18242 Main St.* *209/782–5122* *jamestownservicestation.com.*

Hotels

1859 Historic National Hotel

$$ | B&B/INN | In business since 1859, the National has survived the gold rush, gambling, prostitution, at least two fires, a ghost named Flo, and Prohibition, and stands today a well-maintained property with all the authentic character and charm its storied past suggests. **Pros:** authentic character—feels straight out of a Western movie; views from odd-numbered rooms (plus Room 2); popular restaurant (good brunches). **Cons:** some rooms are small; most even-numbered rooms have no view; some noise issues. *Rooms from: $180* *18183 Main St.* *209/984–3446* *www.national-hotel.com* *9 rooms* *Free breakfast.*

Jamestown Hotel

$ | HOTEL | The spacious, light-filled rooms above this century-old hotel's saloon and restaurant are decorated simply but with flair, and all have updated bathrooms with a period feel. **Pros:** convenient to shops, restaurants, and tasting rooms; balcony overlooking Main Street; on-site dining. **Cons:** rooms lack refrigerators, microwaves, TVs, and other amenities; noise from restaurant and saloon bleeds through in some rooms; no elevator. *Rooms from: $140* *18153 Main St.* *209/984–3902* *www.thejamestownhotel.com* *8 rooms* *No meals.*

Chapter 17

LAKE TAHOE

WITH RENO, NEVADA

Updated by
Cheryl Crabtree

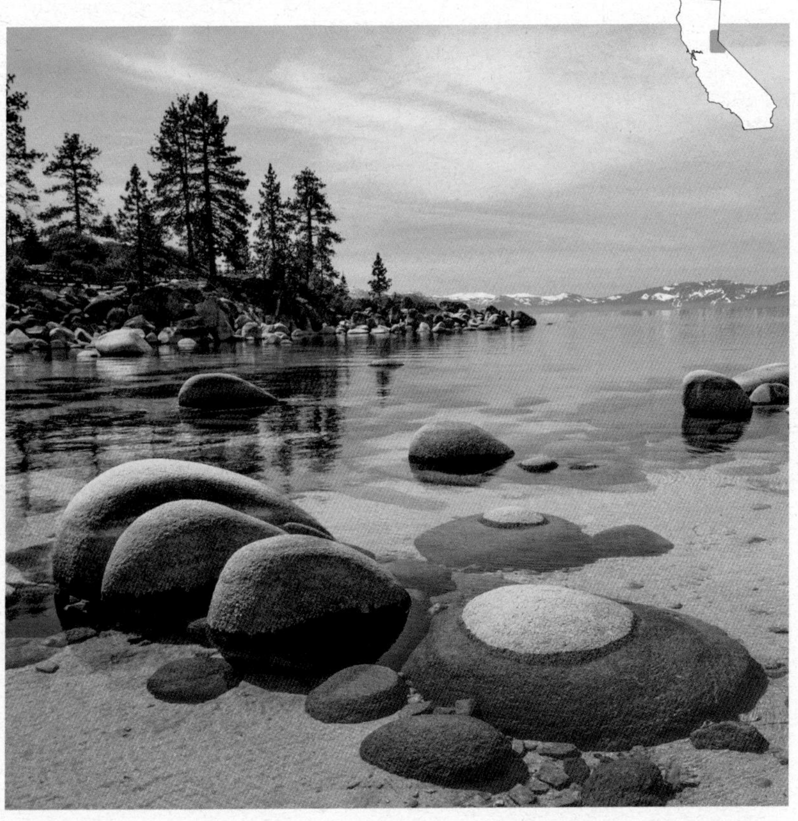

Sights	Restaurants	Hotels	Shopping	Nightlife
★★★★★	★★★★☆	★★★★★	★☆☆☆☆	★☆☆☆☆

WELCOME TO LAKE TAHOE

TOP REASONS TO GO

★ **The lake:** Blue, deep, and alpine pure, Lake Tahoe is far and away the main reason to visit this High Sierra paradise.

★ **Skiing:** Daring black-diamond runs or baby-bunny bumps—whether you're an expert, a beginner, or somewhere in between, the numerous Tahoe-area ski parks abound with slopes to suit your skills.

★ **The great outdoors:** A ring of national forests and recreation areas linked by miles of trails makes Tahoe excellent for nature lovers.

★ **Dinner with a view:** You can picnic lakeside at state parks or dine in restaurants perched along the shore.

★ **A date with lady luck:** Whether you want to roll dice, play the slots, or hope the blackjack dealer goes bust before you do, you'll find round-the-clock gambling at the casinos on the Nevada side of the lake and in Reno.

1 **South Lake Tahoe.** This small city is a gateway to nature: swoosh down slopes at Heavenly Mountain, hike or bike scenic trails, or embark on a lake cruise.

2 **Pope-Baldwin Recreation Area.** Protected forests and several of the west shore's best beaches line the shores here.

3 **Emerald Bay State Park.** Named for the glistening green waters in its shallow, emerald-shaped cove, this state park is a favorite spot to recreate.

4 **D.L. Bliss State Park.** Hike the Rubicon Trail along 6 miles of shoreline to access white-sand beaches and spectacular views.

5 **Ed Z'berg Sugar Pine Point State Park.** Lake Tahoe's largest state park encompasses dense forests and nearly 2 miles of shoreline.

6 **Tahoma.** This serene lakeshore village reflects early Lake Tahoe, where rustic cottages housed vacationers who sought refuge from urban commotion.

7 **Tahoe City.** The Truckee River begins its journey to Nevada in this small town, a convenient place to shop and dine.

8 **Olympic Valley.** The area that hosted the 1960 Winter Olympics is now the north shore's year-round recreation center.

9 **Truckee.** This Old West city is a trendy town with a historic depot.

10 **Carnelian Bay to Kings Beach.** Many north shore amenities and services line this scenic stretch.

11 **Incline Village.** The draws of this ritzy Nevada-side community include Mount Rose and Diamond Peak in winter and beaches and lush hillsides in summer.

12 **Zephyr Cove.** This tiny Nevada resort occupies a secluded spot edging the eastern shore.

13 **Stateline.** Towering casinos and 24/7 action give this small city a border-town feel.

14 **Reno.** This busy city has the Tahoe region's main airport and a revitalized downtown.

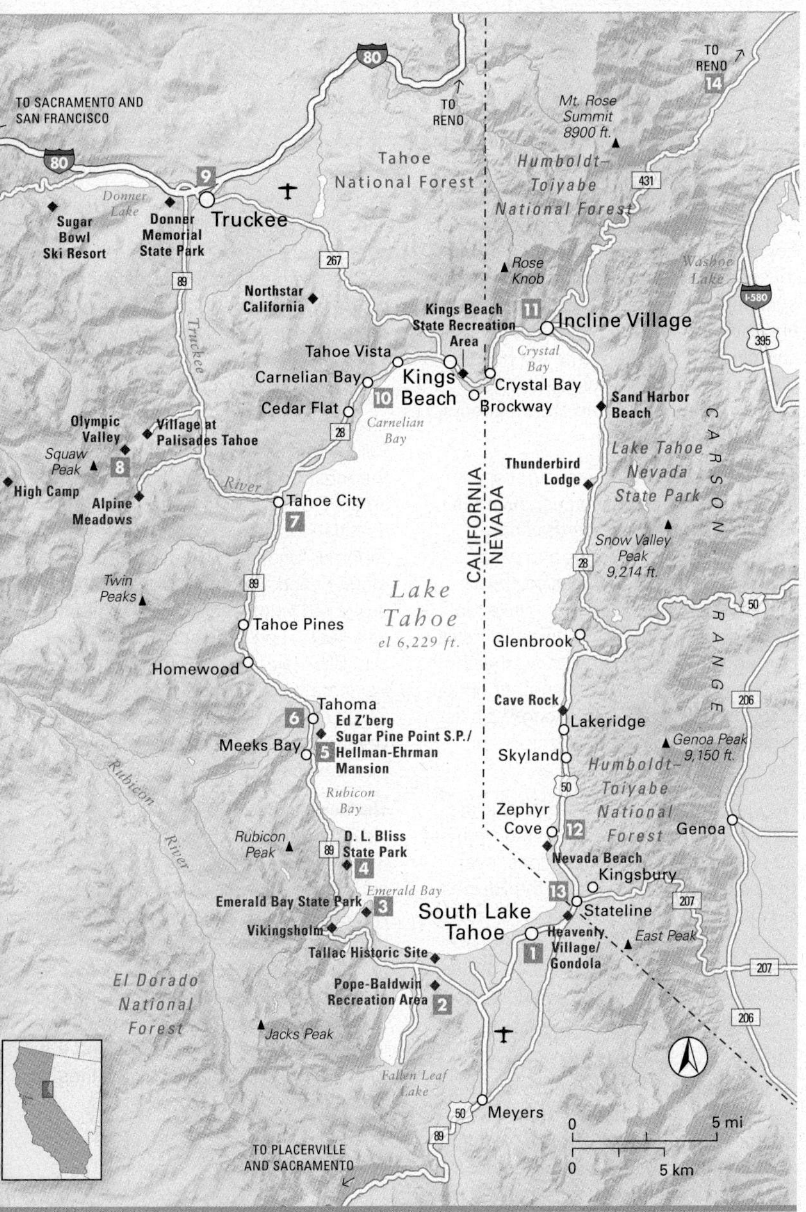
TO SACRAMENTO AND
SAN FRANCISCO
80
TO
RENO
TO
RENO
14
Mt. Rose
Summit
8900 ft.
Tahoe
National Forest
Humboldt–
Toiyabe
National Forest
431
9
Truckee
Donner
Lake
Sugar
Bowl
Ski Resort
Donner
Memorial
State Park
267
89
Rose
Knob
Washoe
Lake
I-580
395
Northstar
California
Kings Beach
State Recreation
Area
11
Incline Village
Crystal
Bay
Tahoe Vista
Carnelian Bay
Kings
Beach
10
Crystal Bay
Brockway
Cedar Flat
Sand Harbor
Beach
Carnelian
Bay
28
Olympic
Valley
Village at
Palisades Tahoe
Squaw
Peak
8
High Camp
Alpine
Meadows
River
Truckee
Tahoe City
7
Thunderbird
Lodge
Lake Tahoe
Nevada
State Park
CARSON
RANGE
CALIFORNIA
NEVADA
Snow Valley
Peak
9,214 ft.
28
Twin
Peaks
89
Lake
Tahoe
el 6,229 ft.
50
Tahoe Pines
Glenbrook
Homewood
Tahoma
6
Ed Z'berg
Sugar Pine Point S.P./
Hellman-Ehrman
Mansion
5
Meeks Bay
Cave Rock
Lakeridge
206
Genoa Peak
9,150 ft.
Skyland
Humboldt–
Toiyabe
National
Forest
50
Rubicon
Bay
Rubicon
River
Zephyr
Cove
12
Genoa
Rubicon
Peak
89
D. L. Bliss
State Park
4
Nevada Beach
Kingsbury
13
Stateline
207
Emerald Bay
Emerald Bay State Park
3
South Lake
Tahoe
Vikingsholm
Heavenly
Village/
Gondola
1
East Peak
Tallac Historic Site
207
El Dorado
National
Forest
Pope-Baldwin
Recreation Area
2
206
Jacks Peak
Fallen Leaf
Lake
Meyers
50
89
0
5 mi
0
5 km
TO PLACERVILLE
AND SACRAMENTO

Whether you swim, fish, sail, or simply rest on its shores, you'll be wowed by the overwhelming beauty of Lake Tahoe, which is famous for its cobalt-blue water and surrounding snowcapped peaks.

One of the world's largest, clearest, and deepest alpine lakes straddles the border of California and Nevada, giving this popular Sierra Nevada resort region a split personality. About half of its visitors are intent on low-key sightseeing, hiking, camping, and boating; the rest head directly to the Nevada side, lured by bargain dining, big-name entertainment, and glittering casinos.

To explore the lake area and get a feel for its differing communities, drive the 72-mile road that follows the shore through wooded flatlands and past beaches, climbing to vistas on the rugged southwest side of the lake, and passing through busy commercial developments and casinos on its northeastern and southeastern edges. Another option is to travel *on* the 22-mile-long, 12-mile-wide lake via a sightseeing cruise or kayaking trip.

Note, however, that in fall of 2021, the Caldor Fire burned its way along Highway 50 on the western Sierra slopes, over the peaks, and eastward to the Nevada border, coming dangerously close to the lake's southwestern shore. South Lake Tahoe was spared, but evidence of the fire is visible for miles as you drive along Highways 50 and 89.

Although the lake and the region's protected tracts of wilderness are the main draws, other nearby destinations are gaining popularity. Truckee, with an Old West feel and innovative restaurants, entices visitors looking for a relaxed pace and easy access to Tahoe's north shore and Olympic Valley ski parks. And Reno, once known only for its casinos, attracts tourists with its buzzing arts scene, downtown riverfront, and campus events at the University of Nevada.

MAJOR REGIONS

The California Side. The most hotels, restaurants, and ski resorts are on the California side, but you'll also encounter the most congestion and developed areas. From south to north, lakeshore destinations include South Lake Tahoe, Tahoma, Tahoe City, Carnelian Bay, and Kings Beach. Also near the shore are protected lands such as the Pope-Baldwin Recreation Area and Emerald Bay, D.L. Bliss, and Ed Z'berg Sugar Pine Point state parks. West and north of the lake, Olympic Valley beckons with its year-round recreation opportunities, and Truckee charms with its Old West feel.

The Nevada Side. Top stops along the Nevada-side's southern shore include Stateline and its casinos, Zephyr Cove, and Nevada Beach. To the north are Lake Tahoe–Nevada State Park and Sand Harbor Beach as well as the resort area of Incline Village. From there, it's just a short drive northeast to Reno, a long-time gambling town whose revitalized downtown includes interesting museums and the Riverwalk District of shops, galleries, and restaurants.

Planning

When to Go

Christmas week and July 4th are the busiest times, and prices go through the roof, so plan accordingly. If you don't ski, the best times to visit are early fall and late spring. The crowds thin, prices dip, and you can count on Lake Tahoe being beautiful.

In summer, it's crisper and cooler here than in the scorched Sierra Nevada foothills, and the lake's surface temperature is an invigorating 65°F to 70°F (compared with 40°F to 50°F in winter). That said, summer is when visitors—100,000 on peak weekends—clog the lake, its lodgings, and area roads, especially Highway 89 just south of Tahoe City, Highway 28 east of Tahoe City, and U.S. 50 in South Lake Tahoe.

Most Lake Tahoe accommodations, restaurants, and even a handful of parks are open year-round, but many visitor centers, mansions, state parks, and beaches are closed from October through May. During these months, winter-sports enthusiasts pack Tahoe's many downhill resorts and cross-country centers. Note, though, that storms often close roads and force chain requirements on the interstate.

Getting Here and Around

AIR

The nearest airport is Reno–Tahoe International Airport (RNO), in Reno, 50 miles northeast of the closest point on the lake. Airlines serving RNO include Alaska, Allegiant, American, Delta, Frontier, JetBlue, JSX, Southwest, United, and Volaris. Except for Allegiant, these airlines plus Aeromexico, Air Canada, Boutique Air, Contour Airlines, Horizon, Hawaiian, Spirit, and Sun Country serve Sacramento International Airport (SMF), 112 miles from South Lake Tahoe. North Lake Tahoe Express runs buses ($49 each way) between RNO and towns on the western and northern shores, plus Incline Village, Truckee, Palisades Tahoe, and Northstar. South Tahoe Airporter runs buses ($32.75 one-way, $59 round-trip) between Reno–Tahoe Airport and resort hotels in the South Lake Tahoe area.

AIRPORT CONTACTS Reno Tahoe International Airport. (*RNO*) ✉ *2001 E. Plumb La., off U.S. 395/I–580, Reno* ☎ *775/328–6400* 🌐 *www.renoairport.com.* **Sacramento International Airport.** (*SMF*) ✉ *6900 Airport Blvd., Sacramento* ✥ *Off I–5, 12 miles northwest of downtown* ☎ *916/929–5411* 🌐 *www.sacramento.aero/smf.*

TRANSFER CONTACTS North Lake Tahoe Express. ☎ *833/709–8080* 🌐 *www.northlaketahoeexpress.com.* **South Tahoe Airporter.** ☎ *775/325–8944* 🌐 *southtahoeairporter.com.*

BUS

Greyhound stops in San Francisco, Sacramento, Truckee, and Reno. Tahoe Transportation District ($2 per ride) provides year-round local service in South Lake Tahoe, Stateline, and along the eastern shore to Sand Harbor. On the north shore, Tahoe Area Regional Transit (TART; $1.75) operates buses between Tahoma and Incline Village and runs shuttles to Truckee. RTC RIDE buses ($2) serve the Reno area. All local rides require exact change.

In winter, Tahoe Transportation District provides free ski-shuttle service from South Lake Tahoe hotels and resorts to various Heavenly Mountain ski lodge locations. Most of the major ski resorts offer shuttle service to nearby lodging.

BUS CONTACTS RTC RIDE. ☎ *775/348–7433* 🌐 *www.rtcwashoe.com.* **Tahoe Transportation District.** ☎ *775/ 589–5500, 530/541–7149* 🌐 *www.tahoetransportation.org.* **Tahoe Truckee Area**

Regional Transit (TART). ☎ *530/550–1212, 800/736–6365* 🌐 *tahoetruckeetransit.com/contact-us.*

CAR

Lake Tahoe is 198 miles northeast of San Francisco, a drive of less than four hours in good weather and light traffic—if possible avoid heavy weekend traffic, particularly leaving the San Francisco area for Tahoe on Friday afternoon and returning on Sunday afternoon. The major route is I–80, a four-lane freeway that cuts through the Sierra Nevada about 14 miles north of the lake. From there Highway 89 and Highway 267 reach the west and north shores, respectively.

U.S. 50, much of which is only two lanes with no center divider, is the more direct route to the south shore, a two-hour drive from Sacramento. From Reno you can get to the north shore by heading south on U.S. 395/I–580 for 10 miles, then west on Highway 431 for 25 miles. For the south shore, head south on U.S. 395/I–580 through Carson City, and then turn west on U.S. 50 (56 miles total).

The scenic 72-mile route around the lake is marked Highway 89 (southwest and west shores), Highway 28 (north and northeast shores), and U.S. 50 (east and southeast shores). During snowy periods, occasional closures along Highway 89 (usually at Emerald Bay because of avalanche danger) make it impossible to complete the lake loop. Interstate 80, U.S. 50, and U.S. 395/I–580 are all-weather highways, but expect snow-removal delays during major storms. Carry tire chains from October through May, though, if you're renting a car, check that the rental agency allows their use. If not, rent a four-wheel-drive vehicle.

TRAIN

Amtrak's cross-country rail service makes stops in Truckee and Reno. Amtrak also operates several buses daily between Reno and Sacramento to connect with coastal train routes.

Restaurants

On weekends and in high season, expect long waits at popular restaurants—and higher prices almost everywhere. In the April–May and September–November "shoulder seasons," some places close or limit their hours, but local papers and websites often feature deals, such as two-for-one coupons.

To attract gamblers, casino marquees often tout "$9.99 prime rib dinners" or "$5.99 breakfast specials." Some of these meals are downright lousy, and they're usually available only in coffee shops or at buffets. The higher prices at finer casino restaurants are offset by reasonable service and a bit of atmosphere. Unless otherwise noted, even the most expensive area restaurants welcome customers in casual clothes.

Hotels

Waterfront inns, slope-side slodges, suburban-style motels, casino hotels, and house and condo rentals constitute Tahoe's lodging choices. In summer and during ski season, reserve as far ahead as possible, especially for holiday periods when prices skyrocket. Spring and fall offer more leeway and lower rates, especially at casinos.

Head to South Lake Tahoe for the most activities and the widest range of lodging options. Heavenly Village, in the heart of town, has an ice rink, cinema, shops, cafés, fine-dining restaurants, and a gondola that will whisk you up to the ski park. Walk two blocks south from downtown, and you can hit the casinos.

Tahoe City, on the west shore, has a small-town atmosphere and is accessible to several ski resorts. A few miles northwest of the lake, Palisades Tahoe has its own self-contained village, an aerial tram to the slopes, and year-round outdoor activities.

Looking for a taste of Old Tahoe? The north shore is your best bet, with Carnelian Bay and Tahoe Vista on the California side. Across the border in Nevada you'll find casino resorts where Hollywood stars once romped.

Restaurant and hotel reviews have been shortened. For full information, visit Fodors.com. Restaurant prices are the average cost of a main course at dinner, or if dinner is not served, at lunch. Hotel prices are the lowest cost of a standard double room in high season.

What It Costs

$	$$	$$$	$$$$
RESTAURANTS			
under $17	$17–$26	$27–$36	over $36
HOTELS			
under $150	$150–$250	$251–$350	over $350

Tours

★ Cruise Tahoe

BOAT TOURS | The captain of the *Tahoe*, a classic wooden boat, takes passengers on an east shore cruise whose highlights are a walking tour and picnic lunch at the Thunderbird Lodge, a historic mansion. A tour of Emerald Bay and Vikingsholm Castle (Sun.–Wed., late May–Sept.) is also available. ✉ *Departures from Zephyr Cove Pier, 760 U.S. 50, Zephyr Cove* ☎ *775/230–8907* 🌐 *www.cruisetahoe.com/public-cruises* 🎫 *$169 Thunderbird Lodge Cruise, $135 Emerald Bay Cruise.*

Lake Tahoe Balloons

AIR EXCURSIONS | Take a hot-air balloon flight over the lake from mid-May through mid-October with this company that launches and lands its balloons on a boat. The four-hour excursion (the flight is 45–60 minutes) begins shortly after sunrise and ends with a traditional champagne toast. ✉ *Tahoe Keys Marina, 2435 Venice Dr. E, South Lake Tahoe* ✣ *Tahoe Keys Blvd. off Lake Tahoe Blvd.* ☎ *530/544–1221, 800/872–9294* 🌐 *www.laketahoeballoons.com* 🎫 *From $325.*

MS *Dixie II*

BOAT TOURS | The 520-passenger MS *Dixie II*, a stern-wheeler, sails year-round from Zephyr Cove to Emerald Bay on sightseeing and dinner cruises. ✉ *Zephyr Cove Marina, 760 U.S. Hwy. 50, near Church St., Zephyr Cove* ☎ *800/238–2463* 🌐 *www.zephyrcove.com/cruises* 🎫 *From $68.*

North Lake Tahoe Ale Trail

SELF-GUIDED | Bike or walk one of North Lake Tahoe's dozens of trails, then reward yourself with a craft brew at an alehouse near the end of your chosen route. The largest concentration of beer stops is around Incline Village, but you'll find places to stop for a pint from Tahoma to Zephyr Cove. A dedicated website has an interactive map, descriptions, and short videos pairing trails and drinking spots. There are also suggestions for paddleboarders and kayakers. 🌐 *www.gotahoenorth.com/lake-tahoe-activities/north-lake-tahoe-ale-trail.*

Sierra Cloud

BOAT TOURS | The *Sierra Cloud*, a 41-passenger catamaran, departs from the Hyatt Regency beach at Incline Village and cruises the north and east shore areas for two hours. ✉ *Hyatt Regency Lake Tahoe, 111 Country Club Dr., Incline Village* ☎ *775/831–4386* 🌐 *www.awsincline.com* 🎫 *From $100* ⏲ *Closed Oct.–Apr.*

South Tahoe Beer Trail

SELF-GUIDED | Download a handy map to find your way to nearly a dozen craft breweries along Lake Tahoe's south shore, from Tahoe Keys to Stateline. 🌐 *tahoesouth.com/beer-trail.*

Tahoe Gal

BOAT TOURS | Docked in Tahoe City this old-style 120-passenger paddle wheeler departs—daily from June through September and some days in May—on brunch, lunch, happy-hour, and sunset tours of Emerald Bay and Lake Tahoe's north and west shores. Specialty excursions feature live music or other entertainment. ✉ *Departures from Lighthouse Center, 952 N. Lake Blvd., Tahoe City* ☎ *800/218–2464* 🌐 *www.tahoegal.com* 🎫 *From $42.*

Tahoe Cruises *Safari Rose*
BOAT TOURS | This outfit operates year-round cruises on the *Safari Rose*, an 80-foot, wooden motor yacht. Options between mid-May and mid-October include barbecue-lunch, happy-hour, sunset, and champagne cruises. Shuttle-bus pickup service is available. ✉ *Ski Run Marina, 900 Ski Run Blvd., South Lake Tahoe* ☎ *775/588–1881* 🌐 *www.tahoecruises.com* 🎫 *From $90.*

★ **Tahoe Tastings**
BOAT TOURS | Taste eight Northern California wines aboard the *Golden Rose*, a 1953 Chris-Craft Venetian Water Taxi, on two-hour cruises from Tahoe Keys to Emerald Bay and back. Charcuterie boards are available for purchase with advance reservation, or you can bring your own snacks along. Tours depart midday, later in the afternoon, and at sunset. ✉ *2435 Venice Dr., South Lake Tahoe* ✣ *Rubicon Dock, Tahoe Keys Marina* ☎ *530/494–9222* 🌐 *www.tahoetastings.com* 🎫 *From $65.*

Visitor Information

CONTACTS Go Tahoe North. ☎ *530/581–6900* 🌐 *www.gotahoenorth.com.* **Tahoe South.** ☎ *775/542–4637 California, 800/588–4591 Nevada* 🌐 *tahoesouth.com.*

South Lake Tahoe

60 miles south of Reno, 198 miles northeast of San Francisco.

The city of South Lake Tahoe's raison d'être is tourism: the casinos of adjacent Stateline, Nevada; the ski slopes at Heavenly Mountain; the beaches, docks, bike trails, and campgrounds all around the south shore; and the backcountry of Eldorado National Forest and Desolation Wilderness. The small city's main attributes are its convenient location, bevy of services, and gorgeous lake views.

GETTING HERE AND AROUND

The main route into and through South Lake Tahoe is U.S. 50; signs say "Lake Tahoe Boulevard" in town. Arrive by car or, if coming from Reno airport, take the South Tahoe Express bus. Tahoe Transportation District operates daily bus service in the south shore area year-round.

ESSENTIALS

VISITOR INFORMATION Visit Lake Tahoe South. ✉ *Visitor Center, 169 U.S. Hwy. 50, at Kingsbury Grade, Stateline* ☎ *775/588–4591* 🌐 *tahoesouth.com* ✉ *Visitor Center, 4114 Lake Tahoe Blvd.* ☎ *530/542–4637* 🌐 *tahoesouth.com.*

Sights

★ **Heavenly Gondola**
VIEWPOINT | **FAMILY** | Whether you ski or not, you'll appreciate the impressive view of Lake Tahoe from the Heavenly Gondola. Its eight-passenger cars travel from Heavenly Village 2.4 miles up the mountain in 15 minutes. When the weather's fine, you can take one of three hikes around the mountaintop and then have lunch at Tamarack Lodge. ✉ *4080 Lake Tahoe Blvd.* ☎ *775/586–7000, 800/432–8365* 🌐 *www.skiheavenly.com* 🎫 *$61.*

Skiing and Snowboarding

The mountains around Lake Tahoe are bombarded by blizzards throughout the winter, and, sometimes, in the fall and spring, as well. Indeed, the Sierras often have the continent's deepest snowpack (10- to 12-foot bases are common), though it can be very heavy and wet owing to relatively mild temperatures over the Pacific. The upside is that you can sometimes ski (either downhill or cross-country) and snowboard (allowed at all Tahoe ski areas) as late as May. Check conditions at OntheSnow.com, or get the inside scoop by talking to waiters and bartenders, many of whom are ski bums.

On weekends, avoid moving with the masses by arriving early and quitting early, with a lunch break at 11 am or 1:30 pm rather than noon. Also consider skiing at areas with few high-speed lifts or limited lodging and real estate at their bases, namely Sugar Bowl, Homewood, Mt. Rose, Sierra-at-Tahoe, Diamond Peak, and Kirkwood.

Cross-country skiing at resorts can be costly, but you get the benefits of machine grooming and trail preparation. If it's bargain Nordic you're after, take advantage of thousands of acres of public forest and parkland trails.

Heavenly Village

STORE/MALL | This lively complex at the base of the Heavenly Gondola has good shopping, an arcade for kids, a cinema, a brewpub, a skating rink in winter, miniature golf in summer, and the Loft for magic shows and other live entertainment. Base Camp Pizza Co., Azul Latin Kitchen, and Kalani's for seafood stand out among the several restaurants. ✉ *1001 Heavenly Village Way, at U.S. 50* 🌐 *www.theshopsatheavenly.com.*

Restaurants

Artemis Lakefront Cafe

$$ | **MEDITERRANEAN** | A festive marina restaurant with a heated outdoor patio, Artemis reveals its Greek influences in breakfast dishes like baklava French toast and gyros and egg pita wraps. All day, though, the menus encompass more familiar options (eggs Benedict in the morning, burgers and grilled mahimahi later on). **Known for:** heated outdoor patio; outgoing staff; marina location. *Average main: $21* ✉ *900 Ski Run Blvd.* ☎ *530/542–3332* 🌐 *www.artemislakefrontcafe.com.*

★ Evan's American Gourmet Cafe

$$$$ | **ECLECTIC** | Its excellent service, world-class cuisine, and superb wine list make this intimate restaurant the top choice for high-end dining in South Lake. Inside a converted cabin, Evan's serves creative American cuisine that might include pan-seared day boat scallops and meat dishes such as rack of lamb marinated with rosemary and garlic and served with raspberry demi-glace. **Known for:** intimate atmosphere; world-class cuisine; superb wine list. *Average main: $38* ✉ *536 Emerald Bay Rd., Hwy. 89, at 15th St.* ☎ *530/542–1990* 🌐 *evanstahoe.com* ⏲ *No lunch. Closed Sun. and Mon.*

Kalani's at Lake Tahoe

$$$$ | **ASIAN** | The white-tablecloth dining room at Heavenly's sleekest (and priciest) restaurant is decked out with carved bamboo, a burnt-orange color palette, and a modern-glass sculpture, all of which complement Pacific Rim–influenced dishes like fillet of beef with miso-garlic butter and the signature Chilean sea bass with Thai-basil mash, wilted balsamic greens, and ponzu butter sauce. Sushi selections with inventive rolls and sashimi combos, plus less expensive vegetarian dishes, add depth to the menu. **Known for:** fresh-off-the-plane Hawaiian seafood; thoughtful wine selections; upscale setting. $ *Average main: $38 ✉ 1001 Heavenly Village Way, #26, at U.S. 50 ☎ 530/544–6100 🌐 www.kalanis.com.*

My Thai Cuisine

$ | **THAI** | Fantastic flavors and gracious owners have earned this humble roadside restaurant with river-stone columns, pine-paneled walls and ceilings, Thai statues and ornamentation the loyalty of Tahoe residents and regular visitors. The aromatic dishes include crab pad Thai, basil lamb, sizzling shrimp, and numerous curries. **Known for:** many vegetarian options; lunch specials a steal; lively atmosphere. $ *Average main: $15 ✉ 2108 Lake Tahoe Blvd., ¼ mile northeast of "Y" intersection of U.S. 50 and Hwy. 89 ☎ 530/544–3232 🌐 www.mythaitahoe.com.*

Red Hut Café

$ | **AMERICAN** | A vintage-1959 Tahoe diner, all chrome and red plastic, the Red Hut is a tiny place with a wildly popular breakfast menu: huge omelets; banana, pecan, and coconut waffles; and other tasty vittles. A second South Lake branch has a soda fountain and is the only one that serves dinner, and there's a third location in Stateline. **Known for:** huge omelets; variety of waffles; old-school feel. $ *Average main: $12 ✉ 2723 Lake Tahoe Blvd., near Blue Lake Ave. ☎ 530/541–9024 🌐 www.facebook.com/TheRedHut ⊗ No dinner.*

Scusa! Italian Ristorante

$$ | **ITALIAN** | This longtime favorite turns out big plates of veal scaloppine, chicken piccata, and garlicky linguine with clams—straightforward Italian American food (and lots of it), served in an intimate dining room warmed by a crackling fire on many nights. There's an outdoor patio that's open in warm weather. **Known for:** classic Italian American recipes; fritto misto, grilled radicchio, and fresh-baked mozzarella appetizers; sticky-bun bread pudding for dessert. $ *Average main: $25 ✉ 2543 Lake Tahoe Blvd., at Sierra Blvd. ☎ 530/542–0100 🌐 www.scusalaketahoe.com ⊗ No lunch.*

★ **Sprouts Natural Foods Cafe**

$ | **AMERICAN** | If it's in between normal mealtimes and you're hungry for something healthful, head to this order-at-the-counter café for salads, overstuffed wraps, hot sandwiches, homemade vegan soups, all-day breakfasts, and the best smoothies in town. Dine at wooden tables in the cheery contemporary indoor space or out front on the patio, or just order food to go. **Known for:** fresh, healthy cuisine; vegan and vegetarian friendly; congenial staff. $ *Average main: $12 ✉ 3123 Harrison Ave., U.S. 50 at Alameda Ave. ☎ 530/541–6969 🌐 www.sproutscafetahoe.com.*

Hotels

Base Camp South Lake Tahoe

$ | **HOTEL** | This three-floor boutique hotel near the Heavenly Gondola, Stateline casinos, and several good restaurants provides solid value in a hip yet family-friendly setting. **Pros:** convenient location; great for groups; cool public spaces include rooftop hot tub with mountain views. **Cons:** communal dinners won't appeal to all travelers; near a busy area; not on the lake. $ *Rooms from: $143 ✉ 4143 Cedar Ave., off U.S. 50 ☎ 530/208–0180 🌐 www.basecamptahoesouth.com 74 rooms Free breakfast.*

★ **Black Bear Lodge**

$$ | **B&B/INN** | Built in the 1990s with meticulous attention to detail, this entire complex feels like a grand old Adirondack lodge, with rooms and kitchenette-equipped cabins that feature 19th-century American antiques, fine art, and fireplaces. **Pros:** near Heavenly skiing; within walking distance of good

restaurants; wine and beer bar. **Cons:** no room service; lacks big-hotel amenities; social types may find setting too sedate. *$ Rooms from: $199 ✉ 1202 Ski Run Blvd. ☎ 530/544–4451 🌐 www.tahoe-blackbear.com ⇨ 9 units 🍽 No meals.*

Camp Richardson

$ | RESORT | FAMILY | An old-fashioned family resort on 120 acres fronting Lake Tahoe, Camp Richardson earns retro cred for its 1920s, log cabin–style lodge, its few dozen cabins, and its small inn—all tucked beneath giant pine trees—but wins no style points for its straightforward accommodations with a dearth of amenities. **Pros:** lakeside location with wide choice of lodgings; great for families; inexpensive daily and weekly rates. **Cons:** dated style; lacks upscale amenities (and even phones and TVs in some rooms); some cabins available in summer only. *$ Rooms from: $115 ✉ 1900 Jameson Beach Rd. ☎ 530/541–1801, 800/544–1801 🌐 www.camprichardson.com ⇨ 74 units 🍽 No meals.*

Hotel Azure

$$$ | HOTEL | High-end motel meets boutique hotel at this totally revamped (to the tune of $3.5 million) property across the road from a beach. **Pros:** clean, spacious rooms; good work spaces and tech amenities; short drive to Heavenly Mountain. **Cons:** on busy Lake Tahoe Boulevard; no bell or room service; some sound bleed-through from room to room. *$ Rooms from: $262 ✉ 3300 Lake Tahoe Blvd. ☎ 530/542–0330, 800/877–1466 🌐 www.hotelazuretahoe.com ⇨ 99 rooms 🍽 No meals.*

The Landing Resort & Spa

$$$$ | RESORT | Perched at the edge of a semi-private beach that's less than a ½ mile from Heavenly Village, The Landing provides luxe rooms and resort amenities in a prime location—removed from, but close to the Stateline action. **Pros:** across the street from the beach and lake; full-service spa with six treatment rooms, pool, hot tub, fitness center; spacious rooms, most over 450 square feet. **Cons:** lack of resort grounds; small lobby; busy beach in peak season. *$ Rooms from: $449 ✉ 4104 Lakeshore Blvd. ☎ 855/700–5263, 530/541–5263 🌐 www.thelandingtahoe.com ⇨ 82 rooms 🍽 No meals.*

Marriott's Grand Residence and Timber Lodge

$$$ | RESORT | You can't beat the location of these two gigantic, modern condominium complexes right at the base of Heavenly Gondola, smack in the center of town. **Pros:** central location; great for families; near excellent restaurants. **Cons:** can be jam-packed on weekends; no room service; lacks serenity. *$ Rooms from: $245 ✉ 1001 Heavenly Village Way ☎ 530/542–8400 Marriott's Grand Residence, 800/845–5279, 530/542–6600 Marriott's Timber Lodge 🌐 www.marriott.com ⇨ 431 rooms 🍽 No meals.*

★ Wylder Hope Valley

$$$$ | RESORT | You can lie on a hammock beneath the aspens, or sit in a rocker on your own front porch at this woodsy, 165-acre resort within the Eldorado National Forest and 20 minutes south of town. **Pros:** gorgeous rustic setting; good on-site café serves three meals a day (nonguests welcome); outdoor activities. **Cons:** nearest nightlife is 20 miles away; lacks amenities of larger properties; basic furnishings. *$ Rooms from: $325 ✉ 14255 Hwy. 88, Hope Valley ☎ 530/694–2203, 800/423–9949 🌐 wylderhotels.com ⇨ 36 units 🍽 No meals.*

Nightlife

Most of the area's nightlife is concentrated in the casinos over the border in Stateline. To avoid slot machines and blinking lights, try the California-side nightspots in and near Heavenly Village.

BARS

The Loft

THEMED ENTERTAINMENT | Crowd-pleasing magic shows and other entertainment and a casual-industrial setting keep patrons happy at this Heavenly Village bar and lounge where kids aren't out of place. The mood is upbeat, the specialty cocktails are potent, and if you're in the mood for dinner the kitchen turns out Italian fare more tasty than one might expect at such a venue. ✉ *1001 Heavenly Village Way* ☎ *530/523–8024* 🌐 *www.thelofttahoe.com.*

Mc P's Taphouse & Grill

BARS/PUBS | You can hear live bands—rock, jazz, blues, alternative—on most nights at Mc P's while you sample a few of the 40 beers on draft. Lunch and dinner (pub grub) are served daily. ✉ *4125 Lake Tahoe Blvd., Suite A, near Friday Ave.* ☎ *530/542–4435* 🌐 *www.mcpstahoe.net.*

FISHING

Tahoe Sport Fishing

FISHING | One of the area's largest and oldest fishing-charter services offers morning and afternoon trips. Outings include all necessary gear and bait, and the crew cleans and packages your catch. ✉ *900 Ski Run Blvd., off Lake Tahoe Blvd.* ☎ *530/541–5448* 🌐 *www.tahoesportfishing.com* 🎫 *From $160.*

HIKING

Desolation Wilderness

HIKING/WALKING | Trails within the 63,960-acre wilderness lead to gorgeous backcountry lakes and mountain peaks. It's called Desolation Wilderness for a reason, so bring a topographic map and compass, and carry water and food. You need a permit for overnight camping (☎ *877/444–6777*). In summer you can access this area by boarding a boat taxi ($18 one-way) at **Echo Chalet** (*9900 Echo Lakes Rd., off U.S. 50,* ☎ *530/659–7207,* 🌐 *www.echochalet.com*) and crossing Echo Lake. The Pacific Crest Trail also traverses Desolation Wilderness. ✉ *El Dorado National Forest Information Center* ☎ *530/644–2349* 🌐 *www.fs.usda.gov/eldorado.*

Pacific Crest Trail

HIKING/WALKING | Hike a couple of miles on this famous mountain trail that stretches from Mexico to Canada. ✉ *Echo Summit, about 12 miles southwest of South Lake Tahoe off U.S. 50* ☎ *916/285–1846* 🌐 *www.pcta.org.*

ICE-SKATING

Heavenly Village Outdoor Ice Rink

ICE SKATING | **FAMILY** | If you're here in winter, practice your jumps and turns at this rink between the gondola and the cinema. ✉ *1001 Heavenly Village Way* ☎ *530/542–4230* 🌐 *www.theshopsatheavenly.com* 🎫 *$22, includes skate rental.*

South Lake Tahoe Ice Arena

ICE SKATING | For year-round fun, head to this NHL regulation–size indoor rink where you can rent equipment and sign up for lessons. **■ TIP→ Hours vary; call or check website for public skate times.** ✉ *1176 Rufus Allen Blvd.* ☎ *530/544–7465* 🌐 *www.tahoearena.co* 🎫 *$15; includes skate rental.*

KAYAKING

Kayak Tahoe

KAYAKING | Sign up for lessons and excursions (to the south shore, Emerald Bay, and Sand Harbor), offered from May through September. You can also rent a kayak and paddle solo on the lake. ✉ *Timber Cove Marina, 3411 Lake Tahoe Blvd., at Balbijou Rd.* ☎ *530/544–2011* 🌐 *www.kayaktahoe.com* 🎫 *Rentals from $35, tours from $80.*

MOUNTAIN BIKING

Tahoe Sports Ltd.

BICYCLING | You can rent road and mountain bikes and get tips on where to ride from the friendly staff at this full-service sports store. ✉ *Tahoe Crescent*

V Shopping Center, 4000 Lake Tahoe Blvd., Suite 7 ☎ *530/542–4000* 🌐 *www.tahoesportsltd.com.*

SKIING

★ Heavenly Mountain Resort

SKIING/SNOWBOARDING | Straddling two states, vast Heavenly Mountain Resort—composed of nine peaks, two valleys, and four base-lodge areas, along with the largest snowmaking system in the western United States—pairs terrain for every skier with exhilarating Tahoe Basin views. Beginners can choose wide, well-groomed trails, accessed from the California Lodge or the gondola from downtown South Lake Tahoe; kids have short and gentle runs in the Enchanted Forest area all to themselves. The Sky Express high-speed quad chair whisks intermediate and advanced skiers to the summit for wide cruisers or steep tree-skiing. Mott and Killebrew canyons draw experts to the Nevada side for steep chutes and thick-timber slopes.

The ski school is big and offers everything from learn-to-ski packages to canyon-adventure tours. Call about ski and boarding camps. Skiing lessons are available for children ages four and up; there's day care for infants older than six weeks. Summertime thrill seekers participate in Epic Discovery—fun for the whole family that includes a mountain coaster, zip lines, a climbing wall, ropes courses, hiking opportunities, and a learning center. **Facilities:** 97 trails; 4,800 acres; 3,500-foot vertical drop; 28 lifts. ✉ *Ski Run Blvd., off U.S. 50* ☎ *775/586–7000, 800/432–8365* 🌐 *www.skiheavenly.com* 🎟 *Day pass from $67.*

Kirkwood Ski Resort

SKIING/SNOWBOARDING | Thirty-six miles south of Lake Tahoe, Kirkwood is the hard-core skiers' and boarders' favorite south-shore mountain, known for its craggy gulp-and-go chutes, sweeping cornices, steep-aspect glade skiing, and high base elevation. But there's also fantastic terrain for newbies and intermediates down wide-open bowls, through wooded gullies, and along rolling tree-lined trails. Families often head to the Timber Creek area, a good spot to learn to ski or snowboard. Tricksters can show off in two terrain parks on jumps, wall rides, rails, and a half-pipe. The mountain gets hammered with an average of 354 inches of snow annually. If you're into out-of-bounds skiing, check out Expedition Kirkwood, a backcountry-skills program that teaches basic safety awareness. If you're into cross-country, the resort has 80 km (50 miles) of superb groomed-track skiing, with skating lanes, instruction, and rentals. Nonskiers can snowshoe, snow-skate, and go dogsledding or snow-tubing. The children's ski school has programs for ages 3 to 12. **Facilities:** 86 trails; 2,300 acres; 2,000-foot vertical drop; 15 lifts. ✉ *1501 Kirkwood Meadows Dr., Kirkwood* ✣ *Off Hwy. 88, 14 miles west of Hwy. 89* ☎ *209/258–6000* 🌐 *www.kirkwood.com* 🎟 *Day pass from $67.*

Sierra-at-Tahoe

SKIING/SNOWBOARDING | Wind-protected and meticulously groomed slopes, excellent tree-skiing, and gated backcountry skiing are among the draws at this low-key but worthy resort. Extremely popular with snowboarders, Sierra has several terrain parks, including Halfpipe, with 18-foot walls and a dedicated chairlift. For beginners, Sierra-at-Tahoe has more than 100 acres of learning terrain, and there are two snow-tubing lanes. **Facilities:** 46 trails; 2,000-plus acres; 2,250-foot vertical drop; 14 lifts. ✉ *1111 Sierra-at-Tahoe Rd., Twin Bridges* ✣ *12 miles from South Lake Tahoe off U.S. 50, past Echo Summit* ☎ *530/659–7453 information, 530/659–7475 snow phone* 🌐 *www.sierraattahoe.com* 🎟 *Lift ticket $125.*

Pope-Baldwin Recreation Area

5 miles west of South Lake Tahoe.

To the west of downtown South Lake Tahoe, U.S. 50 and Highway 89 come together, forming an intersection nicknamed "the Y." If you head northwest on Highway 89, also called Emerald Bay Road, and follow the lakefront, commercial development gives way to national forests and state parks. One of these is Pope-Baldwin Recreation Area.

GETTING HERE AND AROUND

The entrance to the Pope-Baldwin Recreation Area is on the east side of Emerald Bay Road. The area is closed to vehicles in winter, but you can cross-country ski here.

Sights

★ Tallac Historic Site

HISTORIC SITE | At this site you can stroll or picnic lakeside year-round, and then in late spring and summer you can also explore three historic estates. The **Pope House** is the magnificently restored 1894 mansion of George S. Pope, who made his money in shipping and lumber and played host to the business and cultural elite of 1920s America. The **Baldwin Museum** is in the estate that once belonged to entrepreneur "Lucky" Baldwin; today it houses a collection of family memorabilia and Washoe Indian artifacts. The **Valhalla** (*valhallatahoe.com*), with a spectacular floor-to-ceiling stone fireplace, was occupied for years by Walter and Claire Heller (tidbit: after their divorce, each visited the property on alternate weekends, though she held the title). Its Grand Hall, Grand Lawn, and a lakeside boathouse refurbished as a theater, host the summertime Valhalla Art, Music and Theatre Festival of concerts, plays, and cultural activities. Docents conduct tours of the Pope House in summer; call for tour times. *Pope Baldwin Recreation Area Hwy. 89 530/541–5227 late May–mid-Sept., 530/544–7383 year-round tahoeheritage.org Free, summer guided site walk $5, Pope House tour $10 House and museum closed late Sept.–late May.*

Taylor Creek Visitor Center

INFO CENTER | **FAMILY** | At this center operated by the U.S. Forest Service you can visit the site of a Washoe Indian settlement; walk self-guided trails through meadow, marsh, and forest; and inspect the Stream Profile Chamber, an underground display with windows right into Taylor Creek. In fall you may see spawning kokanee salmon digging their nests. In summer Forest Service naturalists organize discovery walks and evening programs. *Hwy. 89, 3 miles north of junction with U.S. 50 530/543–2674 late May–Oct., 530/543–2600 year-round www.fs.usda.gov Free.*

Emerald Bay State Park

4 miles west of Pope-Baldwin Recreation Area.

You can hike, bike, swim, camp, scuba dive, kayak, or tour a look-alike Viking castle at this state park. Or you can simply enjoy the most popular tourist stop on Lake Tahoe's circular drive: the high cliff overlooking Emerald Bay, famed for its jewel-like shape and color.

GETTING HERE AND AROUND

The entrance to Emerald Bay State Park is on the east side of a narrow, twisting section of Highway 89. Caution is the key word for both drivers and pedestrians. The park is closed to vehicles in winter.

Fjord-like Emerald Bay is possibly the most scenic part of Lake Tahoe.

Sights

★ Emerald Bay State Park

NATIONAL/STATE PARK | A massive glacier millions of years ago carved this 3-mile-long and 1-mile-wide fjord-like inlet. Famed for its jewel-like shape and colors, the bay surrounds Fannette, Tahoe's only island. Highway 89 curves high above the lake through Emerald Bay State Park; from the Emerald Bay lookout, the centerpiece of the park, you can survey the whole scene. This is one of the don't-miss views of Lake Tahoe. The light is best in mid- to late morning, when the bay's colors really pop. ✉ *Hwy. 89* ☎ *530/525–7232* 🌐 *www.parks.ca.gov* 🎫 *$10 parking fee.*

Vikingsholm

HOUSE | This 38-room estate was completed in 1929 and built as a precise copy of a 1,200-year-old Viking castle, using materials native to the area. Its original owner, Lora Knight, furnished it with Scandinavian antiques and hired artisans to build period reproductions. The sod roof sprouts wildflowers each spring. There are picnic tables nearby and a gray-sand beach for strolling. A steep 1-mile-long trail from the Emerald Bay lookout leads down to Vikingsholm, and the hike back up is hard (especially if you're not yet acclimated to the elevation), although there are benches and stone culverts to rest on. At the 150-foot peak of Fannette Island are the ruins of a stone structure known as the Tea House, built so that Knight's guests could have a place to enjoy afternoon refreshments after a motorboat ride. The island is off-limits from February through mid-June to protect nesting Canada geese. The rest of the year it's open for day use—kayak and paddleboard rentals are available at Emerald Bay State Park's beach. ✉ *Hwy. 89* ☎ *530/525–7232* 🌐 *www.vikingsholm.com* 🎫 *Day-use parking fee $10; mansion tour $15* ⏲ *Closed late Sept.–late May.*

Activities

HIKING

Eagle Falls

HIKING/WALKING | To reach these falls, leave your car in the parking lot of the Eagle Falls picnic area (near Vikingsholm; arrive early for a good spot), and walk up the short but fairly steep canyon nearby. You'll have a brilliant panorama of Emerald Bay from this spot near the boundary of Desolation Wilderness. For a strenuous full-day hike, continue 5 miles, past Eagle Lake (a good spot for an alpine swim), to Upper and Middle Velma lakes. Pick up trail maps at Taylor Creek Visitor Center in summer, or year-round at the main U.S. Forest Service Office in South Lake Tahoe, at 35 College Drive. ✉ *Hwy. 89 at Emerald Bay State Park.*

D.L. Bliss State Park

3 miles north of Emerald Bay State Park, 17 miles south of Tahoe City.

This park shares 6 miles of shoreline with adjacent Emerald Bay State Park and has two white-sand beaches. Hike the Rubicon Trail for stunning views of the lake.

GETTING HERE AND AROUND

The entrance to D.L. Bliss State Park is on the east side of Highway 89 just north of Emerald Bay. No vehicles are allowed in when the park is closed for the season.

Sights

D.L. Bliss State Park

NATIONAL/STATE PARK | This park takes its name from Duane LeRoy Bliss, a 19th-century lumber magnate. At one time Bliss owned nearly 75% of Tahoe's lakefront, along with local steamboats, railroads, and banks. The park shares 6 miles of shoreline with Emerald Bay State Park; combined the two parks cover 1,830 acres, 744 of which the Bliss family donated to the state. At the north end of Bliss is Rubicon Point, which overlooks one of the lake's deepest spots. Short trails lead to an old lighthouse and Balancing Rock, which weighs 250,000 pounds and balances on a fist of granite. The 4.5-mile Rubicon Trail—one of Tahoe's premier hikes—leads to Vikingsholm and provides stunning lake views. Two white-sand beaches front some of Tahoe's warmest water. ✉ *Hwy. 89* ✣ *Entrance east side of Hwy. 89, 3 miles north of Emerald Bay State Park* ☎ *530/525–3384 visitor information (summer), 530/525–9528 Lake Tahoe sector ranger station/winter conditions, 530/525–7277 D.L. Bliss kiosk (summer)* 🌐 *www.parks.ca.gov* 🎫 *$10 per vehicle, day-use.*

Ed Z'berg Sugar Pine Point State Park

8 miles north of D. L. Bliss State Park, 10 miles south of Tahoe City.

Visitors love to hike, swim, and fish here in the summer, but this park is also popular in winter, when a small campground remains open. Eleven miles of cross-country ski and snowshoe trails allow beginners and experienced enthusiasts alike to whoosh through pine forests and glide past the lake.

GETTING HERE AND AROUND

The entrance to Sugar Pine Point is on the east side of Highway 89, about a mile south of Tahoma. A bike trail links Tahoe City to the park.

Sights

Ed Z'Berg Sugar Pine Point State Park

NATIONAL/STATE PARK | Visitors love to hike, swim, and fish in the summer at this park named for a state lawmaker who sponsored key conservation legislation, but it's also popular in winter, when a

A classic lake view at Ed Z'berg Sugar Pine Point State Park.

small campground remains open. Eleven miles of cross-country ski and snowshoe trails allow beginners and experienced enthusiasts alike to whoosh through pine forests and glide past the lake. Rangers lead full-moon snowshoe tours from January to March. With 2,000 densely forested acres and nearly 2 miles of shore frontage, this is Lake Tahoe's largest state park. ✉ *Hwy. 89, 1 mile south of Tahoma* ☎ *530/525–7982 summer, 530/525–9528 year-round* 🌐 *www.parks.ca.gov* 🎫 *$10 per vehicle, day-use.*

Hellman-Ehrman Mansion

HOUSE | The main attraction at Sugar Pine Point State Park is the Hellman-Ehrman Mansion, a 1903 stone-and-shingle summer home furnished in period style. In its day the height of modernity, the mansion had electric lights and full indoor plumbing. Also in the park are a trapper's log cabin from the mid-19th century, a nature preserve with wildlife exhibits, a lighthouse, the start of the 10-mile biking trail to Tahoe City, and an extensive system of hiking and cross-country skiing trails. If you're feeling less ambitious, you can relax on the sun-dappled lawn behind the mansion and gaze out at the lake. ■ **TIP→ Purchase tour tickets at the Sugar Pine nature center.** ✉ *Hwy. 89* ☎ *530/525–7982 summer, 530/525–9528 year-round, 530/583–9911 house tours* 🌐 *www.parks.ca.gov* 🎫 *$10 per vehicle, day-use; mansion tour $10.*

Tahoma

1 mile north of Ed Z'berg Sugar Pine Point State Park, 23 miles south of Truckee.

With its rustic waterfront vacation cottages, Tahoma exemplifies life on the lake in its quiet early days before bright-lights casinos and huge crowds proliferated. In 1960, Tahoma was host of the Olympic Nordic-skiing competitions. Today, there's little to do here except stroll by the lake and listen to the wind in the trees, making it a favorite home base for mellow families and nature buffs.

GETTING HERE AND AROUND

Approach Tahoma by car on Highway 89, called West Lake Boulevard in this section. From the northern and western communities, take a TART bus to Tahoma. A bike trail links Tahoe City to Tahoma.

Hotels

Tahoma Meadows B&B Cottages

$ | **B&B/INN** | **FAMILY** | With 16 individually decorated little red cottages sitting beneath towering pine trees, it's hard to beat this serene property for atmosphere and woodsy charm. **Pros:** lovely setting; good choice for families; close to Homewood ski resort. **Cons:** far from the casinos; may be too serene for some guests; old-style decor. *Rooms from: $149* *6821 W. Lake Blvd.* *530/525–1553* *www.tahomameadows.com* *16 rooms* *No meals.*

Activities

SKIING

Homewood Mountain Resort

SKIING/SNOWBOARDING | Schuss down these slopes for fantastic views—the mountain rises across the road from the Tahoe shoreline. This small, usually uncrowded resort is the favorite area of locals on a snowy day, because you can find lots of untracked powder. It's also the most protected and least windy Tahoe ski area during a storm; when every other resort's lifts are on wind hold, you can almost always count on Homewood's to be open. There's only one high-speed chairlift, but there are rarely any lines. The resort may look small as you drive by, but most of it isn't visible from the road. **Facilities:** 67 trails; 1,260 acres; 1,650-foot vertical drop; 8 lifts. *5145 W. Lake Blvd., Homewood* *Hwy. 89, 5 miles south of Tahoe City* *530/525–2992 information, 530/525–2900 snow phone* *www.skihomewood.com* *Lift ticket $129.*

Tahoe City

9 miles north of Tahoma, 14 miles south of Truckee.

Tahoe City is the only lakeside town with a charming downtown area good for strolling and window-shopping. Stores and restaurants are all within walking distance of the Outlet Gates, where water is spilled into the Truckee River to control the surface level of the lake.

GETTING HERE AND AROUND

Tahoe City is at the junction of Highway 28, also called North Lake Boulevard, and Highway 89 where it turns northwest toward Palisades Tahoe and Truckee. TART buses serve the area.

ESSENTIALS

VISITOR INFORMATION Go Tahoe North. *530/581–6900* *www.gotahoenorth.com.*

Sights

Gatekeeper's Museum

MUSEUM | This museum preserves a little-known part of the region's history. Between 1912 and 1968 the gatekeeper who lived on this site was responsible for monitoring the level of the lake, using a winch system (still used today and visible just outside the museum) to keep the water at the correct level. Also here, the fantastic Marion Steinbach Indian Basket Museum displays intricate baskets from 85 tribes. *130 W. Lake Blvd.* *530/583–1762* *www.northtahoemuseums.org* *$5* *Closed Mon.–Wed. early-Sept.–late May.*

Watson Cabin Living Museum

MUSEUM | In the middle of Tahoe City sits a 1909 hand-hewn log cabin, the town's oldest structure still on its original site. Now a museum open during the summer, it's filled with century-old furnishings and many reproductions. *560 N. Lake Blvd.* *530/583–1762* *www.northtahoemuseums.org*

Free Closed Tues. and Wed. and early Sept.–May.

Restaurants

Cafe Zenon

$ | **ECLECTIC** | Straightforward Vietnamese pho noodle soup is served all day at this restaurant at Tahoe City's public golf course, but the chef also prepares everything from poutine and kimchi hot dogs to green beans with pork or prawns. The Vietnamese French Dip, a local favorite, substitutes pho broth for the traditional beef. **Known for:** roasted-chicken, Polish sausage, and other sides; Hawaiian buns and gravy with fried egg at weekend brunch; golf course setting (skating rink in winter). *Average main: $13 251 N. Lake Blvd. Behind Bank of America building 530/583–1517 www.cafezenon.com.*

★ Christy Hill

$$$$ | **MODERN AMERICAN** | Huge windows reveal stellar lake views at this Euro–Cal restaurant serving seafood, beef, and vegetarian entrées, along with small-plate offerings. The extensive wine list and exceptional desserts earn accolades; the atmosphere is casual. **Known for:** tasting menu a good deal; romantic choice; dinner on the deck in fine weather. *Average main: $40 115 Grove St., at N. Lake Blvd. 530/583–8551 www.christyhill.com No lunch. Closed Mon. and Tues.*

Fire Sign Cafe

$ | **AMERICAN** | There's often a wait for breakfast and lunch at this great little diner with pine paneling, hardwood floors, and an exposed-beam ceiling, but it's worth it. The pastries are made from scratch, the salmon is smoked in-house, the salsa is hand cut, and there's real maple syrup for the many types of pancakes and waffles. **Known for:** pastries from scratch; many pancakes and waffles; fruit cobbler for dessert. *Average main: $14 1785 W. Lake Blvd. Hwy. 89, 2 miles south of downtown Tahoe City at Fountain Ave. 530/583–0871 www.firesigncafe.com No dinner.*

Wolfdale's

$$$$ | **ECLECTIC** | Consistent, inspired cuisine served in an elegantly simple dining room makes Wolfdale's one of the top restaurants on the lake, albeit among the most expensive. The imaginative entrées, many involving seafood, merge Asian and European cooking, and everything from teriyaki glaze to smoked fish is made in-house. **Known for:** multiple martinis and other cocktails; lake-view setting; happy hour wines and small plates (5–6:30 except Saturday and holidays). *Average main: $44 640 N. Lake Blvd., near Grove St. 530/583–5700 www.wolfdales.com Closed Tues. No lunch.*

Hotels

Basecamp Tahoe City

$$ | **B&B/INN** | **FAMILY** | A downtown motel for the 21st century, Basecamp charms with a combination of industrial, retro, and rustic styles. **Pros:** lively public spaces; stylish rooms; convenient to commercial strip with restaurants and grocery stores. **Cons:** some road noise; lacks amenities of large properties; eight-minute walk to local beach. *Rooms from: $161 955 N. Lake Blvd. 530/580–8430 www.basecamptahoecity.com 24 rooms Free breakfast.*

Cottage Inn

$$ | **B&B/INN** | Avoid the crowds by staying in one of these charming circa-1938 log cottages under the towering pines on the lake's west shore. **Pros:** romantic, woodsy setting; all rooms have gas fireplaces, some two-person tubs; private beach access. **Cons:** guests must be older than 12; most cottages accommodate two people maximum; minimum weekend- and multiple-day stays required in peak. *Rooms from: $194 1690 W. Lake Blvd. 530/581–4073, 800/581–4073 www.thecottageinn.com 22 rooms Free breakfast.*

Granlibakken Tahoe

$$ | **RESORT** | A condo community with its own snow-play area in winter, this secluded 74-acre resort's name means "a hillside sheltered by fir trees" in Norwegian. **Pros:** range of lodging options, from studio condos to town houses; secluded location; pool and spa treatments. **Cons:** some guests find the location too secluded; more for families than romantic interludes; conference activities and weddings. *Rooms from: $171* *725 Granlibakken Rd.* *530/583–4242 front desk, 800/543–3221 reservations* *granlibakken.com* *165 rooms* *Free breakfast.*

★ **Sunnyside Restaurant and Lodge**

$$ | **HOTEL** | The views are superb and the hospitality gracious at this lakeside lodge 3 miles south of Tahoe City. **Pros:** complimentary continental breakfast and afternoon tea; most rooms have balconies overlooking the lake; lively bar and restaurant. **Cons:** can be pricey for families; noisy in summer; pricey entrées at restaurant. *Rooms from: $199* *1850 W. Lake Blvd.* *530/583–7200, 800/822–2754* *www.sunnysideresort.com* *23 rooms* *Free breakfast.*

RAFTING

Truckee River Rafting

WHITE-WATER RAFTING | **FAMILY** | In summer you can take a self-guided raft trip down a gentle 5-mile stretch of the Truckee River. This outfitter will shuttle you back to Tahoe City at the end of your two- to three-hour trip. **TIP→ On a warm day this makes a great family outing.** *175 River Rd., near W. Lake Blvd.* *530/583–1111* *www.truckeeriverrafting.com* *From $60.*

SKIING

AREAS

Alpine Meadows Ski Area

SKIING/SNOWBOARDING | With an average 450 inches of snow annually, Alpine (part of Palisades Tahoe) has some of Tahoe's most reliable conditions. It's usually one of the first areas to open in November and one of the last to close in May or June. Alpine isn't the place for show-offs; instead, you'll find down-to-earth alpine fetishists. The two peaks here are well suited to intermediate skiers, with a number of runs for experts only. Snowboarders and hot-dog skiers will find a terrain park with a super-pipe, rails, and tabletops, as well as a boarder-cross course. Alpine is a great place to learn to ski and has a ski school for kids and adults. On Saturday, because of the limited parking, there's more acreage per person than at other resorts. Lift tickets are good at neighboring Palisades Tahoe; a free shuttle runs all day between the two ski parks. **Facilities:** 100-plus trails; 2,400 acres; 1,802-foot vertical drop; 13 lifts. *2600 Alpine Meadows Rd.* *Off Hwy. 89, 6 miles northwest of Tahoe City, 13 miles south of Truckee* *530/583–4232, 800/403–0206* *www.palisadestahoe.com* *Lift ticket $169.*

EQUIPMENT RENTALS

Tahoe Dave's Skis and Boards

SKIING/SNOWBOARDING | You can rent skis, boards, and snowshoes at this shop, which has the area's best selection of downhill rental equipment. *590 N. Lake Blvd.* *530/583–6415* *www.tahoedaves.com.*

Palisades Tahoe has runs for skiers of all abilitiy levels, from beginner to expert.

Olympic Valley

7 miles north of Tahoe City to Palisades Tahoe Rd., 8½ miles south of Truckee.

Olympic Valley got its moniker in 1960, when its ski resort, Palisades Tahoe, hosted the Winter Olympics. Snow sports remain the primary activity, but once summer comes, you can hike into the adjacent Granite Chief Wilderness, explore wildflower-studded alpine meadows, or lie by a swimming pool in one of the Sierra's prettiest valleys.

GETTING HERE AND AROUND

Palisades Tahoe Road, the only way into Olympic Valley, branches west off Highway 89 about 8 miles south of Truckee. TART connects the Palisades Tahoe ski area with the communities along the north and west shores, and Truckee, with year-round public transportation. Palisades Tahoe provides a free shuttle to many stops in those same areas.

Sights

High Camp

VIEWPOINT | Ride the Palisades Tahoe Aerial Tram to this activity hub, which at 8,200 feet commands superb views of Lake Tahoe and the surrounding mountains. In summer, go for a hike, sit by the pool, or have a cocktail and watch the sunset. In winter you can ski or snow-tube. There's also a restaurant, a lounge, and a small Olympic museum. Pick up trail maps at the tram building. *Aerial Tram Bldg., Palisades Tahoe 800/403–0206 www.palisadestahoe.com Aerial Tram, $46.*

Village at Palisades Tahoe

COMMERCIAL CENTER | **FAMILY** | The centerpiece of Olympic Valley is a pedestrian mall at the base of several four-story ersatz Bavarian stone-and-timber buildings, where you'll find restaurants, high-end condo rentals, boutiques, and cafés. *1750 Village East Rd. 530/584–1000, 800/403–0206 information www.palisadestahoe.com.*

Restaurants

Fireside Pizza Company

$$ | **PIZZA** | **FAMILY** | Adults might opt for the signature pear-and-Gorgonzola pizza at this modern Italian restaurant, but most kids clamor for the house favorite: an Italian-sausage-and-pepperoni combo with a bubbly blend of four cheeses. Salads and pasta dishes round out the menu at this family-friendly spot. **Known for:** inventive pizzas; good, inexpensive dining option in a pricey area; family-friendly. *Average main: $17* *The Village at Palisades Tahoe, 1985 Palisades Tahoe Rd., #25* *530/584–6150* *www.firesidepizza.com.*

★ **PlumpJack Cafe**

$$$$ | **AMERICAN** | The menu at this silver-tone white-tablecloth restaurant whose wide windows reveal Palisades Tahoe in all its glory changes seasonally, but look for rib-eye steak, seared diver scallops with risotto, and a filling, inventive vegetarian dish. Rather than complicated, heavy sauces, the chef uses simple reductions to complement a dish, resulting in clean, dynamic flavors. **Known for:** specialty cocktails; less expensive but equally adventurous bar menu; varied, reasonably priced wines. *Average main: $42* *1920 Palisades Tahoe Rd.* *530/583–1586* *www.plumpjackcafe.com* *No lunch (except at bar).*

Hotels

★ **PlumpJack Inn**

$$ | **HOTEL** | Stylish and luxurious, this two-story, cedar-sided inn has a snappy, sophisticated look and laid-back sensibility, perfect for the Bay Area cognoscenti who flock here on weekends. **Pros:** small and intimate; loaded with amenities; personable and attentive service. **Cons:** not the best choice for families with small children; not all rooms have tubs; laid-back sensibility may not work for some guests. *Rooms from: $225* *1920 Palisades Tahoe Rd.* *530/583–1576, 800/323–7666* *plumpjackinn.com* *56 rooms* *Free breakfast.*

Resort at Squaw Creek

$$$ | **RESORT** | This Palisades Tahoe multifacility offers restaurants, a golf course, spa, heated swimming pool, ice skating rink, chairlift to the mountain, and groomed cross-country ski tracks on the property, plus all the amenities and services you could possibly want in the Tahoe area. **Pros:** every conceivable amenity; chairlift to Palisades Tahoe for ski-in, ski-out; attractive furnishings. **Cons:** so large it can feel impersonal; high in-season rates; a lot of hubbub during ski season. *Rooms from: $299* *400 Squaw Creek Rd.* *530/412–7034, 800/404–8006 reservations* *www.destinationhotels.com/squawcreek* *405 rooms* *No meals.*

The Village at Palisades Tahoe

$$ | **HOTEL** | **FAMILY** | Right at the base of the slopes, at the center point of Olympic Valley, the Village's condominiums (from studio to three bedrooms) come complete with gas fireplaces, daily maid service, and heated slate-tile bathroom and kitchen floors. **Pros:** each condo sleeps at least four people; near Village restaurants and shops; at base of slopes. **Cons:** village often gets crowded on weekends; nicely appointed but not high style; lacks room service and other hotel amenities. *Rooms from: $209* *1750 Village East Rd.* *530/584–1000, 888/259–1428* *www.palisadestahoe.com* *198 rooms* *No meals.*

Activities

GOLF

Resort at Squaw Creek Golf Course

GOLF | For beautiful views of Palisades Tahoe's surrounding peaks, play this narrow, challenging championship course designed by Robert Trent Jones Jr. The design emphasizes accuracy over distance, especially on the front nine. All fees include a golf cart plus valet parking;

rates drop after noon and again after 3 pm. ✉ *400 Squaw Creek Rd.* ☎ *530/583–6300, 530/581–6637 pro shop* 🌐 *www.destinationhotels.com/squawcreek/recreation* 🎟 *From $127* ⛳ *18 holes, 6931 yards, par 71.*

SKIING

AREAS

★ Palisades Tahoe

SKIING/SNOWBOARDING | Known for some of the toughest skiing in the Tahoe area, this park was the centerpiece of the 1960 Winter Olympics. Today it's the definitive North Tahoe ski resort and among the top-three megaresorts in California (the other two are Heavenly and Mammoth). Although Palisades Tahoe has changed significantly since the Olympics, the skiing is still world-class and extends across vast bowls stretched between six peaks. Experts often head directly to the untamed terrain of the infamous KT-22 face, which has bumps, cliffs, and gulp-and-go chutes, or to the nearly vertical Palisades, where many famous extreme-skiing films have been shot. Fret not, beginners and intermediates: you have plenty of wide-open, groomed trails at High Camp (which sits at the *top* of the mountain) and around the more challenging Snow King Peak. Snowboarders and show-off skiers can tear up the five fantastic terrain parks, which include a giant super-pipe. Ski passes are good at neighboring Alpine Meadows, which is part of Palisades Tahoe; free shuttles run all day between the Alpine and Olympic Valley base camps. (By early 2022, a gondola will connect them.) **Facilities:** 178 trails; 3,600 acres; 2,840-foot vertical drop; 30 lifts. ✉ *1960 Palisades Tahoe Rd.* ✣ *Off Hwy. 89, 7 miles northwest of Tahoe City* ☎ *800/403–0206* 🌐 *www.palisadestahoe.com* 🎟 *Lift ticket $179.*

EQUIPMENT RENTALS

Tahoe Dave's Skis and Boards

SKIING/SNOWBOARDING | If you don't want to pay resort prices, you can rent and tune downhill skis and snowboards at this shop. ✉ *3039 Hwy. 89, at Palisades Tahoe Rd.* ☎ *530/583–5665* 🌐 *www.tahoedaves.com.*

Truckee

13 miles northwest of Kings Beach, 14 miles north of Tahoe City.

Formerly a decrepit railroad town in the mountains, Truckee is now the trendy first stop for many Tahoe visitors. The town was officially established around 1863, and by 1868 it had gone from a stagecoach station to a major stopover for trains bound for the Pacific via the new transcontinental railroad. Every day, freight trains and Amtrak's *California Zephyr* still idle briefly at the depot in the middle of town. The visitor center inside the depot has a walking-tour map of historic Truckee.

Across from the station, where Old West facades line the main drag, you'll find galleries, gift shops, boutiques, a wine-tasting room, old-fashioned diners, and several good restaurants.

GETTING HERE AND AROUND

Truckee is off Interstate 80 between Highways 89 and 267. Greyhound and Amtrak stop here, and TART buses serve the area.

ESSENTIALS

VISITOR INFORMATION Truckee Donner Chamber of Commerce and the California Welcome Center. ✉ *Amtrak depot, 10065 Donner Pass Rd., near Spring St.* ☎ *530/587–8808* 🌐 *www.truckee.com.*

Sights

Donner Memorial State Park and Emigrant Trail Museum

NATIONAL/STATE PARK | The park and museum commemorate the 89 members of the Donner Party, westward-bound pioneers who became trapped in the Sierra in the winter of 1846–47 in snow 22 feet deep. Barely more than half survived, some by resorting to cannibalism. The absorbing Emigrant Trail Museum in the visitor center contains exhibits about the Donner Party, regional Native Americans, and railroad and transportation development in the area. In the park, you can picnic, hike, camp, and go boating, fishing, and waterskiing in summer; winter brings cross-country skiing and snowshoeing on groomed trails. ✉ *12593 Donner Pass Rd.* ✣ *Off I–80, Exit 184, 2 miles west of Truckee* ☎ *530/582–7892* 🌐 *www.parks.ca.gov/donnermemorial* 🎫 *$10 parking, day-use ($5 in winter).*

Restaurants

★ Cottonwood Restaurant & Bar

$$$ | **ECLECTIC** | Perched above town on the site of North America's first chairlift, this local institution has a bar decked out with old wooden skis, sleds, skates, and photos of Truckee's early days. The ambitious menu includes grilled steak, baby-back short ribs with chipotle barbecue jus, and house-special pasta dishes like chicken linguine. **Known for:** early-bird three-course dinner except in high season; wine selection; hilltop views from atmospheric bar. $ *Average main: $31* ✉ *10142 Rue Hilltop Rd., off Brockway Rd., ¼ mile south of downtown* ☎ *530/587–5711* 🌐 *www.cottonwoodrestaurant.com* ⏱ *No lunch Sept.–May or weekdays in summer.*

FiftyFifty Brewing Company

$$ | **AMERICAN** | In this brewpub, the warm red tones and comfy booths, plus a pint of the Donner Party porter (or a shot of bourbon), will take the nip out of a cold day on the slopes. The menu includes salads, burgers, inventive pizzas, barbecued ribs, pan-seared salmon, and the house specialty: a pulled-pork sandwich. **Known for:** high-quality burger beef; 2018 Brewery Group of the Year honors at top beer fest; après-ski action. $ *Average main: $24* ✉ *11197 Brockway Rd., near Martis Valley Rd.* ☎ *530/587–2337* 🌐 *www.fiftyfiftybrewing.com.*

Moody's Bistro, Bar & Beats

$$$ | **ECLECTIC** | Head here for contemporary-Cal cuisine in a sexy dining room with pumpkin-color walls, burgundy velvet banquettes, and art-deco fixtures. The earthy, sure-handed cooking features organically grown ingredients: look for ahi poke, snazzy pizzas bubbling-hot from a brick oven, braised lamb shanks, pan-roasted wild game, fresh seafood, and organic beef. **Known for:** lighter fare for lunch; summer alfresco dining; live music in bar some nights. $ *Average main: $32* ✉ *10007 Bridge St., at Donner Pass Rd.* ☎ *530/587–8688* 🌐 *www.moodysbistro.com.*

Pianeta Ristorante

$$$ | **ITALIAN** | A longtime town favorite, Pianeta serves high-style Italian cuisine in a warmly lit bi-level redbrick space on Truckee's historic main drag. Start with a beef carpaccio antipasto plate or perhaps house-made spicy-fennel and mild sausages, following up with a pasta course of ravioli Bolognese (both pasta and sauce made in-house), an entrée of ragout with spicy sausage and Mexican prawns—or both. **Known for:** welcoming atmosphere; tiramisu and panna cotta for dessert; West Coast and Italian wine selections. $ *Average main: $30* ✉ *10096 Donner Pass Rd.* ☎ *530/587–4694* 🌐 *www.pianetarestauranttruckee.com* ⏱ *No lunch.*

Squeeze In

$ | **AMERICAN** | Meet the locals at Truckee's top choice for breakfast, thanks to the dozens of omelets and several variations on eggs Benedict along with banana-walnut pancakes and French toast oozing with cream cheese. At lunch savor homemade soups and sandwiches. **Known for:** cheeseburger omelet; homemade soups; gluten-free variations. $ *Average main: $15* ✉ *10060 Donner Pass Rd., near Bridge St.* ☎ *530/587–9814* 🌐 *www.squeezein.com* ⏱ *No dinner.*

Truckee Tavern and Grill

$$$ | **AMERICAN** | The wood-fired grill in this second-floor downtown restaurant turns out steaks, chicken, and chops along with fish dishes that might include Mt. Lassen trout with white beans and mushrooms. As with the food, the decor is New West contemporary—bricks line the wall behind the bar, where mixologists craft wiggy drinks like the Salvador (as in Dalí, with rye, mescal, blood orange, and egg white), and, in tribute to Truckee's bootlegging past, pour artisanal small-batch gin and whiskey. **Known for:** buffalo tri-tip; pasta and fish entrées; deck overlooking downtown action. *Average main: $29 10118 Donner Pass Rd., near Spring St. 530/587–3766 www.truckeetavern.com No lunch Wed.*

Hotels

Cedar House Sport Hotel

$$ | **HOTEL** | The clean, spare lines of the Cedar House's wooden exterior evoke a modern European feel, while energy-saving heating, cooling, and lighting systems emphasize the owners' commitment to sustainability. **Pros:** environmentally friendly; hip yet comfortable; heated-tile bathroom floors. **Cons:** some bathrooms on the small side; not all bathrooms have tubs; about a mile from historic downtown Truckee. *Rooms from: $215 10918 Brockway Rd. 530/582–5655, 866/582–5655 www.cedarhousesporthotel.com 40 rooms Free breakfast.*

Northstar California Resort

$$ | **RESORT** | The area's most complete destination resort entices families with its sports activities and concentration of restaurants, shops, and accommodations. **Pros:** array of lodging types; on-site shuttle; several dining options in Northstar Village. **Cons:** family accommodations can be pricey; lacks intimacy; some units not as attractive as others. *Rooms from: $220 5001 Northstar Dr. Off Hwy. 267, 6 miles southeast of Truckee 530/562–1010, 800/466–6784 www.northstarcalifornia.com 250 units No meals.*

★ **Ritz-Carlton Highlands Court, Lake Tahoe**

$$$$ | **RESORT** | Nestled mid-mountain on the Northstar ski resort, the four-story Ritz-Carlton has plush accommodations with floor-to-ceiling windows, fireplaces, cozy robes, and down comforters. **Pros:** superb service; gorgeous setting; ski-in, ski out convenience. **Cons:** in-season prices as breathtaking as the views; resort fee and mandatory valet parking add to cost of stay; must go off-site for golf and tennis. *Rooms from: $382 13031 Ritz-Carlton Highlands Court 530/562–3000, 800/241–3333 www.ritzcarlton.com 170 rooms No meals.*

River Street Inn

$$ | **B&B/INN** | On the banks of the Truckee River, this 1882 wood-and-stone inn has uncluttered, comfortable rooms that are simply decorated, with attractive, country-style wooden furniture and extras like flat-screen TVs. **Pros:** tidy rooms; good value; in historic downtown Truckee. **Cons:** parking is a half block from inn; decor is simple; noise from on-site restaurant and bar and nearby trains. *Rooms from: $165 10009 E. River St. 530/550–9290 inn, 530/550–9222 restaurant www.riverstreetinntruckee.com 7 rooms Free breakfast.*

Truckee Hotel

$$ | **HOTEL** | A four-story hotel in business in various forms since 1873, the Truckee Hotel attracts history buffs and skiers, the latter for the reasonable rates when in-season prices skyrocket at Northstar, Sugar Bowl, and other nearby resorts. **Pros:** historic atmosphere; convenient to shops and restaurants; same owners operate a modern Hampton Inn nearby. **Cons:** no pool, fitness center, elevator; train and other noise issues (when booking ask for a quiet room); most rooms share bathrooms (though all have a sink). *Rooms from: $189 10007 Bridge St.*

☎ 530/587–4444 🌐 www.truckeehotel.com 🛏 32 rooms 🍽 Free breakfast.

GOLF

Coyote Moon Golf Course

GOLF | With pine trees lining the fairways and no houses to spoil the view, this course is as beautiful as it is challenging. Fees include a shared cart; the greens fee drops at 1 pm and dips again at 3. ✉ *10685 Northwoods Blvd., off Donner Pass Rd.* ☎ *530/587–0886* 🌐 *www.coyotemoongolf.com* 🎟 *$185* ⛳ *18 holes, 7177 yards, par 72* ⏲ *Closed late fall–late spring.*

Northstar Golf

GOLF | Robert Muir Graves designed this course that combines hilly terrain and open meadows. The front nine holes here are open-links style, while the challenging back nine move through tight, tree-lined fairways. Rates, which include a cart, drop successively after 11, 1, and 4. ✉ *168 Basque Dr.* ✣ *Off Northstar Dr., west off Hwy. 267* ☎ *530/562–3290 pro shop* 🌐 *www.northstarcalifornia.com* 🎟 *$110 for 18 holes* ⛳ *18 holes, 6781 yards, par 72.*

MOUNTAIN BIKING

Cyclepaths Mountain Bike Adventures

BICYCLING | This combination full-service bike shop and bike-adventure outfitter offers instruction in mountain biking, guided tours, tips for self-guided bike touring, bike repairs, and books and maps on the area. ✉ *Pioneer Center, 10825 Pioneer Trail, Suite 105* ☎ *530/582–1890* 🌐 *cyclepaths.com.*

Northstar California Bike Park

BICYCLING | From late May through September Northstar's ski slopes transform into a magnificent lift-served bike park with 100 miles of challenging terrain, including the aptly named Livewire trail. Guided tours, multiday retreats, and downhill, cross-country, and endurance races are available for riders of all abilities. ✉ *Northstar Dr., off Hwy. 267* ☎ *530/562–1010* 🌐 *www.northstarcalifornia.com* 🎟 *Lift $70.*

SKIING

AREAS

★ Northstar California

SKIING/SNOWBOARDING | Meticulous grooming and long cruisers make this resort a paradise for intermediate skiers and a fine choice for families. Although the majority of the trails are intermediate in difficulty, advanced skiers and riders have access to Lookout Mountain's more than two dozen expert trails and 347 acres of gated terrain and steeps. The diversity of terrain in proximity makes it easier for families and groups with varying skills to hang out with each other. As for terrain parks, the ones here are considered among North America's best, with features that include a 420-foot-long super-pipe, a half-pipe, rails and boxes, and lots of kickers. The Cross Country, Telemark and Snowshoe Center, located mid-mountain, is the starting point for a network of 35 km (22 miles) of groomed trails, including double-set tracks and skating lanes. The trails are also fat-bike friendly, so nonskiers can enjoy the park, too. The school has programs for skiers ages three and up, and on-site care is available for tots two and older. **Facilities:** 100 trails; 3,170 acres; 2,280-foot vertical drop; 20 lifts. ✉ *5001 Northstar Dr.* ☎ *530/562–2267* 🌐 *www.northstarcalifornia.com* 🎟 *day pass from $67.*

★ Royal Gorge

SKIING/SNOWBOARDING | If you love to cross-country, don't miss Royal Gorge, which serves up 140 km (124 miles) of track for all abilities, six trail systems on a whopping 6,000 acres, a ski school, and nine warming huts. Because the complex, affiliated with Sugar Bowl, sits right on the Sierra Crest, the views are drop-dead gorgeous. ✉ *9411 Pahatsi Dr., Soda Springs* ✣ *Off I–80, Soda Springs/Norden exit* ☎ *530/426–3871, 530/426–3871* 🌐 *www.royalgorge.com* ☞ *All-day pass $40.*

Sugar Bowl Ski Resort

SKIING/SNOWBOARDING | Opened in 1939 by Walt Disney, this is the oldest—and one of the best—resorts at Tahoe. Atop Donner Summit, it receives an incredible 500 inches of snowfall annually. Four peaks are connected by 1,650 acres of skiable terrain, with everything from gentle groomed corduroy to wide-open bowls to vertical rocky chutes and outstanding tree skiing. Snowboarders can hit two terrain parks with numerous boxes, rails, and jumps. Because it's more compact than some of the area's megaresorts, there's a gentility here that distinguishes Sugar Bowl from its competitors, making this a great place for families and a low-pressure, low-key place to learn to ski. It's not huge, but there's some very challenging terrain (experts: head to the Palisades). There is limited lodging at the base area. Facilities: 100 trails; 1,650 acres; 1,500-foot vertical drop; 12 lifts. ✉ *629 Sugar Bowl Rd., Norden* ✣ *Off Donner Pass Rd., 3 miles east of I–80 Soda Springs/Norden exit, 10 miles west of Truckee* ☎ *530/426–9000, 530/426–1111 snow phone* 🌐 *www.sugarbowl.com* 🎫 *Lift ticket from $118.*

Tahoe Donner Cross Country Ski Center

SKIING/SNOWBOARDING | Just north of Truckee, the center, which ranks among the nation's best cross-country venues for the skiing and the magnificent Sierra Crest views, includes 65 trails on 100 km (62 miles) of groomed tracks on more than 2,800 acres. In addition to cross-country skiing, there are fat-biking, dog, and snowshoeing trails. ✉ *15275 Alder Creek Rd.* ☎ *530/587–9484* 🌐 *www.tahoedonner.com/xc.*

EQUIPMENT RENTALS

BackCountry

SKIING/SNOWBOARDING | If you plan to ski or board the backcountry, you'll find everything from crampons to transceivers at this shop. ✉ *11400 Donner Pass Rd.* ☎ *530/582–0909* 🌐 *www.thebackcountry.net.*

Tahoe Dave's

SKIING/SNOWBOARDING | You can save money by renting skis and boards at this shop, which has the area's best selection and also repairs and tunes equipment. ✉ *10200 Donner Pass Rd., near Spring St.* ☎ *530/582–0900* 🌐 *www.tahoedaves.com.*

Carnelian Bay to Kings Beach

5–10 miles northeast of Tahoe City.

The small lakeside commercial districts of Carnelian Bay and Tahoe Vista service the thousand or so locals who live in the area year-round and the thousands more who have summer residences or launch their boats here. Kings Beach, the last town heading east on Highway 28 before the Nevada border, is full of basic motels and rental condos, restaurants, and shops.

GETTING HERE AND AROUND

To reach Kings Beach and Carnelian Bay from the California side, take Highway 89 north to Highway 28 north and then east. From the Nevada side, follow Highway 28 north and then west. TART provides public transportation in this area.

Beaches

Kings Beach State Recreation Area

BEACH—SIGHT | **FAMILY** | The north shore's 28-acre Kings Beach State Recreation Area, one of the largest such areas on the lake, is open year-round. The 700-foot-long sandy beach gets crowded in summer with people swimming, sunbathing, Jet Skiing, riding in paddleboats, spiking volleyballs, and tossing Frisbees. If you're going to spend the day, come early to snag a table in the picnic area; there's also a good playground. **Amenities:** food and drink; parking (fee); toilets; water sports. **Best for:** sunrise; sunset; swimming; windsurfing. ✉ *8318 N. Lake Blvd., Kings Beach* ☎ *530/523–3203* 🌐 *www.parks.ca.gov* 🎫 *$10 parking fee.*

Restaurants

Gar Woods Grill and Pier

$$$ | **ECLECTIC** | The view's the thing at this lakeside stalwart, where you can watch the sun shimmer on the water through the dining room's plateglass windows or from the heated outdoor deck. Price wise, this is a better bet for lunch or weekend breakfast than for dinner, at which grilled steak and fish are menu mainstays, but specialties like crab chiles rellenos and pomegranate braised pork ribs also merit consideration. **Known for:** lake views; grilled steak and fish; specialty cocktails. *Average main: $36* *5000 N. Lake Blvd., Carnelian Bay* *Hwy. 28, 2 miles west of Tahoe Vista* *530/546–3366* *www.garwoods.com.*

Jason's Beachside Grille

$$ | **AMERICAN** | If the kids want burgers but you want bourbon, area mainstay Jason's has a full bar as well as steaks, 10 kinds of burgers, teriyaki chicken, and a big salad bar. The whole place is wood, from floor to ceiling, lending it an ultrarustic feel. **Known for:** salad bar; summer dining on deck overlooking the lake; tables by fireplace in winter. *Average main: $21* *8338 N. Lake Blvd., Kings Beach* *530/546–3315* *jasonsbeachsidegrille.com.*

Soule Domain

$$$ | **ECLECTIC** | Rough-hewn wood beams, a vaulted wood ceiling, and in winter, a roaring fireplace, lend high romance to this cozy, 1927, pine-log cabin. Chef-owner Charlie Soule's specialties include curried almond chicken; sea scallops poached in Champagne with a kiwi-and-mango cream sauce; and a vegan sauté judiciously flavored with ginger, jalapeños, sesame seeds, and teriyaki sauce. **Known for:** romance by candlelight; skillfully prepared cuisine; suave service. *Average main: $30* *9983 Cove St., ½ block up Stateline Rd. off Hwy. 28, Kings Beach* *Restaurant is just west of Tahoe Biltmore casino at California–Nevada border.* *530/546–7529* *www.souledomain.com* *No lunch.*

Spindleshanks American Bistro and Wine Bar

$$$ | **AMERICAN** | A local favorite on the Old Brockway Golf Course, Spindleshanks serves mostly classic American cooking—ribs, steaks, and seafood updated with adventurous sauces—as well as house-made ravioli. Savor a drink from the full bar or choose a wine from the extensive list while you enjoy views of Lake Tahoe or the historic greens where Bing Crosby hosted his first golf tournament in 1934. **Known for:** classic American cooking; Lake Tahoe views; patio dining. *Average main: $28* *400 Brassie Ave., Kings Beach* *At Hwy. 267 and N. Lake Tahoe Blvd.* *530/546–2191* *www.spindleshankstahoe.com.*

Hotels

Ferrari's Crown Resort

$ | **HOTEL** | **FAMILY** | Great for families with kids and all travelers on a budget willing to trade style and amenities for below-average rates and (from some rooms) impressive water views, the family-owned Ferrari's has straightforward rooms in two formerly separate vintage-1950s motels, sitting side-by-side on the lake. **Pros:** family-friendly; lakeside location; a few rooms value-priced. **Cons:** older facility with unappealing exterior; thin walls; uninspired breakfast. *Rooms from: $115* *8200 N. Lake Blvd., Kings Beach* *530/546–3388, 800/645–2260* *www.tahoecrown.com* *72 rooms* *Free breakfast.*

Mourelatos Lakeshore Resort

$$ | **B&B/INN** | At first glance this family-run waterfront property looks like a slightly above-average two-story motel, but with a private beach, two hot tubs, ceaselessly alluring lake and mountain vistas, and summertime barbecuing, kayaking, and other extras it legitimately lays claim to the title of resort. **Pros:**

private beach; some rooms have full kitchens; summertime barbecuing and kayaking. **Cons:** decor a tad dated; books up quickly for summer; some rooms lack sufficient heat in winter. *Rooms from: $220 ✉ 6834 N. Lake Blvd., Tahoe Vista ☎ 530/546–9500 🌐 www.mlrtahoe.com 32 rooms Free breakfast.*

Rustic Cottages

$ | HOTEL | FAMILY | These charming clapboard cottages sit clustered beneath tall pine trees across the road from Lake Tahoe and a little beach. **Pros:** woodsy Old Tahoe feel; expanded continental breakfast; good value. **Cons:** older facility; some rooms are very small; lacks big-hotel amenities. *Rooms from: $134 ✉ 7449 N. Lake Blvd., Tahoe Vista ☎ 530/546–3523, 888/778–7842 🌐 www.rusticcottages.com 20 rooms No meals.*

Activities

KAYAKING

Wild Society

KAYAKING | FAMILY | Gaze at the underwater world while paddling a clear-bottom kayak around Kings Beach. Rentals incude (on request) wireless waterproof speakers with a USB plug, waterproof phone cases, binoculars, goggles, snorkels, cooler, cup holders, selfie sticks, and safety equipment. Guided kayak tours from Sand Harbor and SUP rentals (Kings Beach only) are also available. *✉ 8612 N. Lake Blvd., Kings Beach ✣ At Raccoon St. ☎ 530/553–1771 🌐 www.wildsocietylt.com one-hour single $60, tandem $80.*

Incline Village

5½ miles northeast of Kings Beach.

Incline Village dates from the early 1960s, when an Oklahoma developer bought 10,000 acres north of Lake Tahoe. His idea was to sketch out a plan for a town without a central commercial district, hoping to prevent congestion and to preserve the area's natural beauty. One-acre lakeshore lots originally cost $12,000 to $15,000; today you couldn't buy the same land for less than several million.

GETTING HERE AND AROUND

From the California side, reach Incline Village via Highway 89 or 267 to Highway 28. From South Lake Tahoe, take U.S. 50 north to Highway 28 north. TART serves the communities along Lake Tahoe's north and west shores from Incline Village to Tahoma.

ESSENTIALS

VISITOR INFORMATION Lake Tahoe Incline Village/Crystal Bay Visitors Bureau. *✉ 969 Tahoe Blvd. ☎ 775/832–1606, 800/468–2463 🌐 www.gotahoenorth.com.*

Sights

Lakeshore Drive

SCENIC DRIVE | Take this beautiful drive to see some of the most expensive real estate in Nevada. The route is discreetly marked: to find it, start at the Hyatt hotel and drive westward along the lake. *✉ Incline Village.*

★ Tahoe Science Center

MUSEUM | FAMILY | Learn how Lake Tahoe was formed, why it's so blue, and how its ecosystem is changing at Tahoe's only science center, which is affiliated with UC Davis researchers. Hands-on exhibits include aquariums, a virtual ecology lab and research boat, a watershed map with the 63 streams that flow into the lake (and the only one that flows out, the Truckee River), tables that teach how to identify trees, and a 3D theater. Visitors ages 8 and older will gain the most from the experience. *✉ 291 Country Club Dr. ✣ At Tahoe Center for Environmental Sciences, Sierra Nevada University campus ☎ 775/881–7560 🌐 tahoesciencecenter.com $5 Closed Sat.–Mon.*

★ Thunderbird Lodge

HOUSE | George Whittell, a San Francisco socialite who once owned 40,000 acres of property along the lake, began building this lodge in 1936, completing it in 1941. You can tour the mansion and the grounds by reservation only, and though it's pricey to do so, you'll be rewarded with a rare glimpse of a time when only the very wealthy had homes at Tahoe. The lodge is accessible via a bus from the Incline Village–Crystal Bay Visitors Bureau, several boats from the Hyatt in Incline Village, and a 1950 wooden cruiser from Zephyr Cove. ✉ *5000 Hwy. 28* ☎ *800/468–2463 tours, 775/832–8750 lodge* 🌐 *www.thunderbirdtahoe.org/tours* 🎟 *From $50 for bus tour, $169 for boat tours.*

Beaches

Lake Tahoe–Nevada State Park and Sand Harbor Beach

BEACH—SIGHT | Protecting much of the lake's eastern shore from development, this park comprises several sections that stretch from Incline Village to Zephyr Cove. Beaches and trails provide access to a wilder side of the lake, whether you're into cross-country skiing, hiking, or just relaxing at a picnic. With a gently sloping beach for lounging, crystal-clear water for swimming and snorkeling, and a picnic area shaded by cedars and pines, **Sand Harbor Beach** sometimes reaches capacity by 11 am on summer weekends. A handicap-accessible nature trail has interpretive signs and beautiful lake views. Pets are not allowed on the beach from mid-April through mid-October. **Amenities**: food and drink; parking ($10, $15 for non-NV license plates); toilets; water sports. **Best for**: boating; snorkeling; sunset; swimming; walking. ✉ *Sand Harbor Beach, Hwy. 28, 3 miles south of Incline Village* ☎ *775/831–0494* 🌐 *parks.nv.gov/parks/lake-tahoe-nevada-state-park.*

Restaurants

Azzara's

$$ | ITALIAN | This dependable if not fabulous Italian family restaurant serves a dozen pasta dishes and many pizzas, as well as chicken, veal, shrimp, and beef. Prices initially might seem high, but once you factor in soup or salad and garlic bread, it's a pretty good value. **Known for:** family run; daily specials; excellent tiramisu. $ *Average main: $22* ✉ *Raley's Shopping Center, 930 Tahoe Blvd., near Village Blvd.* ☎ *775/831–0346* 🌐 *www.azzaras.com* ⏲ *Closed Mon. No lunch.*

Le Bistro

$$$$ | FRENCH | Incline Village's hidden gem (this restaurant is hard to find, so ask for directions when you book) serves French-country cuisine in a romantic dining room with single-stem roses adorning linen-dressed tables. The five-course prix-fixe menu may include starters like flame-broiled eggplant with ratatouille or escargots, followed by one of several salads (try the gem lettuce Caesar) and lamb loin with lentils and tomato chutney or *coquille St.-Jacques* (scallops in cream sauce), paired with award-winning wines if you choose. **Known for:** romantic setting; five-course prix-fixe meal with wine pairings; gracious, attentive service. $ *Average main: $65* ✉ *120 Country Club Dr., #29* ✣ *Off Lakeshore Blvd.* ☎ *775/831–0800* 🌐 *www.lebistrotahoe.com* ⏲ *Closed Sun. and Mon. No lunch.*

★ Mountain High Sandwich Company

$ | AMERICAN | A casual plank-floored all-natural deli serving breakfast and lunch, Mountain High may well be the only place in Tahoe to find coconut chia seed pudding and similar delicacies. More familiar fare—biscuits and sausage gravy for breakfast, house-smoked tri-tip sandwiches for lunch—is also on the menu, with many selections gluten-free and vegan or vegetarian friendly. **Known for:** grab-and-go items; inventive soups; sustainable practices. $ *Average main: $11* ✉ *120 Country*

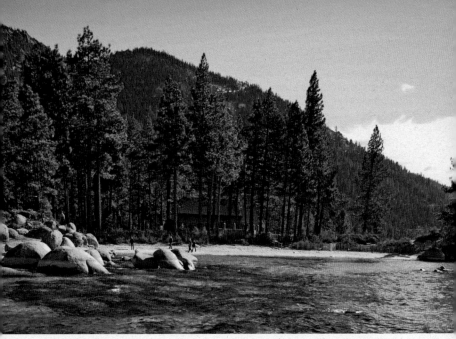

Get to Sand Harbor Beach in Lake Tahoe–Nevada State Park early; the park sometimes fills to capacity before lunchtime in summer.

Club Dr., Suite 28 ☎ *775/298–2636* 🌐 *www.mountainhighsandwichco.com* 🕒 *Closed Mon. No dinner.*

Hotels

Hyatt Regency Lake Tahoe

$$$$ | **RESORT** | A full-service destination resort on 26 acres of prime lakefront property, the Hyatt has a range of luxurious accommodations, from tower-hotel rooms to lakeside cottages. **Pros:** incredible views; low-key casino; luxurious accommodations. **Cons:** pricey (especially for families); feels corporate; smallish beach. *Rooms from: $379* ✉ *111 Country Club Dr.* ☎ *775/832–1234, 888/899–5019* 🌐 *www.hyatt.com* *422 rooms* *No meals.*

Activities

GOLF

Incline Championship

GOLF | Robert Trent Jones Sr. designed this challenging course of tightly cut, tree-lined fairways laced with water hazards that demand accuracy as well as distance skills. Greens fee includes a cart. ✉ *955 Fairway Blvd., at Northwood Blvd., north off Hwy. 28* ☎ *775/832–1146 pro shop* 🌐 *www.yourtahoeplace.com/golf-incline* *$199 weekdays, $220 weekends* *18 holes, 7106 yards, par 72.*

Incline Mountain

GOLF | Robert Trent Jones Jr. designed this executive (shorter) course that requires accuracy more than distance skills. The greens fee includes a cart. ✉ *690 Wilson Way, at Golfer's Pass, south off Hwy. 431* ☎ *866/925–4653 reservations, 775/832–1150 pro shop* 🌐 *www.yourtahoeplace.com/golf-incline* *From $70* *18 holes, 3527 yards, par 58.*

MOUNTAIN BIKING

Flume Trail Bikes

BICYCLING | You can rent bikes and get helpful tips from this company, which also operates a bike shuttle to popular trailheads. ✉ *1115 Tunnel Creek Rd., at Ponderosa Ranch Rd., off Hwy. 28* ☎ *775/298–2501* 🌐 *www.flumetrailtahoe.com* *From $50.*

SKIING

Diamond Peak

SKIING/SNOWBOARDING | Diamond Peak has affordable rates and many special programs. Snowmaking covers 75% of the mountain, and runs are groomed nightly. The ride up the 1-mile Crystal Express rewards you with fantastic views. Diamond Peak is less crowded than Tahoe's larger ski parks and provides free shuttles to nearby lodgings. A great place for beginners and intermediates, it's appropriately priced for families. Though there are some steep-aspect black-diamond runs, advanced skiers may find the acreage too limited. For snowboarders there's a small terrain park. **Facilities:** 30 trails; 655 acres; 1,840-foot vertical drop; 7 lifts. ✉ *1210 Ski Way, off Country Club Dr.* ☎ *775/832–1177* 🌐 *www.diamondpeak.com* 🎟 *Lift ticket from $114.*

Mt. Rose Ski Tahoe

SKIING/SNOWBOARDING | At this park, ski some of Tahoe's highest slopes and take in bird's-eye views of Reno, the lake, and Carson Valley. Though more compact than the bigger Tahoe resorts, Mt. Rose has the area's highest base elevation and consequently the driest snow. The mountain has a wide variety of terrain. The most challenging is the Chutes, 200 acres of gulp-and-go advanced-to-expert vertical. Intermediates can choose steep groomers or mellow, wide-open boulevards. Beginners have their own corner of the mountain, with gentle, wide slopes. Boarders and tricksters have several terrain parks to choose from, on opposite sides of the mountain, allowing them to follow the sun as it tracks across the resort. The mountain gets hit hard in storms; check conditions before heading up during inclement weather or on a windy day. **Facilities:** 61 trails; 1,200 acres; 1,800-foot vertical drop; 8 lifts. ✉ *22222 Mt. Rose Hwy., Reno* ✣ *Hwy. 431, 11 miles north of Incline Village* ☎ *800/754–7673* 🌐 *www.skirose.com* 🎟 *Lift ticket $145.*

Tahoe Meadows Snowplay Area

SKIING/SNOWBOARDING | This is the most popular area near the north shore for noncommercial cross-country skiing, sledding, tubing, snowshoeing, and snowmobiling. ✉ *Off Hwy. 431* ✣ *From Hwy. 28 at Incline Village, head north about 6½ miles on Hwy. 431 toward Mt. Rose Ski Area.*

Zephyr Cove

22 miles south of Incline Village.

The largest settlement between Incline Village and the Stateline area is Zephyr Cove, a tiny resort. It has a beach, marina, campground, picnic area, coffee shop in a log lodge, rustic cabins, and nearby riding stables.

GETTING HERE AND AROUND

From the north shore communities, reach Zephyr Cove by following Highway 28 along the eastern side of the lake. From South Lake Tahoe, take U.S. 50 north and then west. Public transportation isn't available in Zephyr Cove.

Cave Rock

NATURE SITE | Near Zephyr Cove, this 75 feet of solid stone at the southern end of Lake Tahoe–Nevada State Park is the throat of an extinct volcano. The impressive outcropping towers over a parking lot, a lakefront picnic ground, and a boat launch. The views are some of the best on the lake; this is a good spot to stop and take a picture. ⚠ **Cave Rock is a sacred burial site for the Washoe Indians. Climbing to it or through it is prohibited.** ✉ *U.S. 50, 4 miles north of Zephyr Cove* ☎ *775/588–7975* 🌐 *parks.nv.gov/parks* 🎟 *$10 ($15 for non-NV vehicles).*

Restaurants

Capisce?

$$$ | **ITALIAN** | The signature mushroom-and-tomato sauce is so thick it's called "gravy" at this roadside restaurant whose menu emphasizes old favorites from the Italian-American side of the family that runs it. The mildly spicy concoction adds zest to cioppino (seafood stew), lasagna, and pasta dishes that include house-made ravioli that some diners prefer slathered instead with a velvety butter-and-Parmesan-cheese sauce. **Known for:** old family recipes; full bar patronized by many locals; desserts including gooey-wonderful cinnamon bun. *Average main: $29 178 U.S. 50 775/580–7500 www.capiscelaketahoe.com Closed Mon. No lunch.*

Hotels

Zephyr Cove Resort

$$ | **RENTAL** | **FAMILY** | Beneath towering pines at the lake's edge stand 28 cozy, modern, vacation cabins with peaked knotty-pine ceilings. **Pros:** family-friendly; cozy cabins; old-school ambience. **Cons:** lodge rooms are basic; can be noisy in summer; not all cabins have fireplaces. *Rooms from: $220 760 U.S. 50, 4 miles north of Stateline 775/589–4906, 800/238–2463 www.zephyrcove.com 32 units No meals.*

Stateline

5 miles south of Zephyr Cove.

Stateline is the archetypal Nevada border town. Its four high-rise casinos are as vertical and contained as the commercial district of South Lake Tahoe, on the California side, is horizontal and sprawling. And Stateline is as relentlessly indoors-oriented as the rest of the lake is focused on the outdoors. This small strip is where you'll find the most concentrated action in Lake Tahoe: restaurants (including typical casino buffets), showrooms with semi-famous headliners and razzle-dazzle revues, tower-hotel rooms and suites, and 24-hour casinos.

GETTING HERE AND AROUND

From South Lake Tahoe take U.S. 50 north across the Nevada border to reach Stateline and its casinos. If coming from Reno's airport, take U.S. 395/I–580 south to Carson City, and then head west on U.S. 50 to the lake and head south. Or take the South Tahoe Express bus. Tahoe Transportation District operates daily bus service.

Beaches

Nevada Beach

BEACH—SIGHT | Although less than a mile long, this is the widest beach on the lake and especially good for swimming (many Tahoe beaches are rocky). You can boat and fish here, and there are picnic tables, barbecue grills, and a campground beneath the pines. This is the best place to watch the July 4th or Labor Day fireworks, but most of the summer the subdued atmosphere attracts families and those seeking a less-touristy spot. **Amenities:** parking; water sports; toilets. **Best for:** sunrise; swimming; walking. *Elk Point Rd., off U.S. 50, 3 miles north of Stateline 530/543–2600 www.fs.usda.gov/recarea/ltbmu/recarea/?recid=11757 $10 day-use fee Dogs permitted on leash in picnic areas but not on beach.*

Restaurants

★ Edgewood Tahoe

$$$ | **AMERICAN** | The three restaurants at Stateline's classy resort, all in impeccably designed spaces that make the most of the lakeside setting, offer some of the area's best dining, if on the pricey side. Head to the Bistro for casual-fancy breakfast, lunch, and dinner; Brooks Bar & Grill for inventive comfort food during lunch and dinner; and the Edgewood

Restaurant for evening fine dining with views across the lake to Mt. Tallac. **Known for:** a venue for all moods; vegan and gluten-free options; golf-course views from outdoor deck at Brooks. *Average main: $30* *Edgewood Tahoe, 100 Lake Pkwy.* *775/588–2787* *www.edgewoodtahoe.com/dine-imbibe.*

Hotels

Harrah's Tahoe Hotel/Casino

$ | **HOTEL** | The 18-story hotel's major selling point is that every room has two full bathrooms, a boon if you're traveling with family. **Pros:** lake and mountain views from upper-floor rooms; good midweek values; top-floor steak house with good views from all tables. **Cons:** can get noisy; uneven housekeeping; lacks intimacy. *Rooms from: $119* *15 U.S. 50, at Stateline Ave.* *775/588–6611, 800/427–7247* *www.caesars.com/harrahs-tahoe* *512 rooms* *No meals.*

Harveys Lake Tahoe Resort Hotel and Casino

$ | **HOTEL** | This resort began as a cabin in 1944, and now it's Tahoe's largest casino-hotel, where premium rooms have custom furnishings, oversize marble baths, minibars, and excellent lake views. **Pros:** live entertainment; great on-site restaurants; lake views from upper-floor rooms. **Cons:** can get loud at night; high summer rates; large property. *Rooms from: $119* *18 U.S. 50, at Stateline Ave.* *775/588–2411, 800/648–3361* *www.caesars.com/harveys-tahoe* *742 rooms* *No meals.*

★ The Lodge at Edgewood Tahoe

$$$$ | **RESORT** | On a prime lakefront parcel, this hotel makes a bold impression with its stone-and-walnut Great Hall, whose four-story wall of windows frames views across Lake Tahoe to grand Mt. Tallac. **Pros:** prime lakefront location; haute-rustic design; all rooms have balconies and fireplaces. **Cons:** high rates in-season; some rooms have no lake views; long walk to pool and hot tub from some rooms. *Rooms from: $410* *100 Lake Pkwy.* *775/588–2787, 888/769–1924* *www.edgewoodtahoe.com/lodge* *154 rooms* *No meals.*

Nightlife

Each of the major casinos has its own showroom, featuring everything from comedy to magic acts to sexy floor shows to Broadway musicals.

LIVE MUSIC

Harveys Outdoor Summer Concert Series

CONCERTS | Headliners such as Trevor Noah, Miranda Lambert, Blake Shelton, and Jackson Browne perform at this weekend concert series. *Harveys Lake Tahoe, 18 U.S. 50* *775/588–2411* *www.caesars.com/harveys-tahoe/shows.*

South Shore Room

CABARET | Classic acts like Chris Botti and Todd Rundgren play Harrah's big showroom, along with the psychedelic Pink Floyd Laser Spectacular show and comedians like Sinbad. *Harrah's Lake Tahoe, 15 U.S. 50* *775/586–6244 tickets, 775/588–6611* *www.caesars.com/harrahs-tahoe/shows.*

Activities

GOLF

Edgewood Tahoe

GOLF | Golfers of all skill levels enjoy this scenic lakeside course that has four sets of tees, offering a variety of course lengths. The greens fee includes an optional cart. *100 Lake Pkwy., at U.S. 50* *775/588–3566* *www.edgewood-tahoe.com/golf* *From $150 (varies throughout season)* *18 holes, 7529 yards, par 72.*

Reno

38 miles northeast of Incline Village.

Established in 1859 as a trading station at a bridge over the Truckee River, Reno grew along with the silver mines of nearby Virginia City and the transcontinental railroad that chugged through town. Train officials named it in 1868, but gambling—legalized in 1931—put Reno on the map. This is still a gambling town, with most of the casinos crowded into five square blocks downtown, but a thriving university scene and outdoor activities also attract visitors.

Parts of downtown are sketchy, but things are changing. Reno now touts family-friendly activities like kayaking on the Truckee, museums, and a downtown climbing wall. With more than 300 days of sunshine annually, temperatures year-round in this high-mountain-desert climate are warmer than at Tahoe, though rarely as hot as in Sacramento and the Central Valley, making strolling around town a pleasure.

GETTING HERE AND AROUND

Interstate 80 bisects Reno east–west, U.S. 395 north–south (south of town the road is signed U.S. 395/I–580). Greyhound and Amtrak stop here, and several airlines fly into Reno-Tahoe International Airport. RTC Ride provides bus service.

ESSENTIALS

BUS CONTACT RTC Ride. ✉ *Transit Center, E. 4th and Lake Sts.* ☎ *775/348–7433* 🌐 *www.rtcwashoe.com.*

VISITOR INFORMATION Reno Tahoe Visitor Center. ✉ *135 N. Sierra St.* ☎ *775/682–3800* 🌐 *www.visitrenotahoe.com.*

Sights

★ National Automobile Museum

MUSEUM | **FAMILY** | One of the best of museums of its kind is filled with antique and classic cars made by obscure and familiar companies like Packard, Studebaker, Maxwell, Oldsmobile, and Lincoln. Celebrity vehicles include the Lana Turner Chrysler (one of only six made), an Elvis Presley Cadillac, and a Mercury coupe driven by James Dean in the movie *Rebel Without a Cause*. Hard to miss are the experimental and still futuristic-looking 1938 Phantom Corsair and a gold-plated 1980 DeLorean. ✉ *10 S. Lake St., at Mill St.* ☎ *775/333–9300* 🌐 *www.automuseum.org* 🎫 *$12.*

Nevada Museum of Art

MUSEUM | A dramatic four-level structure designed by Will Bruder houses this splendid museum's collection, which focuses on themes such as the Sierra Nevada/Great Basin and altered-landscape photography. The building's exterior torqued walls are sided with a black zinc-based material that has been fabricated to resemble textures found in the Black Rock Desert. Inside the building, a staircase installed within the central atrium is lit by skylights and suspended by a single beam attached to the atrium ceiling. ✉ *160 W. Liberty St., and Hill St.* ☎ *775/329–3333* 🌐 *www.nevadaart.org* 🎫 *$10* ⊙ *Closed Mon. and Tues.*

Riverwalk District

PROMENADE | A formerly dilapidated section of Reno's waterfront is now the toast of the town. The Riverwalk itself is a half-mile promenade on the north side of the Truckee River, which flows around Wingfield Park, where festivals and other events take place. On the third Saturday of each month, local merchants host a **Wine Walk** between 2 and 5. For $30 you receive a glass and can sample fine wines at participating shops, bars, restaurants, and galleries. In July, look for outdoor art, opera, dance, and kids' performances as part of the monthlong **Artown festival** (🌐 *artown.org*), presented mostly in Wingfield Park. Also at Wingfield is the **Truckee River Whitewater Park.** With activities for all skill levels, it's become a major attraction for water-sports enthusiasts. ✉ *North side of Truckee River between Lake and Ralston Sts.* 🌐 *www.renoriver.org.*

Restaurants

Beaujolais Bistro

$$$$ | **FRENCH** | Across from the Truckee River, this Reno favorite serves earthy, country-style French food—escargots, steak frites with red wine sauce, cassoulet, and crisp sweetbreads with Madeira, along with fish and vegetarian selections—with zero pretension. Wood floors, large windows, and brick walls with a fireplace create a welcoming and intimate atmosphere. **Known for:** inventive cocktails; intimate atmosphere; more casual experience at the bar. *Average main: $36* ⊠ *753 Riverside Dr., near Winter St.* ☎ *775/323–2227* *www.beaujolaisbistro.com* *Closed Mon. No lunch.*

Hotels

Eldorado Resort Casino

$ | **HOTEL** | In the middle of glittering downtown, this resort's huge tower has rooms overlooking either the mountains or the lights of the city. **Pros:** spacious rooms; skywalk connects hotel to casinos; amusingly kitschy decor. **Cons:** noisy atmosphere; some housekeeping lapses; faux-everything decor can overwhelm. *Rooms from: $60* ⊠ *345 N. Virginia St.* ☎ *775/786–5700, 800/879–8879* *www.eldoradoreno.com* *816 rooms* *No meals.*

Peppermill Reno

$ | **HOTEL** | A few miles removed from downtown's flashy main drag, this property set a high standard for luxury in Reno, especially in the Tuscany Tower, whose 600 baroque suites have plush king-size beds, marble bathrooms, and European soaking tubs. **Pros:** luxurious rooms; casino decor; good coffee shop. **Cons:** deluge of neon may be off-putting to some; enormous size; mostly expensive dining. *Rooms from: $119* ⊠ *2707 S. Virginia St.* ☎ *775/826–2121, 866/821–9996* *www.peppermillreno.com* *1623 rooms* *No meals.*

Nightlife

CASINOS

Eldorado Resort Casino

CASINOS | Action-packed, with lots of slots and popular bar-top video poker, this casino also has good coffee-shop and food-court fare. Don't miss the Fountain of Fortune with its massive Florentine-inspired sculptures. ⊠ *345 N. Virginia St., at W. 4th St.* ☎ *775/786–5700, 800/879–8879* *www.eldoradoreno.com.*

Peppermill

CASINOS | A few miles from downtown, this casino is known for its excellent restaurants and neon-bright gambling areas. The Fireside cocktail lounge is a blast. ⊠ *2707 S. Virginia St., at Peppermill La.* ☎ *775/826–2121, 866/821–9996* *www.peppermillreno.com.*

Silver Legacy

CASINOS | A 120-foot-tall mining rig and video poker games draw gamblers to this razzle-dazzle casino. ⊠ *407 N. Virginia St., at W. 4th St.* ☎ *775/325–7411, 800/215–7721* *www.silverlegacyreno.com/gaming.*

Chapter 18

SAN FRANCISCO

Updated by
Trevor Felch, Monique Peterson,
Coral Sisk, and Ava Liang Zhao

Sights	Restaurants	Hotels	Shopping	Nightlife
★★★★★	★★★★☆	★★★★★	★☆☆☆☆	★☆☆☆☆

WELCOME TO SAN FRANCISCO

TOP REASONS TO GO

★ **The bay:** It's hard not to gasp as you catch sight of sunlight dancing on the water when you crest a hill, or watch the Golden Gate Bridge vanish and reemerge in the summer fog.

★ **The food:** San Franciscans are serious about what they eat, and with good reason. Home to some of the nation's best chefs, top restaurants, and finest local produce, it's hard not to eat well here.

★ **The shopping:** Shopaholics visiting the city will not be disappointed—San Francisco is packed with browsing destinations, everything from quirky boutiques to massive malls.

★ **The good life:** A laid-back atmosphere, beautiful surroundings, and oodles of cultural, culinary, and aesthetic pleasures … if you spend too much time here, you might not leave.

★ **The great outdoors:** From Golden Gate Park to sidewalk cafés in North Beach, San Franciscans relish their outdoor spaces.

1 **Union Square.** Has hotels and upscale stores aplenty.

2 **Chinatown.** A dense neighborhood full of shops and restaurants.

3 **SoMa and Civic Center.** A once-industrial, still-in-transition district anchored by SFMOMA and Yerba Buena Gardens.

4 **Civic Center.** Marked by monumental government buildings.

5 **Tenderloin.** Situated just north of the Civic Center.

6 **Hayes Valley.** West is this chic neighborhood.

7 **Nob Hill.** Old-money San Francisco.

8 **Russian Hill.** Steep streets lace this classy, au courant district.

9 **Polk Gulch.** A tiny area next door to Russian Hill.

10 **Pacific Heights.** Has some of the city's grand Victorians.

11 **Japantown.** A tight-knit Japanese American community with shopping and dining.

12 **Western Addition.** South of Japantown is this vibrant residential neighborhood.

13 **North Beach.** The city's small, historically Italian neighborhood.

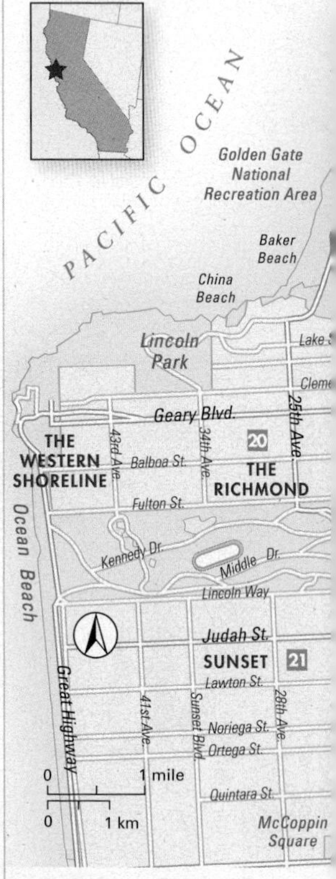

14 **Fisherman's Wharf.** A tourist mecca.

15 **Embarcadero.** The famous Ferry Building is at the foot of Market Street.

16 **Financial District.** A district of towering buildings inland from Embarcadero.

17 **The Marina.** Home to many young professionals.

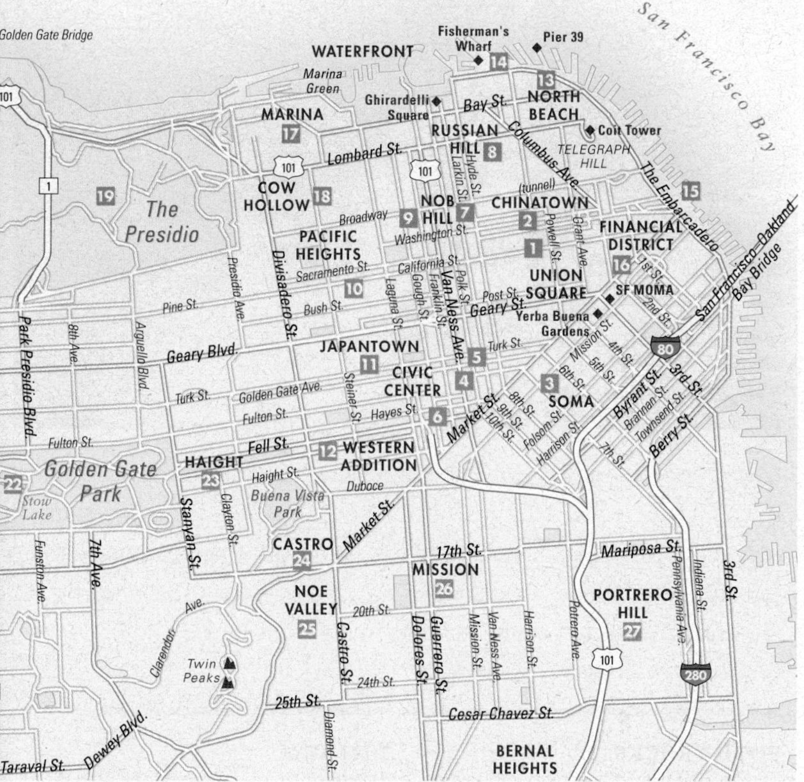

18 Cow Hollow. Affluent and residential.

19 The Presidio. A huge, wooded, shoreline park in the shadow of the Golden Gate Bridge.

20 The Richmond. Residential district north of Golden Gate Park.

21 The Sunset. The city's largest residential and commercial area.

22 Golden Gate Park. San Francisco's backyard.

23 The Haight. Still marked by a '60s atmosphere.

24 The Castro. Rainbow-flagwaving, in-your-face fab.

25 Noe Valley. A cute, pricey neighborhood favored by young families.

26 Mission District. A prime destination for restaurants and hip bars.

27 Potrero Hill. East of the Mission and off the tourist path.

HOW TO EAT LIKE A LOCAL

Several farmers' markets occupy the Ferry Building

San Francisco may well be the most piping-red-hot dining scene in the nation now. After all, with a booming tech industry, there are mouths to feed. Freedom to do what you want. Innovation. Eccentricity. These words define the culture, the food, and the cuisine of the city by the bay. Get in on what locals know by enjoying their favorite foods.

FOOD TRUCKS

This is where experimentation begins, where the overhead is low, and risk-taking is fun. From these mobile kitchens careers are launched. A food meet-up called "Off the Grid" happens in season at Fort Mason where you can have a progressive dinner among the 25 or so trucks. Year-round the convoy roams to different locations, selling things like Korean poutine, Indian burritos, and Vietnamese burgers. Each dish seems to reflect a refusal to follow the norm.

DIM SUM

The tradition of dim sum took hold in San Francisco when Chinese immigrants from Guangdong Province arrived with Cantonese cuisine. These earlier settlers eventually established teahouses and bakeries that sold dim sum, like the steamed dumplings stuffed with shrimp (*har gow*) or pork (*shao mai*). Now carts roll from table to table in Chinatown restaurants—and other parts of the city. Try the grilled and fried bite-size savories but also the sweets like *dan tat,* an egg custard tart.

BARBECUE

Whaaa? San Francisco barbecue? And what would that be? You can bet it's meat from top purveyors nearby. The city is surrounded by grazing lands, where the animals and their minders, the ranchers, are king. Until now, meats came simply plated. Now it's messy, with smokiness, charred crusts, and gorgeous marbling. But you may never hear of a San-Fran-style barbecue because, in the words of one chef, we're "nondenominational." You'll see it all: Memphis, Texas, Carolina, and Kansas City.

ICE CREAM

How ice cream became so popular in a place that spends many of its 365 days below the 75 degree mark is a mystery. But the lines attest to the popularity of the frozen dessert that gets its own San Francisco twist. This is the vanilla-bean vanilla and Tcho chocolate crowd. Bourbon and cornflakes? Reposado tequila? Cheers to that. Diversity and local produce is blended into flavors like ube (purple yam), yuzu, and Thai latte.

BURRITOS

This stuffed tortilla got its Bay Area start in the 1960s in the Mission District. Because the size and fillings distinguish it from other styles, it became known as the Mission burrito. Look for rice (Southern Californians are cringing), beans, salsa, and enough meat in the burrito for two meals. The aluminum foil keeps the interior neat, in theory. Popular choices are *carne asada* (beef) and *carnitas* (pork). But then there's *lengua* (beef tongue) and *birria* (goat). This is a hands-on meal.

Dim sum

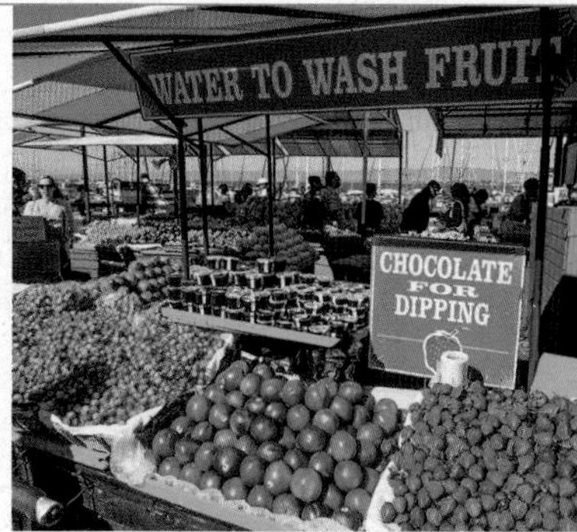

The food truck

COFFEE

Coffee roasters here are like sports teams in other cities. You pick one of the big five or six to be loyal to, and defend it tirelessly. San Francisco favorites source impeccably and blend different beans as if they were wine making. In addition, a few of the big names—Four Barrel, Sightglass, Ritual, Blue Bottle—roast their own to control what they grind and pour at their outlets across the city—and now nationally and internationally.

FARMERS' MARKETS

These are our new grocery stores. They're the places to discover the latest in fruits, vegetables, and dried beans—much of it grown within a 60-mile radius. Cheeses, cured salami, breads, and nuts are sampled. Then there are the local ready-to-eat snacks, like pizza and *huevos rancheros*. The most popular market is the one on Saturday at the Ferry Plaza.

On a 46½-square-mile strip of land between San Francisco Bay and the Pacific Ocean, San Francisco has charms great and small. Residents cherish it for the same reasons visitors do: proximity to the bay, rows of hillside Victorian homes, sunsets framed by the Golden Gate Bridge, world-class cuisine.

You can spend hours exploring downtown, Chinatown, North Beach, the northern and western waterfronts, and Golden Gate Park, along with colorful neighborhoods like the Haight, the Mission murals, and the Castro. The city's attraction, though, goes much deeper than its alluring physical space, from the diversity of its neighborhoods to its free-spirited tolerance. All these things together explain why many San Franciscans—despite the dizzying cost of living and the chilly summers—can't imagine calling any place else home.

The City by the Bay's highlights include a cable car ride over Nob Hill, a walk down the Filbert Street Steps, gazing at the thundering Pacific from the cliffs of Lincoln Park, cheering the San Francisco Giants to *beat L.A.* in lively Oracle Park, and eating freshly shucked oysters at the Ferry Building. The diverse wonders of this beautiful metropolis inspire at every turn.

Planning

When to Go

Possibly the best time is September and October, when the city's summer-like weather brings outdoor concerts and festivals. The climate here always feels Mediterranean and moderate, with a foggy, sometimes chilly bite. The temperature rarely drops below 40°F, and anything warmer than 80°F is considered a heat wave. Be prepared for rain in winter, especially December and January. Winds off the ocean can add to the chill factor. That old joke about summer in San Francisco feeling like winter is true at heart, but once you move inland, it gets warmer. (And some locals swear that the thermostat has inched up in recent years.)

Getting Here and Around

AIR

The major gateway to San Francisco is San Francisco International Airport (SFO), 15 miles south of the city. It's off U.S. 101 near Millbrae and San Bruno. Oakland International Airport (OAK) is across the bay, not much farther away from downtown San Francisco (via Interstate 80 east and Interstate 880 south), but rush-hour traffic on the Bay Bridge may lengthen travel times considerably. San Jose International Airport (SJC) is about 40 miles south of San Francisco; travel time depends largely on traffic flow, but plan on an hour and a half with moderate traffic.

AIRPORTS Oakland International Airport. *(OAK) ✉ 1 Airport Dr., Oakland ☎ 510/563–3300 🌐 www.oaklandairport.com.* **San Francisco International Airport.** *(SFO) ✉ McDonnell and Links Rds., San Francisco ☎ 800/435–9736, 650/821–8211 🌐 www.flysfo.com.* **San Jose International Airport.** *(SJC) ✉ 1701 Airport Blvd., San Jose ☎ 408/392–3600 🌐 www.flysanjose.com.*

BART

BART (Bay Area Rapid Transit) trains, which run until midnight, travel under the bay via tunnel to connect San Francisco with Oakland, Berkeley, and other cities and towns beyond. Within San Francisco, stations are limited to downtown, the Mission, and a couple of outlying neighborhoods.

Trains travel frequently from early morning until evening on weekdays. After 8 pm weekdays and on weekends, there's often a 20-minute wait between trains on the same line. Trains also travel south from San Francisco as far as Millbrae. BART trains connect downtown San Francisco to San Francisco International Airport; the ride costs $9.65. Intracity San Francisco fares are $2.10; intercity fares are $3.70 to $11.45. BART bases its ticket prices on miles traveled and doesn't offer price breaks by zone. The easy-to-read maps posted in BART stations list fares based on destination, radiating out from your starting point of the current station.

During morning and evening rush hour, trains within the city are crowded—even standing room can be hard to come by. Cars at the far front and back of the train are less likely to be filled to capacity. Smoking, eating, and drinking are prohibited on trains and in stations.

CONTACTS Bay Area Rapid Transit. *(BART) ☎ 510/465–2278 🌐 www.bart.gov.*

BOAT

Several ferry lines run out of San Francisco. Blue & Gold Fleet operates a number of routes, including service to Sausalito ($13 one-way) and Tiburon ($13 one-way). Tickets are sold at Pier 39; boats depart from Pier 41 nearby. Alcatraz Cruises, owned by Hornblower Cruises and Events, operates the ferries to Alcatraz Island ($42, including audio tour and National Park Service ranger-led programs) from Pier 33, about a half-mile east of Fisherman's Wharf. Boats leave 14 times a day (more in summer), and the journey itself takes 30 minutes. Allow at least 2½ hours for a round-trip jaunt. Golden Gate Ferry runs daily to and from Sausalito and Larkspur ($13.50 and $13 one-way), leaving from Pier 1, behind the San Francisco Ferry Building. The Alameda/Oakland Ferry operates daily between Alameda's Main Street Terminal, Oakland's Jack London Square, and San Francisco's Pier 41 and the Ferry Building ($7.20 one-way); some ferries go only to Pier 41 or the Ferry Building, so ask when you board. Purchase tickets on board.

CONTACTS Alameda/Oakland Ferry. ☎ *877/643–3779* 🌐 *sanfranciscobayferry.com.* **Alcatraz Cruises.** ☎ *415/981–7625* 🌐 *www.alcatrazcruises.com.* **Blue & Gold Fleet.** ☎ *415/705–8200* 🌐 *www.blueandgoldfleet.com.* **Ferry Building Marketplace.** ✉ *1 Ferry Bldg., at foot of Market St. on Embarcadero, San Francisco* 🌐 *www.ferrybuildingmarketplace.com.* **Golden Gate Ferry.** ☎ *415/923–2000* 🌐 *www.goldengateferry.org.*

BUS

Outside the city, AC Transit serves the East Bay, and Golden Gate Transit serves Marin County and a few cities in southern Sonoma County.

CABLE-CAR

Don't miss the sensation of moving up and down some of San Francisco's steepest hills in a clattering cable car. Jump aboard as it pauses at a designated stop, and wedge yourself into any available space. Then just hold on. At this writing, cable-car service is set to resume later in fall 2021, but not all lines; check sfmta.com for updates.

The fare (for one direction) is $8. Buy tickets in advance at the kiosks at the cable-car turnarounds at Hyde and Beach Streets and at Powell and Market Streets. Or consider MuniMobile or a Clipper Card; see 🌐 *sfmta.com.* Cash purchases require exact change.

The heavily traveled Powell–Mason and Powell–Hyde lines begin at Powell and Market Streets near Union Square and terminate at Fisherman's Wharf; lines for these routes can be long, especially in summer. The California Street line runs east and west from Market and California Streets to Van Ness Avenue; there's often no wait to board this route.

CAR

Driving in San Francisco can be a challenge because of the one-way streets, snarly traffic, and steep hills. The first two elements can be frustrating enough, but those hills are tough for unfamiliar drivers. ■ **TIP→ Remember to curb your wheels when parking on hills—turn wheels away from the curb when facing uphill, toward the curb when facing downhill. You can get a ticket if you don't do this.**

MUNI

The San Francisco Municipal Railway, or Muni, operates light-rail vehicles, the historic F-line streetcars along Fisherman's Wharf and Market Street, buses, and the world-famous cable cars. Light-rail travels along Market Street to the Mission District and Noe Valley (J line), Ingleside (K line), and the Sunset District (L, M, and N lines) while also passing through the West Portal, Glen Park, and Castro neighborhoods. The N line continues around the Embarcadero to the Caltrain station at 4th and King Streets; the T-line light-rail runs from the Castro, down Market Street, around the Embarcadero, and south past Mission Bay and Hunters Point to Sunnydale Avenue and Bayshore Boulevard. Muni provides 24-hour service on select lines to all areas of the city.

On buses and streetcars, the fare is $2.50. Exact change is required, and dollar bills are accepted in the fare boxes. For all Muni vehicles other than cable cars, 90-minute transfers are issued free upon request at the time the fare is paid. These are valid for unlimited transfers in any direction until they expire (time is indicated on the ticket). Cable cars cost $8 and include no transfers *(see Cable-Car Travel)*.

One-day ($13), three-day ($31), and seven-day ($41) Visitor Passports valid on the entire Muni system can be purchased at several outlets, including the cable-car ticket booth at Powell and Market Streets and the visitor information center downstairs in Hallidie Plaza. A monthly ticket is available for $81, which can be used on all Muni lines (including cable cars) and on BART within city limits. The San Francisco CityPass ($76), a discount ticket booklet to several major city attractions, also covers all Muni travel for seven consecutive days.

■ **TIP→ Save money by purchasing your Passports on MuniMobile, the mobile ticketing app of the San Francisco Metropolitan Transportation Authority (SFMTA).**

BUS AND MUNI CONTACTS San Francisco Municipal Transportation Agency . *(Muni)* ☎ *311, 415/701–3000* 🌐 *www.sfmta.com.*

TAXI

Taxi service is notoriously bad in San Francisco, and finding a cab can be frustratingly difficult. Popular nightlife locales, such as the Mission, SoMa, North Beach, and the Castro, are the easiest places to hail a cab off the street; hotel taxi stands are also an option. If you're going to the airport, make a reservation or book a shuttle instead. Taxis in San Francisco charge $3.50 for the first 0.5 mile (one of the highest base rates in the United States), 55¢ for each additional 0.2 mile, and 55¢ per minute in stalled traffic; a $4 surcharge is added for trips from the airport. There's no charge for additional passengers; there's no surcharge for luggage. For trips farther than 15 miles outside city limits, multiply the metered rate by 1.5; tolls and tip are extra.

That said, San Francisco's poor taxi service was a direct factor in the creation of ridesharing services, such as Uber and Lyft, which are easy to use and prominent throughout the city and its surrounding areas. San Franciscans generally regard taxis as a thing of the past and use ridesharing on a day-to-day basis. If you're willing to share a car with strangers, a trip within the city can run as low as $4; rates go up for private rides and during peak-demand times. These services are especially economical when going to or from the airport, where a shared ride starts at about $25—half the cost of a cab.

CONTACTS Flywheel Taxi. ☎ *415/970–1300* 🌐 *flywheeltaxi.com.* **Luxor Cab.** ☎ *415/282–4141* 🌐 *www.luxorcab.com.* **National Veterans Cab.** ☎ *415/648–4444.* **Yellow Cab.** ☎ *415/333–3333* 🌐 *yellowcabsf.com.*

COMPLAINTS San Francisco Police Department Taxi Complaints. ☎ *415/701–4400.*

TRAIN

Amtrak trains travel to the Bay Area from some cities in California as well as the greater United States. The Coast Starlight travels north from Los Angeles to Seattle, passing the Bay Area along the way, but contrary to its name, the train runs inland through the Central Valley for much of its route through Northern California; the most scenic stretch is in Southern California, between San Luis Obispo and Los Angeles. Amtrak also has several routes between San Jose, Oakland, and Sacramento. The California Zephyr travels from Chicago to the Bay Area, with spectacular alpine vistas as it crosses the Sierra Nevada range. San Francisco doesn't have an Amtrak train station but does have an Amtrak bus stop at the Ferry Building, from which shuttle buses transport passengers to trains in Emeryville, just over the Bay Bridge. Shuttle buses also connect the Emeryville train station with BART and other points in downtown San Francisco. You can buy a California Rail Pass, which gives you 7 days of travel in a 21-day period, for $159.

Caltrain connects San Francisco to Palo Alto, San Jose, Santa Clara, and many smaller cities en route. In San Francisco, trains leave from the main depot, at 4th and Townsend Streets, and a rail-side stop at 22nd and Pennsylvania Streets. One-way fares are $3.75 to $15, depending on the number of zones through which you travel; tickets are valid for four hours after purchase time. A ticket is $8.25 from San Francisco to Palo Alto, at least $10.50 to San Jose. You can also buy a day pass ($7.50–$30) for unlimited travel in a 24-hour period. It's worth waiting for an express train for trips that last from 1 to 1¾ hours. On weekdays, trains depart three or four times per hour during the morning and evening, but only once or twice per hour during daytime non-commute hours and late night. Weekend trains run once per hour, though there are two bullet trains per day, one in late morning and one in early evening The system shuts down after midnight. There are no onboard ticket sales. You must buy tickets before boarding the train or risk paying up to $230 for fare evasion.

CONTACTS Amtrak. ☎ *800/872–7245* 🌐 *www.amtrak.com.* **Caltrain.** ☎ *800/660–4287* 🌐 *www.caltrain.com.* **San Francisco Caltrain station.** ✉ *700 4th St., near Townsend St., SoMa* ☎ *800/660–4287* 🌐 *www.caltrain.com/stations.*

Restaurants

Make no mistake, San Francisco is one of America's top food cities. Some of the biggest landmarks are restaurants. In fact, on a Saturday, the Ferry Building—a temple to local eating—may attract more visitors than the Golden Gate Bridge: cheeses, breads, "salty pig parts," homemade delicacies, and sensory-perfect vegetables and fruits attract rabidly dedicated aficionados. You see, San Franciscans are a little loco about their edibles. If you ask them what their favorite season is, don't be surprised if they respond, "tomato season."

Some renowned restaurants are booked weeks or even months in advance. But you can get lucky at the last minute if you're flexible—and friendly. Most restaurants keep a few tables open for walk-ins and VIPs. Show up for dinner early (5:30 pm) or late (after 9 pm) and politely inquire about any last-minute vacancies or cancellations.

The impact of the COVID-19 pandemic on the restaurant scene in the Bay Area, as in many other parts of the globe, has been widespread and severe. Many restaurants and bars have responded with adjusted hours, changed menus, and limited indoor or only outdoor seating. Call the restaurant or check their website for the latest information. One upside is that temporary parklets and pedestrian-friendly slow streets may become permanent fixtures, lending an air of alfresco European leisure to the streets of San Francisco.

Restaurant reviews have been shortened. For full information, visit Fodors.com. Prices are the average cost of a main course at dinner or, if dinner is not served, at lunch.

What It Costs

	$	$$	$$$	$$$$
RESTAURANTS	under $16	$16–$22	$23–$30	over $30

Hotels

San Francisco accommodations are diverse, ranging from cozy inns and kitschy motels, to chic little inns and true grande dames, housed in century-old structures and sleek high-rises (though some closed temporarily or permanently due to COVID 19). While the tech boom has skyrocketed the prices of even some of the most dependable low-cost options, luckily, some Fodor's faves still offer fine accommodations without the jaw-dropping prices to match those steep hills. In fact, the number of reasonably priced accommodations is impressive.

Hotel reviews have been shortened. For full information, visit Fodors.com. Prices are the lowest cost of a standard double room in high season.

What It Costs

	$	$$	$$$	$$$$
HOTELS	under $150	$150–$249	$250–$350	over $350

Nightlife

After hours, the city's business folk and workers give way to costume-clad partygoers, hippies and hipsters, downtown divas, frat boys, and those who prefer something a little more clothing-optional. Downtown and the Financial District remain pretty serious even after dark, and Nob Hill is staid, though you can't beat views from penthouse lounges, the most famous being the Top of the Mark (in the InterContinental Mark Hopkins). Nearby North Beach is an even better starting point for an evening out.

Always lively, North Beach's options include family-friendly dining spots, historic bars from the city's bohemian past (among them Jack Kerouac's old haunts), and even comedy clubs where stars like Robin Williams and Jay Leno cut their teeth. In SoMa there are plenty of places to catch a drink before a Giants game and brewpubs to celebrate in afterward. SoMa also hosts some of the hottest dance clubs, along with some saucy gay bars. While Union Square can be a bit trendy, even the swanky establishments have loosened things up in recent years.

Heading west to Hayes Valley, a more sophisticated crowd dabbles in the burgeoning "culinary cocktail movement." Up-and-coming singles gravitate north of here to Cow Hollow and the Marina. Polk Gulch was the city's gay mecca before the Castro and still hosts some wild bars, but things get downright outlandish in the Castro District. Indie hipsters of all persuasions populate the Mission and Haight Districts by night. Keep in mind, though, that some of the best times San Francisco has to offer are off the beaten path. And a good party can still be found in even the sleepiest of neighborhoods, such as Bernal Heights and Dogpatch.

Sports bars and hotel bars tend to be open on Sunday, but others may be closed. A few establishments—especially wine bars and bars attached to restaurants—also close on Monday.

Performing Arts

The heart of the mainstream theater district lies on or near Geary Street, mostly west of Union Square, though touring Broadway shows land a little farther afield at big houses like the Orpheum and the Golden Gate. But theater can be found all over town. For a bit of culture shock, slip out to eclectic districts, maybe the Mission or the Haight, where smaller theater companies reside and short-run and one-night-only performances happen on a regular basis.

The city's opera house and symphony hall present the musical classics, and venues like the Fillmore and the Warfield host major rock and jazz talents, but the city's extensive festival circuit broadens the possibilities considerably. Stern Grove presents a popular, free summer music festival; Noise Pop is the premier alt-rock showcase; and Hardly Strictly Bluegrass is a beloved celebration of bluegrass, country, and roots music, attracting hundreds of thousands of attendees from all over every year.

Shopping

Each neighborhood has its own distinctive finds, whether it's 1960s housewares, cheeky stationery, or vintage Levi's. If shopping in San Francisco has a downside, it's that real bargains can be few and far between. Sure, neighborhoods like the Lower Haight and the Mission have thrift shops and other inexpensive stores, but you won't find many discount outlets in the city, where rents are sky-high and space is at a premium.

Serious shoppers head straight to Union Square, San Francisco's main shopping area and the site of most of its department stores, including Macy's, Neiman Marcus, and Saks Fifth Avenue. Nearby are such platinum-card international boutiques as Yves Saint Laurent, Cartier, Emporio Armani, Gucci, Hermès, and Louis Vuitton.

Seasonal sales, usually in late January and late July into August, are good opportunities for finding deep discounts on clothing. The *San Francisco Chronicle* and *San Francisco Examiner* advertise sales. For smaller shops, check the free *SF Weekly,* which can be found on street corners every Wednesday. Sample sales are usually held by individual manufacturers, so check your favorite company's website before visiting.

Visitor Information

CONTACTS San Francisco Visitor Information Center. ✉ *Moscone Center, 749 Howard St. , between 3rd and 4th Sts., SoMa* ☏ *415/391–2000* 🌐 *www.sftravel.com.*

Union Square

The city's finest department stores put on their best faces in Union Square, along with such exclusive emporiums as Tiffany & Co. and Bulgari, and such big-name retailers as Nike, Apple, H&M, and Disney. Visitors lay their heads at several dozen hotels within a three-block walk of the square, and the downtown theater district is nearby. Union Square is shopping-centric; nonshoppers will find fewer enticements here.

Sights

Maiden Lane

NEIGHBORHOOD | Known as Morton Street in the raffish Barbary Coast era, this former red-light district reported at least one murder a week during the late 19th century, though things cooled down after the 1906 fire: these days Maiden Lane is a chic, designer-boutique-lined pedestrian mall stretching two blocks, between Stockton and Kearny Streets. Wrought-iron gates close the street to traffic most days between 11 and 5, when the lane becomes an alfresco hot spot dotted with umbrella-shaded tables. It's also popular with photographers and Instagrammers for its quaint-chic aesthetic. At **140 Maiden Lane** is the only Frank Lloyd Wright building in San Francisco, fronted by a large brick archway. The curving ramp and skylights of the interior, which houses exclusive Italian menswear boutique Isaia, are said to have been his model for the Guggenheim Museum in New York. ✉ *Between Stockton and Kearny Sts., Union Sq.*

Union Square

PLAZA | The marquee destination for big-name shopping in the city and within walking distance of many hotels, Union Square is home base for many visitors. The Westin St. Francis hotel and Macy's line two of the square's sides, and Saks, Neiman Marcus, and Tiffany & Co. edge the other two. Four globular contemporary lamp sculptures by the artist R. M. Fischer preside over the landscaped, 2½-acre park anchored by the monument to Admiral George Dewey. The area also has a café with outdoor seating, an open-air stage, and the city's favorite holiday season ice-skating rink—along with a kaleidoscope of characters: office workers sunning and brown-bagging, street musicians, shoppers taking a rest, kids chasing pigeons, and a fair number of homeless people. The constant clang of cable cars traveling up and down Powell Street helps maintain a festive mood. ✉ *Bordered by Powell, Stockton, Post, and Geary Sts., Union Sq.*

The epicenter of high-end shopping, Union Square is lined with department stores.

The Westin St. Francis San Francisco on Union Square

HOTEL—SIGHT | Built in 1904 and barely established as the most sumptuous hotel in town before it was ravaged by fire following the 1906 earthquake, this grande-dame hotel designed by Walter Danforth Bliss and William Baker Faville reopened in 1907 with the addition of a luxurious Italian Renaissance–style residence designed to attract loyal clients from among the world's rich and powerful. The hotel's checkered past includes the ill-fated 1921 bash in the suite of the silent-film superstar Fatty Arbuckle, at which a woman became ill, leading to her death. Arbuckle endured three sensational trials for rape and murder before being acquitted, by which time his career was kaput. In 1975, Sara Jane Moore, standing among a crowd outside the hotel, attempted to shoot then-President Gerald Ford. Of course, the grand lobby contains no plaques commemorating these events. ■ **TIP→ Some visitors make the St. Francis a stop whenever they're in town, soaking up the lobby ambience or enjoying a cocktail at the Clock Bar or lunch at the Oak Room Restaurant.** ✉ *335 Powell St., at Geary St., Union Sq.* ☎ *415/397–7000* 🌐 *westinstfrancis.com.*

Restaurants

★ Liholiho Yacht Club

$$$$ | MODERN AMERICAN | Inspired but not defined by the chef's native Hawaii, Ravi Kapur's lively restaurant is known for big-hearted, high-spirited cooking, including contemporary riffs on poke and Spam but also squid served with crispy tripe and manila clams in coconut curry. The dining room and front bar area are perpetually packed, and are dominated by an enormous photo of a beaming woman who happens to be none other than the chef's mother. **Known for:** beef tongue on poppy-seed steamed buns "bao"; giant mains that serve two to four people; beautifully composed cocktails. *[$] Average main: $42* ✉ *871 Sutter St., Union Sq.* ☎ *415/440–5446* 🌐 *lycsf.com* ⏲ *Closed Sun. No lunch.*

Sights

1 Chinatown Gate.......... **C4**

2 Golden Gate Fortune Cookie Factory........... **C2**

3 Maiden Lane............ **D5**

4 Portsmouth Square...... **C2**

5 Tin How Temple.......... **C3**

6 Union Square............ **C5**

7 The Westin St. Francis San Francisco on Union Square............ **B5**

Restaurants

1 Liholiho Yacht Club..... **A5**

2 Mister Jiu's............... **C3**

3 Sam Wo Restaurant..... **C3**

Hotels

1 Cornell Hotel De France................ **B4**

2 Hotel Adagio, Autograph Collection... **A5**

3 Hotel Emblem San Francisco........... **B4**

4 Hotel Triton............... **C4**

5 The Westin St. Francis San Francisco on Union Square............ **B5**

Hotels

★ Cornell Hotel de France

$ | **HOTEL** | In their six-story, 1910 structure, hosts Claude and Micheline Lambert have created a bit of Paris a few blocks from Union Square, with rooms individually decorated with pastel colors, a stenciled ceiling, and prints of works by Picasso, Chagall, Klimt, and other European artists. **Pros:** excellent room quality and design for the price; updated bathrooms; special packages and discounts. **Cons:** several blocks from the center of things; surrounding area mildly dodgy after dark; small lobby. *$ Rooms from: $144 ✉ 715 Bush St., Union Sq. ☎ 415/421–3154 🌐 www.cornellhotel.com 🛏 50 rooms 🍽 Free breakfast.*

Hotel Adagio, Autograph Collection

$ | **HOTEL** | The Spanish-colonial facade of this 16-story theater-row hotel complements its chic interior, with good-size rooms that have beautiful sea-blue carpets and plenty of tech amenities for working or relaxing after sightseeing. **Pros:** Marriott-run property with boutique-hotel charm; central location for lots of sightseeing; good drinks and scene at lobby bar, the Mortimer. **Cons:** street noise; area can be dicey at night; adjacent to a popular outdoor bar. *$ Rooms from: $159 ✉ 550 Geary St., Union Sq. ☎ 415/775–5000 🌐 www.hoteladagiosf.com 🛏 171 rooms 🍽 No meals.*

Hotel Emblem San Francisco

$ | **HOTEL** | Inspiration is everywhere at this intimate hotel, with a prominent literary theme that celebrates San Francisco's Beat poets, from its lobby wall of books and poetry-laced carpet to in-room libraries and typewriters. **Pros:** fun, creative vibe; excellent eating and drinking options; amenities available by request include diffusers, a humidifier, and bath bombs. **Cons:** some guests might feel the hotel is trying too hard to be hip; no on-site fitness option; some rooms on the small side. *$ Rooms from: $159 ✉ 562 Sutter St., Union Sq. ☎ 415/433–4434 🌐 www.viceroyhotelsandresorts.com/en/emblem 🛏 96 rooms 🍽 No meals.*

Cable Car Terminus

Two of the three cable-car lines begin and end their runs at Powell and Market streets, a couple blocks south of Union Square. These two lines are the most scenic, and both pass near Fisherman's Wharf, so they're usually clogged with first-time sightseers. The wait to board a cable car at this intersection is longer than at any other stop in the system. If you'd rather avoid the mob, board the less-touristy California line at the bottom of Market Street, at Drumm Street.

Hotel Triton

$ | **HOTEL** | With a strong location at the convergence of Chinatown, the Financial District, and Union Square, this boutique anchor attracts a design-conscious crowd and is highlighted by its intricately decorated lobby featuring marble floors, a wood-beam ceiling, and art from around the world. **Pros:** arty environs; Carrara marble bathrooms and showers; beautiful Café de la Presse next door offers discount for guests. **Cons:** rooms and baths are on the small side; hallways feel cramped; room decor feels a bit dated to some guests. *$ Rooms from: $160 ✉ 342 Grant Ave., Union Sq. ☎ 415/394–0500 🌐 www.hoteltriton.com 🛏 140 rooms 🍽 No meals.*

The Westin St. Francis San Francisco on Union Square

$$ | **HOTEL** | The survivor of two major earthquakes, some headline-grabbing scandals, and even an attempted presidential assassination, this richly appointed and superbly located grande

dame dating to 1904 is comprised of the landmark building, renovated in 2018, and a modern 32-story tower whose glass elevators reveal Union Square views from the upper floors. **Pros:** prime Union Square location; correctly named Heavenly Bed; Chateau Montelena wine-tasting room and the excellent Clock Bar. **Cons:** rooms in original building can be small; public spaces lack the panache of days gone by; no dinner at on-site Oak Room Restaurant. $ *Rooms from: $209* ✉ *335 Powell St., Union Sq.* ☎ *415/397–7000, 888/627–8546* ⊕ *www.marriott.com* *1,195 rooms* *No meals.*

Nightlife

Mikkeller Bar San Francisco

BARS/PUBS | Beer nerds rejoice every time they step through the door from the dicey sidewalk of Mason Street and are greeted by 40 shiny taps serving the celebration creations of the namesake Danish brewer plus some of the world's most in-demand small production beers. This is hardly a proper pub or beer dive—the exposed-brick interior and zigzag-shape bar are as chic as any fashionable drinking spot in town. Don't miss the house-made sausages. ✉ *34 Mason St., Union Sq.* ☎ *415/984–0279* ⊕ *mikkeller.com.*

Redwood Room

BARS/PUBS | Opened in 1933 and updated many times, including in 2019, this lounge at the Clift Hotel is a San Francisco icon. The art-deco bar itself and the wood-paneled room are constructed from a single old redwood tree, giving a distinct only-in-California sense of place. Cocktails are a mix of high-quality classics and slightly creative newcomers. ✉ *The Clift Royal Sonesta Hotel, 495 Geary St., at Taylor St., Union Sq.* ☎ *415/929–2372 for table reservations* ⊕ *redwoodroomsf.com.*

Performing Arts

TIX Bay Area

TICKETS | Half-price, same-day tickets for many local and touring shows go on sale (cash only) at the TIX booth in Union Square, which is open daily from 10 to 6. Discount purchases can also be made online. ✉ *350 Powell St., at Geary St., Union Sq.* ☎ *415/433–7827* ⊕ *www.tixbayarea.org.*

THEATER

American Conservatory Theater

THEATER | One of the nation's leading regional theater companies presents about eight plays a year, from classics to contemporary works, often in repertory. The season runs from early fall to late spring. In December ACT stages a beloved version of Charles Dickens's *A Christmas Carol.* ✉ *415 Geary St., Union Sq.* ☎ *415/749–2228* ⊕ *www.act-sf.org.*

Shopping

Union Square is still San Francisco's main shopping area and the site of most of its department stores, including Macy's, Neiman Marcus, and Saks Fifth Avenue. Nearby are such platinum-card international boutiques as Yves Saint Laurent, Cartier, Emporio Armani, Gucci, Hermès, and Louis Vuitton.

The **Westfield San Francisco Centre,** anchored by Bloomingdale's and Nordstrom, is notable for its gorgeous atriums and top-notch dining options.

■ TIP→ Most retailers in the square don't open until 10 am or later, so there isn't much advantage to getting an early start unless you're grabbing breakfast nearby. If you're on the prowl for art, be aware that many galleries are closed on Sunday and Monday.

ART GALLERIES

Hang Art

ART GALLERIES | A spirit of fun imbues this inviting space that showcases local, emerging artists. Prices range from a few hundred dollars to several thousand, making it an ideal place for novice collectors to get their feet wet. ✉ *567 Sutter St., 2nd fl., near Mason St., Union Sq.* ☎ *415/434–4264* 🌐 *hangart.com*.

Chinatown

A few blocks uphill from Union Square is the abrupt beginning of dense and insular Chinatown—the oldest such community in the country. When the street signs have Chinese characters, produce stalls crowd pedestrians off the sidewalk, and whole roast ducks hang in deli windows, you'll know you've arrived. (The neighborhood huddles together in the 17 blocks and 41 alleys bordered roughly by Bush, Kearny, and Powell streets and Broadway.) A number of neighborhood businesses closed or struggled during the COVID-19 pandemic, and, as in other parts of San Francisco and in cities around America, the community is seeing an unfortunate rise in anti–Asian American incidents. The city is trying hard to support this landmark neighborhood and keep its largely elderly population safe.

Sights

Chinatown Gate

BUILDING | At the official entrance to Chinatown, stone lions flank the base of the pagoda-topped gate; the lions, dragons, and fish up top symbolize wealth, prosperity, and other good things. The four Chinese characters immediately beneath the pagoda represent the philosophy of Sun Yat-sen, the leader who unified China in the early 20th century. Sun Yat-sen, who lived in exile in San Francisco for a few years, promoted the notion of friendship and peace among all nations based on equality, justice, and goodwill. The vertical characters under the left pagoda read "peace" and "trust," the ones under the right pagoda "respect" and "love."

Look Up!

When wandering around Chinatown, don't forget to look up! Above the chintziest souvenir shop might loom an ornate balcony or a curly pagoda roof. The best examples are on the 900 block of Grant Avenue (at Washington Street) and at Waverly Place.

The whole shebang telegraphs the internationally understood message of "photo op." Immediately beyond the gate, dive into souvenir shopping on Grant Avenue, Chinatown's tourist strip. ✉ *Grant Ave. at Bush St., Chinatown.*

Golden Gate Fortune Cookie Factory

FACTORY | **FAMILY** | Follow your nose down Ross Alley to this tiny but fragrant cookie factory. Two workers sit at circular motorized griddles and wait for dollops of batter to drop onto a tiny metal plate, which rotates into an oven. A few moments later, out comes a cookie that's pliable and ready for folding. It's easy to peek in for a moment, and hard to leave without getting a few free samples and then buying a bagful of fortune cookies for snacks and wisdom later. ✉ *56 Ross Alley, between Washington and Jackson Sts., west of Grant Ave., Chinatown* ☎ *415/781–3956* 🌐 *www.goldengatefortunecookies.com* 🎟 *Free.*

Portsmouth Square

PLAZA | Chinatown's living room buzzes with activity: the square, with its pagoda-shape structures, is a favorite spot for morning tai chi, and by noon dozens of men huddle around Chinese chess tables, engaged in competition. Kids scamper about the square's two grungy playgrounds. Back in the late 19th century this land was near the waterfront. The square is named for the USS *Portsmouth*, the ship helmed by Captain John Montgomery, who in 1846 raised the American flag here and claimed the then-Mexican land for the United States. A couple of years later, Sam Brannan kicked off the gold rush at the square when he waved his loot and proclaimed, "Gold from the American River!" Robert Louis Stevenson, the author of *Treasure Island,* often dropped by, chatting up the sailors who hung out here. Some of the information he gleaned about life at sea found its way into his fiction. A bronze galleon sculpture, a tribute to Stevenson, anchors the square's northwest corner. A plaque marks the site of California's first public school, built in 1847. ✉ *Bordered by Walter Lum Pl. and Kearny, Washington, and Clay Sts., Chinatown* 🌐 *sfrecpark.org.*

★ Tin How Temple

RELIGIOUS SITE | In 1852, Day Ju, one of the first three Chinese to arrive in San Francisco, dedicated this temple to the Queen of the Heavens and the Goddess of the Seven Seas, and the temple looks largely the same today as it did more than a century ago. Duck into the inconspicuous doorway, climb three flights of stairs, and be surrounded by the aroma of incense in this tiny, altar-filled room. In the entryway, elderly ladies can often be seen preparing "money" to be burned as offerings to various Buddhist gods or as funds for ancestors to use in the afterlife. Hundreds of red-and-gold lanterns cover the ceiling; the larger the lamp, the larger its donor's contribution to the temple. Gifts of oranges, dim sum, and money left by the faithful, who kneel while reciting prayers, rest on altars to different gods. Tin How presides over the middle back of the temple, flanked by one red and one green lesser god. Taking photographs is not allowed. ✉ *125 Waverly Pl., between Clay and Washington Sts., Chinatown* 🎫 *Free, donations accepted.*

Restaurants

Mister Jiu's

$$$ | **CHINESE** | Brandon Jew's ambitious, graceful restaurant offers the chef's delicious contemporary, farm-to-table interpretation of Chinese cuisine that sometimes tweaks classic dishes with a California spin (hot-and-sour soup with nasturtiums) or enhances fresh produce with unique Chinese flavors (local asparagus with smoked tofu). The elegant dining room—accented with plants and a chrysanthemum chandelier—provides beautiful views of Chinatown, while the menu breathes new life into it. **Known for:** sea urchin cheong fun (rice noodle rolls); standout cocktails; large-format roast duck with pancakes. 💲 *Average main: $29* ✉ *28 Waverly Pl., Chinatown* ☎ *415/857–9688* 🌐 *misterjius.com* 🕒 *Closed Sun. and Mon. No lunch.*

Sam Wo Restaurant

$ | **CHINESE** | Few restaurants in San Francisco—or the country—can match the history of this city treasure that has been around since 1908 (with a brief closure in 2012) and now resides in a narrow, two-story space across the street from Portsmouth Square. You'll want to try as much as possible from the menu, which is a unique mix of Cantonese dishes, a few items from other regions of China, a couple Southeast Asia–inspired noodles, and more familiar Chinese American fare. **Known for:** iconic sign; jook (rice porridge); BBQ pork noodle roll, a great appetizer to share. 💲 *Average main: $11* ✉ *713 Clay St., Chinatown* ☎ *415/989–8898* 🌐 *samworestaurant.com* 🕒 *Closed Tues.*

SoMa

SoMa is less a neighborhood than a sprawling area of wide, traffic-heavy boulevards lined with office skyscrapers and ultrachic condo high-rises. Aside from the fact that many of them work in the area, locals are drawn to the cultural offerings, destination restaurants, and concentration of bars and restaurants. In terms of sightseeing, gigantic and impressive SFMOMA tops the list, followed by the specialty museums of the Yerba Buena arts district.

Sights

Contemporary Jewish Museum (CJM)
MUSEUM | Noted architect Daniel Libeskind designed the postmodern CJM, whose impossible-to-ignore diagonal blue cube juts out of a painstakingly restored power substation. A physical manifestation of the Hebrew toast *l'chaim* (to life), the cube may have obscure philosophical origins, but Libeskind created a unique, light-filled space that merits a stroll through the lobby even if the current exhibits (the museum is non-collecting and does not have permanent holdings, so they change regularly) don't entice you into the galleries. Exhibits, usually two or three at a time, vary, from a look at the history of Levi Strauss to an immersive series about the 19th-century Jewish immigrant and photographer Shimmel Zohar. **■ TIP→ San Francisco's best Jewish deli, Wise Sons, operates a counter in the museum. Try the company's popular smoked salmon bagel sandwich or a slice of chocolate babka.** ✉ *736 Mission St., between 3rd and 4th Sts., SoMa* ☎ *415/655–7800* 🌐 *www.thecjm.org* 🎟 *$16* 🕑 *Closed Mon.–Wed.*

Museum of the African Diaspora (MoAD)
MUSEUM | Dedicated to the influence that people of African descent have had in places all over the world, MoAD focuses on temporary exhibits in its four galleries over three floors. With floor-to-ceiling windows onto Mission Street, the museum fits perfectly into the cultural scene of Yerba Buena and is well worth a 30-minute foray. Most striking is its front-window centerpiece: a three-story mosaic, made from thousands of photographs, that forms the image of a young girl's face. **■ TIP→ Walk up the stairs inside the museum to view the mosaic photographs up close—Malcolm X is there, Muhammad Ali, too, along with everyday folks—but the best view is from across the street.** ✉ *685 Mission St., SoMa* ☎ *415/358–7200* 🌐 *www.moadsf.org* 🎟 *$10* 🕑 *Closed Mon. and Tues.*

★ San Francisco Museum of Modern Art (SFMOMA)
MUSEUM | Opened in 1935, the San Francisco Museum of Modern Art was the first museum on the West Coast dedicated to modern and contemporary art, and after a three-year expansion designed by Snøhetta, it emerged in 2016 as one of the largest modern art museums in the country and the revitalized anchor of the Yerba Buena arts district. With gallery space over seven floors, the museum displays only a portion of its more than 33,000-work collection and has numerous temporary exhibits. You could spend a day here, but allow at least two hours; three is better. The museum's holdings include art from the Doris and Donald Fisher Collection, one of the world's greatest private collections of modern and contemporary art. Highlights here include deep collections of works by German abstract expressionist Gerhard Richter and American painter Ellsworth Kelly and an Agnes Martin gallery. The third floor is dedicated to photography. Also look for seminal works by Diego Rivera, Alexander Calder, Matisse, and Picasso. Don't miss the third-floor sculpture terrace. The first floor is free to the public and contains four large works as well as the museum's shop and expensive restaurant. Ticketing, information, and one gallery are on the second floor; save time and reserve timed tickets online. ✉ *151 3rd St., SoMa* ☎ *415/357–4000* 🌐 *www.sfmoma.org* 🎟 *$25.*

A
B
C
D
E
F
1
2
3
4
5
6
7
8
9
Broadway
Pacific Avenue
Jackson Street
Washington Street
Clay Street
Sacramento Street
California Street
Lafayette Park
101
Cable Car
CHINATOWN
Cable Car Barn
Hyde Street
Leavenworth Street
Jones Street
Taylor Street
Mason Street
Powell Street
Pleasant St.
Huntington Park
Cable Car
NOB HILL
Cable Car
Van Ness Avenue
Polk Street
Larkin Street
POLK GULCH
Pine Street
Bush Street
Sutter Street
Post Street
Geary Street
O'Farrell Street
Gough Street
Franklin Street
Larkin Street
Hyde Street
Leavenworth Street
O'Farrell Street
Ellis Street
Eddy Street
Cleary Ct.
Ellis Street
TENDERLOIN
101
Eddy Street
Turk Street
Van Ness Avenue
Turk Street
Jefferson Square
Golden Gate Ave.
Market Street
6th Street
Jessie St.
Stevenson St.
7th Street
Mission St.
McAllister Street
Fulton St.
CIVIC CENTER
Polk Street
CIVIC CENTER
Fulton St.
Grove Street
8th Street
Julia St.
HAYES VALLEY
9th Street
Mission St.
Minna St.
Natoma St.
Laguna St.
Hayes Street
Linden St.
Fell Street
10th Street
Howard Street
Washburn St.
Grace St.
Tehama St.
Clementina St.
Hickory St.
Oak St.
Octavia Blvd.
Lily St.
Page St.
Rose St.
Market Street
Van Ness Avenue
11th Street
Minna St.
Natoma St.
Lafayette St.
Dore St.
Folsom Street
Ringold St.
Harrison Street
Brady St.
Gough St.
12th St.
Kissling St.
Valencia St.
Mission St.
101
KEY
Exploring Sights
Restaurants
Hotels
BART station
0
300m
0
1,000 ft

SoMa, Civic Center, The Tenderloin, and Hayes Valley

Sights

1 Asian Art Museum................. **D6**
2 City Hall.............................. **C6**
3 Contemporary Jewish Museum (CJM)..................... **H4**
4 Museum of the African Diaspora (MoAD)......... **H4**
5 San Francisco Museum of Modern Art (SFMOMA)............ **I4**
6 Yerba Buena Gardens............. **H4**

Restaurants

1 Benu................................. **I4**
2 Californios........................... **E8**
3 In Situ................................ **I4**
4 Marlowe............................. **J7**
5 Rich Table.......................... **B8**
6 Suppenküche....................... **I4**
7 Zuni Café........................... **B8**

Hotels

1 Four Seasons Hotel San Francisco...................... **G4**
2 Hotel Zetta San Francisco........ **G5**
3 Inn at the Opera.................... **B7**
4 San Francisco Proper Hotel....... **E6**
5 The St. Regis San Francisco **H4**

Yerba Buena Gardens

CITY PARK | FAMILY | Not much south of Market Street encourages lingering outdoors, with this notable exception: these two blocks encompass the Yerba Buena Center for the Arts, the Metreon, and Moscone Convention Center, but the gardens themselves are the everyday draw. Office workers and convention-goers escape to the green swath of the East Garden, the focal point of which is the memorial to Martin Luther King Jr. Powerful streams of water surge over large, jagged stone columns, mirroring the enduring force of King's words, which are carved on the stone walls and on glass blocks behind the waterfall. Moscone North is behind the memorial, and an overhead walkway leads to Moscone South and its rooftop attractions. **■ TIP→ The gardens are liveliest during the week and especially during the Yerba Buena Gardens Festival, from May through October (www.ybgfestival.org), with free performances.**

Atop the Moscone Center perch a few lures for kids. The historic Looff carousel (*$5 for two rides; $3 with museum admission*) twirls daily 10–5. The carousel is attached to the Children's Creativity Museum (☎ *415/820–3320* 🌐 *creativity.org*), a high-tech, interactive arts-and-technology center (*$13*) geared to children ages 3–12. Just outside, kids adore the slides, including a 25-foot tube slide, at the play circle. Also part of the rooftop complex are gardens, an ice-skating rink, and a bowling alley. ✉ *Bordered by 3rd, 4th, Mission, and Folsom Sts., SoMa* 🌐 *yerbabuenagardens.com* 🎟 *Free.*

Restaurants

★ Benu

$$$$ | MODERN AMERICAN | Chef Corey Lee's three-Michelin-star fine dining mecca is a must-stop for those who hop from city to city collecting memorable meals. At this tasting menu–only restaurant, each course is impossibly meticulous, a marvel of textures and flavors. **Known for:** high-end dining; phenomenal wine pairings and list of bottles; stellar service. 💲 *Average main: $325* ✉ *22 Hawthorne St., SoMa* ☎ *415/685–4860* 🌐 *www.benusf.com* ⏱ *Closed Sun. and Mon. No lunch.*

★ Californios

$$$$ | MODERN MEXICAN | Most restaurant discussion in San Francisco during the COVID-19 pandemic sadly revolved around the closings, except for a few exciting openings like this Californian-Mexican tasting-menu concept by chef Val M. Cantu that relocated in 2021 from its Mission District digs to a larger, ultrachic home in SoMa's former Bar Agricole space. **Known for:** house-made tortillas used in brilliant ways; wonderful patio; hard to get reservations. 💲 *Average main: $223* ✉ *355 11th St., SoMa* ☎ *415/757–0994* 🌐 *www.californiossf.com* ⏱ *Closed Sun. and Mon. No lunch.*

★ In Situ

$$$ | CONTEMPORARY | Benu chef Corey Lee's restaurant at SFMOMA is an exhibition of its own, with a rotating menu comprised of dishes from 80 famous chefs around the world. You might taste David Chang's sausage and rice cakes, René Redzepi's wood sorrel granita, or Wylie Dufresne's shrimp grits. **Known for:** global culinary influences; sleek space that fits the modern art vibe; most refined daytime option in an area without many sit-down lunch choices. 💲 *Average main: $30* ✉ *151 3rd St., SoMa* ☎ *415/941–6050* 🌐 *insitu.sfmoma.org* ⏱ *Closed Tues. and Wed. No dinner Mon.*

Marlowe

$$$ | AMERICAN | Hearty American bistro fare and hip design draw crowds to this Anna Weinberg–Jennifer Puccio enterprise. The menu boasts one of the city's best burgers, and the dining room gleams with white penny-tile floors and marble countertops. **Known for:** refined takes on comfort food like roast chicken and deviled eggs; strong drinks; festive atmosphere. [$] *Average main: $29* ✉ *500 Brannan St., SoMa* ☎ *415/777–1413* 🌐 *marlowesf.com.*

 Hotels

Four Seasons Hotel San Francisco
$$$$ | HOTEL | Occupying floors 5 through 17 of a skyscraper, the Four Seasons delivers subdued elegance in rooms with contemporary artwork, fine linens, floor-to-ceiling windows that overlook Yerba Buena Gardens or downtown, and bathrooms with soaking tubs and glass-enclosed showers. **Pros:** near museums, galleries, restaurants, shopping, and clubs; terrific fitness facilities; luxurious rooms and amenities. **Cons:** in-house restaurant/bar has delicious eats and drinks but lacks personality; rooms can feel sterile; Market Street entrance can have aggressive street life outside. [$] *Rooms from: $490* ✉ *757 Market St., SoMa* ☎ *415/633–3000* 🌐 *www.fourseasons.com/sanfrancisco* *277 rooms* *No meals.*

★ Hotel Zetta San Francisco
$ | HOTEL | With a playful lobby lounge, London-style brasserie The Cavalier, and slick-yet-homey tech-friendly rooms, this trendy redo behind a stately 1913 neoclassical facade is a leader on the SoMa hotel scene. **Pros:** tech amenities and arty design; in-room spa services; noteworthy fitness center. **Cons:** lots of hubbub and traffic; no bathtubs; aesthetic too frenetic for some guests. [$] *Rooms from: $198* ✉ *55 5th St., SoMa* ☎ *415/543–8555* 🌐 *hotelzetta.com* *116 rooms* *No meals.*

★ The St. Regis San Francisco
$$$$ | HOTEL | Across from Yerba Buena Gardens and SFMOMA, the luxurious and modern St. Regis is favored by celebrities, such as Lady Gaga and Al Gore, and others drawn to guest rooms and suites decorated with subdued cream colors, leather-textured walls, and window seats offering city views. **Pros:** excellent views; stunning lap pool and luxe spa; art by local artists on display. **Cons:** expensive rates; restaurant isn't on par with the rest of the hotel; cramped space for passenger unloading. [$] *Rooms from: $489* ✉ *125 3rd St., SoMa* ☎ *415/284–4000* 🌐 *st-regis.marriott.com* *260 rooms* *No meals.*

★ City Beer Store
BARS/PUBS | Called CBS by locals, this friendly tasting room meets liquor mart has a wine bar's sensibility. Perfect for both connoisseurs and the merely beer curious, CBS stocks hundreds of different bottled beers, and more than a dozen are on tap to enjoy on the patio or the bar seats in front of a whimsical mural depicting aquatic animals flying around the Bay Bridge. ✉ *1148 Mission St., between 7th and 8th Sts., SoMa* ☎ *702/941–0349* 🌐 *www.citybeerstore.com.*

Terroir
WINE BARS—NIGHTLIFE | The focus at this quaint wine bar is on natural (and mostly old-world) vintages, though it's not impossible to find local offerings, too. The space may be small, but the selection is not: hundreds of different wines, stacked along the walls, compete for your attention. Not sure about Jura wines or the difference between Poulsard and Trousseau? The staff is always eager to help. The bar also serves a small selection of artisanal cheeses and charcuterie to pair with the wines. **■ TIP→ Go on a weekday and head to the candlelit loft above the bar. It's the best seat in the house.** ✉ *1116 Folsom St., at 7th St., SoMa* ☎ *415/558–9946* 🌐 *terroirsf.com.*

21st Amendment Brewery
BREWPUBS/BEER GARDENS | Known for its range of beer types, this popular brewery has multiple taps going at all times. In the summer, the Hell or High Watermelon—a wheat beer—gets rave reviews.

■ TIP→ Serious beer drinkers should try the Back in Black, a black IPA-style beer this brewpub helped pioneer. The space has an upmarket warehouse feel, though exposed wooden ceiling beams, framed photos, whitewashed brick walls, and hardwood floors help keep it cozy. It's a good spot to warm up before a Giants game and an even better place to party after they win. ✉ *563 2nd St., between Bryant and Brannan Sts., SoMa* ☎ *415/369–0900* 🌐 *www.21st-amendment.com.*

Performing Arts

Yerba Buena Center for the Arts

ARTS CENTERS | Across the street from SFMOMA and abutting a lovely urban garden, this performing arts complex schedules interdisciplinary art exhibitions, touring and local dance troupes, music, film programs, and contemporary theater events. You can depend on the quality of the productions at Yerba Buena. Film buffs often come here for screenings by the San Francisco Cinematheque (🌐 *www.sfcinematheque.org*), which showcases experimental film and digital media. And dance enthusiasts can attend concerts by a roster of city companies that perform here, including Smuin Ballet (🌐 *www.smuinballet.org*), ODC/Dance (🌐 *www.odcdance.org*), and Alonzo King's LINES Ballet (🌐 *www.linesballet.org*). Lamplighters (🌐 *www.lamplighters.org*), an alternative opera that specializes in Gilbert & Sullivan, also performs here. ✉ *701 Mission St., SoMa* ☎ *415/978–2787* 🌐 *ybca.org.*

Shopping

BOOKS

★ Chronicle Books

BOOKS/STATIONERY | A local beacon of publishing produces inventively designed fiction, cookbooks, art books, and other titles, as well as diaries, planners, and address books—all of which you can purchase at its home near Oracle Park in an old maritime machine shop and warehouse. ✉ *680 2nd St., SoMa* ☎ *415/537–4200* 🌐 *www.chroniclebooks.com.*

FOOD AND DRINK

K&L Wine Merchants

WINE/SPIRITS | More than any other wine store in the city, this one has an ardent cult following around town. The friendly staffers promise not to sell what they don't taste themselves, and weekly events—on Friday from 5 pm to 6:30 pm and Saturday from noon to 3 pm—open the tastings to customers. The best-seller list for varietals and regions for both the under- and over-$30 categories appeals to the wine lover in everyone. ✉ *855 Harrison St., near 4th St., SoMa* ☎ *415/896–1734* 🌐 *www.klwines.com.*

Civic Center

The eye-catching, gold-domed City Hall presides over this patchy neighborhood bordered roughly by Franklin, McAllister, Hyde, and Grove streets. The optimistic "City Beautiful" movement of the early 20th century produced the Beaux Arts–style complex for which the area is named, including City Hall, the War Memorial Opera House, the Veterans Building, and the old public library, now the home of the Asian Art Museum. The wonderful Main Library on Larkin Street between Fulton and Grove streets is a modern variation on the Civic Center's architectural theme.

Sights

★ Asian Art Museum

MUSEUM | You don't have to be a connoisseur of Asian art to appreciate a visit to this museum whose monumental exterior conceals a light, open, and welcoming space. The fraction of the museum's collection on display (about 2,500 pieces out of 18,000-plus total) is laid out thematically and by region, making it easy to follow historical developments.

Begin on the third floor, where highlights of Buddhist art in Southeast Asia and early China include a large, jewel-encrusted, exquisitely painted 19th-century Burmese Buddha and clothed rod puppets from Java. On the second floor you can find later Chinese works, as well as exquisite pieces from Korea and Japan. The ground floor is devoted to temporary exhibits and the museum's wonderful gift shop. During spring and summer, visit on Thursday evenings for extended programs and sip drinks while a DJ spins tunes. ✉ *200 Larkin St., between McAllister and Fulton Sts., Civic Center* ☎ *415/581–3500* 🌐 *asianart.org* 🎫 *$15, free 1st Sun. of month; $8 Thurs. 5–8* ⏲ *Closed Tues. and Wed.*

★ City Hall

GOVERNMENT BUILDING | This imposing 1915 structure with its massive gold-leaf dome—higher than the U.S. Capitol's—is about as close to a palace as you're going to get in San Francisco: the classic granite-and-marble behemoth was modeled after St. Peter's Basilica in Rome. Architect Arthur Brown Jr., who was also behind Coit Tower and the War Memorial Opera House, designed an interior with grand columns and a sweeping central staircase. The 1899 structure it replaced had taken 27 years to erect, but it collapsed in about 27 seconds during the 1906 earthquake.

City Hall was seismically retrofitted in the late 1990s, but the sense of history remains palpable, and you can learn about it on a tour. Some noteworthy events that have taken place here include the hosing of civil-rights and freedom-of-speech protesters (1960); the assassinations of Mayor George Moscone and openly gay supervisor Harvey Milk (1978); the torching of the lobby by angry members of the gay community in response to the light sentence given to the former supervisor who killed both men (1979); and the first domestic partnership registrations of gay couples (1991). In 2004, Mayor Gavin Newsom took a stand against then-current state and federal law by issuing marriage licenses to same-sex partners.

Across Polk Street from City Hall is **Civic Center Plaza,** with lawns, walkways, seasonal flower beds, a playground, and an underground parking garage. This sprawling space is generally clean but somewhat grim, as many homeless people hang out here. ✉ *1 Dr. Carlton B. Goodlett Pl. , bordered by Van Ness Ave. and Polk, Grove, and McAllister Sts., Civic Center* ☎ *415/554–4000, 415/554–6139 tour reservations* 🌐 *sfgov.org/cityhall/city-hall-tours* 🎫 *Free* ⏲ *Closed weekends.*

Performing Arts

DANCE

★ San Francisco Ballet

DANCE | For ballet lovers, the nation's oldest professional company is reason alone to visit the Bay Area, as SFB's performances under the direction of Helgi Tomasson have won critical raves. The primary season runs from February through May. The repertoire includes full-length ballets such as *Don Quixote* and *Sleeping Beauty*; the December presentation of *The Nutcracker* is truly spectacular. The company also performs bold new dances from star choreographers such as William Forsythe and Mark Morris, alongside modern classics by George Balanchine and Jerome Robbins. Tickets are available at the **War Memorial Opera House.** ✉ *War Memorial Opera House, 301 Van Ness Ave., at Grove St., Civic Center* ☎ *415/865–2000* 🌐 *www.sfballet.org.*

MUSIC

★ San Francisco Symphony

MUSIC | One of America's top orchestras performs from September through May, with additional summer performances of light classical music and show tunes.

The symphony is known for its daring programming of 20th-century American works, often performed with soloists of the caliber of André Watts, Gil Shaham, and Renée Fleming. Legendary maestro Michael Tilson Thomas retired in 2020, and music lovers are eager to listen to the opening postpandemic concerts of the new music director, Esa-Pekka Salonen. ✉ *Louise M. Davies Symphony Hall, 201 Van Ness Ave., at Grove St., Civic Center* ☎ *415/864–6000* 🌐 *www.sfsymphony.org.*

OPERA

★ San Francisco Opera

OPERA | Founded in 1923, this internationally recognized organization has occupied the War Memorial Opera House since the building's completion in 1932. From September through December and June through July, the company presents a wide range of operas, from *Carmen* to an operatic version of *It's a Wonderful Life* . The opera often takes on ambitious world premieres and sometimes presents unconventional, edgy projects designed to attract younger audiences. Translations are projected above the stage during most non-English productions. ✉ *War Memorial Opera House, 301 Van Ness Ave., at Grove St., Civic Center* ☎ *415/864–3330 tickets* 🌐 *sfopera.com.*

The Tenderloin

Stretching west of Union Square and north of Civic Center, the Tenderloin is not an attractive neighborhood. So why would anyone go out of their way to come here? Trendy watering holes and coffee shops are springing up, with a handful of intrepid hipsters moving into the hood after them. The Tenderloin may be on its way to becoming the next Mission, but for now it remains a gritty slice of San Francisco.

Hotels

★ San Francisco Proper Hotel

$$ | **HOTEL** | Inside the magnificent, flatiron-shape Beaux-Arts building—given a modern refresh in the mid-2010s—is one of the city's most spectacular places to stay, a sharp, upscale, ultra-hip boutique hotel; in contrast, outside is one of the roughest intersections for streetlife in San Francisco. **Pros:** gorgeous lobby; excellent restaurant and cocktails; tech elements like wireless speakers and smart TV. **Cons:** price may seem high for difficult location; too cool for many tastes; $30 daily fee for amenities. [$] *Rooms from: $220* ✉ *1100 Market St., Tenderloin* ✥ *Entrance at 45 McAllister St.* ☎ *415/737–7777, 888/730–4299 reservations* 🌐 *properhotel.com/san-francisco* *131 rooms* *No meals.*

Nightlife

★ Bourbon & Branch

BARS/PUBS | Although this spot reeks of Prohibition-era speakeasy cool, it's not exclusive: everyone is granted a password, though it's *highly* recommended to book a reservation. The place has sex appeal, with tin ceilings, bordello-red silk wallpaper, intimate booths, and low lighting; loud conversations and cell phones are not allowed. The menu of expertly mixed cocktails and quality bourbon and whiskey is substantial, with cocktails leaning more in the spirit-forward direction. A speakeasy within the speakeasy called Wilson & Wilson is more exclusive, but just as funky. ✉ *501 Jones St., at O'Farrell St., Tenderloin* ☎ *415/346–1735* 🌐 *www.bourbonandbranch.com.*

Great American Music Hall

MUSIC CLUBS | You can find top-drawer entertainment at this eclectic concert venue. Acts range from the best in blues, folk, and jazz to up-and-coming college-radio and American-roots artists to indie rockers. The colorful marble-pillared club, built in 1907 as a bordello, also accommodates dancing at some shows. Pub grub is available most nights. ✉ *859 O'Farrell St., between Polk and Larkin Sts., Tenderloin* ☎ *415/885–0750* 🌐 *slimspresents.com/great-american-music-hall.*

Hayes Valley

A chic neighborhood due west of Civic Center, Hayes Valley has terrific eateries, cool watering holes, and great browsing in its funky clothing, home-decor, and design boutiques. Locals love this quarter, but without any big-name draws it remains off the radar for many visitors.

Restaurants

★ Rich Table

$$$ | MODERN AMERICAN | Sardine chips and porcini doughnuts are popular bites at co-chefs (and husband and wife) Evan and Sarah Rich's lively, creative restaurant; mains are also clever stunners, including pastas like the sea urchin *cacio e pepe*. The room's weathered-wood wallboards repurposed from a Northern California sawmill give it a homey vibe. **Known for:** tough-to-get reservations; freshly baked bread; seasonal ingredients. $ *Average main: $34* ✉ *199 Gough St., Hayes Valley* ☎ *415/355–9085* 🌐 *www.richtablesf.com* ⏲ *No lunch.*

Suppenküche

$$ | GERMAN | Nobody goes hungry—and no beer drinker goes thirsty—at this lively, hip outpost of simple German cooking in Hayes Valley. The hearty food—bratwurst and sauerkraut, potato pancakes with house-made applesauce, meat loaf, braised beef, pork loin, schnitzel, spaetzle—is tasty and kind to your wallet, and the imported brews are first-rate. **Known for:** seating at common tables; any of the sausages; quick service. $ *Average main: $26* ✉ *525 Laguna St., Hayes Valley* ☎ *415/252–9289* 🌐 *www.suppenkuche.com* ⏲ *Closed Mon. No lunch weekdays.*

★ Zuni Café

$$$ | MODERN AMERICAN | After one bite of Zuni's succulent brick-oven-roasted whole chicken with warm bread salad, you'll understand why the two-floor café is a perennial star. Its long copper bar is a hub for a disparate mix of patrons who commune over oysters on the half shell and cocktails and wine. **Known for:** seasonal Californian cooking at its best; under-the-radar lunch and late-night burger; beloved margarita. $ *Average main: $35* ✉ *1658 Market St., Hayes Valley* ☎ *415/552–2522* 🌐 *zunicafe.com* ⏲ *Closed Mon. and Tues.*

Hotels

Inn at the Opera

$$ | B&B/INN | Within walking distance of Davies Symphony Hall and the War Memorial Opera House, this inn with small rooms with dark wood furnishings caters to season-ticket holders for the opera, ballet, and symphony; it's also been the choice for stars of the music, dance, and opera worlds, from Luciano Pavarotti to Mikhail Baryshnikov. **Pros:** staff goes the extra mile; good on-site dining; prime location but a quiet block. **Cons:** no air-conditioning; sold out far in advance during opera season; difficult parking. $ *Rooms from: $215* ✉ *333 Fulton St., Hayes Valley* ☎ *415/863–8400* 🌐 *www.shellhospitality.com/inn-at-the-opera* *48 rooms* *Free breakfast.*

Nightlife

The Mint Karaoke Lounge

BARS/PUBS | A mixed gay-straight crowd that's drop-dead serious about its karaoke—to the point where you'd think an *American Idol* casting agent was in attendance—comes here seven nights a week. Regulars sing everything from Simon and Garfunkel songs to disco classics in front of an attentive audience. Do *not* walk onstage unprepared! Check out the songbook online to perfect your debut before you attempt to take the mic. Hit the ATM beforehand, as everything here is cash-only. ✉ *1942 Market St., between Duboce Ave. and Laguna St., Hayes Valley* ☎ *415/626–4726* 🌐 *themint.net.*

★ Smuggler's Cove

BARS/PUBS | With the decor of a pirate ship and a slew of rum-based cocktails, you half expect Captain Jack Sparrow to sidle up next to you at this offbeat, Disney-esque hangout. But the folks at Smuggler's Cove take rum so seriously they've even had it made for them from distillers around the world, which you can sample along with more than 550 other offerings. A punch card is provided so you can try the entire menu (featuring 80-plus cocktails). The small space fills up quickly, so arrive early. The same owner also has a gin-centric cocktail bar, Whitechapel, a few blocks away on Polk Street, where the cocktails are equally special and the outrageous decor echoes a vintage London Underground station. ✉ *650 Gough St., at McAllister St., Hayes Valley* ☎ *415/869–1900* 🌐 *www.smugglerscovesf.com.*

Performing Arts

★ SFJAZZ Center

MUSIC | Jazz legends Branford Marsalis and Herbie Hancock have performed at the snazzy center, as have Rosanne Cash, Dianne Reeves, and world-music favorite Esperanza Spalding. The sight lines and acoustics here are impressive, as are the second-floor tile murals. Shows often sell out quickly. ✉ *201 Franklin St., Hayes Valley* ☎ *866/920–5299* 🌐 *www.sfjazz.org.*

Shopping

BOOKS

Isotope Comic Book Lounge

BOOKS/STATIONERY | For full-frontal nerdity in a chic modern setting, pay a visit to SF's premier comic book hangout. You'll find a great selection of graphic novels and artwork by popular and local artists, as well as lively after-hours events. ✉ *326 Fell St., at Gough St., Hayes Valley* ☎ *415/621–6543* 🌐 *www.isotopecomics.com.*

FOOD AND DRINK

Miette Patisserie & Confiserie

FOOD/CANDY | There is truly nothing sweeter than a cellophane bag tied with colorful ribbon and filled with malt balls or floral meringues from this Insta-friendly candy and pastry store. Grab a gingerbread cupcake or a tantalizing macaron or some shortbread. The pastel-color cake stands make even window-shopping a treat. It's open Thursday–Sunday. ✉ *449 Octavia Blvd., between Hayes and Linden Sts., Hayes Valley* ☎ *415/626–6221* 🌐 *www.miette.com.*

Nob Hill

Nob Hill was officially dubbed during the 1870s when the "Big Four"—Charles Crocker, Leland Stanford, Mark Hopkins, and Collis P. Huntington, who were involved in the construction of the transcontinental railroad—built their hilltop estates. The lingo is thick from this era: those on the hilltop were referred to as "nabobs" (originally meaning a provincial governor from India) and "swells," and the hill itself was called Snob Hill, a term that survives to this day. By 1882 so many estates had sprung up on Nob Hill that Robert Louis Stevenson called it "the hill of palaces." The 1906 earthquake and fire, though, destroyed all the palatial mansions except for portions of the James Flood brownstone. History buffs may choose to

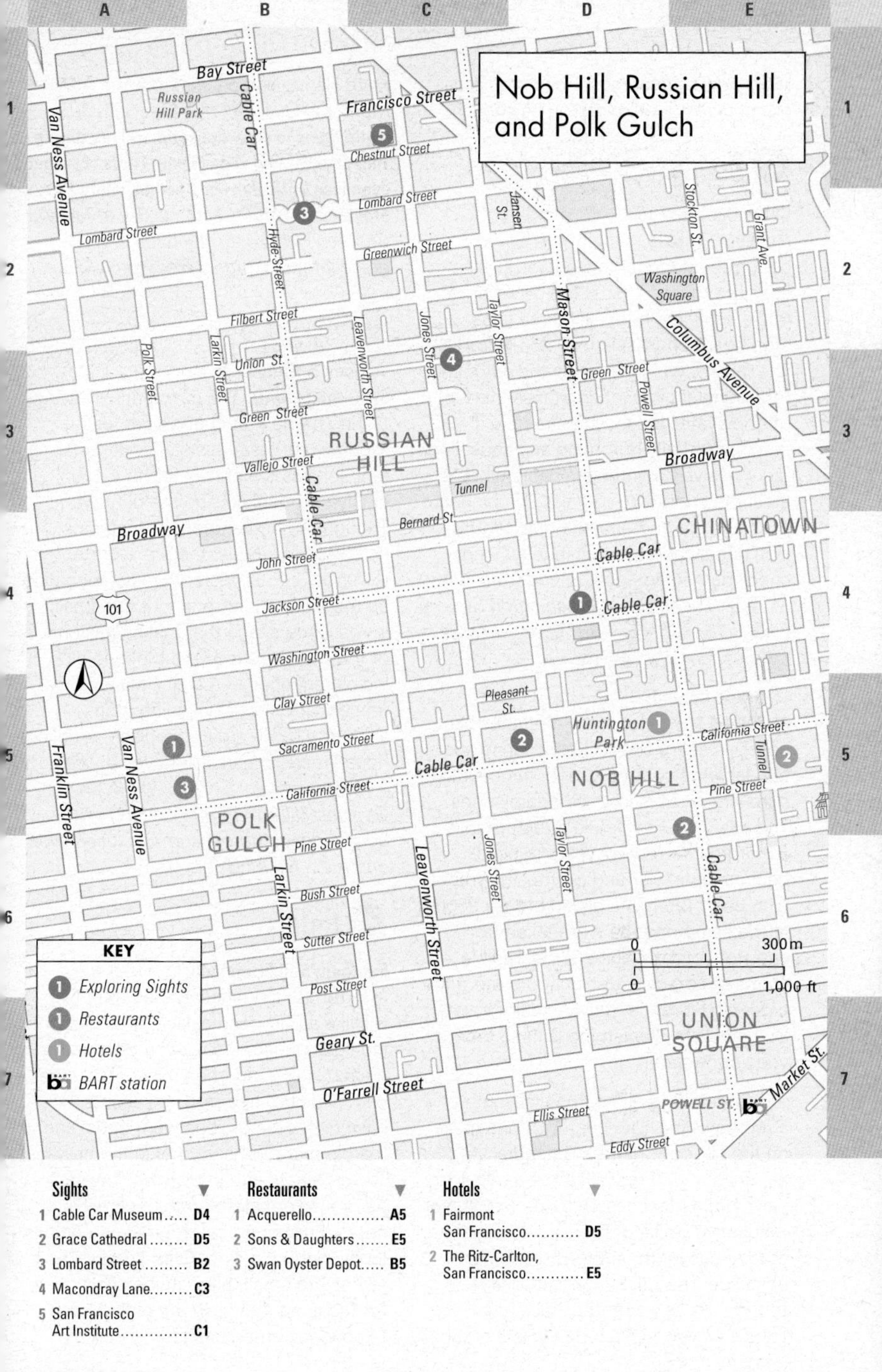

Sights

1 Cable Car Museum **D4**

2 Grace Cathedral **D5**

3 Lombard Street **B2**

4 Macondray Lane......... **C3**

5 San Francisco Art Institute **C1**

Restaurants

1 Acquerello............... **A5**

2 Sons & Daughters....... **E5**

3 Swan Oyster Depot..... **B5**

Hotels

1 Fairmont San Francisco........... **D5**

2 The Ritz-Carlton, San Francisco............ **E5**

linger here, but for most visitors, a casual glimpse from a cable car will be enough.

Sights

Cable Car Museum
MUSEUM | **FAMILY** | One of the city's best free offerings, this museum is an absolute must for kids. You can even ride a cable car here—all three lines stop between Russian Hill and Nob Hill. The facility, which is inside the city's last remaining cable-car barn, takes the top off the system to let you see how it all works. Eternally humming and squealing, the massive powerhouse cable wheels steal the show. You can also climb aboard a vintage car and take the grip, let the kids ring a cable-car bell (briefly), and check out vintage gear dating from 1873. ✉ *1201 Mason St., at Washington St., Nob Hill* ☎ *415/474–1887* 🌐 *www.cablecarmuseum.org* 🎫 *Free.*

★ Grace Cathedral
RELIGIOUS SITE | Not many churches can boast an altarpiece by Keith Haring and two labyrinths, but this one, the country's third-largest Episcopal cathedral, does. The soaring Gothic-style structure took 14 (often interrupted) years to build, beginning in 1927 and eventually wrapping up in 1964. The gilded bronze doors at the east entrance were taken from casts of Lorenzo Ghiberti's incredible *Gates of Paradise*, designed for the Baptistery in Florence, Italy. A sculpture of St. Francis by Beniamino Bufano greets you as you enter.

The 34-foot-wide limestone labyrinth is a replica of the 13th-century stone maze on the floor of Chartres Cathedral. All are encouraged to walk the 1/8-mile-long labyrinth, a ritual based on the tradition of meditative walking. There's also a granite outdoor labyrinth on the church's northeast side. The AIDS Interfaith Chapel, to the right as you enter Grace, contains a bronze triptych by the late artist Keith Haring and panels from the AIDS Memorial Quilt. **■ TIP→ Especially dramatic times to view the cathedral are during Tuesday-evening yoga (6 pm), Thursday-night evensong (5:15 pm), and special holiday programs.** ✉ *1100 California St., at Taylor St., Nob Hill* ☎ *415/749–6300* 🌐 *www.gracecathedral.org* 🎫 *Free; tours $25.*

Restaurants

★ Sons & Daughters
$$$$ | **AMERICAN** | The constantly evolving tasting menu that chef-owner Teague Moriarty serves at his standout restaurant serves as a primer for how to do highly seasonal cuisine the right way. Though the preparations are intricate and often luxurious, there is a pretension-free, contemporary type of elegance on the plate and throughout the small, immaculate space that makes this one of the most relaxed (and fun) fine-dining experiences in the city. **Known for:** refined, cozy but chic dining room anchored by an ornate fireplace; excellent house-made bread; attentive service. 💲 *Average main: $175* ✉ *708 Bush St., Nob Hill* ☎ *415/994–7933* 🌐 *www.sonsanddaughterssf.com* ⏲ *Closed Mon. and Tues. No lunch.*

Hotels

Fairmont San Francisco
$$$ | **HOTEL** | Dominating the top of Nob Hill like a European palace, the Fairmont indulges guests in luxury: rooms in the main building, adorned in sapphire blues with platinum and pewter accents, have high ceilings, decadent beds, and marble bathrooms; rooms in the newer Tower, many with fine views, have a neutral color palette with bright-silver notes. **Pros:** huge bathrooms; stunning lobby; great location. **Cons:** some older rooms are small; hills can be challenging for those on foot; $30 per night Urban Experience amenities fee. 💲 *Rooms*

Continued on page 635

SAN FRANCISCO'S CABLE CARS

The moment it dawns on you that you severely underestimated the steepness of the San Francisco hills will likely be the same moment you look down and realize those tracks aren't just for show—or just for tourists.

Sure, locals rarely use the cable cars for commuting these days. (That's partially due to the $8 fare—hear that, Muni?) So you'll likely be packed in with plenty of fellow sightseers. You may even be approaching cable-car fatigue after seeing its image on so many souvenirs. But if you fear the magic is gone, simply climb on board, and those jaded thoughts will dissolve. Grab the pole and gawk at the view as the car clanks down an insanely steep grade toward the bay. Listen to the humming cable, the clang of the bell, and the occasional quip from the gripman. It's an experience you shouldn't pass up, whether on your first trip or your fiftieth.

HOW CABLE CARS WORK

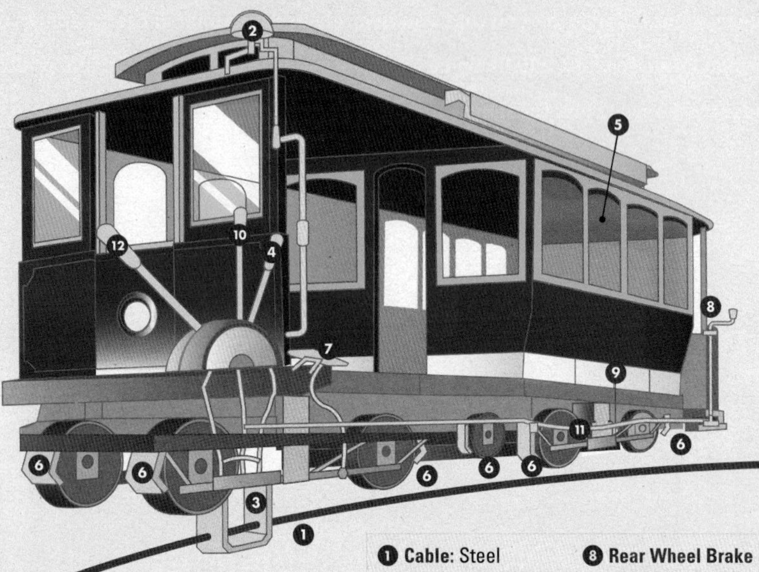

The mechanics are pretty simple: cable cars grab a moving subterranean cable with a "grip" to go. To stop, they release the grip and apply one or more types of brakes. Four cables, totaling 9 miles, power the city's three lines. If the gripman doesn't adjust the grip just right when going up a steep hill, the cable will start to slip and the car will have to back down the hill and try again. This is an extremely rare occurrence—imagine the ribbing the gripman gets back at the cable car barn!

Gripman: Stands in front and operates the grip, brakes, and bell. Favorite joke, especially at the peak of a steep hill: "This is my first day on the job, folks . . ."

Conductor: Moves around the car, deals with tickets, alerts the grip about what's coming up, and operates the rear wheel brakes.

❶ **Cable:** Steel wrapped around flexible sisal core; 2 inches thick; runs at a constant 9½ mph.

❷ **Bells:** Used for crew communication; alerts other drivers and pedestrians.

❸ **Grip:** Vice-like lever extends through the center slot in the track to grab or release the cable.

❹ **Grip Lever:** Left-hand lever; operates grip.

❺ **Car:** Entire car weighs 8 tons.

❻ **Wheel Brake:** Steel brake pads on each wheel.

❼ **Wheel Brake Lever:** Foot pedal; operates wheel brakes.

❽ **Rear Wheel Brake Lever:** Applied for extra traction on hills.

❾ **Track Brake:** 2-foot-long sections of Monterey pine push down against the track to help stop the car.

❿ **Track Brake Lever:** Middle lever; operates track brakes.

⓫ **Emergency Brake:** 18-inch steel wedge, jams into street slot to bring car to an immediate stop.

⓬ **Emergency Brake Lever:** Right-hand lever, red; operates emergency brake.

ROUTES

Cars run at least every 15 minutes, from around 6 am to about 1 am.

Powell–Hyde line: Most scenic, with classic Bay views. Begins at Powell and Market streets, then crosses Nob Hill and Russian Hill before a white-knuckle descent down Hyde Street, ending near the Hyde Street Pier.

Powell–Mason line: Also begins at Powell and Market streets, but winds through North Beach to Bay and Taylor streets, a few blocks from Fisherman's Wharf.

California line: Runs from the foot of Market Street, at Drumm Street, up Nob Hill and back. Great views (and aromas and sounds) of Chinatown on the way up. Sit in back to catch glimpses of the bay. **■ TIP➜ Take the California line if it's just the cable-car experience you're after—the lines are shorter, and the grips and conductors say it's friendlier and has a slower pace.**

RULES OF THE RIDE

Tickets. There are ticket booths at all three turnarounds. You must purchase your ticket in advance.

■ TIP➜ If you're planning to use public transit a few times, or if you'd like to ride back and forth on the cable car without worrying about the price, consider a one-day (or multiday) Muni Visitor Passport. You can get passports online, at the Powell Street turnaround, the TIX booth on Union Square, or the Fisherman's Wharf cable-car ticket booth at Beach and Hyde streets. Also consider Muni Mobile or a Clipper Card; see sfmta.com. Cash purchases require exact change.

All Aboard. You can board on either side of the cable car. It's legal to stand on the running boards and hang on to the pole, but keep your ears open for the gripman's warnings. **■ TIP➜ Grab a seat on the outside bench for the best views.**

Most people wait (and wait) in line at one of the cable car turnarounds, but you can also hop on along the route. Board wherever you see a white sign showing a figure climbing aboard a brown cable car; wave to the approaching driver, and wait until the car stops.

Riding on the running boards can be part of the thrill.

CABLE CAR HISTORY

HALLIDIE FREES THE HORSES

In the 1850s and '60s, San Francisco's streetcars were drawn by horses. Legend has it that the horrible sight of a car dragging a team of horses downhill to their deaths roused Andrew Smith Hallidie to action. The English immigrant had invented the "Hallidie Ropeway," essentially a cable car for mined ore, and he was convinced that his invention could also move people. In 1873, Hallidie and his intrepid crew prepared to test the first cable car high on Russian Hill. The anxious engineer peered down into the foggy darkness, failed to see the bottom of the hill, and promptly turned the controls over to Hallidie. Needless to say, the thing worked . . . but rides were free for the first two days because people were afraid to get on.

SEE IT FOR YOURSELF

The Cable Car Museum (✉ 1201 Mason St, 🌐 cablecarmusem.org) is one of the city's best free offerings and an absolute must for kids. (You can even ride a cable car there, since all three lines stop between Russian Hill and Nob Hill.) The museum, which is inside the city's last cable-car barn, takes the top off the system to let you see how it all works. Eternally humming and squealing, the massive powerhouse cable wheels steal the show. You can also climb aboard a vintage car and take the grip, let the kids ring a cable-car bell (briefly, please!), and check out vintage gear dating from 1873.

■ TIP→ The gift shop sells cable car paraphernalia, including an authentic gripman's bell (it'll sound like Powell Street in your house every day). For significantly less, you can pick up a key chain made from a piece of worn-out cable. Books, T-shirts, hats, and models are also on sale.

CHAMPION OF THE CABLE CAR BELL

Each fall (though the month can vary widely : check 🌐 sfmta.com for update) the city's best and brightest come together to crown a bell-ringing champion at Union Square. The crowd cheers gripmen and conductors as they stomp, shake, and riff with the rope. But it's not a popularity contest; the ringers are judged by former bell-ringing champions and others who take each ping and gong very seriously.

from: $301 ✉ 950 Mason St., Nob Hill ☎ 415/772–5000, 866/550–4491 🌐 www.fairmont.com/san-francisco 🛏 606 rooms 🍽 No meals.

★ **The Ritz-Carlton, San Francisco**
$$$ | **HOTEL** | A tribute to beauty and attentive, professional service, the Ritz-Carlton emphasizes luxury and elegance, which are evident in the Ionic columns that grace the neoclassical facade and the crystal chandeliers that illuminate marble floors and walls in the lobby. **Pros:** terrific service; beautiful furnishings throughout; lobby wine-tasting lounge. **Cons:** nothing is a bargain; hilly location; no pool. *$ Rooms from: $364 ✉ 600 Stockton St., at Pine St., Nob Hill ☎ 415/296–7465, 800/542–8680 🌐 www.ritzcarlton.com/sanfrancisco 🛏 336 rooms 🍽 No meals.*

Russian Hill

Essentially a tony residential neighborhood of spiffy pieds-à-terre, Victorian flats, Edwardian cottages, and boxlike condos, Russian Hill has some of the city's loveliest stairway walks, hidden garden ways, and steepest streets—not to mention those bay views.

Sights

★ **Lombard Street**
NEIGHBORHOOD | The block-long "Crookedest Street in the World" makes eight switchbacks down the east face of Russian Hill between Hyde and Leavenworth Streets. Residents bemoan the traffic jam outside their front doors, but the throngs continue. Join the line of cars waiting to drive down the steep hill, or avoid the whole mess and walk down the steps on either side of Lombard. You take in super views of North Beach and Coit Tower whether you walk or drive—though if you're the one behind the wheel, you'd better keep your eye on the road lest you become yet another of the many folks who ram the garden barriers. **■ TIP→ Can't stand the traffic? Thrill seekers of a different stripe may want to head two blocks south of Lombard to Filbert Street. At a gradient of 31.5%, the hair-raising descent between Hyde and Leavenworth Streets is one of the city's steepest. Go slowly!** *✉ Lombard St. between Hyde and Leavenworth Sts., Russian Hill.*

★ **Macondray Lane**
NEIGHBORHOOD | San Francisco has no shortage of impressive, grand homes, but Macondray Lane is the quintessential hidden garden. Enter under a lovely wooden trellis and proceed down a quiet, cobbled pedestrian lane lined with Edwardian cottages and flowering plants and trees. A flight of steep wooden stairs at the end of the lane leads to Taylor Street—on the way down you can't miss the bay views. If you've read any of Armistead Maupin's *Tales of the City* books, you may find the lane vaguely familiar. It's the thinly disguised setting for parts of the series' action. *✉ Between Jones and Taylor Sts., and Union and Green Sts., Russian Hill.*

San Francisco Art Institute
COLLEGE | The number-one reason for a visit to this art college is Mexican master Diego Rivera's *The Making of a Fresco Showing the Building of a City* (1931), in the student gallery to your immediate left inside the entrance. Rivera himself is in the fresco—his broad behind is to the viewer—and he's surrounded by his assistants. They in turn are surrounded by a construction scene, laborers, and city notables, such as sculptor Ralph Stackpole and architect Timothy Pflueger. *Making* is one of three San Francisco murals painted by Rivera. The school itself has seen substantial changes on the academic side because of budget issues and the COVID-19 pandemic, but the mural still remains, as does the panoramic view from the courtyard café.

The **Walter & McBean Galleries** (*☎ 415/749–4563; ⏲ closed Sun. and Mon.*) exhibit the often provocative works of established artists. *800 Chestnut St., Russian Hill 415/771–7020 sfai.edu Galleries free.*

Polk Gulch

Polk Gulch, the microhood surrounding north–south Polk Street, hugs the western edges of Nob Hill and Russian Hill but is nothing like either. It's actually two microhoods: Upper Polk Gulch, fairly classy in its northern section, runs from about Union Street south to California Street; Lower Polk Gulch, the rougher southern part, continues south from California to Geary or so. Polk Gulch was the Castro before the Castro. It was the city's gay neighborhood into the 1970s, hosting San Francisco's first pride parade in 1972 and several festive Halloween extravaganzas.

Restaurants

★ Acquerello

$$$$ | **ITALIAN** | At this true San Francisco dining gem, chef and co-owner Suzette Gresham has elicited plenty of swoons over the years with high-end but soulful Italian cooking that is worth every penny. Her cuttlefish "tagliatelle" is a star of the menu, which features both classic and cutting-edge dishes. **Known for:** sensational prix-fixe dining with a variety of options; city's premier Italian cheese selection; extensive Italian wine list. *Average main: $115 1722 Sacramento St., Polk Gulch 415/567–5432 www.acquerellosf.com Closed Sun., Mon. and Tues. No lunch.*

★ Swan Oyster Depot

$$ | **SEAFOOD** | Half fish market and half diner, this small, slim, family-run seafood operation, open since 1912, has no tables, just a narrow marble counter with about 18 stools. Some locals come in to buy perfectly fresh salmon, halibut, crabs, and other seafood to take home; everyone else hops onto one of the rickety stools to enjoy a dozen oysters, other shellfish, or a bowl of clam chowder—the only hot food served. **Known for:** memorable Dungeness crab Louie salad; long lines; payment is cash only. *Average main: $26 1517 Polk St., Polk Gulch 415/673–1101 swanoysterdepot.us No credit cards Closed Sun. No dinner.*

Pacific Heights

Pacific Heights defines San Francisco's most expensive and dramatic real estate. Grand Victorians line the streets, mansions and town houses are priced in the millions, and there are magnificent views from almost any point in the neighborhood. Old money and new, personalities in the limelight and those who prefer absolute media anonymity live here, and few outsiders see anything other than the pleasing facades of Queen Anne charmers, English Tudor imports, and baroque bastions. Nancy Pelosi and Dianne Feinstein, Larry Ellison, and Gordon Getty all own impressive homes here, but not even pockets as deep as those can buy a large garden—space in the city is simply at too much of a premium. Luckily, two of the city's most spectacular parks are located in the area. The boutiques and restaurants along Fillmore Street, which range from glam to funky, are a draw for the whole city as well.

Sights

Haas-Lilienthal House

HOUSE | A small display of photographs on the bottom floor of this elaborate, gray 1886 Queen Anne house makes clear that despite its lofty stature and striking, round third-story tower, the house was modest compared with some of the giants that fell victim to the 1906 earthquake and fire. San Francisco Heritage, a foundation to preserve San Francisco's architectural history, operates the home, whose carefully kept rooms provide a glimpse into late-19th-century life through period furniture, authentic details (like the antique dishes in the kitchen built-in), and photos of the Haas family, who occupied the house for three generations until 1972. **■TIP→ You can admire hundreds of gorgeous San Francisco Victorians from the outside, but this is the only one that's open to the public, and it's worth a visit.** You can download free maps of two nearby walking tours highlighting the neighborhood's historic architecture on the house's website. ✉ *2007 Franklin St., Pacific Heights* ✥ *Between Washington and Jackson Sts.* ☎ *415/441–3000* 🌐 *www.haas-lilienthalhouse.org* 🎟 *Tours $10.*

Restaurants

★ Octavia

$$$ | MODERN AMERICAN | Regardless of the time of year, Melissa Perello's second and more upscale restaurant (Frances is the first) is a perennial favorite for diners seeking out what California cuisine really tastes like. The warm, immaculate dining room is a perfect setting for edgier dishes like the popular chilled squid ink noodles starter, along with more comforting produce-driven small plates and entrées. **Known for:** exciting preparations with peak-of-season produce; spicy deviled egg starter; truly professional service. $ *Average main: $32* ✉ *1701 Octavia St., at Bush St., Lower Pacific Heights* ☎ *415/408–7507* 🌐 *www.octavia-sf.com* ⏲ *No lunch.*

Sociale

$$$ | NORTHERN ITALIAN | The COVID-19 pandemic's outdoor dining requirement led San Francisco diners to discover the city's premier patios—like the one that regulars have known about for years at this Presidio Heights stalwart, hidden from the street down a little alley, almost like a posh, aboveground speakeasy. Whether you're dining on that patio or in the elegant dining room, Italian and seasonal Californian cooking mingle together on the menu. **Known for:** fantastic pastas; chocolate oblivion cake for dessert; Barolo and Barbaresco wine choices. $ *Average main: $28* ✉ *3665 Sacramento St., Presidio Heights* ☎ *415/921–3200* 🌐 *sfsociale.com* ⏲ *Closed Sun. and Mon.*

Hotels

★ Hotel Drisco

$$$$ | HOTEL | You can pretend you're a denizen of one of San Francisco's wealthiest residential neighborhoods while you stay at this understated, elegant Edwardian hotel built in 1903. **Pros:** gorgeous rooms and public spaces; great service and many amenities; quiet residential neighborhood retreat. **Cons:** not a close walk to restaurants or major sights; room prices are as steep as nearby hill; no complimentary chauffeur service in the afternoon or evening. $ *Rooms from: $499* ✉ *2901 Pacific Ave., Pacific Heights* ☎ *415/346–2880, 800/634–7277* 🌐 *hoteldrisco.com* *48 rooms* 🍽 *Free breakfast.*

Nightlife

The Snug

BARS/PUBS | A welcoming yet refined drinking destination, this Lower Pac Heights bar is exactly what the well-heeled and fun-loving neighborhood needed. It's the rare bar that emphasizes clever cocktails, in-high-demand local craft beer, and smartly selected wine in equal parts. Come hungry, as well, because elevated takes on bar bites like yellowtail poke and sesame naan with shiitake mushroom hummus are created by a chef formerly at some of the country's gastronomic heavyweights (Benu, Alinea). ✉ *2301 Fillmore St., Lower Pacific Heights* 🌐 *www.thesnugsf.com.*

Shopping

Browser Books

BOOKS/STATIONERY | FAMILY | Opened in 1976, one of the city's most beloved independent bookstores resides quietly among the chic fashion boutiques lining Fillmore Street. All ages will find ample choices for their next reading material, from contemporary fiction to children's books to a large selection of Buddhist Dharma literature. The store was recently sold to the small, local Green Apple Books group (with two other bookstores in the city), but barely anything has changed at the store with the transition. ✉ *2195 Fillmore St., Lower Pacific Heights* ☎ *415/567–8027* 🌐 *www.greenapplebooks.com.*

★ Verve Wine

WINE/SPIRITS | Wine nerds will fall in love with this trendy, upscale destination from one of the country's few master sommeliers, Dustin Wilson. Many wine drinkers will also recognize him from the popular 2012 documentary *Somm* (and its sequels). High-quality, smaller producers from prominent and lesser-known regions share wall space in this exceptionally organized boutique. ✉ *2358 Fillmore St., between Washington St. and Jackson St., Lower Pacific Heights* ☎ *415/896–4935* 🌐 *vervewine.com.*

Japantown

Though still the spiritual center of San Francisco's Japanese American community, Japantown feels somewhat adrift. The Japan Center mall, for instance, comes across as rather sterile, and whereas Chinatown is densely populated and still largely Chinese, Japantown struggles to retain its unique character.

Sights

Japan Center

STORE/MALL | FAMILY | Cool and curious trinkets, noodle houses and sushi joints, a destination bookstore, and a peek at Japanese culture high and low await at this 5-acre complex designed in 1968 by noted American architect Minoru Yamasaki. The Japan Center includes the shop- and restaurant-filled Kintetsu Mall and Kinokuniya Building; the excellent Kabuki Springs & Spa; the Hotel Kabuki; and the AMC Kabuki reserved-seating cinema/restaurant complex. ✉ *Bordered by Geary Blvd. and Fillmore, Post, and Laguna Sts., Japantown* 🌐 *www.japancentersf.com.*

★ Kabuki Springs & Spa

SPA—SIGHT | The serene spa is one Japantown destination that draws locals from all over town, from hipsters to grandmas, Japanese American or not. Balinese urns decorate the communal bath area of this house of tranquility. The extensive service menu includes facials, salt scrubs, and mud and seaweed wraps, in addition to massage. You can take your massage in a private room with a bath or in a curtained-off area. The communal baths ($30) contain hot and cold tubs, a large Japanese-style bath, a sauna, a steam room, and showers. Bang the gong for quiet if your fellow bathers are speaking too loudly. The clothing-optional baths are open for men only on Monday, Thursday, and Saturday; women bathe on Wednesday, Friday, and Sunday. Bathing suits are required on Tuesday, when the baths are coed. Men and women can reserve a private room daily. ✉ *1750 Geary Blvd., Japantown* ☎ *415/922–6000* 🌐 *kabukisprings.com.*

Restaurants

Marufuku Ramen

$$ | RAMEN | Hakata-style *tonkotsu* (pork) and extra-intense chicken *paitan* ramen are the specialties of this modern-looking Japan Center restaurant that serves what many San Franciscans consider the city's finest bowl of ramen. As a result, long lines can be daunting, but luckily tables move pretty quickly inside the bustling yet relaxed space decorated with wood design elements and dangling Edison bulbs. **Known for:** no reservations, but there's an online wait list; gyoza (pan-fried dumplings) and pork buns to snack on; lively, contemporary vibe. *Average main: $18* *Kinokuniya Bldg., 1581 Webster St., #235, Japantown* *415/872–9786* *www.marufukuramen.com* *Closed Mon.*

Sasa

$$ | SUSHI | Japantown has a host of sushi options at all price points, but this longtime staple on the second floor of the Japan Center stands out from the crowd for its excellent rolls, nigiri, and sashimi. The *omakase* (selections chosen by the chef) menu, with eight pieces of sushi and nigiri, is a fraction of the cost of its downtown peers, but close to equal in quality and diner satisfaction. **Known for:** "mystery box" mini chirashi (rice and raw fish) bowl; uni spoon with quail egg and ikura (cured salmon roe); an oasis in a busy mall. *Average main: $26* *Japan Center East Mall, 22 Peace Plaza, Suite 530, Japantown* *628/600–6945* *sasasf.com.*

Shopping

BOOKS

Kinokuniya Bookstore

BOOKS/STATIONERY | FAMILY | The selection of English-language books about Japanese culture—everything from medieval history to origami instructions—is one of the finest in the country. Kinokuniya is also the city's biggest seller of Japanese-language books. Dozens of glossy Asian fashion magazines attract the young and trendy; the manga and anime books and magazines are wildly popular, too. *Kinokuniya Bldg., 1581 Webster St., at Geary Blvd., Japantown* *415/567–7625* *usa.kinokuniya.com.*

Western Addition

Part of the Western Addition, the Lower Fillmore in its post–World War II heyday was known as the Harlem of the West for its profusion of jazz night spots, where such legends as Billie Holliday, Duke Ellington, and Charlie Parker would play. These days the neighborhood tries to maintain its African American core and its link to that heritage; one success is the annual Fillmore Jazz Festival in June. More live music rings at the Fillmore Auditorium, made famous in the 1960s by Bill Graham and the iconic bands he booked there, and at the blues-centric Boom Boom Room.

Sights

★ Alamo Square Park

CITY PARK | FAMILY | Whether you've seen them on postcards or on the old TV show *Full House,* the colorful "Painted Ladies" Victorian houses are some of San Francisco's world-renowned icons. The signature view of these beauties with the downtown skyline in the background is from the east side of this hilly park. Tourists love the photo opportunities, but locals also adore the park's tennis courts, dog runs, and ample picnic area—with great views, of course. After taking plenty of photos, swing by the park's northwest corner and admire the William Westerfeld House (*1198 Fulton St.*), a splendid five-story late-19th-century Victorian mansion. **■ TIP→ If it's a sunny day, grab picnic provisions from Bi-Rite Market (*550 Divisadero St., at Hayes St.*). On Fridays and weekends, the Lady Falcon Coffee**

A
B
C
D
E
F
1
2
3
4
5
6
7
8
9
Green Street
Vallejo Street
Broadway
Pacific Avenue
Jackson Street
Washington Street
Baker St.
Clay Street
Sacramento Street
California Street
Lyon St.
Pine Street
Bush Street
Sutter Street
Post Street
Geary Blvd.
Kaiser
Med. Ctr.
O'Farrell Street
Terra Vista Ave.
Encanto Ave.
Fortuna Ave.
Baker St.
Josephs Ave.
Anza Vista Ave.
Turk St.
Golden Gate Ave.
McAllister St.
Fulton St.
Grove St.
Hayes Street
Fell Street
Panhandle
Oak Street
Page Street
Haight Street
HAIGHT
ASHBURY
Presidio Avenue
Lyon Street
Baker Street
Broderick St.
Divisadero Street
Lyon St.
PACIFIC
HEIGHTS
Alta Plaza
Divisadero Street
Scott Street
Pierce St.
Streetiner Street
Fillmore Street
Webster St.
Buchanan Street
Laguna Street
FILLMORE
Mt. Zion
Hosp.
Hamilton
Square
Kimball
Playground
Ellis Street
Eddy Street
Elm St.
WESTERN
ADDITION
Alamo
Square
Grove St.
Pierce Street
Waller St.
Broadway
Pacific Avenue
Jackson Street
Washington St.
Pacific
Med.
Center
Lafayette
Park
Geary Street
St. Francis
Square
Cleary Ct.
Hollis
Ellis St.
Willow St.
Western
Addition
Cultural Center
Laguna Street
Haight St.
Germania St.
Herman St.
0
300 m
0
1,000 ft

Sights

1 Alamo Square Park D7
2 Cathedral of Saint Mary of the Assumption G5
3 Haas-Lilienthal House G1
4 Japan Center E4
5 Kabuki Springs & Spa D4

Restaurants

1 Che Fico C7
2 4505 Burgers & BBQ B7
3 Marufuku Ramen E4
4 Merchant Roots D5
5 The Mill C7
6 Nopa C8
7 Octavia F3
8 SaSa E4
9 Sociale A3
10 State Bird Provisions D5

Hotels

1 Hotel Drisco A2

Club truck is stationed in the park, offering a great caffeine pick-me-up. ✉ *Western Addition* ✣ *Bordered by Steiner, Hayes, Scott, and Fulton Sts.* 🌐 *sfrecpark.org.*

Cathedral of Saint Mary of the Assumption
RELIGIOUS SITE | Residing at the prominent intersection of two busy thoroughfares (Geary Boulevard and Gough Street), this striking cathedral stands out with its sweeping contemporary design. Italian architects Pietro Belluschi and Pier Luigi Nervi intended to create a spectacular cathedral that reflects both the Catholic faith and modern technology. It was controversial when it opened in 1971, yet now is applauded for its grand, curving roof that rises to a height of 190 feet, with sections that form a cross highlighted with intricate stained-glass work. The cathedral is open daily for visitors other than during Mass, and it usually has docents on duty in the late morning hours. ✉ *1111 Gough St., at Geary St., Western Addition* 🌐 *smcsf.org.*

Restaurants

Che Fico
$$$ | **MODERN ITALIAN** | In a city full of Italian restaurants, this consistently popular Divisadero spot on the second floor of a revamped auto body shop sets itself apart with homemade charcuterie, plus antipasti, pastas, and pizza that often take traditional standbys for a creative spin or a California slant from local produce. The clever, beautifully balanced cocktails and fun twists on homey desserts are both must-orders. **Known for:** pineapple pizza; loud space and hard-to-get reservations; Roman Jewish specialties. $ *Average main: $32* ✉ *838 Divisadero St., Western Addition* ☎ *415/416–6959* 🌐 *www.chefico.com* ⏲ *Closed Sun. and Mon. No lunch.*

4505 Burgers & BBQ
$$ | **BARBECUE** | **FAMILY** | The smoker works overtime from noon to night at this hipster-chic barbecue shack, churning out an array of succulent meats that can be had by the plate, the pound, or as a sandwich. Every plate comes with two sides, and you should certainly make the frankaroni one of them: possibly the work of the devil, this is macaroni-and-cheese with pieces of hot dog ... deep fried. **Known for:** partially outdoor seating in shipping containers; decadent sides; self-named and possibly correct "Best Damn Cheeseburger." $ *Average main: $20* ✉ *705 Divisadero St., between Grove and Fulton Sts., Western Addition* ☎ *415/231–6993* 🌐 *www.4505burgersandbbq.com.*

Merchant Roots
$$$$ | **CONTEMPORARY** | After starting as part grocer/part lunch café/part tasting menu, this tiny Fillmore spot is now fully devoted to the elaborate tasting menus of chef-owner Ryan Shelton. Themes and dishes change every few months (it could be "flowers" or "Alice in Wonderland"), but the one constant is Shelton's incredible imagination and ability to transform those themes into elaborate, technique-driven composed dishes. **Known for:** SF's best chocolate chip cookies available as a takeout supplement; warm and welcoming ambience; excellent wine program. $ *Average main: $128* ✉ *1365 Fillmore St., Western Addition* ☎ *530/574–7365* 🌐 *www.merchantroots.com* ⏲ *Closed Sun. and Mon. No lunch.*

★ The Mill
$ | **BAKERYBAKERY** | "Four-dollar toast" is a phrase used around San Francisco referring to gentrification—and it was inspired by this sun-drenched, Wi-Fi-less café. At this project between one of the city's leading bakers, Josey Baker (yes, that's really his last name and profession!), and the Mission's Four Barrel Coffee, toasts slathered with jam or spreads are the specialty during the day. **Known for:** stellar loaves of bread; precious, post-yoga vibe; one pizza topping served most nights. $ *Average main: $8* ✉ *736 Divisadero*

St., Western Addition ☎ *415/345–1953* 🌐 *www.themillsf.com.*

★ Nopa

$$$ | AMERICAN | This is the good-food granddaddy of the hot corridor of the same name (it's hard to tell which came first—Nopa the restaurant or NoPa the North of the Panhandle neighborhood). The Cali-rustic fare here draws dependable crowds regardless of the night, with attractions including a beloved Moroccan vegetable tagine; crisp-skin rotisserie chicken; a juicy hamburger with thick-cut fries; and an outstanding weekend brunch. **Known for:** high-quality comforting food with smart twists; actually good food after 11 pm; a constant and diverse crowd. *Average main: $28* ✉ *560 Divisadero St., Western Addition* ☎ *415/864–8643* 🌐 *nopasf.com* *No lunch weekdays.*

★ State Bird Provisions

$$ | MODERN AMERICAN | It's more or less impossible to score a reservation for a normal dinner hour at Lower Fillmore's game-changing restaurant, but once you nab a golden ticket, you'll be rewarded with fascinating bites served from roving carts and an à la carte printed menu. The food has an artsy bent to it, and the colorful dining room with pegboard walls adds to a vibe that's part high-school art room, part bohemian dinner party. **Known for:** "State Bird" namesake buttermilk fried quail; long lines at opening time for the no-reservation tables; "World Peace" peanut milk dessert drink. *Average main: $26* ✉ *1529 Fillmore St., Western Addition* ☎ *415/795–1272* 🌐 *www.statebirdsf.com* *No lunch.*

Nightlife

Boom Boom Room

MUSIC CLUBS | One of San Francisco's liveliest music spots is this Fillmore blues favorite, opened in 1997 by the "King of the Boogie," John Lee Hooker. The club has a fun blend of blues, funk, and hip-hop shows most nights of the week. ✉ *1601 Fillmore St., at Geary Blvd., Western Addition* ☎ *415/673–8000* 🌐 *boomboomroom.com.*

The Fillmore

MUSIC CLUBS | This is *the* club that all the big names, from Coldplay to Clapton, want to play. San Francisco's most famous rock-music hall presents national and local acts: rock, reggae, grunge, jazz, folk, acid house, and more. Go upstairs to view the amazing collection of rock posters lining the walls. At the end of each show, free apples are set near the door, and staffers hand out collectible posters. **TIP→ Avoid steep service charges by purchasing tickets at the club's box office on Sunday from 10 to 4.** ✉ *1805 Geary Blvd., at Fillmore St., Western Addition* ☎ *415/346–6000* 🌐 *www.thefillmore.com.*

Horsefeather

BARS/PUBS | Creative, produce-driven cocktails and a chic, low-key vibe make this Divisadero drinking destination a locals' frequent top choice for a fun night out. The always interesting (but never too bizarre) cocktails range from a breezy California Cooler with celery juice to the rum-and-whiskey-based Breakfast Punch featuring clarified Cinnamon Toast Crunch–infused milk. Weekend brunch is excellent, as is the delightfully messy double cheeseburger. As an added bonus, the kitchen stays open late nightly. ✉ *528 Divisadero St., Western Addition* ☎ *415/817–1939* 🌐 *www.horsefeatherbar.com.*

North Beach

San Francisco novelist Herbert Gold called North Beach "the longest-running, most glorious, American bohemian operetta outside Greenwich Village." Indeed, to anyone who has spent some time in its eccentric old bars and cafés, North Beach evokes everything from the Barbary Coast days to the no-less-rowdy Beatnik era.

Sights

Beat Museum

MUSEUM | "Museum" might be a stretch for this tiny storefront that's half bookstore, half memorabilia collection. You can see the 1949 Hudson from the movie version of *On the Road* and the shirt Neal Cassady wore while driving Ken Kesey's Merry Prankster bus, "Further." There are also manuscripts, letters, and early editions by Jack Kerouac, Allen Ginsberg, and Lawrence Ferlinghetti; but the true treasure here is the passionate and well-informed staff, which often includes the museum's founder, Jerry Cimino: your short visit may turn into an hours-long trip through the Beat era. **■ TIP→ The excellent Saturday walking tour goes beyond the museum to take in favorite Beat watering holes and hangouts in North Beach.** ✉ *540 Broadway, North Beach* ☎ *415/399–9626* 🌐 *www.thebeatmuseum.org* 🎫 *$8* 🕒 *Closed Tues. and Wed.*

★ City Lights Bookstore

STORE/MALL | The exterior of this famous literary bookstore is iconic in itself, from the replica of a revolutionary mural destroyed in Chiapas, Mexico, by military forces to the art banners hanging above the windows. Designated a landmark by the city, the hangout of Beat-era writers and independent publishers remains a vital part of San Francisco's literary scene. Browse the three levels of poetry, philosophy, politics, fiction, history, and local zines, to the beat of creaking wood floors.

Back in the day, writers like Allen Ginsberg and Jack Kerouac would do their reading here (and even receive mail in the basement). The late poet Lawrence Ferlinghetti, who cofounded City Lights in 1953, cemented its place in history by publishing Ginsberg's *Howl and Other Poems* in 1956. The small volume was ignored in the mainstream ... until Ferlinghetti and the bookstore manager were arrested for obscenity and corruption of youth. In the landmark First Amendment trial that followed, the judge exonerated both men. *Howl* went on to become a classic.

Stroll Kerouac Alley, branching off Columbus Avenue next to City Lights, to read the quotes from Ferlinghetti, Maya Angelou, Confucius, John Steinbeck, and the street's namesake embedded in the pavement. ✉ *261 Columbus Ave., North Beach* ☎ *415/362–8193* 🌐 *www.citylights.com.*

Coit Tower

VIEWPOINT | Among San Francisco's most distinctive skyline sights, this 210-foot tower is often considered a tribute to firefighters because of the donor's special attachment to the local fire company. As the story goes, a young gold rush–era girl, Lillie Hitchcock Coit (known as Miss Lil), was a fervent admirer of her local fire company—so much so that she once deserted a wedding party and chased down the street after her favorite engine, Knickerbocker No. 5, while clad in her bridesmaid finery. When Lillie died in 1929, she left the city $125,000 to "expend in an appropriate manner ... to the beauty of San Francisco." You can ride the elevator to the top of the tower to enjoy the 360° view of the Bay Bridge and the Golden Gate Bridge; due north is Alcatraz Island. Most visitors saunter past the 27 fabulous Depression-era murals inside the tower that depict California's economic and political life, but take the time to appreciate the first New Deal art project, supported by taxpayer money. It's also possible to walk up and down (if you're in shape): a highlight is the descent toward the Embarcadero via the **Filbert Steps,** a series of stairways that are a shaded green oasis in the middle of the city. ✉ *Telegraph Hill Blvd., at Greenwich St. or Lombard St., North Beach* ☎ *415/362–0808* 🌐 *sfrecpark.org* 🎫 *Free; elevator to top $9.*

Grant Avenue

NEIGHBORHOOD | Originally called Calle de la Fundación, Grant Avenue is the oldest street in the city, but it's got plenty of young blood. Here, dusty bars such as the Saloon mix with independent boutiques and odd curio shops, as well as curated gourmet shops such as Italian Slow Food import store Sotto Casa and fancy wine and cheese shop Little Vine. While the street runs from Union Square through Chinatown, North Beach, and beyond, the fun stuff in this neighborhood is jammed into the four blocks from Columbus Avenue north to Filbert Street. ✉ *North Beach.*

★ Telegraph Hill and the Filbert Steps

NEIGHBORHOOD | Residents here have some of the city's best views, as well as the most difficult ascents to their aeries. The hill rises from the east end of Lombard Street to a height of 284 feet and is capped by Coit Tower. If you brave the slope, though, you can be rewarded with a "secret treasure" San Francisco moment. Filbert Street starts up the hill, then becomes the **Filbert Steps** when the going gets too steep. You can cut between the Filbert Steps and another flight, the **Greenwich Steps,** on up to the hilltop. As you climb, you pass some of the city's oldest houses and are surrounded by beautiful, flowering private gardens. In some places the trees grow over the stairs, so it feels like you're walking through a green tunnel; elsewhere, you'll have wide-open views of the bay. The cypress trees that grow on the hill are a favorite roost of local avian celebrities, the wild parrots of Telegraph Hill; you'll hear the cries of the cherry-headed conures if they're nearby. And the telegraphic name? It comes from the hill's status as the first Morse code signal station back in 1853. ✉ *Bordered by Lombard, Filbert, Kearny, and Sansome Sts., North Beach.*

Washington Square

PLAZA | Once the daytime social heart of San Francisco's Italian district, this grassy patch has changed character numerous times over the years. The Beats hung out here in the 1950s, hippies camped out in the 1960s and early '70s, and nowadays you're more likely to see picnickers and residents doing community dance, yoga, or tai chi. You might also see homeless people hanging out on the benches and young locals sunbathing or running their dogs. Lillie Hitchcock Coit, in yet another show of affection for San Francisco's firefighters, donated the statue of two firemen with a rescued child. Camera-toting visitors focus on the Romanesque splendor of **Saints Peter and Paul Church** (Filbert St. side of square), a 1924 building with Disneyesque stone-white towers that are local landmarks. Mass reflects the neighborhood; it's given in English, Italian, and Chinese. ✉ *Bordered by Columbus Ave. and Stockton, Filbert, and Union Sts., North Beach* 🌐 *sfrecpark.org.*

Restaurants

The Italian Homemade Company

$ | **ITALIAN** | **FAMILY** | In Italy, the bastion of fresh pasta is Emilia-Romagna, and a trio of entrepreneurs hailing from the region give respect to its claim to carb fame in a mini-empire of fast-casual pasta eateries, with the one in North Beach as its flagship. Come for treats like slabs of lasagna that fool you into thinking you're calorie loading in Bologna, as well as stuffed ravioli and gnocchi. **Known for:** varieties of piadina (Italian flatbreads with meats, cheeses, and vegetables); mix-and-match pastas and sauces; great quality for the price. $ *Average main: $13* ✉ *716 Columbus Ave., North Beach* ☎ *415/712–8874* 🌐 *italianhomemade.com.*

Tony's Pizza Napoletana

$$ | **PIZZA** | **FAMILY** | Repeatedly crowned the World Champion Pizza Maker at the World Pizza Cup in Naples, Tony

A
B
C
D
E
F
1
2
3
4
5
6
7
8
9
Pier 45
Pier 43
Pier 41
Pier 39
Pier 35
Pier 47
Aquatic Park
Maritime Museum
Ghirardelli Square
NORTH BEACH
Jefferson Street
Beach Street
North Point St.
Bay Street
Columbus Avenue
Russian Hill Park
Cable Car
San Francisco Art Institute
Chestnut Street
Francisco Street
Pfeiffer St.
Streetckton Street
TELEGRAPH HILL
Lombard Street
Greenwich Street
Filbert Street
Union Street
Hyde Street
Jansen St.
Jones Street
Taylor Street
Mason Street
Powell Street
Kearny St.
Grant Ave.
Kearny Street
Vallejo Street
Green Street
Larkin Street
Polk Street
Van Ness Avenue
Leavenworth Street
Union St.
RUSSIAN HILL
Tunnel
Bernard St.
CHINATOWN
Broadway
John Street
Jackson Street
Washington Street
Clay Street
Pleasant St.
Huntington Park
Sacramento Street
POLK GULCH
California Street
NOB HILL
Pine Street
St. Mary's Sq.
Chinatown Gate
Grant Avenue
Bush Street
Sutter Street
Post Street
Geary St.
UNION SQUARE
MONT
101
KEY
Exploring Sights
Restaurants
Hotels
BART station

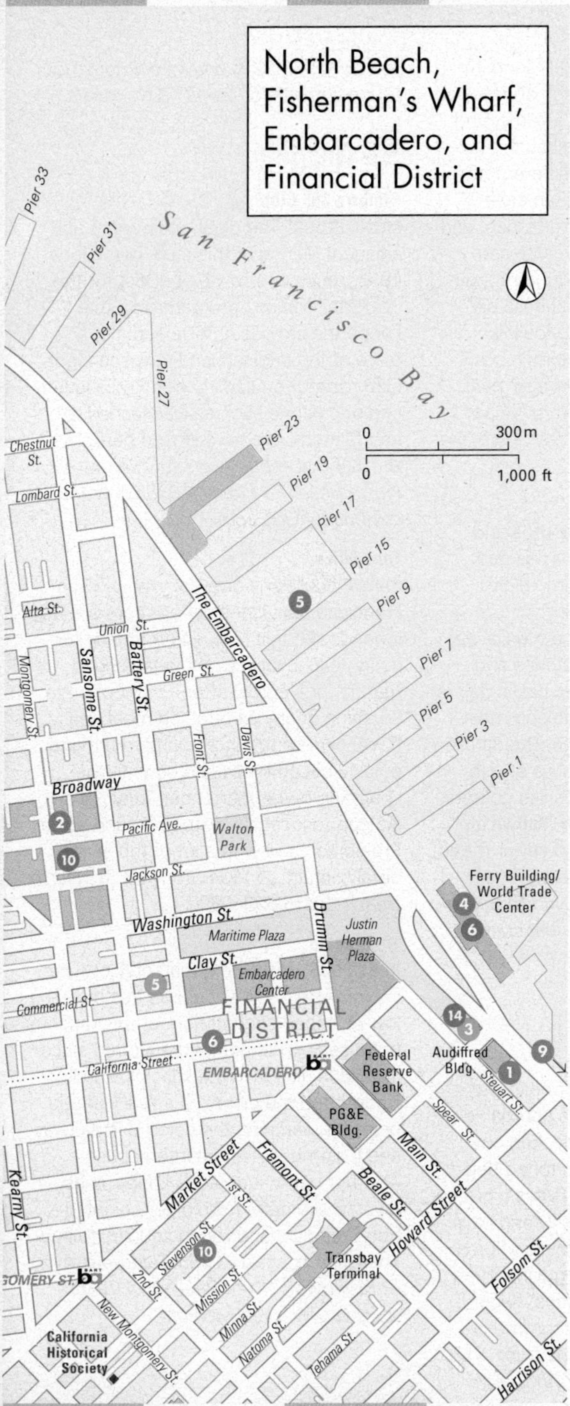

North Beach, Fisherman's Wharf, Embarcadero, and Financial District

Sights

1	Alcatraz	F1
2	Beat Museum	F6
3	City Lights Bookstore	F6
4	Coit Tower	F4
5	Exploratorium	I4
6	Ferry Building	J6
7	F-line	C2
8	Grant Avenue	F6
9	Hyde Street Pier	B2
10	Jackson Square Historic District	G6
11	Musée Mécanique	C2
12	Pier 39	E1
13	San Francisco National Maritime Museum	A2
14	San Francisco Railway Museum	J7
15	Telegraph Hill and the Filbert Steps	F4
16	Washington Square	E5

Restaurants

1	Angler	J7
2	Cotogna	G6
3	Gary Danko	B3
4	Hog Island Oyster Company	J6
5	The Italian Homemade Company	D4
6	Perbacco	H7
7	Tony's Pizza Napoletana	E5
8	Tosca Cafe	F6
9	Waterbar	J7
10	Yang Sing	H8

Hotels

1	Argonaut Hotel	B2
2	Columbus Motor Inn	C4
3	Hotel Vitale	J7
4	Hotel Zoe Fisherman's Wharf	D3
5	Le Méridien San Francisco	H7

Gemignani is a carb-friendly legend in the city for his flavorful dough and myriad versions. The multiple gas, electric, and wood-burning ovens in his casual, modern pizzeria turn out many different styles of pies—the famed Neapolitan-style Margherita, but also Sicilian, Roman, and Detroit styles—with salads, antipasti, homemade pastas, and calzone rounding out the menu. **Known for:** Cal-Italia pie with aged balsamic drizzle; vibes like an NYC pizza parlor; slice stand next door if you can't wait. *Average main: $26* *1570 Stockton St., North Beach* *415/835–9888* *tonyspizzanapoletana.com.*

Tosca Cafe

$$$$ | **ITALIAN** | The leather booths and chairs are in high demand at this dark and clubby boho classic from 1919, where well-heeled locals and visitors delight in food that skews to the Cal-Italian genre, meaning local catches and seasonal produce as well as Italian flair in dishes such as halibut crudo and meatballs swimming in red sauce. The dinner menu is prix fixe, and there's a stylish Sunday brunch with choices like polenta pancakes and salt cod hash. **Known for:** Italian cocktails; raw bar and caviar menu; Tuscan fried chicken. *Average main: $75* *242 Columbus Ave., North Beach* *415/986–9651* *toscacafesf.com* *No lunch.*

Hotels

Columbus Motor Inn

$ | **HOTEL** | **FAMILY** | Close to Chinatown and Fisherman's Wharf, this affordable lodging with basic rooms decked out with oversize pillows, earth-toned bedding, and large flat-screen TVs is a great pick if you brought your family and have a car to park. **Pros:** free parking; affordable rooms deep-cleaned regularly; lively location. **Cons:** lacks amenities; decor is not stylish; street-facing accommodations can be noisy. *Rooms from: $120* *1075 Columbus Ave., North Beach* *415/885–1492* *www.columbusmotorinn.com* *45 rooms* *No meals.*

Nightlife

Bimbo's 365 Club

MUSIC CLUBS | The plush main room and adjacent lounge of this club, here since 1951, retain a retro vibe perfect for the "Cocktail Nation" programming that keeps the crowds entertained. For a taste of the original San Francisco nightclub scene, you can't beat it. Indie low-fi and pop bands such as Mustache Harbor and Tainted Love have played here. *1025 Columbus Ave., at Chestnut St., North Beach* *415/474–0365* *www.bimbos365club.com.*

Tony Nik's

BARS/PUBS | For a dive bar with old San Francisco soul (considering there are few legends like this left), go no further for a nightcap involving an old-fashioned, martini, or Negroni after a night of pizza crushing or any carb-fueled meal, really. If you can, hang out at the bar with and quickly become acquainted with the charming owner/bartender. Tony Nik's is an icon to local bar history, around since Prohibition and with a lot of the same details intact. *1534 Stockton St., North Beach* *415/693–0990.*

★ **Vesuvio**

BARS/PUBS | If you're hitting only one bar in North Beach, it should be this one. The low-ceilinged second floor of this raucous boho saloon hangout, little altered since its 1960s heyday (when Jack Kerouac frequented the place), is a fine vantage point for watching the colorful Broadway and Columbus Avenue intersection. Another part of Vesuvio's appeal is its diverse clientele, from older neighborhood regulars and young couples to bacchanalian posses. *255 Columbus Ave., at Broadway, North Beach* *415/362–3370* *www.vesuvio.com.*

Thousands of visitors take ferries to Alcatraz each day to walk in the footsteps of the notorious criminals who were held on "The Rock."

Shopping

Knitz and Leather

CLOTHING | Local artisans Julia Relinghaus and Katharina Ernst have been producing one-of-a-kind and custom products of extraordinary craftsmanship for over 30 years. Ernst's bold knitted sweaters and accessories will help you stand out from the crowd, and Relinghaus's exquisite, high-quality leather jackets for men and women are the kind of investment you make for fine leather. ✉ *1453 Grant Ave., North Beach* ☎ *415/391–3480*.

Fisherman's Wharf

The crack of fresh Dungeness crab, the aroma of sourdough warm from the oven, the cry of the gulls—in some ways you can experience Fisherman's Wharf today as it has been for more than 100 years.

Sights

★ Hyde Street Pier

MUSEUM | **FAMILY** | If you want to get to the heart of the Wharf, there's no better place to do it than at this pier. Don't pass up the centerpiece collection of historic vessels, part of the **San Francisco Maritime National Historical Park,** almost all of which can be boarded. The *Balclutha,* an 1886 full-rigged three-masted sailing vessel that's more than 250 feet long, sailed around Cape Horn 17 times. Kids especially love the *Eureka*, a side-wheel passenger and car ferry, for her onboard collection of vintage cars. The *Hercules* is a steam-powered tugboat, and the *C. A. Thayer* is a beautifully restored three-masted schooner.

Across the street from the pier and a museum in itself is the maritime park's **Visitor Center** (*499 Jefferson St., 415/447–5000*), whose fun, large-scale exhibits make it an engaging stop. See a huge First Order Fresnel lighthouse lens and a shipwrecked boat. Then stroll through time in the exhibit "The Waterfront," where you can touch the timber from a gold rush–era ship recovered from below the Financial District, peek into 19th-century storefronts, and see the sails of an Italian fishing vessel. ⊠ *Hyde and Jefferson Sts., Fisherman's Wharf* ☎ *415/561–7100* 🌐 *www.nps.gov/safr* 🎫 *Ships $15 (ticket good for 7 days).*

Musée Mécanique

MUSEUM | **FAMILY** | Once a staple at Playland at the Beach, San Francisco's early 20th-century amusement park, the antique mechanical contrivances at this time-warp arcade—including peep shows and nickelodeons—make it one of the most worthwhile attractions at the Wharf. Some favorites are the giant and rather creepy "Laffing Sal"; an arm-wrestling machine; the world's only steam-powered motorcycle; and mechanical fortune-telling figures that speak from their curtained boxes. Note the depictions of race that betray the prejudices of the time: stoned Chinese figures in the "Opium-Den" and clown-faced African Americans eating watermelon in the "Mechanical Farm." **■TIP→ Admission is free, but you'll need quarters to bring the machines to life.** ⊠ *Pier 45, Shed A, Fisherman's Wharf* ☎ *415/346–2000* 🌐 *museemecaniquesf.com* 🎫 *Free.*

Pier 39

STORE/MALL | **FAMILY** | The city's most popular waterfront attraction draws millions of visitors each year, who come to browse through its shops and concessions hawking every conceivable form of souvenir. The pier can be quite crowded, and the numerous street performers may leave you feeling more harassed than entertained. Arriving early in the morning ensures you a front-row view of the sea lions that bask here, but if you're at Pier 39 to shop, be aware that most stores don't open until 9:30 or 10 (later in winter).

Follow the sound of barking to the northwest side of the pier to view the **sea lions** flopping about the floating docks. During the summer, orange-clad naturalists answer questions and offer fascinating facts about the playful pinnipeds—for example, that most of the animals here are males.

At the **Aquarium of the Bay** (☎ *415/623–5300 or 888/732–3483* 🌐 *www.aquariumofthebay.org* 🎫 *$29.95*), moving walkways transport you through a space surrounded on three sides by water filled with indigenous San Francisco Bay marine life, from fish and plankton to sharks. ⊠ *Beach St., at Embarcadero, Fisherman's Wharf* 🌐 *www.pier39.com.*

San Francisco National Maritime Museum

MUSEUM | **FAMILY** | You'll feel as if you're out to sea when you step aboard, er, inside this sturdy, ship-shape (literally), Streamline-Moderne structure, dubbed the Bathhouse Building and built in 1939 as part of the New Deal's Works Progress Administration. The first floor of the museum, part of the **San Francisco Maritime National Historical Park,** has stunningly restored undersea dreamscape murals and some of the museum's intricate ship models. The first-floor balcony overlooks the beach and has lovely WPA-era tile designs. **■TIP→ If you've got young kids in tow, the museum makes a great quick, free stop. Then pick up ice cream at Ghirardelli Square across the street and enjoy it on the beach or next door in Victorian Park, where you can watch the cable cars turn around.** ⊠ *Aquatic Park, foot of Polk St., Fisherman's Wharf* ☎ *415/447–5000* 🌐 *www.nps.gov/safr* 🎫 *Donation suggested.*

Restaurants

Gary Danko

$$$$ | **AMERICAN** | This San Francisco classic for prix-fixe dining has earned a legion of fans—and a Michelin star—for its namesake chef's refined and creative seasonal California cooking, displayed in dishes like glazed oysters with Ossetra caviar and juniper-crusted bison. The banquette-lined rooms, with stunning floral arrangements, are as memorable as the food and impeccable service. **Known for:** tableside cheese cart; soufflé for dessert; reservations are hard to get. *Average main: $97 800 N. Point St., Fisherman's Wharf 415/749–2060 garydanko.com No lunch Jacket required.*

Hotels

★ Argonaut Hotel

$$ | **HOTEL** | **FAMILY** | The nautically themed Argonaut's spacious guest rooms have exposed-brick walls, wood-beam ceilings, and best of all, windows that open to the sea air and the sounds of the waterfront; many rooms enjoy Alcatraz and Golden Gate Bridge views. **Pros:** hotel's seafood restaurant is above average for the neighborhood; near Hyde Street cable car; toys for the kids. **Cons:** nautical theme isn't for everyone; cramped public areas; far from crosstown attractions. *Rooms from: $269 495 Jefferson St., at Hyde St., Fisherman's Wharf 415/563–0800, 800/790–1415 reservations www.argonauthotel.com 252 rooms No meals.*

Hotel Zoe Fisherman's Wharf

$$ | **HOTEL** | A little removed from the heart of the wharf area craziness, this smart-looking boutique hotel with guest-room interiors inspired by luxury Mediterranean yachts aims for subtle contemporary elegance in the form of lightly stained woods and soft-brown and cream fabrics and walls. **Pros:** cozy feeling; nice desks and sitting areas in rooms; open-air courtyard with firepits. **Cons:** rather congested touristy area; smaller rooms can feel too tight; resort fee catches some guests off guard. *Rooms from: $239 425 N. Point St., at Mason St., Fisherman's Wharf 415/561–1100, 800/648–4626 www.hotelzoesf.com 221 rooms No meals.*

Nightlife

★ Buena Vista Cafe

BARS/PUBS | At the end of the Hyde Street cable-car line, the Buena Vista packs 'em in for its famous Irish coffee—which, according to owners, was the first served stateside (in 1952). The place oozes nostalgia with its white-jacketed bartenders and timeless atmosphere, drawing devoted locals as well as out-of-towners relaxing after a day of sightseeing. It's narrow and can get crowded, but this spot is a sip of history and provides a fine alternative to the overpriced tourist joints nearby. *2765 Hyde St., at Beach St., Fisherman's Wharf 415/474–5044 www.thebuenavista.com.*

Embarcadero

Stretching from below the Bay Bridge to Fisherman's Wharf, San Francisco's flat, accessible waterfront invites you to get up close and personal with the bay, the picturesque and constant backdrop to this stunning city. For decades the Embarcadero was obscured by a raised freeway and known best for the giant buildings on its piers that further cut off the city from the water. With the freeway gone and a few piers restored for public access, the Embarcadero has been given a new lease on life. Millions of visitors may come through the northern waterfront every year, lured by Fisherman's Wharf and Pier 39, but locals tend to stop short of these, opting instead for the gastronomic pleasures of the Ferry Building or using the palm-tree-lined sidewalks as a jogging route. Between the wharf and South Beach Park, though, you'll find tourists and San Franciscans alike soaking up the sun, walking out over the water on a long pier to see the sailboats, savoring the excellent restaurants and old-time watering holes, and watching the street performers that crowd Embarcadero Plaza on a sunny day—these are the simple joys that make you happy you're in San Francisco, whether for a few days or a lifetime.

★ Alcatraz

JAIL | FAMILY | Thousands of visitors come every day to walk in the footsteps of Alcatraz's notorious criminals. The stories of life and death on "the Rock" may sometimes be exaggerated, but it's almost impossible to resist the chance to wander the cell block that tamed the country's toughest gangsters and saw daring escape attempts. Some infamous inmates included Al "Scarface" Capone, Robert "The Birdman" Stroud, and George "Machine Gun Kelly." The boat ride to the island is brief (15 minutes) but affords beautiful views, and the audio tour is highly recommended. Allow at least three hours for the visit and boat rides combined. Tour options include a regular daytime one, plus a Night Tour and an evening Behind the Scenes Tour. ■ **TIP→ Booking your tour ahead is absolutely essential to avoid disappointment.** ✉ *Pier 33, Embarcadero* ☎ *415/981–7625* 🌐 *www.nps.gov/alca* 🎫 *From $41.*

★ Exploratorium

MUSEUM | FAMILY | Walking into this fascinating "museum of science, art, and human perception" is like visiting a mad-scientist's laboratory, but one in which most of the exhibits are supersize and you can play with everything. Signature experiential exhibits include the Tinkering Studio and a glass Bay Observatory building, where the exhibits inside help visitors better understand what they see outside. Get an Alice-in-Wonderland feeling in the Distorted Room, where you seem to shrink and grow as you walk across the slanted, checkered floor. In the Shadow Box, a powerful flash freezes an image of your shadow on the wall; jumping is a favorite pose. More than 650 other exhibits focus on sea and insect life, computers, electricity, patterns and light, language, the weather, and more. One surefire hit is the pitch-black, hands-on Tactile Dome ($15 extra; reservations required): crawl through ladders, slides, and tunnels, relying solely on your sense of touch. Don't miss a walk around the outside of the museum afterward for superb views and a lesson about the bay's sediment and water motion in the Bay Windows presentation. ✉ *Piers 15–17, Embarcadero* ☎ *415/528–4444 general information, 415/528–4407 Tactile Dome reservations* 🌐 *www.exploratorium.edu* 🎫 *$30.*

★ Ferry Building

MARKET | The jewel of the Embarcadero, erected in 1896 and now home to an outstanding food marketplace, is topped by a 230-foot clock tower modeled after the campanile of the cathedral in Seville, Spain. On the morning of April 18, 1906, the tower's four clock faces stopped at 5:17—the moment the great earthquake struck—and stayed still for 12 months.

Today San Franciscans flock to the street-level marketplace, stocking up on supplies from local favorites, such as Acme Bread, Blue Bottle Coffee, El Porteño (empanadas), the gluten-free Mariposa Baking Company, and Humphry Slocombe (ice cream). The Slanted Door, the city's beloved high-end Vietnamese restaurant, is the fine dining favorite here, along with Hog Island Oyster Company and the seasonal Californian duo of Bouli Bar and Boulette's Larder. On the plaza side, the outdoor tables at Gott's Roadside offer great people-watching and famous burgers. On Saturday morning the plazas outside the building buzz with an upscale farmers' market. Extending south from the piers north of the building to the Bay Bridge, the waterfront promenade out front is a favorite among joggers and picnickers, with a view of sailboats plying the bay. True to its name, the Ferry Building still serves actual ferries: from its eastern flank they sail to Sausalito, Larkspur, Tiburon, and the East Bay. ✉ *Embarcadero , 1 Ferry Bldg., at foot of Market St.,*

Embarcadero ☎ *415/983–8030* 🌐 *www.ferrybuildingmarketplace.com.*

F-line

TRANSPORTATION SITE (AIRPORT/BUS/FERRY/TRAIN) | The city's system of vintage electric trolleys, the F-line, gives the cable cars a run for their money as a beloved mode of transportation. The beautifully restored streetcars—some dating from the 19th century—run from the Castro District down Market Street to the Embarcadero, then north to Fisherman's Wharf. Each car is unique, restored to the colors of its city of origin, from New Orleans and Philadelphia to Melbourne and Milan. **■ TIP→ Pay with a Clipper card or purchase tickets on board; exact change is required.** ✉ *San Francisco* 🌐 *www.streetcar.org* 🎫 *$3.*

San Francisco Railway Museum

MUSEUM | FAMILY | A labor of love brought to you by the same vintage-transit enthusiasts responsible for the F-line's revival, this one-room museum and store celebrates the city's streetcars and cable cars with photographs, models, and artifacts. The permanent exhibit includes the replicated end of a streetcar with a working cab—complete with controls and a bell—for kids to explore; the cool, antique Wiley birdcage traffic signal; and models and display cases to view. Right on the F-line track, just across from the Ferry Building, this is a great quick stop. ✉ *77 Steuart St., Embarcadero* ☎ *415/974–1948* 🌐 *www.streetcar.org/museum/* 🎫 *Free* ⏲ *Closed Mon.*

Restaurants

Angler

$$$ | SEAFOOD | Immaculately fresh seafood and a wood-burning hearth are the centerpieces of this bustling yet luxurious Embarcadero sibling to Saison. The menu descriptions might be brief, but it's really all about the ingredients—whether it's "fresh from the live tank" geoduck (a large Pacific clam) or peak seasonal baby artichokes—fulfilling their full potential on the plate with a few smart embellishments. **Known for:** taxidermy-filled back room with Bay Bridge views; bigeye tuna tartare; Instagram-favorite radicchio salad. 💲 *Average main: $36* ✉ *132 The Embarcadero, Embarcadero* ☎ *415/872–9442* 🌐 *anglerrestaurants.com/san-francisco* ⏲ *Closed Sun. and Mon. No lunch.*

Hog Island Oyster Company

$$ | SEAFOOD | A thriving oyster farm north of San Francisco in Tomales Bay serves up its harvest at this raw bar and restaurant in the Ferry Building, where devotees come for impeccably fresh oysters and clams on the half shell. Other mollusk-centered options include a first-rate seafood stew, grilled oysters, clam chowder, and "steamer" dishes, but the bar also turns out one of the city's best grilled cheese sandwiches, made with three artisanal cheeses on artisanal bread. **Known for:** crowds slurping dozens of oysters; local produce salads; superior Bloody Mary. 💲 *Average main: $21* ✉ *1 Ferry Bldg., Embarcadero at Market St., Embarcadero* ☎ *415/391–7117* 🌐 *hogislandoysters.com.*

Waterbar

$$$$ | SEAFOOD | You come for seafood with a view: sky-high aquariums dominate the dining room, and the bay is just beyond, but the biggest attraction is the food. Every fin and shell of the sea, from the oak-roasted Petrale sole to the roasted Sacramento sturgeon, is sustainably sourced. **Known for:** cured fish starters; ample oyster bar; delightful Pat Kuleto–designed interior. 💲 *Average main: $38* ✉ *399 The Embarcadero, between Folsom and Harrison Sts., Embarcadero* ☎ *415/284–9922* 🌐 *www.waterbarsf.com.*

Hotels

Hotel Vitale

$$$ | HOTEL | The emphasis on luxury and upscale relaxation at this eight-story property across the street from the bay is apparent: limestone-lined baths stocked with top-of-the-line products; the penthouse-level day spa with soaking tubs set in a rooftop bamboo forest; terraces on the fifth, seventh, and eighth floors with great waterfront views. **Pros:** excellent Americano Restaurant & Bar; spacious rooms; well-designed work-from-room setups with ergonomic chairs. **Cons:** not close to much nightlife; steep $40 per day amenities fee adds expense to an already pricey property; yet another charge for Wi-Fi beyond basic. $ *Rooms from: $319* ✉ *8 Mission St., Embarcadero* ☎ *415/278–3700* 🌐 *www.hotelvitale.com* *200 rooms* *No meals.*

Hard Water

BARS/PUBS | The waterfront restaurant and bar with a stunning horseshoe-shape bar centerpiece pays homage to America's most iconic spirit—bourbon—with a wall of whiskeys and a lineup of specialty cocktails. The menu, crafted by Charles Phan of Slanted Door fame, is an ode to New Orleans cuisine and includes spicy pork-belly cracklings, BBQ oysters, must-try Nashville hot fried chicken, and other fun snacks. ✉ *Pier 3, at The Embarcadero, Embarcadero* ☎ *415/392–3021* 🌐 *www.hardwaterbar.com.*

FARMERS' MARKETS

★ **Ferry Plaza Farmers' Market**

OUTDOOR/FLEA/GREEN MARKETS | The partylike Saturday edition of the city's most upscale and expensive farmers' market places baked goods, gourmet cheeses, smoked fish, and fancy pots of jam alongside organic basil, specialty mushrooms, heirloom tomatoes, and juicy-ripe locally grown fruit. Smaller markets also take place on Tuesday and Thursday year-round, rain or shine—and the many passionate San Francisco home cooks who frequent them will come even in a rainstorm. ✉ *Ferry Plaza, at Market St., Embarcadero* ☎ *415/291–3276* 🌐 *www.ferrybuildingmarketplace.com.*

Financial District

During the latter half of the 19th century, when San Francisco was a brawling, extravagant gold-rush town, today's Financial District (FiDi, for short) was underwater. Yerba Buena Cove reached all the way up to Montgomery Street, and what's now Jackson Square was the heart of the Barbary Coast, bordering some of the roughest wharves in the world.

These days, Jackson Square is a genteel and upscale neighborhood wedged between North Beach and the Financial District, but buried below Montgomery Street lie remnants of those wild days: more than 100 ships abandoned by frantic crews and passengers caught up in gold fever rest under the foundations of buildings here. The Financial District of the 21st century is a decidedly less exciting affair: it's all office towers with mazes of cubicles now. When the sun sets, this quarter empties out fast. The few sights here will appeal mainly to gold-rush history enthusiasts; others can spend time elsewhere.

Jackson Square Historic District

NEIGHBORHOOD | This was the heart of the Barbary Coast of the Gay '90s—the 1890s, that is. Although most of the red-light district was destroyed in the fire that followed the 1906 earthquake, the remaining old redbrick buildings, many of them now occupied by advertising agencies, law offices, and antiques firms, retain hints of the romance and rowdiness of San Francisco's early days.

With its gentrified gold rush–era buildings, the 700 block of **Montgomery Street** just barely evokes the Barbary Coast days, but this was a colorful block in the 19th century and on into the 20th. Writers Mark Twain and Bret Harte were among the contributors to the spunky *The Golden Era* newspaper, which occupied No. 732 (now part of the building at No. 744).

Restored 19th-century brick buildings line Hotaling Place, which connects Washington and Jackson Streets, named for the **A. P. Hotaling Company whiskey distillery** (*451 Jackson St., at Hotaling Pl.*), the largest liquor repository on the West Coast in its day. The exceptional Gold Rush City walking tour offered by City Guides (☎ *415/557–4266* 🌐 *www.sfcityguides.org*) covers this area and brings its history to life. ✉ *Bordered by Columbus Ave., Broadway, and Washington and Sansome Sts., Financial District.*

Restaurants

Cotogna

$$$ | ITALIAN | The draw at this urban trattoria—just as in demand as its fancier big sister, Quince, next door—is chef Michael Tusk's flavorful, rustic, seasonally driven Italian cooking, headlined by pastas, beautifully grilled or spit-roasted meats, and homemade gelato. The look is comfortably chic, with wood tables, quality stemware, and fantastic Italian and under-the-radar Californian wines by the bottle and glass. **Known for:** raviolo with brown butter and egg in center; very tough to get prime reservations; peak seasonal produce in antipasti. $ *Average main: $29* ✉ *490 Pacific Ave., Financial District* ☎ *415/775–8508* 🌐 *www.cotognasf.com* ⏲ *Closed Mon. and Tues.*

Perbacco

$$ | ITALIAN | From the complimentary basket of skinny, brittle breadsticks to the pappardelle with short rib *ragù*, chef Staffan Terje's entire menu is a delectable paean to northern Italy. With a long marble bar and open kitchen, this brick-lined two-story space oozes big-city charm, attracting business types and Italian food aficionados alike to the FiDi well after evening rush hour ends. **Known for:** agnolotti del plin (a type of pasta filled with meat); house-made cured meats; vitello tonnato (cold veal with a tuna-flavored sauce) appetizer. $ *Average main: $26* ✉ *230 California St., Financial District* ☎ *415/955–0663* 🌐 *www.perbaccosf.com* ⏲ *Closed Sun.–Tues. No lunch Sat.*

Yank Sing

$$ | CHINESE | FAMILY | This bustling, lunch-only restaurant serves some of San Francisco's best dim sum to office workers on weekdays and boisterous families on weekends, and the take-out counter makes a meal on the run a satisfying compromise when office duties—or sightseeing—won't wait. The several dozen varieties prepared daily include the classic and the creative; steamed pork buns, shrimp dumplings, scallion-skewered prawns tied with bacon, and basil seafood dumplings are among the many delights. **Known for:** Peking duck; Shanghai soup dumplings; energetic vibe in dining room. $ *Average main: $18* ✉ *49 Stevenson St., Financial District* ☎ *415/541–4949* 🌐 *yanksing.com* ⏲ *No dinner.*

Hotels

Le Méridien San Francisco

$ | HOTEL | The stylishly contemporary Le Méridien scores well on both form and function, with compelling artwork throughout the lobby and guest rooms outfitted with polished granite sinks, wall-size San Francisco maps, and floor-to-ceiling windows. **Pros:** spacious rooms; interesting artwork throughout; accommodating staff. **Cons:** this FiDi neighborhood grows sleepy after dark; restaurant and bar merely adequate; not a lot of amenities. $ *Rooms from: $169* ✉ *333 Battery St., Financial District* ☎ *415/296–2900* 🌐 *lemeridiensanfrancisco.com* *360 rooms* *No meals.*

The Marina

Well-funded postcollegiates and the nouveau riche flooded the Marina after the 1989 Loma Prieta earthquake had sent many residents running for more-solid ground, changing the tenor of this formerly low-key neighborhood. The number of yuppie coffee emporiums skyrocketed, a bank became a Williams-Sonoma store, and the local grocer gave way to a Pottery Barn. On weekends a young, fairly homogeneous, well-to-do crowd floods the cafés and bars.

Sights

★ Palace of Fine Arts

BUILDING | At first glance this stunning, rosy rococo palace on a lagoon seems to be from another world, and indeed, it's the sole survivor of the many tinted-plaster structures (a temporary neoclassical city of sorts) built for the 1915 Panama-Pacific International Exposition, the world's fair that celebrated San Francisco's recovery from the 1906 earthquake and fire. The expo buildings originally extended about a mile along the shore. Bernard Maybeck designed this faux-Roman classic beauty, which was reconstructed in concrete and reopened in 1967. A victim of the elements, the Palace required a piece-by-piece renovation that was completed in 2008.

The pseudo-Latin language adorning the Palace's exterior urns continues to stump scholars. The massive columns (each topped with four "weeping maidens"), great rotunda, and swan-filled lagoon have been used in countless fashion layouts, films, and wedding photo shoots. Other than its use for major events and exhibitions inside the building, it's really an outdoor architecture attraction that's perfect for an hour of strolling and relaxing. After admiring the lagoon, look across the street to the house at 3460 Baker Street. If the statues out front look familiar, they should—they're original casts of the "garland ladies" you can see in the Palace's colonnade. ✉ *3301 Lyon St., at Beach St., Marina* ☎ *415/886–1296* 🌐 *palaceoffinearts.com* 🎫 *Free.*

Restaurants

A16

$$$ | ITALIAN | Named after a highway that runs through southern Italy, this trattoria specializes in the food from that region, done very, very well. The menu is stocked with pizza and rustic pastas like *maccaronara* with *ragù Napoletano* (a meat sauce) and house-made salted ricotta, as well as entrées like roasted chicken with caper salsa *verde*. **Known for:** spicy arrabbiata pizza; one of the city's best Italian wine programs; dark chocolate budino tart. 💲 *Average main: $36* ✉ *2355 Chestnut St., Marina* ☎ *415/771–2216* 🌐 *www.a16pizza.com* 🕒 *Closed Mon.*

Causwells

$$ | AMERICAN | There are two personalities to Chestnut Street's sleek grown-up diner—the double-stack burger that draws burger hounds from dozens of miles away, and the rest of the honest, spruced-up comfort-food menu. It's a local institution that feels partially like a bistro and partially like a modern tavern, and a place where the buzz from signature mezcal paloma cocktails and delicious eats never disappears. **Known for:** house-made ricotta; excellent wine list full of bottles from lesser-known regions; feels like a party even on weeknights. 💲 *Average main: $24* ✉ *2346 Chestnut St., Marina* ☎ *415/447–6081* 🌐 *www.causwells.com* 🕒 *Closed Mon. No lunch Tues.–Thurs.*

Greens

$$$ | VEGETARIAN | Owned and operated by the San Francisco Zen Center, this legendary vegetarian restaurant gets some of its fresh produce from the center's organic Green Gulch Farm. Despite the lack of meat, the hearty and often creative dishes—such as root vegetable *biryani* (mixed rice) with tamarind chutney—really satisfy, and floor-to-ceiling windows give diners a sweeping view of the Marina and the Golden Gate Bridge. **Known for:** magnificent wood-heavy decor headlined by a large redwood sculpture; mesquite-grilled tofu entrée; seasonal produce–driven pizzas. 💲 *Average main: $27* ✉ *Bldg. A, Fort Mason, 2 Marina Blvd., Marina* ☎ *415/771–6222* 🌐 *greens-restaurant.com* 🕑 *Closed Mon.*

California Wine Merchant

WINE BARS—NIGHTLIFE | Part cluttered shop, part cozy bar, Chestnut Street's marquee wine destination is a longtime favorite for grabbing a glass or three. Wines featured always come from some of the state's most highly regarded vintners of all sizes and celebrity standings. The neighborhood has many wine bars, but this is where the locals go when the focus is on the wine itself. ✉ *2113 Chestnut St., Marina* ☎ *415/567–0646* 🌐 *www.californiawinemerchant.com.*

The Interval

BARS/PUBS | Even many locals don't realize that the Fort Mason Center is home to one of the city's most impressive and scene-free cocktail bars. As part of the Long Now Foundation, a nonprofit devoted to long-term thinking, the bar serves cocktails that reflect the group's approach, finding innovative ways to serve tried-and-true libations. The Navy Gimlet with clarified lime juice is a modern-day San Francisco classic. ✉ *Fort Mason Center, 2 Marina Blvd., Bldg. A, Marina* ☎ *415/496–9187* 🌐 *www.theinterval.org.*

Cow Hollow

Between old-money Pacific Heights and the well-heeled, postcollegiate Marina lies comfortably upscale Cow Hollow. The neighborhood's name harks back to the 19th-century dairy farms whose owners eked out a living here despite the fact that there was more sand than grass.

Restaurants

★ Atelier Crenn

$$$$ | **MODERN FRENCH** | Dinner at the spectacularly inventive flagship of San Francisco's most celebrated chef of the moment, Dominique Crenn, starts with the presentation of a poem. Each course, many of which include produce from Crenn's own Bleu Belle Farm, and some of which have a slight French influence, is described by a line in the poem: the "Hidden beneath the bluffs" might be whole grilled Monterey abalone with a purée of its own liver and a grilled mussel sauce. **Known for:** extraordinary, whimsical tasting menu with fish and seafood but no meat; stellar desserts; hip-elegant atmosphere. 💲 *Average main: $365* ✉ *3127 Fillmore St., Cow Hollow* ☎ *415/440–0460* 🌐 *www.ateliercrenn.com* 🕑 *Closed Sun. and Mon. No lunch.*

Bar Crenn

$$$ | **FRENCH** | Dominique Crenn's sumptuous salon decked out with fur-draped bar stools, chandeliers, and lush velvet drapes is really a bar only in name. Yes, there's a bar pouring outstanding wines and it's possible to graze on warm *gougères* (savory cheese puffs) and oysters. **Known for:** Versailles-style furnishings; canelés de Bordeaux (a type of small pastry); fine Champagne. 💲 *Average main: $36* ✉ *3131 Fillmore St., Cow Hollow* ☎ *415/440–0460* 🌐 *www.barcrenn.com* 🕑 *Closed Sun. and Mon. No lunch.*

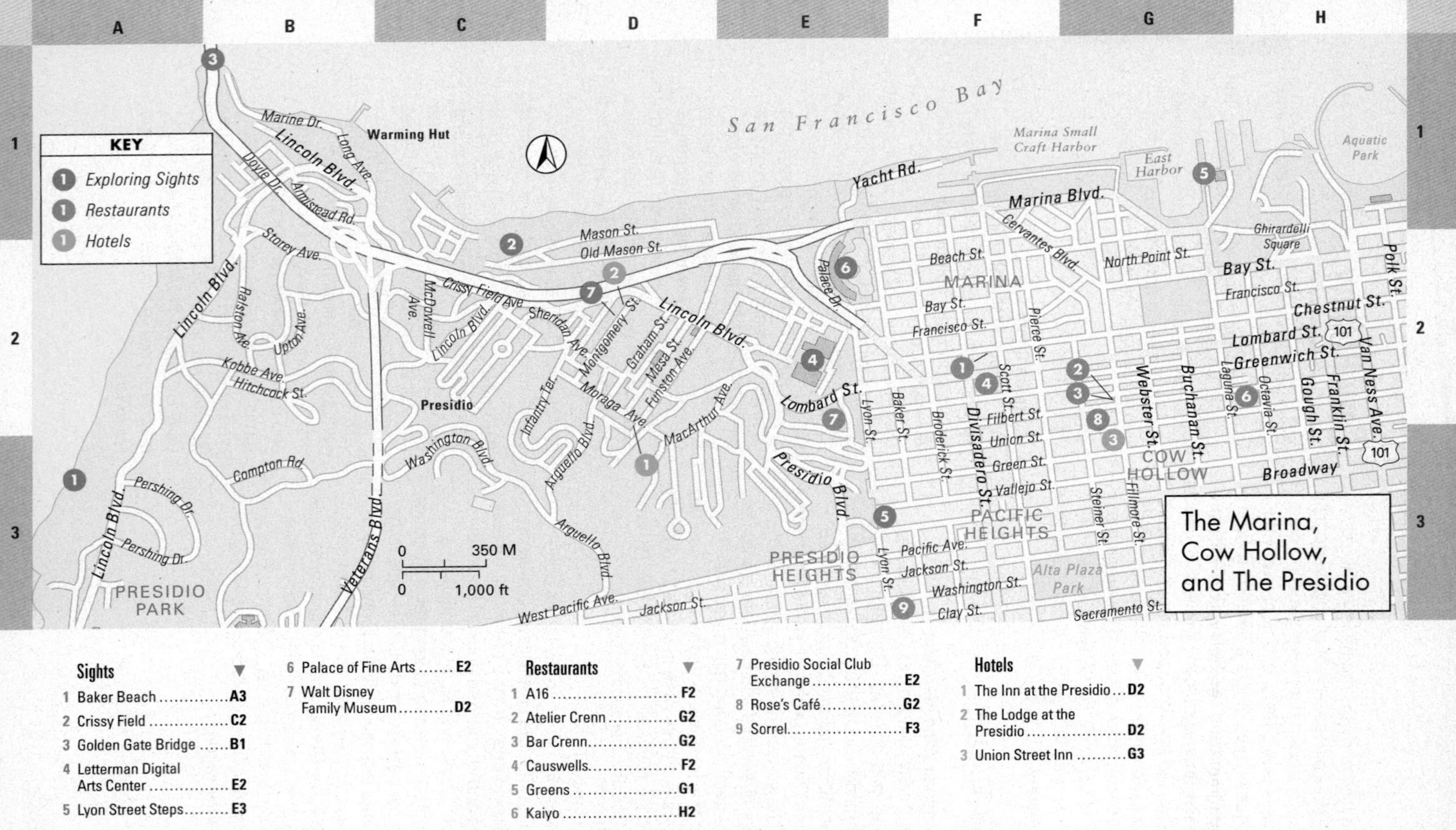

The Marina, Cow Hollow, and The Presidio
KEY
1 Exploring Sights
1 Restaurants
1 Hotels
San Francisco Bay
Marina Small Craft Harbor
East Harbor
Aquatic Park
Ghirardelli Square
Warming Hut
MARINA
COW HOLLOW
PACIFIC HEIGHTS
PRESIDIO HEIGHTS
PRESIDIO PARK
Presidio
Alta Plaza Park
Marine Dr.
Lincoln Blvd.
Long Ave.
Doyle Dr.
Armistead Rd.
Storey Ave.
Ralston Ave.
Upton Ave.
Kobbe Ave.
Hitchcock St.
Compton Rd.
Pershing Dr.
Veterans Blvd.
McDowell Ave.
Crissy Field Ave
Washington Blvd.
Mason St.
Old Mason St.
Sheridan Ave.
Montgomery St.
Graham St.
Mesa St.
Funston Ave.
Infantry Ter.
Moraga Ave.
Arguello Blvd.
MacArthur Ave.
West Pacific Ave.
Jackson St.
Palace Dr.
Lombard St.
Presidio Blvd.
Yacht Rd.
Marina Blvd.
Cervantes Blvd.
Beach St.
Bay St.
Francisco St.
North Point St.
Lyon St.
Baker St.
Broderick St.
Divisadero St.
Scott St.
Pierce St.
Filbert St.
Union St.
Green St.
Vallejo St.
Pacific Ave.
Washington St.
Clay St.
Sacramento St.
Steiner St.
Fillmore St.
Webster St.
Buchanan St.
Laguna St.
Octavia St.
Gough St.
Franklin St.
Van Ness Ave.
Greenwich St.
Chestnut St.
Polk St.
Broadway
101
0 350 M
0 1,000 ft
Sights
1 Baker Beach A3
2 Crissy Field C2
3 Golden Gate Bridge B1
4 Letterman Digital Arts Center E2
5 Lyon Street Steps E3
6 Palace of Fine Arts E2
7 Walt Disney Family Museum D2
Restaurants
1 A16 .... F2
2 Atelier Crenn G2
3 Bar Crenn G2
4 Causwells F2
5 Greens G1
6 Kaiyo H2
7 Presidio Social Club Exchange E2
8 Rose's Café G2
9 Sorrel F3
Hotels
1 The Inn at the Presidio D2
2 The Lodge at the Presidio D2
3 Union Street Inn G3

Kaiyo

$$ | **PERUVIAN** | San Francisco has a handful of Peruvian restaurants, but this uber-hip Union Street spot is the first "Nikkei" (Japanese-Peruvian) cuisine restaurant for diners to explore. Skip the pedestrian *pollo a la brasa* (rotisserie chicken) and have fun sampling around the *tiraditos* (dishes with raw fish) and sushi rolls. **Known for:** creative pisco cocktails; shrimp tempura and yellowtail Lima roll; no reservations, so lines can be long. *Average main: $18 1838 Union St., Cow Hollow 415/525–4804 kaiyosf.com Closed Mon.*

Rose's Café

$$ | **AMERICAN** | **FAMILY** | Although it's open morning until night, this cozy café is most synonymous with brunch. Sleepy-headed locals turn up for delights like the smoked ham, fried egg, and Gruyère breakfast sandwich, and evening favorites lean toward roast chicken, pastas, and seasonal-rustic fare. **Known for:** pizzas for the morning and night; house-baked goods; wonderful sidewalk patio. *Average main: $25 2298 Union St., Cow Hollow 415/775–2200 rosescafesf.com.*

Hotels

★ Union Street Inn

$$ | **B&B/INN** | Antiques, unique artwork, fine linens, and windows opening to a lovely courtyard or Union Street view make this charming Edwardian inn popular with honeymooners and those looking for a romantic getaway with an English countryside ambience. **Pros:** personal service; afternoon wine and cheese; beautiful secret garden. **Cons:** parking garage is two blocks away; old-fashioned decor not for all tastes; no elevator. *Rooms from: $270 2229 Union St., Cow Hollow 415/346–0424 unionstreetinn.com 6 rooms Free breakfast.*

Nightlife

The Black Horse London Pub

BARS/PUBS | Barely seven stools fit in San Francisco's smallest bar. Plus, there are just as many bottled beers (no taps) as seats, and be sure to bring some cash since credit cards aren't accepted. It's as bare-bones as it gets, but there's sports on TV, a fun dice game, and most important, a neighborhood camaraderie that is increasingly hard to find. *1514 Union St., Cow Hollow 415/678–5697 www.blackhorselondon.com.*

West Coast Wine & Cheese

WINE BARS—NIGHTLIFE | Whether you're in the mood for a Mendocino County rosé or an Oregon Pinot Noir, as the name suggests, you'll find it at this narrow, sleek locals' favorite. The kitchen isn't much more than a stovetop but does some pretty impressive work beyond cheese and charcuterie. Take advantage of the ability to order half pours and sample more wines. *2165 Union St., Cow Hollow 415/376–9720 www.westcoastsf.com.*

Shopping

The Caviar Company

FOOD/CANDY | "The Caviar Sisters" Petra and Saskia Bergstein created this sustainability-minded brand that has developed a cult following among caviar connoisseurs and chefs in the Bay Area. Their chic above-street-level boutique on Union Street allows the public to pick out some of the finest caviar products in town—and feel good about it. *1954 Union St., Cow Hollow 415/580–7986 thecaviarco.com.*

Presidio

At the foot of the Golden Gate Bridge, one of city residents' favorite in-town getaways is the 1,400-plus-acre Presidio, which combines accessible nature-in-the-raw with a window into the past.

Sights

★ Baker Beach

BEACH—SIGHT | FAMILY | West of the Golden Gate Bridge is a mile-long stretch of soft sand beneath steep cliffs, beloved for its spectacular views and laid-back vibe (read: good chance you'll see naked people here on the northernmost end). Its isolated location makes it rarely crowded, but many San Franciscans know that there is no better place to take in the sunset than this beach. Kids love climbing around the old Battery Chamberlin. This is truly one of those places that inspires local pride. **Amenities:** parking (free); toilets. **Best for:** nudists; solitude; sunsets. ✉ *Baker Beach, Presidio* ✣ *Accessed from Bowley St. off Lincoln Blvd.* 🌐 *www.parksconservancy.org* 🎫 *Free.*

Crissy Field

NATIONAL/STATE PARK | FAMILY | One of the most popular places for San Franciscans to get fresh air is this stretch of restored marshland along the sand of the bay, part of the Golden Gate National Recreation Area. Kids on bikes, folks walking dogs, and joggers share the paved path along the shore, often winding up at the Warming Hut, a combination café and fun gift store at its end, for a hot chocolate in the shadow of the Golden Gate Bridge. Midway along the Golden Gate Promenade that winds along the shore is the Greater Farallones National Marine Sanctuary Visitor Center, where kids can get a close-up view of small sea creatures and learn about the rich ecosystem offshore. Alongside the main green of Crissy Field, several renovated airplane hangars and warehouses are now home to the likes of rock-climbing gyms, an air trampoline park, and a craft brewery (the latter is not open to the public). The Quartermaster Reach Marsh by Crissy Field was reclaimed as wetland ecosystem in 2020 after being asphalt. It nicely connects the Presidio with Crissy Field for pedestrians. ✉ *1199 E. Beach, Presidio* ✣ *Area north of Mason St. between Baker St. and Marine Dr.* 🌐 *www.presidio.gov/places/crissy-field.*

★ Golden Gate Bridge

BRIDGE/TUNNEL | Instantly recognizable as an icon of San Francisco, the two reddish-orange towers of the majestic Golden Gate Bridge rise 750 feet over the Golden Gate at the mouth of San Francisco Bay, linking the city and Marin County. Designed in simple but powerful art-deco style and opened in 1937, the 1.7-mile suspension span and the towers were built to handle winds of more than 100 mph. Crossing the bridge under your own power, by foot or bicycle, is exhilarating, a bit scary—and definitely chilly. From the bridge's eastern-side walkway, the panoramic views of the city skyline, Marin Headlands, and Pacific Ocean are magnificent. ✉ *Lincoln Blvd., near Doyle Dr. and Fort Point, Presidio* ☎ *415/921–5858* 🌐 *www.goldengate.org* 🎫 *Free.*

Letterman Digital Arts Center

LOCAL INTEREST | FAMILY | Bay Area filmmaker George Lucas's 23-acre **Letterman Digital Arts Center,** a digital studio "campus" along the eastern edge of the land, is exquisitely landscaped and largely open to the public. If you have kids in tow or are a *Star Wars* fan yourself, make the pilgrimage to the **Yoda Fountain** (*Letterman Dr. at Dewitt Rd.*), between two of the arts-center buildings, then take your picture with the life-size Darth Vader statue in the lobby, open to the public on weekdays. The center's public restaurant, **Sessions,** is a good stop for a craft beer and some satisfying eats that often include produce or beef from

Lucas's Skywalker Ranch. ✉ *1 Letterman Dr., Presidio* 🌐 *www.presidio.gov/places/letterman-digital-arts-center* ⏲ *Lobby closed weekends.*

Lyon Street Steps

VIEWPOINT | Get ready for a workout—and a spectacularly rewarding view at the top—when tackling the 332 steps at the eastern edge of the Presidio. There will likely be no shortage of exercise seekers bounding up the steps, but feel free to conquer the climb slowly. The trimmed hedge landscaping is worthy of its own visit, but the views of the Presidio forests and the bay are the reason these steps are a top attraction. Equally stunning, though, are the opulent mansions surrounding them. ✉ *2545 Lyon St., Presidio Heights* ✣ *Between Green St. and Broadway* 🌐 *www.nps.gov/places/000/lyon-street-steps.htm.*

Walt Disney Family Museum

MUSEUM | **FAMILY** | This beautifully refurbished brick barracks is a tribute to the man behind Mickey Mouse, the Disney Studios, and Disneyland. The smartly organized displays include hundreds of family photos, and well-chosen videos play throughout. Disney's legendary attention to detail becomes evident in the cels and footage of Fantasia, Sleeping Beauty, and other animation classics. "The Toughest Period in My Whole Life" exhibit sheds light on lesser-known bits of history: the animators' strike at Disney Studios, the films Walt Disney made for the U.S. military during World War II, and his testimony before the U.S. House Un-American Activities Committee during its investigation of Communist influence in Hollywood. The liveliest exhibit, and the largest gallery, documents the creation of Disneyland with a fun, detailed model of what Disney imagined the park would be. Teacups spin, the Matterhorn looms, and that world-famous castle leads the way to Fantasyland. You won't be the first to leave humming "It's a Small World." In the final gallery, titled simply "December 15, 1966," a series of cartoons chronicles the world's reaction to Disney's sudden death. Worth checking for are periodic special exhibitions that take a deep dive into film themes or historical periods surrounding Disney's life. ✉ *Main Post, 104 Montgomery St., off Lincoln Blvd., Presidio* ☎ *415/345–6800* 🌐 *www.waltdisney.org* 🎟 *$25* ⏲ *Closed Mon.–Wed.*

Restaurants

Presidio Social Club Exchange

$$ | **AMERICAN** | **FAMILY** | American comfort classics meet seasonal California cooking in this restaurant in an old barracks building at the eastern edge of the Presidio. Like the military base/national park itself, the restaurant has a blend of the nostalgic past and the trendy present (spice-fried Cornish game hen; a Thursday prime rib special; shrimp cocktail), as well as a substantial "exchange" shop/takeout café and ample patio seating that allows diners to soak up the Presidio outdoor beauty. **Known for:** East–West chicken soup; French onion burger; barrel-aged cocktails. 💲 *Average main: $26* ✉ *563 Ruger St., Presidio* ☎ *415/885–1888* 🌐 *www.presidiosocialclub.com* ⏲ *Closed Mon.–Wed. No brunch Thurs.–Fri. No dinner Sun.*

★ Sorrel

$$$ | **MODERN AMERICAN** | After a long run as one of San Francisco's most important dining pop-ups, Alex Hong's refined seasonal Californian cooking can be found in one of San Francisco's most dramatic dining settings, with a skylight and floral arrangements that epitomize California "good life" architecture. That vibe is reflected in dishes like a springtime dry-aged duck with green garlic and kumquat, where Hong beautifully blends contemporary techniques and local ingredients. **Known for:** exemplary pastas; beautifully composed tasting menu; upscale dinner party vibe. 💲 *Average main: $36* ✉ *3228 Sacramento*

St., Presidio Heights ☎ 415/525–3765 🌐 www.sorrelrestaurant.com ⏲ Closed Mon. and Tues.

Hotels

The Inn at the Presidio

$$$ | B&B/INN | Built in 1903, this two-story, Georgian revival–style structure once served as officers' quarters but these days is a standout boutique hotel where the rooms and suites have a nice sense of modern refinement and historical touches varying by the room, such as wrought-iron beds, vintage black-and-white photos, and Pendleton blankets. **Pros:** beautifully designed rooms, some with gas fireplaces; peaceful place away from the city's frenetic vibe; evening wine-and-cheese reception by firepits. **Cons:** lack of noise blocking because of old building; 2-night minimum on weekends; challenging to get a taxi/ride-share. *$ Rooms from: $320 ✉ 42 Moraga Ave., Presidio ☎ 415/800–7356 🌐 www.presidiolodging.com 26 rooms 🍽 Free breakfast.*

★ The Lodge at the Presidio

$$$ | B&B/INN | The three-story Lodge occupies former Army barracks, built in the 1890s, and is at the Main Post green's northwestern edge, allowing some rooms to have Golden Gate Bridge views; all rooms are far more upscale and chic than military accommodations, with large flat-screen TVs, well-appointed bathrooms, work stations, and dreamy, custom-made pillow-top mattresses. **Pros:** gorgeous, spacious rooms; charming staff; feels like a vacation from the city but within the city. **Cons:** traffic noise is fairly loud in rooms facing the Golden Gate Bridge; isolated from restaurants and nightlife; similar prices to downtown's more lavish luxury hotels. *$ Rooms from: $320 ✉ 105 Montgomery St., Presidio ☎ 415/561–1234 🌐 www.presidiolodging.com 42 rooms 🍽 Free breakfast.*

The Richmond

In the mid-19th century, the western section of town just north of Golden Gate Park was known as the Outer Lands, covered in sand dunes and seen fit for cemeteries and little else. Today it's the Richmond, comprised of two distinct neighborhoods: the Inner Richmond, from Arguello Boulevard to about 20th Avenue, and the Outer Richmond, from 20th to the ocean.

Sights

★ Legion of Honor

MUSEUM | Built to commemorate soldiers from California who died in World War I and set atop cliffs overlooking the ocean, the Golden Gate Bridge, and the Marin Headlands, this beautiful Beaux Arts building in Lincoln Park displays an impressive collection of 4,000 years of ancient and European art. A pyramidal glass skylight in the entrance court illuminates the lower-level galleries, which exhibit prints and drawings, European porcelain, and ancient Assyrian, Greek, Roman, and Egyptian art. The 20-plus galleries on the upper level display European art (paintings, sculpture, decorative arts, and tapestries) from the 14th century to the present day. The noteworthy Auguste Rodin collection includes two galleries devoted to the master and a third with works by Rodin and other 19th-century sculptors. An original cast of Rodin's *The Thinker* welcomes you as you walk through the courtyard. Also impressive is the 4,526-pipe Spreckels Organ; live concerts take advantage of the natural sound chamber produced by the building's massive rotunda. As fine as the museum is, the setting and view outshine the collection and also make a trip here worthwhile. *✉ 100 34th Ave., at Clement St., Richmond ☎ 415/750–3600 🌐 legionofhonor.famsf.org $15, free 1st Tues. of month; free Sat. for Bay Area residents ⏲ Closed Mon.*

Armed with only helmets, safety harnesses, and painting equipment, a full-time crew of 38 painters keeps the Golden Gate Bridge clad in International Orange.

★ Lincoln Park

CITY PARK | Although many of the city's green spaces are gentle and welcoming, Lincoln Park is a wild, 275-acre park in the Outer Richmond with windswept cliffs and panoramic views. The **Coastal Trail,** the park's most dramatic one, leads out to **Lands End**; pick it up west of the Legion of Honor (at the end of El Camino del Mar) or from the parking lot at Point Lobos and El Camino del Mar. Time your hike to hit Mile Rock at low tide, and you might catch a glimpse of two wrecked ships peeking up from their watery graves. ⚠ **Be careful if you hike here; landslides are frequent, and people have fallen into the sea by standing too close to the edge of a crumbling bluff top.**

Lincoln Park's 18-hole golf course (🌐 *www.lincolnparkgolfcourse.com)* is on land that in the 19th century was the Golden Gate Cemetery. (When digging has to be done in the park, human bones still occasionally surface.) Next door to the golf course on 33rd Avenue and California Street are the dazzling, mosaic Lincoln Park Steps, which rival the 16th Avenue Steps and the Hidden Garden Steps in the Sunset District. They provide a delightful backdrop for contemplation or an Instagram photo op. ✉ *Entrance at 34th Ave. at Clement St., Richmond* 🌐 *sfrecpark.org.*

Sutro Baths

LOCAL INTEREST | Along the oceanfront, to the north of the Cliff House, lie the ruins of the once-grand glass-roof Sutro Baths. Today visitors can explore this evocative historical site and listen to the pounding surf. Adolph Sutro, eccentric onetime San Francisco mayor and Cliff House owner, built the bath complex in 1896 so that everyday folks could enjoy the benefits of swimming. Six enormous baths—freshwater and seawater—and more than 500 dressing rooms plus several restaurants covered 3 acres and accommodated 25,000 bathers. Likened to Roman baths in a European glass palace, the baths were for decades a favorite destination of San Franciscans. The complex fell into disuse after World War II, was closed in

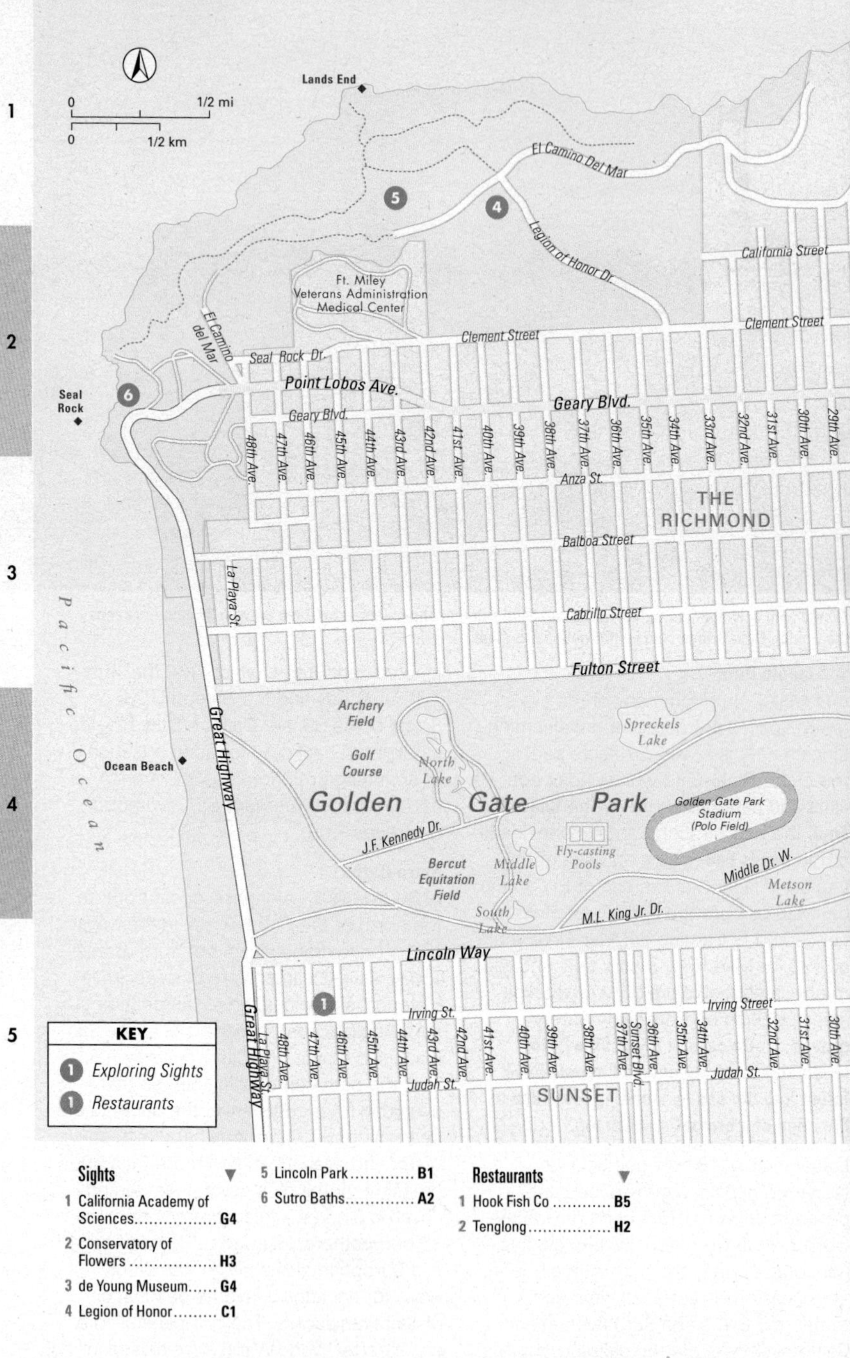

Sights

1 California Academy of Sciences........ **G4**

2 Conservatory of Flowers........ **H3**

3 de Young Museum...... **G4**

4 Legion of Honor......... **C1**

5 Lincoln Park............. **B1**

6 Sutro Baths.............. **A2**

Restaurants

1 Hook Fish Co **B5**

2 Tenglong................. **H2**

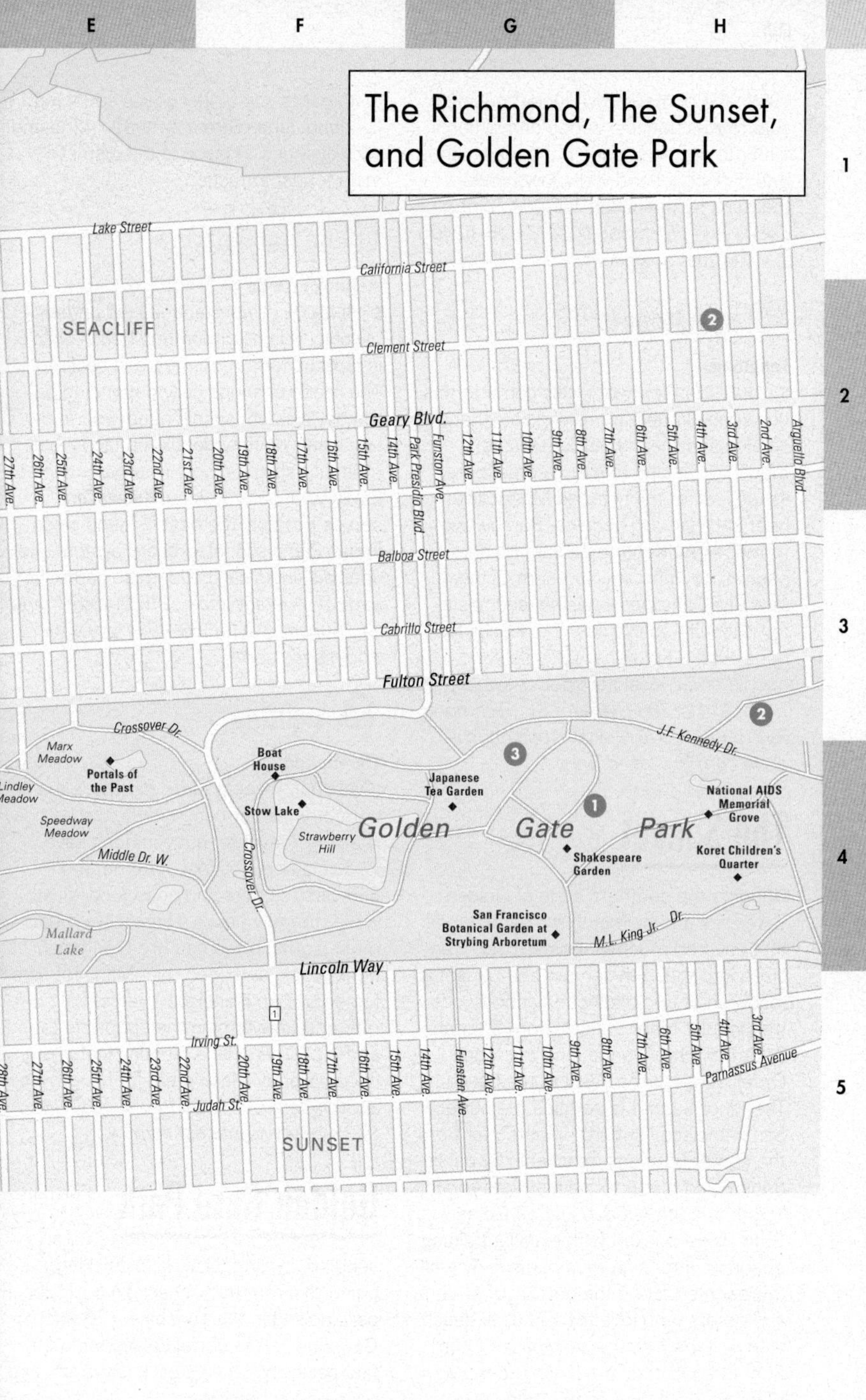

E
F
G
H
1
2
3
4
5
The Richmond, The Sunset, and Golden Gate Park
Lake Street
California Street
SEACLIFF
Clement Street
Geary Blvd.
27th Ave.
26th Ave.
25th Ave.
24th Ave.
23rd Ave.
22nd Ave.
21st Ave.
20th Ave.
19th Ave.
18th Ave.
17th Ave.
16th Ave.
15th Ave.
14th Ave.
Park Presidio Blvd.
Funston Ave.
12th Ave.
11th Ave.
10th Ave.
9th Ave.
8th Ave.
7th Ave.
6th Ave.
5th Ave.
4th Ave.
3rd Ave.
2nd Ave.
Arguello Blvd.
Balboa Street
Cabrillo Street
Fulton Street
Crossover Dr.
J.F. Kennedy Dr.
Marx Meadow
Portals of the Past
Lindley Meadow
Boat House
Japanese Tea Garden
National AIDS Memorial Grove
Stow Lake
Speedway Meadow
Strawberry Hill
Golden Gate Park
Shakespeare Garden
Koret Children's Quarter
Middle Dr. W.
Crossover Dr.
San Francisco Botanical Garden at Strybing Arboretum
M.L. King Jr. Dr.
Mallard Lake
Lincoln Way
Irving St.
28th Ave.
27th Ave.
26th Ave.
25th Ave.
24th Ave.
23rd Ave.
22nd Ave.
Judah St.
20th Ave.
19th Ave.
18th Ave.
17th Ave.
16th Ave.
15th Ave.
14th Ave.
Funston Ave.
12th Ave.
11th Ave.
10th Ave.
9th Ave.
8th Ave.
7th Ave.
6th Ave.
5th Ave.
4th Ave.
3rd Ave.
Parnassus Avenue
SUNSET

1952, and burned down (under questionable circumstances) during demolition in 1966. To get here, park in the main Lands End parking lot and walk down toward the ruins by the ocean. ✉ *1004 Point Lobos Ave., Richmond* ☎ *415/426–5240* 🌐 *www.nps.gov/goga.*

Tenglong

$ | CHINESE | Plenty of locals come to this tidy space known for remarkably friendly service and the dry chicken wings, fried in garlic and roasted red peppers, as well as for thinly sliced Mongolian beef and *dan dan* noodles. Run by two former Hong Kong restaurant owners, it specializes in mostly southern Chinese fare, like Cantonese cuisine, and has a few Sichuan specialties, too. **Known for:** honey-walnut prawns; spicy seafood noodle soup; local hot spot. $ *Average main: $14* ✉ *208 Clement St., Richmond* ☎ *415/666–3515* 🌐 *www.tenglongchinese.com* ⏲ *Closed Tues.*

The Sunset

Hugging the southern edge of Golden Gate Park and built atop the sand dunes that covered much of western San Francisco into the 19th century, the Sunset is made up of two distinct neighborhoods—the popular Inner Sunset, from Stanyan Street to 19th Avenue, and the foggy Outer Sunset, from 19th to the beach. The Inner Sunset is perhaps the perfect San Francisco "suburb": not too far from the center of things, reachable by public transit, and home to main streets—Irving Street and 9th Avenue just off Golden Gate Park—packed with excellent dining options, with Asian food particularly well represented. Long the domain of surfers and others who love the laid-back beach vibe and the fog, the slow-paced Outer Sunset finds itself newly on the radar of locals, with high-quality cafés and restaurants and quirky shops springing up along Judah Street between 42nd and 46th avenues. The zoo is the district's main tourist attraction.

★ Hook Fish Co

$ | SEAFOOD | Unpretentious yet undeniably chic, this neighborhood beach shack is famous for its simple, fresh seafood. The menu changes daily depending on the day's catch, so join hungry surfers and locals as they gobble up tacos, burritos, or fish-and-chips; wash your choice down with beer or wine. **Known for:** serves possibly the best fish-and-chips in San Francisco; blackboard oysters and specials; lines can be long, so come early. $ *Average main: $16* ✉ *4542 Irving St., Sunset* ☎ *415/569–4984* 🌐 *www.hookfishco.com.*

The Riptide

BARS/PUBS | A cozy cabin bar that's the perfect finale for beachgoers, the Riptide is a surfer favorite, but you don't have to own a board to feel at home. You'll find classic beers and good food, all at wallet-friendly prices. There's live music most nights, often country, bluegrass, honky-tonk, and open mic. Many tourists fooled by San Francisco's version of summer end up warming their popsicle toes at the bar's fireplace. Sunday features a bacon Bloody Mary, great for hangovers. ✉ *3639 Taraval St., Sunset* ☎ *415/681–8433* 🌐 *www.riptidesf.com.*

Golden Gate Park

Jogging, cycling, skating, picnicking, going to a museum, checking out a concert, dozing in the sunshine ... Golden Gate Park is the perfect playground for fast-paced types, laid-back dawdlers, and everyone in between.

Sights

★ California Academy of Sciences

MUSEUM | FAMILY | With its native plant–covered living roof, retractable ceiling, three-story rain forest, gigantic planetarium, living coral reef, and frolicking penguins, the California Academy of Sciences is one of the city's most spectacular treasures. Dramatically designed by Renzo Piano, it's an eco-friendly, energy-efficient adventure in biodiversity and green architecture. Moving away from a restrictive role as a museum that cataloged natural history, the academy these days is all about sustainability and the future, but the locally beloved dioramas in African Hall remain.

It's best to look at the academy's floor plan to design your visit before you arrive. Here's the quick version: head left from the entrance to the wooden walkway over otherworldly rays in the Philippine Coral Reef, then continue to the Swamp to see Claude, the famous albino alligator. Swing through African Hall and study the penguins, take the elevator up to the living roof, then return to the main floor and get in line to explore the Rainforests of the World. You'll end up below ground in the Amazonian Flooded Rainforest, where you can explore the academy's other aquarium exhibits. The popular adults-only NightLife event, held every Thursday evening, includes after-dark access to all exhibits, as well as special programming and a full bar. **■ TIP→ Considering the hefty price of admission, start early and take advantage of in-and-out privileges to take a break.** ✉ *55 Music Concourse Dr., Golden Gate Park* ☎ *415/379–8000* 🌐 *www.calacademy.org* 🎫 *From $30; free one Sun. per quarter; save $3 if you bike, walk, or take public transit here.*

Conservatory of Flowers

GARDEN | FAMILY | Whatever you do, be sure to at least drive by the Conservatory of Flowers—it's too darn pretty to miss. The gorgeous, white-framed 1878 glass structure is topped with a 14-ton glass dome. Stepping inside the giant greenhouse is like taking a quick trip to the rain forest, with its earthy smell and humid warmth. The undeniable highlight is the Aquatic Plants section, where lily pads float and carnivorous plants dine on bugs to the sounds of rushing water.

On the east side of the conservatory (to the right as you face the building), cypress, pine, and redwood trees surround the **Dahlia Garden,** which blooms in summer and fall. Adding to the allure are temporary special exhibits; a recurring holiday-season model-train display punctuated with mini buildings, found objects, and dwarf plants; night blooms; and a butterfly garden that returns periodically. To the west is the **Rhododendron Dell,** which contains 850 varieties, more than any other garden of its kind in the country. It's a favorite local Mother's Day picnic spot. ✉ *100 John F. Kennedy Dr., at Conservatory Dr., Golden Gate Park* ☎ *415/831–2090* 🌐 *conservatoryofflowers.org* 🎫 *$10 Tues.–Thurs., $12 Fri.–Sun., free 1st Tues. of month* ⊗ *Closed Mon.* ☞ *No food, drink, tripods, or strollers are allowed inside.*

de Young Museum

MUSEUM | It seems that everyone in town has a strong opinion about the de Young museum: some adore its striking copper facade, while others just hope that the green patina of age will mellow the effect. Most maligned is the 144-foot tower, but the view from its ninth-story observation room, ringed by floor-to-ceiling windows and free to the public, is worth a trip here by itself. The building almost overshadows the de Young's respected collection of American, African, and Oceanic art. The museum also plays host to major international exhibitions; there's often an extra admission charge for these. The annual Bouquets to Art is a fanciful tribute to the museum's collection by notable Bay Area floral designers. On many Friday evenings in the fall, admission is free and the museum hosts fun events, with live music and a wine and beer bar (the café stays open late, too). ✉ *50 Hagiwara Tea Garden Dr., Golden Gate Park* ☎ *415/750–3600* 🌐 *deyoung.famsf.org* 🎫 *$15, good for same-day admittance to the Legion of Honor; free 1st Tues. of month, free Sat. for Bay Area residents* ⏱ *Closed Mon.*

Nightlife

BARS

Beach Chalet

BARS/PUBS | Renovated in 2021, this restaurant-microbrewery, on the second floor of a historic building filled with 1930s Works Project Administration murals (on the first floor), has a stunning view of the Pacific Ocean. It's open for lunch and dinner, but you may want to time your visit and a drink to coincide with the sunset. **■ TIP→ Arrive at least 30 minutes before sunset to beat the dinner crowd.** The house brews are rich and flavorful, and there's a good selection of California wines by the glass. ✉ *1000 Great Hwy., near John F. Kennedy Dr., Golden Gate Park* ☎ *415/386–8439* 🌐 *www.beachchalet.com.*

The Haight

During the 1960s the siren song of free love, peace, and mind-altering substances lured thousands of young people to the Haight, a neighborhood just east of Golden Gate Park. By 1966 the area had become a hot spot for rock artists, including the Grateful Dead, Jefferson Airplane, and Janis Joplin. Some of the most infamous flower children, including Charles Manson and People's Temple founder Jim Jones, also called the Haight home.

Sights

Haight-Ashbury Intersection

NEIGHBORHOOD | On October 6, 1967, hippies took over the intersection of Haight and Ashbury Streets to proclaim the "Death of Hip." If they thought hip was dead then, they'd find absolute confirmation of it today, what with the only tie-dye in sight on the famed corner being a Ben & Jerry's storefront. ✉ *Haight.*

Restaurants

Parada 22

$$ | PUERTO RICAN | A small, colorful space sandwiched between larger restaurants on either side, Parada 22 serves up heaping plates of home-style Puerto Rican cuisine—think plantains, seafood, and slow-roasted pork. This still being the Haight, there's also plenty of vegetarian fare on offer. **Known for:** delicious yuca fries; marinated meats and vegetables; lunch specials. 💲 *Average main: $17* ✉ *1805 Haight St., near Shrader St., Haight* ☎ *415/750–1111.*

Nightlife

Magnolia Brewing Company

BREWPUBS/BEER GARDENS | Known for its food as much as its beers, Magnolia is a San Francisco institution, thanks in part to its prime location one block away from the famous Haight-Ashbury intersection. Come for the smoked trout croquettes, falafel salad, and famed burgers, or just grab any one of the over a dozen beers on tap, many made right here in the in-house brewery. There is also a second popular location on 3rd Street in the Dogpatch. ✉ *1398 Haight St., at Masonic St., Haight* ☎ *415/864–7468* 🌐 *magnolia-brewing.com.*

Shopping

MUSIC

★ Amoeba Music

MUSIC STORES | With well over a million new and used CDs, DVDs, and records at bargain prices, this warehouselike offshoot of the Berkeley original carries titles you likely can't find on Amazon. No niche is ignored—from electronica and hip-hop to jazz and classical—and the stock changes frequently. **■ TIP→ Weekly in-store performances attract large crowds.** ✉ *1855 Haight St., between Stanyan and Shrader Sts., Haight* ☎ *415/831–1200* 🌐 *www.amoeba.com.*

The Castro

The Castro district—the social, political, and cultural center of San Francisco's thriving gay community— stands at the western end of Market Street. This neighborhood is one of the city's liveliest and most welcoming, especially on weekends. Streets teem with folks out shopping, pushing political causes, heading to art films, and lingering in bars and cafés. It's also one of the city's most expensive neighborhoods to live in, with an influx of tech money exacerbating an identity crisis that's been simmering for a couple of decades.

Sights

★ Castro Theatre

ARTS VENUE | Here's a classic way to join in a beloved Castro tradition: grab some popcorn and catch a flick at this 1,500-seat art-deco theater built in 1922, the grandest of San Francisco's few remaining movie palaces. The neon marquee, which stands at the top of the Castro strip, is the neighborhood's great landmark. The Castro was the fitting host of 2008's red-carpet preview of Gus Van Sant's film *Milk*, starring Sean Penn as openly gay San Francisco supervisor Harvey Milk. The theater's elaborate Spanish baroque interior is fairly well preserved. Before many shows, the theater's pipe organ rises from the orchestra pit and an organist plays pop and movie tunes, usually ending with the Jeanette MacDonald standard "San Francisco" (go ahead, sing along). The crowd can be enthusiastic and vocal, talking back to the screen as loudly as it talks to them. Flicks such as *Who's Afraid of Virginia Woolf?* take on a whole new life, with the assembled beating the actors to the punch and fashioning even snappier comebacks for Elizabeth Taylor. There are often family-friendly sing-alongs to classics like *Mary Poppins*, as well as the occasional niche film festival. ✉ *429 Castro St., Castro* ☎ *415/621–6120* 🌐 *www.castrotheatre.com* 🎫 *$14.*

Harvey Milk Plaza

PLAZA | An 18-foot-long rainbow flag, the symbol of gay pride, flies above this plaza named for the man who electrified the city in 1977 by being elected to its Board of Supervisors as an openly gay candidate. In the early 1970s, Milk's camera store on Castro Street became the center for his campaign to open San Francisco's social and political life to gays and lesbians.

The liberal Milk hadn't served a full year of his term before he and Mayor George Moscone, also a liberal, were shot to death in November 1978 at City Hall. The murderer was a conservative ex-supervisor named Dan White, who had resigned his post and then became enraged when Moscone wouldn't reinstate him. Milk and White had often been at odds on the board. The gay community became infuriated when the "Twinkie defense"—that junk food had led to diminished mental capacity—resulted in only a manslaughter verdict for White. During the so-called White Night Riot of May 21, 1979, gays and their allies stormed City Hall, torching its lobby.

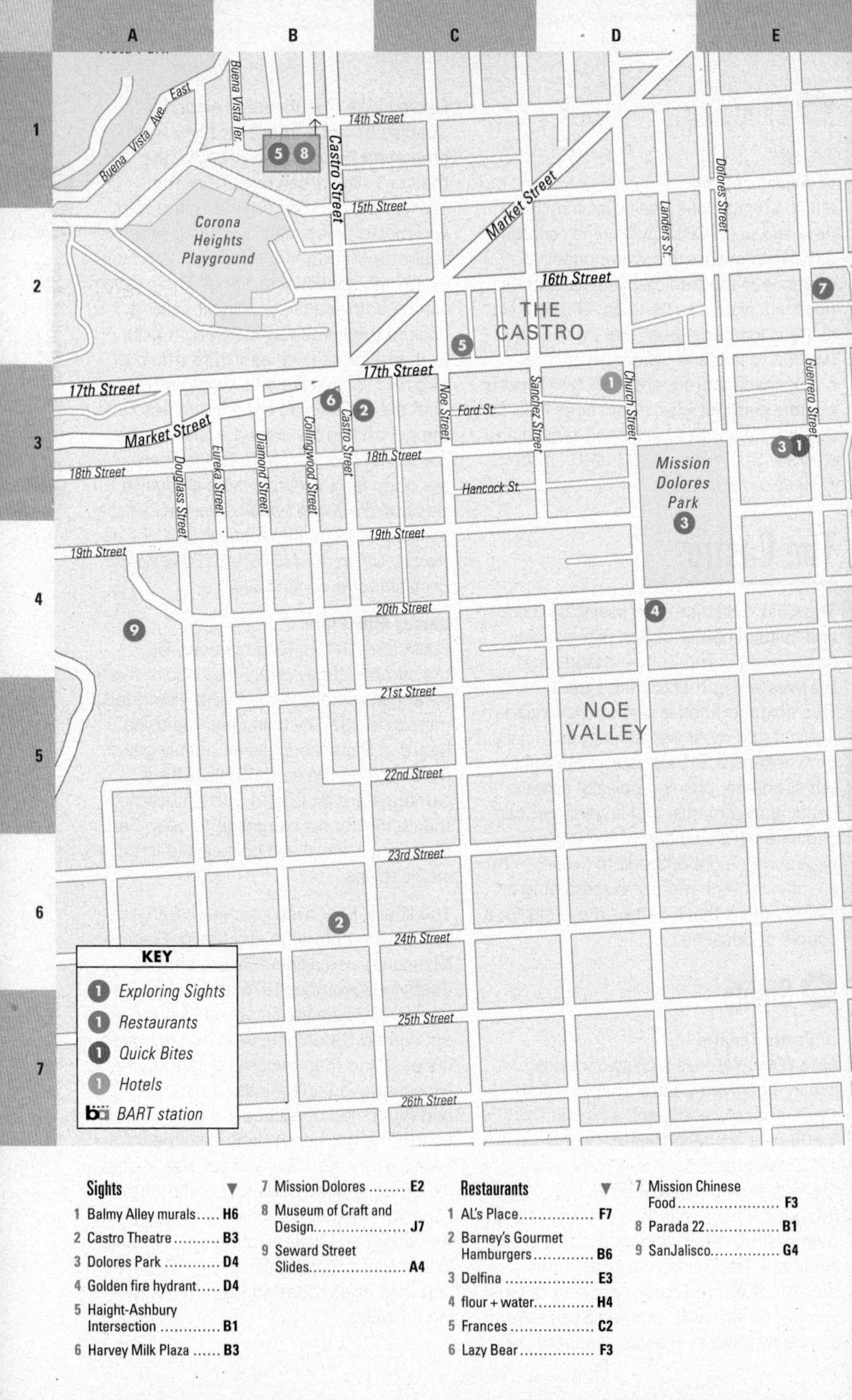

Sights

1 Balmy Alley murals H6
2 Castro Theatre B3
3 Dolores Park D4
4 Golden fire hydrant D4
5 Haight-Ashbury Intersection B1
6 Harvey Milk Plaza B3
7 Mission Dolores E2
8 Museum of Craft and Design.................... J7
9 Seward Street Slides..................... A4

Restaurants

1 AL's Place................ F7
2 Barney's Gourmet Hamburgers............ B6
3 Delfina E3
4 flour + water............ H4
5 Frances C2
6 Lazy Bear F3
7 Mission Chinese Food F3
8 Parada 22................ B1
9 SanJalisco............... G4

Quick Bites ▼

1 Tartine Bakery **E3**

Hotels ▼

1 The Parker Guest House............. **D3**

Milk, who had feared assassination, left behind a tape recording in which he urged the community to continue his work. His legacy is the high visibility of gay people throughout city government; a bust of him was unveiled at City Hall in 2008, and the 2008 film *Milk* gives insight into his life. Keep your visiting expectations in check: sandwiched between SoulCycle and a Muni bus stop, this is more of a historical site than an Instagrammable spot. ✉ *Southwest corner of Castro and Market Sts., Castro.*

Restaurants

Frances

$$$ | MODERN AMERICAN | Still one of the hottest tickets in town, chef Melissa Perello's simple, sublime restaurant is a consummate date-night destination. Perello's seasonal California-French cooking is its own enduring love affair, with menu standouts including the savory *bavette* steak, grilled Sakura pork chop, and *panisse frites.* For dessert, the lumberjack cake is a perennial favorite. **Known for:** lumberjack cake for dessert; neighborhood gem; tough reservation due to intimate size. $ *Average main: $34* ✉ *3870 17th St., Castro* ☎ *415/621–3870* 🌐 *www.frances-sf.com* ⏲ *Closed Mon. No lunch.*

Performing Arts

FILM

★ Castro Theatre

FILM | A large neon sign marks the exterior of this 1,400-plus-seat art-deco movie palace whose exotic interior transports you back to 1922, when the theater first opened. High-profile festivals present films here, along with classic revivals and foreign flicks. There are a few cult-themed drag shows every month. **■ TIP→ Lines for the Castro's popular sing-along movie musicals often trail down the block.** ✉ *429 Castro St., near Market St., Castro* ☎ *415/621–6120* 🌐 *www.castrotheatre.com.*

Noe Valley

This upscale but relaxed enclave just south of the Castro is among the city's most desirable places to live, with laid-back cafés, kid-friendly restaurants, and comfortable, old-time shops along Church Street and 24th Street, its main thoroughfares. You can also see remnants of Noe Valley's agricultural beginnings: Billy Goat Hill (at Castro and 30th streets), a wild-grass hill often draped in fog and topped by one of the city's best rope-swinging trees, is named for the goats that grazed here right into the 20th century.

Sights

Seward Street Slides

CITY PARK | FAMILY | A teenager designed these two long, concrete slides back in 1973, saving this mini park from development. Aimed at older kids and adults rather than little ones, the slides offer a fun, steep ride down, so wear sturdy pants. ✉ *Seward Mini Park, 30 Seward St., Noe Valley* 🌐 *www.sfrecpark.org* ⏲ *Closed Mon.*

Restaurants

Barney's Gourmet Hamburgers

$ | AMERICAN | FAMILY | The Noe Valley location of this family-friendly California burger chain offers a cozy indoor-outdoor dining area, the latter really a patio encased in glass windows for watching foot traffic along 24th Street. The ample menu is loaded with fancier versions of diner classics—think the Gastropub burger, with a fried egg and a pretzel bun, or the Maui Waui, with a teriyaki glaze and grilled pineapple. **Known for:** all kinds of fries; vegetarian options; delicious milk shakes. $ *Average main: $14* ✉ *4138 24th St., near Castro St., Noe Valley* ☎ *415/282–7770* 🌐 *www.barneyshamburgers.com.*

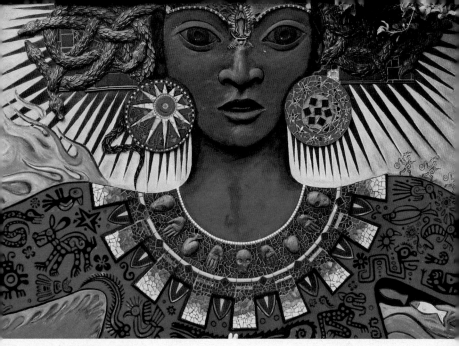

A colorful mosaic mural in the Castro

Mission District

The Mission has a number of distinct personalities: it's the Latino neighborhood, where working-class folks raise their families and where gangs occasionally clash; it's the hipster hood, where tattooed and pierced twenty- and thirtysomethings hold court in the coolest cafés and bars in town; it's a culinary epicenter, with the strongest concentration of destination restaurants and affordable ethnic cuisine; it's the face of gentrification, where high-tech money prices out longtime commercial and residential renters; and it's the artists' quarter, where murals adorn literally blocks of walls long after the artists have moved to cheaper digs. It's also the city's equivalent of the Sunshine State—this neighborhood's always the last to succumb to fog.

 Sights

Balmy Alley murals

PUBLIC ART | Mission District artists have transformed the walls of their neighborhood with paintings, and Balmy Alley is one of the best-executed examples. Many murals adorn the one-block alley, with newer ones continually filling in the blank spaces. In 1971, artists began teaming with local children to create a space to promote peace in Central America, community spirit, and (later) AIDS awareness; since then dozens of muralists have added their vibrant works. The alley's longtime popularity has grown exponentially thanks to its Instagram appeal. ⚠ **Be alert here: the 25th Street end of the alley adjoins a somewhat dangerous area.**

Once you're done at Balmy Alley, head a couple blocks west on 24th Street to another prominent alley of murals on Cypress Street (also between 24th and 25th Streets). ⊠ *24th St. between and parallel to Harrison and Treat Sts., alley runs south to 25th St., Mission District* 🌐 *balmyalley.org.*

★ Dolores Park

CITY PARK | A two-square-block microcosm of life in the district, Mission Dolores Park is one of San Francisco's liveliest green spaces: dog lovers and their pampered pups congregate, kids play at the extravagant playground, and hipsters hold court, drinking beer and rosé cans on sunny days. (Fair warning: if it's over 70°, the place can get packed like traffic at rush hour for picnic-blanket space.) During the summer, Dolores Park hosts movie nights, performances by the San Francisco Mime Troupe, and any number of pop-up events and impromptu parties. Spend a warm day here—maybe sitting at the top of the park with a view of the city and the Bay Bridge —surrounded by locals and that laid-back, still-abundant San Francisco energy, and you may well find yourself plotting your move to the city. The best views are in the southeast corner, near the historic **golden fire hydrant** that saved the neighborhood after the 1906 earthquake. ✉ *Between 18th and 20th Sts. and Dolores and Church Sts., Mission District* 🌐 *sfrecpark.org.*

Golden fire hydrant

LOCAL INTEREST | When all the other fire hydrants went dry during the fire that followed the 1906 earthquake, this one kept pumping. Noe Valley and the Mission District were thus spared the devastation wrought elsewhere in the city, which explains the large number of prequake homes here. Every year on April 18th (the anniversary of the quake), folks gather here to share stories about the disaster, and the famous hydrant gets a fresh coat of gold paint. ✉ *Church and 20th Sts., southeastern corner of intersection, across from Dolores Park, Mission.*

Mission Dolores

RELIGIOUS SITE | Two churches stand side by side here, a newer multidomed basilica and the small adobe **Mission San Francisco de Asís,** the latter being the city's oldest standing structure along with the Presidio Officers' Club. Completed in 1791, it's the sixth of the 21 California missions founded by Franciscan friars in the 18th and early 19th centuries. Its ceiling depicts original Ohlone Indian basket designs, executed in vegetable dyes. The tiny chapel includes frescoes and a hand-painted wooden altar.

There's a hidden treasure here, too, a mural forgotten and rediscovered: an original 20-by-22-foot mural with images including a dagger-pierced Sacred Heart of Jesus, painted with natural dyes by Native Americans in 1791, was found in 2004 behind the altar. Interesting fact: Mission San Francisco de Asís was founded on June 29, 1776, five days before the Declaration of Independence was signed.

The small museum in the mission complex covers its founding and history, and the pretty cemetery—which appears in Alfred Hitchcock's film *Vertigo*—contains the graves of mid-19th-century European immigrants. The remains of an estimated 5,000 Native Americans who died at the mission lie in unmarked graves. ✉ *3321 16th St., at Dolores St., Mission District* ☎ *415/621–8203* 🌐 *www.missiondolores.org* 🎫 *Suggested donation $7.*

Museum of Craft and Design

MUSEUM | Right at home in this once-industrial neighborhood now bursting with creative energy, this small, four-room space—definitely a quick view—mounts temporary art and design exhibitions. The focus might be sculpture, metalwork, furniture, or jewelry, though it might also be industrial design, architecture, or very on-trend 2020s subjects like data and computer encoding. The beautifully curated shop is a perfect place for unique souvenirs and imagination-spurring items for the home office. ✉ *2569 3rd St., near 22nd St., Dogpatch* ☎ *415/773–0303* 🌐 *sfmcd.org* 🎫 *$10* 🕓 *Closed Mon. and Tues.*

Did You Know?

These pastel Victorian homes in Pacific Heights are closer to the original hues sported back in the 1900s. It wasn't until the 1960s that the bold, electric colors now seen around San Francisco gained popularity. Before that, the most typical house paint color was a standard gray.

Restaurants

★ AL's Place

$$ | **MODERN AMERICAN** | AL is chef Aaron London, and his place is a sunny, whitewashed corner spot that serves Michelin-starred, vegetable-forward cooking. London's menu changes frequently, but some dishes, like yellow eye bean stew and grits with goat's milk curd and seasonal produce, stick around, and the wine list is packed with some of the world's finest, largely under-the-radar small producers. **Known for:** fries with a cult following; inventive, vegetable-heavy menu; wonderful sherry and vermouth cocktails. *Average main: $22 1499 Valencia St., Mission 415/416–6136 www.alsplacesf.com Closed Mon. and Tues. No lunch.*

★ Delfina

$$$ | **ITALIAN** | Crowds are a constant fixture at Craig and Annie Stoll's cultishly adored northern Italian spot, where aluminum-topped tables are squeezed into a casual chic interior with hardwood floors, a room-length mirror, and a tile bar that seems to radiate happiness. Deceptively simple, exquisitely flavored dishes include excellent pastas and consistently great roast chicken; the *panna cotta* is best in class. **Known for:** signature spaghetti with plum tomatoes; hard to get reservations; Monterey Bay calamari with white bean salad. *Average main: $29 3621 18th St., Mission District 415/552–4055 www.delfinasf.com No lunch.*

★ flour + water

$$ | **MODERN ITALIAN** | This handsome and boisterous hot spot with slate-gray walls, sturdy wooden tables, and a tiny bar is synonymous with pasta and also serves top-notch, blistery thin-crust Neapolitan pizzas, but the grand experience here is the seven-course pasta-tasting menu (extra charge for wine pairings). Pastas on both menus change constantly with the seasons, but the one standby is a meatless Taleggio *scarpinocc* with aged balsamic drizzled over the bow tie–shaped pasta. **Known for:** difficult-to-get reservations; rarely seen pasta shapes; Italian wines from small producers. *Average main: $25 2401 Harrison St., Mission District 415/826–7000 www.flourandwater.com No lunch.*

★ Lazy Bear

$$$$ | **MODERN AMERICAN** | There's no end to the buzz around chef David Barzelay's 12-plus-course prix-fixe seasonal and imagination-driven dinners, which might include grilled lamb covered in spring herbs and flowers or delicate San Francisco coast king salmon with English peas and cured roe. An ode to the Western lodge, the high-ceilinged, spacious dining room includes a fireplace, charred wood walls, and wooden rafters. **Known for:** brown bread rolls with butter cultured in-house; sensational friendly yet formal service; dinner-party vibe. *Average main: $245 3416 19th St., Mission District 415/874–9921 www.lazybearsf.com Closed Mon. and Tues.*

Mission Chinese Food

$$ | **CHINESE** | While the setting is a bit confusing (the awning still bears the name of its predecessor) and notably informal, the food draws throngs for its bold, cheerfully inauthentic riffs on Chinese cuisine made with quality meats and ingredients, including the fine and super-fiery kung pao pastrami, salt cod fried rice with mackerel confit, and sour chili chicken. Some of the food spikes hot (Chongqing chicken wings), while milder dishes (Westlake rice porridge) are homey and satisfying. **Known for:** thrice-cooked bacon and rice cakes; mapo tofu (tofu in a spicy sauce); party vibe. *Average main: $20 2234 Mission St., Mission District 415/863–2800 www.missionchinesefood.com.*

SanJalisco

$ | **MEXICAN** | **FAMILY** | This colorful old-time, sun-filled, family-run restaurant has been a neighborhood favorite since 1988, and not only because it serves breakfast all day—though the hearty *chilaquiles* always hits the spot. On weekends, longtime regulars opt for *birria*, a spicy barbecued goat stew, or *menudo*, a tongue-searing soup made from beef tripe, complemented by beer and sangria. **Known for:** huevos "con amor"; soups change based on day of the week; friendly service. *$ Average main: $13 ✉ 901 S. Van Ness Ave., Mission District ☎ 415/648–8383 🌐 www.sanjaliscorestaurant.com.*

Coffee and Quick Bites

★ Tartine Bakery

$ | BAKERY | FAMILY | Chad Robertson is America's first modern cult baker, and this tiny Mission District outpost is where you'll find his famed loaves of tangy country bread, beloved pastries like croissants and morning buns, and near-constant lines out the door—good luck finding a seat. They're longest in the morning when locals (and plenty of tourists) need a pastry punch to start the day, and later in the afternoon when the famed loaves emerge freshly baked. **Known for:** anything bread-related; chocolate soufflé cake; indecisive guests who want to order everything. *$ Average main: $15 ✉ 600 Guerrero St., at 18th St., Mission District ☎ 415/487–2600 🌐 tartinebakery.com ⏲ No dinner.*

Hotels

★ The Parker Guest House

$$ | B&B/INN | Two yellow 1909 Edwardian houses enchant travelers wanting an authentic San Francisco experience; dark hallways and steep staircases lead to bright, earth-toned rooms with tiled baths (most with tubs), comfortable sitting areas, and cozy linens. **Pros:** handsomely designed, affordable rooms; close to the Castro and Dolores Park; evening wine social hour. **Cons:** long walk or short car ride from the main Mission nightlife; economy rooms have private baths in a hallway; standard rooms are a little tight. *$ Rooms from: $229 ✉ 520 Church St., Mission District ☎ 415/621–3222 🌐 www.parkerguesthouse.com 21 rooms 🍽 Free breakfast.*

Nightlife

ABV

BARS/PUBS | One of the city's top cocktail bars offers elevated small plates (the burger has a devoted following) late into the night to pair with the excellent cocktail menu, which includes such favorites as a Mumbai Mule featuring saffron vodka. A knowledgeable and friendly staff serves a diverse, energetic crowd that knows their drinks, in a smart modern setting with hard surfaces, bar-stool seating, and a giant mural. The sidewalk tables are popular on sunny days. **■ TIP→ Pay attention to the schedule of the upstairs loft, Over Proof. When open, it's one of the city's best themed cocktail–pairing dinner experiences.** *✉ 3174 16th St., Mission District ☎ 415/294–1871 🌐 www.abvsf.com.*

★ El Rio

BARS/PUBS | A dive bar in the best sense, El Rio has a calendar chock-full of events, from free bands and films to Salsa Sunday (seasonal), all of which keep Mission kids coming back. No matter what day you attend, expect to find a diverse gay and straight crowd enjoying local beers and margaritas. When the weather's warm, the large patio out back is especially popular, and the midday dance parties are *the* place to be. *✉ 3158 Mission St., between César Chavez and Valencia Sts., Mission District ☎ 415/282–3325 🌐 www.elriosf.com.*

Martuni's

BARS/PUBS | A mixed crowd enjoys cocktails in the semi-refined environment of this piano bar where the Castro, the Mission, and Hayes Valley intersect; variations on the martini and different fruit-flavored lemon drops are a specialty. This is not the place for innovative mixology. In the intimate back room a pianist plays nightly, and patrons take turns boisterously singing show tunes. Martuni's often gets busy after symphony and opera performances—Davies Hall and the Opera House are both within walking distance. ✉ *4 Valencia St., at Market St., Mission District* ☎ *415/241–0205.*

★ Zeitgeist

BARS/PUBS | It's a dive but one of the city's best beer bars—there are almost 50 on tap—and a great place to relax with a cold one or an ever-popular Bloody Mary in the large "garden" (there's not much greenery) on a sunny day. Burgers and brats are available, and if you own a trucker hat, a pair of Vans, and a Pabst Blue Ribbon T-shirt, you'll fit right in. This is one of the city's quintessential experiences, both in terms of bars and of simply having fun. ✉ *199 Valencia St., at Duboce Ave., Mission District* ☎ *415/255–7505* 🌐 *www.zeitgeistsf.com.*

Shopping

FURNITURE, HOUSEWARES, AND GIFTS

★ Paxton Gate

GIFTS/SOUVENIRS | Elevating gardening to an art, this serene shop offers beautiful earthenware pots, amaryllis and narcissus bulbs, decorative garden items, and coffee-table books, such as a composting book called *Let It Rot!* The collection of taxidermy and preserved bugs provides more unusual gift ideas. A couple storefronts away is too-cute Paxton Gate Curiosities for Kids, jam-packed with retro toys, books, and other stellar finds. ✉ *824 Valencia St., between 19th and 20th Sts., Mission District* ☎ *415/824–1872* 🌐 *paxtongate.com.*

Potrero Hill

Tucked between two freeways east of the Mission and south of SoMa, warm and sunny Potrero Hill is a laid-back, family-friendly neighborhood that can feel like a place apart from the rest of the city. The longtime music club Bottom of the Hill has always been a draw, but the area is still off the tourist radar.

Nightlife

Bottom of the Hill

MUSIC CLUBS | This is a great live-music dive—in the best sense of the word—and truly the epicenter of Bay Area indie rock. The club has hosted some great acts over the years, including the Strokes and the Throwing Muses. Rap and hip-hop acts occasionally make it to the stage. ✉ *1233 17th St., at Missouri St., Potrero Hill* ☎ *415/626–4455* 🌐 *www.bottomofthehill.com.*

Chapter 19

THE BAY AREA

Updated by
Monique Peterson

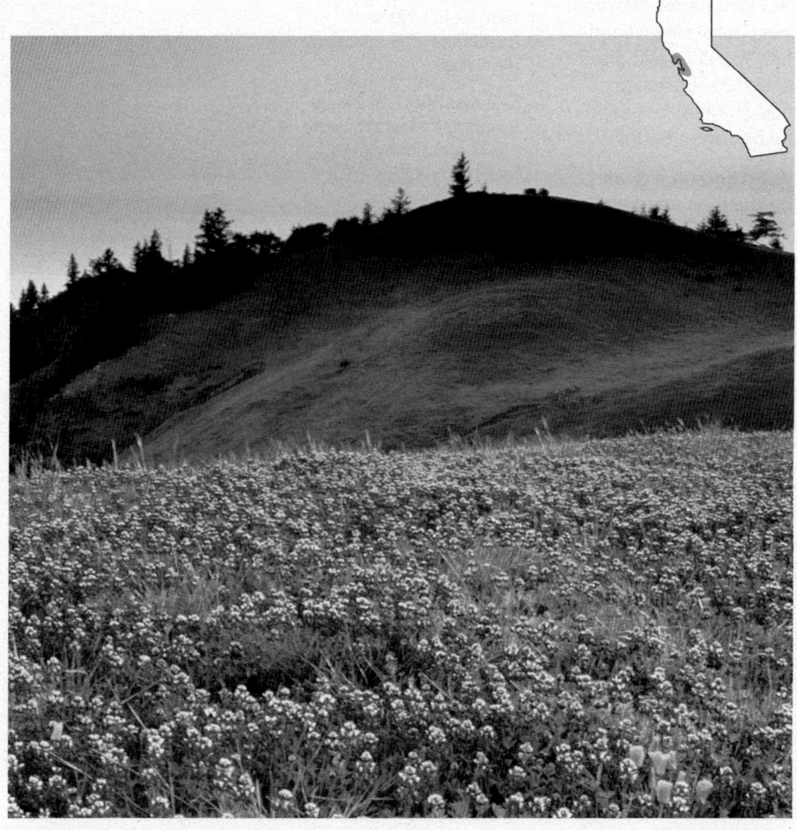

Sights ★★★★☆

Restaurants ★★★★☆

Hotels ★★☆☆☆

Shopping ★★☆☆☆

Nightlife ★★★★☆

WELCOME TO THE BAY AREA

TOP REASONS TO GO

★ **Berkeley's culinary mecca:** Eat your way through this area of North Berkeley, starting with a slice of perfect pizza from Cheese Board Pizza (just look for the line).

★ **Point Reyes National Seashore:** Hike beautifully rugged—and often deserted—beaches at one of the most beautiful places on Earth.

★ **Sitting on a dock by the bay:** Admire the beauty of the Bay Area from the rocky, picturesque shores of Sausalito or Tiburon.

★ **"Beer-hopping" in Oakland's hippest hoods:** Spend time discovering the wealth of unique brewers and award-winning craft-beer makers along the Oakland Ale Trail in a city that takes its beer seriously.

★ **Giant redwoods:** Walking into Muir Woods National Monument, a mere 12 miles north of the Golden Gate Bridge, is like entering a cathedral built by God.

1 **Berkeley.** Independent bookstores, excellent coffee spots, and thousands of cyclists.

2 **Oakland.** A diverse, multifaceted city with a lively arts, nightlife, and food scene.

3 **The Marin Headlands.** Stretching from the Golden Gate Bridge to Muir Beach, these headlands offer spectacular vistas.

4 **Sausalito.** This Marin County city has stunning views and a bohemian feel.

5 **Tiburon.** Scenic and quaint, this town has good dining and hiking.

6 **Mill Valley.** A superb natural setting with a bustling downtown area. Nearby are the towering redwoods of Muir Woods National Monument and breathtaking panoramas of the entire Bay Area from Mt. Tamalpais State Park.

7 **Muir Beach.** The quiet beach here has a distinctly local feel.

8 **Stinson Beach.** An expansive stretch of beach and a town with a nonchalant surfer vibe.

9 **Point Reyes National Seashore.** A dramatic and rocky coastline with miles of sandy beaches.

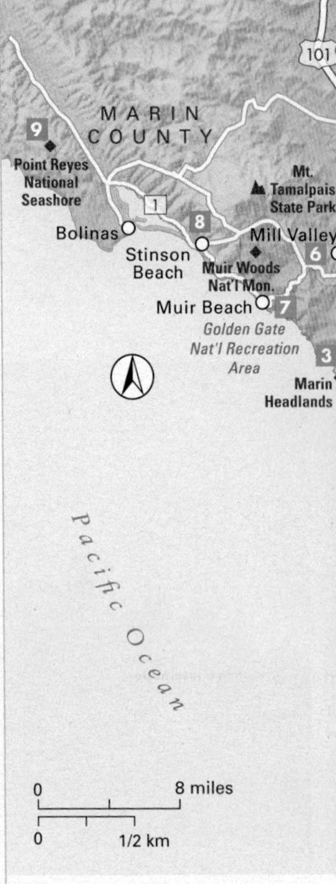

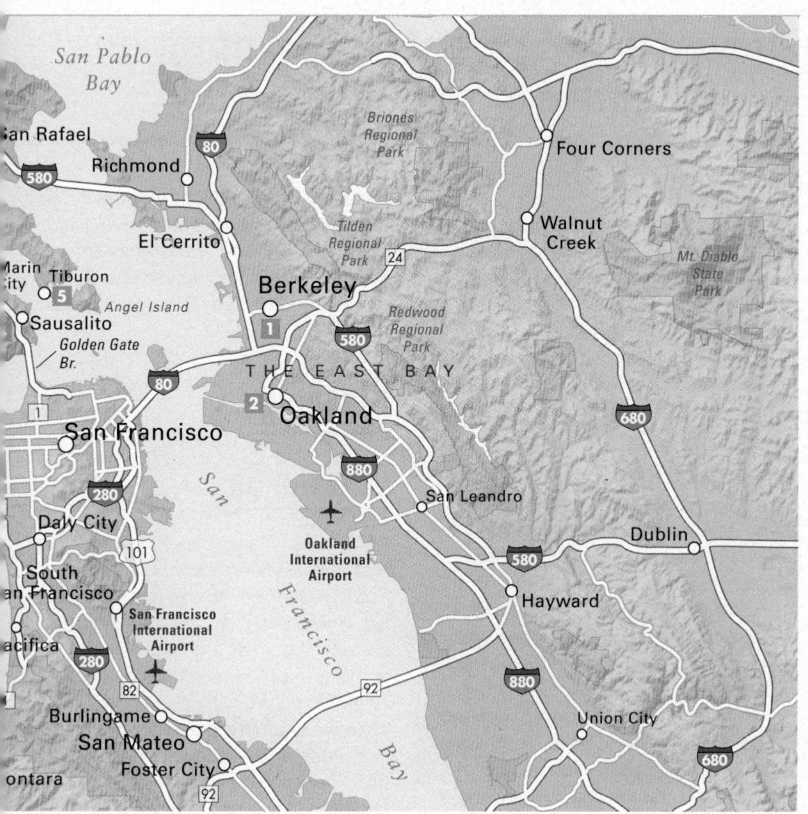
San Pablo Bay
Richmond
El Cerrito
Tiburon
Angel Island
Sausalito
Golden Gate Br.
Berkeley
Briones Regional Park
Tilden Regional Park
Redwood Regional Park
Four Corners
Walnut Creek
Mt. Diablo State Park
THE EAST BAY
Oakland
San Francisco
San Leandro
Daly City
South
Oakland International Airport
San Francisco Bay
Dublin
Hayward
San Francisco International Airport
Burlingame
San Mateo
Foster City
Union City
580
80
24
680
880
280
101
1
82
92
1
2
5

It's rare for a metropolis to compete with its suburbs for visitors, but the view from any of San Francisco's hilltops shows that the Bay Area's temptations extend far beyond the city limits.

MAJOR REGIONS

East of the city are the energetic urban centers of Berkeley and Oakland. Famously radical Berkeley is also comfortably sophisticated, while Oakland has an arts and restaurant scene so hip that it pulls San Franciscans across the bay. To the north is Marin County with its dramatic coastal beauty and chic, affluent villages.

The East Bay. The college town of Berkeley has long been known for its liberal ethos, stimulating university community (and perhaps even more stimulating coffee shops), and activist streak. But these days, the lively restaurant and arts scenes are luring even those who wouldn't be caught dead in Birkenstocks. Meanwhile, life in the diverse, harborfront city of Oakland is strongly defined by a turbulent history. Today, progressive Oakland is an incubator for artisans of all kinds, and the thriving culinary and creative scenes are taking off.

Marin County. Marin is considered the prettiest of the Bay Area counties, primarily because of its wealth of open space. Anchored by water on three sides, the county is mostly parkland, including long stretches of undeveloped coastline along the Marin Headlands, recognizable by the distinguished peak of Mt. Tamalpais. The coastal treasures of Muir Woods National Monument, "Mt. Tam," Stinson and Muir Beaches, and the entire Point Reyes National Seashore are among the country's greatest natural beauties. It's no wonder that the picturesque small towns here—Sausalito, Tiburon, Mill Valley, and Bolinas among them—may sometimes look rustic, but most are home to a dizzyingly high tax bracket.

Planning

When to Go

As with San Francisco, you can visit the rest of the Bay Area any time of year, and it's especially nice in late spring and fall. Unlike San Francisco, though, the surrounding areas are reliably sunny in summer—it gets hotter as you head inland. Even the rainy season has its charms, as otherwise golden hills turn a rich green and wildflowers become plentiful. Precipitation is usually the heaviest between November and March. Berkeley is a university town, so it's easier to navigate the streets and find parking near the university between semesters, but there's also less buzz around town then.

Getting Here and Around

Seamless travel from train to ferry to bus with one fare card is possible—and often preferable to driving on congested freeways and over toll bridges. For trips from one city to the next across the bay, take a tip from locals and save time and money with a Clipper card. They work with BART, Muni, buses, and ferries. ■ **TIP→ Order a Clipper card before you travel:** 🌐 *www.clippercard.com.*

BART

Using public transportation to reach Berkeley or Oakland is ideal. The under- and aboveground BART (Bay Area Rapid Transit) trains make stops in both cities as well as other East Bay destinations. Trips to either take about a half hour one-way from the center of San Francisco. BART does not serve Marin County. ■ **TIP→ Check ahead for safety measures and service advisories.**

CONTACTS BART. ☎ *510/465–2278* 🌐 *www.bart.gov.*

BOAT AND FERRY

For sheer romance, nothing beats the ferry; there's service from San Francisco to Sausalito, Tiburon, and Larkspur in Marin County, and to Alameda and Oakland in the East Bay.

The Golden Gate Ferry crosses the bay to Larkspur and Sausalito from San Francisco's Ferry Building (✉ *Market St. and the Embarcadero*). Blue & Gold Fleet ferries depart daily for Sausalito and Tiburon from Pier 41 at Fisherman's Wharf; weekday commuter ferries leave from the Ferry Building for Tiburon. The trip to either Sausalito or Tiburon takes from 25 minutes to an hour. Purchase tickets from terminal vending machines.

The Angel Island–Tiburon Ferry sails to the island daily from April through October and on weekends the rest of the year. Call ahead to book and to check schedules.

The San Francisco Bay Ferry runs several times daily between San Francisco's Ferry Building or Pier 41 and Oakland's Jack London Square, by way of Alameda. The trip lasts from 25 to 45 minutes and leads to Oakland's waterfront shopping and restaurant district. Purchase tickets on board.

CONTACTS Angel Island–Tiburon Ferry. ☎ *415/435–2131* 🌐 *angelislandferry.com.* **Blue & Gold Fleet.** ☎ *415/705–8200* 🌐 *www.blueandgoldfleet.com.* **Golden Gate Ferry.** ☎ *415/921–5858* 🌐 *www.goldengate.org.* **San Francisco Bay Ferry.** ☎ *707/643–3779, 877/643–3779* 🌐 *sanfranciscobayferry.com.*

BUS

Golden Gate Transit buses travel north to Sausalito, Tiburon, and elsewhere in Marin County from Perry and 3rd Streets and other points in San Francisco. For Mt. Tamalpais State Park and West Marin (Stinson Beach, Bolinas, and Point Reyes Station), take any route to Marin City and then transfer to the West Marin Stagecoach. San Francisco Muni buses primarily serve the city. ■ **TIP→ Several other bus options exist for local and regional travel throughout the Bay Area, including Amtrak, Greyhound, California Shuttle, and more (www.bayareatransit.net/regional).**

Though less speedy than BART, more than 30 AC Transit bus lines provide service to and from San Francisco throughout the East Bay, even after BART shuts down. The F and FS lines will get you to Berkeley, while lines C, P, B, and O take you to Oakland and Piedmont. Many lines have been temporarily suspended due to COVID-19, so check ahead. At this writing, face masks are required.

CONTACTS AC Transit. ☎ *510/891–4777* 🌐 *www.actransit.org.* **Golden Gate Transit.** ☎ *511* 🌐 *www.goldengate.org.* **SamTrans.** ☎ *800/660–4287* 🌐 *www.samtrans.com.* **San Francisco Muni.** ☎ *311* 🌐 *www.sfmta.com.* **West Marin Stagecoach.** ☎ *511* 🌐 *marintransit.org/stagecoach.*

CAR

To reach the East Bay from San Francisco, take Interstate 80 East across the San Francisco–Oakland Bay Bridge. For U.C. Berkeley, merge onto Interstate 580 West and take Exit 11 for University Avenue. For Oakland, merge onto Interstate 580 East. To reach downtown Oakland, take Interstate 980 West from Interstate 580 East and exit at 14th Street. Travel time varies depending on traffic but should take about 30 minutes (or more than an hour if it's rush hour).

For all points in Marin, head north on U.S. 101 and cross the Golden Gate Bridge. Sausalito, Tiburon, the Marin Headlands, and Point Reyes National Seashore are all accessed off U.S. 101. The scenic coastal route, Highway 1, also called Shoreline Highway (and briefly, Panoramic Highway) for certain stretches, can be accessed off U.S. 101 as well. Follow this road to Muir Woods, Mt. Tamalpais State Park, Muir Beach, Stinson Beach, and Bolinas. From Bolinas, you can continue north on Highway 1 to Point Reyes.

Restaurants

The Bay Area is home to many popular and innovative restaurants, such as Chez Panisse in Berkeley and Commis in Oakland—for which reservations must be made well in advance. There are also many casual but equally tasty eateries to test out; expect an emphasis on organic seasonal produce, locally raised meats, craft cocktails, and curated wine menus. Marin's dining scene trends toward the sleepy side, so be sure to check hours ahead of time.

Hotels

With a few exceptions, hotels in Berkeley and Oakland tend to be standard-issue, but many Marin hotels package themselves as cozy retreats. Summer in Marin is often booked well in advance, despite weather that can be downright chilly. Check for special packages during this season.

Restaurant and hotel reviews have been shortened. For full information, visit Fodors.com. Restaurant prices are the average cost of a main course at dinner or, if dinner is not served, at lunch. Hotel prices are the lowest cost of a standard double room in high season.

What It Costs

$	$$	$$$	$$$$
RESTAURANTS			
under $17	$17–$26	$27–$36	over $36
HOTELS			
under $200	$200–$300	$301–$400	over $400

Tours

★ **Best Bay Area Tours**
SPECIAL-INTEREST | FAMILY | Morning and afternoon tours of Muir Woods and Sausalito include at least 90 minutes in the redwoods before heading on to Sausalito. On returning to the city, tours make a scenic stop in the Marin Headlands to enjoy fantastic views. Knowledgeable guides lead small tours in comfortable vans, and hotel pickup is included, though park entrance is not. Another tour option includes a visit to Muir Woods plus Wine Country exploration. ☎ *415/543–8687* 🌐 *bestbayareatours.com* 🎫 *From $110.*

Berkeley

2 miles northeast of Bay Bridge.

Berkeley is the birthplace of the Free Speech Movement, the radical hub of the 1960s, the home of arguably the nation's top public university, and a frequent site of protests and political movements. The city of 103,000 is also a culturally diverse breeding ground for social trends, a bastion of the counterculture, and an important center for Bay Area writers, artists, and musicians. Berkeley residents, students, and faculty spend hours nursing coffee concoctions while they read, discuss, and debate at the dozens of cafés that surround campus. It's the quintessential university town, with numerous independent bookstores, countless casual eateries, myriad meet-ups, and thousands of cyclists.

Oakland may have the edge over Berkeley when it comes to ethnic diversity and cutting-edge arts, but unless you're accustomed to sipping hemp-milk lattes while taking in a spontaneous street performance prior to yoga, you'll likely find Berkeley charmingly offbeat.

GETTING HERE AND AROUND

BART is the easiest way to get to Berkeley from San Francisco. Exit at the Downtown Berkeley Station, and walk a block up Center Street to get to the western edge of campus. AC Transit buses F and FS lines stop near the university and Fourth Street shopping. By car, take Interstate 80 East across the Bay Bridge, merge onto Interstate 580 West, and take the University Avenue exit through downtown Berkeley or take the Ashby Avenue exit and turn left on Telegraph Avenue. Once you arrive, explore on foot. Berkeley is very pedestrian-friendly.

TOURS

Edible Excursions

WALKING TOURS | For an unforgettable foodie experience in Berkeley, book a culinary walking tour, maybe one of North Berkeley. Come hungry for knowledge and noshing. Tours take place Thursday, Saturday, and Sunday. The company also offers tours of San Francisco and Oakland. ☎ *415/806–5970* 🌐 *www.edibleexcursions.net* 🎫 *From $114.*

ESSENTIALS

VISITOR INFORMATION Koret Visitor Center. ✉ *2227 Piedmont Ave., at California Memorial Stadium, Downtown* ☎ *510/642–5215* 🌐 *visit.berkeley.edu.* **Visit Berkeley.** ✉ *2030 Addison St., Suite 102, Downtown* ☎ *510/549–7040, 800/847–4823* 🌐 *www.visitberkeley.com.*

Sights

★ BAMPFA (Berkeley Art Museum and Pacific Film Archive)

MUSEUM | This combined art museum, repertory movie theater, and film archive, known for its extensive collection of some 28,000 works of art and 18,000 films and videos, is now also home to the world's largest collection of African American quilts, thanks to the bequest of art scholar Eli Leon. Artworks span five centuries and include modernist notables Mark Rothko, Jackson Pollock, David Smith, and Hans Hofmann. The Pacific Film Archive includes the largest selection of Japanese films outside Japan and specializes in international films, offering regular screenings, programs, and performances. ✉ *2155 Center St., Downtown* ☎ *510/642–0808* 🌐 *bampfa.org* 🎫 *$14; free 1st Thurs. of month* ⏲ *Closed Mon. and Tues.*

Fourth Street

NEIGHBORHOOD | Once an industrial area, this walkable stretch of Fourth Street north of University Avenue has transformed into the busiest few blocks of refined shopping and eating in Berkeley. A perfect stop for lovers of design, curated taste experiences, artful living, and fashion, the vibrant district boasts more than 70 shops, specialty stores, cafés, and restaurants. See creation and find inspiration at Castle in the Air, Builders Booksource, and Stained Glass Garden, or sip a "live roast" at Artís, where you can watch small-batch coffee roasting in progress—one pound at a time. ✉ *4th St. between University Ave. and Virginia St., 4th Street* 🌐 *www.fourthstreet.com.*

★ Shattuck & Vine Street Neighborhood

NEIGHBORHOOD | The success of Alice Waters's Chez Panisse defined California cuisine and attracted countless food-related enterprises to a stretch of Shattuck Avenue. Foodies will do well here poking around the shops, grabbing a quick bite, or indulging in a feast.

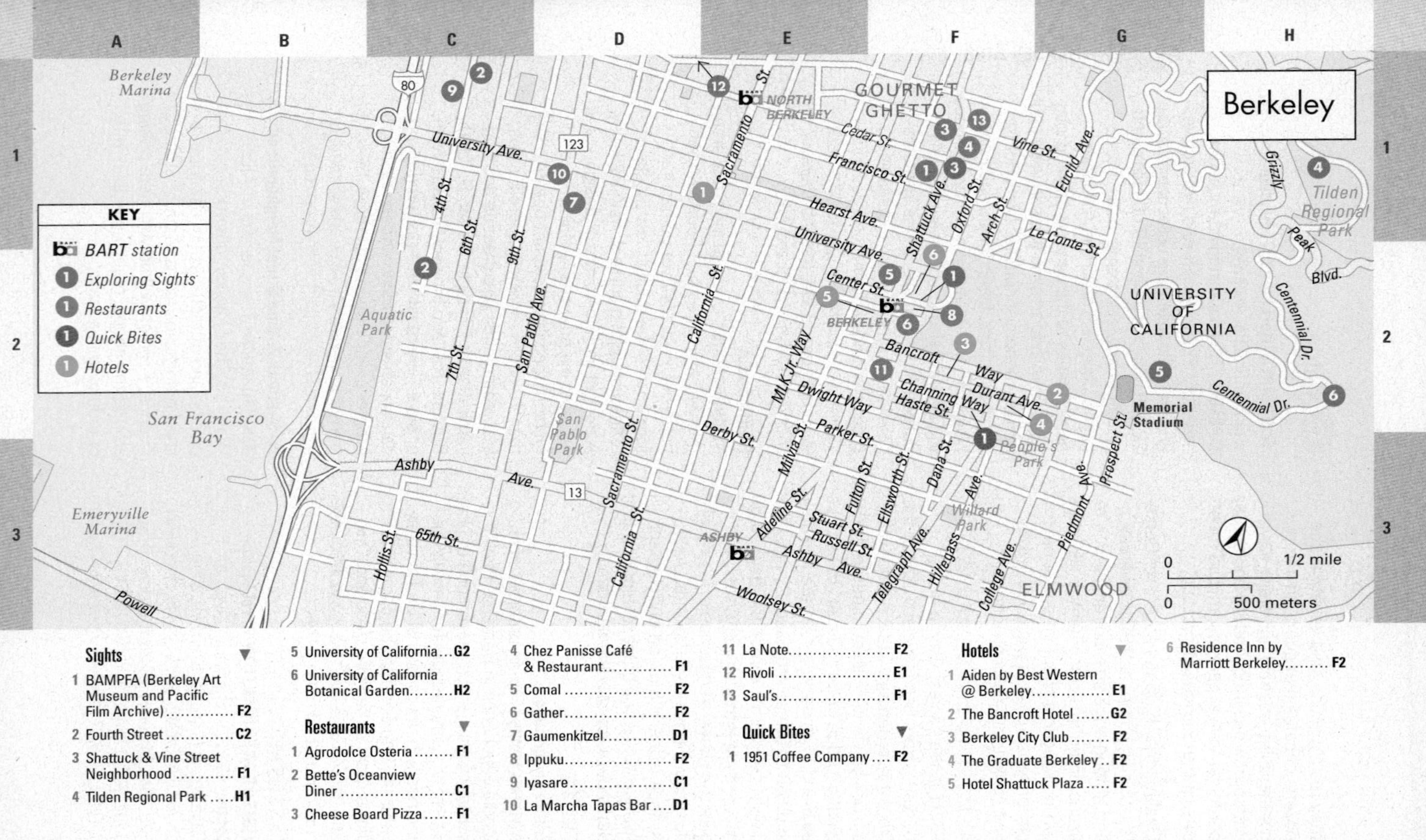

Berkeley
KEY
BART station
Exploring Sights
Restaurants
Quick Bites
Hotels
A B C D E F G H
1 2 3
Berkeley Marina
Emeryville Marina
San Francisco Bay
Aquatic Park
San Pablo Park
People's Park
Willard Park
Tilden Regional Park
UNIVERSITY OF CALIFORNIA
Memorial Stadium
GOURMET GHETTO
ELMWOOD
NORTH BERKELEY
BERKELEY
ASHBY
80
123
13
University Ave.
4th St.
6th St.
7th St.
9th St.
San Pablo Ave.
Sacramento St.
California St.
MLK Jr. Way
Milvia St.
Shattuck Ave.
Oxford St.
Arch St.
Euclid Ave.
Vine St.
Cedar St.
Francisco St.
Hearst Ave.
Le Conte St.
Center St.
Bancroft Way
Durant Ave.
Channing Way
Haste St.
Dwight Way
Parker St.
Derby St.
Ashby Ave.
65th St.
Hollis St.
Powell
Woolsey St.
Adeline St.
Stuart St.
Russell St.
Fulton St.
Ellsworth St.
Dana St.
Telegraph Ave.
Hillegass Ave.
College Ave.
Piedmont Ave.
Prospect St.
Centennial Dr.
Grizzly Peak Blvd.
0 1/2 mile
0 500 meters
Sights
1 BAMPFA (Berkeley Art Museum and Pacific Film Archive) F2
2 Fourth Street C2
3 Shattuck & Vine Street Neighborhood F1
4 Tilden Regional Park H1
5 University of California G2
6 University of California Botanical Garden H2
Restaurants
1 Agrodolce Osteria F1
2 Bette's Oceanview Diner C1
3 Cheese Board Pizza F1
4 Chez Panisse Café & Restaurant F1
5 Comal F2
6 Gather F2
7 Gaumenkitzel D1
8 Ippuku F2
9 Iyasare C1
10 La Marcha Tapas Bar D1
11 La Note F2
12 Rivoli E1
13 Saul's F1
Quick Bites
1 1951 Coffee Company F2
Hotels
1 Aiden by Best Western @ Berkeley E1
2 The Bancroft Hotel G2
3 Berkeley City Club F2
4 The Graduate Berkeley F2
5 Hotel Shattuck Plaza F2
6 Residence Inn by Marriott Berkeley F2

Tigerlily (✉ *1513 Shattuck*) dishes up authentic modern Indian cuisine along with signature cocktails and light fare on the patio. Neighboring **Epicurious Garden** (✉ *1509–1513 Shattuck*) food stands sell everything from sushi to gelato. A small terraced garden winds up to the **Imperial Tea Court,** a Zen-like teahouse rife with imports and teaware.

Across Vine Street, the **Vintage Berkeley** (✉ *2113 Vine*) wine shop offers regular tastings and reasonably priced bottles within the walls of a historic former pump house. Coffee lovers can head to the original **Peet's Coffee & Tea** at the corner of Walnut and Vine (*2124 Vine*).

South of Cedar Street, **The Local Butcher Shop** (✉ *No. 1600*) sells locally sourced meat and hearty sandwiches of the day. For high-end food at takeout prices, try the salads, sandwiches, and signature potato puffs at **Grégoire,** around the corner on Cedar Street (✉ *No. 2109*). **Masse's Pastries** (✉ *No. 1469 Shattuck*) is a museum of edible artwork. We could go on, but you get the idea. ✉ *Shattuck Ave. between Delaware and Rose Sts., North Berkeley* 🌐 *www.northshattuckassociation.org.*

★ Tilden Regional Park

NATIONAL/STATE PARK | **FAMILY** | Stunning bay views, a scaled-down steam train, and a botanic garden with the nation's most complete collection of California plant life are the hallmarks of this 2,077-acre park in the hills just east of the U.C. Berkeley campus. The garden's visitor center offers tours as well as information about Tilden's other attractions, including its picnic spots, Lake Anza swimming site, golf course, and hiking trails (the paved **Nimitz Way,** at Inspiration Point, is a popular hike with wonderful sunset views). ■ **TIP→ Children love Tilden's interactive Little Farm and vintage carousel.** ✉ *Tilden Regional Park, 2501 Grizzly Peak Blvd., Tilden Park* ☎ *510/544–2747 park office* 🌐 *www.ebparks.org* 🎫 *Free parking and botanic garden.*

University of California

COLLEGE | Known simply as "Cal," the founding campus of California's university system is one of the leading intellectual centers in the United States and a major site for scientific research. Chartered in 1868, the university sits on 178 oak-covered acres split by Strawberry Creek; it's bounded by Bancroft Way to the south, Hearst Avenue to the north, Oxford Street to the west, and Gayley Road to the east. Campus highlights include bustling and historic **Sproul Plaza** (✉ *Bancroft Way and Sather Rd.*), the seven floors and 61-bell carillon of **Sather Tower** (✉ *Campanile Esplanade*), the nearly 3 million artifacts in the **Phoebe A. Hearst Museum of Anthropology** (Kroeber Hall), hands-on **Lawrence Hall of Science** (✉ *1 Centennial Dr.*), the vibrant 34-acre **Botanical Gardens** (✉ *200 Centennial Dr.*), and the historic **Hearst Greek Theatre** (✉ *2001 Gayley Rd.*), the classic outdoor amphitheater designed by John Galen Howard. ✉ *Downtown* ☎ *510/642–6000* 🌐 *www.berkeley.edu.*

University of California Botanical Garden

GARDEN | **FAMILY** | Thanks to Berkeley's temperate climate, more than 10,000 types of plants from all corners of the world flourish in the 34-acre University of California Botanical Garden. Free garden tours are given regularly with paid admission. Benches and shady picnic tables make this a relaxing place for a snack with a breathtaking view. Call or go online before you travel to reserve your visit. ✉ *200 Centennial Dr., Downtown* ☎ *510/643–2755* 🌐 *www.botanicalgarden.berkeley.edu* 🎫 *$15* 🕒 *Closed 1st Tues. every month.*

Restaurants

Dining in Berkeley may be low-key when it comes to dress, but it's top-of-class in quality, even in less fancy spaces. Late diners beware: Berkeley is an "early to bed" kind of town.

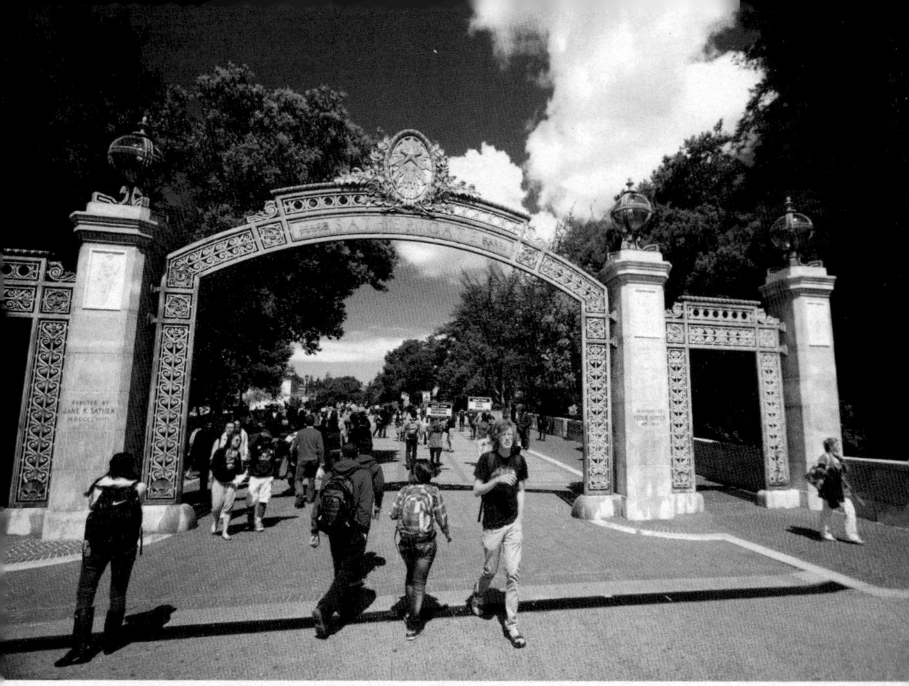

The University of California is the epicenter of Berkeley's energy and activism.

Agrodolce Osteria

$$ | **ITALIAN** | **FAMILY** | Angelo D'Alo's family brings Sicilian flavors and their love for preparing them freshly to the heart of the Shattuck & Vine Street neighborhood, in a setting with black-and-white photos and Italian home decor that add to the old-world atmosphere. The menu features local, sustainable, and organic ingredients in such dishes as house-made orecchiette, seafood risotto, and free-range *pollo allo scarpariello*. **Known for:** oven-roasted heritage pork shoulder; spicy arrabiata; antipasti specialties. *Average main: $22* *1730 Shattuck Ave., North Berkeley* *510/848–8748* *www.agrodolceberkeley.com* *Closed Tues. No lunch.*

Bette's Oceanview Diner

$ | **DINER** | **FAMILY** | Checkered floors, vintage burgundy booths, and an old-time jukebox set the scene at this retro-chic diner in the heart of Berkeley's fashionable Fourth Street shopping district. The wait for a seat at breakfast can be quite long; luckily Bette's To Go is always an option. **Known for:** soufflé pancakes; poached egg specialties; meat loaf and gravy. *Average main: $13* *1807 4th St., near Delaware St., 4th Street* *510/644–3230* *bettesdiner.com* *No dinner.*

★ Cheese Board Pizza

$ | **PIZZA** | A jazz combo often entertains the line that usually snakes down the block outside Cheese Board Pizza; it's that good. The cooperatively owned vegetarian and vegan takeout spot and restaurant draws devoted customers with the smell of just-baked garlic on the pie of the day. **Known for:** cheese varieties; green sauce; live music. *Average main: $12* *1504–1512 Shattuck Ave., at Vine St., North Berkeley* *510/549–3183* *cheeseboardcollective.coop/pizza* *Pizza closed Sun. and Mon., bakery closed Sun.*

★ Chez Panisse Café & Restaurant

$$$$ | **MODERN AMERICAN** | Alice Waters's legendary eatery, the birthplace of California cuisine, first opened its doors on August 28, 1971. It's still known for a

passionate dedication to locally sourced heirloom varieties of fruits and vegetables, heritage breeds, and ethically farmed or foraged ingredients. **Known for:** sustainably sourced meats; attention to detail; simpler fare in upstairs café. *Average main: $150 ✉ 1517 Shattuck Ave., at Vine St., North Berkeley ☎ 510/548–5525 restaurant, 510/548–5049 café ⊕ www.chezpanisse.com ⊙ Closed Sun. No lunch in restaurant.*

★ Comal

$ | MODERN MEXICAN | Relaxed yet trendy, Comal's cavernous indoor dining space and intimate back patio and firepit draw a diverse, decidedly casual crowd for creative Oaxacan-inspired fare and well-crafted cocktails. The modern Mexican menu centers on small dishes that lend themselves to sharing and are offered alongside more than 100 tequilas and mezcals. **Known for:** margaritas and mezcal; house-made chicharróns; wood-fired entrées. *Average main: $16 ✉ 2020 Shattuck Ave., near University Ave., Downtown ☎ 510/926–6300 ⊕ www.comalberkeley.com ⊙ No lunch.*

Gather

$ | MODERN AMERICAN | All things local, organic, seasonal, and sustainable reside harmoniously under one roof at Gather. This haven for vegans, vegetarians, and carnivores alike serves up market and grain salads, shareable grilled local vegetables or cheese plates, roast chicken, and more in a vibrant, well-lit space that boasts funky light fixtures, shiny wood furnishings, and banquettes made of recycled leather belts. **Known for:** heirloom varietals; wood-fired pizzas; house-made liqueurs. *Average main: $16 ✉ 2200 Oxford St., at Allston Way, Downtown ☎ 510/809–0400 ⊕ www.gatherberkeley.com.*

Gaumenkitzel

$$ | GERMAN | FAMILY | This award-winning, convivial locale for organic, slow-food German fare is also the spot for the Bay Area's best variety of German beers. With dishes like spätzle and caramelized onions, house-made *brezel* with bratwurst, *jägerschnitzel* with braised red cabbage, and panfried rainbow trout, this kitchen puts a fresh stamp on traditional German favorites. **Known for:** German wine and beer selection; house-made German breads; fresh, sustainable, zero-waste ingredients. *Average main: $20 ✉ 2121 San Pablo Ave., Downtown ☎ 510/647–5016 ⊕ www.gaumenkitzel.net ⊙ Closed Mon.*

★ Ippuku

$$ | JAPANESE | More Tokyo street chic than standard sushi house, this *izakaya*—the Japanese equivalent of a bar with appetizers—is decked with bamboo-screen booths. Servers pour an impressive array of sakes and *shōchū* and serve up surprising fare. **Known for:** shōchū selection; charcoal-grilled yakitori skewers; selection of small dishes. *Average main: $18 ✉ 2130 Center St., Downtown ☎ 510/665–1969 ⊕ ippuku-berkeley.com ⊙ Closed Mon. No lunch.*

Iyasare

$$ | JAPANESE | Reservations are recommended at this Fourth Street hot spot where the outdoor seating is ideal for people-watching and the Japanese country food is uniquely prepared. Locals come back for seasonally changing, eclectic dishes made with a blend of local ingredients, such as burdock root tempura and tamari-kombu cured salmon or sake-steamed Asari clams with squid-ink pasta. **Known for:** Japanese whiskey and specialty sakes; donburi (rice-bowl dishes) and small plates; cured salads. *Average main: $20 ✉ 1830 4th St., 4th Street ☎ 510/845–8100 ⊕ iyasare-berkeley.com ⊙ Closed Sun. and Mon.*

La Marcha Tapas Bar

$$ | SPANISH | Delectable samplings of Spanish cuisine and a lively setting with expanded outdoor seating keep this tapas bar brimming with energy amid savory smells of seafood dishes and small plates of peel-and-eat prawns, wild

Famed Berkeley restaurant Chez Panisse focuses on seasonal local ingredients.

boar meatballs, or goat cheese–stuffed *piquillos rellenos.* The bar's passion for Spanish cuisine and culture is evident in the wines, the Mediterranean flavors, and the cozy setting. **Known for:** paella varieties; happy hour specials; churros con chocolate. *Average main: $18* *2026 San Pablo Ave., Downtown* *510/647–9525* *www.lamarchaberkeley.com.*

★ La Note

$$ | **FRENCH** | A charming taste of Provence in a 19th-century locale with stone floors, country tables, and a seasonal flowering patio, La Note serves rustic French food that is as thoughtfully prepared as the space is lovely. Enjoy breakfast and brunch outdoors with fresh, crusty breads and pastries, eggs Lucas with house-roasted tomatoes, and lemon gingerbread pancakes, or romantic dinners including mussels *mouclade,* ratatouille, and fondue. **Known for:** rustic sandwiches; house-made Merguez sausage; brioche pain perdu. *Average main: $20* *2377 Shattuck Ave., Downtown* *Between Channing Way and Durant Ave.* *510/843–1525* *www.lanoterestaurant.com* *No dinner Sun.–Wed.*

Rivoli

$$$ | **MODERN AMERICAN** | Italian-inspired dishes using fresh California ingredients star on a menu that changes regularly. Inventive offerings are served in a Zen-like modern dining room with captivating views of the lovely back garden. **Known for:** line-caught fish and sustainably sourced meats; curated wine list and specialty cocktails; thoughtfully combined ingredients. *Average main: $30* *1539 Solano Ave., at Neilson St., North Berkeley* *510/526–2542* *www.rivolirestaurant.com* *Closed Mon. and Tues. No lunch.*

★ Saul's

$ | **AMERICAN** | **FAMILY** | High ceilings and red-leather booths add to the friendly, retro atmosphere of Saul's deli, a Berkeley institution that is well known for its house-made celery tonic sodas and enormous sandwiches made with Acme bread. Locals swear by the pastrami Reubens, stuffed-cabbage rolls, and challah French toast. **Known for:** hand-rolled organic bagels; chicken schnitzel; corned beef brisket. *Average main: $14 1475 Shattuck Ave., near Vine St., North Berkeley 510/848–3354 www.saulsdeli.com.*

 Coffee and Quick Bites

★ 1951 Coffee Company

$ | **CAFÉ** | Taking its name from the 1951 Refugee Convention at which the United Nations first set guidelines for refugee protections, 1951 Coffee Company is a nonprofit coffee shop inspired and powered by refugees. In addition to crafting high-caliber coffee drinks and dishing out local pastries and savory bites, the colorful café also serves as an inspiring advocacy space and barista training center for refugees. Just three blocks south of campus, this community hub is a favorite meetup spot for locals and students alike. **Known for:** hand-roasted blends; Third Culture Bakery mochi doughnuts and muffins; matcha lattes. *Average main: $8 2410 Channing Way, at Dana St., Downtown 510/280–6171 www.1951coffee.com No dinner.*

 Hotels

For inexpensive lodging, investigate University Avenue, west of campus. The area can be noisy, congested, and somewhat dilapidated, but it does include a few decent motels and chain properties. All Berkeley lodgings are strictly mid-range.

Aiden by Best Western @ Berkeley

$ | **HOTEL** | One of Berkeley's newest hotels, the Aiden is the first of Best Western's boutique lines to open in California; within a mile of campus and the heart of downtown, it celebrates the culture of Berkeley with posters and wall art that showcase the campus life and spirit the town is known for. **Pros:** private parking; rooftop terrace with firepits and San Francisco Bay views; free bikes. **Cons:** no pets; no capacity for cribs or extra beds; congested area. *Rooms from: $189 1499 University Ave., Downtown 800/528–1234 toll-free www.bestwestern.com 39 rooms No meals.*

The Bancroft Hotel

$$ | **HOTEL** | This eco-friendly boutique hotel—across from the U.C. campus—is quaint, charming, and completely green. **Pros:** closest hotel in Berkeley to U.C. campus; friendly staff; many rooms have good views. **Cons:** some rooms are quite small; despite renovation, the building shows its age with thin walls; no elevator. *Rooms from: $230 2680 Bancroft Way, Downtown 510/549–1000, 800/549–1002 bancrofthotel.com 22 rooms Free breakfast.*

★ Berkeley City Club

$$ | **HOTEL** | Moorish design and Gothic architecture join with modern amenities at this historic locale steps from the campus, arts venues, and eateries. **Pros:** art gallery and courtyard seating; laundry facilities; on-site salon and skin care. **Cons:** no nonservice pets allowed; limited, fee-only parking; no televisions in rooms. *Rooms from: $245 2315 Durant Ave., Downtown www.berkeleycityclub.com 38 rooms Free breakfast.*

The Graduate Berkeley

$ | **HOTEL** | Fresh, colorful design and Bohemian flair set the tone at this hotel in one of Berkeley's registered historic places, just steps from campus and downtown eating, shopping, and entertainment. **Pros:** convenient location; pet-friendly; complimentary bikes. **Cons:** rooms can be noisy; rooms can be small; fee parking only. *Rooms from: $159 2600 Durant Ave., Downtown 510/845–8981 www.graduatehotels.com/berkeley 144 rooms No meals.*

★ **Hotel Shattuck Plaza**
$ | **HOTEL** | This historic boutique hotel sits amid Berkeley's downtown arts district, just steps from the U.C. campus and a short walk from North Berkeley's best bites. **Pros:** central location near public transit; special date night and B&B packages; modern facilities. **Cons:** public and street parking only; limited on-site fitness center; street-facing rooms may be noisy. *Rooms from: $173* ✉ *2086 Allston Way, at Shattuck Ave., Downtown* ☎ *510/845–7300* *www.hotelshattuck-plaza.com* *199 rooms* *No meals.*

Residence Inn by Marriott Berkeley
$$$ | **HOTEL** | **FAMILY** | One of Berkeley's newest hotels (planned opening is September 2021), in the heart of the city's arts and cultural district, this Residence Inn reflects the community's dedication to green living, as evident in its Gold LEED certification, use of recycled materials, organic design, and vibrant art that celebrates the city and campus life. **Pros:** views from bar and terrace on 12th floor; steps from campus, arts, fine dining, and sights; state-of-the-art technology. **Cons:** no swimming pool; no free parking; traffic gets very congested in the area. *Rooms from: $301* ✉ *2121 Center St., Downtown* ☎ *510/982–2100* *www.marriott.com* *331 suites* *Free breakfast.*

Nightlife

★ **The Freight & Salvage Coffeehouse**
MUSIC CLUBS | Since 1968, the Freight has been a venue for some of the world's finest practitioners of folk, jazz, gospel, blues, world-beat, bluegrass, and storytelling. The nonprofit organization grew from an 87-seat coffee house to a thriving, 500-seat venue in the heart of Berkeley's Arts District. Many tickets cost less than $30. ✉ *2020 Addison St., between Shattuck Ave. and Milvia St., Downtown* ☎ *510/644–2020* *thefreight.org.*

★ **Tupper & Reed**
BARS/PUBS | Housed in the former music shop of John C. Tupper and Lawrence Reed, this music-inspired cocktail haven presents a symphony of carefully crafted libations, which are mixed with live music performed by local musicians. The historic 1925 building features a balcony bar, cozy nooks, antique fixtures, a pool table, and romantic fireplaces. ✉ *2271 Shattuck Ave., at Kitteredge St., Downtown* ☎ *510/859–4472* *www.tupperandreed.com.*

Performing Arts

Aurora Theatre Company
ARTS CENTERS | Known for critically acclaimed productions like David Mamet's *American Buffalo* and Toni Morrison's *The Bluest Eye*, the Aurora is at the heart of Berkeley storytelling and community engagement. The theater's Alafi Auditorium seats 150 on three sides of the stage for premium viewing, and the smaller Harry's UpStage offers a more intimate experience for 49. New play development and storytelling continue beyond the stage with collaborative audio dramas broadcast weekly. ✉ *2081 Addison St., Downtown* ☎ *510/843–4822* *www.auroratheatre.org.*

Berkeley Repertory Theatre
THEATER | One of the region's most highly respected and innovative repertory theaters, Berkeley Rep performs the work of classic and contemporary playwrights. Well-known pieces mix with world premieres and edgier fare, like steamy Afro-jazz musicals. The theater's complex, which includes the 400-seat Peet's Theatre and the 600-seat Roda Theatre, is in the heart of downtown Berkeley's arts district, near BART's Downtown Berkeley station. ✉ *2025 Addison St., near Shattuck Ave., Downtown* ☎ *510/647–2949* *www.berkeleyrep.org.*

★ California Jazz Conservatory

MUSIC | What started as a music education program in 1977, offering classes with the Bay Area's best jazz players, has become the area's top concert venue for the freshest sounds in jazz from around the world. Two 100-seat performance venues across the street from each other, Hardymon Hall (*2087 Addison St.*) and Rendon Hall (*2040 Addison St.*), offer intimate viewing of some of the world's most influential musicians. Classes and workshops continue to serve as the foundation of the conservatory, with regular, affordably priced weekend concerts and weekly performances for the public. ✉ *2087 Addison St., Downtown* ☎ *510/845–5373* 🌐 *cjc.edu.*

Cal Performances

ARTS CENTERS | Based out of U.C. Berkeley, this autumn and spring series runs from September/October through May/June. It features a varied bill of internationally acclaimed artists ranging from classical soloists to the latest jazz, world-music, theater, and dance ensembles. ✉ *101 Zellerbach Hall , Suite 4800, Downtown* ✣ *Dana St. and Bancroft Way* ☎ *510/642–9988* 🌐 *calperformances.org.*

The UC Theatre Taube Family Music Hall

MUSIC | One of Berkeley's oldest theaters opened its doors in 1917 as a first-run movie house with seating for 1,466 filmgoers. For years it served as a famous venue for foreign and domestic classics, closing in 2001. The theater's programming and ongoing renovation are now run by the nonprofit Berkeley Music Group, dedicated to bringing local, national, and international talent to Berkeley's arts district. Limited outdoor drinks and dining are available at the street bar, Out Front at the UC. ✉ *2036 University Ave., Downtown* ☎ *510/356–4000* 🌐 *theuctheatre.org.*

Shopping

★ ACCI Gallery

ART GALLERIES | The Arts & Crafts Coöperative, Inc., a collective of Berkeley artists and artisans, has been a stalwart gallery and retail store showcasing ceramics, textiles, paintings, photography, jewelry, and various media since 1959. Explore the amazing range of local talent in a well-lit historic space, and find truly one-of-a-kind gems to take home. ✉ *1652 Shattuck Ave., North Berkeley* ✣ *At Lincoln St.* ☎ *510/843–2527* 🌐 *www.accigallery.com.*

★ Amoeba Music

MUSIC STORES | Heaven for audiophiles and movie collectors, this legendary Berkeley favorite is *the* place to head for new and used CDs, vinyl, cassettes, VHS tapes, Blu-ray discs, and DVDs. The massive and ever-changing stock includes thousands of titles for all music tastes, as well as plenty of Amoeba merch. There are branches in San Francisco and Hollywood, but this is the original. ✉ *2455 Telegraph Ave., at Haste St., Downtown* ☎ *510/549–1125* 🌐 *www.amoeba.com.*

Hammerling Wines

WINE/SPIRITS | Offering a curated taste of Central Coast sparkling wines, winemaker Josh Hammerling sources his grapes from responsibly farmed vineyards with distinctive fruit. Old-world techniques are part of the practice for these wines made entirely by hand. Drop in on weekends for wines by the glass; it's first come, first served. ✉ *1350 5th St., 4th Street* ☎ *510/984–0340* 🌐 *www.hammerling-wines.co.*

★ Moe's Books

BOOKS/STATIONERY | The spirit of Moe—the creative, cantankerous, cigar-smoking late proprietor—lives on in this world-famous four-story house full of new and used books. Since its doors first opened in 1959, students and professors have flocked here to browse the large selection, which includes literary and cultural criticism, art titles, and literature in foreign languages. ✉ *2476 Telegraph Ave., near Haste St., Downtown* ☎ *510/849–2087* 🌐 *www.moesbooks.com.*

Oakland

East of Bay Bridge.

In contrast to San Francisco's buzz and beauty and Berkeley's storied counterculture, Oakland's allure lies in its amazing diversity. Here you can find a Nigerian clothing store, a Gothic revival skyscraper, a Buddhist meditation center, and a lively salsa club, all within the same block.

Oakland's multifaceted nature reflects its colorful and tumultuous history. Once a cluster of Mediterranean-style homes and gardens that served as a bedroom community for San Francisco, the town had a major rail terminal and port by the turn of the 20th century. Already a hub of manufacturing, Oakland became a center for shipbuilding and industry when the United States entered World War II. New jobs in the city's shipyards, railroads, and factories attracted thousands of laborers from across the country, including sharecroppers from the Deep South, Mexican Americans from the Southwest, and some of the nation's first female welders. Neighborhoods were imbued with a proud but gritty spirit, along with heightened racial tension. In the wake of the civil rights movement, racial pride gave rise to militant groups like the Black Panther Party, but they were little match for the economic hardships and racial tensions that plagued Oakland. In many neighborhoods the reality was widespread poverty and gang violence—subjects that dominated the songs of such Oakland-bred rappers as the late Tupac Shakur. The protests of the Occupy Oakland movement in 2011 and 2012 and the Black Lives Matter movement more recently illustrate just how much Oakland remains a mosaic of its past.

Oakland's affluent reside in the city's hillside homes and wooded enclaves like Claremont, Piedmont, and Montclair, which provide a warmer, more spacious alternative to San Francisco. A constant flow of newcomers ensures continued diversity, vitality, and growing pains. Neighborhoods to the west and south of the city center show signs of gentrification as the renovated downtown and vibrant arts scene continue to inject new life into the city. Even San Franciscans, often loath to cross the Bay Bridge, come to Uptown and Temescal for the nightlife, arts, and restaurants.

Everyday life here revolves around the neighborhood. In some areas, such as Piedmont and Rockridge, you'd swear you were in Berkeley or San Francisco's Noe Valley. Along Telegraph Avenue just south of 51st Street, Temescal is littered with hipsters and pulsing with creative culinary and design energy. These are perfect places for browsing, eating, or relaxing between sightseeing trips to Oakland's architectural gems, rejuvenated waterfront, and numerous green spaces.

GETTING HERE AND AROUND

Driving from San Francisco, take Interstate 80 East across the Bay Bridge, then take Interstate 580 East to the Grand Avenue exit for Lake Merritt. To reach downtown and the waterfront, take Interstate 980 West from Interstate 580 East and exit at 12th Street; exit at 18th Street for Uptown. For Temescal, take Interstate 580 East to Highway 24 and exit at 51st Street.

By BART, use the Lake Merritt Station for the Oakland Museum and southern Lake Merritt; the Oakland City Center–12th Street Station for downtown, Chinatown, and Old Oakland; and the 19th Street Station for Uptown, the Paramount Theatre, and the north side of Lake Merritt.

By bus, take the AC Transit's C and P lines to get to Piedmont in Oakland. The

O bus stops at the edge of Chinatown near downtown Oakland.

Oakland's Jack London Square is an easy hop on the ferry from San Francisco. Those without cars can take advantage of the free Broadway Shuttle, which runs from Jack London Square to Grand Avenue weekdays, with continued service to 27th Street weeknights from 7 to 10 pm. There's no weekend service.

Be aware of how quickly neighborhoods can change. Walking is generally safe downtown and in the Piedmont and Rockridge areas, but be mindful when walking west and southeast of downtown, especially at night.

CONTACTS Broadway Shuttle. ⊕ *www.oaklandca.gov*.

ESSENTIALS

VISITOR INFORMATION Visit Oakland. ✉ *481 Water St., near Broadway, Jack London Square* ☎ *510/839–9000* ⊕ *www.visitoakland.com*.

Sights

★ Lake Merritt

NATURE PRESERVE | In the center of Oakland just east of downtown, this tidal lagoon with its unique habitat for more than 100 bird species became the country's first wildlife refuge in 1870. Today the 3.1-mile path around the lake is also a free refuge for walkers, bikers, joggers, and nature lovers. **Lakeside Park** has **Children's Fairyland** (✉ *699 Bellevue*) and the **Rotary Nature Center** (✉ *600 Bellevue*), where monthly bird walks commence every fourth Wednesday. For views from the water, the **Lake Merritt Boating Center** (✉ *568 Bellevue*) rents kayaks and rowboats (⊕ *www.lakemerritt.org*). Venetian gondolas cruise from the Oakland Boathouse (🎫 *Basic tours start at $75 for 45 mins* ⊕ *gondolaservizio.com*), where visitors can also indulge in local artisanal chocolates.

On the lake's south side, the **Camron-Stanford House** (✉ *1418 Lakeside Dr.*) is the last of the grand Victorians that once dominated the area; it's open Sundays for tours. Nearby, bold **Oakland mural art** offers a more modern feast for the eyes (✉ *Between Madison and Webster Sts. and 7th and 11th Sts.*).

The lake's necklace of lights adds allure for diners heading to the art-deco **Terrace Room** (✉ *1800 Madison St.*) or **Lake Chalet** (✉ *1520 Lakeside Dr.*), as well as to a host of tasty options along Grand Avenue, from Ethiopian cuisine at **Enssaro** (✉ *357a*) and Korean BBQ at **Jong Ga House** (✉ *372*) to comfort gourmet at **Grand Lake Kitchen** (✉ *576*). ✉ *Lake Merritt* 🎫 *Free*.

★ Oakland Museum of California (*OMCA*)

MUSEUM | **FAMILY** | Designed by Kevin Roche, this museum is one of the country's quintessential examples of mid-century modern architecture and home to a capacious collection of nearly 2 million objects in three distinct galleries celebrating California's history, natural sciences, and art. Listen to native species and environmental soundscapes in the Library of Natural Sounds and engage in stories of the state's past and future, from Ohlone basket making to emerging technologies and current events. Not to be missed are the photographs from Dorothea Lange's personal archive and a worthy collection of Bay Area figurative painters, including David Park and Joan Brown. The museum is also home to Oakland's freshest culinary destination—star chef Tanya Holland's Town Fare café. Experience vegetable-centric California soul food raised to an art form. **■ TIP→ On Friday evening, the museum bustles with live music, food trucks, and after-hours gallery access.** ✉ *1000 Oak St., at 10th St., Downtown* ☎ *510/318–8400, 888/625–6873 toll-free* ⊕ *museumca.org* 🎫 *$16, free 1st Sun. of month* ⏲ *Closed Mon.–Thurs.*

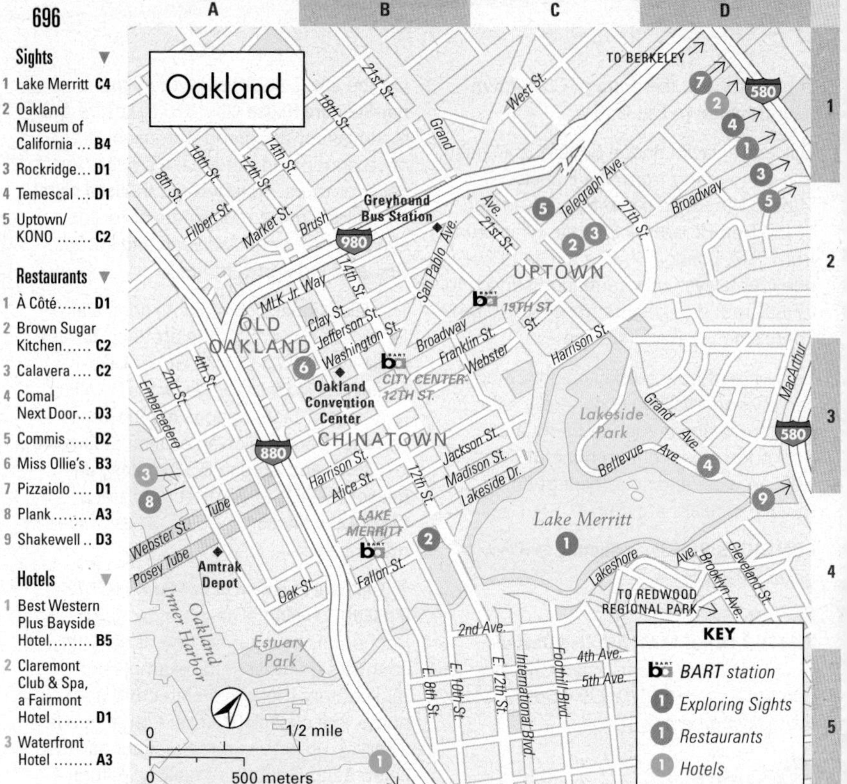

Rockridge

NEIGHBORHOOD | **FAMILY** | One of Oakland's most desirable places to live is this fashionable, upscale neighborhood. Explore the tree-lined streets that radiate out from **College Avenue,** just north and south of the Rockridge BART station for a look at California Craftsman bungalows at their finest. By day, College Avenue between Broadway and Alcatraz Avenue is crowded with shoppers buying fresh flowers, used books, and clothing; by night, the same folks are back for handcrafted meals, artisanal wines, and locally brewed ales. With its specialty food shops and quick bites to go, **Market Hall,** an airy European-style marketplace at Shafter Avenue, is a hub of culinary activity. ✉ *Market Hall, 5655 College Ave., between Alcatraz Ave. and Broadway, Rockridge* 🌐 *www.rockridgedistrict.com.*

★ Temescal

NEIGHBORHOOD | Centering on Telegraph Avenue between 40th and 51st Streets, Temescal (the Aztec term for "sweat house") is a low-pretension, moneyed-hipster hood with young families and middle-aged folks thrown into the mix. Newly redesigned protected bike lanes, bus islands, and a pedestrian plaza add to the vibrancy of this neighborhood. A critical mass of excellent eateries draws diners from around the Bay Area; there are newer favorites like **Co Nam Noodle Bar** (✉ *3936 Telegraph Ave.*) and **Smokin Woods BBQ** (✉ *4307 Telegraph Ave.*), as well as standbys like **Pizzaiolo** (✉ *5008 Telegraph Ave.*) and **Rose's Taproom** (✉ *4930 Telegraph Ave.*). Old-time dive bars and smog-check stations share space with public art installations of murals, sculptures, and mosaic trash cans.

Temescal Alley (✉ *Off 49th St.*), a tucked-away lane of tiny storefronts, crackles with the creative energy of local makers. Find botanical wonders at **Crimson Horticultural Rarities** (✉ *No. 470*) or get an old-fashioned straight-edge shave at **Temescal Alley Barbershop** (✉ *No. 470B*). Don't miss grabbing a sweet scoop at **Curbside Creamery** (✉ *No. 482*). ✉ *Temescal* ✣ *Telegraph Ave. between 40th and 51st Sts.* 🌐 *www.temescaldistrict.org.*

Uptown/KONO

NEIGHBORHOOD | Uptown and KONO (Koreatown/Northgate) is where nightlife and cutting-edge art merge. Dozens of galleries cluster around Telegraph Avenue and north of Grand Avenue into KONO, exhibiting everything from photography and installations to glasswork and fiber arts. The first Friday of each month, thousands of people descend for **Art Murmur** (🌐 *www.oaklandartmurmer.org*), a late-night gallery event that has expanded into **First Fridays** (🌐 *www.oaklandfirstfridays.org*), a festival of food trucks, street vendors, and live music along Telegraph Avenue.

Restaurants with a distinctly urban vibe make Uptown/KONO a dining destination every night of the week. Favorites include eclectic Japanese-inspired fare at **Hopscotch** (✉ *1915 San Pablo Ave.*), ramen and *izakaya* offerings at **Shinmai** (✉ *1825–3 San Pablo Ave.*), Oaxacan cuisine at **Agave Uptown** (✉ *2135 Franklin St.*), and soul food with a French-inspired twist at **Brown Sugar Kitchen** (✉ *2295 Broadway*), to name just a few.

Toss in the bevy of bars and there's plenty within walking distance to keep you busy all evening, such as **Drake's Dealership** (✉ *2325 Broadway*), with its spacious, hipster-friendly beer garden, and **Somar** (✉ *1727 Telegraph Ave.*), a bar, music lounge, and art gallery in one. ✉ *Uptown* ✣ *Telegraph Ave. and Broadway from 14th to 27th Sts.*

Restaurants

À Côté

$$ | **MEDITERRANEAN** | This Mediterranean hot spot is all about seasonal small plates, cozy tables, family-style eating, and excellent wine. Heavy wooden tables, intimate dining nooks, natural light, and a heated patio make this an ideal destination for couples, families, and the after-work crowd. **Known for:** Pernod mussels; Wed. and Thurs. happy hour specials; global and regional wine list. $ *Average main: $23* ✉ *5478 College Ave., at Taft Ave., Rockridge* ☎ *510/655–6469* 🌐 *www.acoterestaurant.com* ⏲ *No lunch.*

★ **Brown Sugar Kitchen**

$$ | **SOUTHERN** | **FAMILY** | Distinguished chef Tanya Holland dishes up soul food flavored by her African American heritage and French culinary training. This bright, airy, modern Uptown venue is a beloved and bustling community-favorite dining spot, serving local, organic ingredients and sweet and savory dishes—from sweet potato pie to Creole meat loaf—paired with house cocktails and sumptuous wines. **Known for:** fried chicken and cornmeal waffles; bacon-cheddar-scallion biscuits; catfish and oyster po'boys. $ *Average main: $17* ✉ *2295 Broadway, Uptown* ☎ *510/839–7685* 🌐 *www.brownsugarkitchen.com* ⏲ *Closed Mon. No dinner Tues. and Wed.*

Calavera

$$ | **MODERN MEXICAN** | **FAMILY** | This Oaxacan-inspired hot spot offers inventive and elevated plates in an industrial-chic space with lofty ceilings, warm wooden tables, exposed brick walls, and heated outdoor dining. Innovative cocktails like the salt-air margarita come from a beautiful bar with a library of more than 100 agaves. **Known for:** fresh ceviches with shrimp or mushrooms; family-style, wood-fired chicken and whole fish; carnitas tacos in nixtamal heirloom-corn tortillas. $ *Average main: $22* ✉ *2337 Broadway, at 24th*

St., Uptown ☎ *510/338–3273* 🌐 *calaveraoakland.com* ⏲ *Closed Mon.*

Comal Next Door

$ | **MEXICAN** | A sister restaurant to Berkeley's creative, Oaxacan-inspired Comal, this modern Mexican taqueria centers on mouthwatering, quick-service dishes with freshly grilled ingredients and house-made tortillas, sauces, and salsas. It's easy to see why the lines can be long, thanks to unique bottled mezcal libations and takeaway favorites like *cenas televisiónes*—frozen TV dinners of chicken enchiladas with mole or *rajas* (sliced poblano peppers) and zucchini tamales. **Known for:** burrito bowls and tortas; bottled cocktails and house-made frescas; buttermilk fried chicken and chipotle aioli. [$] *Average main: $11* ✉ *550 Grand Ave., Grand Lake* ☎ *510/422–6625* 🌐 *comalnextdoor.com.*

★ Commis

$$$$ | **AMERICAN** | A slender, unassuming storefront houses the first East Bay restaurant with a Michelin star (two of them, in fact). The room is minimalist and polished: nothing distracts from the artistry of chef James Syhabout, who creates a multicourse prix-fixe dining experience based on the season and his distinctive vision of modern and classic creations. **Known for:** inventive tasting menu; dizzying variety of wines from around the world; reservations needed well in advance. [$] *Average main: $73* ✉ *3859 Piedmont Ave., at Rio Vista Ave., Piedmont* ☎ *510/653–3902* 🌐 *commisrestaurant.com* ⏲ *Closed Sun. and Mon. No lunch.*

Miss Ollie's

$ | **CARIBBEAN** | **FAMILY** | Centrally located in the city's historic district, Miss Ollie's is a colorful, community-minded Afro-Caribbean gem in Swan's Market that packs in mouthwatering flavors. Lunch specialties include the likes of Bajan fried chicken or eggplant sandwiches and Creole salads with persimmon and jicama, while heartier dishes are jerk hen with coconut rice, spicy goat curry, and split-pea and okra fritters. **Known for:** skillet-fried chicken and collard greens; Caribbean meat and vegetable patties; pea and pumpkin soups. [$] *Average main: $16* ✉ *901 Washington St., Old Oakland* ☎ *510/285–6188* 🌐 *www.realmissolliesoakland.com* ⏲ *Closed Tues.*

Pizzaiolo

$$ | **ITALIAN** | **FAMILY** | Chez Panisse alum Charlie Hallowell helms the kitchen of this rustic-chic Oakland institution. Diners of all ages perch on wooden chairs with red-leather backs and nosh on farm-to-table Italian fare from a daily-changing menu. **Known for:** seasonal wood-fired pizza; daily house-made breads; California-Italian entrées. [$] *Average main: $21* ✉ *5008 Telegraph Ave., at 51st St., Temescal* ☎ *510/652–4888* 🌐 *www.pizzaiolooakland.com* ⏲ *No lunch. Closed Mon. and Tues.*

Plank

$$ | **AMERICAN** | **FAMILY** | Food and entertainment come together in an expansive indoor-outdoor space with a waterfront view. Sip from more than 50 handcrafted local beers while playing boccie in the beer garden, lunch on Cuban sandwiches and Cajun mahi tacos during a bowling or billiards match, or try your hand at the arcade before biting into baby back ribs. **Known for:** fun outdoor space with firepits; generous portions; burgers and pizzas with local ingredients. [$] *Average main: $17* ✉ *98 Broadway, Jack London Square* ☎ *510/817–0980* 🌐 *www.plankoakland.com.*

★ Shakewell

$$ | **MEDITERRANEAN** | Two *Top Chef* vets opened this stylish Lakeshore restaurant, which serves creative and memorable Mediterranean small plates in a lively setting that features an open kitchen, wood-fired oven, communal tables, and snug seating. As the name implies, well-crafted cocktails are shaken (or stirred) and poured with panache. **Known for:** wood-oven paella; Spanish and

Mediterranean small plates; vegetarian options. $ *Average main: $20* ✉ *3407 Lakeshore Ave., near Mandana Blvd., Grand Lake* ☎ *510/251–0329* 🌐 *www.shakewelloakland.com* ⊗ *Closed Mon.*

Hotels

Best Western Plus Bayside Hotel
$ | **HOTEL** | Sandwiched between the serene Oakland Estuary and an eight-lane freeway, this all-suites property has handsome accommodations with balconies or patios, many overlooking the water. **Pros:** attractive, budget-conscious choice; estuary walkways and views; easy access to and from airport, Jack London Square, and downtown. **Cons:** few shops or restaurants in walking distance; freeway-side rooms can be noisy; some rooms have no views or patios/balconies. $ *Rooms from: $189* ✉ *1717 Embarcadero, off I–880, at 16th St. exit, San Antonio* ☎ *510/356–2450* 🌐 *www.baysidehoteloakland.com* *81 rooms* *Free breakfast.*

★ **Claremont Club & Spa, a Fairmont Hotel**
$$$ | **HOTEL** | **FAMILY** | Straddling the Oakland–Berkeley border, this amenities-rich property dating from 1915 beckons like a gleaming white castle in the hills. **Pros:** amazing spa and outdoor fitness pavilion; daily events and special programs for children; solid business amenities. **Cons:** parking is pricey; mandatory facilities charge; remote from shops and restaurants. $ *Rooms from: $339* ✉ *41 Tunnel Rd., at Ashby and Domingo Aves., Claremont* ☎ *510/843–3000, 800/257–7544 reservations* 🌐 *www.fairmont.com/claremont-berkeley* *276 rooms* *No meals.*

★ **Waterfront Hotel**
$$ | **HOTEL** | **FAMILY** | Thoroughly modern and pleasantly appointed, this JdV by Hyatt hotel sits among the many high-caliber restaurants of Jack London Square and is both a favorite place for locals' family members and a sweet spot for business travelers with its proximity to the square and downtown. **Pros:** outdoor dining in Jack London Square; lovely views, including some water views; free shuttle service to downtown and easy access to SF ferry. **Cons:** passing trains can be noisy on the city side; parking is pricey; limited amenities. $ *Rooms from: $200* ✉ *10 Washington St., Jack London Square* ☎ *510/836–3800 front desk, 888/842–5333 reservations* 🌐 *www.jdvhotels.com* *145 rooms* *No meals.*

Nightlife

BARS

★ **Heinold's First and Last Chance Saloon**
BARS/PUBS | Arguably California's longest continuously active saloon since it opened in 1884, this watering hole, built from the hull of a flat-bottomed stern-wheeler, is the famous place where young Jack London got his start as a writer. Historic photos, artifacts, and turn-of-the-20th-century curios hang from the crooked walls and ceilings, which have been atilt since the 1906 earthquake. Get a peek at the slanted bar, where beers on tap and bottomless stories of Oakland history abound. If the proprietor is in, you'll be in for a treat: a trip through time into the Oakland of old is well worth a visit. ✉ *48 Webster St., Jack London Square* ☎ *510/839–6761* 🌐 *www.heinoldsfirstandlastchance.com.*

Make Westing
BARS/PUBS | Named for a short story by Oakland native Jack London, this sprawling industrial-chic space is always abuzz with hipsters playing bocce, the postwork crowd sipping old-fashioneds, or pretheater couples passing Mason jars of unexpected delectables like Cajun shrimp boil. The patio's your best bet for a conversation on a busy evening. ✉ *1741 Telegraph Ave., at 18th St., Uptown* ☎ *510/251–1400* 🌐 *makewesting.com.*

BREWPUBS AND BEER GARDENS

★ Brotzeit Lokal

BREWPUBS/BEER GARDENS | Wonderfully situated, this tucked-away German *biergarten* is in Oakland's Brooklyn Basin along the waterfront Bay Trail, with lovely views of the marina, estuary, and Coast Guard Island. Known for its select German beers and a delectable offering of Bavarian dishes, including house-made sausage, schnitzel, sauerkraut, and sandwiches, this family-friendly spot is especially popular on nice days. ✉ *1000 Embarcadero, at 10th Ave., Lake Merritt* ☎ *510/ 645–1905* 🌐 *brotzeitbiergarten.com.*

Buck Wild Brewing

BREWPUBS/BEER GARDENS | Oakland's Jack London District is home to a luxurious taproom that is California's first 100%-gluten-free brewery, specializing in craft beers made without rye, wheat, or barley. The brewery has also partnered with San Francisco's Kitava, which provides a menu with fare (such as fish and chips, loaded fries, Cuban bowls, and small bites) completely free of inflammatory ingredients. ✉ *401 Jackson St., at 4th St., Jack London Square* ☎ *510/350–7938* 🌐 *www.buckwildbrew.com.*

Federation Brewing Company

BREWPUBS/BEER GARDENS | Part of Oakland's Ale Trail, the brewery has a convivial tasting room in the Jack London District with plenty of games for extended sipping of their pilsners, saisons, sours, and hoppy IPAs. Wednesday happy hours and regular rotating comedy and music entertainment usually pack the place, so it's good to check ahead and reserve advance tickets. ✉ *420 3rd St., Jack London Square* ☎ *510/496–4228* 🌐 *www.federationbrewing.com.*

Line 51 Brewing—The Terminal Taproom

BREWPUBS/BEER GARDENS | The bright, airy, 7,500-square-foot brewery and taproom is in many ways a tribute to its early history, when the brewers hauled their kegs on public transit line 51 to their warehouse. Now, Oakland Ale Trail explorers can enjoy freshly tapped beer from a vintage 1971 AC transit bus that serves as a refrigeration unit for their brews. Fermentation tanks are on full display: the owners are passionate about their Red Death ale, IPAs, Short Dog ale, and porters. ✉ *303 Castro St., at 3rd St., Jack London Square* ☎ *510/985–4181* 🌐 *www.line51beer.com.*

Original Pattern Brewing

BREWPUBS/BEER GARDENS | The love for beer of all varieties is evident in the selection of award-winners at this employee-owned brewery in a brick warehouse space in the Jack London District. The list of IPAs, lagers, sours, fruit-infused beers, Belgian-style ales, and porters is ever changing as the latest brews are tapped. Food pop-ups from Good to Eat Dumplings make outdoor dining possible with dumplings, wontons, and noodles. ✉ *292 4th St., Jack London Square* ☎ *510/844–4833* 🌐 *www.originalpatternbeer.com.*

★ The Trappist

BREWPUBS/BEER GARDENS | Brick walls, dark wood, soft lighting, and a hum of conversation set a warm and mellow tone inside this Old Oakland Victorian space that has been renovated to resemble a traditional Belgian pub. The setting (which includes two bars and a back patio) is a draw, but the real stars are the artisanal beers—more than 100 Belgian, Dutch, and North American brews. Experience guided tastings and curated offerings by passionate staff well versed in the styles of Trappist and European craft brewing. ✉ *460 8th St., near Broadway, Old Oakland* ☎ *510/238–8900* 🌐 *www.thetrappist.com.*

CAFÉS

Mua

CAFES—NIGHTLIFE | Cuisine, cocktails, and culture—husband-and-wife-owned Mua puts it all together in an airy converted garage decked out with works by owner/artist Hi-Suk Dong as well as pieces from his personal collection. The chefs serve up beautifully crafted dishes like blackened catfish and garlic prawns; the bartenders shake up elegant cocktails; and a lively crowd enjoys cultural offerings that include community sketch nights, art shows, and weekend DJ music. This is the perfect stop for any foodie who supports the arts. ✉ *2442a Webster St., between 24th and 26th Sts., Uptown* ☎ *510/238–1100* 🌐 *muaoakland.com.*

ROCK, POP, HIP-HOP, FOLK, AND BLUES CLUBS

Fox Theater

MUSIC CLUBS | This renovated 1928 theater, Oakland's favorite performance venue, is a remarkable feat of Mediterranean Moorish architecture and has seen the likes of Willie Nelson, the Magnetic Fields, Rebelution, and B.B. King, to name a few. The venue boasts good sight lines, a state-of-the-art sound system, brilliant acoustics, and a restaurant and bar, among other amenities. ✉ *1807 Telegraph Ave., between 18th and 19th Sts., Uptown* ☎ *510/302–2250* 🌐 *thefoxoakland.com.*

★ Yoshi's

MUSIC CLUBS | Opened in 1972 as a sushi bar, Yoshi's has evolved into one of the area's best jazz and live music venues. The full Yoshi's experience includes traditional Japanese and Asian fusion cuisine in the adjacent restaurant. ✉ *510 Embarcadero W, between Washington and Clay Sts., Jack London Square* ☎ *510/238–9200* 🌐 *yoshis.com.*

Performing Arts

Paramount Theatre

ARTS CENTERS | A glorious art-deco specimen, the Paramount operates as a venue for concerts and performances of all kinds, from the Oakland Ballet and Oakland Symphony to Jerry Seinfeld and Elvis Costello. The popular classic movie nights start off with a 30-minute Wurlitzer concert. **■ TIP→ Docent-led tours ($5), offered the first and third Saturday of the month, are fun and informative.** ✉ *2025 Broadway, at 20th St., Uptown* ☎ *510/465–6400* 🌐 *paramounttheatre.com.*

Shopping

Bay-Made

GIFTS/SOUVENIRS | Owned and operated by women artists, this gift shop showcases the delightful works of more than 120 Oakland artisans and makers. Browse offerings such as handcrafted paper and print art, collage art, chocolate, waxworks, jewelry, ceramics, herbs and oils, and quality art and printing supplies. A rotating gallery wall features the latest works from local artists. ✉ *3295 Lakeshore Ave., Grand Lake* ☎ *510/520–4600* 🌐 *www.bay-made.com.*

Maison d'Etre

GIFTS/SOUVENIRS | Close to the Rockridge BART station, this store epitomizes the Rockridge neighborhood's funky-chic shopping scene. Look for high-end housewares along with impulse buys like whimsical watches, imported fruit-tea blends, one-of-a-kind gifts, and funky slippers. ✉ *5640 College Ave., at Keith Ave., Rockridge* ☎ *510/658–2801* 🌐 *www.maisondetre.com.*

★ Oaklandish

CLOTHING | The ultimate place for Oakland swag started in 2000 as a public art project of local pride and has become a celebrated brand around the bay, with clothing and accessories for men, women, and kids. A portion of the proceeds from hip Oaklandish-brand T-shirts and accessories supports grassroots nonprofits committed to bettering the local community. It's good-looking stuff for a good cause. ✉ *1444 Broadway, near 15th St., Uptown* ☎ *510/251–9500* 🌐 *oaklandish.com.*

Oakland Athletics

BASEBALL/SOFTBALL | FAMILY | Baseball's Oakland Athletics, also called the Oakland A's, has a loyal following among locals in Oakland and enjoys a fierce rivalry with the San Francisco Giants just across the bay. The team hopes to move from its RingCentral Coliseum stadium to a proposed new waterfront ballpark at Jack London Square, perhaps in 2023, but Major League Baseball is also allowing the team to consider relocating to another city; stay tuned. ✉ *RingCentral Coliseum, 7000 Coliseum Way* ☎ *877/493–2255 box office* 🌐 *mlb.com/athletics.*

The Marin Headlands

Due west of the Golden Gate Bridge's northern end.

The term "Golden Gate" has become synonymous with the world-famous bridge, but it was first given to the narrow waterway that connects the Pacific and San Francisco Bay. To the north of the Golden Gate Strait lie the Marin Headlands, part of the Golden Gate National Recreation Area (GGNRA), with some of the area's most dramatic scenery.

GETTING HERE AND AROUND

Driving from San Francisco, head north on U.S. 101. Just after you cross the Golden Gate Bridge, take Exit 442 for Alexander Avenue. Keep left at the fork and follow signs for San Francisco/U.S. 101 South. Go through the tunnel under the freeway, and turn right up the hill. On weekends and major holidays, Muni bus 76X runs hourly from Sutter and Sansome Streets in the city to the Marin Headlands Visitor Center.

Marin Headlands

NATIONAL/STATE PARK | FAMILY | The stunning headlands stretch from the Golden Gate Bridge to Muir Beach, drawing photographers who perch on the southern heights for spectacular shots of the city and bridge. Equally remarkable are the views north along the coast and out to the ocean, where the Farallon Islands are visible on clear days. Hawk Hill (accessed from Conzelman Rd.) has a trail with panoramic views and is a great place to watch the fall raptor migration; it's also home to the mission blue butterfly.

The headlands' strategic position at the mouth of San Francisco Bay made them a logical site for military installations from 1890 through the Cold War. Today you can explore the crumbling concrete batteries where naval guns once protected the area. Main attractions are centered on Forts Barry and Cronkhite, which are separated by Rodeo Lagoon and Rodeo Beach, a dark stretch of sand that attracts sandcastle builders and dog owners.

The visitor center is a worthwhile stop for its exhibits on the area's history and ecology, and kids enjoy the educational installations and small play area inside. You can pick up guides to historic sites and wildlife and get information about programming and guided walks. ✉ *Golden Gate National Recreation Area, Visitor Center, Fort Barry Chapel, Fort Barry, Bldg. 948, Field and Bunker Rds., Sausalito* ☎ *415/331–1540* 🌐 *www.nps.gov/goga* 🎫 *Free* 🕒 *Closed Tues.*

Sausalito

2 miles north of Golden Gate Bridge.

Bougainvillea-covered hillsides and an expansive yacht harbor give Sausalito the feel of an Adriatic resort. The town sits on the northwestern edge of San Francisco Bay, where it's sheltered from the ocean by the Marin Headlands; the mostly mild weather here is perfect for strolling and outdoor dining. Nevertheless, morning fog and afternoon winds can roll over the hills without warning, funneling through the central part of Sausalito once known as Hurricane Gulch.

South of Bridgeway, which snakes between the bay and the hills, a waterside esplanade is lined with restaurants on piers that lure diners with good seafood and even better views. Stairs along the west side of Bridgeway and throughout town climb into wooded hillside neighborhoods filled with both rustic and opulent homes. Back on the northern portion of the shoreline, harbors shelter a community of more than 400 houseboats. As you amble along Bridgeway past shops and galleries, you'll notice the absence of basic services. Find them and more on Caledonia Street, which runs parallel to Bridgeway and inland a couple of blocks. While ferry-side shops flaunt kitschy souvenirs, smaller side streets and narrow alleyways offer eccentric jewelry and handmade crafts.

■ TIP→ The ferry is the best way to get to Sausalito from San Francisco; you get more romance (and less traffic) and disembark in the heart of downtown.

First occupied by the Coast Miwok tribe and later visited by Spanish explorers who called the area Saucito (Little Willow) for the trees growing along its streams, Sausalito was developed as a ranch in 1838 under the ownership of English mariner William Richardson. It served as a port for whaling ships during the 19th century and became a major terminus for transport by rail, ferry, and, eventually, car. By the mid-1800s, wealthy San Franciscans had made Sausalito their getaway across the bay and built lavish Victorian summer homes in the hills. Meanwhile, an influx of hardworking, fun-loving merchants and working-class folk populated the waterfront area, which grew thick with saloons, gambling dens, and bordellos. Bootleggers flourished during Prohibition, and shipyard workers swelled the town's population in the 1940s, at the height of World War II.

Sausalito developed its bohemian flair in the 1950s and '60s, when creative types, including artist Jean Varda, poet Shel Silverstein, and madam Sally Stanford, established an artists' colony and a houseboat community here (this is Otis Redding's "Dock of the Bay"). Both the spirit of the artists and the neighborhood of floating homes persist. For a close-up view of the quirky community, head north on Bridgeway, turn right on Gate Six Road, park where it dead-ends, and enter through the unlocked gates.

GETTING HERE AND AROUND

From San Francisco by car or bike, follow U.S. 101 North across the Golden Gate Bridge and take Exit 442 for Alexander Avenue, just past Vista Point; continue down the winding hill toward the water to where the road becomes Bridgeway. Golden Gate Transit buses will drop you off in downtown Sausalito, and the ferries dock downtown as well. The center of town is flat, with plenty of sidewalks and bay views. It's a pleasure and a must to explore on foot.

ESSENTIALS

VISITOR INFORMATION Sausalito Chamber of Commerce. ✉ *1913 Bridgeway* ☎ *415/331–7262* 🌐 *www.sausalito.org.*

Sights

The Marine Mammal Center

COLLEGE | FAMILY | This hospital for distressed, sick, and injured marine animals is a leading center for ocean conservancy in the Bay Area and the largest rehabilitation center of its kind in the world. Dedicated to pioneering education, rehabilitation, and research, the center is free and open daily to the public. Tour the facilities and see how elephant seals, sea lions, and pups are cared for and meet the scientists who care for them. Bonus: you'll catch some of the best views of the

Marin Headlands and San Francisco Bay along the way. ■ **TIP→ Call ahead or check their website for tour availability.** ✉ *2000 Bunker Rd.* ☎ *415/289–7325* 🌐 *www.marinemammalcenter.org* 🎟 *Free.*

Sally Stanford Drinking Fountain

FOUNTAIN | There's an unusual historic landmark on the Sausalito Ferry Pier—a drinking fountain inscribed "Have a drink on Sally" in remembrance of Sally Stanford, the former San Francisco brothel madam who became Sausalito's mayor in the 1970s. Sassy Sally would have appreciated the fountain's eccentric attachment: a knee-level basin with the inscription "Have a drink on Leland," in memory of her beloved dog. ✉ *Sausalito Ferry Pier, Anchor St. at Humboldt St., off southwest corner of Gabrielson Park* 🌐 *www.oursausalito.com.*

Sausalito Ice House Museum and Visitor Center

INFO CENTER | The local historical society operates this dual educational exhibit and visitor center, where you can get your bearings, learn some history, and find out what's happening around town. The artifacts of indigenous Miwok peoples and photography of turn-of-the-20th-century Sausalito are worth a peek. ✉ *780 Bridgeway, at Bay St.* ☎ *415/332–0505* 🌐 *www.sausalitohistoricalsociety.com* 🕓 *Closed Mon.*

Viña del Mar Plaza and Park

PLAZA | The landmark Plaza Viña del Mar, named for Sausalito's sister city in Chile, marks the center of town. Adjacent to the parking lot and ferry pier, the plaza is flanked by two 14-foot-tall statues of elephants, which were created for the Panama–Pacific International Exposition world's fair held in San Francisco in 1915. A picture-perfect fountain here is great for people-watching. ✉ *Bridgeway and El Portal St.* 🌐 *www.oursausalito.com.*

Restaurants

Arawan Thai

$ | **THAI** | Tucked along the restaurant row of Caledonia Street for decades, Arawan Thai has been a stalwart destination for some of the tastiest Thai dishes in Marin County. The elegant and cozy interior lends an intimate quality to this hidden gem known for its generous variety of authentic soups, salads, and grilled specialties, along with shareable dishes, such as spicy angel wings (stuffed chicken wings) and prawn and cream cheese puffs. **Known for:** panang, red, and green coconut curries; papaya and mango salads; sizzling wok dishes. $ *Average main: $14* ✉ *47 Caledonia St.* ☎ *415/729–9395* 🌐 *www.arawansausalito.com.*

Fast Food Français

$ | **BISTRO** | **FAMILY** | F3, as it's known, puts a French twist on classic American fast food and dishes up some French nibbles, too, in this casual bistro. The same folks who started Le Garage branch out here with quick bites like French onion burgers with cheddar fondue and double-cream mac-and-cheese, along with Brussels sprouts chips, deviled eggs, and ratatouille. **Known for:** fries and frites; spacious locale; excellent brunch spot. $ *Average main: $16* ✉ *39 Caledonia St.* ☎ *415/887–9047* 🌐 *www.eatf3.com.*

★ Fish

$$ | **SEAFOOD** | **FAMILY** | Unsurprisingly, fish—specifically, fresh, sustainably caught fish—is the focus at this gleaming dockside fish house a mile north of downtown. Order at the counter—cash only—and then grab a seat by the floor-to-ceiling windows or at a picnic table on the pier, overlooking the yachts and fishing boats. **Known for:** taco plate; barbecued oysters; fire-grilled entrées. $ *Average main: $23* ✉ *350 Harbor Dr., at Gate 5 Rd., off Bridgeway* ☎ *415/331–3474* 🌐 *www.331fish.com* 💳 *No credit cards.*

The Joinery

$$ | **AMERICAN** | Sausalito's popular beer hall and rotisserie offers ample, open, airy indoor seating at long tables and expanded outdoor deck dining with exceptional views of the bay. It's a relaxing spot to enjoy burgers, sandwiches, soups, and salads along with a selection of Belgian beers, IPAs, lagers, and ciders on tap. **Known for:** fried chicken sandwich and grilled cheese; Joinery burger with special sauce; dirty fries and fried Brussels sprouts. $ *Average main: $18* ✉ *300 Tourney St.* ☎ *415/766–8999* 🌐 *www.joineryca.com.*

Le Garage

$$$ | **FRENCH** | Brittany-born Olivier Souvestre serves traditional French bistro fare in a relaxed, bayside setting that feels more sidewalk café than the converted garage that it is. The restaurant seats only 35 inside and 15 outside, so make reservations or arrive early. **Known for:** PEI mussels and house-cut fries; no-reservation weekend brunch; outstanding bouillabaisse. $ *Average main: $27* ✉ *85 Liberty Ship Way, Suite 109* ☎ *415/332–5625* 🌐 *www.legarage-sausalito.com.*

Poggio

$$ | **ITALIAN** | A hillside dining destination, Poggio serves modern Tuscan-style comfort food in a handsome, old world–inspired space whose charm spills onto the sidewalks. An extensive and ever-changing menu, with ingredients sourced from the restaurant's garden and local farms, features house-made capellini, grilled fish, and wood-fired pizzas. **Known for:** traditional northern Italian dishes; rotisserie chicken with property-grown organic herbs and vegetables; lobster-roe pasta. $ *Average main: $25* ✉ *777 Bridgeway, at Bay St.* ☎ *415/332–7771* 🌐 *www.poggiotrattoria.com.*

Sausalito Seahorse

$$ | **ITALIAN** | Live music and dancing complement Tuscan seafood and pasta specialties here and make the Seahorse one of Sausalito's most spirited supper clubs. Sample an abundant antipasti menu and homemade focaccia on outdoor patios or enjoy the band inside with traditional seafood stew or lasagna *classica*. **Known for:** happy hour; schiacciata (a type of Tuscan bread) panini; fun atmosphere. *Average main: $23* *305 Harbor Dr.* *415/331–2899* *www.sausalitoseahorse.com.*

★ Sushi Ran

$$ | **JAPANESE** | Sushi aficionados swear that this tiny, stylish restaurant—in business since 1986—is the Bay Area's finest option for raw fish, but don't overlook the excellent Pacific Rim fusions, a melding of Japanese ingredients and French cooking techniques. Book in advance or expect a wait, which you can soften by sipping one of the bar's 30 by-the-glass sakes. **Known for:** fish imported from Tokyo's famous Tsukiji market; local miso-glazed black cod; outstanding sake and wine list. *Average main: $25* *107 Caledonia St., at Pine St.* *415/332–3620* *sushiran.com* *No lunch Mon.–Thurs.*

Taste of Rome

$$ | **ITALIAN** | **FAMILY** | From early-morning espresso and frittatas to late-night wine and marsalas, there's something just right at Taste of Rome any time of day. With spacious indoor and outdoor seating and a bountiful menu of fresh and homemade Italian specialties, it's easy to see why this family-owned café is beloved among locals. **Known for:** coffee drinks and desserts; locally sourced organic produce and sustainable seafood; house-made pasta. *Average main: $17* *1000 Bridgeway* *415/332–7660* *tasteofrome.co.*

Coffee and Quick Bites

★ Hamburgers Sausalito

$ | **BURGER** | Patrons queue up daily outside this tiny street-side shop for organic Angus beef patties that are made to order on a wheel-shaped grill. Brave the line (it moves fast) and take your food to the esplanade to enjoy fresh air and bayside views. **Known for:** legendary burgers; bay views; local following. *Average main: $9* *737 Bridgeway, at Anchor St.* *415/332–9471* *No dinner.*

Venice Gourmet Deli & Pizza

$ | **ITALIAN** | The traditional Italian deli sandwiches, pizzas made daily, and a shop filled with gourmet delectables, wines, kitchenware, and local flavor have enticed taste buds along picturesque Bridgeway since 1969. Enjoy a meal alfresco at the sidewalk tables, or take a picnic a few steps away to Yee Toch Chee Park for a waterside bite. **Known for:** picnic-perfect sandwiches; service and quality from family owners; plentiful selections. *Average main: $12* *625 Bridgeway* *415/332–3544* *www.venicegourmet.com.*

Hotels

The Inn Above Tide

$$$$ | **B&B/INN** | The balconies at the inn literally hang over the water, and each of its rooms has a "perfect 10" view that takes in wild Angel Island as well as the city lights across the bay. **Pros:** generous continental breakfast; free bikes to tour the area; in-room spa services available. **Cons:** costly daily parking; some rooms are on the small side; ferry-side rooms can be noisy. *Rooms from: $425* *30 El Portal* *415/332–9535, 800/893–8433* *www.innabovetide.com* *33 rooms* *Free breakfast.*

Tiburon

7 miles north of Sausalito, 11 miles north of Golden Gate Bridge.

On a peninsula that was named Punta de Tiburón (Shark Point) by 18th-century Spanish explorers, this beautiful Marin County community retains the feel of a village—it's more low-key than Sausalito—despite the encroachment of commercial establishments from the downtown area. The harbor faces Angel Island across Raccoon Strait, and San Francisco is directly south across the bay, making the views from the decks of harbor restaurants major attractions. Since 1884, when the San Francisco and North Pacific Railroad relocated their ferry terminal facilities to the harbor town, Tiburon has centered on the waterfront. The ferry is the most relaxing (and fastest) way to get here and allows you to skip traffic and parking problems.

One of the bay's best secrets in plain sight, Angel Island State Park (☎ *415/435–1915* 🌐 *www.parks.ca.gov*) offers 13 miles of roads and trails from the perimeter up to Mt. Livermore (788 feet), with magnificent panoramic views. The 12-minute ferry ride to Angel Island from Tiburon ($15 round-trip) includes the cost of park admission. **■ TIP→ To see the sites by bike, rent on the island (www.angelisland.com/bike-rentals) or in Tiburon at Pedego Electric Bikes (10 Main St.).**

GETTING HERE AND AROUND

Blue & Gold Fleet ferries travel between San Francisco and Tiburon daily. By car, head north from San Francisco on U.S. 101 and get off at CA 131/Tiburon Boulevard/ East Blithedale Avenue (Exit 447). Turn right onto Tiburon Boulevard and drive just over 4 miles to downtown. Golden Gate Transit serves downtown Tiburon from San Francisco; watch for changes during evening rush hour. Tiburon's Main Street is perfect for wandering, as are the footpaths that frame the water's edge.

ESSENTIALS

VISITOR INFORMATION destination: Tiburon. ✉ *Town Hall, 1505 Tiburon Blvd.* ☎ *415/435–2298* 🌐 *www.destinationtiburon.org.*

Sights

Ark Row

NEIGHBORHOOD | The historic second block of Main Street is known as Ark Row and has a tree-shaded walk lined with antiques shops, restaurants, and specialty stores. The quaint stretch gets its name from the 19th-century ark houseboats that floated in Belvedere Cove before being beached and transformed into stores. **■ TIP→ If you're curious about architectural history, the Tiburon Heritage & Arts Commission has a self-guided walking-tour map, available online and at local businesses.** ✉ *Ark Row, Main St., south of Juanita La.* 🌐 *www.townoftiburon.org.*

Old St. Hilary's Landmark and John Thomas Howell Wildflower Preserve

HISTORIC SITE | The architectural centerpiece of this attraction is a stark-white 1888 Carpenter Gothic church that overlooks the town and the bay from its hillside perch. Surrounding the church, which was dedicated as a historical monument in 1959, is a wildflower preserve that's spectacular in May and June, when the rare Tiburon paintbrush and Tiburon black jewel flower bloom. Expect a steep walk uphill to reach the preserve. The Landmarks Society will arrange guided tours by appointment. **■ TIP→ The hiking trails behind the landmark wind up to a peak that has views of the entire Bay Area.** ✉ *201 Esperanza St., off Mar West St. or Beach Rd.* ☎ *415/435–1853* 🌐 *landmarks-society.com* ⏲ *Church closed Mon.–Sat. and Nov.–Mar.*

Railroad & Ferry Depot Museum

MUSEUM | A short waterfront walk from the ferry landing, this free museum in Shoreline Park is a well-preserved time capsule of the city's industrial history, complete with working trains. The landmark building has a detailed scale model of Tiburon and its 43-acre rail yard at the turn of the 20th century, when the city served as a major railroad and ferry hub for San Francisco Bay. The Depot House Museum on the second floor showcases a restoration of the stationmaster's living quarters. ✉ *1920 Paradise Dr.* ☎ *415/435–1853* 🌐 *landmarkssociety.com* ⏲ *Closed Mon.–Sat. and Oct.–Apr.*

 Restaurants

Caffè Acri
$ | **CAFÉ** | This Italian espresso bar and café at the end of the Tiburon Ferry dock is a sweet spot to enjoy a leisurely breakfast or lunch with a cup of locally roasted coffee while waiting for the ferry. In addition to daily-baked pastries and desserts, the menu ranges from omelets and toasted sandwiches to smoothies. **Known for:** farm-fresh salads; espresso drinks; soups and paninis. $ *Average main: $10* ✉ *1 Main St.* ☎ *415/435–8515* 🌐 *www.caffeacri.com* ⏲ *No dinner.*

★ Luna Blu
$$ | **SICILIAN** | Friendly, informative staff serve Sicilian-inspired seafood in this lively Italian restaurant just a stone's throw from the ferry. Recent renovations have opened up 1,000 square feet of new patio and tripled the capacity of the original dining space. **Known for:** sustainably caught seafood and local, organic ingredients; homemade pastas; rock crab bisque. $ *Average main: $20* ✉ *35 Main St.* ☎ *415/789–5844* 🌐 *lunablurestaurant.com* ⏲ *Closed Tues. No lunch weekdays.*

Salt & Pepper
$$ | **AMERICAN** | **FAMILY** | Bright and welcoming, this American bistro on Ark Row is known for its seafood starters (oyster poppers, crab stacks, scallops, and steamers) and salads as well as shareable dishes and burgers, chops, and ribs. The airy, rustic space has a pleasant café-like atmosphere that makes it easy to stay and even consider returning for a breakfast of Dungeness crab omelet or ricotta pancakes. **Known for:** clam chowder; kabocha squash and vegetable curry; Mongolian pork chops and rib-eye steaks. $ *Average main: $24* ✉ *38 Main St.* ☎ *415/435–3594* 🌐 *www.saltandpeppertiburon.com.*

★ Sam's Anchor Cafe
$$ | **AMERICAN** | Open since 1920, this beloved dockside restaurant is the town's most famous eatery, and after 99 years, a bright remodel includes floor-to-ceiling sliding-glass doors and an 80-foot heated bench for deck views on cool days. Remnants of Sam's history are evident in some vintage decor, the hamburger and champagne specials, and the free popcorn. **Known for:** excellent raw bar; pink lemonade and margarita "bowls"; hurricane fries. $ *Average main: $22* ✉ *27 Main St.* ☎ *415/435–4527* 🌐 *samscafe.com.*

Servino Ristorante
$$ | **SOUTHERN ITALIAN** | **FAMILY** | This family-owned eatery specializes in southern Italian recipes, including lobster agnolotti, seafood stew, pork sausage fondue, house-made pastas, and pizza made with local, sustainable ingredients. With spacious indoor and outdoor seating and waterfront views, the scene is cozy and welcoming even in cooler weather, when there's heated patio dining. **Known for:** alfresco waterfront dining; wines from Italy and California; black truffle raviolacci. $ *Average main: $23* ✉ *9 Main St.* ☎ *415/435–2676* 🌐 *www.servino.com.*

 Coffee and Quick Bites

Waypoint Pizza
$ | **PIZZA** | **FAMILY** | A nautical theme and a tasty "between the sheets" pizza-style sandwich are signatures of this creative pizzeria, which is housed in the 19th-century landmark building that was once home to the Pioneer Boathouse and is now owned by two sailing aficionados. Booths

are brightened with blue-checkered tablecloths, and a playful air is added by indoor deck chairs and a picnic table complete with umbrella. **Known for:** pizza-style sandwiches; wild shrimp pesto pizza; soft-serve organic ice cream. *$ Average main: $15 ✉ 15 Main St. ☎ 415/435–3440 🌐 www.waypointpizza.com.*

Hotels

Waters Edge Hotel

$$$ | B&B/INN | Checking into this stylish downtown hotel feels like tucking away into an inviting retreat by the water—the views are stunning, and the lighting is perfect. **Pros:** complimentary wine and cheese for guests every evening; restaurants and sights are steps away; free bike rentals for guests. **Cons:** downstairs rooms lack privacy and balconies; paid self-parking; 2-night minimum weekends, 3-night minimum holidays. *$ Rooms from: $309 ✉ 25 Main St., off Tiburon Blvd. ☎ 415/789–5999, 877/789–5999 🌐 www.marinhotels.com ⇆ 23 rooms 🍴 Free breakfast.*

Shopping

Local Spicery

FOOD/CANDY | This is the place for spices of all varieties from around the world, from adobo to za'atar. Where historic Ark Row curves uphill, the apothecary-like storefront features an aromatic library of assorted loose teas and spices milled in small quantities and prepared in small-batch hand blends to obtain maximum freshness and quality. Not sure where to begin? Ask about pairing flavors with your favorite ingredients and ways of cooking. *✉ 80 Main St. ☎ 415/435–1100 🌐 www.localspicery.com.*

Schoenberg Guitars

MUSIC STORES | Small, narrow, and chockablock with handmade guitars alongside fine vintage classics, this shop is a treat even for those who don't play music. Dozens, if not hundreds, of guitars varying in size, shape, and color hang from the walls and stand against the polished wood floor. There is an organized beauty to the layout of this place and a comforting sense of musical harmony. You may even enjoy an impromptu concert or workshop. *✉ Ark Row Shopping Center, 106 Main St. ☎ 415/789–0846 🌐 www.om28.com.*

Tiburon Wine

WINE/SPIRITS | Some 200 regional and international wines as well as local Marin Rieslings and pinot noirs line the walls of this cozy shop, which has an indoor tasting room where you can sample more than two dozen. There's also an outdoor seating space for sipping by the glass or bottle. *✉ 84 Main St. ☎ 415/435–3499 🌐 tiburonwine.net.*

Mill Valley

2 miles north of Sausalito, 4 miles north of Golden Gate Bridge.

Chic and woodsy Mill Valley has a dual personality. Here, as elsewhere in the county, the foundation is a superb natural setting. Virtually surrounded by parkland, the town lies at the base of Mt. Tamalpais and contains dense redwood groves traversed by countless creeks. But this is no lumber camp. Smart restaurants and chichi boutiques line streets that have been roamed by more rock stars than one might suspect.

The rustic village flavor isn't a modern conceit, but a holdover from the town's early days as a center for the lumber industry. In 1896, the Mt. Tamalpais Scenic Railroad—dubbed the "Crookedest Railroad in the World" because of its curvy tracks—began transporting visitors from Mill Valley to the top of Mt. Tam and down to Muir Woods, and the town soon became a vacation retreat for city slickers. The trains stopped running in the 1930s as cars became more popular, but the old railway depot still serves as the center of town:

the 1929 building has been transformed into the popular Depot Café & Bookstore, at 87 Throckmorton Avenue.

The small downtown area has the constant bustle of a leisure community; even at noon on a Tuesday, people are out shopping for fancy cookware, eco-friendly home furnishings, and boutique clothing.

GETTING HERE AND AROUND

By car from San Francisco, head north on U.S. 101 and get off at CA 131/Tiburon Boulevard/East Blithedale Avenue (Exit 447). Turn left onto East Blithedale Avenue and continue west to Throckmorton Avenue; turn left to reach Depot Plaza, then park. Golden Gate Transit buses serve Mill Valley from San Francisco. Once here, explore the town on foot.

ESSENTIALS

VISITOR INFORMATION Mill Valley Chamber of Commerce & Visitor Center. ✉ *85 Throckmorton Ave.* ☎ *415/388–9700* 🌐 *www.millvalley.org.*

Sights

Lytton Square

PLAZA | **FAMILY** | Mill Valley locals congregate on weekends to socialize in the coffeehouses and cafés near the town's central square, but it's buzzing most of the day. The Mill Valley Depot Café & Bookstore at the hub of it all is the place to grab a coffee and sweet treat while reading or playing a game of chess. Shops, restaurants, and cultural venues line the nearby streets. ✉ *Miller and Throckmorton Aves.*

★ Marin County Civic Center

BUILDING | A wonder of arches, circles, and skylights just 10 miles north of Mill Valley, the Civic Center was Frank Lloyd Wright's largest public project and has been designated a national and state historic landmark, as well as a UNESCO World Heritage Site. It's a performance venue and the locale for the fun and funky Marin County Fair. One-hour docent-led tours leave from the café on the second floor Wednesday and Friday morning at 10:30. ✉ *3501 Civic Center Dr., off N. San Pedro Rd., San Rafael* ☎ *415/473–6400 Cultural Services department* 🌐 *www.marincounty.org* 🎫 *Free; tour $10* 🕒 *Closed weekends; no tours Mon., Tues., Thurs.*

★ Mill Valley Lumber Yard

HISTORIC SITE | **FAMILY** | The lumber yard, once a vital center of the region's logging industry, is now a vibrant micro-village of craftsfolk, bread bakers, textile makers, and lifestyle designers, and their boutiques and restaurants. You'll even find a chocolate art studio where custom-designed chocolates and truffles may look almost too good to eat. The preserved brick-red historic structures are hard to miss along Miller Avenue, and with plenty of parking in the area, plus picnic tables and outdoor space, it's well worth a visit. ✉ *129 Miller Ave.* 🌐 *www.millvalleylumberyard.com.*

★ Mt. Tamalpais State Park

NATIONAL/STATE PARK | **FAMILY** | The view of Mt. Tamalpais from all around the bay can be a beauty, but that's nothing compared to the views *from* the mountain, which take in San Francisco, the East Bay, the coast, and beyond. Although the summit of Mt. Tamalpais is only 2,571 feet high, the mountain rises practically from sea level, dominating the topography of Marin County. For years the 6,300-acre park has been a favorite destination for hikers, with more than 200 miles of trails. The park's major thoroughfare, Panoramic Highway, snakes its way up from U.S. 101 to the **Pantoll Ranger Station** and down to Stinson Beach. Parking is free along the roadside, but there's an $8 fee (cash or check only) at the ranger station and additional charges for walk-in campsites and group use.

The **Mountain Theater,** also known as the Cushing Memorial Amphitheatre, is a natural 3,750-seat amphitheater that has showcased summer "Mountain Plays" since 1913.

The **Rock Spring Trail** starts at the Mountain Theater and gently climbs for 1½ miles to the **West Point Inn,** where you can relax at picnic tables before forging ahead via Old Railroad Grade Fire Road and the Miller Trail to Mt. Tam's Middle Peak.

From the Pantoll Ranger Station, the precipitous **Steep Ravine Trail** brings you past stands of coastal redwoods. Hike the connecting **Dipsea Trail** to reach Stinson Beach. ■ **TIP→ If you're too weary to make the 3½-mile trek back up, Marin Transit Bus 61 takes you from Stinson Beach back to the ranger station.** ✉ *Pantoll Ranger Station, 3801 Panoramic Hwy., at Pantoll Rd.* ✣ *on Mt. Tamalpais* ☎ *415/388–2070* 🌐 *www.parks.ca.gov.*

★ **Muir Woods National Monument**

NATIONAL/STATE PARK | FAMILY | One of the last old-growth stands of redwood (*Sequoia sempervirens*) giants, Muir Woods is nature's cathedral: awe-inspiring and not to be missed. The nearly 560 acres of Muir Woods National Monument contain some of the most majestic redwoods in the world—some more than 250 feet tall.

Part of the Golden Gate National Recreation Area, Muir Woods is a pedestrian's park. The popular 2-mile main trail begins at the park headquarters and provides easy access to streams, ferns, azaleas, and redwood groves. Summer weekends can prove busy, so consider taking a more challenging route, such as the **Dipsea Trail,** which climbs west from the forest floor to soothing views of the ocean and the Golden Gate Bridge. For a complete list of trails, check with rangers.

Picnicking and camping aren't allowed, and neither are pets. Crowds can be large, especially from May through October, so come early in the morning or late in the afternoon. The **Muir Woods Visitor Center** has books and exhibits about redwood trees and the woods' history as well as the latest info on trail conditions; the **Muir Woods Trading Company** serves hot food, organic pastries, and other tasty snacks, and the gift shop offers plenty of souvenirs. ■ **TIP→ Muir Woods has no cell service or Wi-Fi, so plan directions and communication ahead of time.**

For parking reservations (required) and shuttle information, visit 🌐 *gomuirwoods.com.* To drive directly from San Francisco, take U.S. 101 North across the Golden Gate Bridge to Exit 445B for Mill Valley/Stinson Beach, then follow signs for Highway 1 North and Muir Woods. ✉ *1 Muir Woods Rd., off Panoramic Hwy.* ☎ *415/561–2850 park reservations,* 🌐 *www.nps.gov/muwo* 🎫 *$15.*

Old Mill Park

CITY PARK | FAMILY | To see one of the numerous outdoor oases that make Mill Valley so appealing, follow Throckmorton Avenue a quarter mile west from Lytton Square to Old Mill Park, a shady patch of redwoods that shelters a playground and reconstructed sawmill. The park also hosts September's annual Mill Valley Fall Arts Festival. From the park, Cascade Way winds its way past creek-side homes to the trailheads of several forest paths. ✉ *Throckmorton Ave. and Cascade Dr.* ☎ *415/383–1370 for rental information.* 🌐 *www.millvalleyrecreation.org.*

Restaurants

Boo Koo

$ | ASIAN | Southeast Asian street food with local flair is fired up in this hip and modern street café, where there's outdoor seating and a 10-tap bar. Summer rolls, satays, and skewers complement pho and wok specialties, and the locally sourced, vegan-based menu still has plenty for carnivores, who can customize dishes with grass-fed beef, wild salmon, and free-range chicken. **Known for:** green curry noodles; mint salad; Asian Brussels

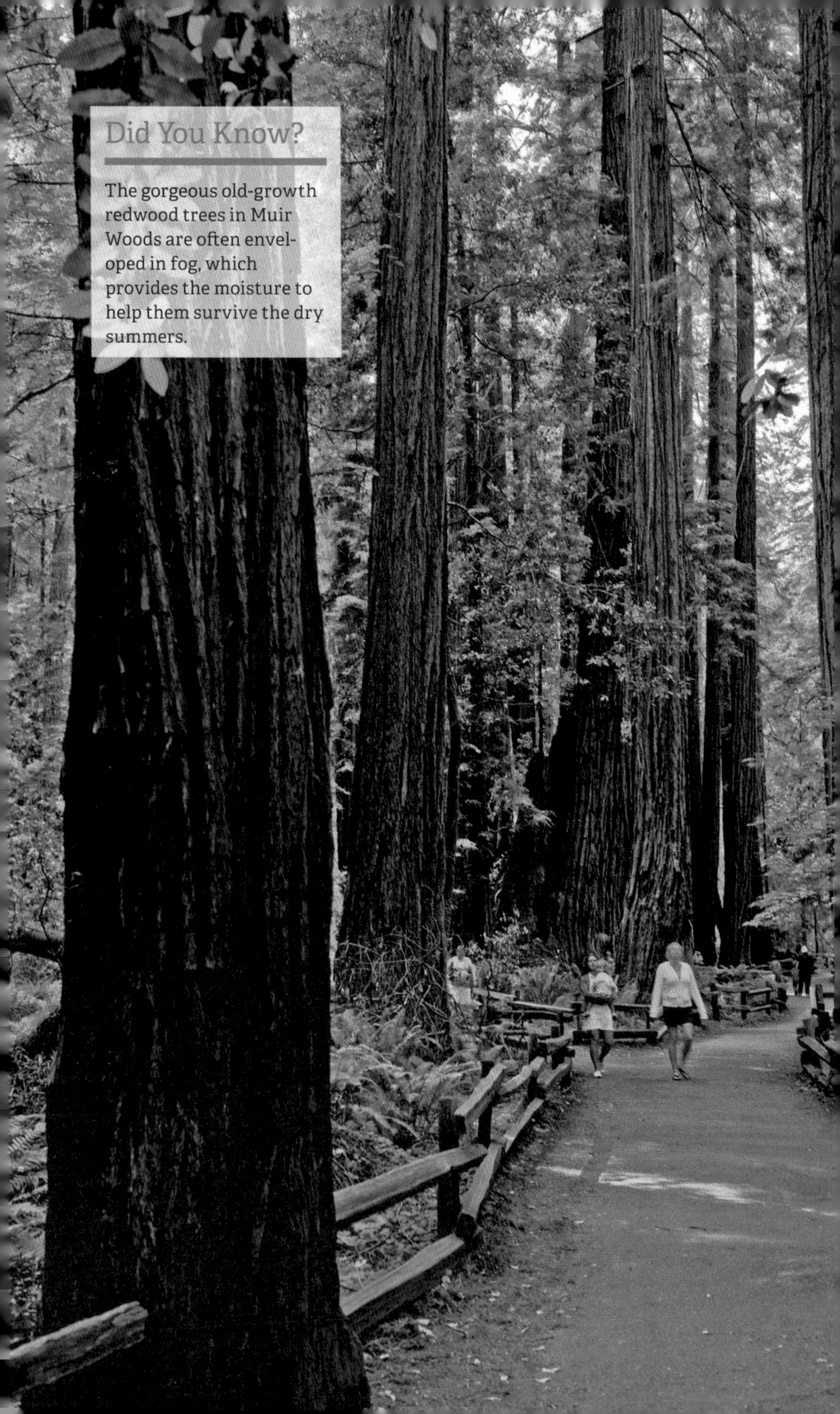

Did You Know?

The gorgeous old-growth redwood trees in Muir Woods are often enveloped in fog, which provides the moisture to help them survive the dry summers.

sprouts. $ *Average main: $11* ✉ *25 Miller Ave.* ☎ *415/888–8303* 🌐 *eatbookoo.com.*

Buckeye Roadhouse
$$$ | **AMERICAN** | House-smoked meats and fish, grilled steaks, classic salads, and decadent desserts bring locals and visitors back again and again to this 1937 lodge-style roadhouse. Enjoy a Marin martini at the cozy mahogany bar or sip local wine beside the river-rock fireplace. **Known for:** oysters bingo; chili-lime "brick" chicken; ribs and chops. $ *Average main: $29* ✉ *15 Shoreline Hwy., off U.S. 101* ☎ *415/331–2600* 🌐 *www.buckeyeroadhouse.com.*

Bungalow 44
$$ | **AMERICAN** | An open, well-lit space with booths and countertop seating from which diners can watch the cooks in action sets the scene at this lively eatery, which serves contemporary California cuisine and inventive cocktails. The menu focuses on locally sourced veggies and seafood. **Known for:** $1 oyster daily happy hour; fresh Marin Farmers' Market ingredients; kickin' fried chicken. $ *Average main: $24* ✉ *44 E. Blithedale Ave., at Sunnyside Ave.* ☎ *415/381–2500* 🌐 *www.bungalow44.com* ⏲ *No lunch.*

La Ginestra
$$ | **ITALIAN** | **FAMILY** | In business since 1964, La Ginestra—named for the flowers that grow on Mt. Vesuvius, in the owners' homeland—is a Mill Valley institution renowned for its no-pretense, family-style Italian meals and impressive wine list. The Sorrento Bar, off the dining room, serves up a delectable array of bar bites, pizzas, and sweets to enjoy while sipping wines and cocktails inspired by the Aversa family's home country. **Known for:** handmade pasta and gnocchi; excellent ravioli; daily fish and small plates. $ *Average main: $20* ✉ *127 Throckmorton Ave., off Miller Ave.* ☎ *415/388–0224* 🌐 *www.laginestramv.com* ⏲ *Closed Mon. and Tues. No lunch.*

Piazza D'Angelo
$$ | **ITALIAN** | **FAMILY** | In the heart of downtown, busy D'Angelo's is known for its authentic and fresh pastas; there are even gluten-free options. Another draw is the scene, especially in the lounge area, which hosts a lively cocktail hour in a traditional trattoria setting. **Known for:** fresh seafood; homemade pasta; top-notch tiramisu. $ *Average main: $22* ✉ *22 Miller Ave., off Throckmorton* ☎ *415/388–2000* 🌐 *www.piazzadangelo.com.*

Playa
$$ | **MODERN MEXICAN** | Modern Mexican farm-to-table creations and inspired cocktails are the focus of this festive indoor-outdoor space that's popular for its firepit, made-to-order masa station, and happy hour. An open kitchen serves up locally sourced, organic, and sustainable dishes like ceviche and flautas, grilled octopus tacos, and braised pork tortas. **Known for:** taco Tuesdays; rare tequilas and mezcals; moles and salsas. $ *Average main: $18* ✉ *41 Throckmorton Ave.* ☎ *415/384–8871* 🌐 *www.playamv.com.*

Vasco
$ | **ITALIAN** | With its wood-fired pizza oven, wine bar, and live music in the evening, this lovely corner restaurant has serious neighborhood charm. Authentic Italian specialties include chicken marsala, seafood stew, and calamari steak. **Known for:** great atmosphere; gluten-free pizza and pasta; memorable tiramisu. $ *Average main: $16* ✉ *106 Throckmorton Ave.* ☎ *415/381–3343* 🌐 *vascorestaurantmillvalley.com* ⏲ *No lunch.*

Coffee and Quick Bites

Avatar's Restaurant
$ | **INDIAN** | The lines can get long at this hole-in-the-wall, no-frills kitchen, where Indian curries are served burrito style while you wait (note: it's cash only). Punjabi burritos or rice plates come with savory lamb, chicken, fish, vegetarian, and vegan ingredients flavored with

seasonal fruit chutneys, tamarind sauce, and aromatic blends. **Known for:** curried pumpkin; smoked eggplant; mostly take-out dining. *Average main: $8* *15 Madrona St.* *415/381–8293* *Closed Sun.* *No credit cards.*

Equator Coffees

$ | **CAFÉ** | This is the prime spot for a pick-me-up (and people-watching) over a picturesque view of downtown Mill Valley and Mt. Tam. The owners are as serious about coffee as they are about social responsibility, from their fair-chain single-origin beans and organic loose teas down to the locally recycled wood and metal decor. **Known for:** espresso and cappuccino drinks; breakfast sandwiches; strawberry and chocolate waffles. *Average main: $9* *2 Miller Ave.* *415/383–1651* *www.equatorcoffees.com* *No dinner.*

Hotels

Acqua Hotel

$$ | **HOTEL** | Alongside Richardson Bay, this stylish boutique hotel has modern, elegant rooms decorated in soft Zen-like color schemes. **Pros:** evening wine service; free parking and Wi-Fi; hearty breakfast buffet. **Cons:** next to freeway; traffic audible in rooms facing east; limited amenities within walking distance. *Rooms from: $259* *555 Redwood Hwy., off U.S. 101* *415/388–9353* *www.marinhotels.com* *49 rooms* *Free breakfast.*

Mill Valley Inn

$$$ | **B&B/INN** | The only hotel in downtown Mill Valley is comprised of one of the area's first homes, the Creek House, which has smart-looking Victorian rooms, and two small cottages nestled in a grove beyond a creek. **Pros:** unique rooms in private yet central location; some rooms have balconies, soaking tubs, and fireplaces; free mountain bikes. **Cons:** limited room service; dark in winter because of surrounding trees; some rooms are not accessible via elevator. *Rooms from: $329* *165 Throckmorton Ave., near Miller Ave.* *415/389–6608, 855/334–7946* *millvalleyinn.com* *25 rooms* *Free breakfast.*

Mountain Home Inn

$$ | **B&B/INN** | Abutting 40,000 acres of state and national parks, this airy wooden inn sits on the skirt of Mt. Tamalpais, where you can follow hiking trails all the way to Stinson Beach. **Pros:** amazing terrace and views; peaceful, remote setting; cooked-to-order breakfast. **Cons:** nearest town is a 12-minute drive away; restaurant can get crowded on sunny weekend days; some rooms are tiny and have no TVs. *Rooms from: $243* *810 Panoramic Hwy., at Edgewood Ave.* *415/381–9000* *www.mtnhomeinn.com* *10 rooms* *Free breakfast.*

Nightlife

BREWPUBS AND BEER GARDENS

The Junction Beer Garden & Bottle Shop

BREWPUBS/BEER GARDENS | With more than a hundred styles of canned and bottled beers and 30 beers on tap, plus wine and hard kombucha, this enormous indoor and outdoor beer garden is perfectly situated along the Dipsea Trail for a visit before or after a Mt. Tam hike or Tennessee Valley beach visit. The brewers partnered with PizzaHacker, a cult-favorite pizzeria in San Francisco's Bernal Heights, to provide classic pies like their "top-shelf" Margherita, as well as salads and meatballs. The landscaped outdoor space is lined with picnic tables, Adirondack chairs, and firepits. *226 Shoreline Hwy.* *415/888–3544* *thejunc.com.*

Performing Arts

★ Throckmorton Theatre

ARTS CENTERS | A vibrant cultural hub in the region, the restored cinema and vaudeville house in Mill Valley is known for fostering exceptional arts and education. The darling playhouse seats upward of 260 and features live theater, comedy, and concerts. Two smaller street-side halls, the Tivoli and Crescendo, feature free classical concerts on Wednesday, along with Sunday evening sessions, jazz performances, and new art exhibits every month. ✉ *142 Throckmorton Ave.* ☎ *415/383–9600* 🌐 *www.throckmortontheatre.org.*

 Shopping

Mill Valley Market

FOOD/CANDY | This family-owned market has been the go-to stop for specialty foods, groceries, deli items, and hot food since 1929. Known for the notable beer and wine selection alongside local and organic produce and healthy grab-and-go foods, this is an ideal place to prepare for a picnic or seek out gourmet gifts, like imported chocolates and 100-year-old balsamic vinegars. ✉ *12 Corte Madera Ave.* ☎ *415/388–3222* 🌐 *millvalleymarket.com.*

Muir Beach

12 miles northwest of Golden Gate Bridge, 6 miles southwest of Mill Valley.

Except on the sunniest of weekends, Muir Beach is relatively quiet, but the drive to this community and beach is a scenic adventure.

GETTING HERE AND AROUND

A car is the best way to reach Muir Beach. From Highway 1, follow Pacific Way southwest ¼ mile.

 Beaches

Muir Beach

BEACH—SIGHT | **FAMILY** | Small but scenic, this beach—a rocky patch of shoreline off Highway 1 in the northern Marin Headlands—is a good place to stretch your legs and gaze out at the Pacific Ocean. Locals often walk their dogs here; families and cuddling couples come for picnicking and sunbathing. At the northern end of the beach are waterfront homes (and occasional nude sunbathers), and at the other are the bluffs of the Golden Gate National Recreation Area. A land bridge connects directly from the parking lot to the beach, as well as to a short trail that leads to a scenic overlook and connects to other coastal paths. There are no lifeguards on duty and the currents can be challenging, so swimming is not advised. **Amenities:** parking (free); toilets. **Best for:** solitude; sunset; walking. ✉ *100 Pacific Way, off Shoreline Hwy.* 🌐 *www.nps.gov/gogo.*

 Hotels

The Pelican Inn

$$ | **B&B/INN** | From its slate roof to its whitewashed plaster walls, this Tudor-style inn built in the 1970s is English to the core, with its cozy upstairs guest rooms (no elevator) and draped half-tester beds, a sun-filled solarium, and bangers and grilled tomatoes for breakfast. **Pros:** five-minute walk to the beach; great bar and restaurant; peaceful setting. **Cons:** 20-minute drive to nearby attractions; rooms are quite small and rustic; workout and steam room access not on-site. $ *Rooms from: $224* ✉ *10 Pacific Way, off Hwy. 1* ☎ *415/383–6000* 🌐 *www.pelicaninn.com* *7 rooms* *Free breakfast.*

Stinson Beach

20 miles northwest of Golden Gate Bridge.

This laid-back hamlet is all about the beach, and folks come from all over the Bay Area to walk its sandy, often windswept shore. An ideal day trip would include a morning hike at Mt. Tamalpais followed by lunch at one of Stinson's unassuming eateries and a leisurely beach stroll.

GETTING HERE AND AROUND

If you're driving, take U.S. 101 to the Mill Valley/Stinson Beach/Highway 1 exit and follow the road west and then north. By bus, take Golden Gate Transit to Marin City and then transfer to the West Marin Stagecoach (61) for Bolinas.

Beaches

Stinson Beach

BEACH—SIGHT | FAMILY | When the fog hasn't rolled in, this expansive stretch of sand is about as close as you can get in Marin to the stereotypical feel of a Southern California beach. There are several clothing-optional areas, among them a section south of Stinson Beach called Red Rock Beach. ⚠ **Swimming at Stinson Beach can be dangerous; the undertow is strong, and shark sightings, though infrequent, have occurred; lifeguards are on duty May–September.** Pets are not allowed on the national park section of the beach.

On any hot summer weekend, roads to Stinson are packed and the parking lot fills, so factor this into your plans. The town itself—population 600, give or take—has a nonchalant surfer vibe, with a few good eating options and pleasant hippie-craftsy browsing. **Amenities:** food and drink; lifeguards (summer); parking (free); showers; toilets. **Best for:** nudists; sunset; surfing; swimming; walking, windsurfing. ✉ *Hwy. 1, 1 Calle Del Sierra* ☎ *415/868–0942 lifeguard tower* 🌐 *www.nps.gov/goga.*

Restaurants

Parkside Cafe

$$ | AMERICAN | FAMILY | Though this place is popular for its 1950s beachfront snack bar, the adjoining café, coffee bar, marketplace, and bakery shouldn't be missed either. The full menu serves up fresh ingredients, local seafood, and wood-fired pizzas. **Known for:** espresso and pastry bar; tasty fish-and-chips; rustic house-made breads. $ *Average main: $26* ✉ *43 Arenal Ave., off Shoreline Hwy.* ☎ *415/868–1272* 🌐 *www.parksidecafe.com.*

Stinson Beach Breakers Cafe

$$ | AMERICAN | Hard to miss along the tiny stretch of Main Street, this café is an easy prebeach destination for coffee and griddle specialties or postsurf bar bites and cocktails on the heated patio in the afternoon. Beach-cottage hardwood floors and a woodstove add to the warmth of the rustic seaside interior, while a mountain view and firepit enhance the deck. **Known for:** hearty egg breakfast dishes with a Latin twist; fresh oysters; fish tacos. $ *Average main: $19* ✉ *3465 Hwy. 1* ☎ *415/868–2002* ⏲ *Closed Tues. and Wed. Nov.–Mar.*

Hotels

Sandpiper Lodging

$$ | B&B/INN | FAMILY | Recharge, rest, and enjoy the local scenery at this ultrapopular lodging that books up months, even years, in advance. **Pros:** beach chairs, towels, and toys provided; lush garden with grill; minutes from the beach and town. **Cons:** walls are thin; limited amenities; charge for rollaway beds and extra persons. $ *Rooms from: $262* ✉ *1 Marine Way, off Arenal Ave.* ☎ *415/868–1632* 🌐 *www.sandpiperstinsonbeach.com* *11 rooms* 🍽 *No meals.*

Point Reyes National Seashore

Bear Valley Visitor Center is 14 miles north of Stinson Beach.

With sandy beaches stretching for miles, a dramatic rocky coastline, a gem of a lighthouse (Point Reyes Lighthouse: closed at this writing, but check online), and idyllic, century-old dairy farms, Point Reyes National Seashore is one of the most varied and strikingly beautiful corners of the Bay Area.

GETTING HERE AND AROUND

From San Francisco, take U.S. 101 North, head west at Sir Francis Drake Boulevard (Exit 450B) toward San Anselmo, and follow the road just under 20 miles to Bear Valley Road. From Stinson Beach or Bolinas, drive north on Highway 1 and turn left on Bear Valley Road. If you're going by bus, take one of several Golden Gate Transit buses to Marin City; in Marin City, transfer to the West Marin Stagecoach (you'll switch buses in Olema). Once at the visitor center, the best way to get around is on foot.

Sights

Bear Valley Visitor Center

INFO CENTER | FAMILY | Tucked in the Olema Valley, this welcoming center is a perfect point of orientation for trails and roads throughout the region's unique and diverse ecosystem. It offers a rich glimpse of local cultural and natural heritage with engaging exhibits about the wildlife, history, and ecology of the Point Reyes National Seashore. The rangers at the barnlike facility share their in-depth knowledge about beaches, whale-watching, hiking trails, and camping. Restrooms are available, as well as trailhead parking and a picnic area with barbecue grills. Winter hours may be shorter and summer weekend hours may be longer; call or check the website for details. ✉ *Bear Valley Visitor Center, 1 Bear Valley Visitor Center Access Rd., west of Hwy. 1, off Bear Valley Rd., Point Reyes Station* ☎ *415/464–5100* 🌐 *www.nps.gov/pore.*

★ Duxbury Reef

NATURE PRESERVE | FAMILY | Excellent tide pooling can be had along the 3-mile shoreline of Duxbury Reef; it's the most extensive tide pool area near Point Reyes National Seashore, as well as one of the largest shale intertidal reefs in North America. Look for sea stars, barnacles, sea anemones, purple urchins, limpets, sea mussels, and the occasional abalone. But check a tide table (🌐 *tidesandcurrents.noaa.gov*) or the local papers if you plan to explore the reef—it's accessible only at low tide. The reef is a 30-minute drive from the Bear Valley Visitor Center. Take Highway 1 South from the center, turn right at Olema Bolinas Road (keep an eye peeled; the road is easy to miss), left on Horseshoe Hill Road, right on Mesa Road, left on Overlook Drive, and then right on Elm Road, which dead-ends at the Agate Beach County Park parking lot.

Excellent tide pooling can be had along the 3-mile shoreline of Duxbury Reef; it's the most extensive tide pool area near Point Reyes National Seashore, as well as one of the largest shale intertidal reefs in North America. Look for sea stars, barnacles, sea anemones, purple urchins, limpets, sea mussels, and the occasional abalone. But check a tide table (🌐 *tidesandcurrents.noaa.gov*) or the local papers if you plan to explore the reef—it's accessible only at low tide. The reef is a 30-minute drive from the Bear Valley Visitor Center. Take Highway 1 South from the center, turn right at Olema Bolinas Road (keep an eye peeled; the road is easy to miss), left on Horseshoe Hill Road, right on Mesa Road, left on Overlook Drive, and then right on Elm Road, which dead-ends at the Agate Beach County Park parking lot. ✣ *At Duxbury Point, 1 mile west of Bolinas* 🌐 *www.ptreyes.org* 🎫 *Free.*

Palomarin Field Station & Point Reyes Bird Observatory

NATURE PRESERVE | FAMILY | Birders adore Point Blue Conservation Science, which maintains the Palomarin Field Station and the Point Reyes Bird Observatory that are located in the southernmost part of Point Reyes National Seashore. The Field Station has excellent interpretive exhibits, including a comparative display of real birds' talons. The surrounding woods harbor some 200 bird species. As you hike the quiet trails through forest and along ocean cliffs, you're likely to see biologists banding birds to aid in the study of their life cycles. ■ **TIP→ Visit Point Blue's website for detailed directions and to find out when banding will occur.** ✉ *999 Mesa Rd., Bolinas* ☎ *415/868–0655 field station, 707/781–2555 headquarters* 🌐 *www.pointblue.org.*

★ **Point Reyes National Seashore**

NATIONAL/STATE PARK | **FAMILY** | One of the Bay Area's most spectacular treasures and the only national seashore on the West Coast, the 71,000-acre Point Reyes National Seashore encompasses hiking trails, secluded beaches, and rugged grasslands, as well as Point Reyes itself, a triangular peninsula that juts into the Pacific. The Point Reyes Lighthouse occupies the peninsula's tip and is a scenic 21-mile drive from Bear Valley Visitor Center; at this writing it is closed for renovations, but check online. The town of **Point Reyes Station** is a one-main-drag affair, with some good places to eat.

When explorer Sir Francis Drake sailed along the California coast in 1579, he allegedly missed the Golden Gate Strait and San Francisco Bay, but he did land at what he described as a convenient harbor. In 2012 the federal government recognized Drake's Bay, which flanks the point on the east, as that harbor, designating the spot a National Historic Landmark.

The infamous San Andreas Fault runs along the park's eastern edge; take the **Earthquake Trail** from the visitor center to see the impact near the epicenter of the 1906 earthquake that devastated San Francisco. A half-mile path from the visitor center leads to **Kule Loklo,** a reconstructed Miwok village of the region's first known inhabitants.

You can experience the diversity of Point Reyes's ecosystems on the scenic **Coast Trail** through eucalyptus groves and pine forests and along seaside cliffs to beautiful and tiny Bass Lake.

The 4.7-mile-long (one-way) **Tomales Point Trail** follows the spine of the park's northernmost finger of land through the Tule Elk Preserve, providing spectacular ocean views from high bluffs. ✉ *Bear Valley Visitor Center, 1 Bear Valley Visitor Center Access Rd., Point Reyes Station* ✥ *West of Hwy. 1, off Bear Valley Rd.* ☎ *415/464–5100* 🌐 *www.nps.gov/pore*  *Free.*

Restaurants

Cafe Reyes

$ | **PIZZA** | **FAMILY** | Sunny patio seating, hand-tossed pizza, and organic local ingredients are the selling points of this laid-back café. The semi-industrial dining room, built around a brick oven, features glazed concrete floors, warm-painted walls, and ceilings high enough to accommodate full-size market umbrellas. **Known for:** wood-fired pizza; Tomales Bay fresh oysters; good salads. $ *Average main: $15* ✉ *11101 Hwy. 1, Point Reyes Station* ☎ *415/663–9493* 🌐 *cafe-reyes.com* ⏲ *Closed Mon. and Tues.*

Due West

$$ | **AMERICAN** | A convivial atmosphere and local, sustainable culinary provisions keep this classic Point Reyes tavern a favorite stop among locals. Refurbished and modernized since its days as a horse-and-wagon stop in the 1860s, it now has a farm-to-fork seasonal menu including American classics from burgers and brick-roasted chicken to seafood specialties like shrimp scampi and steamed mussels. **Known for:** artisanal cheese plate; steak frites; regional wine list. $ *Average main: $23* ✉ *10021 Coastal Hwy. 1, Olema* ☎ *415/663–1264* 🌐 *olemahouse.com/due-west-restaurant/.*

Eleven

$$ | **WINE BAR** | For a true taste of local culture, this sisters-owned venture welcomes you to sit back, relax, sip some wine, and enjoy the flavors and scene Bolinas is known for, from the town's laid-back lifestyle and quirky decor to the natural beauty and the fresh coastal air. The wine bar and bistro's short but ever-changing creative and thoughtful menus change daily based on what's available and reflect the richness of this region's foodshed—considered one of the nation's most diverse. **Known for:** house-made, locally sourced ingredients; local natural wine selections; pizzas and oysters. *Average main: $17 11 Wharf Rd., Bolinas 415/868–1133 www.11wharfroad.com Closed Sun.–Wed.*

★ Hog Island Oyster Co. Marshall Oyster Farm and the Boat Oyster Bar

$$ | SEAFOOD | FAMILY | Take a short trek north on Highway 1 to the gritty mecca of Bay Area oysters—the Hog Island Marshall Oyster Farm. For a real culinary adventure, arrange to shuck and barbecue your own oysters on one of the outdoor grills (all tools supplied, reservations required); or for the less adventurous, the Boat Oyster Bar is an informal outdoor café that serves raw and grilled oysters, local snacks, and tasty beverages. **Known for:** fresh, raw, and grilled oysters; farm tours; Hog Shack shellfish to go. *Average main: $24 20215 Shoreline Hwy. 415/663–9218 hogislandoysters.com Oyster Bar closed Tues.–Thurs. No dinner.*

Inverness Park Market & Tap Room

$$ | AMERICAN | An organic oasis in the region, this deli, restaurant, and taproom offers a true taste of the Point Reyes foodshed. Classic sandwiches, breakfast bites, burritos, grilled Niman Ranch beef, wild-caught salmon, and vegan burgers are all prepared with fresh local ingredients. **Known for:** Tuesday tacos and Wednesday sushi specials; house-cooked tri-tip and smoked pastrami; grilled oysters. *Average main: $18 12301 Sir Francis Drake Blvd., Inverness Park 415/663–1491 invernessparkmarket.com.*

Saltwater Oyster Depot

$$ | SEAFOOD | Oysters shucked moments after they're taken out of Tomales Bay and French and California wines sourced from small producers are the keystones of this neighborhood oyster bar. True to the spirit of the region, it is dedicated to sustainable farming, foraging, and fishing. **Known for:** broiled, baked, and chili oysters; clam chowder; natural wines. *Average main: $20 12781 Sir Francis Drake Blvd., Inverness www.saltwateroysterdepot.com Closed Mon.–Wed.*

★ Side Street Kitchen

$ | AMERICAN | FAMILY | Rotisserie meats and veggies sourced from local farms steal the show at this former mid-20th-century truck stop and diner. It's a go-to for tri-tip and pork belly sandwiches or house-seasoned roasted chicken, best eaten with a host of sides, sips, and sweets, like crispy Parmesan Brussels sprouts, ginger lemonade, and butterscotch pudding. **Known for:** cold smoked seafood and rotisserie chicken; dog-friendly outdoor patio; apple fritters. *Average main: $16 60 4th St., Point Reyes Station 415/663–0303 sidestreet-prs.com No dinner after 6 pm.*

★ Station House Café

$$ | AMERICAN | Relocated to the space where the restaurant originally opened its doors in 1974, the Station House Café has been a stalwart venue for local music and a staunch supporter of local farms and food artisans. The community-centric eatery serves a blend of modern and classic California dishes comprised of organic seasonal ingredients, sustainable hormone-free meats, and wild-caught seafood. **Known for:** signature popovers and bread pudding; hearty breakfast items; fresh local seafood. *Average main: $17 11285 Hwy. 1, at 3rd St., Point Reyes Station 415/663–1515 www.stationhousecafe.com Closed Wed. and Thurs.*

Hotels

★ Olema House

$$$$ | B&B/INN | FAMILY | Once a historic 1860s stagecoach stopover, this renovated, luxurious getaway offers just as many reasons to stay on property—with its views of Mt. Wittenberg and garden setting—as to explore the 71,000 acres of national seashore just steps away. **Pros:** steps from trails; convenient parking and horse hitching; friendly and informative staff. **Cons:** steps to some rooms may be steep; street-facing rooms above restaurant may be noisy; Wi-Fi and cell service may be spotty. *Rooms from: $480* ✉ *10021 Coastal Hwy. 1, Olema* ☎ *415/663–9000* 🌐 *olemahouse.com* *25 rooms* *Free breakfast.*

Shopping

★ Cowgirl Creamery

FOOD/CANDY | FAMILY | In this former hay barn, a couple of Berkeley foodies (from Chez Panisse and Bette's Oceanview Diner) started their original creamery for artisanal cheeses. In addition to more than 200 specialty cheeses—local, regional, and international—you'll find Tomales Bay Foods offerings featuring West Marin farm wares. Cowgirl Creamery cheeses harness flavors unique to Point Reyes, such as their award-winning Red Hawk and Mt. Tam made with Straus Family organic milk. Sample seasonal cheeses and see how the cheese is made or order a hot mac-and-cheese at the cantina and stay for a bite at the picnic tables. Abundant deli items, gourmet goodies, and wine selections are perfect for picnicking. ✉ *80 4th St., Point Reyes Station* ☎ *415/663–9335* 🌐 *cowgirlcreamery.com.*

Gospel Flat Farm Stand

LOCAL SPECIALTIES | This combination art gallery, farm stand, and flower shop captures the true essence of the Bolinas and Olema area, with its dedication to community arts and a bounty of local organic vegetables, fruits, and eggs. The colorful self-serve site is open 24 hours, but what makes it truly special is that the entire stand operates on the honor system. Weigh and log your produce, and slip your payment (cash or check) in the box. The ever-rotating local art on exhibit adds to the allure of this roadside treasure. ✉ *140 Olema-Bolinas Rd., Bolinas* ☎ *415/868–0921* 🌐 *gospelflatfarm.com.*

★ Toby's Feed Barn

LOCAL SPECIALTIES | The heart of the community since 1942, the barn has a bounty of local gifts and produce, plus an art gallery, yoga studio, and Toby's Coffee Bar for espresso drinks and sell-out pastries. See and hear what's happening locally, catch a live band or literary event, and explore the garden. The internationally renowned all-local, all-organic Point Reyes Farmers' Market is held here on Saturdays during the growing season. ✉ *11250 Hwy. 1, Point Reyes Station* ☎ *415/663–1223* 🌐 *www.tobysfeedbarn.com.*

Chapter 20

NAPA AND SONOMA

Updated by
Daniel Mangin

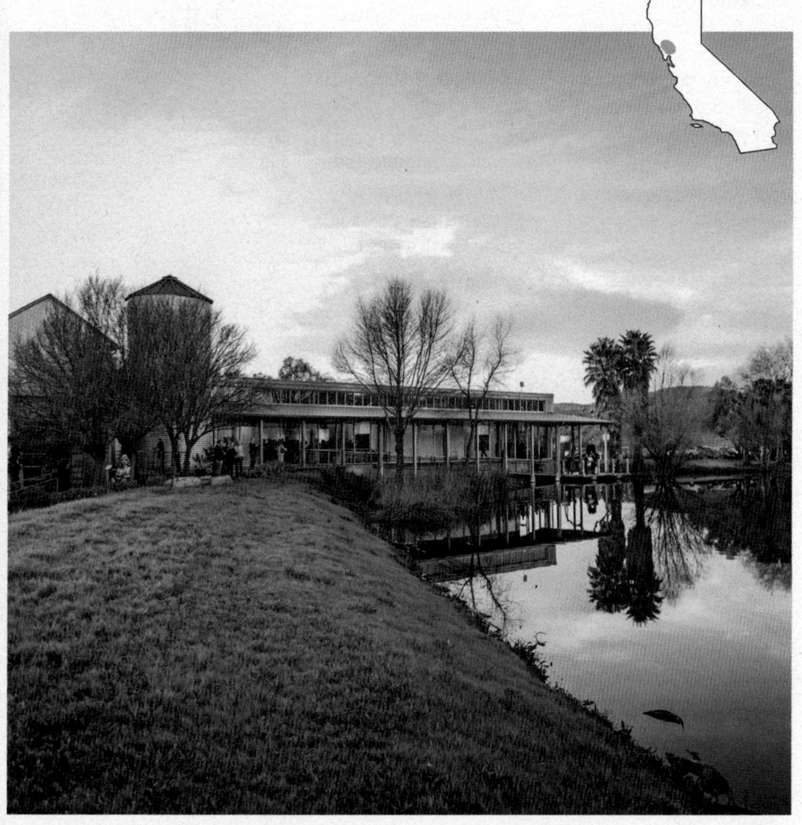

Sights ★★★★★ | Restaurants ★★★★★ | Hotels ★★★★☆ | Shopping ★★★☆☆ | Nightlife ★★★☆☆

WELCOME TO NAPA AND SONOMA

TOP REASONS TO GO

★ **Touring wineries:** Let's face it: this is the reason you're here, and the range of excellent sips to sample would make any oenophile (or novice drinker, for that matter) giddy.

★ **Biking:** Gentle hills and vineyard-laced farmland make Napa and Sonoma perfect for combining leisurely back-roads cycling with winery stops.

★ **Spa treatments:** Work-hard, play-hard types and inveterate sybarites flock to Wine Country spas for pampering.

★ **Fine dining:** A meal at a top-tier restaurant can be a revelation about the level of artistry intuitive chefs can achieve and how successfully quality wines pair with food.

★ **Viewing the art:** Several wineries, among them the Hess Collection in Napa, The Donum Estate in Sonoma, and Hall St. Helena, display museum-quality artworks indoors and on their grounds.

1 **Napa.** Good base, with tasting rooms, dining, shopping, nightlife.

2 **Yountville.** Walkable downtown, must-visit restaurants.

3 **Oakville.** Cabernet central.

4 **Rutherford.** Find out what "Rutherford dust" is.

5 **St. Helena.** Genteel downtown amid wineries.

6 **Calistoga.** Spas—from rustic to chic.

7 **Sonoma.** Anchored by a historic mission and plaza.

8 **Glen Ellen.** Creekside village with a rural flavor.

9 **Kenwood.** Top of Sonoma Valley.

10 **Petaluma.** Farming town, proud of it.

11 **Healdsburg.** Northern Sonoma's swank hub.

12 **Geyserville.** Alexander Valley wineries, fun downtown.

13 **Forestville.** Woodsy river enclave.

14 **Guerneville.** A Russian River vacation spot.

15 **Sebastopol.** West County's HQ.

16 **Santa Rosa.** Sonoma County's largest city.

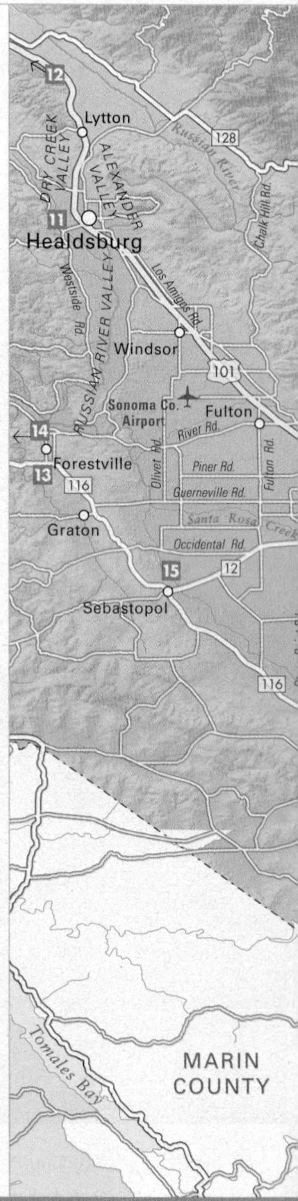

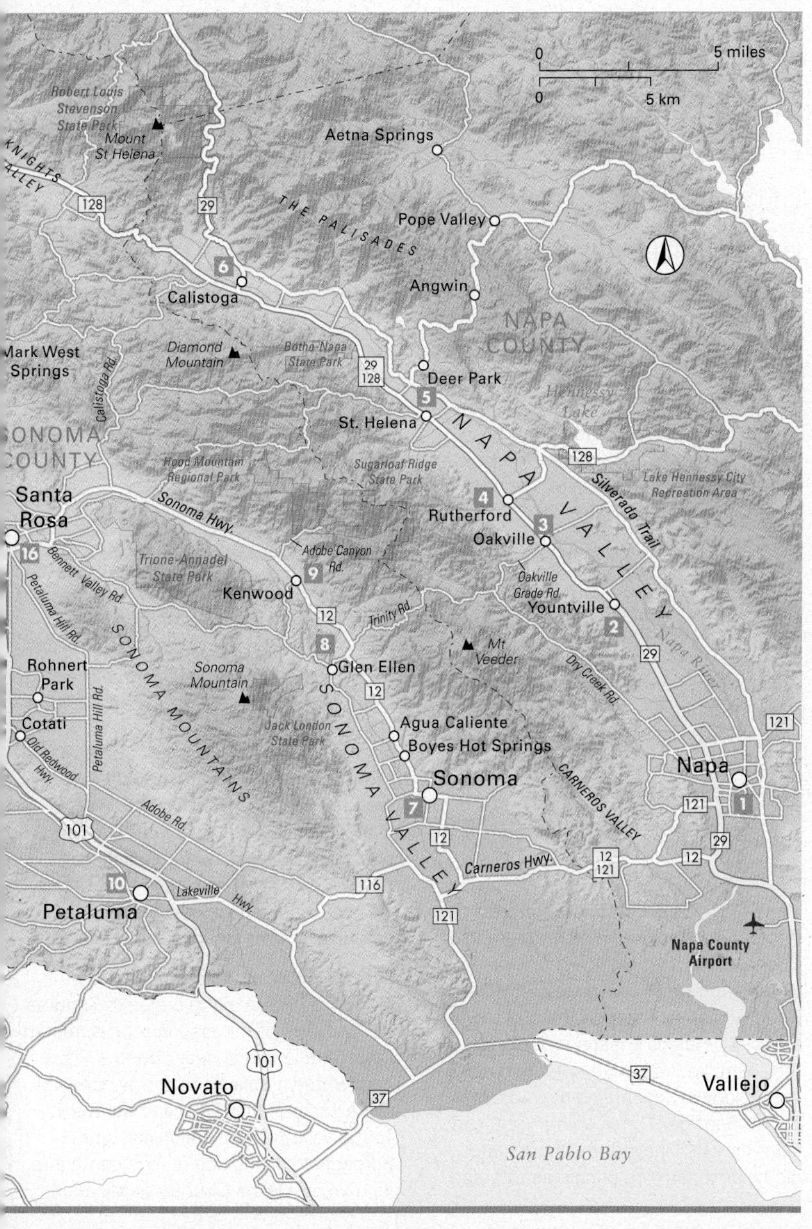

0
5 miles
0
5 km
Robert Louis Stevenson State Park
Mount St Helena
KNIGHTS VALLEY
Aetna Springs
THE PALISADES
Pope Valley
Angwin
Calistoga
NAPA COUNTY
Diamond Mountain
Botha-Napa State Park
Mark West Springs
Calistoga Rd.
Deer Park
Hennessy Lake
St. Helena
SONOMA COUNTY
NAPA VALLEY
Hood Mountain Regional Park
Sugarloaf Ridge State Park
Silverado Trail
Lake Hennessy City Recreation Area
Santa Rosa
Sonoma Hwy.
Rutherford
Oakville
Adobe Canyon Rd.
Trione-Annadel State Park
Bennett Valley Rd.
Petaluma Hill Rd.
Kenwood
Oakville Grade Rd.
Yountville
Trinity Rd.
Napa River
SONOMA MOUNTAINS
Mt Veeder
Rohnert Park
Sonoma Mountain
Glen Ellen
Dry Creek Rd.
Cotati
Old Redwood Hwy.
Petaluma Hill Rd.
Jack London State Park
SONOMA VALLEY
Agua Caliente
Boyes Hot Springs
Napa
Sonoma
CARNEROS VALLEY
Adobe Rd.
Carneros Hwy.
Petaluma
Lakeville Hwy.
Napa County Airport
Novato
Vallejo
San Pablo Bay

In California's premier wine region, the pleasures of eating and drinking are celebrated daily. It's easy to join in at famous wineries and rising newcomers off country roads, or at trendy in-town tasting rooms. Chefs transform local ingredients into feasts, and gourmet groceries sell perfect picnic fare.

Yountville, Healdsburg, and St. Helena have small-town charm as well as luxurious inns, hotels, and spas. Yet the natural setting is equally sublime, whether experienced from a canoe on the Russian River or the deck of a winery overlooking endless rows of vines.

The Wine Country is also rich in history. In Sonoma you can explore California's Spanish and Mexican pasts at the Sonoma Mission, and the origins of modern California wine making at Buena Vista Winery. Some wineries, among them St. Helena's Beringer and Rutherford's Inglenook, have cellars or tasting rooms dating to the late 1800s. Calistoga is a flurry of late-19th-century Steamboat Gothic architecture, though the town's oldest-looking building, the medieval-style Castello di Amorosa, is a 21st-century creation.

Visits to the Napa Valley's Beringer, Robert Mondavi, and Inglenook—and at Buena Vista in the Sonoma Valley—provide an entertaining overview of Wine Country history. Through the glass walls at Hall St. Helena's tasting room you may glimpse 21st-century wine-making technology in action, and over in Glen Ellen's Benziger Family Winery you can learn how its vineyard managers apply biodynamic farming principles to grape growing. At numerous facilities you can play winemaker at seminars in the fine art of blending wines. If that strikes you as too much effort, you can always pamper yourself at a luxury spa.

To delve further into the fine art of Wine Country living, pick up a copy of *Fodor's Napa and Sonoma*.

MAJOR REGIONS

Napa Valley. Practically speaking, the valley can be divided into its southern and northern parts. The southern Napa Valley encompasses cooler grape-growing areas and the tasting rooms, restaurants, and hotels of **Napa** and **Yountville**, along with slightly warmer **Oakville.** The northern valley begins around **Rutherford,** like Oakville blessed with Cabernet-friendly soils. Beyond it lies hotter **St. Helena,** whose downtown entices with boutiques, galleries, and restaurants. Warmer still is **Calistoga,** known for spas and hot springs.

Sonoma Valley and Petaluma. Modern California wine making began in Sonoma Valley. North of the tasting rooms, restaurants, and lodgings near Sonoma Plaza in downtown **Sonoma** lie the wineries of more pastoral **Glen Ellen** and **Kenwood.** To the valley's west, **Petaluma,** with a burgeoning dining scene, has come into its own as a Wine Country destination.

Northern Sonoma, Russian River, and West County. Its walkable downtown, swank hotels, and restaurant scene make **Healdsburg** the tourist hub of Sonoma County's northern section. North of Healdsburg, mostly rural **Geyserville** has a small, engaging downtown. The Russian River winds through or near **Forestville, Guerneville,** and **Sebastopol,** three West County towns where Chardonnay and Pinot Noir grow well. The county's largest city, **Santa Rosa,** contains nonwine attractions and affordable lodgings.

Planning

When to Go

High season extends from late May through October. In summer, expect the days to be hot and dry. Hotel rates are highest during the height of harvest, in September and October. Then and in summer, book lodgings well ahead. November, except for Thanksgiving week, and December before Christmas are less busy. The weather in Napa and Sonoma is pleasant nearly year-round. Daytime temperatures average from about 55°F during winter to the 80s and 90s (occasionally 100s) in summer. April, May, and October are milder but still warm. The rainiest months are usually from December through March.

Getting Here and Around

AIR

Wine Country regulars often bypass San Francisco and Oakland and fly into Santa Rosa's Charles M. Schulz Sonoma County Airport (STS), which receives direct flights from several western cities. The airport is 15 miles from Healdsburg. **■ TIP→ Alaska Airlines allows passengers flying out of STS to check up to one case of wine for free.**

BUS

Bus travel is an inconvenient way to explore the Wine Country, though it is possible. Take Golden Gate Transit from San Francisco to connect with Sonoma County Transit buses. VINE connects with BART commuter trains in the East Bay and the San Francisco Bay Ferry in Vallejo. VINE buses serve the Napa Valley.

CAR

A car is the most convenient way to navigate Napa and Sonoma. If you're flying into the area, it's almost always easiest to pick up a car at the airport. You'll also find rental companies in major Wine Country towns. A few rules to note: smartphone use for any purpose is prohibited, including mapping applications unless the device is mounted to a car's windshield or dashboard and can be activated with a single swipe or finger tap. A right turn after stopping at a red light is legal unless posted otherwise.

If you base yourself in the Napa Valley towns of Napa, Yountville, or St. Helena, or in Sonoma County's Healdsburg or Sonoma, you can visit numerous tasting rooms and nearby wineries on foot or by bicycle on mostly flat terrain. The free Yountville trolley loops through town, and ride-sharing is viable there and in Napa. Sonoma County sprawls more, but except for far west the public transit and ride-sharing generally work well.

■ TIP→ When wine tasting, select a designated driver or monitor your intake—the police keep an eye out for tipsy drivers.

Restaurants

Top Wine Country chefs tend to apply French and Italian techniques to dishes incorporating fresh, local products. Menus are often vegan- and vegetarian-friendly, with gluten-free options. At pricey restaurants you can save money by having lunch instead of dinner. With a few exceptions (noted in individual restaurant listings), dress is informal.

Hotels

The fanciest accommodations are concentrated in the Napa Valley towns of Yountville, Rutherford, St. Helena, and Calistoga; Sonoma County's poshest lodgings are in Healdsburg. The cities of Napa, Petaluma, and Santa Rosa are the best bets for budget hotels and inns. On weekends, two- or even three-night minimum stays are commonly required at smaller lodgings. Book well ahead for stays at such places in summer or early fall. Some accommodations aren't suitable for kids, so ask before you book.

Restaurant and hotel reviews have been shortened. For full information, visit Fodors.com. Restaurant prices are the average cost of a main course at dinner, or if dinner is not served, at lunch. Hotel prices are the lowest cost of a standard double room in high season.

What It Costs

$	$$	$$$	$$$$
RESTAURANTS			
under $17	$17–$26	$27–$36	over $36
HOTELS			
under $200	$200–$300	$301–$400	over $400

Napa

46 miles northeast of San Francisco.

After many years as a blue-collar burg detached from the Wine Country scene, the Napa Valley's largest town (population about 80,000) has evolved into one of its shining stars. Masaharu Morimoto and other chefs of note operate restaurants here, swank hotels and inns can be found downtown and beyond, and the nightlife options include the West Coast edition of the famed Blue Note jazz club. A walkway that follows the Napa River has made downtown more pedestrian-friendly, and the Oxbow Public Market, a complex of high-end food purveyors, is popular with locals and tourists. The market is named for the nearby oxbow bend in the Napa River, a bit north of where Napa was founded in 1848. The first wood-frame building was a saloon, and the downtown area still projects an old-river-town vibe.

GETTING HERE AND AROUND

Downtown Napa lies a mile east of Highway 29—take the 1st Street exit and follow the signs. Ample parking, much of it free for the first three hours and some for the entire day, is available on or near Main Street. Several VINE buses serve downtown and beyond.

Sights

★ Ashes & Diamonds

WINERY/DISTILLERY | Barbara Bestor's sleek white design for this appointment-only winery's glass-and-metal tasting space evokes mid-century modern architecture and with it the era and wines predating the Napa Valley's rise to prominence. Two much-heralded pros lead the wine-making team assembled by record producer Kashy Khaledi: Steve Matthiasson, known for his classic, restrained style and attention to viticultural detail, and Diana Snowden Seysses, who draws on experiences in Burgundy, Provence, and California. Bordeaux varietals are the focus, most notably Cabernet Sauvignon and Cabernet Franc but also the white blend of Sauvignon Blanc and Sémillon and even the rosé (of Cabernet Franc). With a label designer who was also responsible for a Jay-Z album cover and interiors that recall the *Mad Men* in the Palm Springs story arc, the pitch seems unabashedly intended to millennials, but the wines, low in alcohol and with high acidity (good for aging the wines), enchant connoisseurs of all stripes. ✉ *4130 Howard La., Napa* ✥ *Off Hwy. 29* ☎ *707/666–4777* 🌐 *ashesdiamonds.com* 🎫 *Tastings from $75.*

CIA at Copia

COLLEGE | Full-fledged foodies and the merely curious achieve gastronomical bliss at the Culinary Institute of America's Oxbow District campus, its facade brightened by a wraparound mural inspired by the colorful garden that fronts the facility. When everything's going full tilt, you could easily spend a few hours dining at the indoor and outdoor restaurants; checking out the shop, themed exhibitions, and Vintners Hall of Fame wall; or attending (book ahead) classes and demonstrations. If it's open, head upstairs to the Chuck Williams Culinary Arts Museum. Named for the Williams-Sonoma kitchenwares founder, it holds a fascinating collection of cooking, baking, and other food-related tools, tableware, gizmos, and gadgets, some dating back more than a century. ✉ *500 1st St., Napa* ✥ *Near McKinstry St.* ☎ *707/967–2500* 🌐 *www.ciaatcopia.com* 🎫 *Facility/museum free, class/demo fees vary.*

★ Domaine Carneros

WINERY/DISTILLERY | A visit to this majestic château is an opulent way to enjoy the Carneros District—especially in fine weather, when the vineyard views are spectacular. The château was modeled after an 18th-century French mansion owned by the Taittinger family. Carved into the hillside beneath the winery, the cellars produce sparkling wines reminiscent of those made by Taittinger, using only Los Carneros AVA grapes. Enjoy flights of sparkling wine or Pinot Noir with cheese and charcuterie plates, caviar, or smoked salmon. Tastings are by appointment only. ✉ *1240 Duhig Rd., Napa* ✥ *At Hwy. 121* ☎ *707/257–0101, 800/716–2788* 🌐 *www.domainecarneros.com* 🎫 *Tastings from $40.*

Etude Wines

WINERY/DISTILLERY | You're apt to see or hear hawks, egrets, Canada geese, and other wildlife on the grounds of Etude, known for sophisticated Pinot Noirs. Although the winery and its light-filled tasting room are in Napa County, the grapes for its flagship Carneros Estate Pinot Noir come from the Sonoma portion of Los Carneros, as do those for the rarer Heirloom Carneros Pinot Noir. Longtime winemaker Jon Priest also excels at single-vineyard Napa Valley Cabernets. In good weather, hosts pour Priest's reds, plus Chardonnay, Pinot Gris, and a few others, on the patio outside the contemporary tasting room. ✉ *1250 Cuttings Wharf Rd., Napa* ✥ *1 mile south of Hwy. 121* ☎ *707/257–5782* 🌐 *www.etudewines.com* 🎫 *Tastings from $30* ⏲ *Closed Tues. and Wed.*

★ Fontanella Family Winery

WINERY/DISTILLERY | Six miles from the downtown Napa whirl, husband-and-wife Jeff and Karen Fontanella's hillside spread seems a world apart. In addition to his formal studies, Jeff learned about wine making at three prestigious wineries before he and Karen, a lawyer, established their own operation on 81 south-facing Mt. Veeder acres. The couple braved an economic recession, an earthquake, and wildfires in the first decade but emerged tougher, if no less gracious to guests lucky enough to find themselves tasting Chardonnay, Zinfandel, and Cabernet Sauvignon on the patio here. Tastings often end with a Zinfandel-based port-style wine. With the barnlike production facility in the foreground and nearby Cabernet vines ringing a large irrigation pond, the setting represents the very picture of Napa Valley life many visitors imagine. ■ **TIP→ If offered the chance to stroll the estate, take it—the views south to San Francisco and east to Atlas Peak reward the exertion.** ✉ *1721 Partrick Rd., Napa* ✥ *1st St. to Browns Valley Rd. west of Hwy. 29* ☎ *707/252–1017* 🌐 *www.fontanellawinery.com* 🎫 *Tasting $45.*

Continued on page 732

WINE
TASTING in
NAPA and
SONOMA

Whether you're a serious wine collector making your annual pilgrimage to Northern California's Wine Country or a newbie who doesn't know the difference between a Merlot and Mourvèdre but is eager to learn, you can have a great time touring Napa and Sonoma wineries. Your gateway to the wine world is the tasting room, where staff members are happy to chat with curious guests.

(opposite page) Carneros vineyards in autumn, Napa Valley. (top) Pinot Gris grapes. (bottom) Bottles from Far Niente winery.

VISITING WINERIES

Tasting rooms range from the grand to the humble, offering everything from a few sips of wine to in-depth tours of facilities and vineyards. Some are open for drop-in visits, usually daily from around 10 or 11 am to 5 pm. Many require guests to make reservations. First-time visitors frequently enjoy the history-oriented focus at Charles Krug, Inglenook, and Buena Vista. The environments at some wineries reflect their owners' or founders' other interests: art at The Donum Estate and Hall St. Helena, movie making at Francis Ford Coppola, and medieval history at the Castello di Amorosa.

Many wineries describe their pourers as "wine educators," and indeed some of them have taken online or other classes and have passed an exam to prove basic knowledge of appellations, grape varietals, vineyards, and wine-making techniques. The one constant, however, is a deep, shared pleasure in the experience of wine tasting.

Fees. Most wineries charge for tasting. In the Napa Valley, expect to pay \$35–\$65 to sample current releases, \$75–\$100 or more for reserve, estate, or library wines. Sonoma County tastings generally cost \$20–\$40 for the former, \$40–\$75 for the latter. To experience wine making at its highest level, consider splurging for at least one special tasting.

Some wineries waive tasting fees if you join the wine club, purchase a few bottles, or spend a particular dollar amount. At others, the fees are "exclusive of purchase."

Tipping. Many guests tip out of instinct, but it isn't required. Instances when you might consider tipping include when your server has given a few extra pours or a discount on your purchases or has otherwise provided outstanding service. For a basic tasting, \$5–\$10 per couple will suffice; for a hosted seated tasting, \$5–\$10 per person, perhaps a little more for extra attention.

WINE TASTING 101

TAKE A GOOD LOOK.

Hold your glass by the stem, raise it to the light, and take a close look at the wine. Check for clarity and color. (This is easiest to do if you can hold the glass in front of a white background.) Any tinge of brown usually means that the wine is over the hill or has gone bad.

BREATHE DEEP.

1. Sniff the wine once or twice to see if you can identify any smells.

2. Swirl the wine gently in the glass. Aerating the wine this way releases more of its aromas. (It's called "volatilizing the esters," if you're trying to impress someone.)

3. Take another long sniff. You might notice that experienced wine tasters spend more time sniffing the wine than drinking it. This is because this step is where the magic happens. The number of scents you might detect is almost endless, from berries, apricots, honey, and wildflowers to leather, cedar, or even tar. Does the wine smell good to you? Do you detect any "off" flavors, like wet dog or sulfur?

AT LAST! TAKE A SIP.

1. Swirl the wine around your mouth so that it makes contact with all your taste buds and releases more of its aromas. Think about the way the wine feels in your mouth. Is it watery or rich? Is it crisp or silky? Does it have a bold flavor, or is it subtle? The weight and intensity of a wine are called its body.

2. Hold the wine in your mouth for a few seconds and see if you can identify any developing flavors. More complex wines will reveal many different flavors as you drink them.

SPIT OR SWALLOW.

The pros typically spit, since they want to preserve their palate (and sobriety) for the wines to come, but you'll find that swallowers far outnumber the spitters in the winery tasting rooms. Whether you spit or swallow, notice the flavor that remains after the wine is gone (the finish).

Swirl

Sniff

Sip

MAKE AN APPOINTMENT

Most Napa and Sonoma wineries accept visitors by appointment only to serve patrons better, though some welcome walk-ins if space is available. To avoid disappointment, make reservations at least a day or two ahead. In summer and early fall, try to visit on weekdays or before 11 am or so when it's less crowded. Also look for wineries off the main drags of Highway 29 in Napa and Highway 12 in Sonoma.

HOW WINE IS MADE

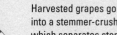

1. CRUSHING
Harvested grapes go into a stemmer-crusher, which separates stems from fruit and crushes the grapes to release "free-run" juice.

2. PRESSING
Remaining juice is gently extracted from grapes. Usually done by pressing grapes against the walls of a tank with an inflatable bladder.

3. FERMENTING
Extracted juice (and also grape skins and pulp, when making red wine) goes into stainless-steel tanks or oak barrels to ferment. During fermentation, sugars convert to alcohol.

4. AGING
Wine is stored in stainless-steel or oak casks or barrels, or sometimes in concrete vessels, to develop flavors.

5. RACKING
Wine is transferred to clean barrels; sediment is removed. Wine may be filtered and fined (clarified) to improve its clarity, color, and sometimes flavor.

6. BOTTLING
Wine is bottled either at the winery or at a special facility, then stored again for bottle-aging.

WHAT'S AN APPELLATION?

American Viticultural Area (AVA) or, more commonly, an appellation. What can be confusing is that some appellations encompass smaller subappellations. The Rutherford, Oakville, and Mt. Veeder AVAs, for instance, are among the Napa Valley AVA's 16 subappellations. Wineries often buy grapes from outside their AVA, so their labels might reference different appellations. A winery in the warmer Napa Valley, for instance, might source Pinot Noir grapes from the cooler Russian River Valley, where they grow better. The appellation listed on a label always refers to where a wine's grapes were grown, not to where the wine was made. By law, if a label bears the name of an appellation, 85% of the grapes must come from it.

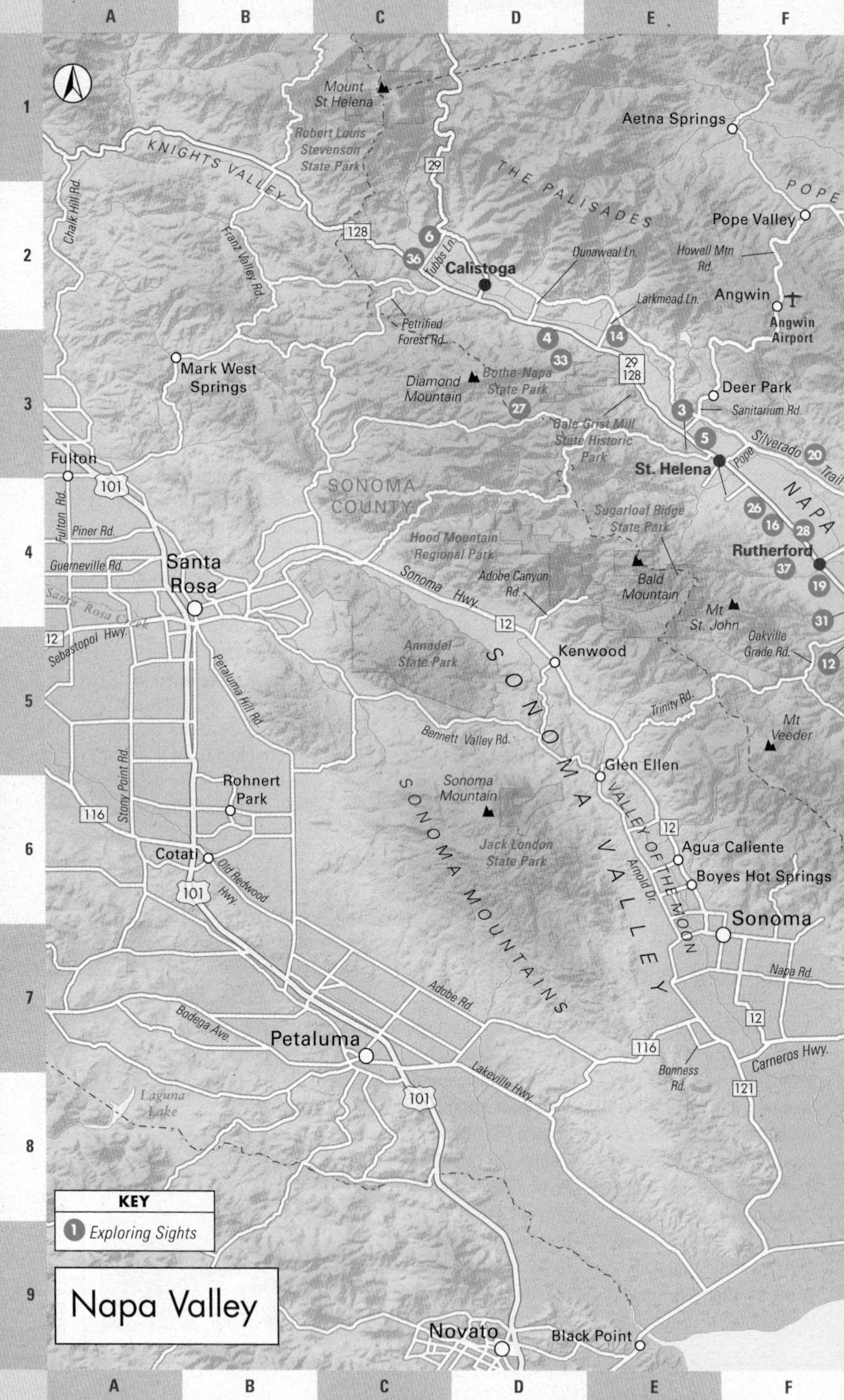

A B C D E F
1 2 3 4 5 6 7 8 9
Mount St Helena
Robert Louis Stevenson State Park
KNIGHTS VALLEY
THE PALISADES
Aetna Springs
POPE
Pope Valley
Chalk Hill Rd.
Franz Valley Rd.
Tubbs Ln.
Calistoga
Dunaweal Ln.
Howell Mtn Rd.
Larkmead Ln.
Angwin
Angwin Airport
Petrified Forest Rd.
Mark West Springs
Diamond Mountain
Bothe-Napa State Park
Deer Park
Sanitarium Rd.
Bale Grist Mill State Historic Park
Silverado Trail
Pope
Fulton
St. Helena
NAPA
SONOMA COUNTY
Fulton Rd.
Sugarloaf Ridge State Park
Piner Rd.
Hood Mountain Regional Park
Rutherford
Guerneville Rd.
Santa Rosa
Adobe Canyon Rd.
Sonoma Hwy
Bald Mountain
Santa Rosa Creek
Mt St. John
Sebastopol Hwy.
Oakville Grade Rd.
Annadel State Park
Kenwood
Petaluma Hill Rd.
Trinity Rd.
Mt Veeder
Bennett Valley Rd.
Glen Ellen
Stony Point Rd.
Rohnert Park
Sonoma Mountain
VALLEY OF THE MOON
SONOMA VALLEY
SONOMA MOUNTAINS
Jack London State Park
Agua Caliente
Cotati
Arnold Dr.
Boyes Hot Springs
Old Redwood Hwy.
Sonoma
Napa Rd.
Adobe Rd.
Bodega Ave.
Petaluma
Carneros Hwy.
Bonness Rd.
Lakeville Hwy.
Laguna Lake
KEY
1 Exploring Sights
Napa Valley
Novato
Black Point

Sights

1	Ashes & Diamonds	H6
2	B Cellars	G4
3	Beringer Vineyards	E3
4	Castello di Amorosa	D3
5	Charles Krug Winery	E3
6	Chateau Montelena	C2
7	CIA at Copia	I6
8	Cliff Lede Vineyards	H4
9	Domaine Carneros	G7
10	Elyse Winery	G5
11	Etude Wines	H7
12	Far Niente	F5
13	Fontanella Family Winery	G6
14	Frank Family Vineyards	E3
15	Frog's Leap	G4
16	Hall St. Helena	F4
17	Heron House Yountville	G5
18	Hess Collection	G6
19	Inglenook	F4
20	Joseph Phelps Vineyards	F3
21	Mayacamas Downtown	H6
22	Mumm Napa	G4
23	Napa Valley Wine Train	I6
24	Oasis by Hoopes	G5
25	Oxbow Public Market	I6
26	Prager Winery & Port Works	F4
27	Pride Mountain Vineyards	D3
28	The Prisoner Wine Company	F4
29	RH Wine Vault	G5
30	Robert Biale Vineyards	H6
31	Robert Mondavi Winery	F4
32	Robert Sinskey Vineyards	H5
33	Schramsberg	D3
34	Silver Oak	G4
35	Stag's Leap Wine Cellars	H5
36	Tamber Bey Vineyards	C2
37	Tres Sabores Winery	F4
38	ZD Wines	G4

Hess Collection

WINERY/DISTILLERY | About 9 miles northwest of Napa, up a winding road ascending Mt. Veeder, this winery is a delightful discovery. The limestone structure, rustic from the outside but modern and airy within, contains Swiss founder Donald Hess's world-class art collection, including large-scale works by contemporary artists such as Andy Goldsworthy, Anselm Kiefer, and Robert Rauschenberg. Cabernet Sauvignon and Chardonnay are strengths, along with small-lot reds (Petite Sirah, Pinot Noir, Syrah, and blends). All visits are by appointment. **■ TIP→ Guided or self-guided gallery tours are part of most tastings.** ✉ *4411 Redwood Rd., Napa* ✣ *West off Hwy. 29 at Trancas St./Redwood Rd. exit* ☎ *707/255–1144* 🌐 *www.hesscollection.com* 🎫 *Tastings from $45.*

★ **Mayacamas Downtown**

WINERY/DISTILLERY | Cabernets from Mayacamas Vineyards placed second and fifth respectively on *Wine Spectator* magazine's 2019 and 2020 "Top 100" lists of the world's best wines, two accolades among many for this winery founded atop Mt. Veeder in 1889. One of Napa's leading viticulturists, Annie Favia farms the organic vineyards, elevation 2,000-plus feet, without irrigation; her husband, Andy Favia, is the consulting winemaker. The grapes for the Chardonnay come from 40-year-old vines. Aged in mostly neutral (previously used) French oak barrels to accentuate mountain minerality, the wine is a Napa Valley marvel. The Cabernet Sauvignon ages for three years, spending part of the time in oak barrels more than a century old. Erin Martin, a Napa Valley resident with a hip international reputation, designed the light-filled storefront tasting space. **■ TIP→ Experiencing these magnificent wines at this downtown tasting room may entice you to visit the estate.** ✉ *First Street Napa, 1256 1st St., Napa* ✣ *At Randolph St.* ☎ *707/294–1433* 🌐 *www.mayacamas.com* 🎫 *Tastings from $35* ⊙ *Closed Mon. and Tues.*

Napa Valley Wine Train

TOUR—SIGHT | Guests on this Napa Valley fixture ride the same 150-year-old rail corridor along which trains once transported passengers as far north as Calistoga's spas. The rolling stock includes restored Pullman cars and a two-story Vista Dome coach with a curved glass roof. The train travels a leisurely, scenic route between Napa and St. Helena. Patrons on some tours enjoy a multicourse meal and tastings at one or more wineries. Some rides involve no winery stops, and themed trips are occasionally scheduled. **■ TIP→ It's best to make this trip during the day, when you can enjoy the vineyard views.** ✉ *1275 McKinstry St., Napa* ✣ *Off 1st St.* ☎ *707/253–2111, 800/427–4124* 🌐 *www.winetrain.com* 🎫 *From $160.*

★ **Oxbow Public Market**

MARKET | The 40,000-square-foot market's two dozen stands provide an introduction to Northern California's diverse artisanal food products. Swoon over decadent charcuterie at the Fatted Calf (great sandwiches, too), slurp oysters at Hog Island, enjoy empanadas at El Porteño, or chow down on vegetarian, duck, or salmon tacos at C Casa. Sample wine (and cheese) at the Oxbow Cheese & Wine Merchant, ales at Fieldwork Brewing's taproom, and barrel-aged cocktails at the Napa Valley Distillery. The owner of Kara's Cupcakes operates the adjacent Bar Lucia for (mostly) sparkling wines and rosés. Napa Bookmine is among the few nonfood vendors here. **■ TIP→ Five Dot Ranch and Cookhouse sells quality steaks and other meat to go; if you don't mind eating at the counter, you can order from the small menu and dine on the spot.** ✉ *610 and 644 1st St., Napa* ✣ *At McKinstry St.* 🌐 *www.oxbowpublicmarket.com.*

★ **Robert Biale Vineyards**

WINERY/DISTILLERY | Here's a surprise: a highly respected Napa Valley winery that doesn't sell a lick of Cabernet. Zinfandel from heritage vineyards, some with vines more than 100 years old, holds the spotlight, with luscious Petite Sirahs in supporting roles. Nearly every pour comes with a fascinating backstory, starting with the flagship Black Chicken Zinfandel. In the 1940s, the Biale family sold eggs, walnuts, and other farm staples, with bootleg Zinfandel a lucrative sideline. Because neighbors could eavesdrop on party-line phone conversations, "black chicken" became code for a jug of Zin. These days the wines are produced on the up-and-up by valley native Tres Goetting, whose vineyard and cellar choices bring out the best in two unsung varietals. The 10-acre property's open-air tasting setting—a stone's throw from Zinfandel vines, with far-off views of two mountain ranges—has a back-porch feel. Visits are by appointment; call ahead for same-day. ✉ *4038 Big Ranch Rd., at Salvador Ave., Napa* ☎ *707/257–7555* 🌐 *biale.com* *Tastings from $35.*

Stag's Leap Wine Cellars

WINERY/DISTILLERY | A 1973 Stag's Leap Wine Cellars S.L.V. Cabernet Sauvignon put this winery and the Napa Valley on the enological map by placing first in the famous Judgment of Paris tasting of 1976. The grapes for that wine came from a vineyard visible from the stone-and-glass Fay Outlook & Visitor Center, which has broad views of a second fabled Cabernet vineyard (Fay) and the promontory that gives both the winery and the Stags Leap District AVA their names. The top-of-the-line Cabernets from these vineyards are poured at appointment-only tastings (call ahead for same-day visits), some of which include perceptive food pairings by the winery's executive chef. **■ TIP→ When the weather's right, two patios with the same views as the tasting room fill up quickly.** ✉ *5766 Silverado Trail, Napa* ✣ *At Wappo Hill Rd.* ☎ *707/261–6410* 🌐 *www.stagsleapwinecellars.com* *Tastings from $50.*

Restaurants

Angèle

$$$ | **FRENCH** | A vaulted wood-beamed ceiling and paper-topped tables set the scene for romance at this softly lit French bistro inside an 1890s boathouse. Look for clever variations on classic dishes such as croque monsieur (grilled Parisian ham and Gruyère) and Niçoise salad for lunch, with veal sweetbreads and, in season, steamed mussels with white wine–and–saffron broth for dinner. **Known for:** classic bistro cuisine; romantic setting; outdoor seating under bright-yellow umbrellas. 💲 *Average main: $33* ✉ *540 Main St., Napa* ✣ *At 5th St.* ☎ *707/252–8115* 🌐 *www.angelerestaurant.com.*

★ Compline

$$$ | **MODERN AMERICAN** | The full name of this enterprise put together by master sommelier Matt Stamp and restaurant wine vet Ryan Stetins is Compline Wine Bar, Restaurant, and Merchant, and indeed you can just sip wine or purchase it here. The place evolved into a hot spot, though, for its youthful vibe and eclectic small and large plates that might include shrimp lumpia (essentially a type of fried spring roll) and citrus-brined chicken but always the Compline burger, best enjoyed with duck-fat fries—and, per Stamp, champagne. **Known for:** upbeat vibe; pastas and vegetarian dishes; by-the-glass wines. 💲 *Average main: $29* ✉ *1300 1st St., Suite 312, Napa* ☎ *707/492–8150* 🌐 *complinewine.com* 🕙 *Closed Tues.*

Grace's Table

$$ | **ECLECTIC** | A dependable, varied menu makes this modest corner restaurant occupying a brick-and-glass storefront many Napans' go-to choice for a simple meal. Fish tacos and iron-skillet corn bread with lavender honey and butter show up at all hours, with buttermilk pancakes and chilaquiles scrambled eggs among the brunch staples and cassoulet and roasted young chicken popular for

dinner. **Known for:** congenial staffers; good beers on tap; eclectic menu focusing on France, Italy, and the Americas. *Average main: $26 1400 2nd St., Napa At Franklin St. 707/226–6200 www.gracestable.net.*

★ La Toque

$$$$ | **MODERN AMERICAN** | Chef Ken Frank's La Toque is the complete package: his imaginative French-inspired cuisine, served in a formal dining space, is complemented by a wine lineup that consistently earns the restaurant a coveted *Wine Spectator* Grand Award. Ingredients appearing on the prix-fixe multicourse tasting menu often include caviar, sea scallops, squab, and lamb saddle, in dishes prepared and seasoned to pair with wines jointly chosen by the chefs and master sommelier. **Known for:** chef's tasting menu (à la carte also possible); astute wine pairings; vegetarian tasting menu. *Average main: $150 Westin Verasa Napa, 1314 McKinstry St., Napa Off Soscol Ave. 707/257–5157 www.latoque.com Closed Mon. and Tues. No lunch.*

Morimoto Napa

$$$$ | **JAPANESE** | *Iron Chef* star Masaharu Morimoto is the big name behind this downtown Napa restaurant where everything is delightfully over the top, including the desserts. Organic materials such as twisting grapevines above the bar and rough-hewn wooden tables seem simultaneously earthy and modern, creating a fitting setting for the gorgeously plated Japanese fare, from straightforward sashimi to more elaborate seafood, chicken, pork, and beef entrées. **Known for:** theatrical ambience; gorgeous plating; cocktail and sake menu. *Average main: $42 610 Main St., Napa At 5th St. 707/252–1600 www.morimotonapa.com.*

Oenotri

$$ | **ITALIAN** | Often spotted at local farmers' markets and his restaurant's gardens, Oenotri's ebullient chef-owner and Napa native Tyler Rodde is ever on the lookout for fresh produce to incorporate into his rustic southern-Italian cuisine. His restaurant, a brick-walled contemporary space with tall windows and wooden tables, is a lively spot to sample housemade salumi and pastas, thin-crust pizzas, and entrées that might include seared fresh fish or grilled skirt steak. **Known for:** lively atmosphere; Margherita pizza with San Marzano tomatoes; desserts with flair. *Average main: $26 1425 1st St., Napa At Franklin St. 707/252–1022 www.oenotri.com.*

★ Torc

$$$ | **MODERN AMERICAN** | *Torc* means "wild boar" in an early Celtic dialect, and owner-chef Sean O'Toole, who formerly helmed kitchens at top Manhattan, San Francisco, and Yountville establishments, occasionally incorporates the restaurant's namesake beast into his eclectic offerings. A recent menu featured baked-stuffed Maine lobster, nettle risotto, three hand-cut pasta dishes, and pork-belly with pole beans, all prepared by O'Toole and his team with style and precision. **Known for:** gracious service; specialty cocktails; Bengali sweet-potato pakora and deviled-egg appetizers. *Average main: $36 1140 Main St., Napa At Pearl St. 707/252–3292 www.torcnapa.com Closed Sun. and Mon.*

★ ZuZu

$$$ | **SPANISH** | At festive ZuZu the focus is on cold and hot tapas, paella, and other Spanish favorites often downed with cava or sangria. Regulars revere the paella, made with Spanish *bomba* rice, and small plates that might include garlic shrimp, jamón Ibérico, lamb chops with Moroccan barbecue glaze, and white anchovies with sliced egg and rémoulade on grilled bread. **Known for:** singular flavors and spicing; Spanish jazz on the stereo; sister restaurant La Taberna three doors south for beer, wine, and bar bites. *Average main: $32 829 Main St., Napa Near 3rd St. 707/224–8555 www.zuzunapa.com Closed Mon. and Tues.*

Hotels

Andaz Napa

$$$ | **HOTEL** | Part of the Hyatt family, this boutique hotel with an urban-hip vibe has spacious guest rooms with white-marble bathrooms stocked with high-quality products. **Pros:** casual-chic feel; proximity to downtown restaurants, theaters, and tasting rooms; cheery, attentive service. **Cons:** unremarkable views from some rooms; expensive on weekends in high season; some room show wear and tear. *Rooms from: $304 1450 1st St., Napa 707/687–1234 andaznapa.com 141 rooms No meals.*

★ Archer Hotel Napa

$$$ | **HOTEL** | Ideal for travelers seeking design pizzazz, a see-and-be-seen atmosphere, and first-class amenities, this five-story downtown Napa property fuses New York City chic and Las Vegas glamour. **Pros:** restaurants and room service by chef Charlie Palmer; Sky & Vine rooftop bar; great views from upper-floor rooms (especially south and west). **Cons:** not particularly rustic; expensive in high season; occasional service, hospitality lapses. *Rooms from: $324 1230 1st St., Napa 707/690–9800, 855/200–9052 archerhotel.com/napa 183 rooms No meals.*

★ Carneros Resort and Spa

$$$$ | **RESORT** | A winning combination of glamour, service, and pastoral seclusion makes this resort with freestanding board-and-batten cottages the perfect getaway for active lovebirds or families and groups seeking to unwind. **Pros:** cottages have lots of privacy; beautiful views from hilltop pool and hot tub; heaters on private patios. **Cons:** long drive to upvalley destinations; least expensive accommodations pick up highway noise; pricey pretty much year-round. *Rooms from: $749 4048 Sonoma Hwy./Hwy. 121, Napa 707/299–4900, 888/400–9000 www.carnerosresort.com 100 rooms No meals.*

★ The Inn on First

$$ | **B&B/INN** | Guests gush over the hospitality at this inn where the painstakingly restored 1905 mansion facing 1st Street contains five rooms, with five additional accommodations, all suites, in a building behind a secluded patio and garden. **Pros:** full gourmet breakfast by hosts-with-the-most owners; gas fireplaces and whirlpool tubs in all rooms; away from downtown but not too far. **Cons:** no TVs; owners "respectfully request no children"; lacks pool, fitness center, and other amenities of larger properties. *Rooms from: $225 1938 1st St., Napa 707/253–1331 www.theinnonfirst.com 10 rooms Free breakfast.*

★ Inn on Randolph

$$$ | **B&B/INN** | A few calm blocks from the downtown action on a nearly 1-acre lot with landscaped gardens, the Inn on Randolph—with a Gothic Revival–style main house and its five guest rooms plus five historic cottages out back—is a sophisticated haven celebrated for its gourmet gluten-free breakfasts and snacks. **Pros:** quiet residential neighborhood; spa tubs in cottages and two main-house rooms; romantic setting. **Cons:** a bit of a walk from downtown; expensive in-season; weekend minimum-stay requirement. *Rooms from: $339 411 Randolph St., Napa 707/257–2886 www.innonrandolph.com 10 rooms Free breakfast.*

Nightlife

Blue Note Napa

MUSIC CLUBS | The famed New York jazz room's intimate West Coast club hosts national headliners such as Kenny Garrett, KT Tunstall, and Jody Watley. There's a full bar, and you can order a meal or small bites from the kitchen. The larger JaM Cellars Ballroom upstairs books similar artists. *Napa Valley Opera House, 1030 Main St., Napa At 1st St. 707/880–2300 www.bluenotenapa.com.*

Cadet Wine + Beer Bar

WINE BARS—NIGHTLIFE | Cadet plays things urban-style cool with a long bar, high-top tables, and a low-lit, generally loungelike feel. When they opened their bar, the two owners described their outlook as "unabashedly pro-California," but their wine-and-beer lineup circles the globe. The crowd here is youngish, the vibe festive. ✉ *930 Franklin St., Napa* ✥ *At end of pedestrian alley between 1st and 2nd Sts.* ☎ *707/224–4400* 🌐 *www.cadetbeerandwinebar.com* ☞ *Closed Mon. and Tues.*

Shopping

First Street Napa

SHOPPING CENTERS/MALLS | The Archer Hotel Napa anchors this open-air downtown complex of mostly ground-level restaurants, tasting rooms, and national (Anthropologie, Lululemon) and homegrown (Bennington Napa Valley, Habituate Lifestyle + Interiors, Napa Stäk) design, clothing, housewares, and culinary shops. Copperfield's Books and the Visit Napa Valley Welcome Center are also here, along with Milo and Friends for pet necessities and accessories. ✉ *1300 1st St., Napa* ✥ *Between Franklin and Coombs Sts.* ☎ *707/257–6900* 🌐 *www.firststreetnapa.com.*

Activities

Napa Valley Gondola

TOUR—SPORTS | Rides in authentic gondolas that seat up to six depart from downtown Napa's municipal dock. You'll never mistake the Napa River for the Grand Canal, but on a sunny day this is a diverting excursion that often includes a serenade. ✉ *Main Street Boat Dock, 680 Main St., Napa* ✥ *Riverfront Promenade, south of 3rd St. Bridge* ☎ *707/373–2100* 🌐 *napavalleygondola.com* ☞ *From $145 (up to 6 people).*

Yountville

9 miles north of the town of Napa.

Yountville (population 3,000) is something like Disneyland for food lovers. You could stay here several days and not exhaust all the options—a few of them owned by The French Laundry's Thomas Keller—and the tiny town is full of small inns and high-end hotels that cater to those who prefer to walk (not drive) after an extravagant meal. It's also well located for excursions to many big-name Napa wineries, especially those in the Stags Leap District, from which big, bold Cabernet Sauvignons helped make the Napa Valley's wine-making reputation.

GETTING HERE AND AROUND

Downtown Yountville sits just off Highway 29. Approaching from the south take the Yountville exit—from the north take Madison—and proceed to Washington Street, home to the major shops and restaurants. Yountville Cross Road connects downtown to the Silverado Trail, along which many noted wineries do business. The free Yountville Trolley serves the town daily 10 am–7 pm (on-call service until 11 pm except on Sunday).

Sights

★ Cliff Lede Vineyards

WINERY/DISTILLERY | Inspired by his passion for classic rock, owner and construction magnate Cliff Lede named the blocks in his Stags Leap District vineyard after hits by the Grateful Dead and other bands. Rock memorabilia and contemporary art like Jim Dine's outdoor sculpture *Twin 6' Hearts,* a magnet for the Instagram set, are two other Lede obsessions. The vibe at his efficient, high-tech winery is anything but laid-back, however. Cutting-edge agricultural and enological science informs the vineyard management and wine making here. Lede produces Sauvignon Blanc, Cabernet Sauvignon, and Bordeaux-style red blends; tastings often include a Chardonnay, Pinot Gris, or Pinot Noir from sister winery FEL. All the wines are well crafted, though the Cabs really rock. ✉ *1473 Yountville Cross Rd., Yountville* ✣ *Off Silverado Trail* ☎ *707/944–8642* 🌐 *cliffledevineyards.com* 🎫 *Tastings from $60 (sometimes $40 for weekend garden tastings).*

★ Elyse Winery

WINERY/DISTILLERY | One of his colleagues likens Elyse's winemaker, Russell Bevan, to "a water witch without the walking stick" for his ability to assess a vineyard's weather, soil, and vine positioning and intuit how particular viticultural techniques will affect wines' flavors. Bevan farms judiciously during the growing season, striving later in the cellar to preserve what nature and his efforts have yielded rather than rely on heavy manipulation. Under previous owners for three-plus decades (until 2018), Elyse became known for single-vineyard Zinfandels and Cabernet Sauvignons, with Merlot, Petite Sirah, and red blends other strong suits. A country lane edged by vines leads to this unassuming winery, whose tastings, often outdoors, have a backyard-casual feel. ■ **TIP→ Costing much less than the average Napa Valley Cab, Elyse's Holbrook Mitchell Cabernet Sauvignon holds its own against peers priced appreciably higher.** ✉ *2100 Hoffman La., Napa* ✣ *1¾ miles south of central Yountville, off Hwy. 29 or Solano Ave.* ☎ *707/944–2900* 🌐 *elysewinery.com* 🎫 *Tastings from $50.*

★ Heron House Yountville

WINERY/DISTILLERY | Nine family-owned wineries specializing in small-batch Cabernet Sauvignon showcase their output at this southern Yountville tasting space that doubles as a boutique for contemporary art, fashion accessories, and household items. Several heavy-duty Napa names are involved, starting with Richard Steltzner, who began growing grapes here in 1965. His daughter, Allison, Heron House's founder, represents his Steltzner Vineyards and her Bench Vineyards, and well-known vintners and winemakers are behind the other operations: Eponymous, Hobel, Lindstrom, Myriad, Perchance, Switchback Ridge, and Zeitgeist. The wineries also make whites, rosés, and other reds. Tasting fees vary depending on the flight, which hosts are happy to adjust to match guests' preferences. Visits are by appointment, but walk-ins are accommodated when possible. ■ **TIP→ The King of Kings Cabernet Experience suits collectors and Napa Valley Cab lovers eager to up their game.** ✉ *6484 Washington St., Suite G, Yountville* ✣ *At Oak Circle* ☎ *707/947–7039* 🌐 *heronhouseyountville.com* 🎫 *Tastings from $65* ⊙ *Closed Tues. and Wed.*

★ Oasis by Hoopes

WINERY/DISTILLERY | Vineyards surround the walk-through organic garden and corral for rescue animals that anchor second-generation vintner Lindsay Hoopes's playfully pastoral, cool-bordering-on-chic wine venue. In conceiving this family- and dog-friendly outdoor-oriented spot—with ample patio and garden seating, an Airstream trailer Instagrammers love, and even a tent—Hoopes aimed to expand the notion of what a Napa Valley wine tasting can entail. To that end, each group or solo visitor pays a table charge the hosts apply to bottles purchased for sipping on-site or later. If you prefer a traditional flight, the fee can go toward that, too. Lindsay's father started Hoopes Vineyard in the 1980s, selling his Oakville AVA Cabernet Sauvignon grapes to A-list producers before starting his boutique label in 1999. The lineup now includes Sauvignon Blanc, Chardonnay, rosé, Merlot, and Syrah. Most are gems, particularly two Oakville Cabs and a Howell Mountain Merlot. ✉ *6204 Washington St., Yountville* ✣ *1 mile south of downtown* ☎ *707/944–1869* 🌐 *hoopesvineyard.com/oasis-by-hoopes* 🎫 *Tastings from $75.*

RH Wine Vault

WINERY/DISTILLERY | Gargantuan crystal chandeliers, century-old olive trees, and strategically placed water features provide visual and aural continuity at Restoration Hardware's quadruple-threat food, wine, art, and design compound. An all-day café fronts two steel, glass, and concrete home-furnishings galleries, with a bluestone walkway connecting them to a reboot of the former Ma(i) sonry wine salon here. Centered on a two-story 1904 manor house constructed from Napa River stone, it remains an excellent spot to learn about small-lot Napa and Sonoma wines, served by the glass, flight, or bottle. Collector-revered labels like Corison, Fisher, Lail, Matthiasson, Melka, and Spottswoode are all represented, the wines in good weather poured in "outdoor living rooms" behind the stone structure. Oozing RH fabulousness as it does, the Wine Vault can feel like a scene on a busy day, but the wines are the real deal. All tastings are by appointment. ✉ *6725 Washington St., Yountville* ✣ *At Pedroni St.* ☎ *707/339–4654* 🌐 *www.restorationhardware.com* *Tastings from $50.*

Robert Sinskey Vineyards

WINERY/DISTILLERY | Although the winery produces a Stags Leap Cabernet Sauvignon (SLD Estate), two Bordeaux-style red blends (Marcien and POV), and white wines, Sinskey is best known for its intense, brambly Carneros District Pinot Noirs. All the grapes are grown in organic, certified biodynamic vineyards. The influence of Robert's wife, Maria Helm Sinskey—a chef and cookbook author and the winery's culinary director—is evident during the tastings, all of which are accompanied by at least a few bites of food. The elevated Terroir Tasting explores the winery's land and farming practices. Chef's Table takes in the winery's culinary gardens and ends with a seated wine-and-food pairing. All visits require an appointment, wisely made a day or two ahead. ✉ *6320 Silverado Trail, Napa* ✣ *At Yountville Cross Rd.* ☎ *707/944–9090* 🌐 *www.robertsinskey.com* *Tastings from $40.*

Restaurants

Ad Hoc

$$$$ | **MODERN AMERICAN** | At this low-key dining room with zinc-top tables and wine served in tumblers, superstar chef Thomas Keller offers a single, fixed-price, nightly menu that might include smoked beef short ribs with creamy herb rice and charred broccolini or sesame chicken with radish kimchi and fried rice. Ad Hoc also serves a small but decadent Sunday brunch, and Keller's Addendum annex, in a separate small building behind the restaurant, sells boxed lunches to go (including moist buttermilk fried chicken) from Thursday to Saturday except in winter. **Known for:** casual cuisine at great prices for a Thomas Keller restaurant; don't-miss buttermilk-fried-chicken night; Burgers & Half Bottles (of wine) pop-up. *Average main: $56* ✉ *6476 Washington St., Yountville* ✣ *At Oak Circle* ☎ *707/944–2487* 🌐 *www.thomaskeller.com/adhoc* *Closed Tues. and Wed. No lunch Mon. and Thurs.* ☞ *Check website or call a day ahead for next day's menu.*

★ Bistro Jeanty

$$$ | **FRENCH** | Escargots, cassoulet, *steak au poivre* (pepper steak), and other French classics are prepared with the utmost precision inside this tan-brick country bistro whose flower-filled window boxes, extra-wide shutters, and red-and-white-striped awning hint at the Old World flair and joie de vivre that infuse the place. Regulars often start with the rich tomato soup in a flaky puff pastry before proceeding to sole meunière or coq au vin, completing the French sojourn with a lemon meringue tart or other authentic dessert. **Known for:** traditional preparations; oh-so-French atmosphere; patio seating. *Average main: $30* ✉ *6510 Washington St., Yountville* ✣ *At Mulberry St.* ☎ *707/944–0103* 🌐 *www.bistrojeanty.com.*

★ Bouchon Bistro

$$$ | **FRENCH** | The team that created The French Laundry is also behind this place, where everything—the zinc-topped bar, antique sconces, suave waitstaff, and traditional French onion soup—could have come straight from a Parisian bistro. Pan-seared rib eye with béarnaise and mussels steamed with white wine, saffron, and Dijon mustard—both served with crispy, addictive fries—are among the perfectly executed entrées. **Known for:** bistro classics; raw bar; Bouchon Bakery next door. *Average main: $35* *6534 Washington St., Yountville* *Near Humboldt St.* *707/944–8037* *thomaskeller.com/bouchonyountville.*

Ciccio

$$ | **MODERN ITALIAN** | The ranch of Ciccio's owners, Frank and Karen Altamura, supplies some of the vegetables and herbs for the modern Italian cuisine prepared in the open kitchen of this remodeled former grocery store. Seasonal growing cycles dictate the menu, with fried-seafood appetizers (calamari, perhaps, or softshell crabs), a few pasta dishes, herb-crusted fish, and several pizzas among the likely offerings. **Known for:** Negroni bar; pizzas' flavorful cheeses; mostly Napa Valley wines, some from owners' winery. *Average main: $23* *6770 Washington St., Yountville* *At Madison St.* *707/945–1000* *www.ciccionapavalley.com* *Closed Mon. and Tues. No lunch.*

Coqueta Napa Valley

$$$ | **SPANISH** | From *pintxos* (small plates) and paellas to Iberian cheeses and fish *a la plancha* (flat-grilled), the chefs at this Wine Country offspring of Michael Chiarello's successful San Francisco restaurant Coqueta reimagine Spanish classics with a 21st-century farm-to-table sensibility. The frenetic pace in the flame-happy open kitchen, inside Yountville's redbrick former railroad depot, keeps the mood lively in the relatively small dining space, with the vibe on the patio out back even more so. **Known for:** sensual flavors; dynamic spicing; seasonal cocktails inspired by Spain and the Napa Valley. *Average main: $32* *6525 Washington St., Yountville* *Near Yount St.* *707/244–4350* *www.coquetanv.com/home* *Closed Tues. and Wed.*

★ The French Laundry

$$$$ | **AMERICAN** | An old stone building laced with ivy houses chef Thomas Keller's destination restaurant. Some courses on the two prix-fixe menus, one of which highlights vegetables, rely on luxe ingredients such as *calotte* (cap of the rib eye); others take humble elements like carrots or fava beans and elevate them to art. **Known for:** signature starter "oysters and pearls"; sea urchin, black truffles, and other "supplements"; superior wine list. *Average main: $350* *6640 Washington St., Yountville* *At Creek St.* *707/944–2380* *www.frenchlaundry.com* *No lunch Mon.–Thurs.* *Jacket required* *Reservations essential wks ahead.*

Mustards Grill

$$$ | **AMERICAN** | Cindy Pawlcyn's Mustards Grill fills day and night with fans of her hearty cuisine, equal parts updated renditions of traditional American dishes—what Pawlcyn dubs "deluxe truck stop classics"—and fanciful contemporary fare. Barbecued baby back pork ribs and a lemon-lime tart piled high with brown-sugar meringue fall squarely in the first category, and sweet corn tamales with tomatillo-avocado salsa and wild mushrooms represent the latter. **Known for:** roadhouse setting; convivial mood; hoppin' bar. *Average main: $30* *7399 St. Helena Hwy./Hwy. 29, Napa* *1 mile north of Yountville* *707/944–2424* *www.mustardsgrill.com.*

North Block

$$$ | **MODERN AMERICAN** | In his California debut, chef Nick Tamburo, previously of two Manhattan locations of celeb chef David Chang's Momofuku, prepares farm-to-table cuisine with intriguing

flavors and ingredients. A recent starter paired oro blanco (a grapefruitlike citrus) and ever-so-thinly sliced kohlrabi (a type of turnip) spiced to marvelous effect with the mildly minty Japanese herb shiso, the chef's artistry repeating itself on the menu's wood-fired pizzas and fish and meat entrées. **Known for:** courtyard patio seating; cocktails and wine list; atmospheric interior. *Average main: $35 North Block Hotel, 6757 Washington St., Yountville Near Madison St. 707/944–8080 www.northblockhotel.com/dining.*

★ Perry Lang's

$$$$ | STEAKHOUSE | An 1870 redbrick former mansion holds this contemporary chophouse whose art-deco accents recall an old-school gentlemen's club—the kind of place to order a stiff cocktail, a wedge salad topped with thick maple-glazed bacon, and a dry-aged rib eye or tomahawk. Chef Adam Perry Lang, a grilling and barbecue artiste, seduces patrons with culinary drama and hand-tooled steak knives so exquisite it's a felony to swipe them, delivering the goods with an experience that satisfies appetite and soul. **Known for:** St. Louis pork ribs with peach barbecue sauce; Cabernet bone-marrow jus and béarnaise and horseradish sauces for steaks; potent craft cocktails. *Average main: $40 6539 Washington St., Yountville Just south of Vintage House 707/945–4522 perrylangs.com No lunch.*

Hotels

★ Bardessono

$$$$ | RESORT | Tranquillity and luxury with a low carbon footprint are among the goals of this ultragreen wood, steel, and glass resortlike property in downtown Yountville, but there's nothing spartan about the accommodations, arranged around four landscaped courtyards. **Pros:** large rooftop lap pool; in-room spa treatments; three luxury villas for extra privacy. **Cons:** expensive year-round; limited view from some rooms; a bit of street traffic on hotel's west side. *Rooms from: $750 6526 Yount St., Yountville 707/204–6000, 855/232–0450 www.bardessono.com 65 rooms No meals.*

Maison Fleurie

$$ | B&B/INN | A stay at this comfortable, reasonably priced inn, said to be the oldest hotel in the Napa Valley, places you within walking distance of Yountville's fine restaurants. **Pros:** smallest rooms a bargain; outdoor hot tub and pool; free bike rental. **Cons:** lacks amenities of a full-service hotel; some rooms pick up noise from nearby Bouchon Bakery; hard to book in high season. *Rooms from: $229 6529 Yount St., Yountville 707/944–2056 www.maisonfleurienapa.com 13 rooms Free breakfast.*

Napa Valley Lodge

$$ | HOTEL | Clean rooms in a convenient motel-style setting draw travelers willing to pay more than at comparable lodgings in the city of Napa to be within walking distance of Yountville's tasting rooms, restaurants, and shops. **Pros:** well-maintained rooms; vineyard-view rooms on north and west sides; large pool area. **Cons:** no elevator; nice enough but lacks panache; pricey on weekends in high season. *Rooms from: $285 2230 Madison St., Yountville 707/944–2468, 888/944–3545 www.napavalleylodge.com 55 rooms Free breakfast.*

★ North Block Hotel

$$$$ | HOTEL | A two-story boutique property near downtown Yountville's northern edge, the North Block attracts sophisticated travelers who appreciate the clever but unpretentious style and offhand luxury. **Pros:** extremely comfortable beds; personalized service; spacious bathrooms. **Cons:** outdoor areas get some traffic noise; weekend minimum-stay requirement; rates soar on high-season weekends. *Rooms from: $540 6757 Washington St., Yountville 707/944–8080 northblockhotel.com 20 rooms No meals.*

Vintage House

$$$$ | **RESORT** | Part of the 22-acre Estate Yountville complex—other sections include sister lodging Hotel Villagio, the 13,000-square-foot Spa at the Estate, and shops and restaurants—this downtown hotel consists of two-story brick buildings along verdant landscaped paths shaded by mature trees. **Pros:** aesthetically pleasing accommodations; private patios and balconies; secluded feeling yet near shops, tasting rooms, and restaurants. **Cons:** highway noise audible in some exterior rooms; very expensive on summer and fall weekends; weekend minimum-stay requirement. *Rooms from: $429 ✉ 6541 Washington St., Yountville ☎ 707/944–1112, 877/351–1153 🌐 www.vintagehouse.com 80 rooms Free breakfast.*

Shopping

The Conservatory

CLOTHING | The New York City–based lifestyle company's heavily curated "considered luxury" comes in the form of clothing, accessories, and decor and well-being items created by small, quality-oriented brands for a discerning clientele. Local products include Vintner's Daughter Active Botanical Serum face oil, whose adherents swear nearly stops time. *✉ 6540 Washington St., Yountville ✣ Near Humboldt St. ☎ 707/415–5015 🌐 theconservatorynyc.com/pages/napa-store.*

Activities

BALLOONING

Napa Valley Aloft

BALLOONING | Passengers soar over the Napa Valley in balloons that launch from downtown Yountville. Flights are from 40 minutes to an hour-plus, depending on the wind speed, with the entire experience taking from three to four hours. *✉ The Estate Yountville, 6525 Washington St., Yountville ✣ Near Mulberry St. ☎ 707/944–4400, 855/944–4408 🌐 www.nvaloft.com $250 per person.*

BICYCLING

Napa Valley Bike Tours

BICYCLING | With dozens of wineries within 5 miles, this shop makes a fine starting point for guided and self-guided vineyard and wine-tasting excursions. Rental bikes are also available. *✉ 6500 Washington St., Yountville ✣ At Mulberry St. ☎ 707/251–8687 🌐 www.napavalleybiketours.com From $124 (½-day guided tour).*

SPAS

The Spa at The Estate

FITNESS/HEALTH CLUBS | The joint 13,000-square-foot facility of Vintage House and the Hotel Villagio is a five-minute walk from the former's lobby, even less from the latter's. Private spa suites are popular with couples, who enjoy the separate relaxation areas, indoor and outdoor fireplaces, steam showers, saunas, and extra-large tubs. Many treatments involve Omorovicza products based on Hungarian thermal waters and minerals. For a quick uplift, book 20 minutes in the spa's oxygen chair, designed to optimize breathing and promote relaxation. Facials, lip plumping, and massages are among the other à la carte services. The ground-floor retail area, open to the public, is well stocked with beauty products. *✉ The Estate Yountville, 6481 Washington St., Yountville ✣ At Oak Circle ☎ 707/948–5050 🌐 www.villagio.com/spa Treatments from $85.*

Oakville

2 miles northwest of Yountville.

A large butte that runs east–west just north of Yountville blocks the cooling fogs from the south, facilitating the myriad microclimates of the Oakville AVA, home to several high-profile wineries.

GETTING HERE AND AROUND

Driving along Highway 29, you'll know you've reached Oakville when you see the Oakville Grocery on the east side of the road. You can reach Oakville from the Sonoma County town of Glen Ellen by heading east on Trinity Road from Highway 12. The twisting route, along the mountain range that divides Napa and Sonoma, eventually becomes the Oakville Grade. The views on this drive are breathtaking, though the continual curves make it unsuitable for those who suffer from motion sickness.

Sights

B Cellars

WINERY/DISTILLERY | The chefs take center stage in the open-hearth kitchen of this boutique winery's hospitality house, and with good reason: creating food-friendly wines is B Cellars's raison d'être. Visits to the Oakville facility—all steel beams, corrugated metal, and plate glass yet remarkably cozy—often begin with a tour of the winery's culinary garden and vineyard, with a pause for sips of wine still aging in barrel. A seated tasting of finished wines paired with small bites follows the tour. Kirk Venge, whose fruit-forward style suits the winery's food-oriented approach, crafts red and white blends and single-vineyard Cabernets from estate fruit and grapes from Beckstoffer and other noteworthy vineyards. All visits are strictly by appointment. ✉ *703 Oakville Cross Rd., Oakville* ✣ *West of Silverado Trail* ☎ *707/709–8787* 🌐 *www.bcellars.com* 🎫 *Tastings from $80* ⏲ *Closed Tues. and Wed.*

Far Niente

WINERY/DISTILLERY | Hamden McIntyre, a prominent winery architect of his era also responsible for Inglenook and what's now the Culinary Institute of America at Greystone, designed the centerpiece 1885 stone winery here. Abandoned in the wake of Prohibition and only revived beginning in 1979, Far Niente now ranks as one of the Napa Valley's most beautiful properties. Guests participating in the Estate Tasting learn some of this history while sipping the flagship wines, a Chardonnay and a Cabernet Sauvignon blend, along with Russian River Valley Pinot Noir from the affiliated EnRoute label and Dolce, a late-harvest Sémillon and Sauvignon Blanc wine. The Extended Estate Tasting takes in the winery and its aging caves, while the Library Wine Tasting compares older vintages. ✉ *1350 Acacia Dr., Oakville* ✣ *Off Oakville Grade Rd.* ☎ *707/944–2861* 🌐 *www.farniente.com* 🎫 *Tastings from $80.*

Robert Mondavi Winery

WINERY/DISTILLERY | Arguably the most influential participant in the Napa Valley's rise to international prominence, the late Robert Mondavi established his namesake winery in the 1960s after losing a battle with his brother over the direction of their family's Charles Krug Winery. In an era when tasting rooms were mostly downscale affairs, Mondavi commissioned architect Cliff May to create a grand Mission-style space to receive visitors. May's design still resonates, the graceful central arch framing the lawn and the vineyard behind, inviting a stroll under the arcades. The Estate Tour & Tasting and Vintner's Tasting provide an introduction to the winery, its portfolio, and Mondavi's life. Another offering focuses on whites and caviar, with a third involving Cabernet Sauvignon from the Mondavi section of the famed To Kalon Vineyard. All visits require a reservation, with last-minute requests often granted. ✉ *7801 St. Helena Hwy./Hwy. 29, Oakville* ☎ *888/766–6328* 🌐 *www.robertmondaviwinery.com* 🎫 *Tastings and tours from $40.*

★ Silver Oak

WINERY/DISTILLERY | The first review of this winery's Napa Valley Cabernet Sauvignon declared the debut 1972 vintage not all that good and, at $6 a bottle, overpriced. Oops. The celebrated Bordeaux-style

Cabernet blend, still the only Napa Valley wine bearing its winery's label each year, evolved into a cult favorite, and founders Ray Duncan and Justin Meyer received worldwide recognition for their signature use of exclusively American oak to age the wines. At the Oakville tasting room, constructed out of reclaimed stone and other materials from a 19th-century Kansas flour mill, the Silver Oak Tasting includes sips of the current Napa Valley vintage, its counterpart from Silver Oak's Alexander Valley operation in Sonoma County, and a library wine. Hosts of vertical tastings pour six Cabernet vintages. All visits require an appointment. ✉ *915 Oakville Cross Rd., Oakville* ✣ *Off Hwy. 29* ☎ *707/942–7022* 🌐 *www.silveroak.com* 🎫 *Tastings from $30.*

Rutherford

2 miles northwest of Oakville.

With its singular microclimate and soil, Rutherford is an important viticultural center, with more big-name wineries than you can shake a corkscrew at. Cabernet Sauvignon is king here. The well-drained, loamy soil is ideal for those vines, and since this part of the valley gets plenty of sun, the grapes develop exceptionally intense flavors.

GETTING HERE AND AROUND

Wineries around Rutherford are dotted along Highway 29 and the parallel Silverado Trail north and south of Rutherford Road/Conn Creek Road, on which wineries can also be found.

Sights

★ Frog's Leap

WINERY/DISTILLERY | If you're a novice, the tour at eco-friendly Frog's Leap is a fun way to begin your education. Conducted by hosts with a sense of humor, the tour stops by a barn built in 1884, 5 acres of organic gardens, and a frog pond topped with lily pads. The winery produced its first vintage, small batches of Sauvignon Blanc and Zinfandel, in 1981, adding Chardonnay and Cabernet Sauvignon the next year. These days Chenin Blanc is another white, with Merlot, Petite Sirah, and the Heritage Blend of classic Napa Valley varietals among the other reds. All visits require a reservation. ■ **TIP→ The tour is recommended, but you can forgo it and taste on a garden-view porch.** ✉ *8815 Conn Creek Rd., Rutherford* ☎ *707/963–4704* 🌐 *www.frogsleap.com* 🎫 *Tastings from $45, tour and tasting $75.*

★ Inglenook

WINERY/DISTILLERY | *Wine Enthusiast* magazine bestowed a lifetime-achievement award on vintner-filmmaker Francis Ford Coppola, whose wine-world contributions include resurrecting the historic Inglenook estate. Over the decades he reunited the original property acquired by Inglenook founder Gustave Niebaum, remodeled Niebaum's ivy-covered 1880s château, and purchased the rights to the Inglenook name. The winery's place in Napa Valley history is among the topics discussed at tastings, some of which involve cheese, charcuterie, or other wine-food pairings. Most sessions see a pour of the signature Rubicon wine, a Cabernet Sauvignon–based blend. All visits require an appointment; call the winery or check at the visitor center for same-day. ■ **TIP→ In lieu of a tasting, you can book a table at The Bistro, a wine bar with a picturesque courtyard, to sip wine by the glass or bottle.** ✉ *1991 St. Helena Hwy./Hwy. 29, Rutherford* ✣ *At Hwy. 128* ☎ *707/968–1100* 🌐 *www.inglenook.com* 🎫 *Tastings from $60* ⊙ *Closed Mon.–Wed.*

Mumm Napa

WINERY/DISTILLERY | When Champagne Mumm of France set about establishing a California sparkling-wine outpost, its winemaker chose the Napa Valley, where today the winery sources grapes from more than 50 local producers. Made

Frog's Leap's picturesque country charm extends all the way to the white picket fence.

in the *méthode traditionelle* style from Chardonnay, Pinot Noir, Pinot Meunier, and occasionally Pinot Gris, the wines are all fermented in the bottle. Most guests enjoy them alfresco, by the glass or flight, on a patio above the surrounding vineyards or one at eye level. Book an Oak Terrace Tasting to sample top-of-the-line cuvées under the sprawling branches of a blue oak nearly two centuries old. Tasting is by appointment only. ✉ *8445 Silverado Trail, Rutherford* ✣ *1 mile south of Rutherford Cross Rd.* ☎ *707/967–7700* 🌐 *www.mummnapa.com* 🎫 *Tastings from $40.*

ZD Wines

WINERY/DISTILLERY | Founded in 1969 and still run by the same family, this winery specializing in Chardonnay, Pinot Noir, and Cabernet Sauvignon is respected for its organic practices, local philanthropy, and Abacus blend. Made "solera-style," Abacus contains wine from every ZD Reserve Cabernet Sauvignon vintage since 1992. The Chardonnay and Pinot Noir come from a Carneros property, the Cabernet from the winery's Rutherford estate, where the wines are made and presented to the public. Appointment-only tastings (same-day often possible) take place in a second-floor space with broad valley views west to the Mayacamas Mountains. For an introduction to ZD and its wine-making philosophy, book a current-release flight. Barrel tastings, small bites, and small-batch reserve wines are all part of the Abacus Experience, which concludes with a current and older Abacus blend. ✉ *8383 Silverado Trail, Rutherford* ☎ *800/487–7757* 🌐 *www.zdwines.com* 🎫 *Tastings from $40.*

Restaurants

★ Restaurant at Auberge du Soleil

$$$$ | **MODERN AMERICAN** | Possibly the most romantic roost for brunch or dinner in all the Wine Country is a terrace seat at the Auberge du Soleil resort's illustrious restaurant, and the Mediterranean-inflected cuisine more than matches the dramatic vineyard views. The prix-fixe dinner menu (three or four courses), which relies mainly on local produce, might include caviar or diver scallop starters, delicately prepared fish or vegetable middle-course options, and mains like prime beef pavé with béarnaise, spiced lamb loin, or Japanese Wagyu. **Known for:** polished service; comprehensive wine list; special-occasion feel. *$ Average main: $135 ✉ Auberge du Soleil, 180 Rutherford Hill Rd., Rutherford ✣ Off Silverado Trail ☎ 707/963–1211, 800/348–5406 ⊕ www.aubergedusoleil.com.*

Rutherford Grill

$$$ | AMERICAN | Dark-wood walls, subdued lighting, and red-leather banquettes make for a perpetually clubby mood at this Rutherford hangout where the patio, popular for its bar, fireplace, and rocking chairs, opens for full meal service or drinks and appetizers when the weather's right. Many entrées—steaks, burgers, fish, rotisserie chicken, and barbecued pork ribs—emerge from an oak-fired grill operated by master technicians. **Known for:** iron-skillet corn bread direct from the oven; signature French dip sandwich and grilled jumbo artichokes; reasonably priced wine list with rarities. *$ Average main: $29 ✉ 1180 Rutherford Rd., Rutherford ✣ At Hwy. 29 ☎ 707/963–1792 ⊕ www.rutherfordgrill.com.*

Hotels

★ Auberge du Soleil

$$$$ | RESORT | Taking a cue from the olive-tree-studded landscape, this hotel with a renowned restaurant and spa cultivates a luxurious look that blends French and California style. **Pros:** stunning valley views; spectacular pool and spa areas; Deluxe-category suites fit for a superstar. **Cons:** stratospheric prices; least expensive rooms get some noise from the bar and restaurant; weekend minimum-stay requirement. *$ Rooms from: $925 ✉ 180 Rutherford Hill Rd., Rutherford ☎ 707/963–1211, 800/348–5406 ⊕ www.aubergedusoleil.com 52 rooms Free breakfast.*

★ Rancho Caymus Inn

$$$ | HOTEL | A romantic hacienda-away-from-home that off-season may well be the Napa Valley's best value in its price range, this upscale-contemporary boutique hotel near Inglenook and the Rutherford Grill contains rooms whose decor and artworks evoke the area's Mexican heritage. **Pros:** courtyard pool area; smallest rooms are 400 square feet, with several 600 or more; well-trained staff. **Cons:** all rooms have only showers (albeit nice ones); king beds in all rooms (no sofa beds, though a few rollaways available); no spa or fitness center. *$ Rooms from: $396 ✉ 1140 Rutherford Rd., Rutherford ☎ 707/200–9300 ⊕ www.ranchocaymusinn.com 26 rooms Free breakfast.*

St. Helena

2 miles northwest of Oakville.

Downtown St. Helena is the very picture of good living in the Wine Country: sycamore trees arch over Main Street (Highway 29), where visitors flit between boutiques, cafés, and storefront tasting rooms housed in sun-faded redbrick buildings. The genteel district pulls in rafts of tourists during the day, though like most Wine Country towns St. Helena more or less rolls up the sidewalks after dark.

The Napa Valley floor narrows between the Mayacamas and Vaca mountains around St. Helena. The slopes reflect heat onto the vineyards below, and since there's less fog and wind, things get pretty toasty. This is one of the valley's hottest AVAs, with midsummer temperatures often reaching the mid-90s. Bordeaux varietals are the most popular grapes grown here—especially Cabernet Sauvignon but also Merlot, Cabernet Franc, and Sauvignon Blanc.

GETTING HERE AND AROUND

Downtown stretches along Highway 29, called Main Street here. Many wineries lie north and south of downtown along Highway 29. More can be found off Silverado Trail, and some of the most scenic spots are on Spring Mountain, which rises southwest of town.

Sights

Beringer Vineyards

WINERY/DISTILLERY | Brothers Frederick and Jacob Beringer opened the winery that still bears their name in 1876. One of California's earliest bonded wineries, it's the oldest one in the Napa Valley never to have missed a vintage—no mean feat, given Prohibition. Reserve tastings of a limited release Chardonnay, a few big Cabernets, and a Sauterne-style dessert wine take place on the veranda (also inside when possible) at Frederick's grand Rhine House Mansion, built in 1884 and surrounded by mature landscaped gardens. Beringer is known for several widely distributed wines, but many poured here are winery exclusives. Visits require a reservation; same-day guests are accommodated if possible. ✉ *2000 Main St./Hwy. 29, St. Helena* ✥ *Near Pratt Ave.* ☎ *707/963–8989* 🌐 *www.beringer.com* 🎟 *Tastings from $35.*

Charles Krug Winery

WINERY/DISTILLERY | A historically sensitive renovation of its 1874 Redwood Cellar Building transformed the former production facility of the Napa Valley's oldest winery into an epic hospitality center. Charles Krug, a Prussian immigrant, established the winery in 1861 and ran it until his death in 1892. Italian immigrants Cesare Mondavi and his wife, Rosa, purchased Charles Krug in 1943, operating it with their sons Peter and Robert (who later opened his own winery). Still run by Peter's family, Charles Krug specializes in small-lot Yountville and Howell Mountain Cabernet Sauvignons plus Sauvignon Blanc, Chardonnay, Merlot, and Pinot Noir. All visits are by appointment. ✉ *2800 Main St./Hwy. 29, St. Helena* ✥ *Across from Culinary Institute of America* ☎ *707/967–2229* 🌐 *www.charleskrug.com* 🎟 *Tasting $45, tour $75 (includes tasting).*

Hall St. Helena

WINERY/DISTILLERY | The Cabernet Sauvignons produced here are works of art born of the latest in organic-farming science and wine-making technology. A glass-walled tasting room allows guests to see some of the high-tech equipment winemaker Megan Gunderson employs to craft wines that also include Merlot, Cabernet Franc, and Sauvignon Blanc. Looking westward from the second-floor tasting area, rows of neatly spaced Cabernet vines capture the eye, beyond them the tree-studded Mayacamas Mountains. Hard to miss as you arrive along Highway 29, Lawrence Argent's 35-foot-tall *Bunny Foo Foo,* a stainless-steel sculpture of a rabbit leaping out of the vineyard, is one of many museum-quality artworks on display at appointment-only Hall (call for same-day). ■ **TIP→ Sister winery Hall Rutherford hosts an exclusive wine-and-food pairing atop a Rutherford hillside.** ✉ *401 St. Helena Hwy./Hwy. 29, St. Helena* ✥ *Near White La.* ☎ *707/967–2626* 🌐 *www.hallwines.com* 🎟 *Tastings from $40.*

★ Joseph Phelps Vineyards

WINERY/DISTILLERY | An appointment is required for tastings at the winery started by the late Joseph Phelps, but it's worth the effort—all the more so after an inspired renovation of the main redwood structure, a classic of 1970s Northern California architecture. Phelps produces very fine whites, along with Pinot Noir from its Sonoma Coast vineyards, but the blockbusters are the Bordeaux reds, particularly the Cabernet Sauvignons and Insignia, a luscious-yet-subtle Cab-dominant blend. Insignia, which often receives high-90s scores from respected wine publications, is always among the current releases poured at the one-hour seated Terrace Tasting overlooking grapevines and oaks. Several other experiences involve food pairings; participants in the blending seminar mix the varietals that go into Insignia. ✉ *200 Taplin Rd., St. Helena* ⊕ *Off Silverado Trail* ☎ *707/963–2745, 800/707–5789* 🌐 *www.josephphelps.com* 🎫 *Tastings from $90.*

Prager Winery & Port Works

WINERY/DISTILLERY | "If door is locked, ring bell," reads a sign outside the weathered-redwood tasting shack at this family-run winery known for red, white, and tawny ports. The sign, the bell, and the thousands of dollar bills tacked to the walls and ceilings inside are your first indications that you're drifting back in time with the old-school Pragers, who have been making regular and fortified wines in St. Helena since the late 1970s. Five members of the second generation, along with two spouses, run this homespun operation founded by Jim and Imogene Prager. In addition to ports the winery makes Petite Sirah and Sweet Claire, a late-harvest Riesling dessert wine. Some tastings take place in a garden outside the tasting room or on the crush pad. ✉ *1281 Lewelling La., St. Helena* ⊕ *Off Hwy. 29* ☎ *707/963–7678* 🌐 *www.pragerport.com* 🎫 *Tastings $40 (includes glass).*

★ Pride Mountain Vineyards

WINERY/DISTILLERY | This winery 2,200 feet up Spring Mountain straddles Napa and Sonoma counties, confusing enough for visitors but even more complicated for the wine-making staff: government regulations require separate wineries and paperwork for each side of the property. It's one of several Pride Mountain quirks, but winemaker Sally Johnson's "big red wines," including a Cabernet Sauvignon that earned 100-point scores from a major wine critic two years in a row, are serious business. On a visit, by appointment only, you can learn about the farming and cellar strategies behind Pride's acclaimed Cabs (the winery also produces Syrah, a Cab-like Merlot, Viognier, and Chardonnay among others). ■ **TIP→ The views here are knock-your-socks-off gorgeous.** ✉ *4026 Spring Mountain Rd., St. Helena* ⊕ *Off St. Helena Rd. (extension of Spring Mountain Rd. in Sonoma County)* ☎ *707/963–4949* 🌐 *www.pridewines.com* 🎫 *Tastings from $30* ⊗ *Closed Tues.*

The Prisoner Wine Company

WINERY/DISTILLERY | The iconoclastic brand opened an industrial-chic space with interiors by the wildly original Napa-based designer Richard Von Saal to showcase its flagship The Prisoner red blend. "Getting the varietals to play together" is winemaker Chrissy Wittmann's mission with that wine (Zinfandel, Cabernet Sauvignon, Petite Sirah, Syrah, Charbono) and siblings like the Blindfold white (Chardonnay plus Rhône and other varietals). The Line-up Tasting of current releases unfolds either in the Tasting Lounge (more hip hotel bar than traditional tasting room) or outside in the casual open-air The Yard. When offered, The Makery Experience (indoors) involves boldly flavored plates that pair well with Wittman's fruit-forward wines. The Prisoner's tasting space is quite the party, for which a reservation is required. ✉ *1178 Galleron Rd., St. Helena* ⊕ *At Hwy. 29* ☎ *707/967–3823, 877/283–5934* 🌐 *www.theprisonerwinecompany.com* 🎫 *Tastings from $45.*

★ Tres Sabores Winery

WINERY/DISTILLERY | A long, narrow lane with two sharp bends leads to splendidly workaday Tres Sabores, where the sight of sheep, golden retrievers, guinea hens, pomegranate and other trees and plants, a slew of birds and bees, and a heaping compost pile reinforce a simple point: despite the Napa Valley's penchant for glamour this is, first and foremost, farm country. Owner-winemaker Julie Johnson specializes in single-vineyard wines that include Cabernet Sauvignon and Zinfandel from estate-grown certified-organic Rutherford bench vines. She also excels with Petite Sirah from dry-farmed Calistoga fruit, Sauvignon Blanc, and the zippy ¿Por Qué No? (Why not?) red blend. *Tres sabores* is Spanish for "three flavors," which to Johnson represents the land, her vines, and, as she puts it, "the spirit of the company around the table." Tastings by appointment only are informal and usually held outside. *1620 S. Whitehall La., St. Helena* *West of Hwy. 29* *707/967–8027* *www.tressabores.com* *Tasting $50.*

Restaurants

Brasswood Bar + Bakery + Kitchen

$$$ | **ITALIAN** | After Napa Valley fixture Tra Vigne lost its lease, many staffers regrouped a few miles north at the restaurant (the titular Kitchen) of the Brasswood complex, which also includes a bakery, shops, and a wine-tasting room. Along with dishes developed for the new location, chef David Nuno incorporates Tra Vigne favorites such as mozzarella-stuffed *arancini* (rice balls) into his Mediterranean-leaning menu. **Known for:** mostly Napa-Sonoma wine list; no corkage on first bottle; Tra Vigne favorites. *Average main: $31* *3111 St. Helena Hwy. N, St. Helena* *Near Ehlers La.* *707/968–5434* *www.brasswood.com.*

The Charter Oak

$$$ | **MODERN AMERICAN** | Christopher Kostow's reputation rests on his swoonworthy haute cuisine for The Restaurant at Meadowood, but he and his Charter Oak team adopt a more straightforward approach—fewer ingredients chosen for maximum effect—at this high-ceilinged, brown-brick downtown restaurant. On the ever-evolving menu this strategy might translate into dishes like celery-leaf chicken with preserved lemon, herbs, and pan drippings, and red kuri squash with caramelized koji and goat cheese (or just go for the droolworthy cheeseburger and thick fries). **Known for:** exceedingly fresh produce from nearby Meadowood farm; patio dining in brick courtyard; top chef's affordable cuisine. *Average main: $29* *1050 Charter Oak Ave., at Hwy. 29, St. Helena* *707/302–6996* *www.thecharteroak.com* *No lunch Mon. and Tues.*

★ Cook St. Helena

$$ | **ITALIAN** | A curved marble bar spotlit by contemporary art-glass pendants adds a touch of style to this downtown restaurant whose northern Italian cuisine pleases with understated sophistication. Mussels with house-made sausage in a spicy tomato broth, chopped salad with pancetta and pecorino, and the daily changing risotto are among the dishes regulars revere. **Known for:** top-quality ingredients; reasonably priced local and international wines; intimate dining. *Average main: $26* *1310 Main St., St. Helena* *Near Hunt Ave.* *707/963–7088* *www.cooksthelena.com* *Closed weekends (check website for updates).*

★ Farmstead at Long Meadow Ranch

$$$ | **MODERN AMERICAN** | In a high-ceilinged former barn with plenty of outside seating, Farmstead revolves around an open kitchen whose chefs prepare meals with grass-fed beef and lamb, fruits and vegetables, and eggs, olive oil, wine, honey, and other ingredients from nearby Long Meadow Ranch. Entrées might include wood-grilled trout with fennel, mushroom, onion, and bacon-mustard vinaigrette; caramelized beets with goat cheese; or a wood-grilled heritage pork chop with jalapeño grits. **Known for:** Tuesday fried-chicken night; house-made charcuterie; on-site general store, café, and Long Meadow Wines tasting space. *Average main: $27* *738 Main St., St. Helena* *At Charter Oak Ave.* *707/963–4555* *www.longmeadowranch.com/eat-drink/restaurant.*

Goose & Gander

$$$ | **MODERN AMERICAN** | A Craftsman bungalow whose 1920s owner reportedly used the cellar for bootlegging during Prohibition houses this restaurant where the pairing of food and drink is as likely to involve a craft cocktail as a sommelier-selected wine. Main courses such as brick-cooked chicken, a heritage-pork burger, and dry-aged New York steak with black-lime and pink-peppercorn butter follow starters that might include blistered Brussels sprouts and roasted octopus. **Known for:** intimate main dining room with fireplace; alfresco patio dining; basement bar among Napa's best watering holes. *Average main: $31 ✉ 1245 Spring St., St. Helena ✣ At Oak St. ☎ 707/967–8779 ⊕ www.goosegander.com ⊙ No lunch.*

Gott's Roadside

$ | **AMERICAN** | A 1950s-style outdoor hamburger stand goes upscale at this spot whose customers brave long lines to order breakfast sandwiches, juicy burgers, root-beer floats, and garlic fries. Choices not available a half century ago include ahi tuna and Impossible burgers and kale and Vietnamese chicken salads. **Known for:** tasty 21st-century diner cuisine; shaded picnic tables (arrive early or late for lunch to get one); second branch at Napa's Oxbow Public Market. *Average main: $14 ✉ 933 Main St./Hwy. 29, St. Helena ✣ Near Charter Oak Ave. ☎ 707/963–3486 ⊕ www.gotts.com ☞ Reservations not accepted.*

★ Press

$$$$ | **MODERN AMERICAN** | For years this cavernous restaurant with a contempo-barn interior and wraparound patio steps from neighboring vineyards was northern Napans' preferred stop for a top-shelf cocktail, grass-fed dry-aged steak, and high-90s-scoring local Cabernet. It still is, but since arriving in 2019, chef Philip Tessier, formerly of Yountville's The French Laundry and Bouchon Bistro and New York City's Le Bernardin, has expanded the menu to include more refined preparations, much of whose produce is grown nearby. **Known for:** extensive wine cellar; impressive cocktails; casual-chic ambience. *Average main: $45 ✉ 587 St. Helena Hwy./Hwy. 29, St. Helena ✣ At White La. ☎ 707/967–0550 ⊕ www.pressnapavalley.com ⊙ No lunch Mon.–Thurs.*

Hotels

Alila Napa Valley

$$$$ | **HOTEL** | An upscale-casual ultracontemporary adults-only resort formerly known as Las Alcobas Napa Valley but as of 2021 in the Hyatt Alila brand's fold, this hillside beauty sits adjacent to Beringer Vineyards six blocks north of Main Street shopping and dining. **Pros:** vineyard views from most rooms; Acacia House restaurant; pool, spa, and fitness center. **Cons:** expensive much of the year; per website no children under age 18 permitted; no self-parking. *Rooms from: $700 ✉ 1915 Main St., St. Helena ☎ 707/963–7000 ⊕ www.alilanapavalley.com 68 rooms No meals.*

El Bonita Motel

$ | **HOTEL** | A classic 1950s-style neon sign marks the driveway to this well-run roadside motel that—when it isn't sold out—offers great value to budget-minded travelers. **Pros:** cheerful rooms; family-friendly; microwaves and mini-refrigerators. **Cons:** noise issues in roadside and ground-floor rooms; expensive on high-season weekends; lacks amenities of fancier properties. *Rooms from: $160 ✉ 195 Main St./Hwy. 29, St. Helena ☎ 707/963–3216 ⊕ www.elbonita.com 52 rooms Free breakfast.*

Harvest Inn

$$$ | **HOTEL** | Although this inn sits just off Highway 29, its patrons remain mostly above the fray, strolling 8 acres of gardens, enjoying views of the vineyards adjoining the property, partaking in spa services, and drifting to sleep in beds

adorned with fancy linens and down pillows. **Pros:** garden setting; spacious rooms; near choice wineries, restaurants, and shops. **Cons:** some lower-price rooms lack elegance; high weekend rates; occasional service lapses. *Rooms from: $359* *1 Main St., St. Helena* *707/963–9463* *www.harvestinn.com* *81 rooms* *No meals.*

Inn St. Helena

$$$ | **B&B/INN** | A large room at this spiffed-up downtown St. Helena inn is named for author Ambrose Bierce *(The Devil's Dictionary),* who lived in the main Victorian structure in the early 1900s, but sensitive hospitality and modern amenities are what make a stay worth writing home about. **Pros:** aim-to-please staff and owner; outdoor porch and swing; convenient to shops, tasting rooms, restaurants. **Cons:** no pool, gym, room service, or other typical amenities; two-night minimum on weekends (three with Monday holiday); per website "children 16 and older are welcome". *Rooms from: $309* *1515 Main St., St. Helena* *707/963–3003* *www.innsthelena.com* *8 rooms* *Free breakfast.*

Meadowood Napa Valley

$$$$ | **RESORT** | This elite 250-acre resort's celebrated restaurant and more than half its accommodations were destroyed in the 2020 Glass Fire, but the spa, pools, tennis courts, fitness center, and a fair number of cottages in one part survived and reopened in 2021, with reconstruction in other areas not expected to affect the guest experience. **Pros:** scrupulously maintained rooms; all-organic spa; gracious service. **Cons:** still recovering from fire; far from downtown St. Helena; weekend minimum-stay requirement. *Rooms from: $825* *900 Meadowood La., St. Helena* *707/963–3646, 866/987–8212* *www.meadowood.com* *36 rooms* *No meals.*

Wine Country Inn

$$$ | **B&B/INN** | Vineyards flank the three buildings, containing 24 rooms, and five cottages of this pastoral retreat, where blue oaks, maytens, and olive trees provide shade, and gardens feature lantana (small butterflies love it) and lavender. **Pros:** staff excels at anticipating guests' needs; good-size swimming pool; vineyard views from most rooms. **Cons:** some rooms let in noise from neighbors; expensive in high season; weekend minimum-stay requirement. *Rooms from: $329* *1152 Lodi La., St. Helena* *East of Hwy. 29* *707/963–7077, 888/465–4608* *www.winecountryinn.com* *29 rooms* *Free breakfast.*

★ Wydown Hotel

$$$ | **HOTEL** | This smart boutique hotel near downtown shopping and dining delivers comfort with a heavy dose of style: the storefront lobby's high ceiling and earth tones, punctuated by rich-hued splashes of color, hint at the relaxed grandeur owner-hotelier Mark Hoffmeister and his design team achieved in the rooms upstairs. **Pros:** well run; eclectic decor; downtown location. **Cons:** lacks the amenities of larger properties; large corner rooms pick up some street noise; two-night minimum on weekends. *Rooms from: $339* *1424 Main St., St. Helena* *707/963–5100* *www.wydownhotel.com* *12 rooms* *No meals.*

Nightlife

The Saint

WINE BARS—NIGHTLIFE | This high-ceilinged downtown wine bar benefits from the grandeur and gravitas of its setting inside a stone-walled late-19th-century former bank. Lit by chandeliers and decked out in contemporary style with plush sofas and chairs and Lucite stools at the bar, it's a classy, loungelike space to expand your enological horizons. *1351 Main St., St. Helena* *Near Adams St.* *707/302–5130* *www.*

thesaintnapavalley.com ☞ Closed Mon.–Wed. (but check).

Calistoga

3 miles northwest of St. Helena.

With false-fronted, Old West–style shops and 19th-century inns and hotels lining its main drag, Lincoln Avenue in Calistoga comes across as more down-to-earth than its more polished neighbors. Don't be fooled, though. On its outskirts lie some of the Wine Country's swankest (and priciest) resorts and its most fanciful piece of architecture, the medieval-style Castello di Amorosa winery.

Calistoga was developed as a spa-oriented getaway from the start. Sam Brannan, a gold rush–era entrepreneur, planned to use the area's natural hot springs as the centerpiece of a resort complex. His venture failed, but old-time hotels and bathhouses—along with some glorious new spas—still operate. You can come for an old-school mud bath, or go completely 21st century and experience lavish treatments based on the latest innovations in skin and body care.

GETTING HERE AND AROUND

Highway 29 heads east (turn right) at Calistoga, where in town it is signed as Lincoln Avenue. If arriving via the Silverado Trail, head west at Highway 29/Lincoln Avenue.

Sights

Castello di Amorosa

WINERY/DISTILLERY | An astounding medieval structure complete with drawbridge and moat, chapel, stables, and secret passageways, the Castello commands Diamond Mountain's lower eastern slope. Some of the 107 rooms contain artist Fabio Sanzogni's replicas of 13th-century frescoes (cheekily signed with his website address), and the dungeon has an iron maiden from Nuremberg, Germany. You must pay for a tour, when offered, to see most of Dario Sattui's extensive eight-level property, though with general admission you'll have access to part of the complex. Bottlings of note include several Italian-style wines, including La Castellana, a robust "super Tuscan" blend of Cabernet Sauvignon, Sangiovese, and Merlot; and Il Barone, a deliberately big Cab primarily of Rutherford grapes. All visits are by appointment. ✉ *4045 N. St. Helena Hwy./Hwy. 29, Calistoga* ⊕ *Near Maple La.* ☎ *707/967–6272* 🌐 *www.castellodiamorosa.com* 🎫 *Check with winery for tasting and tour prices.*

Chateau Montelena

WINERY/DISTILLERY | Set amid a bucolic northern Calistoga landscape, this winery helped establish the Napa Valley's reputation for high-quality wine making. At the pivotal Paris tasting of 1976, the Chateau Montelena 1973 Chardonnay took first place, beating out four white Burgundies from France and five other California Chardonnays, an event immortalized in the 2008 movie *Bottle Shock*. A 21st-century Napa Valley Chardonnay is always part of A Taste of Montelena—the winery also makes Sauvignon Blanc, Riesling, a fine estate Zinfandel, and Cabernet Sauvignon—or you can opt for the Montelena Estate Collection tasting of Cabernets from several vintages. When tours are offered, there's one that takes in the grounds and covers the history of this stately property whose stone winery building was erected in 1888. All visits require a reservation. ✉ *1429 Tubbs La., Calistoga* ⊕ *Off Hwy. 29* ☎ *707/942–5105* 🌐 *www.montelena.com* 🎫 *Tastings from $40.*

Frank Family Vineyards

WINERY/DISTILLERY | As a former Disney film and television executive, Rich Frank knows a thing or two about entertainment, and it shows in the chipper atmosphere that prevails in the winery's bright-yellow Craftsman-style tasting room. The site's wine-making history dates from the 19th century, and portions of an original 1884 structure, reclad in stone in 1906, remain standing today. From 1952 until 1990, Hanns Kornell made sparkling wines on this site. Frank Family makes sparklers itself, but the high-profile wines are the Carneros Chardonnay and several Cabernet Sauvignons, particularly the Rutherford Reserve and the Winston Hill red blend. Tastings are sit-down affairs, indoors, on the back veranda, or under 100-year-old elms. Reservations are required. ✉ *1091 Larkmead La., Calistoga* ✣ *Off Hwy. 29* ☎ *707/942–0859* 🌐 *www.frankfamilyvineyards.com* 🎫 *Tastings from $50.*

★ Schramsberg

WINERY/DISTILLERY | On a Diamond Mountain site the German-born Jacob Schram planted to grapes in the early 1860s, Schramsberg pours its esteemed *méthode traditionnelle* (aka *méthode champenoise*) sparkling wines. Author Robert Louis Stevenson was among Schram's early visitors. After the vintner's death in 1905 the winery closed and fell into disrepair, but in 1965 Jack and Jamie Davies purchased the 200-acre Schramsberg property and began restoring its buildings and caves. Chinese laborers dug some of the latter in the 1870s. In the 1990s, the family set about replanting the vineyard to Cabernet Sauvignon and other Bordeaux varietals for the Davies Vineyards label's still red wines. Tastings at Schramsberg can include pours of only sparkling wines, only still wines, or a combination of the two. All visits are by appointment. ✉ *1400 Schramsberg Rd., Calistoga* ✣ *Off Hwy. 29* ☎ *707/942–4558, 800/877–3623* 🌐 *www.schramsberg.com* 🎫 *Tastings from $50.*

Tamber Bey Vineyards

WINERY/DISTILLERY | Endurance riders Barry and Jennifer Waitte share their passion for horses and wine at their glam-rustic winery north of Calistoga. Their 22-acre Sundance Ranch remains a working equestrian facility, but the site has been revamped to include a state-of-the-art winery with separate fermenting tanks for grapes from Tamber Bey's vineyards in Yountville, Oakville, and elsewhere. The winemakers produce Chardonnay, Sauvignon Blanc, and Pinot Noir, but the showstoppers are several subtly powerful reds, including the flagship Oakville Cabernet Sauvignon and a Yountville Merlot. The top-selling wine, Rabicano, is a Cabernet Sauvignon-heavy Bordeaux-style blend. Visits here require an appointment. ✉ *1251 Tubbs La., Calistoga* ✣ *At Myrtledale Rd.* ☎ *707/942–2100* 🌐 *www.tamberbey.com* 🎫 *Tastings from $45.*

Restaurants

★ Lovina

$$$ | **MODERN AMERICAN** | A vintage-style neon sign outside this bungalow restaurant announces "Great Food," and the chefs deliver with imaginative, well-plated dishes served on two floors or a streetside patio that in good weather is especially festive during weekend brunch. Entrée staples on the seasonally changing menu include cioppino and slow-roasted half-chicken, with heirloom-tomato gazpacho a summer starter and chicken-dumpling soup its warming winter counterpart. **Known for:** imaginative cuisine; weekend brunch scene; Wine Wednesdays no corkage, discounts on wine list. $ *Average main: $34* ✉ *1107 Cedar St., Calistoga* ✣ *At Lincoln Ave.* ☎ *707/942–6500* 🌐 *www.lovinacalistoga.com* ⏲ *No lunch weekdays.*

Sam's Social Club

$$$ | **MODERN AMERICAN** | Tourists, locals, and spa guests—some of the latter in bathrobes after treatments—assemble inside this resort restaurant or on its extensive patio for breakfast, lunch, bar snacks, or dinner. Lunch options include thin-crust pizzas, sandwiches, an aged-cheddar burger, and entrées such as chicken paillard, with the burger reappearing for dinner along with pan-seared

The astounding Castello di Amorosa has 107 rooms.

fish, rib-eye steak frites, and similar fare. **Known for:** casual atmosphere; cocktail-friendly starters; hearty salads. *Average main: $31 Indian Springs Resort and Spa, 1712 Lincoln Ave., Calistoga At Wappo Ave. 707/942–4969 www.samssocialclub.com.*

★ Solbar

$$$$ | MODERN AMERICAN | The restaurant at Solage attracts the resort's clientele, upvalley locals, and guests of nearby lodgings for sophisticated farm-to-table cuisine served in the high-ceilinged dining area or alfresco on a sprawling patio warmed by shapely heaters and a mesmerizing fire pit. Dishes on the lighter side might include house-made pasta or well-executed sole, with duck breast, crispy pork, or prime New York steak among the heartier options. **Known for:** artisanal cocktails; festive patio; Sunday brunch. *Average main: $40 Solage, 755 Silverado Trail, Calistoga At Rosedale Rd. 866/942–7442 solage.aubergeresorts.com/dine.*

Hotels

★ Embrace Calistoga

$$$ | B&B/INN | Extravagant hospitality defines the Napa Valley's luxury properties, but Embrace Calistoga takes the prize in the "small lodging" category. **Pros:** attentive owners; marvelous breakfasts; restaurants, tasting rooms, and shopping within walking distance. **Cons:** light hum of street traffic; no pool or spa; two-night minimum some weekends. *Rooms from: $309 1139 Lincoln Ave., Calistoga 707/942–9797 embracecalistoga.com 5 rooms Free breakfast.*

Four Seasons Resort and Residences Napa Valley

$$$$ | RESORT | Opened in 2021, this suave luxury resort entices high rollers with farmhouse-eclectic interiors and amenities that include a spa, a destination restaurant, two pools, 7-plus acres of vines, and a working winery. **Pros:** estate villa and one-bedroom suites offer maximum luxury and privacy; destination restaurant

Truss; on-site vineyard and winery. **Cons:** expensive year-round; casual-chic yet may feel too formal for some guests; minimum two-night weekend requirement. *Rooms from: $1400 ✉ 400 Silverado Trail N, Calistoga ☎ 707/709–2100, 800/819–5053 for reservations ⊕ www.fourseasons.com/napavalley ⇨ 83 rooms ⊛ No meals.*

Indian Springs Calistoga

$$$ | **RESORT** | Palm-studded Indian Springs—operating as a spa since 1862—ably splits the difference between laid-back and chic in accommodations that include lodge rooms, suites, cottages, stand-alone bungalows, and two houses. **Pros:** palm-studded grounds with outdoor seating areas; on-site Sam's Social Club restaurant; enormous mineral pool. **Cons:** lodge rooms are small; many rooms have showers but no tubs; two-night minimum on weekends (three with Monday holiday). *Rooms from: $309 ✉ 1712 Lincoln Ave., Calistoga ☎ 707/709–8139 ⊕ www.indianspringscalistoga.com ⇨ 113 rooms ⊛ No meals.*

★ Solage

$$$$ | **RESORT** | The aesthetic at this 22-acre property, where health and wellness are priorities, is Napa Valley barn meets San Francisco loft: guest rooms have high ceilings, sleek contemporary furniture, all-natural fabrics in soothingly muted colors, and an outdoor patio. **Pros:** great service; complimentary bikes; separate pools for kids and adults. **Cons:** vibe might not suit everyone; longish walk from some lodgings to spa and fitness center; expensive in-season. *Rooms from: $749 ✉ 755 Silverado Trail, Calistoga ☎ 866/942–7442, 707/226–0800 ⊕ www.solagecalistoga.com ⇨ 89 rooms ⊛ No meals.*

Mad Mod Shop

CLOTHING | Find the new polka-dotted, patent-leathered you at this quirky stop for vintage-inspired dresses, skirts, tops, and accessories in all sizes. *✉ 1410 Lincoln Ave., Calistoga ✣ At Washington St. ☎ 707/942–1059 ⊕ madmodshop.com.*

BICYCLING

Calistoga Bikeshop

BICYCLING | Options here include regular and fancy bikes that rent for $28 and up for two hours, and there's a self-guided Cool Wine Tour ($110) with stops for tastings at three or four small wineries. *✉ 1318 Lincoln Ave., Calistoga ✣ Near Washington St. ☎ 707/942–9687 ⊕ www.calistogabikeshop.net.*

SPAS

Indian Springs Spa

FITNESS/HEALTH CLUBS | Even before Sam Brannan constructed a spa on this site in the 1860s, the Wappo Indians built sweat lodges over its thermal geysers. Treatments include a Calistoga-classic, pure volcanic-ash mud bath followed by a mineral bath, after which clients are wrapped in a flannel blanket for a 15-minute cool-down session or until called for a massage if they've booked one. Oxygen-infusion facials are another specialty. Before or following a treatment, guests unwind at the serene Buddha Pool, fed by one of the property's four geysers. *✉ 1712 Lincoln Ave., Calistoga ✣ At Wappo Ave. ☎ 707/942–4913 ⊕ indianspringscalistoga.com/spa-overview ⊡ Treatments from $95.*

★ Spa Solage

FITNESS/HEALTH CLUBS | This 20,000-square-foot eco-conscious spa reinvented the traditional Calistoga mud-and-mineral-water regimen with the hour-long "Mudslide." The three-part treatment includes a mud body mask applied in a heated lounge, a soak in a thermal bath, and a power nap in a sound-vibration chair. The mud here, less gloppy than at other resorts, is a mix of clay, volcanic ash, and essential oils. Traditional spa services—combination Shiatsu-Swedish and other massages, foot reflexology, facials, and waxes—are available, as are yoga and wellness sessions. ✉ *755 Silverado Trail, Calistoga* ✣ *At Rosedale Rd.* ☎ *707/226–0825* 🌐 *solage.aubergeresorts.com/spa* 🎫 *Treatments from $110.*

Sonoma

14 miles west of Napa, 45 miles northeast of San Francisco.

One of the few towns in the valley with multiple attractions unrelated to food and wine, Sonoma has plenty to keep you busy for a couple of hours before you head out to tour the wineries. And you needn't leave town to taste wine. About three dozen tasting rooms are within steps of tree-filled Sonoma Plaza. The valley's cultural center, Sonoma was founded in 1835 when California was still part of Mexico.

GETTING HERE AND AROUND

Highway 12 (signed as Broadway near Sonoma Plaza) heads north into Sonoma from Highway 121 and south from Santa Rosa into downtown Sonoma. Parking is relatively easy to find on or near the plaza, and you can walk to many restaurants, shops, and tasting rooms. Signs point the way to several wineries a mile or more east of the plaza. Sonoma County Transit buses serve the town.

Sights

★ Bedrock Wine Co.

WINERY/DISTILLERY | Zinfandel and other varietals grown in heritage vineyards throughout California are the focus of Bedrock, a young winery whose backstory involves several historical figures. Tastings take place in a home east of Sonoma Plaza owned in the 1850s by General Joseph Hooker. By coincidence, Hooker planted grapes at what's now the estate Bedrock Vineyard a few miles away. General William Tecumseh Sherman was his partner in the vineyard (a spat over it affected their Civil War interactions), which newspaper magnate William Randolph Hearst's father, George, replanted in the late 1880s. Some Hearst vines still produce grapes, whose current owner-winemaker, Morgan Twain-Peterson, learned about Zinfandel from his dad, Ravenswood founder Joel Peterson. Twain-Peterson's bottlings, many of them field blends containing multiple varietals grown and fermented together, are as richly textured as his winery's prehistory. ✉ *General Joseph Hooker House, 414 1st St. E, Sonoma* ✣ *Near E. Spain St.* ☎ *707/343–1478* 🌐 *www.bedrockwine-co.com* 🎫 *Tastings from $30* 🕒 *Closed Mon. and Tues.*

Buena Vista Winery

WINERY/DISTILLERY | A local actor in top hat and 19th-century garb often greets guests as Count Agoston Haraszthy at this entertaining homage to the birthplace of modern California wine making. Haraszthy's rehabilitated former press house (used for pressing grapes into wine), completed in 1864, is the architectural focal point, with photos, banners, plaques, and artifacts providing historical context. Chardonnay, Pinot Noir, and several red blends are the strong suits among the two-dozen-plus wines produced. During appointment-only visits (walk-ins sometimes possible), you can taste some of them solo or preorder a box lunch from the affiliated Oakville Grocery. ✉ *18000 Old Winery Rd., Sonoma* ✣ *Off E. Napa St.* ☎ *800/926–1266* 🌐 *www.buenavistawinery.com* 🎫 *Tastings from $20.*

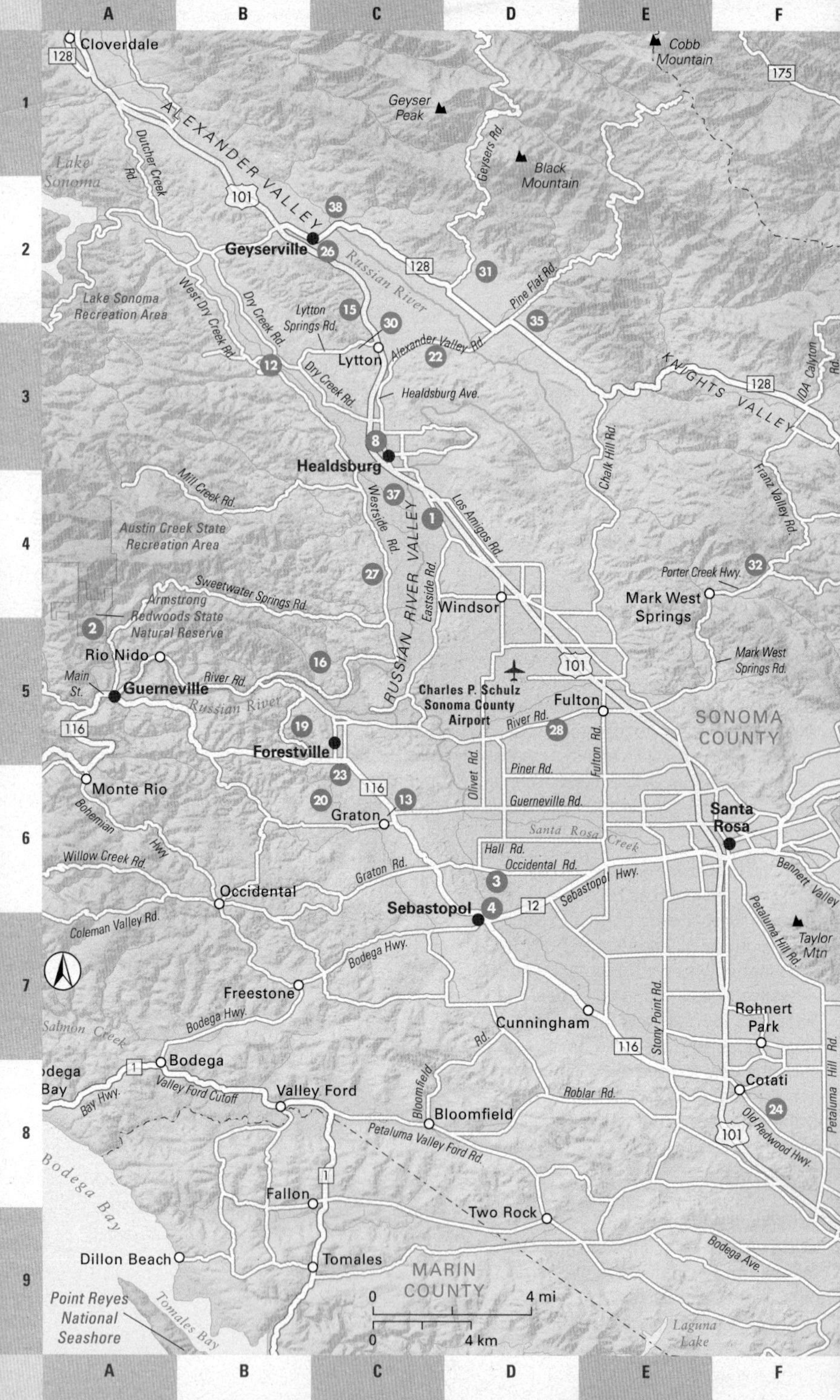
A
B
C
D
E
F
1
2
3
4
5
6
7
8
9
Cloverdale
128
Cobb Mountain
175
Geyser Peak
Alexander Valley
Dutcher Creek Rd.
Lake Sonoma
Geysers Rd.
Black Mountain
101
38
Geyserville
26
Russian River
128
31
West Dry Creek Rd.
Dry Creek Rd.
Lake Sonoma Recreation Area
Pine Flat Rd.
Lytton Springs Rd.
15
30
35
Lytton
Alexander Valley Rd.
22
12
Dry Creek Rd.
Knights Valley
128
Ida Calyton Rd.
Healdsburg Ave.
Chalk Hill Rd.
8
Healdsburg
Mill Creek Rd.
Westside Rd.
37
Los Amigos Rd.
1
Franz Valley Rd.
Russian River Valley
Austin Creek State Recreation Area
Eastside Rd.
27
Porter Creek Hwy.
32
Sweetwater Springs Rd.
Armstrong Redwoods State Natural Reserve
Windsor
Mark West Springs
2
Rio Nido
16
Mark West Springs Rd.
101
Main St.
River Rd.
Guerneville
Charles P. Schulz Sonoma County Airport
Fulton
Russian River
116
19
River Rd.
28
Sonoma County
Forestville
Olivet Rd.
Fulton Rd.
Piner Rd.
Monte Rio
23
116
13
20
Guerneville Rd.
Graton
Santa Rosa
Bohemian Hwy
Santa Rosa Creek
Hall Rd.
Willow Creek Rd.
Occidental Rd.
Graton Rd.
Bennett Valley
3
Sebastopol Hwy.
Occidental
Sebastopol
4
12
Coleman Valley Rd.
Petaluma Hill Rd.
Taylor Mtn
Bodega Hwy.
Freestone
Stony Point Rd.
Rohnert Park
Salmon Creek
Bodega Hwy.
Cunningham
Rd.
116
Bodega
1
Bodega Bay
Valley Ford Cutoff
Cotati
Bay Hwy.
Valley Ford
Roblar Rd.
Bloomfield Rd.
24
Bloomfield
Old Redwood Hwy.
101
Petaluma Valley Ford Rd.
Petaluma Hill Rd.
1
Bodega Bay
Fallon
Two Rock
Bodega Ave.
Dillon Beach
Tomales
Marin County
Point Reyes National Seashore
Tomales Bay
0
4 mi
0
4 km
Laguna Lake

G
H
I
J
Sonoma County
KEY
1 Exploring Sights
Middletown
LAKE COUNTY
Butts Canyon Rd.
Mount St Helena
Robert Louis Stevenson State Park
Aetna Springs
THE PALISADES
Pope Valley
Calistoga
Angwin
Angwin Airport
Petrified Forest Rd.
Bothe-Napa State Park
Diamond Mountain
Calistoga Rd.
Deer Park
Silverado Trail
St. Helena
NAPA COUNTY
Hood Mountain Regional Park
Bald Mountain
Rutherford
Sonoma Hwy.
Adobe Canyon Rd.
Sugarloaf Ridge State Park
Oakville Grade Rd.
Annadel State Park
SONOMA VALLEY
Kenwood
Trinity Rd.
BENNETT VALLEY
Bennett Valley Rd.
Mt Veeder
Glen Ellen
Sonoma Mountain
SONOMA MOUNTAINS
VALLEY OF THE MOON
Jack London State Park
Gehricke Rd.
Agua Caliente
Boyes Hot Springs
Arnold Dr.
Sonoma
E. Napa St.
Napa Rd.
Adobe Rd.
Washington
Carneros Hwy.
Petaluma
Lakeville Hwy.
Bonness Rd.

Sights

Corner 103

WINERY/DISTILLERY | After leading an effort to revive a troubled local winery, Lloyd Davis, an African American financier and oenophile, turned his attention to a new passion: making the experience of learning about wine and food-wine pairings less daunting. To that end he opened a light-filled space, diagonally across from Sonoma Plaza, for tastings of Sonoma County wines usually paired with cheeses or other pertinent bites. The lineup includes a Brut Rosé sparkler, Chardonnay and Marsanne-Roussanne whites, a rosé of Pinot Noir, and several reds. Corner 103's welcoming atmosphere, which earned it the top slot on *USA Today's* Best Tasting Room list for 2020, makes it an excellent choice for wine novices seeking to expand their knowledge. Visits are by appointment only, though hosts usually accommodate drop-ins seeking wine-only tastings. ✉ *103 W. Napa St., Sonoma* ✣ *At 1st St. W* ☎ *707/931–6141* 🌐 *www.corner103.com* 🎫 *Tastings from $20.*

★ The Donum Estate

WINERY/DISTILLERY | The wine-making team of this prominent Chardonnay and Pinot Noir producer prizes viticulture—selecting vineyards with superior soils and microclimates, planting compatible clones, then farming with rigor—over wine-making wizardry. The Donum Estate, whose white board-and-batten tasting room affords guests hilltop views of Los Carneros, San Pablo Bay, and beyond, farms two vineyards surrounding the structure, one in the Russian River Valley, and another in Mendocino County's Anderson Valley. All the wines exhibit the "power yet elegance" that sealed the winery's fame in the 2000s. Tastings are by appointment only. Forty large-scale museum-quality contemporary sculptures placed amid the vines, including works by Ai Weiwei, Lynda Benglis, Louise Bourgeois, Keith Haring, and Anselm Kiefer, add a touch of high culture to a visit here. ■ **TIP→ The winery offers an invigorating 1½-hour guided stroll past the artworks without the tasting.** ✉ *24500 Ramal Rd., Sonoma* ✣ *Off Hwy. 121/12* ☎ *707/732–2200* 🌐 *www.thedonumestate.com* 🎫 *Tastings from $95, art tour $50.*

Gloria Ferrer Caves and Vineyards

WINERY/DISTILLERY | On a clear day this Spanish hacienda–style winery's Vista Terrace lives up to its name as guests at seated tastings sip delicate sparkling wines while taking in views of gently rolling Carneros hills and beyond them San Pablo Bay. The Chardonnay and Pinot Noir grapes from the vineyards in the foreground are the product of old-world wine-making knowledge—generations of the founding Ferrer family made cava in Spain—but also contemporary soil management techniques and clonal research. Hosts well-acquainted with the winery's sustainability practices and history as the Carneros District's first sparkling-wine house serve the wines accompanied by food that varies from cheese and charcuterie to caviar or a full lunch. All visits are by appointment. ■ **TIP→ For the cheese-and-charcuterie option you can upgrade from the standard flight, which includes still wines, to an all-bubbles one.** ✉ *23555 Carneros Hwy./Hwy. 121, Sonoma* ☎ *707/933–1917* 🌐 *www.gloriaferrer.com* 🎫 *Tastings from $55.*

Hanson of Sonoma Distillery

WINERY/DISTILLERY | The Hanson family makes grape-based organic vodkas, one traditional, the rest infused with cucumbers, ginger, mandarin oranges, Meyer lemons, or habanero and other chili peppers. A surprise to many visitors, the Hansons make a blended white wine before distilling it into vodka. The family pours its vodkas, along with single-malt whiskey, in an industrial-looking tasting room heavy on the steel, with wood reclaimed from Deep South smokehouses adding a rustic note. In good weather some sessions take place on the landscaped shore of a small pond. Per state law, there's a limit to the amount poured, but it's sufficient to get to know the product. ✉ *22985 Burndale Rd., Sonoma ✢ At Carneros Hwy. (Hwy. 121)* ☎ *707/343–1805* 🌐 *hansonofsonoma.com* 🎫 *Tastings from $25, tours from $50 (includes tasting).*

★ Sangiacomo Family Wines

WINERY/DISTILLERY | Several dozen wineries produce vineyard-designate Chardonnays and Pinot Noirs from grapes grown by the Sangiacomo family, whose Italian ancestors first started farming in Sonoma in 1927. The family didn't establish its own label until 2016, but its cool-climate wines and a Napa Valley Cabernet are already earning critical plaudits. Chardonnay vines and the Carneros District's western hills form the backdrop for tastings, usually outdoors, at the 110-acre Home Ranch, the first of a dozen-plus vineyards the Sangiacomos acquired or lease. At appointment-only visits you're apt to encounter one or more third-generation members, all of whom enjoy meeting guests and sharing their family's legacy. ■ **TIP→ On Fridays, the winery hosts Sunset on the Terrace, with wines served by the glass or bottle from 3:30 pm until sundown.** ✉ *21545 Broadway, Sonoma ✢ 2½ miles south of Sonoma Plaza* ☎ *707/934–8445* 🌐 *www.sangiacomowines.com* 🎫 *Tastings from $30.*

Sonoma Mission

RELIGIOUS SITE | The northernmost of the 21 missions established by Franciscan friars in California, Sonoma Mission was founded in 1823 as Mission San Francisco Solano. These days it serves as the centerpiece of **Sonoma State Historic Park,** which includes several other sites in Sonoma and nearby Petaluma. Some early mission structures fell into ruin, but all or part of several remaining buildings date to the era of Mexican rule over California. The **Sonoma Barracks,** a half block west of the mission at 20 East Spain Street, housed troops under the command of General Mariano Guadalupe Vallejo, who controlled vast tracts of land in the region. **General Vallejo's Home,** a Victorian-era structure, is a few blocks west. ✉ *114 E. Spain St., Sonoma ✢ At 1st St. E* ☎ *707/938–9560* 🌐 *www.parks.ca.gov* 🎫 *$3, includes same-day admission to other historic sites.*

Restaurants

★ Cafe La Haye

$$$ | AMERICAN | In a postage-stamp-size open kitchen (the dining room, its white walls adorned with contemporary art, is nearly as compact), chef Jeffrey Lloyd turns out understated, sophisticated fare emphasizing seasonably available local ingredients. Meats, pastas, and seafood get deluxe treatment without fuss or fanfare—and the daily risotto special is always worth trying. **Known for:** Napa-Sonoma wine list with French complements; signature butterscotch pudding; owner Saul Gropman on hand to greet diners. $ *Average main: $27* ✉ *140 E. Napa St., Sonoma ✢ East of Sonoma Plaza* ☎ *707/935–5994* 🌐 *www.cafelahaye.com* ⏲ *Closed Sun. and Mon. No lunch.*

El Dorado Kitchen

$$$ | MODERN AMERICAN | This restaurant owes its visual appeal to its clean lines and handsome decor, but the eye inevitably drifts westward to the open kitchen, where longtime chef Armando Navarro and his team craft dishes full of subtle surprises. The menu might include cod ceviche or fried calamari with spicy marinara sauce as starters and pan-roasted salmon or paella awash with seafood and dry-cured Spanish chorizo sausage among the entrées. **Known for:** subtle tastes and textures; truffle-oil fries with Parmesan; bar menu's pizzas and burger. $ *Average main: $29* ✉ *El Dorado Hotel, 405 1st St. W, Sonoma ✢ At W. Spain St.* ☎ *707/996–3030* 🌐 *eldoradokitchen.com.*

★ Girl & the Fig

$$ | **FRENCH** | At this hot spot for inventive French cooking inside the historic Sonoma Hotel bar, you can always find a dish with the signature figs on the menu, whether it's a fig-and-arugula salad or an aperitif blending sparkling wine with fig liqueur. Also look for duck confit, a burger with matchstick fries, and wild flounder meunière. **Known for:** Rhône-wines emphasis; artisanal cheese platters; Sunday brunch. *$ Average main: $26 ✉ Sonoma Hotel, 110 W. Spain St., Sonoma ✥ At 1st St. W ☎ 707/938–3634 ⊕ www.thegirlandthefig.com.*

★ LaSalette Restaurant

$$$ | **PORTUGUESE** | Born in the Azores and raised in Sonoma, chef-owner Manuel Azevedo serves cuisine inspired by his native Portugal in this warmly decorated spot. The wood-oven-roasted fish is always worth trying, and there are usually boldly flavored pork dishes, along with stews, salted cod, and other hearty fare. **Known for:** authentic Portuguese cuisine; sophisticated spicing; local and Portuguese wine flights. *$ Average main: $29 ✉ 452 1st St. E, Sonoma ✥ Near E. Spain St. ☎ 707/938–1927 ⊕ www.lasaletterestaurant.com ⊙ Closed Wed.*

Taub Family Outpost

$$ | **AMERICAN** | Its varied initiatives and location across from Sonoma Plaza's southwest corner ensure steady traffic to this combination all-day restaurant, gourmet marketplace, wine shop, café, bar, and wine-tasting space whose updated-country-store decor suits its 1912 building's Mexican period/Old West flourishes. Items that might appear on the menu range from the healthful (ancient-grain burgers; smoked-beet salad) to the sinfully delicious (grilled cheese with bacon; fried chicken) and in-between (prosciutto with honeydew melon). **Known for:** coffee and cocktails; wines from many lands; patio dining. *$ Average main: $22 ✉ 497 1st St. W, Sonoma ✥ At W. Napa St. ☎ 707/721–1107 ⊕ taubfamilyoutpost.com ⊙ Closed Mon.*

★ Wit & Wisdom Tavern

$$$ | **MODERN AMERICAN** | A San Francisco culinary star with establishments worldwide, Michael Mina debuted his first Wine Country restaurant in 2020, its interior of charcoal grays, browns, and soft whites dandy indeed, if by evening vying with outdoor spaces aglow with fire pits and lighted water features. Seasonal regional ingredients—Pacific Coast fish, pasture-raised meats, freshly plucked produce—go into haute-homey dishes, prepared open-fire, that include pizzas, handmade pastas, and the signature lobster potpie with brandied lobster cream and black truffle. **Known for:** shellfish and duck-wing apps; extensive local wines; large outdoor patio. *$ Average main: $35 ✉ The Lodge at Sonoma, 1325 Broadway, Sonoma ✥ At Leveroni Rd. ☎ 707/931–3405 ⊕ www.witandwisdomsonoma.com.*

Hotels

Inn at Sonoma

$$ | **B&B/INN** | Little luxuries delight at this well-run inn ¼-mile south of Sonoma Plaza whose guest rooms, softly lit and done in pastels, have comfortable beds topped with feather comforters and plenty of pillows. **Pros:** last-minute specials are a great deal; afternoon wine, cheese, and freshly baked cookies; good soundproofing blocks out Broadway street noise. **Cons:** on a busy street rather than right on the plaza; pet-friendly rooms book up quickly; some rooms on the small side. *$ Rooms from: $259 ✉ 630 Broadway, Sonoma ☎ 707/939–1340 ⊕ www.innatsonoma.com ⇨ 27 rooms ¶ Free breakfast.*

★ Ledson Hotel

$$$ | **B&B/INN** | With just six rooms the Ledson feels intimate, and the furnishings and amenities—down beds, mood lighting, gas fireplaces, whirlpool tubs,

and balconies for enjoying breakfast or a glass of wine—stack up well against Wine Country rooms costing more, especially in high season. **Pros:** convenient Sonoma Plaza location; spacious, individually decorated rooms; whirlpool tub in all rooms. **Cons:** two people maximum occupancy in all rooms; children must be at least 12 years old; front rooms have plaza views but pick up some street noise. *Rooms from: $350 ✉ 480 1st St. E, Sonoma ☎ 707/996–9779 www.ledsonhotel.com 6 rooms No meals.*

★ MacArthur Place Hotel & Spa

$$$$ | HOTEL | Guests at this 7-acre boutique property five blocks south of Sonoma Plaza bask in ritzy seclusion in plush accommodations set amid landscaped gardens. **Pros:** verdant garden setting; restaurant among Sonoma's best; great for a romantic getaway. **Cons:** a bit of a walk from the plaza; some traffic noise audible in street-side rooms; pricey in high season. *Rooms from: $459 ✉ 29 E. MacArthur St., Sonoma ☎ 707/938–2929, 800/722–1866 www.macarthurplace.com 64 rooms Free breakfast.*

Nightlife

Sigh!

WINE BARS—NIGHTLIFE | From the oval bar and walls the color of a fine Blanc de Blancs to retro chandeliers that mimic champagne bubbles, everything about this sparkling-wine bar's frothy space screams "have a good time." That owner Jayme Powers and her posse are trained in the fine art of *sabrage* (opening a bottle of sparkling with a saber) only adds to the festivity. **TIP→ Sigh! opens at noon, so it's a good daytime stop, too.** *✉ 120 W. Napa St., Sonoma ✣ At 1st St. W ☎ 707/996–2444 www.sighsonoma.com.*

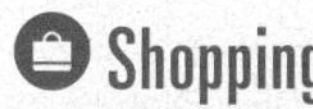

Shopping

Chateau Sonoma

HOUSEHOLD ITEMS/FURNITURE | The fancy furniture, lighting fixtures, and objets d'art at this upscale shop make it a dangerous place to enter: within minutes you may find yourself reconsidering your entire home's aesthetic. The owner's keen eye for French style makes a visit here a pleasure. *✉ 453 1st St. W, Sonoma ✣ Between W. Napa and W. Spain Sts. ☎ 707/309–1993 www.chateausonoma.com.*

Activities

SPAS

Willow Stream Spa at Fairmont Sonoma Mission Inn & Spa

FITNESS/HEALTH CLUBS | By far the Wine Country's largest spa, the Fairmont resort's 40,000-square-foot facility provides every amenity you could want, including pools and hot tubs fed by local thermal springs. Each of the three signature treatments achieves a specific objective. Starting with a lavender bubble bath, followed by a botanical body wrap and a massage, the Couples Lavender Kur focuses on pampering, whereas the Neroli Blossom Kur—a body polish, a full-body massage, a moisture mask, and a facial and scalp massage—is all about restoring balance. For clients in need of a detox, the Wine Country Kur begins with exfoliation, a soak, and a wrap, concluding with a grape-seed oil massage. *✉ 100 Boyes Blvd./Hwy. 12, Sonoma ✣ 2½ miles north of Sonoma Plaza ☎ 707/938–9000 www.fairmont.com/sonoma/willow-stream Treatments from $79.*

Glen Ellen

7 miles north of Sonoma.

Craggy Glen Ellen epitomizes the difference between the Napa and Sonoma valleys. Whereas small Napa towns like St. Helena get their charm from upscale boutiques and restaurants lined up along well-groomed sidewalks, Glen Ellen's crooked streets are shaded with stands of old oak trees and occasionally bisected by the Sonoma and Calabazas creeks. Tucked among the trees of a narrow canyon where Sonoma Mountain and the Mayacamas pinch in the valley floor, Glen Ellen looks more like a town of the Sierra foothills gold country than a Wine Country village.

GETTING HERE AND AROUND

Glen Ellen sits just off Highway 12. From the north or south, take Arnold Drive west and follow it south less than a mile. The walkable downtown straddles a half-mile stretch of Arnold Drive. Sonoma County Transit buses serve Glen Ellen.

Sights

Benziger Family Winery

WINERY/DISTILLERY | One of the best-known Sonoma County wineries sits on a sprawling estate in a bowl with 360-degree sun exposure. Hosts conducting popular tram tours explain the benefits of the vineyard's natural setting and how biodynamic farming yields healthier, more flavorful fruit. The eco-friendly agricultural practices include extensive plantings to attract beneficial insects and the deployment of sheep to trim vegetation between the vines while simultaneously tilling the soil with their hooves and fertilizing to boot. Known for Chardonnay, Cabernet Sauvignon, Merlot, Pinot Noir, and Sauvignon Blanc, the winery is a beautiful spot for an alfresco tasting, whether you take the tour or not. All visits are by appointment; in summer and early fall, reserve a tram tour at least a day or two ahead. ✉ *1883 London Ranch Rd., Glen Ellen* ✣ *Off Arnold Dr.* ☎ *888/490–2739* 🌐 *www.benziger.com* *Tasting $30, tram tour and tasting $60* ⏲ *Closed Tues. and Wed.*

★ Jack London State Historic Park

NATIONAL/STATE PARK | The pleasures are pastoral and intellectual at author Jack London's beloved Beauty Ranch, where you could easily spend the afternoon hiking some of the 30-plus miles of trails that loop through meadows and stands of oaks, redwoods, and other trees. Manuscripts and personal artifacts depicting London's travels are on view at the House of Happy Walls Museum, which provides an overview of the writer's life, literary passions, humanitarian and conservation efforts, and promotion of organic farming. A short hike away lie the ruins of Wolf House, which burned down just before London was to move in. Also open to visitors are a few outbuildings and the restored wood-framed cottage where London penned many of his later works. He's buried on the property. **■ TIP→ The park's Broadway Under the Stars series, a hot summer ticket, is expected to resume in 2021.** ✉ *2400 London Ranch Rd., Glen Ellen* ✣ *Off Arnold Dr.* ☎ *707/938–5216* 🌐 *www.jacklondonpark.com* *Parking $10 ($5 walk-in or bike), includes admission to museum; cottage $4.*

★ Lasseter Family Winery

WINERY/DISTILLERY | Immaculately groomed grapevines dazzle the eye at John and Nancy Lasseter's secluded winery, and it's no accident: Phil Coturri, Sonoma Valley's premier organic vineyard manager, tends them. Even the landscaping, which includes an insectary to attract beneficial bugs, is meticulously maintained. Come harvest time, the wine-making team oversees gentle processes that transform the fruit into wines of purity and grace, among them a Sémillon–Sauvignon Blanc blend, two rosés, and Bordeaux and Rhône reds. Evocative labels illustrate the tale behind each wine. In good weather, guests enjoy these well-told stories at tastings on the winery's outdoor patio, whose views include the vineyard and the Mayacamas Mountains. All visits are by appointment. ✉ *1 Vintage La., Glen Ellen* ✣ *Off Dunbar*

Benziger tram tours take to the fields to show biodynamic farming techniques in action.

Rd. ☎ *707/933–2814* 🌐 *www.lasseter-familywinery.com* 🎫 *Tastings from $25.*

Restaurants

★ Glen Ellen Star

$$$ | ECLECTIC | Chef Ari Weiswasser honed his craft at The French Laundry, Daniel, and other bastions of culinary finesse, but at his Wine Country outpost he prepares haute-rustic cuisine, much of it emerging from a wood-fired oven that burns a steady 600°F. Crisp-crusted, richly sauced Margherita and other pizzas thrive in the torrid heat, as do tender whole fish entrées and vegetables roasted in small iron skillets. **Known for:** outdoor dining area; prix-fixe Wednesday "neighborhood night" menu with free corkage; Weiswasser's sauces, emulsions, and spices. 💲 *Average main: $30* ✉ *13648 Arnold Dr., Glen Ellen* ✣ *At Warm Springs Rd.* ☎ *707/343–1384* 🌐 *glenellenstar.com* 🕒 *No lunch.*

★ Les Pascals

$ | FRENCH | A bright-yellow slice of France in downtown Glen Ellen, this combination pâtisserie, boulangerie, and café takes its name from its husband-and-wife owners, Pascal and Pascale Merle. Pascal whips up croissants, breads, turnovers, and sweet treats like Napoleons, galettes, and eclairs, along with quiches, potpies, and other savory fare; Pascale creates an upbeat environment for customers to enjoy them. **Known for:** memorable French onion soup; shaded back patio; high-test French and Italian coffee drinks. 💲 *Average main: $10* ✉ *13758 Arnold Dr., Glen Ellen* ✣ *Near London Ranch Rd.* ☎ *707/934–8378* 🌐 *www.lespascalspatisserie.com* 🕒 *Closed Wed. No dinner.*

Hotels

★ Gaige House + Ryokan

$$$ | B&B/INN | There's no other place in Sonoma or Napa quite like the Gaige House + Ryokan, which blends the best elements of a traditional country inn, a boutique hotel, and a longtime expat's classy Asian hideaway. **Pros:** short walk to Glen Ellen restaurants, shops, and tasting rooms; freshly baked cookies; full breakfasts, afternoon wine and appetizers. **Cons:** sound carries in the main house; the least expensive rooms are on the small side; oriented more toward couples than families with children. *$ Rooms from: $302 ✉ 13540 Arnold Dr., Glen Ellen ☎ 707/935–0237, 800/935–0237 ⊕ www.thegaigehouse.com 23 rooms 🍽 Free breakfast.*

★ Olea Hotel

$$$ | B&B/INN | Husband-and-wife team Ashish and Sia Patel operate this down-home country casual yet sophisticated boutique lodging. **Pros:** beautiful style; complimentary wine; filling two-course breakfasts. **Cons:** minor road noise in some rooms; fills up quickly on weekends; weekend minimum-stay requirement. *$ Rooms from: $309 ✉ 5131 Warm Springs Rd., Glen Ellen ✥ West off Arnold Dr. ☎ 707/996–5131 ⊕ www.oleahotel.com 15 rooms 🍽 Free breakfast.*

Kenwood

4 miles north of Glen Ellen.

Tiny Kenwood consists of little more than a few restaurants, shops, tasting rooms, and a historic train depot, now used for private events. But hidden in this pretty landscape of meadows and woods at the north end of Sonoma Valley are several good wineries, most just off the Sonoma Highway. Varietals grown here at the foot of the Sugarloaf Mountains include Sauvignon Blanc, Chardonnay, Zinfandel, and Cabernet Sauvignon.

GETTING HERE AND AROUND

To get to Kenwood from Glen Ellen, head northeast on Arnold Drive and north on Highway 12. Sonoma Transit buses serve Kenwood from Glen Ellen and Sonoma.

Sights

★ En Garde Winery

WINERY/DISTILLERY | Sommeliers, critics, and collectors extol the Pinot Noirs and Cabernet Sauvignons of Csaba Szakál, En Garde's Hungarian-born winemaker and owner. Striving to create what he describes as "aromatic, complex, lush, and juicy" wines, Szakál selects top Sonoma County vineyards for the Pinots and the Napa Valley's Diamond Mountain, Mt. Veeder, and other high-elevation sites for the Cabernets. Not afraid to heavy up the oak on the Cabernets, he nevertheless achieves elegance as well. The winemaker is equally precise about hiring staffers for his modest highway's-edge tasting room along Kenwood's brief commercial strip. Well-acquainted with his goals and methods, they provide a wealth of knowledge about wine making and California viticulture. If you're lucky, Szakál himself will be around to discuss his wines (he loves to), which also include Chardonnay, Viognier, and rosé of Pinot Noir. Visits are by reservation, with same-day appointments sometimes possible. *✉ 9077 Sonoma Hwy., Kenwood ✥ At Shaw Ave. ☎ 707/282–9216 ⊕ www.engardewinery.com Tastings from $25.*

St. Francis Winery

WINERY/DISTILLERY | Nestled at the foot of Mt. Hood, St. Francis has earned national acclaim for its pairings of wines and small bites. With its red-tile roof and bell tower and views of the Mayacamas Mountains to the east, the winery's California Mission–style visitor center occupies one of Sonoma County's most scenic locations. The charm of the surroundings is matched by the mostly red wines, among them rich, earthy Zinfandels from the Dry Creek, Russian River, and Sonoma valleys. The five-course pairings might include Chardonnay with lobster bisque or Cabernet Sauvignon with wine-braised beef ribs. *✉ 100 Pythian Rd., Kenwood ✥ Off Hwy. 12*

☏ *707/538–9463, 888/675–9463* ⊕ *www.stfranciswinery.com* *Tastings from $20* ⊙ *Closed Tues. and Wed.*

Restaurants

Salt & Stone

$$$ | **MODERN AMERICAN** | The menu at this upscale roadhouse with a sloping wood-beamed ceiling focuses on seafood and meat—beef, lamb, chicken, duck, and other options—with many dishes in both categories grilled. Start with the classics, perhaps a martini and oysters Rockefeller, before moving on to well-plated contemporary entrées that might include crispy-skin salmon or duck breast, a fish stew, or grilled rib-eye. **Known for:** mountain-view outdoor seating area; weekend brunch; weekday happy hour 2:30–5:30 except holidays. [$] *Average main: $29* ✉ *9900 Sonoma Hwy., Kenwood* ✣ *At Kunde Winery Rd.* ☏ *707/833–6326* ⊕ *www.saltstonekenwood.com* ⊙ *No lunch Tues. and Wed.*

Hotels

★ Kenwood Inn and Spa

$$$ | **B&B/INN** | Fluffy feather beds, custom Italian furnishings, and French doors in most cases opening onto terraces or balconies lend this inn's uncommonly spacious guest rooms a romantic air—more than a few guests are celebrating honeymoons or anniversaries. **Pros:** large rooms; lavish furnishings; romantic setting. **Cons:** far from nightlife; expensive in high season; geared more to couples than families with children. [$] *Rooms from: $381* ✉ *10400 Sonoma Hwy./Hwy. 12, Kenwood* ☏ *707/833–1293, 800/353–6966* ⊕ *www.kenwoodinn.com* *29 rooms* *Free breakfast.*

Petaluma

24 miles southwest of Kenwood, 39 miles north of San Francisco.

The first thing you should know about Petaluma is that this is a farm town—with more than 62,500 residents, a large one—and the residents are proud of it. Recent years have seen an uptick in the quality of Petaluma cuisine, fueled in part by the proliferation of local organic and artisanal farms and boutique wine production. With the 2018 approval of the Petaluma Gap AVA, the city even has its name on a wine appellation.

GETTING HERE AND AROUND

Petaluma lies west of Sonoma and southwest of Glen Ellen and Kenwood. From Highway 12 or Arnold Drive, take Watmaugh Road west to Highway 116 west. Sonoma Transit buses serve Petaluma. From San Francisco take U.S. 101 (or Golden Gate Transit Bus 101) north.

Sights

Lagunitas Brewing Company

WINERY/DISTILLERY | These days owned by Heineken International, Lagunitas began as a craft brewery in Marin County in 1993 before moving to Petaluma in 1994. In addition to its large facility, the company operates a taproom, the Schwag Shop for gifts, and an outdoor beer garden that in good weather bustles even midday. Guides leading the brewery tour, which when offered includes a beer flight, provide an irreverent version of the company's rise to international acclaim. An engaging tale involves the state alcohol board's sting operation commemorated by Undercover Investigation Shut-down Ale, one of several small-batch brews made here. ■ **TIP→ The taproom closes on Monday and Tuesday, but the gift shop stays open and tours may take place.** ✉ *1280 N. McDowell Blvd., Petaluma* ✣ *½ mile north of Corona Rd.* ☏ *707/769–4495* ⊕ *lagunitas.com/*

taproom/petaluma 🎫 *Tour free* ⏲ *Taproom closed Mon. and Tues.*

★ McEvoy Ranch

WINERY/DISTILLERY | The late Nan McEvoy's retirement project after departing as board chair of the *San Francisco Chronicle,* the ranch produces organic extra virgin olive oil as well as Pinot Noir and other wines, the estate ones from the Petaluma Gap AVA. Relaxing tastings of oils or wines unfold on a pond's-edge flagstone patio with views of alternating rows of Syrah grapes and mature olive trees. Two wine tastings include a simple lunch; the Taste of the Season spread involves wine served with artisanal cheeses, charcuterie, and other items. Walkabout Ranch Tours of four guests or more take in vineyards, gardens, and a Chinese pavilion. All visits require an appointment. ✉ *5935 Red Hill Rd., Petaluma* ✥ *6½ miles south of downtown* ☎ *866/617–6779* 🌐 *www.mcevoyranch.com* 🎫 *Tastings from $25 (olive oil), $35 (wine); tours from $55.*

Restaurants

★ Central Market

$$ | **MODERN AMERICAN** | A participant in the Slow Food movement, Central Market serves creative, upscale Cal-Mediterranean dishes—many of whose ingredients come from the restaurant's organic farm—in a century-old building with an exposed brick wall and an open kitchen. The menu, which changes daily depending on chef Tony Najiola's inspiration and what's ripe and ready, might include smoked duck wings as a starter, a slow-roasted-beets salad, pizzas, stews, two or three pasta dishes, and wood-grilled fish and meat. **Known for:** chef's tasting menus; superior wine list; historic setting. 💲 *Average main: $26* ✉ *42 Petaluma Blvd. N, Petaluma* ✥ *Near Western Ave.* ☎ *707/778–9900* 🌐 *www.centralmarketpetaluma.com* ⏲ *Closed Mon. and Tues. No lunch.*

★ Pearl Petaluma

$$ | **MEDITERRANEAN** | Regulars of this southern Petaluma "daytime café" with indoor and outdoor seating rave about its eastern Mediterranean–inflected cuisine—then immediately downplay their enthusiasm lest this unassuming gem become more popular. The menu changes often, but mainstays include *shakshuka* (a tomato-based stew with baked eggs) and a lamb burger dripping with tzatziki. **Known for:** weekend brunch; fun beverage lineup, both alcoholic and non; menu prices include gratuity. 💲 *Average main: $20* ✉ *500 1st St., Petaluma* ✥ *At G St.* ☎ *707/559–5187* 🌐 *pearlpetaluma.com* ⏲ *Closed Tues. No dinner.*

Healdsburg

17 miles north of Santa Rosa, 32 miles northwest of Petaluma.

Sonoma County's ritziest town and the star of many a magazine spread or online feature, Healdsburg is located at the intersection of the Dry Creek Valley, Russian River Valley, and Alexander Valley AVAs. Several dozen wineries bear a Healdsburg address, and around downtown's plaza you'll find fashionable boutiques, spas, hip tasting rooms, and art galleries, and some of the Wine Country's best restaurants.

Especially on weekends, you'll have plenty of company as you tour the downtown area. You could spend a day just exploring the tasting rooms and shops surrounding Healdsburg Plaza, but be sure to allow time to venture into the surrounding countryside. With orderly rows of vines alternating with beautifully overgrown hills, this is the setting you dream about when planning a Wine Country vacation.

GETTING HERE AND AROUND

Healdsburg sits just off U.S. 101. Heading north, take the Central Healdsburg exit to reach Healdsburg Plaza; heading south, take the Westside Road exit and pass east under the freeway. Sonoma County Transit buses serve Healdsburg from Santa Rosa.

Sights

★ Aperture Cellars

WINERY/DISTILLERY | As a youth, Jesse Katz tagged along with his photographer father, Andy Katz, to wineries worldwide, stimulating curiosity about wine that led to stints at august operations like the Napa Valley's Screaming Eagle and Bordeaux's Petrús. In 2009, still in his 20s, Katz started Aperture, a success from the get-go for his single-vineyard Cabernets and Bordeaux blends. Among the whites are Sauvignon Blanc and an old-vine Chenin Blanc that's one of California's best. Katz's wines, which benefit from rigorous farming and cellar techniques, are presented by appointment only in an ultracontemporary hospitality center that opened in 2020 about 2½ miles south of Healdsburg Plaza. One tasting explores Aperture's various wine-growing sites, the other the single-vineyard wines. The center's shutterlike windows and other architectural elements evoke Andy Katz's photography career; his images of the Russian River Valley and beyond hang on the walls. ✉ *12291 Old Redwood Hwy.* ✣ *¼ mile south of Limerick La.* ☎ *707/200–7891* 🌐 *www.aperture-cellars.com* 🎫 *Tastings from $50.*

Breathless Wines

WINERY/DISTILLERY | The mood's downright bubbly (pardon that pun) at the oasis-like garden patio of this sparkling-wine producer tucked away in an industrial park northwest of Healdsburg Plaza. Established by three sisters in memory of their mother, Breathless sources grapes from appellations in Sonoma, Napa, and Mendocino counties that find their way into sparklers and a few still wines. The small indoor tasting area, decorated flapper-era-style, was ingeniously fashioned out of shipping containers, though nearly everyone sips in the umbrella-shaded garden in fine weather. You can sample wine by the glass, flight, or bottle; all visits require an appointment, with same-day reservations sometimes possible. **■ TIP→ Splurge on the Sabrage Experience to learn how to open a bottle with a saber, a tradition supposedly initiated by Napoléon's soldiers.** ✉ *499 Moore La.* ✣ *Off North St.* ☎ *707/395–7300* 🌐 *www.breathless-wines.com* 🎫 *Tastings from $13 per glass, $20 per flight* ⏲ *Closed Tues. and Wed. (sometimes changes).*

Dry Creek Vineyard

WINERY/DISTILLERY | Loire-style Sauvignon Blanc marketed as Fumé Blanc brought instant success to the Dry Creek Valley's first new winery since Prohibition, but this stalwart established in 1972 also does well with Zinfandel and Cabernet Sauvignon and other Bordeaux-style reds. Founder David Stare's other contributions include leading the drive to develop the Dry Creek Valley appellation and coining the term "old-vine Zinfandel." The winery's history and wine-making evolution are among the topics addressed at tastings—outdoors under the shade of a magnolia and several redwood trees or in the nautical-themed tasting room. ✉ *3770 Lambert Bridge Rd.* ✣ *Off Dry Creek Rd.* ☎ *707/433–1000, 800/864–9463* 🌐 *www.drycreekvineyard.com* 🎫 *Tastings from $25.*

Gary Farrell Vineyards & Winery

WINERY/DISTILLERY | Pass through an impressive metal gate and wind your way up a steep hill to reach this winery with knockout Russian River Valley views from the elegant two-tiered tasting room and terrace outside. In 2017 *Wine Enthusiast Magazine* named a Gary Farrell Chardonnay wine of the year, one among many accolades for this winery known for sophisticated single-vineyard Chardonnays and Pinot Noirs. Farrell departed in the early 2000s, but current winemaker Theresa Heredia acknowledges that her philosophy has much in common with his. For the Pinots, this means picking on the early side to preserve acidity and focusing on "expressing the site." The Elevation Tasting of single-vineyard wines provides a good introduction. All visits are by appointment; same-day reservations are possible during the week, but call ahead. ✉ *10701 Westside Rd.* ☎ *707/473–2909* 🌐 *www.garyfarrellwinery.com* 🎫 *Tastings from $35.*

★ Jordan Vineyard and Winery

WINERY/DISTILLERY | Founders Tom and Sally Jordan erected the French-style château here in part to emphasize their goal of producing Sonoma County Chardonnays and Cabernet Sauvignons—one of each annually—to rival those from the Napa Valley and France itself. Their son John, now at the helm, has instituted numerous improvements, among them the replanting of many vines and a shift to all-French barrels for aging. Most tastings revolve around executive chef Todd Knoll's small bites, whose ingredients come mainly from Jordan's organic garden. The Library Tasting of current releases concludes with an older Cabernet for comparison. An enchanting themed lunch and wine pairing, Paris on the Terrace, unfolds on the château's terrace from spring to early fall, when the winery often hosts a three-hour Estate Tour & Tasting. The latter's pièce de résistance is the stop at a 360-degree vista point overlooking the 1,200-acre property's vines, olive trees, and countryside. Visits are strictly by appointment. ✉ *1474 Alexander Valley Rd.* ✥ *1½ miles east of Healdsburg Ave.* ☎ *800/654–1213, 707/431–5250* 🌐 *www.jordanwinery.com* 🎫 *Tastings from $45* ⏲ *Closed Tues. and Wed. Dec.–Mar.*

MacRostie Estate House

WINERY/DISTILLERY | A driveway off Westside Road curls through undulating vineyard hills to the steel, wood, and heavy-on-the-glass tasting space of this longtime Chardonnay and Pinot Noir producer. Moments after you've arrived and a host has offered a glass of wine, you'll already feel transported to a genteel, rustic world. Hospitality is clearly a priority, but so, too, is seeking out top-tier grape sources—30 for the Chardonnays, 15 for the Pinots—among them Dutton Ranch, Sangiacomo, and owner Steve MacRostie's Wildcat. With fruit this renowned, current winemaker Heidi Bridenhagen downplays the oak and other tricks of her trade, letting the vineyard settings, grape clones, and vintage do the talking. Tastings, inside or on balcony terraces with views across the Russian River Valley, are all seated and by appointment. ✉ *4605 Westside Rd.* ✥ *Near Frost Rd.* ☎ *707/473–9303* 🌐 *macrostiewinery.com* 🎫 *Tastings from $35.*

★ Ridge Vineyards

WINERY/DISTILLERY | Ridge stands tall among local wineries, and not merely because its 1971 Monte Bello Cabernet Sauvignon rated second-highest among California reds competing with French ones at the famous Judgment of Paris blind tasting of 1976. The winery built its reputation on Cabernets, Zinfandels, and Chardonnays of unusual depth and complexity, but you'll also find blends of Rhône varietals. Ridge makes wines using grapes from several California locales—including the Dry Creek Valley, Sonoma Valley, Napa Valley, and Paso Robles—but the focus is on single-vineyard estate wines such as the Lytton Springs Zinfandel from fruit grown near the tasting room. In good weather you can sit outside, taking in views of rolling vineyard hills while you sip. ✉ *650 Lytton Springs Rd.* ✥ *Off U.S. 101* ☎ *408/867–3233* 🌐 *www.ridgewine.com/visit/lytton-springs* 🎫 *Tastings from $20.*

★ Silver Oak

WINERY/DISTILLERY | The views and architecture are as impressive as the wines at the Sonoma County outpost of the same-named Napa Valley winery. In 2018, six years after purchasing a 113-acre parcel with 73 acres planted to grapes, Silver Oak debuted its ultramodern, environmentally sensitive winery and glass-walled tasting pavilion. As in Napa, the Healdsburg facility produces just one wine each year: a well-balanced Alexander Valley Cabernet Sauvignon aged in American rather than French oak barrels. One tasting includes the current Alexander Valley and Napa Valley Cabernets plus an older vintage. Two or more wines of sister operation Twomey Cellars, which produces Sauvignon Blanc, Pinot Noir, and Merlot, begin a second offering that concludes with the current Cabernets. Hosts at a third pour current and older Cabernets from either Napa or Sonoma. Make a reservation for all visits. *7300 Hwy. 128 Near Chaffee Rd. 707/942–7082 www.silveroak.com Tastings from $40.*

★ Tongue Dancer Wines

WINERY/DISTILLERY | Down a country lane less than 2 miles south of Healdsburg Plaza, James MacPhail's modest production facility seems well away from the upscale fray. MacPhail makes wines for The Calling, Sangiacomo, and other labels, but Tongue Dancer's Chardonnays and Pinot Noirs are his handcrafted labors of love. Made from small lots of grapes from choice vineyard sites, the wines impress, sometimes stun, with their grace, complexity, and balance. The flagship Sonoma Coast Pinot Noir, a blend from two or more vineyards, is poured at most tastings, in a mezzanine space above oak-aging barrels or on an outdoor patio. Either the winemaker or his co-owner and wife, Kerry Forbes-MacPhail—she's credited on bottles as the "Knowledgeable One" (and she is)—will host you. As James describes it, they aim to "create an approachable experience for guests we hope will leave as friends." Appointment-only visits are best made a day or more ahead. *851 Magnolia Dr. Off Westside Rd. 707/433–4780 tonguedancerwines.com Tastings from $25 Closed Sun.*

Restaurants

★ Barndiva

$$$$ | **AMERICAN** | Music plays quietly in the background while servers carry inventive seasonal cocktails at this restaurant that abandons the homey vibe of many Wine Country spots in favor of a more urban feel. Make a light meal out of yellowtail tuna crudo or homemade linguine, or settle in for the evening with pan-seared day scallops or a grass-fed strip loin. **Known for:** good cocktails; stylish cuisine; open-air patio. *Average main: $38 231 Center St. Near Matheson St. 707/431–0100 www.barndiva.com Closed Mon. and Tues. No lunch weekdays.*

Bravas Bar de Tapas

$$$ | **SPANISH** | Spanish-style tapas and an outdoor patio in perpetual party mode make this restaurant, headquartered in a restored 1920s bungalow, a popular downtown perch. Contemporary Spanish mosaics set a perky tone inside, but unless something's amiss with the weather, nearly everyone heads out back for flavorful croquettes, paella, jamón, *pan tomate* (tomato toast), grilled octopus, skirt steak, and crispy fried chicken. **Known for:** casual small plates; specialty cocktails, sangrias, and beer; sherries from dry to sweet. *Average main: $28 420 Center St. Near North St. 707/433–7700 www.barbravas.com Closed Mon. and Tues.*

Campo Fina

$$ | **ITALIAN** | Chef Ari Rosen serves up contemporary-rustic Italian cuisine at this converted storefront that once housed a bar notorious for boozin' and brawlin'. Sandblasted red brick, satin-smooth walnut tables, and old-school lighting fixtures (and a large back patio) strike a retro note for a menu built around pizzas and gems such as Rosen's variation on his grandmother's tomato-braised chicken with creamy-soft polenta. **Known for:** outdoor patio's boccie court out of an Italian

movie set; lunch sandwiches; wines from California and Italy. *Average main: $23* *330 Healdsburg Ave.* *Near North St.* *707/395–4640* *www.campofina.com.*

Costeaux French Bakery
$ | **FRENCH** | Breakfast, served all day at this bright-yellow French-style bakery and café, includes the signature omelet (sun-dried tomatoes, bacon, spinach, and Brie) and French toast made from thick slabs of cinnamon-walnut bread. French onion soup and cranberry-turkey, French dip, and (on the cinnamon-walnut bread) Monte Cristo sandwiches are among the lunch favorites. **Known for:** breads, croissants, and fancy pastries; quiche and omelets; front patio. *Average main: $15* *417 Healdsburg Ave.* *At North St.* *707/433–1913* *www.costeaux.com* *Closed Mon. and Tues. (check to be sure). No dinner.*

★ SingleThread Farms Restaurant
$$$$ | **ECLECTIC** | The seasonally oriented, multicourse Japanese dinners known as *kaiseki* inspired the prix-fixe vegetarian, meat, and seafood menu at the spare, elegant restaurant—redwood walls, walnut tables, mesquite-tile floors, muted-gray yarn-thread panels—of internationally renowned culinary artists Katina and Kyle Connaughton (she farms, he cooks). As Katina describes the endeavor, the microseasons of their nearby farm (ask about visiting it) plus SingleThread's rooftop garden of fruit trees and greens dictate Kyle's rarefied fare, prepared in a theatrically lit open kitchen. **Known for:** culinary precision; instinctive service; impeccable wine pairings. *Average main: $295* *131 North St.* *At Center St.* *707/723–4646* *www.singlethreadfarms.com* *No lunch weekdays.*

★ Valette
$$$ | **MODERN AMERICAN** | Northern Sonoma native Dustin Valette opened this homage to the area's artisanal agricultural bounty with his brother, who runs the high-ceilinged dining room, where the playful contemporary lighting tempers the austerity of the exposed concrete walls and butcher-block-thick wooden tables. Charcuterie is an emphasis, but also consider the signature day-boat scallops *en croûte* (in a pastry crust) or dishes that might include Szechuan-crusted duck breast or a variation on Niçoise salad with albacore poached in olive oil. **Known for:** "Trust me" (the chef) tasting menu; mostly Northern California and French wines; chef's nearby The Matheson for wine tasting, pairings, and rooftop dining. *Average main: $36* *344 Center St.* *At North St.* *707/473–0946* *www.valettehealdsburg.com* *No lunch.*

Hotels

★ Harmon Guest House
$$$ | **HOTEL** | A boutique sibling of the h2hotel two doors away, this downtown delight debuted in late 2018 having already earned LEED Gold status for its eco-friendly construction and operating practices. **Pros:** rooftop bar's cocktails, food menu, and views; connecting rooms and suites; similarly designed sister property h2hotel two doors south. **Cons:** minor room-to-room noise bleed-through; room gadgetry may flummox some guests; minimum-stay requirements some weekends. *Rooms from: $389* *227 Healdsburg Ave.* *707/922–5262* *harmonguesthouse.com* *39 rooms* *Free breakfast.*

Hotel Trio Healdsburg
$$ | **HOTEL** | Named for the three major wine appellations—the Russian River, Dry Creek, and Alexander valleys—whose confluence it's near, this Residence Inn by Marriott 1¼ miles north of Healdsburg Plaza caters to families and extended-stay business travelers with spacious rooms equipped with full kitchens. **Pros:** cute robot room service; full kitchens; rooms sleep up to four or six. **Cons:** 30-minute walk to downtown; slightly corporate feel; pricey in high

season. $ *Rooms from: $242 ✉ 110 Dry Creek Rd. ☎ 707/433–4000 🌐 www.hoteltrio.com 🛏 122 rooms 🍽 Free breakfast.*

★ Montage Healdsburg

$$$$ | RESORT | Its bungalowlike guest rooms deftly layered into oak- and Cabernet-studded hills a few miles north of Healdsburg Plaza, this architectural sensation that opened fully in 2021 significantly upped Sonoma County's ultraluxury game. **Pros:** vineyard views from spa, restaurant, and swimming pool; outdoor living spaces with daybeds and fire pits; recreational options on-property or nearby. **Cons:** expensive year-round; hefty resort fee; car trip required for off-property visits. $ *Rooms from: $845 ✉ 100 Montage Way ☎ 707/979–9000 🌐 www.montagehotels.com/healdsburg 🛏 130 bungalows 🍽 No meals.*

★ River Belle Inn

$$ | B&B/INN | An 1875 Victorian with a storied past and a glorious colonnaded wraparound porch anchors this boutique property along the Russian River. **Pros:** riverfront location near a dozen-plus tasting rooms; cooked-to-order full breakfasts; attention to detail. **Cons:** about a mile from Healdsburg Plaza; minimum-stay requirement on weekends; lacks on-site pool, fitness center, and other amenities. $ *Rooms from: $280 ✉ 68 Front St. ☎ 707/955–5724 🌐 www.riverbelleinn.com 🛏 12 rooms 🍽 Free breakfast.*

Shopping

ART GALLERIES

★ Gallery Lulo

ART GALLERIES | A collaboration between a local artist and jewelry maker and a Danish-born curator, this gallery presents changing exhibits of jewelry, sculpture, and objets d'art. *✉ 303 Center St. ✥ At Plaza St. ☎ 707/433–7533 🌐 www.gallerylulo.com.*

FOOD AND WINE

Dry Creek General Store

FOOD/CANDY | For breakfasts, sandwiches, bread, cheeses, and picnic supplies, stop by the general store, established in 1881 and still a popular spot for locals to hang out on the porch or in the bar. Beer and wine are also for sale, along with artisanal sodas, ciders, and juices. *✉ 3495 Dry Creek Rd. ✥ At Lambert Bridge Rd. ☎ 707/433–4171 🌐 www.drycreekgeneralstore1881.com.*

Activities

SPAS

★ A Simple Touch Spa

FITNESS/HEALTH CLUBS | Skilled in Swedish, deep-tissue, sports, and other massage modalities, this soothing but unpretentious day spa's therapists routinely receive post-session raves. The most popular treatment involves heated basalt stones applied to the client's body, followed by a massage of choice. Foot reflexology, reiki, and facials are among the other specialties. **■ TIP→ Couples can enjoy any of the massages performed side-by-side by two therapists.** *✉ 239 Center St., Suite C ✥ Near Matheson St. ☎ 707/433–6856 🌐 asimpletouchspa.com 🎟 Treatments from $55.*

Geyserville

8 miles north of Healdsburg.

Several high-profile Alexander Valley AVA wineries, including the splashy Francis Ford Coppola Winery, can be found in the town of Geyserville, a small part of which stretches west of U.S. 101 into northern Dry Creek. Not long ago this was a dusty farm town, and downtown Geyserville retains its rural character, but the restaurants, shops, and tasting rooms along the short main drag hint at Geyserville's growing sophistication.

GETTING HERE AND AROUND

From Healdsburg, the quickest route to downtown Geyserville is north on U.S. 101 to the Highway 128/Geyserville exit. Turn right at the stop sign onto Geyserville Avenue and follow the road north to the small downtown. For a more scenic drive, head north from Healdsburg Plaza along Healdsburg Avenue. About 3 miles north, jog west (left) for a few hundred feet onto Lytton Springs Road, then turn north (right) onto Geyserville Avenue. In town the avenue merges with Highway 128. Sonoma County Transit buses serve Geyserville from downtown Healdsburg.

 Sights

Francis Ford Coppola Winery

WINERY/DISTILLERY | The fun at what the film director has called his "wine wonderland" is all in the excess. You may find it hard to resist having your photo snapped standing next to Don Corleone's desk from *The Godfather* or beside other memorabilia from Coppola films (including some directed by his daughter, Sofia). A bandstand reminiscent of one in *The Godfather Part II* is the centerpiece of a large pool area where you can rent a changing room, complete with shower, and spend the afternoon lounging poolside, perhaps ordering food from the adjacent café. A more elaborate restaurant, Rustic, overlooks the vineyards. As for the wines, the excess continues in the cellar, where Coppola's team produces several dozen varietal bottlings and blends. ✉ *300 Via Archimedes* ✣ *Off U.S. 101* ☎ *707/857–1400* 🌐 *www.franciscoppolawinery.com* 🎫 *Tastings from $35.*

★ Locals Tasting Room

WINERY/DISTILLERY | If you're serious about wine, Carolyn Lewis's tasting room is worth the trek 8 miles north of Healdsburg Plaza to downtown Geyserville. Connoisseurs who appreciate Lewis's ability to spot up-and-comers head here regularly to sample the output of a dozen or so small wineries, most without tasting rooms of their own. There's no fee for tasting—extraordinary for wines of this quality—and the extremely knowledgeable staff are happy to pour you a flight of several wines so you can compare, say, different Cabernet Sauvignons. ✉ *21023A Geyserville Ave.* ✣ *At Hwy. 128* ☎ *707/857–4900* 🌐 *www.localstastingroom.com* 🎫 *Tasting free.*

★ Robert Young Estate Winery

WINERY/DISTILLERY | Panoramic Alexander Valley views unfold at Scion House, the stylish yet informal knoll-top tasting space of this longtime Geyserville grower. The first Youngs began farming this land in the mid-1800s, raising cattle and growing wheat, prunes, and other crops. In the 1960s the late Robert Young, of the third generation, began cultivating grapes, eventually planting two Chardonnay clones now named for him. Grapes from them go into the Area 27 Chardonnay, among the best whites. The reds—small-lot Cabernet Sauvignons plus individual bottlings of Cabernet Franc, Malbec, Merlot, and Petit Verdot—shine even brighter. Tastings at Scion House, named for the fourth generation, whose members built on Robert Young's legacy and established the winery, are by appointment. Call ahead for same-day reservations. **■ TIP→ Cab fanatics should consider the Ultimate Cabernet Lovers Experience of top-tier estate wines.** ✉ *5120 Red Winery Rd.* ✣ *Off Hwy. 128* ☎ *707/431–4811* 🌐 *www.ryew.com* 🎫 *Tastings from $30* ⏲ *Closed Tues.*

★ Zialena

WINERY/DISTILLERY | Sister-and-brother team Lisa and Mark Mazzoni (she runs the business, he makes the wines) debuted their small winery's first vintage in 2014, but their Italian American family's wine-making heritage stretches back more than a century. Named for the siblings' great aunt Lena, known for her hospitality, Zialena specializes in estate-grown Zinfandel and Cabernet Sauvignon, some of whose lush mouthfeel derives from techniques Mark absorbed while working for the international consultant Philippe Melka. The Zin and Cab grapes, along with those for the Chardonnay and seductive rosé of Sangiovese, come from the 120-acre Mazzoni Vineyard, from which larger labels like Jordan also source fruit. Tastings are by appointment only, with same-day visits often possible. ✉ *21112 River Rd.* ✥ *Off Hwy. 128* ☎ *707/955–5992* 🌐 *www.zialena.com* 🎫 *Tastings from $15.*

Restaurants

Diavola Pizzeria & Salumeria

$$ | ITALIAN | A dining area with hardwood floors, a pressed-tin ceiling, and exposed-brick walls provides a fitting setting for the rustic cuisine at this Geyserville mainstay. Chef Dino Bugica studied with artisanal cooks in Italy before opening this restaurant specializing in wood-fired pizzas and house-cured meats, with a few salads and meaty main courses rounding out the menu. **Known for:** talented chef; smoked pork belly, pancetta, and spicy Calabrese sausage; casual setting. 💲 *Average main: $23* ✉ *21021 Geyserville Ave.* ✥ *At Hwy. 128* ☎ *707/814–0111* 🌐 *www.diavolapizzeria.com.*

Hotels

Geyserville Inn

$$ | HOTEL | Clever travelers give the Healdsburg hubbub and prices the heave-ho but still have easy access to outstanding Dry Creek and Alexander Valley wineries from this modest, motel-like inn with a boutique-hotel sensibility. **Pros:** outdoor pool; vineyard-view decks from second-floor rooms in back; picnic area. **Cons:** rooms facing pool or highway can be noisy; weekend two-night minimum requirement; not for party types. 💲 *Rooms from: $209* ✉ *21714 Geyserville Ave.* ☎ *707/857–4343, 877/857–4343* 🌐 *www.geyservilleinn.com* *41 rooms* 🍴 *No meals.*

Forestville

13 miles southwest of Healdsburg.

To experience the Russian River Valley AVA's climate and rusticity, follow the river's westward course to the town of Forestville, home to a highly regarded restaurant and inn and a few wineries producing Pinot Noir from the Russian River Valley and well beyond.

GETTING HERE AND AROUND

To reach Forestville from U.S. 101, drive west from the River Road exit north of Santa Rosa. From Healdsburg, follow Westside Road west to River Road and then continue west. Sonoma County Transit buses serve Forestville.

Sights

★ **Hartford Family Winery**

WINERY/DISTILLERY | Pinot Noir lovers appreciate the subtle differences in the wines Hartford's team crafts from grapes grown in several Sonoma County AVAs, along with fruit from nearby Marin and Mendocino counties and Oregon. The winery also produces highly rated Chardonnays and old-vine Zinfandels. If the weather's good, enjoy a flight on the patio outside the opulent main winery building. At private library tastings, guests sip current and older vintages. All visits are by appointment; call ahead on the same day. ✉ *8075 Martinelli Rd.* ✥ *Off Hwy. 116 or River Rd.* ☎ *707/887–8030* 🌐 *www.hartfordwines.com* 🎫 *Tastings from $25* ⊙ *Closed Tues. and Wed.*

Joseph Jewell Wines

WINERY/DISTILLERY | Pinot Noirs from the Russian River Valley and Humboldt County to the north are the strong suit of this winery sourcing from prestigious vineyards like Bucher and Hallberg Ranch. Owner-winemaker Adrian Manspeaker, a Humboldt native, spearheaded the foray into Pinot Noir grown in the coastal redwood country. His playfully rustic storefront tasting room in downtown Forestville (visits by appointment) provides the opportunity to experience what's unique about the varietal's next Northern California frontier. There are plenty of whites here, too—Sauvignon Blanc, two Chardonnays, Pinot Gris, and Vermentino—plus rosé of Pinot, and Zinfandel from 1970s vines. **■ TIP→ In 2021 the winery expects to begin offering outdoor tastings and vineyard tours at Raymond Burr Vineyards in Healdsburg.** ✉ *6542 Front St.* ✣ *Near 1st St.* ☎ *707/820–1621* 🌐 *www.josephjewell.com* 🎫 *Tastings from $25* ⏲ *Closed Mon.–Wed.*

Backyard

$$$ | **MODERN AMERICAN** | The couple behind this casually rustic modern American restaurant, who met while working at Thomas Keller restaurants in Yountville, regard Sonoma County's farms and gardens as their "backyard." Dinner entrées, which change seasonally, usually include buttermilk fried chicken with buttermilk biscuits, coleslaw, and honey butter. **Known for:** husband-and-wife chef-owners; ingredients from high-quality local purveyors; poplar-shaded outdoor front patio. *Average main: $28* ✉ *6566 Front St./Hwy. 116* ✣ *At 1st St.* ☎ *707/820–8445* 🌐 *backyardforestville.com* ⏲ *Closed Tues.–Thurs.*

★ The Farmhouse Inn

$$$$ | **B&B/INN** | With a farmhouse-meets-modern-loft aesthetic, this low-key but upscale getaway with a pale-yellow exterior contains spacious rooms filled with king-size four-poster beds, whirlpool tubs, and hillside-view terraces. **Pros:** fantastic restaurant; luxury bath products; full-service spa. **Cons:** mild road noise audible in rooms closest to the street; two-night minimum on weekends; pricey, especially during high season. *Rooms from: $518* ✉ *7871 River Rd.* ☎ *707/887–3300, 800/464–6642* 🌐 *www.farmhouseinn.com* *25 rooms* *Free breakfast.*

Burke's Canoe Trips

CANOEING/ROWING/SKULLING | You'll get a real feel for the Russian River's flora and fauna on a leisurely 10-mile paddle downstream from Burke's to Guerneville. A shuttle bus returns you to your car at the end of the journey, which is best taken from late May through mid-October and, in summer, on a weekday—summer weekends can be crowded and raucous. ✉ *8600 River Rd.* ✣ *At Mirabel Rd.* ☎ *707/887–1222* 🌐 *www.burkescanoetrips.com* 🎫 *$75 per canoe.*

Guerneville

7 miles northwest of Forestville, 15 miles southwest of Healdsburg.

Guerneville's tourist demographic has evolved over the years—Bay Area families in the 1950s, lesbians and gays starting in the 1970s, and these days a mix of both groups, plus techies and outdoorsy types—with coast redwoods and the Russian River always central to the town's appeal. The area's most famous winery is Korbel Champagne Cellars, established nearly a century and a half ago. Even older are the stands of trees that except on the coldest winter days make Armstrong Redwoods State Natural Reserve such a perfect respite from wine tasting.

GETTING HERE AND AROUND

To get to Guerneville from Healdsburg, follow Westside Road south to River Road and turn west. From Forestville, head west on Highway 116; alternatively, you can head north on Mirabel Road to River Road and then head west. Sonoma County Transit buses serve Guerneville.

Sights

★ Armstrong Redwoods State Natural Reserve

NATIONAL/STATE PARK | FAMILY | Here's your best opportunity in the western Wine Country to wander amid *Sequoia sempervirens,* also known as coast redwood trees. The oldest example in this 805-acre state park, the Colonel Armstrong Tree, is thought to be more than 1,400 years old. A half mile from the parking lot, the tree is easily accessible, and you can hike a long way into the forest before things get too hilly. **■ TIP→ During hot summer days, Armstrong Redwoods's tall trees help the park keep its cool.** ✉ *17000 Armstrong Woods Rd.* ✣ *Off River Rd.* ☎ *707/869–2958 for visitor center, 707/869–2015 for park headquarters* 🌐 *www.parks.ca.gov* 🎫 *$8 per vehicle, free to pedestrians and bicyclists.*

Restaurants

★ boon eat+drink

$$ | MODERN AMERICAN | A casual storefront restaurant on Guerneville's main drag, boon eat+drink has a menu built around salads, smallish shareable plates, and entrées that might include a vegan bowl, chili-braised pork shoulder, and local cod with beluga lentils. Like many of chef-owner Crista Luedtke's dishes, the signature polenta lasagna—creamy ricotta salata cheese and polenta served on greens sautéed in garlic, all of it floating upon a spicy marinara sauce—deviates significantly from the lasagna norm but succeeds on its own merits. **Known for:** adventurous culinary sensibility; Sonoma County wine selection; local organic ingredients. 💲 *Average main: $23* ✉ *16248 Main St.* ✣ *At Church St.* ☎ *707/869–0780* 🌐 *eatatboon.com* ⏲ *Closed Mon. and Tues.*

Hotels

boon hotel+spa

$$ | HOTEL | Redwoods, Douglas firs, and palms supply shade and seclusion at this lushly landscaped resort ¾ mile north of downtown Guerneville. **Pros:** filling breakfasts; pool area and on-site spa; complimentary bikes. **Cons:** lacks amenities of larger properties; pool rooms too close to the action for some guests; can be pricey in high season. 💲 *Rooms from: $213* ✉ *14711 Armstrong Woods Rd.* ☎ *707/869–2721* 🌐 *boonhotels.com* 🛏 *15 rooms* 🍽 *Free breakfast.*

Sebastopol

14 miles southeast of Guerneville.

A stroll through downtown in Sebastopol—formerly known more for Gravenstein apples than for grapes but these days a burgeoning wine hub—reveals glimpses of the past and, perhaps, the future, too. Many hippies settled here in the '60s and '70s and, as the old Crosby, Stills, Nash & Young song goes, they taught their children well: the town remains steadfastly countercultural.

GETTING HERE AND AROUND

From Guerneville, take Highway 116 south. From Santa Rosa, head west on Highway 12. Sonoma County Transit buses serve Sebastopol.

Sights

The Barlow

MARKET | A multibuilding complex on a former apple-cannery site, The Barlow celebrates Sonoma County's "maker" culture with tenants who produce or sell wine, beer, spirits, crafts, clothing, art, and artisanal food and herbs. The anchor wine tenant, Kosta Browne, receives only club members and allocation-list guests, but other tasting rooms are open to the public, and Region wine bar promotes small Sonoma County producers. Crooked Goat Brewing makes and sells ales, Golden State Cider pours apple-driven beverages, and you can have a nip of vodka, gin, sloe gin, or wheat and rye whiskey at Spirit Works Distillery. Over at Fern Bar, the zero-proof (as in nonalcoholic) cocktails entice as much as the traditional ones. The bar serves food, as do Sushi Koshō, Blue Ridge Kitchen (Southern-influenced comfort fare), and a few other spots. ✉ *6770 McKinley St.* ✣ *At Morris St., off Hwy. 12* ☎ *707/824–5600* 🌐 *www.thebarlow.net* 🎫 *Complex free; fees for tasting.*

★ **Dutton-Goldfield Winery**

WINERY/DISTILLERY | An avid cyclist whose previous credits include developing the wine-making program at Hartford Court, Dan Goldfield teamed up with fifth-generation farmer Steve Dutton to establish this small operation devoted to cool-climate wines. Goldfield modestly strives to take Dutton's meticulously farmed fruit and "make the winemaker unnoticeable," but what impresses the most about these wines, which include Chardonnay, Gewürztraminer, Riesling, Pinot Noir, and Zinfandel, is their sheer artistry. Among the ones to seek out are the Angel Camp Pinot Noir, from Anderson Valley (Mendocino County) grapes, and the Morelli Lane Zinfandel, from fruit grown on the remaining 1.8 acres of an 1880s vineyard Goldfield helped revive. One tasting focuses on current releases, another on single-vineyard Pinot Noirs. ✉ *3100 Gravenstein Hwy. N/Hwy. 116* ✣ *At Graton Rd.* ☎ *707/827–3600* 🌐 *www.duttongoldfield.com* 🎫 *Tastings from $30.*

★ **Iron Horse Vineyards**

WINERY/DISTILLERY | A meandering one-lane road leads to this winery known for its sparkling wines and estate Chardonnays and Pinot Noirs. The sparklers have made history: Ronald Reagan served them at his summit meetings with Mikhail Gorbachev; George H. W. Bush took some along to Moscow for treaty talks; and Barack Obama included them at official state dinners. Despite Iron Horse's brushes with fame, a casual rusticity prevails at its outdoor tasting area (large heaters keep things comfortable on chilly days), which gazes out on acres of rolling, vine-covered hills. Tastings are by appointment only. ✉ *9786 Ross Station Rd.* ✣ *Off Hwy. 116* ☎ *707/887–1507* 🌐 *www.ironhorsevineyards.com* 🎫 *Tasting $30.*

Restaurants

★ **Handline Coastal California**

$ | **MODERN AMERICAN** | **FAMILY** | Sebastopol's former Foster's Freeze location, now a 21st-century fast-food palace, won design awards for its rusted-steel frame and translucent panel-like windows. The menu, a paean to coastal California cuisine, includes oysters raw and grilled, fish tacos, ceviche, tostadas, three burgers (beef, vegetarian, and fish), and, honoring the location's previous incarnation, chocolate and vanilla soft-serve ice cream. **Known for:** upscale comfort food; outdoor patio; sustainable seafood and other ingredients. 💲 *Average main: $14* ✉ *935 Gravenstein Hwy. S* ✣ *Near Hutchins Ave.* ☎ *707/827–3744* 🌐 *www.handline.com.*

Ramen Gaijin

$$ | **JAPANESE** | Inside a tall-ceilinged, brick-walled, vaguely industrial-looking space with reclaimed wood from a coastal building backing the bar, the chefs at Ramen Gaijin turn out richly flavored ramen bowls brimming with crispy pork belly, woodear mushrooms, seaweed, and other well-proportioned ingredients. *Izakaya* (Japanese pub grub) dishes like *donburi* (meat and vegetables over rice) are another specialty, like the ramen made from mostly local proteins and produce. **Known for:** artisanal cocktails, beer, wine, and cider; gluten-free, vegetarian dishes; karage (fried chicken) and other small plates. 💲 *Average main: $18* ✉ *6948 Sebastopol Ave.* ✣ *Near Main St.*

☎ *707/827–3609* 🌐 *www.ramengaijin.com* ⊙ *Closed Sun. and Mon. No lunch.*

Santa Rosa

6 miles east of Sebastopol, 55 miles north of San Francisco.

Urban Santa Rosa isn't as popular with tourists as many Wine Country destinations—not surprising, as there are more office parks than wineries within its limits. Still, this hardworking town has a couple of interesting cultural offerings and a few noteworthy restaurants and vineyards. The city's chain motels and hotels can be handy if everything else is booked, especially since Santa Rosa is roughly equidistant from Sonoma, Healdsburg, and the western Russian River Valley, three of Sonoma County's most popular wine-tasting destinations.

GETTING HERE AND AROUND

From Sebastopol, drive east on Highway 12. From San Francisco, cross the Golden Gate Bridge and continue north on U.S. 101. Santa Rosa's hotels, restaurants, and wineries are spread over a wide area; factor in extra time when driving around the city, especially during rush hours. From San Francisco or Marin County, take Golden Gate Transit Bus 101. Sonoma County Transit buses serve Santa Rosa and the surrounding area.

Sights

Balletto Vineyards

WINERY/DISTILLERY | A few decades ago Balletto was known more for quality produce than grapes, but the new millennium saw vineyards emerge as the core business. About 90% of the fruit from the family's 650-plus acres goes to other wineries, with the remainder destined for Balletto's estate wines. The house style is light on the oak, high in acidity, and low in alcohol content, a combination that yields exceptionally food-friendly wines. Sipping a Pinot Gris, rosé of Pinot Noir, or brut rosé sparkler on the outdoor patio can feel transcendent on a warm day, though the Chardonnays and Pinot Noirs, starting with the very reasonably priced Teresa's Unoaked Chard and flagship Estate Pinot, steal the show. ✉ *5700 Occidental Rd.* ✣ *2½ miles west of Hwy. 12* ☎ *707/568–2455* 🌐 *www.ballettovineyards.com* 🎫 *Tastings from $15.*

★ Belden Barns

WINERY/DISTILLERY | Experiencing the enthusiasm this winery's owners radiate supplies half the pleasure of a visit to Lauren and Nate Belden's Sonoma Mountain vineyard, where at elevation 1,000 feet they grow fruit for their all-estate lineup. Grüner Veltliner, a European white grape, isn't widely planted in California, but the crisp yet softly rounded wine they produce from it makes a case for an increase. Critics also hail the Grenache, Pinot Noir, Syrah, and a nectarlike late-harvest Viognier, but you're apt to like anything poured. Tastings take place in a high-ceilinged former milking barn whose broad doorway frames a view of grapevines undulating toward a hilltop. The Beldens tailor visits to guests' interests but will nearly always whisk you into the vineyard, past a 2-acre organic garden, and over to a wishing tree whose results Lauren swears by. **■ TIP→ The tasting fee here is a two-bottle purchase per adult.** ✉ *5561 Sonoma Mountain Rd.* ✣ *10 miles south of downtown off Bennett Valley Rd.; 5½ miles west of Glen Ellen off Warm Springs Rd.* ☎ *415/577–8552* 🌐 *www.beldenbarns.com* 🎫 *Tastings from $50 (for two bottles).*

★ Martinelli Winery

WINERY/DISTILLERY | In a century-old hop barn with the telltale triple towers, Martinelli has the feel of a traditional country store, but sophisticated wines are made here. The winery's reputation rests on its complex Pinot Noirs, Syrahs, and Zinfandels, including the Jackass Hill Vineyard Zin, made with grapes from vines planted mostly in the 1880s. Noted winemaker Helen Turley set the Martinelli style—fruit-forward, easy on the oak, reined-in tannins—in the 1990s, and the current team continues this approach. Tastings held (weather permitting) on a vineyard's-edge terrace survey the current releases. All visits are by appointment, best made online. **TIP→ Call the winery directly about library or collector flights.** *3360 River Rd., Windsor ⊕ East of Olivet Rd. 707/525–0570, 800/346–1627 www.martinelliwinery.com Tastings from $25 Closed days may vary; check with winery.*

Safari West

NATURE PRESERVE | FAMILY | An unexpected bit of wilderness in the Wine Country, this preserve with African wildlife covers 400 acres. Begin your visit with a stroll around enclosures housing lemurs, cheetahs, giraffes, and rare birds like the brightly colored scarlet ibis. Next, climb with your guide onto open-air vehicles that spend about two hours combing the expansive property, where more than 80 species—including gazelles, cape buffalo, antelope, wildebeests, and zebras—inhabit the hillsides. **TIP→ If you'd like to extend your stay, lodging in swank Botswana-made tent cabins is available.** *3115 Porter Creek Rd. ⊕ Off Mark West Springs Rd. 707/579–2551, 800/616–2695 www.safariwest.com From $93 Sept.–May, from $108 June–Aug.*

Restaurants

Grossman's Noshery and Bar

$$ | DELI | The menu at this homage to Jewish delicatessens plays the greatest hits—blintzes, latkes, lox, chopped liver, and knishes, plus pastrami, corned beef, and Reuben sandwiches—but mashes things up with chicken shawarma kebabs, fish-and-chips, and other atypical deli dishes. It's all executed with panache, and the retro-eclectic decor (black-and-white ceramic tile floors, colorful tropical-bird-print wallpaper, chunky stone fireplace) feels nostalgic yet of the moment. **Known for:** baked goods; happy-hour (daily 3–5) frozen vodka shots; picnic-table seating beside the building. *$ Average main: $18 Hotel La Rose, 308½ Wilson St. ⊕ Near 4th St. 707/595–7707 grossmanssr.com.*

★ Walter Hansel Wine & Bistro

$$$ | FRENCH | Tabletop linens and lights softly twinkling from this ruby-red roadhouse restaurant's low wooden ceiling raise expectations the Parisian-style bistro cuisine consistently exceeds. A starter of cheeses or lobster bisque in a puff pastry awakens the palate for entrées like chicken cordon bleu, steak au poivre, or what this place does best: seafood dishes that might include scallops in white-truffle cream sauce or subtly sauced wild Alaskan halibut. **Known for:** romantic setting for classic cuisine; prix-fixe option; vegan and vegetarian dishes. *$ Average main: $35 3535 Guerneville Rd. ⊕ At Willowside Rd., 6 miles northwest of downtown 707/546–6462 walterhanselbistro.com Closed Mon. and Tues. No lunch.*

Hotels

★ Vintners Resort

$$$$ | HOTEL | With a countryside location, a reserved sense of style, and spacious rooms with comfortable beds, the Vintners Resort further seduces with a slew of amenities and a scenic vineyard landscape. **Pros:** John Ash & Co. restaurant; vineyard jogging path; personalized service. **Cons:** occasional noise from adjacent events center; trips to downtown Santa Rosa or Healdsburg require a car; pricey on summer and fall weekends. *$ Rooms from: $415 4350 Barnes Rd. 707/575–7350, 800/421–2584 www.vintnersresort.com 78 rooms No meals.*

Chapter 21

THE NORTH COAST

FROM SONOMA TO THE REDWOODS

Updated by
Daniel Mangin

Sights	Restaurants	Hotels	Shopping	Nightlife
★★★★★	★★★★☆	★★★★★	★☆☆☆☆	★☆☆☆☆

WELCOME TO THE NORTH COAST

TOP REASONS TO GO

★ **Scenic coastal drives:** There's hardly a road here that *isn't* scenic.

★ **Wild beaches:** This stretch of California is one of nature's masterpieces. Revel in the unbridled, rugged coastline, without a building in sight.

★ **Dinnertime:** When you're done hiking the beach, refuel with delectable food; you'll find everything from fresh-off-the-boat seafood to haute French-inspired cuisine.

★ **Fine wine:** Sip wines at family-owned tasting rooms—cool-climate Pinot Noirs and Chardonnays in the Anderson Valley, then wines from Zinfandel and other heat-loving varietals as you move inland.

★ **Wildlife:** Watch for migrating whales, sunbathing sea lions, and huge Roosevelt elk with majestic antlers.

It's all but impossible to explore the Northern California coast without a car. Indeed, you wouldn't want to—driving here is half the fun. The main road is Highway 1, two lanes that twist and turn (sometimes 180 degrees) up cliffs and down through valleys in Sonoma and Mendocino counties, with U.S. 101 proceeding parallel inland until the two roads join northward in the Redwood Country of Humboldt County.

1 **Bodega Bay.** Harbor seals bask on Bodega Bay's windswept beaches.

2 **Jenner.** Cliffs here overlook the estuary where the Russian River empties into the Pacific.

3 **Elk.** Perched high above the ocean, Elk entices with a downscale roadhouse café and an ultraluxurious resort.

4 **Little River.** Bask in breathtaking ocean views at inns and restaurants in Little River and nearby Albion.

5 **Mendocino.** Artsy Mendocino is all about aesthetics, from sweeping coastal vistas to stylishly plated cuisine

6 **Ft. Bragg.** Travelers love this down-to-earth town for its botanical garden, working harbor, and water's-edge trail.

7 **Philo.** Chardonnay and Pinot Noir star in scenic Philo.

8 **Boonville.** Sip beer at a famous brewery or drop by family-owned wineries at this town with a certified language all its own.

9 **Hopland.** This wisp of a town has acquired a hip cachet for its tasting rooms, restaurants, and lodgings.

10 **Ukiah.** Wine making in and around Mendocinio County's largest city dates back a century-plus.

11 **Avenue of the Giants.** This glorious stretch of redwoods passes through tiny Weott.

12 **Eureka.** Ornate Victorians line downtown blocks of this gateway to national and state parks.

13 **Trinidad.** A former trading post, Trinidad trades these days on its beauty and proximity to ocean and redwoods.

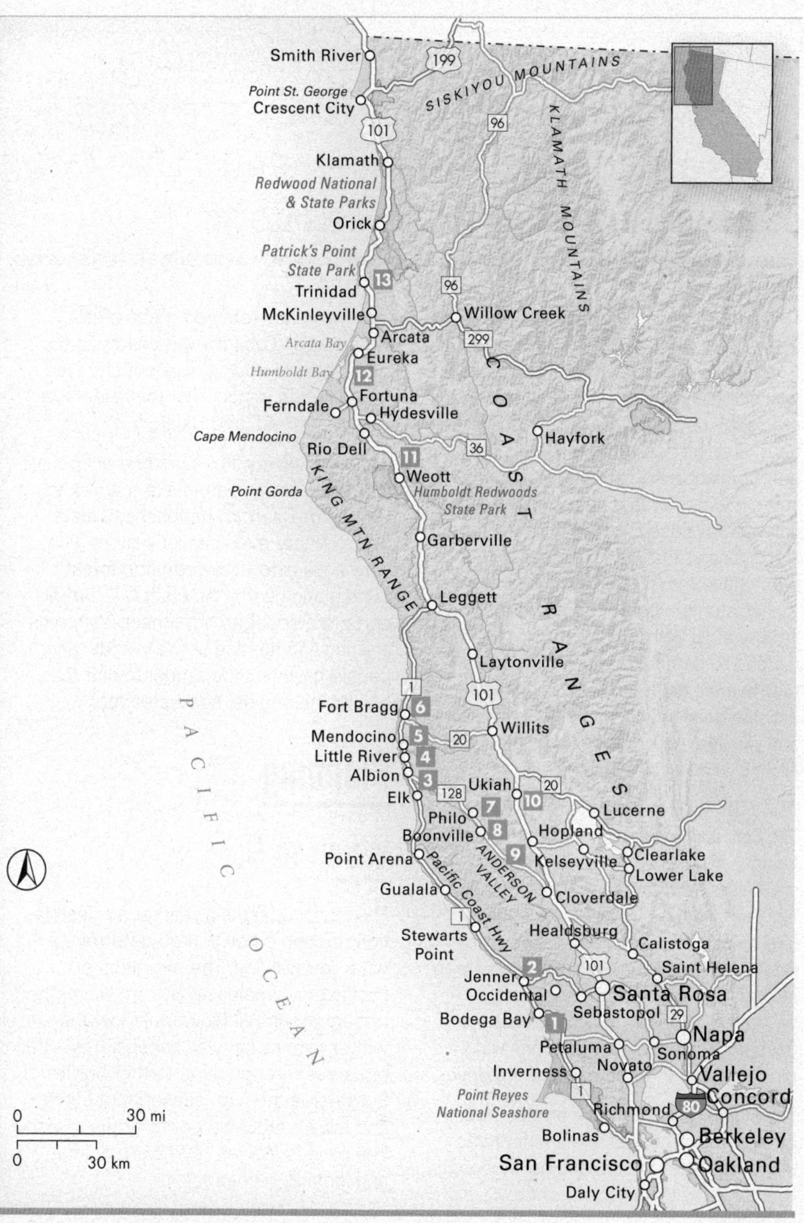
Smith River
Point St. George
Crescent City
Klamath
Redwood National & State Parks
Orick
Patrick's Point State Park
Trinidad
McKinleyville
Arcata
Arcata Bay
Eureka
Humboldt Bay
Fortuna
Ferndale
Hydesville
Cape Mendocino
Rio Dell
Weott
Point Gorda
Humboldt Redwoods State Park
KING MTN RANGE
Garberville
Leggett
Laytonville
Fort Bragg
Mendocino
Little River
Albion
Elk
Ukiah
Philo
Boonville
Point Arena
ANDERSON VALLEY
Pacific Coast Hwy
Gualala
Stewarts Point
Jenner
Occidental
Bodega Bay
Willits
Lucerne
Hopland
Kelseyville
Clearlake
Lower Lake
Cloverdale
Healdsburg
Calistoga
Saint Helena
Santa Rosa
Sebastopol
Napa
Petaluma
Sonoma
Novato
Inverness
Vallejo
Concord
Point Reyes National Seashore
Richmond
Bolinas
Berkeley
San Francisco
Oakland
Daly City
Willow Creek
Hayfork
SISKIYOU MOUNTAINS
KLAMATH MOUNTAINS
COAST RANGES
PACIFIC OCEAN
0 30 mi
0 30 km

The spectacular coastline of Sonoma, Mendocino, and Humboldt counties defies expectations. The Pacific Ocean defines the landscape, but instead of boardwalks and bikinis there are ragged cliffs and pounding waves—and the sunbathers are mostly sea lions.

Two-lane Highway 1 follows the fickle shoreline. Although coastal towns vary from deluxe spa retreat to hippie hideaway, all are reliably sleepy—and that's precisely why many Californians escape here to enjoy nature unspoiled. On a detour inland, you can explore redwoods and sip wines at tasting rooms rarely too crowded or pricey. When you travel the North Coast, turn off your phone; you won't have much of a signal anyway, and this stretch of Highway 1 has numerous little worlds, each different from the last, waiting to be discovered. ■ **TIP→ Don't plan to drive too far in one day. Some drivers stop frequently to appreciate the views, and you can't safely drive faster than 30 or 40 mph on many stretches.**

MAJOR REGIONS

The Sonoma Coast. As you enter Sonoma County from the south on Highway 1, you pass through rolling pastureland. North of Bodega Bay dramatic shoreline takes over. The road snakes up, down, and around sheer cliffs and steep inclines—some without guardrails—where cows seem to cling precariously. Stunning vistas (or cottony fog) and hairpin turns make for an exhilarating drive.

The Mendocino Coast. The timber industry gave birth to most of the small towns along this stretch of coastline. Although tourism now drives the economy, the region has retained much of its old-fashioned charm. The beauty of the landscape, of course, has not changed. Inland lie the wineries of the Anderson Valley, Hopland, and Ukiah.

Redwood Country. For a pristine encounter with giant redwoods, make the trek to Humboldt County's national and state parks, where even casual visitors have easy access to thick redwood forests. Eureka and nearby Arcata, both former ports, are sizeable, but otherwise towns are tiny and nestled in the woods, and people have an independent spirit that recalls the original homesteaders.

Planning

When to Go

The North Coast is a year-round destination, though when you go determines what you will see. The migration of Pacific gray whales lasts from November through April. Wildflowers follow the winter rain, as early as January in southern areas through June farther north. Summer is the high season, but spring and fall are arguably better times to visit. The pace is slower, towns are quieter, and lodging is cheaper.

The coastal climate is similar to San Francisco's, although winter nights are colder than in the city. In July and August, thick fog can drop temperatures to the high 50s, but fear not: you need only drive inland a few miles to find temperatures that are often 20 degrees higher.

Getting Here and Around

AIR

Arcata/Eureka Airport (ACV), 14 miles north of Eureka in McKinleyville, is served by United Express and a few other small carriers. Most visitors rent a car, with ride-sharing (starting at $25 or so to Eureka) the next best option.

AIRPORT CONTACTS Arcata/Eureka Airport. ✉ *3561 Boeing Ave., McKinleyville* ☎ *707/445–9651* 🌐 *flyhumboldt.org.*

GROUND TRANSPORTATION CONTACTS City Cab. ☎ *707/442–4551* 🌐 *citycab-humboldt.com.* **Door-to-Door Airporter.** ☎ *707/839–4186* 🌐 *www.doortodoorairporter.com.*

BUS

Greyhound buses serve Eureka. Mendocino Transit Authority serves its county plus a few Sonoma County towns. Humboldt Transit Authority connects Eureka and Trinidad.

BUS CONTACTS Humboldt Transit Authority. ☎ *707/443–0826* 🌐 *www.hta.org.* **Mendocino Transit Authority.** ☎ *707/462–1422* 🌐 *mendocinotransit.org.*

CAR

U.S. 101 has excellent services, but long stretches separate towns along Highway 1. ■ **TIP→ If you're running low on fuel and see a gas station, stop for a refill.** Twisting Highway 1 is the scenic route to Mendocino from San Francisco, but the fastest one is U.S. 101 north to Highway 128 west (from Cloverdale) to Highway 1 north. The quickest route to the far North Coast is straight up U.S. 101 past Cloverdale to Hopland and Ukiah and on into Humboldt County.

Restaurants

Restaurants here entice diners with dishes fashioned from fresh seafood and locally grown vegetables and herbs. Attire is usually informal, though at pricier places dressy casual is the norm. Most kitchens close at 8 or 8:30 pm, and few places serve past 9:30 pm.

Hotels

Restored Victorians, rustic lodges, country inns, and vintage motels are among the accommodations available here. Few have air-conditioning (the ocean breezes make it unnecessary), and many lack in-room phones or TVs. Except in Fort Bragg and a few other towns, budget accommodations are rare, but in winter you're likely to find reduced rates. In summer and on weekends, make reservations at small inns as far ahead as possible—rooms at the best ones often sell out months in advance.

Restaurant and hotel reviews have been shortened. For full information, visit Fodors.com. Restaurant prices are the average cost of a main course at dinner, or if dinner is not served, at lunch. Hotel prices are the lowest cost of a standard double room in high season.

What It Costs

$	$$	$$$	$$$$
RESTAURANTS			
under $17	$17–$26	$27–$36	over $36
HOTELS			
under $150	$150–$250	$251–$350	over $350

Visitor Information

CONTACTS Humboldt County Visitors Bureau. ☎ *707/443–5097, 800/346–3482* 🌐 *www.visitredwoods.com.* **Sonoma County Tourism.** ☎ *707/522–5800, 800/576–6662* 🌐 *www.sonomacounty.com.* **Visit Mendocino County.** ☎ *707/964–9010, 866/466–3636* 🌐 *www.visitmendocino.com.*

Bodega Bay

23 miles west of Santa Rosa.

Pockets of modernity notwithstanding, this commercial fishing town retains the workaday vibe of its cinematic turn in Alfred Hitchcock's *The Birds* (1963). Little from the film's era remains save the windswept bay and ocean views. (For the ocean ones, drive west from Highway 1, Eastshore to Bay Flat to Westshore.) To the east in the town of Bodega, the film's schoolhouse still stands, at Bodega Lane off Bodega Highway.

GETTING HERE AND AROUND

To reach Bodega Bay, exit U.S. 101 at Santa Rosa and take Highway 12 west (called Bodega Highway west of Sebastopol) 23 miles to the coast. A scenic alternative is to take U.S. 101's East Washington Street/Central Petaluma exit and follow signs west to Bodega Bay; just after you merge onto Highway 1, you'll pass through down-home Valley Ford. Mendocino Transit Authority buses serve Bodega Bay.

Sights

Sonoma Coast Vineyards

WINERY/DISTILLERY | This winery with an ocean-view tasting room makes small-lot wines from grapes grown close to the Pacific. The Petersen Vineyard Chardonnay and Antonio Mountain Pinot Noir stand out among cool-climate bottlings that also include Sauvignon Blanc, rosé of Pinot Noir, and a Blanc de Noirs sparkler. ✉ *555 Hwy. 1* ☎ *707/921–2860* 🌐 *www.sonomacoastvineyards.com* 🎟 *Tastings from $10 glass.*

Beaches

★ Sonoma Coast State Park

BEACH—SIGHT | The park's gorgeous sandy coves stretch for 17 miles from Bodega Head to 4 miles north of Jenner. **Bodega Head** is a popular whale-watching perch in winter and spring, and **Rock Point, Duncan's Landing,** and **Wright's Beach,** at about the halfway mark, have good picnic areas. Rogue waves have swept people off the rocks at Duncan's Landing Overlook, so don't stray past signs warning you away. Calmer **Shell Beach,** about 2 miles north, is known for beachcombing, tidepooling, and fishing. Walk part of the bluff-top **Kortum Trail** or drive about 2½ miles north of Shell Beach to **Blind Beach.** Near the mouth of the Russian River just north of here at **Goat Rock Beach,** you'll find harbor seals; pupping season is from March through August. Bring binoculars and walk north from the parking lot to view the seals. During summer, lifeguards are on duty at some beaches, but strong rip currents and heavy surf keep most visitors onshore. **Amenities:** parking (fee); toilets. **Best for:** solitude; sunset; walking. ✉ *Park Headquarters/Salmon Creek Ranger Station, 3095 Hwy. 1* ✣ *2 miles north of Bodega Bay* ☎ *707/875–3483* 🌐 *www.parks.ca.gov* 🎟 *$8 per vehicle.*

Restaurants

Spud Point Crab Company

$ | **SEAFOOD** | Crab sandwiches, New England or Manhattan clam chowder, and homemade crab cakes with roasted red-pepper sauce star on this food stand's brief menu. Place your order and enjoy your meal to go or, when possible, at one of the marina-view picnic tables outside. **Known for:** family operation;

opens at 9 am; seafood cocktails, superb chowder. *Average main: $10* *1910 Westshore Rd.* *West off Hwy. 1, Eastshore Rd. to Bay Flat Rd.* *707/875–9472* *www.spudpointcrabco.com* *No dinner.*

★ Terrapin Creek Cafe & Restaurant
$$$ | MODERN AMERICAN | Intricate but not fussy cuisine based on locally farmed ingredients and *fruits de mer* has made this casual yet sophisticated restaurant with an open kitchen a West County darling. Start with raw oysters, rich potato-leek soup, or (in season) Dungeness crab before moving on to halibut or other fish pan-roasted to perfection. **Known for:** intricate cuisine of chefs Liya and Andrew Truong; Bay Area food-lovers' choice; great starters and salads. *Average main: $34* *1580 Eastshore Rd.* *Off Hwy. 1* *707/875–2700* *www.terrapincreekcafe.com* *Closed Mon.–Wed. No lunch Thurs.*

Hotels

Bodega Bay Lodge
$$$ | HOTEL | Looking out to the ocean across a wetland, the lodge's shingle-and-river-rock buildings contain Bodega Bay's finest accommodations. **Pros:** spacious rooms with ocean views; on-site Drakes Sonoma Coast restaurant for seafood; fireplaces and patios or balconies in most rooms. **Cons:** pricey in-season; parking lot in foreground of some rooms' views; fairly long drive to other fine dining. *Rooms from: $349* *103 Coast Hwy. 1* *707/875–3525* *www.bodegabaylodge.com* *83 rooms* *No meals.*

Jenner

10 miles north of Bodega Bay.

The Russian River empties into the Pacific Ocean at Jenner, a wide spot in the road where houses dot a mountainside high above the sea. Facing south, the village looks across the river's mouth to Sonoma Coast State Park's Goat Rock Beach. North of the village, Fort Ross State Historic Park provides a glimpse into Russia's early-19th-century foray into California. South of the fort a winery named for it grows Chardonnay and Pinot Noir above the coastal fog line. North of the fort lie more beaches and redwoods to hike and explore.

GETTING HERE AND AROUND

Jenner is north of Bodega Bay on Highway 1. From Guerneville head west on Highway 116 (River Road). Mendocino Transit Authority buses serve Jenner.

Sights

Fort Ross State Historic Park
NATIONAL/STATE PARK | FAMILY | With its reconstructed Russian Orthodox chapel, stockade, and officials' quarters, Fort Ross looks much the way it did after the Russians made it their major California coastal outpost in 1812. Russian settlers established the fort on land they leased from the native Kashia people. The Russians hoped to gain a foothold in the Pacific coast's warmer regions and to produce crops and other supplies for their Alaskan fur-trading operations. In 1841, with the local marine mammal population depleted and farming having proven unproductive, the Russians sold their holdings to John Sutter, later of gold-rush fame. The land, privately ranched for decades, became a state park in

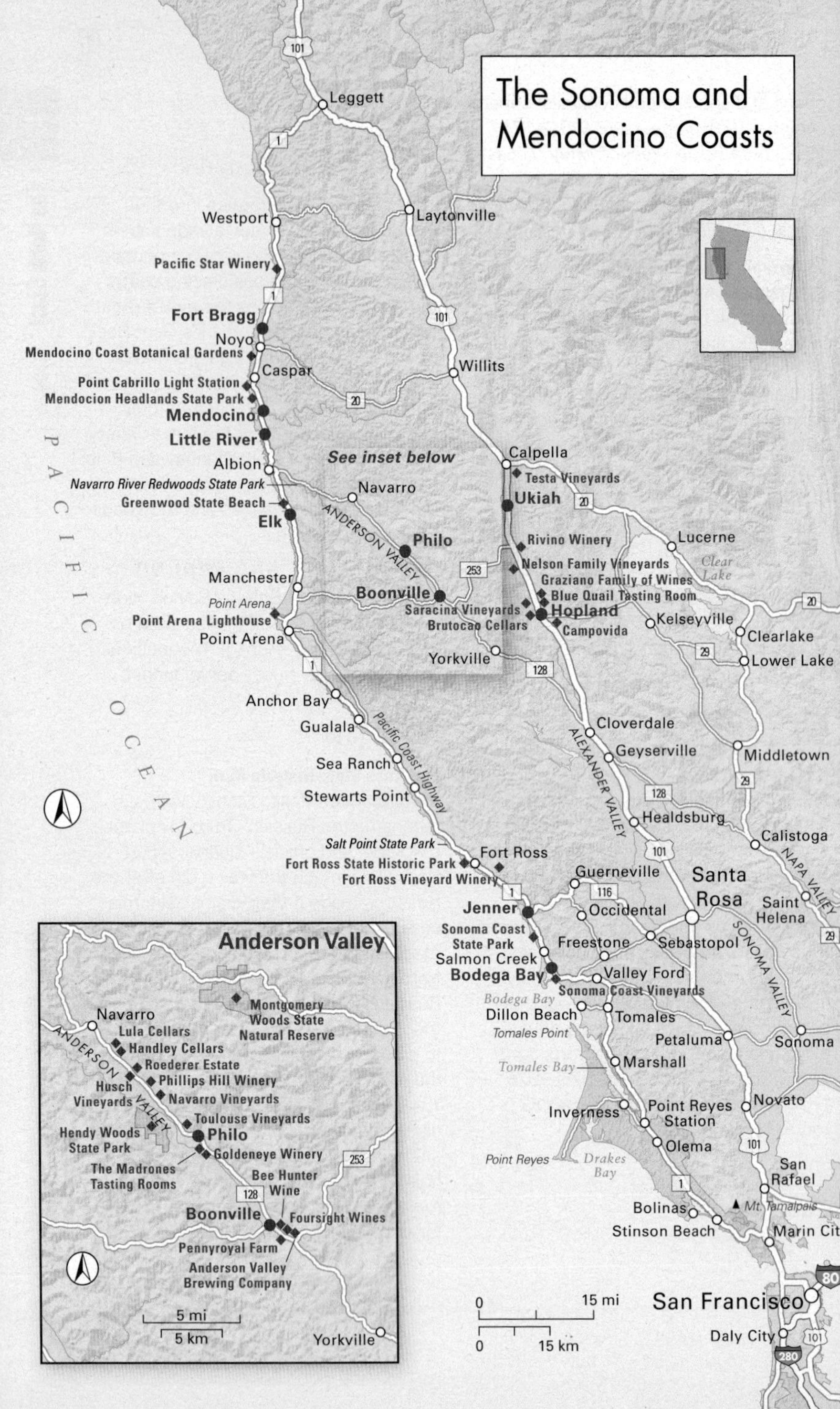

The Sonoma and Mendocino Coasts
Leggett
Westport
Laytonville
Pacific Star Winery
Fort Bragg
Noyo
Mendocino Coast Botanical Gardens
Caspar
Point Cabrillo Light Station
Mendocion Headlands State Park
Mendocino
Little River
Willits
Albion
Navarro River Redwoods State Park
Greenwood State Beach
Elk
See inset below
Navarro
Anderson Valley
Philo
Boonville
Calpella
Testa Vineyards
Ukiah
Rivino Winery
Nelson Family Vineyards
Graziano Family of Wines
Blue Quail Tasting Room
Saracina Vineyards
Hopland
Brutocao Cellars
Campovida
Lucerne
Clear Lake
Kelseyville
Clearlake
Lower Lake
Manchester
Point Arena
Point Arena Lighthouse
Point Arena
Yorkville
Pacific Ocean
Anchor Bay
Gualala
Sea Ranch
Stewarts Point
Pacific Coast Highway
Cloverdale
Geyserville
Alexander Valley
Middletown
Healdsburg
Calistoga
Napa Valley
Salt Point State Park
Fort Ross State Historic Park
Fort Ross
Fort Ross Vineyard Winery
Guerneville
Santa Rosa
Jenner
Occidental
Saint Helena
Sonoma Coast State Park
Freestone
Sebastopol
Salmon Creek
Sonoma Valley
Bodega Bay
Valley Ford
Sonoma Coast Vineyards
Bodega Bay
Dillon Beach
Tomales
Tomales Point
Petaluma
Sonoma
Tomales Bay
Marshall
Inverness
Point Reyes Station
Novato
Olema
Point Reyes
Drakes Bay
San Rafael
Mt. Tamalpais
Bolinas
Stinson Beach
Marin City
San Francisco
Daly City
0
15 mi
0
15 km
Anderson Valley
Navarro
Lula Cellars
Handley Cellars
Roederer Estate
Husch Vineyards
Phillips Hill Winery
Navarro Vineyards
Montgomery Woods State Natural Reserve
Toulouse Vineyards
Hendy Woods State Park
Philo
Goldeneye Winery
The Madrones Tasting Rooms
Bee Hunter Wine
Boonville
Foursight Wines
Pennyroyal Farm
Anderson Valley Brewing Company
5 mi
5 km
Yorkville

1909. One original Russian-era structure remains, as does a cemetery. The rest of the compound has been reconstructed to look much as it did during Russian times. An excellent small museum documents the history of the fort, the Kashia people, and the ranch and state-park eras. No dogs are allowed past the parking lot and picnic area. ✉ *19005 Hwy. 1* ✣ *11 miles north of Jenner village* ☎ *707/847–3437* 🌐 *www.fortross.org* 🎫 *$8 per vehicle.*

Fort Ross Vineyard & Winery

WINERY/DISTILLERY | The Russian River and Highway 116 snake west from Guerneville through redwood groves to the coast, where Highway 1 twists north past rocky cliffs to this windswept ridgetop winery. Until recently many experts deemed the weather this far west too chilly even for cool-climate varietals, but Fort Ross Vineyard and other Fort Ross–Seaview AVA wineries are proving that Chardonnay and Pinot Noir can thrive above the fog line. The sea air and rocky soils here produce wines generally less fruit-forward than their Russian River Valley counterparts but equally sophisticated and no less vibrant. With its rustic-chic, barnlike tasting room and outdoor patio overlooking the Pacific, Fort Ross provides an appealing introduction to its region's wines. Tastings include a cheese and charcuterie plate (vegetarian option possible). Appointments are required; for same-day visits call before 11 am. ✉ *15725 Meyers Grade Rd.* ✣ *Off Hwy. 1, 6 miles north of Jenner* ☎ *707/847–3460* 🌐 *www.fortrossvineyard.com* 🎫 *Tastings from $55* ⏲ *Closed Tues. and Wed.*

Restaurants

River's End

$$$ | **AMERICAN** | The hot tip at this low-slung cliff's-edge restaurant is to come early or reserve a window table, where the Russian River and Pacific Ocean views alone, particularly at sunset, might make your day (even more so if you're a birder). Seafood is the specialty—during the summer the chef showcases local king salmon—but filet mignon, duck, elk, a vegetarian napoleon, and pasta with prawns are often on the dinner menu. **Known for:** majestic setting; international wine list; burgers, fish-and-chips for lunch. $ *Average main: $34* ✉ *11048 Hwy. 1* ✣ *1½ miles north of Hwy. 116* ☎ *707/865–2484* 🌐 *www.ilovesunsets.com.*

Hotels

★ Timber Cove Resort

$$$ | **RESORT** | Restored well beyond its original splendor, this resort anchored to a craggy oceanfront cliff is by far the Sonoma Coast's coolest getaway. **Pros:** dramatic sunsets; grand public spaces; patio dining at Coast Kitchen restaurant. **Cons:** some service lapses; pricey ocean-view rooms; far from nightlife. $ *Rooms from: $340* ✉ *21780 Hwy. 1* ☎ *707/847–3231* 🌐 *www.timbercoveresort.com* *46 rooms* *No meals.*

Elk

70 miles north of Jenner, 17 miles south of Mendocino.

In this quiet town on the cliff above Greenwood Cove, just about every spot has a view of the rocky coastline and stunning Pacific sunsets. There's a museum, and few restaurants and inns do business here, but the main attraction is highly walkable Greenwood State Beach, accessed via a trail that starts across Highway 1 from the town's general store.

GETTING HERE AND AROUND

Elk is along Highway 1, 6 miles south of Highway 128. Mendocino Transit Authority buses serve Elk.

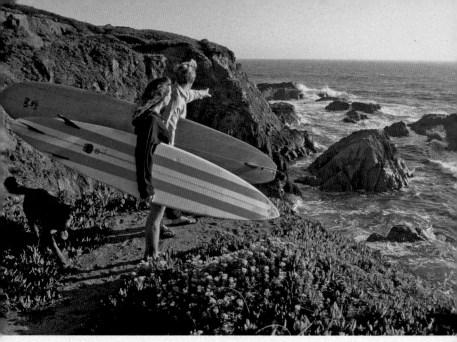

Surfers check out the waves near Bodega Bay on the Sonoma Coast.

Sights

Greenwood State Beach

BEACH—SIGHT | If you're not staying at one of Elk's cliff-top lodgings, the easiest access to the sandy shore below them is at this state beach whose parking lot sits across Highway 1 from the town's general store. A trail leads from the lot down to the beach, where the waves crashing against the huge offshore rocks are the perfect backdrop. **Amenities:** parking (free). **Good for:** sunset; walking. ✉ *6150 Hwy. 1* ☎ *707/937–5804* 🌐 *www.parks.ca.gov* 🎫 *Free.*

★ Point Arena Lighthouse

LIGHTHOUSE | For an outstanding view of the ocean and, in winter, migrating whales, take the marked road off Highway 1 to this 115-foot lighthouse, completed in 1908. If the structure is open, climb the 145 steps, and a 360-degree panorama unfolds. The ground-level museum displays the original Fresnel lens and other maritime artifacts. Six cottages with full kitchens can be booked for overnight stays. ✉ *45500 Lighthouse Rd., Point Arena* ✥ *Off Hwy. 1, 19 miles south of Elk* ☎ *707/882–2809, 877/725–4448* 🌐 *www.pointarenalighthouse.com* 🎫 *Tour $8 ($5 if no tour).*

Restaurants

★ Harbor House Inn Restaurant

$$$$ | **MODERN AMERICAN** | The chef at this ocean-bluff inn's redwood-paneled dining room describes the Mendocino Coast's most intricate meal—an 8- to 12-course, prix-fixe extravaganza—as "hyperlocal" seasonal cuisine revolving around seafood and vegetables (many of the latter grown on-site). The artistry displayed in every dish lives up to the raves the restaurant has received from local and national food writers. **Known for:** breathtaking views; swoonworthy cuisine; astute wine pairings. 💲 *Average main: $220* ✉ *5600 S. Hwy. 1* ☎ *707/877–3203* 🌐 *theharborhouseinn.com/dine* ⏲ *Closed Tues. and Wed.* ☞ *Reservations essential.*

Queenie's Roadhouse Cafe
$ | **AMERICAN** | If the day's sunny, grab one of the picnic tables in front of this beloved hangout for big breakfasts (served until closing, at 3) and lunches that include blue-cheese burgers topped with onions browned in bourbon and butter. The café's deck and wide windows provide Pacific views to enjoy with your meal. **Known for:** omelets, huevos rancheros, waffles, and pancakes; burgers, salads, and sandwiches; local wines and microbrews. *Average main: $15* *6061 S. Hwy. 1* *707/877–3285* *www.queeniesroadhousecafe.com* *Closed Tues. and Wed. and late Dec.–mid-Feb. No dinner.*

Hotels

Elk Cove Inn & Spa
$$ | **B&B/INN** | Perched on a bluff above pounding surf and a driftwood-strewn beach, this property has stunning views from most of its accommodations, which include seven rooms, five suites, and four cottages. **Pros:** gorgeous views; filling breakfast; steps to the beach. **Cons:** rooms in main house are smallish; not suitable for young children; spa's massage calendar often full. *Rooms from: $199* *6300 S. Hwy. 1* *707/877–3321, 800/275–2967* *www.elkcoveinn.com* *16 units* *Free breakfast.*

★ **Harbor House Inn**
$$$$ | **B&B/INN** | Prepare to be bowled over by every aspect of this showcase property with a rugged Pacific-cliff setting, destination restaurant, sterling hospitality, and luxurious accommodations in a 1916 redwood Craftsman-style house and a few newer cottages. **Pros:** romantic, ocean-view setting; luxurious base for wine tasting and outdoor activities; destination restaurant. **Cons:** not ideal for kids; 16 miles from Mendocino; best accommodations expensive for the area. *Rooms from: $399* *5600 S. Hwy. 1* *707/877–3203, 800/720–7474* *www.theharborhouseinn.com* *11 rooms* *Free breakfast.*

Little River

13½ miles north of Elk.

The town of Little River is not much more than a post office and a convenience store; Albion, its neighbor to the south, is even smaller. Along this winding portion of Highway 1 you'll find numerous inns and restaurants, all situated to take advantage of the breathtaking ocean views.

GETTING HERE AND AROUND

Little River is along Highway 1, 7 miles north of Highway 128. Mendocino Transit Authority buses serve the area.

Sights

Van Damme State Park
NATIONAL/STATE PARK | Best known for its quiet beach, a prime diving spot, this park is also popular with day hikers. A ¼-mile stroll on a boardwalk leads to the bizarre **Pygmy Forest,** where acidic soil and poor drainage have produced mature cypress and pine trees that are no taller than a person. For more of a challenge, hike the moderate 4¼-mile Pygmy Forest and Fern Canyon Loop past the forest and sword ferns that grow as tall as 4 feet. The visitor center has displays on ocean life and the historical significance of the redwood lumber industry along the coast. *Little River Park Rd., off Hwy. 1* *707/937–5804* *www.parks.ca.gov* *$8 per vehicle, walk-ins free (park at beach).*

Restaurants

Ledford House
$$ | **FRENCH** | The only thing separating this bluff-top wood-and-glass restaurant from the Pacific Ocean is a great view. Entrées evoke the flavors of southern France and include hearty bistro dishes—stews, cassoulet, and pastas—and large portions of grilled meats and freshly caught fish (though the restaurant also is vegetarian

friendly). **Known for:** outdoor deck; Mendocino-centric wine list; three-course bistro special. *Average main: $26 3000 N. Hwy. 1, Albion 707/937–0282 www.ledfordhouse.com Closed Mon. and Tues. and late-Feb.–early Mar. and mid-Oct.–early Nov. No lunch.*

Little River Inn

$$$ | **AMERICAN** | Straightforward seafood preparations and seasonal cocktails (best sipped from the ocean-view Whale Watch Bar) rank high among the pleasures of a visit to the Little River Inn resort, opened in 1939 and still run by members of the same family. Start with clam chowder, fried calamari, or Dungeness crab cakes before settling into cioppino, the day's catch, a 12-ounce rib eye, or red-wine-braised short ribs. **Known for:** step-back-in-time feel; alfresco dining in garden courtyard; olallieberry cobbler from founder's wife's recipe. *Average main: $32 7901 N. Hwy. 1 707/937–5942 littleriverinn.com No lunch.*

Albion River Inn

$$ | **B&B/INN** | Contemporary, New England–style cottages at this inn overlook the dramatic bridge and seascape where the Albion River empties into the Pacific. **Pros:** ocean views; great bathtubs; romantic glassed-in restaurant. **Cons:** often foggy in summer; no TV in rooms; 2-night weekend minimum. *Rooms from: $195 3790 N. Hwy. 1, Albion 707/937–1919, 800/479–7944 albionriverinn.com 22 rooms Free breakfast.*

★ **Glendeven Inn & Lodge**

$$$ | **B&B/INN** | If Mendocino is the New England village of the West Coast, then Glendeven—an 1867 farmhouse and several other buildings—is the local country manor, with sea views and 8 acres of gardens, complete with llamas and chickens that provide eggs for three-course breakfasts served in-room. **Pros:** romantic setting with acres of gardens; owners' attention to detail; ocean views. **Cons:** no TVs in two buildings; per website no guests under age 18; weekend minimum-stay requirement. *Rooms from: $255 8205 N. Hwy. 1 707/937–0083, 800/822–4536 glendeven.com 21 rooms Free breakfast.*

Mendocino

3 miles north of Little River.

A flourishing logging town in the late-19th century, Mendocino seduces 21st-century travelers with windswept cliffs, phenomenal Pacific Ocean views, and boomtown-era New England–style architecture. Following the timber industry's mid-20th-century decline, artists and craftspeople began flocking here, and so did Hollywood: Mendocino served as a backdrop for *East of Eden* (1955), starring James Dean, and the town stood in for fictional Cabot Cove, Maine, in the TV series *Murder, She Wrote.* Today, shops, galleries, inns, and cafés predominate in the small downtown area.

GETTING HERE AND AROUND

Main Street is off Highway 1 about 10 miles north of Highway 128. Mendocino Transit Authority buses serve the area.

★ **Mendocino Headlands State Park**

NATIONAL/STATE PARK | A 3-mile easy-to-walk trail leads across the spectacular seaside cliffs bordering Mendocino. The restored Ford House, built in 1854, serves as the visitor center for the park and the town. The house has a scale model of Mendocino as it looked in 1890, when it had 34 water towers and a 12-seat public outhouse. *45035 Main St. 707/937–5397 mendoparks.org/mendocino-headlands Park and visitor center free, museum $2.*

Point Cabrillo Light Station

LIGHTHOUSE | Completed in 1909 and noteworthy for its original, third-order, Fresnel lens that glows like a jewel day or night, the still-active station inhabits a breezy plateau 3 miles north of Mendocino village. Dirt and paved paths lead downhill from the parking lot to the station. **TIP→ The lighthouse museum and other historic buildings are worth a peek if open, but the park merits a visit for its views alone.** *45300 Lighthouse Rd. Point Cabrillo Dr. off Hwy. 1 707/937–6123 pointcabrillo.org Park free, museum $5.*

Restaurants

Cafe Beaujolais

$$$ | **AMERICAN** | A garden of heirloom and exotic plantings surrounds this popular restaurant inside a yellow Victorian cottage. Local ingredients find their way into dishes that might include Oaxacan-style ceviche, smash burgers, pizzas from a wood-fired brick oven, fish and prawn tacos, beef bourguignon, and oven-roasted cauliflower with house-made mole verde. **Known for:** garden dining in fine weather; bowls and other vegan and vegetarian selections; "Waiting Room" for morning pastries and other grab-and-go fare. *Average main: $28 961 Ukiah St. 707/937–5614 www.cafebeaujolais.com Closed Mon. and Tues.*

Fog Eater Cafe

$$ | **VEGETARIAN** | The culinary influences are Deep South and Californian at this vegetarian (mostly vegan) restaurant with salmon-colored walls, teal tables, and white trim. The chefs' flair for the dramatic might exhibit itself in carrot-cake waffles at Sunday brunch; hush-puppies and beet-dyed deviled eggs as happy-hour nibbles; and dinnertime fried-green-tomato biscuit sliders and Mississippi Delta–style hot tamales. **Known for:** all-organic Mendocino and Sonoma produce; outdoor dining; natural wines and local beers. *Average main: $20 45104 Main St. At Albion St. 707/397–1806 fogeatercafe.com Closed Mon. and Tues. No lunch Wed.–Sat. No dinner Sun.*

Trillium Cafe

$$$ | **AMERICAN** | The term "light rustic" applies equally well to this comely café's decor—plank flooring, wood-top tables, gas fireplace with brick hearth—and its cuisine, which emphasizes local produce and seafood. The menu changes seasonally, with the grilled flatbread, albacore appetizer, Point Reyes blue cheese salad, and grilled organic pork chop among the year-round crowd-pleasers. **Known for:** outdoor patio area with garden and ocean views; wine list favoring Northern California wines, particularly Mendocino; organic grass-fed meats. *Average main: $33 10390 Kasten St. 707/937–3200 www.trilliummendocino.com Closed Wed. and Thurs. (but check).*

Hotels

Blue Door Inns

$$ | **B&B/INN** | Each of the three Victorian properties operated by California-based Four Sisters Inns has its appeal—Blue Door for its garden, Packard House for its serene setting, JD House for its ocean views—with all three worth consideration for their proximity to restaurants, shops, and the Mendocino Headlands. **Pros:** historic properties with modern decor; service-oriented staff; range of prices and room types. **Cons:** some rooms are on the small side; lacks personal touch of on-site owner-innkeeper; best rooms are pricey. *Rooms from: $175 10481 Howard St. 707/937–4892, 800/234–1425 www.bluedoorgroup.com 19 rooms Free breakfast.*

★ Brewery Gulch Inn

$$$$ | **B&B/INN** | The feel is modern yet tasteful at this inn with stained-wood and leather furnishings and plush beds; two rooms have whirlpool tubs with views. **Pros:** luxury in tune with nature; peaceful ocean views; complimentary wine hour and light dinner buffet. **Cons:** a mile from Mendocino village; expensive in-season; 2-night minimum on weekends. *$ Rooms from: $425 ✉ 9401 N. Hwy. 1 ☎ 707/937–4752, 800/578–4454 ⊕ www.brewerygulchinn.com ⇆ 11 rooms 🍽 Free breakfast.*

Stanford Inn by the Sea
$$$$ | HOTEL | This woodsy yet luxurious family-run property a few minutes south of town feels like the Northern California version of an old-time summer resort, with an ecologically friendly twist. **Pros:** lovely grounds; on-site bike and kayak rentals; on-site vegetarian restaurant. **Cons:** New Age feel won't appeal to everyone; carnivores may find menus challenging; least expensive rooms lack ocean views. *$ Rooms from: $351 ✉ 44850 Comptche Ukiah Rd. ☎ 707/937–5615, 800/331–8884 ⊕ www.stanfordinn.com ⇆ 41 rooms 🍽 Free breakfast.*

Fort Bragg

10 miles north of Mendocino.

Fort Bragg is a working-class town that many feel is the most authentic place on the coast. The city maintains a local vibe since most people who work at the area hotels and restaurants also live here, as do many artists and commercial anglers. The pleasures of a visit are mainly outdoors, a stroll through the botanical gardens or along the town's coastal trail, touring by train or boat, tidepooling or fishing at the state park, or tasting wine within steps of the ocean.

GETTING HERE AND AROUND

Highway 20 winds west 33 miles from Willits to Highway 1 just south of Fort Bragg. Mendocino Transit Authority buses serve the town.

Sights

Fort Bragg Coastal Trail
TRAIL | A multiuse path, much of it flat and steps from rocky and highly photogenic shoreline, stretches the length of Fort Bragg. A particularly pleasant section, lined with benches created by local artists, follows the coast north about 2 miles between Noyo Headlands Park in southern Fort Bragg and Glass Beach. From the beach you can continue well into MacKerricher State Park. **■ TIP→ There's free parking at both Noyo Headlands Park and Glass Beach.** *✉ Fort Bragg ↔ Noyo Headlands Park, W. Cypress St. off S. Main St. (Hwy. 1); Glass Beach, W. Elm St. off N. Main St.*

★ **Mendocino Coast Botanical Gardens**
GARDEN | Something beautiful is always abloom in these marvelous gardens. Along 4 miles of trails, including pathways with ocean views and observation points for whale-watching, lie a profusion of flowers. The rhododendrons are at their peak from April through June; the dahlias begin their spectacular show in July and last through September. In winter the heather and camellias add more than a splash of color. The main trails are wheelchair accessible. *✉ 18220 N. Hwy. 1, 2 miles south of Fort Bragg ☎ 707/964–4352 ⊕ www.gardenbythesea.org 🎫 $15.*

★ **Noyo Harbor Tours with Captain Dan**
TOUR—SIGHT | The genial Captain Dan has piloted commercial fishing boats on the high seas, but, for his gentle tours of Noyo Harbor from the river up to (but not into) the ocean, he ordered a custom-built, 18-foot, eco-friendly Duffy electric boat. Having been in Fort Bragg for decades he knows everyone and everyone's story, including those of the harbor seals, sea lions, birds, and other wildlife you'll see on his excursion. *✉ 32399 Basin St. ↔ From S. Main St. (Hwy. 1), take Hwy. 20 east ¼ mile, S. Harbor Dr. north ¼ mile, and Basin St. northeast 1*

mile ☎ *707/734–0044* 🌐 *www.noyoharbortours.com* 🎫 *From $35.*

Pacific Star Winery

WINERY/DISTILLERY | When the sun's out and you're sipping wine while viewing whales or other sea creatures swimming offshore, this bluff-top winery's outdoor tasting spaces feel mystical and magical. Equally beguiling on a brooding stormy day, Pacific Star has still more aces up its sleeve: its engaging owner-winemaker, Sally Ottoson, whose cheery staffers pour a lineup of varietals that includes Charbono and Sangiovese. The wines, among them a vibrant blend of Mendocino County Zinfandel, Barbera, Charbono, and Petite Sirah, are good, and they're reasonably priced. ✉ *33000 N. Hwy. 1* ✥ *12 miles north of downtown* ☎ *707/964–1155* 🌐 *www.pacificstarwinery.com* 🎫 *Tasting $10* ⏲ *Closed Dec. and Mon.–Wed.*

Skunk Train and Rail Bikes

TOUR—SIGHT | **FAMILY** | A reproduction train travels a few miles of the route of its 1920s predecessor, a fume-spewing gas-powered motorcar that shuttled passengers along a rail line dating from the 1880s logging days. Nicknamed the Skunk Train, the original traversed redwood forests inaccessible to automobiles. There are also excursions from the town of Willits as well as seasonal and holiday-themed tours. **■TIP→ For a separate fee you can pedal the same rails as the Skunk Train on two-person, side-by-side, reclining bikes outfitted for the track, an experience many patrons find more diverting (albeit pricier) than the train trip.** ✉ *100 W. Laurel St.* ✥ *At Main St.* ☎ *707/964–6371* 🌐 *www.skunktrain.com* 🎫 *Train rides from $42; rail bikes from $195 for 2 people (no single-rider fee)* ⏲ *Days, hrs vary; call or check website.*

Beaches

MacKerricher State Park

NATIONAL/STATE PARK | This park begins at **Glass Beach,** its draw an unfortunately dwindling supply of sea glass (remnants from the city dump once in this area), and stretches north for 9 miles, beginning with rocky headlands that taper into dunes and sandy beaches. The headlands are a good place for whale-watching from November through April. Fishing, canoeing, hiking, tidepooling, jogging, bicycling, beachcombing, camping, and harbor seal watching at Laguna Point are among the popular activities, many accessible to the mobility-impaired. ⚠ **Be vigilant for rogue waves—don't turn your back on the sea.** **Amenities:** parking; toilets. **Best for:** solitude; sunset; walking. ✉ *24100 MacKerricher Park Rd.* ✥ *Off Hwy. 1, 3 miles north of town* ☎ *707/937–5804* 🌐 *www.parks.ca.gov* 🎫 *Free.*

Restaurants

North Coast Brewing

$$ | **AMERICAN** | Clam chowder, pork chili, and nachos are among the beer-friendly starters at the brewing company's expansive restaurant, whose headlining entrées include burgers, pulled-pork sandwiches, shrimp po'boys, and beer-batter fish-and-chips. The beers, award-winners worldwide, run the gamut from pilsners and the flagship Red Seal amber ale to the heavier Russian-style Rasputin stout and Old Stock Ale. **Known for:** seasonal beers; sampler flights; beer-wise staffers. 💲 *Average main: $18* ✉ *444 N. Main St.* ☎ *707/964–3400* 🌐 *northcoastbrewing.com/brewery-taproom* ⏲ *Closed Tues. and Wed. (but check).*

Noyo River Grill

$$ | **SEAFOOD** | The Noyo River Bridge looms high above this family-owned harborside restaurant whose outdoor tables have views of the river emptying (via Noyo Bay) into the Pacific. No surprises with the straightforward, beer-friendly, seafood-oriented cuisine—fried calamari, fish-and-chips, prawns scampi, and the like—but it's executed well, especially the grilled local salmon. **Known for:** harbor-watching from outdoor tables; po'boys and homemade tacos at lunch; shellfish apps at lunch and dinner. *Average main: $24 32150 N. Harbor Dr. Off S. Main St. (Hwy. 1) almost 1 mile 707/962–9050 Closed Thurs.*

★ Princess Seafood Market & Deli

$ | **SEAFOOD** | Captain Heather Sears leads her all-woman crew of "girls gone wild for wild-caught seafood" that heads oceanward on the *Princess* troller, returning with some of the seafood served at this shanty astride the vessel's Noyo Harbor dock. Order chowder (might be clam, crab, or salmon), crab rolls and shrimp po'boys, raw or barbecued oysters, or other sturdy fare at the counter, dining under the all-weather tent kept toasty by heaters and a firepit when the wind's ablowin'. **Known for:** fresh, sustainable seafood; canned wines and beer; crew members who clearly love their jobs. *Average main: $16 32410 N. Harbor Dr. Off S. Main St. (Hwy. 1) about ½ mile 707/962–3123 fvprincess.com/p/fish-market Closed Tues.–Thurs. (but check). No dinner.*

Hotels

★ Inn at Newport Ranch

$$$$ | **B&B/INN** | Attention to detail in design and hospitality makes for an incomparable stay at this 2,000-acre working cattle ranch with 1½ miles of private coastline. **Pros:** over-the-top design; mesmerizing Pacific views; UTV ranch tour, horseback riding, ocean-side cocktails by a firepit, and other diversions. **Cons:** all this design and glamour comes at a price; lengthy drive back from Mendocino and Fort Bragg restaurants at night; coast can be foggy in summer. *Rooms from: $475 31502 N. Hwy. 1 707/962–4818 theinnatnewportranch.com 11 rooms Free breakfast.*

★ Noyo Harbor Inn

$$$ | **HOTEL** | Craftsman touches abound in this luxury inn's lavishly restored, 1868 main structure, which overlooks Noyo Harbor, and a nearby newer wing with Pacific Ocean views. **Pros:** landscaped grounds; warm service; brunch or dinner on harbor-view deck. **Cons:** barking of sea lions in harbor at certain times of year; expensive during high season; some rooms lack water views. *Rooms from: $255 500 Casa del Noyo Dr. 707/961–4200 noyoharborinn.com 15 rooms No meals.*

Surf and Sand Lodge

$$ | **HOTEL** | As its name implies, this five-building, two-story property, whose owners run two similar lodgings nearby, sits practically on the beach; pathways lead from the accommodations down to the rock-strewn shore. **Pros:** beach location; gorgeous sunsets from decks and patios of ocean-side rooms; very affordable in the off-season. **Cons:** motel style; no restaurants close by; least expensive rooms lack view. *Rooms from: $159 1131 N. Main St. 707/964–9383 www.surfsandlodge.com 30 rooms No meals.*

Activities

All Aboard Adventures

FISHING | Captain Tim of All Aboard operates whale-watching trips from late December through April. He also heads out to sea for salmon, crab, rock cod, and other excursions. *Noyo Harbor, 32410 N. Harbor Dr. 707/964–1881 www.allaboardadventures.com From $50.*

Philo

34 miles southeast of Mendocino, 5 miles west of Boonville.

Many wineries straddle Highway 128 in Philo, where the tasting rooms are more low-key than their counterparts in Napa. The wineries here, however, produce world-class Pinot Noirs, Chardonnays, Rieslings, and Gewürztraminers, whose grapes thrive in the moderate coastal climate.

GETTING HERE AND AROUND

Highway 128 travels east from coastal Highway 1 south of Mendocino and west from Boonville to Philo. Mendocino Transit Authority buses serve the area.

Sights

Goldeneye Winery

WINERY/DISTILLERY | Established in 1996 by the founders of the Napa Valley's well-respected Duckhorn Wine Company, Goldeneye makes Pinot Noirs from estate and other local grapes, along with a Brut Rosé sparkling wine, Gewürztraminer, Pinot Gris, Chardonnay, and a blush Vin Gris of Pinot Noir. Leisurely tastings, some by appointment only, take place in either a restored farmhouse or on a patio with vineyard views. ✉ *9200 Hwy. 128, Philo* ☎ *800/208–0438, 707/895–3202* 🌐 *www.goldeneyewinery.com* 🎟 *Tastings from $15* ⏲ *Closed Wed.*

Handley Cellars

WINERY/DISTILLERY | International folk art collected by founding winemaker the late Milla Handley adorns the tasting room at this Anderson Valley pioneer whose lightly oaked Chardonnays and Pinot Noirs earn high praise from wine critics. The winery, which has an arbored outdoor patio picnic area, also makes Gewürztraminer, Pinot Gris, Riesling, Zinfandel, sparklers, and several other wines. Reservations are recommended, but walk-ins are accommodated when possible. ✉ *3151 Hwy. 128, Philo* ☎ *707/895–3876, 800/733–3151* 🌐 *www.handleycellars.com* 🎟 *Tasting $15* ⏲ *Closed Tues. and Wed. Dec.–Mar.*

Hendy Woods State Park

NATIONAL/STATE PARK | Two groves of ancient redwoods accessible via short trails from the parking lot are the main attractions at this park that's also perfect for a picnic or a summer swim. ✉ *18599 Philo Greenwood Rd., Philo* ✥ *Entrance ½ mile southwest of Hwy. 128* ☎ *707/937–5804* 🌐 *www.parks.ca.gov* 🎟 *$8 per vehicle.*

Husch Vineyards

WINERY/DISTILLERY | A century-old former pony barn houses the tasting room of the Anderson Valley's oldest winery, founded in 1971. Wines of note include Gewürztraminer, Chardonnay, Pinot Noir, and old-vine Zinfandel. You can picnic on the deck or at tables under grape arbors. ✉ *4400 Hwy. 128, Philo* ☎ *800/554–8724* 🌐 *www.huschvineyards.com* 🎟 *Tasting free.*

★ Lula Cellars

WINERY/DISTILLERY | Seventeen miles inland from Highway 1, the fun, relaxing, and pet-friendly Lula is among the Anderson Valley wineries closest to the coast. Lula produces Sauvignon Blanc, Gewürztraminer, Zinfandel, and a rosé of Pinot Noir, but the several Pinot Noirs, each flavorful and with its own personality, are the highlights. ✉ *2800 Guntly Rd., Philo* ✥ *At Hwy. 128* ☎ *707/895–3737* 🌐 *www.lulacellars.com* 🎟 *Tastings from $10.*

★ The Madrones Tasting Rooms

WINERY/DISTILLERY | Expand your palate at this 2-acre complex's trio of tasting rooms pouring wines from a dozen varietals. Chardonnay and Pinot Noir are the focus at **Long Meadow Ranch,** where you can also order well-brewed espresso or tea. Next door, **Drew Family Wines** specializes in Pinot Noir and Syrah beloved by sommeliers. Nearby **Smith Story** makes Anderson Valley Pinots plus wines from Sonoma County grapes.

Across from Smith Story, the owner-chefs at Wickson bake bread and roast meat and vegetables in a wood-fired oven. ■ **TIP→ The Bohemian Chemist bills itself as a "curated cannabis apothecary" and spa for sun-grown marijuana products and CBD skin-care treatments and facials.** *9000 Hwy. 128, Philo* *707/895–2955* *www.themadrones.com/tasting-rooms* *Tastings from $15* *Days closed vary.*

Navarro Vineyards

WINERY/DISTILLERY | A visit to this family-run winery, opened in 1974, is a classic Anderson Valley experience, with tastings in fine weather on several perches overlooking sustainably farmed vineyards. Best known for Alsatian varietals such as Gewürztraminer and Riesling, Navarro also makes Chardonnay, Pinot Noir, and other wines. *5601 Hwy. 128, Philo* *707/895–3686, 800/537–9463* *www.navarrowine.com* *Tasting $10.*

★ Phillips Hill Winery

WINERY/DISTILLERY | You're apt to meet owner-winemaker Toby Hill on a visit to this winery whose tasting room occupies the upper floor of a weatherworn former apple dryer barn. The grapes for the Pinot Noirs here come from the Anderson Valley's floor and hillsides. Hill also makes whites that include Gewürztraminer and Riesling. ■ **TIP→ Picnic tables on the willow-shaded lawn below the tasting room invite lingering.** *5101 Hwy. 128, Philo* *707/895–2209* *www.phillipshill.com* *Tastings $12* *Closed Tues. and Wed.*

Roederer Estate

WINERY/DISTILLERY | The Anderson Valley is particularly hospitable to Pinot Noir and Chardonnay grapes, the two varietals used to create Roederer's sparkling wines. The view of vineyards and rolling hills from the patio is splendid. *4501 Hwy. 128, Philo* *707/895–2288* *www.roedererestate.com* *Tasting $10.*

Toulouse Vineyards & Winery

WINERY/DISTILLERY | The view west across the Anderson Valley from this winery's tasting room and deck is captivating enough to warrant a visit, but the wines don't disappoint either. Tastings begin with whites that might include Pinot Gris, Riesling, or Gewürztraminer—there's also a rosé of Pinot Noir that sells out quickly each spring—followed by Pinot Noir from estate and sourced fruit and perhaps another red. *8001 Hwy. 128, Philo* *707/895–2828* *www.toulousevineyards.com* *Tasting $15.*

 Restaurants

★ The Bewildered Pig

$$$$ | MODERN AMERICAN | Chef Janelle Weaver cooked for seven years at a prestigious appointment-only Napa Valley winery, perfecting skills that serve her well at this low-key yet polished roadside restaurant. Her prix-fixe menu, which varies with the season, might include smoked trout or extraordinary Peking duck breast from a local provider, with miso deviled eggs (all the better with sparkling wine) among the tantalizing starters. **Known for:** garden dining area; phenomenally fresh salads; inspired wine pairings. *Average main: $105* *1810 Hwy. 128, Philo* *707/895–2088* *www.bewilderedpig.com* *Closed Sun.–Thurs. (but check). No lunch.*

Wickson Restaurant

$$$ | MODERN AMERICAN | A wood-fired oven anchors the small kitchen of this contempo-rustic restaurant whose chefs' deeply held views about environmentally sensitive food sourcing influence their seasonally oriented menu. Small plates might include marinated olives, a citrus and avocado salad, or smoked trout with crème fraîche and pickled onions, with spinach lasagna and quail with roasted carrots and chimichurri sauce typical of the entrées. **Known for:** wood-fired bread and focaccia; pizza Mondays; alfresco dining, especially at lunch. *Average* *main: $27 ✉ 9000 Hwy. 128, Philo ☎ 707/895–2955 🌐 wicksonrestaurant.com ⏲ Closed Tues. and Wed. (occasionally other days).*

Hotels

★ The Madrones Guest Quarters

$$$ | B&B/INN | The centerpiece of a 2-acre spread that includes tasting rooms, a gift shop, an apothecary-style cannabis dispensary, and a restaurant, this property has nine eclectically decorated accommodations that range from apartment-like studios to duplex cottages, some with patios or balconies facing landscaped gardens. **Pros:** location near wineries and Hendy Woods State Park; on-site Wickson Restaurant; nearby sister property The Brambles set among redwoods for a more casual experience. **Cons:** weekend minimum-stay requirement; pricey on summer weekends; yogurt, cereal, and coffee/tea provided in-room but no breakfast served. *$ Rooms from: $255 ✉ 9000 Hwy. 128, Philo ☎ 707/895–2955 🌐 www.themadrones.com 🛏 9 rooms 🍴 No meals.*

Boonville

6 miles east of Philo, 28 miles northwest of Hopland.

At first glance Boonville, population a little more than 1,000, looks pretty much as it has for decades, with the 19th-century Boonville Hotel anchoring the few blocks downtown and sheep farms and fruit orchards fanning out on either side of Highway 128, albeit with more grapevines these days. The founding of the Anderson Valley Brewing Company in the late 1980s and the revitalization of the hotel by its current owners, the Schmitt family, jump-started the transformation of Boonville into a haven of artisanal food, wine, and beer. Despite this, the town retains its old-school character—listen carefully and you may hear fragments of the academically recognized Boontling argot, which dates to the time when this stretch of the valley was even more isolated.

GETTING HERE AND AROUND

Boonville lies along Highway 128 at its junction with Highway 253. Mendocino Transit Authority buses serve the area.

Sights

Anderson Valley Brewing Company

WINERY/DISTILLERY | Brewery tours, tastings, and cornhole, bocce, and disc golf provide an entertaining and diversified, mainly outdoor experience at the home of Boont Amber Ale, double and triple Belgian style ales, and other brews. Local winemakers clear their palates with the Bourbon Barrel Stout, aged in Tennessee whiskey barrels. *✉ 17700 Hwy. 253, Boonville ✣ At Hwy. 128 ☎ 707/895–2337 🌐 www.avbc.com 🎫 Tastings from $15.*

Bee Hunter Wine

WINERY/DISTILLERY | Winemaker Andy DuVigneaud of Bee Hunter Wine prefers vineyards close to the ocean because the cool climate requires that grapes stay longer on the vine, preventing them from ripening before their flavors have fully developed. His restrained yet delicious wines, which he pours with enthusiasm in a former car repair shop in Boonville, include Sauvignon Blanc, Chardonnay, dry Riesling, a dry and light rosé of Pinot Noir, several Pinot Noirs, and a few other reds. *✉ 14251 Hwy. 128, Boonville ☎ 707/895–3995 🌐 www.beehunterwine.com 🎫 Tasting free.*

★ Foursight Wines

WINERY/DISTILLERY | Four generations of the Charles family have farmed the land that produces this winery's vegan-friendly all-estate lineup of Sauvignon Blanc, Semillon, Vin Gris of Pinot Noir (aka rosé), and Pinot Noir. With the Pinots, winemaker Joe Webb employs various techniques to produce four very different wines, from the light Zero, aged solely in used oak barrels, to the "richer, riper" Paraboll, its flavors heightened by new French oak. ■ **TIP→ After a tasting, you can picnic outside the casual wood-frame tasting room, enjoying a glass or bottle.** ✉ *14475 Hwy. 128, Boonville* ☎ *707/895–2889* 🌐 *www.foursightwines.com* 🎫 *Tastings $25* ⏲ *Closed Tues. and 3rd wk of June.*

★ Pennyroyal Farm

WINERY/DISTILLERY | **FAMILY** | At this ranch with a contemporary-barn tasting room and vineyard-view patio you can sample Sauvignon Blanc, velvety Pinot Noirs, and other wines from estate and sourced grapes, along with cheeses made on the premises from goat and sheep milk. Engaging tours of the farmstead should have resumed by the time you read this. The wines, cheeses, pastoral setting, and adorable animals win most guests' hearts. All visits require a reservation. ✉ *14930 Hwy. 128, Boonville* ☎ *707/895–2410* 🌐 *www.pennyroyalfarm.com* 🎫 *Tastings from $25* ⏲ *Closed Tues. and Wed. (check for updates).*

Restaurants

Disco Ranch Wine Bar + Specialty Market

$ | **WINE BAR** | In a rough-hewn structure that for years housed a beloved coffee haunt called the Horn of Zeese—the local "Boontling" lingo for a cup (horn) of coffee (zeese)—international wine expert Wendy Lamer operates this combination wine bar and gourmet mini-mart. Well versed in the local wine scene and generous with advice, she pours wines by the glass or bottle and serves up sliders and other "disco snacks." **Known for:** wines by Anderson Valley producers without tasting rooms; European and other wines complementing local selection; good stop for light lunch. $ *Average main: $8* ✉ *14025 Hwy. 128, Boonville* ☎ *707/901–5002* 🌐 *discoranch.com* ⏲ *Closed Tues. and Wed. No dinner.*

Lauren's

$ | **AMERICAN** | Boonville locals and frequent visitors love Lauren's for its down-home vibe and healthful comfort food—vegetarian and ground-beef burgers, pizzas, chicken tostadas, meat loaf, and curry noodle bowls. Chocolate brownie sundaes and (seasonally) apple tarts and honey-baked pears are among the desserts worth a trip on their own. **Known for:** "made-from-scratch American-International cooking"; many ingredients grown or produced nearby; Taco Tuesdays. $ *Average main: $16* ✉ *14081 Hwy. 128, Boonville* ☎ *707/895–3869* 🌐 *laurensgoodfood.com* ⏲ *Closed Wed. No lunch Tues.*

★ Restaurant at The Boonville Hotel

$$$$ | **AMERICAN** | This stylishly funky restaurant's chef, Perry Hoffman, got his start (at age five) working in the kitchen of Napa Valley's The French Laundry, which his grandmother founded and later sold to Thomas Keller. As an adult, Hoffman made a name for himself at three highly praised Napa and Sonoma spots before returning to Boonville in 2019 to prepare prix-fixe, California farm-to-table cuisine (including a few original French Laundry dishes) at his extended family's hotel. **Known for:** many ingredients grown on-site or nearby; superior protein sources; alfresco patio dining. $ *Average main: $75* ✉ *Boonville Hotel, 14050 Hwy. 128, Boonville* ☎ *707/895–2210* 🌐 *www.boonvillehotel.com/eats* ⏲ *Closed Mon.–Thurs. Nov.–Apr., closed Tues. and Wed. May–Oct. No lunch.*

Hotels

★ The Boonville Hotel

$$ | **HOTEL** | From the street, this looks like a standard small-town hotel with nine freestanding cottages and a two-room, two-story building in the back garden, but once you cross the threshold you begin to sense the laid-back sophistication that makes the entire Anderson Valley so

You'll find excellent wines and great places to taste them in the laid-back Anderson Valley.

appealing. **Pros:** stylish yet homey; beautiful gardens and grounds; restaurant's excellent prix-fixe meals. **Cons:** minimum-stay requirement most weekends; no TVs or phones, no a/c in some rooms; lacks big-hotel amenities. *Rooms from: $185* *14050 Hwy. 128, Boonville* *707/895–2210* *www.boonvillehotel.com* *17 rooms* *Free breakfast.*

Hopland

28 miles east of Boonville, 14 miles south of Ukiah, 32 miles north of Healdsburg.

U.S. 101 briefly narrows to one lane in each direction to become this small town's main drag. For many years a center for the cultivation and drying of beer hops—the source of its name—Hopland these days is a center of grape growing and wine making and a pleasant stop for tastings and a meal.

GETTING HERE AND AROUND

Car travelers from Sonoma and Humboldt counties arrive in Hopland via U.S. 101. Highway 253 will get you here from Boonville. Mendocino Transit Authority buses serve the area.

ESSENTIALS

VISITOR INFORMATION Destination Hopland. *707/564–2582* *destination-hopland.com.*

Sights

Campovida

WINERY/DISTILLERY | Wines from Italian and Rhône varietals grown in Mendocino County organic, biodynamic, and sustainable vineyards are the focus of Campovida, on a historic 56-acre property whose previous owners include local railroad magnate A.W. Foster and the Fetzer wine-making clan. The Rhônes are the strong suit, especially the estate organic Viognier and the Grenache and rosé of Grenache from the biodynamically farmed Dark Horse Vineyard. All visits are by appointment only. ■ **TIP→ Sister property Stock Farm in downtown Hopland provides prepared foods for a picnic amid the landscaped gardens (no outside food).** ✉ *13601 Old River Rd., Hopland* ✣ *Head east ¾ mile from U.S. 101 on Hwy. 175* ☎ *707/744–8797* 🌐 *www.campovida.com* 🎫 *Tastings from $25.*

Graziano Family of Wines
WINERY/DISTILLERY | A winemaker who never met a grape he didn't want to transform in the cellar, Gregory Graziano creates wines for four separate labels, one devoted to Burgundian grapes like Pinot Noir, two to Italian varietals, and the last to Zinfandel, Rhône, and a few other types. The winery's oldest Mendocino County vineyard was planted just before Prohibition by Gregory's grandfather. The lineup poured in the downtown Hopland tasting space might include Pinot Gris and Arneis whites and Dolcetto and Nebbiolo reds. ✉ *13275 U.S. 101, Hopland* ☎ *707/744–8466* 🌐 *grazianofamilyofwines.com* 🎫 *Tasting free.*

★ **Saracina Vineyards**
WINERY/DISTILLERY | Guests at this boutique winery's contemporary, stone-and-glass hospitality center enjoy views of landscaped outdoor picnic and tasting areas and the olive grove and vineyards beyond. Tastings sometimes begin with a Sauvignon Blanc that helped establish Saracina. Some of the wine's organic grapes come from California's oldest Sauvignon Blanc vines (1945). The standout reds include Zinfandel, Cabernet Sauvignon, and Malbec. ■ **TIP→ Wine caves are rare in Mendocino, but there's one here, and it's sometimes open by appointment for free tours.** ✉ *11684 U.S. 101, Hopland* ☎ *707/670–0199* 🌐 *www.saracina.com* 🎫 *Tastings from $15.*

Restaurants

★ **Golden Pig**
$$ | **AMERICAN** | Grass-fed burgers, pulled-pork and pork-schnitzel sandwiches, and cod ceviche are among the popular items this hip-casual restaurant serves all day, with bone-in pork chops, rotisserie chicken, and similar plates appearing for dinner. Well-selected breads and buns, crispy fries with the burgers, perfect pickles with the sandwiches, and slivers of fresh ginger in the ceviche elevate the farm-to-table comfort fare, much of it showcasing ingredients from local purveyors. **Known for:** Northern California beers, Mendocino County wines; everything on menu made gluten-free if desired; tastings at affiliated wine shop 200 feet south. 💲 *Average main: $24* ✉ *13380 U.S. 101, Hopland* ☎ *707/670–6055* 🌐 *www.thegoldenpig.com.*

Hopland Tap and Grill
$ | **AMERICAN** | A plaque out front hints at the layers of history that have unfolded in this hangout's redbrick 1880s structure. The mood's invariably upbeat in the bar, even more so in the courtyard beer garden, where patrons chow down on burgers, sandwiches (including four griddled-cheese options), chicken wings, and other pub grub. **Known for:** California brews on tap; down-home atmosphere; live rock on Saturday night. 💲 *Average main: $11* ✉ *13351 U.S. 101, Hopland* ☎ *707/510–9000* 🌐 *hoplandtap.com* ⏲ *Closed Mon. and Tues. (but check).*

Stock Farm
$$ | **MODERN AMERICAN** | Gourmet wood-fired pizzas, many with ingredients grown a mile away at Campovida winery, are the main attraction at this country-casual restaurant and bar whose owners also operate the seven-room Stock Farm Inn upstairs and the Thatcher Hotel next door. Menu staples include burgers; grilled vegetables; pasta dishes; and seasonal soups, stews, and salads. **Known for:**

rustic-chic bar's specialty cocktails; street-side patio dining; well-made coffee drinks. *$ Average main: $20 ✉ 13441 U.S. 101, Hopland ☎ 707/744–1977 🌐 www.stockfarmhopland.com ⏲ Closed Mon.–Wed.*

Hotels

Stock Farm Inn

$$$$ | B&B/INN | Atop the same-named pizzeria and bar, this inn—whose owners also operate Campovida winery less than a mile away and the boutique 1890s Thatcher Hotel next door—sits along Hopland's main drag near shops, tasting rooms, and other restaurants. **Pros:** plush furnishings; two rooms with pullout couches sleep four; fireplaces, wet bars, whirlpool tubs, refrigerators, and balconies in all rooms. **Cons:** single-person whirlpool tubs in two rooms; more self-serve than pampering; weekend minimum-stay requirement. *$ Rooms from: $370 ✉ 13441 U.S. 101, Hopland ☎ 707/744–1977 🌐 www.stockfarmhopland.com/inn 🛏 7 rooms 🍽 No meals.*

Ukiah

14 miles north of Hopland, 21 miles northeast of Boonville.

About 16,000 people live in Ukiah, the Mendocino County seat and largest town. Logging and beer hops were two prominent industries starting in the late-19th century and continuing well into the 20th. Grape plantings date from the late 1800s, though many of the head-trained (no trellising) old vines were planted in the early 1900s and during and just after Prohibition. Warmer than the Anderson Valley, the Ukiah area is known for Zinfandel, Cabernet Sauvignon, and other varietals that thrive in high heat. Should you need to cool off, you can repair to the redwoods of Montgomery Woods State Natural Reserve.

GETTING HERE AND AROUND

Ukiah is off U.S. 101; if coming from Boonville, take Highway 253 northeast to U.S. 101 and head north. Mendocino Transit Authority buses serve the area.

ESSENTIALS

VISITOR INFORMATION Ukiah Visitor Center. *✉ 200 S. School St. ☎ 707/467–5766 🌐 www.visitukiah.com.*

Sights

Montgomery Woods State Natural Reserve

NATIONAL/STATE PARK | Narrow Orr Springs Road winds 13 miles west from Ukiah to this secluded park whose 2-mile loop trail leads to serene old-growth redwood groves. Only the intermittent breezes, rustling of small wildlife, and calls of resident birds punctuate the prehistoric quiet of the most remote one. The reserve (no dogs allowed) is a place like few others in all of California. **■ TIP→ From the town of Mendocino you can access the park by taking the Comptche Ukiah Road to Orr Springs Road.** *✉ 15825 Orr Springs Rd., Ukiah ✥ 13 miles west of N. State St. ☎ 707/937–5804 🌐 www.parks.ca.gov 🎟 Free.*

Nelson Family Vineyards

WINERY/DISTILLERY | The grandparents of the current winemaker moved to Mendocino County in the early 1950s, establishing a ranch just north of Hopland that now encompasses 2,000 acres. About 10% of the land is devoted to grapes (Chardonnay and Cabernet Sauvignon are two strong suits), with olives and pears among the other plantings. Tastings take place inside the former family home or in an outdoor area with views of grapevines and a redwood grove. *✉ 550 Nelson Ranch Rd., Ukiah ☎ 707/462–3755 🌐 www.nelsonfamilyvineyards.com 🎟 Tastings from $10.*

Rivino Winery

WINERY/DISTILLERY | The open-air tasting room and outdoor spaces at Rivino are oriented to maximize the views of the 215-acre estate's vineyard and pond. As with the architecture, owner-winemaker Jason McConnell takes a minimalist approach with his wines, all from grapes grown on-site. The Sangiovese and Sedulous blend of Merlot, Cabernet Sauvignon, and a touch of Viognier stand out, as does the Amber Eve rosé, a brisk seller. All visits are by appointment. **■ TIP→ Talented local musicians perform some days from April through October.** ✉ *4101 Cox Schrader Rd., Ukiah* ✣ *Exit 545 off U.S. 101* ☎ *707/293–4262* 🌐 *www.rivino.com* 🎫 *Tastings from $10.*

★ Testa Vineyards
WINERY/DISTILLERY | This family-owned winery sells most of its grapes—some from vines planted in the 1930s and 1940s—to notable Napa, Sonoma, and Mendocino brands but withholds some of its certified organic and biodynamic output for its small label. Winemaker Maria Testa Martinson, whose great-grandparents established Testa Ranch in 1912, makes Charbono, Carignane, Petite Sirah, old-vine Zinfandel, Cabernet Sauvignon, and other reds from grapes grown on the estate, with a few whites from outside sources. Tastings, preferably by appointment (though walk-ins might be possible), take place in or just outside in a spiffed-up former chicken coop with views of a pond and rolling vineyards. ✉ *6400 N. State St., Calpella* ✣ *From Ukiah take U.S. 101 north to Exit 555A, turning right on Moore St. and left on N. State* ☎ *707/485–7051* 🌐 *testaranch.com* 🎫 *Tastings from $15* ⏲ *Closed Sun.*

Restaurants

Cultivo
$$ | **AMERICAN** | An oasis of low-key sophistication in downtown Ukiah, Cultivo is known for inventive wood-fired pizzas (try the braised-pork or wild-boar-sausage pie or go meatless with one starring trumpet mushrooms) but also plates up oysters on the half shell, fish tacos, a kale Caesar salad (sourdough croutons make it work), and a heritage pork chop. Meals are served on thick wooden tables in the downstairs bar area and in the mezzanine; there's also sidewalk dining out front. **Known for:** something for everyone; California beers on tap; gluten-free options. $ *Average main: $21* ✉ *108 W. Standley St., Ukiah* ☎ *707/462–7007* 🌐 *cultivorestaurant.com* ⏲ *Closed Sun. No lunch Mon.–Wed.*

Hotels

Vichy Springs Resort
$$$ | **RESORT** | The cottages and multiunit one-story buildings of this historic hot-springs resort—luminaries from Ulysses S. Grant to Nancy Pelosi have unwound here—surround a broad lawn shaded by mature manzanitas and oaks. **Pros:** rural solitude; naturally carbonated hot springs; some accommodations have full kitchens. **Cons:** pool is only heated part of the year; not a pampering-type spa; noise from nearby gun range. $ *Rooms from: $275* ✉ *2605 Vichy Springs Rd., Ukiah* ☎ *707/462–9515* 🌐 *www.vichysprings.com* 🛏 *26 rooms* 🍽 *Free breakfast.*

Avenue of the Giants

74 miles northeast of Fort Bragg, 98 miles north of Ukiah.

Conservationists banded together a century ago as the Save the Redwoods League and scored a crucial victory when a memorial grove was dedicated in 1921. That grove is now part of Humboldt Redwoods State Park. About a third of the park's more than 53,000 acres contain untouched old-growth coast redwoods most easily viewed while driving the 32-mile Avenue of the Giants.

GETTING HERE AND AROUND

The Avenue of the Giants is off U.S. 101 between Exits 645 and 674. Southern Humboldt Intercity (hta.org) buses serve the area.

Sights

★ Avenue of the Giants

NATIONAL/STATE PARK | FAMILY | Some of the tallest trees on Earth tower over this magnificent 32-mile stretch of two-lane blacktop, also known as Highway 254, that follows the south fork of the Eel River through Humboldt Redwoods State Park. The highway runs more or less parallel to U.S. 101 from Phillipsville in the south to the town of Pepperwood in the north. A brochure available at either end of the highway or the visitor center, 2 miles south of Weott, contains a self-guided tour, with short and long hikes through various redwood groves. A trail at **Founders Grove** passes by several impressive trees, among them the fallen 362-foot-long Dyerville Giant, whose root base points skyward 35 feet. The tree can be reached via a short trail that begins 4 miles north of the visitor center. About 6 miles north of the center lies Rockefeller Forest. The largest remaining old-growth coast redwood forest, it contains more than a third of the 100 tallest trees in the world. ✉ *Humboldt Redwoods State Park Visitor Center, 17119 Ave. of the Giants, Weott* ☎ *707/946–2263* 🌐 *www.parks.ca.gov/humboldtredwoods* 🎟 *Free; $8 day-use fee for Williams Grove.*

Briceland Vineyards

WINERY/DISTILLERY | Lean yet flavorful Humboldt County Pinot Noirs are the specialty of this winery set amid the trees. In good weather, the low-key tastings take place in front of the weathered original winery building. Guests sip Chardonnay, Sauvignon Blanc, or other whites before sampling Pinots and perhaps Syrah or Zinfandel. ■ **TIP→ From late May through August, drop-ins are welcome 3–6 on weekends; otherwise tastings are by appointment.** ✉ *5959 Briceland Rd., 10½ miles southwest of Ave. of the Giants southern entrance* ✣ *Take Briceland Rd. 5½ miles west from Redwood Dr. in Redway (from north, U.S. 101 Exit 642; from south, Exit 639B)* ☎ *707/923–2429* 🌐 *bricelandvineyards.com* 🎟 *Tastings $20.*

Hotels

Scotia Lodge

$$ | HOTEL | Eureka-based entrepreneurs passionate about providing safe legal places for patrons to enjoy cannabis products renovated a century-old logging hotel near the northern Avenue of the Giants entrance into a hip, stylish hub welcoming all travelers. **Pros:** snappy reboot of historic property; some adjoining rooms; restaurant's comfort food includes vegan- and gluten-free items. **Cons:** some rooms a little dark; pot vibe may not work for all travelers; a tad pricey for the area. [$] *Rooms from: $185* ✉ *100 Main St.* ☎ *707/783–3059* 🌐 *www.scotia-lodge.com* *22 rooms* *No meals.*

Eureka

33 miles north of Avenue of the Giants north entrance.

An excellent place to fuel up, buy groceries, and learn a little about the region's mining, timber, and fishing pasts, historic Eureka was named after a gold miner's hearty exclamation. The county visitor center has maps of self-guided walking tours of the town's nearly 100 Victorians. Art galleries and antiques stores liven up the Old Town district from C to N Street between the waterfront and 4th Street, and a walking pier extends into the harbor.

GETTING HERE AND AROUND

Eureka is set along the North Coast's main north–south highway, U.S. 101. Give yourself about 45 minutes to drive to Kuchel Visitor Center, at the park's south end.

ESSENTIALS

VISITOR INFORMATION Humboldt County Visitors Bureau. ✉ *322 1st St.* ☎ *707/443–5097, 800/346–3482* 🌐 *www.visitredwoods.com.*

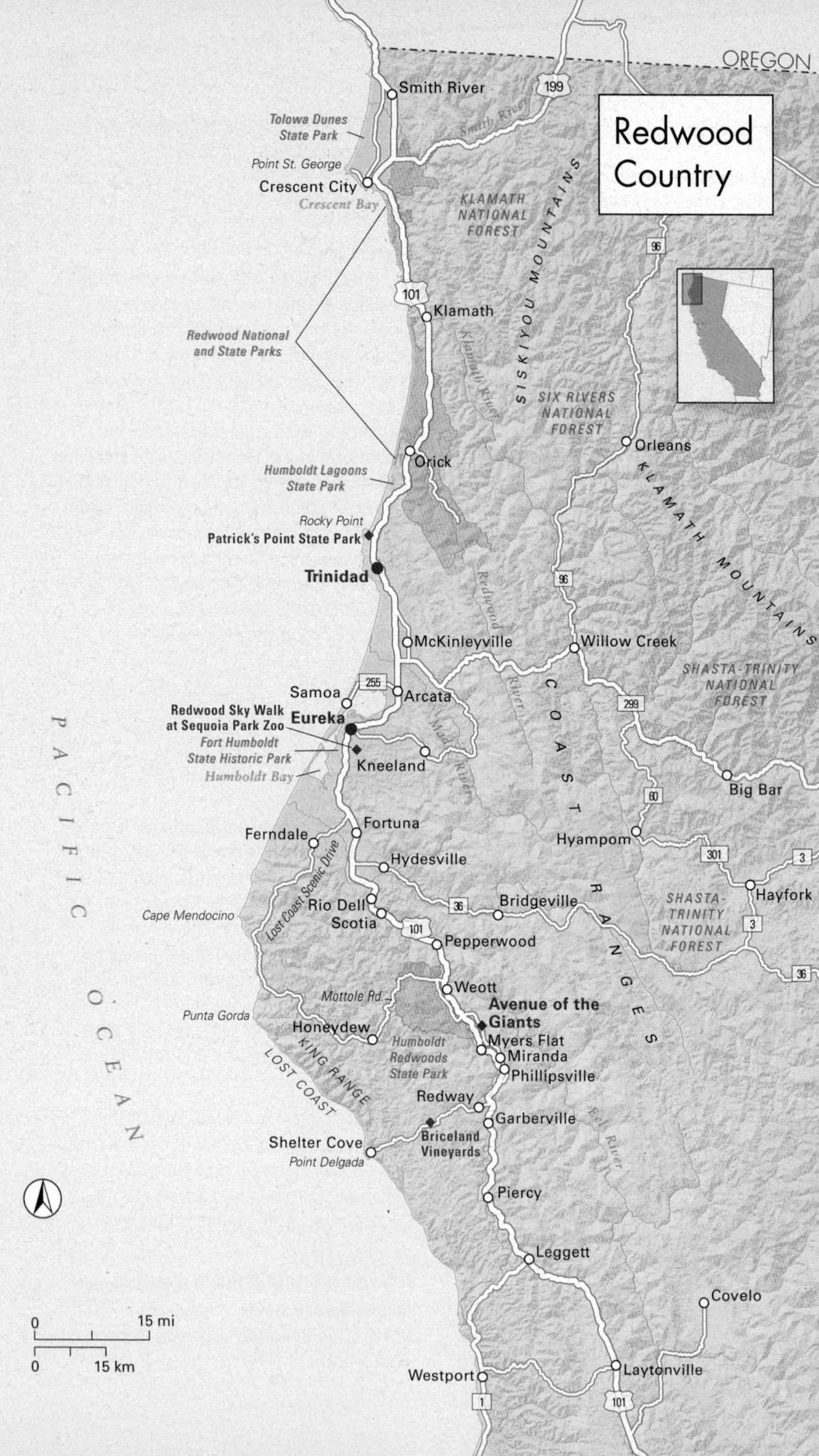

Redwood Country
OREGON
Smith River
199
Smith River
Tolowa Dunes State Park
Point St. George
Crescent City
Crescent Bay
KLAMATH NATIONAL FOREST
SISKIYOU MOUNTAINS
96
101
Klamath
Redwood National and State Parks
Klamath River
SIX RIVERS NATIONAL FOREST
Orleans
Orick
Humboldt Lagoons State Park
KLAMATH MOUNTAINS
Rocky Point
Patrick's Point State Park
Trinidad
Redwood Creek
96
McKinleyville
Willow Creek
SHASTA-TRINITY NATIONAL FOREST
255
Samoa
Arcata
299
Redwood Sky Walk at Sequoia Park Zoo
Eureka
Fort Humboldt State Historic Park
Kneeland
Mad River
Humboldt Bay
COAST RANGES
Big Bar
60
PACIFIC OCEAN
Fortuna
Ferndale
Hyampom
301
3
Hydesville
Lost Coast Scenic Drive
Hayfork
Rio Dell
Scotia
36
Bridgeville
Cape Mendocino
SHASTA-TRINITY NATIONAL FOREST
3
101
Pepperwood
36
Weott
Mottole Rd.
Avenue of the Giants
Punta Gorda
Honeydew
Humboldt Redwoods State Park
Myers Flat
Miranda
Phillipsville
KING RANGE
LOST COAST
Redway
Garberville
Eel River
Briceland Vineyards
Shelter Cove
Point Delgada
Piercy
Leggett
Covelo
0
15 mi
0
15 km
Westport
Laytonville
1
101

Sights

Blue Ox Millworks

FACTORY | This woodshop is among a handful in the country specializing in Victorian-era architecture, but what makes it truly unique is that its craftspeople use antique tools to do the work. Visitors can watch artisans use printing presses, lathes, and other equipment to create gingerbread trim, fence pickets, and other signature Victorian embellishments. The shop is less interesting on Saturday, when most craftspeople take the day off. *1 X St. 707/444–3437 www.blueoxmill.com $12 Closed Sun. and Dec.–Mar., Sat.*

Lost Coast Scenic Drive

SCENIC DRIVE | A loop drive counterclockwise from the town of Ferndale, 20 miles south of Eureka, yields astounding ocean views and winds through forests and small towns before heading into Humboldt Redwoods State Park and then back up U.S. 101 toward the starting point. The road has numerous curves and some rugged stretches are in need of repair, but driving this 100-or-so-mile route is exhilarating. **TIP→ Allot four hours for this excursion.** *From Ferndale, head southwest on Wildcat Ave., which soon becomes Mattole Rd. Follow Mattole west to the coast, south to Petrolia, and east to Honeydew and the park. At U.S. 101 return north to Ferndale or Eureka. visitredwoods.com/listing/lost-coast-scenic-drive/148.*

★ **Redwood Sky Walk at Sequoia Park Zoo**

ZOO | **FAMILY** | Stroll as high as 100 feet above the forest floor on the elevated walkway, an instant hit following its 2021 debut at California's oldest zoo. Although relatively small, Sequoia Park, which opened in 1907, is conservation-focused and fully accredited. Favorite areas for wildlife viewing include the red panda exhibit, a barnyard petting zoo, and a walk-in aviary with local and exotic birds. *3414 W St. 707/441–4263 redwoodskywalk.com $25 Closed Mon.*

Restaurants

★ **Brick & Fire Bistro**

$$ | **MODERN AMERICAN** | Nearly every seat in this urbane downtown bistro has a view of its most important feature—a wood-fired brick oven used to prepare everything from local Kumamoto oysters and creatively topped pizzas to wild-mushroom cobbler. Even the "fries," char-roasted potatoes tossed in olive oil and spices, come out of the oven, with grilled meats and seafood rounding out the menu. **Known for:** house-made sausage pizzas; polenta lasagna and (lunch only) vegetarian eggplant "blt"; affiliated 2 Doors Down wine bar is just steps away. *Average main: $23 1630 F St. 707/268–8959 www.brickandfirebistro.com Closed Tues. No lunch weekends.*

Café Waterfront

$$ | **SEAFOOD** | Amid Old Town's vibrant dining district, this rollicking spot in what served as a saloon and brothel in the 1950s turns out consistently fresh locally caught seafood. Steamed clams, grilled snapper, oyster burgers, and chowders are all on the menu—one of the West Coast's top oyster beds, in the bay across the street, supplies the oysters on the half shell. **Known for:** historic vibe and Old Town setting; excellent locally sourced oysters (raw and grilled); homemade clam chowder. *Average main: $21 102 F St. 707/443–9190 www.cafewaterfronteureka.com.*

Hotels

★ **Carter House Inns**

$$ | **HOTEL** | Richly painted and aglow with wood detailing, the rooms, in two main Victorian buildings and several historic cottages, contain a mix of modern and antique furnishings; some have whirlpool tubs and separate sitting areas. **Pros:** elegant ambience; attention to detail; superb on-site Restaurant 301. **Cons:** not suitable for children; restaurant is a bit pricey; two-night

minimum on weekends. *Rooms from: $195* *301 L St.* *707/444–8062, 800/404–1390* *www.carterhouse.com* *33 rooms* *Free breakfast.*

Trinidad

23 miles north of Eureka.

A mellow base for exploring the southern portion of Redwood National and State Parks, coastal Trinidad got its name from the Spanish mariners who entered the bay on Trinity Sunday, June 9, 1775. Formerly the principal trading post for mining camps along the Klamath and Trinity rivers, these days Trinidad is a quiet and genuinely charming community with several beaches and a small but impressive selection of restaurants and romantic inns.

GETTING HERE AND AROUND

Trinidad sits right off U.S. 101, about 10 miles north of Highway 299.

Sights

Patrick's Point State Park

BEACH—SIGHT | This park on a forested plateau almost 200 feet above the surf offers stunning views of the Pacific, great whale- and sea lion–watching spots, campgrounds, picnic areas, bike paths, and hiking trails through old-growth spruce forest. There are also tidal pools at Agate Beach, a re-created Yurok Indian village, and a small visitor center with exhibits. It's uncrowded and sublimely quiet here. Dogs are not allowed on trails or the beach. *4150 Patricks Point Dr.* *Off U.S. 101, 5 miles north of town* *707/677–3570* *www.parks.ca.gov* *$8 parking.*

Restaurants

★ Larrupin' Cafe

$$$$ | **AMERICAN** | Set in a two-story house on a quiet country road north of town, this casually sophisticated restaurant—one of the North Coast's best places to eat—is often packed with people enjoying mesquite-grilled fresh seafood, beef brisket, St. Louis–style ribs, and vegetarian dishes. The garden setting and candlelight stir thoughts of romance. **Known for:** refined but friendly service; rosemary-crusted garlic, Cambozola cheese, and toast points appetizer; superb wine list. *Average main: $37* *1658 Patricks Point Dr.* *707/677–0230* *www.larrupin.com* *No lunch.*

Trinidad Bay Eatery & Gallery

$$ | **SEAFOOD** | A short stroll from Trinidad's bayfront, this unpretentious combination gallery and seafood-oriented restaurant cooks up tasty meals, starting with breakfast's buttermilk pancakes and Dungeness crab Benedict. Burgers, crab Louie salads, and clam chowder star at lunch; for dinner, consider the starter of ahi poke with crème fraîche, followed by lemon-caper calamari steak, red-coconut-curry scallops, or cioppino in chipotle broth. **Known for:** well-curated wine list; cioppino in chipotle broth; blackberry cobbler. *Average main: $21* *607 Parker St.* *707/677–3777* *www.trinidadeatery.com.*

Hotels

Lost Whale Inn

$$$ | **B&B/INN** | For a romantic, special-occasion getaway, look to this intimate, luxurious inn perched on a seaside bluff near Patrick's Point State Park. **Pros:** stunning ocean views; elaborate and delicious breakfast spread; spa services, in-room or out on the lawn, are offered. **Cons:** no pets allowed (but you'll find a few adorable pets residing at the inn); 2-night minimum on summer weekends; sometimes books up fully for weddings. *Rooms from: $300* *3452 Patricks Point Dr.* *707/677–3425* *www.lostwhaleinn.com* *8 rooms* *Free breakfast.*

Chapter 22

REDWOOD NATIONAL AND STATE PARKS

Updated by
Andrew Collins

Camping ★★★☆☆

Hotels ★★★★☆

Activities ★★★★☆

Scenery ★★★★★

Crowds ★★★★☆

WELCOME TO REDWOOD NATIONAL AND STATE PARKS

TOP REASONS TO GO

★ **Giant trees:** These mature coastal redwoods, which you can hike beneath in numerous groves throughout the park, are the tallest trees in the world.

★ **Hiking along the sea:** The park offers many miles of ocean access, including the Coastal Trail, which runs along the western edge of the park.

★ **Rare wildlife:** Mighty Roosevelt elk favor the park's flat prairie and open lands; seldom-seen black bears roam the backcountry; trout and salmon leap through streams; and Pacific gray whales swim along the coast during their spring and fall migrations.

★ **Stepping back in time:** Hike mossy and mysterious Fern Canyon Trail and explore a prehistoric scene of lush vegetation and giant ferns—a memorable scene in *Jurassic Park 2* was shot here.

★ **Getting off-the-grid:** Amid the majestic redwoods you're usually out of cell phone range and often free from crowds, offering a rare opportunity to disconnect.

1 **South.** The highlights of the parks' southern section are the hikes and scenic driving along Bald Hills Road, including the Lady Bird Johnson Grove, and the beautiful coastal scenery at Thomas H. Kuchel Visitor Center and the estuarial lagoons to the south. This section encompasses much of the original Redwood National Park and is where you'll find the small village of Orick, which has a gas station and a few other basic services.

2 **Middle.** Here in the span of park that extends from north of Orick to the Yurok tribal community of Klamath, you'll find some of the most magnificent and accessible stands of old-growth redwoods. Start your adventures at Prairie Creek Redwoods State Park's visitor center, from which several trails emanate. Also set aside time to explore the meadows inhabited by Roosevelt elk, the trail to Fern Canyon from Gold Bluffs Beach, and the gorgeous drives along Newton B. Drury Scenic Parkway and Klamath's Coastal Drive Loop

3 **North.** Anchored by the region's largest community, Crescent City, the park's northern third encompasses the rugged, pristine forests of Jedediah Smith Redwoods State Park, which is slightly inland, and Del Norte Coast Redwoods State Park, which also offers visitors the chance to visit stretches of windswept beaches, steep sea cliffs, and forested ridges. On a clear day it's postcard-perfect; with fog, it's mysterious and mesmerizing.

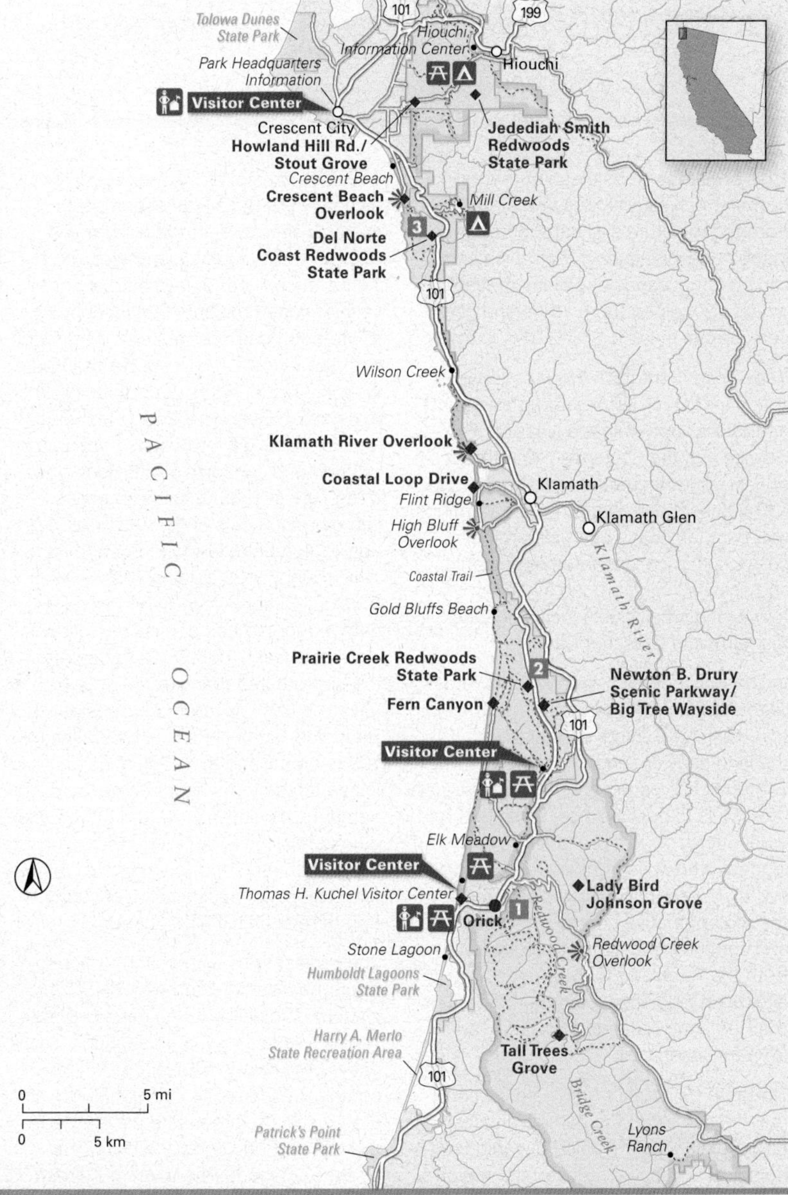

101
199
Tolowa Dunes State Park
Hiouchi Information Center
Hiouchi
Park Headquarters Information
Visitor Center
Crescent City
Howland Hill Rd./ Stout Grove
Jedediah Smith Redwoods State Park
Crescent Beach
Crescent Beach Overlook
Mill Creek
3
Del Norte Coast Redwoods State Park
Wilson Creek
PACIFIC OCEAN
Klamath River Overlook
Coastal Loop Drive
Klamath
Flint Ridge
Klamath Glen
High Bluff Overlook
Klamath River
Coastal Trail
Gold Bluffs Beach
Prairie Creek Redwoods State Park
2
Newton B. Drury Scenic Parkway/ Big Tree Wayside
Fern Canyon
Visitor Center
Elk Meadow
Visitor Center
Thomas H. Kuchel Visitor Center
Lady Bird Johnson Grove
Orick
1
Redwood Creek
Redwood Creek Overlook
Stone Lagoon
Humboldt Lagoons State Park
Harry A. Merlo State Recreation Area
Tall Trees Grove
Bridge Creek
0
5 mi
0
5 km
Patrick's Point State Park
Lyons Ranch

Soaring more than 375 feet high, California's coastal redwoods are miracles of efficiency—some have survived hundreds of years, a few more than two millennia.

These massive trees glean nutrients from the rich alluvial flats at their feet and from the moisture and nitrogen trapped in their uneven canopy. Their thick bark can hold thousands of gallons of water, which has helped them withstand centuries of fires.

Redwood differs from other national parks, in that it's administered by a joint partnership between the National Park Service and the California Department of Parks and Recreation. This sprawling 139,000-acre park system has a footprint that extends nearly 50 miles up the coast, encompasses three state parks, and snakes in and around a handful of towns and small cities, including Orick, Klamath, and Crescent City.

Indigenous people have been stewards of this special ecosystem for millennia—hunting, fishing, and foraging the land early on, and in more recent centuries harvesting timber from downed redwoods to build homes. Despite the cruel efforts of gold prospectors and loggers who in the 1850s arrived and swiftly began trying to eradicate them, the region's native communities survived and continue to this day to thrive here. Both the Yurok and Tolowa tribes have large land holdings within the borders of the Redwood National and State Parks (RNSP) system.

Northern California's gold rush immediately transformed the natural landscape. Large-scale logging, aided by rapid technological advances, reduced the region's 2 million acres of old-growth redwoods by nearly 90% in a little over a century—only about 5% of the old-growth forest remains today. Fortunately, by the 1910s, a small but determined conservation-minded minority began lobbying to protect these special trees, beginning with the formation of the Save-the-Redwoods League, whose efforts helped to establish Del Norte Coast Redwoods and Prairie Creek Redwoods state parks in 1925, and Jedediah Smith Redwoods State Park in 1939 (these successes came on the heels of the 1921 designation of Humboldt Redwoods State Park, which is about 30 miles southeast of Eureka and not part of RNSP). A huge demand for lumber, particularly following World War II, continued to deplete the unprotected tracts of forest, which led the federal government to establish Redwood National Park in 1968. Finally, in 1994, federal and state agencies officially joined forces to manage the newly designated Redwood National and State Parks, whose mission is both to preserve uncut old-growth redwood forest and to restore and replant some significant sections that have already been logged.

The easiest way to approach exploring the rather vast and complex RNSP system is to divide it geographically into North, Middle, and South sections, each of which contains at least one visitor center. Crescent City is in the North, as are two of the three state parks—Jedediah Smith Redwoods and Del Norte Coast Redwoods. The town of Klamath is

AVERAGE HIGH/LOW TEMPERATURES					
JAN.	FEB.	MAR.	APR.	MAY	JUNE
54/39	56/41	57/41	59/42	62/45	65/48
JULY	AUG.	SEPT.	OCT.	NOV.	DEC.
67/51	67/51	68/49	64/46	58/43	55/40

in the Middle section, as is Prairie Creek Redwoods State Park. And the village of Orick is in the South, which also contains much of the original national park, although you'll find other sections of it in the Middle and North sections, too. Additionally, there are four coastal parks just south of RNSP: Humboldt Lagoons State Park, Harry A. Merlo State Recreation Area, Big Lagoon Beach and County Park, and Patrick's Point State Park. U.S. 101 is the main north–south route through the park, but the northern section is also bisected by a short stretch of U.S. 199 east of Crescent City.

Some park attractions, scenic drives, and trails are in the national park, and others are in state parks, but as you explore, it's difficult—and not particularly important—to know which section you're in. Just adhere to the excellent map in the free park brochure and visitor guide newspaper, and you'll easily figure out where you're going and how to get around this magnificent preserve that aims to protect one of the world's oldest and largest living things.

Planning

When to Go

Campers and hikers flock to the park from mid-June to early September. The crowds disappear in winter, but you'll have to contend with frequent rains and nasty potholes and even occasional closures on side roads. Temperatures fluctuate widely: the foggy coastal lowland is much cooler than the higher-altitude interior.

The average annual rainfall is between 60 and 80 inches, most of it falling between November and April. During the dry summer, thick fog rolling in from the Pacific can veil the forests, providing the redwoods a large portion of their moisture intake.

Getting Here and Around

AIR

United Airlines flies a few times daily between San Francisco and the most practical gateway, California Redwood Coast–Humboldt County Airport, between Trinidad and Arcata, about 16 miles north of Eureka. The regional carrier Contour offers daily service from Oakland to Del Norte County Regional Airport in Crescent City. Another option is Oregon's Rogue Valley International Medford Airport, which is served by Alaska, Allegiant, American, Delta, and United, and is about a two-hour drive from the northern end of the park in Crescent City.

CAR

U.S. 101 runs north–south nearly the entire length of the park. You can access all the main park roads via U.S. 101 and U.S. 199, which runs east–west through the park's northern portion. Many roads within the park aren't paved, and winter rains can turn them into obstacle courses; sometimes they're closed completely. Motor homes/RVs and trailers aren't permitted on some routes. The drive from San Francisco to the park's southern end takes about six hours via U.S. 101. From Portland it takes roughly the same

Redwood in One Day

From Crescent City head south on U.S. 101, pausing for a stroll overlooking the ocean either at **Crescent Beach** or a little farther south with a short stroll along the **Yurok Loop Trail.** A mile south of Klamath, detour onto the 9-mile-long, narrow, and mostly unpaved **Coastal Drive** loop. Along the way, you'll pass the old **Douglas Memorial Bridge,** destroyed in the 1964 flood. Coastal Drive turns south above Flint Ridge. In less than a mile you'll reach the **World War II B-71 Radar Station,** which looks like a farmhouse, its disguise in the 1940s. Continue south to the intersection with Alder Camp Road, stopping at the **High Bluff Overlook**—keep an eye out for whales during the winter and spring migrations.

Back on U.S. 101, head south to reach **Newton B. Drury Scenic Parkway,** a 10-mile drive through one of the park's best and most accessible expanses of old-growth redwood forest. Stop at **Prairie Creek Visitor Center,** housed in a small redwood lodge. Enjoy a picnic lunch and an engaging tactile walk in a grove behind the lodge on the Revelation Trail, which was designed for vision-impaired visitors, or if you have an hour or two, hike the stunning 3½-mile **Prairie Creek–Big Tree–Cathedral Trees Loop.** Return to U.S. 101, and turn west on mostly unpaved **Davison Road,** checking out **Elk Meadow** on your left, where you'll sometimes see a portion of the park's Roosevelt elk herd roaming about. In about 30 minutes you'll curve right to **Gold Bluffs Beach.** Continue north a short way and make the hike into lush and spectacular **Fern Canyon.** Return to U.S. 101, and drive south to the turnoff onto **Bald Hills Road,** and follow it for 2 miles to the **Lady Bird Johnson Grove Nature Loop Trail.** Take the footbridge to the easy 1.4-mile loop, which follows an old logging road through a mature redwood forest. If you have an extra hour, continue south on Bald Hills Road to **Redwood Creek Overlook** or even all the way to 3,097-foot **Schoolhouse Peak,** before backtracking to U.S. 101 and driving south through Orick to the **Thomas H. Kuchel Visitor Center.** This is a beautiful spot late in the day to watch the sunset over the ocean. Note that if you're approaching the park from Trinidad or Eureka, it's easy to undertake this itinerary in reverse. ■ TIP→ **Motor homes/RVs and trailers are not allowed on Coastal Drive or Davison Road and are not advised on Bald Hills Road. Conditions on these roads can sometimes lead to closures or the requirement of high-clearance vehicles—check with the visitor centers before you set out.**

amount of time to reach the park's northern section via Interstate 5 to U.S. 199. ■ TIP→ **Don't rely solely on GPS, which is inaccurate in parts of the park; closely consult official park maps.**

Park Essentials

PARK FEES AND PERMITS

Admission to Redwood National Park is free; a few areas in the state parks collect day-use fees of $8, including the Gold Bluffs Beach and Fern Canyon sections of Prairie Creek Redwoods State Park, and the day-use areas accessed via the campground entrances in Jedediah Smith and Del Norte Coast state parks (the fee for camping overnight is $35). To visit the popular Tall Trees Grove, you must get a free permit at the Kuchel Visitor Center in Orick. Free permits, available at the Kuchel, Crescent City, and (summer only) Hiouchi visitor centers, are needed to stay at all designated backcountry camps.

PARK HOURS

The park is open year-round, 24 hours a day.

CELL PHONE RECEPTION

It's difficult to pick up a signal in much of the park, especially in the camping areas and on many hiking trails. The Prairie Creek and Jedediah Smith visitor centers have pay phones.

Hotels

The only lodgings within park grounds are the Elk Meadow Cabins, near Prairie Creek Redwoods Visitor Center. Orick, to the south of Elk Meadow, and Klamath, to the north, have basic motels, and in Klamath there's also the charming and historic Requa Inn. Elegant Victorian inns, seaside motels, and fully equipped vacation rentals are among the options in Crescent City to the north, and Eureka and to a more limited extent Trinidad and Arcata to the south. In summer, try to book at least a week ahead at lodgings near the park.

Restaurants

The park has no restaurants, but Eureka and Arcata have diverse dining establishments—everything from hip oyster bars to some surprisingly good ethnic restaurants. The dining options are more limited, though decent, in Crescent City and Trinidad, and there are just a couple of very basic options in Klamath and tiny Orick. Most small-town restaurants close early, around 7:30 or 8 pm.

Hotel and restaurant reviews have been shortened. For full information visit Fodors.com. Hotel prices are the lowest cost of a standard double room in high season. Restaurant prices are the average cost of a main course at dinner, or if dinner is not served, at lunch

What It Costs

	$	$$	$$$	$$$$
RESTAURANTS				
	under $17	$17–$26	$27–$36	over $36
HOTELS				
	under $150	$150–$250	$251–$350	over $350

Visitor Information

CONTACTS Redwood National and State Parks Headquarters. ✉ *1111 2nd St., Crescent City* ☎ *707/465–7306* 🌐 *www.nps.gov/redw*.

South

19 miles north of Trinidad, 8 miles south of Prairie Creek Visitor Center, 44 miles south of Crescent City.

This is the section of the park system that you'll reach if driving up the coast from Eureka and Trinidad, and it's home to one of the largest visitor information resources, the beachfront Thomas H. Kuchel Visitor Center, which is on U.S. 101 shortly after you enter the park. For the purposes of this chapter, this section includes the town of Orick and everything else south of the turnoff onto Bald Hills Road, which leads to some of the largest stands of redwoods in the park, including the Lady Bird Johnson and Tall Trees groves.

Sights

SCENIC DRIVES

Bald Hills Road

SCENIC DRIVE | A winding, steep, and dramatic road that stretches into the park's southernmost section and highest elevations, Bald Hills Road accesses some great hikes—Lady Bird Johnson Grove and Lyons Ranch among them—as well as the access road to the Tall Trees Grove. But it's also wondrously scenic route all on its own, passing through sometimes misty patch of redwoods before entering a stretch of open meadows with wildflowers in spring and the chance to see Roosevelt elk and bears any time of year. Do stop at Redwood Creek Overlook, a 2,100-foot elevation pullout at mile 6.6. Bald Hills Road is paved for the first 13 miles. It continues another 4 miles unpaved to the park's southern boundary, and it's then possible to continue another 20 miles or so to the small village of Weitchpec and then onward inland toward Redding or Yreka. ✉ *Off U.S. 101, Orick.*

TRAILS

★ Lady Bird Johnson Grove Trail

TRAIL | One of the park's most accessible spots to view big trees, this impressive grove just a short drive northeast of Orick was dedicated by, and named for, the former first lady. A level 1.4-mile nature loop crosses a neat old wooden footbridge and follows an old logging road through this often mist-shrouded forest of redwoods. *Easy.* ✉ *Orick* ✢ *Trailhead: Bald Hills Rd., 2 miles east of U.S. 101.*

Lyons Ranch Trail

TRAIL | You won't see redwoods on this open upper-elevation 3.7-mile round-trip trail, but on summer days when the coast is socked in with rain or fog, an adventure to this typically sunny prairie at the park's southeastern boundary is highly rewarding, as is the steep—but slow—17-mile drive on Bald Hills Road. The trail leads hikers to a former sheep and cattle ranch with a few interesting old outbuildings that date to the turn-of-the-20th-century. *Moderate.* ✉ *Redwood National Park* ✢ *Trailhead: Off Bald Hills Rd., 17 miles south of U.S. 101.*

Tall Trees Trail

TRAIL | Although every bit as beautiful as the other stands of old-growth redwood in the park, getting to this roughly 30-acre grove requires a steep and windy 14-mile drive, followed by a somewhat rigorous 4-mile round-trip hike that involves an 800-foot descent into the Redwood Creek flood plain. Additionally, you must obtain a free permit at the Kuchel Visitor Center to access the unpaved road off of Bald Hills Road. Rangers dispense a limited number per day, first come, first served. No trailers or RVs. Given the effort required, if you don't have a lot of time, it's best to save this one for your second or third visit. *Moderate.* ✉ *Orick* ✢ *Trailhead: Tall Trees Access Rd., off Bald Hills Rd., 7 miles from U.S. 101, then 6½ miles to trailhead.*

VISITOR CENTER

★ Thomas H. Kuchel Visitor Center

INFO CENTER | **FAMILY** | The park's southern section contains this largest and best of the Redwoods visitor centers. Rangers here dispense brochures, advice, and free permits to drive up the access road to Tall Trees Grove. Whale-watchers find the center's deck an excellent observation point, and bird-watchers enjoy the nearby Freshwater Lagoon, a popular layover for migrating waterfowl. Many of the center's exhibits are hands-on and kid-friendly. ✉ *U.S. 101, Orick* ✢ *Redwood Creek Beach County Park* ☎ *707/465–7765* 🌐 *www.nps.gov/redw.*

Middle

8 miles north of Thomas H. Kuchel Visitor Center, 34 miles south of Crescent City.

Encompassing a relatively narrow band of coastal forest that extends north of Orick (starting around Elk Meadow) to north of Klamath (up to Requa Road), the park's middle section is home to one of the most magical places to stroll through a redwood forest, Prairie Creek State Park, which is laced with both easy and challenging trails and traversed by the stunning Newton B. Drury Scenic Parkway. Near the visitor center and in nearby Elk Meadow, you can often view herds of Roosevelt elk. The state park extends west to famously spectacular Gold Bluffs Beach and Fern Canyon on the coast. The middle section's other highlight are the sections of the park along both sides of the Klamath River, including Coastal Drive and Klamath River Overlook.

Sights

SCENIC DRIVES

★ Coastal Drive Loop

SCENIC DRIVE | The 9-mile, narrow, and partially unpaved Coastal Drive Loop takes about 45 minutes to traverse. Weaving through stands of redwoods, the road yields close-up views of the Klamath River and expansive panoramas of the Pacific. Recurring landslides have closed sections of the original road; this loop, closed to trailers and RVs, is all that remains. Hikers access the Flint Ridge section of the Coastal Trail off the drive. ✉ *Klamath* ⊕ *Off Klamath Beach Rd. exit from U.S. 101.*

★ Newton B. Drury Scenic Parkway

SCENIC DRIVE | This paved 10-mile route threads through Prairie Creek Redwoods State Park and old-growth redwoods. It's open to all noncommercial vehicles. Great stops along the route include the 0.8-mile walk to Big Tree Wayside and observing Roosevelt elk in the prairie—both of these are near the Prairie Creek Visitor Center. ✉ *Orick* ⊕ *Entrances off U.S. 101 about 5 miles south of Klamath and 5 miles north of Orick.*

SCENIC STOPS

★ Fern Canyon

CANYON | Enter another world and be surrounded by 50-foot canyon walls covered with sword, deer, and five-finger ferns. Allow an hour to explore the ¼-mile-long vertical garden along a 0.7-mile loop. From the northern end of Gold Bluffs Beach it's an easy walk, although you'll have to wade across or scamper along planks that traverse a small stream several times (in addition to driving across a couple of streams on the way to the parking area). But the lush, otherworldly surroundings, which appeared in *Jurassic Park 2,* are a must-see when creeks aren't running too high. Motor homes/RVs and all trailers are prohibited. You can also hike to the canyon from Prairie Creek Visitor Center along the challenging West Ridge–Friendship Ridge–James Irvine Loop, 12½ miles round-trip. ✉ *Orick* ⊕ *2¾ miles north of Orick, take Davison Rd. northwest off U.S. 101 and follow signs to Gold Bluffs Beach.*

Klamath River Overlook

VIEWPOINT | This grassy, windswept bluff rises 650 feet above the confluence of the Klamath River and the Pacific. It's one of the best spots in the park for spying migratory whales in early winter and late spring, and it accesses a section of the Coastal Trail. Warm days are ideal for picnicking at one of the tables. ✉ *End of Requa Rd., Klamath* ⊕ *2¼ miles west of U.S. 101.*

TRAILS

★ Coastal Trail

TRAIL | This gorgeous 70-mile trail, much of it along dramatic bluffs high above the crashing surf, can be tackled in both short, relatively easy sections and longer, strenuous spans that entail backcountry overnight camping. Here are some of the most alluring smaller sections, listed in order from north to south, which are

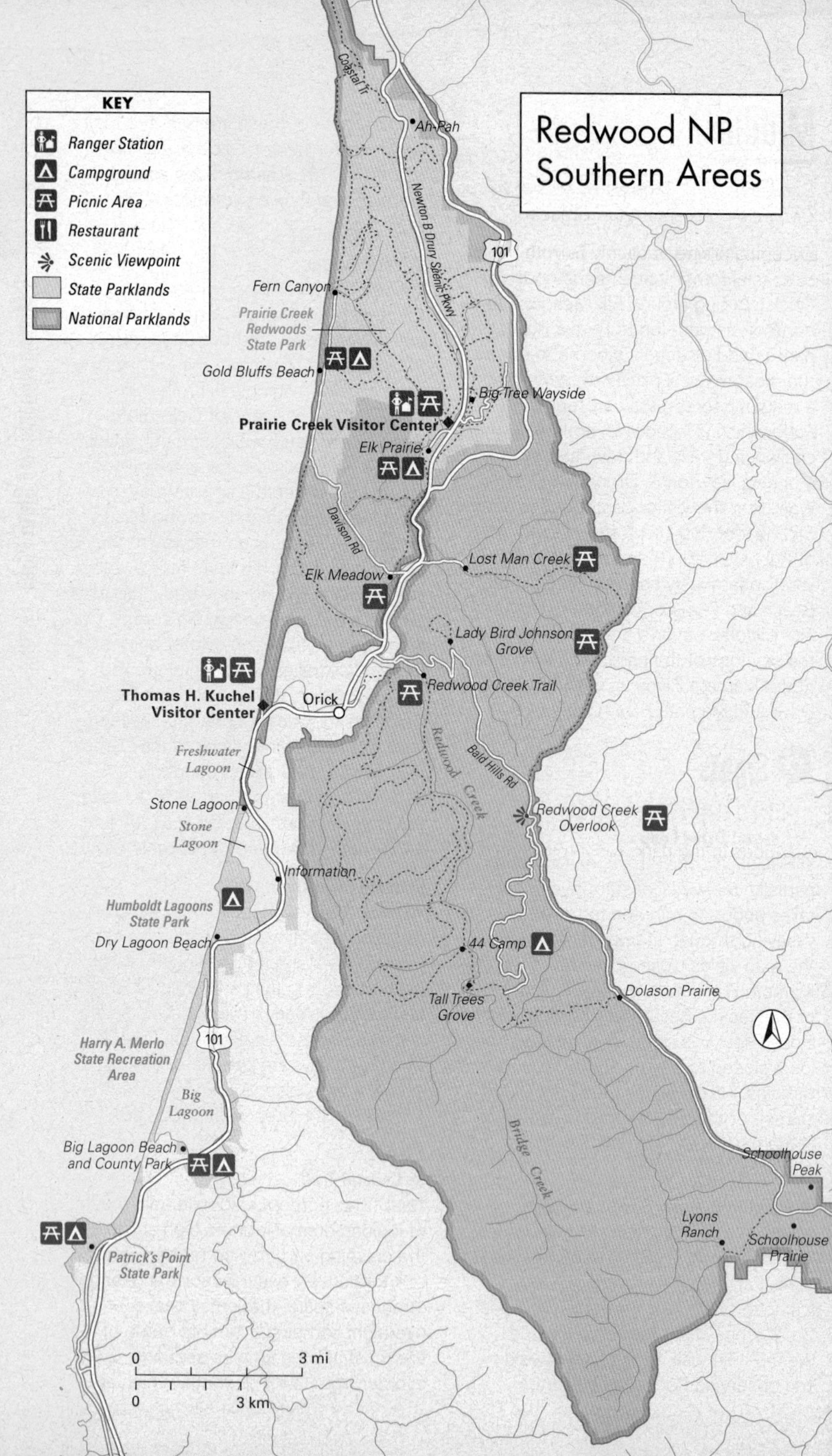

Redwood NP
Southern Areas
KEY
Ranger Station
Campground
Picnic Area
Restaurant
Scenic Viewpoint
State Parklands
National Parklands
Coastal Tr
Ah-Pah
Newton B Drury Scenic Pkwy
101
Fern Canyon
Prairie Creek Redwoods State Park
Gold Bluffs Beach
Big Tree Wayside
Prairie Creek Visitor Center
Elk Prairie
Davison Rd
Lost Man Creek
Elk Meadow
Lady Bird Johnson Grove
Thomas H. Kuchel Visitor Center
Orick
Redwood Creek Trail
Redwood Creek
Bald Hills Rd
Freshwater Lagoon
Stone Lagoon
Stone Lagoon
Redwood Creek Overlook
Information
Humboldt Lagoons State Park
Dry Lagoon Beach
44 Camp
Tall Trees Grove
Dolason Prairie
Harry A. Merlo State Recreation Area
Big Lagoon
Big Lagoon Beach and County Park
Bridge Creek
Schoolhouse Peak
Lyons Ranch
Schoolhouse Prairie
Patrick's Point State Park
0
3 mi
0
3 km

accessible at well-marked trailheads. The moderate-to-difficult **DeMartin section** (accessed from mile marker 15.6 on U.S. 101) leads south past 6 miles of old-growth redwoods and through sweeping prairie. It connects with the moderate 5½-mile-long **Klamath section,** which proceeds south from Wilson Creek Picnic Area to Klamath River Overlook, with a short detour to Hidden Beach and its tide pools, providing coastal views and whale-watching opportunities. If you're up for a real workout, hike the brutally difficult but stunning **Flint Ridge section** (accessed from the Old Douglas Memorial Bridge Site on Klamath Beach Rd.), with its 4½ miles of steep grades and numerous switchbacks past Marshall Pond and through stands of old-growth redwoods. There are additional spans at the northern and southern ends of the park. *Moderate.* ✉ *Klamath.*

★ Prairie Creek–Big Tree–Cathedral Trees Loop

TRAIL | **FAMILY** | This flat, well-maintained 3½-mile loop starts and ends at the Prairie Creek Visitor Center and passes beneath some of the most awe-inspiring redwoods in the park. The 1-mile section along the Prairie Creek Trail fringes a babbling brook; you then cross Newton B. Drury Scenic Parkway, turn south onto the Cathedral Trees Trail and make a short detour along the 0.3-mile Big Tree Loop before meandering south and west through yet more gorgeous old-growth forest. Options for extending your hike include walking 1½ miles up Cal-Barrel Road (an old, unpaved logging route), and then looping back 2 miles on the Rhododendron Trail to rejoin Cathedral Trees. *Easy–Moderate.* ✉ *Orick* ✣ *Trailhead: Prairie Creek Visitor Center.*

Trillium Falls Trail

TRAIL | **FAMILY** | On this lush trek through a mix of old-growth redwoods, ferns, smaller deciduous trees, and some clusters of trillium flowers, you'll encounter the pretty cascades that give the hike its name after the first ½ mile. It's worth continuing on, though, and making the full 2.8-mile loop, as the southern end of the hike offers the best views of soaring redwoods. Herds of elk sometimes roam in the meadow by the trailhead. *Easy–Moderate.* ✉ *Orick* ✣ *Trailhead: Elk Meadow parking lot, Davison Rd., just west of U.S. 101.*

VISITOR CENTER

★ Prairie Creek Visitor Center

INFO CENTER | **FAMILY** | A massive stone fireplace anchors this small redwood lodge with wildlife displays that include a section of a tree a young elk died beside. Because of the peculiar way the redwood grew around the elk's skull, the tree appears to have antlers. The center has information about interpretive programs as well as a gift shop, a picnic area, restrooms, and exhibits on flora and fauna. Roosevelt elk often roam the vast field adjacent to the center, and several trailheads begin nearby. Stretch your legs with an easy stroll along **Revelation Trail,** a short loop that starts behind the lodge. ✉ *Prairie Creek Rd., Orick* ✣ *Off southern end of Newton B. Drury Scenic Pkwy.* ☎ *707/488–2039* 🌐 *www.nps.gov/redw.*

Hotels

★ Elk Meadow Cabins

$$$ | **B&B/INN** | **FAMILY** | From the porches of these beautifully restored 1,200-square-foot former mill workers' cottages, guests often see Roosevelt elk meandering in the meadows—or even their backyards. **Pros:** elks frequently congregate on the grounds; perfect for groups or families; adjacent to stunning Prairie Creek State Park. **Cons:** a bit of a drive from most area restaurants; expensive for just two occupants, though reasonable for families or groups; furnishings are comfortable but plain. $ *Rooms from: $314* ✉ *7 Valley Green Camp Rd., off U.S. 101 north of Davison Rd., Orick* ☎ *707/488–2222, 866/733–9637* 🌐 *www.elkmeadowcabins.com* *9 cabins* *No meals.*

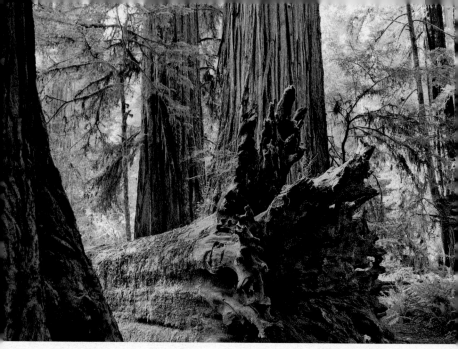

Redwood trees, and the moss that often coats them, grow best in damp, shady environments.

North

34 miles north of Prairie Creek Redwoods State Park, 84 miles north of Eureka, 73 miles south of Grants Pass, OR, 133 miles south of Coos Bay, OR.

Home to the small city of Crescent City, which is also where you'll find the Redwood National and State Parks headquarters, the North is home to two state parks: Del Norte Redwoods and Jedediah Smith Redwoods. Del Norte lies 5 miles south of Crescent City on U.S. 101 and contains 15 memorial redwood groves and 8 miles of pristine coastline, which you can most easily access at Crescent Beach and Wilson Beach. Jedediah Smith is 5 miles east of Crescent City on U.S. 199 and is home to the legendary Stout Memorial Grove, along with some 20 miles of hiking and nature trails. The park is named after a trapper who in 1826 became the first white man to explore Northern California's interior. If coming from interior Oregon, this is your first chance to drive and hike among stands of soaring redwoods.

Sights

SCENIC DRIVES

★ Howland Hill Road through Stout Grove

SCENIC DRIVE | Take your time as you drive this 10-mile route along Mill Creek, which meanders within inches of the hulking trunks of old-growth redwoods and past the Smith River. Trailers and RVs are prohibited on this route, which is unpaved but well maintained for the roughly 7 miles that pass through Jedediah Smith Redwoods State Park. There are several pull-outs along the route, including the trailheads for the Stout Grove and Boy Scout Tree trails. You can enter either from downtown Crescent Road or off U.S. 199, via South Fork and Douglas Park Roads. ✣ *Western access from Elk Valley Rd. in Crescent City.*

Plants and Wildlife in Redwood

Coast redwoods, the world's tallest trees, grow in the moist, temperate climate of California's North Coast. The current record holder, named Hyperion, tops out at 380 feet and was found in the Redwood Creek watershed in 2006. These ancient giants thrive in an environment that exists in only a few hundred coastal miles along the Pacific Ocean. They commonly live 600 years—though some have been around for more than 2,000 years.

Diverse, Complex

A healthy redwood forest is diverse and includes Douglas firs, western hemlocks, tan oaks, and madrone trees. The complex soils of the forest floor support a profusion of ferns, mosses, and fungi, along with numerous shrubs and berry bushes. In spring, California rhododendron bloom all over, providing a dazzling purple and pink contrast to the dense greenery.

Old-Growth Forests

Redwood National and State parks hold nearly 50% of California's old-growth redwood forests, but only about a third of the forests in the park are old-growth. Of the original 3,125 square miles (2 million acres) in the Redwoods Historic Range, only 4% survived logging that began in 1850. A quarter of these trees are privately owned and on managed land. The rest are on public tracts.

Wildlife Species

In the park's backcountry, you might spot mountain lions, black bears, black-tailed deer, river otters, beavers, and minks. Roosevelt elk roam the flatlands, and the rivers and streams teem with salmon and trout. Gray whales, seals, and sea lions cavort near the coastline. More than 280 species of birds have been recorded in the park, which is located along the Pacific Flyway. A plan is also underway to reintroduce California condors to the park by 2022.

SCENIC STOPS

Crescent Beach Overlook

VIEWPOINT | The scenery here includes views of the ocean and, in the distance, Crescent City and its working harbor. In balmy weather this is a great place for a picnic. You may spot migrating gray whales between November and April. ✉ *Enderts Beach Rd.* ✥ *4½ miles south of Crescent City.*

TRAILS

★ Boy Scout Tree Trail

TRAIL | This is the most challenging but also the most rewarding of the hikes along Howland Hill Road. Give yourself about three hours to complete this 5.6-mile round-trip trek to verdant Fern Falls, as the old-growth redwoods along this tranquil trek are absolutely magnificent. If you don't have as much time, the easy ½-mile-loop Stout Grove Trail is a good alternative along this route. *Moderate.* ✉ *Crescent City* ✥ *Trailhead: Howland Hill Rd., 3.7 miles east of Elk Valley Rd.*

Simpson-Reed Trail

TRAIL | **FAMILY** | Of the redwood hikes in Jedediah Smith Redwoods State Park, this flat and easy 1-mile loop through an incredibly dense forest is the best fit if you have only an hour or so. The trailhead is a short hop off U.S. 199 between Crescent City and Hiouchi, and interpretative signs tell a bit about the diverse flora—you'll encounter hemlocks, huckleberries, and lots and lots of ferns along this route. *Easy.* ✉ *Crescent City* ✥ *Trailhead: Walker Rd., off U.S. 199, 2.5 miles east of U.S. 101.*

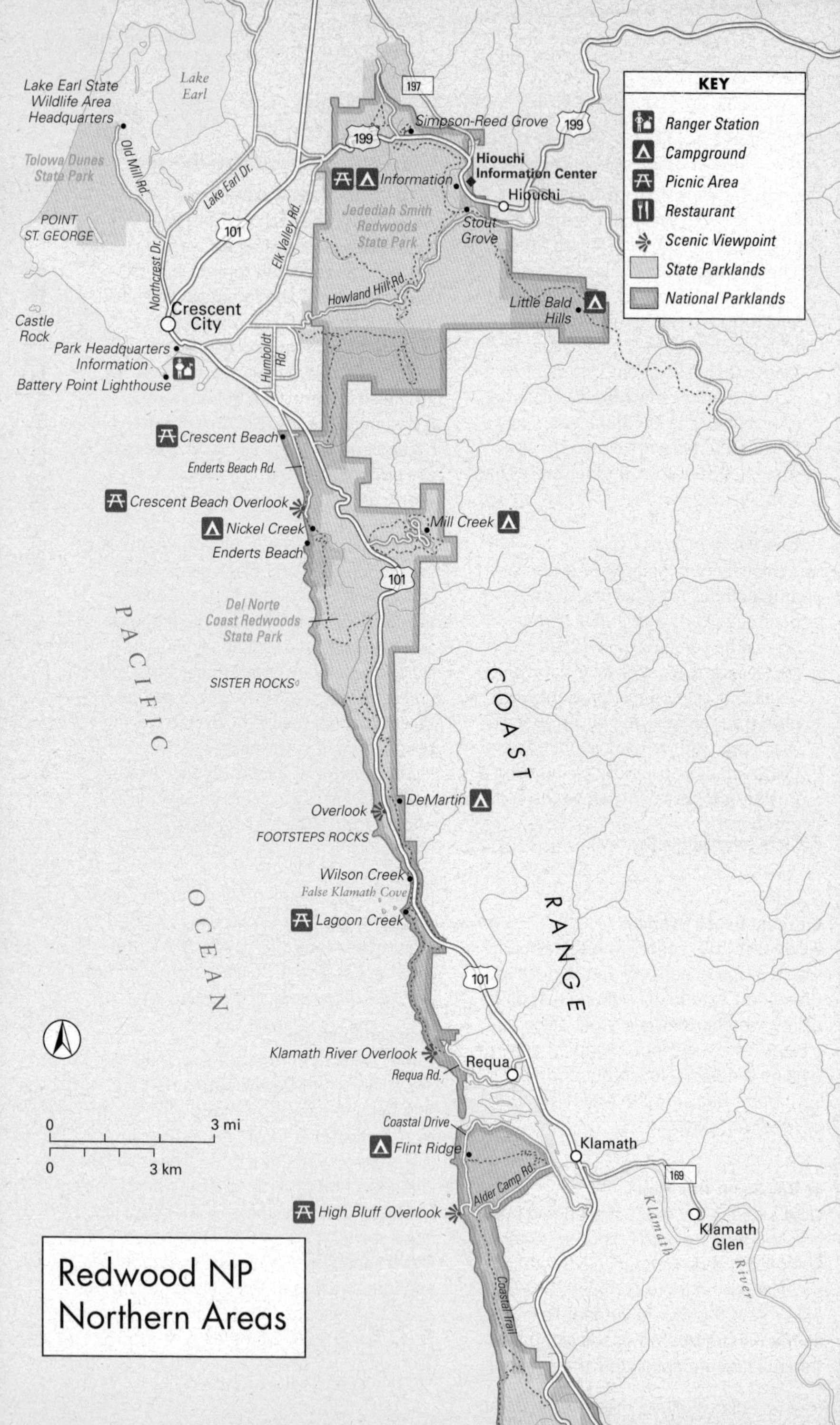
Redwood NP
Northern Areas
KEY
Ranger Station
Campground
Picnic Area
Restaurant
Scenic Viewpoint
State Parklands
National Parklands
Lake Earl State
Wildlife Area
Headquarters
Lake
Earl
Tolowa Dunes
State Park
Old Mill Rd.
POINT
ST. GEORGE
Lake Earl Dr.
Northcrest Dr.
Elk Valley Rd.
Castle
Rock
Crescent
City
Park Headquarters
Information
Battery Point Lighthouse
Humboldt
Rd.
197
199
Simpson-Reed Grove
Hiouchi
Information Center
Hiouchi
Information
Jedediah Smith
Redwoods
State Park
Stout
Grove
Howland Hill Rd.
Little Bald
Hills
Crescent Beach
Enderts Beach Rd.
Crescent Beach Overlook
Nickel Creek
Enderts Beach
Mill Creek
101
Del Norte
Coast Redwoods
State Park
SISTER ROCKS
PACIFIC
OCEAN
COAST
RANGE
DeMartin
Overlook
FOOTSTEPS ROCKS
Wilson Creek
False Klamath Cove
Lagoon Creek
Klamath River Overlook
Requa
Requa Rd.
Coastal Drive
Flint Ridge
Klamath
169
Alder Camp Rd.
High Bluff Overlook
Klamath Glen
Klamath
River
Coastal Trail
0
3 mi
0
3 km

Yurok Loop Trail

BEACH—SIGHT | FAMILY | Providing a lovely opportunity to stretch your legs and breathe in the fresh sea air, this 1.2-mile loop starts at the Lagoon Creek Picnic Area on U.S. 101, at the very southern end of Del Norte Coast Redwoods State Park, and follows a short stretch of the California Coastal Trail. It then forks off toward False Klamath Cove, providing sweeping views of the ocean—keep an eye out for shore birds and migrating whales. Just to the north of False Klamath Cove, there's great beachcombing to be had along Wilson Creek Beach. *Easy. ✉ Klamath ✥ Trailhead: Lagoon Creek Picnic Area on U.S. 101, 6.5 miles north of Klamath.*

VISITOR CENTERS

Crescent City Information Center

INFO CENTER | At the park's headquarters, this downtown Redding visitor center with a gift shop and picnic area is the main information stop if you're approaching the Redwoods from the north. *✉ 1111 2nd St., Crescent City ☎ 707/465–7335 🌐 www.nps.gov/redw ⏲ Closed Tues. and Wed. in Nov.–Mar.*

Hiouchi Information Center

INFO CENTER | This small center at Jedediah Smith Redwoods State Park has exhibits about the area flora and fauna and screens a 12-minute park film. A starting point for ranger programs, the center has restrooms and a picnic area. *✉ U.S. 199 ✥ Opposite Jedediah Smith Campground, 9 miles east of Crescent City ☎ 707/458–3294 🌐 www.nps.gov/redw.*

Jedediah Smith Visitor Center

INFO CENTER | Adjacent to the Jedediah Smith Redwoods State Park main campground, this seasonal center has information about ranger-led walks and evening campfire programs. Also here are nature and history exhibits, a gift shop, and a picnic area. *✉ U.S. 199, Hiouchi ✥ At Jedediah Smith Campground ☎ 707/458–3496 🌐 www.nps.gov/redw ⏲ Closed Oct.–May.*

Activities

BIKING

Besides the roadways, you can bike on several trails, many of them along former logging roads. Best bets include the 11-mile Lost Man Creek Trail, which begins 3 miles north of Orick; the 12-mile round-trip Coastal Trail (Last Chance Section), which starts at the southern end of Enderts Beach Road and becomes steep and narrow as it travels through dense slopes of foggy redwood forests; and the 19-mile, single-track Ossagon Trail Loop in Prairie Creek Redwoods State Park, on which you're likely to see elk as you cruise through redwoods before coasting ocean side toward the end.

■ TIP→ You can rent electric bikes, which are especially nice for riding the hilly Lost Man Creek Trail, from Redwood Adventures (see Hiking).

BIRD-WATCHING

Many rare and striking winged specimens inhabit the area, including chestnut-backed chickadees, brown pelicans, great blue herons, pileated woodpeckers, northern spotted owls, and marbled murrelets. By 2022, California condors are planned to be reintroduced to the park.

CAMPING

Within a 30-minute drive of Redwood National and State parks, you'll find roughly 60 public and private camping facilities. None of the primitive or backcountry areas in Redwood—DeMartin, Elam Creek, Flint Ridge, 44 Camp, Little Bald Hills, or Redwood Creek—is a drive-in site, although Flint Ridge is just a ¼-mile from the road. You must obtain a free permit from the Kuchel or Hiouchi visitor centers before camping in these areas; all are first come, first served. Bring your own drinking water—there are no sources at the sites.

Redwood has four developed, drive-in campgrounds—Elk Prairie, Gold Bluffs Beach, Jedediah Smith, and Mill

Creek, all of them within the state-park boundaries. None has RV hookups, but Jedediah Smith and Mill Creek have dump stations. Fees are $35 nightly. For reservations, contact ☎ *800/444–7275* or 🌐 *www.reserveamerica.com*.

DEVELOPED CAMPGROUNDS

Elk Prairie Campground. Roosevelt elk frequent this popular campground adjacent to a prairie and old-growth redwoods. ✉ *Newton B. Drury Scenic Pkwy., Prairie Creek Redwoods State Park.*

Gold Bluffs Beach Campground. You can camp in tents right on the beach at this Prairie Creek Redwoods State Park campground near Fern Canyon. ✉ *End of Davison Rd., off U.S. 101.*

Jedediah Smith Campground. This is one of the few places to camp—in tents or RVs—within groves of old-growth redwood forest. ✉ *9 miles east of Crescent City on U.S. 199.*

Mill Creek Campground. Redwoods tower over large Mill Creek, in the remote and quiet interior of Del Norte Coast Redwoods State Park. Open mid-May–September. ✉ *U.S. 101, 7 miles southeast of Crescent City.*

EDUCATIONAL PROGRAMS

RANGER PROGRAMS

All summer long, ranger-led programs explore the mysteries of both the redwoods and the sea. Topics include how the trees grow from fleck-size seeds to towering giants, what causes those weird fungi on old stumps, why the ocean fog is so important to redwoods, and exactly what those green-tentacled creatures are that float in tide pools. Campfire programs can include slide shows, storytelling, music, and games. Check with visitor centers for offerings and times.

Junior Ranger Program

LOCAL SPORTS | **FAMILY** | Kids earn a badge by completing activity books, which are available from visitor centers. Additionally, rangers lead programs for kids throughout the summer, including nature walks and lessons in bird identification and outdoor survival.

Ranger Talks

LOCAL SPORTS | From mid-May through mid-September, state park rangers regularly lead discussions on the redwoods, tide pools, geology, and Native American culture. Check schedules at the visitor centers.

Redwood EdVentures

TOUR—SIGHT | **FAMILY** | Fun and engaging Redwood EdVentures nature scavenger hunts for kids, called Quests, include ones in the park. Visit the website for "treasure map" PDFs detailing the Quests, which typically take no more than an hour. Participants receive a patch upon completion. 🌐 *www.redwood-edventures.org.*

FISHING

Deep-sea and freshwater fishing are popular here. Anglers often stake out sections of the Klamath and Smith rivers seeking salmon and trout. A single state license (🌐 *www.wildlife.ca.gov/licensing/fishing*) covers both ocean and river fishing. A two-day license costs about $27. You can go crabbing and clamming on the coast, but check the tides carefully: rip currents and sneaker waves can be deadly. No license is needed to fish from the long B Street Pier in Crescent City.

HIKING

The park has miles of trails, including quite a few short, level treks just off the main roads and easily managed even if you have limited experience. Avid hikers will find plenty of fantastic rambles with serious elevation gains and thrilling flora and fauna. Note that some of the park's most delightful treks don't actually pass any big trees but rather hug Northern California's pristine and wild shoreline. Most famous is the Coastal Trail, which runs for about 70 miles from the northern to southern ends of the park.

★ Redwood Adventures

HIKING/WALKING | Operated by and run out of the office of Elk Meadow Cabins, this small agency with a highly knowledgeable, passionate staff offers half- and full-day hikes through some of the park's most stunning stands of redwoods, as well as adventures exploring coastal tidepools and Fern Canyon. Backpacking with overnight camping options are also available, as are electric-bike rentals, which are great for touring around the park, especially the Lost Man Creek Trail. ✉ *7 Valley Green Camp Rd., Orick* ☎ *866/733–9637* 🌐 *www.redwoodadventures.com.*

KAYAKING

With many miles of often shallow rivers, streams, and estuarial lagoons, kayaking is a popular pastime in the park, especially in the southern end of the park near Kuchel Visitor Center, on Arcata and Humboldt bays near Eureka, up north along the Klamath and Smith rivers, and on the ocean in Crescent City.

Humboats Kayak Adventures

KAYAKING | You can rent kayaks and book kayaking tours that from December to June include whale-watching trips. Half-day river kayaking trips pass beneath massive redwoods; the whale-watching outings get you close enough for good photos. ✉ *Woodley Island Marina, 601 Startare Dr., Dock A, Eureka* ☎ *707/443–5157* 🌐 *www.humboats.com* 🎫 *From $30 rentals, $55 tours.*

★ Kayak Trinidad

KAYAKING | This respected outfitter rents kayaks and stand-up paddleboards, good for touring the beautiful estuarial and freshwater lagoons of Humboldt Lagoons State Park or sea kayaking out at sea. You can also book guided half-day paddles around Big Lagoon and Stone Lagoon, and along Trinidad Bay. The lagoons are stunning. Herds of Roosevelt elk sometimes traipse along the shoreline of Big Lagoon; raptors, herons, and waterfowl abound in both lagoons; and you can paddle across Stone Lagoon to a spectacular secluded Pacific-view beach. ✉ *Trinidad* ☎ *707/329–0085* 🌐 *www.kayaktrinidad.com.*

WHALE-WATCHING

Good vantage points for whale-watching include Crescent Beach Overlook, the Kuchel Visitor Center in Orick, points along the Coastal Trail, Klamath Beach Road, and Klamath River Overlook. From late November through January is the best time to see their southward migrations; from February through April the whales return, usually passing closer to shore.

What's Nearby

Arcata

8 miles north of Eureka, 33 miles south of Kuchel Visitor Center.

Begun in 1850 as a base camp for miners and lumberjacks, Arcata is today an artsy, progressive college town. Activity centers on the grassy Arcata Plaza, which is surrounded by restored buildings containing funky bars, cafés, and indie shops.

GETTING HERE AND AROUND

Set along U.S. 101, Arcata also lies just south of the junction with the main road, Highway 299, that connects the region to the east with Redding and Interstate 5. Highway 299 is a windy, hilly route—allow about two hours and 45 minutes to make the 135-mile drive to Redding.

ESSENTIALS

VISITOR INFORMATION Arcata Humboldt Visitor Center. ✉ *1635 Heindon Rd., Arcata* ☎ *707/822–3619* 🌐 *www.arcatachamber.com.*

Restaurants

Cafe Brio

$ | **AMERICAN** | With an inviting indoor dining room and outside seating overlooking bustling Arcata Plaza, this artisan bakery and restaurant is known for its savory and sweet breads. Notable noshes include ham-and-cheese breakfast croissants, focaccia sandwiches with avocado and Humboldt Fog goat cheese from Arcata's Cypress Grove creamery, and farm-to-table dinner fare. **Known for:** lemon cream tarts and other pastries available all day; small but terrific wine selection; Blue Bottle coffees. *Average main: $14* *791 G St., Arcata* *707/822–5922* *www.cafebrioarcata.com* *No dinner.*

★ **Salt Fish House**

$$ | **SEAFOOD** | Just a couple of blocks from Arcata's festive Plaza, this hip seafood restaurant inside a beautifully converted old machine shop offers seating in both an airy dining room and on a large side patio. Specialties include classic panko-crusted cod and chips and seared-rare steelhead with polenta cakes, but you could also make a meal of small plates from the raw bar—octopus ceviche, scallop crudo, and grilled Pacific oysters with *nuoc cham* (dipping sauce) among them. **Known for:** sharable raw-seafood trays and towers; superb wine and cocktail list; house-made ice cream in seasonal flavors. *Average main: $25* *935 I St., Arcata* *707/630–5300* *www.saltfishhouse.com* *Closed Mon. No lunch.*

Coffee and Quick Bites

Wildberries Marketplace

$ | **DELI** | This market with juice and salad bars and a small café carries a great selection of deli items, cheeses, and picnic provisions, many of them produced regionally. There's a good selection of local wine and beer, too. **Known for:** burgers and jerk chicken sandwiches; organic produce; excellent pizzas, tarts, pies, and other baked goods. *Average main: $8* *747 13th St., Arcata* *707/822–0095* *www.wildberries.com* *No credit cards.*

Klamath

13 miles north of Prairie Creek Redwoods Visitor Center, 22 miles south of Crescent City, 64 miles north of Eureka.

A low-key, unincorporated community surrounded by Redwood parkland on all sides, Klamath is a hub of the Yurok indigenous tribe, which makes up nearly 50% of the town's population and operates a casino resort in its center. There are a few mostly inexpensive, no-frills motels and eateries in town and nearby along with the inviting and historic Requa Inn.

ESSENTIALS

VISITOR INFORMATION **Yurok Country Visitor Center.** *101 Klamath Blvd., Klamath* *707/482–1555* *www.visityurokcountry.com.*

Sights

Trees of Mystery

FOREST | **FAMILY** | Since opening in 1946, this unabashedly goofy but endearing roadside attraction has been doling out family fun. From the moment you pull your car up to the 49-foot-tall talking statue of Paul Bunyan (alongside Babe the Blue Ox), the kitschy thrills begin. You can then explore a genuinely informative museum of Native American artifacts, admire intricately carved redwood figures, and browse tacky souvenirs. For a fee you can ride a six-passenger gondola over the redwood treetops for a majestic view of the forest canopy, and stroll along several mostly easy trails through the adjacent forest of redwoods, Sitka spruce, and Douglas firs. *15500 U.S. 101 N, between Klamath and Del Norte Coast Redwoods State Park, Klamath*

800/638–3389 *www.treesofmystery.net* *Museum free, trails and gondola $20.*

Restaurants

Woodland Villa Restaurant

$ | **AMERICAN** | This homey diner-style café just north of Klamath serves the sort of hearty American fare that'll fuel you up before a big day of hiking. There's breakfast sandwiches, Belgian waffles, and chicken-fried steaks in the morning, and deli sandwiches, salads, and pizzas offered throughout the rest of the day. **Known for:** big portions; good selection of craft beer and cider; local smoked-salmon in the adjacent market. *Average main: $9* *15870 U.S. 101, Klamath* *707/482–2081* *www.woodlandvillacabins.com* *Closed Mon.*

Hotels

★ Historic Requa Inn

$ | **B&B/INN** | This serene 1914 inn overlooks the Klamath River a mile east of where it meets the ocean. **Pros:** serene; relaxing yet central location with river views; excellent restaurant. **Cons:** least expensive rooms are quite small; not a good choice for families with kids; not many dining options in the area. *Rooms from: $132* *451 Requa Rd., Klamath* *707/482–1425* *www.requainn.com* *16 rooms* *Free breakfast.*

Motel Trees

$ | **HOTEL** | Operated by and adjacent to the joyfully kitschy Trees of Mystery roadside attraction, this casual mid-century motel has simply furnished rooms brightened with paintings and in some cases wall-length photographic murals of local redwoods and coastal scenes. **Pros:** very affordable; close to park beaches and trails; fun retro-'50s vibe. **Cons:** not a lot of frills; on-site restaurant is just so-so; some highway noise from U.S. 101. *Rooms from: $89* *15495 U.S. 101, Klamath* *707/482–3152, 800/848–2982* *www.moteltrees.com* *23 rooms* *No meals.*

Crescent City

5 miles north of Del Norte Coast Redwoods State Park, 5 miles west of Jedediah Smith Redwoods State Park, 25 miles south of Brookings, OR, 82 miles southwest of Grants Pass, OR.

The northern gateway to and headquarters of Redwood National and State Parks, this small oceanfront city just below the Oregon border offers close access to many of the park's key features, from the redwoods of Stout and Simpson-Reed groves in Jedediah Smith park to the sweeping, boulder-strewn beaches of Del Norte Coast park. The town itself enjoys a remarkable scenic setting overlooking the Pacific and contains several mostly mid-priced places to eat and stay, although it's often socked in by fog in summer or pelted by big storms in winter.

ESSENTIALS

VISITOR INFORMATION Visit Del Norte County. *1001 Front St., Crescent City* *707/464–3174* *www.visitdelnortecounty.com.*

Sights

Battery Point Lighthouse

LIGHTHOUSE | Only during low tide, you can walk from the pier across the ocean floor to this working lighthouse, which was built in 1856. It houses a museum with nautical artifacts and photographs of shipwrecks. There's even a resident ghost. *Lighthouse parking, 235 Lighthouse Way, Crescent City* *707/464–3089* *www.delnortehistory.org* *$5* *Closed weekdays Oct.–Mar.*

Northcoast Marine Mammal Center

ZOO | The nonprofit center rescues and rehabilitates stranded, sick, and injured seals, sea lions, dolphins, and porpoises. Its facility isn't a museum or an aquarium, but placards and kiosks provide information about marine mammals and coastal ecosystems, and even when the place is closed you can observe the rescued animals through a fence enclosing individual pools. The gallery and gift shop is open on most weekends and some weekdays, especially in summer, and volunteers are often on hand to answer questions. It's worth calling the day of your visit to find out when feedings will take place. ✉ *424 Howe Dr., Crescent City* ☎ *707/465–6265* 🌐 *www.northcoastmmc.org* *Free.*

Restaurants

Good Harvest Cafe

$$ | **AMERICAN** | **FAMILY** | This cheerful café, which serves great breakfasts and espresso drinks, lives up to its name with ample use of locally grown and organic ingredients. For lunch and dinner there are salads, burgers, sandwiches, vegetarian specialties, and several fish entrées, plus a nice range of local beers and West Coast wines. **Known for:** fish-and-chips and other local seafood; hearty, delicious breakfasts; plenty of vegetarian items. *Average main: $17* ✉ *575 U.S. 101 S, Crescent City* ☎ *707/465–6028* 🌐 *www.goodharvest-cafe.com.*

★ **SeaQuake Brewing**

$ | **PIZZA** | Water from the cool and clean Smith River goes into the dozen or so beers poured at this microbrewery with a spacious modern-industrial interior. They pair well with wood-fired thin-crust pizzas that include one with grilled chicken, bacon, artichoke hearts, garlic cream sauce, and cheeses from the local Rumiano Cheese Company. **Known for:** attractive patio with heat lamps; well-crafted beers on tap; the caramel stout sundae. *Average main: $15* ✉ *400 Front St., Crescent City* ☎ *707/465–4444* 🌐 *seaquakebrewing.com* *Closed Sun. and Mon.*

Hotels

Curly Redwood Lodge

$ | **HOTEL** | A single redwood tree produced the 57,000 board feet of lumber used to build this budget 1957 motor lodge. **Pros:** large rooms; several restaurants within walking distance; cool retro furnishings. **Cons:** road noise can be bothersome; very basic amenities; no breakfast. *Rooms from: $75* ✉ *701 U.S. 101 S, Crescent City* ☎ *707/464–2137* 🌐 *www.curlyredwoodlodge.com* *36 rooms* *No meals.*

Ocean View Inn & Suites

$ | **HOTEL** | This clean, comfortable, and reasonably priced hotel doesn't have a lot of bells and whistles, but it does enjoy a great location on the edge of downtown Crescent City very close to the water. **Pros:** views of the water; many restaurants nearby; good value. **Cons:** on a busy road; cookie-cutter furnishings; nearby foghorn can be a little noisy. *Rooms from: $125* ✉ *270 U.S. 101, Crescent City* ☎ *707/465–1111, 855/623–2611* 🌐 *www.oceanviewinncrescentcity.com* *65 rooms* *Free breakfast.*

Chapter 23

THE FAR NORTH

WITH LAKE SHASTA, MT. SHASTA, AND LASSEN VOLCANIC NATIONAL PARK

Updated by
Daniel Mangin

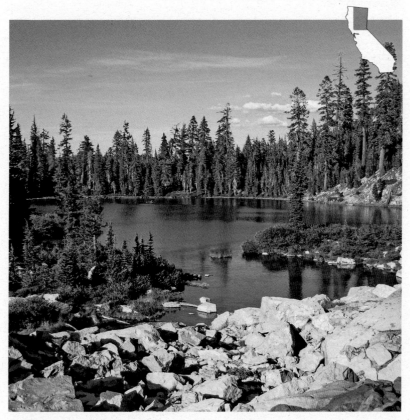

Sights
★★★★☆

Restaurants
★★★☆☆

Hotels
★★★☆☆

Shopping
★★★☆☆

Nightlife
★★★☆☆

WELCOME TO THE FAR NORTH

TOP REASONS TO GO

★ **Mother Nature's wonders:** California's Far North has more rivers, streams, lakes, forests, and mountains than you'll ever have time to explore.

★ **Volcanoes:** With two volcanoes to view—Lassen and Shasta—you can learn firsthand what happens when a mountain blows its top.

★ **Fantastic fishing:** Whether you like casting from a riverbank or letting your line bob beside a boat, you'll find fabulous fishing in all the northern counties.

★ **Cool hops:** On a hot day there's nothing quite as inviting as a visit to Chico's world-famous Sierra Nevada Brewery. Take the tour, and then savor a chilled glass on tap at the adjacent brewpub.

★ **Shasta:** Wonderful in all its forms: lake, dam, river, mountain, forest, and town.

1 **Chico.** A state university and a famous brewery help set the mood in this city also known for its artisans and farmers.

2 **Corning.** Olive-oil tasting rooms make this small town a fun stop for travelers along I–5.

3 **Redding.** This northern gateway to Lassen Volcanic National Park, has several points of interest within city limits, and day trips to Weaverville, Shasta Dam, and Lake Shasta Caverns National Natural Landmark are easily undertaken from here.

4 **Weaverville.** A 19th-century temple erected by Chinese miners is the centerpiece of this laid-back town's historic district.

5 **Shasta Lake.** Caverns, Shasta Dam, and vacation houseboats count among this quiet town's draws.

6 **Dunsmuir.** The upper Sacramento River near Dunsmuir consistently ranks among the country's best fishing spots. Most of the accommodations at a popular resort here were formerly cabooses.

7 **Mt. Shasta.** The town named for the peak that towers above it lures outdoorsy types year-round—hikers and golfers in summer, skiers in winter.

8 **Chester.** The southern gateway to Lassen Volcanic National Park sits on the forested edge of Lake Almanor.

9 **Mineral.** Lassen's official address is this town within the 165-square-mile national treasure.

10 **Burney.** President Theodore Roosevelt was among the fans of two magnificent waterfalls here.

11 **Tulelake.** Hundreds of underground lava tube caves make this town's Lava Beds National Monument well worth the remote drive.

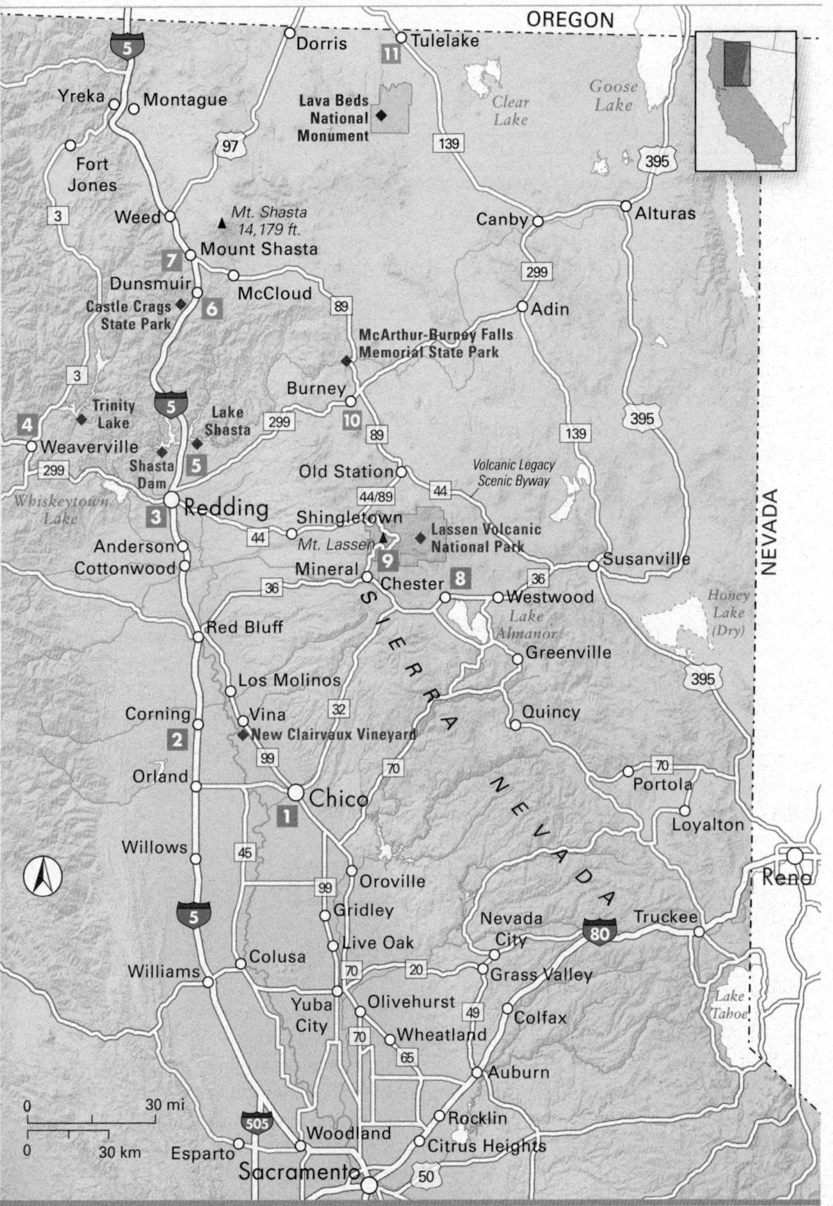
OREGON
NEVADA
Dorris
Tulelake
Lava Beds National Monument
Clear Lake
Goose Lake
Yreka
Montague
Fort Jones
Weed
Mt. Shasta 14,179 ft.
Mount Shasta
Dunsmuir
McCloud
Castle Crags State Park
McArthur-Burney Falls Memorial State Park
Canby
Alturas
Adin
Burney
Trinity Lake
Lake Shasta
Weaverville
Shasta Dam
Old Station
Volcanic Legacy Scenic Byway
Whiskeytown Lake
Redding
Shingletown
Mt. Lassen
Lassen Volcanic National Park
Anderson
Cottonwood
Mineral
Chester
Susanville
Westwood
Lake Almanor
Honey Lake (Dry)
Red Bluff
Greenville
SIERRA NEVADA
Los Molinos
Corning
Vina
New Clairvaux Vineyard
Quincy
Orland
Chico
Portola
Loyalton
Willows
Oroville
Reno
Gridley
Nevada City
Truckee
Live Oak
Colusa
Williams
Grass Valley
Yuba City
Olivehurst
Colfax
Lake Tahoe
Wheatland
Auburn
Rocklin
Woodland
Citrus Heights
Esparto
Sacramento
0 30 mi
0 30 km

The Far North's soaring mountain peaks, trail-filled national forests, alpine lakes, and wild rivers teeming with trout make it the perfect destination for outdoor enthusiasts, including hikers, cyclists, kayakers, and bird-watchers.

You won't find many hot nightspots or cultural enclaves in this region, but you will discover crowd-free national and state parks, crystal-clear mountain streams, superlative hiking and fishing, plus small towns worth exploring. And the spectacular landscapes of Lassen Volcanic National Park and Mt. Shasta are sure to impress.

The wondrous landscape of California's northeastern corner is the product of volcanic activity. At the southern end of the Cascade Range, Lassen Volcanic National Park is the best place to witness the Far North's fascinating geology. Beyond the sulfur vents and bubbling mud pots, the park owes much of its beauty to 10,457-foot Mt. Lassen and 50 wilderness lakes. Mt. Lassen and another volcano, Mt. Shasta, draw amateur geologists, weekend hikers, and avid mountain climbers to their rugged terrain. An intricate network of high-mountain watersheds feeds lakes large and small, plus streams and rivers that course through several forests.

The most enduring image of the region, though, is Mt. Shasta, whose 14,179-foot snowcapped peak beckons outdoor adventurers of all kinds. There are many versions of Shasta to enjoy—the mountain, the lake, the river, the town, the dam, and the forest—all named after the Native Americans known as the Shatasla, or Sastise, who once inhabited the region.

MAJOR REGIONS

From Chico to Mt. Shasta. The Far North is bisected, south to north, by I–5, which passes through several historic towns and state parks, as well as miles of mountainous terrain. Halfway to the Oregon border is Lake Shasta, a favorite recreation destination, and farther north stands the spectacular snowy peak of Mt. Shasta.

The Backcountry. East of I–5, the Far North's main corridor, dozens of scenic two-lane roads crisscross the wilderness, leading to dramatic mountain peaks and fascinating natural wonders. Small towns settled in the second half of the 19th century seem frozen in time, except that they are well equipped with tourist amenities.

Planning

When to Go

Heat scorches the valley in summer. Temperatures above 110°F are common, but the mountains provide cool respite. Fall throughout the Far North is beautiful, rivaled only by spring, when wildflowers bloom and mountain creeks fed by the snowmelt splash through the forests. Winter is usually temperate in the valley, but cold and snowy in the high country. As a result, some tourist attractions are closed in winter or have sharply curtailed hours.

Getting Here and Around

AIR

For the cheapest fares, fly into Sacramento, rent a car (you'll need one anyway), and drive north. United Express and Avelo serve Redding's small airport, which has no shuttle service. Ride-sharing (starting at about $15 to downtown) is the best option.

AIR CONTACTS Redding Municipal Airport. ✉ *6751 Woodrum Circle, off Airport Rd., Redding* ☎ *530/224–4320* 🌐 *www.cityofredding.org/departments/airports.*

BUS

Greyhound buses stop in Chico and Redding. STAGE buses serve Dunsmuir and Mt. Shasta. Various other agencies provide local public transit.

BUS CONTACTS STAGE. ☎ *530/842–8220* 🌐 *www.co.siskiyou.ca.us/generalservices/page/stage-schedule.*

CAR

Interstate 5 runs up the center of California through Redding and Mt. Shasta. Chico is east of I–5 where Highways 32 and 99 intersect. Lassen Volcanic National Park can be reached off I–5 by Highway 36 from Red Bluff or (except in winter) Highway 44 from Redding. Highway 299 connects Weaverville and Redding. Check weather reports and carry detailed maps, warm clothing, and tire chains if you head into mountainous terrain in winter.

TRAIN

Amtrak serves Chico, Redding, and Dunsmuir.

Restaurants

Redding and Chico have the most varied restaurant options. Cafés and simple eateries are the norm in smaller towns. Dress is always informal.

Hotels

Chain properties predominate in this region, with the occasional inn or restored hotel. Wilderness resorts close in fall and reopen in mid-spring after snow season ends. Book well ahead for summer visits to Mt. Shasta, Dunsmuir, Mineral, and Chester and to ensure state or national park campsite availability.

Restaurant and hotel reviews have been shortened. For full information, visit Fodors.com. Restaurant prices are the average cost of a main course at dinner, or if dinner is not served, at lunch. Hotel prices are the lowest cost of a standard double room in high season.

What It Costs

	$	$$	$$$	$$$$
RESTAURANTS				
	under $17	$17–$26	$27–$36	over $36
HOTELS				
	under $150	$150–$250	$251–$350	over $350

Visitor Information

CONTACTS Shasta Cascade Wonderland Association. ✉ *Shasta Outlets, 1699 Hwy. 273, off I–5, Exit 667, Anderson* ☎ *530/365–7500* 🌐 *www.shastacascade.com.* **Visit Trinity County.** ✉ *509 Main St., Weaverville* ☎ *530/623–6101* 🌐 *www.visittrinity.com.*

Chico

86 miles north of Sacramento.

Its name is Spanish for "small," but with a 40% increase in population between censuses, Chico outpaced Redding as the Far North's largest city. Chico State University, the scores of local artisans, and area agriculture all influence life here, but the Sacramento Valley city's main claim to fame—and the premier tourist attraction—is the nationally renowned Sierra Nevada Brewery.

GETTING HERE AND AROUND

Highway 99, off I–5 from the north or south, and Highway 32 east off the interstate, intersect Chico. Amtrak and Greyhound stop here, and Butte Regional Transit's B-Line buses serve the area. Chico's downtown neighborhoods are walkable.

BUS CONTACT B-Line. ☎ *530/342–0221* 🌐 *www.blinetransit.com.*

ESSENTIALS

VISITOR INFORMATION Chico Chamber of Commerce. ✉ *180 E. 4th St., Suite 120* ☎ *530/891–5556, 800/852–8570* 🌐 *www.chicochamber.com.*

Sights

Bidwell Mansion State Historic Park

HOUSE | Built between 1865 and 1868 by General John Bidwell, the founder of Chico, this mansion was designed by Henry W. Cleaveland, a San Francisco architect. Bidwell and his wife, Annie, welcomed many distinguished guests to their pink Italianate home, including President Rutherford B. Hayes, naturalist John Muir, suffragist Susan B. Anthony, and General William T. Sherman. When offered, a one-hour tour takes you through most of the three-story mansion's 26 rooms. ✉ *525 Esplanade, at Memorial Way* ☎ *530/895–6144* 🌐 *bidwellmansionpark.com* 🎫 *$6* 🕒 *Closed Tues.–Fri.*

Bidwell Park

CITY PARK | The sprawling 3,670-acre Bidwell Park is a community green space straddling Big Chico Creek, where scenes from *Gone With the Wind* and the 1938 version of *Robin Hood* (starring Errol Flynn) were filmed. The region's recreational hub, it includes a golf course, swimming areas, and biking, hiking, horseback riding, and skating trails. Chico Creek Nature Center serves as the official information site for Bidwell Park. ✉ *1968 E. 8th St., off Hwy. 99* ☎ *530/891–4671* 🌐 *chicorec.com/chico-creek-nature-center* 🎫 *Park free, nature center $4* 🕒 *Nature center closed Sun.–Tues.*

Chico Museum

MUSEUM | Immerse yourself in all things Chico at this small but engaging museum near Chico State University. Past exhibits have surveyed the city's Native American legacy, its former Chinatowns and agricultural past, and area movers and shakers. ✉ *141 Salem St., at 2nd St.* ☎ *530/891–4336* 🌐 *www.chicohistorymuseum.org* 🎫 *$5* 🕒 *Closed Mon.–Wed.*

Museum of Northern California Art

MUSEUM | After several years of successful pop-up exhibitions around town, this engaging museum found a permanent home in the Veterans Memorial Building, a handsome 1927 Classical Revival structure designed by the local architecture firm of Cole & Brouchaud. The focus is contemporary art produced from San Jose north to Oregon, some of it by area artists. ✉ *900 Esplanade, at E. Washington Ave.* ☎ *530/487–7272* 🌐 *www.monca.org* 🎫 *$5* 🕒 *Closed Mon.–Wed.*

National Yo-Yo Museum

MUSEUM | Cast aside images of a grand edifice and curators of renown: this yo-yo collection spanning multiple decades occupies the back of a downtown toy and novelty shop, itself a throwback to some era or another. If you've ever aspired to Walk the Dog or venture Around the World, you'll find this a diverting 15-minute stop. Highlights include the 256-pound No-Jive 3-in-1 yo-yo and comedian Tom Smothers's collection. ■ **TIP→ In the shop, don't miss the posters for years of Chico events.** ✉ *Bird in Hand, 320 Broadway, near W. 3rd St.* ☎ *530/893–0545* 🌐 *nationalyoyo.org* 🎫 *Free.*

★ Sierra Nevada Brewing Company

WINERY/DISTILLERY | This pioneer of the microbrewery movement still has a hands-on approach to beer making. Take the free Brewery Tour and see how the beer is produced—from sorting hops through fermentation and bottling, and concluding with a tasting. Other tours, for which there is a fee, focus on topics like hops, the brewery's history, and sustainability initiatives. ■ **TIP→ When offered, tours fill up fast; reserve by phone or online before you visit.** ✉ *1075 E. 20th St., at Sierra Nevada St.* ☎ *530/345–2739 taproom, 530/899–4776 tours* 🌐 *www.sierranevada.com* 🎫 *Tours free–$50 (includes tasting).*

Restaurants

★ Bidwell Perk

$ | AMERICAN | A clean and tidy, many-windowed chain alternative for coffee (several different roasts daily) and pastries, Bidwell Perk also serves full breakfasts and light lunches. Bagels, French toast, quiche, and croissant sandwiches in the morning give way to small plates, salads, panini, and sliders as the day moves along. **Known for:** mostly small-batch beers and wines; outdoor patio; well-crafted espresso drinks. 💲 *Average main: $9* ✉ *664 E. 1st Ave., at Mangrove Ave.* ☎ *530/899–1500* 🌐 *bidwellperk.com* 🕒 *No dinner.*

★ 5th Street Steakhouse

$$$$ | STEAKHOUSE | Hand-cut steak is the star in this refurbished early 1900s building, the place to come when you're craving red meat, a huge baked potato, or some fresh seafood. Exposed redbrick walls warm the dining rooms, and a long mahogany bar catches the overflow crowds that jam the place on weekends. **Known for:** alfresco dining on outdoor patio; weekend crowds; prime cuts of beef with white-tablecloth service. 💲 *Average main: $37* ✉ *345 W. 5th St., at Normal Ave.* ☎ *530/891–6328* 🌐 *www.5thstreetsteakhouse.com* 🕒 *Closed Mon. No lunch Sat.–Thurs.*

Red Tavern

$$$ | MEDITERRANEAN | With its burgundy carpet, white linen tablecloths, and mellow lighting, this is one of Chico's coziest restaurants. The Mediterranean-influenced menu, inspired by fresh local produce, with vegetarian and pescatarian fare in addition to meat and poultry dishes, changes seasonally—fettuccine with beef short-rib ragout and seared salmon with citrus beurre blanc are among recent offerings. **Known for:** California wine list; nightly specials; patio seating. 💲 *Average main: $29* ✉ *1250 Esplanade, at E. 3rd Ave.* ☎ *530/894–3463* 🌐 *www.redtavern.com* 🕒 *Closed Mon. No lunch Tues.–Sat.*

Sierra Nevada Brewery Taproom

$$ | AMERICAN | An easy choice, especially if you've just done a tour and are steeped in company lore, the famous brewery's high-ceilinged, heavy-on-the-wood taproom bustles day and night with patrons washing down well-conceived gastropub grub with the best-selling Pale Ale and smaller-batch offerings, some of which are only available here. The open kitchen turns out burgers, wood-oven pizzas, and fish-and-chips (the fish's batter made with Pale Ale) with remarkable speed. **Known for:** beer cheese and pretzels with mustard; soups and salads; beer flights on patio. 💲 *Average main: $17* ✉ *1075 E. 20th St.* ✣ *½ mile west of Hwy. 99, Exit 384* ☎ *530/345–2739* 🌐 *www.sierranevada.com/brewery/california/taproom.*

Hotels

Hotel Diamond

$$ | **HOTEL** | Crystal chandeliers and gleaming century-old wood floors and banisters welcome guests into the foyer of this restored 1904 gem near Chico State University. **Pros:** downtown location; refined rooms, some with bay windows and fireplaces; Diamond Steakhouse. **Cons:** street scene can be noisy on weekends; some rooms are small; some rooms lack tubs. *Rooms from: $151* *220 W. 4th St., near Broadway* *530/893–3100, 866/993–3100* *www.hoteldiamondchico.com* *43 rooms* *No meals.*

Corning

29 miles northwest of Chico, 50 miles south of Redding.

Signs along Highway 99 and I–5 beckon travelers to Corning, whose favorable soil and plentiful sunshine have made the town a center of olive cultivation and olive-oil manufacturing. At several tasting rooms you can sample olives, olive oil, and other products.

GETTING HERE AND AROUND

Corning lies just off I–5 at Exit 631. From Chico take Highway 99 for 17½ miles and follow signs west to Corning. TRAX provides weekday bus service.

CONTACTS TRAX. *530/385–2877* *www.taketrax.com.*

Sights

New Clairvaux Vineyard

WINERY/DISTILLERY | History converges in fascinating ways at this winery and vineyard whose tale involves pioneer-rancher Peter Lassen (Mt. Lassen is named for him), railroad baron Leland Stanford, newspaper magnate William Randolph Hearst, the Napa Valley's five-generation Nichelini wine-making family, and current owners the Trappist-Cistercian monks. In the 1890s the rambling redbrick tasting room, erected by Stanford, stored 2 million gallons of wine. These days the hosts pour Albariño, Tempranillo, Barbera, and other small-lot bottlings from grapes mostly grown nearby. The Syrah and Cabernet stand out, but everything's well made. The on-site chapel (the Hearst connection) has a convoluted story all its own. *26240 7th St., Vina* *10 miles from Corning, South Ave. east off I–5 or Hwy. 99 to Rowles Rd. north to 7th St. west* *530/839–2434* *www.newclairvauxvineyard.com* *Tastings $10.*

Olive Pit

LOCAL INTEREST | Three generations of the Craig family run this combination café, store, and tasting room where you can learn all about California olive production and sample olive products, craft beers and small-lot wines, and artisanal foods. Sandwich selections at the café include muffulettas and olive burgers. Wash your choice down with a balsamic shake in flavors that include peach, coconut, strawberry, and chocolate. *2156 Solano St., Corning* *Off I–5, Exit 631 (Corning Rd.)* *530/824–4667* *www.olivepit.com* *Tastings free for olive oil, fee (varies) for beer and wine.*

Redding

50 miles north of Corning.

A handy gateway to Lassen Volcanic National Park, Redding, population about 95,000, sits along the busy I–5 corridor, with attractions that include the photogenic Sundial Bridge in Turtle Bay Exploration Park. The city makes a good base for visiting Shasta Lake and Lake Shasta Caverns to the north. It's also a good stopover if you're traveling between Lassen and Redwood National and State Parks on the coast.

GETTING HERE AND AROUND

Interstate 5 is the major north–south route through Redding. Highway 299 bisects the city east–west, and Highway 44 connects Redding and Lassen Park's northwest entrance.

ESSENTIALS

VISITOR INFORMATION Visit Redding. ✉ *1448 Pine St.* ☎ *530/225–4100* 🌐 *www.visitredding.com.*

Sights

Moseley Family Cellars

WINERY/DISTILLERY | Although its street name conjures up pastoral images, this appointment-only winery whose grapes come from vineyards as far afield as Napa, Sonoma, Lodi, and Oregon's Rogue Valley is actually in an industrial park. Despite the location, it's worth a visit for its Chardonnay and Viognier whites and Syrah, Mourvèdre, old-vine Zinfandel, and other reds. ✉ *4712 Mountain Lakes Blvd., Suite 300* ☎ *530/229–9463* 🌐 *www.moseleyfamilycellars.com* *Tastings $10* *Closed Mon.–Wed. (sometimes Thurs.) except by appointment.*

Shasta State Historic Park

HISTORIC SITE | Six miles west of downtown and straddling Highway 299 lies the former town of Shasta City, which thrived in the mid- to late 1800s. The park's 19 acres of half-ruined brick buildings, accessed via trails, are a reminder of the glory days of the California gold rush. The former county courthouse building (whose exhibits include rare California landscape paintings), jail, and gallows have been restored to their 1860s appearance. The Litsch General Store (1850–1950), now a museum, displays items once sold here. **■ TIP→ Next to the store in a wooden shack, family-run Shorty's Eatery serves up good sandwiches and Filipino dishes.** ✉ *15312 Hwy. 299* ☎ *530/243–8194* 🌐 *www.parks.ca.gov/shastashp* *Free to park, $3 Courthouse Museum* *Courthouse Museum closed Mon.–Wed.*

★ Turtle Bay Exploration Park

CITY PARK | FAMILY | This peaceful downtown park has 300 acres of walking trails, an aquarium, an arboretum and botanical gardens, and many interactive exhibits for kids. The main draw is the stunning Santiago Calatrava–designed **Sundial Bridge,** a metal and translucent glass pedestrian walkway, suspended by cables from a single tower, spanning a broad bend in the Sacramento River. On sunny days the 217-foot tower lives up to the bridge's name, casting a shadow on the ground below to mark time. Access to the bridge and arboretum is free, but there's a fee for the museum and gardens. ✉ *844 Sundial Bridge Dr.* ☎ *530/243–8850* 🌐 *www.turtlebay.org* *Museum $18* *Museum closed Mon. and Tues. early Sept.–mid-Mar.*

Restaurants

From the Hearth Artisan Bakery & Café

$ | AMERICAN | A homegrown variation on the Panera theme, this extremely popular operation (as in expect a wait at peak dining hours) serves pastries, eggs and other hot dishes, and good coffee drinks, juices, and smoothies for breakfast. The chefs whip up a diverse selection of wraps, panini, sandwiches, burgers, rice bowls, and soups the rest of the day. **Known for:** baked goods; pork breakfast tacos; two other Redding locations (one downtown) plus a Shasta Lake drive-through. *Average main: $11* ✉ *2650 Churn Creek Rd.* ☎ *530/424–2233* 🌐 *www.fthcafe.com.*

Jack's Grill

$$$ | STEAKHOUSE | The original Jack opened his grill (and an upstairs brothel) in 1938. Tamer these days, this place is famous for its 16-ounce steaks and deep-fried shrimp and chicken dishes. **Known for:** 1930s atmosphere; great martinis; thick slabs of beef. *Average main: $29*

1743 California St. *530/241–9705* *www.jacksgrillredding.com* *Closed Sun. No lunch.*

View 202

$$$ | **MODERN AMERICAN** | The view at this glass-walled hilltop restaurant is of the Sacramento River below the wide outdoor patio and well beyond the waterway to snowcapped mountains. It's best to stick with the least complicated preparations on the New American menu, which emphasizes grilled meats and fish from noted California purveyors but also includes Asian-tinged appetizers and house-made ravioli. **Known for:** Friday and Saturday prime rib; specialty cocktails; wine list. *Average main: $29* *202 Hemsted Dr., off E. Cypress Ave.* *530/226–8439* *www.view202redding.com.*

Vintage Public House

$$ | **AMERICAN** | Patrons of this comfort-food haven across from downtown's 1935 Cascade movie palace wash down elevated pub grub with classic and craft cocktails and an international selection of wines and beers. The fare includes homemade soups, a few salads, rice bowls, jalapeño wonton nachos, a locally revered mac and cheese, plenty of burgers (one grilled with a whiskey glaze and topped with candied bacon), and heartier entrées like lasagna and chicken marsala. **Known for:** patio dining; weekly appetizer special; artisanal spirits. *Average main: $22* *1790 Market St., at Sacramento St.* *530/229–9449* *vintageredding.com* *Closed Sun. and Mon. No lunch Sat.*

★ Bridgehouse Bed & Breakfast

$ | **B&B/INN** | In a residential area a block from the Sacramento River and a ½-mile from downtown Redding, this inn contains six rooms in two side-by-side homes. **Pros:** easygoing hospitality; proximity to downtown and Turtle Bay; freshly baked scones at full breakfast. **Cons:** lacks pool, fitness center, and other standard hotel amenities; the two least expensive rooms are small; books up well ahead in summer. *Rooms from: $119* *1455 Riverside Dr.* *530/247–7177* *www.bridgehousebb.com* *6 rooms* *Free breakfast.*

★ Sheraton Redding Hotel at Sundial Bridge

$$ | **HOTEL** | **FAMILY** | Stylish and modern, this hotel at the entrance to Sundial Bridge and Turtle Bay Exploration Park makes a great, family-friendly base for visiting Lassen, Whiskeytown and Shasta lakes, and other area attractions. **Pros:** pool and gym; excellent restaurant; patio dining. **Cons:** parking fee; neighborhood not very walkable; nearly an hour's drive to Lassen Volcanic NP. *Rooms from: $209* *820 Sundial Bridge Dr.* *530/364–2800* *www.marriott.com* *130 rooms* *No meals.*

Nightlife

Final Draft Brewing Company

BREWPUBS/BEER GARDENS | This spacious brick-walled brewpub receives high acclaim for its accessible ales and above-average pub grub. Try the beer-battered Sidewinder Fries instead of regular ones. While they're cooking, order a sampler flight to decide which of the brews to wash them down with. *1600 California St., at Placer St.* *530/338–1198* *www.finaldraftbrewingcompany.com.*

Woody's Brewing Company

BREWPUBS/BEER GARDENS | A fun downtown hangout with a party vibe, Woody's has built a loyal following for its Polish nachos (kettle chips, beer cheese, smoked sausage, and sauerkraut), special-recipe tater tots, and range of beers from fruited wheat ales to an unfiltered dry-hopped IPA and the Pray for Powder porter. *1257 Oregon St., at Shasta St.* *530/768–1034* *www.woodysbrewing.com.*

Activities

The Fly Shop

FISHING | This store that bills itself as "Northern California's fly-fishing headquarters" sells gear and other products and has information about guides, conditions, and fishing trips. *4140 Churn Creek Rd., at Denton Way 530/222–3555, 800/669–3474 www.theflyshop.com.*

Weaverville

46 miles west of Redding on Hwy. 299.

Chinese miners erected the 1874 Joss House that anchors Weaverville's downtown historic district. The town, population about 3,200, is a popular headquarters for family vacations and hiking, fishing, and gold-panning excursions.

GETTING HERE AND AROUND

Highway 299, east from the Pacific Coast or west from Redding, becomes Main Street in central Weaverville. Trinity Transit provides bus service.

ESSENTIALS

VISITOR INFORMATION Trinity County Visitors Bureau. *509 Main St. 530/623–6101 www.visittrinity.com.*

Sights

Hal Goodyear Historical Park

HISTORIC SITE | For a vivid sense of Weaverville's past, visit this outdoor park of old mining equipment, and step inside the adjacent **Jake Jackson Memorial Museum.** A blacksmith shop and a stamp mill (where ore is crushed) from the 1890s are still in use during certain community events. *780 Main St. 530/623–5211 www.trinitymuseum.org Museum closed various days Jan.–Apr. and Oct.–Dec.*

★ Weaverville Joss House State Historic Park

HISTORIC SITE | Weaverville's main attraction is the Joss House, a Taoist temple built in 1874 and called Won Lim Miao ("the temple of the forest beneath the clouds") by Chinese miners. The oldest continuously used Chinese temple in California, it attracts worshippers from around the world. With its golden altar, antique weaponry, and carved wooden canopies, the Joss House is a piece of California history best appreciated on a guided 30-minute tour. *630 Main St., at Oregon St. 530/623–5284 www.parks.ca.gov Museum free; guided tour $4 Closed Mon.–Wed.*

Restaurants

Mamma Llama Eatery & Café

$ | **AMERICAN** | Tap into the spirit of 21st-century Weaverville at this mellow café that serves breakfast (all day) and lunch and in winter specializes in hot soups to warm body and soul. Expect all the usual suspects at breakfast along with Country Cheesy Potatoes (topped with green chili) and sausage between two biscuits topped with homemade sausage gravy; a spicy club wrap and several vegetarian sandwiches are among the lunch offerings. **Known for:** mellow vibe; good soups; espresso drinks. *Average main: $9 490 Main St. 530/623–6363 www.mammallama.com Closed weekends. No dinner.*

Trinity County Brewing Company

$ | **AMERICAN** | Craft brews, from pale ales to stout, and pub grub a cut above the expected made this 2020 newcomer with a cavernous industrial interior an instant hit despite opening during difficult times. The cheese-curd and chicken-wing starters and burger and grilled-chicken sandwich are the best sellers. **Known for:** community feel; mellow outside patio; garlic fries with secret sauce. *Average main: $11 301 Main St. 530/423–4114*

⊕ *trinitycountybrewery.com* ⊙ *Closed Mon. and Tues. (but check).*

Hotels

Weaverville Hotel

$ | HOTEL | Originally built during the gold rush, this beautifully restored hotel is filled with antiques and period furniture. **Pros:** gracious on-site owners; in heart of town's historic district; beautifully restored. **Cons:** no breakfast on-site; children under 12 not permitted; only one room has a TV. *Rooms from: $140* ✉ *481 Main St., near Court St.* ☎ *530/623–2222, 800/750–8853* ⊕ *www.weavervillehotel.com* *7 rooms* *No meals.*

Activities

Weaverville Ranger Station

HIKING/WALKING | Check here for maps, free wilderness and campfire permits, and information about local fishing and the 600 miles of hiking trails in the 500,000-acre Trinity Alps Wilderness. ✉ *360 Main St.* ☎ *530/623–2121.*

Shasta Lake

10 miles north of Redding.

The city of Shasta Lake, population about 10,000, is a portal to water, wilderness, and dazzling stalagmites, with the monolithic Shasta Dam in the midst of it all.

GETTING HERE AND AROUND

Shasta Lake lies at the intersection of I–5 and Highway 151. There is no local bus service.

Sights

Lake Shasta

BODY OF WATER | Created when Shasta Dam corraled the Sacramento River in the 1940s, Lake Shasta evolved into a habitat for numerous types of fish, including rainbow trout, salmon, bass, brown trout, and catfish. The lake region also supports a large nesting population of bald eagles. You can rent fishing boats, ski boats, sailboats, canoes, paddleboats, Jet Skis, and windsurfing boards at marinas and resorts along the 370-mile shoreline. ✉ *Shasta Lake* ⊕ *www.shastacascade.com.*

★ Lake Shasta Caverns National Natural Landmark

NATURE SITE | FAMILY | Stalagmites, stalactites, flowstone deposits, and crystals entice visitors to the Lake Shasta Caverns. To see this impressive spectacle, you must take the two-hour tour, which includes a catamaran ride across the McCloud arm of Lake Shasta and a bus ride up North Grey Rocks Mountain to the cavern entrance. The temperature in the caverns is 58°F year-round, making them a cool retreat on a hot summer day. The most awe-inspiring of the limestone rock formations is the glistening Cathedral Room, which appears to be gilded. **■ TIP→ In summer it's wise to purchase tickets online a day or more ahead of your visit.** ✉ *20359 Shasta Caverns Rd., Lakehead* ↔ *20 miles north of Redding (take I–5 Exit 695 and follow signs)* ☎ *530/238–2341, 800/795–2283* ⊕ *www.lakeshastacaverns.com* *$32.*

Shasta Dam

DAM | Road-trippers traveling along I–5 often stop at the second-largest concrete dam in the United States—only Grand Coulee in Washington is bigger. Shasta Dam was completed in 1945 by a crew that included many women because potential male workers were fighting World War II. Exhibits at the visitor center explain the engineering and construction, but even if the facility isn't open, the photogenic view north to snowcapped Mt. Shasta makes the landmark worth the detour. Hour-long guided tours, suspended in 2020, may resume by 2022, but you can tour the top of the dam on your own. ✉ *16349 Shasta Dam Blvd.,*

Shasta Lake ✣ From I–5 Exit 685, take Hwy. 151/Shasta Dam Blvd. west to Lake Blvd. north ☎ 530/247–8555 🌐 www.usbr.gov/mp/ncao/dam-tours.html 🎟 Free ⏲ Closed Tues. and Wed. (but check).

Activities

Shasta Marina at Packers Bay

BOATING | FAMILY | Trips aboard this highly regarded operator's amenities-packed houseboats, which sleep up to 20 people, qualify as waterborne glamping. Some boats even have a hot tub on board. The outfit conducts pre-trip lessons in the basics for first-time houseboaters. ✉ *16814 Packers Bay Rd., Lakehead ✣ West from I–5, Exit 693 (see directions on website) ☎ 800/959–3359 🌐 shastalake.net 🎟 From $350 per night (more in summer), 3-night minimum.*

Dunsmuir

10 miles south of Mt. Shasta.

Surrounded by towering forests and boasting world-class upper Sacramento River fly-fishing, Dunsmuir acquired its current moniker when a Scottish coal baron built a fountain in exchange for the town renaming itself in his honor. An upscale restaurant and a boutique hotel do business downtown. Farther out lie the restored-caboose lodgings of the fun Railroad Park Resort.

GETTING HERE AND AROUND

Reach Dunsmuir via exits off I–5 at the north and south ends of town. Amtrak stops here. On weekdays, STAGE buses serve Dunsmuir.

ESSENTIALS

VISITOR INFORMATION Dunsmuir Chamber of Commerce. ✉ *5915 Dunsmuir Ave., Suite 100 ☎ 530/235–2177 🌐 dunsmuir.com.*

Fine Fishing

The upper Sacramento River near Dunsmuir is consistently rated one of the best fishing spots in the country. Check with the chamber of commerce for local fishing guides.

Sights

★ Castle Crags State Park

NATIONAL/STATE PARK | Named for its 2,000–6,500-foot glacier-polished crags, formed by volcanic activity centuries ago, this park offers fishing on the upper Sacramento River, hiking in the backcountry, and a view of Mt. Shasta. The 4,350-acre park has 28 miles of hiking trails, including a 2¾-mile access trail to **Castle Crags Wilderness,** part of the **Shasta-Trinity National Forest.** The excellent trails at lower altitudes include the ¼-mile Vista Point Trail (near the entrance), which leads to views of Castle Crags and Mt. Shasta. ✉ *20022 Castle Creek Rd., Castella ✣ I–5, Exit 724, 6 miles south of Dunsmuir ☎ 530/235–2684 🌐 www.castlecragspark.org 🎟 $10 per vehicle, day-use.*

Restaurants

Café Maddalena

$$$ | MEDITERRANEAN | The chef here gained experience working in top San Francisco restaurants before moving north to prepare adventurous Mediterranean fare with a French influence. Appetizers like a recent menu's crispy quail and pea-and-mint croquettes hint at the level of refinement on display, as do entrées that might include sea bass served with Meyer lemon risotto or rabbit-and-porcini ragout atop pappardelle. **Known for:** elevated cuisine; artisanal small-lot wines; outdoor dining under an arbor. 💲 *Average main: $29 ✉ 5801 Sacramento Ave. ☎ 530/235–2725 🌐 www.*

cafemaddalena.com ⌚ Closed Mon.–Wed. and Jan.–mid-Feb. No lunch.

Dunsmuir Brewery Works

$$ | **AMERICAN** | Travelers mingle with locals at this downtown spot for microbrews and pub fare that includes vegetarian-nut, elk, and ½-pound Angus-beef burgers, along with pesto-cream mussels, baby back ribs, and bratwurst in a brioche bun with kraut and cheese sauce. The house brews range from pale ale to a porter, with growlers available to go. **Known for:** outdoor patio; house-made beer cheese bread; clam chowder Fridays. *Average main: $19 ✉ 5701 Dunsmuir Ave. ☎ 530/235–1900 🌐 www.dunsmuirbreweryworks.com ⌚ Closed Mon. early Sept.–late May.*

Yaks on the 5

$$ | **AMERICAN** | Beloved on social media for its sticky buns, addictive two-cheese tater tots, and bacon-jalapeño and other 100% grass-fed burgers, this festive, brightly painted joint wins most diners' hearts with its house-made ingredients, dozens of beers, and upbeat staff. You'll pay more than expected but will likely leave feeling you got your money's worth. **Known for:** murals and artworks; smoked wings and ribs with house barbecue sauce; Yaks Shack in Mt. Shasta. *Average main: $19 ✉ 4917 Dunsmuir Ave. ☎ 530/678–3517 🌐 www.yaks.com ⌚ Closed Wed.*

Hotels

★ Mossbrae Hotel

$$ | **HOTEL** | Patrons of this urbane, two-story, boutique hotel bask in au courant comfort in guest rooms with kitchenettes and either queen or California king beds. **Pros:** luxury feel; queen rooms, though small, are a good value; easy walk to Dunsmuir Brewing, Cafe Maddalena, art venues. **Cons:** costs a bit more than town's other properties (but outshines them); no elevator (one ground-floor ADA suite); some rooms have no tubs. *Rooms from: $159 ✉ 5734 Dunsmuir Ave. ☎ 530/235–7019 🌐 mossbraehotel.com 7 rooms No meals.*

Railroad Park Resort

$ | **HOTEL** | **FAMILY** | The antique cabooses here were collected over more than three decades and converted into 23 cozy motel rooms in honor of Dunsmuir's railroad legacy; there are also four cabins. **Pros:** gorgeous setting; unique accommodations; kitschy fun. **Cons:** cabooses can feel cramped; must drive to Dunsmuir restaurants; some guests find location too remote. *Rooms from: $135 ✉ 100 Railroad Park Rd. ☎ 530/235–4440 🌐 www.rrpark.com 27 rooms No meals.*

Mt. Shasta

34 miles north of Lake Shasta.

While a snow-covered dormant volcano is the area's dazzling draw, the town of Mt. Shasta charms visitors with its small shops, friendly residents, and beautiful scenery in all seasons.

GETTING HERE AND AROUND

Three exits off I–5 lead to the town of Mt. Shasta. When snow hasn't closed Highway 89, you can take it northwest from the Lassen Park area to Mt. Shasta. Greyhound stops at Weed, 10 miles north; Amtrak stops at Dunsmuir, 10 miles south. STAGE provides bus service.

ESSENTIALS

VISITOR INFORMATION Visit Mt. Shasta. *✉ Visitor Center, 300 Pine St., at W. Lake St. ☎ 530/926–4865 🌐 visitmtshasta.com.*

Sights

★ Mt. Shasta

VOLCANO | The crown jewel of the 2.5-million-acre Shasta-Trinity National Forest, Mt. Shasta, a 14,179-foot-high dormant volcano, is a mecca for day hikers. It's especially enticing in spring, when fragrant Shasta lilies and other flowers adorn the rocky slopes. A paved road, the Everitt Memorial Highway, reaches only as far as the timberline; the final 6,000 feet are a tough climb of rubble, ice, and snow (the summit is perpetually ice-packed). Hiking enthusiasts include this trek with those to the peaks of Kilimanjaro and Mt. Fuji in lists of iconic must-do mountain hikes. **■TIP→ Always check weather predictions; sudden storms—with snow and freezing temperatures—have trapped climbers.** ✉ *Mt. Shasta* 🌐 *visitmtshasta.com/activities/mountaineering.*

Restaurants

Lilys

$$ | ECLECTIC | This restaurant in a white-clapboard home, framed by a picket fence and arched trellis, offers an eclectic menu, starting with bananas Foster French toast for breakfast. The varied lunch and dinner selections might include a Brussels sprout salad, herb-stuffed fresh trout, pad Thai, filet mignon, and always several burgers. **Known for:** patio dining; Wednesday sushi night; weekend brunch. $ *Average main: $24* ✉ *1013 S. Mt. Shasta Blvd., at Holly St.* ☎ *530/926–3372* 🌐 *www.lilysrestaurant.com* ⏲ *Per website, hrs "subject to change".*

Poncho & Lefkowitz

$ | MEXICAN | The cuisine is Mexican and American at this small stand popular for its quesadillas, fish tacos, tamales, sausages, Seattle dogs (bratwurst with cream cheese, cabbage, and jalapeños), and filling Big Nasty burritos. Order at the window, and enjoy your meal at outdoor picnic tables with Mt. Shasta views. **Known for:** fish tacos; strawberry lemonade; vegetarian offerings. $ *Average main: $9* ✉ *401 S. Mt. Shasta Blvd.* ☎ *530/926–1505* ⏲ *Closed Sun. No dinner.*

Seven Suns Coffee and Cafe

$ | CAFÉ | A favorite gathering spot for locals, this small coffee shop in a stone building serves specialty wraps and burritos for breakfast and lunch (both served all day), plus soups and salads. Pastries, made daily, include muffins, cookies, and scones (great blackberry ones in season). **Known for:** coffee, tea, chai, spiced cider, Italian sodas; outside patio; vegetarian offerings. $ *Average main: $11* ✉ *1011 S. Mt. Shasta Blvd., at Holly St.* ☎ *530/926–9701* ⏲ *No dinner.*

Hotels

Best Western Tree House Motor Inn

$$ | HOTEL | The clean, standard rooms at this motel less than a mile from downtown Mt. Shasta are decorated with natural-wood furnishings. **Pros:** close to ski park; heated indoor pool; lobby's roaring fireplace is a big plus on winter days. **Cons:** not all lodging buildings have elevators; pricier than other chain properties (though it delivers more); doesn't offer free breakfast like much of BW chain. $ *Rooms from: $175* ✉ *111 Morgan Way* ☎ *530/926–3101, 800/545–7164* 🌐 *www.bestwesterncalifornia.com/hotels/best-western-plus-tree-house* *98 rooms* *No meals.*

Inn at Mount Shasta

$$ | HOTEL | This two-story, motel-style property on Mt. Shasta's main drag wins points for its cleanliness, comfortable beds, and spacious (325 square feet minimum) rooms with Wi-Fi, microwaves, refrigerators, hair dryers, and flat-screen TVs with satellite HDTV. **Pros:** solicitous hosts; 500-square-foot family suite with three beds; convenient location. **Cons:** minimal style; some street and room-to-room noise; no elevator to second-floor rooms. $ *Rooms from: $169* ✉ *710 S. Mt. Shasta Blvd.* ☎ *530/918–9292* 🌐 *innatmountshasta.com* *30 rooms* *No meals.*

Mount Shasta Resort

$$ | RENTAL | The private chalets, all with gas-log fireplaces, are nestled among tall pine trees along the shore of Lake Siskiyou. **Pros:** romantic woodsy setting with incredible views; full kitchens in many lodgings; largest chalets sleep up to six people. **Cons:** kids may get bored; must drive to Mt. Shasta restaurants; some hospitality lapses. *Rooms from: $189* *1000 Siskiyou Lake Blvd.* *530/926–3030, 800/958–3363* *www.mountshastaresort.com* *65 rooms* *No meals.*

Activities

Fifth Season Mountaineering Shop
CLIMBING/MOUNTAINEERING | This shop rents bicycles and skiing and climbing equipment, and operates a recorded 24-hour climber-skier report. *300 N. Mt. Shasta Blvd.* *530/926–3606, 530/926–5555 mountain report* *www.thefifthseason.com.*

Jack Trout Fly Fishing
FISHING | The upper Sacramento River is a world-class fly-fishing destination, and few anglers have as much experience fishing it as Jack Trout. He and his guides also book trips to several other Northern California rivers. *Mt. Shasta* *530/926–4540* *www.jacktrout.com* *Rates vary depending on trip, number of guests.*

Mt. Shasta Board & Ski Park
SKIING/SNOWBOARDING | **FAMILY** | Three-quarters of the trails at this ski park on Mt. Shasta's southeast flank are for beginning or intermediate skiers. A package for children, available through the ski school, includes a lift ticket, ski rental, and a lesson. There's twilight skiing on some nights for those who want to see the moon rise as they schuss. The base lodge has a bar, a few dining options, a ski shop, and a ski-snowboard rental shop. **Facilities:** 32 trails; 425 skiable acres; 1,435-foot vertical drop; 5 lifts. *4500 Ski Park Hwy.* *Hwy. 89 exit east from I–5, south of Mt. Shasta City* *530/926–8610 winter only, 530/926–8686 snow phone* *www.skipark.com* *Lift ticket $74.*

Mt. Shasta Forest Service Ranger Station
HIKING/WALKING | Check here for current trail conditions and avalanche reports. *204 W. Alma St., at Pine St.* *530/926–4511, 530/926–9613 avalanche conditions* *www.fs.usda.gov/main/stnf.*

Mt. Shasta Nordic Center
SKIING/SNOWBOARDING | This center, run by a nonprofit, maintains 15 miles of groomed cross-country ski trails, plus a short snowshoeing trail. *Ski Park Hwy.* *North off Hwy. 89, 7 miles southeast of Mt. Shasta City* *530/925–3495, 530/925–3494 grooming report* *mtshastanordic.org.*

Chester

30 miles southeast of Lassen's southwest entrance, 71 miles east of Red Bluff.

A gateway to Lassen Volcanic National Park on Lake Almanor's north shore, Chester, population 2,200, supports locals and tourists with modest restaurants, hotels, and shops. The Dixie Fire of 2021, the second-largest wildfire in California's history, consumed much of the lake's western shore, but firefighters saved Chester. Expect to see evidence of the conflagration and recovery efforts when traveling in the area, though.

GETTING HERE AND AROUND

Chester is on Highway 36, the main route east from I–5 at Red Bluff, at the junction of Highway 89, which leads northwest to Lassen.

ESSENTIALS

VISITOR INFORMATION Lake Almanor Area Chamber of Commerce. *278 Main St.* *530/258–2426* *www.lakealmanorarea.com.*

Sights

★ Volcanic Legacy Scenic Byway

SCENIC DRIVE | A 500-mile scenic drive, the byway connects Lassen with Oregon's Crater Lake National Park. The route's **southern loop** begins in Chester and winds for about 185 miles through the forests, volcanic peaks, hydrothermal springs, and lava fields of Lassen National Forest and Lassen Volcanic National Park. The all-day excursion into dramatic wilderness includes a detour north to 129-foot-tall Burney Falls. The Dixie Fire of 2021 scorched the forested areas along Highway 36 and Lassen National Park Highway near Chester. Damage is likely to remain visible for a few years at least. ✣ *From Chester, take Hwy. 36 west to Hwy. 89 (Lassen Nat'l Park Hwy. within the park) north to Burney Falls. Backtrack south on Hwy. 89, turning southeast on Hwy. 44. At Hwy. 36 head west past Lake Almanor back to Chester* 🌐 *www.volcaniclegacybyway.org* ⏲ *In most yrs, snow closes parts of the byway from mid-fall to mid-spring.*

Restaurants

★ Cravings Cafe Espresso Bar & Bakery

$ | CAFÉ | This casual breakfast and lunch place inside a white clapboard house satisfies diners' cravings with dishes like homemade slow-cooked corned-beef hash topped with two eggs and accompanied by a slice of sourdough or gluten-free bread. You can get breakfast and excellent pastries all day, with soups, salads, sandwiches, and burgers on the menu for lunch. **Known for:** waffles with applewood-smoked bacon in the batter; attached bookstore's hiking and nature titles; outdoor patio. $ *Average main: $10* ✉ *278 Main St.* ☎ *530/258–2229* ⏲ *Closed Tues. and Wed. No dinner.*

The Ranch House

$$ | AMERICAN | FAMILY | This convivial neighborhood pub stands out because of its abundance of shaded patio seating—and full horseshoes pit—set in the restaurant's landscaped backyard. It's a reliable bet for filling up on hearty comfort fare after a long day of hiking and exploring—consider the decadent "loaded" fries with cheese, bacon, and pulled pork. **Known for:** substantial kids' menu; garlic and sweet potato fries; molten lava chocolate cake. $ *Average main: $17* ✉ *669 Main St.* ☎ *530/258–4226* ⏲ *Closed Mon. and Tues. No dinner Sun.*

Hotels

Antlers Motel

$ | HOTEL | A spotlessly clean, simple, and affordable option in downtown Chester, this homey, two-story motel is a handy base for exploring Warner Valley and the southern end of Lassen Park Highway. **Pros:** reasonable rates; coffeemakers and refrigerators in every room; short walk to restaurants and bars. **Cons:** no breakfast; basic decor; parking tight when motel is fully booked. $ *Rooms from: $90* ✉ *268 Main St.* ☎ *530/258–2722* 🌐 *www.antlersmotel.com* *20 rooms* *No meals.*

Mineral

58 miles east of Redding, 42 miles east of Red Bluff.

Fewer than 200 people live in Mineral, which serves as Lassen Volcanic National Park's official address.

GETTING HERE AND AROUND

Reach the park's southern entrance by turning north off Highway 36 onto Highway 89. Access the northwest entrance via Highway 44 from Redding. No buses serve the area.

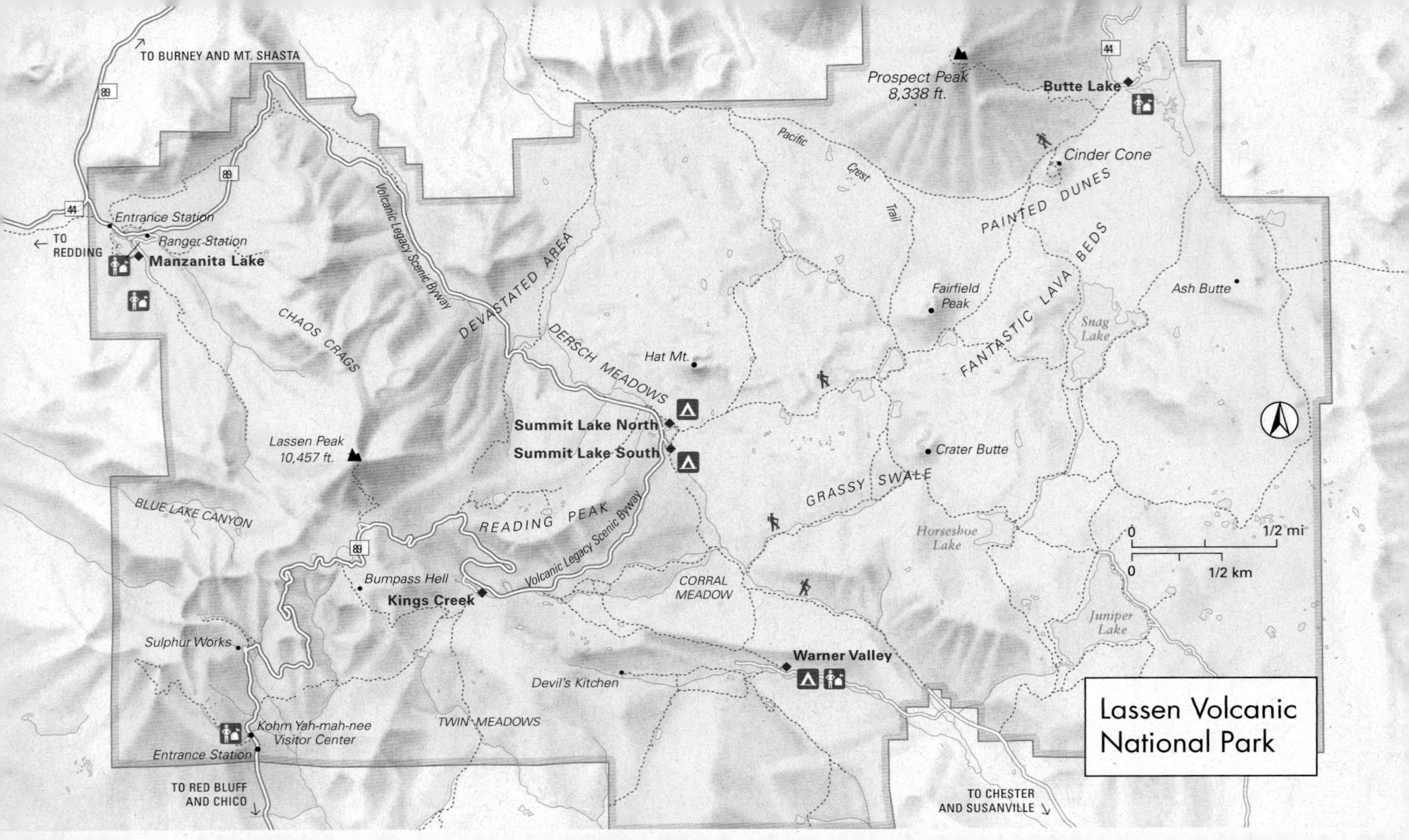
Lassen Volcanic National Park
TO BURNEY AND MT. SHASTA
89
44
Entrance Station
Ranger Station
TO REDDING
Manzanita Lake
CHAOS CRAGS
Volcanic Legacy Scenic Byway
DEVASTATED AREA
DERSCH MEADOWS
Hat Mt.
Summit Lake North
Summit Lake South
Lassen Peak
10,457 ft.
BLUE LAKE CANYON
READING PEAK
Bumpass Hell
Kings Creek
CORRAL
MEADOW
Sulphur Works
Devil's Kitchen
Warner Valley
Kohm Yah-mah-nee
Visitor Center
TWIN MEADOWS
Entrance Station
TO RED BLUFF
AND CHICO
TO CHESTER
AND SUSANVILLE
Prospect Peak
8,338 ft.
Butte Lake
Pacific
Crest
Trail
Cinder Cone
PAINTED DUNES
FANTASTIC LAVA BEDS
Fairfield
Peak
Ash Butte
Snag
Lake
Crater Butte
GRASSY SWALE
Horseshoe
Lake
Juniper
Lake
0
1/2 mi
0
1/2 km

Sights

★ Lassen Volcanic National Park

NATIONAL/STATE PARK | A plug dome, Lassen Peak is the main focus of Lassen Volcanic National Park, but this 166-square-mile tract of coniferous forests and alpine meadows also abounds with memorable opportunities for hiking, camping, and wildlife photography. The famed peak began erupting in May 1914, sending pumice, rock, and snow thundering down the mountain and gas and hot ash billowing into the atmosphere. Lassen's most spectacular outburst occurred in 1915, when it blew a cloud of ash almost 6 miles high. The resulting mudflow destroyed vegetation for miles, and the evidence is still visible today. The volcano finally came to rest in 1921 but is not considered dormant: frothy mud pots, steamy fumaroles, and boiling springs create a fascinating if dangerous landscape that can be viewed throughout the park, especially via a hiked descent into Bumpass Hell. Because of its significance as a volcanic landscape, Lassen became a national park in 1916. Several volcanoes—the largest of which is now Lassen Peak—have been active in the area for roughly 600,000 years. Lassen Park Road (the continuation of Highway 89 within the park) and numerous hiking trails provide access to many of these wonders. The café at the main Kohm Yah-mah-nee Visitor Center, in the park's southern section, serves pizza, salads, sandwiches, burgers, and the like, along with coffee, hot cocoa, beer (some of it from local producer Lassen Ale Works), and wine. Although the Dixie Fire of 2021 ravaged more than half the park, the visitor center, Bumpass Trail, and other popular spots survived. ⚠ **Heed signs warning visitors to stay on the trails and railed boardwalks to avoid falling into boiling water or through thin-crusted areas.** ✉ *Mineral* ☎ *530/595–4480* 🌐 *www.nps.gov/lavo* 🎫 *$30 car, $25 motorcycle, $15 person not in motor vehicle (fees good for 7 days)* ⏲ *Visitor center closed Mon. and Tues. Nov.–Apr. except Mon. nat'l holidays.*

Sulphur Works Thermal Area

NATURE SITE | FAMILY | Proof of Lassen Peak's volatility becomes evident shortly after you enter the park at the southwest entrance. Sidewalks skirt boiling springs and sulfur-emitting steam vents. This area is usually the last site to close in winter, but even when the road is closed, you can access the area via a 2-mile round-trip hike through the snow. ✉ *Lassen Park Hwy., Lassen Volcanic National Park* ✣ *1 mile from southwest entrance.*

Restaurants

★ Highlands Ranch Restaurant and Bar

$$$ | AMERICAN | Dining at the Highlands Ranch Resort's contemporary roadhouse restaurant is in a stained-wood, high-ceilinged indoor space or out on the deck, which has views of a serene meadow and the hillside beyond. Among the few sophisticated eating options within Lassen Volcanic National Park's orbit, the restaurant serves updated classics like rib-eye steak (up to 24 ounces), balsamic-marinated Muscovy duck, and blackened ahi. **Known for:** striking views inside and out; small plates and burgers in the bar; inventive sauces and preparations. $ *Average main: $32* ✉ *41515 Hwy. 36, Mill Creek* ☎ *530/595–3388* 🌐 *www.highlandsranchresort.com/restaurant* ⏲ *Closed Mon.–Wed. Nov.–late May.*

Hotels

★ Highlands Ranch Resort

$$$ | B&B/INN | On a gorgeous 175-acre alpine meadow 10 miles from Lassen's southwest entrance, this cluster of smartly designed upscale bungalows is peaceful and luxurious. **Pros:** stunning views; most luxurious accommodations near the park; friendly and helpful staff. **Cons:** pricey for the area; remote location; books up months ahead for summer stays. 💲 *Rooms from: $299* ✉ *41515 Hwy. 36, Mill Creek* ☎ *530/595–3388* 🌐 *www.highlandsranchresort.com* 🕑 *Closed Mon.–Wed. Nov.–late May* 🛏 *7 cottages* 🍽 *Free breakfast.*

Mill Creek Resort

$ | RESORT | FAMILY | Set amid towering evergreens in a tranquil patch of Lassen National Forest, this delightfully unfussy 1930s cabin and camping resort feels as though it could be inside the national park, although it's actually about 10 miles south, on a scenic country road. **Pros:** utterly peaceful, wooded setting; one of the closest lodging options to Lassen's southwest entrance; old-fashioned, family-friendly summer-camp vibe. **Cons:** remote location is a bit of a drive from other restaurants and services; bedrooms and bathrooms in each cabin are quite cozy; there's no cell reception or Wi-Fi (although cell phones work 2 miles away). 💲 *Rooms from: $120* ✉ *40271 Hwy. 172, Mill Creek* ☎ *530/595–4449* 🌐 *www.millcreekresort.net* 🕑 *Closed mid-Oct.–Apr.* 🛏 *9 cabins* 🍽 *No meals.*

Activities

★ Bumpass Hell Trail

TRAIL | FAMILY | This 3-mile round-trip hike leads to arguably the park's most mesmerizing feature, a wondrous landscape of hydrothermal activity characterized by boiling springs, hissing steam vents, and roiling gray mud pots. Allow two hours to complete the loop, which involves a gradual 300-foot descent into the Bumpass Hell basin, and be sure to venture to the basin's several upper viewpoints, which provide amazing views of the entire scene. Stay on trails and boardwalks near the thermal areas, as what appears to be firm ground may be only a thin crust over scalding mud. From the basin, you have the option of continuing another 1.9 miles along a scenic ridge to Cold Boiling Lake, from which you can trek farther to Kings Creek Picnic Area or Crumbaugh Lake. *Moderate.* ✉ *Lassen Park Hwy., Lassen Volcanic National Park* ✥ *Trailhead: 6 miles from southwest entrance.*

★ Lassen Peak Trail

TRAIL | This trail winds 2½ miles to the mountaintop. It's a tough climb—2,000 feet uphill on a steady, steep grade—but the reward is a spectacular view. At the peak you can see into the rim and view the entire park (and much of California's Far North). Give yourself about five hours to complete this climb, and bring sunscreen, water, snacks, a first-aid kit, and a jacket—it can be windy and cold at the summit. *Difficult.* ✉ *Lassen Park Hwy., Lassen Volcanic National Park* ✥ *Trailhead: 7 miles north of southwest entrance.*

Burney

62 miles southeast of Mt. Shasta, 41 miles north of Lassen Volcanic National Park.

One of the most spectacular sights in the Far North is Burney Falls, where countless ribbon-like streams pour from moss-covered crevices. The park's beauty is well worth the trek along two forested highways.

GETTING HERE AND AROUND

To get to the falls, head east off I–5 on Highway 89 at Mt. Shasta. From Redding, head east on Highway 299 to Highway 89; follow signs 6 miles to the park.

Sights

★ McArthur–Burney Falls Memorial State Park

NATIONAL/STATE PARK | FAMILY | Just inside this park's southern boundary, Burney Creek wells up from the ground and divides into two falls that cascade over a 129-foot cliff into a pool below. Countless ribbon-like streams pour from hidden moss-covered crevices; resident bald eagles are frequently

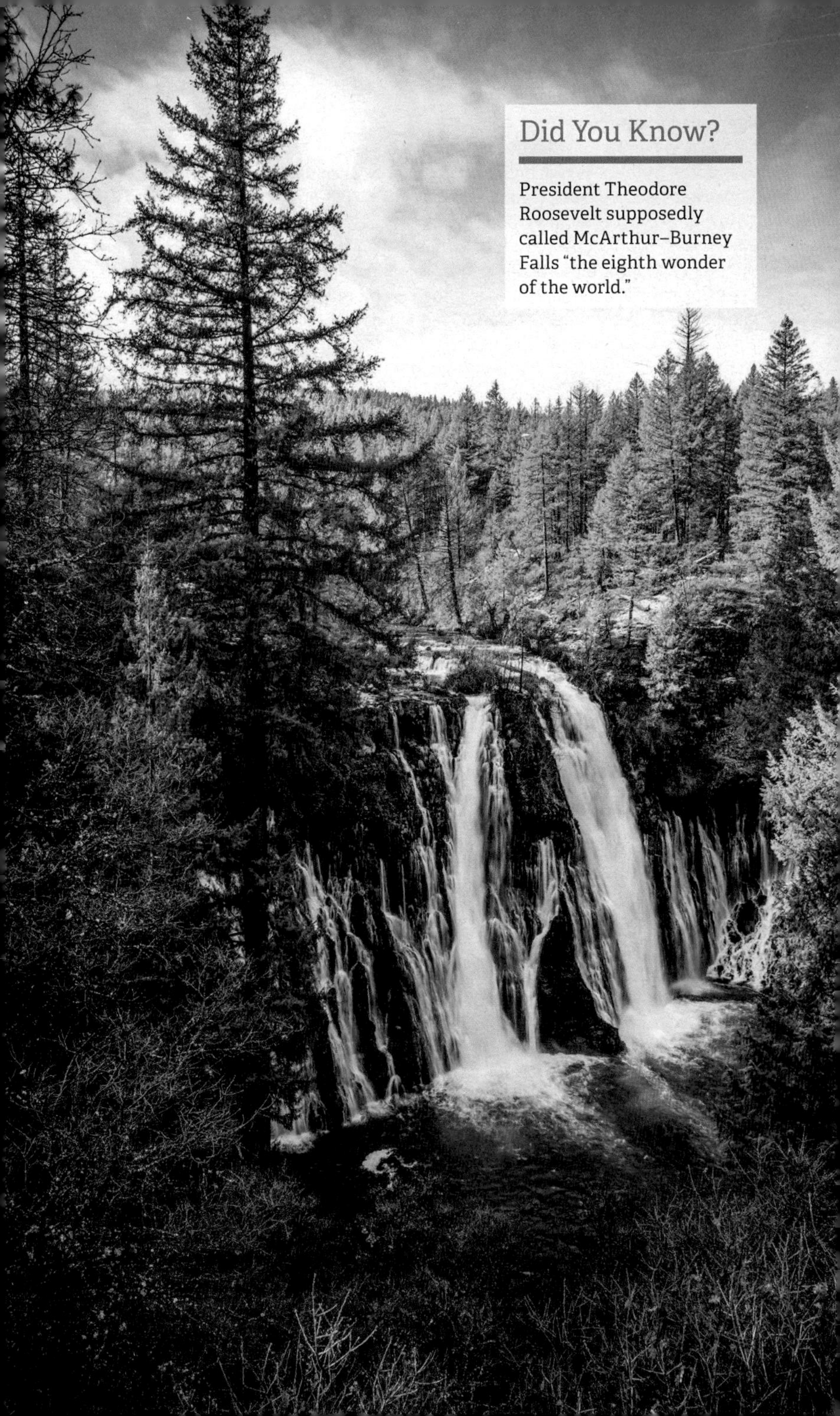

Did You Know?

President Theodore Roosevelt supposedly called McArthur–Burney Falls "the eighth wonder of the world."

seen soaring overhead. You can walk a self-guided nature trail that descends to the foot of the falls, which Theodore Roosevelt—according to legend—called "the eighth wonder of the world." On warm days, swim at Lake Britton; lounge on the beach; rent motorboats, paddleboats, and canoes; or relax at one of the campsites or picnic areas. ✉ *24898 Hwy. 89, 6 miles north of Hwy. 299, Burney* ☎ *530/335–2777* 🌐 *www.burneyfallspark.org* *$10 per vehicle, day-use.*

Tulelake

89 miles from Burney, 85 miles from Mt. Shasta City.

Lava Beds National Monument, the chief attraction of Tulelake, is so far north that one of the two main routes to it briefly passes into Oregon before looping back south into California. Stunning underground lava tube caves make the trip to this off-the-beaten-path geological site well worth the detour.

GETTING HERE AND AROUND

From McArthur-Burney state park, take Highway 89 south to Highway 299 east to Bieber-Lookout Road and Highway 139 north. At Forest Service Rte. 97 turn left (west) and follow signs. From Mt. Shasta City, take Highway 89 to Forest Service Routes 97 and 10. There's no public transportation.

Sights

★ Lava Beds National Monument

NATURE SITE | FAMILY | Thousands of years of volcanic activity created this rugged landscape; distinguished by cinder cones, lava flows, spatter cones, pit craters, and more than 400 underground lava tube caves. During the Modoc War (1872–73), Modoc Indians under the leadership of their chief "Captain Jack" Kintpuash took refuge in a natural lava fortress now known as Captain Jack's Stronghold. They managed to hold off U.S. Army forces, which outnumbered them 20 to 1, for five months. When exploring this area, be sure to wear hard-soled boots and a bump hat. Bring a flashlight with you, although some are available for borrowing at the Indian Well Visitor Center, at the park's southern end. This is the departure point for summer activities such as guided walks, cave tours, and campfire programs. As you drive through Lava Beds you may see the effects of a 2020 wildfire that destroyed more than half the monument, though not its main attractions. **■ TIP→ Lava Beds is extremely remote; visit the website for detailed driving instructions.** ✉ *1 Indian Well, Tulelake* ✣ *Take Forest Rte. 97 to Forest Rte. 10* ☎ *530/667–8113* 🌐 *www.nps.gov/labe* *$25 per vehicle, good for 7 days.*

Index

A

B

D

E

F

G

Y

Z

Photo Credits

Front Cover: Mariusz Blach/Agefotostock [Description: Lake Tahoe]. **Back cover, from left to right:** David Chang/iStockphoto, choness/iStockphoto, Marcelo Araujo/iStockphoto. Spine: Gordon Swanson/Shutterstock. **Interior, from left to right:** Daniel Sanchez/istockphoto (1). Frank DeBonis/istockphoto (2). Robert Holmes (5). **Chapter 1: Experience California:** Jaime Espinosa de los Monteros/iStockphoto (8-9). Max Whittaker/Visit California (10-11). Jill Krueger (11). Charlie Blacker/istockphoto (11). Matt Morris/Joseph Phelps Vineyards (12). California Travel and Tourism Commission dba Visit California.All rights reserved. (12). Visit California/Carol Highsmith (12). Hamilton Pytluk/Universal Studios Hollywood (12). David Livingston/The Hollywood Sign Trust (13). Visit California/Andreas Hub (13). JillKrueger (14). Disney Enterprises, Inc. All Rights Reserved. For editorial news use only. (14). TraceRouda/istockphoto (14). Jose Angel Astor Rocha/Shutterstock (14). Jill Krueger (15). Visit California/Bongo (16). Sergey Didenko/Shutterstock. (16). Kelly vanDellen/istockphoto (16). Amanda Marsalis/Chez Panisse (16). Michael Lauffenburger/shutterstock (17). Los Angeles Dodgers/Courtesy L.A. Tourism (17). Visit California/thatgirlproductions.com/Jamie Williams (18). Visit California/Robert Holmes (18). Briana Edwards/Paramount studios (18). Visit California/Blaise (18). Jill Krueger (19). Joshua Resnick/Shutterstock (26). Courtesy_Din Tai Fung USA (27). Matt Morris/Joseph Phelps Vineyards (28). Emma Morris/Ashes & Diamonds (28). Ridge Vineyards (28). Jordan Vineyard & Winery (28). Damion Hamilton Photographer (29). Courtesy of Domaine Carneros (29). The Donum Estate (29). Inglenook (29). joseph s giacalone/Alamy Stock Photo (30). Dancestrokes/Shutterstock (30). Sebastien Burel/Shutterstock (30). Marcel Fuentes/Shutterstock (31). Julia Hiebaum/Alamy Stock Photo (31). Jill Krueger (32). TJ Muzeni (32). Jemny/Shutterstock (32). ESB Professional/Shutterstock (32). Morenovel/Shutterstock (33). MNStudio/Shutterstock (33). Eug Png/Shutterstock (33). kropic1/Shutterstock (33). travelview/Shutterstock (34). Pinz Bowling Center (34). www.nicholasnicholas.com (34). LMWH/Shutterstock (34). ROB STARK (35). Henry Hargreaves (35). Catch Hospitality Group (35). Courtesy of Los Angeles Tourism (35). **Chapter 3: California's Best Road Trips:** PauloZimmermann/istockphoto (47). **Chapter 4: San Diego:** Sierralara/shutterstock (67). Americanspirit/Dreamstime.com (93). alisafarov/Shutterstock (93). Robert Holmes (94). Steve Snodgrass [CC BY 2.0]/Flickr (95). Lequint/Dreamstime.com (96). Edward Fielding/Shutterstock (96). fPat [CC BY 2.0]/Flickr (96). fPat [CC BY 2.0]/Flickr (96). Chris Gotz/Shutterstock (96). Jose Angel Astor Rocha/Shutterstock (97). Howard Sandler/iStockphoto (110). **Chapter 5: Disneyland and Orange County:** Beach Media/shutterstock (121). Eric Castro [CC BY-NC-SA 2.0]/Flickr (132). Robert Holmes (142). f00sion/iStockphoto (145). www.rwongphoto.com/Alamy (148). Brett Shoaf/Artistic Visuals Photography (152). Lowe Llaguno/Shutterstock (155). Steve Heap/shutterstock.com (160). **Chapter 6: Los Angeles:** Jill Krueger (165). Paper Cat/shutterstock (173). Carl Yu (189). Adam Latham (200). **Chapter 7: Palm Springs:** Carol M. Highsmith/Visit California (239). Danielschreurs/Dreamstime.com (248). David Falk/iStockphoto (259). **Chapter 8: Joshua Tree National Park:** Eric Foltz/iStockphoto (275). Dennis Silvas/shutterstock (284). miroslav_1/istockphoto (288). Greg Epperson/shutterstock (290). **Chapter 9: Mojave Desert:** Sierralara/shutterstock (293). mlgb/Fodors.com Member (299). DebsG/shutterstock (302). Maksershov/Dreamstime.com (306). **Chapter 10: Death Valley National Park:** Bryan Brazil/Shutterstock (311). kavram/shutterstock (319). **Chapter 11: The Central Coast:** jamesh1977/istockphoto (327). Davidmschrader/Dreamstime.com (351). Aimee M Lee/Shutterstock (385). lucky-photographer/istockphoto (388-389). **Chapter 12: Monterey Bay Area:** haveseen/shutterstock (393). Nadezhdasarkisian/Dreamstime.com (402). Artyart/Shutterstock (410). Wolterk/Dreamstime.com (419). Mike Brake/Dreamstime (429). **Chapter 13: Sequoia and Kings Canyon National Park:** Robert Holmes (439). urosr/Shutterstock (454). **Chapter 14: Yosemite National Park:** Ershov_Maks/istockphoto (467). Sky_Sajjaphot/istockphoto (482). Jane Rix/Shutterstock (486). Simon Dannhauer/iStockphoto (492). Katrina Leigh/Shutterstock (494-495). **Chapter 15: Eastern Sierra:** Glenn Pettersen/shutterstock (501). Mark Sayer/shutterstock (511). **Chapter 16: Sacramento and the Gold Country:** heyengel/istockphoto (521). RickC [CC BY 2.0]/Flickr (547). Ambient Images Inc./Alamy (555). **Chapter 17: Lake Tahoe:** MariuszBlach/istockphoto (565). Mblach/Dreamstime.com (579). thetahoeguy/Shutterstock (581). Tom Zikas/North Lake Tahoe (585). Christopher Russell/iStockphoto (595). **Chapter 18: San Francisco:** Jill Krueger (601). Scott Chernis/San Francisco Travel Association (604). Walleyelj/Dreamstime.com (605). T photography/Shutterstock (605). San Francisco Travel Association/Scott Chernis (613). canadastock/Shutterstock (631). Pius Lee/Shutterstock (633). San Francisco Municipal Railway Historical Archives (634). Andresr/Dreamstime.com (649). Robert Holmes (663). aprillilacs/Fodors.com Member (673). rramirez125/iStockphoto (675). **Chapter 19: The Bay Area:** Gary Crabbe/Alamy Stock Photo (679). Bongo/California Travel and Tourism Commission (688). Nancy Hoyt Belcher/Alamy (690). Robert Holmes (712). **Chapter 20: Napa and Sonoma:** Israel Valencia/Infinity Visuals (721). Robert Holmes (728). kevin miller/iStockphoto (729). Far Niente+Dolce+Nickel & Nickel (729). Gemenacom/Shutterstock (730). Gemenacom/Shutterstock (730). Gemenacom/Shutterstock (730). Napa Valley Conference Bureau (Top) (731). Wild Horse Winery/ Forrest L. Doud (Second and Third from Top) (731). Napa Valley Conference Bureau (Fourth from Top) (731). Panther Creek Cellars/Ron Kaplan (Fifth from Top) (731). Clos du Val (Marvin Coffin). (Sixth from Top) (731). Panther Creek Cellars/ Ron Kaplan (Seventh from Top) (731). Warren H. White (731). Terry Joanis/Frog's Leap (746). Courtesy of Castello di Amorosa (755). Robert Holmes (765). **Chapter 21: The North Coast:** MWP/istockphoto (781). Robert Holmes (790). Robert Holmes (801). **Chapter 22: Redwood National and State Parks:** Ericliu08/istockphoto (809). westphalia/iStockphoto (820). **Chapter 23: The Far North:** NPS (829). Stephen Moehle/shutterstock (849). **About Our Writers:** All photos are courtesy of the writers.

*Every effort has been made to trace the copyright holders, and we apologize in advance for any accidental errors. We would be happy to apply the corrections in the following edition of this publication.

Notes

Fodor's CALIFORNIA

Publisher: Stephen Horowitz, *General Manager*

Editorial: Douglas Stallings, *Editorial Director*; Jill Fergus, Amanda Sadlowski, Caroline Trefler, *Senior Editors*; Kayla Becker, Alexis Kelly, *Editors;* Angelique Kennedy-Chavannes, *Assistant Editor*

Design: Tina Malaney, *Director of Design and Production*; Jessica Gonzalez, *Graphic Designer*

Production: Jennifer DePrima, *Editorial Production Manager*; Elyse Rozelle, *Senior Production Editor;* Monica White, *Production Editor*

Maps: Rebecca Baer, *Senior Map Editor*; Mark Stroud (Moon Street Cartography), David Lindroth, *Cartographers*

Photography: Viviane Teles, *Senior Photo Editor;* Namrata Aggarwal, Payal Gupta, Ashok Kumar, *Photo Editors;* Rebecca Rimmer, *Photo Production Associate;* Eddie Aldrete, *Photo Production Intern*

Business and Operations: Chuck Hoover, *Chief Marketing Officer*; Robert Ames, *Group General Manager*; Devin Duckworth, *Director of Print Publishing*

Public Relations and Marketing: Joe Ewaskiw, *Senior Director of Communications & Public Relations*

Fodors.com: Jeremy Tarr, *Editorial Director;* Rachael Levitt, *Managing Editor*

Technology: Jon Atkinson, *Director of Technology;* Rudresh Teotia, *Lead Developer*; Jacob Ashpis, *Content Operations Manager*

Writers: Andrew Collins, Cheryl Crabtree, Claire Deeks van der Lee, Paul Feinstein, Trevor Felch, Marlise Kast-Myers, Daniel Mangin, Sabrina Medora, Kai Oliver-Kurtain, Monique Peterson, Coral Sisk, Jeff Terich, Michelle Rae Uy, Clarissa Wei, Jill Weinlein, Candice Yacono, and Ava Liang Zhao

Editor: Laura M. Kidder

Production Editor: Elyse Rozelle

34th Edition

ISBN 978-1-64097-409-8

ISSN 0192–9925

Library of Congress Control Number 2019938463

SPECIAL SALES

This book is available at special discounts for bulk purchases for sales promotions or premiums. For more information, e-mail SpecialMarkets@fodors.com.

PRINTED IN THE UNITED STATES OF AMERICA

10 9 8 7 6 5 4 3 2 1

About Our Writers

Native Californian **Cheryl Crabtree** has worked as a freelance writer since 1987 and regularly travels up, down, and around the state for work and fun. She has contributed to *Fodor's California* since 2003, and she also contributes regularly to the *Fodor's Oahu* and *National Parks* guides. Cheryl is editor of *Montecito Magazine* and co-author of *The California Directory of Fine Wineries* hardcover book series (Napa-Sonoma and Central Coast editions). Her articles have appeared in many regional and national magazines, and she has also authored travel apps for mobile devices and content for travel websites. For this edition, Cheryl updated the Palm Springs, Joshua Tree National Park, Mojave Desert, Death Valley National Park, Central Coast, Monterey Bay Area, Sequoia and Kings Canyon National Parks, Yosemite National Park, Eastern Sierra, and Lake Tahoe chapters.

Daniel Mangin has been a Fodor's Travel writer and editor for more than a quarter century. The author of all four editions of *Fodor's Napa and Sonoma,* he has also written about wine and wineries for *The California Directory of Fine Wineries, Napa Valley Life,* and other print and online outlets. For this edition, Daniel updated the Napa and Sonoma, North Coast, Sacramento and the Gold Country, Far North, California's Best Road Trips, and Travel Smart chapters.

Our San Diego chapter was updated by a team of Fodor's San Diego writers: **Claire Deeks van der Lee, Marlise Kast-Myers, Sabrina Medora, Kai Oliver-Kurtin, Jeff Terich.**

Our Los Angeles and Orange County chapters were updated by a team of Fodor's Los Angeles writers: **Paul Feinstein, Michelle Rae Uy, Jill Weinlein,** and **Candice Yacono.**

San Franciso and Bay Area chapters were updated by a team of Fodor's San Francisco writers: **Trevor Felch, Monique Peterson, Coral Sisk,** and **Ava Liang Zhao.**

The Redwood National and State Parks chapter was updated by: **Andrew Collins.**